...iday, 18th March, 1966,

...unched at home with Franco Zeffirelli, Alessandro de Paris, Irene Sharaff and Dick McWhirter. Irene is a funny... And enormously concerned with her own dignity.

After lunch I saw some tests of the film for which etc which seemed to be splendid and then we had a press conference. The usual stupid answers to the inevitable stupid questions. What a bore they are.

Dinner at home alone and fried chicken. Must read script and original version of Shrew again before Monday. Rebecca coming to lunch tomorrow we think. We are to dine with Edward Albee on Sat (tomorrow) night. I hope he's more articulate than the last time I met him in N.Y.

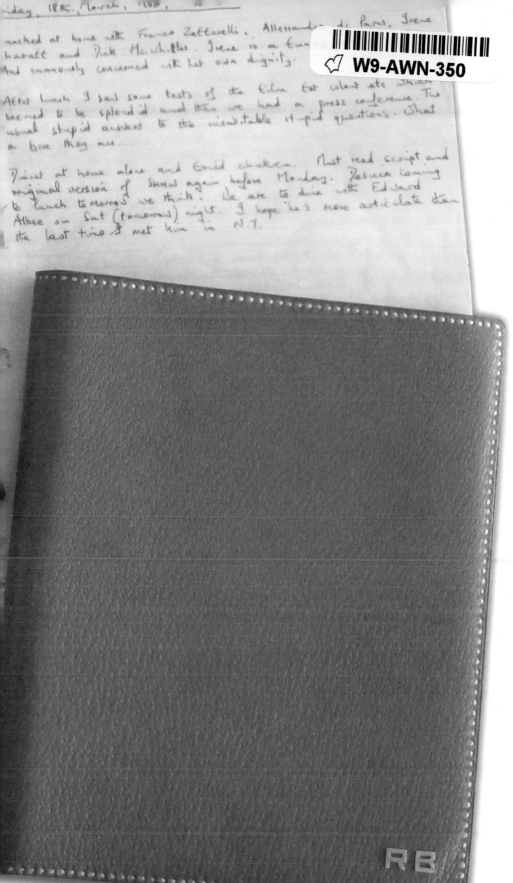

RB

THE RICHARD BURTON DIARIES

THE
RICHARD BURTON DIARIES

EDITED BY CHRIS WILLIAMS

YALE UNIVERSITY PRESS
NEW HAVEN AND LONDON

For information about this and other Yale University Press publications, please contact:
U.S. Office: sales.press@yale.edu   www.yalebooks.com
Europe Office: sales @yaleup.co.uk   www.yalebooks.co.uk

Set in Minion Pro by IDSUK (Data Connection) Ltd.
Printed in the United States of America.

Library of Congress Cataloging-in-Publication Data

Burton, Richard, 1925–1984.
   The Richard Burton diaries/edited by Chris Williams.
      p. cm.
   ISBN 978-0-300-18010-7 (cl: alk. paper)
1. Burton, Richard, 1925–1984—Diaries. 2. Actors—Great Britain—Diaries.
I. Williams, Chris. II. Title.
   PN2598.B795A3 2012
   792.02′8092—dc23
   [b]   2012023966

A catalogue record for this book is available from the British Library.

10 9 8 7 6 5 4 3 2 1

CONTENTS

THE RICHARD BURTON DIARIES

ILLUSTRATIONS

ACKNOWLEDGEMENTS

My primary thanks go to Sally Burton, whose gift of the diaries to Swansea University made this publication possible and who has taken a very keen and sympathetic interest in the project at every stage of its development. Kate Burton has also been wonderfully supportive, and I am very grateful to her for her enthusiasm and understanding. Other family members whose help has been vital to the work's completion include Graham Jenkins, Hilary Jenkins and Christopher Wilding.

The acquisition of the diaries and of the wider collection of Burton papers by Swansea University would not have been possible without the sustained commitment of Dr Hywel Francis, MP for Aberavon, and of Professor Richard B. Davies, Vice-Chancellor of Swansea University. Key roles have also been played by Professors Noel Thompson, John Spurr, Kevin Williams, M. Wynn Thomas OBE, all of the university's College of Arts and Humanities, and Professor Helen Fulton (now of the University of York). Jasmine Donahaye and Diane Green carried out some critical early work on the diaries, and Dr Louise Miskell and Dr Martin Johnes, friends in the Department of History and Classics, have said and done the right things at the right times to keep the whole show on the road. I am also very grateful to Dr Elaine Canning, Helen Baldwin and Sara Robb of the Research Institute for Arts and Humanities with whom I have worked closely in the final stages.

It is difficult to overstate the vital part that has been played and will continue to be played in the entire Richard Burton enterprise at Swansea by colleagues in the university's library and archives. Chris West and Kevin Daniels have provided encouragement and backing from the top. Elisabeth Bennett, the university archivist, has been deeply involved in all things Burton from the very beginning and continues to provide crucial advice and support at every juncture, ably supported by Sue Thomas. Dr Katrina Legg undertook the transcription of the diaries and carried it out with a painstaking professionalism that I suspect I could not, even with unlimited time, have matched. Her labours represent the solid foundation on which so much else rests. I also thank Lee Fisher and Emyr Lewis of the university's solicitors Morgan Cole for their legal expertise, Gordon Andrews and Emma Wilcox of Neath Port Talbot County Borough Council, Bethan Jones and Judith Winnan of BBC Cymru Wales, and Catrin Brace of the Department of the First Minister of the Welsh Government in New York.

Plenty of people have responded to my enquiries for assistance and advice on various aspects of Richard Burton's life and times, or have volunteered valuable information. They include Professor Gino Bedani, David Leslie Davies, Gerwyn Davies, Hubert Davies, Rona Davies, Geoffrey Evans, Keith Evans, Paul Ferris, Mrs Llewella Gibbon, John Julian, Jack Lowe, Dr Gethin Matthews, Glen Parkhouse, Dr Rees Pryce, Dr Robert Shail, Hilary Smith and the cultural commentator Peter Stead.

It has been a very pleasant experience to work with Yale University Press. I am especially thankful to have been dealing with Robert Baldock who has shown such interest and faith in the project from the outset. He has been wonderfully supported by Candida Brazil, Tami Halliday, Katie Harris and Stephen Kent in the London office and by Jennifer Doerr in the United States. Also to the copy-editor Beth Humphries, the proofreader Loulou Brown and Douglas Matthews for the index my many thanks.

Friends have provided invaluable support at so many junctures that it seems entirely inadequate to reduce that to a brief listing. I am, as ever, profoundly indebted to my good friend and former doctoral supervisor, Professor Dai Smith. Others who have helped significantly are Alun Burge, Professor Trevor Herbert of the Open University in Wales, Professor Angela V. John, Professor Gareth Williams of the University of Glamorgan, Siân Williams of the South Wales Miners' Library and the late Professor Nina Fishman.

If friends contribute, through all kinds of encouraging words and messages of goodwill, then my father Peter Williams's informal press clippings service on Burtonmania has kept me up to date with the latest developments in the media circus, and my mother Josephine Williams's bakestones (Welsh cakes to most of the world) has fuelled many a late night editing session. I also thank my adult sons Philip Watt and the Reverend Harri Williams, who have been through all of this before, and my younger children Samuel Williams (7) and Owen Williams (5), who are now experts at identifying Richard Burton on screen or in audio. My most profound thanks and my deepest love go to my wife Sara Spalding, without whom I would not get to the start line, let alone the finishing tape.

Chris Williams, Pontypridd, July 2012.

NOTE ON THE PRINT VERSION

The version of the diaries that has been prepared here for print is shorter than the full version (which will be made available online). While the introduction, linking passages, bibliography and the vast majority of the footnotes are all identical, the total volume of the text (of Burton's own words, very largely, although this also includes a small number of footnotes) has been reduced by one-quarter. In a very few cases this has meant the excision of the entire entry for a day. Mostly, however, it has involved the removal of less interesting, repetitious or apparently inconsequential material. Such editorial excisions are indicated by the sign [. . .] and should not be confused with Burton's occasional practice of entering – . . . – an ellipsis. All material removed from the print version will be found in the online version, with the exception of elements of a dozen entries that include material of a sensitive nature in respect of family members still living. Occasionally it has also been necessary to reorder or reorganize footnotes in order for the presentation of material to be consistent with the print version.

INTRODUCTION

He is a deeply educated and remarkably unself-conscious man. He combines education with intuition to an unusual degree. He is a brilliant actor (in fact, he is all actor), but he is also an enemy to vulgarity and a man at war with boredom. He does not believe in a social elite nor will he take lodging in an ivory tower. He is a worker with a mind, but the worker remains. Happily, he is not snobbish in any direction. . . . He sincerely likes all manner of humanity, and I envy the characteristic. He is sophisticated without being cynical. He is generous without aggrandizing himself. He is a first-class acting companion, and I admire his personality without reservation.

William Redfield, writing about Richard Burton, 1964[1]

Diaries? Autobiography? Time will tell, and may surprise.

Emlyn Williams, speaking at the Memorial Service for
Richard Burton, St Martin-in-the-Fields, London, 30 August 1984

This introduction to Richard Burton's diaries performs a number of functions. First, it offers a sketch of the life of Richard Jenkins, later Richard Burton, from his birth in 1925 through to the beginning of what may be called the 'diary years', in 1965. During these first four decades Burton did keep two diaries which are reproduced in this volume: one in 1939/40, when he was still Richard Jenkins, and one in 1960, when he was married to his first wife, Sybil. Both are interesting, but neither offers anything in the way of a continuous narrative which might replace a broader overview of the subject's life in these years.

Once we arrive at the beginning of 1965, however, the diaries are sufficiently substantial and sequential to render any biographical sketching redundant. Linking passages, situated chronologically amidst the text itself, perform the vital function of connecting those parts of the diaries kept between January 1965 and March 1972 with each other.

After March 1972 the diaries are more fragmented. Further passages, also situated in the text, contextualize the primary materials for 1975, 1977, 1980 and 1983, and the last months of Richard Burton's life.

The second section of this introduction addresses the question of the provenance and purpose of the diaries. Why did Burton keep them? Who was their intended audience? To what extent can one explain the lapses in making entries, or even the many months and years that separate some of the diaries that have survived?

The third section extends this analysis by considering the value of the diaries, particularly when set against the context of the many biographies of Burton and of Elizabeth Taylor that purport to tell the story of the same period of time. To what extent, one has to enquire, do they represent a corrective to previously published accounts? Is it possible to see the diaries as harbouring a greater 'truth' than the many interviews given by Burton, or are they exercises in self-deception, no more reliable than any other source?

Finally, the principles by which these diaries have been edited and prepared for publication will be explained.

Richard Burton: A Biographical Sketch, 1925–1965

Richard Walter Jenkins was born on 10 November 1925 at the family home, 2, Dan-y-bont, Pontrhydyfen in the Afan valley, Glamorgan, Wales. His father, also named Richard Walter Jenkins and born in the same place in 1876, was a collier. His mother, born Edith Maud Thomas in 1883, had been a barmaid, and was originally from Llangyfelach north of Swansea, six miles to the west. Richard Sr and Edith had married in 1900. Their eldest child, Thomas Henry, had been born in 1901, and by 1925 there were four more sons – Ivor (born 1906), William (born 1911), David (born 1914) and Verdun (born 1916) – and four daughters: Cecilia (born 1905), Hilda (born 1918), Catherine (born 1921) and Edith (born 1922). Two other daughters, both named Margaret Hannah, had died in infancy (in 1903 and 1908, respectively). So Richard junior was the twelfth child and the sixth son of a prolific union, even by the standards of coal miners' families in the early twentieth century.[2]

Pontrhydyfen was a mining village. The coal industry was the primary employer, although a greater diversity of industrial jobs existed a few miles to the south at Cwmafan and Port Talbot. At its immediate pre-war peak there had been a large pit in Pontrhydyfen and an associated drift mine together named the Cynon colliery, employing around 700 men, as well as the Merthyr Llantwit and the Argoed collieries, both of which employed around a hundred men each. Smaller concerns employing about twenty men operated at Graig Lyn and Wern Afon. There were other collieries within relatively easy travelling distance to the north, around Cymmer, and to the south, at Cwmafan.

The steep valley sides were, and remain, the dominant landscape motif and give the area an Alpine feel. The dramatic atmosphere is enhanced by two large viaducts: a seven-arch railway viaduct of red brick, and, looming above the Jenkins family home, what had originally been the Bont Fawr aqueduct, powering waterwheels at the long-closed Oakwood ironworks. This four-spanned structure in Pennant sandstone by 1925 carried a minor road.

Pontrhydyfen enjoyed the standard facilities of South Wales mining communities. There was a pub (the Miners' Arms), a Co-operative store, a primary school, an Anglican church (St John's) and two Nonconformist chapels. Bethel Welsh Baptist was the one favoured by the Jenkins family. Welsh was the language of the home, although all but the youngest children would also have been fluent in English.

By 1925 the South Wales coal industry was on the cusp of decline. South Wales coal had always been high in quality but also high in price, owing mainly to geological factors. Many of its favoured export markets had been lost during the First World War, or were now threatened by competitors able to undercut prices. Long-standing structural difficulties were exacerbated by Britain's return to the Gold Standard in 1925, which raised the prices of exports, by the facility given to Germany to pay some of its reparations under the Paris Peace Settlement in the form of coal, and by a succession of industrial disputes, including a three-month stoppage in 1921. A major dispute was narrowly postponed in 1925, but a showdown between the coal industry's notoriously intransigent employers and its equally robust trade unions appeared inevitable.

The crisis in the coal industry would have profound consequences for the Jenkins family, for not only did Richard Sr work underground but so did sons Tom, Ivor, Will, David and Verdun. The year after Richard's birth, 1926, was a profoundly traumatic one in the coal industry. A seven-month-long industrial dispute wrought havoc in areas such as South Wales, and plunged many families into serious poverty and debt. Richard Jenkins Sr's colliery closed, along with most in the immediate area, and he was forced to seek employment in a series of casual jobs.

But whatever the troubles in coalfield society at large, a more profound tragedy would befall the Jenkins family in 1927. Richard's mother Edith gave birth to her thirteenth child, Graham, on 25 October. Six days later she was dead, aged forty-four, having succumbed to septicaemia.

The response of the Jenkins family to this catastrophe revealed both its strengths and its weaknesses. Richard Sr – always a heavy drinker, a gambler and someone who was incapable of exercising control over his spending patterns – appears not to have had the sense of responsibility that, fortunately, his older children did possess. New baby Graham was sent to live a few miles away in Cwmafan with brother Tom and his wife Cassie. Two-year-old Richard moved further again: to Taibach, a district of Port Talbot, on the coast, and into the home of sister Cecilia ('Cis' or 'Cissie') and her husband Elfed James.

Cis was twenty years older than her brother. She was old enough to be his mother, and in many respects embraced that role. She and Elfed had been married for only four months when Edith died, and they were living in a terraced house in Caradog Street, Taibach. Elfed James was, like so many others, a miner, working mainly at Goitre colliery, just to the north of Taibach. He and Cis had met at Gibeon Welsh Independent (Congregationalist) Chapel, where Elfed's father was a deacon. Elfed, it seems, though competent in Welsh, was happiest speaking English, and this was the language of the James household, as it was of much of Taibach and Port Talbot generally. A year after taking Richard in, Cis and Elfed's first child, Marian, was born, in November 1928. A second daughter, Rhianon, followed in December 1931.

Although Richard would become most closely associated in the public mind with his birthplace of Pontrhydyfen, it is more accurate to see him as a product of Port Talbot, as this was where he lived from the age of two until he left South Wales altogether at the age of twenty-one.

Port Talbot took its name both from docks that were opened in 1839 and from the Talbot family that had lived at the nineteenth-century Tudor-style home of Margam Castle, further to the south. It embraced the older village centre of Aberafan, and was home to tinplate works and (from 1907) steel-works. The docks served both industries, as well as the copper works of the Cwmafan area and the coal mines of the Afan valley. The Great Western Railway passed through the town on the South Wales Railway, providing easy connections to both Cardiff (30 miles to the east) and Swansea (12 miles to the west), while the Rhondda and Swansea Bay railway line brought coal from the upper Rhondda Fawr through the Rhondda Tunnel (the longest in Wales) down the Afan valley to the docks. New docks were opened in 1898. The main occupations for men were in the metal industries, mining and transport. Women comprised less than a sixth of the officially recorded labour force, and most were to be found in the personal service, commercial and financial sectors, although there were some jobs for women in the tinplate industry. The majority of women were fully occupied in the home.

The 1921 census recorded Port Talbot's population as 40,005. That it grew to only 40,678 by 1931 indicates a certain amount of economic stagnation, although given that the population of the county of Glamorgan in which it stood declined in the same decade from 1,252,481 to 1,225,717, one might say that it fared better than settlements uniquely identified with the coal industry. Like many of the industrial towns of South Wales, it was characterized by left-wing politics. The Member of Parliament for Aberavon at the time of Richard's birth was Labour's J. Ramsay MacDonald, the former, and future, Prime Minister, while another scion of the town was George Thomas, who would become a long-serving Labour MP for the constituency of Cardiff West and, eventually, a famous Speaker of the House of Commons. Labour voting rested on strong traditions of trade unionism. William Abraham ('Mabon' to give him his bardic name), the leader of the South Wales miners in the late nineteenth and early twentieth centuries, had been born at Cwmafan, while Clive Jenkins, born in Port Talbot a few months later than his namesake Richard, would become a leading light of the Trades Union Congress in the 1970s.

Neither the strength of such working-class credentials, nor the fact that Port Talbot society was increasingly dominated by the English language, inhibited the flourishing of Welsh national sentiment in the town. The National Eisteddfod, the major cultural festival of Wales, visited during

Richard Jenkins's time in primary school – 1932 – and the suggestion was even advanced in 1943 that Port Talbot be made the capital of Wales, given that half the population of the country could be found within a 30-mile radius.[3] Notwithstanding the economic difficulties of the inter-war years, this was still a proud, self-confident society.

At the age of five Richard began attending the Eastern Primary School. At eight he passed on to the Eastern Boys' School. He was an able, if not exceptional, pupil, with strong interests in sport (particularly rugby union) and in books. He made great use of the local public library on Station Road. Richard's interests were encouraged by one of his teachers at the Boys' School, Meredith Jones, and in June 1937 he passed the scholarship examination that would take him to Port Talbot Secondary School, one of two grammar schools in the town (the other being the 'County'). This was a significant achievement: most boys, especially working-class boys as Richard undoubtedly was, did not take this step, even if they had the ability.

Richard appears to have continued to develop and flourish in his new environment. Academically he had potential, but it was probably his sporting talents that were most apparent in his early years in the 'Sec'. His qualities as a wing forward in rugby union were recognized, but he was also an able cricketer. The first of his diaries provides ample evidence of his sustained focus both on his studies and on his attainments on the playing field.

School, of course, was just one element in a boy's life. Richard was being brought up in a household where religious observance was taken seriously, and where attendance at chapel on a Sunday was expected, often more than once. In 1933 a split had occurred in Gibeon Chapel: Cis and Elfed had followed their disgruntled pastor, the Reverend Dr John Caerau Rees, to a new cause named Noddfa ('Refuge'), initially in his own home but subsequently located in the library in Taibach. In 1939 Noddfa had finally opened its own premises, on Station Road, and the 1940 diary reveals that this would be regularly visited by Richard on most Sabbaths. Chapel-going involved much more than theology, of course. In many respects it was more important as a vehicle for social and cultural activities. Richard learned to play the organ and developed a talent for singing and recitation, which could be exhibited in the many Eisteddfodau that were staged in the Afan and nearby valleys.

Money was, it seems, an issue in the James household when Richard was a boy. The family moved a couple of hundred yards up Caradog Street, to a more attractive, semi-detached house, entirely their own, at the start of the 1930s. Their previous home had been rented accommodation: this was now on a mortgage. But regular and well-paid employment was not easy to find or to keep and finance was often difficult. In order to provide himself with pocket money Richard pursued a number of avenues. He delivered newspapers, and collected old papers to wrap fish and chips, and he collected animal dung from the hillsides above Taibach for sale as garden fertilizer. He spent his income on almost weekly visits to the cinema (there are forty-two recorded in his first diary), on books, and on clothes.

If 1940 catches Richard at a time when he is looking forward to a brighter future, despite the war that is raging in Europe and in the skies above Port Talbot, 1941 was to be much more disruptive. For in April of that year Richard suddenly left the Port Talbot Secondary School and, temporarily at least, abandoned his academic ambitions. His intention of taking the School Certificate examinations in June was put aside, and instead he began work in the men's outfitting department of the Taibach Co-operative Wholesale Society, just across the road from both the library and Noddfa chapel in Station Road. What prompted this appears to have been a financial crisis in the James household occasioned by Richard's brother-in-law Elfed falling ill and being out of work, although it is possible that it was partly explained by the disruption in the coal trade brought about by the fall of France in 1940. The James family had influence in the Co-op – Elfed would later serve on its management committee – which was a powerful institution with over 6,500 members in the locality and nine different premises.

Fortunately for Richard, this hiatus in his scholarly progress was temporary. His old teacher Meredith Jones continued to watch out for him, and urged him to return to school. Other supporters included County Councillor Llewellyn Heycock, a governor of the Port Talbot Sec and also chairman of the Glamorgan Education Committee, and Leo Lloyd, drama director of the Taibach Youth Club. Headmaster C. T. Reynolds was not enthusiastic about welcoming Richard back, but he did so in September 1941.

It was in this last phase of Richard's schooling that the influence of the English teacher Philip Burton became most profound. Richard had encountered Burton before – he is mentioned in the 1940 diary, most notably in connection with Richard's participation in the school production of George Bernard Shaw's *The Apple Cart* – but it was only after his return to school in the autumn of 1941 that the two began to work closely together.

Philip Burton had been born on 30 November 1904 in Mountain Ash, in the Cynon valley, Glamorgan. His parents were of English stock and the family were Anglican in religion. Burton's father had been killed underground when Philip was fourteen, but he had nonetheless studied at the University College of South Wales and Monmouthshire in Cardiff, obtaining a double honours degree in mathematics and history. On graduation in 1925 he had become a teacher at Port Talbot Secondary School, and had developed strong interests in drama and youth development. He was a published playwright, had had work dramatized on BBC radio, and produced and directed a series of accomplished productions both at the Sec and through the Port Talbot YMCA, of which he had become chairman. During the early stages of the Second World War he had taken a lead in establishing the Port Talbot Squadron of the Air Training Corps (ATC), becoming a Flight Lieutenant and its commanding officer.

Between the autumn of 1941 and the spring of 1943, a strong and mutually beneficial relationship developed between Richard Jenkins and Philip Burton. Burton was a man of pronounced learning who was generous with his time. Richard possessed a very considerable drive to achieve, succeed, get on in life. At one time sport had appeared to offer the best way forward, but, with the encouragement and guidance of Philip Burton, a more academic avenue now opened up. Perhaps as well, in some respects Philip Burton appeared to Richard as a surrogate father – at a time when his relationship with his brother-in-law Elfed might have been strained.

Burton gained great pleasure from nurturing and championing young talent. An earlier protégé, Owen Jones, had won a scholarship to the Royal Academy of Dramatic Art and appeared in Shakespearean productions alongside Laurence Olivier at the Old Vic in London.

Richard and Philip began to spend much time together outside as well as inside school. Richard was cast in a number of dramatic productions at school, the YMCA and the ATC, and Burton advised him on vocal projection, and on how to adapt his accent. Then, in March 1943, a room became vacant at Philip Burton's lodgings, in Connaught Street, Port Talbot, and Richard moved in.

The relationship between Richard and Philip was formalized in December 1943 when Richard became Philip's ward and Philip his legal guardian until Richard reached the age of twenty-one. Adoption had been considered but Philip was twenty days short of the minimum age difference of twenty-one years required in law. Henceforth Richard used the surname Burton, and it was as Richard Burton that he became known to the wider world.

From this point on, Richard's world changed and his horizons were immensely broadened. He passed the School Certificate examinations (in English, history, geography, Welsh, mathematics and chemistry) in the summer of 1943, reaching the standard necessary for matriculation to university. Under the auspices of the Royal Air Force, he was accepted on to a short course programme at Oxford University, to run for six months from the spring of 1944. In the meantime, he made his professional debut as an actor.

Philip Burton had arranged an audition for Richard with the playwright and actor Emlyn Williams, who was seeking Welsh speaking actors for a production of The Druid's Rest. Richard got the part, and appeared at the Royal Court Theatre, Liverpool from 22 November 1943, and in London from 26 January 1944. When at Oxford he then starred in the Friends of Oxford University Dramatic Society production of Measure for Measure, staged in the cloisters at Christ Church, where he was directed by Nevill Coghill.

Richard's dramatic career was interrupted by the exigencies of wartime service. When his brief stint at Exeter College, Oxford came to an end he began training as a navigator at RAF Babbacombe near Torquay. There were other postings, including to Heaton Park near Manchester, and occasionally Richard obtained leave of absence to appear in some of Philip Burton's productions for

BBC Radio. But by May 1945 he was on a ship bound for further training in Canada, when the war in Europe came to an end. Burton remained in Canada, training for potential bombing campaigns against Japan, but by the time the war ended in August 1945 he had not seen active service.

It would take twenty-eight months after the war's end for Richard Burton to part company with the Royal Air Force. Most of that time was spent on RAF bases in the United Kingdom – in Norfolk, Gloucestershire and Wiltshire – and he did manage to keep his acting ticking over with occasional work for radio and television.

Demobilization eventually came on 16 December 1947. Pursuing an offer made to him in Oxford in 1943, Burton approached Hugh 'Binkie' Beaumont, of the H. M. Tennent casting agency, and his full-time stage career, with a contract of £10 a week, was launched. From 24 February 1948 Burton was directed by Daphne Rye as Mr Hicks in a production of *Castle Anna* at the Lyric, Hammersmith. Other parts followed – in *Dark Summer*, and *Captain Brassbound's Conversion*. And Burton's activities were not confined to the stage, for Emlyn Williams cast him in the part of Gareth in his film *The Last Days of Dolwyn*, which would appear in 1949.

While filming *Dolwyn* Burton met his first wife, Sybil Williams. She was five years younger than Burton, but also from the South Wales coalfield. Her father had been a colliery under-manager at Tylorstown, in the Rhondda Fach, and she had attended the London Academy of Music and Dramatic Art. She was appearing in *Dolwyn* as an extra. Richard and Sybil married on 5 February 1949 at the Kensington Registry Office, and started married life in a rented room in Daphne Rye's house in Fulham. Later they would move to Lyndhurst Road, Hampstead. Not long after marrying, Sybil gave up her acting career.

From the very beginning Richard Burton had pursued a dual acting career, on stage and in film, as well as appearing on radio, and all of this continued as his career prospered. He was highly successful in Christopher Fry's plays *The Boy with a Cart* and *The Lady's not for Burning*, the last of which enjoyed a successful run in New York as well as in London. He received lucrative sums for appearances in British film productions such as *Now Barabbas*, *Waterfront*, *The Woman with No Name* and *Green Grow the Rushes*. But what truly propelled Burton into the ranks of great actors were the Shakespearean parts that he took – first at Stratford-upon-Avon, later at the Old Vic in London – from 1951 onwards. Burton made his mark as Prince Hal and Henry V in the history cycle under Anthony Quayle at Stratford in 1951, and this brought him to the attention of Twentieth Century-Fox, who subsequently secured his services from Alexander Korda.

Burton went to Hollywood in 1952, playing opposite Olivia de Havilland in *My Cousin Rachel*, which earned him his first Academy Award nomination. This was followed by *The Desert Rats* and then another Academy Award nomination (this one for Best Actor rather than Best Supporting Actor) for

The Robe. It was at this time that Burton first met Elizabeth Taylor, then married to fellow actor Michael Wilding.

For the next three years Burton juggled his film career with a continuing commitment to the stage. He was immensely successful in the Old Vic productions of *Hamlet* and *Coriolanus* in 1953 and 1954, of *Henry V* in 1955, and of *Othello* in 1956. His record on film was more mixed: the series of films he made with Twentieth Century-Fox between 1954 and 1956 – *Prince of Players, Alexander the Great, The Rains of Ranchipur, Sea Wife* and *Bitter Victory* – were not as successful as had been anticipated and he failed to establish himself as a Hollywood 'leading man'. Perhaps his greatest tangible achievement from this period (tangible in that we still have a record of it, unlike his stage performances), was his performance in his friend Dylan Thomas's *Under Milk Wood*, first broadcast in January 1954.

The year 1957 was one of major changes in Burton's life. Early in the year he and Sybil moved to the small Swiss village of Céligny, near Geneva, where they bought a villa, naming it Le Pays de Galles ('Wales' in French). This would remain Burton's home to his death, notwithstanding that he would often live elsewhere. The move was undertaken for tax reasons, and ensured that he could henceforth spend just 90 days in any given year in the United Kingdom. Effectively this curtailed his stage career in Britain and committed him more firmly to film projects, especially those that could be shot outside the UK. In March 1957 his natural father Richard died (at the age of eighty-one) back in Wales, but Richard did not attend the funeral. Six months later and, after some years of frustrated waiting, Richard and Sybil became parents: daughter Kate was born on 10 September. A second child, Jessica, would be born on 26 November 1959.

Though resident in Switzerland Burton would continue to work mainly in the USA and, to a lesser extent, in Britain. There were more undistinguished films – *The Bramble Bush, Ice Palace* – but also a notable success: the part of Jimmy Porter in the film adaptation of John Osborne's *Look Back in Anger*. Osborne wrote the play *A Subject of Scandal and Concern* in which Burton played the lead for BBC Television in 1960, mentioned in the brief diary he kept during the early months of that year.

What is not covered in the 1960 diary is any of Burton's work for the production of the musical *Camelot*, in which he would play King Arthur, and which opened on Broadway, following some weeks in Toronto and Boston, on 3 December. This was an enormous success, chiming with the zeitgeist of the presidency of John F. Kennedy (Burton was invited to the White House and became particularly friendly with Bobby Kennedy). It gave Burton a level of public exposure in the USA (including an appearance on the *Ed Sullivan Show*) that he had not enjoyed since 1953, and he won a New York Drama Critics' Circle award (a Tony) in 1961 for the best performance in a musical. Burton's credentials for 'star quality' and panache were effectively re-established, and his prowess in *Camelot* led directly to an approach from Twentieth Century-Fox to take the part of Mark Antony (originally allocated to Stephen Boyd) in the troubled mega-production of *Cleopatra*.

In September 1961 Burton flew out to Rome to join the cast, which included Elizabeth Taylor in the title role and Rex Harrison as Julius Caesar. Sybil and the children joined him, the family sharing a villa with Roddy McDowall, who had also made the transition from *Camelot*. In January 1962 Burton played his first scenes opposite Taylor, and a romance swiftly developed between them.

Taylor, six and a half years younger than Burton, was the supreme female Hollywood star of the moment, rivalled only by Marilyn Monroe. She was in the third year of her marriage to her fourth husband, the singer Eddie Fisher. Previously she had been married to Conrad 'Nicky' Hilton (1950–1), Michael Wilding (1952–6) and Mike Todd (1957–8), the last marriage ending with Todd's death in a plane crash in March 1958. She was a mother of three children: Michael (born 1953) and Christopher (born 1955) by Michael Wilding; and Liza (born 1957) by Mike Todd. She and Fisher were in the process of trying to adopt a German girl, Maria.

Burton was certainly no stranger to extramarital liaisons, some of which, such as those with Claire Bloom and Susan Strasberg, had been quite serious. Sybil had apparently tolerated this state of affairs, confident that Richard would never leave the security of his marriage, or risk losing his children. This time, however, things turned out differently. The Taylor–Fisher marriage was more brittle, and Taylor did not hesitate long before effectively ending it. Burton was undoubtedly torn. Racked by guilt, yet captivated by Taylor, he lived a very public double life throughout the first half of 1962, repeatedly making public statements that denied any serious intention in his relationship with Taylor, yet equally repeatedly being caught on camera in her company.

Contemporary and subsequent accounts of the Burton–Taylor romance are legion. Biographers' accounts are often more sympathetic to, or indulgent of, their subject's position during this time. Various levels of calculation are ascribed to the protagonists. Burton's diaries offer virtually no comment on, or insight into, this phase in his relationship with Taylor, but on the evidence therein it is difficult to agree with those who see his choice of Elizabeth over Sybil as motivated by a desire for fame and fortune. Quite what Burton's state of mind was at any given point in what was eventually a fifteen-month period when he hovered between his wife, his children and his lover is probably impossible to judge. It would appear, however, that his hesitation, vacillation and apparently heavy drinking were all indications of his recognition that the decision he would have to take would be momentous.

The decision was finally taken, and Burton chose Taylor. They had separated at the end of the filming of *Cleopatra* in July 1962, but after some weeks began meeting again in Switzerland (Taylor having recently taken possession of a chalet in Gstaad). Their liaison continued throughout the autumn and winter in London, where they occupied adjoining suites at the Dorchester Hotel while filming *The V.I.P.s*. By this time Sybil, Kate and Jessica were also in London, living at the house Burton had bought in Squire's Mount, on the edge of Hampstead Heath. Only in April 1963 were matters resolved, when Sybil left with her children for New York. On 5 December she divorced Richard on the grounds of abandonment and cruel and inhuman treatment, took custody of Kate and Jessica, and obtained a $1 million settlement.

In the meantime Burton had made two of his best films – *Becket*, alongside Peter O'Toole, in London, and *The Night of the Iguana*, alongside Ava Gardner and Deborah Kerr, in Mexico. Taylor, putting her career temporarily on hold, had been at his side throughout both productions. While in Mexico they had lived in the small town of Puerto Vallarta, and subsequently they bought the property they had rented – Casa Kimberley – renovating it and adding to it over the months and years that followed. The adoption procedures for Maria continued, with Burton as adoptive father in place of Eddie Fisher, from whom Elizabeth obtained a divorce in March 1964.

By this time Burton and Taylor were in Toronto, where Burton was rehearsing for the role of Hamlet in a production directed by John Gielgud. On 15 March, a week after Taylor's divorce from Fisher was granted, Burton and Taylor married in Montreal. By early April *Hamlet* was playing on Broadway, beginning a record run of seventeen weeks, and attracting enormous publicity. A filmed version – the only record of Burton in a Shakespearean stage performance – survives. When the run was over, in August 1964, Burton and Taylor appeared in their third film together: *The Sandpiper*, shot in California and Paris. Although this was forgettable, they also laid plans to work jointly once more in *Who's Afraid of Virginia Woolf?*

It is at this point, between *The Sandpiper* and *Woolf*, that what one might term Richard Burton's 'diary years' begin, in January 1965 Burton himself is about to play one of his finest screen roles – Alec Leamas in *The Spy Who Came in from the Cold* – shot in London, Dublin, Germany and the Netherlands. After this Burton and Taylor would take a delayed honeymoon in France and Switzerland before travelling to the USA to make *Woolf*. For the next seven and a quarter years Burton kept a diary, and it is through his words that we may best follow his continuing adventure.

The Provenance and Purpose of the Diaries

For whom, it suddenly occurred to him to wonder, was he writing this diary? For the future, for the unborn.

George Orwell, *Nineteen Eighty-Four*[4]

'no one ever kept a diary for just himself'

Thomas Mallon, *A Book of One's Own*[5]

Richard Burton kept diaries that cover all or part of fifteen years of his life. They do not form a consecutive sequence.[6] The first is a pocket diary given to the then Richard Walter Jenkins when he was fourteen, in November 1939, and kept until the end of 1940. The next, that of 1960, when Burton was living in Switzerland with his first wife, Sybil, is little more than an incomplete appointments diary, some entries written in (rather imperfect) French. Then, 1965 sees the first of a series of diaries running up to March 1972. The earlier ones are handwritten, the later typed. The first is in a bound volume, the others loose-leaved and kept together in folders or binders. In total this sequence amounts to almost 350,000 words and constitutes the central core of Burton's writing. After 1972 there are fragments: one diary running for eight months in 1975, a couple of pages from March 1977, a more substantial diary covering the latter half of 1980, and one for the early spring of 1983. Taken together, from November 1939 to April 1983 there are approximately 390,000 words covering 93 months, spread over 44 years.

The phrase 'taken together' imposes an artificial coherence on disparate bodies of work. The 1940 diary was kept not by Richard Burton but by Richard Walter Jenkins, who had little idea at the age of fourteen what awaited him in life. That, naturally, is the source of its charm and its power, but it was not part of any conscious series. While the 1965 to 1972 diaries do form a coherent whole, they vary enormously from year to year: that of 1965 totals fewer than 5,000 words; that of 1971 runs to more than 105,000. And as for those that come after, they may not be the only ones ever to have existed, even if it appears that they are the only ones to have survived.[7]

The diaries that are published here were given to Swansea University in 2006 by Richard Burton's widow Sally. They form the core of the Richard Burton collection, which also includes correspondence, film posters, press cuttings, photographs, a collection of Burton's books, and a variety of audio-visual materials.

An important consideration in assessing the diaries is the extent to which their existence was known to others, and whether their contents were kept entirely private.

As to the first question, it seems highly unlikely that anyone close to Richard would not have known that he was keeping a diary. It may well be that his 1940 diary was a birthday gift, and we know that Elfed James wrote (abusively) in it. The 1960 diary was probably viewed by Burton's wife Sybil. The 1965 diary was a gift from Elizabeth Taylor, who also contributed some entries. Thereafter, although Burton remains almost the only person to write in his diaries (Elizabeth Taylor contributes a handful more entries, and there is one – 'Richard is the best' – by Brook Williams in 1970) he usually typed up his day's account on one of his portable typewriters, often in full view of family and household members. The fact that Richard kept a diary, for certain periods of his life at least, was a matter of public record – commented on in interviews and noted in correspondence.

If Burton was disinclined to secrecy in the matter of diary-keeping, to what degree did he seek to keep their contents private? As already noted, Elizabeth Taylor herself wrote in some of the diaries. Thereafter, there is no evidence that Richard sought to conceal the contents of his diaries from his second wife. In fact he appears to have encouraged her to dip in and out as she wished, remarking on 31 December 1968 that Taylor had 'free access' and that the diary's contents 'normally gave her a giggle'. And, in August 1980, we find Burton reading passages from his diary out to his third wife Susan.

If Burton's diaries were open, at least to his wives, then one would think this must have affected what he chose to include in them. We have some evidence of self-censorship: in August 1971 he refrained from committing to paper his worries about Elizabeth's mother's state of health for fear of Elizabeth coming across his entries. Yet at the same time Burton could be remarkably frank about the state of his relationship with Taylor, and unabashed about detailing some of her medical conditions. The explanation may be that Burton felt comfortable with a 'warts and all' portrait of his marriage, providing he was reassured that his writing would not be studied by anyone other than himself and Taylor. There is very little evidence, for example, of the children, members of the entourage, or of friends reading the diaries.[8]

In January 1969 Burton noted that he could not find 'the last volume of my diary', and thinks he must have put it 'in such a safe place ... that I cannot remember'. This turns out to be the case – the diaries were in the wine cellar at Chalet Ariel. But he worried '[i]t wouldn't be very nice if it got into the wrong hands. It's too revealing about other people, but above all about myself. It's supposed to be for the old age of E and myself.'[9]

If this suggests that Burton had a very restricted sense of the audience for the diaries, at least at the time of writing, and perhaps for the foreseeable future, it also raises the question of why Burton was keeping a diary in the first place. The answer here necessarily excludes the 1940 and 1960 diaries, which would not appear to have been kept as part of any grand design. And there is very little direct evidence: when Burton starts the 1965 diary he does not open with any kind of prospectus or justification. This raises the possibility that there was an earlier diary begun in 1964, perhaps following his marriage to Taylor, but we have no evidence of that. Perhaps, rather than attempting to set out a rationale for what he was doing, Burton just got on and did it. He may well not have been entirely clear in his own mind precisely what his objective was.

If one confines oneself to the 'diary years' sequence of 1965 to 1972, then it may be argued that they were not kept with a view to being published in their raw state. They were written in relatively fluent English (though with typing errors and a surprisingly haphazard grasp of spelling), substantially free of abbreviations or coded messages, and, as a consequence, are rarely difficult to decipher. But they were not written in the polished, carefully crafted style of Burton's published articles for newspapers and magazines. Instead they read as rough notes, ideas, memories, a daily catalogue of people and places, meals and conversations. They functioned as a private record of his life, an aide-memoire to which he presumably intended to return at some future, unspecified date.

For precisely what purpose he would return was nowhere made explicit – but it seems that Burton regarded writing the diary as a good habit, a corrective to what he believed was his latent idleness, a way of forcing himself to 'keep my mind in some kind of untidy order' (9 January 1969). In such comments we may discern an awareness of the redemptive value of labour, and an obeisance to a Nonconformist work ethic. Burton was not someone who was content with his personality, with his achievements or his prospects. He was undeniably restless, predominantly dissatisfied, measuring himself against his ambitions and against the achievements of others. Diary-keeping was one record of that persistent itch, that yearning to achieve, to become, to realize.

But Burton could also be dismissive of his diary-writing efforts, referring to 'today's entry for the idiot stakes' (13 November 1968), 'this pathetic journal' (20 March 1969) which was 'stupendously tedious' (15 June 1970). Sometimes he struggled to complete a single page of typescript; on other days the words kept flowing. When he stopped keeping the diary the reasons were occasionally given in retrospect – too many things happening ('when events tumble over each other I don't write it down' – 1 November 1969), 'acute unhappiness' (20 March 1969), drinking too much, sleeping too late, not feeling he had anything worth recording ('[w]hen faced with this machine latterly I feel as dull as drinkwater' – 31 May 1970). But often there was no explanation provided for the gaps, and there is no comment at all in the diaries from 1975 or later in the more substantial run of diaries dating from 1965 to 1972. The only extraneous evidence in these later years comes from an interview conducted by the talk-show host Dick Cavett in 1980. Asked about his diaries, Burton responded:

They are virtually unreadable . . . I have occasionally had a glance back . . . but in actual fact I haven't only very sporadically [sic] written the diary for the last three or four years . . . and I said to a great friend of mine he said 'how's the journal?' because occasionally I take bits from the journal and elaborate on them and they get published you know *Ladies' Home Journal*, *Vogue* magazine, the people who pay the most money, *Cosmopolitan*, that stuff, but very rarely, I've only published about ten pieces in my life. But I said . . . why do you think the impulse to write has temporarily I hope just died, and he said it's perfectly obvious, you're too happy. And I thought but

I've been happy before and I kept on writing and I still can't work it out it.
Anyway it does continue occasionally.

Rarely, it would appear, did Burton re-read his entries or attempt to develop a
narrative that spanned successive days. On 23 July 1969 he commented that he
'must start putting this diary together. I just slide it into the nearest drawer and
so can't look back and find out what I wrote or didn't write about what or who
or which.'

There is the possibility that Burton thought he would some day write his
autobiography. In October 1968 he recorded that he had been offered a million
dollars for a month's worth of the diary. He was not entirely convinced that it
would be interesting, and thought the notion 'mad'. In August 1976 agent
Robbie Lantz wrote to Burton concerned by a report that had reached him
that Burton might be writing a book, presumably an autobiography; there is
no record of Burton's reply.[10] Burton was lukewarm, from the evidence
contained within the diaries themselves, about any autobiographical project,
uncertain whether there was really an audience for his life, and suspicious of
the genre of actors' autobiographies. Of course, had he lived longer, he might
well have come to feel that such a project was worthwhile: that he had some
flair for autobiographical writing is evident from his published output, particularly his pieces *A Christmas Story, Meeting Mrs Jenkins*, and his writings on
rugby union.

Burton's sudden, unanticipated death at the age of fifty-eight meant that
his intentions for his diaries were not made clear. At the time of the publication of Melvyn Bragg's biography in 1988 various claims were made to the
effect that Burton had intended them to be destroyed, or that they should have
been closed for at least twenty years after his death.[11] Burton himself may have
had what was then the 'thirty-year rule' for the closure of official records in
mind. In his papers there is an undated telegram sent to his solicitor Aaron
Frosch, explaining in response to an apparent enquiry concerning an autobiography that:

My diary is my own personal possession and is read by nobody else except
Elizabeth. It is for obvious reasons not publishable except in an emasculated
form for a hundred years after we are all dead. I don't even reread it myself. It
is merely a daily exercise in the obviation of frustration.[12]

Reading the diaries today, one is struck by the incongruity of the sentiments
expressed in this telegram. There is relatively little that was libellous, even at
the time of writing (when most of the subjects being written about were still
alive). Burton does not provide the reader with a list of his female conquests
or shed light on the hitherto concealed sexual preferences of some of his fellow
actors. There are no great revelations of corruption or of criminality. Instead

the diaries tell us about the life and thoughts of Richard Burton. But do they tell the truth?

Diaries, Biography and 'Truth'

> Here he speaks as truthfully as he can. (Melvyn Bragg)[13]
> I never lie when I write. Honest. Though I'm not sure of that!
> (Diary, 25 May 1969)

At one level, the appeal of the diary as a 'truthful' source is straightforward. It is a record kept by an individual of their activities, feelings and opinions. If the author is the only reader, then no legitimate purpose, one might argue, would be served by the compiling of an inaccurate, insincere or otherwise false account. Diaries may be presented as unmediated, unreflective and natural commentaries, offering a direct route to consciousness and events not enjoyed by most rival source materials.

Yet it is clear that such a depiction of diary-writing as a genre is one-dimensional and misleading. The very process of remembering, most certainly of writing, is itself an editorial process, offering many opportunities for self-censorship. Diarists, it can be argued, always have one eye on a readership, even if that readership is to be found after their own death, or even if it is only themselves. There is no sense in which diaries (written at the time) are any more 'natural' than autobiographical memoirs written years after the events being described, although obviously they offer different kinds of information and are subject to their own genre conventions.

Not everything in the diaries, it has to be acknowledged, would pass muster in a court of law. Yet it is possible to agree with Robert Fothergill that these diaries, like other diaries, are 'true to life' if not necessarily 'truthful'. As Fothergill writes, '[e]ven in their disguises, evasions, and lies diarists are responding to the pressure of first-hand experience; they are being, for better or worse, themselves.'[14]

The extent to which Burton's diaries were accessible to his wives, and more generally known to exist by his family, friends and entourage, has already been discussed. That Burton knew that Elizabeth, or Susan, or Sally, might read his entries may have encouraged a certain degree of self-censorship. That should not surprise: all diarists, even those who keep diaries written in code and in locked vaults, must edit themselves and their testimonies to some degree.

The fact that Richard did not write about something in the diary does not mean it did not happen. There were days, weeks, sometimes months, even during the 'diary years', when he did not write. From July 1965 to March 1966, from November 1967 to July 1968, and from September 1970 to June 1971, he appears to have kept no record.[15] And, of course, he decided how much to write, which could vary enormously. Variations in the length of the diaries means that the nature of the record kept is quite different. Although he kept a diary in 1975, ostensibly over a period of eight months, this amounted to only a little over 8,000 words. Most of the entries are quite short.

Furthermore, at times Richard did not, or could not, remember what had happened even though he was keeping a diary. There are days in some years when the only entry is the word 'booze'. That might cover a multitude of sins! One must ask whether Richard was always fully honest with himself in entering his record of the previous day's proceedings. He sometimes records that he and Elizabeth rowed, or that he behaved badly in a public or social context, but rarely does he go into any great detail. He chose not to relive those episodes beyond a brief mention. Equally there were other events and episodes which do not reflect badly on Richard but which also fail to appear in the diaries.

Melvyn Bragg's view was that the diaries were the place where Burton could detach himself from the celebrity whirlwind, the gossip columns and mischievously playful interviews, and be serious, honest with himself. They were his record of truth – 'He swore on the Bible of these Notebooks'.[16] One certainly senses in the diaries a level of disengagement, a distancing from his public persona. Burton would have been aware that there was someone called 'Richard Burton' who existed in the press, on the television screen, in the cinema, who millions of people thought they knew (and still do). It was not always someone he recognized. In his diary, he could construct his own sense of himself, of who he was, what he valued, and where he was going.

In pursuing the question of the diaries' 'truth' one example may be considered. Much speculation at the time and since has surrounded his relationship with the French-Canadian actor Geneviève Bujold, with whom he appeared in *Anne of the Thousand Days*. Taylor evidently suspected Burton of having had some kind of fling with Bujold, and this was a matter of contention between them. Yet Burton offers no support whatsoever for such suspicion in his diaries; quite the opposite.[17] Richard's own testimony in one of his last entries in the 'diary years' sequence, on 15 March 1972, was that he and Elizabeth had been faithful to each other throughout their marriage, and there is nothing in the diaries to contradict this. Sceptics will point out, particularly as Taylor had access to the diaries, that that is exactly what one would suspect, and of course one cannot prove a negative. But the available evidence for any relationship with Bujold is exceedingly slender – despite the generalized claim, for example, that Burton slept with 'all his leading ladies' (with exceptions made, presumably, for Sue Lyon, Ava Gardner and Deborah Kerr at the time of *The Night of the Iguana*; Claire Bloom at the time of *The Spy Who Came in from the Cold*; and Rex Harrison at the time of *Staircase!*), or the suggestion that Burton gave nicknames to all his conquests, so that the fact that he called Bujold 'Gin' was proof of sexual congress.

Part of the difficulty here is that Burton's reputation both preceded him and has survived him; that there is a public appetite for believing the most outlandish claims about his life; and that many of those who have written about Burton prefer the sensationalism of a 'good story' to more sober evaluation of the evidence. Much of what passes for biographical writing is badly researched and heedless of the obligation of any serious writer to corroborate testimonies. Instead, the many lurid, sensational and improbable stories about Burton's drinking and private life are recycled and embellished. As a consequence, Burton's personality, achievement and importance continue to be regularly misrepresented and misunderstood. All too often he appears as a caricature: brawling, drinking, womanizing, throwing his talent away in an orgy of self-destruction. In reading such books one is reminded of John Updike's comment that most biographies are 'novels with indexes'.[18]

Of course, Burton himself was guilty of telling tall tales about his life and times, sometimes, it would appear, simply to see whether he would be believed, sometimes because he feared being thought boring and thus strove for maximum dramatic effect, employing considerable poetic licence in the process. As John Cottrell and Fergus Cashin noted, 'Burton the story-teller has never been one to let concern for accuracy outweigh his concern for effect. . . . Burton tells and retells so many stories that they grow or become confused, but so marginally that he does not realize it and sincerely believes he is reproducing the original.'[19]

Among those who knew Burton, often it is individuals who were most peripheral to the man who are relied on most heavily for 'authoritative' quotations about his escapades, or even insert themselves into the narrative of his life.[20] Even those who may be counted as friends good and true, can fall into the trap of colouring their reminiscences for dramatic effect, of conflating episodes, of imposing their own explanations and interpretations on Burton's life and, naturally enough in the process, casting themselves in the best possible light.

Burton's diaries have no automatic claim to 'truth'.[21] But they are surely one of the most important sources, if not the most important, for Burton's life, at least during the years when they were kept. They allow Burton to speak for himself.

Editing the Diaries

No editor can be trusted not to spoil a diary.

(Ponsonby, *English Diaries*)[22]

Melvyn Bragg, who published the authorized biography of Burton – *Rich* – in 1988, had access to most of the diaries presented here.[23] In his work, Bragg drew substantially on Burton's own words, citing about one-fifth of what he had access to at the time of writing. Inevitably he was forced to be highly selective, and could not provide the level of contextual information and referencing that is possible in a fuller scholarly edition.

It is not suggested that Melvyn Bragg, in any significant way, mishandled or misrepresented the diaries' contents. There are a few places in which the transcription differs from his but, for the most part, the spirit in which Richard Burton's words are rendered in Bragg's biography are faithful to what one might feel to be the original and intended meaning. Yet it is only through publication of the diaries as they were written that one will be able fully to appreciate Burton's own words and the insights the diaries offer into his life. Rather than Bragg, like any biographer, allowing Burton's words to appear at a time in the book and on a subject both of Bragg's own choosing, the diaries allow Burton's voice to be heard unmediated, direct, clear and in full.

The first principle adopted in editing the diaries has been to refrain from doing anything that might alter the meaning of the text. Where the text is ambiguous, then it has been left ambiguous, and the reader may make up his or her mind as to its meaning. However, where Richard Burton crossed out or altered words or passages these reconsiderations have been respected.

A second principle, clearly subordinate to the first, is to remove any unnec-essary obstacles to readability and accessibility. There seems little point in irri-tating or confusing readers by retaining typing errors or misspellings when no such ambiguity exists. (It cannot be said of Richard Burton, as it has been said of Virginia Woolf, that his spelling was 'so consistently good that [his] rare aberrations are preserved'.)[24] Abbreviations have been bodied out and capi-talization and punctuation have been rationalized, providing no damage is done thereby to the meaning of the text. Ampersands, unless integral to the title of (for instance) a business, have been replaced by 'and', the occasional '∴' replaced by 'therefore'. Where handwriting places the title of a film or a book in inverted commas, that has been changed to italics. Where double quotation marks were used it has often been possible to render these as single quotation marks, more in tune with current practice. Such transformations have been made silently, that is, without the need for a footnote to mark them. The text has also been formatted in a consistent manner, so that dates are presented in standardized form.

As for referencing, the primary objective followed in referencing the diaries has been to provide such information as is necessary or helpful for the reader in allowing him or her to understand the text. Thus, individuals mentioned have been given their full name, profession, vital dates (where known) and any other information of relevance (such as previous or future connections with Richard Burton). This has been provided once, on first mention (the reader will need to consult the index if they seek further information following a second or subse-quent mention). Where no clarificatory footnote is provided, that is because no further information about that individual or location has been found.

Book and film references have been clarified, where possible. Where Burton quoted from a poem, play or book it has usually been possible to identify the relevant line or passage and provide contextual (sometimes corrective) information. Where he referred to current affairs or historical events, brief explanatory notes have been provided. Where he mentioned locations, places, hotels or restaurants, again, clarification has been supplied wherever possible. Specialist terms have also been explained where this has been thought necessary.

Except in very few cases it has not been thought necessary to provide references to the references, as it were. It should also be noted that the professional historian's caution has been rendered implicit rather than explicit, otherwise the word 'presumably' would make regular and tedious appearances throughout the notes. For some references at least, an element of guesswork and conjecture is involved, and corrections and further information will be welcomed for any future editions.

Distances are given in the form appropriate to the location described. Thus, in the UK and the USA they are given as miles, but in Switzerland and France as kilometres.

Virginia Woolf wrote that it was the role of the biographer to 'admit contradictory versions of the same face'.[25] Neither the diarist nor, most certainly, the diarist's editor, may be thought a biographer, and there are significant differences between diarists and autobiographers, whatever claims may be made for the all-embracing genre of 'life writing'. Yet Woolf's observation pushes us to recognize the fragmented nature of the individual life, the constructed character of any would-be coherent personal identity, and the difficulties that face any attempt to approach the 'essence' of any one person.[26]

Richard Burton was a complex, conflicted, and contradictory character. There is ample evidence of this in his diaries, as in other aspects of his turbulent life. It would be rash to claim that the diaries reveal the 'true' Richard Burton, not least because it is not clear why the Burton who sits quietly at his typewriter assembling his account of his previous day's activities should automatically be considered any more genuine than the Burton whose antics filled newspaper column inches.

Nevertheless, it is possible to suggest that a more varied Burton emerges from his own writings than the one currently circulating in the public domain. We find here Richard Burton the acclaimed actor, the international film star and the jet-set celebrity, but we also find Richard Burton the family man, father and husband. The diaries reveal the melancholic, afflicted, troubled and introspective Richard Burton struggling to come to terms with the missed opportunities and unfulfilled potential of his life and talent, and they show us the Richard Burton justly proud of his achievements, of his journey in life, hungry to scale greater heights. In the pages of his diaries we see Richard

Burton watching his weight, watching his drinking, watching other men watching *his* Elizabeth. We have a Richard Burton who reads, who thinks, who longs to write. On the many pages of his diaries Richard Burton displays his multiple selves.

Notes

1. William Redfield, *Letters from an Actor* (New York: Viking, 1967), p. 20.
2. Data collected by the 1911 population census revealed that women aged between 20 and 24 averaged 7.36 children if they married coal miners, but only 3.48 children if they married doctors. Coal miners also enjoyed one of the earliest average ages of marriage of any occupational group, a function of the relatively high wages that could be earned by young men underground.
3. *Port Talbot Guardian*, 5 February 1943. Wales had no officially recognized capital until 1955, when the city of Cardiff was accorded that honour.
4. George Orwell, *Nineteen Eighty-Four* (1949; Guild Publishing, 1989), p. 434.
5. Thomas Mallon, *A Book of One's Own: People and their Diaries* (St Paul, Minnesota: Hungry Mind Press, 1995 edn), xvii.
6. Burton uses the terms 'diary', 'journal' and 'notebook' at various times to describe what he is doing. Here the term 'diary' has been chosen as more accurately reflective of the entire sequence and the fact that Burton did keep dated entries confined to single days.
7. There are scattered references, in the diaries and elsewhere, which suggest the existence of other diaries or other forms of writing. Hollis Alpert, *Burton* (New York: G. P. Putnam's Sons, 1986), p. 90, refers to Burton keeping a diary, written 'in his own invented hieroglyphics' in about 1960. Perhaps Burton meant his schoolboy French. Alpert also suggests that Burton was writing a novel and had written 20,000 words which he lost when in Hollywood in 1970 (p. 197).
8. There does not appear to be any supporting evidence for the suggestion made by Penny Junor, in *Burton: The Man Behind the Myth* (London: Sphere, 1986), p. 143, that Burton read his diary 'out loud to friends'.
9. In fact most, perhaps all, of the diaries covering this period have survived.
10. Lantz to Burton, 11 August 1976, Richard Burton Archives, RWB 1/2/1175.
11. *Sunday Express*, 4 December 1988; *Sunday Times*, 18 December 1988.
12. RWB 1/2/1/3 – Weissburger and Frosch [Box 19/3]. Although undated, this evidently dates from the period 1964–75.
13. Melvyn Bragg, *Rich: The Life of Richard Burton* (London: Hodder & Stoughton, 1988), p. 211.
14. Robert A. Fothergill, *Private Chronicles: A Study of English Diaries* (London: Oxford University Press, 1974), p. 10.
15. There is very limited evidence of wilful destruction of the diaries. On 24 June 1965 Burton records that 'in fury' he had torn out the preceding page of the diary, covering 17–23 June. The page has not survived. There is no other comment of this kind, but this does not rule out the possibility that he destroyed other pages and did not leave evidence of such destruction.
16. Bragg, *Rich*, p. 369. See further assessments on pp. 108, 165, 210–11, 216–17, 290.
17. A similar case is that of Burton and Raquel Welch. Taylor was suspicious of Welch's interest in her husband, and there is speculation to this day (not quashed by Welch herself) that Burton and Welch may have been lovers during the making of *Bluebeard*. Yet the diaries (which admittedly end in March 1972, before the cessation of filming) offer no evidence for this.
18. Cited in Hermione Lee, *Biography* (Oxford: Oxford University Press, 2009), p. 7. This is not the place to list the failings of specific Burton biographies and biographers (or, indeed, those of Elizabeth Taylor). For readers seeking further enlightenment and relatively sure-footed narrative, my advice would be to consult the works by Bragg, Ferris and Stead on Richard Burton, and by Alexander Walker on Elizabeth Taylor.
19. John Cottrell and Fergus Cashin, *Richard Burton: A Biography* (London: Arthur Barker, 1971), pp. 345–6.
20. The most recent example being Michael Munn, in his *Richard Burton: Prince of Players* (London: JR Books, 2008). Munn is not named in any of the diaries.
21. Bragg, perhaps subconsciously, appears to accept this when he writes (*Rich*, p. 375) 'As in many autobiographies there is self-justification as well as self-revelation.'
22. Arthur Ponsonby, *English Diaries* (London: Methuen, 1923), p. 5.
23. The exceptions are the diaries of 1940 (Bragg had some kind of indirect knowledge of this) and 1975.

24. *The Diary of Virginia Woolf*, volume II: *1920–1924*, ed. Anne Olivier Bell (Luda: Hogarth, 1978), Editor's preface, p.ix.
25. Virginia Woolf, 'The Art of Biography' (1939), in *The Death of the Moth and other essays* (New York: Harcourt, Brace, 1942), p. 195.
26. See Lee, *Biography*, p. 16: 'The idea that there is such a thing as an innate, essential nature, often vies in biographical narrative with the idea that the self is formed by accidents, contingencies, education and environment. The belief in a definable, consistent self, an identity that develops through the course of a life and that can be conclusively described, breaks down, to a great extent, in the late 19th and early 20th centuries.' Elizabeth Podnieks develops this further: 'The self is always to some degree invented, so the diary that contains this self is at least partially fictive' (*Daily Modernism: The Literary Diaries of Virginia Woolf, Antonia White, Elizabeth Smart and Anaïs Nin* (Montreal and Kingston: McGill-Queen's University Press, 2000), p. 5.

1939

DECEMBER

10 *Sunday* Cassie died today. Graham came to sleep with me.[1]

18 *Monday* I am keeping notes of *Richard II*.[2] I am keeping homework time-table.

25 *Monday* Went down Mrs Pike's for a party not bad had great fun playing darts.[3]

26 *Tuesday* Went to another party down Mrs Davies. Had a ragtime band. Colin Wherle was there.[4]

27 *Wednesday* Went to Cach in the evening and *Stranded in Paris* and *Bulldog Drummond Secret Police* was there.[5]

28 *Thursday* Went to Regent to see *I Met a Murderer* and *Exile Express* starring Anna Sten.[6] The first picture was very boring.

29 *Friday* Waiting for result of the job I applied for last Wednesday. Sis has been canvassing for me.

---

[1] Richard's brother, Thomas Henry Jenkins (1901–80), a coal miner by occupation, was widowed when his wife Cassie (born 1905) died, leaving him with a daughter (Mair (1938–2008). Tom and Cassie lived at Cwmafan, an industrial settlement located in the Afan valley two miles north (as the crow flies) of Richard's home in Taibach. They had taken in the youngest of the Jenkins children, Graham, following his mother's death shortly after giving birth to him in 1927.
[2] William Shakespeare's *Richard II, King* (c.1595).
[3] Mrs Pike, the mother of Raymond Pike, one of Richard's friends, who later emigrated to Australia.
[4] Colin Wherle, a fellow pupil, lived in Heol-yr-Orsedd, Port Talbot.
[5] The 'Cach' was the local name given to the Picturedrome, the cinema in Taibach, located between Gallipoli Row and Alma Terrace. It mainly showed films well after their first release (i.e. not film premieres), the programme starting at 6 p.m. Before it became a cinema it had been the local drill hall for the Territorial Force (after 1920 Territorial Army). *Cach* is Welsh for 'shit'. *Stranded in Paris* was the UK title of *Artists and Models Abroad* (1938), directed by Mitchell Leisen (1898–1972), starring Jack Benny (1894–1974). *Bulldog Drummond's Secret Police* (1939), directed by James P. Hogan (1890–1943), starring John Howard (1913–95) and H. B. Warner (1876–1958) was the latest in a long series of films featuring the eponymous hero.
[6] The Regent was a cinema in Taibach located on Commercial Road. *I Met A Murderer* (1939), directed by Roy Kellino (1912–56), starred James Mason (1908–94) and Pamela Kellino (1916–96). *Exile Express* (1939), directed by Otis Garrett (1905–41), starred the Russian-born actor Anna Sten (1908–93).

30 Saturday Played football yesterday – Mr Nicky said to turn up next Friday.[7]
Went to Cach with Ray Pike.

31 Sunday We had a party down Aunt Edie's and I went out to greet the New
Year to people.[8] I went with Dillwyn.[9] We had 2/3 each.

---

[7] Although Richard writes 'football' he means rugby football rather than association football. Mr Nicky
was Mr Jack N. Nicholas, the maths teacher, who also coached the school rugby team.
[8] Aunt Edith Evans, the sister of Richard's brother-in-law Elfed James. Edith, usually 'Ede' but sometimes 'Edie', who lived at 9, Geifr Road, Taibach, ran (together with her brother, Ivor James) a fish and
chip shop, located in the front room of her house. Richard would collect newspapers (used for wrap-
ping purposes) for her for money.
[9] Dillwyn is Dillwyn Dummer, one of Richard's childhood friends, a second cousin once removed, and
just a few months younger than Richard. Dillwyn's mother Margaret Ann was Elfed James's sister.

1940

JANUARY

1 Monday I went up Cwmafan to Tom Henry's. I had 2/6 today. Reached up there about 10.30 came home by 2.30. Played football in the Park.[1] Went to Regent to see *Oklahoma Kid* with James Cagney and H. Bogart.[2]

2 Tuesday Rode Boyo Jenkins up town yesterday and he went to Lloyds.[3] Went down the Library after.[4] Played football, in the afternoon, it was a decent game. Stayed in to-night and listened to *ITMA*.[5] It's very cold.[6]

3 Wednesday Went shopping for Cis yesterday.[7] I have got to have an interview with the Co-op committee tomorrow.[8] Played football today. There is a terrific wind. Went to Cach to see Sandy Powell.[9]

4 Thursday Went to see the old boys beating the school yesterday. Not a bad game at all. Went to have an interview tonight for the job in the co-op. Everything went splendidly and I have been told that I have had the job.

---

[1] The Talbot Memorial Park, located between Taibach and Port Talbot.
[2] *The Oklahoma Kid* (1939), directed by Lloyd Bacon (1889–1955), starred James Cagney (1899–1986) and Humphrey Bogart (1899–1957). Richard was to become friendly with Bogart in the 1950s.
[3] Arthur 'Boyo' Jenkins, a fellow pupil, who lived in Varna Terrace, Taibach, and who later played first-class rugby for Aberavon RFC. Lloyd's bicycle and sports shop, Station Road, Port Talbot.
[4] The Carnegie Free Public Library, Taibach, situated on Commercial Road, opposite the Co-operative store.
[5] *ITMA*, an abbreviation for *It's That Man Again*, was a very popular wartime radio show, starring Tommy Handley (1894–1949).
[6] Britain suffered its severest frost for 45 years in 1940. Snow remained on the hills around Port Talbot until the end of February.
[7] Cecilia or 'Cis' James, née Jenkins (1905–93), Richard's sister, married to Elfed James (1900–79), with whom he lived at 73 Caradog Street, Taibach.
[8] This refers to the Taibach and Port Talbot Co-operative Society. Their central premises were at 4–16 Commercial Road, Taibach. Elfed James was to serve on its management committee. Richard was to work there as a draper's assistant after leaving school in April 1941.
[9] Albert 'Sandy' Powell (1898–1982) was a British comedian and film actor famous for his catchphrase, 'Can you hear me, mother?'

5 *Friday* Had football practice on the Plough and left my brown coat behind.[10] My diary and 2d cash were inside. Had the 2d off Mrs Jackson for going to Dr Marshall's for her.[11]

6 *Saturday* Went to see Cardiff beating Aberavon.[12] Went to Cach in the night and saw. . . .[13] Afterwards went to Joe's and had hot milk pop and chocolates.[14] Had chips after.

7 *Sunday* Used Mam James presented book for the 1st time.[15] Went to Chapel all day.[16] Went up Baglan for a walk.[17]

8 *Monday* Elementary school started today. Went down to see school playing in the yard. Had no money so I stayed in the house with my mother.[18] I haven't done much today. We are short of coal. Very cold.

9 *Tuesday* Ray and I went to play billiards down Glen Parkhouse's.[19] Going to try to have a game of football with Eastern practice team.[20] Went to Cach to see *Inspector Hornby*.[21]

---

[10] The Plough field is a sports ground, immediately north of and adjacent to the Talbot Memorial Park.
[11] Mrs Jackson was Richard's next-door neighbour in Caradog Street, and was originally from Gloucestershire. Richard was friends with her son Billy. Dr Marshall was the local general practitioner, who lived at 1, Grange Street, his house both consulting room and dispensary.
[12] A rugby union match. Aberavon lost 7 points to 16 in a match the *Port Talbot Guardian* thought 'one of the most exciting and interesting played on the ground this season'.
[13] Dots in the original.
[14] Joe's was Joe Morozzi's ice-cream parlour on Talbot Road, officially known as 'Berni's'.
[15] 'Mam James' – Elfed James's mother. She lived at 3 Inkerman Row (since demolished), immediately behind (uphill from) Caradog Street.
[16] Noddfa Welsh Congregational Chapel on Commercial Road, Taibach. Noddfa had been established in 1933 following a schism in Gibeon Welsh Congregational Chapel (which was near the Picturedrome, between Gallipoli Row and Alma Terrace) and had moved into its new premises in November 1939. Both chapels were Welsh in language.
[17] Baglan is a settlement lying to the north-west of Port Talbot, approximately three miles from Richard's home in Taibach.
[18] 'My mother' must refer not to Richard's natural mother (who had died in 1927) but to his sister Cis. Cis and Elfed were second cousins, both great-grandchildren of Rees Morgan and Hannah Davis, who had lived in Pontrhydyfen. They shared common membership of Gibeon Welsh Congregational Chapel, Taibach, and married in 1927, only four months before they took in Richard following his mother's death. Cis had worked as a housemaid for the Handford family, drapers by occupation, who had a shop opposite the Talbot Arms Hotel, later a store on Station Road (afterwards the site of Woolworths). Elfed was a coal miner who worked at a colliery at Goytre. This was probably the Glenhafod Level, owned by the Glenhafod Collieries Limited of Port Talbot. Glenhafod Colliery was located in the bottom of the valley below the present cemetery.
[19] 'Ray' is Richard's friend Raymond Pike. Glen Parkhouse lived at 8, Mill Row, Taibach.
[20] 'Eastern' refers to Richard's former school, the Eastern Boys' School, Margam Road, Port Talbot.
[21] Richard means *Inspector Hornleigh* (1938), directed by Eugene Forde (1898–1986), starring Gordon Harker (1885–1967) and Alastair Sim (1900–76).

10 Wednesday Uncle Ben has a new game about land, buying and selling houses etc.[22] He broke Elfed after about 2 hours I was undefeated but I did not stay on. Fetched sticks.

11 Thursday Went down Uncle Ben's again. I was broke early. Dillwyn was winning with a tremendous amount of money. Then Uncle Ben broke him. Uncle Ben hasn't lost yet.

12 Friday Went over the woods to fetch some blocks sawed off the wood. I met Afan and Gwylfa Powell.[23] Went down Uncle Ben's again. Was beaten.

13 Saturday Done all shopping. Had a haircut in Sandies.[24] Had a bath in the afternoon. Went to Regent in the night saw *Vernon and Irene Castle*.[25] Went to Joe's and had hot milk.

14 Sunday Went to chapel all day. Nice dinner after chapel went for a walk with Ray Pike up to town.[26]

15 Monday Went down Eastern School chasing Eddie Miles and Plum.[27] Went up the park afterwards. Tapped shoes afterwards.[28] Stayed in and read the book brought from the Library by our Marian.[29] Went to bed 10.20.

16 Tuesday Started school today. Played football in yard. Went to school in the afternoon. Had an easy day. Stayed in tonight and started to read *Martin Chuzzlewit* written by Dickens.[30]

17 Wednesday Woke about 8.20. Went to school. Fairly good morning. Had dinner then went to school. It was bitterly cold so I wore my overcoat. Only had a bit of Geog to do and I did not do it. Had stew for supper.

---

[22] Uncle Ben James (1900–70) was Elfed's brother. His back had been broken in an underground accident at Newlands colliery and he was paralysed from the waist down. The game referred to is Monopoly, which began life in the USA and which was being produced by John Waddington Ltd in the United Kingdom from the late 1930s onwards.

[23] Afan W. and Gwylfa P. Powell were identical twins who lived at 40 Caradog Street, Taibach. The Powells also attended Noddfa Chapel.

[24] 'Sandies' is Sanderson's barbershop, Commercial Road, Taibach.

[25] Richard saw *The Story of Vernon and Irene Castle* (1939) directed by H. C. Potter (1904–77), starring Fred Astaire (1899–1987) and Ginger Rogers (1911–95).

[26] 'Town': Port Talbot.

[27] Eddie Miles was a fellow pupil who lived in Somerset Street, Taibach, and who later served in the Royal Navy. Plum was the nickname of Royston Palmer, another pupil, who lived in Brook Street, Taibach, and who later became a teacher.

[28] Repairing shoes using a cast-iron last.

[29] Richard's cousin Marian James (1928—), the eldest child of Elfed and Cis.

[30] Charles Dickens, *Martin Chuzzlewit*, first published 1843–4.

18 Thursday Went to school as usual. Went up the Side and helped to carry water for Elfed's glass house.[31] Freezing today. Went down Uncle Ben's – played darts and won after a poor start. Lost again in Monopoly. I was doing well for a time.

19 Friday Went to school. I thought that my name would have been up on the board. But probably the ground was too hard.[32] Went down Uncle Ben's and won the 1st game. No good 2nd game.

20 Saturday Snow has frozen on the ground. Bitterly cold today. Ground like glass. Went out on my bike. Went to Cach and saw very good picture *Union Pacific*.[33] Went to Joe's then had chips.

21 Sunday Went to Chapel afternoon and night did not go in morning. Cis had row with Elfed. Graham and Edie came down.[34]

22 Monday Sis was bilious today so I stayed home today.[35] We can get no water from the tap because of ice. Went down the Co-op in the afternoon. Gave note to Tom Henry. Went to Uncle Ben's had two good games.

23 Tuesday Went down to fetch papers. Had Gym fell down hurt my knee. Very nearly finished my model in woodwork. Did my homework and went up the Side. Fetched chips for Mam James had 1d for it.

24 Wednesday Went to school as usual in the morning as usual. Had hot dinner [. . .]. Went down the Co-op for Sis when I came home from school went down G. Parkhouse to play Monopoly. Lost again.

25 Thursday Great drowning tragedy in Cwmafan. 4 people drowned.[36] Parkhouse asked me down again but I refused and went down Uncle Ben's and for once I won. Dillwyn was runner up.

---

[31] 'The Side': the mountainside up behind Caradog Street. Elfed owned a glasshouse up above Inkerman Row East on the mountainside.

[32] This probably refers to the practice of posting the team sheet for sports teams on the noticeboard. It is not clear whether Richard was simply not selected for the team in question or whether the game was cancelled because of the state of the pitch.

[33] *Union Pacific* (1939), directed by Cecil B. DeMille (1881–1959), and starring Barbara Stanwyck (1907–90).

[34] 'Edie' is Edith Jenkins (1922–66), Richard's sister.

[35] 'Sis' is what is written. He might have meant 'Cis', but as she was his sister (although he had already referred to her elsewhere as his mother) it is possible he meant 'Sis[ter]'.

[36] In fact four boys (aged between five and seven) had drowned when the ice on Dankyr Pond, on which they were playing, gave way, and one man (Mr Jenkin Powell, aged 58), who attempted to rescue them, also died.

26 Friday Went to school in the morning. Had an uneventful day. Soon as I had tea I went down Uncle Ben's to play Monopoly – Uncle Ben won the 1st game and Alan the 2nd game.[37] Had great fun.

27 Saturday Went to fetch papers then I went down Co-op. I was there for ages. Uncle Evan just gobbed on my book.[38] Went down the Library to pay my debt. Went down Uncle Ben's in the night.

28 Sunday Went to chapel in the morning. There was a tremendous congregation of 12. Very windy. There was about 60 people in chapel in the Noon.[39]

29 Monday Went down to fetch papers none there so I waited for some time and then went to school. Then in the noon I fetched the papers. Went down Uncle Ben's we did not play Monopoly. Auntie was ironing blast her.[40]

30 Tuesday Finished my model in woodwork. Papers did not come properly yesterday or today. So I took them out in the afternoon.[41] Went down Uncle Ben's to play the usual lost twice. Auntie Win went out early. Got some good books.

31 Wednesday Papers did not arrive in time again today. Had geometry for homework. Did all my homework. I kidded Glen Parkhouse that he had lost my book for me. Went down house to play Monopoly. I won once then he won. [. . .]

FEBRUARY

1 Thursday Went down to fetch papers yesterday but they were not there, as usual. Played football after school with the seniors. Went down Ben's afterwards to play Monopoly. Hope to be picked for the Middles to pay B. County on Saturday.[42] Very bad cold.

2 Friday Went to school. No papers. Went to school on bike this afternoon. Fetched papers for the chip shop but Auntie Ede was not in so I will have to go down tomorrow. Went down to play Monopoly down Ben's. Lost twice.

---

[37] Alan James was Elfed and Ben's nephew.
[38] Evan Dummer, whose brother Edwin was married to Margaret Ann, Elfed James's eldest sister. 'Gob' is a slang term for spitting.
[39] 'Noon' often appears as short for 'afternoon'.
[40] Ben's wife, referred to by Richard as 'Winifred', 'Winnie', 'Win' and even 'Wyn'.
[41] Richard may be referring here to a part-time job as a newspaper delivery boy, which he had started at the age of eight.
[42] 'Middles' probably refers to the 'Middle School' team, as opposed to the 'Seniors'. 'B. County' is Bridgend County School. Bridgend is a town 10 miles to the south-east of Taibach (1931 population 10,029).

3 Saturday Went down to fetch papers and lent my togs to Trevor George.[43] Had 1/-off Davey.[44] Had bath in the afternoon did a little homework. Went to Regent to see *Spies of the air*.[45] Had food in Joe's hot milk toffolux.[46]

4 Sunday Went to Chapel all day. After chapel in the night I went down Alan Dummer's.[47] I had a lend of a book off him. It is about school life in the Council school of Britain.[48]

5 Monday Was very late for the papers this morning. I jumped on the bike the tyres were not far from the rims. When I pumped it up lunch hour the tyre burst. Played football with the firsts it was a bit muddy but all right. Did all my homework tonight. Shorthand.

6 Tuesday Started to make a tray in woodwork [. . .]. Had a fine afternoon especially with Burton who talked about Astronomy.[49] Went down Uncle Ben's and played the usual. I won 1st then Alan 2nd.

7 Wednesday My name was upon the board for practice with the middles. Did my homework then I went down Uncle Ben's to play Monopoly. The best game I've had for some time although Uncle Ben won. I gave him a good run though.

8 Thursday Played with the seniors tonight. I had a fine game. Went down Uncle Ben's and I lost to him after a very good hand. He held all the Blues and all the 'Pall Mall' etc. block. I owned Reds but I lost.[50]

9 Friday Went to school and we started what Mr Burton called Telegrams. There was a definite score at the end of each telegram.[51] I had a pleasant surprise today. I was picked to play for the Seniors against Tonyrefail in Ton.[52]

---

[43] Trevor George was a close school friend of Richard who went on to become a headmaster. He played rugby for Aberavon and was also a talented cricketer.

[44] David Jenkins (1914–94), Richard's brother, a policeman, lived in the small town of Llantwit Major, 18 miles to the south-east.

[45] *Spies of the Air* (1939), directed by David MacDonald (1904–83).

[46] Toffolux: a tube of toffees, made by Mackintosh's.

[47] Alan Dummer, a relative of Dillwyn Dummer.

[48] Presumably should be 'Council schools'.

[49] This is the first reference to Philip Burton (1904–95), teacher of English at Richard's school, who was to have a profound influence over Richard during the next few years, becoming his legal guardian in December 1943.

[50] 'Blues' and 'Reds' refer to blocks of streets in Monopoly. 'Pall Mall' is another street (coloured purple).

[51] A précis-writing exercise.

[52] Tonyrefail was a mixed industrial and market centre 16 miles due east of Taibach.

10 Saturday Woke up about 7.40 and rushed with my papers round – Bus was some time coming. When we reached Tonyrefail we found that we could not play because the ground was too hard. I went up Cwmafan I collected 1/9.

11 Sunday Went to chapel all day. In the night while Dr Rees was giving his sermon there was thunderous knocking on the door of the church.[53] It was two boys probably.

12 Monday Went to school as usual. Played Football with the Seniors in the afternoon had a few good runs. Stayed in tonight and did my homework. I am now keeping a Home-diary. Sis went to Neath with Hilda.[54] I hope to go down Uncle Ben's tomorrow.

13 Tuesday Still doing my model in woodwork. I went up Mayne's to fetch a bottle of dark oak for Mr Owens.[55] Went down Uncle Ben's. I played two games and lost both. Mog has brought darts for Uncle Ben and about time too.

14 Wednesday Name is upon the board for practice tomorrow I suppose I will turn out. I had a new pair of shoes. A pair of Brogues. Stayed in tonight and did my homework. Went to fetch milk for Sis rode back on the trucks.

15 Thursday Played football in the afternoon with the Middle XV. I had great fun. Went down Uncle Ben's in the night and played Darts with Dad James and Uncle Ben and Allan.[56] I lost both times. Fetched chips for Dad James had 2d.

16 Friday My name was up on the board to play for the middle XV. We had a fall of snow again today I went down the Co-op for Sis it was bitter. Went down Uncle Ben's to play the usual.

17 Saturday Did all shopping. The snow is quite thick on the ground. Had 1/- off Mrs Hibberd. Did not go to Pictures but went down Ben's and played Monopoly with Uncle Ben.

18 Sunday Went to chapel all day. Blinding wind and rain. Went home straight after chapel to do my homework. We did not have a sermon in the morning.

---

[53] Dr John Caerau Rees DD, minister of Noddfa Chapel.
[54] Richard's sister Hilda Jenkins (1918–95), who by this time was married and known as Hilda Owen. Neath is a town (1931 population 33,340) six miles to the north-west of Port Talbot.
[55] W. H. Mayne was a local ironmonger, located on Station Road. Mr Owens was the woodwork teacher.
[56] 'Dad James' – Ben and Elfed's father. He was a deacon at Noddfa Chapel and also on the committee of the Taibach Co-operative Wholesale Society. Allan here but usually Alan.

19 Monday Went to school. Played football this afternoon with the seniors. Mr Smith said that I might play for the seniors against Neath County and County School.[57] Stayed in and did my homework. Went down the Co-op for Sis. I've got 4/- on the club.[58]

20 Tuesday Did my model in woodwork. Had some fun going home from school with Afan and Gwylfa. Mr Wellington came up our house tonight [...].[59] I went down to fetch Rhianon's shoes and so I watched them being done.[60]

21 Wednesday Went down Uncle Ben's in the night and had one game of Monopoly. Then I went down the chip shop for Auntie Win with Peggy and Dillwyn: Just before going out Mr Rossiter and son came in and his son said that a vet was a very good job.[61]

22 Thursday We had to do a lousy drawing for Miss Best this afternoon and I was glad when the lesson ended.[62] Played footer with the seniors and we had a decent game. I stayed in tonight and did my homework.[63]

23 Friday I am supposed to play for seniors tomorrow if the weather holds out. Supposed to be in Tonyrefail. Pop saw all the boys without their caps on except me.[64] Pop was very surprised when I told him my age.

24 Saturday [...] Played for the Seniors in Tonyrefail. We won 13–0.[65] Felt awful sick after the match. Went to Cach in the night. Went up Cwm in the afternoon.[66] Ivor went to Swansea [...].[67]

25 Sunday Went to chapel all day. Dr Rees gave a good sermon in the evening. Went home straightway. I left my stuff in the bus yesterday.

---

[57] 'County School' – Port Talbot County School, the other grammar school in the town. Mr Smith was PE master at Port Talbot Secondary School.
[58] The Co-op's savings scheme.
[59] Mr Wyndham Wellington.
[60] Richard's cousin Rhianon James, Elfed and Cis's second child (1931—).
[61] Mr Rossiter's son was Bernard Rossiter. Peggy Davies was daughter of Ben and Win James.
[62] Miss M. E. Best taught geography at Port Talbot Secondary School.
[63] 'Footer' would seem to suggest association football, as distinct from 'rugger' (rugby football).
[64] 'Pop' the headmaster (1935–43) of Port Talbot Secondary School, Mr Christopher T. Reynolds.
[65] The scoreline suggests this was a rugby match.
[66] 'Cwm' meaning Cwmafan.
[67] Richard's brother Ivor Jenkins (1906–72), a coal miner. Swansea (1931 population 164,797), then the largest town in Wales (Cardiff, the largest urban settlement, having acquired city status in 1905), is eight miles north-west of Taibach.

26 Monday Went to school all day. Played football in the Gym this afternoon. Had a Saint book from the library it is OK.[68] We are going to play the County Juniors tomorrow. We have a much weakened team.

27 Tuesday The team was picked this morning. We are five forwards less than usual. Mahoney says that he will not play again.[69] I scored a try against the County and Phillips converted.[70] They had a penalty. So we won 5–3.[71] Went down Ben's.

28 Wednesday School as usual. Our house is well up. Keen competition among the houses. I am very stiff. Many people say that it was a dirty try against the County but it is all in the game. [. . .]

29 Thursday Some very good entries for the poem section of the Eisteddfod. Played football with the seniors. Playing Saturday for the seniors in the front row.[72] We are playing one of the best teams in Wales Saturday so here's luck.

MARCH

1 Friday St David's day Eisteddfod today. Iestyn won. We came a close second and Morgan 3rd.[73] My name was up on the board to play for the seniors against Swansea Grammar.

2 Saturday Played against Grammar school in Swansea. It was a very hard game and a hopeless ref. They won 11–5. Went to Plaza in the night.[74] I paid 1/3 to go in George Formby in *Come on George*.[75]

3 Sunday Went to chapel all day. It is a lovely day today. Went for a walk with Prince over the woods this morning.[76] It is light until about 7.30 now.

---

[68] Leslie Charteris (1907–93) wrote a series of books featuring 'The Saint', later adapted for radio, film and television.
[69] Gerry A. Mahoney, a fellow pupil, lived at 44, Brynheulog.
[70] Brinley Phillips, a fellow pupil. Later played rugby football for Aberavon as a centre three-quarter.
[71] At this time a try was worth three points, a conversion two, and a penalty goal three.
[72] The front row consists of two props and a hooker.
[73] Iestyn and Morgan were the names of school houses. Leisan was the name of Richard's house, Caradog the name of another. All were named after medieval Lords of Glamorgan.
[74] The Plaza cinema was located at Station Road, Port Talbot.
[75] *Come on George* (1939), directed by Anthony Kimmins (1901–64), starring George Formby (1904–61).
[76] Prince was a dog.

4 Monday Went to school per usual. Played football today and when we were dressing in the gym a plane came over and parted my hair for me. Had a Bindle book from the library but it is not such a good book.[77]

5 Tuesday Finished my model in woodwork today and I have only to buy handles for it now. Worked in the garden tonight and sawed up a pit prop which I found in the railway line and it was very large. We used the two man saw.

6 Wednesday Went to see the hockey house match between Leisan and Caradog. We won. We went down to Uncle Ben's and played Monopoly. Dillwyn won under my managership. I had no ink so I did not do my homework.

7 Thursday Played for the house against Caradog today. We won 8–3. I played sideman to the hooker.[78] The tries were scored by C. Owen and G. Parkhouse.[79] Trevor kicked the goal and I held the ball. It was an easy victory.

8 Friday Dillwyn birthday today and of course I forgot to buy the card for him. He was 14 years old today. We had a last minute fixture with Eastern and it was found that Mahoney, Jones, Phillips and Lambourne are unable to play.[80]

9 Saturday Played Eastern today with two more absentees. Butt and F. Williams.[81] It was a hard game and we were beat 8–0. I went to the Cach in the Evening. Graham came down to see me playing. England won today.[82]

10 Sunday Went to chapel all day. After chapel this morn I went with Plum over the woods (played for the Eastern against me yesterday).

11 Monday Played footer with the seniors. But only a runabout and a bit of scrummaging. We are having the hard game tomorrow on the Athletic field.[83] I have an idea that I will be playing for the seniors against Neath on Thursday.

---

[77] Herbert George Jenkins (1876–1923) wrote a series of books featuring the character 'Bindle'.
[78] 'Sideman to the hooker' – what is usually termed a prop forward.
[79] Cliff W. Owen or Owens, a fellow pupil.
[80] Eric Lambourne, a fellow pupil who later became a teacher and a headmaster.
[81] Ronald Butt, a fellow pupil, lived in Cwmafan. Freddie Williams (1926—) was to enjoy a highly successful career as a speedway rider with the Wembley Lions team in London, becoming world champion twice, in 1950 and 1953.
[82] A special wartime rugby international was arranged to raise money for various charities. Wales played England at Cardiff Arms Park, losing by 9 points to 18. A return match at Gloucester in April saw another English victory, this time by 17 points to 3.
[83] Talbot Athletic Ground, home of Aberavon Rugby Football Club, which was shortly to be converted into a site for barrage balloons.

12 Tuesday Went to bed early tonight about 9.15. Played rugger with the firsts. Walter Vickery turned out with us and could he play.[84] Revised some English. Started woodwork test this morning a dove tail joint.

13 Wednesday My name was up on the board to play against Neath County in Neath. Dillwyn and I fetched stones for Uncle Ben to make a bed for the cement. After that we broke a box for him. We both had a tanner and a game of Monopoly.

14 Thursday Played football in Neath County. We lost 20–0. This is the biggest defeat I have ever played in. They were much superior to us. I went down Ben's in the night to play Monopoly. Peggy won for the 1st time.

15 Friday We had a filthy time in school today. Everyone booed us cause we lost to Neath. Last night when I went down Ben's Miss Griffith saw me walking with Peggy and she told me to do my homework.[85]

16 Saturday Went to Majestic to see *Stanley and Livingstone*.[86] I had a new trousers off Tom Henry and Graham had one too. Did all my errands in the morning had a 1/- off Tom and I went to the 1/3 in the Majestic.[87]

17 Sunday Went up Cwmafan with Rhianon and I went to hear the Party rehearsing [. . .]

18 Monday Feeling very ill today but I took up Tom's clothes and heard him sing in the choir. They sang fairly well. I came straight down and went to bed. I did some swotting in bed but I was still pretty bad.

19 Tuesday Went to school this morning but I felt so ill that I did not go in the afternoon and so I missed Chem exam. Did a little swotting for Geog and Welsh. I did not do much as I couldn't concentrate.

20 Wednesday We had a not too good Geog paper and a lousy Welsh one. But I managed in both. Went down Uncle Ben's in the night and he ticked me off for not taking the planks back to T.H.[88]

---

[84] Walter Vickery (1909–2000) was capped four times (as a Number 8) by Wales in 1938 and 1939, and captained Aberavon in the 1936–7 and 1945–6 seasons. Father George Vickery (1879–1970) had played for Aberavon and England.

[85] Miss E. E. Griffiths (not Griffith) taught Welsh at Port Talbot Secondary School.

[86] *Stanley and Livingstone* (1939), directed by Henry King (1886–1982), starring Spencer Tracy (1900–67).

[87] The Majestic cinema in Bethany Square in the centre of Port Talbot had opened in 1938. It may be what is today the Job Centre building.

[88] 'T.H.' – Thomas Henry, Richard's brother.

21 Thursday Had English exam this morning and it was a fairly good one I did an essay on 'My Brother' and didn't I give it socks. Went down the park to play football with Wherle and co.

22 Friday Sis went to Cymanfa tonight.[89] All the Boys went down the Beach this afternoon and we found a barrel of Guinness stout but, the Coastguard tipped it into the sea. There might be a reward.

23 Saturday Not looking forward to exams at all but they must come. Did not go to pictures because I went yesterday I stayed in the house and had a good read. There will be no school Monday again the same as yesterday. Saw Phipps playing tennis in the Park.[90]

24 Sunday Went to chapel all day.[91] There was a good crowd in school today and in chapel in the evening [. . .]

25 Monday Went down Uncle Ben's this morning to fetch stones for the cement bed Dillwyn came with me. Went to Majestic to see *King of the River*.[92] Plaza opened today and it was all crowded out.[93]

26 Tuesday Had exams today Geom and Physics. Physics was better than expected and Geom was good too but I just couldn't remember the necessary things. Went to the park to play with my ball. There is a terrific wind up today. [. . .]

27 Wednesday Had exams today. Algebra in the morning but nothing in the afternoon. Went down the park in the night. Have got a new lace to my football off D. and had a row off Sis for playing football with my school shoes on but I can take it.

28 Thursday We had a trigonometry exam this morning and no exam this afternoon because the timetable was changed. I had an afternoon off reading *Realities of War* by P. Gibbs.[94] Went down Park and ripped my nail. Did not play football.

---

[89] 'Cymanfa' is a reference to a Gymanfa Ganu, a Welsh singing festival.
[90] Possibly Nettie Phipps. There were tennis courts in the Talbot Memorial Park.
[91] This was Easter Sunday.
[92] There is no record of this film or anything resembling it showing in Port Talbot at this time.
[93] The Plaza cinema had undergone refurbishment and was reopened (as Port Talbot's 'new luxury super-cinema') on Easter Monday. The building still stands in Station Road, although now derelict.
[94] Sir Philip Hamilton Gibbs, *Realities of War* (1920, revised edn 1929).

29 Friday We had arithmetic and history today the last thank goodness. My name is upon the list as reserve but I will play probably against Maesteg.[95] Graham and Edie were down. I had 3d off Edie. Went down Ben's for a game of Monopoly.

30 Saturday Played Maesteg and lost 6–3 and we couldn't blame the ref. this time. Went over the park – all the boys were pinching tennis balls. Went to Cach to see Gracie Fields in *Shipyard Sally*.[96] All Propaganda.

31 Sunday Now that we've finished exams, I'm looking forward to a week of rest. Went all day to Chapel. Mr Bowen absent tonight.[97]

APRIL

1 Monday I had a shock today I only had 19 in Welsh but I can take it. Had footer in the gym and had a great time tackling the mattress which was tied in the middle by a string. I had a nasty smack on my neck.

2 Tuesday Ran in the road race and finished 11th out of entry of 28 people. Our house was last in the race. We are going to play the County juniors tomorrow [. . .]. I had a fairly good tennis racket off Mr Smith.

3 Wednesday Played County and lost 5–0. Alun Thomas was the County star.[98] Our forwards were outplayed and our backs were slow to force home an advantage. The try they scored was not a very good one and I thought it not.

4 Thursday Went to see the seniors playing and they lost 3–0 and though they were much the better team. Only about twice they hooked the ball all through the match. Eifion did very well and hooked almost 100%.[99]

5 Friday Had a sing song in the Hall and I had to sing alone before the whole school. The song was 'Clementine'.[100] Broke up today. Had tennis in the school courts with Royston Palmer. He won.

---

[95] Maesteg (1931 population 25,570), an industrial town in the Llynfi valley, about five miles east of Taibach.
[96] *Shipyard Sally* (1939), directed by Monty Banks (1897–1950), starring Gracie Fields (1898–1979).
[97] Rees Bowen, a deacon at Noddfa.
[98] Alun Thomas (1926–91) went on to play first-class rugby for Swansea, Cardiff and Llanelli. He was capped 13 times by Wales, went on tour with the British Lions to South Africa in 1955, and returned as tour manager for the Lions in 1974.
[99] Eifion H. N. Davies, a sixth-former, who went on to become a headteacher.
[100] Presumably 'Oh My Darling, Clementine'.

6 Saturday Went up Cwmafan. Went to Ivor's and we went for a walk up on top road. There was a car smash on top road last night. Nobody was killed.[101]

7 Sunday Went to chapel morn afternoon and night.

8 Monday Took my bat over in the morning to have 5 strings put in. I went back in the evening (5) and it was done – cost me 3/-. I had a lend of 2/6 off Sis. Bucket of D.[102]

9 Tuesday Went up Mountain and had a bucket of D. Went again afternoon and had another. Played tennis in the park this afternoon with Wherle and co. stayed in tonight.

10 Wednesday Went up to fetch dung and I washed by the farmer. But he didn't catch me. Played tennis in the park with Roy Palmer in the noon and night. Stinks and D. Walters played with us in the night. Hopeless game.

11 Thursday Fetched a bucket of D. Prince was chasing the sheep and Daddy James saw him so I can't take Prince up the mountain again. Played football with Eastern in the noon and with Wherle and co. in the night.

12 Friday Helped to chuck in a load of coal for Auntie Hannah.[103] Then I went over Mary Ann Jones to clean her chimney for her.[104] We had 1/0. Went up the colliery in the noon to fetch Elfed's pay for him.

13 Saturday Did all my errands in the morning and read a library book in the noon. Went to Cach to see *Four Daughters*.[105] Came home and read a bit before going to bed.

14 Sunday The papers has been in a week now only another 51. Went to chapel [. . .] They are planing the chapel floor so I took my hymn book home.

15 Monday Played football today with Stan Williams' ball. There was only about 5 aside. We won easily. I had a row off Sis for getting home late. Played with C. Eynon in the afternoon.[106] Played cricket and football [. . .]

---

[101] A Maesteg to Port Talbot bus crashed on Tydraw Hill. One passenger died two days later from injuries suffered.
[102] Bucket of dung, or cow and horse manure. Richard would collect this from the mountainside and sell it.
[103] Auntie Hannah Oates, Richard's first cousin once removed.
[104] Mary Ann Jones was an elderly neighbour who lived on Inkerman Row East.
[105] *Four Daughters* (1938), directed by Michael Curtiz (1886–1962), starring Claude Rains (1889–1967) and John Garfield (1913–52).
[106] Colin T. C. Eynon, a fellow pupil.

16 Tuesday Went up Pontrhydyfen this morning to fetch a tennis press but it was needed so I did not have it. About 11.0 I went down to Tom's and had dinner there. Went to see Cassie's grave. Rode to park – played football.

17 Wednesday Played tennis with Ron Butt, B. Fallows and Tr Cound.[107] We had a fine game. That was in the noon. Went up Cwm in the night and met Ivor. He gave me a tanner. Had a bob off Dai. Went ½ with Sis. [. . .]

18 Thursday It has been raining pouring for hours. It started delightfully. Went down Ben's this afternoon with Dillwyn. Ben won easily. But we'll have him back. Dai Owen went to the Army today.[108] Hitler can stop when he likes.

19 Friday Fetched a bucket of D. There was another man up there but I was very keen today I could smell D. a mile off. This mountain is nothing but D. Played tennis with A. and G. Powell. They are hopeless players. Went down Ben's.

20 Saturday Did all my errands. I plucked up courage to ask all the people on my round to keep papers for me. Most of them agreed. Went to the Cach. Supposed to play tennis with Ivor. But it was too wet. [. . .]

21 Sunday [. . .] Went to Chapel morn afternoon and night. School coming nearer and nearer. Very good Sermon.

22 Monday Did not play tennis with Colin or anybody. Went up the park in the night and played football with Colin Wherle and Co. Did not play all night as usual. Finished about 7.30. G. Parkhouse and Bonehead went to flicks.[109]

23 Tuesday Took papers for wall up Cwmafan. Had money and went to Cach to see *Gorilla*.[110] School a week today. Called in Neville Williams and borrowed his pump as my tyres were soft.[111] *Gorilla* was good.

24 Wednesday Played with J. Beynon T. George and C. Eynon in morn and with R. Butt in noon.[112] Went for my first dip of the season it was cold but nice. It is a glorious day. Walked back and fore went over park after.

---

[107] Truda Cound was a fellow pupil and a skilled tennis player.
[108] Dai Owen, Richard's sister Hilda's husband.
[109] Presumably Arthur 'Bonehead' Jenkins. 'Flicks' is a colloquial term for the cinema.
[110] *The Gorilla* (1939), directed by Allan Dwan (1885–1981).
[111] Arthur Neville Williams, a fellow pupil, who lived in Cwmafan.
[112] J. Beynon was a fellow pupil and a talented cricketer.

25 Thursday Went to fetch D. and had to wait ages for it. I met G. Powell up there. Went down the park about 11.0 and played cricket with the practice teams. Went to the park. Played football.

26 Friday Sis went up Cwmafan to paper again. I fetched Elfed's pay. In the morn I went over to the paper hangers and told them to pack up for Sis. Went over the park and took papers for Auntie Edie. More than usual.

27 Saturday Collected all papers from the people and they came to quite a pile. Anyway I had 6d extra off Auntie Ede. I went up Pont and took Gerwyn for a walk.[113] I had 2/6 off Pop.[114] He was drunk. It is clearance.[115]

28 Sunday Went to chapel per usual. Only 1 more day of hols. Went for a walk with D. D. and J. Williams and Hubert David [. . .][116]

29 Monday Went down to change my library book this morning and helped Uncle Evan and Edwin to carry blackout to Mrs Hopkins – Had two glasses of Pop.[117] I am determined to work hard in school this term. Letter for Sis from Dai Jenkins but not for me. Also Dai Owen.

30 Tuesday School started today. Had wood work all morning and did not take Gym. After starting a tie box I converted my labour into a knife box. Had usual lessons this afternoon. Did a little swotting of *Richard II* our new play. It is interesting homework. Real work tonight.

MAY

1 Wednesday Did my Geog and tried my Geometry but I was beaten. Played football against Bowditch's team.[118] We won 6–5. Scored a goal. The farmer came and tried to find my name but I argued that he did not have a notice up. He asked my name and I told him to find out.

---

[113] Pont, meaning Pontrhydyfen and sometimes written as 'Ponty', Richard's birthplace, about three and a half miles north of Taibach. Gerwyn Owen, eldest child of Dai and Hilda Owen, and Richard's nephew.
[114] Richard's father, also named Richard Walter Jenkins (1876–1957), and sometimes referred to as 'Dic Bach' (little Dick).
[115] 'Clearance' refers to the quarterly clearance of personal debt at the Co-op. After clearance, members were allowed to trade again.
[116] 'D.D.' – Dillwyn Dummer. Jack Williams and Hubert Davies (not David), who both lived in Brook Street, Taibach.
[117] Edwin Dummer, Elfed James's brother-in-law, who was married to Margaret Ann, and father of Dillwyn. A Mr and Mrs Hopkins ran a baker's shop nearby in Taibach: their son Anthony had been born in 1937.
[118] Bowditch was a fellow pupil who lived in Margam.

2 Thursday Tried to do my Geom homework but I couldn't. Went down Park and played footer. We had art today and I am starting to copy old English Printing with D. H. Lodwig.[119] I have not heard anything about farmer.

3 Friday Went to school as usual. Did my Geom in Phys with the help of THM I was the only one to do it and have it right. Went down the park in the night and played football. Scored 2 goals. 1st time that Boyo has been on my side.

4 Saturday Did all my errands and went down the park in the noon and played putting. Did a little homework and went to Social. Had tea then went up Park and played putting again with Allan and Dillwyn. Dillwyn won most. I won one. In 25.

5 Sunday Went to Chapel all day. Went for a walk in the evening with Plum and Dill. Nelson had a fight with Palmer.[120] They were stopped.

6 Monday Played football with the Boys tonight. Our Davey is home on hols. and he sleeps with me. What a life. I helped Sis to shift the bed from one room to another and a bed off Mrs Turner over to our house.[121] Sis now sleeps in the front room upstairs.

7 Tuesday Played Dai Rees's team and we won.[122] Just in time by 5 goals to 4. I scored a penalty with my special. Ron Butt was picked as Captain of the Cricket team Juniors and I as vice captain. It came as great shock to us all. We expected B. Phillips to be Captain.

8 Wednesday Only another 5 days before Whitsun. I am writing this in the cold hours of Thursday morning. Davey is going to play Tennis with me on Friday. I wonder if he is very hot. Went down the Park. [. . .] Played putting with R. Palmer and we drew twice. He won the rest.

9 Thursday 4 more days to Whitsun. Great debate in the Commons over the conduct of the War by Chamberlain. Lloyd George made fiery speech. Norway now is lost or practically so. Capture of Narvik imminent by Britain.[123]

---

[119] David Henry Lodwig was a fellow pupil and a talented cricketer.
[120] Eric Nelson, whose family ran a coal merchant's business in Margam.
[121] Mrs Turner was a neighbour in Caradog Street and a member of Noddfa Chapel.
[122] David Rees lived in Taibach. He was to die during active service in the Second World War.
[123] In fact Narvik, in northern Norway, was not taken by Allied forces until 27 May, by which time the situation in France and the Low Countries had become so desperate as to render its capture irrelevant. Accordingly, Allied forces were evacuated from Norway by 7 June.

10 Friday Holland, Luxembourg and Belgium invaded by Adolph and his crazy gang. They arc being held. I think this is Germany's great and first mistake. Played Tennis with Dai. He won. When reached home he was called back.

11 Saturday Germany claims that Holland and Belgium were making alliance with GB. Went to baths this afternoon. Chamberlain resigned yesterday. Churchill new premier Just heard. Attlee Greenwood Eden Sinclair and Alexander and Chamber in cab.[124]

12 Sunday Went to chapel all day and had tickets for Whitsun Treat. Elfed is not having his annual hols next week not even his 1 day bank holiday. Roy Palmer is coming to Ogmore.[125]

13 Monday Holiday. News on wireless says we go back to school tomorrow. Very shocked. Went to Ogmore lovely weather. Palmer and I had a pile of fun. Met feller named Josie Jenkins who owned a farm there. Knew all the sheep's names by heart. Had 1/- left.

14 Tuesday No holiday today as per usual. Went to school. Our form put the nets up. After much struggling with it we had a game of cricket which was a refreshing reward. Saw Form IV rehearsing their play in the Hall. Played cricket with Wherle. We bought a new ball.

15 Wednesday Went to school. War improving for us. Dutch stopped fighting. Stayed in and did my homework. Had a cricket practice with the Juniors. Some of the boys were not there because of the play but we had a good game. Everybody had a knock and a bowl.

16 Thursday Played cricket with Wherle and Co. Had a knock with the Seniors. Eastern lost to Centrals by an innings. Ivor Jones bowled them all out.[126] I scored 34 not out against Wherley's bowling. We won by 20 runs. I cannot bowl good length at all.

17 Friday Played cricket. D. H. Lodwig has left school to work in the steel works. In a way I'm sorry. Played cricket with the 'boys'. I scored 24 clean

---

[124] Presumably 'in [the] cabinet'. Winston Churchill (1874–1965) replaced Neville Chamberlain (1869–1940) as Prime Minister on 10 May 1940 and included in his new cabinet Clement Attlee (1883–1967), Arthur Greenwood (1880–1954), Anthony Eden (1897–1977), Archibald Sinclair (1890–1970), A. V. Alexander (1885–1965) and Chamberlain himself.

[125] Ogmore by Sea is a coastal settlement four miles south of Bridgend, a popular destination for holidaymakers.

[126] Ivor Jones, a fast bowler and first-class cricketer, lived in Brook Street, Taibach.

bowled. My average is now 58 as I was not out in my 1st innings. Left my whites strap and coat in school.

18 Saturday Went to Cach to see Will Fyffe and D. Fairbanks Junior in *Rulers of the sea*.[127] Went down the park and had a game of putting with B. Phipps. I won most of the games. Highlight of Cach was Billy Bennett with his great poem 'Out in the Jungle where men are men'.[128]

19 Sunday Went to chapel morn afternoon and night. Dr Rees gave a good sermon and after it all he made a nasty wisecrack about Uncle Charles.[129] Absent.

20 Monday Played cricket with Wherle and Co. I had 3 inns 12, 1 and 23 which made my average 24. Went down the Sandfields to play cricket with the Seniors.[130] Archie bowled me.[131] School as usual. Weygand now instead of Gamelin in the War.[132]

21 Tuesday At four o Clock Richard Walter shits his Pants.[133]

This entry was written by Elfed in an attempt to spoil the Book but it will remain if I live to be a 100.

22 Wednesday Went to see *As you like it* as performed by Form IV. It was very good. T. George was the star of the evening as Touchstone the Clown.[134] The War has taken a serious turn against us. The Huns are only 15 miles from the Channel. But am confident that we'll pull up.[135]

23 Thursday Played tennis with Jakeweed Williams.[136] Went up the park and played cricket with Stan Walter of international and Rydal School fame.[137] He is a beautiful bat. The war is going badly for us but am confident of victory.

---

[127] *Rulers of the Sea* (1939), directed by Frank Lloyd (1886–1960), starring Douglas Fairbanks Jr. (1909–2000), Will Fyffe (1884–1947) and Margaret Lockwood (1916–90).

[128] Billy Bennett (1887–1942) was a comedian, film actor and monologuist.

[129] Uncle Charles Thomas was Richard's mother's brother.

[130] Sandfields, to the immediate north-west of Aberavon, now covered by housing and industrial estates.

[131] 'Archie' Richard Davies.

[132] Maxime Weygand (1897–1965) replaced Maurice Gamelin (1872–1958) as Commander-in-Chief of the Allied Forces following Gamelin's dismissal on 15 May.

[133] This sentence is written in pencil and in a different hand.

[134] It was presented in modern dress. Trevor George had had a small part in the school's 1939 production of *The Doctor's Dilemma*.

[135] Bragg (*Rich*, 34), apparently citing Philip Burton's then unpublished manuscript, misquotes as 'am confident we'll pull through'.

[136] Jake Williams, a fellow pupil, who later became a teacher.

[137] Rydal School, Colwyn Bay. Stanley T. J. Walter, who lived in Abbey Road, Port Talbot, also played full back for Aberavon RFC.

24 Friday The King made a speech today and made Sunday a day of National Prayers for the boys in France. Big meeting coming nearer now. Am looking forward to seeing preacher Mr J. Derlwyn Evans of Ynysmeudwy.[138]

25 Saturday Went to Cach and saw *Rose of Washington Square*.[139] T. Henry came down and I had very acceptable dough off him. I have bought a tick off T. George to go to play the next Tuesday.[140] Mr Wellington was in our house when I reached home tonight.

26 Sunday What a rousing sermon of Derlwyn Evans tonight when he said that our country's sheet is not too clean also.

27 Monday Went to school all day. Had a knock in the nets this afternoon with Smite and Tadpole bowling for me.[141] I'm afraid that I am rather weak on the off side, but should score runs this season. Ron Butt had knock.

28 Tuesday Went to Regent to see *Captain Fury*.[142] It was a jolly good show. Illustrating the liberation of the settlers in Australia by Captain Fury who was a convict. [...]

29 Wednesday I keep a War Diary now. Played tennis with T. George, D. Parr and J. Beynon.[143] We had a jolly game but not a good one. Don tried continually to beat the altitude record. We lost the ball about 7 times.

30 Thursday Had a letter from Will my soldier brother.[144] In it he said that cinema war pictures were nothing to reality. It wasn't a very long letter. Went to see the County sports. Saw K. Cordy win the ½ mile with plenty to spare.[145] Tudor won.[146]

31 Friday Had preliminaries for sports. After going around with P. Lane etc. in the 440 I was surprised that I could stick it so.[147] I am going to enter for the middle 440 yards. And I am sure I ought to win it.

---

[138] Ynysmeudwy, an industrial settlement two miles north-east of Pontardawe, in the Tawe or Swansea valley.

[139] *Rose of Washington Square* (1939), directed by Gregory Ratoff (1897–1960), starring Al Jolson (1886–1950).

[140] 'tick' – ticket.

[141] 'Smite' and 'Tadpole' were nicknames given to teachers. 'Tadpole' was Mr Jack Nicholas.

[142] *Captain Fury* (1939), directed by Hal Roach (1892–1992), starring Brian Aherne (1902–86) in the title role.

[143] Don Parr lived at 10, Mill Row.

[144] Will Jenkins (1911–86), Richard's brother, had been in the Army for over nine years. He served in the Machine Gun Corps, and would be evacuated from Dunkirk.

[145] The spelling is Cordey in the local press.

[146] Tudor was the name of the house in the County School.

[147] Patrick A. Lane, a fellow pupil and talented athlete, who later rose to a senior position in the National Coal Board.

JUNE

1 Saturday Did all my errands as usual and changed my library book in the noon. Went to the Regent and I saw a picture called *Four Feathers*.[148] Showed what family tradition can do to a man. This man was sent four white feathers. But he proved them wrong.

2 Sunday Went to chapel all day and Dr Rees gave his usual sermon. I am afraid that Dr Rees goes terribly sometimes.

3 Monday Sports nearing. Not very confident in our House's victory in the Sports. Road race has been run today. Morgan came 2nd Caradog 1st Iestyn 3rd. Have entered the 440 in the sports and putting the shot and javelin.

4 Tuesday I have already won the long jump and the second place in the high jump. Ran with Haffield for honour of representing house in school sports. I won by about 30 yards in the quarter. Hope I can repeat it.

5 Wednesday Straight after school I went up the field and practice the 440. I have worked out the positions as to where I go all out for the finish. Am afraid that Tanner can stick it. I hope not.

6 Thursday Sports. I won the putt the shot by 18 ins (from R. Butt) with a throw of 31ft 7 ins. I came third in the Javelin through bad luck. I came first in the 440. My worked out spurt came off. Total 17 points.

7 Friday Today Mr Smith said that I was to run the 440 yards and putt the shot and long jump in M. Ash.[149] I am very nervous about the result. I hope there are no crack runners there because I'm no crack.

8 Saturday Went to M. Ash. I came 6th in shot out of 23. 7th in long jump out of 30. Bridgend won senior sports again. J. Beynon and B. Phillips both won their heats in the hurdles. But lost in the finals. Did not run.

9 Sunday Went to Chapel all day. After Chapel I went down the beach. Have been expecting our Will home. I had a dip.[150] First I ever had on Sunday.

---

[148] *The Four Feathers* (1939), directed by Zoltan Korda (1895–1961), starring John Clements (1910–88) and Ralph Richardson (1902–83). Richard was later to work for Alexander Korda (1893–1956) and with Ralph Richardson.
[149] Mountain Ash, a colliery town (1931 population 38,386) in the Cynon valley, 17 miles north-east of Taibach.
[150] In the sea.

10 Monday Italy declared war on us. Don Parr and I went down the beach. We had great fun I had a knock in cricket at the nets. Tadpole heard THM swearing and made a joke out of it.

11 Tuesday Had Woodwork and finished my model but I'll spend next Tuesday polishing it up. [. . .] Had cricket practice but I didn't have a knock all through.

12 Wednesday Went to School as usual. We had a P Study last lesson because Burton is not here.[151] We have the usual rotten singing now that he is gone. The newcomer can not do it half so good as he can.

13 Thursday We will play County and Eastern tomorrow and Saturday morning. If we can't beat Eastern we ought to be shot. Army doing badly in France.

14 Friday Played Eastern and after getting them all out for 46 we went in and beat them by 2 wickets. I. Williams and K. Williams being top scores with 17 and 15 respectively.[152] I scored 1 bowled by the 4th ball I received.

15 Saturday Played County lost by 2 runs. I played badly scored 0 bowled second ball. Went up the park and saw Jack Nicholas with his niece and a little baby. Also Swansea beat GKB in tennis.[153] There was two blackmen playing.

16 Sunday Went to chapel all day as usual. After chapel in the night I went up the park with 'Jakeweed' Williams. [. . .]

17 Monday The French have asked Hitler for Peace Terms. We played cricket with Jack Nicholas. Had some fun too. I think there is to be practice tomorrow on the concrete pitch again.

18 Tuesday We did not play cricket afterwards but we are going to play tomorrow. Finished my model and brought it home and am going to use it in my bed-room.

19 Wednesday We had a T. Trial today and they gave me a bowl. I took 2 wickets for 7 runs. I scored 2 run out. My average is now .75 which is not very good but I haven't started yet. Todd said everything OK.[154]

---

[151] Private study. Philip Burton, *Early Doors: My Life and the Theatre* (New York: The Dial Press, 1969), 81, notes that he 'spent most of the summer of 1940 in bed, suffering from a rheumatic complaint that affected the heart'.
[152] Ken Williams was from Pantdu, and a good cricketer.
[153] GKB being Guest Keen and Baldwins, the local steel company.
[154] 'Todd' is A. Leslie Evans, a teacher at Central School and a keen local historian.

20 *Thursday* Jake Williams myself and Brin Phillips took a ball and bat and went for a knock up the nets. [. . .] I am in the running for captaincy of the Town Team. There was an air raid over here last night.

21 *Friday* I went to the Cach to see *Frontier Marshal*.[155] I am starting swotting this weekend for the exams week next Monday. [. . .] There are rumours of an air raid on Bridgend.

22 *Saturday* I went to the pictures tonight and I saw a great picture a bit on the sob stuff side. I had a 1/- off Edie. Sis went to Pyle to an Eisteddfod.[156] I saw a broken aeroplane being towed on a lorry. I think it was the Cwm crash.

23 *Sunday* I swotted very hard today and learned Chem practically off by heart. I stayed home from chapel.

24 *Monday* I bowled in games at the nets and I am improving tremendously now. I can keep a dead length for about 10 overs which is good. I swotted Geom tonight but not so much as Chemistry.

25 *Tuesday* This morning at 2.30 I had experienced and survived my first air raid. Fortunately the plane did not come over P. Talbot at all. We all went into Mrs Jackson's cellar where space was a bit cramped. I did not hear anything.

26 *Wednesday* Found out that I was captain of the Town Team to play against Neath schoolboys on Friday. We have never beaten Neath and it would be a great honour if we could pull it off this year.

27 *Thursday* It is rumoured that German planes flew over Port Talbot but owing to a muddle the siren was not used. We had a practice (school team) tonight and members of the Town Team also turned up for a knock

28 *Friday* Sis's Birthday – After looking forward to playing against Neath I found that when I got down there it was too late for me to play. The Town lost by about 6 wickets. It was a time limit match. The sec did well.

---

[155] *Frontier Marshal* (1939), directed by Allan Dwan, starring Randolph Scott (1898–1987).
[156] Pyle, an industrial settlement five miles to the south-east of Taibach.

29 Saturday I went up the Ynys cricket ground to play Trefelin but rain stopped it.[157] Last night saw the biggest air raid in South Wales and the 1st in Port Talbot. Franchis and a house on Tydraw Hill are in a mess.[158] Others too.

30 Sunday Iona Gwen and Thomas Henry and Graham were down here. We are playing Trevelin tomorrow. Elfed is not going to work because he disagrees with pay for it.[159]

JULY

1 Monday We had our first exams today and 1 this afternoon because there was an air raid in here and 9 bombs were dropped. One just missed the gasometer and another some munitions trucks.[160]

2 Tuesday We won our match with Trefelin yesterday and we are now in the semi-final for the shield. It is rumoured that we are playing Neath on Saturday in Neath and Cardiff the following Friday.

3 Wednesday I am sleeping in Mrs Jackson's tonight with Bill.[161] I have slept all the week up the Side. Marian and Rhian are staying in Ponty and Sis is staying in Cwm while Elfed is working nights.

4 Thursday We played Central and lost by about 10 runs. We could have won easily if we had only played carefully but we all went in to have a knock and so failed. I scored 2 caught very well.

5 Friday Played Neath in the Ferry today and as usual we lost but we did not do wholly bad.[162] I scored my usual but I can [be] sure that I could have done better if I had only taken my time.

---

[157] Trefelin (sometimes Trevelin) was a school in the Velindre area of Port Talbot, north of the town centre, on the west bank of the Afan. The Ynys cricket ground was at Ynys y Gored, on the east bank of the Afan, between Velindre and Cwmafan.

[158] The west window of Franchi Bros. confectioners, situated at Huddersfield Buildings, Station Road, Port Talbot, was shattered when a bomb exploded in the street outside. A pair of houses on Tydraw Hill was split in two by another bomb. Nine bombs in all were dropped on Port Talbot, but no one was killed.

[159] Additional Sunday shifts in the coal industry had been adopted so as to maximize production, although with the fall of France the market for South Wales coal collapsed.

[160] The gasometer, which actually had been emptied earlier in the war, was a regular target for German attacks.

[161] Billy Jackson.

[162] The Ferry meaning Briton Ferry, south of Neath on the east bank of the Nedd and about four miles north-west of Taibach.

6 Saturday Did all my errands and went up Cwm in the morn where I met Ivor and T. Henry. A very serious thing has happened. Money has been stolen by someone from T. Henry to the extent of £5–0–0.

7 Sunday Went to chapel as usual and had 6d off Edie who came down with Graham to tea.

8 Monday Everything has been very quiet lately but another air raid is not far off. We had our last exam this morning. It was trigonom and it was alright. I went up Cwmafan to see TH after going up Pont.

9 Tuesday We had an air raid warning last night and we could distinctly hear the plane. It was for this reason that I did not go to school, as I slept late. I went to see *I am the law* with E. G. Robinson.[163] [. . .]

10 Wednesday Put up cardboard all morn in school to stop blast. There was an aerial battle over here today which was very one sided. 3 Spitfires and 1 German.[164] I don't know the result of the battle yet.

11 Thursday No exams or anything in school today and we just muck about. We have had a quiet time lately regarding air raids but not for long I suppose – I must remember to take Dai's clothes to Llantwit Major.

12 Friday Had an air raid today or should I say tonight and we were in the shelters for ¾ of hour. When we went to bed it was quarter to one. Don Parr and I helped to nail up blast stoppers in Form II.

13 Saturday I am writing this during an air raid warning. Sis is down the cellar with Mrs Jackson and Olive Rees. Did all my errands etc. and went down the road to fetch papers during the raid. Longest raid yet.

14 Sunday Gerwyn is down again this weekend and can he talk. Went to chapel morn noon and night as usual.

15 Monday We had 3 air raid warnings today. Two of them during school hours. Played cricket tonight with Wherle. I had a scrap with Dai Lodwig. I thought I was going up Cwm. I had 73 in arith.

---

[163] *I Am the Law* (1938), directed by Alexander Hall (1894–1968), starring Edward G. Robinson (1893–1973). Richard was a great admirer of Robinson.
[164] The Spitfire was the Royal Air Force's best-known fighter aircraft, heavily used during the Battle of Britain.

16 Tuesday Today after clamouring for History marks Mr Davies unbent so far as to tell me I was top which is good enough.[165] I think I have done well in Trig also as Tom Lane saw 22 marks on the 1st two pages.[166]

17 Wednesday I found out that though I was top in History I only had 53 marks. Playing football and cricket anagrams with Parkhouse. Played with the boys and scored 19. Central are playing County tomorrow.

18 Thursday Have not had any more marks. We are only having 3 weeks hols. County beat Central by 100 odd runs. Helped 'Happy' and Bobby to erect blast stoppers.[167] Had air raid last night.

19 Friday Have had Trig marks. I had 56 which makes my average for five exams 55.6. With luck I might have a final average of about 50. The reason for drop in average is 39 in Phys. But even that was more than expected.

20 Saturday Did my errands quickly this morning as the Town played Aberdare this afternoon. When we reached Aberdare I had the shock of my life when I found I was not picked but it learned me not to be too cocksure.[168]

21 Sunday Went to chapel all day. Today there are three balloons up in Taibach and one down Margam.[169] [. . .]

22 Monday Went to school as usual I had 67 in Chemistry and I must truly say that I was disappointed. I expected more. My average is now about 57.5. I played tennis with John Beynon tonight. [. . .]

23 Tuesday We had yet another air raid yesterday or should I say last night. This was the longest on record and the 4th air raid in successive nights.[170] Went to the Cach to see *I lost a Million*.[171]

---

[165] Mr J. Vyrnwy Davies, history teacher at the Sec, who later became Headmaster at Dyffryn Comprehensive, and whose nickname was 'Tout', a reference to the distinguished professional historian Thomas Frederick Tout (1855–1929).

[166] Tom or Tommy Lane, also to be involved in the YMCA drama club.

[167] 'Happy' is Mr George M. Hapgood, 'Bobby' is Mr Robert M. Owen. Both were teachers at Port Talbot Secondary School. George Hapgood was a talented amateur actor and appeared in a number of P. H. Burton's productions. He also served as an air raid warden, and as a Flight Commander in the Air Training Corps.

[168] Aberdare, the major town in the Cynon valley (1931 population 48,746), 16 miles north-east of Taibach.

[169] Margam is the area immediately to the south-east of Taibach, including Margam Park.

[170] The air raid sirens sounded on 17 occasions in the Port Talbot area in July 1940.

[171] This may refer to either *I'll Give a Million* (1938), directed by Walter Lang (1896–1972), starring Warner Baxter (1891–1951) and Peter Lorre (1904–64), or to *I Stole a Million* (1939), directed by Frank Tuttle (1892–1963) starring George Raft (1895–1980) and Claire Trevor (1909–2000).

21 Wednesday Went to school per usual. Another air raid last night. Breaking up tomorrow for 3 weeks. Played cricket for Wherle's team against Bonehead's team. We are going to play the 2nd inns tomorrow.

25 Thursday Had my report this morning and it was very good compared with last term's report. I realized an average of 56.5. We have broken up for 3 weeks. No air raid Went to play down shelter with Jake.

26 Friday When Jake and I went walking over the Brombil valley we found a delightful little tributary valley which was very beautiful.[172] It was made of all hidden waterfalls [. . .]

27 Saturday We had a two hour air raid last night. 11–1 o'clock. Only 5 people were down there. Three Jacksons and Sis and Elfed. I stayed in bed. Went [to] the Regent to see *Naughty Marrietta*.[173]

28 Sunday Did not go to Chapel this morning – the 1st time for ages. During my walk down Margam I ripped my leg and my trousers.

29 Monday Ivor's Birthday. Played another of those Colin v Arthur matches. We won easily. I took 5 wickets for 9 runs and I scored 22. I was top in both cases. It is a job to find something to do in these days.

30 Tuesday Went up mountain to help Jake carry and cut grass clotches for the top of his air raid shelter.[174] I was offered 6d but I refused it. Went to Cach to see D. Wakefield and J. Benny.[175]

31 Wednesday This morning Dillwyn came up and told that there was a job down the Coop for me. When I went down I was detailed for a boy to shout 'Baker' in the Streets.[176]

AUGUST

1 Thursday Dug up the spare patch in the garden and stoned it. Went down Margam park to see Eastern play Central. Found that I and Phillip and Wherle had game.[177] I scored 1 not out.

---

[172] The Brombil valley opens out on to the coastal plain at Margam, south of Taibach.
[173] *Naughty Marietta* (1935), directed by W. S. Van Dyke (1889–1943), starring Jeanette MacDonald (1906–65) and Nelson Eddy (1901–67).
[174] A protective cover.
[175] Duggie Wakefield (1899–1951). Jack Benny. One imagines they were starring in different films.
[176] Dillwyn Dummer had left school to work as a baker's roundsman for the Co-op.
[177] 'Phillip': Brinley Phillips.

2 Friday Went up the Colliery to fetch Elfed's pay. He gave me 6d and Verdun gave me a 1/-.[178] As soon as I came home I had a haircut in Sandies. Later on I had 6d off Dad James. Went to Cach to see *Arsenal St*.[179]

3 Saturday Had a lot more money again today. 6d off Charles and 6d off Mam James. Went to Regent to see *The Flying Deuces*.[180] I spent 2/7 in the night's entertainment. Air raids every night.

4 Sunday We had a new preacher in Chapel today. His name was A. E. Lewis. I have his autograph. He was good.

5 Monday I had 1/5 off Sis today and I spent it all. Went to Regent to see *Q Planes*.[181] Roy Palmer came with me and afterwards we went up the park to muck around.

6 Tuesday Holiday – Went to baths with Brin Phillips and Chas Hockin.[182] There weren't many there [. . .] Had much fun. Went up the park to play cricket scored 6 and 11 not out.

7 Wednesday Went to the bath with Brin Phillips and his cousin. We had a fine time there. I had an argument with Mr Bragg the manager.[183] Went to fetch blackberries with Elfed. We filled his work box.

8 Thursday Went down the Coop for Sis and met Susie Preece down there.[184] Went down Glen Parkhouse's this afternoon to play billiards. I won 2d then lost a 1d again Went to Cach. Davey came down.[185]

9 Friday Went down Glen Parkhouse's all day today and I had a deficiency of 2d at the end of the pool play. Sis went up Cwm. When I got home there was a terrible smell of tar all over Taibach.

---

[178] Verdun Jenkins (1916–2002), Richard's brother.

[179] *The Arsenal Stadium Mystery* (1939), directed by Thorold Dickinson (1903–84), starring Leslie Banks (1890–1952).

[180] *The Flying Deuces* (1939), directed by Edward Sutherland (1895–1973), starring Stan Laurel (1890–1965) and Oliver Hardy (1892–1957).

[181] *Q Planes* (1939), directed by Tim Whelan (1893–1957), starring Ralph Richardson and Laurence Olivier (1907–89). Richard was to become a good friend of Olivier.

[182] Charles Hockin, a friend of Richard's, who later became a schoolmaster in Taibach.

[183] George Henry Bragg was caretaker/manager of the public baths (erected in 1900 but refurbished or rebuilt in 1938) on Forge Road.

[184] Susie Preece was a fellow pupil at Port Talbot Secondary School. She would later be Richard's girlfriend.

[185] Richard's brother David.

10 Saturday Did all my errands etc. and I went to the baths this afternoon with Charlie Hockin. In the evening I went to the Regent. I contemplated giving up my job with Auntie Ede because I cannot get enough papers.

11 Sunday Had a new preacher who gave us a very long winded sermon but which was quite nice.

12 Monday Went down the Coop for Sis and changed my library book the same time. Cleaned the windows also. Went to Cach to see Will Hay in *Where's That Fire?*[186]

13 Tuesday I was supposed to fit for a suit but I came home too late from Glen Parkhouse's. Did a lot of work today for Sis. Helped Peter Dan to push his cart up the hill. I won 2d off Eddie Miles and 2d off 'Bonehead' Jenkins.

14 Wednesday Went down Parkhouse's again this morn. Played Monopoly with Palmer, Plum and Parkhouse, Parkhouse won. We have been having many raids. We had 4 last night and at least one every night previous to it for 4 or 5 weeks.

15 Thursday This morning I had a letter off Davey asking me to take his bag and kit down to Llantwit Major for him. So I decided to go down there tomorrow. He sent 3/- for expenses. Went down Glen Parkhouse's practically all day. I came away all square with everyone.

16 Friday Caught the 11.30 bus to Bridgend and the 1.52 from Bridgend to Llantwit. Went to Police Station and met Davey and his pals – They are a jolly lot.[187] Inspected the Town and the new cinema. Davey gave 10/- to Sis and 1/2 crown to me – I took it all.

17 Saturday Last night I walked up to Ponty with Hilda all the way, during which walk, which was at the dead of night, there was an air raid. Will and Cassie came home [. . .][188] I had some fine ties this week off Dai and Ivor. Pair of shoes too.

18 Sunday Dr Rees back today. He gave us a decent sermon but not very enjoyable. Will came to Chapel. He is home on leave. Cassie came too.

---

[186] *Where's That Fire?* (1939), directed by Marcel Varnel (1894–1947), starring Will Hay (1888–1949).
[187] For a while Richard considered joining the police force.
[188] Cassie is Richard's sister Catherine (1921–2011).

19 Monday Started school.[189] I am in Form Vm.[190] Gerwyn Williams has stayed on and the prospects of a good rugby team are much brighter.[191] At least ten of last year's team are eligible, while there are some good youngsters who might fill in the gaps. Brin Phillips etc.

20 Tuesday Met the new Gym master who is the Tout's brother. His name is of course Mr Davies but most of the boys call him the second Tout.[192] Had a decent day. Voted for Gerwyn Williams for Captain but Clifford Owen was picked. He is alright but not so good as Gin.

21 Wednesday Cliff Owen has arranged a football practice for tomorrow night. The team is up on the board. If Archie Davies comes back to school we should have a very strong team this season. I have had a new or practically new pair of shoes off Ivor (once Will's).

22 Thursday Had the football practice on the Plough – formerly destined for the Island (Margam) because there is a balloon in the Park. The Gym master picked me as leader of the pack. I have my best shoes a fortnight now. This is in case of arguments.

23 Friday Had training in the Gym after school. We had about ¾ hr of Post-ball.[193] We won 15–13. Form Vt won't play us in Post-ball. Had the steel frame of an incendiary bomb which was dropped in Llantwit Major. Cassie went to see Dai and brought it back.

24 Saturday Went to Pictures – Saved 2/- to put in the fund for Co-op Clearance. Met Eric Nelson and we went to the shelter in the Park when the Siren went. There was much fun there. There were many bombs dropped. There were six air raids today.

25 Sunday Went to chapel as usual. I am going to put 2/- in the penny bank tomorrow if all goes well. Started Chocolate club with Auntie Win. Gave 6d.

26 Monday Had football practice with the new gym master. He has put me leader of the pack. Put 2/- in the bank. Went to the Regent with Will to see

---

[189] In 1940 the summer holiday was reduced to three weeks, to compensate for the fact that school hours were shortened (from 0945 to 1545) as a result of the blackout.

[190] Year V was divided into two forms: Vm and Vt.

[191] Gerwyn Williams (1924–2009) was already capped at rugby football by Wales at under-15 level and went on to win 13 senior caps between 1950 and 1954, including one against New Zealand in the victory of 1953. He was also a talented cricketer who represented South Wales.

[192] Mr V. Davies, brother of J. Vyrnwy Davies or 'Tout'.

[193] A form of basketball.

Juarez.[194] It was an enjoyable picture. Bette Davis and Paul Muni were the stars. John Garfield was also in it.

27 Tuesday We had Gym today and it was very enjoyable. Will went back today. He went at 9.20. He has left his overcoat here probably for me. Later Thomas Henry came and told Sis [. . .] that Will had said that I was to have the coat.

28 Wednesday School as usual. Life and work in Vm is much the same as usual. I have been flaunting different ties every day. I have about 40 ties all different.[195] My suit will be ready a fortnight Saturday. I picked a blue striped one double breast.

29 Thursday Just as we were going to go out for football practice after school the air raid warning went and we had to stop practice. Was I angry? Went down Parkhouse's to play Monopoly. We played 3 games. I won two.

30 Friday Sis, Elfed and I went to fetch blackberries. We collected about 9½ pints all together. I went by myself and I had nearly 3 pints. Sis and Elfed are supposed to have found a fine spot somewhere in the Goytre Valley.[196] I'm thinking of going up tomorrow.

31 Saturday At first I did not intend going to the pictures as it would alter my budget but as Hilda and Edie contributed 9d to me and my fund and [I] went. I did not go to fetch blackberries as I thought. [. . .]

SEPTEMBER

1 Sunday Did not go to Chapel as usual in the morning but went and read a psalm to start school in the noon.

2 Monday Last night we had the worst air raid of the war. Over 200 people were killed in Swansea, and Ben Evans, the market and Marks and Spencers were hit while Swansea Station was completely wrecked.[197]

---

[194] *Juarez* (1939), directed by William Dieterle (1893–1972), starring Brian Aherne, Bette Davis (1908–89), Paul Muni (1896–1967) and John Garfield.

[195] P. Burton (*Richard and Philip*, 14) quotes this line but misdates it as Wednesday 25 August.

[196] The Goytre valley, today known as Cwm Dyffryn, opens out on to the coastal plain at the northern end of Taibach.

[197] Over 1,000 incendiary bombs were dropped on Swansea in the most serious attack in the area until then. High Street station was badly damaged. The death toll was actually 33, although another 100 people were injured.

3 Tuesday I am going to try hard in school this year. We are having continued air raids. Skewen oil works is still burning and there is a black pall of smoke over the sky.[198] There are now 42 barrage balloons within sight.[199]

4 Wednesday Oil works still burning. Final trial on school field tomorrow. [...] Mr Burton has not come back yet. We had chem practical today. It was jolly interesting too. Had an excellent result.

5 Thursday We had films in school describing the production of oil. In parts interesting. In other parts it was dry. Had games. I think that it is going to be a massacre Saturday for the Old Boys. Let's hope not.

6 Friday Argument in school whether to play Cochlin or Parkhouse on the wing Saturday. I voted for Parkhouse but Cochlin played.[200] Mitched school and went with Sis to fetch blackberries.[201] Had 9½ pints. Farmer warned us off.

7 Saturday Led the pack against the Old Boys. They much too heavy for us. We lost 22–3. It was a good game but Elwyn Bowen stand off half for the other team simply tore through our Team.[202] Colin Eynon scored our try [...]

8 Sunday Did not go to chapel all day because Sis said I was not fit to go until I have my new suit next Sunday.

9 Monday Played football at blind side wing forward.[203] I am wondering whether he intends keeping me in that position. I hope so. Tom Mainwaring is back in school again.[204] Played football with us. Pretty good too.

10 Tuesday I intended stopping in and doing homework but Phillips came and sent a little boy up later, so I went with him. Papers did not come in until 6 o'clock tonight. It is very annoying. London bombed fiercely from end to end.

11 Wednesday School as usual except that we are having films by Gas companies and Ford motors etc. which are not very interesting but offer

---

[198] Skewen is on the west bank of the Nedd, two miles from Neath itself. The oil refinery was at Llandarcy, south-west of Skewen. The fires continued for four days, and smoke drifted as far as Cardiff.
[199] Barrage balloons were used in an attempt to defend Swansea Bay from air attack.
[200] D. A. Cochlin, a fellow pupil.
[201] 'Mitch' is a colloquial expression for playing truant.
[202] 'Stand off half' often referred to today as 'fly half' or 'outside half'. Elwyn Bowen was a talented athlete.
[203] In the back row, often referred to as a 'flank forward' or 'flanker' today.
[204] Thomas H. (often 'Tom' or 'Tommy') Mainwaring, a friend of Richard's.

a relief from the monotony of school life. Mr Burton says there's a long new film coming.

12 Thursday This morning Stanley Jones gave me a letter from Edie.[205] Inside it was another letter from Will. It contained half a crown. That night I went to the Cach and did not tell Sis. It was quite a good show starring Richard Green and Dix.[206]

13 Friday This morning the milkboy told Sis that he had seen me in the Cach eating chocolates etc. but I denied it and she believed me – at least I think so – although it was no crime. We had Burton today – very interesting talk on Essays.

14 Saturday Fetched 6 pints of blackberries this morning and I sold them all. The sale realized 1/6 each for Sis and I. Went to Regent in the night – it was pretty good. Uncle Charles gave me 6d. I am not going to get papers for Aunt Ede again.

15 Sunday Determined to work hard at school and break all records by passing matric 1st time.[207] Very few Vm boys have ever done it.

~~16~~ 23rd Monday[208] I am practically certain of being in the school play. We had football down Margam. It was a jolly game. Mr Sanderson was there and his remarks were not complimentary.[209]

17 Tuesday We are supposed to play Cardiff Saturday. In the play I am the American ambassador, Mr Vanhattan, to London.[210] [. . .]

18 Wednesday Mr Burton had the rest of the people there but he didn't want me as I am only in one act that is the last one.

---

[205] Stanley Jones, a fellow pupil and a talented athlete, who lived in Cwmafan.

[206] Richard Dix (1894–1949) and Richard Greene (1918–85) both featured in the 1939 films *Man of Conquest* and *Here I Am Stranger*.

[207] 'matric' refers to the School Certificate examination of the Central Welsh Board. Eventually, in September 1943, after a brief hiatus in his formal education, Richard would pass this examination.

[208] '23rd' in circle, written in pencil, above deleted '16'. It would appear that Richard transposed the entries for the two weeks concerned but only made this obvious on the Monday (the first day of the week to view) in both cases.

[209] Mr Mervyn Sanderson, a teacher, who also ran a dancing school.

[210] Richard played the part of the American Ambassador Mr Vanhattan in *The Apple Cart* (1929) by George Bernard Shaw (1856–1950), produced and directed by Philip Burton, which would be staged by the Port Talbot Secondary School players in January 1941. In previous years Burton had produced a number of Shaw's plays at the school, including *Captain Brassbound's Conversion, Saint Joan* and *The Doctor's Dilemma*. *The Apple Cart* was the players' 14th production. Because of blackout restrictions and safety regulations it had to be staged in the YMCA rather than in the school hall. See also Burton, *Early Doors*, 39–41.

19 Thursday Supposed to play football but went to Burton instead. Had a nice time. He told me to modulate my voice a little more as I sounded like a gangster not an American who has been educated.[211]

20 Friday Whitchurch cancelled their match. – Very disappointed but as they are a lot of Swanks it is not so important.[212]

21 Saturday Edie came down today and gave me a 1/- which was very acceptable under the circumstances in which I was in. She asked me if I had the letter from Will.

22 Sunday Went to Chapel as usual. Gave a 1/- to Peggy from Mrs Rees which I had last Sunday.

23 16th Monday[213] I am writing now just to fill up space as I haven't written for a fortnight and it is very difficult to fill up space. We are playing against Tonyrefail home on Saturday. They have a poor team this year.

24 Tuesday Had Chem and other lessons as usual. All the boys are going to put up the football posts tomorrow night down Eastern Ground. Ginger is persuading me to help.[214]

25 Wednesday We all went down and you should have seen the try lines they were more like a briar stick than a straight line. We made a miscalculation by making the top try line 67 yards long and the bottom 70 yards.[215]

26 Thursday Most of the boys went down again to 'dig for victory'. I am not sure but I think I went to the pictures. Simeon Jones is a great support.[216] He'll turn up anywhere.

27 Friday Although the boys have been working all the week only today did they put the posts up while we had Geography. Cliff Owen put up the team but I made him change it and put Mog Griffiths in.[217]

---

[211] Burton (*Richard and Philip*, 15) quotes this as 'who had been educated'.
[212] Whitchurch is an affluent suburb in north-west Cardiff.
[213] '16th' in circle, written in pencil, above deleted '23'.
[214] 'Ginger' was Gerwyn Williams.
[215] Both try lines should have been the same length. The maximum permissible was 75 yards.
[216] Simeon Jones was an (older) fellow pupil who acted the part of Cutler Walpole in *The Doctor's Dilemma*.
[217] Morgan 'Mog' Griffiths, a fellow pupil, who was to have the role of King Magnus in *The Apple Cart*.

28 Saturday Played Tonyrefail. I led the pack fairly well. We only played 25 minutes each way but that was enough. We won 14–0. We had them beaten in every way. Went to pictures with the gang including T. George.

29 Sunday Went to chapel all day as I have had my new suit. I have written on the wrong page.

30 Monday I sneaked away today from school and did not play football. Joe James was caught and was made to do graphs by Tadpole and so I think he will take games from now on.[218]

OCTOBER

1 Tuesday We had an air raid siren during Chemistry which was very welcome. When we came back we had films so missing nearly all the morning. It is rumoured that we have a fortnight holiday.

2 Wednesday We had two air raids today and they were very welcome. I am afraid that this business will stop from now on and air raids will be given only during greatest danger.

3 Thursday Had 3 air raids during school hours today and they were very acceptable. I forgot to say that Dai sent Sis a quid and weren't we glad. Played football up the field with Mr Davies. He has a fine kick on him. G.W. broke his shoulder.[219]

4 Friday Team picked. Alb Morris in pack although he does not turn out for practice. Did a pile of homework tonight. Uncle Charles was there. I meant to have my togs mended but it is too late now.

5 Saturday Played Ogmore today.[220] Wore good overcoat. We won, after a shaky [start] in first half, when we were losing 3–nil, to finally win 12–3. We had a good meal and milk was quite a surprise.

6 Sunday Went to Chapel. Will came home yesterday bringing his wife and children with him.

---

[218] Joe James, a fellow pupil and talented athlete.
[219] Gerwyn Williams.
[220] This probably refers to the colliery settlement of Ogmore Vale, in the Ogwr valley north of Bridgend.

7 Monday Did not go down to play football on the Eastern ground. I went up the Plough and Mr Davies (Hist) told me that we did not shove enough in the scrums (i.e. the W-forwards[221]) [...]

8 Tuesday We haven't had any long air raids lately during school hours. Rain is coming now. Pelting down and filling up the reservoirs for us. For the last three months we haven't had any water in the nights – a very dry summer.

9 Wednesday I heard Burton tell 'Pop' that he was going to London to see a Mr Shaw. I wonder if it is the Great G.B.[222] Possibly. We had a doubles of geom instead with Pop and couldn't he teach. We have a fortnight's hols. this week.

10 Thursday Had a terrible row today. Elfed told me to go back to Pontrhydyfen. I walked up to Cwmafan. I hate the sight of Elfed. I am going to ask Daddy to take me back home where I can go to work.[223] I could never stay home now. Sis went to Dad James.

11 Friday I intended to go to Ponty but I have cooled off a bit now. Sis wants me to go if I want to. But I am sure that where ever I go I will be not wanted the same as here.[224]

12 Saturday Elfed's Birthday. Marian gave him a packet of his own cigarettes and he took them. Went down Margam to see Eastern play our Juniors. It was a drawn game 3–3. [...]

13 Sunday Went to chapel in the noon and night. I went down Ben's in the morn and picked my chocs.

14 Monday Uncle Charles came up and took me to the Cach in the 9d. It was a decent show a bit on the sad side. He was very pleased with himself. Sis told me to go to Ponty tomorrow.

15 Tuesday Had a row with Elfed. I dressed up to go but he would not let me go after all. I then went to play football with the boys. 1st we went down Margam then we came to Plough.

---

[221] Wing forwards.
[222] George Bernard Shaw.
[223] Richard's second reference to his father.
[224] Interestingly, Bragg (*Rich*, 35, citing Burton) and Burton (*Richard and Philip*, 14) have a comma between 'wanted' and 'the same', which alters the meaning, and they reverse the order from 'be not wanted' to 'not be wanted'. Obviously this is open to differences of emphasis and interpretation, but it would seem to be potentially a case of editorial transformation on the part of Philip Burton.

16 Wednesday Went to Cwm and Tom gave me 6d. Sis came up too. Ivor was up there also but he gave me nothing and so I was rather surprised.

17 Thursday Went down Plough to play football with Sec but they would not turn out. Went to Cymalog this noon and Dill and I had about 4lbs each.[225] I had more than Dill.

18 Friday Went up Ponty. Hilda was in Swansea. Daddy bought me a pair of shoes 16/6 although he hadn't been working all this week. He gave me money too. Went to Cach.

19 Saturday Gave Auntie Win 6d for the Chocolate Club. I am buying an 8/- present for Sis. I went to the Regent to see *Andy Hardy* (M. Rooney).[226] No one came with me. I will have to find 1/6 a week for Auntie Win on account.

20 Sunday Went to chapel all day per usual. Our yearly big meeting is on Fortnight Sunday. [. . .]

21 Monday Air blitzkrieg still continues over London. At least 3800 people have been killed.[227] Things have quietened down here at home. – Sis is still grumpy and Elfed still gets his black moods. Walled up shelter.[228]

22 Tuesday Forgot to say I went to Cach last night. Had a 1/- off Sis for doing shelter. Did not do any today. Just for argument Sis had her 'navy' shoes last week and so did Marian. Clearance in a fortnight.

23 Wednesday I am reading on average about 3 books in two days. Went down Library to change my books and Elfed was shouting because he wanted to read one of them. Not so many air raids lately.

24 Thursday Walled up shelter again today as one side had not a very good foundation and did ½ the other side. Dad James said it was a good bit of walling. Uncle Charles has not been up our house for ages.

---

[225] Cymalog – today written as Cwm Maelwg, a valley behind Margam Castle.

[226] This probably refers to *Andy Hardy Gets Spring Fever* (1939), directed by W. S. Van Dyke, starring Mickey Rooney (1920—), or another of the Hardy Family series of films.

[227] The Luftwaffe's bombing of London in particular had begun in early September 1940 and continued, barely without a pause, until mid November, when the focus shifted to a wider range of targets. The estimate of 3,800 civilian deaths by early November does not seem excessive. In total 13,596 civilians were killed as a result of enemy action in the London civil defence region (admittedly more extensive than the city itself) in the course of 1940.

[228] Anderson shelters for individual households had arrived in the district in September.

25 Friday Went down the Co-op for Sis and took all I could. Went up the side in the evening to help Mam James cut out black-out for lamps for the chapel. Elfed said I'll have to wear strap shoes next week for school.

26 Saturday Went down Co-op again and Brin Phillips came with me. We both went down the Park in the afternoon and we played football. Went to the pictures in the evening. *Hunch-back of Notre Dame* [...][229]

27 Sunday Went to chapel all day as usual. Our big meeting next Sunday. Gwilym Rees will be preaching.[230]

28 Monday Back to school after a fortnight's hols and I wasn't sorry to go back. I worked hard at my homework tonight. Played football down Margam. H. Owen and V Hughes were watching us. They are football selectors.

29 Tuesday Went to school. My feet fit easier in to the shoes than they did yesterday. as I have corn remover on and I hope they will succeed. I am going to take them off Thursday night probably. Did a lot of homework.

30 Wednesday Cassie came home yesterday and she is 'llawn o twang'.[231] I don't think I'll ever get a credit in Welsh and am doubtful if I'll get a pass.[232] Of the rest I'm pretty sure. Worked all night at Chem.

31 Thursday Did heaps of Chem swotting. I think I will swot Geom next week. We had football in the Gym. I had a little fight with Don Parr. – Quite spirited. Gerry Mahoney was there too. Mr Davies came near the end to stop us.

NOVEMBER

1 Friday Did homework all night. Those corn removers came up trumps and I am now corn free. We are playing Garw tomorrow.[233] Mr Davies is not coming so we are having 'Bumf' (Mr Evans) Instructions.[234]

---

[229] *The Hunchback of Notre Dame* (1939), directed by William Dieterle, starring Charles Laughton (1899–1962).

[230] The Revd Gwilym Rees MA, of Cardiff, brother of Dr J. Caerau Rees.

[231] Welsh for 'full of twang', or 'speaking posh'. Cassie had been nursing in England.

[232] Gethin Matthews is perhaps stretching a point when he argues (*Richard Burton*, 29) that '*mae nodiadau Richard yn ei ddyddiadur o 1940 yn dangos yn amlwg ei fod yn rhoi mwy o bwys ar ei ganlyniadau yn y Gymraeg nag mewn unrhyw bwnc arall*' (Richard's notes in his 1940 diary show clearly that he placed more importance on his results in Welsh than in any other subject' [my translation]).

[233] Garw School, Pontycymer, a colliery settlement in the Garw valley, north of Bridgend.

[234] Mr Evans, the physics teacher.

2 Saturday Got up about 20 to 8 o'clock and made arrangements about papers. Went to Gar w although it was pouring down and played during drenching rain. We lost a hard game 5–nil. They had a heavy pack. Here hoping for next time.

3 Sunday Big meeting today. G. Rees gave three beautiful sermons. Could not work today. Working hard.

4 Monday Last day of the Cwrdd mawr.[235] I was told that Gwil Rees today was good. I had a row with Sis – she went to cry. She was bad during church this afternoon. We had no football this 'noon. Nick is now A.F.S. head.[236]

5 Tuesday Did chem swotting tonight as usual. I am well on in the book now and should get about 70 in chem. I am worried about Welsh. I am afraid I will not do very well in it. Still rather stiff with Sis.

6 Wednesday Leisan house had a meeting today. I was picked Captain of football in Leisan house. We have a fairly good team. Cliff Owen and I both had equal votes and the chairman Mr Burton came my way.[237]

7 Thursday Had rehearsal today for the play. I am confident I can play my part well enough. Three girls tried for Queen position. Glenys Hare a form VI girl won and she can do it very well.[238]

8 Friday Team was picked to play against Maesteg. Roy Vincent in the team as Joe James has dropped out.[239] It doesn't look as if we will play as it is very wet. Had rehearsal with Burton. Pretty hot work.

9 Saturday Played Maesteg. We won 7–6. It was a fine match although it poured down. The lead swung from side to side. Brin Phillips and I went to Pictures on Sat night and afterwards to Joe's.

10 Sunday It seemed that the chapel had about £31 last Sunday which is not bad at all for a small chapel.

11 Monday Swotted chem all night and did a little English. It is hard work. Watched the cabinet rehearsing tonight and when I was going through the hall saw films.[240] I was 15 years old yesterday. Had 2/-.

---

[235] *Cwrdd mawr* is Welsh for 'big meeting', in this context a religious gathering.
[236] Auxiliary Fire Service. 'Nick' was Mr Jack Nicholas.
[237] Philip Burton was Head of Leisan House.
[238] Glenys Hare played the part of Queen Jemima in *The Apple Cart*.
[239] Roy Vincent, a fellow pupil, also participated in the YMCA dramatic productions.
[240] Burton is referring here to the 'bevy of . . . Cabinet Ministers' who feature in *The Apple Cart*.

12 Tuesday Swotted English. Did not do so much work as usual. Did my English play. It is very interesting. Mr Wellington came here and stopped me for a bit from going up stairs. Finished about 10.30.

13 Wednesday Got home early today. I am very worried about Welsh. I am certain that it is going to let me down in Matric. I must try and see what she accents on this term and swot them up.

14 Thursday Did a lot of Homework. I only want to finish one act of Shakespearean play. (*Twelfth Night*). Played football. I scored. Tommy Mainwaring has a terrific swerve on him. [. . .]

15 Friday I had to take John Davies' part in rehearsal today and so I could not go in to Gym.[241] Verdun it seems has come into money (£450) and he left ½ crown for me.[242] He gave Sis 10/- for the Bike. I have to take it up tomorrow.

16 Saturday Left Marian to do the papers. Started walking up with the bike. I was drenched when I got by Cwm. Verdun and I came down Town and he bought a 2nd hand machine. He bought me two mouth organs.

17 Sunday Went to Chapel. We had special collection (17/-). Total collection was £1 odd.

18 Monday Played football in the Gym. Only 5 of us there. Did a lot of swotting tonight. I should get a fairly good result at Terminals especially in Chem.[243] I am still worried about Welsh. I am afraid Geog is not going to be a great help.

19 Tuesday Did Homework as usual. Mr Burton wanted to see me for rehearsal I thought but he changed his mind afterwards and sent me home. I was glad and did a whack of homework. Glad when exams are over.

20 Wednesday Had a rehearsal today. Had a good tea when I got home. I have got to learn my words in 10 days. I practically know them so everything will be alright. [. . .] Swotted a lot tonight.

21 Thursday Played football in the Gym tonight. We had great fun. Went home and Verdun's wife and mother-in-law were there. Swotted and worked out a possible average. I calculated about 50%. Probably more though.

---

[241] John Eaton Davies, a fellow pupil from Cwmafan, who later became a teacher.
[242] Verdun had been disabled in a mining accident, for which he received compensation.
[243] Terminals meaning end of term examinations.

22 Friday We are playing Neath tomorrow and I am not confident of holding them as they have a good team. Did a bit of homework but not much. I will do more over the next few days. I played a little on the mouth organ.

23 Saturday I wore Elfed's hat over to school and Don Parr and I went running around yelling like Red Indians (I found a tambourine). We lost to Neath as I expected by 20 points. Went up Ive's. He is going next Thurs to RASC.[244]

24 Sunday Went to chapel in the noon and night. Had a lend of 1/3 off Sis and paid off my debt of 3/9 to Auntie Wyn.

25 Monday At first I was not going to take football but I changed my mind borrowed a bike and went home to get my stuff. We had an enjoyable game. We won of course. Did a lot of homework and learned characters of Shakespeare.

26 Tuesday Did a lot of homework. I had to put the blackout up in the dark and I had to count money for Marian and Nan Morse.[245] Mr Reynolds was seen in school today although he wasn't actually on the job.[246]

27 Wednesday We did revision of Chemistry all (almost) of the afternoon and about 3.15 Mr Burton came in and told us that there was to be an English exam tomorrow and were we shocked.

28 Thursday Had English exam. I did a fairly good paper. I should get about 40%. I wrote an essay on 'The Atlantic Ocean'. The exam time table is up. We have History first I think, so I must learn it hard.

29 Friday Our Ivor should be at his billet by now. I worked hard at Geog all I could today. I have a rehearsal tomorrow. I think I will do well in History and fairly well in Welsh I am feeling more cocky.

30 Saturday Had rehearsal today. I forgot my book and had to go back for it. Stayed in the YM for a bit and then went home to get my stuff to play for them.[247] We lost 5-3. I played badly.

---

[244] Ivor served in the Royal Army Service Corps during the Second World War.

[245] Nan Morse was a friend, member of Noddfa Chapel, and lived at 1, Constant Road.

[246] Mr Christopher 'Pop' Reynolds the headmaster had been absent from school through illness. He would retire in 1943.

[247] The Port Talbot YMCA (chairman: P. H. Burton) was by this time located in its new premises (which had opened in April) on Talbot Road. Its Boys' Club had a membership of about 100 and catered for boys between the ages of 12 and 16.

DECEMBER

1 Sunday Went to chapel all day as usual. Went up Auntie's after evening chapel and played with Edwina.[248]

2 Monday School as usual. We had no football today because of rain. Hist is our first exam and I learned quite a bit about it. Mr Burton said to be prepared for a shock about one Lit Paper. Mr Reynolds is back.

3 Tuesday Went to school as usual. We have a woodwork theory exam. Learned Hist all night. Lord Haw-Haw is talking now.[249] The Greeks are beating the Italians, who are retreating at every step.[250]

4 Wednesday Exams tomorrow. I am not looking forward to Welsh but I am feeling a little better about the result. I did no Hist tonight but let it go. I will learn some tomorrow. We are playing Garw tomorrow.

5 Thursday Had Hist – I did fairly well although I did not finish I should get about 50. 45 at least. Just finished Welsh – I have done very well in the last 3 questions but in the Trans and Essay hopeless.[251] Should get 60%.

6 Friday Had Chem this morning and it was an easy paper although on the long side. I finished however and I think I had the problems all right. We had Arith. Not so good I will be lucky If I get 60%. We are playing Garw tomorrow.

7 Saturday I joined the Y.M.C.A. this afternoon.[252] Paid 6d down. We played Garw and won 8–nil. Thus we avenged our defeat further in the season. It was the first time they have been defeated this season.

8 Sunday Stayed home all day and tried to swot but I am sorry that I did stay home because I will not do much better after all.

9 Monday We had Welsh today and indeed it was better than I expected and I think I ought to get about 45% between the two. Had Algebra this morning but I did it badly. I should think I will get about 35%. Geog tomorrow.

---

[248] Edwina Dummer: the youngest daughter of Margaret Ann and Edwin Dummer.
[249] 'Lord Haw-Haw' was William Joyce (1906–46), who delivered radio broadcasts of Nazi propaganda to British audiences.
[250] Italian troops had invaded Greece on 28 October 1940 and within a week were being repulsed.
[251] Trans meaning translation.
[252] Philip Burton was co-founder of the YMCA amateur dramatic society, and had produced a number of his own plays under their auspices, including *Granton Street* (1934) and *White Collar* (1938). See Burton, *Early Doors*, 44–51.

10 *Tuesday* Had Geography and it was something better than I expected. I have given myself 43% but I shouldn't be surprised if I had more. We had Woodwork Theory and if it wasn't that Bobby is a good marker I wouldn't expect much.

11 *Wednesday* Christmas only fortnight off but I'm not half so thrilled as usual. We had English today. I wanted to stay home from Phys tomorrow so I stayed home this noon as well to avert suspicion. We have no exam this noon.

12 *Thursday* Stayed home this morning but went this afternoon. Took the opportunity to swot up Geom. Confident of a good mark in Geom. Went up the YMCA and had a bit of fun. Col Eynon and etc. Went to see play.

13 *Friday* Had geom this morning and it was very good and two of the very things I asked him about came up. I expect 65 at least for Geom. I worked out my prob av: 50%. If I do have this it will be very good.

14 *Saturday* Went up YM Pressed my trousers before I went and aired it. Went to pictures tonight with Brin Phillips and Strawb. I bought a pipe for a bit of fun and a smoked it for a bet.

15 *Sunday* I was made a member today and I drank my first drop of wine and ate my first lump of bread.[253]

16 *Monday* Went to school as usual. I expected some marks but I did not get any. We had films this afternoon and one of them was pretty good. Dillwyn and I went out singing carols and we realized 4/- i.e. 2/- each.

17 *Tuesday* Had my History mark (58) and Woodwork mark (43). As I was going home John Davies told me my chem mark was 70 odd. Later George Dear told me I had 50 odd in Lit and 40 odd in grammar.[254]

18 *Wednesday* I had 55 in Eng Lit and 44 in Grammar. I did well in Maths. 2nd in Geom with 78 5th in Arith 65 and about 10th in alg. with 49 making a maths average of 64. My average is now a very good one.

19 *Thursday* Had my Welsh marks – 54 – which were more than expected. I found that I had most of my marks were for grammar [*sic*] in which I had 57% but in Literature I only had 29 out of 60.

---

[253] Richard was received into membership of Noddfa Chapel and took his first communion.
[254] George Dear (sometimes Deer) was a fellow pupil, who later became a teacher of English.

23 Monday Went up Cwmafan. Edie was thrown out yesterday morn for raising the Elbow.[255] I had 2/- off Tom. Took Edie's clothes up Pont with Graham. Edie was very sullen.

24 Tuesday Had 1/- off Hilda through the post. Davey was home – gave me 1/4. Dick Bach gave me 2/6. Went to Cach with Dill Dummer. Looking forward to Christmas Dinner.

25 Wednesday Went to chapel this morning. After chapel went for a walk down Margam and visited. Had dinner – went up Goytre for a walk. Went to Regent in night. Felt ill Christmas night. [. . .]

26 Thursday Went up the side in morning. Brin Phillips told me he'll meet me at 5.15 to go to Pics. Played football this afternoon with Dill and Phillips. Went to Regent but didn't meet Phillips.

27 Friday Went up Goytre to fetch Elfed's pay. Verdun gave me 1/-. Went down Uncle Ben's to play Monopoly. Dillwyn came too. We blackened Auntie Win's face. [. . .]

28 Saturday Went down Edith's for a party. Dill was bad. He was sick. Morwen Edwina were also sick.[256] Milly Gronow had a fit.[257] They gave me a bladder also Rowntree's sweets.

29 Sunday Went to Chapel all day. We had £5 collection in Sunday School. We had £15 collection in the evening.

30 Monday Did some shopping. Went up YM in the afternoon. Don Parr had ripped the cloth on the table.[258] Went to Regent in the evening to see *Devil on Wheels*.[259]

---

[255] Edie had a sometimes difficult relationship with her older brother Tom, who disapproved of her smoking.
[256] Morwen is Morwen Gronow, the daughter of Elfed's sister Ethel.
[257] Milly Gronow was the sister of Elfed's sister Ethel. She suffered from epilepsy.
[258] The YMCA had a billiard room with three tables.
[259] *Indianapolis Speedway* (1939), directed by Lloyd Bacon, also known as *Devil on Wheels*.

1960

Friday 1st, New York In New York. I arrived on 29 December.

Saturday 2nd Rehearsal. *Fifth Column*.[1] We have begun without Max Schell.[2] He will arrive in two or three days. George Rose and Betsy Von Furstenberg are also with us.[3] The director Frankenheimer is a typical American – a Jew, a genius type. He swears all the time, he curses and he's always afraid.[4]

Wednesday 20th I have seen the tape. I hate myself and my face in particular. I have spoken with Sybil in Geneva.[5]

Thursday 21st Tape *Fifth Column*. I made mischief between Max Schell and Sally Ann Howes.[6] I told him that she adores Max and that after an argument she had told me this. It's true. Max has done nothing.

Friday 22nd Tape *Fifth Column*. L. Harvey, Hugh Griffith, Dekin, Hugh French have drunk with me in my room at the Navarro.[7]

Saturday 23rd I saw B. Bogart in her play – only the last act.[8] She goes well but the play is awful.

---

[1] *The Fifth Column* (1960), a television adaptation of the novel by Ernest Hemingway. It screened on 29 January 1960 on CBS in the USA.
[2] Maximilian Schell (1930—), actor. Schell was to play a part in finding Maria (1961—), who was to be adopted by Elizabeth Taylor in 1962.
[3] George Rose (1920–88), actor, who was to play the part of first gravedigger in the 1964 production of *Hamlet*. Betsy von Furstenberg (1931—), actor.
[4] John Frankenheimer (1930–2002), television and film director.
[5] Sybil Burton (1929—), Richard's wife.
[6] Sally Ann Howes (1930—), actor.
[7] L. Harvey is Burton's friend Laurence Harvey (1928–73), actor, who later that year would star in *Butterfield 8* alongside Elizabeth Taylor. Harvey would also appear with Taylor in *Night Watch* (1973). Hugh Griffith (1912–80), actor and friend of Richard's, who had appeared alongside him in *The Last Days of Dolwyn*, in the summer 1951 Stratford productions of *Henry IV (Part I)*, *The Tempest* and *Henry V*, and in *Legend of Lovers* in New York in 1951. Hugh French (1910–76), formerly an actor, by this time an agent for Richard. The Hotel Navarro, on Central Park South, New York.
[8] B. Bogart is Lauren 'Betty' Bacall (1924—), the widow of Humphrey Bogart, who had died in 1957. The production to which Burton refers may have been *Goodbye, Charlie*, staged on Broadway, in which Lauren Bacall starred.

Sunday 24th I went to PHB's place to eat, drink and watch Su Str on television.[9] She was very good, but otherwise, as with Betty Bacall, the play stank.

Monday 25th, New York I leave for France. TWA. When we arrived at the airport the police told us that a maniac had telephoned to say that he had put a bomb on our plane. We had a nervous and restless trip.

Tuesday 26th, Paris We could not land at Paris Orly – fog – and we continued to Geneva. Sybil left Geneva yesterday so that we would meet in Paris. I returned to Paris in the afternoon. [. . .] K.J.W. and Syb are well.[10]

Wednesday 27th I hope to see P. Brook today.[11]
     I went to see Brook at 6 o'clock at 14 Avenue Hoche, Production Vienna, 3rd floor. I saw him and also Miss Jeanne Moreau.[12] I didn't like her much. Pretty enough but . . . I will not do the film.[13]

Thursday 28th We arrived at Geneva where Kate and Berenice were waiting for us.[14] Kate loves The Station. In the evening we will stay at home with Berenice who is going to sleep in the new little house.[15] Not true. We have visited and eaten at Paul's.[16]

Friday 29th The washing machine doesn't work. The heater is always smoking. Paul arrived and fixed everything. What a man. In the evening we stay at home with René and Berenice.[17] René has returned from Zurich.

Saturday 30th I visited the bank this morning with K. I bought her a little red car. We ate in the airport restaurant waiting for Bernard and Claire.[18] They arrived at ten past one. At home – we stayed (with a visit to Nyon to buy ski wear) for the rest of the day.[19]

---

[9] PHB is Philip Burton, Richard's former guardian. Su Str is Susan Strasberg (1938–99). Burton and Strasberg had enjoyed a passionate affair in 1957–8.
[10] K refers to Kate Burton, Richard and Sybil's eldest child (born 1957). J. is Jessica Burton, Richard and Sybil's youngest child (born 1959). W is Wendy, their nurse.
[11] Peter Brook (1925—), director.
[12] Jeanne Moreau (1928—), actor.
[13] Peter Brook was to direct Jeanne Moreau in *Seven Days . . . Seven Nights* (also titled *Moderato Cantabile*, based on the novel of the same name by Marguerite Duras) in 1960. It is possible that Burton was considering the part of Chauvin, played in due course by Jean-Paul Belmondo (1933—).
[14] Berenice Weibel, a friend and neighbour in Céligny.
[15] The chalet that Richard and Sybil had built in the grounds of their house in Céligny.
[16] Paul Fillistorf, chef and proprietor of Café de la Gare, Céligny.
[17] René Weibel, Berenice's husband.
[18] Bernard Greenford, Sybil's brother-in-law, and his daughter Claire.
[19] Nyon is a small town and port 5 km from Céligny, on the north shore of Lake Geneva.

Notes

J'espere fait le ski dans dix on deux jours.[20] It is an exotic, romantic and snobby sport. We will try.

FEBRUARY

Monday 1st We left for Villars.[21] The journey took 1½ hours. Everything is fine.

Tuesday 2nd The first skiing lesson with Herr Von Stump. I tried my first slope on my own. Disaster.

Wednesday 3rd I have not been skiing because I fell yesterday.

Thursday 4th No skiing.

Friday 5th I start skiing again at Bretaye.[22]

Saturday 6th Skiing all day.
     We have beaten the Scots 8–0.[23] I saw it on TV at Villars. Bebb one try.[24] Penalty from N. Morgan – back-row forward from Newport.[25]

Thursday 11th I did a Christie for the first time.[26]

Friday 12th We returned to Céligny. It snowed in the morning and we had some difficulty with the cloud getting down to Aigle.[27]
     We ate at Paul's with René, Berenice, Rene and Osian Ellis, Bern and Claire.[28] Osian played the harp, when we got back home.

Saturday 13th Rene and Osian Ellis arrived yesterday evening. In the afternoon Osian played the harp for Radio Geneva. The English have beaten the Irish 8–5.[29] I won 18000 French francs from Divonne.[30]

---

[20] I hope to learn to ski in ten or two days.
[21] Villars is a ski resort south-east of the eastern end of Lake Geneva, high above the Rhône valley, in the area known as the Alpes Vaudoises.
[22] Bretaye is the name of a col and of one of the main skiing areas around Villars.
[23] At rugby union, at Cardiff Arms Park.
[24] Dewi Iorwerth Ellis Bebb (1938–96), Welsh rugby player.
[25] Norman Morgan (1935—), Welsh rugby player, was actually a full-back, not a back-row forward. He kicked one penalty and converted Bebb's try.
[26] A 'stem Christie' is a particular kind of skiing turn.
[27] Aigle is a Swiss town near the Rhône valley floor.
[28] Osian Gwynn Ellis (1928—), Professor of Harp at the Royal Academy of Music, and his wife Rene. Ellis was in Switzerland performing at the invitation of the British Council.
[29] The match was played at Twickenham.
[30] There is a casino at Divonne-les-Bains, a French spa town and resort 4 km west of Céligny.

Sunday 14th Bernard and Claire left at 2.55.

In the evening, Osian and I played in Chateau Bossy for the Church school.[31] We ate at Café du Soleil.[32]

Monday 15th Prince Michael Vashinski arrives; he has not arrived. He's in London. He telephoned and we discussed the film *Son of Man*. We'll see. I left the car at Fleury's.[33] Rene and Osian have left.

Tuesday 16th We visited Penny Moyes at Vervier and we ate well at Café Mirdy.[34]

In the morning I went to Geneva for the car.

Snow remains but not on the major roads.

Wednesday 17th Michael Benthall from the Old Vic arrives.[35] [. . .]

We ate at Coppet and spent the afternoon drinking there.[36] M. Benthall told me that I should play *Peer Gynt* and Macbeth. We'll see.

Thursday 18th Michael has left for Milan. We had a drink with the Koesslers at their place.[37] Nice and pretty.

Saturday 20th We ate at the Restaurant La Pergola on the Bargue with Rene and Berenice.[38] Very pretty.

In the morning we bought lots of books at Naville's.[39] And a machine for cutting film.

---

[31] The Ecumenical Institute located at the Château de Bossey, Bogis-Bossey, 2 km west of Céligny. Burton read poetry, Ellis played the harp.

[32] Now the Hôtel du Soleil, Céligny.

[33] Garage Fleury et Cie, Rue du Nant, Geneva.

[34] Patricia 'Penny' Moyes (1923–2000), author of crime novels featuring the character Henry Tibbett (the first, *Dead Men Don't Ski*, was published in 1959). She had also translated Jean Anouilh's *Leocadia*, which as *Time Remembered*, ran on Broadway in 1957–8 with Richard Burton in the role of Prince Albert. Formerly a personal assistant to Peter Ustinov, she lived at Verbier, a ski resort in the Valais above the Vallée de Bagnes east of Martigny. Burton has definitely written Vervier but he may have made an error.

[35] Michael Benthall (1919–74), theatre director, and artistic director of the Old Vic, who had directed Burton in *Hamlet* in Edinburgh in 1953 and at the Old Vic in London in 1953–4, also Burton in *Coriolanus* (1953–4), *Henry V* (1955–6), and *Othello* (1955–6).

[36] Coppet, 5km south along the shore of Lake Geneva from Céligny.

[37] Edouard Koessler was a partner with the Genevan bank Bordier & Cie, where Burton banked. He lived in Céligny.

[38] *Une barque* is a small boat, so presumably this is a restaurant on a boat on Lake Geneva. There has been but is no longer a La Pergola restaurant at Geneva's Inter Continental Hotel.

[39] A Swiss bookstore chain.

Sunday 21st Nothing to do. Books all day. Hornblower – novels, detective stories etc.[40] The weather is fine every day at the moment. I met P. Ustinov at Geneva. He is leaving for Hollywood.[41]

Monday 22nd I wrote letters in the morning and in the afternoon we went to Nyon where I bought a present for Wendy the nurse – a camera with a flash attachment.

Tuesday 23rd This evening we ate at Berenice's and had a very interesting conversation with Dobrynski, the dentist, and his wife.

Wednesday 24th We ate in a little restaurant at Versoix with Penny Moyes and her friend Jim.[42] He struck me as intelligent.

I spoke with Richardson about John Osborne's play which begins next Monday.[43]

Monday 29th Yeats.[44] Dinner.

MARCH

Tuesday 8th John Ormond.[45]

Saturday 12th Dublin. Wales beat the Irish 10–9.[46] We have returned from Great Britain.

---

[40] Hornblower refers to the series of novels by C. S. Forester (1899–1966).

[41] Peter Ustinov (1921–2004), actor, author, director, playwright, raconteur. He would act alongside Richard Burton and Elizabeth Taylor in *The Comedians* (1967) and *Hammersmith is Out* (1972), which he also directed. From 1969 he was a Goodwill Ambassador for UNICEF and enlisted the support of Taylor and Burton for UNICEF ventures.

[42] Jim is James Haszard (died 1994), lawyer, interpreter, whom Penny Moyes subsequently married. Versoix is 10km south along the shore of Lake Geneva from Céligny.

[43] Tony Richardson (1928–91), director. Richardson and Burton had worked together on the film *Look Back in Anger*, and were now to collaborate on *A Subject of Scandal and Concern* (BBC TV, 1960). They would later fall out bitterly in 1968 over *Laughter in the Dark*. John Osborne (1929–94), playwright, actor, writer. Author of *Look Back in Anger* (play) and co-author of the screenplay for the film starring Burton. Author of *A Subject of Scandal and Concern*, and later involved in the prelude to the film *Divorce His, Divorce Hers* (1973).

[44] Presumably a reference to the poet William Butler Yeats (1865–1939).

[45] John Ormond (1923–90), Swansea-born director and television producer for the BBC, later an accomplished poet. Burton would narrate Ormond's half-hour documentary *Borrowed Pasture* which screened on BBC Television in 1960.

[46] At Ireland's home ground at Lansdowne Road.

Sunday 13th Nick Ray arrived from Hollywood.[47] 'Lucius' star of *King of Kings* perhaps.[48]

Monday 14th I went to Divonne. I won 40,000 francs.

Tuesday 15th Emlyn and Molly.[49]
    Nick Ray left.

Wednesday 16th Emlyn and Molly.

Sunday 20th Christening K. and J.[50]
    D. Wms arrives.[51]

Wednesday 23rd I have begun to study Russian.

APRIL

Saturday 2nd D. Wms and Liz Hardy have left.[52]
    I am going to London but I don't know the exact date, to do a new play by John Osborne. It's an interesting play.

Sunday 3rd We ate at the Café du Soleil with Kate, Ivor and Gwen.[53]

Saturday 9th To London at 11 o'clock.

Sunday 10th I have arrived in London.

Monday 25th We did *A Matter of Scandal and Concern*.

Wednesday 27th I left London at 2 o'clock by train.

---

[47] Nicholas Ray (1911–79), director. He and Burton had worked together on *Bitter Victory* (1957).
[48] Ray went on to direct *King of Kings* (1961). Presumably Burton was considering the part of Lucius, which was in due course played by Ron Randell (1918–2005), who also appeared in *The Longest Day*.
[49] Emlyn Williams (1905–87), playwright, actor, director. Emlyn Williams had been critical to Richard Burton's emergence as an actor in Britain in the 1940s. He had cast him in the stage production of *The Druid's Rest* (1943: Burton's stage debut), and directed him in *The Last Days of Dolwyn* (1949: Burton's film debut). He married Molly Shan in 1935. In 1952 he had played alongside Elizabeth Taylor in *Ivanhoe* (1952). In March 1960 he was performing in Geneva, Lausanne and Vevey.
[50] The joint christening of Kate and Jessica.
[51] David William (real name Williams) (1926–2010), actor and director.
[52] Liz Hardy. Former wife of Robert Hardy (1925—), actor.
[53] Ivor Jenkins, Richard's brother, and his wife Gwen.

Thursday 28th I arrived at Lausanne at 7 o'clock.[54]

Saturday 30th Dinner at Paul's.

MAY

Tuesday 3rd Paul Joy arrive [. . .][55]

Wednesday 4th [. . .]
    Phil 3.45.[56]
    [. . .]

Saturday 7th Paul has left.

Tuesday 10th 3.0. Pierre Folliet.[57]

Wednesday 11th P.H.B. has arrived.

Thursday 12th Guy Green arrives.[58]

Monday 16th TV Rehearsals start – oh boy, I miss Syb already!![59]

Tuesday 17th Harvey to Paris.[60]

JUNE

Thursday 9th Bernard.[61]

Monday 13th Paul opens Oxford.[62]

---

[54] Lausanne, Swiss city on the north shore of Lake Geneva.
[55] Paul Scofield (1922–2008), actor, and his wife Joy Parker (1924—).
[56] Philip Burton.
[57] Pierre Folliet was a Genevan lawyer who acted for Burton in Switzerland.
[58] Guy Green (1913–2005), cinematographer and director.
[59] Different hand; pencilled sad face. Could have been drawn by Sybil.
[60] Probably Harvey Orkin (1918–75), theatrical agent, with whom Burton was in correspondence at the time.
[61] Presumably Bernard Greenford.
[62] Paul Scofield first played the part of Sir Thomas More in the stage production of *A Man For All Seasons*, written by Robert Bolt (1924–2005), in 1960. It seems likely that this refers to its pre-London tour.

Monday 20th Mark starts

Monday 27th Gareth Moira arrives.[63]

JULY

Wednesday 6th Elfed and Cis arrive.

Thursday 7th Gareth Moira left.

---

[63] Gareth Owen, Richard's nephew, and his first wife Moira.

1965

JANUARY

1 Friday Recovered from crapulousness.

Read *Britannica* with E.[1] She's a good little girl. Picked up Sara last night in Palace Hotel swung her around and charmingly shouted 'I hate Old Women.'[2]

Putting J. Sullivan under some sort of contract.[3] He and his future Daliah Lavi leave tomorrow.[4]

2 Saturday Sara and Francis leaving tomorrow for London.[5] Out to Park hotel for make-up dinner.[6] Successful. Sara still harping on Francis' heart condition in whispers looks and sometimes so directly and in the third person so that E said once: 'You talk as if Daddy were <u>not here</u>.'

3 Sunday Lunched with Sara and Francis. Dined with Natalie Wood and Young Niven.[7] She emaciated and looks riddled with TB.[8] Pekinese eyes. Sad case. Went to Chesery – horrible noisy place.[9]

4 Monday Went to Berne to Consulate to register, also to Police at Saanen to obtain permit de séjour.[10] E unable to come. Cracked her head against open cupboard door in middle of night. Mother and Father of all black eyes. Nobody will believe I didn't hit her – such is my reputation – so we pretend she fell on slopes. [...] E and I in box-office thing of year me 10 E 11th. Ha-ha. She did not of course make a film! Not strictly fair.[11]

---

[1] *Encyclopaedia Britannica.*
[2] Sara Taylor (née Sara Viola Warmbrodt) (1896–1994) Elizabeth's mother. 'Palace Hotel': the Gstaad Palace Hotel.
[3] John Sullivan was aspiring to a career as a film producer.
[4] Daliah Lavi (1942—), actor and singer.
[5] Francis Taylor (1897–1968), Elizabeth's father.
[6] Grand Hotel Park, Gstaad.
[7] Natalie Wood (1938–81), actor. 'Young Niven' is David Niven Jr., a talent agent for the William Morris Agency, and son of the actor. He and Natalie Wood were enjoying a brief fling, staying at the Niven family home at Château d'Oex, 15 km west of Gstaad.
[8] Tuberculosis.
[9] Hostellerie Chesery, Gstaad.
[10] Berne or Bern, Switzerland. Saanen is 3 km west of Gstaad. A *permit de séjour* was an official document required by non-Swiss nationals.
[11] Burton had been ranked 10th in the *Motion Picture Herald* list of the top box-office stars in America, Taylor 11th.

5 Tuesday E. unable (Doctors' orders) to travel so caught 3.34 from Lausanne. [. . .] The train was comically irritating. A small boy, a smaller boy and a huge dog that took up two-thirds of the floor space, also two men and [. . .] voluble lady [. . .]. Arrived Paris 9.45. Met by Gaston and was taken to the Meurice <u>not</u> Lancaster as expected.[12] Wrote note authorizing Rene Weibel to take Syb's 'affaires' from Céligny. André had requested it![13] She wants home movies too. Seems a little masochistic. Paris snowless and a nice change.

6 Wednesday Left Paris 12.34 on *Golden Arrow*. Splendid train surely one of the best in the world.[14] Arrived London [. . .]. Met by Heyman and Rolls Royce.[15] Called E. who will come tomorrow by air. Had drinks in smart pub near Dorchester with Heyman.[16] Later joined by Sullivan and Daliah. Went home and so to read and so to bed à la Pepys.[17] (Had haircut in Alexandre's before leaving Paris).[18]

7 Thursday Went to Berman's at 10 and walked to Wardour Street afterwards with M. Ritt.[19] We 'kicked the script around a bit' for about an hour. Talked to Oskar Werner on the phone.[20] Sounds young and enthusiastic. Had lunch at Isow's with Ritt and Claire Bloom.[21] She was nervous but was alright. For this relief <u>much</u> thanks. Met my good girl at London airport. Her face looks extremely bruised poor old dab. Nerves made me rather snappy partner and we went earliesh to bed after bangers and mash.[22]

---

[12] Gaston Sanz was Burton's driver and bodyguard. Hôtel Le Meurice, Rue de Rivoli, Paris. Lancaster Hotel, Rue de Berri, Paris.

[13] André 'Bobo' Besançon, the caretaker and housekeeper at Pays de Galles (d. 1968).

[14] The *Golden Arrow* was a Pullman rail service linking London and Paris.

[15] John Heyman (1933—) was Burton and Taylor's British agent (as head of the International Artists Agency) and adviser on tax havens. He was also a film producer, having produced the film version of Burton's *Hamlet* (he also co-produced the stage production in New York) and would produce *Boom!*, the Taylor film *Secret Ceremony* and *Divorce His, Divorce Hers*.

[16] Burton and Taylor stayed at the Dorchester Hotel, Park Lane, London, while Burton worked on the London filming of *The Spy Who Came in from the Cold*.

[17] Samuel Pepys (1633–1703), English diarist. 'And so to bed' was a phrase Pepys commonly used.

[18] Louis Alexandre de Raimon (1922–2008) was a renowned Parisian hairdresser, known as Alexandre de Paris. Taylor was one of his regular and most celebrated clients.

[19] Bermans was a professional costumiers (owned by Monty Berman, 1912–2002), supplying film, television and theatre companies located on Shaftesbury Avenue. Wardour Street, off Oxford Street, central London. Martin or Marty Ritt (1914–90) was producing and directing *The Spy Who Came in from the Cold*.

[20] Oskar Werner (1922–84) played Fiedler in *The Spy Who Came in from the Cold*. Werner was older than Burton by three years!

[21] Isow's restaurant, Brewer Street, Soho. Claire Bloom (1931—) played Nan Perry in *The Spy Who Came in from the Cold*. She and Burton had played opposite each other in the stage play *The Lady's Not for Burning* (1949, 1950), in the Old Vic productions in 1953–54 of *Hamlet, Twelfth Night, Coriolanus* and *The Tempest*, and in the films *Alexander the Great* (1956) and *Look Back in Anger* (1959). They had been lovers during the 1950s.

[22] Sausages and mashed potato.

13 Wednesday Battersea Park at 8.15 to rehearse with Michael Hordern. [23]
Very very cold and particularly so as I am totally immobile during the scene
and Marty shot take after freezing take. Springer arrived with Hugh French.[24]
Also journalist called Palmer from AP.[25] He didn't seem like a journalist at all.
Perhaps he isn't. Hoped to have E for lunch but didn't. Ended work lunch time
(in Six Bells, King's Road) went home met E in lobby with her dad and
P. Sellers.[26] Cis and Elfed arrived (cut Ivor dead at Paddington!) and had
dinner.[27] I had mine in bed. Cold very bad.

[There are no further entries in the diary from mid-January to early May.
On 16 January 1965 Richard and Elizabeth travelled to Cardiff to see Wales
defeat England at rugby union by 14 points to 3. Filming of *The Spy Who
Came in from the Cold* continued in Dublin, Bavaria and in the Netherlands
as well as in London. During this period Richard was nominated for an
Academy Award as Best Actor for his performance in *Becket*, but the Oscar
was won by Rex Harrison for his performance in *My Fair Lady*. Burton
also made a single – 'A Married Man' – taken from the musical *Baker
Street*, and recorded some war poems by the British poet Wilfred Owen
(1893–1918). While in Dublin Burton and Taylor were visited by Franco
Zeffirelli (1923–) and a friendship developed between them that would
result in Zeffirelli directing *The Taming of the Shrew* the following year.]

MAY

5 Wednesday Operation for E.[28] Went in to see her after finishing work.
Worked at Mansion House Tube and opposite Telegraph buildings in Fleet
Street.[29] Visited Mirror Building [. . .][30] Nervous all day long worrying about
her. Went there slightly sloshed and they allowed her home as long as she

---

[23] Battersea Park, on the south bank of the River Thames, opposite the Chelsea Embankment. Michael
Hordern (1911–95) played the part of Ashe in *The Spy Who Came in from the Cold*. He had played with
both Burton and Taylor in *The VIPs* (1963), would do so again in *The Taming of the Shrew* (1967), and
alongside Burton alone in *Where Eagles Dare* (1968), *Anne of the Thousand Days* (1970) and *The
Medusa Touch* (1978). He and Burton had appeared on stage together in the Old Vic productions of
Hamlet, King John, Twelfth Night and *The Tempest*.
[24] John Springer (1916–2001) was a publicist who headed the East Coast branch of the Arthur P. Jacobs
public relations company, and worked as a press agent for Burton and Taylor. Hugh French was
Burton's London agent who also became Taylor's agent, and who later moved to Hollywood.
[25] Raymond E. Palmer of the Associated Press's London office.
[26] The Six Bells was at 195–7, King's Road, Chelsea. Peter Sellers (1925–80), actor. Burton was to make
a fleeting appearance in the Sellers film *What's New Pussycat?*
[27] Paddington station is the terminal for railway lines entering London from Wales and the west of
England.
[28] Taylor underwent minor surgery of an undisclosed nature. From the evidence of her note on 6 May
it might have been something gynaecological.
[29] Mansion House tube station is on the District and Circle lines, located on Cannon Street. Telegraph
buildings were the offices of the *Daily Telegraph* and *Sunday Telegraph*, then on Fleet Street.
[30] Mirror Building was the offices of the *Daily Mirror* and *Sunday Mirror*.

didn't move about too much. Watched TV in bed. Rode on bus round and round Kensington Tube Station.[31] [. . .]

6 Thursday Last day *Spy.*

> Husband was sweet to me. And I know how much he hates 'ill people' and avoids any and <u>all</u> signs of pain in someone he likes and loves. But he has been wonderful with me. Spoiled me like mad!! I adore it!! Maybe – (they told me) after another operation I could give him a baby. I want that more than anything in the whole world. <u>Please</u> let him <u>know</u> nothing will happen to me. <u>Please</u> make him say 'Yes'. (Please God). [Elizabeth Taylor's hand.]

8 Saturday Party Spy.

11 Tuesday Dinner at Mirabelle.[32]

16 Sunday

> Lunch with Peter Glenville and Bill – saw a wild and crazy house next door.[33] 'Poofsville' should be the name of it. Peter sweet and excited about R. in G. I.[34] Then I had to go alone to see Sandpiper! It is not quite as bad as I thought. R. looks better than I have ever seen him (he's so bloody beautiful – and sexy) and he takes words, so mundane, and turns them into something deeply moving and real – No one else in the world could have done what he does. He made me cry. I'm not even ashamed of what I did – but only when I acted with him. He makes us all look better than we are. [Elizabeth Taylor's hand.]

17 Monday

> I was supposed to do all kinds of things today – like buy dresses (and things and stuff) Things I would ordinarily have loved and indulged in – buying clothes and jewels. I still have over 5 thou' to spend on my allowance and 45 thous of insurance money for jewelery – but we did something else – Something more beautiful than anything in the world. My God it was lovely! Then we had a late dinner at 'Mediterannée' and talked about all the things

---

[31] South Kensington tube station.

[32] Mirabelle, Curzon Street, Piccadilly, London.

[33] Peter Glenville (1913–96), stage and film director. He had directed Burton in *Becket* and would direct him again in *The Comedians*. Hardy William ('Bill') Smith (d. 2001) was a theatrical producer, and Glenville's lover. Glenville had also sacked Richard from *Adventure Story* in 1949.

[34] *Reflections in a Golden Eye* was to be made in 1967, starring Taylor and Marlon Brando (1924–2004), directed by John Huston (1906–87), based on the novel by Carson McCullers (1917–67).

we are going to do on our honeymoon – It's almost 5 years long now.[35] Better every day! [Elizabeth Taylor's hand.]

18 Tuesday First night of honeymoon (?) by leaving Paris driving ourselves in R.R.[36] Followed, for a time by two press. E. has bangs.[37] Can't make up mind whether like or not. E called Baron E. Rothschild to make intro to J. Heyman.[38] Lunched (pizza) at Bas Bréau Barbizon.[39] Lovely. Then went on to Avallon and are staying at 'La Poste'.[40] E. behaving as if it really were the first time for us both to be married to each other. Have to be careful. I might become idolatrous. Wish I knew her well enough to tell her how exciting life is with her about.

19 Wednesday Visited chateau 'Roche Pot' seen from the road.[41] Chilled to the bone.
     Left about 1.0 pm. Talked Glenville re *Man to be King* and *Golden Eye*.[42] Curious Ray Stark.[43] Napoleon stayed at 'Poste' from Elba before he met Ney.[44] 'Girl' enjoys everything including ugliness. Very worth-while woman. Lunched at Cote d'Or at Saulieu.[45] Splendid. She spoiled by everyone. Enjoy it, donkey, while it lasts says he enviously. Love her. What a Lune de miel.[46] Staying here at hotel called 'de France' which makes Copper House look like Savoy.[47] But with usual perversity E thinks it romantic. The sheets are clean. Manager inarticulate with excitement. Press came to restaurant de Bressanne.[48] Two photographers. One's flash refused to work. (Memo write about reaction to fame or lack of it).

20 Thursday

Last night the room became beautiful! When we woke up it <u>looked</u> ugly but had already become a 'lovely experience'. The manager was so touching that it made us both feel all kind of funny. The way he kept smiling and nodding over the heads of the two locals photographers it was like he'd given birth to

---

[35] La Méditerranée Place de l'Odéon, Paris.
[36] Rolls-Royce.
[37] Bangs: a hairstyle involving fringes across the forehead.
[38] Baron Elie de Rothschild (1917–2007), financier.
[39] Hôtellerie du Bas Bréau, Barbizon, Fontainebleau, France.
[40] Hôtellerie de la Poste, Avallon, Yonne, France.
[41] Chateau de la Rochepot, south of Breaune, Côte d'Or.
[42] *The Man Who Would Be King*, based on the short story by Rudyard Kipling (1865–1936), which would eventually appear in 1975 starring Sean Connery (1930—) and Michael Caine (1933—).
[43] Ray Stark (1915–2004), producer, 7 Arts films. He was to produce *Reflections in a Golden Eye*.
[44] The Emperor Napoleon (1769–1821), on escaping from exile on Elba, stayed at the Hôtel de la Poste, Saulieu, before his confrontation with Marshal Ney (1769–1815) at Auxerre, some 90km to the north-west, on 14 March 1815.
[45] La Côte d'Or, Saulieu.
[46] Literally, 'honeymoon'.
[47] Hôtel de France, Chalon-sur-Saône. The Copperhouse is a pub in Cwmafan. The Savoy Hotel, the Strand, London, is a five-star establishment.
[48] Auberge Bressanne, Chalon-sur-Saône.

us. Drove 40 kms to Nantua for lunch, sweet woman told the route to avoid long line of customs – it worked![49] Saw Geneva for first time – beautiful! Saw R.'s house, met André – felt very funny – as I knew I would – So did R. got over it <u>soon</u> – Thank God. Stopped at Chateau De C. and and the 'Other Place' – Home! Kids! Home!![50] [Elizabeth Taylor's hand.]

21 Friday Got up late midday! Went tramping with Michael, Christopher, Liza after having watched them at the Riding School.[51] Liza and Mike splendid but Christoph started to show panic and with my usual hatred of watching others humiliated I left with Maria for a stroll to the river. E, feeling the same, came out shortly afterwards. Chris obviously upset at the end of the ride. Asked me if I would ride for pleasure. I said no I'd rather read a good book. I think he agrees heartily but he mustn't be stopped. The shame of it. Dined at home. Fried chicken.

22 Saturday Bad day. Woke in foul temper. Read *Woolf* in the sun then went for walk with boys and Liza to neighbouring village.[52] Leg-weary. Went to Olden with E.[53] Started picking on her – dined at home on turkey – then went on to a rip and tear quarrel with no holds barred. Slept <u>alone</u>! <u>Fools</u>!

23 Sunday Woke up in wrong bed! Took E to Alte Post at Weissenburg for lunch.[54] Drove back with top down. For a time. Played Liar Poker Dice with E in Olden with many variations.[55] Maria fell backwards off dining chair. Waiting invitation for Wednesday to go Côte d'Azur arranged P. Glenville.[56] Splendid etc!

24 Monday Still sleeping too much – must be altitude – woke at 10.30.[57] Got word that house in St Tropez OK but wait for invitation which should arrive tomorrow.[58] Had lunch at Olden where we were taught a dice game called 'Yatsee' – most interesting.[59] Taught it at 1pm (approximately) and were still

[49] The town of Nantua, west of Geneva.

[50] This refers to Taylor's house, the Chalet Ariel, at Gstaad. Sold in 2001 'Chateau De C' may mean Chateau D'Oex.

[51] Michael Wilding (1953—) and Christopher Wilding (1955—): Elizabeth's two sons by her marriage to Michael Wilding Sr (1912–79). Liza Todd (1957—), Elizabeth's daughter by her marriage to Mike Todd (1907–58).

[52] 'Woolf' refers to the script of *Who's Afraid of Virginia Woolf?* that Burton and Taylor were to film (later that year). Initially, in 1964, Taylor had been approached to act the part of Martha. Subsequently it was agreed that Burton would also play the part of George.

[53] Hotel Olden, Gstaad.

[54] The Hotel Alte Post, Weissenburg, near Darstetten. Weissenburg is 30 km from Gstaad.

[55] A dice game, this version using poker dice.

[56] The Côte d'Azur, or French Riviera, on the Mediterranean coast of south-east France.

[57] Gstaad is 1,100 m above sea level.

[58] St Tropez, Provence, France.

[59] Yahtzee, a dice game, first released in 1965.

playing it 6.45pm (approximately). Children joined us at about 4.30. Dined at home on pork etc. Ate with enjoyment for the first time. Will probably leave for South of France on Wednesday if all goes well. Can't think what stages to do the journey in. Eli Roths. calling E.[60] What for? What a funny fellow. And so to bed.

25 Tuesday

Received invitation to South of France. Packed for California and S. of Fr. And the boat – Pooped! Went to 'Olden' played 'Yahtesee' (?) for hours just the two of us then Paul and his girl – it was great fun.[61] The kids are even better than any of us – Cheeky bags!

What a funny night = starting a honeymoon! It's so soppy! We don't really know <u>where</u> we're going! (Keep fingers crossed about House – that it really happened!!) [Elizabeth Taylor's hand.]

26 Wednesday 'You write,' She said, 'because you must tell how lovely this day has been and how it's so honeymooney.' What,' I said, 'What if I write that I am bitterly angry because so sharply lovely a day could come to me only in my 39th year?' Anyway, we're in a place called Talloires in the High Savoy in an old monastery called L'Abbeye, and we arrived at 9.00, and we loved the room, and we had the two beds put together, and we saw Liston knocked out by Clay in slow motion, and [. . .] we walked along the lapping shore, and we came back to our cell and we loved being here and we talked about a stood-up lonely boy and so to bed.[62]

27 Thursday Went to lunch at 'Père Bise.'[63] Very good but all the menus are so similar. Had poularde de bresse.[64] A family at next table gave E a bunch of 'Lily of the Valley.' Love in the afternoon. Then dozed and read K. Allott's anthology of modern poetry.[65] What a little pussycat he is in his comments. Wrote PCs to the children in Gstaad.[66] Read some more. Had drinks and dinner and so to bed and reading. I am drinking too steadily – lunch time and dinner time. Will stop when we get to La Reine Jeanne for a few days.[67] Am still a bundle of nerves. Wish I didn't have to work so soon.

---

[60] Elie de Rothschild.

[61] Paul Neshamkin was the children's tutor.

[62] L'Abbaye is in Talloires, on the eastern shore of Lac d'Annecy, Haute Savoie, France. Cassius Clay, later Muhammad Ali (1942—), knocked out Sonny Liston (1932–71) in controversial circumstances in a world heavyweight championship bout in Lewiston, Maine, USA, on 25 May 1965.

[63] L'Auberge du Père Bise at Talloires.

[64] *Poularde de bresse* is a celebrated chicken dish.

[65] *The Penguin Book of Contemporary Verse*, selected with an introduction and notes by Kenneth Allott (1912–73), published in 1950.

[66] Postcards.

[67] Villa La Reine Jeanne, Les Baux de Provence, Provence. South of Avignon.

28 Friday 'What's your name?'
  'Elizabeth Taylor'
  'Prove it.'
  'My father's name was Taylor.'
  'Prove it.'
  'I love him that's all'
  'Prove it.'
  'Where were you born?'
  'Hampstead, England'
  'Prove it'
  'I have a birth thing'
  'Show it.'
  'I don't have it with me'
  'Find it.'
  'I am alone and defenceless'
  'Why?'
  'I argue.'
  'Whom with?'
  'You'
  'Why'
  'Because we love each other.'
  'Prove it!'
  Just be<u>cau</u>se that's all! [Elizabeth Taylor's hand.]

29 Saturday

Woke up feeling very contrite – both of us – what a stupid waste of energy and time! Quietly and gently we became us again – had lunch at Les Baux, Baumaniére, almost ran out of Gas – had a hell of a time finding our way here.[68] I tried to be R's navigator – but the map and the roads are so poorly marked that we both became screaming 'things'. Anyway, we are finally Home. Already the strings of nerves are loosening. It's a really lovely place and the dearest people are taking care of us. 'Honeymoon' is back with us. God, I love him so! Make me a better wife (Please) [Elizabeth Taylor's hand.]

30 Sunday This establishment we stay at is like a hotel but is not. Its owner Cmdr. Weiller lets us use it and his servants and his food and wine for nothing.[69] Yet there are signs as in a hotel. 'Put out lights.' 'Please use this bag for sanitary towels. Do not flush down toilet.' We must find out more. Downstairs

---

[68] Probably L'Oustau de Baumanière, Les Baux.
[69] Commandant Paul-Louis Weiller (1893–1993), aviator, engineer, industrialist and philanthropist. Owner of the Villa La Reine Jeanne, built for him in 1928.

in the Salon Burt has found scrapbooks of guests in past years.[70] The Chaplins. D. Fairbanks Jr. Merle Oberon, Margot Fonteyn etc.[71] We shopped in Lavandou today and drove around a bit.[72] Cold pork for dinner and 'William' to finish.[73] I played piano, read Sundays. Burt beat me at Yahtsee. Teach her! Weather unfriendly. Hope to bathe soon. Burt looking very pretty today.

31 Monday Rose late. Can't understand this continual late sleeping. [. . .] Day is gone before one looks around. Took first dip in sea. Cold. Went for walk with Burt to local which is a bar on the sand a mile and a bit from the house. Burt walked there and back. What next? Paced the return. Fish and omelette 'porquerolle' for dessert.[74] Read Orwell's *Clergyman's Daughter*.[75] Uneven.

JUNE

1 Tuesday Got up 9.50 went to Lavandou. Bought cigs, books, sandals (lots of tar on beach) b. costume.[76] Woke Burt up at 12.00. Meantime workmen were mending gate so couldn't get in. Had coffee in local. Nice people. Swam? sun bathed, lunched, bed read, ate, slept. Whew! Burt a bit sarky today.

He should frigging talk! [Elizabeth Taylor's hand.]

2 Wednesday Rose 10 o'clock but weather dull. Went downstairs and began Grenier's M.S. 'Yes and back again'.[77] Very flatly written, ridden with clichés and so far difficult to get through. But it has been accepted so there. I wouldn't have accepted it either as commercial or artistic possibility but there's no knowing. We then visited Bormez which is enchanting and were photographed.[78] Then we sought 'pizza' and found it in a rather drab little place on the main road. With it we drank Pernod and later vin blanc. We called at our local on way home. Deserted. Apparently the estate is 70 hectares and the price after the war was 2 sous sq. metre! Had good row with Burt and accused her, among other things, of lousy taste. She accused me among other things of snobbery. I said the only thing we had in common was Yahtsee. I forgot some other things.

---

[70] 'Burt': one of Burton's many nicknames for Taylor.
[71] Charlie Chaplin (1889–1977), actor; other famous family members and actors include Sydney (1885–1965), Charles's older brother; Sydney Earl (1926–2009) Charles's son; and Geraldine (1944—) his daughter. Merle Oberon (1911–79), actor; Margot Fonteyn (1919–91), ballerina.
[72] Le Lavandou, east of Toulon.
[73] Possibly the liqueur Poire William.
[74] The Ile de Porquerolles is an island just off the French coast, south of Hyères.
[75] The novel *A Clergyman's Daughter* (1935) by George Orwell (1903–50).
[76] Bathing costume.
[77] Richard Grenier (1923–2002), newspaper correspondent, screenwriter, and novelist. *Yes and Back Again*, novel, (1966).
[78] Probably Bormes-les-Mimosas, inland from Le Lavandou.

3 Thursday [. . .] For the first time today the phone rang! Twice! Gaston being officious. R. Hanley calling at our request from Greece.[79] He goes to London tomorrow. We did nothing all day. I read papers from cover to cover. Endlessly. Weather good but windy and therefore impossible to do anything except crosswords and eat endless cherries (delicious) and irritate Burt. I drank nothing and pilled nothing. But still I'm lethargic. Where went my energy? Read delightful 'tec novel by ?. Very good anyway.

4 Friday Sat and sunbathed most of the day but wind still a little cold for swimming. Went into Lavandou to replenish book supply. We stopped at local on way home and drank beer (me) pernod (Burt). Learned to our horror that Dick Merriman's adopted baby girl died. We don't know the cause. This means he will work with Burt on the boat instead of here. We had sole for supper. [. . .] Poor Merriman. There's nowt one can do. More adoption is the answer I suppose.

5 Saturday

> Lingering Day! R. went to town after washing the car (with the top down, which caused all kinds of wolf calls) to buy me a present – a bikini – It turned out to be small for my boobs – so he went back (stores were closed). I was washing my hair so could not go with him Then he went back after lunch to get it. I think he <u>enjoyed</u> the rides in the Rolls with the top down. I must say they do look dishy together! We got all dressed up for dinner, went to Le Lavendou and had our first dinner out – marvelous! [*sic*] Strange people around the village most of them are young but weird looking R. got more whistles than I did. Stopped at Pizza Place for desert [*sic*]. R. lost <u>beautifully</u> at Yahtzee! Oi givalt![80] [Elizabeth Taylor's hand.]

6 Sunday Stayed at home and ate lunch – salad and roquefort dressing. Stayed in the sun almost all the time. We are both getting quite brown but prefer the mornings on the balcony to the beach in the noon. It's so boring sunbathing on sand. We drank little and ate a lot for dinner. [. . .]

7 Monday Whitsun Monday and pouring tropically with rain. We went to lunch [. . .] place called Les Roches Fleuries.[81] Very nicely situated. Food OK. Talked nonsense pleasantly with some people at the next table and so to the bar. A little shopping for Kleenex and so home.[82] Dinner at home and sleep.

---

[79] Richard (often 'Dick') Hanley (1909–71) was Taylor's secretary, who became press secretary for both Burton and Taylor. He had been Mike Todd's secretary's assistant. He performed a wide variety of tasks for the Burton/Taylor household, including helping to look after the children.
[80] A Yiddish expression conveying shock or amazement. Often written 'oy gevalt'.
[81] Hôtel Les Roches Fleuries at Aiguebelle, east along the coast from Le Lavandou.
[82] Kleenex: tissues.

8 Tuesday Woke fitfully at 10. Sat on balcony until lunch reading newspapers. Learned to our relief that the 'Gemini Twins' were back from the Cosmos safely.[83] For some reason we both felt oddly nervous about them. It is odd, too, that I almost always think – no condescension intended – of Americans as being gifted and brave but almost always child-like. White, the man who walked for 20 minutes in space, when asked how it was replied 'It was really something.' How deep was Columbus' mind? Wasn't Churchill a boy with a gift for man's words? What was Alexander?[84] Who Caesar? Not Rex Harrison.[85] Idiot. Strange love affair this afternoon. Tolerable agony. Agonizing Love. Lovely pain.

9 Wednesday Lunch at home and then we packed a week-end bag and left for Roches Fleuries, a Hotel at place called Aiguebelle four kms on from Lavandou. We obtained a room overlooking the sea. Nice enough. [. . .] Went to dinner at Lavandou and both had moules maranieres.[86] Had a quarrel again. Nasty habit we have. Home and to Yahtsee and bed in sullen silence. It's always (nearly) alright in the morning.

10 Thursday Called R. Hanley this morn to have him send some money from Antibes where he is staying at the Hotel du Cap.[87] Told us that Sybil is getting married on Sunday next to a member of a 'Pop' group called 'The Wild Ones!' We don't know his name yet but we <u>do</u> know that he's only 24. This makes him 11 years younger than Syb I think.[88] I hope to God he's a tidy bloke and will be good for Kate as well as Syb.[89] Maybe I'll see K a bit more often now. How I love that child. Tubby old thing as she thinks she is. What sort of a telegram should we send? Witty, serious. (Lots of puns available on 'Wild Ones'.)

11 Friday Returned home today to La Reine Jeanne. We shall be leaving on Monday for Hotel du Cap at Antibes then away on Wednesday to USA. Sybil's boyfriend disapproved of by all who know her and of the marriage. She has known him apparently only three months and they have been serious, as 'twere, only three weeks. I hope she knows what she's doing. Burt points out that she knows quite a few people who have happily remained married to men years and years younger than themselves. Let us pray. Weather continually brilliant though everyone native complains of the mistral.[90] Not us!

---

[83] This refers to the second manned spaceflight by the US spacecraft *Gemini 4*. The astronauts were James Alton McDivitt (1929–) and Edward Higgins White (1930–67). White was the first American to walk in space.

[84] Alexander the Great.

[85] Rex Harrison (1908–90) had played Julius Caesar in *Cleopatra* and would play alongside Richard Burton in *Staircase* (1969).

[86] Moules marinières: mussels.

[87] Hôtel du Cap-Eden-Roc, Antibes, on the Cap d'Antibes, west of Nice.

[88] Richard's former wife Sybil married the musician Jordan Christopher (born Jordan Zankoff, Youngstown, Ohio, 1942–96), lead singer of The Wild Ones.

[89] 'Tidy' is a South Walian colloquialism (in this context) for 'decent', 'good'.

[90] The mistral is a strong wind associated with the Provence region.

12 Saturday Old Burt ill with tooth trouble and aching bones. Fussed over her a bit and she had food upstairs for a change – at least lunch. We dined downstairs [...] chicken and tomato salad. No drink at all today. Talk of drink – Michel Jazy has just broken the mile world's record and, according to *Figaro*, drinks a quart of red wine a day!!?[91] No way of finding out anymore about Sybil's feller. The Press (English) have been hounding us a bit – *Mirror* and *Express* – probably about Sybil. Talked to nobody. 'Phoning here is impossible a sort of Olympian shouting match.

13 Sunday Talked to Aaron today who was dourly opposed to Sybil's marriage.[92] The chap's name is Zaroff. Greek American from Ohio. 'Is 24 looks 18' says Aaron. Penniless. Syb retains $200,000. Rest goes into trust for Children. Roddy furious.[93] Helen Greenford refuses to go to Wedding.[94] Ivor delighted! Phil not caring.[95] I talked to Kate for a moment. She sounded awfully Yankee.

14 Monday Left for Antibes. Much farewelling [...] at the local (called the Paillotte).[96] Lunched in Leï Mouscadins at St Tropez.[97] Stopped for a drink at Carlton in Cannes.[98] Went for a walk. Met editor of *Sunday Mirror*.[99] Got sloshed.

15 Tuesday Woke late (around 11.00) and lunched on hors d'oeuvres at Eden Roc which is of course the restaurant for the Hotel.[100] We then went to Nice airport to pick up kids flying from Geneva with Bea.[101] Later I took the kids swimming on the rock and gave Michael and Christopher two key-ring compasses which they adore. For early dinner we all went to Juan les Pins to eat pizza.[102] We watched with fascination how many people were fascinated by the old Rolls-R. I don't recollect any car getting such attention – particularly in France. Rather a savage game of Yahtsee which I lost.

---

[91] Michel Jazy (1936–), silver medallist in the 1500m at the Rome Olympics in 1960, set a new world record for the mile of 3 min. 53.6 sec. on 9 June 1965. *Le Figaro* is a French daily newspaper.
[92] Aaron Frosch (1925–89), Richard's lawyer.
[93] Roddy McDowall (1928–98), actor, friend of Richard, Sybil and Elizabeth. He had played alongside Burton in an adaptation of *The Tempest* for NBC television in 1960, also in the New York production of *Camelot* (1960–1), had shared a villa with Richard and Sybil in Rome during the making of *Cleopatra*, and had had a part in *The Longest Day*.
[94] Helen Greenford (b. 1941): Sybil's niece, daughter of her half-sister Linda, who had married Bernard Greenford.
[95] Philip Burton had moved to the USA in 1954.
[96] La Paillotte, Avenue Gavine, Hyères.
[97] Leï Mouscardins, 1 Rue de Portalet, St Tropez, east along the coast from Le Lavandou.
[98] Carlton Hotel, Cannes, just west of Antibes.
[99] The editor of the *Sunday Mirror* at the time was Michael Christiansen (1926–84).
[100] Hôtel du Cap Eden Roc, Antibes.
[101] 'Bea' interlined. Bea was the children's governess. Nice is a short distance east of Antibes.
[102] Juan les Pins, between Antibes and Cannes.

16 Wednesday E had fittings for her clothes from Dior today.[103] They look very good. I packed for myself and Dick and Bea packed for Burt.[104] We went to catch the tender for the *Michelangelo* and sat for over an hour on the open deck (no place to hide) while the whole South of France took photographs.[105] The boat, compared with the Cunard Lines, is surprisingly utilitarian and appallingly decorated.[106] Everything looks very cheap and chromy. Photographer scrambling to snap us as we boarded from the Tender hit Maria in the face with a shoulder hanging camera. I slashed him across the neck and back. Impertinent sod.

The page for 17–23 June is missing. The next entry is:

24 Thursday In fury one night I tore out the preceding page of diary. Silly of course but there you are. Tomorrow we arrive in NY. J. Springer will meet the boat [. . .]. We shan't see him or his press friends until much much later. I will leave the rest of this day's journal until tomorrow's over.!

Arrived NY. Usual Press. Usual idiotic questions usual idiotic answers. Tomorrow have arranged to go out into the country to place called Quogue to see Kate, Ivor and Gwen.[107] E. very nervous but as much as I.

28 Monday Left NY for LA today.

29 Tuesday Had lunch with Kup in the pump room of the Ambassador.[108]

30 Wednesday Met Hermes Pan on train and also he was on the boat![109]

JULY

1 Thursday Arrived LA from Chicago and NY. Lovely journey on the train. Read biography of Dylan by Fitzgibbon which I am enjoying if an account of so desperate a life can be described as enjoyable.[110]

We disembarked at Pomona in the hope that it would beat the Press but they were there.[111] Drove back home with J. Springer. [. . .] The house is alright. Lots of things don't work but the grounds are beautiful and there are <u>two</u>

---

[103] Christian Dior the fashion house.
[104] Dick being Dick Hanley.
[105] The SS *Michelangelo*, a liner built for the North Atlantic crossing in 1962.
[106] Burton had previously travelled on the Cunard Lines' *Queen Mary*.
[107] Quogue, Long Island. Home of Aaron Frosch.
[108] Irv 'Kup' Kupcinet (1912–2003), newspaper columnist and television talk show host, married to Esther 'Essee' Solomon (d. 2001). The Pump Room, restaurant, in the Ambassador East Hotel, Chicago.
[109] Hermes Pan (1910–90), American choreographer and dancer, who worked closely with Fred Astaire and Ginger Rogers, and who had been the choreographer for *Cleopatra*.
[110] Constantine Fitzgibbon, *The Life of Dylan Thomas* (1965). Burton, who had been a friend of Thomas, would write a review of this volume for the *New York Herald Tribune*.
[111] Pomona, Los Angeles.

swimming pools. The kids love it of course. Went to see Francis. He moves badly but his brain's OK.

2 Friday Swam in the pool all morning and searched for Shanni who has got herself lost or stolen.[112] She is so minute that she might be stuck in the undergrowth for all I know. Had lunch with Francis and Sara at Scandia[113] [. . .] Saw Mike Nichols and girl called Rosemary Forsythe.[114] Mike loves fairly dumb girls. Taught E. to play billiards. Did some good shots.

3 Saturday Spent day in and around pool. Stiff with sun and playing football with Thomas à Becket.[115] Dick and John showed us delicious new car from Italy – a Fiat about the size of a Mini Cooper with chains, four doors and a canopied top.[116] Took E for drive around Holmby Hills.[117]

4 Sunday Had Francis and Sara for barbecue lunch [. . .] Two boys went down the beach with their father and Maggie.[118] Mike Snr more incoherent than ever. Rex came over[119] [. . .] and taught me new word game. We taught him Yahtsee. Nice guy.

5 Monday Poolside again. E read *V. Woolf* for first time – at least new script. Val came over for lunch and dinner.[120] We visited her place and tried pool chair with turbulent water. Seems splendid but we shall know tomorrow if it makes us stiff. Waiting anxiously for reply from Syb re. Kate. I hope she'll be alright about letting her come out to stay with us. What will I do if she doesn't comply amiably? Have written letters to Kate, Graham, Gwyneth, Ivor, Syb. Whew!

[This is the last entry, apart from a table of scores from Yahtzee!. Work on *Who's Afraid of Virginia Woolf?* began the following day with three weeks of rehearsals at the Warner Studios, Burbank, Los Angeles.]

---

[112] A pet.
[113] Scandia restaurant, Sunset Boulevard.
[114] Mike Nichols (1931—), at this point renowned as a theatre director. He was to make his directorial debut on film with *Who's Afraid of Virginia Woolf?* (1966). Rosemary Forsyth (sometimes Forsythe, Forsyth-Yuro) (1944–), actor.
[115] Their Yorkshire Terrier.
[116] John Lee, Dick Hanley's secretary.
[117] A district to the immediate west of Beverly Hills.
[118] 'Their father': Michael Wilding Sr, actor and agent. 'Maggie': Dame Margaret Leighton (1922–76), by this time married to Michael Wilding Sr, and who would appear with Taylor in *X, Y and Zee*.
[119] Dr Rexford Kennamer, a doctor at the Hollywood Presbyterian hospital, often treated Taylor and Burton when they were in California. He had met Taylor at the time of Montgomery Clift's car accident in 1956, and had become part of Taylor's wider entourage, occasionally accompanying her on trips abroad, including to Rome during the filming of *Cleopatra*. He was physician to many famous Hollywood stars.
[120] Valerie Douglas, at this time Burton's publicist in Beverly Hills.

1966

Richard stopped keeping his 1965 diary in July, and did not start making entries for 1966 until mid-March. From July to August 1965 he and Elizabeth lived on Carolwood Drive, in the Holmby Hills in Bel Air, while rehearsing and filming *Who's Afraid of Virginia Woolf?* In late August they moved from Los Angeles to Smith College, Northampton, Massachusetts, for location filming. In the meantime their film *The Sandpiper* was released. In late September they returned to Hollywood, where Richard celebrated his fortieth birthday on 10 November 1965. On this occasion *Woolf*'s producer and screenwriter Ernest Lehman (1915–2005) presented Richard with an original edition of the essays of Francis Bacon. Elizabeth gave him an Oldsmobile Toronado. Filming on *Woolf* ended on 13 December 1965, after which Richard and Elizabeth visited Elizabeth's brother Howard and his family in Del Mar, San Diego, before spending Christmas in Los Angeles. January saw both embroiled in legal proceedings with Twentieth Century-Fox. In February 1966 Richard and Elizabeth journeyed to Oxford, staying at the Randolph Hotel, to fulfil a promise they had made in 1963 to Richard's former tutor, Nevill Coghill. After ten days of rehearsals they appeared in an Oxford University Dramatic Society production of Christopher Marlowe's *Dr Faustus*, staged at the Oxford Playhouse. The production, which met with a mixed critical response, ran for just one week. Accounts vary of how much money it made – the lowest estimate is £3,000, the highest £17,000. The intention had been that monies raised from the performance (and from the film version that followed) would be put towards a fund-raising initiative (the University Theatre Appeal Fund) designed to provide the university with a new theatre and arts centre. Although these grander designs were not realized, in part because the film itself made a loss, in 1976 the Burton Taylor Studio was added to the Playhouse building.

Following *Faustus*, Burton and Taylor moved on to Rome, where they would begin filming *The Taming of the Shrew* under the direction of Franco Zeffirelli. They stayed in a villa on the Via Appia Antica.

MARCH

Friday 18th, Rome[1] Lunched at home with Franco Zeffirelli, Alexandre de Paris, Irene Sharaff and Dick McWhorter.[2] Irene is a funny contradiction. And enormously concerned with her own dignity.

After lunch [. . .] we had a press conference. The usual stupid answers to the inevitable stupid questions. What a bore they are.

Dinner at home alone and fried chicken. Must read script and original version of *Shrew* again before Monday.[3] De Sica coming to lunch tomorrow we think.[4] We are to dine with Edward Albee on Sat (tomorrow) night.[5] I hope he's more articulate than the last time I met him in NY.

Saturday 19th We dawdled about all day until dinner in Rome at Ranieres (near Spanish Square) with Zeffirelli, Albee and his friend.[6]

Albee was very flattering, especially to E!, about *V. Woolf* and, for him, was very talkative. They were doing a swift tour of Europe – a day here, a day there. He says that he is ⅔ through a new play which should be going on Broadway in the Autumn.[7] It contains 4 men and 2 women. He said that it was 'a very curious play, a very curious play indeed.' After *Tiny Alice* and *V. Woolf* how curious can you, as they say, get.[8] He told us that he thinks about a play for six months approx and then writes it in about three. There is no second draft. It is as it is, and so remains.

We had a hair raising drive to Rome pursued by paparazzi all the way.[9] I think Mario the driver takes too much notice of these butterflies of the gutter. They risk their lives too. Why don't they go where there's real risk. Like a war. Like Viet Nam. Like anywhere.

I finished reading Ugo Betti's play *The Queen and the Rebels*.[10] It is quite good and very actable but weakens quickly at the end. Perhaps they could do something about it. Also some of the dialogue is lamentably old fashioned but all that could be cured.

---

[1] In this diary Burton enters where he is writing from on most days. Here only the initial change of location will be entered.

[2] Franco Zeffirelli, director of *The Taming of the Shrew*. Irene Sharaff (1910–93), Elizabeth Taylor's costume designer for the film, who had also been costume designer for *Cleopatra* and *Who's Afraid of Virginia Woolf?* Richard F. McWhorter, executive producer for the film, had been assistant to the producer on both *The Spy Who Came in from the Cold* and *Becket*.

[3] *The Taming of the Shrew*.

[4] Vittorio De Sica (1901–74), director. De Sica would direct Burton in *The Voyage*.

[5] Edward Albee (1928—), playwright, author of *Who's Afraid of Virginia Woolf?*

[6] Hotel Ranieri, Via Venti Settembre. Albee's partner at this time was William Pennington.

[7] Albee's *A Delicate Balance* would win the Pulitzer Prize in 1966.

[8] *Tiny Alice*; play by Albee, premiered 1964.

[9] Paparazzi – press photographers.

[10] Ugo Betti (1892–1953), *The Queen and the Rebels* (1951).

Sunday 20th So far we had lunch with Vittorio De Sica and his wife and two children (boys).

One boy played the guitar – what a horrible instrument, worse than a mouth-accordion, an accordion, a Jew's harp or a paper-and-comb. Worse than beating on nothing with a nought. But, however, fond parents love the idea of a noise – however absurd – made by their dearest and nearest. De Sica really looked on his son with admiration. He had, I mean the son (and the father too when he, the son, was playing) the face of a demented and somewhat stupefied fish. The Beatles have a lot to pay for. Even my own. Boys I mean. How dull I am.

So. They came to lunch and next Monday we dine with them and we shall also watch *Umberto D*.[11] I must, somehow, get out of that.

And so the day wore inevitably on to another regret in the lost and in future to be recalled days.

What shall we do now. Why not if it's so intolerably wearying. Why not go to bye-byes?

Bugger it then. Let's row.

Tuesday 22nd On Monday, the missing day in this diary, we went to the studios at 6pm to have chat and drinks with crew and cast. We took Liza, Maria and Karen (their nurse) with us. Everybody seemed reasonably pleased and felt that it was a fairly good first day – especially as it was Franco Z's first film.

I had been earlier in the morning, though I was not called, to wish good luck and see how things were. There was a long initial hold-up lasting about 1½ hours waiting for a change of horse. [. . .] Later that morning I went over to the back-lot [. . .] to see the first of the glass shots.[12] That looks good too.

I had lunch with Mr Haggiag.[13] I had been warned that he was a 'wheeler and dealer.' He is, I think, but appears to respond easily to flattery which is always a great weakness in negotiation and a strength if the other gent (for the other gent) can use it.

I took Liza and Maria to school this morning and then went to the bookshop on the Via Veneto and bought some 20 or 30 paperbacks.[14] ½ dozen detective stories, Ludovic Kennedy's *Trial of Stephen Ward* a genuine establishment horror story.[15] And a palpably unjust trial – nightmarishly so. Harry S. Truman's *Memoirs*.[16] Ingenuous to the point of admiration, and also wonder

---

[11] *Umberto D.*; film by Vittorio De Sica, 1952.
[12] A glass shot is the shooting of a scene through glass which may have been painted to represent, for example, scenery.
[13] Robert Haggiag (1913–2009), film producer, who would make *Candy* with Burton in 1968.
[14] Via Vittorio Veneto.
[15] *The Trial of Stephen Ward* (1964).
[16] *Memoirs* by Harry S. Truman: *Year of Decisions* (vol. 1, 1955); *Years of Trial and Hope* (vol. 2, 1956).

that a man of such common (but tough) intellect could ever have become the President. <u>And</u> done so well. Perhaps office really can make the man.

We sat quietly at home for the evening and read. We dined à deux and read and sometimes talked to each other and read out interesting bits to each other even while we ate. It has suddenly become quite summery. For the first time I had to open completely the car windows when driving.

Rome is now, on certain windless days as smog-ridden as any of the really big cities. That deadly miasma is slowly creeping all over this earth. Will no govt. act to stop this immense planetary asphyxiation. Ah well it won't all be the same in a hundred years. Man's inhumanity to himself is stupefying.

The British elections take place on the 31st.[17] It is, to me, a fascinating thing to watch. The mud slinging and pettish accusations of both sides is almost too childish to be believed but yet I am compelled to read it. The unction of the Tory Press, the immense vulgarity of the *Mirror*, the blindness of them both, will not be believed an age from now if, as I mentioned above, there is an age from now.[18] Wilson will win it appears from Polls.[19]

Georgie our Laza Apso is very ill.[20] Poor old boy.

Wednesday 23rd E. had two fittings today for her dress to be worn to the Ballet tomorrow night. What am I doing going to a ballet again? This is the second time in six months. Rudolph Nureyev notwithstanding.[21]

We both had medical examinations for Insurance. It appears to be alright. The doctor sweated a lot and looked as if <u>he</u> could do with a check-up.

We dined at home and E. had her second fitting after dinner. I tried to read Barzini's *The Italians* but found it intolerably prolix and self congratulatory.[22] I'll try it again and will make another desperate attempt to like *The Italians* and the Italians.

Thursday 24th We went to the Opera to see Rudi N dance, and dance he did. How he makes the others look like carthorses, even a brilliant fellow like Bruhn the Dane.[23] Rudi did an extract from Sylphides.[24]

The paparazzi behaved like lunatics, getting inside the theatre and taking snaps even during the performance. The management and the police seem equally helpless. Afterwards we went to the Little Bar in the Via Sistina for a

---

[17] Harold Wilson (1916–95) called a general election in order to secure a larger Labour majority.
[18] 'Tory press' meaning those supporting the Conservative Party. The *Daily Mirror* supported the Labour Party.
[19] Labour won 363 seats at the election, increasing its majority in the House of Commons from 4 to 96 seats.
[20] Lhasa Apso: a breed of dog.
[21] Rudolph Nureyev (1938–93), ballet dancer.
[22] Luigi Barzini, *The Italians: A Full Length Portrait* (1964).
[23] Erik Belton Evers Bruhn (1929–86), ballet dancer.
[24] *Les Sylphides*, the ballet.

quick drink.[25] Met an actor there with Ron Berkeley and his girl Vicky called Coffin![26] [. . .]

Friday 25th The boys arrived from La Suisse.[27] Liza E and I had lunch at Ostia on the edge of the sea.[28] An enormous and terrible lady journalist appeared and asked us questions. I sent her off in a burst of fury.

I felt dreadful all day long – melancholy and distant – and so did E. Georgie died. He must have caught something from some alien dog in the pound he was at. Now E'en so is ill.[29] Pray God she's alright. I love that old Chinese lady.

We dined early with the children and went to bed quite early too. I'm getting nervous about the film and E firmly believes she can't learn her lines. [. . .]

Saturday 26th I woke to my astonishment at 11.00. How late. I would like to awake, until my death, about 6 to 7 in the morning but, life and nerves being what they are, one is lucky to be up and shouting at 4 in the afternoon. There is a kind of lethargy, induced only by vulgarity, which prompts late rising. I remember the days when to sleep more than 5 hours a day was considered self-indulgence. And I am now self-indulgent. It must be booze and age.

The children were about for lunch. They giggled a lot and found great pleasure in being idiotic. They pretended powerful interest in going to the studio. We procured for them ham and cheese sandwiches and sent Maria home. That left us with Michael and Christopher and Liza. We then went to see a film called *The Silencers* starring Dean Martin.[30] It was of an obviousness so anticipatory as to take one's breath away. [. . .] I fell asleep. And the children noticed to my shame.

Wales, I understand, beat France in Rugby and a lot of difference that is going to make to the world.[31]

I also saw a vision of myself on the screen. I was gay stupid and fat. So, as they say, I'm fat, I'm gay I'm stupid and I'm fat and that, as they say, is fat.

I worry enormously about the fact that we have no money. I worry that I will not be able to look after my wife and my children after I'm dead –

[25] The Little Bar is just off the Via Sistina on Via Gregoriana.
[26] Ron Berkeley was Richard's make-up man on many films, including *Taming of the Shrew*. Vicky Tiel (1943—) was at this time a clothes and costume designer who had worked on *What's New Pussycat?*, and who would design clothes and costumes for other films involving Burton, including *Candy* and *Bluebeard*. Berkeley and Tiel would marry in 1971, and divorce in 1986. At this point Tiel was on the verge of establishing herself as a significant fashion designer, with a boutique in Paris.
[27] Switzerland.
[28] Lido di Ostia, 30 km west of Rome.
[29] E'en So: Burton and Taylor's Pekinese.
[30] *The Silencers* (1966), directed by Phil Karlson (1908–85), starring Dean Martin (1917–95).
[31] Wales beat France 9–8 at Cardiff.

nobody else will – and that worries me more than the silliness of Good Gracious Me![32]

Anyway we went to a restaurant over a cow-shed and the food was good. And the children were dying of cold and boredom. And so was I. [. . .]

Sunday 27th and Monday 28th Took E and the children to the beach on Sunday afternoon in the Toronado. We had some fun, for the kids, in beating most other cars.

We then had a 'draw' for the Grand National, run yesterday, and we drew 5 or 6 horses each. Maria won with outsider (50–1) Anglo.[33] [. . .]

Monday lunch with Jack Cardiff and Haggiag.[34] Cardiff seems half-diffident half-cocky – continually mentioning *Sons and Lovers* – presumably his most successful film. I think he was nominated for an Oscar. Or perhaps the film was.[35] Anyway he knows a rather promising sounding process owned by Pinewood.[36] [. . .]

Went to studio and had my hair permed. Ghastly business. Home, supper with the boys, and early bed.

I have to test again tomorrow. Oh happy Day.

We <u>had</u> beaten France. Skin of teeth. 9–8.

Tuesday 29th I went to the studio and made-up and dressed and tested again. E came with me. About 2.30 we went to lunch at the tiny village 10 minutes away – the place with cows called I Streghi or some such name.[37] (The cows are on the right of the restaurant looking at it – not <u>in</u> the restaurant.) The entire village is owned by one of the Borghese family.[38]

Afterwards we had brandy with the proprietor. And then went quietly drinking down the afternoon and home and bed. E very worried about that old internal bleeding that's started up again.

Wednesday 30th At last I began to learn the script. What a dilatory actor I am. How to succeed without really trying.

---

[32] 'Goodness Gracious Me!' was the title of a single released by Peter Sellers and Sophia Loren (1934—) in 1960; it reached no 4 in the charts. Loren would later co-star with Burton in *The Voyage* and *Brief Encounter*.

[33] Anglo, ridden by Tim Norman and trained by Fred Winter.

[34] Cardiff (1914–2009), cinematographer and director, had worked with Robert Haggiag on *The Barefoot Contessa* (1954).

[35] *Sons and Lovers*, (1960) remains his best known film as director. It won an Oscar for cinematography, and was nominated in six other categories, included Best Director.

[36] The 'solarization' process using a so-called 'magic box', was to be utilized in Cardiff's 1968 film, *Girl on a Motorcycle*.

[37] There is today a Ristorante Le Streghe, on the Via Tuscalona, about 2km from the Cinecitta studios in Rome.

[38] A prominent and historic Italian family.

Some agonizing on the part of Franco Z about my initial costume. I hope he's not going to be a bore when we start to work. They are changing or rather adapting the present costume. I wish I had Larry's and John's indeed most actors' love of dressing up and all that goes with it – the fittings, the finicky fussing etc. and always the pouffs.[39] I went to the Studio and played a sort of buffer or mediator between Franco, who is not entirely masculine it seems, and Irene who is not entirely feminine, and so I strode in Limbo for a quarter of an hour. And then came home to old fatty who stayed in bed all day to watch, take care of, that bleeding mentioned above. The election takes place in Britain tomorrow. I've read the political columns until I'm sick of 'em. Shan't read the British ones until the next election. Perhaps not even then.

Thursday 31st [...] Today I received a letter from Franco saying that he felt better able to write his thoughts than speak them as his English is not too reliable. A very good excuse for not facing somebody with something unpleasant. Wasn't it Winston Churchill who always fired his underlings by letter? Who would have thought the Old Man to have had so much milk in him.[40] Anyway, the letter said that he had designed and had had made a new first costume for me and would I come in at 4.00 to try it. I went and of course waited twenty minutes. At first I was dismayed by its weight and size but having tried it on felt better at once. I tested it immediately and will see the result tomorrow at about 11 o'clock. It had better be good. Irene Sharaff is obviously upset and since I find her bone-lazy, inflexible faintly condescending to most people, an intellectual (though she is not overblessed in that department) snob and a crashing bore my sympathy is tempered with discretion. Old Snapshot however adores her and I must use tact and so on to keep her.[41] Lizabet also thinks her talented but I tend to think, as always, that, apart from the odd one here or there, dress designers are like photographers – mere copiers. Take enough snaps, copy enough paintings and some of 'em are bound to be alright.

We learned lines, read books, learned a little Italian (me) in the bedroom suite, had a dinner, both of us ravenous, of roast chicken, potatoes, salad, cheese, and fruit all washed down, in my case with water – I don't fancy drink at the moment – in Snapshot's case with a Vin Rosé. [...]

---

[39] Larry: Laurence Olivier. John: Sir John Gielgud (1904–2000), actor and director, friend of Richard Burton, whom he had directed in *The Lady's Not for Burning* (1949, 1950), *The Boy with a Cart* (1950), *Hamlet* (1964) and with whom he had acted and would again act (*Becket*, *Wagner*). 'always the pouffs' is presumably a derogatory reference to male homosexuals.

[40] A version of the line spoken by Lady Macbeth of Duncan, in *Macbeth* Act V, scene i: 'Yet who would have thought the old man to have had so much blood in him?'

[41] 'Snapshot': one of Richard's nicknames for Elizabeth.

APRIL

Friday 1st What a day! I went in at about 11.30 to see the test of the new costume. It was alright – at least it was better than the other. I then had it refitted and will try it on again tomorrow, Saturday.

Since the atmosphere is now electric I decided to try and do something about it so I took Irene home for lunch and told Zeffirelli I would see him at 6.00. He agreed. The lunch was frightening. Irene really hates the Italian and described my costume as 1930 Opera. She was not, she said, prepared to be a sketch artist for FZ.[42] I don't know what else she is supposed to be. Shumdit says she didn't mean it that way.[43] Finally, at lunch, I was so exasperated by the repetitious complaining that I left the table snarling 'You'll excuse me, I'm in a bad mood.' Shumdit said with her usual immense tact, 'Really, Richard?' I snarled again something witty like 'Shut your mouth' and went tramping furiously over our few acres with E'en So.

When I returned I kissed Shumdit better and then began to attack again because I thought she'd gossiped with the Princess something-or-other who is designing her frock for Mike Todd Junior's TV show about his father.[44] Then we kissed it all better again.

And so to the studio. I told Z that things must be altered, that he shouldn't make costumes behind our backs. He said he had to take the law into his own hands as Irene was so inflexible and that his respect for her had turned into disrespect. He described her costume as 1930 touring version of *Shrew* in America. I said, as far as I was concerned, he could do all the bloody costumes but E Shumdit was adamant re Irene's clothes and that if she turned cold on him that that would be the end of her performance. If there were any more hold-ups I said due to costume problems somebody, I said straight in his eyes, would have to go. We had invested $2,000,000 in this venture and I didn't want another *Cleopatra*.

McWhorter, who was present throughout, asked if he had any other costumes in preparation. Z. said No! No! but I knew he was lying. I suggested that he stop being devious and meet head-on with Irene and scream at her if necessary so that she could scream back. But stop, I begged, being so bloody Machiavellian. He said he would, but only after he'd seen E. Shumdit. So we are to have lunch with him tomorrow. Immediately I was in the car on the way home I realized that Mario had mentioned taking the children to the Spanish Steps to see the flowers and so will cancel the lunch tomorrow when I get up.[45]

---

[42] FZ: Franco Zeffirelli.
[43] 'Shumdit' was another nickname Richard had for Elizabeth.
[44] Mike Todd Jr (1929–2002), the son of Mike Todd by his marriage to Bertha Freeman (1927–46). *Around the World of Mike Todd* would screen in September 1968.
[45] The covering of the Spanish Steps or Piazza di Spagna with flowers is an annual ritual in spring.

I was so fed up I had three glasses of wine and two large brandies in about ½ hour, ate my pasta, and went to bed. We shouted at each other a bit but nothing serious.

Labour won the election easily. Don't know the final count but it's likely to be about a 100 majority. Anyway they're in to stay.

Saturday 2nd And we drove to Rome to the Spanish Steps which wasn't a very good idea as the floral decorations have only just begun; they will obviously be prettier by next weekend. We lunched at a very good restaurant called 'Chianti'.[46] I had an enormous and very good rare T. Bone Steak. E had the speciality chicken. We all (the children were with us) had ravioli to start. Delicious. Maria seemed still asleep at lunch – she had slept all the way in in the car. She suffers, poor dab, from permanent nasal and bronchial irritations.

E + I went to see FZ at the studio. A lot of talk went on but I can't remember much about it. By that time I was sloshed.

We then went to Garden City for Pizza and then home when we talked with Mario about that frightful weekend at Porto Santa Stefano 4 years ago.[47]

It depressed me profoundly and I stared a lot and slept at last.

Sunday 3rd Woke late again at 10.30 largely I suppose because we both woke at 1.30 – 2.00 in the morning and talked until 5–6.

We went for birthday lunch to Richard Hanley's and J. Lee and very nice it was [...] I met Chas Beal the negro pianist.[48] Aaron was there as well as M. Todd Junior, Irene Sharaff, Mai-Mai, MacWhorter and wife, Agnes and Frank Flanagan, Frank LaRue, Ron Berkeley.[49] [...]

We had an early dinner at L'Escargot and went home.[50] Little Liza fell down the stairs, little clown and bruised her face quite badly. She is likely to have a couple of splendid black eyes tomorrow. I asked her if she cried. She said Yes. I could eat her.

Very edgy and cantankerous. No doubt the prospect of working tomorrow is the reason. Always the same before I start a job.

Monday 4th My first day on the film. I was as nervous as a horse at the thought of riding one around a roaring fire with extras all over the place. However I did it reasonably competently.

---

[46] Possibly the Vineria Il Chianti, Via del Lavatore.
[47] Porto Santa Stefano is on the Promontorio dell'Argentario, some 125km from Rome. Burton and Taylor had spent a fraught weekend there in April 1962 during their affair. Burton returns to discuss that weekend's events in his diary for 13 August 1971.
[48] Charles Herbert Beal (1908–91), jazz pianist.
[49] Agnes Flanagan was Elizabeth's hairdresser on *Taming of the Shrew* and would repeat this role for *Doctor Faustus*. Frank Flanagan was her husband. Frank La Rue was Elizabeth's make-up man for *Taming of the Shrew* and for a number of other films.
[50] Ristorante L'Escargot, Via Appia Antica, Rome.

I was at the studio at 7.30 having driven myself in the Toronado (picked up by the Police Car overtaking a lorry over the continuous white line but fortunately I was being followed by our own policeman who arranged everything satisfactorily and amiably) and found that I was 1½ hours too early. My call was for 9.00. I rehearsed with Cyril Cusack and Victor Spinetti but in fact did not appear before the cameras until about 3.30.[51]

E. arrived for lunch with M. Todd. Later we were joined by Johnny Sullivan and new puppy Pekinese white as snow and adorable who is named by us Oh Fie. He is to be, we hope E'en So's husband.

I had a remarkable sex and religion conversation with Cyril who is vastly tempted by some Roman woman. He is, I think, and he thinks so too, immature sexually. He does not have my wide experience of rabid wild oats. I told him that I couldn't, but then I am impervious to that kind of temptation since I fell in love with Cantank.[52]

I became very drunk later and shouted a lot. At E. I don't know what about. Just plain sloshed.

Tuesday 5th Was at work again today, this time at the proper hour. We continued with the scene. FZ sprang some more new lines on us. He mustn't do that. It's very throwing. We got through. E. arrived for lunch. Aaron was there, J. Sullivan, then Mia Farrow and Mike Nichols arrived from NY.[53] That M. Nichols really gets the girls. I wish Farrow would put on 15lbs and grow her hair.

I did one shot after lunch with Cyril and Victor Spinetti and then showered and waited around to do my off-stage lines. I wasn't needed but said I'd be there tomorrow for that purpose. If I appear at all it will be late in the day I imagine. E. is doing her show for M. Todd tomorrow. [. . .]

I read the Capote–Tynan thing in the *Observer*.[54] [. . .] I think Capote was righter than Tynan though I wish it hadn't been so scurrilously written. 'morals of a baboon' 'this faded hipster' etc. I have yet to see Tynan's reply to Capote's reply to Tynan.[55]

We were in bed by 10.00 I think. I was stiff from the horse and irritable as an old man and tired.

Wednesday 6th I went in on Wed by 9.00 and did my off stage lines. Great trouble with the poor dog and the horse. Latter went slightly crazy at one

---

[51] Cyril Cusack (1910–93) was playing the part of Grumio. He had played alongside Richard in *The Spy Who Came in from the Cold* and would do so again in *Tristan and Isolde*. Victor Spinetti (1933–2012), a Welsh actor, was playing the part of Hertensio.
[52] 'Cantank' is another nickname for Elizabeth Taylor.
[53] Mia Farrow (1945—), who was to act alongside Elizabeth Taylor in *Secret Ceremony*.
[54] Kenneth Tynan (1927–80), theatre critic, journalist, literary manager at the National Theatre (1963–73). Truman Capote (1924–84), author. Tynan had reviewed and known Burton since the beginnings of his stage career. Capote was a friend of Taylor.
[55] Tynan's hostile *Observer* review (13 March 1966) of Capote's *In Cold Blood* (1965) provoked Capote into a reply (27 March 1966).

moment and kicked Cyril in the belly. However Cyril (Cusack) was so near the horse that it couldn't really get any purchase. Cyril however will be bruised tomorrow. E who was supposed to TV for M. Todd very ill from that bloody bleeding. We have sent for a doctor from London. I went to bed in a huge depression and nightmares of her dying.

Thursday 7th Took the boys with me to work and they stayed all day. We worked steadily all day long [. . .] M. Nichols and M. Farrow were with E when I came home. Doubtful now if we'll be able to go to Venice this weekend. E feels better and the bleeding has stopped. [. . .]

Friday 8th [. . .] Was called to be ready at 10.00 and was but didn't appear before the cameras until about 11.00. Spinetti said at that time. 'I'd love a glass of cold champagne.' I said 'Bob! Champagne please.' And we had – Cyril, Victor, Bob and myself – champagne. Dom Perignon.

The children arrived for lunch Michael wearing an ear-ring as a nose-ring. [. . .] In the afternoon I was interviewed by the *Daily Mail* man called Barry Norman.[56] I talked too much but it's so tedious to guard one's tongue for four hours.

We had lamb stew for supper and later I told Maria the story of her life. She was very impressed.

E is better. Hooray. She has to have a curetage(?).[57] Diolch iddo byth am gofio llwch y llawr.[58]

Since we were not able to go to Venice I have, to E's disgust, agreed to work tomorrow.

E has blood pressure of 90 – very low apparently – from loss of blood.

Saturday 9th [. . .] I worked with Cyril and Victor Spinetti. Between shots I saw the rushes.[59] They looked very good. However, disturbingly, we are falling behind schedule. I asked MacWhorter why, he said that Franco was slow. He apparently turns up for work only on the stroke of 9am which means he hasn't checked the set etc. I'Z rather lazy I suspect in an energetic way. Does nothing but with great show. I'll give him a couple more days and then I'll have to talk to him. Bloody nuisance.

After work (we were lunchless as we worked straight through) which finished at 3pm I had my usual shower and shampoo and then had drinks with

---

[56] Barry Norman (1933—), film critic and, at this time, show business editor of the *Daily Mail*, in which the interview appeared.
[57] Curettage: a surgical procedure using a curette, a small instrument like a scoop. A rather old-fashioned method of inducing an abortion, but also (and, it seems likely, in this case) a therapeutic procedure that may improve chances of future conception.
[58] Welsh for 'Thanks be to Him / For ever remembering the dust of the earth', a line from the hymn 'Diolch iddo'.
[59] The first, unedited film sequence.

M. Hordern, Alan Webb, Cyril C. and Victor Spin.[60] What a boiling 'of battered' egos in one room, except perhaps for Webb – except that he too must regret the lost stardom of his earlier years. Stories were vied for. Of course I'm not the least offender in that direction though I enjoy immensely a well told, if reasonably believable, theatrical yarn. And there are lots.

At dinner we talked with the children. We talked of the immensity of space. I said that doubtless by their (the children) middle age trips to the moon might be quite common. Maria said, 'Don't go to the moon tomorrow Richard, it's Easter Sunday.' I said I wouldn't bother in that case.

We went to bed quite early though I tried to stay awake reading. E sluggish from those doctor pill. I'll be glad when she doesn't have to take them anymore.

Sunday 10th [. . .] A lovely day sharp and breezy with sun and clouds – they fought all day. Eggs were hidden in the garden by the boys and Gaston for the two girls to find. Suitable finagling went on so that they both ended up roughly equal.[61] Then Gaston hid eggs in the front garden for the boys to find. Same thing. A little finagling again and some cheating. There were quite a lot of presents. Easter is getting more and more like Xmas. We stayed within the grounds all day. I went for two brisk walks with the boys and Liza. [. . .]

I read the Sunday papers and learned some lines. I'm not far from the end now. In about two weeks I should be home.

We dined on a pasta (rigatoni) in the hope that the cook could make, at least, an Italian dish. It wasn't bad and I was hungry so that helped. But she really is an indifferent cook. She used to work for De Sica so we know what <u>he</u> feels about food.

Received a long telegram from Josh Logan asking me to do *Camelot* for Warners.[62] Don't see how I can. And don't want to much anyway. He (Logan) says the new script is magnificent etc. and all that tripe. I'll read it anyway.

Maria very upset when I told her not to be rude to E. She remained silent and hang-dog for the rest of the evening.

Monday 11th [. . .] This is the first time in the writing of this diary that I have done so on the day indicated in the title. Usually it is the next morning or afternoon. Tonight however – it is a quarter to midnight – I am unable to sleep. This is by no means an un-regular occurrence. I frequently wake in the small hours and lie awake sometimes for two or three hrs, sometimes all night.

---

[60] Michael Hordern was playing the part of Baptista. Alan Webb (1906–82) was playing the part of Gremio.

[61] To finagle – to fiddle etc.

[62] Joshua Logan (1908–88), director. He was to direct a film version of *Camelot* starring Richard Harris (1932–2002) for Warner Bros which appeared in 1967.

But tonight is caused by a chemical product called 'FINALGON.' It is German. It was given me when I was in Garmish(?) by Oskar Werner.[63] It is supposed to burn away aching muscles and fibrositic complaints etc. It is applied on external nally and is a pale yellow or ivory white cream. It burns like hell. I applied some tonight about 9.00pm, very little, and it is burning still. I pulled, wrenched or bruised a thigh muscle this afternoon trying to kick a small ball over the garage from the sunken garden. I lost the ball and gained some pain.

So tonight instead of lying there in the near-darkness and sweat from the burning 'Finalgon' I thought I'd kill the burn and the diary with one fell descent. [. . .]

E was visited by the Dr from Rome who says she should have shots for two more days, that the curetage will not be necessary, that she can work on Thursday or Friday. That she may come to the Studio tomorrow for lunch if she limits it to 1½ hours. Hip Hip.

Today we had a letter from Mia Farrow. It is written in a huge childlike hand and is so goody as to invite suspicion of affection. I remember her at lunch forever apologizing, with eyes as round as her fist, for her silly little ability not to know anybody in theatre or films before her time – which she inferred was last week. Or last year. She and M. Nichols appear to be in love and register in hotels as Mr and Mrs N.

I think, now, that, as the tiny Macaulay is reputed to have said to an enquiring lady, the agony is abated. He was four or something.[64] So I'll try to sleep again.

Maria is invested with every conceivable kind of fear, or as her very competent nurse Karen says, 'she scares easy.' She saw a lizard today and cried with fright. What's to do. Leave it to love, I suppose, and time. The other day, with me on a walk, she refused to walk over a line of tiny ants, out of terror. I had to get her over by totally ignoring her and walking on. She was as animated and talkative about this experience as if she'd just crossed the Atlantic single handed in a rubber dinghy.

Work tomorrow. Mickey Rudin arrived today.[65] Nevill Coghill arrives tomorrow.[66] My anti-social tendencies, even with people I know well, are going to be very strained – unless I get drunk. And I don't feel like it.

---

[63] Garmisch, a ski resort in Bavaria.

[64] Thomas Babington Macaulay, 1st Baron Macaulay (1800–59), who is credited with the response (at the age of four), after having hot coffee spilt on his legs: 'Thank you, madam, the agony is abated'.

[65] Milton 'Mickey' Rudin (1920–99), lawyer with Gang, Tyre, Rudin and Brown of Sunset Building, Hollywood. His client list included Elizabeth Taylor and Frank Sinatra. Burton had been using the firm since the early 1960s if not before.

[66] Nevill Coghill (1899–1980), academic. Coghill, then fellow and tutor in English Literature at Exeter College, Oxford, had directed Burton in the 1944 production of *Measure for Measure* and had remained a friend ever since. Coghill, from 1957 to 1966 Merton Professor of English Literature at Oxford, would co-direct *Doctor Faustus* with Richard, having written the screen adaptation.

Tuesday 12th First call and work. [...] Am late this morning so be brief. Telegrammese. E to go into hospital tomorrow for curetage. Came to lunch with me and felt sick and faint. On arrive home bled. [...] Poor little thing. I shouted and bawled at her for being 'unfit' for lack of discipline, for taking too much booze. I think I was talking about myself – out of fear for her. God get tomorrow over rapidly.

Bach gan, I love you.[67] [Elizabeth Taylor's hand.]

Wednesday 13th What a day. I went to work at 7.30 and was made up and learned lines. We shot quite early about 9.30. All the time I waited for the 'phone to ring. E. finally called from the hospital about 11.30 to say that nobody there could speak Italian. I suggested she get Dick's secretary who is bilingual.

I took E'en So for a long walk around the studio. It is a pleasant place. I thought a lot about our lives and shades of mortality grew round me like a mist.

I lunched alone in my room, did some Italian, and waited for the phone to ring. And waited. And waited. I read a whole book, rather precious, by Arthur Machen called *The London Adventure*.[68] Then the blower blew and joy of joys it was herself on the other end and the operation was over and she was in pain but alive and will live to be shouted at another day.

I finished work at 4.00. Showered. Had my vodka and tonic. Sped to the hospital. [...] Read papers with E. Got gruff and bawled a lot about supper's slowness and went home in a typical huff. Before arriving home I stopped (Mario drove) in St Peter's and stared at the whole huge thing and muttered under my breath.[69]

Talked to E on telephone and we went to sleep reasonably happy.

Thursday 14th Elizabeth was expected home at 9.45am. I wasn't called to work and we all [...] waited by the potting shed for her to arrive. Then a message came to say at 10.15 that she had left 10 minutes before. [...] Eventually she did come and sat downstairs for a time and had a drink. She looked pale and wan fond lover and eventually went upstairs to bed.[70] The kids were all embarrassed and awed and sat around like wilting lettuces. E sent them out to show the nurse – Alex – the grounds. I am to sleep with the boys tonight. They are delighted.

---

[67] *Bach gan – bachgen* – Welsh for 'boy'.
[68] *The London Adventure* (1924) was the third and final part of the autobiography of the Welsh writer Arthur Machen (1863–1947).
[69] At the Basilica San Pietro (St Peter's).
[70] 'Why so pale and wan, fond lover?' is the opening line of 'Why so Pale and Wan' by Sir John Suckling (1609–42).

I [. . .] had lunch with Nevill Coghill. We watched some shooting and had lunch with some of the cast – Alan Webb, Hordern, Spinetti, Michael York.[71] M. York was up at Oxford too I discovered his real name is Johnson. Nevill didn't remember him. Afterwards we watched the rushes which appear to be at least very good.

Then home with Nevill to see E, by this time I was somewhat sloshed, and talked around her bed. She tells me that I was nasty again. Obviously I shouldn't drink more than a glass or two of wine, and weak wine at that.

I slept with the boys. At one time we all went downstairs and I made soup for us all. Tinned soup of course. E was furious that we didn't include her but we didn't know she was awake.

I work tomorrow. First call.

Friday 15th, Saturday 16th and Sunday 17th Did two shots only after which, Liza, Mike, Chris, Nevill – Ron Berkeley and I went down to Ron's seaside restaurant and ate and drank until 1.00 in the a.m. Again slept with the boys but also Maria and Liza. Bedlam.

Went into the studio (Sat) with Nevill. Had a fitting and saw the rushes twice, once to show them to Nevill, second time to show them to J. Springer who has been here for a couple of days. I arranged to have them to lunch tomorrow, Sunday. Bought a bike for Maria and skate board for Liza.

Took the children on Sunday morning to Luna Park and a good time was had by all except when I was plagued by Gypsies even after I'd given away something between 15 and 20,000 Lire.[72] How utterly charmless they are.

Nevill and John duly came to lunch after which I took them around the grounds. [. . .] A beautiful day with scudding clouds. England and Wales blanketed with snow!

I read the Sunday papers for the rest of the day.

E. now better and the nurse Alex left on Saturday so I am back in my bed again. E said she was sorry she married me on Sat night and all because I said she was a conyn. (Welsh for moaning hypochondriac) She deserves a good hammering for hurting me like that!

Monday 18th Had the first call for today. I wore the new costume which probably looks splendid on me mounted on the horse but, I think, looks indifferent on the ground. The sheer bulk of it dwarfs my legs from the knee down.

I rode up the street with everyone – extras shouting Petruchio and hurling flowers, cabbage leaves water etc. at me and my poor Rosa, the horse. She,

---

[71] Michael York (real name Michael Hugh Johnson) (1942—) was playing the part of Lucentio. He had read English at Oxford University and had worked with Franco Zeffirelli in the National Theatre prior to making his screen debut in *The Taming of the Shrew*.
[72] Luna Park – Rome's amusement park and funfair.

Rosa, made up to look even uglier than she is, behaved splendidly. Mike and Christopher were dressed and also appeared in the scene. [. . .]

Had dinner at home with M. Todd Junior, the two boys and E. Was fairly uproarious and told endless stories. i.e. literally stories without an ending. Several times the two boys pretended to fall asleep from sheer boredom at my jokes. At least I hope they were pretending.

And so to bed.

Tuesday 19th They shot the TV show on M. Todd today at last. E was very good I thought. I went to the studio about 4.00 to have Nevill see some of the stuff roughly cut in order. Discussed *Faustus* with Nevill. It seems we'll be able to pull it off. He wonders if his younger brother could possibly play in it as an extra and thereby be given an equity card? His younger brother is 60 and does odd-jobs. Nevill said that at the moment he was cleaning lavatories.[73] I said I would do what I could. Poor dab.

Wednesday 20th What a bloody awful day. E was to be tested and into the studio we went. She looked like death. Again some filthy doctor had given her some shot to which she was allergic and therefore she was poisoned instead of helped. I quietly got sloshed, made up, tested with E and got sloshed some more.

I'm sick of these bloody doctors. I'll have to have a really insupportable smash before I'll ever send for one of these ill-trained, drunken, conde-scending, semi-literate sods. The only pain I'd like them to remove is the pain in the arse they give me.

Thursday 21st E much better today – notice that it was achieved without any assistance from a doctor. Again we went to the Studio for further tests on her. I appeared in the test briefly, unmade up and not in costume. In the meantime I worked a little and read a book by Lewes the Victorian dramatic critic on Kean, Macready, Lemaitre, Rachel, Salvini etc.[74] That's the first book about acting and actors I've read since I was about 18. Such books are not really interesting. [. . .]

I'm not sure I like Zeffirelli. I think he's a coward and devious with it. He cannot look you in the eye either physically or mentally. As a mind and person-ality he's not a patch on M. Nichols. But he has flair shall we say. He has a sense of the spectacular. He will succeed. Yesterday he was worried again about his billing. I told him for the umpty ninth time to fix it with Columbia and that whatever was mutually agreeable to them was also so to us.[75] But his grum-bling was put into letter form. He couldn't tell me direct.

[73] Ambrose Coghill would play the part in the film of *Doctor Faustus* (1968) of Avarice/First Professor.
[74] George Henry Lewes (1817–78), *On Actors and the Art of Acting* (1875).
[75] Columbia Pictures were financing *The Taming of the Shrew*.

It was a long day. I didn't drink at all and we had supper at home with the boys.

I read until about 12 – took a long bath and shower and was asleep by 1.00 approx. I may have to work tomorrow. I look forward to it.

You ill tempered bastard! So do I at least you'll be out of my hair! [Elizabeth Taylor's hand.]

Wednesday 27th Here is the longest gap in the diary yet – six days. And what days! Crisis after crisis with Zero a Sharaff over the costumes.[76] E now really loathes him (Z) largely because he is a ruthless selfish multi-faced ego-mad <u>COWARD</u>. It is this last that both of us find most objectionable. I am by no means heroic morally but I can make decisions and accept advice. This chap can do neither.

Some of the scenes have been hilarious. The normally nervous but digni-fied Irene Sharaff opened a meeting with Alexandre, R. Hanley, E and Franco Z with these immortal peace-loving and diplomatic words: 'I would like to say before we go any further that you Franco are a fucking liar.' Good for starters. Later out of the mittel European mask of her face came another qualifier for *Bartlett's Dictionary of Quotations* – 'You are nothing but a fucking fag.'[77] That's my Leslie![78] Pots and kettles turned over in the kitchen of their own accord recognising kinship when they saw it.

Next day on Monday I had a go at Mr Z. It exhausted me spiritually and emotionally (as it did E yesterday) to be so brutally honest with such a tissue of evasions as Franco. But it had to be done.

Yesterday we sort of made up. E hasn't yet but will I suppose for the sake of the film.

Later in the morning Mike Frankovich arrived.[79] Good timing for the situ-ation though it wasn't planned. He was thrilled with the film. The only redeeming thing about Franco Z is that the film seems very good. It's also, perversely, infuriating.

Liza brought a little girl home from school to stay the night. Her name is Jodi Lowell. I asked her what her father did. I had already asked her father's first name which is Robert. She said 'he is a writer and poet.' Could it be the Robert Lowell.[80] Must be I suppose. [. . .]

The cat Charlie disappeared on Sunday evening about 6.00 pm. We called for him in vain. [. . .] At about 4.30–5.00am I thought I heard him cry. [. . .] I

---

[76] Zero meaning Zeffirelli.

[77] A reference to John Bartlett, *Familiar Quotations*, which first appeared in 1855. 'Fag' here being short for 'faggot', a derogatory term for a homosexual.

[78] It is possible that Burton is making a reference here to Sharaff's homosexuality.

[79] Mike Frankovich (1909–92), film producer.

[80] Richard is here referring to Robert Traill Spence Lowell (1917–77), the American poet. Lowell's daughter Harriet was born on 4 January 1957, making her the same age as Liza Todd.

found him up a tree and terrified. It was a pine tree and therefore unclimbable. [. . .] Finally after a frustrated ½ hour looking for a ladder we woke Enzo.[81] He found the ladder on the roof of the potting shed – it had been hidden there to stop the boys climbing, with its aid, onto the roof of the house.

I held the ladder. Enzo climbed. [. . .] At last Enzo got him, descended a few steps and hurled him to the ground. I dived on the cat, Enzo dived from the ladder and the ladder, untended, fell accurately on to E's head. She will have a headache for several days. There was no blood. Phew!

Thursday 28th By our standards of late, today was peaceful. We saw the rushes including E's first shot in the picture. It wasn't very satisfactory. E was fine but the whole set-up is undramatic. She should appear violently like a snarling beast. They will reshoot it.

And they did. In the flesh it looks good. Now we'll wait to see the rushes.

I didn't work today before the camera. I watched E in the re-shooting mentioned above and took her to lunch at a farm house about 1km from the Studio. It was very pleasant.

After lunch Wolf Mankovitz came and we talked of *Faustus*.[82] It will be a good thing to do. [. . .]

Life's Tommy Thomas was sneaked in to see *V. Woolf* and was overwhelmingly impressed.[83] Or so he says. I wonder what will happen when an audience sees it. Will they laugh in the wrong places? Will it disintegrate before derision? We are anxious to know.

We dined at home quietly and made lovely love. The first time for a month because of E's condition. What a magnificent relief and release.

Friday 29th I was called in for make-up at 12.00 noon. E was called for 10.30. But Alexandre didn't get her hairpiece ready till 11.30 and she managed one shot before lunch. As a result of this late start I didn't work at all. I read Auden's latest collection of verse *About the House*.[84] [. . .]

M. Hordern came to dinner with us. [. . .] We work tomorrow. It will be E's only Saturday performance I fancy. I feel dog-tired and need a long sleep but obviously shan't get it for some time.

Tomorrow we shall, out of duty, go and see Chas Beal play his piano.

The film is going smoothly now and E. is beginning to enjoy herself. An wot I says is if yer don't enjoy yerself in yer job wot's the point of it all. That's what I says.

---

[81] Enzo: presumably the housekeeper or caretaker.
[82] Wolf Mankovitz (1924–98), writer, was to write the screenplay for *Faustus* and also work on *The Battle of Sutjeska*.
[83] Burton means Tommy Thompson (1933–82), journalist with *Life*.
[84] W. H. Auden (1907–73), poet. *About the House* (1965).

Saturday 30th A hard day picking up E in the pouring film rain and dumping her on a donkey. Not easy but we managed to do it more or less correctly each time.

Went into town to The Chianti for dinner – took Pamela Brown who is in Rome for a few days because 'the ceilings of my house fell down' – with Bob and Sally Wilson, John Lee, R. Hanley, Frank and Agnes Flanagan.[85] Then on to 'Le Pub' where in the din that always goes on at such places we pretended to listen to Chas Beal play the piano. It is a dull place. Saw Dave Crowley who is very sweet and his 'sportsy' wife who is not.[86] Persuaded P. Brown to stay 'till Tuesday and so see some of the film.

Boy I do not much like Zeff. He didn't want Cyril and Maureen Cusack to come to the party tomorrow night.[87] All the other actors are invited. What a petty little bastard. Some fancied slight from Cyril is behind it I suppose.

Saw E's close-ups etc. at the window. She is splendid now and is bringing up her big guns (no offence). It is one hundred per cent more effective than the previous shots. She is going to be Kate.

I am very worried about Webb's, Lynch's – Biondelle's audibility.[88] It will create ructions among the more 'quality' critics.

MAY

Sunday 1st Having not gone to bed until 5.30 a.m we woke at 9.30 and had a large brunchy breakfast. Fried eggs, bacon, chips, tomatoes and tottered back to bed about 1.00. We slept fitfully till party time. [. . .] The padrone of the restaurant in the Studio came to cook for us. It was a nice enough party though Cyril became very drunk and at one point threatened to shoot Eliz because she told him that of course Maureen, his wife, loved him and that indeed he was generally loved by all. He was however drunkenly determined to be unloved even to the extent of shooting my wife. M. Hordern took them home.

Paul Dehn and friend were very nice.[89] Franco despite the presence of his 'godson' – who looks to be about 104 – was seen kissing and cuddling with

---

[85] Pamela Brown (1917–75) had played alongside both Burton and Taylor in *Cleopatra*, Burton in *Becket* (1964) and would play alongside Taylor in *Secret Ceremony* (1968). She had also acted with Burton in the stage production of *The Lady's Not for Burning* (1949). Sally Wilson (d. 1967) was the wife of Bob Wilson (b. 1905), Richard Burton's dresser and assistant.

[86] Dave Crowley (1910–74), former British lightweight boxing champion, occasional film actor, and proprietor of 'Le Pub'.

[87] Maureen Cusack (died 1977) was Cyril's wife.

[88] Alfred Lynch (1931–2003), playing the part of Tranio, and Roy Holder (1946–), playing the part of Biondello.

[89] Paul Dehn (1912–76), screenwriter for *Taming of the Shrew*. He had also written *The Spy Who Came in from the Cold*.

Natasha Pyne.[90] Spinetti told E and Maureen that he liked women <u>and</u> men as lovers and would never get married for that reason. What is the world coming to?

I told stories and laughed a lot. E very sweet to everybody. She's a good old thing – fair dues.

Liza has 48 hour flu and Maria is very proud that she was able to come to the party while Liza stayed in bed.

Thursday 5th It's actually 10.00 in the morning. [...] It is a glorious day. Indeed all the week we have had glorious weather. I've just come back from a walk. [...] The fallow field is now hip-high with weeds and grass. Poppies, daises, buttercups and an unidentifiable whitish weed that looks like cow parsley or baby's breath but isn't, and a pale blue tiny flower, make a splendid rebellion of colour.

Yesterday E worked but I didn't. She did the mad whipping scene with Natasha Pyne. I sat around all day in my dressing room having first gone to the mini-max (a supermarket) to buy sweets for everybody, particularly me. E was worn out at the end of the day and in the car on the way home she suddenly asked if we could possibly stop at a Trattoria (a sort of roadside cafe restaurant) for a bottle of wine. Gaston, who was driving, stopped at the next one. It was a perfect choice, the kind of place where chickens brood under the table, though there were none here. There was the usual arbour of vines. Two men there intrigued E. One was a distinguished oldish man, well dressed, who sat alone at a terraced table and neither ate nor drank nor moved. The other looked like a mendicant monk of some obscure order. He read from a parchment and ate bread. He didn't look up at all. He had a large beard. At seven-thirty just at dusk a Mass began at the church on the hill the other side of the road. The Church of the Madonna of the Divine Love. The voices of the choir drifted on the air like an invisible mist, like unseen tumbleweed, like a dream. We stopped eating our fave (raw kidney beans) and rough cheese and we stopped drinking the vin de pays to listen. It was one of those moments which are nostalgic before they're over. The two men had gone, the tramp monk maybe to the Mass and the other who knows where. We drove home feeling holy and clean while the moon bright as I've ever seen her and with a whisp of chiffon cloud around her throat (E's image not mine) shone on us from the cloudless night.

On Tuesday I worked in the morning – a couple of extra close-ups – in one costume and then changed to another for our entrance into Baptista's house for the finale.

---

[90] Natasha Pyne (1946—) was playing the part of Bianca.

On Monday we did interminable scenes of entry after pipers etc. Very boring.

Later today I went in to have lunch with E and horror of horrors Kurt Frings was also there.[91] I dislike him a lot [. . .] but E says she's amused by him. Anyway he hung around till we finished [. . .]. I arranged for him to see the rushes and a few bits stuck together.[. . .]

I turned into one of my mad moods last night and went into the spare room to sleep alone. Woke at 4.00 shivering and cold and went back to our bed. [. . .]

Sunday 8th It's 11.00 o'clock in the morning of Sunday. There is a storm going on. We've had thunder and lightning and now there is a high wind and it's raining heavily. We've decided to stay in for the day.

Last night we went to see *The Bible*.[92] I expected to be thoroughly bored but I wasn't. It is a good honest film though it failed to move me at all except at the very opening at the creation of order out of chaos. I hope it's successful. The kids should see it if only for the Noah section with all those animals. Sweetly done.

After it was over we left very quickly. Before it started we met Gore Vidal, a tall dark and handsome fellow.[93] Too handsome, I would have thought, to be a good writer which he is. Also that spoiled Princess Ira von Furstenberg with that feller Patrick O'Neill.[94] I must write a letter to De Laurentiis. His pride in his film is far more touching than anything in the film itself.

We dined at the Fontanella in Rome, E had a turkey slice in batter.[95] I had tripe. Very good too. We drank Frascati and Zambucca with coffee. On the way home we stopped at L'Escargot for another drink. [. . .]

On Friday we began my entrance into Baptista's house. We didn't get very far with it. Saw E in the rushes. She is very good and I'm very proud of her. [. . .]

Tuesday 10th I drank steadily all day long yesterday. Today I shall not drink at all while working. I don't know why I drink so much. I'm not unhappy and I really don't like it very much – I mean the booze itself.

We shot until about 7.00. I allowed it to go so far because I suppose I felt guilty about drinking – not that it affected my performance. And anyway Petruchio in this version is supposed to be semi-sloshed all the time.

---

[91] Kurt Frings (1908–91) was Taylor's Hollywood agent.
[92] *The Bible: In the Beginning* (1966), directed by John Huston and produced by Dino de Laurentiis (1919–2010).
[93] Gore Vidal (1925–2012), novelist, playwright, essayist and satirist.
[94] Princess Virginia Carolina Theresa Pancrazia Galdina von Fürstenberg (1940—), and Patrick O'Neal (1927–94) were making the film *Matchless* (1967) in Italy at the time.
[95] Hotel Fontanella Borghese on the Via della Fontanella di Borghese.

We received the <u>third</u> letter from Chris and still not a word from Michael. I must write to them both today. Also to Kate.

We spent Sunday afternoon down at the beach. It was patchy kind of weather but high summer compared with Wales. The kids and Karen came with us. We ran into Stephen Grimes.[96] He seems prematurely old and hunched.

[...] E. thought she had lost her dragon pin when we arrived home. She had forgotten that she'd given it to R. Hanley. I shouted quite a lot and insisted that the fried chicken and mashed pots tasted like soap. We made up later.

Wednesday 11th Sometimes it is good to write late at night [...]. Out of the idiocy of despair and from lack of discrimination, as I was drunkenly informed by that model of decorum C. Cusack earlier today, one can be ashamed and red-faced, but nevertheless there may be a catchable idea that can in sobriety be expanded into a virtue.

I worked until 10.30 and didn't work again all day [...]. There was a splendidly idiotic memo from that tedious Franco Zeffirelli about his authority to show rushes and/or any part of the film to anybody as he thought within his discretion. It was a puzzling missive. 'Snapshot' guessed immediately that McWhorter had stopped Zeffirelli from showing the 'rushes' and the portions of 'rough cut' to Italian members of the Press. She was absolutely right. [...] It tends, as I used to observe when I was ten, to take one's breath away. What can one do? So at the end of the day we laboured to a Trattoria. We eat some food and we fed the dogs and we drank some wine and we talked about the film. I'm starting to feel afeard about it. We chose, possibly, a bad one. Snapshot is fine, and I think I'm alright, but I worry about the other performers almost all of whom are brilliant but ill-served by the director.

After much thought and many misgivings it seems that there is not <u>one</u> single idea that he has about <u>any</u> one thing that is not mime. After all, as one might say, for Christ's sake, the most important thing about this exercise is that the words are Shakespeare's. And, so far, the only language I'm sure about are my wife's speaking and my own. Everybody else is so busy not being real that the voices die.

Now a great deal of it we can fix or re-arrange but, Arglwydd Mawr, what do we do if only donkey and myself are legitimate.[97]

I worry about the sound. I worry about actors that I think are good and who, if we're not there, descend into inarticulation. And who are also bored. Which is, of course, the greatest sin of all.

---

[96] Stephen Grimes (1927–88), had been the (Academy Award nominated) art director on *The Night of the Iguana* and was also to work on *Reflections in a Golden Eye*.
[97] *Arglwydd Mawr*, Welsh literally for 'great lord', but equivalent here to 'good lord' or 'god in heaven'.

Never again, if ever I have the chance, will I permit anybody to direct something that I know I am better qualified to do.

And anyway it's time to blow my ego. And I have been accused, quite justly, of being bored by films and indeed about and by acting generally but this film is oddly important. I shouldn't care, and of course I don't, but I do.

I watch with exasperation Ossie's and Elaine's continual advice to Zeffirelli that such and such a shot is not necessary because 'Franco you have it already' and 'in any case you must be outside at this point.'[98] But to no, as they say, avail. Might as well fill up the page. We were asked today by M. Cacoyannis to speak poetry at the Acropolis in, guess? Athens.[99] I don't think we can but we will do it, if possible, as a splendid joke. 'I have, of course, played the Acropolis', says milady.

Sunday 15th The gaps in this daily dribble are increasing. On Friday we worked from 9 till 4 without a break for lunch. Zeffirelli worked exclusively on me without Snapshot's being there as she had [. . .] a monumental period. I was eager to work but a combination of a head cold [. . .] and the tedium of close-up after close-up into as 'twere a vacuum bored me to the screaming point. Hovering over us both too was the thought that we must, out of deference to Franco, go into Rome that night by 9.30 to see Anna Magnani in *La Lupa*.[100] She was good we thought but the part was too undonog for her.[101] She turned out, when we met her afterwards to be a charming woman but forthright and not easy. We had not intended to go to the restaurant afterwards but we did and after the initial awkwardness which all such events cause we enjoyed ourselves reasonably well.

On Thursday I did the 'Say that she rail' speech.[102] It was alright I suppose.

Yesterday, Saturday, we lolled about the house all day and had lunch with the children and Karen. Dinner too with them all. I am in one of my lazy moods and do crosswords all the time [. . .]. Tonight we dine with the crew and cast in a sort of celebration for Ossie (Cameraman) Morris' wedding. He is to be married today.

Had a letter and script from Emlyn Williams which took nearly 3 weeks to arrive. Script was *Camelot*. Letter from J. Logan re *Camelot*, also two weeks late. What a postal service.

---

[98] Ossie is Oswald Morris (1915—), Director of Photography on *The Taming of the Shrew*, who had also been photographer on *Look Back in Anger*, director of photography on *The Spy Who Came in from the Cold*, and who would be director of photography on *Equus*. Elaine is Elaine Schreyeck (1924—), responsible for continuity on *The Taming of the Shrew*, who would perform the same role for *Doctor Faustus*. She had been a script supervisor on *Cleopatra*, and responsible for continuity on *Alexander the Great*.

[99] Michael Cacoyannis (or Kakogiannis) (1922—), filmmaker.

[100] *La Lupa*; play by Giovanni Verga, 1896. Anna Magnani (1907–73), actor.

[101] '*Undonog*' – Welsh for monotonous.

[102] Petruchio's speech in Act II, scene i, including the lines, 'Say that she rail, why then I'll tell her plain / She sings as sweetly as a nightingale'.

Tuesday 23rd[103] I must force my intense laziness into a better order. I said the gaps in this journal were getting longer but this is the longest yet. At random [. . .] I'll fiddle about with some things that we, or I, have done in the past ten days or so.

Last weekend [. . .] we borrowed Ron Berkeley's tiny apartment at Corsetti's.[104] It was minuscule and nicely tatty – two small rooms and a sunless balcony. It had some things nevertheless that intrigued Quicktake and myself: The idea of a bed – and a room to go with it – that had been ill-used and used for the most sensual of reasons; one poverty stricken hot-plate on top of a reasonably inefficient refrigerator; no hot water and the idea of sand everywhere. In one's hair, in one's bed, outside the door, hovering on one's eyelashes, under one's nails, caught in the coarse hair that threatens out of one's nostrils. And, of course, the inevitable tar on the soles of the feet.

As Saturday drew towards its burning end (by this time I was bright with red sun) and with the knowledge that we were to listen to Cassius Clay fight Henry Cooper for the heavyweight championship of the world in London on the short-wave radio I became very nervous.[105] I began to think of their fear and, knowing better and not being wise after the event and being chauvinistic frankly and always in favour of the man who couldn't win I predicted a win for the American in 7 rounds. Robert Wilson, who shall be and is nameless said 6. And so he was right. Will they ever believe in one hundred years from now that frightened intelligent cultured people would support such an anachronism as one man beating another man with his fists for MONEY.

On Sunday the babies – Liza and Maria – came down to spend the day. It was unsatisfactory because whereas on Saturday there was reasonable calm on the beach, on Sunday it was somewhat more hectic. More people and a pair of paparazzi.

We left early – about 3.0 – because of their (the paparazzi) presence – and with the haste [. . .] we discovered that we had left 'Oh Fie' behind.

We went home to mourn helplessly his eternal loss and to wish hopefully for his recovery. He was home in half an hour having hidden under the bed of Ron's apartment. E kissed and fussed him a great deal while I, as is my nature, insulted him out of fear for his loveliness and lostness and spoke sharply to all and sundry. Not too nice.

The previous days, like this pen, have nothing to record that can be remembered. The usual awakening at 7.00. The usual arrival at the Studio at 8.00. Franco. Ossie Morris, Carlo, McWhorter with his pretence of camaraderie and

---

[103] Tuesday was the 24th.

[104] Corsetti's is an apartment complex at Tor Vaianica, on the coast some 30km south of Rome.

[105] Henry Cooper (1934–2011) fought the world champion Cassius Clay (later Muhammad Ali) at Arsenal Stadium on 21 May 1966, Clay stopping Cooper in the sixth round. Burton and Taylor had attended the first (non-title) fight between Cooper and Clay at Wembley Stadium in London in 1963, in which Clay had stopped Cooper in the fifth.

fear going hand in hand, as ruthless, unless I am about, as a baked Alaska, boredom, and crossword puzzles.[106]

We had a lunch, as I remember, alone, but invaded by Spinetti who insisted on telling us how abnormal he was. He is fairly worthless. He told us of his being de-virginized by his brother. That is buggered. I don't believe a word he says. 'Four-letter' draws him out as they say. I wish she'd keep him in. I don't know where to look. Unless I'm drunk.

The film is losing ground financially all the time though I don't think it's of immense importance. I don't mean the film, I mean the losing of ground. It has to be understood that this film will be financially a dead loss for us. There is no way out and we, I, may have done immense damage to F. Z. No man could tolerate my insults, when I'm really roused, and survive them without some loss of ego. And not only me but Elisabeth. On our own heads be it.

We have agreed to read Poetry at the Acropolis for 1½ hrs on July 27th. A very eccentric idea of entertainment – two foreigners reading in their own language (therefore foreign) to 5000 Greeks. [. . .]

We had a typical film day today. Two shots of me climbing stairs chasing E before 10am. Next shot of me at 1.30pm. E called for midday, called on set with me for scene in the barn – wool everywhere – at 5.15. Didn't get shot so sent home via our Trattoria and heard the Mass. Wrote some of the above and slept like the dead until 20 minutes ago.

We are being interviewed by a man called Russell Braddon.[107] He appears nice. I wonder if he is. He is an Australian, and he writes books. He is to send me one.

Sunday 29th The end of another working week [. . .] and a rough one. We waded through wool, ran through bats, swung on trapezes, threw each other around. It was a week of visitors too. On Wednesday we had the British Ambassador Sir John Ward and his wife, [. . .] some American who's head of the Film Industry something or other and his wife, McWhorter and wife for lunch.[108] It was noisy and faintly drunken. Lady Ward is a real hard faced toper and quite clearly loathes her husband. I fancy the feeling is mutual. The *NY Times* critic Bosley Crowther and his wife also there.[109] He spent the entire time staring at Booby and saying how beautiful she was.[110] Earlier when we

---

[106] Carlo is probably Carlo Lastricati (1921—), Assistant Director on *Taming of the Shrew*, who would also fill this role on *Boom!* and *The Assassination of Trotsky*. But also working on the film were Carlo Fabianelli, an editor (who was also to work on *Doctor Faustus*), and Carlo Savina, the conductor.

[107] Russell Braddon (1921–95), novelist, journalist and broadcaster, was to publish 'Richard Burton to Liz' in the *Saturday Evening Post*, 3 December 1966. His most famous book was *The Naked Island* (1952), an account of his time as a Japanese prisoner of war.

[108] Sir John Guthrie Ward (1909—) was British Ambassador to Italy from 1962 to 1966. His wife was Daphne Norah Ward (née Mulholland (1915–83).

[109] Bosley Crowther (1905–81), film critic for the *New York Times* from 1940 to 1967, and his wife Florence (née Marks).

[110] 'Booby': one of Richard's nicknames for Elizabeth.

climbed out of the sheep's wool we were lying on, E said that it was full of lice. Crowther said 'You mustn't say you were lousy in *T. of Shrew*.' She said 'No, I'll leave that to you.' Touché.

On Thursday I had lunch with Joseph Levine, monstrously fat and foul-mouthed but oddly likeable and, I think, trustworthy.[111] (I may live to eat those words.) He agreed to supply us with $1,000,000 for *Faustus* and $350,000 to OUDS.[112] Seems alright to me.

After he'd gone Aaron arrived from NY [. . .] tired and plane drunk. Everybody shouted a lot because H. French, who shall be hopeless, had arranged a deal without his, Aaron's, knowledge. Aaron arranged to see Levine that night and again in the morning.

Yesterday, Saturday, I worked until 1pm. Just two shots with M. Hordern and cronies.

Aaron came down and talked business and said rather sadly that he was sorry he bored me, but if he didn't he wouldn't be doing his job as a lawyer. I said he didn't bore me at all but business did.

J. Levine arrived again and there was more amiable obscenity. Anyway we've got the money which is all I care about.

I went home and had brunch at 2.0 with Glorious and swam a few lengths of the pool with Liza. It was cold but refreshing.

We then slept for a couple of hours and set out for the Airport to pick up Chris and Mike who were coming from Switzerland.

We took the two girls with us and stopped at a Trattoria en route. It was pleasant enough. The boys looked lovely in their blazers. And so to bed last night. [. . .]

Continuing the day. We donned bathing costumes about 9.30 and lay in the sun. The servants had all gone to Mass and so I boiled myself a couple of eggs. Later in the morning I swam with Liza, Michael and Chris in the pool – it was cold but exhilarating. The two last had to wear my underpants to swim and sunbathe – they have no swimming costumes if you please and have to borrow them at school! The sun became wilful at about 11.30 and disappeared in an ominous looking cloud about 12 and stayed there 'till 1.30. We lunched on pork chops and chips and hominy grits. I sunbathed for another hour or so and went up to bed. E, already there, was nodding off. After a time we both napped, woke about 5.00 and walked [. . .]

We dined at 7.00 on Southern Fried Chicken. It's been an all-American day for food.

After dinner we walked again with Maria who is too slow to keep up with the others. The others wishing to come with us, having deserted Maria, were

---

[111] Joseph E. Levine (1905–87), film producer and promoter.
[112] OUDS: Oxford University Dramatic Society.

told they couldn't. So they followed us anyway, hiding behind hedges etc. but both the boys had bright red jackets on and were easily detectable.

I rubbed, with Slowtake's assistance, vinegar on my sunburn and smelt like a fried fish and chip shop. Later I took a long slow warm oil bath (a sprinkling in the water of a stuff called 'Sardo') and went to bed. The lights were out at 10.30.

Both Eliz and I agreed solemnly that we never want to work again but simply loll our lives away in a sort of eternal Sunday. Quites right too. We are both bone-lazy. And enjoy it.

Monday 30th One of my awful unaccountable days of savage ill-humour. The day started pleasantly enough. [...] Went down stairs about 8.00 and had some orange juice, returned and wrote some entries in this journal. Went through my lines remaining in the film [...] and took the boys off to the beach. For the rest of the day I snarled at everyone, everything and every idea.

Eliz joined us at lunch. She was gay and sweet but nothing could drag me out of my tantrum. Michael irritated the bejasus out of me. The beach was too sandy, he didn't know how to ask for Coca-Cola, didn't know how to get on the roof to get back his aeroplane, thought the bathing costumes were not 'bitchen' which is the new and horrible word for 'up-to-date', 'modern', 'cool', 'unsquare', 'with it' etc. The latest 'bitchen' bathing costume is apparently made of canvas and comes down to the knees! I'm walking backwards for progress.

Still, little Mike is at an awkward stage, 13, and is a most loveable little feller, and normally I would have joked about it but yesterday. . . . .

I swam quite a bit and talked interminable business with Aaron.

We saw rushes at 4.00 back at the Studio and went to L'Escargot for dinner with Aaron, the two boys, R. Hanley [...] J. Lee, R. and S. Wilson. I started, probably under the benevolent influence of wine, to mellow a little but not much. It is now 3.30am. I have been asleep.

Tuesday 31st My second day off. Eliz left about 8.30 for the studio though we had been up since 4.00am. At 5am we made soup!

I worked on the words a bit first, had some breakfast – two boiled eggs – and did the *Telegraph* crossword in the sun. The boys went into town with Mario and the girls (the girls were going to school) and bought some comics. They are unobtainable in Rolle apparently.[113] Karen prevented them from buying bathing costumes because they were 'improperly dressed' to go shopping.

---

[113] Rolle, on the north shore of Lake Geneva between Nyon and Lausanne, is the location of Institut Le Rosey, the prestigious boarding school attended by Michael and Christopher Wilding.

Went to pick up Eliz for lunch and we went to the 'Barn' to eat with the boys and Joe Roddy (*Look* magazine).[114] It was very pleasant.

Back at the studio I saw the cut film, said goodbye to Frosch – off to Geneva, Paris and NY – and found that Eliz had acquired a bunny rabbit for Liza.

JUNE

Wednesday 1st Work, as usual – The wedding reception. Drank only beer most of the day. Said goodbye to Russ Braddon of the *Sunday Times* (England). Dined at the Trattoria of the Divino Amore. Lost to E at baci (boule). Put out the lights at 11.30 – woke at 1.30 – stayed awake for hours scratching my sunburn. E sprayed me with 'Mediquick'. Killed two mosquitoes. Smoked many cigarettes and listened to trains go by. Went back to sleep at 5.00(?). MacWhorter wrote over zealous letter to Franco Z yesterday. Maybe, however, will do him some good.

Thursday 2nd That hideous costume of Zeff's on again – the one that makes me look as if I have a very nasty and monstrous growth on my right thigh. Apart from its unimaginative ugliness it is also hell to put on and torture to wear. I did my longest speech in the film and took forever to do it. Eliz was very good in her bit. In fact she's very good altogether.

We lunched alone on spaghetti [. . .] and drank a little wine. Joe Roddy there again. Read a long article in *McCall's* about *V. Woolf*.[115] [. . .]

Zeffirelli wrote a reply to McWhorter which was fairly annihilating but McWhorter, impervious to insult, merely said to Eliz. 'Nevertheless he was here at 8.20 this morning.' That's all he cares about.

We are invited to the British Embassy for the Queen's birthday. How posh we are getting. And respectable. We've got to stop that image. [. . .]

There was a national holiday and we stopped at our Trattoria for a glass of wine. Hundreds of people and children there so we didn't stay long. We really need those police around sometimes if only to avoid embarrassment. [. . .]

I am eating a lot.

Friday 3rd I had only one shot to do this morning but, malheureusement, Eliz had three, then of course she had to wash her hair for the weekend so we got away from the studio at 1.30.[116] Down to Corsetti's for lunch – a delicious sole from the Adriatic and Eliz a sea-bass, all with french fries and washed

---

[114] Joe Roddy had written an article, 'Elizabeth Taylor and Richard Burton: The Night of the Brawl', which had appeared in *Look* on 8 February 1966.
[115] *McCall's*: an American monthly magazine aimed at women readers.
[116] *Malheureusement*: French for unfortunately.

down by two bottles of Fontana Candida – a nice white cold wine from Frascati.[117] [. . .]

I was asleep by 9.00 pm. Made myself some cabbage soup at 2.00 am and was joined by Bon Apetito.[118] We eat from the same bowls like two pups.

Saturday 4th We got up early slightly nervous about Maria's school sports. What would she be like? I made Bloody Marys for Karen Eliz and self to steady our nerves.[119] It was a very warm day. We arrived about 5 minutes before the start. Maria, with [. . .] style and grace, and much interest in the other competitors, came last in the 25yd dash. They had sack races, bean-bag throwing, obstacle races. The colours were truly international. From the pinko-grey of N. Europe to Chinese yellow via black-as-nights. I entered the fathers' race which due to the devious machinations of a black Somali, an ambassador, and three Bloody Marys, I lost. We had to pick up a balloon in one corner of the ground, a flag in another, a coca cola bottle at the gate, a chiffon scarf en route and a paper flower elsewhere. I quickly arranged with this black bloody Iago, this coloured Judas, to pick up two balloons, two paper flowers, while he picked up two bottles and two flags which, I rapidly explained, would cut the race in half as we would exchange with each other. But race-memory, atavism, took over inside his boiling black head and I had a double journey for the bottles. His side of the bargain ceased to exist after he'd given me <u>one</u> flag and I had given him one balloon <u>and</u> one paper flower. Such cheating is soul destroying. How can they rule themselves if they are such cheats. No wonder Africa is going to the dogs. Result; the black diplomat nineteenth and me twentieth. From now on I only cheat with Welshmen. I'm starting to train now for next year's race.

We went to the Chianti for lunch. Went home and swam a great deal in the pool. Listened to the BBC and went, worn out, to bed.

Sunday 5th Today is a record equaller. Today is the 7,601st day since the war ended. That number is the exact equal of days between November 11th 1918 and September 3rd 1939. Every day from now on, says the *Sunday Times* cheerfully, should be counted as a bonus.

We spent the 7601st day of uneasy peace peacefully. We sunbathed in the garden, swam in the pool, went for walks across the shorn fields, the hay standing in neat bundles, had an early lunch of Southern Fried Chicken, napped in the afternoon, did our exercises. Dined at 7.00 on pork chops and chips and salad. I played 'boxes' with Liza who is phenomenally quick at

---

[117] Frascati, the important wine-growing area to the south-east of Rome.
[118] Bon Apetito is presumably a nickname for Taylor.
[119] A Bloody Mary is a vodka based cocktail usually including tomato juice, lemon juice and a dash of Worcestershire sauce or Tabasco.

picking up games, read a couple of chapters of Agatha Christie and slept until ½ hour ago.[120]

We had soup for breakfast, out of tin on our private hot plates and soup again for high tea. We are soup mad.

Monday 6th On the way home (it was, surprisingly, raining) we took the Wilsons and the Flanagans and Joe Roddy to our 'Trat'. There were six sergeants Italian there, one from Sicily one from Naples. The last gave bread wine and sausage all made by his mother. I bet Roddy they knew the purple passage from Dante.[121] [. . .] The boys gave me a book of dirty verses. Some of it very funny.

[There are no further entries in the diary from early June to late August. Late in June *Who's Afraid of Virginia Woolf?* was released to considerable critical acclaim. In the same month Burton and Taylor were invited to the home of Princess Luciana Pignatelli (1935–2008) to meet Senator Robert Kennedy (1925–68) and his wife Ethel (1928–). They went to dinner, a night-club, and then returned to the Hotel Eden where Burton and Kennedy competed to see who had the best knowledge of Shakespearean sonnets. Richard watched the Football World Cup Final on 30 July 1966, supporting West Germany against England, with England achieving the final victory.

In August Richard began starring in and co-directing the film production of *Dr Faustus*, using many of the same Oxford University Dramatic Society cast that had appeared in the stage version the previous year. Richard and Elizabeth sank over £300,000 of their own money in the production.]

AUGUST

Tuesday 23rd Yesterday we began shooting *Faustus*. Many things have happened in the missing days in this diary. [. . .] I will try to recapture some of the events. My sister Edith's death and within a few days thereafter Monty Clift's death.[122]

With pre-planning we shot so quickly [. . .] yesterday that we did seven set-ups in the morning and early afternoon. Now to wait for the results!

After shooting E and I attended a press conference with Nevill and the rest of the Oxford lot. Usual inane questions, usual bland answers.

---

[120] Agatha Christie (1890–1976), a prolific author of detective fiction. Burton had played the part of the detective Hercule Poirot in a production of Christie's *Alibi* while a schoolboy in Port Talbot.
[121] A reference to the *Divina Commedia* by Dante Alighieri (1265–1321).
[122] Montgomery Clift (1920–66), actor. He had starred alongside Elizabeth Taylor in *Suddenly Last Summer* (1959) and had been due to act in *Reflections in a Golden Eye*.

Later we went alone for a quiet dinner at a motel on the Raccordo Anulare.[123] Omelette and sauté potatoes and coffee and wine. And so to house and home.

[There are no further entries in the diary until late September. During this period Richard was mainly occupied with the filming of *Dr Faustus*.]

SEPTEMBER

Wednesday 21st Yesterday we began the Garden of Delights – the Seven Deadly Sins – of Faustus. Nevill has gone off to England and then to the USA. So with chubby Nick Young I am alone alone on a wide wide film.[124] I have varying feelings about this project – vague fears that it and I are bad or that it's all going to work.

Roddy Mann of the *Sunday Express* came to interview.[125] He seems lonely and olding. His middle-age is beginning to show – he is 44 and wifeless and childless and of late (two weeks or so ago) motherless. He also writes indifferently.

H. French was there too. Like all potential bullies he is basically vulnerable. He is so anxious to be a big agent, which I suppose technically he is, and for everyone to know it. Every film script I mention he adds 'Yes I told you about that last Feb' or 'As a matter of fact I suggested that to Brando before he called you.' or 'I know I'm a pompous old ass Rich and Eliz hates me but I have made the biggest deals ever for both of you. I am good, I really am good, at making the big deal.'

We adjourned after work to the Trattoria across the Pontina and had wine. We pontificated on the transience of all human affairs and how actors were peculiarly subject to fate [. . .].

Talked to D. F. Zanuck at lunchtime about settling $55,000,000 (or is it $75m) out of court.[126] We shall see.

Thursday 22nd We continued with the 'Sins'. After the first shot (at 9.15) I went to see rushes. They seemed good. Then back to the stage for the second shot, about 10.30, then back to the theatre to see the first ½ of *Shrew*. It's beginning to look like a good 'un.

After lunch with E. (roast beef, roast potatoes, string beans and gravy) saw first H. French about future plans [. . .] Then – Peter Evans of the *Daily Express*

---

[123] The Grande Raccordo Anulare is a motorway encircling Rome.
[124] Nicholas Young was Technical Assistant on *Faustus*.
[125] Roderick Mann (1922–2010), then film critic with the *Sunday Express*.
[126] Darryl Francis Zanuck, (1902–79), a major American film mogul, at this time Executive President of Twentieth Century-Fox, and a man with whom Burton's career had been intertwined since the early 1950s. Zanuck had launched litigation against Burton and Taylor after *Cleopatra*, alleging that their affair had damaged the film's commercial prospects. The case was eventually dropped.

who I am to see again tomorrow.[127] Then – D. Frost of the BBC. [128] I also see him tomorrow.

We stopped at the Trattoria di Divino Amore for a bottle of wine – E and I only. Went home and saw the children who began school today. [...] F. Zeffirelli arrives back from his triumphant disaster at the Met – the one in NY.[129] We should see him shortly. Looking forward to it too. How one changes. He has written many outrageously campy letters from NY.

Thursday 22nd Something wrong with my days or dates – there appear to be two Thursdays this week!

Saw D. Frost and discussed doing life of WSC in five two hour films. It is a fascinating and unique idea – one man, five films. Starting with me as Churchill at 25 approximately to his death. Maybe too big a task to succeed. E just instructed me to say how adorable she looked yesterday so: My God! how adorable she looked yesterday. Gosh.

Had lunch with and was interviewed by P. Evans of the *D. Express*. Same old questions. Desperate searching for new answers. All rubbish. He's writing a book about P. Sellers – all about an actor searching for his identity.[130] Rubbish too. [...]

Drank too much, came home, and fell asleep before supper. E unkindly calls such premature sleep 'passing-out.'

Whew! How adorable E looked yesterday.

Friday 23rd Things that have happened in the empty days of this diary.

My sister Edith (Edie) died at the age of 43. She was the youngest sister and the funniest. She died from an unsuspected clot of blood that formed after she had been operated on for a weak heart. We thought she had recovered from the operation (it seemed she had) but 5 or 6 days later she went out like a candle-light. She is the first child of my parents to die since 1907 approx.[131] The shock was considerable though I was less close to her than to Ivor and Cis for instance. We flew to London for the funeral – all my brothers were there Ivor (who came with us from Rome) Dai, Will, Tom, Graham and Verdun. Will, who is an idiot, when asked in the living room how he felt replied 'In the pink. Never felt better in my life . . .' and then realized he should show suitable decorous sorrow and changed his face into pious conformity. He is almost

---

[127] Peter Evans (1938—), journalist, biographer and novelist.
[128] David Frost (1939—), broadcast journalist, at this time producing *The Frost Report* for the BBC. Frost had had a cameo part as himself in *The V.I.P.s*.
[129] Zeffirelli's production of Samuel Barber's (1910–81) opera *Antony and Cleopatra* was first performed on 16 September at the opening of the new Metropolitan Opera House in New York. It was not well received.
[130] Peter Evans's biography, *Peter Sellers: The Mask Behind the Mask*, appeared in 1968.
[131] Two of Richard's sisters died in infancy, one in 1903 and the other in 1908. Both were named Margaret Hannah.

mindlessly self centred. Ron, the husband, was in a pitiful state.[132] As were all the sisters and Edie's children. All the men, heads carefully bowed so that they could see nothing but neutral dispassionate carpet or chapel floor in the Crematorium, were stoic. I had to harrumph and snort a few times to stop the weeping. E behaved like an angel. She is splendid in a crisis.

Shot the catacombs today and started the day with the end of the Garden of Delights. Mephistopheles (Andreas Teuber) reached a new pitch of intensity in body odour.[133] It is all imagined things dead – rotten seas, decaying books in the tropics, rats trapped dead in drainpipes, forgotten fish, cheese that has become flesh. Between his toes [. . .] is a sort of fungus growth that threatens to turn his feet into webbed feet unless he bathes in the next couple of years. And he is clear-skinned as a girl, while here am I, fanatically clean, pocked, pimpled and carbuncled as a Hogarth.[134] It is not fair!

Franco Zeff arrived at the Studio at lunch time fresh from NY. Looking splendid – he has lost weight – he and E camped about with each other. He seemed to be pleased with the film which he saw this afternoon.

[. . .] Tonight we had dinner with Liza, Maria and Karen. Maria, who wanted to come up to the bedroom with me when I went to bed, said that she loved me and wanted always to be with me at all times.

I am reading a book called *A long way to Shiloh* by Lionel Davidson.[135] Before that a detective story by Agatha Christie. Before that a book called *Utmost Fish*.[136] Not very good though a readable yarn. Before that Randolph Churchill's biography of Winston Churchill, a massive tome which I read in two sittings.[137] It is a perfect illustration of 'the child is father of the man.'[138] I've read some scripts too. *Waterloo* – at least the first ½.[139] *Reflections in a Golden Eye*.[140] *Advice to a married man*.[141] And also the story *Carmen* by Mirameé.[142] Funny little story and totally unbelievable.

---

[132] Ron, Richard's brother-in-law.

[133] Andreas Teuber, actor: formerly an undergraduate at St John's College, Oxford, he had played the part of Mephistophilis in the OUDS production of *Doctor Faustus* earlier in the year, and was now playing the same part (albeit titled Mephistopheles) in the film version. He has since gone on to a distinguished career as a philosopher.

[134] Artist and cartoonist William Hogarth (1697–1764), whose depictions of individuals were often unflattering.

[135] Lionel Davidson, *A Long Way to Shiloh* (1966), a thriller.

[136] Hugh Wray McCann, *Utmost Fish* (1965), a work of fiction (albeit based on a true incident), set during the First World War.

[137] Randolph S. Churchill, *Winston S. Churchill*, Vol. I: *Youth, 1874–1900* (1966).

[138] 'The Child is father of the man': a line from the poem 'My Heart Leaps Up When I Behold' (1802), by William Wordsworth (1770–1850).

[139] Richard was considering the part of Napoleon in *Waterloo* (1970), eventually played by Rod Steiger (1925–2002), who, like Richard, had appeared in *The Longest Day*. They would both appear in *Breakthrough* (1979).

[140] *Reflections in a Golden Eye* appeared in 1967, directed by John Huston, produced by Ray Stark and starring Marlon Brando and Elizabeth Taylor.

[141] This became the film *A Guide for the Married Man* (1967), directed by Gene Kelly (1912–96) and starring Walter Matthau (1920–2000).

[142] Burton means Prosper Mérimée's *Carmen*, (1845).

Saturday 24th Things that happened while these pages were blank:

Monty Clift, possibly E's greatest friend and with whom she was about to start *Reflections* in one month from now, died of a massive heart attack in NY. He died in his sleep. [. . .] The news was told to E by phone from NY by Roddy McDowall. He said, to E's horror, that the death was caused by a combination of drink and drugs. This turned out to be totally untrue.[143] Little Roddy, even when he loves someone, loves their attendant disasters almost as much. He, Monty, left E anything of his possessions in his will. She chose something I don't know what. His companion, nurse and major domo very kindly sent E his (Monty's) handkerchiefs which he had only recently bought in Paris and which he loved, delicate white on white.[144] And to me – Monty's favourite soap! Should I use it or keep it? E was very upset and still cannot believe he's dead. A little Monty Clift cult has started since his death. It would have been more useful when he was alive. He couldn't get a decent job for the last 5 years of his life. Poor sod. I didn't know him very well but he seemed like a good man. [. . .]

We are down at Corsetti's at Tor Vaianica [. . .] for a month of weekends. She cooks, I clean – a little. She does hot dogs and hamburgers and steaks and omelettes and soup. I do salads and I clean – a little. Apart from people staring and the occasional autograph we are not much bothered. One fat young girl last weekend asked me to autograph her behind – only barely covered by a bikini. I declined and signed her arm instead.

We shot the Catacombs and my meeting with Lucifer Belzebub.[145] It's an impressive set [. . .]

I saw the Garden of Delights – at least ½ of it – and was disappointed. It is much too slow. [. . .]

E has bur, arthr, or fibro situs and has great discomfort with her left shoulder and arm. Don't I know it. It is peculiarly maddening because you have nothing to show for it. No swelling, no wound, no bruise to boast of – just nagging infuriating pain.

Sat is an early day so we were here at Corsetti's by 4.45pm. I finished *Long Way to Shiloh*. It is very forgettable and too clever by half. The writer has promise though and I shall look out for his other two books.[146]

I am tackling Italian again. I might as well get it under my belt for the rest of my life. I'm here until the New Year and with my former knowledge of it I should be fairly fluent by then.[147]

---

[143] The official cause of death was 'occlusive coronary artery disease', although it is thought that addiction to alcohol and drugs exacerbated Clift's health problems.

[144] Lorenzo James was Clift's secretary.

[145] The part of Lucifer was played by David McIntosh and that of Belzebub by Jeremy Eccles.

[146] Lionel Davidson (1922–2009) at this point had published two other books (under that name): *The Night of Wenceslas* (1960) and *The Rose of Tibet* (1962), both of which had been very well received.

[147] His past knowledge of Italian had been presumably acquired when in Rome shooting *Cleopatra*.

Ron Berkeley, every night, after I've taken my hot shower and my pores are open, rubs my spotty back with alcohol. It will be interesting to see if it cleans up the skin. [. . .]

Sunday 25th A lazy day by the sea. We both woke in the middle of the night (Saturday) and read. I woke again at 8.30 and [. . .] I took the dogs for a walk along the sand shore. Nobody on the beach except ½ dozen gesticulating Italians trying to launch a boat into the placid sea. Anyone of them could have done it by himself. The sea was so calm its waves could barely break at the water's edge. [. . .]

I made myself a [. . .] sandwich and drank a satisfying cup of tea. I read some Italian, went for a swim about 11am [. . .] I lighted the barbecue fire at 12 and after some frustration [. . .] E. finally cooked the steaks. They were delicious. It is the first time she's ever cooked a steak.

Some film people were about – Basil Fenton Smith (Sound) his wife, Dave Hildyard (Sound) his wife. Robert Jacks (Producer) his wife.[148] [. . .] We exchanged pleasantries but didn't mix.

In the afternoon we read the papers, did crosswords, went for a swim (me) and other things.

[. . .] Gaston told us to change the time back one hour. It is the first time [. . .] that Italy has ever been on summertime and their puzzlement is so great that all trains wherever they were at midnight last night were told to halt for one hour. Is't possible? [. . .]

Monday 26th A thoroughly unpleasant day. It began well enough. We arose early and were in the Studio by 7.45. I did endless pickup shots [. . .] in the Garden of Delights with Gwydion Thomas (R.S. the poet's son.)[149] Infinite tedium. Then E did her bit appearing in the Crystal. [. . .] Then more shots of me and G. Thomas. Then shots of lesbian lovers and normal lovers and acrobats from a Rome circus working on trampolines. Then the set-up for tomorrow. I hate those days in which the script doesn't advance one single line of a page – not even one single stage direction   because these shots are of course added ones (apart from E's) and therefore not in the script. [. . .]

E is at work on the barbecue (We're at Corsetti's). I lighted the fire with one bottle of alcohol, then two, then a third then a fourth and have now decided to leave it to the Gods, E and Ron-next door.

---

148 Basil Fenton Smith (sometimes hyphenated as Fenton-Smith) had been sound mixer on *Sea Wife*, 'sound' on *The Night of the Iguana* and would perform that role again for *Reflections in a Golden Eye*. He would be sound recordist for *Candy*. Dave Hildyard (1916–2008) had been sound mixer on *The Taming of the Shrew* and was performing that role again for *Faustus*. He would later be 'sound' on *Breakthrough*. Robert L. Jacks (1927–87) was a film producer who had worked with Burton on *The Desert Rats* and was the son-in-law of Darryl F. Zanuck.
149 Gwydion Thomas (1945–) who played 'Lechery' and 'Third Scholar' in *Doctor Faustus* was the son of the Welsh poet R. S. Thomas (1913–2000).

Astonishingly I have lost, temporarily I hope, my taste for alcohol in any form. I shall force a campari-soda-vodka between my clenched teeth before dinner or bust. I feel better without it but I look ghastly; great bags under my eyes. E is enjoying her booze as usual and I don't resent it – much. The fire is now, it appears, perfect, and I shall have my hamburgers any minute.

E's delight in cooking is lovely and I think she has a natural gift for it. So far she's done everything right. And has her own pet condiments and sauces. I'm still confined to boiled eggs and salads. I suppose you could live on them if the chips were down. No pun intended.

And now for the Campari-Soda-Vodka – known in this family as 'Goop.'

Have now had my goop and my hamburger. Both delicious. It's extraordinary how one hamburger in a sandwich bun with a slice of raw onion, a slice of tomato, and a couple of lettuce leaves suitably salted and peppered, can be so filling.

Lovely here now. Maybe it's because I've eaten and drunk. [. . .] E's nerves have relaxed; she's frantic when she cooks – Quite incoherent, poised in the dark over the barbecue like a fury.

I shall mutter some Italian and go to bed – After I've had another goop.

I read today ½ of *Don Quixote* (script from Ronny Lubin) and ½ of *Oedipus* – by Lawrence Durrell.[150] Both so far unworthy of their subjects. A standard cowboy script by Carl Foreman called *MacKenna's Gold*.[151] Christ what a lot of rubbish one reads.

Tuesday 27th Things that happened: Kate came to stay with us, from London, (in July?) with Ivor and Gwen as guardians. She looked bonny and long-legged and freckled and slightly pigeon-toed. She is so far physically like us (who's like us?) that she takes my breath away. There is no sign of Syb in her at all except for the mannerisms of proximity. She is loving and clearly loves E and E her. [. . .] They spent one entire gossipy day together in bed, both with temps, both with some 'flu' or other. I had to carry K to her bed at the end of the day because cunningly she thought, perhaps, that she could sleep the whole night with E if she Kate were already asleep. But I was firm and took her away. Neeeeeks! Neeeeeks is Maria's version of the word 'snakes' when she sees worms. Sybil only wanted her Kate to stay for 10 days, but, possession being nine points of the law, we kept her for an extra two weeks. She left, I think, reluctantly and brown and a good girl. Ivor and Gwen are now part of us finally and irrevocably. Were it not for Kate and Jessica I doubt that they would ever see Syb again unless she invited them which she wouldn't. Syb is so odd

---

[150] Ronald A. Lublin (1918–2004), film producer. Lawrence George Durrell (1912–90), poet, novelist, dramatist. *Oedipus the King* was made into a film in 1968, although Durrell is not credited as a scriptwriter.
[151] Carl Foreman (1914–84) would produce *MacKenna's Gold* (1968) starring Gregory Peck (1916–2003) and Omar Sharif (1932—).

now that, notwithstanding 'love changing its property to the sourest and most deadly hate and hell hath no fury etc.,' she did not send any word of commiseration on the death of Edie.[152] And she purported to adore or like Edie. Funny lot those Williams. The odd thing is that nobody in my family ever mentions Syb and when I do, as I must, nobody responds. Nobody. [. . .] It will all resolve itself. Now and again, I look around and wonder how much we give away and realize how little we are given. I and my wife could live for the rest of our lives on what we have given away in the last 5 years. Not to taxes. Not to tax-deductive organisations but to private individual people. I've just discovered that in the last 20 months I have given $76,000 to one person! Over $1,000,000 to another. You have got to be an idiot. Anyway, we are lucky, we can always grow some more. Who's like us?! And anyway sitting on the edge of this central sea what should I write about now? [. . .]

Tea for breakfast and off to work. I have a slightly sore throat. Might be from smoking cigars, which I dislike, but they should stop me (and do stop me) from smoking and inhaling cigarettes [. . .] I mean I smoke less cigs than usual.

I am running out of energy and enthusiasm for *Faustus*. And I mustn't. A/It will show on the screen and B/the big stuff, meeting with Helen of Troy and the descent into hell is yet to be done.[153] I long to laze. I drank some today. Two beers, two vodkas, a goop. [. . .]

We slogged away at the student scene. I didn't feel like working at all, but kept at it anyway. How lovely it would be if one were a highly paid amateur who worked only when he wanted to. But slog it is.

Franco Zeffirelli called in to discuss some cutting and stayed to have a drink. [. . .] E became sentimental and asked Franco to find another film for them to do together as she trusted his taste implicitly.

[. . .] Pasta for supper and having written this entry I will continue to read a book called *The Fixer* by Bernard Malamud.[154] Highly praised. So let's see.

Wednesday 28th 7.15 in the morning. Bright sun. A train passes on to Rome. Sound of traffic on the Raccordo Annulare. A motor horn. I have opened the French window of the 'den' and the dogs are out chasing each other. Birds cheeping. It's difficult to compensate in Britain for instance for the joys of a lovely climate. I doubt if we've had a week's bad weather all told since we arrived in March. Another train passes. And another. I love the sound of trains

---

[152] This is a paraphrase of the lines spoken by the character Sir Stephen Scroop in Shakespeare's *Richard II*, Act III, scene ii: 'Sweet love, I see, changing his property,/Turns to the sourest and most deadly hate', and of the line spoken by the character Zara in Act III Scene viii of William Congreve's *The Mourning Bride* (1697) 'Heaven has no rage like love to hatred turned, Nor hell a fury like a woman scorned'.
[153] A part played by Elizabeth Taylor.
[154] *The Fixer* (1966) by Bernard Malamud (1914–86). It won the National Book Award and the Pulitzer Prize for Fiction.

and hate the sound of jets, that awful high-pitched keening whistling whine. Off to work in 5 minutes. [. . .]

Franco says [. . .] that Fellini has run out of instant inspiration.[155] He woke up one morning [. . .] and found that he couldn't shoot off the cuff anymore. He must prepare a film like other directors. Ah the woolly little genius. Hence the Dino De Laurentiis suit against Fellini.[156] There is a huge set on the back lot which may now be unusable. Dino will figure out a way to come out smiling. Betcha.

3pm. Just had lunch with P. Glenville. [. . .] Lots of gossip [. . .] about Tony Richardson, Jeanne Moreau and a Greek gigolo. Apparently Tony R thought he was in love with Moreau and assumed she was in love with him, left his wife Vanessa Redgrave for that reason.[157] In the meantime Tony Hartley (Tony R's producer, assistant and procureur) had produced a very handsome Greek boy as off-duty entertainment.[158] Glenville then re-enacts the scene of the boy's first appearance on the set: Mouth pursed, eyes narrowed, Moreau says to herself: 'I want that.' And with ten days free from the picture takes the boy to Greece and later announces she will marry him.[159] Peter says. 'Tony R of course doesn't know which way to be jealous or which way turn if you'll pardon l'expression.' He tends to lard his talk with foreign expressions. 'And that Richard is the pozizzioni' etc.[160] Oh prenez garde.

Have also heard that Fellini has found another backer. He will make the film at De L. Studios but as an outsider. I betcha and I was righta!

Finished scenes with three students, Hugh Williams, Gwydion Thomas and Richard Heffer in the morning and began 'was this the face that launched' etc. with E afterwards.[161] We shall finish it tomorrow – I mean the scene.

Saw F. Zeffirelli (and earlier Sheila Pickles his secretary) at the end of the day.[162] He is so camp we'll have to peg him down.

1 a.m. the morning of Thursday 29th Sitting in my dressing room unable to sleep. [. . .] I left the bedroom because my restlessness was obviously disturbing E though no complaint.

---

[155] Federico Fellini (1920–93), director.

[156] On 24 September De Laurentiis had begun to take legal action against Fellini over the future of the film project *Il viaggio di G. Mastorna*. This dispute would be resolved early in 1967, although the film was never made.

[157] Vanessa Redgrave (1937—), actor. Married to Tony Richardson from 1962 to 1967, she was to play alongside Richard Burton in *Wagner* (1983).

[158] Burton means Neil Hartley (1916–94).

[159] The 'Greek gigolo' was Thodoros 'Theo' Roubanis, in 1967 to become the third husband of Lady Sarah Consuelo Spencer-Churchill (1921–2000). They divorced in 1981. Roubanis had a minor acting part in the Richardson-directed film, *The Sailor from Gibraltar* (1967), which is the context referred to here.

[160] Burton presumably means *posizione* – position.

[161] Hugh Williams was playing Second Scholar and Richard Heffer (1946—) First Scholar.

[162] Sheila Pickles was Zeffirelli's personal assistant.

Liza did her homework tonight in our bedroom [. . .] I asked what it was
[. . .] She had to illustrate [. . .] a poem. Teachers haven't changed much. [. . .]
The poem is 'Cargoes?' 'Quinquireme of Nineveh . . . .' Masefield.[163] Well
that's one poem virtually ruined for her unless I can step in and save it.

Shall read a little and try another sleep later. Don't mind really as long as I
don't have to lie there in the dark and chase after my mind.

Thursday 29th Woke to lovely noise of thunder. [. . .] Did my exercises
yesterday morning for the first time for a fortnight and feel stiff as a board this
morning.

Finished 'Was this the face.' And went over to stage 1 for Pope scene. It's
going to be alright I think. Shot 'till six thirty. A very worried John Sullivan
arrived from London. He is in a desperate position poor feller. Daliah is 9
weeks pregnant and they are to marry in three weeks. But that's only part of it.
His script *Osmosis* has been turned down. [. . .] He is also costing me a bloody
fortune. It's a lousy position for both of us. I'm to see Elmo Williams on 27th
October and see if I can salvage something.[164] Nick Young came home with us
last night as he leaves for London tomorrow. E furious that I invited them.

[. . .] N. Young told me that Ruth Blackmore (Phil's niece) had written
letters of passion to himself, to a Welsh boy called Williams whose Dad is a
Socialist MP, and another boy.[165] She had met them all when she stayed with us
in Oxford earlier this year. [. . .] What is the little minx up to? Is she pulling
their legs? Is she a potential nymphomaniac? Her mother would probably have
a fit.

Friday 30th [. . .] Franco Zeffirelli and Pickles came to lunch [they] said
how much they adored Phil. Christian, Phil's friend, is not around much
any more.[166]

Was interviewed by a Mr Lucas of the *Christian Science Monitor*.[167] Might
he say, he said quite seriously, that by example and by making healthy comic
classics like *Shrew* and morality tales like *Faustus*, I was trying to compensate
for the great evils that Films had introduced to the World? My eyes crossed.
[. . .]

Read highly moving very interesting book called, believe it or not, *My Dog
Tulip*. The only decent book on dogs I've ever read.[168] [. . .]

---

[163] 'Cargoes' (1910) by John Masefield (1878–1967). Should be 'Quinquereme'.
[164] Elmo Williams (1913–), President's Representative for Foreign Productions, Twentieth
Century-Fox.
[165] Ruth Blackmore was the granddaughter of Philip Burton's half-brother (18 years older than he), Will
Wilson. Wilson's daughter Megan, a lecturer, had married Fred Blackmore, a school headmaster.
[166] Richard Alderson, known professionally as Christian Alderson, actor, friend and one-time
companion of Philip Burton.
[167] *The Christian Science Monitor* is the newspaper of the Church of Christ, Scientist.
[168] *My Dog Tulip* by J[oe] R[andolph] Ackerley (1956). A film version was released in 2010.

OCTOBER

Saturday 1st Glorious morning. Sea heavy and noisy. Sun in and out but lots of clouds promising lots more rain. [. . .] I cannot imagine what I'm going to do with myself in ten days time when *Faustus* and *Shrew* (extra shots) is over. I can learn *Comedians*.[169] Later I can learn the songs etc. of *Mr. Chips*.[170] Maybe I'll write something other than this diary. Maybe I'll just read and read and read. I have hardly had a drink for about two weeks. An occasional beer and twice I became mildly sloshed on a couple or three goops. Not only do I not miss it I actually feel as if I never want to booze again. Drink yes, booze no.

[. . .] Maria told Karen a story today: Once there were two tiny babies in a hospital and they were herself and Liza and they belonged to nobody. One day Richard (me) saw these two babies and decided to steal them. So he went away and came back at night in his car and stole them. He took them home and put them to bed and then went to Maria and said. 'I've got a surprise for you.' And there we were.

So there you are. If she's adopted Liza's adopted.

[. . .] The children L and M came to lunch today and watched me throw a pie in a friar's face – in the film of course – and managed to get themselves a ride on Pipo the Donkey.[171] [. . .] Steak and kidney pie with Jack Hildyard and wife (future) and drank Mouton 59–60.[172] [. . .]

Sunday 2nd We woke about 9.00, walked on the beach in a light rain and I, sans mac, became somewhat damp. Returned to rooms and changed into dry clothes. Sunday papers arrived per Gaston and I settled down for the day. E cooked splendid steak, quite the most succulent and delicious I've had for a long time. We had Mouton '59 with it.

The Times has been bought by Lord Thomson of Fleet.[173] I wonder if there'll be any more radical changes. The front page changed a few months ago. Now it has news like any other newspaper. The personal columns are on the inside cover.

What a smug little bastard Peregrine Worsthorne (*S. Telegraph*) is.[174] He is so unctuously knowing I could knock his block off. Even when he's right I want him to be wrong.

---

[169] *The Comedians* was Burton's next film project.
[170] Burton was anticipating the role of Arthur Chipping in the musical version of *Goodbye Mr Chips*, which eventually came out in 1969 with Peter O'Toole (1932—) as the lead.
[171] Pipo the donkey appeared in the film.
[172] Jack Hildyard (1908–90), cinematographer, brother of Dave Hildyard. He had been director of photography on *Suddenly Last Summer* and *The V.I.P.s*, and would perform the same role on *The Wild Geese* and *Ellis Island*.
[173] Roy Thomson (1894–76), had become Lord Thomson of Fleet in 1964.
[174] Peregrine Worsthorne (1923—), deputy editor and columnist for the *Sunday Telegraph*.

We took another walk in the afternoon but were followed by a crowd of people who finally drove us to our rooms. We sneaked out later and walked the opposite way on the beach. [. . .] Soup for supper and bed about 11.30.

Last eight or nine days of *Faustus* coming up. Thank God.

Monday 3rd Both E and I felt ghastly, lousy and dull all day long. She with the shivers, me with a headache – very rare for me, two perhaps in 10 years. Ron has the Roman roundabouts. Perhaps it was something we all ate or drank. Anyway we're home and the children are running about with all the decorum and grace of a riot.

We finished the devil-Pope scene. I wonder if it will work. I saw about ½ hour of *Faustus* this morning and I was disappointed. [. . .]

Tomorrow we go to Rome to accept Golden masks or Silver masks or whatever for being rich and infamous, I suppose.[175] That's a splendid fracturing bore to look forward to.

Spent the afternoon browsing through *Oxford Dictionary of Quotations*. I looked up Robert Graves.[176] He still only has one quote 'Goodbye to all that.' What do the compilers have against him? S. Spender has two. R.L. Stevenson about 6 columns, Voltaire 1½. Even Sam Goldwyn has one. One of the quotes accorded to RLS is 'Pieces of Eight.' Come on![177]

Dahomey is 44,000 square miles, roughly same size as Cuba. (Wales is about 13,000 square miles.) So it's quite sizeable. We go there next year for Greene's *Comedians*. Alec Guinness and E co-stars. Glenville directing for MGM.[178] I've never been to Black Africa. I shall be interested. I hated Egyptian and Arabian North Africa. Ah where were those noble sheiks. [. . .]

Listened to World News, News from Britain and Sports News from the BBC, London. I don't listen very often but when I do it gives me a peculiar feeling. The precise over-mellifluous accents, the static noise I love best which is as if the voices were being carried by lonely uncertain winds over the sea and farm and alp. The voice saying: 'that was Sam Longpox talking from Washington,' or 'David Mogs Vaughan from Bechuanaland'[179] It is peculiar to me I think because I remember the 9.00pm news as a child and the remoteness of it. Franco has fallen. Dunkirk. Battle of Britain. One of our aircraft is

---

[175] Silver Masks are the annual Italian awards for achievement in the theatre, cinema, opera and television.

[176] Robert Graves (1895–1985), author, poet. His memoir of wartime service on the Western Front, *Good-bye to All That*, first appeared in 1929.

[177] Sir Stephen Spender (1909–95), poet, critic. Robert Louis Stevenson (1850–94), playwright, novelist, short story writer, essayist. Voltaire, pseudonym of François-Marie Arouet (1694–1778), novelist, poet, critic, philosopher. Samuel Goldwyn (1882–1974), producer. 'Pieces of eight!' is from Stevenson's *Treasure Island* (1883).

[178] *Comedians*. Alec Guinness (1914–2000) was to co-star in *The Comedians*, based on the novel (published in 1965) by Graham Greene (1904–91).

[179] Bechuanaland, now part of Botswana and South Africa.

missing. This is Sandy MacPherson on the Theatre Organ at Blackpool.[180] The Palm Court Orchestra at Bournemouth. ITMA. Munich.[181] Hunger Strikes. Jarrow.[182] All remote. All beyond seeing. All too far away. Still far away but I know that if I picked up the phone I could be in London for late supper tonight and New York for tea and Los Angeles for dinner tomorrow. It is 8pm and we could, if we really tried have a 11.30 supper at D'Chez Eux, and drink a little, and be back for breakfast.[183] It's a short way to Tipperary.[184] But on the radio it still sounds impossibly far.

Tuesday 4th Woke by alarum at seven. Opened shutters in the den and there was a lovely morning with a brilliant sun and wisps of ground mist. [...] We have already done the first shot 15 minutes ago. The War Tent shot, the start. It is now 9.50. I feel immensely better today. The Dodgers play Baltimore in the World Series. Everyone here, i.e. Yankees, very excited. Mostly all of them are Dodgers' Fans. I hope quietly that Baltimore win because I've always liked the American League. We hope to listen to the play on Wednesday night at 9.30 if I can get a good reception. It should be fun.

Lunched with E in the dressing room. [...] E drank Fontana Candida (Frascati). I, nothing though I had a vodka and tonic with Nat and Louise White (Aaron's secretary) who are here for a few days.[185] Nat wants me to join the Players Club in NY. I'm a most unclubbable man as the Good Doctor said of somebody but I may join.[186] It's the thought of those horrible Piper Nights and Founders Nights etc. which give me a turn. Band of Hope and Urdd Gobaith Cymru and Concerts at the YMCA.[187]

Have done the bulk of the war tent scene. Now remains close-ups and one speech. It's about 4.40 so we may only have a couple of shots remaining tomorrow.

Prepared for the Mask of Silver awards. Will write about this later. What a provincial lot the Italians are. Even worse than the Americans or the English. E tells me to say how pretty she looked last night.

---

[180] Sandy MacPherson (1897–1975), theatre organist who broadcast regularly on the BBC during the Second World War.

[181] A reference to the Munich Agreement of September 1938 reached between Britain and France on the one hand, and Hitler's Germany on the other, regarding the fate of the Sudetenland.

[182] Burton presumably means not 'hunger strikes' but the hunger marches of the 1930s, some of which emanated from South Wales, but the most famous of which began in Jarrow in the north-east of England.

[183] D'Chez Eux, Avenue Lowendal, Paris.

[184] A reference to the music hall song 'It's a long way to Tipperary', written in 1912 and made popular during the First World War.

[185] Nat White was Louise's husband.

[186] Samuel Johnson (1709–84), essayist, journalist, author, made this remark of Sir John Hawkins (1719–89).

[187] The Players' social club, Gramercy Park, New York, founded in 1888 by the Shakespearean actor Edwin Booth, whom Burton had portrayed in *Prince of Players*. The Band of Hope was a temperance organization for children, founded in 1847. The Urdd Gobaith Cymru (Welsh League of Youth) was founded in 1922. The Young Men's Christian Association (YMCA), also aimed at young people, was founded in 1844.

The award evening was monstrous. For about ¾ hour endless hard faced breastless models paraded before our bored eyes an extraordinary tasteless concourse of fashions. Then every performer in Italy, old clowns, Alberto Sordi, Marcello Mastroianni, Vittorio Gassman, Virna Lisi, Monica Vita, F. Zeffirelli, Rossana Podesta, TV comics, stage stars, great stage hands were awarded Masks of Silver.[188] We were the last. [. . .]

After the awards we repaired to the Hassler (?) Hotel and talked and drank with Franco Zeffirelli and Sheila Pickles.[189] E was telling us all about her operations when Pickles threw up. All over the carpet. It cleared the bar rather faster than a typhoon.

Eventually home.

Wednesday 5th Did not go into work. Woke late and so ashamed that rather than be late would rather not turn up at all. So not going to turn up. E called and explained, lying like a trooper, that I was desperately ill. It must be the first day of work that I've ever wilfully missed. And I don't care. I have one disease that is incurable. That is, or, as they say in Italian, Cioè, that I am easily bored. I am fascinated by the <u>idea</u> of something but its execution bores me. That is why I think, for instance, that when I explain the particular genius of other actors I impersonate what I think they should have done rather than what they actually did do. I am the best apologist for Gielgud or Swinley, or Ainley or Olivier or Scofield or Brando than they.[190] They are very good but in recollection, in my recollection of them, they are massive Gods.

[. . .] In case there is any mistake. This diary is written for my own benefit. [. . .]

Thursday 6th Brilliant morning again and I left for work feeling somewhat shaky. Arrived about 7.45, shaved, had tea and was made up by 9.00. Baltimore won the ball game 5–2 – the Robinson boys hitting back-to-back homers off Drysdale in the first innings.[191]

For the first shot I was locked into armour with what appears to be swords going right through my body.

Read something in a mag about Syb being a 'late bloomer' in company with ½ dozen other women. With me she was 'dowdy and tubby' but since me she

---

[188] Alberto Sordi (1920–2003), actor. Marcello Mastroianni (1924–96), actor, who was to co-star with Richard in *Massacre in Rome* (1974). Vittorio Gassman (1922–2000), actor and director. Virna Lisi (1937–), actor, who was to co-star with Richard in *Bluebeard* (1972). Monica Vitti (1931–), actor. Rossana Podesta (1934–), actor.
[189] Hassler Hotel, Piazza della Trinità dei Monti, Rome.
[190] Ion Swinley (1891–1937), Shakespearean stage actor. Henry Hinchliffe Ainley (1879–1945), Shakespearean stage and film actor.
[191] Frank Robinson (1935–), and Brooks Robinson (1937–), playing for the Baltimore Orioles. Donald Scott Drysdale (1936–93), pitcher for the LA Dodgers. Baltimore won this, the first game, on 5 October 1966.

has lost 30–5 pounds and is a chic type. Cheek. She was never dowdy and dumpy! Just short that's all. [. . .]

E should work this afternoon I should think. It will be her last but one shot in the picture. Which latter is becoming endless seemingly. Bet E $500 that Orioles would win series. I deliberately bet to lose. Funny giggle if they do.

E found the World Series. Brava! Baltimore won again 6–0. Six errors by Dodgers, 3 to one man Willie Davis.[192] That's a record equalizer. He's probably cut his throat. Worked till 8.30 tonight. Koufax lost.[193]

Friday 7th Started on the dreaded but beautiful last speech of *Faustus* today after cleaning up yesterday's scenes. [. . .]

Slowly we are drawing to the end of the picture but no real immediate respite as we are doing what I guess may be two more days on *Shrew*. Close-ups here there and everywhere.

R. Hanley found me a short history of Africa so that I can find out something more about Dahomey. Sheran Cazalet sent me (us) a copy of her grampa's new book of short stories. He is P. G. Wodehouse.[194] Not vintage so far but readable.

One of the boys from Oxford, one Nick Loukes gave us a dead mounted framed tarantula as a thank you present.[195] Because 'we doubtless had so many beautiful things an ugly one might be welcome.'

I feel jaded and sweaty and unactory today. One of those days when acting seems peculiarly silly. What a sloppy job to have.

[. . .]

Saturday 8th It's now 11am and I have done one shot. Two more and I hope to finish this sequence up to the descent into hell. [. . .]

Received letter from Lord (Richard Rhys) Dynevor about his new art attempt in Dynevor Castle and grounds.[196] It seems to have started rather well. We are to lunch with him next Wednesday. [. . .]

Report in the *Daily American* that the Welsh, under the King of Gwynedd discovered the USA 200 years before Columbus.[197] Can't wait to show Elizabeth

---

[192] Baltimore won the second game, 6–0, on 6 October 1966. Willie Davis (1940–2010) of the LA Dodgers made three errors.

[193] Sanford 'Sandy' Koufax (1935—) of the LA Dodgers.

[194] Ann Sheran Cazalet (1934—), childhood friend of Elizabeth Taylor. P. G. Wodehouse (1881–1975), short story writer, novelist. Possibly the book was *Plum Pie*, an anthology published in September 1966.

[195] Nicholas Loukes (1944–76), who played Pride and Cardinal of Lorraine in *Faustus*.

[196] Richard Charles Uryan Rhys, 9th Baron Dynevor (1935–2008), who had inherited the Llandeilo Estate in 1962. He was at this point attempting to establish an Arts Centre at Newton House, in Dinefwr Park.

[197] This refers to the (historically unsubstantiated) claim that the Welsh Prince Madog ab Owain Gwynedd discovered America *c.*1170.

and must send a copy to Harvey Orkin.[198] Some Welsh maniac has spent 20 years proving it and the results of his researches are to be published in a couple of weeks.[199] I may make it a party piece.

After this next scene I should be able to relax. I don't feel exhausted or anything extreme but simply uninterested in the work however much I double-think myself into enthusiasm. I must arrange more holidays for myself. And for E too.

[. . .]

E's hair in certain lights reveals a lot of grey hair. She accuses me of making all my wives grey haired before their time. (Syb comes from a family of prematurely grey haired people.)

[. . .] Went to the Party. The minute we entered Rome I wanted to leave again. The smell of petrol fumes – a smell I loved as a boy – is now loathsome to me. The Party was given by Ken Muggleston Assistant Art Director I think.[200] It was obviously given for other art directors; there must have been six there. Afterwards we went to Dave's pub where in one hour I had one drink. [. . .]

Dodgers lost again 1–0 but because of the bloody party we were unable to listen to the match.[201] Went to bed about 2.0 I think.

Sunday 9th Woke at 8.30 and dressed, both of us, and went for a short walk as far as the stables. Back at the house I read a detective story by Josephine Tey, not very good, called *A Shilling for Candles*.[202] Gaston brought the barbecue from the beach and E made a tr[ul]y delicious steak. She is really becoming an excellent cook.

After the dinner (5.0 pm) E cooked hotdogs for the kids and Karen. I read another detective story [. . .] by Stanley Ellin.[203] Not very good.

Have now turned into Voice of America or AFM in the hope of listening to the Baseball game from Baltimore. It seems unlikely that the Dodgers can make up lost ground but let's hope they win tonight at least.

They didn't. Frank Robinson hit a home run against Drysdale and that was the only run of the match. 4 straight to Baltimore. It would appear to be a fix if it were not for the last two games. What price the demise of the Dodgers as a great baseball power now.[204]

---

[198] Harvey Orkin, theatrical agent and a good friend of Burton.
[199] A reference to the researches of Richard Deacon, *Madoc* (1966).
[200] Ken Muggleston (1930—) was in charge of properties on both *Taming of the Shrew* and *Faustus*.
[201] Baltimore beat the LA Dodgers 1–0 in the third game on 8 October 1966.
[202] Josephine Tey, pseudonym of Elizabeth Mackintosh, 1896–1952), *A Shilling for Candles* (1936).
[203] Stanley Ellin (1916–86) had published six novels by this time.
[204] Baltimore won the World Series with a 1–0 victory in the fourth game on 9 October 1966.

Monday 10th Woke and arose at 7.00. E works today so we shall go in together, which means I shall be late. [...] Wrote two letters, one Mike, one Chris, saw the rushes. Saw the first reel cut with some music. Impressed for the first time. [...]

Aaron due for lunch today. Lots of business I suppose. I hope he's feeling better.

Aaron very nervous when he arrived but he relaxed after a short while. He has stopped smoking after the warning heart attack in NY. Bobby came later and we lunched on hot dogs.[205] She is a lovely woman. Shot the hell descent about 3.30. And hell it was. The fear of heights conturbat me.[206]

Became thoroughly drunk afterwards and went home and to bed (around 9.30) in silent fury. I really loathe drinking but what's to do if everybody around is drinking. And I don't just mean E but practically everybody Bobby Frosch, John Lee, Bob Wilson, Ron B, The Flanagans.

Tuesday 11th Woke at 6.45 feeling drugged. Splashed myself with cold water. Ran in place for a count of hundred, did 20 push-ups, 20 knees bends, twenty touch-toes, twenty arms fling, twenty sideways bends. And felt better.

Brilliant sunshine to begin but has now clouded over. [...] The Churchill family according to D. Frost ask me to play Winston C on film.[207] And De Laurentiis and J. Huston wish me to play Napoleon. I've already played Alexander the Great, Mark Antony and St. Thomas à Becket. I shall have delusions of reflected grandeur.

Aaron arrived after lunch with E who had just officially become a non-American. She is now British.[208] Hello there Ma'am welcome aboard.

Had lunch with Dave Crowley, former boxing champion, and propr of 'The Pub' in Rome. What a lovely man with all his cockney winks and sly nods. He bewitched me for a couple of hours with stories from his life. [...]

Wednesday 12th Shot gold-making scene with Andy Teuber yesterday.

Today did some pick up shots on *Shrew*. [...] Then on to old age for three pick up shots as Faustus in the afternoon. Saw Richard Dynevor who talked about his castle and grounds and of his scheme to make it a cultural centre. Lovely man. Will try to help him.

Aaron was here all day being very legal. We shot 'till 7.30 and drank 'till 9.00 and home and bed. Dog weary. Last day tomorrow I hope.

---

[205] Bobby Frosch, Aaron's wife.
[206] A reference to William Dunbar (1456–1513), 'Lament for the Makaris, the last line of each verse of which being 'Timor Mortis conturbat me'.
[207] Which Burton eventually would in 1974.
[208] Taylor, who had previously enjoyed dual citizenship, renounced American citizenship in order to become solely a British subject.

Received letter from John Gielgud asking if I'd be interested in *The Tempest* as a film. Have written but not posted him a letter saying yes. He would be a splendid Prospero but persuade money men of that! I would again play Caliban. That would make 3 times. Old Vic and USA TV being the others.[209]

Am thoroughly tired and need relaxation sorely. [. . .]

Thursday 13th Last day at last. Shot the last 4 lines of *Faustus* and finished about 6.30. Tomorrow they will shoot the nudes without me while we're on our way to Positano.[210]

Bobby Frosch saw the rough-cut of *Shrew* and enjoyed it immensely [. . .] if that's the general reaction we'll be very happy.

After the shooting we had drinks with the crew. They have been very nice especially 'Gianni Props.'[211] Everybody likes him.

And so to bed.

Friday 14th – Rome – Positano Woke early, had hot toddies, we both have colds, and slept again until 11.45 or so. [. . .] Stopped for lunch on the Autostrada. [. . .] Then off again to the hotel in Positano. [. . .] Read reminiscences of famous baseball players from the turn of the century. Rather touching and funny sometimes. Read until I couldn't keep my eyes open.

Saturday 15th Positano. Hotel Sirenuse Glorious morning. [. . .] We had café complet for breakfast with bacon. Must go out and buy some dog leads and some books if findable. Couldn't find dog-leads though in frustration bought a pocket dictionary to make sure I hadn't made a mistake in my Italian. I hadn't. [. . .] A lady [. . .] greeted me [. . .] she said we'd met at Ardmore studios, Bray, Ireland with Marty Ritt.[212] Another man, very distingué, asked me if I were R.B. I said yes. He said he was a great admirer etc.

Had lunch down on the beach. [. . .] Walked up the hill home. It's a short walk but steep. We must drop two hundred feet in 400 yards. We went to bed for a time and then, I at least, sat in the sun and read. E. slept. I'm reading Cornelius Ryan's book *The Last Battle*[213] It is very readable but journalese. I'm afraid though I feel sorry for the Germans in Berlin in the last weeks of the war I am not overwhelmed with that passion.

We sat in the bar downstairs and had a couple of negroni vodkas. It's like a goop except for soda instead of tonic water I think.[214] The place gradually

---

[209] Burton had played Prospero in a 1960 production for NBC television, having played Caliban in the Old Vic production in 1953–4.

[210] Positano, a port and resort south of Naples, on the south side of the Sorrentine peninsula.

[211] Possibly the make-up man on both *Faustus* and *The Taming of the Shrew*, Giannetto De Rossi (1942–).

[212] During the making of *The Spy Who Came in from the Cold*.

[213] Cornelius Ryan (1920–74), *The Last Battle* (1964).

[214] A Negroni is made of gin, vermouth and bitters.

filled up with collared and tied gents with ladies in old fashioned dresses – not the remotest relation to a mini skirt. Almost everyone there was English speaking.

We ate in the hotel restaurant. [. . .] I read 'till 11.30 and slept.

Sunday 16th [. . .] I'm sitting on our balcony, with a pair of underpants on only, writing this. [. . .] There's quite a fresh breeze today but it's confortable in the sun.[215] Quite a lot of people on the beach below us. It's a noisy little town. Surf breaking, traffic and horns, church bells, lots of hammering going on, dogs, whistles, boys shouting on the beach playing football, babies, all softened of course by the sea's 'harsh withdrawing roar.'[216] We shall go out for lunch in ½ hour or so. E deeply engrossed in Iris Murdoch's latest.[217] I must say that she writes and (jacket photo) looks like a lesbian. I have the feeling she smokes cigars and wears disfiguring trousers and sweaters.

Lunch today was splendid. Zuppa di Vongole (clam soup with the clams in their shells) and a delicious little pasta called Crepes al formaggio. Light pancakes stuffed with molten cheese and prosciutto. Cake to follow. All good. Rivera to drink. The whole thing was slightly marred by fans, a couple of parties of rowdy ones and a very persistent middle-aged whining female professional photographer. There were amateurs too of course and one frantic woman who ran along beside us screaming: 'If she only takes off her glasses for me to see her beautiful eyes.' [. . .] I loathe Latin fans (any fans for that matter); they make me intensely nervous and self conscious even after all these years.

Later, without F, I took E'en So for a walk up the hill from the hotel but, since I literally stopped traffic, I went back after a couple of hundred yards. Let's hope it's just week-end crowds otherwise we'll have to move on or back. Why do they do it? I never gaped at anybody in my life and much as I admire certain famed people, Churchill, and various writers – R.S. Gwyn and Dylan Thomas, T.S. Eliot, Spender, Greene, MacNeice etc. etc. I have never asked them for an autograph.[218] I actually feel as embarrassed seeing a public figure as being one.

[. . .] Read late a very fat book called *The Detective* – a novel by a man called Thorp.[219] Crashing bore and full of boring middle-brow sex talk but it

[215] Either Burton missed the 'm' on the typewriter and hit the adjacent 'n', or he really meant to use the French for 'comfortable'.
[216] A reference to the 1867 poem 'Dover Beach' by the poet and critic Matthew Arnold (1822–88). The line is 'melancholy, long, withdrawing roar'.
[217] Iris Murdoch (1919–99). The 'latest volume' may have been *The Red and the Green* (1965). She had married John Bayley (1925—) in 1956.
[218] Gwyn Thomas (1913–81), Welsh playwright, novelist, satirist and broadcaster. Dylan Thomas (1914–53), poet and friend of Richard Burton. T. S. Eliot (1888–1965), poet and playwright. Louis MacNeice (1907–63), poet.
[219] Roderick Thorp (1936–99), *The Detective* (1966) made into a 1968 film starring Frank Sinatra (1915–98).

had a plot which I was determined to unravel. I'm afraid, rare for me, I skipped pages here and there. [. . .]

Monday 17th Got up about 9.0. Very cloudy and threatens rain. Walked down to the beach. [. . .] A car stopped and a professional Yankee photographer asked if he could buy E flowers or clothes or something and snap her while she did it [. . .] I was fairly polite as there were children and wife (I guess) in the car with him, but left him no hope except perhaps a short snap of us walking down the street. [. . .] Photographers are all the bloody same. 'It won't take you more than ½ hour <u>Dick</u>!') Ugh.

Got back to the top sweating like a miner. Was hailed by a man with grey hair about my age who said 'Hullo Richard, you won't remember me but we were at a party together at Stratford with Bob Shaw (1950!). I also know your wife through Peter Finch.' I said 'Ah yes old Boozy Finch.' He told me his name was Tony Britton.[220] I remembered the name. I wasn't very polite. I'm sorry now.

[. . .] Slept and read all the afternoon. [. . .] Early to bed, a howling night, rain pelting, high winds. Ah pity all poor sailors. Had a hot toddy and read in bed. Nice and achy all over now – not as earlier.

Tuesday 18th Woke at 9.00 feeling a lot better – lovely day and hot in the sun. We shall go to Sorrento for lunch – in the car.[221] Gaston suggested we go by boat but the sea is quite swelly and getting in and out of small boats is a bore. Especially with 30 people watching your every move. [. . .]

We went by car and lunched in a dreadful little restaurant called Minervetta (?) I think.[222] It was one of those vast featureless restaurants which – upstairs and downstairs – probably seats 500. It was glass enclosed on the edge of the cliffs. The food was indifferent. There were only two waiters. It is recommended in Michelin.[223] So much for that lot. We drank Sambuca and said nasty things to each other. We drove back in silence to Positano. I slept most of the way. We had soup in the room and read and slept. Christ how I hate such days. Beware of Sambuca. It brings out evil things. It is a turner over of stones in damp caves. <u>Mulicribity</u>.[224]

Wednesday 19th Woke early and made friends. Down to the beach by 8.30 to have breakfast. Orange juice, rolls, jam, caffé latte and on the way back home we shopped. That is, E did. It was very pleasant as nobody bothered us at all – Too early perhaps for the tourists or perhaps they're getting used to us. I sat

---

[220] Tony Britton (1924—), actor, who would appear with Taylor in *Night Watch* (1973). Robert Shaw (1927–78), actor. Peter Finch (1916–77), actor, who had initially been cast as Julius Caesar in *Cleopatra*.
[221] Sorrento, a resort town on the north side of the Sorrentine peninsula.
[222] Hotel La Minervetta, Sorrento.
[223] Presumably the Michelin Red Guide to hotels and restaurants.
[224] Presumably Burton means 'muliebrity', the condition of being a woman.

on the balcony and did my Italian – it is coming more and more trippingly off the tongue [. . .] E paraded in her new clothes. [. . .] She adores new clothes. Very few women don't. [. . .] E on a stand-by for Monday. Brando, Huston etc. have all unfortunately arrived from USA therefore there's no delay. We lunched at Saraceni's on the beach.[225] It's a splendid little restaurant. E had what she claims to be the best Cozze (Mussels) she's had outside France and England. I had a few too. They were delicious.

[. . .] Downstairs at cocktails with Ron, Vicky, Gaston. Then, as we've discovered, the fatal error of trying to eat two full meals in one day. We had to abandon the evening meal, apart from soup and totter upstairs. We read in bed and slept. [. . .]

Just before we put the lights out there a tremendous storm. [. . .]

Thursday 20th Woke about 8.00 to a fine morning but threatens storm or rain later on. We walked down to the caffé-bar and had caffé-latte and cream-puffs for breakfast. Ron joined us for a while and showed us pieces of glass in various colours which Vicky Tiel had collected from the beach to make a coffee table. What a wee little thing to do for her wee little apartment in Paris. Wee. Wee. Wee. Ron falls for it.

We were going to have the pork for lunch but changed our minds and dined in the restaurant of the hotel instead. After lunch at about 4.30 E was fitted for her costumes for *Reflections*. They are 1948 period and look odd and awful. 1948 does not seem like a period at all to me. Huston is a simpleton. But believes himself to be a genius. And a self aggrandizing liar. Cunning at it. Dorothy Jeakins is, now that we talk of precious people, the weest girl of them all. She is 80 years old or 50, is 6 feet tall and is wee from head to foot. She has the hallmark of the consummate bore – a sweet half-smile that plays across her self-conscious mouth. The kind of mouth you want to wipe with the back of your hand. Her eyes are dewy with youth and look at you with trusting confidence. She makes me want to fart in public or pee on the carpet. Dorothy Jeakins is the lady who has designed E's clothes for the film.[226] There are worse people in the world I suppose. Like Jack the Ripper.[227]

[. . .] We drank with the *Reflections* party in the bar. I was surprised how little, how really little, Jeakins and Tiziani knew about art.[228] I have an idea that I know more and I know nothing. E put them on a bit.

Later we went up to the room to eat the pork with boiled potatoes which I'd bought that day in the grocer's across the street. I put the stuff on to boil at 20

---

[225] This is a reference to *Hamlet*, Act III, scene ii: 'trippingly on the tongue'. Hotel Covo dei Saraceni, Positano.

[226] Dorothy Jeakins, costume designer (1914–95). She had worked with Richard on *My Cousin Rachel* (1952) and on *The Night of the Iguana* (for each of which she had received an Academy Award).

[227] The serial killer of at least five women in the East End of London in 1888.

[228] Tiziani means Evan Richards (1924—), the founder of the fashion house Tiziani of Rome.

to 8. At ten to 8 all the lights went out. No potatoes. No dinner. Procured the smallest flashlight I've ever seen, from the concierge, and after some debate we walked in the darkness down to the beach.

Gaston was there with Big Nino (our guard from Rome) and two fairly dubious looking ladies. Nino looked embarrassed. Ron and Vicky arrived later and Ron and E bet me I couldn't write a publishable book of not less than 100 pages by Xmas this year. $1000 is the bet. $900 E. $100 Ron. We'll see. I have so many books to write I'll probably end up not writing one.

[. . .] It was very cosy down at the beach. Tony Britton came over and I salved my conscience by chatting a bit.

Friday 21st Woke about 9ish and I had boiled potatoes for breakfast! Later we went to the coffee bar and had doughnuts and caffe latte about 11.00. Delicious. E did some shopping on the way down to the beach and bought some pretty handbags for Vicky – it's her birthday today.

Later, around 1.00, we walked to the other beach [. . .] and two hundred yards from the Restaurant were caught in a downpour of rain. So, somewhat damply, we had a bottle of Ischian wine and soup with pasta in it.[229] [. . .]

Dopo la tempesta we walked back to the main beach.[230] I sat and drank Sambucca and beer with Tony Britton while E went to do more shopping with Mrs (Eva) Britton. She is a Dane but speaks perfect accentless English. The Brittons have a fairly dreadful child called Jasper.[231] Let's hope he grows up nice. His parents certainly are.

Later we tottered up the hill with me complaining all the way that there was no point going all the way up in order to come all the way down again in an hour for Vicky's party. Ah well I lost, and we went down to the party and I spoke bad French and worse Italian to Big Nino and his wife and Gaston's girlfriend. I ate practically nothing, but drank a lot of wine. Quite a heavy drinking day for me today. [. . .]

Saturday 22nd We read today in the Rome *Daily American* that there's been a terrible tragedy in Aberfan.[232] 200 small children 5–12 years old were feared buried under a moving slag-heap that torrential rains had turned into sludge. Christ how many blows have those thin valleys taken. Neither E nor I can get the thing out of our minds. The details are heart rending and I found them so pitiful that I had to stop reading about them. Elizabeth wept. Somebody is at fault. I hope he or they are suitably punished. If not by law then by themselves.

---

[229] Wine from the island of Ischia, in the Bay of Naples.

[230] *Dopo la tempesta*, Italian for 'after the storm'.

[231] Eva Britton, Tony's second wife, is indeed Danish. Jasper Britton (1962–), actor.

[232] Aberfan, a mining community in the Taff valley, South Wales, where on 21 October a coal tip slid down the hillside engulfing a number of buildings, including a primary school. 116 children and 28 adults were killed.

We stayed in all day. I sat in the sun and read and did some Italian.

We had thin, medium-rare, slices of roast beef for dinner with a bottle of Torre Quarto to wash it down. A gorgeous evening with just two tiny boats on the huge sea.

Read in bed and slept. Elizabeth has been given an extra day so we don't go back until Monday. We are delighted.

Sunday 23rd Rose, lazed about, read books. Made myself boiled eggs for breakfast. Gaston brought a leg of lamb from Naples which was cooked for us here at the Sirenuse and we ate it for lunch. It was very good.

Later that day after reading more about the Welsh tragedy we went down the beach and had pizza with Ron and Vicky. Ron was pretty sloshed and repeated himself endlessly. There was an odious American woman who bothered us for a while. Ferdy Mayne and a Welsh actor called Something Griffiths were there when we arrived.[233] They were just leaving. I drank quite a lot but couldn't seem to get drunk so turned to Sambuca. Still no joy of it. The pizza was very good. [. . .]

Monday 24th Positano – Rome We woke about 9.30. I bathed and packed. [. . .] We were going to stop en route for lunch but finally since E, as usual, took an incredible time to bath and make-up we decided to lunch at the beach and leave after lunch. [. . .]

The kids were waiting. E played with them until 10.30. [. . .] She's on stand by tomorrow. And is nervous. I must be nervous for her too. I dreamt the old dream of not knowing my lines on a first night.

Saturday 29th, Rome We went to the Studio on Tuesday and E only rehearsed after all. She didn't film. Marlon B came in for a drink, as did Julie Harris at the end of the day.[234] E suspects the other man Brian Keith has an alcohol problem as he always refuses drink.[235] Met the other protaganist too who plays Williams. Think his name is Forster (Robert?)[236] They all seem very nice and E, after some trepidation initially, now finds J. Huston very easy to work with. Chiefly he doesn't much care if you don't <u>exact</u>ly know the lines which is always a great help. All that fuss about every 'The' 'but' and 'And' being correct is generally unimportant and can, to some people, be quite unnerving. I saw endless people in a seemingly continuous procession: Frosch, John Bryant re *Barbouza*,

---

[233] Ferdy Mayne (1916–98), actor, would appear with Burton in *Where Eagles Dare*. The 'Something Griffiths' was probably Kenneth Griffith (1921–2006), a Welsh actor who was appearing with Mayne in *The Bobo* (1967). Griffith had acted with Burton in *Waterfront*, the 1961 audio production of *King Henry V*, and would appear with him again in *The Wild Geese*.
[234] Julie Harris (1925—) played the part of Alison Langdon in *Reflections in a Golden Eye*.
[235] Brian Keith (1921–97) played the part of Morris Langdon in *Reflections*.
[236] Robert Forster (1941—).

P. Glenville re *Comedians* F. Zeffirelli re *Shrew* Ray Stark re everything.[237] Talked on phone to California to Frankenheimer re *Fixer* by Malamud. McWhorter talked to Wallis re *Anne of the Thousand days* for me [238] [   ]

We've seen a lot of Brando who is very nice – much nicer than he used to be – and very engaging and silly after a couple of small drinks. After 1½ vodkas the other day he said that 'unquestionably, the <u>easiest anquage</u> [*sic*] to learn was Spanish and not' as I had asserted, 'English.'

E seems pretty happy in her work and everybody seems very impressed with her. I think she's probably better than all of 'em.

I saw *Faustus* and *Shrew* all the way through. The latter is very fine. I'm not sure about the former but there's a lot to be done with it and we may have a most interesting piece by the time we've chopped changed and diffused the weaker spots.

The boys arrived from Gstaad today. [. . .] They seem in good form and Mike's standards seem to be improving.

[. . .] Have been reading all kinds of books. *Europe without Baedeker* by that pompous bastard Edmund Wilson.[239] He seems to be wrong about everything – his book deals a lot with immediate post-war Europe. His reflections on national character are puerile. He seems to have talked only to journalists and second rate artistic people (Santayana, an exception) and from them has received these earth shaking impressions.[240] He talks about the overwhelming American influence on English writing for instance and writes more like an Englishman than almost anyone I know. He is also lacking in humour. He is a bore. See his book on Internal Revenue. *Memoirs of Hecate County*, is unreadable.[241]

The above was written in something like impotent fury – he is much better than that – but his determination to prove that the Decline of the West stops its headlong flight just west of the British Isles and Ireland is startling to read. His misunderstanding of the British is colossal. And he doesn't have the courage to say 'I hate the British' but all his stories about them with about two or three exceptions among 100s show them as snob-ridden bores of the traditional, as he describes one Englishman himself, 'Music Hall' kind. He has a mindless short story in it about an English woman and an American woman both working for UNRRA in which the warm homespun democracy of the American and the cold dispassion and cynicism of the Englishwoman are juxtaposed.[242] Need I say who the winner is. He is a sour man who seems to

---

[237] John Bryant (1911–69), producer and production designer.
[238] Hal B. Wallis (1898–1986) had produced *Becket* and would produce *Anne of the Thousand Days*.
[239] Edmund Wilson (1895–1972), *Europe without Baedeker* (1947).
[240] George Santayana (1863–1952), philosopher, writer.
[241] *Memoirs of Hecate County*, Edmund Wilson (1946); banned in USA until 1959 on the grounds of obscenity.
[242] The United Nations Relief and Rehabilitation Agency.

rely for ecstasy entirely on fugitive glimpses of slender women in caught attitudes. He is quite nice for once about an English girl called coyly 'G'. He is, I think, like Hemingway, fascinated by the passionately dispassionate prep-school, finishing school, mater and pater sexiness of the middle and upper-class British woman.[243]

He is, as I have already stated, a bad writer but his single-minded determination to destroy all who are not American is compulsive. Though I fling the book across the room a dozen times (metaphorically) I have to retrieve it and go on reading.

NOVEMBER

Wednesday 2nd I have been more or less drunk for two days. I don't know why but I enjoyed it thoroughly. I didn't do too much harm except that I was rude to Bob Wilson on Monday and he sulked all day yesterday (Tuesday). I also made a feeble pass at Karen, our Maria's nurse, and apologized immediately and straightaway told E who thought it funny but probably harmful to K. I apologized again the next morning in front of E. Now what on earth possessed me to do that? It must be my impending 41st birthday. I think no permanent damage has been done to Karen I hope to God; she's such a very good person.

I also attacked Marlon B for embarrassing R. Stark by taking off his boot to demonstrate that poor Stark wears lifts. I accused Marlon of wearing them too. I think he does though what the devil harm there is in it I don't know. Women wear lifts all the time and I wore them throughout *Shrew* to make myself look bigger. Also I don't much like looking up at people especially those who were born to be looked down on.

It's a glorious Wednesday morn which makes a change – we have had a thunderstorm which seems to have lasted a week. Long low rumbling and sheet lightning. The lights go out all the time of course but we are well prepared with candles. The children love it when the lights go out and prefer flashlights to candles. What a lovely light a candle makes. They take me back at once and unbearably to my bed in the box-room in 73, Caradoc Street.[244] All the books I read, all the things I learned, all my early furtive shame in one little room by candlelight. I was showing *Shrew* yesterday to a group of people including the children when the power failed and stayed failed for about 45 minutes or an hour. Here we are about to land on the moon while it sometimes takes a fortnight, via Airmail, to get a letter from England – One script from Emlyn Williams took over a month – it is virtually impossible nine times out of ten to understand what anyone says on the phone without fantastic concentration, and a lot of rain will put the lights out three times a night. [. . .]

---

[243] Ernest Hemingway (1898–1961), novelist.
[244] 73, Caradoc Street, Taibach, where Richard had lived as a boy.

Thursday 3rd [. . .] For some reason I worried a lot about E this morning, whether she loved me or not and how awful it would be to lose her etc. I worked myself up to a rare state of misery and was absurdly relieved when she telephoned from the Studio. What's the matter with me?

Left for the studio at 12.30 and had lunch with E, the 3 boys and Brando [. . .] Managed to obtain skulls left from *Faustus* for the boys to take back to school. They left the house at 7.40pm to catch their plane. Before going E made hot-dogs on the barbecue. There was a howling wind and the portable barbecue which is on the balcony outside the bedroom flamed and roared like a mad thing. The kids loved it.

I had a couple of drinks and played sad songs on the Joanna.[245] I always worry when somebody close to me goes somewhere in an aeroplane.

I've decided after many years of tolerance that I really don't much care for Ray Stark. He's a very little person I think and is wind blown and windy and, though meaning well, is not to be entirely trusted. He is blindingly transparent and his particular immorality offends me. He is greasy handed. His mind is dirty. I shall probably not work with him again. Short sandy and seventh-rate.

Marlon's immorality, his attitude to it is honest and clean. He is a genuinely good man I suspect and he is intelligent. He has depth. It's no accident that he is such a compelling actor. He puts on acts of course and pretends to be vaguer than he is. Very little misses him as I've noticed.

Monday 7th Tremendous storms hit N. Italy, Switz and Austria last Friday. Over a hundred people have been killed and both Florence and Venice have been severely flooded.[246] There is great fear for the safety, not only of the people but for great works of art. In Florence 6 million precious books are under the deluge. We received only the tail end of the storm here and it was enjoyably wild, not tragic. Two or three trees in the garden were torn out by the roots but Rome is untouched. They are the worst floods in the history of Italy. And that's quite a time.

E finished a little early on Friday and we had planned to go to Venice on the overnight train! But the Gritti Palace was closed for the season so we decided to stay.[247] Just as well. We haven't left the house since, except on Saturday we took the children to lunch at the Flavia and from there to the Zoo.[248] We were soon followed by a small crowd but I was amiable for once.

---

[245] Joanna: cockney rhyming slang for piano.
[246] In Florence the River Arno flooded. Thirty-three people were killed, approximately 5,000 rendered homeless and a large number of valuable books, manuscripts, maps and other artefacts were destroyed or damaged. In Venice it became known as the 'Great Flood', where there was no loss of life, although significant damage to property.
[247] Hotel Gritti Palace, Venice.
[248] Hotel Flavia, Via Flavia, Rome. Rome's zoological gardens, located in the Villa Borghese.

[. . .] Stanley Baker very insistent that we do a TV spectacular for the Aberfan disaster.[249] I think it's a mistake. They have, according to the press, already received £420,000, and don't know what to do with it. It would be silly to add to their embarrassment. E suggests we should turn it over to the Italian disaster fund. Good idea.[250]

Tuesday 8th [. . .] A glorious day – as yesterday, blue skies and sun. I sat outside and got some sun on my face but I became too hot and had to change my sweater for a cooler shirt. [. . .] I cut down smoking cigarettes yesterday from my normal 50 or 60 to 17! It wasn't any great hardship but I wonder if 17 isn't as bad as 50 because I smoked each cigarette thoroughly whereas when I smoke thoughtlessly I probably take no more than two or three real 'drags', the rest simply vaporizing away. My appetite increased too though this may be the effect of not drinking which I haven't for 3 days.

Zeffirelli [. . .] arrived about 3.30. He told us all about going to Florence to get his Auntie and her dog and the impact of the terrible floods on that lovely city. Cows, cats, cars, trees, tapestries, clothes, furniture etc. etc. all piled up in distorted corners of the city. A cow and a calf who had somehow fled before the flood or had been carried along by it finding refuge in the cemetery of Robert and Elizabeth Barrett Browning which is apparently on highish ground.[251] Whole family businesses wiped out and ironically a great shortage of drinking water. [. . .] I am to run *Shrew* again tomorrow at 3.00. I don't like making films. I don't like acting in them and I don't like cutting them – especially the latter.

We dined with the children and Karen on lamb and artichokes and potatoes and salad followed by an apple tart. I made myself a martini before dinner just like a little old American. It tasted awful and put me in slightly bad temper. I read the whole of Anita Loos, *A Girl like I* in one sitting not because it was compulsive reading but feeling that if I stopped at any one place I wouldn't start up again.[252] She tells stories well but they're a little too polished to be true – some of them. She is of course a determined feminist and is kind to her own kind, even going so far as to describe Margalo Gillmore as being one of the great ladies of the American theatre.[253] Poor old talentless intoxicated Margalo. Anyway the book kept me awake until 2.00 in the morn. She is so determined to be witty and different that she succeeds only in becoming anticipated. My

[249] Stanley Baker (1928–76), Welsh actor and a long-time friend of Richard Burton. Richard and Elizabeth were godparents to Stanley and Ellen Baker's daughter Sally.

[250] Burton made this opinion public, which did not go down well with Stanley Baker, but he and Taylor did participate in the television show ('The Heart of Show Business'), which was broadcast on 26 March 1967.

[251] Robert Browning (1812–89), poet, and his wife Elizabeth Barrett Browning (1806–61), poet. Only Elizabeth was buried in the English Cemetery in Florence.

[252] Anita Loos (1891–1981), actor and author. Her autobiography, *A Girl Like I*, was published in 1966.

[253] Margalo Gillmore (1897–1986), actor.

sighs punctuated the whole reading. And what a dreadful story she tells about dead defenceless Alex Woollcott even if it is true.[254] It sounds terribly like what she would like to have happened. It was unforgivable to print it. [. . .]

Wednesday 9th [. . .] E went reluctantly to work an hour ago. I am to join her for lunch.

Tuesday 16th[255] Haven't written for 5–6 days. Since that time I have become 41 years old. I don't seem to feel physically any older and tend to think Well thank God that's another year gone. I'll change my refrain later when I'm 60. If I reach that age.

I received lots of presents, pullovers and shirts and books (one immensely valuable one from E.) a brief case, which I shall now use in preference to the other, a huge writing pad to encourage me to be an author etc. And a splendid movie camera from E.

Sheran Cazalet who has been here since Friday left this morning for England.[256] I wonder if she'll ever get married. It seems unlikely now. She is 33, I think, and is virtually a virgin (one to bed according to her) and probably does not like it much. Perhaps someone could teach her. She seems too not to have any ability in any other direction that could lead her to a career of any outstanding kind. She should be married and lead a life of social ease with a nice husband and a couple of children, a place in the country and a pied-à-terre in Town.

Marlon B and Christian Marquand came to dinner on Saturday night.[257] Everybody became sloshed to the gills and a thoroughly forgettable time (literally 'forgettable' as no two people remember what happened at the same time) was had by all.

Meade Roberts, a writer that I've tried to help, is in an hysteria about something.[258] Money and injured pride. I had asked him to do the screenplay on *Falesa* – Dylan Thomas – but had decided to abandon the project.[259] Therefore he has threatened to kill himself etc. What can I do? [. . .]

We've just heard from the Press that E. Fisher is suing E for divorce, for a property settlement and for custody of Liza.[260] Over my dead body – the latter.

---

[254] Alex Woolcott (1887–1943), critic and writer. The story (*A Girl Like I*, p. 151) is that Woolcott revealed to Loos that 'he had always wanted to be a girl' and 'all my life I've wanted to be a mother!'
[255] Tuesday was 15 November. Burton remains one day out for the rest of the diary.
[256] Sheran Cazalet married Simon Hornby (1934–2010) in 1968.
[257] Christian Marquand (1927–2000), actor and director, who was to direct *Candy* (1968).
[258] Meade Roberts (1930–92), screenwriter.
[259] A reference to the screenplay (part-written by Philip Burton), of Dylan Thomas's *The Beach of Falesa* (1964), based on the 1892 short story by Robert Louis Stevenson.
[260] Eddie Fisher (1928–2010), Elizabeth Taylor's husband prior to her marrying Richard Burton.

I taught Liza to play Gin-Rummy the night before last and she immediately became very good. She is a very clever girl.

I wrote the above [. . .] because she Liza was standing over my shoulder while I wrote. But she is very good at card games and it's all quite true.

[. . .] I tried to comfort E re Eddie – She is so ashamed of herself for having married such an obvious fool. He really is beneath contempt – a gruesome little man and smug as a boot.

Wednesday 17th Woke with Eliz this morning at 7.15. We both took baths in our separate bathrooms – she a short one and a long one for me. And off she went to work. I shaved, and dressed in my new sweater and cardigan (birthday present from E) fawn trousers and fawn desert boots with thick crepe soles [. . .]. I looked rather, I thought like a chocolate mousse. I ran back and asked [. . .] if we had any English kippers left. We did and I had one with salt, pepper and vinegar, toast and butter, and two cups of sweet tea. Delicious and followed by the first cigarette of the day. Equally delicious. I then sat in the sun and read an article in an American magazine by a man who, with a friend, <u>rowed</u> across the Atlantic.[261] Their attitude is one that I think I understand but have no desire to try [. . .] to beat the physical body beyond human reason and still make it go on. But they say what they talked and dreamed of all the time was food and walks in country lanes and magnificent dinners in London etc. In short it must surely be masochistic, like the lunatic who when asked why he knocked his head so much against the wall said that it was so nice when he stopped. Now that they're safely on land and in warmth and comfort they probably think a great deal about the sea and its fascination. They'll try something hazardous again and doubtless one of these days kill themselves in the attempt. Good luck feller-me-lads – I'll content myself with reading about it.

I have just read *Tread Softly for You Tread on my Jokes* – ghastly title by Malcolm Muggeridge.[262] It's a series of articles collected over the years from newspapers and magazines and shows it. He repeats himself quite a bit and is peculiarly engrossed by pornography and sex. I have the feeling that he is not being honest in his reactions. Why does he not like pornography? because, according to the *Oxford Dictionary* it gives rise to lewd thoughts? So what? We'd have lewd thoughts anyway pornography or no pornography. If you're lonely and unwanted it can solace you, and with a companion to share it it can become unimaginably delightful. The unctuous rubbishy shit written about pornography is nonsense. Practically all good pornography is best selling so I understand, and yet I have never found anyone who when asked if they enjoyed it will ever admit so. They will say they've read it – *Fanny Hill*,

---

[261] This is a reference to the exploits of John Ridgway (1938—) and Chay Blyth (1940—), who rowed across the Atlantic in *English Rose III* in 92 days.
[262] Malcolm Muggeridge (1903–90), *Tread Softly for You Tread on my Jokes* (1966).

Chatterley's Lover, Tropics of Capricorn, Cancer, Candy etc.[263] But they're still too inhibited to say it gave them pleasure of a sexual kind. Blah. I know bloody well it did. I've heard too many men talk in too many barracks and Nissen huts and clubs not to know what <u>they</u> think, and too many honest women have confessed to me things they've thought and heard from other women not to know what they think either.[264] There are, doubtless, pure souls who through some act of God are physically neuter, or who have had sexual normality scourged out of them in youth, or are too old to care, who may genuinely be horrified by pornography. I'm sorry for them. Journalists of course are pornography's greatest scourge, working for newspapers who wouldn't dream of having one issue without at least one scantily clad model or actress in the middle pages. Oh how they love to be superior. How they love to pontificate. How they play in the dark we'll never know. They are the real dirt.

There is the argument that pornography can make a man a sex maniac or something perverted. Well now I am I understand a potently sexy man but it hasn't turned me into a sex fiend, a sex killer a sex sadist or a sex masochist and I've been reading the stuff for years – at least twenty. I knew a girl once married to an older man with whom she'd fallen out of physical love but still loved otherwise who relied upon reading pornography urgently and quickly in the bathroom before going in to his bed to satisfy his desires and to inflame her own. The moralists would flay her alive if she had left him for another man to marry. They would excoriate her if she had extra-marital affairs. So? And what's the difference between reading it and thinking it. I myself have had in my time to make love in the dark to women by whom I was bored, desperately trying to imagine they were somebody else. And doubtless some women have had to do the same with me. Muggeridge quotes Kingsmill as saying that the act of love is ludicrous and disgusting. Speak for yourself Kingsmill.[265] I love its disgustingness and comicality. Put some jaundice in your eye and the act of walking is ludicrous and obscene, and swimming and, above all, eating. All those muscles, in most people, 50% atrophied, sluggishly propelling people over land or through water or gulping oysters. Come off it.

I've written the above carelessly but will elaborate on it one day. It is an important thing to kill cant and humbug even if one is a humbug oneself.

I went to the studio for lunch. [. . .] At 2.30 I met Sheila Pickles and the Italian TV man re the documentary on Florence.[266] I have agreed to do it on

[263] John Cleland (?1709–89), *Memoirs of a Woman of Pleasure* (1748–9), often known as *Fanny Hill* after the main character; D. H. Lawrence (1885–1930), *Lady Chatterley's Lover* (1928); Henry Miller (1891–1980), *Tropic of Capricorn* (1938) and *Tropic of Cancer* (1934); Terry Southern (1924–95) (writing as Maxwell Kenton) and Mason Hoffenberg (1922–86), *Candy* (1958).

[264] A Nissen hut was a prefabricated steel building characteristic of military bases and airfields.

[265] Hugh Kingsmill (1889–1949), biographer, novelist, literary critic.

[266] Zeffirelli's documentary on Florence (*Per Firenze* – For Florence, which appeared in 1966), with narration by Burton, is reputed to have raised more than $20m. This appeared on the BBC in English on 11 December 1966 with the title 'Florence: Days of Destruction'.

Friday here in Rome. I will try to do the narration in Italian for the Italians and in English for the UK and USA I fear I'll have to write it too – not in Italian of course, they'll translate that. I looked up Florence and flood in the *Oxford Dictionary of Quotations* – there is practically nothing that is apt except from Inge.[267] I read some more of the Disraeli biography by Robert Blake.[268] I'd no idea he was quite so vain and quite so devious in petty things. So far I'm about up to his 35th year so there's a lot to go. [. . .]

Thursday 18th Rose early bathed and breakfasted at 8.30. [. . .] Finished the diary entry for yesterday had a cup of tea and toast and jelly and took E'en So for a walk. A beautiful warm Autumn day. A horseman on, what looked to my untrained eye, a thoroughbred posted past on the outside hedge. I ran or rather jogged about ½ mile having already done my PT in a fury when I got up.[269] Will my arms ever come back to what they were. I don't so much mean their looks but their strength. Four years of atrophy from pinched nerves? bursitis? arthritis is a long time to make up at 41. Well, keep on trying anyway. Perhaps I should pick up weights. [. . .]

Went to the studio by 1.00 and waited until 2.45 before E came back from location for lunch. I ate like a fiend – roast turkey, beans-and-bacon-and-onions, mashed potatoes and gravy. Still felt bloated at midnight. We went into Rome after work to see the documentary on the disaster in Florence that I am to narrate tomorrow and next week. The force of water is unbelievable – cars bowled along like match boxes, the shops and houses on the Ponte Vecchio smashed to bits though the bridge held, a corpse floating down the street a dead drowned horse with his head over the stall door.[270] Another horse upside down, manuscripts and pages from drowned books in the Uffici plastered to the ceilings.[271] Awful. I drank a little today. One vodka and some Lafitte Roth 1962. Didn't taste like anything. [. . .]

Friday 19th Went into the TV Studios in Rome and worked until 7.15 at night starting at mid-day. All day long – apart from lunch – I read Italian off a tele-prompter. It was torture but I was very patient and so were they. Tomorrow to London.

We lunched in a restaurant which was very Roman and cold of course, flagged floors and damp. It was pouring outside and the traffic was choked. Nauseous fumes from buses. We were stuck for minutes on end between two

---

[267] William Ralph Inge (1860–1954), cleric and journalist. The quotation is: 'The nations which have put mankind and posterity most in their debt have been small states – Israel, Athens, Florence, Elizabethan England.'
[268] Robert Blake, *Disraeli* (1966).
[269] PT: Physical training.
[270] Ponte Vecchio is a medieval bridge over the Arno in Florence.
[271] The Uffizi Gallery, Florence's historic art museum.

diesel-waste-vomiting species of them. The smell of petrol cities is becoming intolerable to me – and especially the diesel smell which is particularly foul. [...]

I don't know quite what I shall do on the Sunday Show – it all seems so band waggoning – the poor people have already had £800,000 and are embarrassed. We can only add to it. The Mayor seems to be the only one who enjoys it.

Went home with Ron Berkeley and B. Wilson, had some drinks and ate some food sole with croquettes and Fontana Candida. Became furious, nerves nerves nerves, because of what I considered to be over packing. For <u>two</u> nights in London we have <u>two</u> large suitcases. But that wasn't the reason really. It was nerves from a hard day and nerves about flying and nerves about the Aberfan show.

Smoked myself furiously to sleep and before doing told E She was not to come with me to London. Leave me alone I screamed as I slammed doors. Give me some peace! What nerves and booze will do. I couldn't go without her.

1967

Richard stopped making entries in his 1966 diary in mid-November. Between then and the start of his 1967 diary he gave an interview to Kenneth Tynan, part of which was broadcast in April 1967, and a transcript of which appeared in print in *Acting in the Sixties* (ed. Hal Burton, London: BBC, 1970). Christmas and New Year were spent in Paris, and early in January Richard and Elizabeth travelled to Dahomey (now known as Benin) in West Africa, to prepare for the filming of *The Comedians*.

JANUARY

Monday 9th, Cotonou[1] Last night we went to Glenville's for cocktails.[2] Most of the people stood outside on the asphalt. It was warm but not oppressive. Alec was there playing the part either of a sweet saint or a great actor charming but removed from the ordinary run of common human beings.[3] We arrived (deliberately) late and left after about an hour. We dined on cold ham, spring onions, radishes, cheese, bread (lovely long loaf) tomatoes.

Gaston works like a dog. He charges around shopping answering telephones, preparing salad, filling thermoses, defleaing the dogs and watching us wherever we go, and all with the greatest good humour. He really is indispensable and, tho' it sounds disloyal, a far better helper than Bob Wilson. There are certain things that are beneath Bob's dignity. Nothing is beneath Gaston's. [. . .]

Today we're off to be officially welcomed by the President of the Republic – events which I dread.[4]

E is looking gorgeous – she blooms in hot climates. It must be that Italian blood. I didn't drink a single drop yesterday and consequently had profound 'shakes'. I must take it easy with the booze.

---

[1] Cotonou, largest city of the Republic of Dahomey (now Republic of Benin), where the filming of *The Comedians* was taking place.
[2] Peter Glenville, director of *The Comedians*.
[3] Alec Guinness, co-starring in *The Comedians*.
[4] President (formerly Colonel and Chief of Staff to the Armed Forces) Christophe Soglo (1909–83), President of the Republic of Dahomey from October 1963 to January 1964 and from November 1965 to December 1967. Soglo, who had fought with distinction for France in the Second World War, had been France's military adviser to the Dahomean government before resigning and acquiring Dahomean citizenship in 1960.

Tuesday 10th Yesterday we went to the Palace to be received by the President called by all his staff 'Mon General.' He is very black (married though to a white wife and has seven children) about 5'8" tall, slightly bow-legged, stockily built. His clothes were ill made though his cabinet members were impeccably dressed.[5] I understand that coups d'états are the thing here, as in most of the new African states, so that he may not be the boss for long. At the moment it is something of a dictatorship – when I asked him how many deputés there were in Congress he said 'aucune.'[6] Whoops! I thought. He obviously likes women and was forever taking E by the arm. She of course was charming and very feminine. We both found the experience oddly moving. Here was this huge mosaiced palace, only completed 3 years ago, and outside the immense Salle de Reception, capable of receiving 3000 people at one time, there was washing on the line.

He showed us with great pride the 'chinese' room which was so cluttered with furniture and bric a brac from, he said proudly, 'Mon grand ami Chiang Kai Shek' that we could barely move between the furniture.[7] With equal pride he showed us his own and his family's living quarters which were poky and small. He showed us his wife's clothes closet and brought a lump to E's throat when with a flourish he opened a cupboard to show a perfectly ordinary rack for shoes.

He asked E to step on to a mat on the way out and chuckled with delight as two wall lights automatically came on. E simulated astonishment and he was very pleased. By this time I was sweating like a bull and was glad to leave.

The English are a cold lot. We had lunch afterwards with Guinness and Glenville and I'm sure that had we not said immediately how impressed and moved we were they were ready to send the whole thing up.

E says that Peter Glenville [. . .] is a right 'bitch.' 'I have yet,' she said, 'to catch him saying a good word about anybody.' She's right I think.

I am madly 'in love' with her at the moment, as distinct from always loving her, and want to make love to her every minute but alas it is not possible for a couple of days. She'll have trouble walking in a couple or three days.

[. . .] Both of us had a hell of a time getting to sleep. The bedroom though air conditioned is the least cold room in the house and there seemed to be scores of minute mosquitoes which even if they didn't bother you made you feel itchy. [. . .]

Wednesday 11th Like all films the first day seems to be the worst. We slept a little last night, perhaps 5–6 hours, and woke unrefreshed. We had Bloody

---

[5] President Soglo had met his wife in French Indochina.
[6] None. Soglo's rule would be brought to an end by an army coup in December 1967. There were to be a total of six coups in Dahomey/Benin during the decade from 1963 to 1972.
[7] Chiang Kai-shek (1887–1975), President of the Republic of China. Soglo had visited Taiwan some time in 1964/65.

Marys for breakfast. There was a mist or fog which hung around for some time. Eventually we shot the first shot at 10.30 approx. Very Hot. We did 3 takes – one of which was my fault. Then we shot 3 close-ups of the same thing. [. . .] Then the President arrived with his wife and entourage. I searched for E. because he quite clearly wanted to see her and not anybody else, though he might strongly deny such a terrible imputation. He was as engaging as ever and wicked. At one time, after a particularly salacious remark he kissed his wife (white) and was given a round of applause by the assembled hangers-on. His wife, who should be used to it, looked perplexed. E adores him. He looks to me like my brother Verdun after a hard day in the pits and before he's washed. He called Christian – our principal servant, one might call him a butler – 'mon petit'. So far it seems that he is beloved. There was a beautiful negro girl, whose name I've forgotten, who never smiled, very chic, who never took her eyes off Elizabeth. There was admiration, envy, malice, hatred and love in her every reaction to my silly old girl.

[. . .] Later we sat at home with the publicity man who is, so far, a bore, and Gaston and Ron and F. La Rue and after the aforesaid pub man had left started talking very seriously and equally very drunkenly of the obligation one has to one's fellow beings. Should one have a child if one has a history of insanity in the family. Should Ron take off with Vicky or stay with his wife Leah. All this laced with profound lectures from me and Elizabeth. Stupendously Smug.

We had lunch with Ron, Claudye, Raymond St Jaques – the latter anxious to prove that he is essentially a stage actor in the Shakespearean tradition.[8] Very American.

[There are no further entries in the diary from mid-January to late March. Burton and Taylor continued filming in Cotonou until mid February. At the end of that month *The Taming of the Shrew* was released, having been selected for the Royal Command Performance at the Odeon in Leicester Square, attended by Princess Margaret and Lord Snowdon, and raising money for the Cinema and Television Benevolent Fund. While in London Burton and Taylor stayed at the Dorchester Hotel, along with many members of Burton's family from South Wales, and on 18 March Richard took the opportunity to see England beat Scotland at rugby union by 27 points to 14 to regain the Calcutta Cup at Twickenham. Further filming for *The Comedians* was carried out at studios in Paris and Nice.]

---

[8] Claudye Ettori was Elizabeth Taylor's hairdresser on *The Comedians* and would become part of the Burton–Taylor entourage in Europe. She also played the small part of the manicurist in the film. Raymond St Jaques (1930–90) played the part of Captain Concasseur in *The Comedians*.

MARCH

Good Friday, 24th, Saint Jean Cap Ferrat[9] What a huge lapse. We spent some more weeks in Dahomey getting hotter and hotter with most people getting sicker and sicker. E won the NY Critics award for *VW*. (I was runner-up to P. Scofield) and cabled M. Brando, who was staying in Gstaad at our house, to ask if he would pick the award up for her.[10] He did and then, if you please, flew to Dahomey to deliver it personally! He apparently made a speech attacking the assembled critics for not acknowledging E before and not giving me the award now. Funny fellow.

[. . .] We still retain a certain amount of nostalgia for Dahomey. The house, the lizards, the palm trees, the unit intrigues, the arrogance of the American negroes with the West Africans, the dangerous fascinating sea only a couple of sand tumps away from the house, the mad palace, the President and his dowdy provincial wife. The Palace receptions and the fetes.

We persuaded PG <u>not</u> to fire an actor called George Stanford Brown – a very beautiful sluggish lethargic negro boy.[11] He always wears tight jeans and sits sprawled with his legs wide open. Gives me a pain but am told to be nice to him by E. And also he's a pupil of PHB's [Philip Burton]. I hope we were right to keep him on – not that it matters, it's only a film.

The food in the two restaurants we went to was good at first and then, through over-familiarity perhaps or boredom or something, became atrocious. We ate mostly at home afterwards. [. . .]

A. Guinness walked around looking very white and pink and read a little note-book which contained his lines for the film. He looks remarkable as a negress.[12] Quite deceived me at first.

P. Ustinov gave a turn at the huge charity benefit for lepers and TB.[13] He is a very good sort but his invention is running out. He is doing the same turns now as he was 10–15 years ago. They are brilliant to the uninitiated. He is very serious when alone with one but must clown with an audience of two. In some vague way, because he seems disturbed, I feel sorry for him. Jack of all trades.

Friday 31st We have been at this house – it's a famous one called 'La Fiorentina' – for 2½ weeks, and for the last 12 days have shot at night, which after the initial adjustment I don't mind.[14] It means a certain amount of sunshine during the day and a game or two of tennis. It has however been quite cold at night

---

[9] Saint Jean Cap Ferrat, port and resort, on the Cap Ferrat peninsula to the east of Nice.
[10] *VW*: *Who's Afraid of Virginia Woolf*. New York Film Critics Circle Award for Best Actress.
[11] George Stanford Brown (1943—) played the part of Henri Philipot in *The Comedians*.
[12] Guinness dressed as a black woman (impersonating Burton's character's cook) for the scene in which his character, Major Jones, finds sanctuary in the embassy.
[13] Peter Ustinov played the part of Ambassador Pineda in *The Comedians*.
[14] Villa La Fiorentina, situated on the Saint Hospice point, Cap Ferrat peninsula. Taylor had previously rented the same property when married to Mike Todd.

and the night before last in the mountains above St Michel it was bitter. We had a soup in St Michel which is well known locally as Potage au Pistou.[15] I think. Very good.

Last Monday night we had drinks at the Palace at Monaco and then went on to the Hotel de Paris to a banquet in aid of the British American Hospital, at which we were the guests of honour.[16] I enjoyed but don't remember too much about it. He was tubby and smiled kindly and seemed nice. She was pretty and young looking and very short-sighted. Her eyes indeed are terribly weak and at the end of the evening were shot bright with blood.[17]

Last night I worked with James Earl Jones – a retake – and then with A. Guinness.[18] We finished by 02.45 – very early for us. A hot bath when I arrived home, a read in bed and asleep by 5.30.

We were roughly 3 weeks in Paris before coming here. We stayed at the Plaza Athenée.[19] So far it's the best hotel we've stayed at in Paris with a splendid restaurant. Things that stick out:

We were both nominated for Oscars for *VW* – the film itself getting 13 nominations.[20]

We had dinner with the Duke and Duchess of Windsor who came back afterwards to our apartment in the Plaza.[21] We all got on famously.

We went to London for the opening night of *Shrew*. A huge success almost totally spoiled by Frank Flanagan's sudden death on the morning of the opening night, which incidentally was E's birthday.[22] He died quickly thank God of a heart attack.

A couple of weeks later Sally Wilson died in NY of leukaemia or a sinister relation.[23]

Bob (Wilson) and Agnes (Flanagan) are both with us here in the house at Saint Jean Cap Ferrat recovering from the terrible shock. Bob is strong and suffers in relative silence. Agnes, poor dab, drinks and drinks and drinks.

---

[15] A garlic and vegetable soup with basil.
[16] The Prince's Palace of Monaco, the official residence of the Prince of Monaco. Hôtel de Paris, Place du Casino, Monaco.
[17] It would appear that Burton is referring here to Prince Rainier of Monaco (1923–2005) and his wife Princess Grace (1928–82), actor.
[18] James Earl Jones (1931—) played the part of Dr Magiot in *The Comedians*.
[19] Hôtel Plaza Athenée, Avenue Montaigne, Paris.
[20] Oscars were won by Elizabeth Taylor (Best Actress); Sandy Dennis (Best Supporting Actress) (1937–92); Haskell Wexler (Best Cinematography) (1922—); Richard Sylbert (Best Art Direction – Black-and-White) (1928–2002); George James Hopkins (Best Set Decoration – Black-and-White) (1896–1985); and Irene Sharaff (Best Costume Design). Nominations were also received for the film as Best Picture; for Ernest Lehman (Best Producer) (1915–2005); Mike Nichols (Best Director); Richard Burton (Best Actor); George Segal (Best Supporting Actor) (1934—); Ernest Lehman (Best Screenplay – Based on Material from Another Medium); Alex North (Best Music) (1910–91); George R. Groves (Best Sound) (1901–76); and Sam Steen (Best Film Editing) (1923–2000).
[21] The Duke of Windsor, formerly King Edward VIII (1894–1972), and his wife, the Duchess of Windsor, formerly Wallis Simpson (1896–1986).
[22] Frank Flanagan, husband of Agnes.
[23] Sally Wilson, wife of Bob.

With the Duke of Windsor in Paris. We went back to our apartment after dinner and the Duke and I sang the Welsh National Anthem in atrocious harmony. I referred disloyally to the Queen as 'her dumpy majesty' and neither the Duke or Duchess seemed to mind.

APRIL

Saturday 1st Went into Nice in the afternoon yesterday to buy books. There wasn't much selection but we bought a lot of thrillers. Afterwards we had cocktails at the Negresco where we ran into Bob Hall (stuntman) and John Lee. Mike (our M.) came with us. I wrote to his headmaster yesterday to try and get him reinstated at Le Rosey from which he has been expelled. Poor boy. Otherwise I'll try and get both boys into Millfield.[24]

[. . .] Wrote to Kate and enclosed $10. She hopes Syb's baby is a boy. He will be called Colin if a boy, Amy if a girl.[25] [. . .]

Telegraphed Franco Z. that he can show *Shrew* at Cannes if he wishes but warned him that he may get royally shrewed! They're a nasty lot around here. [. . .]

[There are no further entries in the diary until late May. During this period work continued on *The Comedians* in the south of France. On 10 April Richard, nominated for Best Actor for his performance in *Who's Afraid of Virginia Woolf*, was beaten to the award by Paul Scofield for his portrayal of Sir Thomas More in *A Man For All Seasons*. Neither Burton nor Taylor attended the awards in California, Taylor collecting her award at a ceremony held at Grosvenor House in London. By late May they were cruising on a chartered yacht in the western Mediterranean.]

MAY

Sunday 21st, on Board Oddyseia *Portofino*[26] We arrived this morning from Corsica where we have been for about a week – 2 days at Ajaccio, two at L'Ile Rousse and two at Calvi.[27] [. . .] We are going to buy this M.Y. It will cost $220,000 and we shall spend 40 or 50,000 dollars on it. It is old – 60 years – is 130 feet long, three engines, 260–80 tons. She will do 14 knots. There are 7 bedrooms two of them with large double beds and will sleep 14 passengers. There are 8 crew, though that includes a cook, maid, waiter. The boat itself

---

[24] Millfield School, Street, Somerset.
[25] Sybil and Jordan's daughter was named Amy.
[26] The *Oddyseia* motor yacht was built in 1906. Richard and Elizabeth had chartered it. Portofino, a resort and port to the east of Genoa, on the Italian Riviera.
[27] Ajaccio, the capital of Corsica on its western coast. L'Ile Rousse and Calvi, both on the north-western coast of Corsica.

needs only 4 – at the most 5 – crew to run it efficiently. I estimate it will cost $25–30000 a year to run it. Not too bad when one considers our last house (rented) cost $10,000 a month plus approx $1000 a week for food and staff etc! If we can use it as much as possible instead of hotels we could actually save money.

Monday 22nd Stayed on board all day yesterday and sunned ourselves. Result – pink all over. Watched the port's traffic which was endless with scores of waterbuses loaded with scores of Sunday tourists from adjacent Genoa, Santa Margherita, Rapallo etc.[28] Thank the lord they didn't know we were here.

This morning however we went shopping and I bought this pen with which I write, a Jockey cap, a couple of pencils and paper while E bought out Pucci's.[29] There were a lot of tourists mostly German and American – the latter being almost exclusively Jewish. They greet one with 'Hi Elizabeth. California.' There are only 20 million people in California. We fled for sanctuary to a splendid restaurant called 'Pitosforo' where we had Vodka Tom Collins, cocktail onions, cheese from Sardinia called Formaggio al Sardo, two kinds of salami and, when I asked for them, fave (spring broad beans sort of).[30] Afterwards, though we'd promised to lunch on board we had steak à la maison and crepes suzette. All delicious. After lunch we went home to the boat and slept and so on.

Must send telegrams tomorrow regarding future plans. Everybody is waiting for decisions. Must make some I suppose or should we? I wish I never had to work again but know I will and suppose we must. I must work out one day how much we have in cash property etc. Must be quite a lot. Perhaps we could stop now if we stopped spending so much.

We think this restaurant 'Pitosforo' – we dined there again tonight to be among the best we know. And the ambience is splendid, the lovely little harbour at your feet.

Wednesday 24th, Portofino Harbour The seas were high and the skies grey and the boat rocked and shivered since we are tied up slightly outside and more subject to the wind and weather. So we locked all doors and settled to read and, in my case, do crossword puzzles. I read E's script *The Old Man and me* and thought it good and a money maker especially with C. Grant but it may by now be unavailable.[31] [. . .] Have read variously since coming on board. *The Whole Truth* a novel about foreign correspondents for a thinly disguised *NY Times*.[32] *Caen* – about the battle of Caen and D-Day (I think I

---

[28] Santa Margherita and Rapallo, both close to Portofino.
[29] Emilio Pucci, fashion house, with a Portofino boutique.
[30] Ristorante Il Pitosforo, Molo Umberto I, Portofino.
[31] Cary Grant (1904–86), actor. Presumably this was a film script based on Elaine Dundy's 1964 novel *The Old Man and Me*. There is no record of the film having been made.
[32] Robert Daley (1930—), *The Whole Truth* (1967). Daley had worked for the *New York Times*.

would have gone mad in that hell).[33] Some detective stories, new original script by Tennessee *Boom!* which E will do as a film.[34] Script of *Shoes of the Fisherman* worst of Hollywood vulgarity and taste, though written by Morris West, an Australian in Rome.[35]

[. . .] E anxious that I write about her so here goes: She is a nice fat girl who loves mosquitos and hates pustular carbuncular Welshmen, loathes boats and loves planes, has tiny blackcurrant eyes and minute breasts and has no sense of humour. She is prudish, priggish and painfully self-conscious. [. . .]

Friday Night, 26th, Santa Margherita Harbour H. French arrived on Wednesday at about 7pm. [. . .] Showed us strange cable in which C. Grant said he would costar with E only if I directed! He must be frightened of her or something. Perhaps he's a little strange in the head.

Hugh came back on Thursday for lunch with news of telephone calls etc. Will hear something shortly I suppose. Told us that James Mason left his agency after 17 years (?) because they [. . .] were getting all the plum parts for me. Well, well.

Suspect that Rex and Rach Harrison are back because I saw a flag on their flag pole.[36] I was right as I've received a note from them this afternoon.

Weather pretty rough so shifted to above harbour as it's safer than Portofino. [. . .]

Stayed on board all day and read and sunbathed. Sky hot and blue but sea a curious milky green from the storm I suppose.

Much threat of war between Israel and U.A.R.[37] Bugger it. Was put in a fury by crowds of staring idiots on Thursday in the square. [. . .] Fury vented on E of course.

JUNE

Thursday 1st, En Route St. Marg – Portofino We were in St Margherita yesterday for watering and fuelling and just as well as it gave us a chance to get away from Rex and Rachel. We had spent Sunday up at their house and, as usual it was very liquid. Rex seems to hold his booze better than he used to but Rachel is still maniacal. We saw them again on Monday evening at La Gritta

---

[33] Alexander McKee, *Caen: Anvil of Victory* (1964).

[34] Both Burton and Taylor would star in *Boom!*

[35] *The Shoes of the Fisherman* was the title both of a novel by Australian writer Morris West (1916–99), and of a 1968 film based on the novel, starring Laurence Olivier and John Gielgud.

[36] Rex Harrison and the Welsh actor Rachel Roberts (1927–80) had married in 1962. Rachel Roberts had played alongside Burton in *A Subject of Scandal and Concern*. The Harrisons had a house – Villa San Genesio – in Portofino.

[37] The United Arab Republic: the official name for Egypt at the time. The Six Day War between Israel on the one hand and Egypt, Syria and Jordan on the other would start on 5 June and end on 10 June 1967, with Israel clearly victorious.

bar in the Port.[38] Fortunately before Rachel became totally demented they left (not without difficulty for Rex) for home and dinner at about 9.30. By this time Tennessee Williams and his friend Bill had arrived and Joe Losey and J. Heyman and H. French.[39] Tennessee, who now prefers to be called Tom, seemed sloshed and spoke in a loud voice, powerful penetrating and incoherent and somewhat embarrassing. E told him to lower his voice a few times. We were in the Pitosforo at the time, and we attract enough attention as it is. Have now decided to do *Boom!* with E. [. . .]

On Tuesday everybody came on board. Rachel became stupendously drunk and was or became totally uncontrollable. The strangers T. Williams, Losey, Bill, French, Heyman, left in disgust. She insulted Rex sexually morally physically and in every way. She lay on the floor in the bar and barked like a dog. At one time she started to masturbate her basset hound – a lovely sloppy old dog called Omar. E lectured her, I did, Rex did. All to no avail. She bitterly harangued the memories of Carole Landis and Kay Kendall, hurled imprecations at Lilli Palmer.[40] Christ.

Yesterday, Wednesday, we left early in the a.m. for S. Marg to fuel and load up. [. . .] Losey came to lunch. He's intelligent but a trifle grim. I hope he has a sense of humour. I found it hard work talking to him for 2 hours. Still one doesn't necessarily have to <u>talk</u> all that much to directors.

Tennessee and Bill came too. Again the former seemed to be tipsy. He is certainly not very prepossessing physically. Heyman told us he tried to kill himself a few weeks ago but was saved by Bill. There were no details. I asked Tenn if diarhyl (?) pills depressed him.

'I have no way of knowing,' he said.

'Because,' I said, 'you're depressed all the time.'

'Right,' he said.

[. . .]

Friday 2nd, Portofino Yesterday afternoon taking a little sun on the after deck (finally driven away by long-focus lens paparazzi who were shooting from the road above) I thought – about 2 o'clock – that I saw Rex Rachel and two other people go by in their boat. E wonders if they think we are snubbing them because of Rachel's behaviour on Tuesday. Perhaps. Must call them today sometime.

---

[38] La Gritta American Bar, Calata Marconi, Portofino.

[39] Bill is William Glavin, Tennessee Williams's paid companion from 1965 to 1970. Joseph Losey (1909–84), director. Losey would direct *Boom!*, *Secret Ceremony*, and *The Assassination of Trotsky*. John Heyman (1933—), agent and producer of *Boom!* Tennessee Williams (1911–83), playwright. Burton and Taylor had played in film adaptations of Williams's *The Night of the Iguana*, *Suddenly, Last Summer* and *Cat on a Hot Tin Roof*. *Boom!* was his own adaptation of his 1962 play *The Milk Train Doesn't Stop Here Anymore*.

[40] Carole Landis (1919–48), actor and former lover of Rex Harrison. Kay Kendall (1926–59), actor and Harrison's third wife (1957–9). Lilli Palmer (1914–86), actor and Harrison's second wife (1943–57).

[. . .] The two dogs have been making love now since last Sunday at least 3 times a day. Who would have thought that dogs in heat went on so long. They remain locked after each coition for about 10–12–15 minutes. They are very serious about it and O Fie's penis is beginning to look the worse for wear.

Saturday 3rd Went on shore yesterday, as promised, to ring R and R. H[arrison]'s keeper told me they were in the harbour so I went to 'La Gritta' and there they were sure enough. They were already somewhat the worse for wear – it was about 2.00 pm. I went with them to a little rest[aurant] and drank some red wine while they ate. [. . .] We talked a lot about death and miraculous recoveries – stemming from Chichester and his cancer and his recovery and his round-the-world voyage.[41] It was pleasant enough.

It was the anniversary of the liberation of Italy by the Allies I gather, and Portofino was crawling with holiday makers.[42]

I took R and R in my new boat and we went for ½ hour spin down the coast. There was so much traffic that we were, until we got clear, soaked with water. I brought the boat back in as one, said Rex, to the manner born.

This coast is unquestionably more interesting than the Côte d'Azur, much more wild and forted. Rex was very anxious to prevent Rach drinking and we managed to keep her off it for an hour but once on board she was on to the Scotch like a homing pigeon. [. . .]

Sunday 4th [. . .] I went on shore to search for Rex Rach and their friend – an Anglo-Portuguese called Arthur Barbosa (E insists on calling him Edward) who is to help E with redecorating the yacht.[43] It is difficult to believe that Barbosa is completely Portuguese by blood – his father was the Portuguese consul in Liverpool which is where I understand Rex met him some centuries ago because he looks talks walks like a caricature of a middle-class, middle-aged public schoolboy. Which he is. He went to St Edward's school near Oxford at the same time as L. Olivier and Douglas (Legless Pilot) Bader.[44] R and R told me that he told them that he'd had a passion all his life to dress up in his wives' nightdresses (He's 4 times married) and be tied to the bed posts. He has however, he languidly assured them, finally cured himself of this mild sexual aberration.

---

[41] Sir Francis Chichester (1901–72), aviator and sailor, had been diagnosed with terminal cancer in 1958. He had won the first single-handed transatlantic yacht race in 1960 and had gone on to circumnavigate the globe from August 1966 to May 1967.
[42] Hostilities between the Germans and the Allies in Italy ceased on 2 May 1945. However, Liberation Day in Italy is celebrated on 25 April, the anniversary of the end of Mussolini's Italian Social Republic.
[43] Arthur Barbosa (1908–95), artist, theatre designer and interior decorator.
[44] St Edward's School is on Woodstock Road, Oxford. Group Captain Sir Douglas Robert Steuart Bader (1910–82), RAF fighter pilot and war hero.

Rach became pretty drunk again on Punt e Mes and Gin and started to strip off at one point.[45] The people on the roadway above started to cheer thinking it was E no doubt. I stopped her.

I can't see – we can't see how Rex can put up with her behaviour if she is continually like this. It has reached a point though, as they both told me, where Rex, after her behaviour last Tuesday (?) wrote her a letter. She's basically a good girl but she should not drink. I was surprised to find she's 40 years old. I thought she was about 37. Rex is fantastically tolerant of her drunken idiocies. She wouldn't last 48 hours with me and he's had it for 7 years.

Monday 5th Kate arrives on the 12th and I am very excited. I haven't seen her for ten months. We shall keep her with us alone for the first five days or so and then take her to Switz to join the girls. I'm missing those little buggers too. It's 9.00 am and I'm sitting on deck waiting for my morning cup of tea while E has her second sleep – what she calls her nightmare sleep. It's a beautiful morning cool and blue. The harbour water barely ruffled by the off-shore breeze. Birds all over the place. Two or three people in dinghys. Buses pass with their klaxons going, on the road above the port. In the harbour, very crowded with craft of all kinds, there is a very august looking sailing yacht with a lot of washing on the line.

Yesterday we stayed on board all day. I read a couple of books one of them called *The Missile Crisis*.[46] It recounts in journalistic documentary form the 1962 confrontation of Kennedy and Khrushchev over the arming of Cuba.[47] The USA handled it very cleverly and bravely it seems to me but Khrushchev comes out of it too with some dignity despite the usual political lying etc. What a monstrous childish arena the political arena is.

[. . .] We heard, two days ago, that we have again been awarded the Donatello David for *T of S*.[48] Both of us. That makes two each. [. . .]

Reading back through this notebook I see that I wasn't writing when we heard that E had won the Oscar and I hadn't! Bloody cheek. But P. Scofield won so that's alright. I sent him a cable and he me. [. . .]

Tuesday 6th [. . .] I stayed in La Gritta with Raj and drank Negronis for a couple of hours while I called R and R. Raj (the owner of the bar) talked a great deal. He said that Rex had altered fantastically – for the better – since he'd become a big film star after *Cleopatra*. He said that he'd told Rex that Rachel must work if she were not to become an alcoholic. He told me how

---

[45] Punt e Mes: an Italian vermouth.
[46] Probably Elie Abel, *The Missile Crisis* (1966).
[47] John F. Kennedy (1917–63), President of the United States of America. Nikita Khrushchev (1894–1971), First Secretary of the Communist Party of the Soviet Union (1953–64).
[48] The David Di Donatello: the Italian version of the Academy Award. *T of S*: *The Taming of the Shrew*.

he (Raj) was an alcoholic and how, voluntarily, he put himself into a clinic in Genoa to cure it. He has been waggonised since January 17. He told me how like the Italians the Welsh were and how his wife had said how Italian I looked!

Later on R and R and Edward Arthur arrived and I talked desultorily with them and finally went back to the boat. E was angry.

Later on, about dusk, R and R and EA approached hailed and were invited on board. They stayed a couple of hours. This time Rach was sober and Rex was drunk (nicely). [. . .]

Raj said war had broken out between Israel and Egypt and other Arab idiots. Shall wait for confirmation. Italians tend to hysteria and it may only be a border incident.

[There would appear to be a missing page or pages at this point. The next entry is . . .]

Monday 12th [. . .] <u>Kate arrives tomorrow and the Israeli war is over</u>. The Israelis completely destroyed the forces against them in <u>3 days</u> with what seems a mopping-up action of two days.

Now for the peace. It's going to be a bugger to settle. That clever idiot Nasser resigned and then 'at the behest of his people' returned to office 16 hours later.[49]

[. . .]

Tuesday 13th, Monte Carlo Kate arrived from NY with Aaron [. . .]. K was, as usual, enchanting and very pretty and excited and she immediately re-established warm 'lovins' with E.

Wednesday 14th [. . .] Kate jumping all over the place and slept with us the night. I finally went to sleep downstairs in K's room. Aaron and Bob came on board and took up Residence.[50] We leave for Portofino tomorrow weather permitting.

Wednesday 21st, Portofino We have been in Portofino a week roughly and leave tomorrow for Monte Carlo. E and K have been shopping like lunatics. E has bought umpty-nine watches, sweaters, 'puccis.' K has bought hats and watches (two I think) and has been giggling steadily from dawn till dusk. Giggling with her has been Elizabeth. What a pair? They each think the other is the funniest comedian in the world. [. . .]

---

[49] Gamal Abdel Nasser (1918–70), President of Egypt (1954–70).
[50] 'Bob' being Bobby Frosch.

Kate was sculpted by one Rocchi and so was I.[51] Kate's sculpture is splendid – mine is too leonine I think but we shall see when he's finished it.

Thursday 22nd, Monte Carlo We sailed from Portofino at approx 11.20 [...] within a short time it was realized (by E and me at least) that it was going to be a sluggish roll and pitch and glug and that our passengers might have some queasiness. Aaron did. Kate did. Bob also did but refused to admit it. Kate threw up twice but was a very good girl and didn't moan and conyn and carry-on as most people do. I was very proud of her. We kept her in our bed and first E then I joined her there and we all fell fast asleep. On both occasions that K vomited she did it onto a towel so there was no mess on the bed.

Eventually to everyone's relief we were in calm waters at Monte Carlo. R. Hanley and Gaston were there to greet us. Later [...] we had dinner at Rampoldi's.[52] By this time K was completely recovered and she and I ate sole meunière with chips, with grapefruit to start with. I still feel odd after so many days in Portofino. It must be lack of exercise. The weather was sticky and warm and no breath of wind. I read and tried to sleep, failed, read again and finally slept about 3.30 am. How I hate that kind of night.

Friday 23rd We all awoke about 9.30 and had tea on deck – K had orange juice.

Finally when all forces had been gathered we repaired to La Ferme where we had an elaborate meal which was [...] absurdly delicious.[53] [...] we took Kate to swim in the Olympic Pool. I sat with Eliz while K swam. Eventually a friend of E's, and a friend of his, joined us for a drink. E has always called him 'Little Abner' so it was rather difficult of myself and Kate to know what he was actually a West Indian called Smatt.[54][...]

Saturday 24th A brilliantly hot day with Kate anxious to swim so we thought we'd kill two birds with one stone and go to La Réserve where K could swim while we ate and drank.[55] This we did going by the Riva speedboat. It was very pleasant K swimming in the sea <u>and</u> the pool. Orson Welles gargantuanly fat joined us for a minute or two.[56] He said that every film he'd directed in his life had cost him money, that he'd never received any money from any of his films and that *Chimes at Midnight* had cost him $75,000 personally out of his own pocket.[57] He left the table suddenly and dramatically with a sotto voce 'darling'

---

[51] Gualberto Rocchi of Milan (1914—), whose bust of Burton was donated to the New Theatre, Cardiff, by Sally Burton in 1989. Kate Burton still owns her Rocchi bust.

[52] Rampoldi's restaurant, Avenue des Spélugues, Monaco.

[53] La Ferme Saint Michel, Avenue La Condamine, Villefranche-sur-Mer.

[54] L'il Abner Yokum was an American comic strip character (1934–77). This may well be Ernie Smatt from Jamaica, a world water-ski champion.

[55] La Réserve de Beaulieu-sur-Mer, on the Côte d'Azur.

[56] Orson Welles (1915–85), actor and director.

[57] *Chimes at Midnight* was a film written, directed and starring Welles that had appeared in 1966.

to E and a conspiratorial squeeze of my shoulder. I wondered to E how he could poooibly make love,

[. . .] We ran into Sam Spiegel and Harry Kurnitz and took them up on the hill for a drink and a cool-off.[58]

Sunday 25th I am sitting on the after-deck at the moment while K writes her diary beside me. She writes well for a 9 year old and needs no help.

[. . .] we went on board the *Southern Breeze* – a big 190 foot MY – to have lunch with a friend of E's mother and her husband. Mr and Mrs Gus Newman.[59] The yacht is very posh and they are obviously stinking rich. Useful people to know and nice with it. Puts our little *Oddyseia* somewhat in the shabby class.

Persuaded E to try and get Howard here instead of going there and to travel to Suisse by car if we can find a big limousine.[60] Here's hoping.

Went to the Port bar and played pin ball machine with Kate, home to supper, Sunday papers and this diary.

Monday 26th – Tuesday 27th – Wednesday 28th, Monte Carlo – San Remy – Talloires [. . .] K suddenly complained of a pain in her back which the doctor-masseur took care of. We suspect the pain will suddenly disappear when swimming is available.

As indeed proved on Tuesday evening at Baumanière.[61] She was into the pool like a trout and jumping and diving without a care. We had a slightly checkered journey. Before we'd left Monte Carlo the power windows blew a fuse and we had to wait in the Negresco over a beer while the car went into the garage.[62] We stopped near a town called Le Luc for lunch at a restaurant called Aux Grillades.[63] [. . .] K slept with E and I slept on a camp bed. Like a log though E says sleeping with K was like trying to embrace an earthquake.

Yesterday Wednesday we left about 10.30 when we were held up for the second day running. E had forgotten her wig box!! We stopped at the Nougat town of Montelimar for lunch at Relais de l'empereur.[64] Very pleasant place with lovely food [. . .]. With it we had the local wine, which is of course Châteauneuf-du-Pape. And playing word games in the car we got to Talloires to stay at L'Abbaye.[65] We dined at Auberge du Pere Bise and I could not eat.[66] One of the truly great restaurants.

[58] Sam Spiegel (1903–85), producer. Harry Kurnitz (1907–68), screenwriter, playwright.
[59] Gus and Frances Newman owned the *Southern Breeze*.
[60] Howard probably refers to Howard Taylor (1929–), Elizabeth's brother, who played the part of the journalist in *Boom!*
[61] L'Oustau de Baumanière, Les Baux de Provence, to the east of Arles.
[62] Hôtel Negresco, Promenade des Anglais, Nice.
[63] Hôtel La Grillade au Feu de Bois, Le Luc, between Fréjus and Brignoles.
[64] Hôtel-Restaurant Le Relais de l'Empereur, Montélimar, in the Rhône valley.
[65] L'Abbaye de Talloires, on the eastern shores of Lake Annecy.
[66] Auberge du Pere Bise, Talloires.

[There are no further entries in the diary until late July. During this time Richard and Elizabeth were at the Chalet Ariel, Gstaad.]

JULY

Thursday, 20th, Gstaad Arrived here on the 29th June [. . .] en route we stopped at Domino's (Rolle) for lunch where Maria and Liza were waiting for us. Hugs and kisses all round and so on to Gstaad. K and Liza travelled ahead with Gaston. We followed with Simon and Maria (Simon is the Gstaad taxi-man.) Stopped at Bulle for a drink of vin blanc.[67] Maria played 'Liza's favourite song' on the Juke-box – 'Puppet on a String.'[68] [. . .]

We have done most of the things we promised each other we'd do. We've eaten raclette, fondue bourgignonne, Steak Diane, Chateaubriands at the madly expensive Palace. We have had the local wines including a rather good one from Sion called Chante Merle Badoud. Sweet and light – not quite a Rosé.

After much cogitation we decided <u>not</u> to go to the USA or Hawaii at all but to have Ive and Gwen take K to NY and to have Howard and Mara come over to Europe.[69] That gives us extra time to relax and also gives K a few more days in Suisse. She and Liza have words now and again but obviously enjoy each other's company.

Kate, surprisingly, though highly intelligent and very charming is I'm afraid a bit of a tale-bearer or tattle-tail as she would say and oddly ungenerous – not in thought but in deed. She finds it intensely difficult to lend something even when she herself doesn't want it. Where the devil does that come from? Syb was never like that and my family loaded with vices as we are don't number lack of generosity among them. Maybe it will pass.

On the 5th July we picked the boys up at the school. A horrible day – Michael has definitely been sacked and Chris is everybody's darling winning two prizes, one for Art. I loathed the headmaster. A very big man, Swiss, with an emaciated wife and, as compensation, a lovely chubby baby daughter.[70] Ava Gardner was there with Ricardo (Madrid) who tends to be a bit of a know-all.[71] He had a son there of 19 who still had not (or just had maybe) graduated. How the hell could Mike be fired and this obvious oaf been allowed to stay on all these years? Mike is lethargic sluggish and graceless but he's very loving and intelligent enough to hold his own in a school as scholastically indifferent as le Rosey. We shall try and get him into Millfield. Fred

---

[67] Bulle, just west of the southern end of Lac de la Gruyère.

[68] Sandie Shaw (1947—) had won the Eurovision Song Contest with 'Puppet on a String' in 1967.

[69] Mara Taylor, Howard's wife.

[70] Colonel Louis Johannot (1919–2009).

[71] Ava Gardner (1922–80), actor, who had played alongside Burton in *The Night of the Iguana*. Ricardo Sicre, a friend of Gardner, whose son, also Ricardo, went on to study at Yale University.

(Heyman's wife) has talked to Meyer, the head, and we might get him in there.[72] [. . .] He's probably a slow starter like his Uncle Howard.

Ivor and Gwen arrived on the 13th and we met them at the Airport K and Liza came with us and we drove to Morges to have lunch with the Yul Brynners.[73] I became a trifle stoned largely as a result of drinking 'Williams' a pear liqueur which is potent. Mrs Brynner is pretty silly sometimes. Her cynicism sometimes verges on the envious.

Ivor and Gwen were delighted with Gstaad and the weather was superb the whole time. We took them to the Olden and the Palace and one night July 14 (Bastille Day) we went, at Gaston's invitation, to the Belle Vue hotel where the barmaid did lots of conjuring tricks.[74] The kids were bewitched and can now do a few of them themselves.

Ivor and Gwen left on the 18th with K for NY. We spent the night before in the Beau Rivage hotel and had dinner with Paul and Janine Fillistorf and their son Roger and his wife.[75] [. . .]

I had woken up in Geneva with a painful left wrist and today as I write it is virtually immovable. I am to see the doctor in an hour's time and for me to see a doctor! The arm from the elbow down seems to be on fire. I hope it's just a sprain and not arthritis again. [. . .] I can't and nobody else can remember my hitting something or falling etc. [. . .]

Maria is being a hell of a nuisance since Gus (the Irish nurse) left. The other kids are too old to play with her [. . .]. Poor little thing. She cries a lot at night and continually wakes up Nella and Claudye in snivelling hysterics.[76] She is a mass of fears. We must get her special treatment.

I went to the doctor in the village – a fellow about my age I think with receding hair and a very clinical look, much washed. I guessed it was arthritis and it was and is. [. . .] Scherz of the Palace Hotel called and asked if we would consent to be televised for Swiss TV.[77] I said we had guests. [. . .]

Victoria Brynner is visiting today – 4 years old approximately and adorable.[78] She is playing with Maria.

Michael is 'dating' a girl called Robin Marlowe. He appears to be much struck by her. She seemed dull and mannerless at first but has improved on acquaintance. Her father Stephen Marlowe writes books and I'm trying to read one of them called The Shining.[79] It is set in Classical Greece and is torture to

---

[72] This may be a jokey reference to Norma Heyman (1940–), John Heyman's wife.

[73] Yul Brynner (1915–85), actor, by this time married to his second wife, Doris Kleiner (the marriage ended in 1967). Morges is 11 km west of Lausanne on the northern shore of Lake Geneva.

[74] Grande Hotel Bellevue, Gstaad.

[75] Hôtel Beau Rivage, Quai du Mont Blanc, Geneva.

[76] Nella was Elizabeth Taylor's maid.

[77] Ernst Andrea Scherz, owner and manager of the Gstaad Palace, with his wife Shiwa. The Scherz family had been running the Gstaad Palace Hotel since 1938.

[78] Victoria Brynner was born in November 1962.

[79] Stephen Marlowe (1928–2008), writer. The Shining appeared in 1961. Marlowe wrote many thrillers.

read. I'd rather a second hand book of sermons or thoughts for the day. E is lucky – his book, sent to her, is a thriller-suspense story. [...]

Vivien Leigh died of TB about a fortnight ago.[80] Jayne Mansfield (big blonde semi-star) was beheaded in a car crash.[81]

Gianni, Claudye's boyfriend, was here when we arrived and is due again tomorrow. I – we – promised him the Mini-Cooper when he marries Claudye and if he stops motor racing. He is a nice Italian boy who has bright red hair – quite startling anywhere but certainly in Italy. They are obviously dotty about each other.[82]

The tennis championship of Suisse is on here at Gstaad and all the big names are here. Emerson, Santana, Osuna etc.[83] I shall watch Saturday and Sunday perhaps.

It seems that the yacht has passed inspection and is now ours and is officially the *KALIZMA*. Kate Liza Maria (Elizabeth included in Liza). It's going to be fun when it's all fitted out. [...]

Friday 21st Yesterday was a medicine and diet day. I had ½ grapefruit (no sugar) two boiled eggs (substitute salt) a piece of bread (no butter) three times, and nothing else at all except water. Result this morning: Lost 3lbs – I am now 180½lbs. It is a sobering thought that the woman who suggested this diet to me – Paula Strasberg, Lee's wife, – is dead.[84]

The effect of these pills on the arthritic arm is fantastic – for about an hour you think somebody is carefully and sadistically slitting open all the veins and that your arm is about to fall off. To counteract this I took ½ tablets of E's empirin and codeine. It helped a little.

Last night, loaded with drugs I fell asleep about 1.00 and didn't wake until 10.30 this morning. E had left to sleep in the other room because my snoring was so heavy. Everything so far re the arm is much better.

Sunday 23rd Yesterday we saw in great trepidation our film of *Dr Faustus*. It is not ½ bad I think and has some moments of genuine quality. There are one or two unalterable vulgarities but generally speaking it is a pretty good achievement to make what appears to be a very expensive film for just over $1 million. Got mildly drunk afterwards in the Olden still sticking vaguely to our diet –

---

[80] Vivien Leigh (1913–67), actor, former wife of Laurence Olivier.
[81] Jayne Mansfield (1933–67), actor. Although she suffered severe head injuries, the rumour that she was decapitated is untrue.
[82] Gianni Bozzacchi, photographer. He and Claudye would marry in June 1968.
[83] Roy Emerson (1936—), Manuel Santana (1938—), and Rafael Osuna (1938–69) were all international tennis stars. Emerson would beat Santana in the final in 1967 for the second year running.
[84] Paula Strasberg (1909–66), actor. Lee Strasberg (1899–1982), drama teacher, founder of the Actors' Studio and guru of 'method' acting. Susan Strasberg (1938–99), actor, was their daughter, and had been Richard's lover in the late 1950s.

hamburger and tomato salad for lunch and a T-bone steak for dinner. My weight (and E's) had dropped 2lbs making me 178½ and E 134½.

[. . .] We went to bed, after feeding MacWhorter and LaRue on barbecued steaks, about 3.0. E very erotic and anche io.[85] It thundered and lightninged all night and was very heavy and stuffy. I finally tried to sleep in the guest bedroom, felt lonely, went back to E – finally went back to the guest bedroom and slept with last thoughts of *Faustus* being a little-regarded failure.

Monday 24th [. . .] We went to the Palace for lunch and had two medium sized entrecotes <u>each</u> for the main course with a tomato and onion salad. Washed down with a rosé (two bottles which we shared with R. McWhorter who lunched with us.)

Afterwards to the tennis where we saw Emerson beat Santana in 3 sets and Emerson and Santana beat McManus and Osborne in 5.[86] The latter looks a very promising boy. Powerful serve. [. . .]

Afterwards to the Olden, where I had a Gibson and E J. Daniels, and played Yahtsee. E beat me 4 out of 5. For dinner we had poached salmon and the inevitable onion and tomato salad. [. . .]

Tuesday 25th Yesterday morning saw the scales drop us ½lb each to 177 for me and 132 for E. Still that's better as E says than being ½lb up.

It was a brilliant day until about 5.00 afternoon when rumbling of thunder was heard, the clouds piling black on the peaks and finally torrential, almost tropical rain. Liza had her wart on her finger burnt off. She was terrified of the needle the contents of which, it seemed to me, the doctor took a devil of a long time to inject. She cried a little but was most interested in the actual burning of the wart. As it sizzled under the heat she said it looked like fried chicken.

[. . .] I retired early and read Gavin Maxwell's *Ring of Bright Water* which I read until, and finished at, 2.00 in the morning.[87] It is a delightful if, now and again in its description pieces, slightly pretentious book of his two otters. They sound delightful but great nuisances.

Wednesday 26th Weight 175¼ for me. 131¼ E. Lost respectively 1¾ and ¾lbs.

[. . .] We stayed in for lunch and had barbecued lamb chops a slice of onion and a slice of tomato. Taught Robin to play Yahtsee. Drove down to the village with Chris who has a girl-friend – his first – a girl of 13 from Neuchatel called Patrice.[88] A nice slow-faced girl solid and Swiss. Speaks no language except

---

[85] 'Anche io' is Italian for 'me too'.
[86] Jim McManus (1940—) and Jim Osborne (1940—), international tennis players, beaten in the men's doubles.
[87] Gavin Maxwell, *Ring of Bright Water* (1960).
[88] Neuchâtel, a city on the northern shore of Lake Neuchâtel, Switzerland.

French which somehow is surprising in Switzerland. Her mother (so I learn from Chris) has recently been divorced and they are living or vacationing at the Rossli Hotel in town.[89]

We went there last night to take the girl home and so met her mother and her aunt. The latter bossy and well-to-do I fancy, broad of face and figure and bespectacled. Patrice's looks are more the aunt's than the mother's who looks like my sister Cis a bit though her face is sharper.

[...] Mike has been to the Marlowes' anniversary (of Marlowe's getting custody of the children!) and came home exhilarated about 11. The girl Robin seems to have given him more vitality and zip. Maybe it will help.

Thursday 27th, Gstaad – London [...] New bookcase arrived and I had it fixed next to the bathroom in guest bedroom and suitably filled it with books. Will have to [...] order another bookcase.

We left Gstaad at 3.25 arrived at Airport driving like mad at 4.15. [...] Left about 6.15 Arrived 1 hour 20 minutes later. Smooth as silk. Did crossword and drank a lot.

Dinner at Salisbury with the boys – cold roast pork etc.[90] Drunken American actor kept on telling me fulsomely that I had 'taken on the mantle of (a) Greatness and (b) Olivier.' I said politely that I wasn't greatly taken with mantles. The boys Mike and Chris, who were with us, enjoyed it greatly. Americans of a certain type are very humourless but rather endearing.

Home and to bed. The boys and E watched TV. I read Agatha Christie.

Friday 28th, London Yesterday we had lunch – the whole purpose of the visit was to see him – with R. J. O. Meyer headmaster of Millfield.[91] He was disappointing. I had imagined a much wiser, more authoritative man. This man was tall, thin very English nervous in gesture and a compulsive talker. One white liar recognizes another and I found some of his stories a little too highly polished. He made E and Michael very nervous but didn't me – perhaps because my respect was mildly tinged with contempt. Anyway it seems that the boys are acceptable. I think they'll be alright there. What bores headmasters generally are. For ½ the year they lord it over children and it must have a distorting effect on their relationship with adults. All their little jokes are laughed at, their little bursts of anger trembled at. Still, he's obviously good at his job. I became a little tetchy once or twice.

We saw Peter Sellers film *Bobo* followed by *Faustus*.[92] *Bobo* is slight but Peter's wife is lovely in it. Sammy Davis Jr came to see *F*.[93] They all seem to be

[89] Posthotel Rössli, Promenade, Gstaad.
[90] Salisbury, Wiltshire, slightly more than halfway between London and Street, Somerset.
[91] R. J. O. Meyer (1905–91), headmaster of Millfield, former captain of Somerset (cricket).
[92] *The Bobo*. Peter Sellers was at this point married to Britt Ekland (1942—).
[93] Sammy Davis Jr (1925–90), entertainer.

impressed by me but not by the film itself – it is of course a one-man show. Wolf Mankovitz wants his name taken off the titles. We agreed. Silly gesture.

Today we leave at 12.55 for Rome – 1½ hours wait – then on to Taormina.[94]

Friday 28th, London – Rome – Taormina – Sicily Am reverting back to writing on the day itself – hence <u>two</u> Fridays in this week.

We left on time and boarded the plane (a woman asked 'sign my autograph please Mr Taylor.') I gave her a look that felled her. That's the first time in 5 years that that's happened. Cheek.

On the plane we found Peter and Sian O'Toole and we proceeded to get drunk.[95] Peter is charming but a real fibber. He asked me how many nominations I'd had. I said truthfully FIVE. He said, holding up his fingers to point it, that he'd had <u>four</u>. I know he's only had two. Does he think we're idiots.[96]

[. . .] I'd forgotten it was 50 kms from Catania to Taormina.[97] We had insisted on an air conditioned car so were driven by a private citizen. Not one word of English could he speak and I kept on speaking French. An unpleasant journey with me stoned.

We were appalled to find that Michael W. senior could not drive the boys to the airport because 'he had to look after Maggie.'[98] E furious. He hasn't seen them for a year, contributes and has contributed nothing to their upbringing or education, and couldn't drive them to the airport. Charming but feckless.

Saturday 29th, Taormina Surrounded by publicity and paparazzi we lived in a blaze of flash lights all day long. At 6.15 we had a press conference with the usual stupid questions and answers. At 9.00 or thereabouts we hied our way to the awards.[99] There we picked up the awards (three this time) and sloshed our way steadily through the night 'till 5.00 in the morning.

As usual E had the biggest hand and Peter O'Toole Vittorio Gassman and I made idiots of ourselves – Gassman without meaning to. The crowds were enormous both in and outside the amphitheatre. We shall not, unless it's <u>very</u> convenient, come here again. It really is a farce.

Started 'Drinking Man's Diet.' Let's see what happens.

Noel Coward is to play the witch in *Boom!* – as a male of course.[100] This makes the film very much more interesting from our point of view, and he

[94] Taormina, a small town on the east coast of Sicily.
[95] Peter O'Toole, actor, who had played alongside Burton in *Becket* and would play alongside both Burton and Taylor in *Under Milk Wood*. Between 1959 and 1979 he was married to the Welsh actor Siân Phillips (1934—), who had also acted in *Becket* and would act in *Under Milk Wood*.
[96] At this point O'Toole had been twice nominated for Oscars (for *Lawrence of Arabia* and *Becket*). His current (2012) tally stands at eight nominations, one higher than Burton.
[97] Catania, city on the east coast of Sicily, and location of the Fontanarossa airport.
[98] Michael Wilding Sr. 'Maggie' refers to Wilding's fourth wife, the actor Margaret Leighton.
[99] Burton and Taylor (and O'Toole) were attending the Taormina Film Festival.
[100] Noël Coward (1899–1973), actor, director and playwright.

should be brilliant. It is 16 years or so since I worked with him and that was for $200 for playing the Marquis de something or other in a recording of *Conversation Piece*.[101] E has never worked with him before. He should be good value. [. . .]

The Israeli Ambassador to Italy anxious that we go to Israel to celebrate this festival week.[102] Might go at the end of the week.

Sunday 30th A slow day, marking time, with a walk in which we bought sunglasses at a little shop. As we left the crowd which had gathered applauded us. E thought it very sweet, which indeed it was. We dined in somnolence and some self-satisfaction as we compared our ancestors and former wives and husbands.

E has become very slim and I can barely keep my hands off her. It turns out that she's not that less in weight but, as a result of massage and exercise the weight has been redistributed. She is at the moment among the most dishiest girls I've ever seen. The most. I mean dishiest.

It is extraordinary how when the festival awards are over, the whole village [. . .] becomes quiet. Nobody in the bar, no paparazzi, and the sea, beneath us and the gardens, hot and misty like a promise of extreme heat. A dredger in the bay moving uneasily on the water as if floating on oil. And churchbells all the time. Millions of saints. Millions of Masses. It is a little hot province Sicily. Everything is a little burned. Even the bougainvillea as E mentioned is yellow and sere.

There were many pictures in the papers, in two of which my child looked good enough to marry. [. . .]

Monday 31st, Rome [. . .] We had not gone to bed until about 2.30 so we were pretty shaky on the road to Catania. Lovely the way the Sicilians decorate their horses – one horse, looked as if he was 17 or 18 hands, a giant, had a really splendid plume which he tossed and nodded with great pride. Many people sitting outside on ordinary kitchen chairs, the houses sun bleached and pinko grey and peeling. Catania is surprisingly large and it took us quite a time to get through it. Mini-skirts are still relatively rare in Sicily and at one moment when we were halted by traffic in a narrow street E's skirts had ridden up and half her (admittedly pretty) thighs were revealed and one young man was so obsessed by the eroticism of the scene that I thought he was going to have an orgasm on the spot. E was too shy to pull her skirt down until we had moved on so the pimply feller had a long long stare. He will dream tonight.

Rome was hot. R. Wilson was there looking and behaving like a new man. Went to the Studio where we had a somewhat pathetic lunch at Dino

---

[101] Burton had played the Marquis of Sheere in Coward's *Conversation Piece*.
[102] Ehud Avriel (1917–80), Israel's ambassador to Italy, 1965–8.

de Laurentiis studio with Tiziani and J. Losey. He is going to be a bore I think.

[...] Staying the night in the Grand Hotel – the most luxurious suite I've seen in Europe.[103] It is the Royal Suite though the service is anything but Royal.

AUGUST

Tuesday 1st Have decided to stay until Friday. All our baggage except hand baggage had gone on to Geneva so I suggested that E raid Pucci's which she did to great effect. I planned to go out and replenish my wardrobe with shirts socks shorts etc. when Jane brought us the news that the bags had turned up.[104] E was allowed to go on anyway.

We stayed in all day. I felt rotten having drank too much the day before. I drank some Martinis which helped temporarily but I was still shaky in the evening. It is hot in Rome but the suite is air conditioned and therefore much more comfortable than outside. I shall go out tomorrow and buy some books.

[...] J. Losey came to chat with E. It is so evident when she dislikes someone. There's a sullen look in the eyes and the face becomes distant and hard. And her language becomes a trifle 4 lettered.

We are both on the 'drinking man's diet' and it seems to be working and unlike some high protein diets with counting of calories it is much more fun to count carbohydrates. Also it allows one to have a few drinks. We'll keep on with it for a few weeks anyway.

Wednesday 2nd What a dreadful and terrible day and good too. All my pettiness and resentment and idiocy all rolled up into one day. I'll blame it on Rome. All the bad things that have happened to me have almost always happened in Rome. Something to do with its elevation perhaps. It is too near sea level. [...]

Nothing worked except for a couple of hours of recording of *La Traviata* with Mckenna and Merrill [105] I didn't move a muscle though I sweated like a worker. When I returned to the hotel with the two M's and their wives we had some drinks and Merrill and his wife took us out to dinner. Elizabeth was at the bar like a real broad and a two-fisted one.

In the middle of the early night Elizabeth and I exchanged insults in which I said that she was not 'a woman but a man' and in which she called me 'little girl'. A lovely charming decadent hopeless couple.

---

[103] Grand Hotel de la Minerve, Plaza della Minerva, Rome.
[104] Jane Swanson, secretary to Burton and Taylor.
[105] Giuseppe Verdi (1813–1901), wrote *La Traviata* (first performance 1853); Robert Merrill (1917–2004), operatic baritone. His second wife was Marion Machno (d. 2010).

I am stupendously disappointed in myself. Something went wrong in my head at the wrong time. Anyway . . . something went wrong. And will never be put right. I am, I think, sublimely selfish.

Thursday 3rd Make-up day when we both kissed and apologies were flying in all directions. We lunched alone together at Capriccio's off the Via Veneto, slept a little in the afternoon and dined around the corner at Taverna Flavia.[106] [. . .]

Tomorrow we leave for Switzerland. It was very hot all day.

Friday 4th, Geneva We flew uneventfully to Geneva arriving about 1.45 leaving Rome at 1.30 (There's an hour's difference in time at this season.) We waited about ½ hour in the Swiss Air Caravelle on the airstrip and it was very hot and sticky until we were airborne. First class on Caravelles is not very comfortable unless you have the VIP seats, which we had booked too late to get. One's knees are around the ears and getting the small tables into position for the lunch is a conjuring feat. However nobody gives a bugger as long as the plane doesn't crash.

We stayed at the Président Hotel which though spacious downstairs is disappointingly box-like – à la Hilton hotels – upstairs.[107] [. . .]

We dined on ham and au gratin potatoes at Cambesy.[108] A charming little restaurant that seems to have burgeoned enormously since I was last there. The food was delicious. Both very excited at the expectation of Howard Mara and the children arriving tomorrow. They are expected at 9.05 from the States.

Thursday 10th, Gstaad The multitude arrived safely after their enormous trip. Leighton immediately fell down the steps of the airport bus and then fell out of the car when we stopped at Rolle for a drink.[109] Later on he was shot by one of the air-rifles. Staying just that one night in Hotel President cost me $3000. E bought me a money-clip watch for $600 and one for herself for $2500. Hers is very very beautiful – a Piaget as thin as a few sheets of paper and jade green face. Hers is a wrist watch of course.

We have all been drinking fairly steadily and not sleeping much the result being that last night we both had a frightful time trying to sleep. [. . .]

Lord Harlech (formerly David Ormsby-Gore) came from Lake Maggiore to have lunch.[110] He and his three children, a boy (12) Francis a girl (13) Alice

[106] Taverna Flavia, Via Flavia 91, Rome.
[107] Hôtel Président Wilson, Quai Wilson, Geneva.
[108] Chambésy, a village on the northern outskirts of Geneva.
[109] Leighton: really Layton. Son of Howard and Mara.
[110] William David Ormsby-Gore, 5th Baron Harlech (1918–85), at this point leading the Harlech Television consortium which would win the franchise from Television Wales and the West.

and a girl (20) Victoria.[111] They were all charming and Alice who is wildly beautiful was extremely sad and inward. She is obviously still affected by her mother's death.[112] She was killed in a car crash about a month ago. She had gone out, Harlech says, to post a letter after a wonderful weekend they'd had at Harlech. [. . .]

We are leaving tomorrow in a chartered plane for Sardinia with all the children and us on board. God help us all. I dread the start of this film as I do all films until we find out how the director works etc. I've only read the script twice and learned not a word. I must learn a few pages today. [. . .]

Lord Derby is still fighting our consortium for the TV Franchise for Wales and the West.[113] We've won I think. In any case I don't think I'm much interested. My bit was to use our names to get it. I don't want to do much more.

Friday 11th, Gstaad – Sardinia A terrible day, frantically disorganized, thousands of bags all over the place, nine children, six adults all on one plane, Howard and Mara's incessant screaming, my and E's pre-film nerves, nine children, plane-fear, Gaston [. . .] has fallen in love again, dwarfly serious, with Patricia's mother (Patricia is Christopher's girl friend) nine children, the *Kalizma* hasn't arrived, nobody at the airport to meet us, nine children, (Dick Hanley, Bob Wilson, John Lee cost us and Mike Todd roughly $1000 a week) and hot and a small room and a multi zillion dollar picture and I screamed 'fuck' out of drunkenness in the hotel lobby, and pasta (not very good) and screaming and heavy stoned sarcasm, and a sloshed memory of fields and farms and towns of France and Italy, and the purple sea, and shame and booze and fear and nine children, and I want to be left alone, and Gaston saying that he has explained to Cecile that he can't marry her because she can't have children, August is the cruellest month, and E making any excuse – not difficult to do since they (the excuses) were handed to her on a platter – not to start the film on Monday, and J. Losey is an arrogant ignorant fool so far and thinks he's a genius and you can't be at his pock-marked age without showing it before, and a frightful day and I hope never to live through another which I will tomorrow and tomorrow and tomorrow.[114]

To scream 'fuck' in the lobby was the only possible way to meet the justice of the day.

---

[111] Francis (1954—), the current Baron Harlech, Alice (1952–95) and Victoria (1945—).
[112] Sylvia Thomas (1940–67).
[113] Lord Derby, chairman of Television Wales and the West.
[114] A reference to T. S. Eliot's poem *The Waste Land* (1922), which opens with the line 'April is the cruellest month'. 'tomorrow and tomorrow and tomorrow', a reference to Shakespeare's *Macbeth*, Act V, scence v.

Wednesday 16th, Hotel Capo Caccia, Alghero, Sardinia[115] The boat has still not arrived and everybody, high and low has his neck permanently cricked towards the horizon. [. . .]

Losey so far is a bit of a crasher and a fusspot interfering with every dept. He keeps on thinking that I must be kept busy. Leave me alone!

On the first night here we frightened him so much that he later, so we're told by the Heymans, cried. Whether it was fright, nerves or disappointment we shall never know.

[. . .] How and Mara are in three rooms with all the children, because our bloody boat is not here. They seem, with the assistance of two guards and a nanny to be coping alright. [. . .]

The boat arrived late this evening. Went on board and found a drunken man in Liza's room unconscious on the bed. Don't trust Barbosa and think the cook is a stirrer. Boat looks pretty though.

Thursday 17th, Sardinia [. . .] Went downstairs this morning and saw Dick Hanley. I wish he would retire to California. He is a semi-invalid and I'm afraid to say anything authoritative to him in case he has a heart attack. We now have John Lee working with Dick, Jane Swanson working for them, and now if you please they have employed a man to look after them. We don't even have a nanny.

Gaston has brought his latest (41 year old) girl friend with him here and her daughter. Was about to order him to send her back to her job in Suisse when it turned out that his brother had died. The telegram arrived 4 days late so the funeral is over. So the lecture will have to wait.

I took Howard to see the locations. By Boat. Speedboat. He is odd when something excites him – he screams, almost like a girl. [. . .] Where E is passively passionate, he is frenetic. [. . .]

[There are no further entries in the diary until early September. It seems probable that at least some of the entries made during this period have been lost. During this period filming began on *Boom!*]

SEPTEMBER

Thursday 7th

[There as appear to be some pages missing here. The diary was being written in Venice, where the party had gone in part to attend a ball, having obtained the agreement of John Heyman and Joseph Losey].

---

[115] Hotel Capo Caccia is on the Capo Caccia peninsula, near Alghero, a port on the north-west coast of Sardinia.

[. . .] All hell broke loose after permission was given – E's Kabuki dress had to be brought from Rome by Evan Roberts Tiziani, her Kabuki headdress was flown from Sardinia by 'Lear' Jet with Jeannette in charge.[116] Alexandre Mara and How went out shopping to buy polo necked sweaters for Howard and myself. We wore them with our dinner jackets with necklaces! The press were all over the place [. . .] But it was all worth it for Mara made the success of her life. And lo and behold the most publicized snap of the evening in the papers next day was one of E, Mara and Princess Grace all sitting side by side and all looking ravishing – especially, of course, E.

Before going to bed tonight a note was handed to me by Pedro.[117] It had been sent from shore by Claudye. It said that Robin Marlowe had approached Gianni (Claudye's boyfriend) and asked him for a contraceptive, as she and Michael intended to make love! Gianni said she was a bit young (she is 13!) and asked if he could see Michael (he is 14!) but Michael refused. I sat up and waited for them and told them to go to bed warning Nella beforehand that they were to be kept apart but the fact is that if they're going to do it, they're going to do it and nothing will stop them. I told Michael a few days ago to be careful. I hope he will be.

Monday 18th, **Kalizma**, *Capo Caccia* A fairly hardworking day. I think, despite weather, we did about 3½ minutes. [. . .]

E talked with Michael about Robin and M was apparently furious with Robin, saying: 'I told her she shouldn't have done it.' He spent the afternoon on the set alone for a time as she Robin presumably had gone back to the hotel in a huff. She came back later and M was terribly sweet with his mother for the rest of the day.

Mary Morgan – W. John Morgan's wife – arrived from the other side of the island where she is staying with an English group of Oxbridge intellectuals – one called Love and somebody who wrote for the *N. Statesman*.[118] Boring, envious, clever and very impressed and, I suspect, just above mediocre and absolutely predictable. I could have written their dialogue for the rest of the hour I was with them after the first 3 minutes.

[. . .] Hell of a job deciding what to do for Liza and Maria regarding school. Liza is 10 and bright. Maria is 6½ and slow. One, the latter, to London? Maria to Ive and Gwen in London where I read they have a very successful machine for teaching slow children? E very depressed. Me too.

---

[116] 'Evan Roberts Tiziani' is a slip – it was Evan Richards. Evan Roberts (1878–1951) was a Welsh evangelist who had led the 1904–05 religious revival in Wales. A Kabuki headdress is an elaborate Japanese wig.

[117] A steward on the *Kalizma*.

[118] W. John Morgan (1929–88), Welsh journalist and television producer, also involved with the establishment of HTV. The *New Statesman* is a British socialist weekly magazine.

Tuesday 19th Worked like dogs and did 7½ minutes – we are nearly 2/3 of the way through the script after only 3½ weeks or 4.

Nasty incident that everyone laughed at when Michael Dunn the dwarf was pulled off his feet by Robbie the Giant Schnauzer dog.[119] He carried it off very well calling the dog a dumb head.

E did a remarkable scene in which she nearly coughed her lungs up. Everybody was impressed.

Noël Coward arrived looking very old and slightly sloshed and proceeded to get more sloshed. He embarrassed us both (separately) and lavished compliments on E about her beauty and her brilliance as an actress. Occasionally he threw a bone to me. He is a most generous man but sadly he is beginning to lose the fine edge of his wit or perhaps like me he repeats himself when tipsy. He moves like an old man but I suddenly remembered that he's always moved like an old man. Stoop-shouldered non-necked he has the curved body of a very tall man but in actual fact he is no taller than I. He is now almost completely bald and the bags under his eyes have made his eyes even more asiatic than hitherto. He calls himself 'the oldest chinese character actress in the world.' Coming off the plane he was asked how his journey was [. . .] and he said peering his way towards customs 'My whole life has been an extravaganza.' He is a delightful man. 'I am completely muddled,' he said, 'by J. Heyman. I have talked to him on the phone and communicated with him by letter and I had firmly made up my mind that J. Heyman was a short hairy greasy Jewish gentleman running rapidly to fat. Instead of which I find a golden boy. It is most off-putting.'

We drank with Noël, his friend Graham Payn, and his secretary Coley until about 9.15 then left for the boat to dine with the children.[120] The boys leave tomorrow for Millfield and everybody is very down in the mouth.

Wednesday 20th, Capo Caccia [. . .] The boys left early in the morning both coming into the stateroom and kissing us in the dark. Very depressing. [. . .] E and N. Coward are madly in love with each other, particularly he with her. He thinks her most beautiful which she is, and a magnificent actress which she also is. We all saw rushes and some assemblage last night. It looks perverse and interesting. I think we are due for another success particularly E. I was worried about her being too young but it doesn't seem to matter at all. Wrote a long letter to Phil which I still haven't finished. [. . .]

Thursday 21st Was first called, though the night before they had said I was on a stand-by. Did two shots talking on the telephone and was finished for the day

---

[119] Michael Dunn (1935–73) played Rudi in *Boom!*
[120] Graham Payn (1918–2005), actor and companion of Coward. 'Coley' was his secretary Cole Lesley (d. 1980).

by lunchtime. Showered and shampooed and then lunched with E and Noël, Coley and G. Payn. Many stories were told. We talked about D. Niven and how, though they had been fact friends, he cut E dead for seven months when she was involved in the 'scandal' with E. Fisher and how though we were still friendly it could never be the same again.[121] [. . .]

E did a retake in the afternoon but it was one of the 'jinxed' shots – there is one in every film – which for various technical reasons (in one take they ran out of film!) took over three hours to do. She was heavy eyed and exhausted when they finally got it at 7.00. She then fitted for clothes with Evan Tiziani for the Paris and Oxford premieres of *Shrew* and *Faustus* respectively while I finished my marathon letter to Phil. We had a few drinks with Noel and Co and repaired to the *Kalizma* and supper about 10.30.

Noel told E after having seen the rushes and assemblage 'My God you have such fantastic authority. I didn't have such authority at your age.' He told me, holding my wrist firmly in his beautiful brown hands which at 67 have a couple of faint liver marks, that E and I were so packed with dynamic personality that he expected us any minute to burst at the seams and flow like volcanic lava. He is a great flatterer if he genuinely likes you.

[. . .] I have decided it's going to cost me more than £50,000 a year to run this ship – more like $100,000. But, if, as we plan to live on it while making films for most of the year, it could be very practical. Anyway it's a splendid toy and a lovely luxurious home.

Friday 22nd [. . .] Norma Heyman was with us all day and stayed to chat with me when E left. We comforted her as best we could re her marriage. It appears that her husband J. Heyman has fallen in love or is infatuated with Joanna Shimkus who plays – very badly – E's secretary in the film.[122] She is a nice enough little girl (of 23 she says) but certainly not the femme fatale and breaker-up-of-homes type. She is tall, auburn haired, pleasant faced, aquiline nosed, nice-eyed, pleasant smiled and breastless. She is also hard work to talk to. From things I hear from Norma she is most definitely on the make for John. She probably thinks he will help in her career. I can't think that she will last very long even if John does marry her.

I became quite tipsy with Norma and went to bed after she'd left – about 11pm I think – and slept until 5.00. Went ashore and found no car to take me to the set but eventually as I was walking to the set, it's about 2½ miles perhaps Valerio the Unit Manager picked me up in his car.[123] He was with Francesca

---

[121] David Niven (1909–83), actor.

[122] Joanna Shimkus (1943–) played the role of Blackie, the secretary to Flora Goforth (played by Taylor).

[123] Valerio DePaolis (1942–), who was to perform again as Unit Manager in *Divorce His, Divorce Hers*.

Roberti who is the step-daughter of Peter Thorneycroft, the MP.[124] E looked dead beat and was. She said that she'd had a terrible time with Noel who was so nervous that he'd dry up again and again. It must have been horrible. Perhaps it was first shot nerves. It would be bad luck if his performance was destroyed by lack of memory.

Saturday 23rd, Capa Caccia – Bonifacio, Corsica Sailed this morning from Sardinia about 9.30 arriving at Bonifacio (It was our second visit we having gone there before a month ago) about 3.30.[125] [. . .] We all napped. I got up about 12.30 and sat and sunbathed with Norma and had a cheese and tomato sandwich. Delicious. Bonifacio was lovely – we tied up exactly where we had last time when the kids had that gorgeous mad hour doing cannon balls etc. from the top deck – and walked to dinner at La Pergola, I think it's called, which is right on the harbour about 200 yards from the mooring. We giggled a lot and drank endless bottles of wine. And so to bed.

Sunday 24th, Bonifacio, Corsica A glorious day with a light breeze ruffling the harbour waters. I got up reasonably early and found that Norma was up before me. It was about 9am I suppose. We sunbathed and read on the upper deck when we heard a lot of shouting as of at a football match so we slipped on some clothes and walked ashore to see it. It was a soccer match played between two teams of foreign legionnaires. After about ½ hour somebody thought he recognized me and went excitedly to his friends. 'Ca c'est Richard Burton c'est vrai, c'est vrai.' Fortunately nobody believed him and we were left undisturbed. There were many snarky remarks to the enthusiast on the general level of 'What would Burton be doing in a shit-house like this?'

Norma and I went for a walk afterwards along the quayside. It is almost entirely cafes, cafe restaurants, restaurants, little general stores, a couple of antique shops, 'live lobsters sold here' etc. The town is a mysterious looking place. The houses are pale grey, or orange, or that peculiarly french blue, and from towering serrated docks the houses go sheer up from the edge. I wouldn't love to live in one. But the harbour is lovely. I bought a bellows for the barbecue, which we've just had sent from Rome, and a wooden pair of tongs to pick up and turn over bangers, hot dogs, hamburgers, steaks and so on.

The harbour master told us of a superb fish restaurant about 9 miles away and offered to drive us there. It appeared though that one could go by speed-boat so off we set. It took us 3½ hours approx to find it. What the harbour

---

[124] Peter Thorneycroft (1909–94), previously Conservative MP for Stafford (1938–45) and Monmouth (1945–66), formerly Chancellor of the Exchequer, had lost his seat at the 1966 general election and become Baron Thorneycroft. His second wife was Carla, Contessa Roberti (1914–2007), by whom he had had a son (Piero) and a daughter (Francesca).
[125] Bonifacio, port on the southern tip of Corsica.

master had not told us was that it was 9 miles by road which is tortuous, but only 2 miles by sea. Eventually however, soaked with spray as there was quite a choppy sea, we found it. It was called 'Le Gaby' and was hidden in a tiny inlet so shallow that the speedboat, having a two foot draft at most, had to be manoeuvred very carefully. But it was worth it. They were expecting us and I had the best Bouillabaisse I've ever had and E and Norma had lobster which they thought the best they'd ever had. And its situation is like a dream. The restaurant is open to the sea which is a gesture away, one could almost spit in it from our table, and gives the impression, perhaps true, of having been built exclusively from flotsam and jetsam thrown up by the sea. In the middle of the room was a hollowed-out log set at about table height which, filled with sea water, had ½ dozen live lobsters in it. One of them was a giant. Elizabeth was looking infinitely sexy. She wore mesh white net leotards and the shortest mini-skirt I've ever seen. It barely, and when she moved didn't, cover her crotch. The beach boys around, who all appeared to be stoned, were beside themselves. And as we left they shouted various invitations to her and offered to kiss her in various parts of her anatomy – the mini-dress was also very low cut – including sundry offers of fornication. They were careful that I was on the boat and moving rapidly away before these generous offers were made. They weren't averse to Norma either, who is also a beautiful girl but built on less generous lines than E.

Later on the ship E barbecued steaks and with her own special sauce it was delicious. Michael Dunn, who is a dwarf – he is 3ft 10ins high, ate a steak almost as big as himself. In the meantime a French deep sea diving ship pulled alongside and moored. It was the French Navy and discovering E was on the next ship they immediately began to get drunk and started to dive into the harbour with all their clothes on. The Captain was in despair but tolerant. Eventually we went on board and E charmed the Captain out of a large fragment of a vase which, the Captain guessed, was about 2000 years old. We tried to get a beautiful anchor which the Captain, who professed to be no expert, guessed to be Phoenician. It was about 3½ – 4 feet high and about perhaps 2ft wide at its base. I lusted after it and so did E but all to no avail. [. . .]

Monday 25th, Capo Caccia Arrived back about 11am to discover that it was actually 10am because the Italians had changed from Summer time to normal time. E went ashore to fit for clothes for the premieres of *Faustus* and *Shrew*, and I went on the speedboat with David Heyman and Michael Dunn and drove them around to the other bay very slowly, almost idling, because David, who is 7 years old and one of the most delectable boys E and I have ever known, wanted to fish.[126] Eventually to my delight he caught a fish which the

---

[126] David Heyman (1961—), more famous today for being the producer of the Harry Potter films.

cook fried for him for lunch. He ate ½ of it but wanted to keep the other half for his father who is not due back from London, or Rome, or Paris, or wherever he is, until Wednesday. [. . .]

About 5 in the afternoon we were awakened by the sounds of a tremendous altercation going on above our heads in the captain's quarters. It seems that the Captain, with my approval, had fired the cook Miquel and his wife Amalia. The cook, who is a balding, middle-aged, holier than thou, long suffering, sweet smiling hypocrite went stark staring mad, broke a glass and jammed it in the Captain's face and smashed the remainder of the glass on the Captain's head – it took 5 stitches we discovered later. In the meantime, and during the screaming and bawling, his boot (the cook's) had come off and when his wife tried to intervene he hit her with it and then, when Pedro the little steward, also tried to intercede he was also belted over the head by the boot. So they all three have nasty headaches. We pretended we knew nothing about it and went ashore as if nothing had happened. I wrote a letter to the cook and his wife saying how sorry I was that they were leaving but, in a choice between the Captain or the Cook, I had no alternative. I am not sorry he's gone. He had the most terrible cough and I always had the feeling that some of the hawking and snorting might get into the soup. Anyway they are leaving tomorrow morning for Monte Carlo.

Tuesday 26th Am writing this at 31,000 feet in a Hawker Siddeley twin-jet on the way from Capo Caccia to Paris.[127]

Last night, out of my usual loyalty (!), stayed up all night with E and N. Coward and Co, I wrote, typed, a long letter to Howard and Mara as to what they should do with the 100G. we gave them as a present. Occasionally I joined E and Noel for chat and gossip. Noel says that the longest he'd ever taken to write a play was 10 days for *Cavalcade*.[128] The shortest 5 days for *Blithe Spirit* which he wrote in Portmeirion.[129] He had the idea on the train journey to Wales and had it written in his head before he sat down to the typewriter. Joyce Carey (actress) was with him and was writing, he says vaguely, something about Keats or something.[130] *Private Lives* took a week.[131] *Hay Fever* 6 days.[132] Astonishing. He has command of his nerves now E says and has become his usual brilliant self. The cook and his wife left for Monte Carlo and, to our astonishment, with Sianni our Yorkshire Terrier, claiming that Liza had said they could have her! It shall be back in two days or they, the cook and wife will

---

[127] Paris was to be the venue for the European premiere of *Taming of the Shrew*.
[128] *Cavalcade* (1931).
[129] The play *Blithe Spirit* (1941). Portmeirion, an Italianate holiday village and architectural flight of fancy in Merionethshire, North Wales.
[130] Joyce Carey (1898–1993), who appeared in the film *Blithe Spirit* (1945).
[131] Burton and Taylor would appear on stage together in 1983 in a production of *Private Lives* (1933).
[132] *Hay Fever* (1925).

be in gaol. Apart from our delight in the dog, who is 4–5 years old, she cost $1200. [. . .] I am very angry about Sianni and shouted and bawled a great deal and was very cantank. Steal money, jewels, anything except living things! Still at 31,000 ft and descending to Paris. Might buy this plane or one like it. 1 hour 35 minutes to Paris which by commercial jet including changes at Rome or Milan would take 5½ hours. It seats 10. Is smooth – so far. And seems to make one feel more secure. I hope. Shall think a lot about it.

Saturday 30th, Paris – Capo Caccia We have had in Paris what is mildly known as a triumph particularly E. Having arrived in Paris on Wednesday, about 5ish we dressed for the dinner at Jacqueline de Ribes and her husband, the Count – a humorous man who quite clearly dotes on E.[133] We went there about 9–9.30. The Duke and Duchess of Windsor were there, Baron Elie (or is it Guy) de Rothschild, Rex and Rachel Harrison etc.[134] There were 24 people in all. I became very sloshed and sang and recited poetry until E decided I was the worse for wear and, like a good boy, I went home with her. I understand from Eliz that I staggered backwards on being confronted by the paparazzi as we left the house. Drunkenly of course. The Duke and Duchess of Windsor were very sarcastic about Rachel Harrison and, when I told them that Rex was wearing a toupée and full make-up, about him too. [. . .]

The following day after about 2 minutes sleep we woke about 8 acutely but excitedly exhausted. We drank beer and talked about the previous evening and the one about to come. We were told that the whole of Paris was agog with expectation and from the point of view of the press it certainly seemed to be true. We had as much, if not more attention as we used to have in Rome, Paris etc. during 'La Scandale.'[135] They had put crush barriers around the streets looking on to the Opera and there must have been several hundred if not thousands of spectators. A lot of people had stayed up all the previous night to ensure a vantage point.

However at about 12 noon this same day I did something beyond outrage. I bought Elizabeth the jet plane we flew in yesterday. It costs, brand new, $960,000. She was not displeased. I think we can operate it at a reasonably practicable rate – perhaps with luck almost nothing. This might sound suspiciously like famous last words but I feel safe in it. It can, in 12 to 15 hours, and with one or two stops depending on weather, cross the Atlantic. It can land on any small airfield including unpaved ones. It can land at Abingdon when we go to Oxford next month. It can land at Saanen. It also means that we never have to land at that horrible London Airport ever again. Hurray!

---

[133] Jacqueline de Ribes (1929—), designer, couturière and socialite. Her husband was Edouard, comte de Ribes.
[134] It could have been either Elie (1917–2007) or his cousin Guy (1909–2007).
[135] 'La Scandale': the affair between Burton and Taylor. It should be 'Le Scandale'.

But about the evening of the film and gala. It was an outstanding success and the Press coverage was enormous. The film is widely praised and apart from a carp or two in the *Herald Tribune* and one French paper – not very important – the critical reaction was joyous. E wore a diadem specially created for her by the De Beers company of Van Cleef and Arpel, designed by Alexandre, which cost $1,200,000. With her other jewellery she wore a total of roughly $1,500,000. When we left the hotel, surrounded by 8 guards, all the hotel guests were forming an aisle to the street. There were many photographers but at the Opera it was a madhouse. Despite the presence of 5 ministers of the Government, one of whom gave us a message purporting to come from De Gaulle himself, and numerous luminaries of the cinema, stage, and society and the arts E was unquestionably the Queen of the evening.[136] They hardly ever photographed anyone else. I did quite well too and the flattery we were subjected to was very rich and heady. It however, I hope, has not gone to our heads. It was nevertheless sweet revenge for the social ostracism we endured such a relatively little time ago.

Later, worn out by the excitement [. . .] we fled with a few friends, Jacqueline de Ribes and husband, Curt Jurgens and wife, two Rothschilds etc. to the hotel where we had a few jars and talked (me) a great deal.[137]

We flew back on 'our' jet in 1.35 minutes and worked through the night though I finished by midnight but stayed up anyway.

OCTOBER

Sunday 1st, Capo Caccia We slept 'till noon while B. Wilson, Ron B and Gaston together with Bob's girl, Judy Hastings, flew in the jet to Nice to try and persuade the idiot chef to give up Sianni. After ten fruitless [. . .] hours arguing and cajoling and threatening – the Police joining in – they gave up. Now I will have to depose and it looks as if the man and his poor wife will go to prison. He has made us both so angry that I feel as if I could strangle him with my bare hands.

We sat in the sun in the afternoon and took Norma and David for a run in the speedboat which I nearly crashed on the way back against the *Kalizma* putting the Riva accidentally into reverse. [. . .]

Friday 20th, Capo Caccia We flew in the 125 to Oxford last Friday landing, by special permission, at Abingdon and went straight to 'The Bear' at Woodstock.[138] We were nerve-racked and nightmared at the prospect of

---

[136] Charles de Gaulle (1890–1970), President of France.

[137] Curd (often Curt) Jurgens (1915–82), actor, who had played alongside Burton in *Bitter Victory*. His wife at this time was Simone Bicheron.

[138] The Bear Hotel, Sunninghill, Woodstock, Oxfordshire.

48 hours of solid public exposure. On Saturday we televised with D. Lewin, Alexander Walker, [. . .] N. Coghill, Lord D. Cecil, and a Professor Rosenberg of Berkeley California.[139] The scholars were fine but the journalists, especially D. Lewin, were quite silly and shaming – on and off TV. Cecil was a joy and both E and I quite fell in love with him. He is the best kind of well-bred eccentric, sane, compassionate but acerbic brilliant maiden aunt – though married and clearly male. Nevill said, upon being asked on TV, that E would have made a fine scholar because she was among 'the most intelligent creatures he'd ever met' and was paradoxically 'an instinctive intellectual.' So there. He said that I was among the three greatest Welshmen he'd known, the other two being Dylan and David (*In Parenthesis*) Jones. He didn't realize – and I didn't correct him – that Jones is a Cockney.[140]

At lunch afterwards at Merton College D. Lewin, quite sober, further disgraced himself. His mind is poverty stricken, and rises only to the lowest levels of the *Daily Mail*, and nevertheless, fool rushing in, he dared to cross scholarly swords with Professors Coghill, Cecil and Rosenberg all of whom treated him with icy politeness. Once or twice his presumptive idiocy drew Nevill to the edge of open anger but like the near-saint that he is he drew back. Not so E. She let him have it with both barrels, both there and on TV. She became almost inarticulate with fury and malapropized freely.

On Sunday morning I read poetry at the Union with Wystan Auden. He read a great deal of his own poetry including his poems to Coghill and MacNeice.[141] Both very fine conversation pieces I thought but read in that peculiar sing-song tonelessness colourless way that most poets have. I remember Yeats and Eliot and MacLeish, who read their most evocative poems with such monotony as to stun the brain. Only Dylan could read his own stuff. Auden has a remarkable face and an equally remarkable intelligence but I fancy, though his poetry like all true poetry is all embracingly and astringently universal, his private conceit is monumental. The standing ovation I got with the 'Boast of Dai' of D. Jones *In Parenthesis* left a look on his seamed face, riven with a ghastly smile, that was compact of surprise, malice and envy. Afterwards he said to me 'How can you, where did you, how did you learn to speak with a Cockney accent?' In the whole piece of some 300 lines only about 5 are in Cockney. He is not a nice man but then only one poet have I ever met was – Archie Macleish.[142] Dylan was uncomfortable unless he was semi-drunk and 'on'. MacNeice was no longer a poet when I got to know him and was

---

[139] David Lewin and James Mossman interviewed Burton and Taylor. Alexander Walker (1920–2003), film critic and writer who would publish a biography of Elizabeth Taylor. Lord David Cecil (1902–86), Professor of English Literature at Oxford, 1948–70. Professor Marvin Rosenberg of the University of California, Berkeley, Shakespearean expert (1912–2003).

[140] Dylan being Dylan Thomas. David Jones (1895–1974), author of *In Parenthesis* (1937).

[141] Louis MacNeice was a friend of Burton.

[142] Archibald MacLeish (1892–1982), poet.

permanently drunk. Eliot was clerically cut with a vengeance. The only nice poets I've ever met were bad poets and a bad poet is not a poet at all – ergo I've never met a nice poet. That may include Macleish. For instance R. S. Thomas is a true minor poet but I'd rather share my journey to the other life with somebody more congenial. I think the last tight smile that he allowed to grimace his features was at the age of six when he realized with delight that death was inevitable. He has consigned his wife to hell for a long time. She will recognize it when she goes there.[143]

And so to Sunday evening and the opening of *Faustus*. It rained like mad, as usual in that splendid climate, and there were lots of people outside the theatre in macs and under umbrellas who applauded etc. A nurse, it was a charity performance for the Nuffield Hospital, and therefore a nurse, presented E with a bouquet of flowers and if you please curtsied.[144] E and I were delighted. I met Quintin Hogg and thinking him to be Boothby asked him 'Where is your Sardinian wife.'[145] He replied that he was not Boothby. I recovered fast, told him I was pulling his leg and asked 'Why aren't you the leader of the Tory Party?' He: 'They had their chance in 1963 and lost it. Now I'm too old at 59.' Me: 'Winston didn't become PM 'til he was 65–66.' He: 'Hmm.'

The Duke and Duchess of Kent arrived and were all presented.[146] The Duchess is adorable and both E and I loved her. She was frantically nervous as we all were but she showed it in close-up. Muscles twitched uncontrollably around her mouth. He was shy. The show went alright.

The party afterwards was alright but exhausting – between us we must have met a 1000 people. Incidentally when we entered the theatre we were greeted by a fanfare of trumpets, then silence as we took our seats and then another fanfare for the D and Duch of Kent. I record that because it shows the idiocy of fame. 5 years ago we'd have had a fanfare of raspberries. If we were lucky.

[. . .] Ken Tynan came up from London to discuss the Churchill play *The Soldiers*.[147] Will write about that later.

The weather was dreadful and made me feel that I never wish to see England again. [. . .] Don't think out of choice that I would live in England again even if they paid me to.

---

[143] Mildred Eldridge (1909–91), artist and wife of R. S. Thomas.
[144] Nuffield Hospital, Woodstock Road, Oxford.
[145] Quintin Hogg (1907–2001), Conservative MP for St Marylebone, formerly (and again after 1970), Lord Hailsham, who had been a contender for the leadership of the Conservative Party in 1963 but had lost out to Edward Heath (1916–2005). Robert Boothby (1900–86), Baron Boothby from 1958, another Conservative politician, who had married earlier that year Wanda Sanna, a Sardinian woman 33 years his junior.
[146] Prince Edward, Duke of Kent (1935—) and Katharine, Duchess of Kent (1933—).
[147] Rolf Hochhuth's play *Soldiers, Necrology on Geneva* (1967). Burton was considering playing the role of Churchill.

Am in a violent temper. E, as usual, has to combat everything I do or say in front of the children. I wish to Christ she'd not contradict me in front of them and wish likewise that I didn't do likewise. But it's the status quo. I'd best shut up.

Saturday 21st, Alghero Bettina and a friend Jorgen Wigmoller (?) stayed with us for two day.[148] She is of course enchanting as ever and very giggly and, despite aging, essentially feminine. He is slim and Danish blond and is I'm afraid a little boring. Largely the latter because he doesn't have the capacity to listen. I also suspect that he's a nose ahead in the white-lying selling plate. [. . .]

Ivor and Gwen and the two girls are with us on the boat and today – J. Losey being ill and therefore no work – we sailed to Alghero. [. . .] We sat around endlessly talking of this and that – mostly about Kate and Sybil. At one point Ivor reached into the depths of his bowels and brought out a cosmic fart that shattered the eardrums. E was delighted and tried to respond but her netherhand [*sic*] was not talking.

[. . .] It's pleasant to sit around on the boat and remember with infinite nostalgia the days when a penny was a penny was a penny, and a green cap with a badge on it and membership of the secondary school was the height of human felicity. And selling papers, dung, blackberries, winberries, dewberries was almost the sum-total of one's life. How I remember that green sweater, that stinking green sweater. And the names of the houses on the way to school are like a roll-call of the dead. 'Pleasant View' for instance had a view of an exactly similar house in Abbey Road called 'Rest Bay' and 'Sans Souci' was a very careful house. And so now to Church and the mumbo-jumbo of Latin imperfectly spoken. And an obeisance to little Liza who bought, out of her allowance, a quite expensive present for Maria – our new Anglo-Welsh stewardess – and the conversation went like this:

Me: You're a good girl Liza. How much did it cost?
She: I'm not going to tell you.
Me: Why not?
She: Because you'll pay me back what I spent.

Now you can't hardly be better than that.

NOVEMBER

Tuesday 7th, Grand Hotel, Rome Two weeks since I wrote during which time we finished the film in Alghero on Sunday morning the 22 October and sailed

---

[148] Bettina Krahmer, Guy Rothschild's stepdaughter by his first marriage.

to Costa Smeralda about 11am.[149] [. . .] We arrived at dusk and, nobody quite knowing whether we had the right landfall, waited for a sign. It came we thought and hoped from a car which flashed its headlights on and off [. . .]. We lowered the *Riva* and crept slowly through the water to the shore. It was Jorgen with a Fiat. Sent Alberto and Raphael back to the boat to get E and Gwen (and the girls) and went in Jorgen's car to Bettina's house.[150] It is lovely and open – except the bedrooms a bit cramped and monastic for my liking – in the living room; a sunbathing roof, several acres of land, a lovely patio, log fireplace and a floor made of log sections set into some sort of stone. A private beach with a small jetty and a fishing boat (converted). Blissful place. We ate well, beef and chips and braised onions and local wine. All immensely pleasant. Bettina is a dear woman.

We decided to stay in the bay (I believe it's called Liscia di Vacco – the place? of the cows) overnight and set sail tomorrow.[151] This after I'd talked with J. Heyman producer.

[. . .] We dine tonight with the Israeli Ambassador to Rome – Ehud Avriel – and his wife. He is, according to Bill Pepper – *Newsweek* correspondent in Rome – 'the wisest man in Israel, much cleverer than the PM or Foreign Secretary.[152] Was ambassador-at-large in Africa and formulated Israeli policy there. Formerly Ambassador to Austria. Goes on special assignments which is why he's in Rome now dealing with the Vatican. Born in Germany. Doctor of Philosophy. Translates Russian poetry.'

We left Costa Smeralda about 2–2.30pm on Monday 23rd October. And for the next 14 hours went through very rough seas on our way to Anzio.[153] [. . .] We reported to Dino de Laurentiis' studios that morning for shooting at 12.00 with Noël. It was his last day. We heard that Phil is to arrive on Friday and we looked forward to seeing him. The girls went reluctantly back to Residence Gardens, where they are staying with Ive and Gwen, and to school.

I like Anzio – it is not pretty but it's a 'working' harbour and everything that works has some kind of attraction even unto a cement mixer. I love the stalls along the quayside where they sell fresh shellfish, oysters mussels etc. It smells very fishy.

And so to cocktails with Ehud Avriel and dinner.

---

[149] Costa Smeralda, on the north-eastern coast of Sardinia.

[150] Alberto and Raphael were crew members on the *Kalizma*.

[151] Liscia di Vacca, a bay between Porto Cervo and Pevero, on the Costa Smeralda. It means 'beach of the cows'.

[152] Curtis Bill Pepper (1917—), war correspondent and head of the Rome bureau for *Newsweek* magazine.

[153] Port city some 60 km south of Rome.

1968

Richard ceased making entries in his 1967 diary in early November, and did not start his 1968 diary until late July. During this period he played the part of Mephisto in *Candy*, filmed in Rome at the end of 1967. He then travelled to Austria and back to the United Kingdom, working on the adventure movie *Where Eagles Dare*. During studio shooting in London Burton and Taylor stayed on a yacht, the *Beatriz of Bolivia*, moored at Tower Pier, which they were renting while the *Kalizma* was being refitted. Early in February they flew to New York for the American premiere of *Doctor Faustus*, attended by Robert and Ethel Kennedy, and later that month they attended the opening of the Paris boutique co-owned by their friend Vicky Tiel, in which they had invested. Elizabeth started work at Elstree Studios in March 1968 for *Secret Ceremony*, other scenes being shot on location in London and in the Netherlands.

In May 1968 Richard purchased the 33.19 carat Krupp diamond for Elizabeth, at a price of $305,000, when it was auctioned in New York. Late that month *Boom!* was released, to poor reviews.

In June Richard was best man to Gianni Bozzacchi at his marriage to Claudye, for whom Elizabeth was maid of honour. The marriage took place at the home of Alexandre de Paris at Saints, to the east of Paris. In the same month Burton and Taylor attended the wedding of Elizabeth's friend Sheran Cazalet to Simon Hornby, held near Tonbridge, Kent. Late in June Burton began working on Tony Richardson's adaptation of Nabokov's *Laughter in the Dark*. In controversial circumstances, the details of which remain disputed, Burton was fired by Richardson on 8 July and subsequently replaced by Nicol Williamson (1938—). Richardson and Burton had worked together before – on *Look Back in Anger* and *A Subject of Scandal and Concern*. But on this occasion their relationship broke down, and an attempt by Taylor to repair the breach was unsuccessful. The diary resumes with Taylor in hospital.

JULY

Tuesday 23rd, Fitzroy-Nuffield Hospital, London[1] I have just spent the two most horrible days of my adult life. There was nothing before, as I recall, no

---

[1] Fitzroy Nuffield Hospital, Bryanston Square, London.

shame inflicted or received, no injustice done to me or by me, no disappoint-ment professional or private that I could not think away in a quarter of an hour. But this is the first time where I've seen a loved one in screaming agony for two days, hallucinated by drugs, sometimes knowing who I was and some-times not, a virago one minute an angel the next and felt completely helpless.

Elizabeth had her uterus removed on Sunday morning. The operation began at 9.30 and ended at 1.00. Three hours and a half. I tried to read Holroyd's book about Lytton Strachey – what a vile, cruel, self-centred man he sounds – but during those hours I read about 5 pages and when I knew she was temporarily safe at least and back in the room I found I had to read them all over again.[2]

But it's the nights that have been so harrowing. I took a room – next door to E's – to be near her until the pain had eased somewhat. The walls are like tissue paper and the first night I heard nothing but her groans throughout the night. It is not a normal hysterectomy – there were great complications – and she is suffering far more than normal. In addition they have given her a drug, which eases the pain, but gives her vivid hallucinations. And extraordinary shafts of clarity at the same time. She thought for a long time yesterday that she was on the yacht and, at one point, when flowers were brought in she told them to 'put the flowers in Liza's room downstairs.' She then sternly told me, looking up from her book (*Public Image* – M. Spark) that I must never shout at Raymond (the steward on the *Kalizma*) again.[3] I said that I wouldn't and she said, 'Hush – he'll hear you.' 'Look', she said at one point, 'they're showing *Faustus* in colour on the TV.' The screen was blank as a blind eye though a greetings telegram had reflected a red into the screen before which it was lying.

Last night she suddenly appeared in my room about midnight supported by a minute Latin nurse and said she was lonesome. She is not supposed to move at all except for the commode. I put her back to bed. Half an hour later I heard her scream 'Jim' – she was in the corridor. Back to bed again. I told her she was a naughty girl and she told me to fuck off. I said I would sit in the room with her. She told me to sit in the hall outside the door as she couldn't stand the sight of my face. She turned away from me. I waited 5 minutes and left the room. Then there was a shout of 'Richard.' The nurse and I arrived together. She was sitting on the edge of the bed. Another time she crashed against a chair in the next room. I shot up and out and she was sitting on the lavatory with the door closed.

I've asked them to give her a drug, if possible, that's not illusion-making. Christ I shall be glad when this week's over. And won't she. She finally fell asleep, or at least remained quiet, at about 4.00 in the a.m. I fell asleep but kept

---

[2] Michael Holroyd (1935—), *Lytton Strachey: The New Biography* (1968).
[3] Muriel Spark, (1918–2006) *The Public Image* (1968). Raymond Vignale, also secretary to Taylor.

waking with the sort of convulsive wide-awakeness of a man who's afraid of having a heart attack in his sleep.

[. . .]

The press has been pestering us night and day and we're in all the papers this morning. What a vile lot they are – especially the English. They're so smirky and sneaky and smug and provincial. They are not honestly scandalous with the awful dirty pornographic glee of the Italians. They are merely snide.

Kate is here – she arrived a week ago, and is as joyous as ever. Within a day Liza was calling me 'Daddy!' I must see her today sometime. Them days are slipping by and she has only 3 weeks left.

The most alarming lesson I learned about this whole thing was the extraordinary effect that hallucinatory drugs have on the brain. E looked at me on occasions yesterday with a malevolence that made a basilisk look like a blood hound. I can only hope that in vino veritas doesn't apply to drugs. She looked at a poster of the Mona Lisa on the wall and said very hostess-like, 'Vicky would you like a drink?' She called me a 'stuffed shirt' at one point – and she's right. That'll teach me to be smug in future.

[. . .] 2.45 and E is awake and perfectly normal. She is completely aware of everything she did last night! God save the mark![4]

Wednesday 24th, Dorchester [Hotel] Have decided to change to typing this diary badly rather than that I should write so hurriedly that sometimes I have difficulty reading my own writing.

[. . .] Janine Filistorf rang today from Geneva with the shocking news that André Besançon, the gardener of Pays de Galles, Céligny and a very dear and honest man, had committed suicide. Poor bugger. How solitary can you get? We, Kate Ivor and I will fly in the jet to Geneva on Friday or Saturday to attend the funeral. He hanged himself. I remembered that he had suffered from a nervous breakdown some 12 or 13 years ago after the death of his wife and before we employed him in 1957. He was about to go into a home this morning at 10 o'clock but it was too late. He killed himself last night. I feel such a bloody fool for not even suspecting it. If I'd known I'm sure I could have helped. I could have had him transferred to Gstaad instead of that amiable but quite useless drunken musician of the mighty name, Johann Sebastian Bach.[5]

K. has a desire to be left alone for a bit, I think, and so tonight she is going to stay in Hampstead with Ivor and Gwen while Liza, Maria and I will stay at the hotel. We took K to the Wells Pub in Hampstead before lunch today while Ivor and I had a couple of pints.[6] [. . .]

---

[4] 'God save the mark!' is a line spoken by Hotspur in *Henry IV* (Part 1), Act III, scene ii.
[5] Johann Sebastian Bach was Burton and Taylor's housekeeper at Chalet Ariel, Gstaad.
[6] The Wells, Well Walk, Hampstead.

I am trying to persuade Elizabeth to postpone her film with F. Sinatra.[7] It starts in only 5 weeks time and it's hardly likely that she'll be properly prepared mentally for such a big job so soon. [. . .]

Just shared a pot of caviare with Ivor and Liza. K. says she doesn't like it. I suspect she has her mother's fear of famous but untried foods. I had it myself for a long time. It's very working class but I was weaned early by PHB. I was reading A. L. Rowse's second volume of biography recently in which he recounts his embarrassment at being offered asparagus when dining with Lord David Cecil and not knowing how to eat them.[8] I know the feeling well.

Thursday 25th Just about to give a lecture to the boys. Apparently they have been playing records in their room until 2.30 in the morning, putting cigarettes out on tables etc. instead of or perhaps including ashtrays. Generally a case of showing off. [. . .]

Friday 26th By the time their explanations had finished it was time for me to go to lunch with Hugh French, who, poor fellow, also had a tale of woe. The only girl he'd ever loved, in his words, had left him. Wealthily married to an impotent old husband she had promised to get a divorce, found herself pregnant by Hugh and suddenly without so much as a by your leave or a kiss me foot had disappeared somewhere in Paris for an abortion. He is looking for her. She's French, youngish, about late twenties, peasant, was on the fringes of the film business. Hugh met her through Terry Young, film director, who'd 'used her' in a film.[9] She sounds as ordinary as a tabloid newspaper but there's no accounting for love lust or taste. [. . .]

I am just about to leave for Geneva with Liza, Kate, Ivor, Gwen and Brook Williams for the funeral of André (Bobo) Besançon.[10]

[. . .] went to the Hospital to see ETB, and there was Norma Heyman who was drunk and who had been turned down by my two stepsons for lunch and proposed to give us, me, E, a lecture on how to talk to the boys and how to keep them interested [. . .]

---

[7] At this point Taylor was planning to make *The Only Game in Town* with Frank Sinatra, singer, actor. The subsequent delay led Sinatra to withdraw from the project, and he was replaced by Warren Beatty (1937—).

[8] Burton means autobiography. A. L. Rowse, *A Cornishman in Oxford* (1965), p. 145: 'He [Cecil] asked me along to lunch: it would have been kinder to ask me to tea, for I foresaw that some fearful social obstacle would rear its ugly head. It did – in the form of asparagus – and I was inwardly vexed. How did one eat it? It was the same conundrum that was raised in an aristocratic Officers' Club under the Nazis: how did the Führer eat his asparagus? I could not bring myself to plunge my fingers into the mess, as my host did without ado; so I proudly left it on the side of my plate.' Burton and Rowse (1903–97) would become friends in the last months of Burton's life, after appearing on American television together.

[9] Terence Young (1915–94) was to direct Burton in *The Klansman* and was also director for the ill-fated film *Jackpot*.

[10] Brook Williams (1938–2005), actor, son of Emlyn and Molly Williams, was a great friend of Burton's and acted alongside him in more than a dozen films starting with *Cleopatra* and ending with *Wagner*.

[There are no further entries in the diary until late September. During this period Richard travelled to Céligny to attend the funeral of André Besançon. He was accompanied by his brother Ivor, Ivor's wife Gwen, Emlyn Williams's son Brook, and daughters Liza and Kate. After the funeral the men dined at the Café de la Gare in Céligny. Initially the intention had been to travel on to Chalet Ariel in Gstaad but, as they had eaten and drunk rather well, it was decided to postpone the journey to the following day. Instead they agreed to stay at Le Pays de Galles, which Burton had not visited for more than two years. Ivor went on ahead to open the house up and put on the heating, and when attempting to gain entry to the property, slipped and struck his neck on a paving slab. In what appears to have been a freak accident he was paralysed from the neck down. Ivor's incapacitation and eventual death in 1972 would cast a considerable shadow over Richard.

Much of August was spent in organizing Ivor's treatment, initially at Stoke Mandeville Hospital, near Aylesbury in Buckinghamshire, but in the last week Burton went to New York. By September he was in Paris to begin work on *Staircase*, co-starring with Rex Harrison, and Elizabeth was to co-star with Warren Beatty in *The Only Game in Town*.]

SEPTEMBER

Thursday 26th, Paris We worked from 7 last night to approx 4 this morning. [. . .] Elizabeth has gone off to work and 'test' costumes. She should be back before I leave I hope. After 7 or is it 8 years I still miss her if she goes to the bathroom. She starts work on Monday, and after a time we shall be working the same hours, 'Continental' hours, so called, which means from mid-day to 8 at night.

Occasionally, as I hopefully continue with this diary I will try and fill in things that happened during the unrecorded days, e.g. We took Kate to NY with us on the *Queen Elizabeth*. With us also we took Liza and my God-Daughter Sally Baker (Stanley's daughter), Nella, and a nurse named Caroline O'Connor for Elizabeth.[11] It was an uneventful crossing, and, having been so often on the big ships, rather sad. [. . .] There was a general air of run-down gentry, frayed at the edges. [. . .] I wondered if after many years of travelling that I had become blasé. Elizabeth said not, and Sally asked me if the ship had always been as shabby. Some of the life-boats and the great steel arms that presumably lower them into the sea were rusty and a great many of the weather-covers were torn. Sally had never been across the Atlantic before and so presumably had nothing to be blasé about.

---

[11] Sally, daughter of Stanley and Ellen Baker.

While at dinner one night in the Verandah Grill, which is the same as ever, I was called to the phone to Ethel Kennedy.[12] I thought it was some sort of crank, because I'd read in the papers as we left England that Ethel was on Onassis's island in Greece.[13] However it later turned out that it was Ethel calling from Hyannis Port to ask me if I would do the narration of a documentary film about Bobby Kennedy. I said yes and did it in Quogue at Aaron's house. It was shown at the end of the disastrous Democratic Convention and was apparently the only thing in those vulgar five days that was well received.[14]

Sunday 29th, Barbizon[15] Last night we dined in the Hotel Restaurant. [. . .] I became very mournful about Ivor, and started blaming myself for not having been with him when he went to open up the house that dreadful night. [. . .]

Back to Paris today. Elizabeth finally got round to reading her script yesterday and likes it, she says. [. . .]

Barry Cooper, Elizabeth's doctor of a few months arrives shortly to examine her.[16] Elizabeth has more examinations in any given month than I've had in my lifetime. [. . .]

Received a letter from Cis and Elfed today thanking us for the 500 quid we sent them and telling us how excited Tom and Hyral were when they received theirs.[17] Cis and Elfed were staying with them when it arrived. Can't wait, said Tom, for the bank to open, they'll hardly be able to get me through the door. Ivor is to be fitted with a collar, which hopefully will enable him to be sat up. This should be of enormous help psychologically. He has finally agreed to see Cis. She's the first so honoured apart from us.

Dr Cooper has been searching, he says, for the origin of Bateau Mouche. And could I tell him, he asked the origin of 'Pumpernickel?' I could, I said. Napoleon's retreat from Moscow. His horse was called Nickel. How it was spelled I don't know. The French soldiery [were] forced to eat off the country, including the black bread of Mittel-Europe. They hated it and groused that it was pain-pour-nickelle.[18] I also told him the etymology of Marmalade. Je voudrais la preserve d'orange pour La Reine <u>Marie qui est malade</u>. This from a courier who had been sent in a hurry from France from Mary Queen of Scots, who, pregnant, was insane to have some of her beloved Scots

---

[12] Ethel Kennedy (1928—), widow of Robert F. Kennedy (1925–68), US Senator, candidate for the Democratic Party's nomination for President, who had been assassinated in June 1968.
[13] Aristotle Onassis (1904–75), shipping magnate, who was to marry Jackie Kennedy (1929–94), widow of President John F. Kennedy, in October 1968.
[14] The documentary film (which won an Oscar for Best Short Subject Documentary) was directed by Charles Guggenheim (1924–2002) and entitled *Robert Kennedy Remembered*.
[15] Hôtellerie du Bas Breau, Grande Rue, Barbizon, Fontainebleau.
[16] Dr Barrington Cooper (1923–2007), who had been introduced to Burton and Taylor by Joseph Losey.
[17] Hyral was Tom's second wife.
[18] This story is not true: the name comes from the German words *pumpern* (to break wind) and *Nickel* (goblin).

marmalade.[19] There's no way of finding out whether these stories are true or not. I like them anyway.

Monday 30th, [Hotel] Plaza, Paris Returned to Paris yesterday having at lunch at Bas-Breau with Caroline and Dr Barry Cooper. It seemed to me that he wasn't bound too strictly by the Hippocratic oath as he might have been when discussing a patient of his and acquaintance of mine called Nick Ray.[20] He talked freely of his drunks, drugs and gambling etc. They lived together for a year he says. He also took a scholarship to Cambridge, and was only the second Jew to win a blue. For rowing. He is very short and tubby so he must have coxed, I suppose.[21] He also asked us and the children to stay with the Butes (Marquise of) in Scotland this winter.[22] He talks carefully and quietly as if afraid that, if he didn't, he would accidentally reveal a non-U accent.[23] He is vocally a bit like a black friend of ours called Roscoe Lee Browne.[24][. . .]

I read P. G. Wodehouse's latest *Do Butlers Burgle Banks?* in one sitting.[25] It's exactly the same as all the others. He's still mining the same vein of gold, but it's as effortlessly entertaining as ever. Then a couple of chapters of Churchill's *World Crisis*, and so to bed for a couple of hours sleep until 12.30, a chat and some more *World Crisis*, and back to sleep again at approx 2.30.[26]

OCTOBER

Tuesday 1st Eliz started work yesterday, but without Beatty. Tomorrow he starts. I continued mine with Rex, and oddly enough he was in sparkling form, not worrying about his lines much, and we got along merrily.[27] Hugh French told me that R. Zanuck was more enthused than he'd ever seen him over the rushes from *Staircase*.[28] [. . .] At Eliz's I saw John (Goulash) Shepridge who told of his favourite restaurant in Paris, known only to a select group, he says.[29] It's called 'L'Ami Louis,' 32, Rue Verte Bois.[30] I think he said it's near the Bastille. [. . .]

I am much happier in Paris than I am in London. It is perhaps that I have a dread of seeing my family, i.e. most of my family? It is because I like acquiring

---

[19] Mary (1542–87), Queen of Scots (1542–67).
[20] Nicholas Ray (1911–79), the director.
[21] Cambridge University has no record of Barry Cooper winning a Blue for rowing.
[22] This refers to the Crichton-Stuarts, Marquesses of Bute, whose family seat is Mount Stuart on the Isle of Bute.
[23] The term 'non-U' means not upper class. The distinction between 'U' and 'non-U' terminology and linguistic usage was popularised in the 1950s by the author Nancy Mitford (1904–73).
[24] Roscoe Lee Browne (1925–2007) had appeared alongside Burton and Taylor in *The Comedians*.
[25] P. G. Wodehouse, *Do Butlers Burgle Banks?* (1968).
[26] Winston Churchill, *The World Crisis, 1911–1918* (1923).
[27] Burton was to co-star with Rex Harrison in *Staircase*.
[28] Richard Zanuck (1934–2012), son of Darryl F. Zanuck and President of Twentieth Century-Fox.
[29] John C. Shepridge had been executive producer of *What's New Pussycat?*
[30] Rue du Vertbois.

new French every day, or that I speak the language, albeit roughly if fluently on occasion? Perhaps I'm ashamed of Britain's weakness. It's awful to see how despised and dismissed she is by the foreign press. Eight in the morning and I must be off to work.

> Darling Nose and Drife
> I miss you like something awful – for some reason especially today – so be all loving and tenderness tonight <u>please</u> – and if you play your cards right I'll take you out to dinner
> All my love
> Wife
> P.S. Call me later
> [Elizabeth Taylor's hand.]

Wednesday 2nd Worked yesterday from 9 to about 4.30 when it became too dark to shoot. We were forced to stop for about two hours around midday because of rain. Went over to see E at lunchtime [...] and the place is like a madhouse. There is a maid to clean up, Dick and John, Frank LaRue, Jeanette, Claudye, Gianni, Vicky and Mia, George Davis and Caroline.[31] [...] In addition, for a lot of the time you have Rocky Brynner.[32] [...]

George Stevens is behaving beautifully, and Beatty worries about whether he should wear a tie or not, according to E.[33] George thinks E is smashing. So that's alright. Richard Zanuck thinks Rex and I are smashing too, according to a telegram we received yesterday. So everybody loves everybody as of this writing. [...]

Picked up E last night and brought her home, and for some reason [...] I suddenly turned from Jekyll into Hyde and went to bed dinnerless in one of my huffs. Eliz ate downstairs with Dick and John. I woke at 4.30 and waited for the world to get up. The world being Elizabeth. Finally decided to wake the world up at 7.00, whereupon it made me a Bloody Mary. That I said is my Vitamin C for the day.

Thursday 3rd Worked all day until about 5 and went to Eliz's studio to pick her up as usual. They seem to be getting on fine. Ours goes well too, though Rex is very funny in his old-fashioned attempts to upstage, get into my close-ups, do funny business on my lines etc. It's rather like acting with a very determined

---

[31] Mia Fonssagrives (1942—), clothes designer on *What's New Pussycat?* and *The Only Game in Town*, partner of Vicky Tiel in the Paris boutique *Mia and Vicky*. George Davis: one of Taylor's secretaries.
[32] Rocky Brynner (1946—), son of Yul Brynner.
[33] George Stevens (1904–75), director of *The Only Game in Town*, who had also directed Taylor in *A Place in the Sun* and *Giant*.

young actress. [. . .] I mentioned it to the director who said first that he hadn't noticed and then that he'd never seen it before in his life. Come to think of it, I never have, on films, and from a man. That is to say if you consider Victor Spinetti to be a Welsh-Italian girl. Because the latter did everything except break wind, and stick his finger up his nose to the knuckle. [. . .]

Last night we stayed up latish to watch a soccer match between Celtic of Glasgow and St Etienne of France. Celtic won by 4 goals.[34] Delighted I was, and always am nowadays at the discomfiture of the French.

My Darling Husband
Just to let you know that going to bed with W.B. hasn't changed my love for you at all – increased it if anything – Aren't you thrilled?
All my love,
Wife
[Elizabeth Taylor's hand.[35]]

Friday 4th We worked inside in the morning and went out in the afternoon. I did only 4 shots all day. The rest of the time I read *L'Express* to improve my French which latter could do with. [. . .] Elliott Kastner came to see me with a carte blanche offer of about ten properties.[36] [. . .] He says that I will realize $7 million from *Eagles*. Now that would be nice.

I am absolutely possessed with the idea of buying a large barge and converting it into a river yacht. My dressing-room windows look over the Seine, and I see a hundred barges a day and beautifully stubby, chuggy, impertinent tugs fussing like bullies. It would be blissful to weigh anchor or whatever one does on barges and motor through the French countryside to Marseilles or Germany or Belgium or Holland. [. . .] I could have a mini-moke on board and a couple of push-bikes for the occasional excursions. I could ask for a lot of films to be done in Paris so that we could live on the barge. I could have a swimming pool put on the deck, and thousands of paperbacks in the library, on every conceivable subject. It shouldn't be all that expensive – much less than a comparable house. I'm told one could buy a 100 ft barge for about 20 or 30 thousand dollars and spend another thirty on it. I would buy hundreds of films in 16mm and have a small projection room. Roddy McDowall told me once that he has a library of several hundred films that cost him very little to buy. [. . .]

---

[34] European Cup Holders Celtic beat St Etienne 4–0 at Celtic Park, Glasgow, in the second leg of their first round tie, winning 4–2 on aggregate.
[35] 'W.B.' is Warren Beatty. Elizabeth is teasing her sometimes jealous husband.
[36] Elliott Kastner (1930—) had produced *Where Eagles Dare* and would also produce *Villain, Absolution*, and the Taylor film *X, Y and Zee*.

Saturday 5th Yesterday we worked desultorily all day until about 5. Rex gave a party for the crew and cast (me) afterwards. [. . .] My turn next week. There was no vodka and Scotch is dangerous, so Jim made Vodka Martinis for us.[37] I have been fairly squiffed three nights in a row, so I'd better watch it.

Pat Newcomb arrived.[38] She is supposed to be head of publicity for the three productions *Staircase, The Only Game in Town* and *Justine*.[39] She looks sun-lamped, and has a pot belly. Is she, one asks oneself, a man or a woman? [. . .]

Hugh French told me that there is a likelihood that I will be getting a telegram or letter from Universal Pictures threatening to sue me if I do not do *Anne of the Thousand Days* next summer, and also informing [me] that they no longer have any intention of backing the film that I really want to do: *The Man From Nowhere*.[40] Now that is very perverse. I shall wait on the events. I wouldn't object to having the whole year off. I could write a book, or dream a lot, or get fit or fat. [. . .] I have an idea that, undemocratic as it may sound, a studio is better and safer when it is run by one man and not a committee. It seems that UP is run by three or four warring factions, all of whom are jealous of the other. Jay Kanter is about the only dependable one.[41] And he is of course subject to the whim of Lou Wasserman and or Ed Henry.[42] Even the names are untrustworthy. And, strictly speaking, I suppose they are only semi-literate. The mind that makes money and the mind that makes or enjoys or appreciates Art and its fellows must be a long way apart. [. . .]

Eliz tells me that the latest scandal about the above-mentioned Pat Newcomb is that she has decided that she is a lesbian and has moved in with Liz Smith who is a journalist of some distinction (she writes for *Cosmopolitan, The New York Times* etc.) and has taken the place of a Diane Judge who oddly enough was cooking chilli for E the other day in E's studio dressing-room when the aforesaid Pat walked in.[43] I think the parts that Rex and I are playing have gone to everybody's heads. [. . .]

Sunday 6th We are lunching with somebody called Alex or Alexis who is Baron (Claudye just told me) de Redé.[44] We are going on afterwards with a party at the running of the Grand Prix d'Arc de Triomphe, the French equivalent of

[37] Jim Benton, Burton's secretary, and partner of George Davis.

[38] Pat Newcomb (1930—), press agent.

[39] *Justine* (Twentieth Century-Fox, 1969), directed by George Cukor (1899–1983).

[40] *The Man From Nowhere* was a screenplay that Joseph Losey was discussing with Burton at this time, but which fell through when Burton decided to act in *Where Eagles Dare* instead.

[41] Jay Kanter, agent of Marlon Brando, who would produce the Burton film *Villain* and the Taylor film *X, Y and Zee* (1971).

[42] Lew Wasserman (1913–2002), head of Universal Pictures. Ed Henry, senior executive at Universal Pictures.

[43] Liz Smith (1923—).

[44] Alexis Rosenberg, 2nd Baron de Redé (1922–2004), collector, socialite.

Ascot or Derby day etc. Though I know very little about horse-racing. It might be interesting. Baron Guy and Marie-Hélène Rothschild invited us.[45] La Callas will probably be there and possibly Ari Onassis.[46] Aren't we posh?

Yesterday I went house-boat hunting, but found nothing suitable. We'll try again later in the week. We did however find a very attractive French trio. A M. Paul-Emile Victor and his wife Collette and her sister.[47] He is an arctic explorer of distinction, about 60 years old I would give a guess, his wife about 35 perhaps, and sister-in-law about 40. He gave me two books, one for E and I and one, which he signed, for Christopher. I shall send it off to Chris today. Paul-Emile told us many fascinating stories about Eskimos, and British Explorers and their entire unflappability. Very amusing.

We must see him again. He has an island of ten acres in the Pacific which has the beautiful island of Buro-Buro right close by.[48] It looks heavenly. We must 'do' the Pacific one of these days. They know Marlon very well. [. . .]

We dined at home and talked about sex with Caroline who seems to be very sensible about it. A lot of passes are made at her it seems. I've seen the come-on from Rex among others. He, by the way when he goes to a Premiere etc. always wears a toupée and makes up with 'ManTan'. Well fancy that. I think I'll try it myself. [. . .]

Monday 7th We went to lunch at the Baron Redé's house, and had a delicious lunch of fish of some kind, followed by partridge, and a magnificent ice-cream with nuts and cake in it. There were three wines, label-less, and brandy equally anonymous, but all very good. Two devastating wars and crippling taxes, and the moneyed Aristocracy still live like Aristos. They must be cleverer than we think. I noticed that every glass still had wine in it when we left. Is it considered impolite to drain your glass when you rise to leave. If so, I was impolite. There must have been about a hundred people for the lunch. [. . .] The house is huge and very lavish and Marie-Hélène said that she considered it the most beautiful in Paris. I said that my favourite house in the world was Ferrières. [. . .]

Later at the Paddock where only the owners are allowed to go in but we were privileged and went in to the ring. So we were standing there with a great lot of them when suddenly a tall man appeared emaciated and ill and stubble-faced and minusculy-moustached and smiled a lot and was quite incoherent, and had a right hand which was burned to the bone between the index finger and the next. It was Peter O'Toole.

I have to write an article about Robert Kennedy. So God help us.

---

[45] Marie-Hélène de Rothschild (1927–96), socialite and wife of Guy de Rothschild.
[46] Maria Callas (1923–77), opera singer.
[47] Paul-Emile Victor (1907–95), explorer, ethnologist.
[48] Burton means Bora-Bora, in the Leeward Islands.

Tuesday 8th I tried like mad to write an article about Bobby Kennedy last night but failed abysmally. I read this morning what I had written and immediately tore it up. I will try again today but I am totally without inspiration. I can't find a peg to hang it on. I've been thinking about it for days too.

[...] Collette and her sister Christianne came to visit but we had finished work, and so I took them over to see E. She too had finished but was rehearsing. Collette's husband Paul Emile joined us later and we had a few drinks and went home.

[...] Maria Callas told us on Sunday that she and Ari had parted. Said he was too destructive and that her singing was affected. I think she's a bit of a bore. She told me how beautiful my eyes were and that they demonstrated a good soul! Said she was a little shy of asking but could she play Lady Macbeth to my Macbeth in the film of it which she had read we were going to do. I suppose she thought Elizabeth was going to play Macduff or Donalbain. Maybe it was merely an off day but she seemed pretty silly to me. [...] She is riddled with platitudes. Was on Sunday anyway. Elizabeth who has eyes in the back of her bum and ears on stalks was aware of everything that was going on.

When E by the way, walked from the paddock to the Loge with Guy and Marie-Hélène the thousands of people applauded her all the way. Not bad for an old woman of 36. I am always pleased and surprised by that sort of thing. We have been expecting it to stop for years but it hasn't. [...]

Wednesday 9th For the past three days I have been going through one of my bouts of melancholy, black as a dirge. It seems I am to be sued by UP which doesn't help. They haven't got a leg to stand on but it's a bloody nuisance. One cheerful note, literally, was a note from Liza written in the new calligraphy, and a pleasant but slightly admonitory note from her form-mistress. I save the comic strips from the *Paris Tribune* and send them to Liza in batches of four or five. I wonder if she's allowed to read them. Liza seems to have decided ever since Kate was here to call me 'dad' while baby Maria still calls me Richard or Rich. [...]

[...] I read yesterday a translation of an article in *Oggi* about Florinda Bolkan who says that she could easily have taken me away from Elizabeth, but thought it would be too tedious to try![49] Now this has been said before but never by a fully matured lesbian. She is desperately trying to be a film star and, poor dear, will never make it.

Yesterday's shooting was uneventful. [...] I'm not sure that Rex on occasions is not over-doing the pansy. I never know whether to tell a fellow actor when I think he's going too far. Especially one as testy as Rex. When I screamed

---

[49] Florinda Bolkan (1937—), actor, had played alongside Burton in *Candy*. *Oggi* (Today) is an Italian magazine.

at him in the street, he did the most elaborate hip shuffle. I think I've got mine under control but one is never sure.

I still cannot write that article about RFK I wonder if I can do it between shots. I wrote *Xmas Story* like that, and a lot of *Meeting Mrs Jenkins*.[50] [. . .]

Peter Evans, who was with the *Daily Express*, and a photographer called I think Terry O'Neill, have been on the set for days writing and taking snaps for some article or other.[51] They are both very little, very scruffy, and wear stupendous lifts. Peter, who is very nice, is a perfect example of a semi-literate who makes a very good living from writing. He is even having a book published shortly!

Thursday 10th Yesterday was unique. I didn't see or talk to Elizabeth for an entire day. I felt desperate all day long and suddenly about 5 o'clock began to drink Martinis. By the time I got home I was so drunk and tired that I fell asleep, euphemism for passed out, almost before I'd managed to get my clothes off. I think perhaps, though it is good for her, that I don't like Elizabeth working without me. [. . .]

I received telegrams threatening to sue me in 'six countries' if I didn't agree to do *Anne of The Thousand Days*. I am so sick of being sued that I shall probably agree today. But I shall never work with that lot again. [. . .]

Terry O'Neill, the photographer, told me yesterday that the most rigid professional he knows is Lester Piggott, the Jockey.[52] He wears a rubber sweatsuit permanently, and drinks nothing but coffee, whereas famous footballers like Bobby Charlton of Manchester United and Billy Bremner of Leeds, I think, drink very heavily after having reached a certain peak of physical fitness.[53] Apparently they confine themselves to beer but nevertheless it's amazing to me that they are able to keep running around for two non-stop periods of 45 minutes. I've seen them on TV and it's tiring just to watch them. [. . .]

Friday 11th [. . .] Yesterday we shot outside on the 'London' lot in the morning and I tested my alopecic bald wig in the afternoon. It's horrifying but effective. I've accepted Henry VIII so there will be no suit. However I may sue them for not doing *The Man From Nowhere* later on. It does mean however that we will have a four or five month holiday, which is something we've fondly dreamed of for years. Might even go to Mexico for a couple of months and roast in the sun.

---

[50] Burton is here referring to his published volumes *A Christmas Story* (1965) and *Meeting Mrs Jenkins* (1966).
[51] Terry O'Neill (1938—), famed photographer of the 1960s.
[52] Lester Piggott (1935—).
[53] Bobby Charlton (1937—), of Manchester United and England. Billy Bremner (1942–97), of Leeds United and Scotland.

Or do a trip around the world like Bettina [Krahmer] has just done. [. . .]

I have worked out that with average luck we should, at the end of 1969, be worth about $12 million between us. About $3 million of that is in diamonds, emeralds, property, paintings (Van Gogh, Picasso, Monet, Utrillo, John etc.) so our annual income will be in the region of a $million.[54] That is God Willing, and no wars, and no '29![55]

We are flying, in the small jet (it's a Hawker-Siddeley De Havilland 125 twin jet) to Nice tonight and going on the *Kalizma* for the weekend. I'm longing to see it again. We could come back on Monday morning. Sheran and Simon Hornby are flying in the same plane from London and picking us up.[56] They are a charming couple. Off to work and more later possibly.

Saturday 12th, St Jean Cap Ferrat Aboard the *Kalizma*. We flew last night from Paris. [. . .] We shall go ashore later and probably go to La Ferme Blanche for lunch. Simon and Sheran are with us. They are delightful and so is the boat. The Monet is in the living room or salon, the Picasso and the Van Gogh are in the dining room. The Epstein bust of Churchill is brooding over the salon and there is a Vlaminck on the wall of the stairwell to the kids' cabins.[57] [. . .] we finished early, about 6.45, and I went to pick up E and the guests at the Boulogne Studios. I saw W. Beatty who gave me a drink and was extremely flattering about Elizabeth. He said how remarkably beautiful she was and great a film actress. [. . .] The flight was as smooth as smooth, and took about an hour and a quarter. No one seemed to be nervous but of course we were stiffened by a few drinks. [. . .]

We didn't go to bed until 3.30 because we were so excited at the joy of the boat. I can't as 'twere stop touching it and staring at it, as if it were a beautiful baby or a puppy-dog. Something you can't believe is your very own.

Kevin McCarthy just appeared swimming, if you please, from the Voile d'Or.[58] [. . .] He is coming for lunch tomorrow. [. . .]

It's fascinating to hear the upper-class English accent. When Sheran told me a story this morning about the Dukes of Abercorn which I will again relate tomorrow. And of course when she says Girl she says not Gel but Geal no it's Geall with the accent on the a.

What a sexy girl, gell, geall, she is. And Good as gold.

---

[54] A reference to paintings owned by Burton and Taylor by Vincent Van Gogh (1853–90), Pablo Picasso (1881–1973), Claude Monet (1840–1926), Maurice Utrillo (1883–1955), and Augustus John (1878–1961). The Monet was *Le Val de Falaise*. The Picasso was *La Famille de saltimbanques*.
[55] A reference to the Wall Street stock market 'crash' of 1929.
[56] Sheran Cazalet had married Simon Hornby on 15 June 1968.
[57] Sir Jacob Epstein (1880–1959) had cast a bust of Churchill in 1946. Maurice de Vlaminck (1876–1958), painter.
[58] Kevin McCarthy (1914–2010), actor. Hôtel La Voile d'Or, Avenue Jean Mermoz, Saint Jean Cap Ferrat.

Sunday 13th, Kalizma, Cap Ferrat Yesterday was a very good day. I'm afraid that I was semi-sloshed for most of the day [. . .] but I don't think I was particularly offensive. What a splendidly intelligent couple the Hornbys are. And he particularly is very well read, in some areas as they say, better read than I. There is lots of delicious space left for delicious books. I must too find a corner for reference books and albums etc., which are very large, and will demand height and depth. The new *Times Atlas of the World* for instance is a couple of square feet or so.

[. . .] Elizabeth has great worries about becoming a cripple because her feet sometimes have no feeling in them. She asked if I would stop loving her if she had to spend the rest of her life in a wheelchair. I told her that I didn't care if her legs bum and bosoms fell off and her teeth turned yellow. And she went bald. I love that woman so much sometimes that I cannot believe my luck. She has given me so much.

It's a day of incomparable beauty. A couple of vagrant clouds, church bells from Beaulieu, half a dozen fishing boats, the ship swinging imperceptibly on her anchor, now towards the Voile d'Or now away. There is a very slight breeze. The flag is as lazy as a cat. There won't be many days as memorable as this. You have to recount them, as young Christopher once said, like diamonds in your pocket.

We are going to Rory Cameron's for a drink before lunch.[59] We were going to ask Lana Turner and her husband to lunch but Kevin said the man is a nasty sort of bloke, and so we changed our minds.[60] Kevin is coming and an actor-socialite called George Hamilton.[61] Very charming they say.

Monday 14th, Studio, Paris This morning [. . .] when we arrived at E's studio we heard the mind-shattering news that Ivor, my brother who is paralysed, is able to move his toenails [. . .] on his left foot. This might mean, and we don't ask much, that he will be able to manipulate himself around in a wheelchair, and go to the lav etc. It is the most exciting news I've heard since I received a letter saying I was going up to Oxford. Even more!

We had quite a lot of people for lunch at Saint Jean Cap Ferrat. George Hamilton [. . .] Hal Polaire and his future wife who seemed out of her depth a bit and was ill to boot, a man called Mr Tinker, who has something to do with Universal Pictures, and is the trouble-shooter for them, and his wife with whom we all fell in love, Mary her name is.[62] And of course one of the nicest

[59] Roderick Cameron, owner of Villa Fiorentina.
[60] Lana Turner (1921–95), actor, at this time married to Robert P. Eaton. She had played alongside Burton in *The Rains of Ranchipur*.
[61] George Hamilton (1939–), actor. Hamilton and Taylor would become companions in the 1980s.
[62] Hal W. Polaire (1918–99), who had been assistant to the producer on *Who's Afraid of Virginia Woolf?* Grant Tinker (1925–), producer and television executive, then married to Mary Tyler Moore (1936–).

fuddliest men in the world, who always reminds me of Eliz's brother, Kevin McCarthy. Mary is the girl we saw in *Thoroughly Modern Millie*. One of these days I'll try to spell when I typewrite. She was also in a TV Series with Dick Van Dyke.[63]

Before lunch I went in the Riva to La Fiorentina with Simon and Sheran to visit with Rory Cameron. He was charming as ever, and said that he thought he was going to sell the house sometime in the Spring to a German, but would keep the house, and change it, presently rented by our metteur-en-scene, Stanley Donen.[64] [...] Simon didn't fancy George Hamilton, though we didn't mind him much but on reflection we tended to agree with Simon. E. and Sheran thought he was greasy looking, and I thought he was bit big-headed. [...]

Tuesday 15th, Plaza, Paris Well yesterday was a practically lost day. I wandered about like a stray cat in a dream or under water, but I managed to get through the work OK. Elizabeth felt similarly and out of pure altruism we were joined towards the end of the nightmare by a certain young nurse called Caroline, who at various and unpredictable times would burst into tears, lament about the injustices in the world and pass out against my knee and repeat all those actions at the drop of a cat. And of course we were all so sloshed that the cat was dropped all night.

Walking Caroline down the corridor to her room was like negotiating the *Kalizma* into a narrow berth. She protested endlessly how much she loved us all and how sweet we were. To make this point clear to us she repeated it several hundred times. John Springer to his astonished delight was included in this vast love-affair. She is a dear girl.

At the end of the day we, Rex, Cathleen Nesbitt (who started work yesterday and is marvellous) and I had to attend a sort of press conference.[65] It was the usual ghastly performance. The idolatrous, the contemptuous, the silly question and the sarcastic and scornful. They are of course for the most part the dregs of their own profession and are here only because it's a free trip provided by Fox. Elizabeth has to face them on Thursday.

I am at the studio and have just done one shot with Cathleen. She is brave enough to take out her teeth for the scene. And this concession from one of the great beauties. She looks remarkable despite her nearly 80 years.

---

[63] Moore had played the part of Laura Petrie, wife of Rob Petrie, played by Dick Van Dyke (1925—) in *The Dick Van Dyke Show* (1961–6) and the part of Miss Dorothy Brown in *Thoroughly Modern Millie* (1967).

[64] Cameron sold the villa in 1969 to Mr and Mrs Harding Lawrence. 'Metteur-en-scene' – scene setter. Stanley Donen (1924—), was producer-director of *Staircase*. He and Taylor had been romantically involved in 1951, from the time that he had directed her in *Love is Better Than Ever*.

[65] Cathleen Nesbitt (1888–1982) played the part of Harry's mother (Burton being Harry) in *Staircase*. She would also act in *Villain*.

James Earl Jones has just had an enormous success in a play on Broadway called the *Great White Hope*.[66] We are all delighted for him and the author Howard Sackler.[67] Jimmy is in his 50s so it's about time.[68]

[. . .] I have been drinking too much recently and will slow down.

Wednesday 16th [. . .] Liz Smith sat most of the afternoon in my dressing-room, and we all swapped stories of English malice etc. particularly in the theatre.[69] [. . .]

Another letter from Liza which we've been puzzling over. She has a word in the letter which is 'irastosable'! I don't know what it means but I shall use it for the rest of my life. A new word has been added to the Anglo-Welsh vocabulary. 'What an irastosable day. I found the film absolutely irastosable.' etc. 'What an irastosable performance.' [. . .]

Friday 18th Yesterday I did a scene in the barber shop in which I blow-waved Rex's hair, steam-towelled and massaged his face. Rex became quite hysterical at my ineptitude but finally after endless takes I got it right. It takes place in total silence. And hopefully will send the film off on a good funny start.

I was a bit harassed yesterday by the number of visitors I had. There were two journalists, Tommy Thompson of yesterday, a round lady called Joan Crosby, a photographer, Collette Victor, Christianne and her daughter Anne, Pat Newcomb who always strikes me as being slightly sinister, and somebody who's name I never got.[70]

[. . .] My typing, hunt and peck, as it is, is getting faster and faster. I reckon that I do about forty words and inaccuracies a minute. I wonder why my spelling which is generally very good falls apart when I type. Perhaps because I don't look at the page when I'm hunting and pecking.

[. . .] We have to go to the first night of Rex's film *A Flea in your Ear* tonight.[71] I hear the film is a bit of a bore and the party afterwards is likely to be even more so. Everybody is dressing up to the nines, whatever that may mean, and the Rainiers, Windsors and every Rothschild in Europe will, so I'm told, be there. [. . .]

Sunday 20th What a curious two days. [. . .] I met my future leading lady, a girl called Geneviève Godjot or something like that.[72] She seems pert and attractive though I suspect somewhat opinionated and not overbright. She'll have to

[66] *The Great White Hope* began a run of 546 performances on Broadway on 3 October 1968.

[67] Howard Sackler (1929–82), screenwriter and playwright.

[68] Jones (born 1931) was in fact in his late thirties.

[69] Smith drew on this for a column that appeared in the *New York Times* on 26 January 1969.

[70] Joan Crosby (1934—), journalist and actor.

[71] *A Flea in Her Ear* (Twentieth Century-Fox, 1968), directed by Jacques Charon (1920–75), starring Rex Harrison and Rachel Roberts.

[72] Geneviève Bujold (1942—), was to play the part of Anne Boleyn in *Anne of the Thousand Days*.

do I suppose though I wish E were playing Anne, but I suppose she is too mature for it. Arne Lindroth came to see me and said that it would take 3 to 5 months to have stabilizers put on the boat, so we'll wait.[73] I was also offered the part of Amundsen (the explorer) in a joint Russo-Italian film which they have been filming since last February.[74] [. . .]

Friday began with the English newspapers and the news in headlines that Jackie Kennedy is to marry Ari Onassis. Everybody is intrigued. He is 69, he claims 62, and she is 39. The youngish Queen of the USA and the aging Greek bandit. He is pretty vulgar and one suspects him of orgies and other dubious things whereas the Kennedy woman seems, though I've never met her, to be a lady. On Friday night I sat beside La Callas who very bravely faced the evening and the Press with a bright if rather forced face. I hugged her when I saw her and said in her ear that he was a son of a bitch. This I said not out of moral outrage or because he'd abandoned her but because she learned the news from the newspapers and he'd left her broke. In all those 10 years he, with all his reputed millions, had not given her a cent. Marie-Hélène said he would never be invited to her house again but I told her that she was fibbing and that after a time they, the Onassises, would be the toast of Europe. Even we would go to see them, I said, out of pure curiosity. Guy de Rothschild agreed.

I am ridiculously (I hope) jealous of E nowadays because I suppose she's working with a young and attractive man who obviously adores her. She tells me I'm a fool and that he's like a younger brother. Ah I say but there have been cases of incest. They have been known. Oh Yes. But of course I trust her as much as I trust myself [. . .]

We are going out tonight with Maria Callas and Warren Beatty. It appears that the former needs our company and comfort and perhaps the attention we attract [. . .]. But I noticed on Friday night that most attention was paid by the Press and Public to Ebeth. She, my girl, looked stunning in a white dress by Dior and, to my surprise as I discovered later, wore for the first time in Paris the great emerald necklace and earrings etc. which I gave her 3 or 4 years ago. My God she's a beauty. Sometimes even now, after nearly 8 years of marriage I look at her when she's asleep at the first light of a grey dawn and wonder at her.

Inevitably this capacity of Ebeth's to attract oohs and ahs didn't go down well with Rex and Rachel Harrison, and inexorably as the evening ground on and as they got drunker and drunker the dam broke. They got into our car by mistake with Rachel screaming at our driver Gaston and shouting insults at us tho' we were out of sight and sound. Then still hustled and bustled by the photographers and carefully protecting Bettina and Cathleen Nesbitt as we made slow progress towards the car, Rex came storming up to us and said

---

[73] Arne Lindroth (1910–85), a marine expert, was advising Burton on the seaworthiness of the *Kalizma*.
[74] The film was *Krasnaya Palatka* (1969: US title *The Red Tent*), which starred Sean Connery (1930—) as Roald Amundsen (1872–1928) the Norwegian explorer, and first man to reach the South Pole.

something like: Come on you Burtons you're deliberately holding everyone up. Get yourselves and your lot into your car and home. Since they were in our car this was not easy so we compromised and went home in theirs. This kind of behaviour from drunken Rex and sotted Rachel is so common now that it is no surprise. What a pair of bores they are when they're drunk. At one point during the evening Rachel who was sitting opposite me and beside Alexis Redé picked up a knife and said that she was going to kill Rex because he had left the table at the same time as an Italian actress called Virna Lisi beside whom he was sitting. I tried to calm her but she took no notice of me. Eventually a very nice girl called Elizabeth Harris, who is the daughter of the Labour no Liberal Peer Lord Ogmore, got the knife away from her.[75] Marie-Hélène was genuinely frightened and said how much she feared drunken people. That endearing young bitch Jacqueline de Ribes was the other side of me during this demonstration of Rachel's and of course enjoyed every minute of it.

The whole evening was a fiasco for everyone except our party. First the film was mediocre. Then the dinner party was catastrophic. [. . .] The place, I still don't know where it is, was so overcrowded that the waiters had difficulty in getting between the tables. A great many people never were served at all. Hair-dos and Tiaras were knocked over or askew by desperately over-worked waiters. Rachel at one point having been jostled from behind by some poor sod of a waiter for the umpteenth time threated to kill him as well as Rex! At another point she started feeling and hugging Alexis de Redé who was aristocratically polite. [. . .] I wouldn't be disenchanted if I never saw Rex and Rachel drunk again. We got to bed about 7.30 in the morning and got up at 10 to go and visit Paul-Emile Victor and his family. We were naturally a bit shaky but they were very kind. We visited with them a houseboat which costs $70,000 and which we might buy. It would cost at least as much again to fix up Beth says. I still yearn for a converted power barge. Why shouldn't I? Life is very short and we give away a great deal of money. [. . .]

Last night we had for what was supposed to be drinks but turned out to be supper as well and went on till 2 in the morning, Linda Mortimer and her husband Henry, an American and a nice young man called Bill who say that they can virtually guarantee us an average of 34% interest on our investments. It seems incredible. Should I give them a million dollars and see what they do with it in a year. An income of $340,000 a year from a million is staggering to the imagination. I told them that my idea of absolute financial bliss was an annual income of a million dollars a year. Without working. They thought that very reasonable. It's a far cry from 1925 and the helpless poverty of the valleys.

---

[75] Elizabeth Harris (1936—), daughter of David Rees-Williams, Baron Ogmore, and at this time married to the actor Richard Harris. She and Rex Harrison would marry in 1971 and divorce in 1976.

A beautiful morning, Bessie still asleep, dogs and cat running around, so now to wake my blissly beautiful animal girl and read the Sunday newspapers together. I am fantastically lucky. Don't spoil it nobody, boys, fellers.

Monday 21st Another beautiful but cold morning. Onassis married Jackie to what appears to be the general disapproval of the USA. At least that's what the papers say. We shall send them a telegram of congratulations today sometime. Dick Hanley says she will be declared a 'public sinner.' I said that she should be declared a public winner. In a comical world the Vatican is sometimes the most comical thing in it. I remember some years ago that the *Osservatore Romano*, however one spells it, recommended that Elizabeth was an unfit mother for her children and that they should be forcibly removed from her![76] Silly pompous asses.

We spent the day quietly and got out of the Callas Beatty dinner. Three nights in a row for people who hardly dine with others or outside more than once a week when we're working is a bit strong. [. . .]

I wrote a longish letter to Kate. The next two tasks are letters to Mike and Chris. I am very bad about letter writing and always have been. I have just acquired a four volume collection of Orwell's papers and he had the same problem but to an agonising degree.[77] For an innately courteous man it is very hard on the conscience to find yourself hiding letters in drawers because of your feeling of guilt. Then suddenly I will write 20 in a morning and then perhaps nothing for a month except absolute musts like letters to the children, especially Kate in New York as I see her less than anyone. [. . .]

Tuesday 22nd I went to work slightly apprehensive of Rex's reaction to Friday night's fiasco. I learned that Rachel and Rex were standing near their car after the supper was over being photographed when suddenly the photographers saw Eliz appearing and abandoned the two Harrisons. Rachel in a red Welsh fury screamed 'I'm the star of this fucking show not that fucking Elizabeth Taylor etc.' The photographers took no notice but it was in the cheaper French papers next day so Tommy Thompson told me. I can understand her feelings but the one way to attract indignity is to shout it to the Press. Ingrid Bergman who was there and who was equally ignored was as calm and regal as ever.[78] She is still very beautiful. Thank God the Windsors and the Rainiers had the sense not to turn up. The film had bad notices. [. . .] Apart from our own first nights, and if possible, not even those, we are not going to such childish affairs again. [. . .]

---

[76] Burton means the Vatican newspaper the *Osservatore della Domenica*, which in 1962 had condemned Taylor for 'erotic vagrancy'.
[77] George Orwell, *The Collected Essays, Journalism and Letters of George Orwell*, edited by Sonia Orwell and Ian Angus (4 vols, 1968).
[78] Ingrid Bergman (1915–82), actor.

The Onassis Kennedy thing still fills the papers. It's odd that you have to search for the news of the three Yanks in orbit in the Apollo.[79] The Vatican says that Mrs Onassis has sinned against her church etc as expected as ever. We sent Onassis a telegram of congratulations yesterday.

Tommy Thompson told me an oddly flat little story yesterday. He said that the American Ambassador Shriver was shooting with the General on his estates with other Ambassadors, when he, Shriver, a self-confessed poor shot brought down a bird.[80] It landed with a thud two feet from the General. And the General said, (wait for it!) 'Splendide.' Now the odd thing is that both Thompson, fairly hard-boiled and very cynical about other public figures and Shriver, who presumably has met a great many Kings and Counsellors of the earth, should consider this nothing story indicative of the courage, sagacity and wit of De Gaulle. The impact of this old fraud's personality must be enormous for that one word to receive the awed report of the head of *Life* Magazine in Europe and the American Ambassador. I'd kick him in the arse if I could reach that high. [. . .]

Wednesday 23rd Elizabeth tells me that Jacqueline de Ribes, Marie Helene, <u>and</u> Baron Alexis are all mad for Warren Beatty. They continually phone E or Warren or each other scheming to get him. Poor bastard. The only really attractive one to my mind is Bettina. But what a world. One's read of the upper-class French morality but never really believed it, or thought it out of date. But not a bit of it. Jacqueline has several lovers and her husband knows it. He has a mistress and his wife knows it. Marie Helene has a lover who is Alexis who has a lover who is a man. Bettina has many lovers but she is rather square in that she is not married. Phew! All this gossip I get from Elizabeth in whom they confide. I have an idea that Marie Helene and Jacqueline were after me for a time about two years ago but gave me up as a bad job.

[. . .] The Onassises have disappeared completely from the front pages and for the most part from the papers altogether. I told Elizabeth that they didn't have our stamina. I also said with great smugness that he had given her a wedding present of only 'slightly less than £100,000 of diamonds precious stones etc.' whereas I had only recently given a £127,000 diamond ring simply because it was a Tuesday. I enjoy being outrageous with Beth. [. . .]

Thursday 24th I have a very tedious couple of days ahead of me I suspect. It is likely to be so because I wear the completely bald alopecian wig. It is not porous and once on cannot be taken off, so I am going to sweat a great great

---

[79] Apollo 7, the first crewed Apollo flight, had launched on 11 October and would splash down on 22 October. The three astronauts were Walter Schirra (1923–2007), Donn Eisele (1930–87) and Walter Cunningham (1932–).
[80] Robert Sargent Shriver (1915–2011), American Ambassador to France (1968–70), and husband of Eunice Kennedy (1921–2009), thus brother-in-law to both John F. and Robert F. Kennedy.

deal. Still for a $1 [million] and a quarter a picture one mustn't grumble. But of course I will. Elizabeth also is receiving $1¼ [million] for her picture. That will mean that this year we will have earned in cash between us $4½ [million]. Which is immoral. In addition to this there are many percentages coming in e.g. $½m from *Shrew*. Roughly a million goes out on living and overheads, yacht and crew, plane and pilots, secretaries and staff chauffeurs. Aaron Frosch once said that between us we created as much business as a small African state. I can believe him. There is, however and plainly, quite a profit. Of course once we stop working the overheads will drop tremendously but even so it will cost about $¼ [million] a year to live on our particular scale. [. . .]

I have been drinking much less lately and feel much better for it. I wish I could stop smoking and get my taste-buds back in order again. It is a pity to be missing on one gastronomic cylinder with such largesse abroad in Paris. However we hardly ever go out to eat and the food in the hotel though splendid in the dining room downstairs is indifferent once carried upstairs. I noticed that at the Savoy and the Dorchester too. I'm told that they are different kitchens. We have now put in a tiny two-burner stove upon which Beth can cook at the weekends and on which I can make my packaged soups and tea in the dead vast and middle of the night.[81]

I awoke this morning at about 5.30, and got up after vainly trying to go back to sleep, at 6.30. I ran over the scenes I have to do today and tomorrow, read the *Herald Tribune*, and went back to bed about 8.30. I fell into a night-mared sleep so profound that E had difficulty in waking me at 10.15. I complained albeit gently that I didn't have to be in work until one o'clock. For some reason I dreamt about Herbert Humphrey and we were riding in a motor-cycle side-car to a place that I think on reflection was either Northampton, England, or an outer featureless suburb like Croydon.[82] I must be worried about the American elections without being all that consciously aware. Cor mate.

Friday 25th Yesterday, because I anticipated the worst, was better than expected and Ron did an excellent job with the bald wig. Judiciously lighted it looks absolutely authentic. Elizabeth thinks it looks lovely and that I look as good as Yul Brynner! [. . .]

Despite being self warned about yesterday's discomforts I was still like a bear all day long, but kept myself under control for the most part until at the end of the day I had a few drinks and started being more and more sarcastic until in the end, by the time I arrived home I was downright boorish and did

---

[81] 'In the dead vast and middle of the night' is a line from *Hamlet*, Act I, scene ii, although it is often rendered 'dead waste and middle of the night'.
[82] Burton must mean Hubert Humphrey (1911–78), Vice-President of the USA and the Democratic Party candidate for the presidency in the 1968 election.

my usual trick of going to bed in the other room alone. Why, as Ivor says, do I do it?

One of the actors in E's film called Charles Braswell called and had a drink in my room.[83] [. . .] Obviously awed that he is acting opposite E, he told stories rather desperately about Lucille Ball and Angela Lansbury, trying to show, no doubt, that ETB was not the only starfish in the sea.[84] I told him not to worry about my lady and that she was infinitely easy to work with. I suspect it is his first film role though he has been around Broadway for years. He is about 45 years old I guess, and that's late to begin in films.[85]

The enemy is insidiously attacking again. Beth read in the papers that Ari Onassis had given Jackie half a million pounds worth of rubies surrounded by diamonds. Now Missy already has, as a result of former battles against useless yours-truly, one of the greatest diamonds in the world and probably the most breathtaking private collection of emeralds surrounded by diamonds also in the world. Now the Battle of the Rubies is on. I wonder who'll win. It will be a long attritive war and the idea has already been implanted that I shouldn't let myself be out-done by a bloody Greek. I can be just as vulgar as he can, I say to myself. Well now to get the money.

Elliott Kastner came from London yesterday and told about flying to the Palace Hotel in Montreux to read Nabokov's new book, which he hasn't yet finished, and for which he asks $1m.[86] All the film boys have been flying into Switzerland in a desperate attempt to be the first to press a million green ones into his hot little Russian palm. How was the book, I said to Kastner? Great, he said. How long is it, I asked? Eight hundred pages. How the devil did you manage to read it in six hours? [. . .] Well, he said, I read half and Alan (his friend and assistant) read the other half. How then, I said, can you tell it's a great book? You've only read half of an unfinished book. He said he trusted Alan's judgement and presumably Nabokov's too. Funny way to buy a book. [. . .]

Saturday 26th Yesterday I finished the scene in which I am wearing the bald wig [   ] It only remains for me to be off-stage for Rex on Monday, who declined to work the full time because he had a series of tongue-twisting speeches and was tiring rapidly he said. [. . .] So we will begin half an hour earlier on Monday.

Elliott Kastner had lunch with us in the dressing room. [. . .] Elliott wants Elizabeth to do a film at the same time as I do *Anne of the Thousand Days*. Since so far he has been a man of his word it might be a good idea [. . .] because Beth plainly enjoys working when the script, people and co-star or stars are

[83] Charles Braswell (1924–74) played the part of Thomas J. Lockwood in *The Only Game in Town*.
[84] Lucille Ball (1911–89), actor, television star. Angela Lansbury (1925—), actor. ETB: Elizabeth Taylor Burton.
[85] This was Braswell's first major film role.
[86] Vladimir Vladimirovich Nabokov (1899–1977), novelist, poet, literary scholar.

congenial. And it's much better for her than sitting at home and twiddling her thumbs. Apart from anything else Bess does no shopping herself. Everything has to be sent to the Hotel as there is a mob scene generally after she's been in a shop for more than twenty minutes. [...] So the common ordinary joys of shopping, which can deliciously, at least for women, waste endless time are denied to the poor little rich girl.

Rachel Harrison came to my room about 6 o'clock and proceeded very quickly to get drunk. While she was there Elizabeth called me from the Hotel, she had a day off yesterday, and I asked Rache if she'd like to speak to her. Yes, she said, and then, without any preamble, began to bark into the phone. Literally. Like her dog – an adorable Basset Hound called Homer. And that's all she did. Barked and barked. Eliz tells me she was so embarrassed that she didn't know what to do. She is a mad case of alcoholism. After the idiocy of her behaviour last Friday night she had the drunken effrontery to ask me if she were allowed to apologise on my behalf for what Rosemary Harris considered to be an insult on that same night, namely that I'd pinched her bottom and said 'I detest you.'[87] Now first of all, I behaved well that night. Secondly, I've never pinched anyone's bottom in my life, I've patted them. Thirdly, from a Welsh miner or his son, 'I detest you' to someone he is very fond of means 'I adore you.' Which in Rosemary's case is true, and which she knows. Rex, hearing the tail-end of Rachel's tale said that she had got it all wrong and that Rosemary was actually not complaining but telling her new husband <u>how sweet and unchanged I was</u>, so there! Anyway Rosemary is 40 years old and I've patted her bottom for about 15 years incessantly telling her how much I loathe her. Rachel was obviously trying to obviate her own guilt.

Sunday 27th It's 10.30 in the morning and a dullish kind of day. We are going out to lunch in the village where Maurice Chevalier lives, somewhere in the forest of St Cloud.[88] The restaurant is called La Tete Negre or something like that.[89]

Yesterday we stayed in all day, read newspapers, did crosswords and read detective stories. I also read part of the first volume of Holroyd's book about Lytton Strachey. I had read the second volume first while E was in hospital this summer. The first volume is obviously not, so far, going to be as enthralling as the second. It is painstakingly copious but may pick up a bit as it gets on. [...]

Earlier on this week in this diary I had said that we might be going down to the yacht this weekend because there was a public holiday on Friday. This is

[87] Rosemary Harris (1925—), who had appeared in *A Flea in Her Ear*, and who had played alongside Burton in the Old Vic production of *Othello*.
[88] Maurice Chevalier (1888–1972), actor and singer, lived at Marnes-la-Coquette in the western suburbs of Paris, close to the Forest of Fausses-Reposes and to the Parc de Saint-Cloud.
[89] Restaurant de la Tête Noire, Place Mairie, Marnes-la-Coquette.

not so. The holiday is next weekend, The following guests are due, and I thought it was going to be a quiet three days: Princess Elizabeth of Jugoslavia and a friend of hers, Bettina, Norma Heyman and her lover, Caroline, Simoleke, a friend of the boys' from Millfield and of course the boys themselves.[90] With us that makes a total of twelve, which is practically a full house. I hope to God the weather's good or it's going to be pretty close quarters for such a mob. I am longing to see the boys and can always slope off with them to Nice, with Elizabeth [. . .]

The Sunday papers are fairly dull today and the Olympics are down to the dreary stage of canoeing and foils etc. and has none of the drama of the demonstrations of 'black power' which we had last week from Tommie Smith and Carlos.[91] Sammy Davis Jun. told me the last time he was in Paris, a couple of weeks ago, that it was no longer considered kosher or 'in' to call Negroes Negroes but blacks. From nigger to negro to black to brown betcha!

Monday 28th Yesterday was a strange and semi-lost one. We went to lunch at a restaurant called Hostellerie de la Tete Noire. Megirl was a little late getting ready which for some reason, and I should be used to it by now, threw me into a fury which I didn't really recover from all day. I tried my damnedest to be nice later on at lunch and later on again when Simoleke arrived but my bloody temper kept on breaking through. I went for a long walk with my little dog and got myself thoroughly lost. As usual I had gone out without money in my pocket and so I couldn't stop and have a drink, which perhaps is just as well. I was in some very deserted street, very odd that it should be so empty and silent while only, as I discovered later, a stone's throw from the Champs Elysees, when a sort of hard-bitten girl came around the corner. I swallowed my pride at being lost and asked her 'Ou est l'avenue Montaigne, s'il vous plait?' 'I don't know,' she replied in English. I thanked her and walked on. Suddenly I realized she had turned and was walking beside me. 'Vous aimez Paris?' she asked. 'Oui, je l'adore,' I replied, picked up E'en So and crossed the road in a sort of urgent half-walk half-trot as if I were the prettiest little virgin in town. I had been made a pass at! First time for years. I wonder if she was a tart.

[. . .] When I arrived back in the hotel I persuaded E to put on some slacks promising that I would take her and Sime to the pizzeria. I of course couldn't find it and we ended up at Fouquet's where we had 'Haddock Poche a L'Anglaise' with 'Pommes Vapeur.'[92] We washed it down with a bottle of Hock.

Simoleke became very tearful because, she said, she felt so guilty about her luck in being adopted by Howard and Mara while the rest of her family, there

[90] Princess Elizabeth of Yugoslavia (1936—), later to enjoy a brief engagement to Burton.
[91] Burton is referring here to the clenched fist salutes given on the podium by Black American sprinters Tommie Smith (1944—) and John Carlos (1945—), who had won gold and bronze medals respectively in the men's 200m at the 1968 Olympic Games in Mexico City.
[92] Fouquet's on the Champs-Elysées.

are 16 in all, were living in uneducated poverty in Samoa. We said that when she started to earn money she could help them out, at least financially, as I have helped my family and Elizabeth hers. But it was hard to console her. [. . .] I suspected that she was something less than loyal to Howard and Mara but E says I am mistaken. I love Howard and Mara so much and admire them so greatly, particularly Howard, that I may be over-protective. And we know how deeply he loves the girl and how much disciplined agony it must cost him to send her half way around the world away from him.

Riots in London yesterday and a front-page picture of a Bobby being kicked in the face.[93] I don't know where my sympathies lie, my own two boys will be on those marches before long, but if either of them kicked somebody else in the face without provocation I would be constrained to kick him sharply in the behind. Not that either of them would ever do such a thing, he said fondly and hopefully. [. . .]

Tuesday 29th I received a letter from Francis Warner yesterday asking if I could or would become a don at St Peter's, Oxford, sometime shortly.[94] I am very excited and am going to write to him suggesting that I should go up for the summer of 1970. He will, he says, give us his chambers and I shall offer to swap them for the yacht and our various houses. He needs a sabbatical he says. How funny it will be to be lecturing at Oxford without a degree! Now I've always had this pregnant woman's yearning for the academic life, probably spurious, and a term of smelly tutorials and pimply lectures should effect a sharp cure. I would like to deal with either the mediaeval poets in English, French, Italian and German and possibly some of the Celtic like Welsh and Irish, or to confine myself to the 'Fantasticks' Donne, Traherne, Henry Vaughn George Herbert. The first poem in English that ever commanded my imagination:

> Sweet day, so cool so calm so bright,
> The Bridal of the earth and sky,
> The dew shall weep thy fall tonight,
> For thou must die.
>
> Sweet Rose whose hue angry and brave,
> Bids the rash gazer wipe his eye,
> Thy root is ever in its grave,
> And thou must die.[95]

---

[93] There were anti-war demonstrations outside the American Embassy in Grosvenor Square, London on 27 October. 'Bobby' is a British term for a police officer.

[94] Francis Warner, tutor in English Literature at St Peter's College, Oxford, and a friend of Burton.

[95] John Donne (1572–1631), Thomas Traherne (1637–94), Henry Vaughan (1621–95) and George Herbert (1593–1633), poets. The poem quoted (first two verses) is Herbert's 'Virtue'. The third verse includes the line 'A box where sweets compacted lie'.

And that's not all. I mean that chap Herbert was indeed a box where sweets compacted lay. I am as thrilled by the English language as I am by a lovely woman or dreams, green as dreams and deep as death.[96] Christ I'm off and running and will lecture them until iambic pentameter comes out of their nostrils. Little do they know how privileged they are to speak and read and think in the greatest language invented by man. I'll learn them.

We went to see a houseboat last night, after finishing work, with Simmy. It was the houseboat 'with the Yellow Roof' as Elizabeth describes it. As usual, her instinct is uncanny. It turned out to be a beauty. We might buy it, if it's for sale. We dined with Paul-Emile and his wife, sister-in-law and niece on board <u>his</u> houseboat. I became rather sloshed but not offensively so, I hope. I told him about the film offer in re Nobile and Amundsen.[97] [. . .]

I have been offered, is that spelled right?, a million dollars for <u>one month</u> of this diary. Somebody is mad. And I is not it. But I wonder if it would be interesting. I would, after all, like to read the diary of an office-worker. Might people be interested in reading a month in the life of an actor, especially one married to such an exotic wife as mine?

Wednesday 30th It's 6 o'clock in the morning and I have been awake since 4.30 approximately. [. . .] I am going to have a bowl of soup in about ten minutes, the kind one makes oneself out of a packet, as it were. We have a couple of hot-plates.

I feel roughly one thousand years old, and have the old familiar arthritis 'old Arthur' back. But not in my shoulders or neck or arms but for a change in my left hip. When I get these little bursts, I realize the stoicism of people like Kathleen Nesbitt and little Gwen, who live with it for years without a complaint. Mine, compared with theirs, is nothing but a kind of mild, dull toothache. [. . .]

[. . .] The piece I wrote, <u>at his request</u>, about Roddy Mann's book called, I think, *The Headliner*, is quoted in the *Evening Standard* against me.[98] 'Burton Lashes Out,' it says in the headlines. They also say, insultingly, that I mix a metaphor. It is quite deliberate. Idiots, but it is extraordinary how sensitive the insensitive press is when it is attacked. But I have to think that like most men Roddy Mann is venal, and will do anything for a mention in the newspapers, and sad it is because he fairly bristles with insignificance. I could write better with my left foot. But what the devil or the dickens or the hell, we have to make a living or die and there are worse things than writing for the popular press,

---

[96] A reference to the poem 'The Old Vicarage, Grantchester', by Rupert Brooke (1887–1915), which includes the line 'Green as a dream and deep as death'.
[97] Peter Finch played the part of General Umberto Nobile (1885–1978), Arctic explorer.
[98] Roderick Mann, *The Headliner* (1968). 'Burton Broadside', *Evening Standard*, 23 October 1968. Burton's mixed metaphor is quoted thus: 'Yet these particular rats, like the worms that Noah forgot to put on the Ark, are necessary. When, as it were, the chips are down, the rats can turn into Rajahs.'

like dying of malnutrition in Biafra.[99] I shall now have my soup and nutrite myself for another day. God save us all and Oscar Wilde.[100]

[. . .] Simmy came to work with me yesterday and nearly ruined a 'take' by laughing in the middle of it. Fortunately her snort was not picked up on the sound-track. She's not the only one. A lot of people apparently find Rex and myself very difficult to watch without laughing. Sometimes indeed we laugh at each other. I hope the paying audience feel the same way.

[. . .] We have a little holiday this weekend. Tomorrow, I mean Friday is a French national holiday. I must find out what for.[101] A letter from Phil yesterday in which he goes into ecstasies over E's performance in *Secret Ceremony*.[102] [. . .]

Thursday 31st An early start today as we have to stop for lunch at 12.15 for the Duke and Duchess of Windsor. They are visiting E's studios and then ours, if the old man is not too tired and are taking lunch there. So this day we have to be ready to start shooting at ten instead of 12 noon. Tonight we fly to Nice in a chartered Mystere. I wonder what she's like. I have become so used to the De Havilland by now. We shall come back by train on the famous Train Bleu.[103] [. . .]

I spent most of yesterday in a bath with a lot of body make-up on, which meant when I came home that Elizabeth had to wash my back. I was back to the mines again, and the wives washing their husbands' backs clean of the grime of the colliery.

[. . .] Must leave for work, it is going on for 9.30 and I mustn't be late or it upsets my whole day. E's still asleep.

NOVEMBER

Friday 1st, Cannes[104] Well here we are on the *Kalizma* in Cannes, and it was silly to make this journey because the weather here is terrible while in Paris it is beautiful and even in England. And in the *Nice-Matin*, to accentuate my terror, there is a headline which says: 'Ramon Novarro, le grand suducteur du [*sic*] cinema muet, ASSASSINE A HOLLYWOOD.'[105] Poor bastard. There but for the grace of God . . .

---

[99] A reference to the starvation crisis and civil war in Biafra, Nigeria that was taking place at the time.
[100] Oscar Wilde (1854–1900), poet, dramatist, novelist, wit.
[101] All Saints' Day (1 November) is a national holiday in France.
[102] *Secret Ceremony*, the film starring Taylor, Mia Farrow and Robert Mitchum (1917–97) which had appeared earlier in the year.
[103] The Train Bleu ran between Paris and Vintimille in Italy.
[104] Cannes, city and port on the French Riviera, to the west of Monaco and Saint Jean Cap Ferrat.
[105] Ramón Novarro (1899–1968), actor, had been murdered at his home in Laurel Canyon, Hollywood. *Nice-Matin*: the Nice daily paper.

[. . .] Everybody on board was charming and gracious except for Norma's boy-friend, who is suffering from a bad attack, which may be permanent, of refusing to be impressed. I feel sorry for him poor bastard. He was one of those pop-singers who didn't survive his first success. He went to Westminster, so he says, which surprised me as he doesn't have a public school accent. He was fired, he says with some pride. His name is Gordon something and I kept on calling him Neil.[106] That didn't help. He is not worthy of Norma.

The boys [. . .] were lovely and Mike is now only an inch away from being my height. Chris is shooting up too. The latter asks such naive and sweet questions that it makes me breathless.

We flew back, instead of taking a train, because we couldn't get proper sleepers on the Wagon Lit of the blue train [. . .]. Mike, reluctant to leave on the second leg of the journey to Bristol and school, said 'Richard, make just one more corny pun before we leave.' Bloody cheek! He genuinely hates school, but I'm afraid he simply has to stay there. At least until next summer.

I took the whole mob to Colombe d'Or, and after a splendid meal with splendid wines the owners refused to let me pay.[107]

Tuesday 5th, Paris The last few paragraphs of the preceding entry were written last night after work. The weekend was so thoroughly disorganized that I couldn't settle down to either read or write. One night for instance none of us went to bed until 4, 5, or six in the morning. And as a result of this behaviour I slept one day until 4.30 in the afternoon! Now I've never done that before in my life, except possibly when I have worked nights, and I doubt it even then.

Yesterday I felt ghastly and found that only the hair of the dog would meet the justice of the case. So I tried Fernet Branca, but couldn't face it.[108] After a time I tried some bacon and eggs which I managed to get down and keep down – I had been throwing up before leaving for work. I was then able to drink slowly a couple of Martinis or so which stopped the shakes. Later on I had a couple more and another two before going home. [. . .]

I took a sleeping pill and didn't get to sleep until 6 in the morning! What a night. [. . .] So I read most of the night, a book on cricket by E. W. Swanton.[109] He's not very evocative and nothing like as good as Cardus and John Arlott.[110] But he helped to while away the night.

Princess Elizabeth came over to the set. She is very pretty but quite impertinent. I am not absolutely sure that she might be a little nasty behind one's back. Tiny touch of the daggers. Just a feeling. She seemed to enjoy Rex's

---

[106] Gordon Waller (1945–2009), formerly combined with Peter Asher in the pop duo 'Peter and Gordon'.
[107] La Colombe d'Or, Saint-Paul-de-Vence, inland from Cagnes-sur-Mer on the Mediterranean coast.
[108] Fernet Branca is an Italian brand of the spirit Fernet, often used for hangovers.
[109] E. W. (Jim) Swanton (1907–2000), cricket writer and commentator. His *Cricket from All Angles* appeared in 1968.
[110] Neville Cardus (1888–1975) and John Arlott (1914–91), both writers on cricket.

inability to remember lines. [...] She was off to dinner with Warren Beatty. She was quite excited but pretended she wasn't.

Off to work in a minute. Oh the smelly man, who is Norma's boyfriend, on the train home from the South of France got drunk and smashed the glasses dishes etc in the train's dining car. He was taken off at some stop en route by the police whereupon he started hitting them. They can keep you for a long time in French gaols if they want to and I was surprised to find that he got out the next morning. Apparently Norma said that it was an act 'passionalle' or whatever it is, and that she'd been insulted by some Arab on the train and her friend was defending her honour. So they took her word for it and he was released. Besides she's a very pretty sexy looking woman.

Election Day today in America, and Guy Fawkes.[111] I hope it's not an omen.

Wednesday 6th Quarter past nine in the morning. Just called Dick Hanley to find out who'd won the Election. Nixon is ahead but they're waiting for the results of the Texas and California voting before they're sure.[112]

Yesterday I worked on and off all day, Rex going mad with his lines again. Maria Callas arrived and since I was in a reading mood she was not welcome. She seems pathetic to me despite her great reputation as an opera singer-actress. She said how she was meeting some Italian in ten days time who wanted her to do *Medea* as a film, but the operatic version, whereas she insists on doing it as in the original, i.e. without singing.[113] [...] I summoned up as much good nature with Callas however as I could and took her on the set a couple of times to watch a couple of snippets that Rex and I were doing. She averred as to how fascinating she found it all, and after a time, much to my relief went to Elizabeth's studio which she'd already visited once. E told me later that she too found her rather sad. She was there when E and Caroline were playing Gin-Rummy and sat and watched like a child. At one moment E was beaten easily by a quick Gin by Caroline and said 'shit'. At this Callas shot up and said in great agitation 'Oh no I've never heard such words, Oh no, no, no, never heard such things.' All this time pacing up and down in great ado. E and Caroline were astonished. Now what was that all about? Next time she comes to see me I'm going to try 'Merde' on her and see what happens. She is not beautiful but her face has a black-eyed animation which can sometimes be very attractive. She has massive legs and what seems a slender body from the

---

[111] A reference to the Gunpowder Plot of 1605 in which an attempt was made by a number of conspirators including Guy Fawkes (1570–1606) to blow up the Houses of Parliament in London.
[112] The Republican candidate Richard Nixon won 43.4% of the popular vote, 32 states, and 301 votes in the electoral college, as against 42.7% of the vote, 13 states (plus the District of Columbia) and 191 votes for the Democratic candidate Hubert Humphrey. George Wallace, running as an Independent, won 13.5% of the vote, 5 states and 46 votes.
[113] Robinson Jeffers's (1887–1962) adaptation of the Greek tragedy of Medea for the stage (1947) and the 1797 opera *Médée* by Luigi Cherubini (1760–1842).

waist up. She has bags under her eyes and wears dark glasses most of the time. Perhaps she cries a lot. She is obviously very lonely after the Onassis marriage. Now she obviously wants to do something that will stagger the artistic world and make him jealous and prove to him that all he's gained is a pretty socialite, while in her he's lost a genius. Quite right too I suppose but without knowing her, and if I had the choice, I'm afraid I'd elect for Jackie Kennedy. She sounds more fun. And in snaps anyway looks prettier.

[. . .] I've had a bad sore throat for the last three days and a blister on my tongue, but this morning both seem better. [. . .] I cut down my smoking yesterday and didn't drink a drop all day.

Thursday 7th The hacking cough that has kept me awake for nights was killed last night by a pill. [. . .] My sore throat is gone. I haven't coughed once since I awoke. I have a bottle of Perrier straight from the fridge at my right hand, cigarettes at my left, the Avenue Montaigne below and in front of me, it's ten to nine in the morning and apart from the fact that Nixon has won the Yankee Election, all's right with the world[114]. Of course a child dies of starvation every minute somewhere in the world, Biafrans are being slaughtered in ambush, napalm is burning babies in Vietnam, and what shall we do about it? 'Good Works' as those hideous upper-class Victorians revelled in. A cauldron of soup and a loaf for Mrs Lewis in the village. She's not too well. Read *Pilgrim's Progress* to dying Mr Jones, illiterate Mr Jones, and go home afterwards to a 7 course dinner, swollen with sanctity.[115] A great house, fifty servants, sweeping lawns, follies and vistas and oak drives and no drainage in the village.

Hullo, and what's the matter with me?

We had a charming and very excited letter from Liza yesterday [. . .]. I have developed a love for that child that is in danger of becoming obsessive. She is so honest about what she wants but generous also. She can of course, as far as I'm concerned, have anything she wants. I have promised her a pony if she gets to Millfield or wherever. I must find out if the school or schools will permit it. I wrote to her yesterday and shall write again shortly.

Yesterday was a miserable working day. [. . .] I am at that stage, which I reach in every film, where everything seems boring and silly. The same thing happens in the theatre with me too. After a month of a run in a play I become suicidally bored, even with parts of infinite variety like Hamlet. And yet I keep on doing it. I'm a rich man. Why don't I pack it in and do some 'Good Works' afore-mentioned? Grow two blades of grass where one grew before and all that. I couldn't grow grass in a window-box or hammer a nail in a wall without hammering a finger in with it. I'd better just continue to give money to charity.

---

[114] Robert Browning (1812–89), *Pippa Passes* (1841), includes the lines 'The lark's on the wing; / The snail's on the thorn; / God's in his Heaven – / All's right with the world!'
[115] John Bunyan (1628–88), *Pilgrim's Progress* (1678–84).

I am reading two books at once: A political biography of de Gaulle and another of Pierre Laval.[116] So far there seems little to choose between them, except height. Scheming, conniving, disloyal monomaniacal monsters, both protesting their love of la belle France. Of the two de Gaulle seems to be the bigger liar. But in politics all men are liars. The squalor of the latest Election campaign in the States has to be read to be disbelieved.

Friday 8th [. . .] After completing yesterday's entry with milady fast asleep in bed as I thought, I was looking through some scenes in the script when suddenly the bedroom door opened and standing there in a near diaphanous nightgown with one shoulder slipped on to her arm was E. So I went back to bed for ten minutes. I was unquestionably seduced and I teased her about it for the rest of the day when we talked on the telephone. She was very beautiful. It is a fact that after all these years the girl can still blush. I lost that latter capacity a long long time ago.

I am reading *My Life* by Sir Oswald Mosley between shots at the Studio, but I fear that I shan't get much done today in that direction as I have John Morgan of the *Sunday Times*, John Sullivan, Elliott Kastner [. . .] all self-invited, coming to visit me at the dressing room.[117] Are they on business, are they on pleasure? I wish they'd all go away.

Yesterday was a hard day physically. Rex and I did innumerable shots fighting on the floor of the living room. Now film fighting is relatively easy because one can cheat on angles etc. but when you have to remember to fight like a queer it complicates things. In addition I had to keep in mind that I must keep my head covered at all costs. It follows that since we rolled around on the floor for most of the day that I am a little grazed and a little sore this morning. Not unpleasantly so. I hope it turns out to be as funny as it seemed to the crew.

[. . .] I have compromised on smoking to the extent that, when I remember, which is most of the time, I don't inhale and only smoke about a ¼ inch of the cigarette and throw it away. Costly, but I feel much better for it already. Occasionally, of course, I cannot resist a deep sensual drag right down to my ankles.

So after this day is over we have three delicious days off. We plan to hide in the hotel and not go out at all, except perhaps for an occasional meal. I shall read and read and read.

Saturday 9th Another rough day physically. I had to pick up a supine para-lysed Cathleen Nesbitt saying to a disgusted Rex Harrison: 'She's seized up

---

[116] Geoffrey Warner (1937—), *Pierre Laval and the Eclipse of France* (1968). Alexander Werth (1901–69), *De Gaulle: A Political Biography* (1966).
[117] Sir Oswald Mosley (1896–1980) *My Life* (1968).

tonight. I'll lift and you pull.' Meaning of course that I would lift her from the sheet while he removed it. Well indeed to God, either Rex or the camera or I, buggered it up every time, so that I had to do it twenty times. I shall have arms like Marlon Brando on my birthday. Which is tomorrow. I'll be forty-three years old. [. . .]

Anyway, John Morgan came to ask me to do an interview for Thames TV. I said I would. With him was a sort of slip of a girl called Foot. Dingle, I said, Michael and Ebbw Vale.[118] [. . .] Give my love, I said to her as she left, give my love, though he will never remember me. We met, I said archly, a thousand years ago in a miners' meeting during the wars of the roses. He'll remember you, she said. Who could forget you? Anyway give my love to Ebbw Vale. She was as mini-skirted as a Californian Palm tree. The hem was only slightly below the neck. [. . .]

Then, in order, I had Shirley MacLaine and a friend, who purports to be a Swede <u>and</u> a Sexologist.[119] That is to say she is a sort of psychologist, so Rex tells me, he knows her, and they show you filthy pornographic photographs and sort of register the mental size of your tink. [. . .]

Then there was Elliott Kastner and somebody called Bick Something, and Bettina for lunch, and John Sullivan. The latter is in a desperate state. He is shrewdly lumpish and his wife is equally so. He cannot match her, except for physical beauty (they are both as handsome as hell) and she has the stamp of failed inordinate ambition written all over her like a Dead Sea scroll. So what does one do. I have given them $100,000 [. . .] about two years ago. So what does one do? Hide.

Sunday 10th I am now 43. It's nine in the morning. The sky is grey but it has a look of turning into sunshine later on. Yesterday was wholly delightful. We drank vodka screwdrivers, but not too many. We taught Caroline to play 'Yahtsee' [. . .]. I'd forgotten how much fun it is. Later we, just E and I, played Gin Rummy for $1,000 a point! I won $648,000! I refused to accept a cheque. It has to be paid in kind, I said.

I received some nice presents. From Gaston, which he can ill afford, a huge tome called *Gloire de la France*. From Ron, an oldish *Oeuvres de Molières* in eight exquisite little volumes.[120] From Bob Wilson a twenty dollar bill when the Americans were still on the Gold Standard. From Jim Benton an old but beautifully preserved sword-stick. From Elliott Kastner an overcoat made out of some kind of leather. [. . .] From Claudye and Gianni a tweed pair of

---

[118] A reference to Michael Foot (1913–2010), Labour Party politician and Member of Parliament for the South Wales constituency of Ebbw Vale at this time.
[119] Shirley MacLaine (1934–), actor, sister of Warren Beatty.
[120] Molière, pseudonym of Jean-Baptiste Poquelin (1622–73), playwright.

trousers which they had copied from a pair they had given me about a year ago. I shall get more today. I mean more presents, not trousers. [. . .]

Two more delicious days off, the French take tomorrow, Armistice Day, as a national holiday. We don't I think. All I seem to remember is two minutes' silence in school and selling penny poppies made out of wire and paper. They were made by blind people, I believe. How quickly the world forgets or doesn't even know. A group of children were recently asked what was the Battle of Britain.[121] They not only didn't know, they didn't know with what weapons it was fought.

Both E and I have had congratulatory telegrams from Richard Zanuck for our 'great' 'brilliant' 'superb etc.' performances in our respective films. Donen and Rex too. It's a long howl to that day in New York, it was actually Shakespeare's birthday, when just about to play *Hamlet* at the Lunt-Fontanne, I was served at the stage door with a writ suing us for $55 million.[122] Settle out of court, of course, after three ghastly years and innumerable depositions.

Monday 11th Armistice Day and cold and grey. We shall probably go out to lunch for the first time for ages, I mean in a restaurant. If open we'll go to Coq Hardy and have some chicken pie.[123] E gave me a mink coat and I shall wear it. A mink coat! It's very dark brown and the nap is close and short and it gleams and catches light as only a mink can. It comes to half way down my thighs. I hope I don't look like a fool of a money-lender! E says not. Any way, short of being robbed, I shall keep it forever. Other presents were three books from Don Waugh, my stand-in, who gave me *Castles of Europe* and *Palaces of Europe* and *A Pictorial History of the Silent Screen*.[124] Dick Hanley and John Lee gave me a thin zip-around briefcase from Hermes. Beautiful to the touch. Nella, E's maid, gave me a silver frame to keep the children's photographs in, and she worried if it was too small. Caroline and Jane clubbed together to give me a jacket, very with it, which zipped up into a roll-top collar. [. . .] Sara and Francis sent me a lovely thick cashmere sweater with a matching scarf. I really could start a boutique with the number of cardigans jumpers and sweaters I have, and yet I never stop giving them away.

We stayed in all day and read. [. . .] I read all the political comment in the 'quality' papers about Nixon as President, *Sunday Times*, *Observer* and *Sunday Telegraph*. I then read in succession my two presents: *Castles of Europe* and *Palaces* of the same. Fascinating little pocket histories but mostly photographs and drawings and reproductions of tapestries like the Bayeux. A [. . .] book

---

121 A conflict in the air between the German Luftwaffe and the Royal Air Force in the summer of 1940 over the UK.
122 A reference to the Zanuck suit against Burton and Taylor in the wake of *Cleopatra*.
123 Café Le Coq Hardy, Rue Notre Dame de Lorette, Paris.
124 Daniel C. Blum, *A Pictorial History of the Silent Screen* (1953).

called *The Double Helix* by a scientist-physicist yclept James D. Watson.[125] It is an account of the search for and discovery of DNA at Cambridge. According to the book DNA is a molecule of heredity and to 'know its structure and method of reproduction enables science to know how the forms of life are ordered from one generation to the next.' On the jacket is a quote from Lord Snow: 'It opens a new world for the general non-scientific reader.' I now append a quotation from the book.[126] It is on p. 190. 'Happily he let out that for years organic chemistry had been arbitrarily favouring particular tautomeric forms over their alternatives on only the flimsiest of grounds. In fact, organic-chemistry textbooks were littered with pictures of highly improbable tauto-meric forms. The guanine picture I was thrusting towards him was almost certainly bogus. All his chemical intuition told him it would occur in the keto form. He was just as sure that thymine was also wrongly assigned an enol configuration. Again he strongly favoured the Keto alternative.' Really milord! Still I stayed up until 2.30 reading it. [. . .]

Tuesday 12th [. . .] We did indeed go to lunch at the Coq d'Or and have chicken pie. And wine, which was my undoing. I came home and slept for about five hours so my mate tells me. Disgraceful. Hence my being able to sit up half the night, writing. In addition, I was in a pub-crawling mood and insisted that we stop and have one. E was very good and complied. [. . .]

I wore my mink coat to everyone's satisfaction, including my own. It really is a splendid fur. [. . .] I shall wear my mink to work and show off and try and make Rex jealous.

E was funny last night. She must have come in to see me ten times during the course of the night, dog-tired as she was, because she said she couldn't sleep without me. She's a funny odd old thing and needs comfort. She could be easily lonely.

I have either lost or mislaid Liza's irastosable letter. I shall go mad if I can't find it. [. . .]

Wednesday 13th I said yesterday that the day might turn out to be irastosable, and it did. E said last night that I behaved just like Rachel Roberts. Probably I did, which is just as well as it means that we'll never be invited again to the Duke and Duchess of Windsor's soirées. And thank God, he said fervently. Rarely have I been so stupendously bored. There were 22 people for dinner and only two names did I know or remember, and that was from history – the Count and Countess of Bismarck.[127] And he, the Count, looks as much like

---

[125] James D. Watson, *The Double Helix: A Personal Account of the Discovery of the Structure of DNA* (1968).

[126] Charles Percy (C. P.) Snow, Baron Snow of Leicester (1905–80), novelist.

[127] Otto Christian Archibald von Bismarck (1897–1975), Prince of Bismarck from 1904 to his death. His wife Anne-Marie (1907–99).

one's mental picture of the iron chancellor as spaghetti. Soft and round and irresolute. He couldn't carve modern Germany out of cardboard. The iron of his grandfather didn't enter his soul.[128]

It is extraordinary how small the Duke and Duchess are. Two tiny figures like Toto and Nanette that you keep on the mantelpiece.[129] Chipped around the edges. Something you keep in the front room for Sundays only. Marred Royalty. The awful majesty that doth hedge around a king is notably lacking in awfulness.[130] Charming and feckless.

I took my coat to work and Rex confessed that he <u>was</u> jealous. Latterly he has been calling me me 'darling.' I call everybody 'love' so I suppose it's rubbed off. He tried on the mink and I had difficulty getting it off him. It, of course, looks superb on him. He wears clothes as only a coathanger can. Clothes, no matter how dreadful, drape themselves around him, knowing that they have come home at last.

E just reminded me that at one point I said to the Duchess last night: 'You are, without any question, the most vulgar woman I've ever met.' Waaaaash! She also just told me that we were the only people at the dinner party who didn't have titles. Little does she know that we've made her the Princess of Pontrhydyfen. The Duke, says E, was furious with everybody that he wasn't sitting next to her, and I was furious that I wasn't sitting next to the Duchess. I was surrounded by two American ladies, one was a Duchess and the other a Countess. They were hard-faced pretty and youngish like ads for Suzy Nickerbocker's column, which I've only read once.[131] One of them said that she had seen me as Hamlet in New York, and actually asked me how could I possibly remember the lines. I told her that I never did actually get them straight and that some of my improvisations on speeches which I hated and therefore could never recall would have been approved by the lousy actor-writer himself. I told her that once I spoke 'To be or not to be' in German to an American audience, but she obviously didn't believe me. I told her there were certain aspects of Hamlet, I mean the man, so revolting that one could only do them when drunk. The frantic self-pity of 'How all occasions do inform against me and spur my dull revenge.' You have to be sloshed to get around that. At least I have to be. I think I must have shocked her.

Another lady, not a day under seventy, who's face had been lifted so often that it was on top of her head asked me if it were true that all actors were queer. I said yes, which was the reason why I was married to Elizabeth who also, because of her profession, was queer, but that we had an arrangement. Her face, in its excitement, nearly joined her chin. 'What,' she said, 'do you do?'

[128] A reference to Germany's 'Iron Chancellor', Otto Christian's grandfather, Otto Eduard Leopold von Bismarck (1815–98). Burton may also be referring to the 1940 novel from *Iron in the Soul* by Jean-Paul Sartre (1905–80).
[129] 'Toto and Nanette' were chalkware figurines popular in the 1930s.
[130] *Hamlet*, Act IV, scene v, when the King speaks the line: 'There's such divinity doth hedge a king'.
[131] Suzy Nickerbocker, the pen name of columnist Aileen Mehle (1921—).

'Well,' I said, as straight as a die, 'she lives in one suite, and I in another, and we make love by telephone.' If she believes that she'll believe anything.

At another moment apparently I picked up the Duchess and swung and swung her around like a dancing singing dervish. Elizabeth was terrified that I'd drop her or fall down and kill her. Christ! I will arise and go now and go home to Welsh miners who understand drink and the idiocies that it arouses.[132] Holy mother, they had to have licensing laws to cure us, and we were incurable. I shall die of drink and make-up.

The reason why there are two pages, instead of one, in today's entry for the idiot stakes, is because I have nothing better to do. [...] I have been up since about eight, and Elizabeth tried to lock me in the spare bedroom, and so I was constrained to try and kick the door down, and nearly succeeded which meant that I spent some time on my hands and knees this morning picking up the battered plaster in the hope that the waiters wouldn't notice that the hotel had nearly lost a door in the middle of the night [...]

Thursday 14th Yesterday was a day as doomed as the Hittites but more delightful, that is to say, nobody died. Many curious things happened. Rachel, who is always pretty good value for a diary, showed everybody her pubic hairs, and as a dessert lay down on the floor in a mini-skirt and showed her bum to anyone who cared to have a glance. Outrage, in Rachel's case, has now become normal. If she had a cup of tea with a ginger-snap and made polite conversation about modern poetry, we would all go mad and display our private parts to visiting tourists. I wasn't much help. She said at one point over my dying body to Rex, hooded-eyed and malevolent, 'I don't care about his hard-faced blondes.' No response. So she said again: 'I don't care about his hard-faced blondes.' 'Neither,' I said with a laugh as false as a dentist's assurance, 'do I.'

I've just received a letter from Cathleen Nesbitt with a poem, 'in his own write' as she says John Lennon would say, written about her by Rupert Brooke.[133] I shall write a poem for her in the next short course of my life or pack in the idea of courtesy for ever. What a lady. They bred 'em good in the old days. She is the only old lady, she is near 80 years old, that I could imagine making love to. [...]

I'd better be off and to work because I behaved with a fair amount of disgrace yesterday. I drank, so I gather from my friends, three bottles of Vodka, during the course of the day. And that, naturally, doesn't include the evening when I think I slowed down. But it is not a good idea to drink so much. I shall miss all the marriages of all my various children, and they'll be angry because there'll be nobody around, apart from their mother, to make bad puns.

---

[132] A reference to the first line of the poem 'The Lake Isle of Innisfree' (1888) by William Butler Yeats (1865–1939): 'I will arise and go now, and go to Innisfree.'
[133] Cathleen Nesbitt and Rupert Brooke (1887–1915) had been engaged to be married prior to his death. Brooke had written sonnets to Nesbitt. John Lennon (1940–80) of The Beatles had published *In His Own Write* in 1964.

Everybody was very kind about me. The director was nice and Rex, feeling himself in the ascendant superior and having received my confession, was good enough to say that with three Hail Marys and a smart visit to the lavatory and a touch of ipepacuana, I would stand a fairish chance of being absolved.[134] [...]

Friday 15th Yesterday passed well enough, though I had a rough time with Aaron who is so sorry for himself that it prevents one from having, temporarily at any rate, any sympathy for him. He has the beginnings of multiple sclerosis, which so the *Oxford Dictionary* says is a 'morbid hardening of tissue'. Lovely. If he turns his head quickly, he loses his balance and is likely to fall down. If I had it, even mildly like Aaron, it would mean the end of my career. One could hardly act if one was going to fall over every time one turned one's head. Aaron can still function and will continue to do so for an ordinary lifetime. So he's lucky in an unlucky way. But it frightens me to see people frightened. I don't think I'll be frightened when the call comes. I hope.

As most days my dressing room was a fishbowl, open to everyone's view. There was Aaron and a drunk James Wishart, and a reporter called Jim Bacon.[135] Cathleen Nesbitt came in for a drink. [...] Rex was in splendid form, giggling and chortling and gurgly. We had the umpty-ninth telegram from Dick Zanuck saying that though he knew he sounded like a broken record he had to tell us again that the latest batch of film was superb etc. In his telegrams he calls Rex and myself 'the boys'. Sixty and Forty-three.

I dread today. First I have to act, which I like doing sometimes, but not today. Second I have Aaron and his endless questions about legal nothings. Third, I'm likely to have a room full of people again. Fourth, I'd like to be alone with E for about two hundred years but can't even get two days – we're off to Guy and Marie-Hélène Rothschild's house for the weekend. I love the house and love them so maybe it will be alright. We don't go until tomorrow and we'll probably come back on Monday morning.

[...] On reflection I realize how dreadful Aaron's disease is. Caroline, who is wise as an old woman, told me that from her experience of it the worst thing is the gradual loss of independence. You have to be guided and manoeuvred [...] wherever you go. I don't think I'd fancy that much.

Saturday 16th Yesterday was alright after all. I pleaded pressure of work and 'important scenes coming up' to cut down Aaron's sesquipedalian questions. Eventually he went off to E's studio but told me later that all he received was a

---

[134] Ipepacuana: a liquid used to induce vomiting.
[135] James Wishart, a chartered accountant with the London firm of W. H. Jack & Co, an authority on tax issues, who had been advising Burton since the 1950s. James Bacon (1914–), journalist and actor, who wrote for the *Hollywood Reporter* and the *Los Angeles Herald-Examiner*.

vague and charming smile and the offer of a drink. So he and James Wishart came back tó my place and eventually came home with me in the car. [. . .] They had a drink with me while I waited for E to come home.

The day went better than expected and I think my acting was good, my weariness giving it a sort of nervous intensity that compensated for lack of enthusiasm. Rex was very good and the sailor too. He doesn't have a word to say but he says them very well, as 'twere. His name is Stephen Lewis, very tall and very cockney.[136] I asked him if my accent was authentic enough. He said it was perfect.

E told me that Princess E called her up yesterday and said that she missed E so much that she was wondering if she could come over next week. E said, 'Come off it, Elisheba, it's not me you miss but Warren Beatty.' My E then turned into the den-mother and dished out advice to the effect that W.B. was a player of the field, and purported at least, to be in love with a film actress called Julie Christie.[137] And that Neil, Elisheba's manfriend of the moment was an infinitely better deal etc. etc., but naturally when a woman is set on a certain course of action, order turns into chaos and logic to insanity.[138] [. . .] Perhaps we should explain to her that the six million dollars he realized out of *Bonnie and Clyde*, as I heard yesterday, because of ill-advice from lawyers, has virtually disappeared like the morning mist before the rising sun.[139] [. . .]

As mentioned before in this writing, I'm not quite sure about Elisheba. Bess says I'm wrong, but I think for a time, until I get to know her, I shall wear armour on my back, where the daggers go in. [. . .]

Aaron said in his cups last night that I was the most intelligent man he'd ever met! And he'd met them all, he went on wildly. Supreme court judges, philosophers, Jack Kennedy, eminent doctors, great actor and Uncle Tom Cobbley and all. I curtsied sweetly but I like the flattery so much that I've gone to the trouble of putting it down in this diary, haven't I? A pebble on the shore of the great sea of knowledge and thank you Sir Isaac Newton.[140] I think I'll try sleeping for an hour to succour my massive brain. [. . .]

Sunday 17th, *Chateau de Ferrières, Seine et Marne* Sunday morning in my favourite house, it is almost midday and the first snow has come in the night [. .]. Yesterday was a bit wearing with a great deal of talk and oddly enough I

---

[136] Stephen Lewis (1936—) played the part of Jack in *Staircase*. He had been a merchant seaman.

[137] Julie Christie (1941—), most famous at this point for her roles in *Billy Liar* (1963) and *Doctor Zhivago* (1965). She had turned down the role of Anne Boleyn in *Anne of the Thousand Days*. Her relationship with Warren Beatty would last until 1974.

[138] Princess Elizabeth would marry Neil Balfour (1944—), merchant banker and Conservative Party candidate in 1969.

[139] *Bonnie and Clyde* (Warner Brothers, 1967), had starred Beatty and Faye Dunaway (1941—).

[140] Sir Isaac Newton (1643–1727), scientist, mathematician, astronomer, who is credited with saying that: 'I do not know what I may appear to the world, but to myself I seem to have been only like a boy playing on the sea-shore, and diverting myself in now and then finding a smoother pebble or a prettier shell than ordinary, whilst the great ocean of truth lay all undiscovered before me.'

was not in a very talky mood but was forced to. We brought Caroline with us to show her the house and grounds, and E says that she was very thrilled, as well she might be. [. . .]

Guy and David were here when we arrived, we met the latter coming out of the trees with a shot rabbit in one hand and a pheasant in the other.[141] The two young boys and a pretty little girl cousin were with. Philippe the youngest had shot the rabbit.[142] It was the first bag of his young life. Also here on arrival was Guy's daughter Lili who has to lie down a great deal as she had a clot on the brain about two months ago.[143] She says that the whole thing was brought on by the unhappy coincidence of a malfunctioning kidney and the famous 'Pill.' The pill that orally taken every day prevents women from having babies. She also said that young girls of eighteen and twenty are struck down by the pill and not having her luck, have died.

The elevator refused to work at the end of the day so Lili's husband and I carried her, fireman fashion, up to her room.[144] I was puffing a bit as it is two floors up.

Most of the conversation before Marie Hélène arrived, was about sexual aberrations. Guy says he knew a man who could only make love if the woman was naked except for bottines-a-boutons, that is old-fashioned fin-de-siecle button-up boots like one's granny used to wear. Sam Spiegel, he said that poor Sam can only get excited if a woman defecates onto his face. [. . .]

Marie Helene arrived in a great state of excitement having had her make-up done for four hours by Alberto de Rossi.[145] It wasn't received very well. She is quite an ugly woman with a large hooked nose and an almost negroid mouth but very beautiful blind eyes, and the vivacity of her manner and her machine gun delivery in both languages makes her very attractive.

I don't know why I find it surprising when rich people are intelligent, after all they have the advantages from birth of superb educations, and the money to hire the best tutors etc., but Guy and his son David are as bright as buttons, especially the former. And they both have a very witty turn of phrase. David makes bad puns which I adore. [. . .]

There were thirteen for dinner so two tables were made up side by side to allay any superstition. At one point I mentioned Onassis's name and a bitter quarrel sprang up between Marie-Hélène and Lili. The former adamant that the Onassises would never be invited to her house, and Lili and myself saying that they <u>would</u> be invited to ours.

---

[141] David René de Rothschild (1942—), Guy de Rothschild's son by his first marriage.
[142] Philippe Sereys de Rothschild (1963—).
[143] Lili Krahmer (1930–96), Guy de Rothschild's stepdaughter by his first marriage.
[144] Lili's husband was Maurice Rheims (1910—2003), photographer.
[145] Alberto de Rossi (d. 1975), make-up artist, who worked on *Cleopatra*, *The Taming of the Shrew* and *Staircase* and who would work on *Divorce His, Divorce Hers*, and on the Taylor film *Ash Wednesday*.

Monday 18th Yesterday was a dream day. We slept until noon and discovered to our delight that lunch was a high tea at 4.30. So we ordered breakfast in our rooms. Bacon and eggs and brioche, homemade, toast from homemade bread, little apples, home grown. Then for me, while E stayed in bed and read a book, a long walk through the woods and the snow. Distantly and occasionally I could hear sounds of the shoot. E waved to me from the window. The lake was starting to freeze over and the ducks and swans were slowly swimming along the still unfrozen channels, very slowly and for some reason, comically.

High Tea was a feast. Chicken in the pot with all kinds of vegetables followed by endless cheeses and desserts. Roasted chestnuts. Raisins. fresh figs, mandarins, oranges, apples, and obviously and deliciously home made preserves. There were about twenty-five people sitting at the table. The minister of the interior whose name I've forgotten talked to me a lot.[146] He said that his job was more important and onerous than our Home Secretary's. He couldn't explain why satisfactorily. I must find out. My ignorance of French politics is pretty stupendous. Perhaps because, all my life until de Gaulle, they seemed so irresponsibly droll. A new Prime Minister every three weeks and one only for a weekend.

Then upstairs to read and sleep a little and take a bath and so dinner in honour of Marie Helene and her birthday. This meal was at many tables instead of one large one. I sat between the Countess of Bardolini(?) and Madame Pompidou wife of de Gaulle's former Prime Minister.[147] She believes, she said, that Georges, her husband, must denounce de Gaulle so that he will stand a chance of returning to power after de Gaulle dies, which she said, perhaps hopefully, cannot be long now. Georges didn't seem very impressive. I took just three words for each and impersonated everyone at our table, vocally that is, which Mme Pompidou found remarkable. So I was told afterwards by Marie Helene and others. They were very easy voices. The Brazilian Ambassador's daughter with a husky voice and a Portuguese French accent, two people with Italian-French accents, an hysterical gent with a very high pitched voice. A German French accent It was a piece of glottal cake.

[. . .] Practically everyone left for Paris after the party, but we sat up with the German Rothschilds and Marie Helene and Alexis Redé and Lili until 3.00 in the morning. I spoke Shakespeare and E and I sang them a Welsh song, 'Ar lan y mor mae rhosys cochion.'[148] Elizabeth looked so beautiful that strong men were awed, and the children came to sit at her feet. She sang sweetly and unaffectedly and impressed everybody, including me. I'm not blasé yet.

---

[146] Raymond Marcellin (1914–2004) was Minister of the Interior from May 1968 to February 1974.
[147] Claude Pompidou (1912–2007), wife of Georges Pompidou (1911–74), who had been Prime Minister of France from 1962 to July 1968 and would become President in June 1969. De Gaulle resigned the presidency in April 1969 and died in November 1970.
[148] A very popular Welsh song, roughly translating as 'Beside the sea red roses growing'.

Tuesday 19th, Paris We left Ferrières late because of my dilatory Liz but miraculously despite driving slowly because of the snow-slushed and verglassed roads, we arrived on time. A man called Flink from *Look* magazine stayed for about an hour in my dressing room.[149] He asked endless questions about homosexuality which I answered traditionally: Live and let live. It takes all sorts to make a world. Judge not lest ye be judged. Cast not the first stone lest ye be stoned. Some of my best friends are homosexuals etc. etc.

Two stories about Sunday's party which I omitted, ommited, ommitted – one of them must be right – from yesterday's entry: There were about perhaps sixty or more people in the room waiting to go in to dinner and cock-tailing, and Elizabeth and I were sitting in a corner of the room with Lili and other assorted odds and sods when Marie Helene came over and said to me: 'Richard will you go over and talk to the dark lady in the corner?' I said, 'For God's sake Marie Helene I don't know her etc. and why should I etc? And Marie-H said, 'She only wants to listen to your voice, which she thinks is heavenly.' And my Elizabeth said in a powerful American accent: 'Tell her I'll be over in a minute and give her an impersonation.' My Broad doesn't muck around. Later when the children, after dinner, had gone up one by one to the head of the head table and made rather self-conscious little speeches, a man sitting next to E said 'How boringly middle-class.' E and I decided that if the Rothschilds and Ferrières and eighty guests for dinner in one wing of the house, where trees in the avenues had been planted by reigning monarchs, where there are a hundred servants, was middle class, then we had just crawled out from underneath a stone. How bored is bored and how middle-class can you be to describe the Rothschilds as middle-class? They are aristos my friend. It's like Syb once describing the Johnsons (President and Lady Bird) as 'suburban'.[150] What the hell does she think Ferndale was?[151] Buck House? Anyway, bugger you stranger, Elizabeth and I, famed as we are, rich as we are, courted and insulted as we are, overpaid as we are, centre of a great deal of attention as we are and have been for nearly a quarter of a century, are not bored or blasé. We are not envious. We are merely lucky.

I have been inordinately lucky all my life but the greatest luck of all has been Elizabeth. She has turned me into a moral man but not a prig, she is a wildly exciting lover-mistress, she is shy and witty, she is nobody's fool, she is a brilliant actress, she is beautiful beyond the dreams of pornography, she can be arrogant and wilful, she is clement and loving, Dulcis Imperatrix, she is Sunday's child, she can tolerate my impossibilities and my drunkenness, she is

149 Stanley Flink, journalist.
150 Lyndon Johnson (1908–73), President of the United States (1963–8), and his wife Lady Bird Johnson (1912–2007).
151 Ferndale, a mining village in the Rhondda Fach in South Wales, adjacent to Tylorstown, birthplace of Richard's first wife Sybil.

an ache in the stomach when I am away from her, <u>and she loves me</u>![152] She is a prospectus that can never be entirely catalogued, an almanack for Poor Richard.[153] And I'll love her 'till I die.

Aaron, Bob Wilson and I went back to the Hotel together and went down to the basement bar for a drink. Hebe Dorsey of the *Tribune* came in and said that she and an American called Dwyer, who she says might be the next Mayor of New York, have fallen in love.[154] She is perhaps 45 and he 61. He is married and she says <u>he</u> says that she transformed his sex life. So there. Later we went to Aaron's room where a woman said, looking at Elizabeth, she's not so beautiful, what's all the fuss about. I asked her why she didn't marry a hatchet and make a perfect match. She was Sam Pisar's the lawyer's wife.[155]

Wednesday 20th It's 7 in the morning, I've been up since 6, and it's still dark. Not, of course as dark as I. Doomed and damned and dissolute and desperate and dull and dying. Alliterative despair. I get a few days off soon. I need them. I was in a mad mood last night and accused E of talking too suspiciously much about Warren Beatty and his various middle-aged amours. She said it was because she loved a good gossip. A likely story, I cackled venomously, you don't have a very good record sweetheart. Christ if you can marry Eddie Fisher you can marry anybody, I said, and having created wounds, rubbed the salt in nicely for an hour or so. The trouble is of course that I love the old bag too much. I must try and be dispassionate. That, of course, will be the day. But it is perfectly obvious to me, I am after all an old hand at the game, that one way to attract a woman is to pay a lot of attention to <u>other</u> women. It drives them mad. I remember screwing everybody in a large company over a year or so to get one woman. I got her. I wish I hadn't now because she was an evil virtuous bitch and filthy minded. But, he said with pride, I got her. There was another woman in a film with me which contained hundreds of good-looking extras. It must have cost me fifty 'crowd artistes' to get the one well-married beautiful lamentable girl. But I got her, he said defiantly. I know them, Dylanesquely, by the thousands. Anyway since <u>this</u> leopard can and has changed his spots I have to believe that the other one can ... and has. Better bloody had.

I had a letter from Kate yesterday. It was sweet and repetitive of my letter to her. She must be a good student, little ape, as she picks up other people's ideas so quickly. I wish I was her teacher. I wish I had the patience. I'd teach

---

[152] Dulcis Imperatrix: charming consort of the emperor. According to the traditional rhyme, 'Sunday's child is full of grace'.
[153] *Poor Richard's Almanack* (1733–58), published by Benjamin Franklin (1706–90).
[154] Hebe Dorsey (1925–87), fashion editor of the *International Herald Tribune*. 'Dwyer' may refer to Paul O'Dwyer (1907–98), unsuccessful Democratic candidate for the Senate for New York, 1968 and 1970. His brother, William (1890–1964), had been Mayor of New York from 1946 to 1950.
[155] Samuel Pisar (1929—).

her to avoid all the pitfalls of my half-baked education. As it is she is stuck with Syb's eighth-baked variety. That won't help. But Syb is as good as gold, fair dues.

[. . .] So now having written myself into an even more melancholy mood I will spritz myself up with a letter to Kate.

I've written a letter to Kate but it hasn't spritzed me up. So bugger it. It was Elizabeth's saint's day yesterday and since so many French people gave her presents she felt obliged to give a party. It was pleasant too and good to see how everybody adores her. She's a good old thing and not bad-looking. She'll be awake in a minute so that's something to look forward to.

Thursday 21st Elizabeth's father died yesterday afternoon and I had to break the news to her. She was like a wild animal even though we've been expecting his death for some years. But of course there is no love comparable to a man's love for his daughter or vicky verka.[156] I know to my cost. My passion for my daughters is ludicrous. Whether it's reciprocated as in Elizabeth's case, is another matter. I feel like one who, stabbed in the back, is dying of his wounds. If you know what I mean. I cannot bear suffering in others. I'd much rather have it myself and I'm no masochist, but suffering at second hand is rough enough in its way. Despite all E's protestations about her mother over the years, like the good girl she is, she now only wants to protect and cherish her. Me too. Death is a son-of-a-bitch. The swinish unpredictable, uncharitable, thoughtless, fuck-pig enemy. [. . .] He's done a lot of mindless damage. One day we'll cure the waster.

We fly over the Pole this afternoon. Francis will probably be buried on Saturday, and we'll probably come back on Sunday. There is, thank God, work to be done. We'll bring Sara back with us. That is if she wants to. I think, after the initial shock, that Sara could find herself a fairly congenial life. That is, I think she might enjoy being with us because we lead relatively exciting lives, and there's my vast family who would consider it an honour to fuss and pamper her. She could very easily be elected, unanimously, on the first count, as Chairwoman of the local whist-drive in any place she wishes to go. Including Pontrhydyfen.

Last night when Elizabeth was talking to her mother, I kept on screaming at her drunkenly and hopelessly to tell her mother to come back to Paris with us after the funeral. Elizabeth ignored me, which infuriated me. What I didn't realize was that Sara was telling E how she'd woken up to find Francis dead, and how she'd massaged his heart frantically, and given him the last agonising kiss-of-life. He'd been dead for an hour. I am illegitimately self-centred and take all tragedy and sins upon myself. Elizabeth's worth glows gooder all the

---

[156] Vice versa: the other way around.

time. She might even make <u>me</u> good one day. Jesus, I sound like a latter-day Christ, if the pun is pardoned.

[. . .] I wish our children were with us. They would distract us a bit perhaps, or perhaps they wouldn't. Children and pups are very good value. Sometimes. I'll be acerbic to the death. That rotten latter bastard.

Ah! what it must feel like to have somebody die, somebody that you genuinely love, somebody of your own blood and bone that you worship with an intensity near to madness, what it must be like. Much worse than one's own death because I'll wrestle with the bastard. But when Ivor or Cis die, somebody hold me down boys. I cannot conceive of life without the knowledge that Ivor and Cis are not [sic] at the end of some tenuous cabled line. And chaps it will be alright if <u>I</u> die, but what's going to happen to me if <u>she</u> dies. I think I'll turn into a tyre on a bus and roll forever and forever over innocent feet.

Friday 22nd, Beverly Hills Hotel[157] [. . .] It's now half past eight in the evening. Howard and Ron and I went to the funeral parlour and picked out the coffin, they call them caskets here, and did it by simply asking which is the most expensive. This one, said the man who was lugubriously invented of course by Charles Dickens. It is copper-lined, he said, to afford protection. Against what? Worms? They are already stirring inside poor Francis. Damp? Graham just arrived from Wales as a combined family representative from the family. I don't know what the hell they think I am. But after all it's a good and typically generous gesture. Whoops there goes my spelling again. [. . .]

DECEMBER

Sunday 1st, Plaza Athenee [Paris] I really must keep this diary up every day. It's hell to start up again once you've missed a few days.

Gaston's youngest brother was killed yesterday in a road accident which completes a splendid ten days. This has been a terrible year so far. Our films have done less well than usual. There was my fracas with Tony Richardson over *Laughter in the Dark*.[158] There was André's suicide. There was and is Ivor's paralysis. There was E's operation which she's still suffering the side effects from. There was her father's death last week. I shan't be sorry when those wild bells ring out the old and ring in the new.[159] And there is a month to go!

The week has been a mixed nightmare. It has taken us both until today to partially recover from the two murderous flights over the Poles. The flight going was long in time – it took about 12 hours – but it was smooth. The flight

---

[157] Beverly Hills Hotel, Sunset Boulevard, Beverly Hills, California.
[158] Director Tony Richardson had sacked Burton from the production of *Laughter in the Dark* for being in breach of contract.
[159] A reference to the poem 'Ring Out, Wild Bells', by Alfred, Lord Tennyson (1809–92).

back was shorter, about ten hours, but the seat belts were on practically all the way. What frightening drunken bores those long flights are. I shall never do one again unless it's, as it was last weekend, a matter of life and death.

We worked well enough last week and are either on or ahead of schedule so I'm told. Rex is a bit worrying latterly. He's become much less queer. In fact he's hardly queer at all – he's almost professor Higgins.[160] However his natural lightness will probably carry him through.

People have been very kind to Sara and Elizabeth about Francis's death. Hundreds of letters telegrams wreaths for the funeral and flowers for suite etc. (Francis received short but good obits in most of the papers.) A notable exception was Frank Sinatra. What a petulant little sod he is. Edie Goetz says that he was annoyed because E had called him on Mia's behalf![161] 'Bleah,' as Peanuts would say.[162]

However, there was some good news even if it was only professional. It appears that *Where Eagles Dare*, a film I made earlier this year is a thrilling film and is likely to be a huge grosser. The few people who've seen it are enraptured. It's a *Boy's Own Paper* fantasy with a vengeance. I kill half the German Army.

[. . .] My brother who had flown over as a representative of the family who had a whip-round for the purpose, was a tower of strength, fetching and carrying and doing a lot of the dirty work and occasionally having to hold me down.

Ron Berkeley and Valerie too were enormously helpful, particularly the former. [. . .]

The funeral was well managed though my gums ached to get hold of the Bible when the old lady whose teeth kept on dropping was reading from it. And the family behaved beautifully. E was dewy-eyed but in control. That old bastard of an Uncle Howard Young, who's been using and robbing Francis all his life was weeping worse than anybody[163] He's 92 and perhaps could feel death's icy hands. He told me later over the funeral baked meats that he had $25,000,000. I hope you're going to leave it to the family, I said. 'No,' he explained, 'You have made your name and Elizabeth hers but I will be forgotten unless I leave my money to an Institution with my name on it.' 'Good luck,' I said with a smile like a death's head. Later Howard, of all people, said he felt sorry for the old robber, and in the car on the way home Eliz said the same thing. Now all these years I've been hearing what a mean monster this Howard

[160] A reference to the role of Professor Henry Higgins which Rex Harrison had played in *My Fair Lady*.
[161] Edie Goetz (1905–87), daughter of Louis B. Mayer (1884–1957), and wife of William Goetz (1903–69), film producer. Frank Sinatra had divorced Mia Farrow earlier in 1968.
[162] A reference to the comic strip *Peanuts* by Charles Schulz (1922–2000).
[163] Howard Young (1878–1972), art dealer and partner in business with Francis Taylor. In his will he bequeathed a sum in the region of $20m for the establishment of the Howard Young Medical Center, Wisconsin.

Young is, so in my inimitable way I blew my top. Irastosably so. Every four-letter word in the book and some that aren't. I do, of course, choose my moments well to shout at my wife, like after her father's funeral. Ah well!

[. . .] We had Thanksgiving Dinner on Thursday night given by E. It went very well it appears, but we left early, me taken out by the ear by E, as we were still living half on California time and half European. Niven was there, smooth urbane witty and nice. [. . .]

Monday 2nd Yesterday I awoke fairly earlyish and mucked around with the diary. I showered and shaved and reheated yesterday's soup for breakfast. Over the weekend, having started and put it down after a few chapters I finished *My Life* by Osbert Sitwell.[164] It is a fascinating account of the political idiocy that was going on in my childhood. And what a brilliant egomaniac it was who could so delude himself about the temper of the naturally conservative British that he could preach Pacifism as his creed on one hand and dress his followers in blackshirts and uniforms, himself included, on the other. The latter to the suspicious and uneducated masses was symbolic of the thing they dreaded most, militancy and war. To add to the fear that everyone in my childhood suffered from, the fool allowed himself to be seen with Mussolini on the balcony of the Piazza Venezia taking the fascist salute in a march-past of the 'might' of the pathetic Italian Army. He let it be known that he had had many interviews with Hitler. But the maniac, and there is no question about it that the man was a little touched, if he'd remained in the Labour Party and become very remotely its leader, if he'd preached the same Pacifism from the by now reasonably staid Labour Platform with no Nazi and Fascist salutes and no private black-shirted army to frighten the ordinary bloke into ridicule, he might quite easily have swept the Tories out of power in 1935. And everything might have been very different. Some of his condescension about my class, the class that I knew so well, is pathetic and a perfect example of the total lack of understanding of the aristocrat of the then-called working class. I think in the end that though he was capable of a dazzling turn of phrase, he was essentially humourless. And the humourless man is in deadly danger, more than any other, of deluding himself. Hitler (1889–1945) and Mussolini (1883–1945), especially the latter with his posturing and his violin, obviously didn't have a grain. And they both deluded themselves cosmically. [. . .]

Tuesday 3rd, Paris This is an entry just for the sake of an entry. Yesterday was desperate. I began alright but suddenly a drunken maudlin Rachel Harrison appeared with a drunk but not maudlin Elizabeth Harris. They both looked battered and both had very cheap looking dyed blonde hair. They both looked

---

[164] Burton means Oswald Mosley. Osbert Sitwell (1892–1969) was a poet and novelist.

like tarts. I fled from them to my room where I found Hebe Dorsey who stayed for <u>four hours</u>. Shortly afterwards Hugh French arrived and both of them plus Bob Wilson proceeded to get drunk. Bob asked me what I was going to do about Ron if I decided to holiday for the next six months. This in front of a journalist. Ron very quietly told him to shut up. During this time I was drinkless. How dumb and boring people are when they're drunk and you're sober. How dumb and boring I must have been for the greater part of my life. Finally in desperation I had a drink which only succeeded in making me cold and nasty. [. . .] I arrived home to find milady playing cards with Caroline. I sat down sullenly to read JBS – an autobiography, correction, biography of Haldane of those initials.[165] Fascinating. [. . .] I felt nicely tired and went to bed about eleven o'clock. At midnight or a little later I was awoken by E who asked me if I wanted a sleeping pill! I nearly went mad. It turned out that I was talking in my sleep and she thought I was awake, but even so she knows I wouldn't take a sleeping pill anyway. Well after shouting at each other for a bit E went and made herself some soup while I continued to read Haldane. We turned out the lights about 2.30 or 3.00. This time I had difficulty in going to sleep but made it around 4.00 I would guess and slept like a log until 10.00. We made it up as, thank God, we invariably do and we cwched and cuddled.[166]

Rex gave me a hard time during the scene. He, in the course of the scene, has to give me artificial respiration and slap my face to bring me round. He is however so uncoordinated that he was really belting me. Since, as usual we had to do it many times, I felt at the end of the day that my jaw was unhinged. [. . .]

I have to see Joe Losey and John Heyman tomorrow about *Man from Nowhere* and I'm going to have to tell them that E is too ill for me to do the film. This will be a nasty blow. [. . .]

Wednesday 4th, Studio Billancourt, Paris A relatively easy day saying goodbye to Rex as he leaves for his trial.[167] No face-slapping, no artificial respiration and only a couple of lines or so. We are now rapidly coming to the end of the picture which with a bit of luck from the weather in England, we should finish ahead of schedule. [. . .]

E cooked supper last night and then cut my hair for the Ball given by Guy and Marie-Hélène tonight at Ferrières. I said we would go only if we could stay the night. Hopefully, I or we might be able to sneak upstairs in the middle of the festivities and tuck into bed with a warm book. Elizabeth has a

[165] J. B. S. Haldane (1892–1964), geneticist, biologist, and member of the Communist Party of Great Britain (1942–50). Ronald Clark's *JBS: The Life and Work of J. B. S. Haldane* appeared in 1968.
[166] Burton means 'cwtched' – the Welsh term for cuddling.
[167] This refers to the trial of the character Charlie Dyer (played by Rex Harrison) in *Staircase*.

magnificent frock made for her by Marc Bohan, glittering all over.[168] She will be the belle I suppose as usual. If not I shall be furious. [. . .]

I continued to read the book about Haldane. Extraordinary how he could be taken in by any ideology when he obviously possessed a mind of such brilliance and <u>common sense</u>. Even I as a child in the valleys knew there was something not quite right about Communism. Mind you, the inertia of the so-called democracies between the wars was likely to drive anybody bonkers. But I would have thought that pure science was above mere politics. He thought differently.

[. . .] It seems that I shall have to fly to Washington to speak at a fund-raising dinner for the Kennedys and in memory of Bobby. I sort of wrote the speech in my head yesterday afternoon between shots and will put it down on paper the first chance I have. I'll base it all on *Henry V* I think and the idea of patriotism in its finest flower and the awful responsibilities of Kingship, and what after all is the office of President of the United States except the possession, even if only for a time of the most powerful Kingship that the world has ever known.

'Upon the King let us our lives our debts our careful wives our children and our sins lay on the King. We must bear all.' Etc.[169]

Thursday 5th, Paris [. . .] It was not, in fact, a good idea to stay the night at Ferrières, because I found myself bidding everybody goodbye and I hope you had a nice time with all the desperation of a lost host. I thought that the Rothschilds had gone to bed, but I am assured by Elizabeth that they were simply in another room. Finally, at about 5 in the morning, having ushered everybody on his or her way to Paris, I managed to crawl my way to bed, wishing that the bed, with E in it, was crawling towards me. Anyway mutually we made it ensemble. I talked to so many people, endlessly, that I shall have to devote another issue to their confessions. Grace of Monaco and her husband, the Duchess of Windsor, Lady Caroline O'Connor, Rich man, Poor man, Beggar-man thief and Lili who has had a massive cerebral stroke, but who of course was not there but in hospital. We must go and see her tomorrow.

Friday 6th Tonight we are entraining for Montreux and then Gstaad by car.[170] I am very excited at the thought of going home and seeing the two girls in their various plays. I wonder if Mrs Trench will let them stay the night with us.[171] Perhaps it's not a good idea as it might break school discipline.

---

[168] Marc Bohan (1926—), fashion designer.
[169] Burton repeats with only one inaccuracy the lines spoken by Henry V in Shakespeare's *The Life of Henry the Fifth*, Act IV, scene i: 'Upon the King! Let us our lives, our souls, / Our debts, our careful wives, / Our children and our sins lay on the king! / We must bear all.'
[170] Montreux, Swiss resort town at the eastern end of Lake Geneva.
[171] Headmistress of the school attended by Liza and Maria.

Guy and Marie Helene have very kindly asked us to stay with them over Xmas but as E and I agreed, there are too many of us – the four children Simmy and her boy-friend, Sara and Caroline. So we are going to suggest that we would be delighted just to come down for the lunch. That will save us the trouble of ordering Turkey and all its trimmings from the Hilton. Also it will be lovely to go for a stroll after lunch in the forest. I hope it snows.

Among other people we met at the Rothschilds' was the writer Romain Gary. He, recently divorced or separated from his actress wife, Jean Seberg, seemed rather sad.[172] We are going to have dinner with him when [. . .] I get back from London. It's going to be very strange without Elizabeth. It will be the first time I've left her for several years. She has had to leave me a couple of times: when her father had his stroke and when Gaston's son was killed in Paris when we were in Dublin. Only death in effect has kept us apart. I went to Geneva because of the suicide of my gardener and left her in a hospital in London. But apart from those few occasions we are constantly together. Fortunately I shall have the boys with me on Wednesday I think and they will stay with me until I return to my baby.

At the Rothschilds' La Baronne Thierry de Zuylen asked me which writer I considered to be the greatest of this century.[173] I said 'James Joyce.' She said: 'You really are the most perverse man, because when I last talked to you of James Joyce you said he was a phony, and that *Finnegans Wake* was a wake only for James Joyce.'[174] I said: 'Try me again next time and I'll attack him again with liberal quotations.' She is very beautiful and is married to a most engaging man, splendidly broken-nosed. They are some connection of the Rothschilds I think. Dutch.

Grace told me that the party was the first <u>private</u> party she and Rainier had ever been to in Paris. Everything else she said was state stuff, receptions charity balls etc. She seemed much more relaxed than usual and nicer, [. . .] The Duchess of Windsor was in splendid form and got nicely tiddly. Elizabeth has [been] a great success with all these people. I am very proud of her and may marry her one of these days.

I dread work today. [. . .] Afterwards we are to be presented with two golden boats or something because we have won, for the second year running apparently, the Parisien award for the most popular actor and actress of the year. Then to see Lili in hospital and then to Gstaad on the sleeper 11.50. [. . .]

Saturday 7th, Gstaad We arrived from Paris this morning [. . .]. We dropped off at Montreux. Simone was waiting for us and we were driven the rest of the

[172] Romain Gary (1914–80). Married to Jean Seberg (1938–79), actor, from 1962 to 1970. Seberg had been romantically involved with Clint Eastwood (1930–), actor, who had played alongside Burton in *Where Eagles Dare*.
[173] La Baronne Thierry de Zuylen, sister-in-law of Marie-Hélène de Rothschild.
[174] James Joyce (1882–1941), novelist. His *Finnegans Wake* was published in 1939.

way to Gstaad. [. . .] There was a very light covering of snow on the lower slopes, hardly more than a suggestion of a heavy frost. How antiseptic La Suisse looks, everything made to order, the streets clean as a table, the mountains in perfect order, everything in careful cautious step. The people all look thoroughly scrubbed, apple-polished, and a bit homely.

The house was as clean as a spitless whistle. How comfy-beautiful it is, and as quiet as a whisper. [. . .]

This is a new typewriter which I bought this morning as I was assured by Jane Swanson that there was a typewriter here. I said there wasn't and I was proved right. So I nipped down to the toy-shop, papeterie, in the village and bought this one. The letters seem very big after the other one.

[. . .] Last night after work I went to E's studio where we were presented with awards. E was the most popular actress in France for 1968, and I was the equivalent male. I wonder if we'd have won if we hadn't been so conveniently in Paris. Two horrid little gilt plaques.

I have a record on of 'five thousand Welsh voices' singing 'Mae d'eisiau di bob awr.' Enough to drive you daft with nostalgia. I need you every hour. Oh yes boys.[175]

[. . .] Christ this hymn is driving me melancholy mad. This is the tenth time I've played it. The dead stand up in rows before my bloodshot eyes. Sod it all. Sod death. Sod age. Sod grief. Sod loneliness. 'Gad i'm teimlo awel o Galfaria fryn.'[176]

Sunday 8th Well then yesterday we went to the school performance. As we walked into the cinema I saw, to my astonishment, Barry Norman of the *Daily Mail*. 'What,' I said, 'in the name of God are you doing here?' 'You have to cover 1st nights,' he said. Then a man from European Radio, we noticed with a stick microphone, was only recording when Liza was on. Obviously they thought that being E's daughter she was like her mother, starting early and was likely to become as great a star as her mother. Can one believe the Press to be as long-looking as this, and as venal. It was a lovely afternoon. When they spoke Shakespeare in American accents it was as much as I could do not to cry, as it was all done with the dreadful authority of innocence. Liza's vehemence against Shylock was murderously good acting. Did she let him have it. 'Oh learned judge.'[177]

And then there were two girls, one negress, and one Chinese doing the French-Language scene from *Henry V*, before the King arrives, elbows, bilbows, fingers, [. . .] who had to be heard to be believed so enchanting.[178] [. . .]

---

[175] A Welsh hymn popular with male voice choirs, translating as: 'I need you every hour'.
[176] Another Welsh hymn – 'Bryn Calfaria' or 'The Hill of Calvary'. This line translates as 'Revive me with a breeze from Calvary'.
[177] A line used frequently in *The Merchant of Venice*, Act IV, scene i.
[178] Act III, scene iv.

Monday 9th, Dorchester [Hotel][179] Another alien typewriter. Jane assumed that I would bring the one from Gstaad.

[...] We helicoptered from Gstaad to Geneva despite the protests of the pilot, who said it was too late and too dark to fly. I forced him to anyway, and the flight was thrilling. To creep over an alp at two hundred feet is a sight indeed.

Little Liza was very tearful when we left. So was her mother. How those two love each other. I quite fancy them myself.

We flew from Geneva to Paris, dropped E and C off and I continued onto London with Jim Benton and Bob Wilson. We used a 'Lear' jet. It is very small and not comparable with the HS 125.[180] No lavatory. No bar. However for such short journeys it doesn't matter I suppose.

I became very drunk and abused people a great deal and insulted E a lot on the telephone when I arrived. One might call the last few days 'The Diary of a Dipsomaniac'.

I miss Elizabeth terribly already. I wish I didn't love people. And I wish I didn't shout at people.

[...] I wrote a letter to Mrs Trench saying how much we'd enjoyed the show. She is very like Phil Burton. She said, as a result of the over-attention paid by the press and radio to Liza and E and myself, 'I suppose nobody cares that I'm the one who's responsible for the excellence of this performance. Some of us must always live in the shade.' Phil to the life. [...]

I feel dazed and hurt, though all I did yesterday was daze and hurt other creatures. Oh bugger it. After all I shall see Ivor tonight.

Thursday 12th We've shot everyday in the unbelievable dreariness of the English weather. If ever I need reminding that I never ever want to live here again, I must turn up this page in the diary. It, the weather, is not dramatically bad, no winds, no tempests, no howling blizzard but simply a low grey cloud that squeezes the spirit like a vice. And the cold is no colder than Paris or Gstaad but it is <u>damp</u> and seems to penetrate the very pith of one's fibres. The French people with us find it difficult to credit the English for wanting to live here. I tell them that some of the Saes actually like it, but that the vast percentage of them have no choice.[181] And again the ordinary people in the street look so pinched and puny and mean. Only the occasional young girl mini-skirted and swinging her bum and breasts give any pleasure. It is rare for me to be made uncomfortable by low temperatures, but [...] I found myself between shots running back to the trailer to warm myself in front of the gas fire. [...] And on top of everything there is no E here to share my discontent and bear the burden

[179] The Dorchester Hotel, Park Lane, London.
[180] H.S. Hawker Siddeley.
[181] 'Saes', abbreviated 'Saeson', Welsh for the English.

of my complaints. I didn't think it possible to miss anybody so much. We talk to each other half a dozen times a day on the blower but it's agony all the same. I miss her like food.

We filmed in Windsor the first two days but it was so dark that we only achieved one shot the first day.[182] It was lucky that there was a warm little pub nearby which is where I spent most of my time. Yesterday we worked at a very gloomy house on the outskirts of a village called East Horsley.[183] [...] It was freezing but the people who worked there (it has been converted into a training college for engineers or something) didn't seem to be affected by the cold at all. Mind you, I think that deep down, atavistically, I loathe the English. They are an admirably lucky lot of clods, that's all. They were lucky, I should say. And they are immeasurably snob-ridden and conceited. All classes.

Today we work somewhere near Kensington Gardens in a moving bus. It should at least be warm as they will have to have lights inside the thing. [...]

The two boys arrived from School yesterday and since I wasn't here they went to [...] Norma Heyman's. I thought Mike looked very thin and pale and after about ¼ hour he fell asleep on the sofa [...]. About an hour later perhaps I saw bubbles come out of his mouth and then, still asleep, he began to vomit. Everything he'd had for days seemed to come up but as Ron and I tried to wake him – it is possible after all to choke on your own puke – and clean him up at the same time we recognized the unmistakeable bouquet of red wine. He was stoned. I was so relieved that it was merely booze. I thought at one time he was having one of his father's epileptic fits which is something E and I have had a secret dread of for years. Finally I rubbed ice on his forehead and half carried him into the bathroom where he was sick again. He was terribly apologetic. I told him that everything was alright but that he should learn how to handle booze. [...]

Chris has a girl-friend! He took her to dinner last night. So that's another worry over, I hope. He's not going to be queer. He's still, despite his age, he is nearly fourteen, a little boy.

I am not very impressed with Millfield. Craig, Ron's son, was wearing pyjamas under his suit and had a big tear in the seat of his trousers, Michael had a big rip in the knee of his and all three boys were absolutely filthy.[184] Their hair was dirty and they'd obviously not changed their underwear or shirts for weeks. I wish I could get them into Eton or Harrow where cleanliness is insisted on.[185] And they would look splendid in Eton collars etc. instead of these bloody Edwardian clothes they wear now, which could of course look marvellous, but not when they're stinking dirty. [...] I wish all children

---

[182] Windsor, Berkshire.

[183] Horsley Towers, East Horsley, Surrey.

[184] Craig Berkeley had a brief career in the 1980s and 1990s as a make-up artist, starting with the Burton mini-series *Wagner*.

[185] Eton and Harrow are considered to be the top public schools in England.

stopped at the age of ten and then vaulted to the age of 21. Puberty and adolescence, smelly sex, wet dreams, ambition and agony and calf-love, fear and examinations and not knowing what you're going to do. A loathsome time.

Saturday 14th, Paris A most extraordinary thing happened yesterday. In the script it says that Charlie and Harry ride on their motor-scooter past Buck House 'while a platoon of Horse Guards canters by'.[186] And it happened. The Horse Guards actually appeared on the dot. How lucky can Donen get!

[. . .] After shooting which was over by 11.30 I sought sanctuary at the Dorchester where I was joined by Rex, Jim, Vicky, Elizabeth Harris, a girlfriend of hers, Tony Pellissier, Hugh French, Sheran, Norma, Bob Wilson, and the two boys.[187] It turned into a party. We left for Gatwick Airport about 3 and got there about 5. The customs man was Welsh and spoke the language. So that was alright. The flight to Le Bourget was smooth and uneventful and took 32 minutes.[188] [. . .]

E seems in great agony. Sara was here when I arrived with Graham and his wife Hilary. Graham and I took the dog Jacob for a walk and stopped in a bistro for ½ dozen oysters for me and ½ dozen snails for Graham. When we returned Ringo Starr and Maureen, his wife, were here.[189] I was rightly stoned.

Elizabeth is in such pain that I fancy she's going to end up in a wheelchair. So I'll have my two favourite people in the world, E and Ivor, tottering around on crutches. Quelle Vie.

We dine tonight with the Duke and Duchess of Windsor at a bistro. I've just read an extraordinary and compelling story about me in the *Telegraph*'s Magazine. It's not me at all but I'd like to meet the man he writes about. I sound idiotically listenable. Which of course I am!

Friday 20th Almost a week since I've written in this. Don't know why. Simply couldn't get round to it.

We did indeed get around to having dinner with the Duke and Duchess. At one point I felt so friendly that I found myself, to my horror, calling His Nibs 'David,' which wasn't well received. There I went again.

[. . .] For the last three days I've been 'dubbing the film. It's my most unfavourite aspect of the job I think. Donen and the cutter who is patently a homosexual, had little giggles between the takes.[190] Sick-making. [. . .] But somehow or other I kept my temper and got through all they asked of me [. . .].

---

[186] By 'Buck House' Burton means Buckingham Palace.
[187] Tony Pellissier (1912–88), actor, screenwriter, producer, director.
[188] Le Bourget airport, Paris.
[189] Ringo Starr (1940—), former Beatle and actor and his wife Maureen (1946–94). Starr had appeared with Burton in *Candy*.
[190] Possibly Richard Marden (d. 2008), the film editor, who would work on *Anne of the Thousand Days*.

Yesterday morning at 9.30 I saw *Where Eagles Dare*. It is in parts the most hair-raising film I've ever seen. Some of it made me shake even though I knew what was coming. The children adored it and went back to see it a second time. And that presumably will be our main audience. [. . .]

I am very worried about E. She is so totally undisciplined about her physical life. The MDs all say she should lie flat on her back for at least a month. The film people have very generously stopped shooting on the film for her to have a rest, and I've yet to see her rest on her back for more than an hour except when asleep. Also she says that the Docs say it's alright for her to drink, but it can't be alright for her to drink and take the doses of drugs that Caroline is forever pumping into her. As a result of the complete lack of auto-care I get impatient when she hobbles around in pain. At this rate her malady will never never get better. And talking to her about it is like talking to the wall. I don't care what the medics say. They've virtually killed her a couple of times, and actually did kill my mother out of sheer neglect. How many really good actors do you get out of a thousand? If you're lucky, about five. The rest are out of work. The same proportion applies to doctors but none of them are out of work – they're all busy somewhere prescribing the wrong drugs, misdiagnosing or butchering some poor unconscious etherized bastard. Oh I could tell you tales that would freeze and harrow.[191]

The children are all here now. Chris is still very handsome and Liza has slimmed down and looks adorable. Mike, as he has now for a couple of years, looks as if he's just crawled through several hedges and got mud in his hair. Maria had her hair cut by someone in Gstaad and looks demented. But they're all very engaging kids, though where it used to be Maria who would never stop talking, now the chatterbox is Liza. Blabbing all day long.

I am delighted the film is over. I was dissipating myself into an early death but when the work is over I don't need artificial stimulants. In fact I don't want them. I plan to get reasonably fit in the next few months, something I haven't been for a long time. I just lighted a cigarette and hastily and guiltily put it out. I'm longing to see and be in Gstaad. I might take up ice-skating again when we have a sufficiently long stay there. I think skiing especially with my recklessness, showing off and long neglect will break me a leg. Which is all I need.

We are worried about Maria. [. . .] Please don't let her be a simpleton. What docs one do with her if she turns out so. I am not a very patient person with intelligent children let alone sub-normal ones. Almost all children, including my own, bore me after a time. Maybe I'm basically selfish.

Saturday 21st We're off to Gstaad today until the 5th of January. We have chartered a large plane, I'm not quite sure what it is but it seats about 16 and is a

---

[191] This is a reference to *Hamlet*, Act I, scene v, where the ghost tells Hamlet 'I could a tale unfold whose lightest word / Would harrow up thy soul, freeze thy young blood'.

turbo-jet. The reason is that we have so many people coming with us: Sara, Michael, Chris, Liza, Maria, Caroline, John Something-or-other who is Simmy's boy-friend from Hawaii, and our two bad selves. Otherwise it's going to be one of those quiet, pipe-smoking, slippered, log-fired Xmasses with a well-loved and well-remembered volume of Dickens. It's going to be a screaming mad-house. I shall lock myself in the bedroom for three days and sneak out for walks in the woods when nobody's looking. Maybe I can read *A Christmas Carol* before the log fire in our bedroom.[192] And do all the Xmas puzzles. I forgot to mention that we are also taking four dogs a cat and a canary. I think I'm going to suggest in future that the family en masse travel without me and I'll go it alone. How lovely it must be to take just the one passport, one bag, a briefcase and a typewriter. And ride in a slow train at night and wake up to cowbells and Swiss chalets. Instead of 'Liza, get a move on for Christ's sake and stop patting that stray dog. Maria, sit down, SIT DOWN. Chris will you for God's sake stop lighting matches all over the bloody airport. Mike get your feet off the pilot's back. He's trying to drive the plane. Watch out for Fatso. Catch the cat. Clean up Jacob's shit somebody. Get that bloody cat's claws out of the canary's cage. Will somebody for the sake of sanity stop Oh Fie from cocking his leg against the navigator's ditto. Oh bugger it, where's the parachute? I'm getting out of here.' I should have said <u>five</u> dogs, I'd forgotten Jacob.

Yesterday, after work, I came straight home and settled in the spare bedroom to read for the rest of the day. [. . .] I read three thrillers, one of which I'd read before but couldn't remember I had until the last few chapters. And then a chunk of a book called *The Bible as History*.[193] Fascinating, the last.

There's a photo today in the *Express* of E kissing the Duke of Windsor, with Sara on the side and the Duke and myself in the background (hullo?) the caption saying. 'The extraordinary breadth of the Windsors' acquaintants.'

Sunday 22nd, Gstaad We arrived yesterday in furious fettle. Dick Hanley had ordered a <u>35 seat</u> aeroplane to carry us to Geneva. I didn't really mind until I discovered from Pierre Alain, who was travelling with us, that there was no bed on the plane for Eliz. Why not? I asked. 'Because nobody asked for one, they asked for a bigger plane for the extra luggage.' Well now. It was a turbo-jet built for tourists so the seats would not even slide back. The result being that today E is a cripple again. The old adage applies: if you want something properly done, you have to do it yourself. A 35 seater plane for 9 people and 32 small bags. Hopeless. [. . .]

We helicoptered from Geneva to Gstaad and it was thrilling as ever. I was in one of my absolutely unstoppably filthy moods, insulting everybody right left and centre. Nobody except Caroline took any notice. Elizabeth screamed a

[192] Charles Dickens, *A Christmas Carol* (1843).
[193] Werner Keller, *The Bible as History* (1955).

bit. I accused her of being a hypochondriac, and that she was ill only when she chose to be. How odd, I said, that when you were in Paris and had to work you were unable to move, but once here in Gstaad you're gambolling around like a spring lamb etc. etc. And I couldn't keep away from the subject. It's like a bloke who nearly kills a child in his car and smacks it for frightening him. I shout at E out of fear for her health. I rarely think of anything else. I miss the days when she was able to move around. Tonight for instance I'm going down to the village to take all the children to dinner <u>without</u> Elizabeth. Inconceivable a month or two ago.

Eventually I went to bed sulking at about 9.30 with Schlesinger's *1000 Days with Jack Kennedy*.[194] I read until 5ish and slept until 1 o'clock after noon. [...]

Now for the long bore of Christmas.

Tuesday 24th [...] Yesterday I went shopping. How I loathe the latter. Put me in a foul mood for the rest of the day. However I just walked around Cadonau's and bought about twenty things in about ten minutes.[195] I may if they're good enough get a ruby or two for Eliz. They sent to Geneva or Zurich or both for all I know, for a selection for me yesterday and they've just phoned to say that they've arrived. So I shall pop down to the village after I've finished this and make my choice, if any. To match the diamonds and the emeralds they have to be pretty good.

There are three men on their way to the moon. Americans. What a hell of a time to send men to the moon.[196] Two of them have 'flu' and one of them is vomiting and has the Tripoli Trots. What a lovely place to have the Aztec Two-Step. I've forgotten what they do with excrement in outer space. Can they jettison it?

Simmy and her boy-friend John Gross announced their engagement last night. He is an extraordinary chap and very likeable. I hope they both know what they're doing. Elisheba came for a drink around 6.30. She's very brittle. We are to have Xmas dinner with them tomorrow night. She said three times that her former husband is an American Jew and that she hoped I would be nice to him.[197] Why the devil shouldn't I? Some of my best friends are Princesses. [...]

Tuesday 31st The last day of the year and I'm not sorry. It's been an upsiddy-downy year, mostly down than up. The list of calamities I've recounted before. There is however one bit of news to welcome in the New Year which I hope

[194] Arthur Schlesinger (1917–2007), *A Thousand Days: John F. Kennedy in the White House* (1965).
[195] Cadonau, Promenade, Gstaad.
[196] The Apollo 8 mission launched on 21 December and returned on 27 December, having orbited the moon. The astronauts were Frank Borman (1928–), James Lovell (1928–) and William Anders (1933–).
[197] Princess Elizabeth's first husband was Howard Oxenberg (1919–2010).

will prove to be propitious. Ivor in the last ten days has been able to stand up three times and has also been swimming three times. Always with assistance of course but at least it's a sign. Give us more signs Oh Lord! I have a bad chest nose and throat cold which I cannot shake off. I seem to be having colds much more frequently of late. I've stopped drinking and cut down on smoking to try and clear it up as it makes me, a cold I mean, very irritable and impatient and vile with everybody. I stayed in the bedroom all day yesterday and read or rather re-read Schlesinger's massive tome on JFK. I must have read without interruption including mealtimes and visits to the lavatory for about 16 hours. The result being that this morning my right eye was bright red. It's the legacy of that fight outside Paddington Station some seven years ago when my eye was so badly kicked by a winkle-pickered boot that I lost the conjunctiva and nearly lost the eye. In middle age those things begin to tell. The base of my spine too gives me hell sometimes, a result of the same fight but perhaps not of the same winkle-picker. There were six of these little monsters against Ivor and myself.[198]

Three days ago we went to Curt Jurgens' house in Saanen for drinks and dinner. It was horrible, full of Germans. I cannot like the latter, much as I try. I feel fine about them for a time and then I meet them en masse or in a group and the old hatred returns. Fortunately David Niven was there and Caroline, Elisheba and of course my E. Everybody became thickly drunk except us and Niven at about midnight took me into the bedroom and said that it would be a good idea to get all my party out of there as he suspected that some sort of exhibitionism or orgy was going to start up any minute. I told him I had the same feeling myself and so we all scarpered fairly rapidly. However, I was now in a drinking mood having only had some very indifferent wine at Curt's, and so we stopped off at the Palace for a night-cap which in my case lasted until 8.15 in the morning. E was furious – she having gone home about 3.30. There was one hysterical interlude when we were joined by four of the squarest Americans I've ever met. The questions they asked were beyond belief. I replied with such seriousness but without their knowing it and for Mike's and Elisheba's benefit with such innuendo and nuance that M and Sheba laughed for about four hours. I spoke *Hamlet Macbeth Antony and Cleopatra Richard II* and *III* all deliberately tongue in cheek. Finally the father of the Americans turned on Elisheba when I'd left the room for a moment and roundly condemned her for giggling when I was speaking this immortal verse with this immortal voice! [. . .]

My chief worry for the New Year among the usual worries about children etc is E's health. It is getting no better and she does maddeningly little to help it. [. . .] If she survives this film she is not going to work for a long time. And if

---

[198] Burton had been involved in a scuffle outside The Load of Hay public house, Praed Street, Paddington, London. Most accounts suggest this took place in January 1963.

she continues to be in trouble with sciatica I'll insist that she <u>never</u> works again It's not fair to her and certainly not to the film companies who employ her. I stayed in bed all day yesterday for instance while she spent the entire day until well after midnight sitting in the main room gossiping etc. And of course inevitably sipping away at the drinks. I dread it at night when she has had her shots etc. of drugs and is only semi articulate. In addition to all this she is being given cortisone which apparently bloats you up and therefore you have to go on a fairly stringent salt free diet to combat it. She lasted <u>two</u> days on the diet. [. . .] The most frightening thing is that as a result of E's total self-indulgence that when she moans and groans in agony I simply become bored. And what is more frightening is she has become bored with everything in life. She never reads a book, at least not more than a couple of pages at a time. It took her over a month to read a cheap thriller by Carter Brown that I could have read in an hour.[199] She hasn't asked to read this diary, to which she has free access and which normally gave her a giggle, for nearly two months. I have always been a heavy drinker but now as a result of this half-life we're leading I am drinking twice as much. The upshot will be that I'll die of drink while she'll go blithely on in her half world. Don't be so depressed Rich, the World will be new tomorrow. I am just praying now that she gets through this film relatively easily. After this one, and if by chance it turns out to be only moderately successful, she'll find it very hard for anybody to pay her a $million a picture again. [. . .]

---

[199] Carter Brown, pseudonym of Alan Geoffrey Yates (1923–85), author of crime fiction.

1969

Saturday 4th, Gstaad We leave in a couple of hours for Geneva by helicopter and from there to Paris by Mystere. [. . .] There are six of us travelling together – Mike, Chris, Sara, Caroline and the two of us. Simmy and John Gross, her intended are staying behind until she has to go to school in about five or six days. E tells me that the former hasn't had a single bath since we arrived and only one hasty shower. Last night Simmy cooked us an Hawaiian dish which was delicious. Some sort of marinated steak and guacamole [. . .]

We stayed in all day and read. I read three books: A history of the *Daily News* journalistically written by somebody called John Chapman 'the distinguished theatre critic'!!!![1] *Lord Hornblower* by C. S. Forester, and *Fair Stood the Wind for France*, by H. E. Bates.[2] I was fascinated by Bates' notices, quoted on the front and back covers. One would have thought he'd written a towering masterpiece. It is abjectly readable and that's about all. I read it only yesterday and already it's forgotten. Competent as the devil but totally without reality. Christ, one has to beware of critics – good or bad, one might be constrained to believe them. [. . .]

Sunday 5th, Paris We arrived back at the Plaza Athenée yesterday. We shall be here for about a month or a bit I suppose, depending on how quickly they set about finishing this monumental film of Elizabeth's. So far, including stoppages for illnesses etc. it has been going on since last September. [. . .] In future, we must try and make sure that, if we work at all, the director is a young man, and if possible, a <u>new</u> young man. They can't afford to muck around. And under no circumstances should they be called by others or themselves 'geniuses' or 'significant' or 'artists in movement'. One ends up with a picture that's over-written by the critics and underseen by the audience.

I cannot find the last volume of my diary which covers about 18 months from last September. Presumably I put it in such a safe place before I left that I cannot remember. It wouldn't be very nice if it got into the wrong hands. It's

---

[1] John Arthur Chapman (1900–72), drama critic of the *Daily News*, 1943–71. *Tell It To Sweeney: The Informal History of the New York Daily News* (1961).
[2] C. S. Forester, pseudonym of Cecil Louis Troughton Smith (1899–1966). *Lord Hornblower* (1946). Herbert Ernest Bates (1905–74), *Fair Stood the Wind for France* (1944).

too revealing about other people, but above all about myself. It's supposed to be for the old age of E and myself.

When we arrived back yesterday we found a present and a couple of notes from The Duchess of Windsor. The letter is rather sad. [. . .] Also was a little china box of two children in bed together. With it the note said that it reminded herself and the Duke of *Staircase*. This was the day that Rex left the set in a huff and I pretended to do a scene with no film in the camera to give the Duke and Duchess something, at least, to see.

I lost my temper with the French Customs and Passport Authorities yesterday in Geneva. A stream of bloodcurdling insults came streaming out of my mouth with infinitely greater fluency in French than I normally command. They said nothing but looked at me with such implacable hatred out of their obsidian French eyes that I was constrained to go further. I told them that they were a nation of women and that without the assistance of Anglo-Saxon <u>men</u> they would have lost three wars instead of just the war of 1871. I doubt that I will be received with Ça va biens the next time I go through Geneva. What a mean avare the normal Frenchman is.[3] I prefer the Italians with all their venality. At least they do not believe in the glory of arms. The French do and fail to practise it except under a foreigner like Napoleon. A Corsican Italian.

Tuesday 7th [. . .] I did stills with Rex yesterday, all of which seem to me to be eminently silly or needless or undignified and all three. However rather than hold things up we went through with them. Rex has a cold and is going back to Portofino until it's better. [. . .]

On Sunday last I took the two boys to Fouquet's for lunch together with Bertrand, E's chauffeur. We then pub-crawled all the way home which meant that we were all pretty squiffy by the time we arrived back at the hotel. To compound matters Kevin McCarthy (actor and brother of Mary, the writer) suddenly hove into view with his future wife, a rather hard little Scandinavian.[4] E wasn't too pleased. I promised I wouldn't do it again, but of course I inevitably will.

[. . .] An odd thing happened last weekend at this hotel which after all is one of the most reputable in Paris. In the lobby beside the lift on the 1st floor John Lee and a friend of his observed, lying on the divan, a completely naked man with a clothed woman 'going down on him.' That is to say she was orally masturbating him. John called the Night Manager (it was quite early – about 10.30 at night) who called the police. After a tremendous struggle in which the naked man threw vases and flower pots etc. into the well of the hotel he was finally overpowered and carried away in a strait-jacket. It turned out that the

---

[3] *Avare*: Miser.
[4] Mary McCarthy (1912–89). Kevin McCarthy (1914–2010), divorced from his first wife in 1961, was not to remarry until 1979. His girlfriend in 1969 was Swedish.

man was high on drugs, probably LSD and the lady was of the streets. It is just the kind of thing that one wishes Liza, Maria and Kate to see. What a world.

I read last night in bed some collected articles of Henry Longhurst, the golf correspondent of the *Sunday Times*.[5] I laughed until the tears poured down my face and became quite uncontrollable.

Wednesday 8th [. . .] Last night I read about a third of a book, which I didn't know he'd written, by Harold Nicolson called *The Age of Reason*.[6] It is very readable, often very funny but also I suspect too easily written. He repeats himself quite a bit which I know his fastidious sense of economy and style would have rejected if he'd had more time, or given it more time. But nevertheless very enjoyable. What a monstrous set of characters the Age of Reason produced. It might have been called the Age of Monomaniacal Monarchs: Fred the Great of Prussia, Catherine the Great of Muscovy and Peter the Great and the Roi de Solieul.[7] Cor! My spelling. Murder and torture, regicide, suicide, infanticide, banishment and all the vices in the book. Catherine the Great had a lady-in-waiting who was known as the 'eprouveuse' who as her name implies tried out the Guards officers in bed first to find out if they would be satisfactory to the Empress of all the Russias. Imagine being found wanting. On second thoughts, imagine being wanted by that raddled old gummy collection of jaded appetites. Peter the Great liked chopping people's heads off and had a long tree trunk laid on the ground so that decapitation of heads as they lay in a row was facilitated. None of that hanging about saying 'next please.' He also fancied orgies and defecated and urinated where he stood. Peter the third, I think, used to tie his Dachsund to the roof-beam with a rope and have a servant hold the hind legs while he flogged the poor little thing. Fragrant lot. Frederick the Great's father used to beat the bejasus out of him with a knout and drag him through mud with his face in it, <u>by the hair</u>. No wonder the man was a screaming homosexual. This, if you please, Fred's father would do to the crown prince in front of the officers. When of course his father died Fred the Great was just as bad. He would rush screaming down the corridors of his castle with a heavy knotted stick and beat anybody who stood within reach. All those servants, there were hundreds, running like mad looking for a hiding place. It must have made the Crazy Gang look sane.[8]

---

[5] Henry Longhurst (1909–78), had published *Only on Sundays* (1964), a collection of his pieces from the *Sunday Times*, and *Talking about Golf* (1966), a collection from *Golf Illustrated*.

[6] Harold Nicolson (1886–1968), *The Age of Reason* (1960).

[7] Frederick II, known as Frederick the Great (1712–86), King of Prussia (1740–86). Catherine II, known as Catherine the Great (1729–96), Empress of Russia (1762–96). Peter I, known as Peter the Great (1672–1725), Emperor of Russia (1682–1725). Louis XIV, also known as the 'Roi Soleil', the Sun King (1638–1715), King of France (1643–1715).

[8] 'The Crazy Gang': British entertainers including Bud Flanagan (1896–1968), and Chesney Allen (1893–1982) active from the mid-1930s to the late 1950s.

I am also reading a book about the French Resistance and so I am fairly up
to the knees in blood. There were a lot of old scores paid off there too I'm sure.
My God the amount of blood that has been needlessly spilt. [. . .]

Thursday 9th Yesterday was a lovely day cold and sparkling. Today is badger-
grey and tired again. I started to dream of Puerto Vallarta and the bedroom
patio and sun-bathing and tacos and frijoles and tequila, and walks through
the cobbled town at dusk and boating to deserted beaches with tuna sandwiches and ice-cold home-made lemon juice and fishing for Dorado and baby
sharks.[9] And the memory of being salt-cleaned and clear-skinned and even
slim. We'll go to Mismaloya and swim in the warm sea and plunge immediately afterwards into the cold, by comparison <u>very</u> cold fresh water river.[10] I
even look forward to the noise and it must surely be the noisiest town per head
of population in the world, church bells and a gun instead of a bell for the poor
church across the river, steel bands, donkeys braying, cocks crowing – the
latter never seeming to know what time of day it is. Serenaders staggering on
marijuana coming to do homage to Elizabeth at four in the morning, children
dancing in the street outside to the rhythm of a fiddle played by the man who
runs the delicatessen next door. But not of course at four in the morning, more
like 8 to 10. And jeeping towards the airport and then up into the hills where
the rivers have to be forded in the jeep as there are no bridges. Once E and I
were temporarily stuck in the middle of such a river and only after waiting
patiently for the engine to dry out were we able to proceed cautiously to the
other bank. Then back to Jack Keyward's bar which is at sand level and only
half a stone's throw from the edge of the sea which is relatively tideless.[11] Lots
of books to read and Spanish Grammars and perhaps the iguanas have come
back to live on the roof. You never know.

I've decided to go on a mild diet, one known as the 'Drinking Man's Diet'
to see if I can lose a few pounds gently. This morning in pyjamas I was [. . .]
13 stone 3 pounds. I'd like to be about 12 stone 7. [. . .]

I took the boys and Sara to lunch at D'Chez Eux and ate myself silly on the
hors d'oeuvres, salami of three different kinds, several terrines and patés and
sweet onions in a sauce and peas and beans and black bread with butter washed
down by the locally made cold sweet wine. [. . .] I returned home and ate half
a pound of liquorice allsorts, a pint of milk. No wonder I'm a little over-weight.
[. . .]

This diary is really no good to anyone but me. It forces me to keep my mind
in some kind of untidy order and is better than nothing for my laziness.

---

[9] Dorado, also known as Mahi-Mahi, commonly known as the dolphin fish.
[10] Mismaloya: a beach 40 miles south of Puerto Vallarta, where much of *The Night of the Iguana* was
shot.
[11] Jack Keyward (possibly Hayward) – also a friend and neighbour in Puerto Vallarta.

Friday 10th Yesterday was a day of funny moods. It began well enough with a blue sky and the promise of taking E to lunch. She finished early and we had a late lunch at La Cascade in the Bois de Boulogne.[12] I stuck to my diet and had a whisky and soda before lunch followed by ½ dozen belons,[13] a steak au poivre, a salad with French dressing and a hefty lump of cheese. I drank Lafite '60, about two glasses, and two or three brandies after the cheese with sugarless and creamless coffee. Later that night I had a couple more whiskies and soda. Apart from water that's all I took in all day. This morning the scale showed a loss of between four and five pounds. I was very surprised. A couple of weeks of this and I shall be belsenic.[14] [. . .] E was astonishingly drunk even as I got to lunch. I don't recollect her before ever being incoherent from drink. I expect it from the drugs she's forced to take, but not from the booze. Christ I hope she's alright. It would be frightful to live the rest of our lives in an alcoholic haze, seeing the world through fumes of spirits and cigarette smoke. Never quite sure what you did or said the day before, or what you read, whether wise or foolish, tardy or too soon. Good I'm going to have a whisky and soda right now. There are few pleasures to match tipsiness in this murderous world especially if, like me, you believe in your bones that it, the world as we know it, is not going to last much longer. This is the age of the abyss and any minute now or dark day we could tumble over the edge into primal chaos. Some frigging foreigner will press a button and gone it will all be. Even the Miners Arms in Pontrhydyfen.[15] Our little lives will be shattered with a cosmic bang. 'These millions of white faces,' as Archie MacLeish says, and then 'nothing, nothing, nothing at all.'[16] But don't let's be stoned all the time. Let's have days and days of brilliant clarity, etched and limpid, cool and surgical.

I think I had an overdose of History lately. The more I read about man and his maniacal ruthlessness and his murdering envious scatological soul the more I realize that he will never change. Our stupidity is immortal, nothing will change it. The same mistakes, the same prejudices, the same injustice, the same lusts wheel endlessly around the parade-ground of the centuries. Immutable and ineluctable. I wish I could believe in a God of some kind but I simply cannot. My intelligence is too muscular and my imagination stops at the horizon, and I have an idea that the last sound to be heard on this lovely planet will be a man screaming. In fear and terror. It might be me. Though I beg that I many go down into the awful dreadful night without a word, like

---

[12] La Grande Cascade au Bois de Boulogne, Allée de Longchamp, Paris.
[13] Belons: flat oysters.
[14] Presumably a reference to the appearance of survivors of the Nazi death camp at Bergen-Belsen.
[15] The pub in Richard's home village.
[16] This is a rather inaccurate borrowing from Archibald MacLeish's (1892–1982) poem 'The End of the World', published in 1935. The relevant lines are 'Those thousands of white faces, those dazed eyes, / There in the starless dark, the poise, the hover / There with vast wings across the canceled skies, / There in the sudden blackness the black pall / Of nothing, nothing, nothing – nothing at all.'

my father Dic Bach Y Saer.[17] Or perhaps just one admonitory and despairing
'Tuck you.'

Saturday 11th Yesterday I went to Alex Maguy's art gallery to try and help Sara
to persuade him to take back a Vuillard which she and Francis had and have
found unsaleable in California, and swap it for a couple of Kislings or
Marquets.[18] He agreed though he has consistently refused for the past few
years. She says that this was entirely due to my presence, my gift of the gab,
even in French, and my fame! [. . .] He's a tiny man who claims to be a great
friend of Picasso's, and indeed he has in his own home an impressive collection of Picassos including one that makes Elizabeth's mouth water. It's a lady in
a blue dress with a dark blue hat with light blue lights in it and she is holding
up what appears to be a train of white feathers. We haven't seen the original,
but he, Alex has promised to invite us to his home to see it. [. . .] Even I like it.
I saw many other paintings and will obviously end up buying one. There is a
charming little Picasso of a Harlequin on a horse for which he's asking $40,000.
[. . .] There's also a medium-sized Marquet, a landscape of Algeria which I like
very much for $24,000 dollars. But the most impressive was two paintings by
Van Gogh painted on both sides of the canvas – one of a man at a loom and
one (the other side) of a man sitting in a chair near a fireplace it seems. But
they are beyond even my purse. There was too, I thought, a very good-looking
Vlaminck of a Cafe de la Gare, but nobody else was impressed.[19] Michael was
with us, he [. . .] unlike me, has a great feeling for art. I hope he becomes an
artist. It seems to go with his dreamy personality. He doesn't seem to pack
enough dynamite to be an actor and he is certainly not literary. He is only just
beyond the comics stage. He wouldn't read Shakespeare or even Dickens from
choice I know. Yesterday he asked me if he might choose a book to read – I
have a small library here in the hotel of about 200 books excluding reference
books – and he chose a History of the Movies. Full of pictures of course. [. . .]
    We stayed in, E didn't get home till 9 o'clock. Yesterday I had the following to
eat and drink: Bloody Mary, Two Scotch and sodas, two softboiled eggs, for tea
½ dozen oysters with a glass of white wine, in the evening three cups of instant
bouillon, for supper a chunk of Chateaubriand and a few stalks of Endive salad.
And two vodka martinis. Result loss of a little less than a pound. Really to
encourage weight losers they should calibrate weighing scales in ounces.

Sunday 12th Yesterday I sustained myself as follows: 2 vodka martinis, 2 slices
of calves liver and bacon, two rashers of bacon, ½ of Spanish Honeydew

---

[17] Dic Bach y Saer – literally 'little Dic the carpenter', Richard's father.
[18] The Galerie d'Elysée of Alex Maguy. Edouard Vuillard (1868–1940); Moise Kisling (1891–1953);
Albert Marquet (1875–1947): painters.
[19] Maurice de Vlaminck (1876–1958), French painter.

melon, two glasses of Riesling (Johannisberger, very good) salad with roquefort dressing. Result a loss in weight of about 3/4 of a pound. I am now something like 12 stone 11 or 179 pounds. [. . .] Fighting fit and hard as iron when
I was playing rugby I was 12 stones 7, but that alas was 20 years ago and weight
has shifted to the wrong parts of the body. [. . .]

We stayed in all day and for the first time I watched French Television,
though we've had the set here for three or four months. I watched
Scotland play France in rugby (the former won against the run of the play
by 6–3) [. . .]

We had Sara for lunch. I cannot make up my mind whether she is a pin-
head or very shrewd. She is certainly very aware of money. Tomorrow I go
with her to some French Government 'expert' to decide whether an Utrillo she
and Francis bought before the war for $1,800 is genuine or not.[20] If he decides
against he apparently has the right to burn it! I offered to buy it from her to
save it at least from that fate but she has some muddled obligation to an art
dealer in LA called Ruth Hatfield.[21] [. . .] The people from whom she and
Francis bought it were apparently all knocked off by the Nazis during the
occupation. They were Jews. [. . .]

Monday 13th My sins have come home to find me! Who would have thought
that a man who had been known in his time to smash windows or fight against
odds as a result of drunkenness should be appalled by it in others? At least
others close to him. And who's closer than E? For the last month now, with
very few exceptions she has gone to bed not merely sozzled or tipsy but <u>stoned</u>.
And I mean stoned, unfocused, unable to walk straight, talking in a slow
meaningless baby voice utterly without reason like a demented child. I
thought, at first, that it was merely drugs but I understand that the stuff she's
having now is merely vitamins so it has to be good old-fashioned booze. I
made a desperate attempt this last weekend, when there was no pressure of
work on her, to see if I could handle it. Result: the same. The awful thing is
that it's turned <u>me</u> off drink! So perhaps it has its virtue. There is very little I
can do about it. It would be a mistake to have a notorious old pet lecture, with
much finger-wagging, a decaying kettle. So I'll continue to pray that it is a
psychological reaction from that bloody removal of the uterus last summer,
that it is only temporary, and that gradually she'll come back to normal. I'll
have to be very careful that I don't allow myself to join her otherwise we'll have
to get a keeper to look after us both. But the boredom, unless I'm drunk too,
of being in the presence of someone to whom you have to repeat everything
twice is like a physical pain in the stomach. If it was anyone else of course I'd
pack my bags, head for the hills and go and live in a Trappist monastery, but

20 Maurice Utrillo (1883–1955), painter.
21 Ruth Hatfield of the Dalzell Hatfield Galleries, Ambassador Hotel, Wilshire Boulevard, Los Angeles.

this woman is my life. I cannot go to work with her though I will try this afternoon and see how she functions on the set. Last night I was so worried about her and us that I didn't get to sleep until well after dawn. I tried to imagine life without her but couldn't. The intolerable dreariness of her life in that studio is hard to watch. Endless long takes from a multitude of angles, surrounded with possibly the dullest collection of sycophants it has ever been my pain to come across. [. . .]

We stayed in all day [. . .] I read a biog auto of Lord Egremont amusing but fatuous.[22] His friends obviously think him a scream. And two detective stories by Michael Innes.[23] [. . .]

Tuesday 14th I went yesterday with Sara to see the 'expert' M. Paul C. Petrides.[24] [. . .] he did his best to sell me a couple of paintings including a dreadful semi-nude by Picasso. It's of a lady with a disgusting figure wearing nothing but a pair of stockings half sitting on a divan. Such is the angle of her body that she appears to have no arms. Her dreadful pubic hairs are well in evidence and she is altogether, Picasso or not, a woman that I would well do without on my gallery wall. [. . .] He tore off the brown paper from Sara's 'Utrillo' and after one swift glance said 'fake'. It was the first time I'd seen it and even I knew it was. [. . .]

After the art gallery I took Sara over to E's studio where we played gin rummy and afterwards watched a scene. E was very good and in total command as usual. Warren Beatty seems very self-conscious and actory. He's not out of the top drawer. He doesn't give that feeling of vibrant power as Rex does or the lethargic dynamism of Marlon. I can feel the power of a top class actor or actress come out in almost palpable waves. I felt nothing from this chap. He is competent and pretty and is doing and will do well. Nice too with it, as they say. [. . .]

Thursday 16th [. . .] [Elizabeth] has managed to persuade her company to give her next Wednesday off and work the following Saturday, so that she can come with me to London for the opening of *Eagles*. So we shall fly on Wednesday morning, see Ivor in the afternoon, attend the opening on Wednesday night and fly back in time for her to work on Thursday. [. . .]

The boys left for Millfield yesterday with very long faces and a great many hints that a phone call from me could quite easily get them an extra couple of days. I thought about it but they are very bored here in Paris, they have no pals and despite their fluent French feel very lost. So it was just as well to pack them off.

---

[22] John Edward Reginald Wyndham, 6th Baron Leconfield and 1st Baron Egremont (1920–72).
[23] Michael Innes, the pseudonym of J. I. M. Stewart (1906–94).
[24] Paul C. Petrides (1901–93), art dealer, sole agent of Utrillo.

I recorded for the BBC the day before yesterday. Instead of four or five poems as promised there were more like fifteen.[25] [. . .]

[Elizabeth] seems to be crashingly bored with everything in the world at the moment. It is virtually impossible to excite her interest in anything: books, gossip, her own film, her mother, her children or me.

Friday 17th [. . .] I stayed in all day yesterday and read and read and read. E came home about 8.30 muttering at the idiocy of a director who wants to shoot a 17 minute scene all in one take and then covers it with umpty-nine different angles. It would seem to me to be an indication of monumental conceit on George's part or, more probably, that he doesn't know what he wants, that he is, in fact, insecure. I am not being wise after the event when I say that it was a mistake to do this film. Let's hope at least that it makes money. E and Caroline and everybody at the studio tell me that suddenly Beatty has suddenly started to come the big star act and is ordering people off the set etc. Ah well.

Monday 20th Yesterday there was an article in the *Daily Mirror* or rather *Sunday Mirror* by that somewhat pompous and humourless *Life* magazine writer Tommy Thompson about E.[26] Among other things, for the most part it was meant to be friendly I think, it said she was 38 while she still is 36, that she was 'thickening' while she's been the same weight for ten years, apart from *Virginia Woolf* period when she deliberately put on weight, and that she was 'greying'. True, the latter but she's been greying for ten years. Ah well. He also says that we never talk about anything but money, so there I've been pouring out my knowledge into his tin ear for days on end in my dressing room and it appears that all I talked about was money. He drank my drinks all day long didn't he? That's money. There is a tendency among certain writers, especially the sententious, to create 'fine' pieces of writing about us. They are all the same. The rich couple, living their lives in a fishbowl glare of publicity, unable to take an ordinary walk in an ordinary city street, mobbed wherever we go, protected by a huge entourage. [. . .] What they don't understand and completely misinterpret is our life-long attitudes to our jobs. I think Mr Thompson was deeply shocked when I told him that acting on stage or films, apart from one or two high moments of nervous excitement, was sheer drudgery. That if I retired from acting professionally tomorrow that I would never appear in the local amateur dramatic society for the sheer love of it. Could he not understand the indignity and the boredom of having to learn the writings of another man, which nine times out of ten was indifferent, when you are 43 years old, are fairly widely read, drag yourself off to work day after day with a long lingering regretful look behind you at the book you're

[25] Possibly for the LP *The World of Dylan Thomas, in Poetry and Prose* (1971).
[26] Thomas Thompson, 'Power and Liz Burton', *Sunday Mirror*, 19 January 1969.

interested in. [. . .] They will never understand that E and I are not 'dedicated' and that my 'first love' (God how many times have I read that?) is not the stage. It is a book with lovely words in it. When I retire which I must do before long I shall write a screaming diatribe against the whole false world of journalism and show business. [. . .]

Wednesday 22nd [. . .] I stayed in all day and read a lot of *Time* capsules. E arrived home from work crocked as a sock, sloshed as a Cossack. I was sober as a Presbyterian, which wasn't a good idea. My sense of humour was not at its best, which also was not a good idea. I have an idea that I am fighting a losing battle.

We leave for London a quarter of an hour ago for the first night of *Eagles*. I couldn't care less but I like Kastner and it's a chance to see Ivor.

I am to see David Harlech at 6 at the Dorchester.[27] I will doubtless see a great many other people. I shall loathe it all. Give me a scallop shell of silence?[28]

[There are no further entries in the diary until late March. During this time Richard and Elizabeth travelled to Caesar's Palace, Las Vegas where filming of *The Only Game in Town* was completed, before going on to Puerto Vallarta. On 26 January Richard bought the pearl La Peregrina for Elizabeth, when it was auctioned at Sotheby's. The jewel had a distinguished history, having been a gift from Philip of Spain to his bride, Mary Tudor, Queen of England, in 1554. In February Elizabeth's first husband, Nick Hilton, died. In March Elizabeth underwent tests in the Cedars of Lebanon hospital, Los Angeles for her chronic back problems.]

MARCH

Thursday 20th, Puerto Vallarta [. . .] Another long silence in this pathetic journal occasioned I suppose by acute unhappiness added to stupendous quantities of guilt, alcohol, laziness, fear for Elizabeth's health and reason, stirred up well with a pinch or two of Celtic pessimism and served as a first class recipe for suicide. It is by no means over. I am still as tightly drawn as a long bow by John of Gaunt, and as touchy as a fretful porpentine but it gets better every day.[29]

The last six or eight months have been a nightmare. I created one half and Elizabeth the other. We grated on each other to the point of separation. I had thought of going to live alone in some remote shack in a rainy place and E had

---

[27] David Ormsby-Gore (1918–95), 5th Baron Harlech.
[28] A reference to the line by Sir Walter Raleigh (c.1552–1618), in 'The Passionate Man's Pilgrimage' (1604): 'Give me my scallop-shell of quiet'.
[29] 'Like quills upon the fretful porpentine', a line spoken by the Ghost in *Hamlet*, Act I, scene v. John of Gaunt, 1st Duke of Lancaster (1340–99), and a character in Shakespeare's *Richard II*.

thought of going to stay with Howard in Hawaii. It is of course quite impossible. We are bound together. Hoop-steeled. Whither thou goest.[30] He said hopefully.

Elizabeth has started to read again and I have started to write so there's hopes isn't there boys? I dread the children coming down here. My temper is still fine-drawn on the edge of impatience and trying to accommodate that with the warring claims of Liza and Maria and, to a lesser extent, with the demands of Chris and Mike is going to stretch my nerves to the limit. The fact is that children bore me. I discovered after a couple of days of fairly close proximity with Kate in Beverly Hills – and after all I don't see very much of her – that I could do without her too. I long for them to grow up and come and see us only at Christmastime, during which festivities I shall build an igloo in the garden and not come out until the New Year. [. . .]

Friday 21st [. . .] E's stay in hospital in Los Angeles started another and inevitable wave of rumours. The *Detroit Free Press* announced that she was in the Cedars of Lebanon because she had cancer of the spine.[31] So much space in print and time of TV was accorded this rumour that I almost began to believe it myself. [. . .]

I will try, as I've tried before in this diary, to fill in some of the things I missed as I write from day to day.

Saturday 22nd [. . .] We were in Las Vegas for about five or six days about 3 weeks ago. It was a horrible place and, if possible, I will never go back there again. Caroline Elizabeth Jim and I seemed to me on reflection to have been permanently drunk from dawn 'til dawn. I only went out once in five days. I suppose if I played golf or liked to gamble I might have enjoyed myself. In daytime it is among the most horrible places I've ever seen. A dirty beige desert with gimcrack houses and a long strip of neon-lighted places of entertainment called indeed 'the Strip'. At night however it was very pretty with all the various coloured lights flashing and winking. But as Chesterton is reputed to have said when he saw Times Square for the first time and at night-time: 'One of the prettiest places on earth if one couldn't read.'[32] A cascade of rippling lights miraculously changing colours and shapes eventually enjoins you to eat Planter's Peanuts. A cunningly contrived and eye-compelling neon fireworks display informs you eventually that it's 'Joe's Diner'. The only time I went out I took E to the Desert Inn, which I remembered from 12 or 15 years ago to be

---

[30] 'Whither thou goest, I will go' – from the Book of Ruth in the Old Testament, Chapter I verse 16.
[31] A reference to what was by this time known as the Cedars-Sinai Medical Center, located at Fountain Avenue, Los Angeles.
[32] G. K. Chesterton (1874–1936), journalist, poet, novelist, critic. The line is usually rendered as 'How beautiful it would be for someone who could not read.'

rather elegant.[33] It no longer is. The food was horrible, the service indifferent, the people automatons. In the whole place E and I decided, and it was a large restaurant called, I think, The Cactus Room, there was only one attractive person – possibly a show-girl walking through or a honeymoon bride. The rest were of an unsurpassable lower-middle-class vulgarity and softly ugly with it. A great many women, all around the forty-five to fifty mark, were dyed blondes with exactly the same hairdos. One of them, obviously thinking she was a dish, made many strutted journeys past our table, ostentatiously not looking at us. At least 50% of them were Jews. What an extraordinary thing that the race which produced Einstein, Marx, Freud and Jesus Christ should also produce these loud-mouthed dumb-bells.

Monday 24th We went to Phil Ober's for drinks and a buffet dinner on Saturday night. The place was packed with the gringo drifters of this town, or perhaps 'escapees' is the word I mean. We must have been the youngest people there. There was a woman called Pantages of the famous Hollywood Pantages Cinema and her brother (a queen), Phil Ober himself, who is a well known character actor on TV etc. and his charming wife.[34] There was a famous news commentator for CBS called Charles Collingwood and his scatty but enchanting wife who used to be quite a well-known actress I understand called Louise Allbritton.[35] Jim and George tell us that though this whole community pretend indifference to these 'movie stars' as they describe us over their booze and drugs, nevertheless the whole room, for a second or two, lost its breath when we walked in and then talked frantically for the rest of the evening, trying desperately not to look at us [. . .].

I became somewhat drunk and was glad to get home. I woke up next morning feeling dreadful and shaky [. . .] to find to my dismay that E had invited Collingwood and wife, the two Pantages and their friend for lunch. I downed two vodkas and limeade to sweeten my disposition. [. . .]

Tuesday 25th It is 4.30 in the morning and I am typing this in the new lower house. Cocks are crowing and an occasional donkey brays. The town itself is silent and no traffic moves. There is a quite large pleasure steamer out in the bay with all its lights blazing. It looks very cosy and safe. The kettle is boiling and it's time for morning tea. [. . .]

I went to the dentist and he X-Rayed my teeth. [. . .] The dentist's operating room was as neat and well equipped as any I have seen in Europe or the States, in complete contrast to the other rooms. This dentist looks as if he's

---

[33] The Desert Inn, hotel and casino, Las Vegas (1950–2000).
[34] The Pantages Theatre, built for the entrepreneur Alexander Pantages (1876–1936) in 1930. Phil Ober (1902–82), actor, married to his third wife, Jane Westover.
[35] Charles Collingwood (1917–85), newscaster and writer. Louise Allbritton (1920–79), actor.

overworked. If he is I think I will arrange to get him an assistant and a second operating room. I will find out these things through Ray Marshall.[36] [. . .]

After the dentist and before dinner I took E out for the first time in the Renault. It's a blue, enclosed car, very small and runs well except that it is much too hot in this climate. I shall sell it after this trip. I've seen a few little open cars around called beach-bugs. I shall get one of those. If possible. We drove down towards Mismaloya on the new road which, when paved is going to be superb. We stopped at a brand new Hotel called Garza Blanca (White Heron) and had a couple of tequilas.[37] [. . .] E is looking gorgeous, though she's still a little tubby. How the sun suits her.

Wednesday 26th [. . .] I worked off and on yesterday at the article for *Look* magazine about Wales.[38] I wrote it in longhand and then laboriously typed it last night until about midnight, so, since I'd been up since 4o'clock the previous morning and awake for two hours before that, it was a weary man who dragged himself to bed. I'm afraid to look at it this morning in case I don't like it and have to do it all over again. It's about 2500–2600 words. I am falling into a trap as a writer that I should guard against very carefully if my ambitions as a minor scribe persist. The trap of talking myself out. I've always known it to be fatal for any writers but particularly the kind who are as glib and articulate as myself. I will frequently reject a fairly fine turn of phrase when writing because I've heard myself say it a couple of times and therefore seems to me to be a cliché. [. . .]

Thursday 27th Got up this morning about nine, though I'd been awake again since 2.30. E and I chatted for three or four hours. [. . .] I told E lots of stories about the Romantic Poets. I dozed a little later, awoke from a frightful nightmare and got up and wrote a letter to Gwyneth asking her to get me some Welsh books and a Grammar and a Dictionary.[39] Syb, who can't read a word of Welsh, took them all to NY when she left. Perhaps Jordan is learning Welsh!

[. . .] Everybody found favour with my piece about Wales though E found the end rather lame so I wrote a more powerful ending. She likes it so there it is. Now we'll wait and see if it's too late for *Look* magazine – the deadline was two, no three weeks ago. If it is I'll sell it to some other mag. *Life* magazine have always said they will publish anything I write. So I could foist it on to them, though they're hardly likely to pay me *Look*'s price which is $2,500. Also they wanted caption writing to go under photographs of Wales rather than an article, so perhaps they'll reject it for that reason. Anyway we'll see.

---

[36] Ray Marshall, house agent in Puerto Vallarta.
[37] Today a resort complex.
[38] Burton's article, 'Who Cares About Wales? I Care', would appear in *Look* on 24 June 1969.
[39] Gwyneth Jenkins, a close friend of Gwen, Ivor's wife and Richard's sister-in-law.

I am enjoying this holiday so much that I am beginning to think I really could retire from acting, and write occasional pieces, I will watch myself over the next five weeks and see how my restlessness goes. [. . .] Perhaps one film, at a reduced fee every three years. And only something really worthwhile.

Friday 28th Another brilliant morning. I awoke at nine. I went to bed about 9 and read a book of Ian Fleming's called *You only live twice*.[40] A clever schoolboy mind and atrociously vulgar. And every so often he stops his narrative to give little homilies about food drink national morals etc. all of excruciating banality. Yet ever since the phenomenal success of the films about his hero James Bond and the books, – I'm not sure which came first, and of course his death, he is actually being treated seriously by serious critics. I put the light out about midnight and slept for a couple of hours, woke and read a short novel by Nathaniel West *Miss Lonelyhearts*.[41] What a contrast between that and Fleming. West's book is taut, spare and agonized while the other is diffuse, urbane and empty. West hates himself and postulates a theory that you are always killed by the thing you love, while Fleming loves only himself, his attraction to women, his sexual prowess, 'the-hint-of-cruelty-in-the-mouth'-sadistic bit, his absurd and comically pompous attitude to food and cocktails 'be sure the martini is shaken not stirred'. He has the cordon-bleu nerve to attack one of my favourite discoveries: American short-order cooking. I remember with watering mouth the soda fountain on 81st Street, one block west of the park in Manhattan, where in a blur of conjuring the cook would produce corned-beef hash with a fried egg on top and french fries on the side and a salad with a choice of about four or five dressings. All this magically produced and whipped on to the table, piping hot before you'd finished the comic strips in the *Herald Tribune*, or read Red Smith's wry column.[42] Yet you cannot help liking Fleming. He is obviously enjoying the creation of his extroverted, Hemingwayese, sadistic, sexually maniacal boy-scout that in the end he becomes likeable. I rather like him too for his death line, if the reports are true. He was about 57 and had known for some time that he had a diseased heart. He is reputed to have said: 'Well, it's been a hell of a bloody lark.'[43] And of course, to that bonviveur, woman-chasing, intelligently-muscled mind it had been. [. . .]

Saturday 29th [. . .] I received a letter, a note more, from Chas Collingwood, saying that he thought I had written a 'hell of a good piece' and enclosing an

[40] Ian Fleming (1908–64), *You Only Live Twice* (1964).
[41] Nathaniel West, *Miss Lonelyhearts* (1933).
[42] Red Smith (1905–82), sports journalist who had worked for the *New York Herald Tribune*.
[43] Another version is that his last words were to ambulancemen: 'Awfully sorry to trouble you chaps'.

article by Denis Brogan in the *Spectator* anent Breton Independence.[44] We are to dine with them in their casa tonight. [. . .]

Elizabeth is now looking ravishingly sun-tanned though the lazy little bugger ought to lose a few pounds or so to look at her absolute best. Looking as critically as I can at her yesterday I could detect no sign of ageing in her at all, except that she has quite a few grey hairs, mostly at the temples. But the skin is as smooth and youthful and unwrinkled as ever it was. The breasts, despite their largeness and considerable weight, sag very slightly but no more than they did 10 years ago. Her bottom is firm and round. She needs weight off her stomach, not so much out of vanity, but because all the medical men say it will ease her bad back if she has less weight to carry for'ard. She swam quite a lot yesterday and if she keeps that up she should be quite firm by the time we get back to London. Dreadful thought, London. [. . .] However it will be a chance to see Ivor more often. And the kids. Might even be time to watch some cricket with Ivor on Sunday afternoons and read books to him and chat. [. . .]

Sunday 30th We roasted in the sun all day and read. E read *Portnoy's Complaint* while I read a book translated from the Spanish called *The Labyrinth of Solitude* written by a poet called Octavio Paz.[45] I am finding it very tough going and one of those assertive books which make me long to argue back. Like most books of self-conscious philosophy it is totally lacking in humour. I like merry philosophers. To relieve my mind I would read a fairly entertaining thriller-with-a-message by Simon Raven, between slabs of the Paz book.[46] It is very difficult to understand how any man can seriously discuss Mexico and Mexicans as if they are all one unit. 'The Mexican is impassive, he is such a prideful man that he will not reveal himself even to his closest friend. etc.'[47] Balls. I know a great many Mexicans and the impassive ones, though the word that is nearer the mark is 'sullen', are almost always uneducated and poor. The educated are like their counterparts in Spain, vivacious and wild and romantic. He is equally sweeping about the Yanks. 'Men and women are subjected from childhood to an inexorable process of adaptation; certain principles in brief formulas are endlessly repeated by the press, the radio, the churches, and the schools . . . They become imprisoned by these schemes like a plant in a flow-erpot too small for it: they cannot grow or mature.'[48] It may be so but it is also

---

[44] Denis Brogan (1900–74), historian, academic, author of *The Development of Modern France, 1870–1939* (1940), *The French Nation, 1814–1940* (1957) and *French Personalities and Problems* (1946).

[45] Philip Roth (1933–), *Portnoy's Complaint* (1969). Octavio Paz (1914–98), poet and essayist. *The Labyrinth of Solitude: Life and Thought in Mexico*, 1950; English translation 1961.

[46] Simon Raven (1927–2001), novelist.

[47] This would appear to be a paraphrase of Paz's argument rather than a direct quotation.

[48] The quotation is not entirely accurate: it should be 'certain principles, contained in brief formulas', and 'A person imprisoned by these schemes . . . he cannot grow or mature' (*Labyrinth of Solitude*, p. 25).

so here in Puerto Vallarta, if P.V. can be assumed to be a typical small town. The Church dominates everything, and from the endless radios that blare from every house as you take a walk the people are only interested in listening to endless noisy bad music. Wouldn't it be awful for Mr Paz if he ever found out that behind the immense 'impassivity' of the Mexican Indian, there was, as we have found in the American Red Indian, nothing nothing nothing at all. Or not very much. I'll keep on ploughing through it. I suppose I feel strongly about this mass lumping of races together from my teens in Oxford and the RAF. 'Taffy was a Welshman, Taffy was a thief.' It's like the myth of the 'fighting Irish'. I was so obsessed by this romantic appellation as compared to ours 'Sly, devious and untrustworthy' that I picked fights with Irishmen wherever I was or whenever I could. It was amazing how few would stand up and fight unless they had the support of a lot of pals. Or again the fable of the cold reserved tight-upper-lip Englishman. Well read his books or his poetry and you'll find that he is riddled with woolly sentimental ideas, and a slush of snob-ridden self pity. I will elaborate on this thesis one day. Or about the crafty penny-pinching Scot and the avaricious Jew. In general I have found them to be generous to the point of folly. [. . .]

Monday 31st [. . .] I am on the 'Drinking Man's Diet' or the 'Low Carbo-hydrate diet' to give it a more respectable title. I rather like dieting. It means I look forward to the next meal whereas normally I'm indifferent. It also means that I don't waste anything. [. . .] Now if only I can get down to what the books say is my proper weight for my height – I am about 5ft 10½ins – and smoke 'à-la-Liza' I shall be among the fittest middle-aged actors in the business. Smokin' 'à-la-Liza' is smoking without inhaling. Just before her last (11th) birthday, which is August 6th, I asked her what she wanted as a present. She said very solemnly that the only present she wanted was for me to give up smoking. I said that was impossible for me to do. I had tried, I said, and had once gone for five months without nicotine but that in the process I became impossible to live with, and even with cigarettes I am not very easy to have around, and found, like Sigmund Freud, who gave up smoking for thirty years and took it up again because he 'couldn't concentrate', that my work was suffering. So she suggested, very sensibly that I should smoke but not inhale. I agreed to try [. . .] The oddest result is that puffing without inhaling tends to give me a sore throat. She is due here any day now and I can't wait to see that determined little face when she sees the donkey which I've hired for her. [. . .]

George Davis told me that Louise [Collingwood] is a lush – she has certainly been drunk every time I've met her so far – and that because of her drunkenness she cost Charles his job as head of CBS (in Paris) in Europe. At one reception she entered the banquet room or whatever and fell flat on her face. She told de Gaulle that she adored the way he spoke French because he was the only Frenchman she understood. She also called him 'honey'. He didn't take it at all well. Poor girl. She says she did a play with Michael Redgrave in London five years ago, that it, the play, had the word 'sun' in its title, that it ran for 15 months and, after much thought, decided that the playwright's name was Hunter. Probably N.C.[49] This was at lunchtime before one had had one's first drink! I hope she's not a drunken liar. She's so gay and nice.

APRIL

April fool's day, Tuesday 1st Well Louise is not a fibber, she is merely a lush. She <u>did</u> do a play in London with Michael and Vanessa Redgrave and it <u>was</u> written by N. C. Hunter, and it <u>did</u> have the word 'sun' in the title. It was in fact called *A Touch of Sun*.[50]

We had the Collingwoods and the three teenage girls to lunch plus Jim, George and two friends called Bronson and Hayes. The latter gets my Oscar for the queerest queer I've ever seen. When I first saw him I genuinely thought he was a woman. He wore an outrageous toupée which he took off later. [. . .]

As usual when surrounded by strangers, I drank far too much. Martini after Martini and later drove E down to the town where I drank tequila after tequila. [. . .] The jeep has turned up freshly painted in lavender and looks very pretty. I am going to paint E's name on the side. Just in case people don't know who she is!

The above is about as far as I could get yesterday. I was just too impossibly lazy and hung-over to muster up the energy.[51]

Wednesday 2nd Yesterday, after failing to finish my daily page, I asked E if she thought we should do a tour of the town and do our duties to the various hostelleries. This was also a sly opportunity to imbibe a few dog's hairs. So about 11.30 we set off [. . .]. We went to La Oceana first which is right close to the sea. It was virtually empty when we went in, but by the time we'd had one drink, and we only had one, the place was packed to standing room only. It was not quite as marked at the next hotel [. . .] but that filled up nicely too. That hotel is called La Rosita.[52] E went to the lavatory there and said it was disgusting. [. . .] The next port of call was an [*sic*] hotel down by Nelly's place on the Muertos Beach. It was horrible and gimcrack and the people equally so. We felt claustrophobic and left in a hurry, not, however, before we had met the Mayor and somebody representing the President and agreed to go to Guadalahara to receive gold medals for being Friends of Mexico or something. Well we surely have been friends to Puerto Vallarta. I remember when Ray

[49] Michael Redgrave (1908–85), actor, father of Vanessa. Norman Charles Hunter (1908–71).
[50] *A Touch of the Sun* (1958).
[51] Presumably typed on the following day.
[52] Hotel Rosita, Paseo Díaz Ordaz, Puerto Vallarta.

Stark told me where the location of *Night of the Iguana* was that we all had to look it up on a map. It wasn't there and we had to get information from the nearest Mexican Embassy. Now there are huge signs in Los Angeles which enjoin one to 'Fly to beautiful unspoilt Puerto Vallarta. Only 2½ hours by Mexicana Jet.' [. . .]

I've been asked with, among others, Noel Coward and John Gielgud, to write a couple of thousand words about Larry Olivier for a pictorial autobiography, I mean biography. E resents my doing it – she takes a long time to forget an insult – but I don't see how I can refuse. I can't say that I think it a bad idea to write about my fellow actors, as Paul Scofield says, because I've done so before.

Thursday 3rd 10 o'clock in the morning and I am sitting in the dining-room cum-kitchen of the lower house. I type every day at the dining room table, a cigarette burning in an ashtray ahead of me and a cup of tea on a dictionary to my right. The tea is on the book to prevent marking the table. The morning is brilliant as usual and E is still asleep but any second the voice will call from the upper balcony, 'Richard' and I will go out on this balcony, wave at her, tell her with signs to come down and see me and the long day will get off to a quiet start. [. . .]

Yesterday we sunned and swam a lot and read a lot. E is reading a long fat novel about the Mafia called *The Godfather* which she says is badly written but un-put-downable.[53] I am reading a paperback history of the Mayans by somebody called Von Hagen, famous Spanish short stories with the English text on one page and the Spanish on the other, and am still ploughing through Senor Paz's *Labyrinths*.[54] In bed I read a rather good detective story set in San Luis, Mexico called the *Rose Window*.[55] A bit in the style of Simenon with a hero called Menendes, a pure Indian.[56] A lot is made of the fact that there is discrimination between Mexicans of Spanish blood and those of pure Indian blood. I didn't realize it was ever apparent. There have been quite a few Indians who are honoured and revered Mexicans. Wasn't Juarez a pure Indian? And Zapata too?[57]

The language is giving me hell. I find myself unless I think slowly and carefully speaking either Italian or French to the servants all the time. I must, since we are hopefully going to spend a long time here in future, God Willing, get a better command of the language. [. . .]

---

[53] Mario Puzo (1920–99), *The Godfather* (1969).
[54] Victor Wolfgang Von Hagen (1908–85), historian, anthropologist and writer. Burton might have been reading his *The World of the Maya* (1960).
[55] Suzanne Blanc, *The Rose Window* (1968).
[56] Georges Simenon (1903–89), author of, amongst other things, the Maigret detective stories.
[57] Benito Pablo Juárez Garcia (1806–72), President of Mexico. Emiliano Zapata (1879–1919), revolutionary leader.

Good Friday, 4th Yesterday was a funny day. It went splendidly for the first half and degenerated into bickering around 3.30 in the p.m. It was largely my fault. I suddenly became testy for no very good reason and remained so for the rest of the day though I tried to get myself better around five but to no avail. E of course was no help at all and bickered back with almost masculine pride. This was some of the dialogue, roughly speaking:

Me: (having gone to read upstairs in the bedroom about 8pm. 'Is the bathroom still smelling?'
She: 'Yes.'
Me: 'I can't smell anything in there. Perhaps it's you.'
She: 'Fuck off.'
(She leaves bedroom and goes downstairs, while me remains reading on bed)
She: (having come back upstairs twenty minutes or so later standing at the door with a look of real loathing on her face): 'I dislike you and hate you' (It may have been 'loathe')
Me: (Getting into a dressing gown.) 'Goodnight, have a good sleep.'
She: 'You too.'
Me exits, and goes to Chris' room where me lies on bed and reads.

N.B. For the benefit of the actors in this little study of home life among the Burtons, it must be emphasized that though the words used are relatively innocuous, the speaking of them is instinct with venomous malice.

The rest of the dialogue which was perfunctory and consisted of similar equally boring exchanges, which took place at four hour silent intervals, culminated in my going back upstairs to finish my detective story in bed. To sleep at 4.30 approx.

The exchanges this morning have been polite but mid-distant. E is now making a 'salty dog' so presumably things will warm up after that. One of E's typically strong-woman-feminine traits is that she's incapable of apologizing unless I apologize first. [. . .] I hated yesterday. I wasn't even drunk and in fact had only had two drinks, one before lunch and one before dinner, all day. Perhaps I should get sloshed.

Sunday 5th Well I did get sloshed yesterday. The damage was done when we arrived at the airport to find that the plane was an hour late and there was nothing to do but sit in the airport bar and drink. Scotch whisky at that which never agrees with me anyway. But I remained in an amiable state all day. The kids all look fine though Liza's hair needs cutting as usual. She has got a certain thin-lipped pointed chinniness (from her father) and she needs a clever hair-style to reduce its slight witchiness.

Michael has become very Anglicized but Chris is still hanging on to his American accent, though his too is fading. [. . .] I drove E and all the kids back in the Beach Buggy which was a success with all. [. . .]

The town is a mad house. Holy week has brought people in by the thousands. Even the Garza Blanca which is normally uncrowded was full and were we not us we might have had difficulty in finding a table. [. . .] Sitting at the next table inevitably it seems nowadays were Chas and Louise Collingwood. He gave me a fragment of a novel he is writing asking me my opinion and saying that if I thought it was any worth he would go on with it. [. . .]

As we arrived back at the house we were hailed by a negro. It turned out to be James Baldwin and a French boy who spoke no English.[58] He was down here escaping from Hollywood he said. We discussed Black Power, Black Panthers, Black is best, Black is beautiful and Black and White. He said quite openly and not at all sneakily: 'Richard, can you let me have 20 dollars?' ('Let me have,' mark you, not 'lend'.)

I was rather surprised, as I would have thought he was fairly affluent and said: 'Twenty dollars?'

'I mean 200 dollars,' he said. I said certainly and Jim is going to give it to him today. We are seeing him again tomorrow.

Wednesday 9th On Sunday we went on the boat for a little fishing and a little sightseeing for Val and Jane. It was not a very successful day as the boat was extremely uncomfortable, cramped and engine-shuddered the whole day. We did catch three Sierra for our supper.[59] [. . .] Small motor-boats [. . .] are the most anti-social means of transportation. Every comment, every conversation, every observation has to be shouted. There are innumerable legs to be tripped over, and all kinds of bits of boat to bark shins on, or stub toes. I loathed it and will never go again except from the *Kalizma* to shore etc. [. . .]

We think that James Baldwin is a thief! Val had $220 or so stolen from her purse when J. Baldwin came to lunch on Monday, and after several reductios ad absurdum have decided that the guilty feller is Baldwin. It may be his French 'friend' but then that's the same thing. [. . .]

Thursday 10th Well, we decided that J. Baldwin had stolen Val's money for the following, mostly psychological, reasons: The servants have not stolen anything in 7 years, despite my habit of leaving money all over the place in trouser pockets etc. and E leaving baubles all over her dressing table and other locations. The children have never stolen anything in their lives. James and George could have robbed us of thousands if they had wished to in the last

---

[58] James Baldwin (1924–87), novelist, playwright, essayist.
[59] Sierra fish, also known as Pacific Sierra or Sierra Mackerel.

many years. It's inconceivable that the Collingwoods would have, and anyway they had no opportunity. Neither E nor I did.

I have already recorded in this diary that Baldwin had asked me for 20, no 200 dollars. Two days later he asked Jim for a further 50. Then a further hundred. Some couple of years ago he had borrowed $10 from Jim (while travelling 1st class on La France) and has never paid him back.[60] He was sitting at the table with us over lunch when he saw me give the money to Jim to give to Val (I had been holding it for her) who put it in her handbag. She had later taken it to her room in the lower house and James had made a tour of the houses alone. We shall never be able to prove it and the money doesn't matter, but why does he do it? Does he also steal from blackmen or does he think that the white man owes him a living? I must find out from others if James has a reputation as a kleptomaniac.[61]

At the same lunch a somewhat sozzled and belligerent Chas said something like how could I continue to do a job as degrading and despicable as being an actor. I said I'd prefer to play Hamlet than read the news. He had prefaced his whole attack on my profession by saying what great potential I had as a writer, and how I was wasting my time on acting etc. His wife later on, so E tells me, embarked on an attack on E. Her back was worse than E's. Liza (E's blood) was sullen while Maria (adopted) was delightful. [. . .] Envy was out in force that day.

Baldwin on the other hand was kind and generous about all and is very intelligent. So he can steal some more if he wishes. [. . .]

Friday 11th [. . .] Yesterday was an indifferent day. First we had a slightly demented and prima donnaish letter from the boring opinionated mediocre headmaster of Michael's school which I enclose.[62] It's almost feminine in its pique. We have decided not to send them back there and a telegram and following letter will be sent off today to that effect. This is not only out of <u>our</u> pique, but because, on reflection, the school has been bad for them. Their values have become tremendously coarsened, Michael started to smoke there and drink there and found jail-bait companions. Though admittedly he might have found them at any other school. Poor Michael, he is a good hearted boy but, outside the family, is incapable of exercising charm. His mother and father both have it and his brother has it in excelsis, but he gives the impression of

[60] Presumably the ocean liner the *SS France*.
[61] James Campbell (1951—), *Talking at the Gates: A Life of James Baldwin* (1991), having read (and quoted) the account of this incident relayed in Bragg's *Rich*, termed it (p. 231) a 'hideous accusation', suggesting that either Burton had made a mistake or that the thief was 'Baldwin's French friend – not quite "the same thing". He goes on (p. 232) to state that all of Baldwin's 'close associates who were asked for their opinion of the incident . . . recoiled at the suggestion that Baldwin could be guilty of simple thieving'. The blame is then placed on the Frenchman, who, we are told, is later discovered to have been gaoled for armed robbery.
[62] Letter not enclosed.

morosely mooning all the time.[63] He cannot for instance sit down in a chair, he sprawls. If his mother asks him to do anything for her it is so charmlessly and apparently unwillingly done that I can understand why masters in school mistake it for spoiled-ness. Since coming here I have seen him read nothing but comic strips. Come to think of it though, I haven't seen Chris read anything else either. Maybe they are just not intellectual and that's that. The truth is though, I suspect, that [...] they are slow starters, and won't really begin to move until they're in their late teens or even their early twenties but unfortunately, unless one is a genius, the modern educational system doesn't cope with the late starters, and their lives are ruined thereafter.

[...] Last night as I lay reading in bed and E was around the corner of the room I asked: What are you doing lumpy?

She said like a little girl and quite seriously: 'Playing with my jewels.'

Thursday 17th I have been so engrossed in the last few days with the letter enclosed from the Millfield headmaster and my reply to it, also enclosed, that I have neglected this daily chore.[64] So the boys are not going back to the school which is a pity really because it means yet another change of school and a lot of bother. And it means searching for another school for Liza. Anyhow, we'll sort it out. So the two boys stay for a bit longer and, as a result of a very important event yesterday the girls are staying for another week also. Liza has had her first 'period' and we feel that she should not do this enormous journey to Europe involving an eight hour time change at this particular point. [...]

Elizabeth has just called down from the upper house to say she's going to take a nap. Can one believe it? She slept for eight hours last night and already wants a 'nap' at 10.30 in the morning. Well maybe she needs it. It's kind of despairing though. [...]

We are beginning to count the days left to us here. Time's winged chariot really hurries along when you would ask him to take it easy.[65] I have no interest in the next film whatsoever. I have been growing a beard for about a week and I loathe it. It is badger grey with smudges of black brown and ginger. Horrible! I must start to learn the part soon, probably tomorrow. We hear news that, despite silly notices where they don't recognize the genre of the picture, *Where Eagles Dare* is making a big gross. [...]

Friday 18th Yesterday we went to Garza Blanca [...] We drank something called Mai-Tais, at least it sounds like that though I don't know how to spell it, and it is a fruit drink with three different kinds of rum, light, medium and

---

[63] In excelsis: to a high degree.
[64] Neither survive.
[65] A reference to the lines from 'To His Coy Mistress' by Andrew Marvell (1621–78): 'But at my back I always hear / Time's wingèd chariot hurrying near'.

black.[66] [. . .] As we were sitting there over lunch Skip Ward and his girl friend Stella Stevens (a film star) arrived from the other hotel in town which they had found impossibly touristy.[67] I was forced by E to leave for home, not without a lot of scowling on my part, before they came out from their suite to join us for a drink. She suspected, not without reason I suppose, that one drink would have led to another and another and another lost day. So I drank at home instead.

[. . .] Tomorrow two people arrive from England to fit me for my costumes for *Anne of the Thousand Days*. The day after, I believe, we are to be given the freedom of Jalisco or whatever it is.[68] So two horrid days loom ahead.

Chas and Louise Collingwood came for a drink before going off to dinner somewhere. I like them both very much when they are sober but both get a little malicious when they've had a few. They come out with the not uncommon resentment of our fame or notoriety when sufficiently into their cups. I wonder if we'll feel the same when our fame has diminished and we are in the company of somebody more known. I don't think so. I have been in the company of your Churchill and Picasso and didn't feel any particular resentment that people stepped on my toes in a blind effort to get near the two 'great' men, and ignored me. [. . .]

Sunday 20th The costume people arrived from London yesterday and I did the fittings in about ½ an hour. Imagine if I'd flown 7000 miles to London for a half hour fitting. I'd have been a pretty picture of a feller, especially, as it turned out that the two fitters <u>had</u> to be in Hollywood anyway to do something for Barbara Streisand.[69]

I have been going through one of my periodic moods of depression for the last three days. Periods when the very thought of seeing anyone except Elizabeth gives me a real physical pain. And when I'm not drinking which I've not been for the last three days it is at its worst. Actually during the last 12 months or so I have become increasingly anti-social and am only really at comparative ease when fairly drunk. [. . .] The fact remains [. . .] I simply don't want people, including my own children whom I love, around. The first two or three weeks here without anyone except E were happy-as-sandboy days. It is the damnedest paradox. I miss the children terribly when they're not here, especially Liza. My heart does several varieties of dance when I first see them coming off the plane or whatever, and within three days I wish them gone. It is very puzzling. [. . .] Time was when my chiefest enjoyment after love-

---

[66] Mai Tai is a white and dark rum based cocktail also including curaçao, syrups and lime juice.
[67] James 'Skip' Ward (1932–2003) had played the part of Hank Prosner in *The Night of the Iguana*. Stella Stevens (1938—), actor, glamour model.
[68] Jalisco, the province in which Puerto Vallarta is situated.
[69] Barbara Streisand (1942—), actor and singer.

making and a good poem was standing at a bar with a convivial few and rambling around poetry and politics and ideas of all kinds - generally second-hand of course - and talking of every subject except the loathed one of acting. And now . . . nothing except to be crouched over a book in our bedroom with the air-conditioning turned on to drown the noises of the outside world. The mood is only temporary of course and even this illiterate apologia may go some way towards dissipating the gloom. [. . .]

The pool is a green pool. Unswimmable. A combination, they say, of acid, chlorine and copper coins dropped into the pool by our intelligent children. The green mantle of the standing pool. Who wrote that?[70]

Monday 21st [. . .] I am reading anything and everything. Most days I read at least 3 books and one day recently I read 5! I read Gavin Maxwell's latest book about his house and otters.[71] Vastly entertaining but a life so alien from urban-ized me as to be unthinkable. Who, in the name of God, wants to walk, some-times through snow and ice and pot-holes up to your behind, two miles to pick up your mail? I suspect that Maxwell is an admirable but not very comfortable or nice man. Still I envy his rapport with animals and his infinite patience with them. Perhaps, in person, he is not as know-allish as he sounds, though I must confess to a weakness for pedagogues. [. . .]

Thursday 24th The children left yesterday at 11 o'clock on time. There was a lot of suspiciously wet eye and the three hugs I had from Liza verged on the desperate, especially the last. E wept freely as we drove to have a drink at the Posada Vallarta to stay our sorrow.[72] I snarled at her to try and stop the flood with a little harshness. It backfired and I was accused of not liking the children as much as she, and it would all have been different if it were Kate who was leaving, blood is thicker than water etc. etc. I left her to ramble on until she ran out of gas. She was alright in a few hours.

The hotel Posada Vallarta is a revelation. It looks as big as the Beverly Hills hotel and is very handsomely appointed. There are little boutiques and acres of space, a large swimming pool and of course the ocean is right at the door with what looks like a fine sand beach. Oddly enough the clientele didn't look as if they could afford the place, and the barmen were slow and all their white jackets were soiled and sweat-marked under the arms. [. . .]

The house is odd without the thunder of children's feet and Liza's exagger-ated screams and the periodic braying of the donkey. The burro was rented for

---

[70] William Shakespeare. *King Lear*, Act III, scene iv, a line spoken by Edgar, son of the Earl of Gloucester.
[71] Gavin Maxwell (1914–69). The book referred to is probably *The Rocks Remain*, first published in 1963.
[72] Posada Vallarta Hotel, Avenue de los Garzas, Puerto Vallarta.

Liza while she was here.[73] His name is what sounds like Pamphilio or Pamphilo. We kept it in what was in the garage of the old house.

[...] Yesterday we had a letter from Prof Truetta now retired and living in his native Spain saying that he had read in a Spanish paper that as a result of his 'saving Maria's leg' (which he did) that we were contributing large lumps of money to the Haemophilia foundation at Oxford.[74] I must write back and tell him that it's true. Lately, as a result of the charity opening of *Eagles* for said Fund we were able to realize something over £3,000. We must do more. Since Uncle Ben's Invalid Miners is now in good shape I think we shall transfer all our British earnings to Haemophilia.[75] [...]

Saturday 26th [...] I read practically all night a biography of Queen Victoria by a lady called Elizabeth Longford (?) who is Lady Longford (?) in private life.[76] I put the question marks because I'm too lazy to go up three flights of stairs in this heat to find out. Anyway, it's a book that has stood on the shelves for a long time staring at me and for a long time I have averted my eyes, since the subject hasn't exactly intrigued me. To my astonishment I find the book, written very racily, and the subject, absolutely absorbing. I am about a third of the way through. I must, when I get to London, read Lytton Strachey's *Victoria*.[77] There was more, obviously, to the dwarf Queen than met the eye. I'd forgotten how German they all were. [...]

We have been invited to stay with Mrs Armstrong-Jones (how reminiscent the name is of Dylan's Mrs Ogmore-Pritchard) and Lord Snowdon and Princess Margaret at Plas Newydd during the investiture of Prince Charles as Prince of Wales at Caernarvon.[78] I would rather have been an onlooker on TV than be on TV myself for the proceedings, but words have been pledged, and anyway it will be something to write about unless some shambling, drivel-mouthed, sideways-moving, sly-boots of a North Welsh imitation of an Irishman might decide to blow everybody to bits.[79]

---

[73] *Burro* is Spanish for donkey, although it may also refer to a Mexican breed of donkey as opposed to those descended from European stock.

[74] Professor Truetta, prominent orthopaedic surgeon.

[75] A reference to a charity championed by Ben James.

[76] Elizabeth, Lady Longford (1906–2002). Her biography, *Victoria RI*, was published in 1964.

[77] Lytton Strachey, *Queen Victoria* (1921).

[78] Antony Charles Robert Armstrong-Jones, 1st Earl of Snowdon (1930—), husband at the time of Princess Margaret, Countess of Snowdon (1930–2002). Mrs Armstrong-Jones is presumably Jennifer, the third wife and widow of the Earl of Snowdon's father Ronald (d. 1966), who was herself to remarry in June 1969. Mrs Ogmore-Pritchard is a character in Dylan Thomas's *Under Milk Wood*. Rather than Plas Newydd, Burton may mean the Armstrong-Jones home at Plas Dinas, Anglesey. Prince Charles (1948—) was invested as Prince of Wales at Caernarfon on 1 July 1969.

[79] The Investiture came at a time when minority elements within the Welsh nationalist movement were active in planting bombs and threatening violence. Two members of Mudiad Amddiffyn Cymru (the Movement for the Defence of Wales) were killed when a bomb they were planting outside government offices in Abergele went off prematurely. Burton acted as narrator for Independent Television's coverage of the Investiture ceremony.

[. . .] Both E and I went mad last night and started eating Callard and Bowsers Liquorice Fingers. I must have eaten a pound or so and E somewhat less. The results were evident this morning. I had put on 3½lbs and E 2lbs. Today we are unrepentant but determined to redress the balance. E longs to be 129lbs and I to be 170. It can be done. But not perhaps by us. [. . .]

Tuesday 29th We drove out to the airport to pick up Caroline expecting the usual hanging around [. . .] when lo! and behold! There was our eldest daughter coming out of the terminal as we arrived. [. . .] We then hustled her off immediately to the Posada Vallarta where we stayed her with a Mai Tai. We stayed only for one drink as the place was, unlike the last time we went, agog with your American tourists who took endless photographs. If the *Origin of Species* is valid then we are certain to see within the next few hundred years American tourists born with built-in cameras.[80] Anyway, by the time we'd got Caroline home and comforted her with a vodka and limeade the two ladies were off and running in a torrent of gossip and reminiscence. You would have thought that they hadn't seen each other for several years. And that they'd grown up together and <u>not</u> that they'd only met last August.

[. . .] A letter and a cheque have just arrived. The letter from Jimmy Baldwin which I enclose and the money order from a lady called Mira L. Waters, also enclosed.[81] Now what does he mean when he says that he doesn't hold a bank account in California? I mean, any old bank account will do. Nova Scotia, National Provincial, The Federal Bank of Dahomey, Calabria, Llanfairpwllgwyngyllgogerychchwyrndrobwllllanfisiliogogogoch, The Chase Manhattan or a postal order.[82] Funny chap. We all, as I've said before, owe him a living because he is black and we are white. Off-White. [. . .]

Wednesday 30th [. . .] It's the last day of the month and reminds us of the dreaded date of departure. I am going to loathe London I suspect. And the film. Why am I doing a film that I so patently am bored by? Why do I allow myself to be talked into doing the mediocre when I could have a choice of the choicest properties on the market? I cannot even bring myself to read the script, let alone learn it. I must! I must! Otherwise I shall feel guilty.

[. . .] Last evening as we were having dinner a school choir stood outside the house in the street and sang to us. It was very pretty and touching. I was particularly pleased that they chose to do so while Caroline was visiting. We wondered why they'd come and E reminded me that we had recently given $2,000 to the school fund. So perhaps it was a thank-you serenade. Jim says that the amount of money needed to make a good school here is

---

[80] Charles Darwin (1809–82), *The Origin of Species* (1859).
[81] Neither enclosed. Mira L. Waters (1945—), actor, singer and songwriter.
[82] Llanfairpwllgwyngyllgogerychwyrndrobwllllantysiliogogogoch: a village on Anglesey in Wales.

about $100,000. How the devil are we going to find that kind of money? And yet we must. [...]

MAY

Thursday 1st E not feeling very well and last night had a temperature of about 102 and a bit. A bit worrying as she doesn't have much resistance, and as I've preached and preached she never takes any exercise. And E is the kind of person who turns a cold of the head nose and throat and common variety into near-death from double-pneumonia. Take out a tooth and she's laid up for a fortnight. Graze her knee and it suppurates for a month. [...]

Last night's sleep seemed to be one continuous dream of great vividness. Most of it was actors' dream, forgetting lines, having the wrong costume on and sometimes none at all. Everybody it seems was in it. A ghost of thousands one might say. John Huston was the director who loomed most large and the action swung from films to stage and back again in the twinkling of an eye. I walked down a long street crowded with extras with Pamela Brown, several times, and could not at the last moment remember the lines which were quite simple. I insisted that I could only do the scene with E and so they were forced to re-write the script so that E could be in that one scene. Then it changed to 73, Caradog Street and the whole family in which, for some reason, my sister Cassie figured predominantly, stood outside the house and implored me to go down to what I think was the Eastern Council School for a booze-up or something.[83] It was the middle of the night and I refused saying that I was going to learn a sonnet or perhaps even write one. Everything and everybody was as vivid as a gaunt tree at the black of night lit by lightning. What does it all mean? I hope my brain hasn't let me down and that when I slope off from this vale of tears I will find that there are dreams after death. Now that <u>would</u> be hell.

So I awoke and lay staring at the ceiling with Elizabeth as quiet as death beside me and reached out for the cool comfort of a cigarette and lighted it and puffed away and tried to decide which period of my life had been most satisfactory. The childhood and teen years I dismissed as total agony. The twenties, riddled with ambition and fear I decided I wouldn't like to live through again. I finally opted for the middle-thirties until now. I'll have another look when I'm 50 and another at 60 and 70. If, of course I don't get killed this afternoon.

Money is a potent old bastard and a great friend of mine. This morning I had a letter from Aaron Frosch saying that Bernard Greenford, Syb's brother-in-law, wanted me to back him to the extent of £45-50,000 with his chain of hairdressing shops. I may well do so. Can't let the family down!

---

[83] Richard's primary school in Taibach.

Friday 2nd Spent the whole day lazing about as usual, while E stayed in bed with a book about the Mafia or Cosa Nostra called *The Valachi Papers*.[84] They are supposed to be the edited confessions of a former 'lieutenant' in that crime syndicate who is the first to talk about the Sicilianos. The first, they claim to break 'omerta' which is the silence unto death or something equally school-boyish. The ramblings of this Joe Valachi are so casually brutal that the book is almost comical instead of being frightening. They seem so stupid that it can only be graft on a high scale in the police forces which can possibly have sustained them. If the police of the US were properly, even lavishly paid so that bribery ceased to be attractive, the Cosa Nostra would die overnight and decline back into ordinary crime with every gang or man for itself. I have read several books lately on the 'hoods', and their grip on American money is something extraordinary. The sums involved apparently go into the hundreds of billions annually. The bribed go from beat-pounding cops right up to the Senate according to all these books. [. . .]

My guilty conscience about the next film and learning the script has now reached an all-time high. I will read it today if I have to stay up all night. It is absolutely disgraceful and very rare for me, and I would be shocked if I discovered such laziness in another actor. I did once, not so long ago when I played Hamlet last. I was amazed at rehearsals in Toronto that Alfred Drake who was playing Claudius did not know a line at the first rehearsals, and while everybody else was bookless at the second rehearsal, he was still muttering around with a book in his hand three weeks later.[85] It meant that he never caught up. The results were obvious in his performance.

Saturday 3rd I've decided that I don't know what poetry is. Last night, in a glut of gloom, I ploughed through the 'collected' poetry, 'all he wishes to preserve', of W. H. Auden. In ten thousand there is hardly one memorable line. Most of it is type-writing. Some of it is scribble. Much of it is indifferent prose cut up. Almost totally it is formless. When is a poem a poem? I will slash away again at Auden since his aura glitters, and find out. I remember reading poetry in tandem with him at Oxford. About three years ago, it was.[86] Among other things I read Dunbar's 'Timor Mortis Conturbat Me' and 'the Boast of Dai' from David Jones' *In Parenthesis*. I doubt if it had ever been heard before at the Union. It was well received. As we walked away afterwards for a drink Auden, a little piqued, asked 'How on earth did you learn to speak Cockney so brilliantly?' His own reading was the usual toneless monotony of the poet reciting his own stuff. Dylan was an exception. But listen to Yeats or T. S. Eliot. Or listen, as we had to once, to Archie MacLeish moan without sense or sound his

[84] Peter Maas (1929–2001), *The Valachi Papers* (1968).
[85] Alfred Drake (1914–92) played Claudius, King of Denmark, in the 1964 production of *Hamlet*.
[86] See diary entry for 20 October 1967.

own lovely verse. E and Ivor and I listened in a tortured agony in a house on a hill in Massachusetts, longing to smash the book out of his hands and read it ourselves. I think that once the mould of form was smashed by a master or series of masters, Pound and Eliot perhaps in poetry and the Impressionists even more perhaps (since I know little about painting) in art, anybody can fool you.[87] And will. And we will never know if they're mucking us about.

The Mexicans today are having a holiday and have decided to fire off explosives all day long. It is almost impossible to speak because of the noise. It is the day of Santa Cruz. The noise is so great that unquestionably they are trying to shoot the Cross to pieces. It is faintly reminiscent of a wartime blitz. There is to be a procession later on at 5 o'clock from one church to another. It has to cross the bridge. What's the betting that somebody is going to blow up the pont when it is packed with small children? Child-chops for dinner with chips? Grilled babies bums. Charcoal-broiled infant with basted brains? Terrine of doting mothers washed down with a sweet liqueur of drunken fathers? I mean Charcoal, of course. A bloody great explosion a second ago has nearly taken my head off. I am essentially unpopular today – everybody has left me and gone to the upper house – which pleases me.

There goes another tremendous explosion, and now we have a brass band playing some god-awful tune with interruptions from a choir and the ineluctable and occasional reply to the atom-bomb. Now a band is playing 'John Brown's Body'. Will somebody tell me why?

There goes another big bang. And another. And another. And me.

Sunday 4th [. . .] Charlie, a divine dirty little cheeky shoe-shine boy from the village came and had a swim in the pool last evening and stayed to have supper with his minute brother. This massive mite is known as Jim. We had tacos with all the trimmings, frijoles and guacamole lettuce and sundry hot sauces. Jim firmly refused all vegetables. Tacos and chicken only thank you. Charlie cleaned my boots for his supper. He is very bright and has picked up English quite well. I would love to pay for his education but we tried that before and the parents are useless. They are so ignorant that they can only see to next week and the handful of pathetic pesos it brings in from boot polish. The working class here have none of the self-sacrificing fanaticism of the Welsh or Scots to get their children educated. David Jones, who lived next door to Gwen in Cunard Cottages worked himself to the bone, denied himself all pleasures except chewing-bacco, went into unpayable debt to put his five or six children in college and then quietly slit his throat.[88] The schools system here is pretty hopeless. The school is so overcrowded that no child gets a full day at school but everyone has a half day. [. . .] The nuns tell us that the school needs roughly

---

[87] Ezra Pound (1885–1972), poet.
[88] Cunard Cottages, Cwmafan.

$100,000. I wonder if we can arrange this somehow. How odd it is that all Roman Catholic countries, including the gifted Irish, are so badly educated. Latin America, Spain, Italy. And yet it was Spanish priests who first brought what we consider to be 'learning' into Latin America for instance. In the last few years two new churches have been built in P.V. but the school has remained the same. So the Lord giveth and he also taketh away.

I have been very unsociable for the last two or three days and recognize it all very well. I am about to start work. Once I'm going all will be fine but from now on until about the fourth of June when the first rushes have been seen and hopefully found adequate, (Will I like the girl? Will I like the Director? Will they bore me? Will I be any good?) I shall be, in E's words, a basket case. [. . .]

Monday 5th [. . .] Some malicious and dangerous little people put sugar in the petrol tank of the B-Buggy and did something to the brakes the night before last. George was putting it away into the garage when he lost control of the Bug, he was driving it in reverse down the hill from the house, and was forced to run it into the house at the bottom of the hill which, though steep, is quite short thank God. Our suspicions are directed towards a couple of men from Guadalahara who came up to the house on Saturday night and said they represented Volks-Vagon [*sic*] cars and were having an exhibition or show in the town, and would we, E and I, pose by exhibits for photographs. Jim said no and they were much piqued. It appears that they bought sugar from La Altena next door. If any of us had been driving the car the other way down where the descent is really precipitous, something like 1 in 4, there could very easily have been a death. Especially as there are usually quite a lot of children playing around at night in these streets. Well the luck holds, but malevolence of that kind is frightening and the world is full of it.

I remember a small incident at Paddington Station during the War. I was on my way home to Port Talbot and had arrived very early at the Station to be sure of a seat. It was the late train leaving about midnight as I remember. I was travelling 3rd Class of course in those days, coming down, I think, from Oxford. I got me a seat and settled down to read a book by the light of a torch. All seats except one were soon taken. Then a soldier, private, arrived followed by a tiny porter who was carrying his kit-bag a suitcase and sundry brown paper parcels. The soldier was of medium height and I suppose in his early twenties. He stood by while the porter stacked his bags on the rack. The Porter waited for the tip and the soldier said in a horrible towny Cardiff accent: 'That's bloody 'ad yew, 'asn't it? You getting no bloody tip from me boyo. Bugger off.' The Porter shrugged and walked away. My hatred for the soldier was so overwhelming that I felt like murdering him. I made myself cool down and then very deliberately and without haste stood up and in total silence opened the door of the carriage and one by one threw all his bags and parcels onto the platform. He looked at me with the hatred of a nightmare but he said nothing and went out to pick up his bags. I closed the door behind him and held it so he couldn't get back in. He must have found a seat elsewhere and I never saw him again. The other occupants of the carriage with typical British taciturnity never referred to the incident at all though we were all together in that compartment for several hours. Odd incident.

Tuesday 6th Well, I broke the ice yesterday and plunged into learning the lines of *Anne*. I learned about ten pages which I will have to re-learn today, while learning another then. By tomorrow yesterday's ten will have fixed themselves in my memory, more or less, while I revise today's ten, and so on. There are quite a few pages of course which contain only a line or two while others, especially in a wordy costume piece of this kind have long uninterrupted monologues. The script is 144 pages long. I do not speak on about 35 of them. That leaves 109. At ten a day that theoretically gives me the whole part of eleven days, though in actual fact it is generally about twice as long because the period of study becomes longer and longer as more and more is committed to memory and the revision extends itself day by day. Also, there are some days when the memory refuses to take in anything at all, and one can only revise.

The script itself is robust and unsubtle but sweeps along at a spanking pace. I hope the direction matches it. Henry is mad, I think. If I continue to think so after I've really got the part into my bones, I shall play him that way. He is certainly demonic. Great charm and stupendous outbursts of rage all co-mixed up with a brilliant cynical intelligence. I might be able to make something of it. Especially if the director and girl are good and help it all along. Since I gather that the other parts, Wolsey, Cromwell, Howard, Thomas Boleyn etc. etc. are being played by Hordern, Colicos and people of their stature I have no worries on that score.[89] Especially Michael Hordern. I think him to be one of the best actors in the world and a rough adversary in a two-handed scene and hard to beat. I don't mean a selfish, spoiled actor like Rex who tries silly old-fashioned things like up-staging, and trying to distract the eye of the audience during a moment which should be yours, but someone who is so deadly perfect and precisely timed that, unless <u>you</u> are too, he is likely to over-balance you.

Just before lunch as we were sitting down here in the lower house George came in looking very apologetic and said that the Governor of Jalisco's daughter was outside with the Director of Tourism for P.V. and would we have a drink with her etc.[90] We said, with a huge groan from E, Caroline and I, ' OK'. It was as smile-fixed a meeting as one could imagine. Platitudes came out from both

---

[89] Michael Hordern was playing Thomas Boleyn in *Anne of the Thousand Days* and John Colicos (1928–2000) was playing Thomas Cromwell. Colicos would also act alongside Burton in *Raid on Rommel*.
[90] The Governor of Jalisco was Francisco Medina Ascencio.

sides with unfailing and desperate regularity. 'And do you like our country?' 'We love it, that's why we live here.' 'Are you here to rest.' 'Yes, I wear a beard because I'm just about to play the English King Henry VIII. 'My father, the Governor, says to say "Hello" to you.' 'Would you say "Hello" back for us?' 'Well I see that you are going to have lunch. It was nice meeting you. If there's anything you need do not hesitate to let us know.' 'Thank you. How kind. We shall.'

She had a face like a double-chinned scimitar. [. . .]

Wednesday 7th [. . .] I went to bed early last night, about 9 and read Waugh's *Put out more Flags* for the umpty-ninth time.[91] I shall have it by heart if I'm not careful. It is astonishing for such a careful writer how often, for a comic effect, he uses the word 'distaste'. The first time he used it was I think in *Decline and Fall* and the line is something like: ' "This is my daughter," said the headmaster, with some distaste.'[92] I remember being convulsed as a small boy. It is a good trick that he uses a lot. 'The Brigadier looked at Basil with revulsion.'[93] But these little lapses apart, he is the writer I'd like to write like most. See Tom Thumb wanting to play Goliath, or the Elephant who dreams of being a ballerina. Anyway I'll never write anything except occasional pieces for the magazines unless I spend four or five hours a day on this diary alone, and not 30 minutes.

[. . .] We are supposed to go to Jim's house for lunch but E is so late – it is now 1.30 and she has been preparing since 12.30. – I may stay here and raid the ice-box and learn some more lines. Have just heard that E has only just gone upstairs to change. Unbelievable. 'Lunch isn't ready over there anyway,' says Caroline stoutly in defence of E. Not the point. We're going to visit the house, the lunch is incidental. E is really fixated about time and her appearance. Even to walk around the corner to a pub for a half of bitter takes an hour's make-up. And nobody needs it less. And imagine how bad it's going to be as she gets older and less good-looking. Start in the morning for dinner at seven, I fancy. [. . .] I've just heard that E is ready. It is 1.45!

Thursday 8th Well, I did not go to Jim's which turned out to be a good idea as I learned quite a lot of lines and thoroughly revised the others. I made myself a huge 'cylffyn' or 'cwlffyn' i.e. a very big sandwich.[94] It consisted of a layer of krafft [*sic*] cheese, a layer of sliced tomato and a layer of crisp ice-cold lettuce between two well buttered thick slices of bread. Chased down by a mug of hot tea. Delicious.

---

[91] Evelyn Waugh (1903–66), *Put Out More Flags* (1942).
[92] Evelyn Waugh, *Decline and Fall* (1928). The actual line (from p. 23 of the Penguin edition of 1937 is ' "That," said Dr Fagan [the headmaster of Llanabba Castle] with some disgust, "is my daughter." '
[93] This is probably a reference to the line 'The Lieutenant-Colonel looked at Basil with detestation, from *Put Out More Flags*, p. 64.
[94] *Cwlffyn* is Welsh for 'hunk' or 'lump'.

[. . .] I cannot stop reading Waugh. In the last two or three days I have read *Scoop, Put Out More Flags, A Little Learning, Officers and Gentlemen* and am just finishing *Men at Arms*.[95] The whole thesis is a lament for the death and dissolution of the Squirearchy. They were tougher than he thought. They are still there, as established as ever. A pity for his theme. A greater pity is that he died before finishing his auto-biography. It would have been interesting to read his reactions to what is in essence a socially unchanged world. The same laws of breeding and background and school still apply. Only, it would seem, in the arts and particularly in sciences, does it not apply. No school, however eminent, can help you as a painter or writer or physicist unless you have the brains or talent. Most of the brilliant new crop of scientists which we have in GB, and are exporting to the USA, have provincial accents, I'm told. But in essence the old order never changeth.

Friday 9th Yesterday we went fishing and trawling.

Tuesday 13th Neither the Governor nor his mate turned up so we were spared that. Today we go to Church to 'stand-up' for a lovely motherless boy who is to be confirmed. His name is Sergio and he is 11 years old. He is extremely polite and his manners are exemplary though he tends to forget himself around E and likes to hug her a lot. I think we have a case of calf love on our hands. I may say it's reciprocated by E. I can just about hugging calf-love abide but draw the line at bull-love. The syntax in the last sentence leaves a lot to be desired. But then I am having a nasty attack of withdrawal from liquor and am not myself at all. I feel as stale as half a loaf in a dust-bin and as tired as a hundredth birthday and do not like going back to Europe at all. We leave for LA tomorrow, spend a day with Sara, then to NY and spend a day with Kate, then to Paris and Versailles to be presented with the Medaille d'Or and spend a night and then to London and the Dorchester and rehearsals. [. . .] That is not to say that I don't like Europe. I love it with a passion and could never exile myself from it for longer than a few months, but I loathe the means of getting there. Flying must be, to the initiated, the most boring and paradoxically the most nerve-wracking method of transport ever devised by mankind for his own torture. In fact show me a man or woman over the age of 20 who likes being flown, I exclude pilots and private plane-owners, and say that they have no fear, and I will show you a LIAR. In any case I have a great fondness for flying-cowards. [. . .] Any man who confesses to me that aeroplanes give him the screaming ab-dabs becomes a friend for life. When I first met Debbie Reynolds' husband, Harry Karl, and when he confessed to me on the *Queen Mary* (I mean, of course, the ocean-going ship and not the late Dowager) that

---

[95] Evelyn Waugh. *Scoop* (1938); *A Little Learning* (1964); *Officers and Gentlemen* (1955); *Men at Arms* (1952).

in the many hundreds of miles, hundreds of thousands of miles rather, that he is forced to travel in the course of his business, he had yet to get on a plane sober, I practically kissed him firmly on the mouth.[96] He showed little taste in marrying Debbie but he obviously has an admirable talent for being craven. [. . .] 'Cowards die many times before their death', said the Swan of Avon.[97] Include me in, Will. [. . .]

Wednesday 14th We went to the church which is brighter and prettier than I remember but like all country R.C. churches is full of hideous but highly coloured plaster images. The boy's uncle Xavier something or other, a pretty Mexican girl, nicely pock-marked, Chas and Louise Collingwood both more plastered than any of the saints in the church, an elderly American who has, I'm told, had his face lifted three times, and Caroline, Jim and George, all left from the house in body, 15 minutes late because of guess who, and en-carred for the church. I carried a massive and quite beautiful candle which is a century or more old, I gather, and proved it by refusing to remain alight. E and I knelt at the altar while for a time a band played the processional march from Aida, which I swore and believed until shown otherwise by Jim and George, was Purcell's Trumpet Voluntory(?).[98] My spelling is bloody awful. The Priest went on quite a bit, seven or eight minutes, but it was rapid Spanish and I only got the random word. I heard our names a couple of times and was told later that the chap had advised the little Sergio that if he brought as much honour and renown to his country as we had to ours, he would have accomplished a great deal in life. I've a feeling that the latter sentiment would meet with general approval only in our immediate families. However it was friendly enough.

I took an already stoned Chas Collingwood to the Oceano for a swift one before going up to the house and the champagne. He told me that Xavier was, is, Sergio's uncle and guardian and that he, Xavier, knowing himself to be a homo-sexual and fearing that the boy might become one too, arranged for him to be seduced, at the age of 12, mark you, by an accommodating Gringa. Not a whore, mind, but an obliging and easy lady. The deed was done and the boy went straight to the Priest and confessed. The same Priest who was trotting out homilies yesterday to the same boy. Charles added that the story goes on to say that this friendly lady left the boy of 12 to go on her weekly

---

[96] Harry Karl (1914–82), businessman, running Karl's Shoe Stores retail chain, married (1960–73) to Debbie Reynolds (1932—), actor, singer, former wife of Eddie Fisher. A reference is also made to Queen Mary (Mary of Teck) (1867–1953), who had become Queen Dowager on the death of her husband, King George V (1865–1936), and to the ocean liner the RMS *Queen Mary*, in service 1936–67. Burton and Taylor had travelled on the *Queen Elizabeth* (not the *Queen Mary*) across the Atlantic in October 1964: Karl and Reynolds had been on the same voyage.
[97] A reference to *Julius Caesar*, Act II, scene ii, where Caesar says 'Cowards die many times before their deaths, / The valiant never taste of death but once.'
[98] *Aida*, opera by Giuseppe Verdi (1813–1901). *Trumpet Voluntary* by Henry Purcell (1659–95).

assignation with Edgar Evans (founder of the famous London String Quartet) who is going on NINETY![99] For a small town there is a lot of action. [. . .]

Thursday 15th, Beverly Hills Hotel [. . .] Having arrived at the bungalow of the B.H. hotel we had a great pleasure of meeting two friends of George Davis. They stayed for not more than two hours and were so fascinating that I fell asleep as they were being introduced. Somebody once said, probably me, that we remember too much. We shall not have our memories over-burdened by the above-mentioned.

Then Hugh French, to add to the general brilliance of the day, told me that the 'sneak-previews' of *Staircase*, except for one, were disastrous. Oddly enough I cared about this film but, what the hell, I'll just grow another callous. I'll end up with a mind like a miner's hands. [. . .]

Monday 19th, Paris, PA [*Plaza Athenée*] Well, I'll tell you, as a result of people and places and Kate and fear and booze and jet-lag, particularly the penultimate, I don't know whether it's the day before yesterday or the day after tomorrow.

Some observations from a scattered survey.

(A) Military heroes are inevitable bores. Yesterday I was stupefied by thousands of such people. They were gonged to the eyebrows but were incapable of syntactically putting a sentence together. I found myself helping them to express their adoration of Elizabeth in a language native to them but foreign to me. I thought about this phenomenon copiously and examined in absentia all the war-heroes I'd ever known and without question they are all bores. Sailor Malan, Douglas Bader, Group-Captain Cheshire, Audie Murphy and 'Mad Jack' Siegfried Sassoon, have, or had, the ability to stop a sentence dead in the middle of its predicate.[100] Bader, said Sailor Malan, was not only fearless, but eliminated the idea of fear in others including myself. Now, any man who lacks fear is a bore. I am not a bore, he said fearlessly. I am not entirely sure that I know what I'm talking about.

(B) Jane Swanson is something that I have missed for a long time. I think that she has been so deeply enwrapped in the mutual envy of Dick and John that I never really had the chance to talk with and to her before.[101] She is very rewarding. She is also a very good listener, which is important in the case of a man who has firmly planned to go down into oblivion shouting new and

---

[99] Burton may mean Charles Warwick Evans (1885–1974), cellist, who founded the London String Quartet, in 1908.

[100] Adolph 'Sailor' Malan (1910–63), RAF fighter pilot in the Second World War. Group-Captain Leonard Cheshire (1917–92), RAF bomber pilot and recipient of the Victoria Cross, also from the Second World War. American Second World War hero Audie Murphy (1925–71). Siegfried Sassoon (1886–1967), First World War poet and recipient of the Military Cross.

[101] Dick Hanley and John Lee.

brilliant stories about R. Richardson, complete with new ones unknown hitherto even to Sir Ralph. She is attractive. She is strange. She is eminently sane. She has an exquisite daughter. She speaks as no other inhabitant of this vale of tears has ever done. But principally she is essentially, quintessentially, seimentally [*sic*] and un-ennuimentally [*sic*] A LADY! [. . .]

Tuesday 20th, Dorchester, London Well we made it to London alright though all of us are suffering from monumental time-lags and today is going to be a relatively full one. I have costume fittings this morning, an aspect of the business which I detest, and a reading with the full cast at 2.30 this afternoon. I know practically everybody there and met the girl yesterday afternoon for the second time so it should be a reasonably affable affair though my old bête noire Tony Quayle will also be there.[102] But I've no doubt that bygones will be bygones and those tiny button eyes in that great arse of a face will be twinkling with false bonhomie. It's toughest on the girl though, having to read cold with all those old pros watching and listening. She seems much more attractive since the first time I met her in Paris. Let's hope she turns out to be not only a good 'un but a nice 'un. Life is too short to work with 'temperamental' people throwing tantrums all the time. The only girl I've had trouble with for years was Mary Ure last year and before that it was Lana Turner about 1955.[103] Otherwise I've been extremely lucky. And I've worked with a great top of ladies. My own E who apart from congenital tardiness is the favourite. Ava Gardner, Deborah Kerr, Olivia de Havilland, Edith Evans, Claire Bloom, Fay Compton, Rosemary Harris, Rachel Roberts, Jean Simmons, Dorothy McGuire, Helen Hayes, Zena Walker and my old darling Pamela Brown et al et al.[104] Perhaps it's something to do with ability because neither Lana can act at all, or Mary. They merely repeat lines by rote. But I think they both think very highly of themselves and are carrying on the mantle of Rachelle and Bernhardt and Duse.[105] They couldn't carry their bloody bags.

I Iugh French came over with us and went on about a TV show for E to do with Mancini, the musician, but I am still a snob about the medium.[106] Thank

---

[102] Anthony Quayle (1913–89) was playing Cardinal Wolsey in *Anne of the Thousand Days*. He had produced and directed Burton at Stratford in a production of *Henry IV (Part 1)*, had played alongside him in that production and in *Henry IV (Part 2)*, and had produced and directed him in *Henry V*.
[103] Mary Ure (1933–75), had played alongside Burton in *Look Back in Anger* and *Where Eagles Dare*.
[104] Ava Gardner and Deborah Kerr (1921–2007) had played alongside Burton in *The Night of the Iguana*. Olivia de Havilland (1916–) had co-starred with him in *My Cousin Rachel*. Edith Evans (1888–1976) had had a part in *Look Back in Anger*. Fay Compton (1894–1978) had appeared on stage with Burton in *Hamlet, King John, Coriolanus* and *The Tempest* in 1953–4. Jean Simmons (1929–2010) co-starred with Burton in *The Robe*. Dorothy McGuire (1916–2001) had co-starred with Burton in *Legend of Lovers*. Helen Hayes (1900–93) had played opposite Burton in *Time Remembered*. Zena Walker (1934–2003) had appeared in a number of productions at the Old Vic, including *Henry V* in 1955–6.
[105] Elisabeth Rachel Felix, known as Rachel (1821–58), Sarah Bernhardt (1844–1923), Eleanora Duse (1858–1924), actors.
[106] Henry Mancini (1924–94), composer and conductor.

God I can afford to be but it still seems to me the cheapest and most vulgar of the performing arts media. I suppose I don't like the thought of any lazy Tom Dick or Harry switching over to Morecambe and Wise while I'm deep in the middle of 'To be or not to be'.[107] Or some 'young man carbuncular' masturbating in a dingy bed-sitter while goggling at E's breasts.[108] Nevertheless we shall have to do something for Harlech one of these days. [. . .]

Wednesday 21st I did my fittings in the morning and it was torture as usual. Though they have very kindly done their best to make the materials as light as possible, they are still very hot and there is going to be a great deal of sweating during the next three or four months. Maggie Furse was there, of course.[109] Costume designers who are not out of the top-drawer are really not worth hiring. The costumes look magnificent but all the great work is done by the two boys who cut and sew. She simply looks up Holbein and illustrated books of costumes about the period in question.[110] I asked if they could change the shape of the shoes and make them come higher up the ankle as I have such idiotic calves. No, this was not possible as they were not the 'period'. So you see she gets all her stuff from the books.

[. . .] I tried to read a detective story by Gore Vidal, writing under the name of Edgar Box but did not make more than two pages before Morpheus claimed me.[111] [. . .]

Quayle was there and behaved exactly as I expected, eyes twinkling, much smiling, speaking his part with measured and unctuous precision. John Colicos too was there and runs Tony a pretty close second for close-set eyes. I doubt whether they could make one of Elizabeth's with both sets put together. His voice too was measured and sonorous. In fact they were both so 'stagey' that I found myself gruffing mine up and speaking at great pace rather than be like them. Still they are well cast – after all both Cromwell and Wolsey were sly and unctuous bastards. Not that Colicos in private life is a double-crossing promiser like Quayle. I'm told he is a very nice man. We had worked together many years ago in *Wuthering Heights* on TV in NY but I don't remember him at all.[112] Fortunately I had been warned by the director before hand so was able to make suitable cries of delighted remembrance.

---

[107] Eric Morecambe (1926–84) and Ernie Wise (1925–99), popular comedians who appeared in the *Morecambe and Wise Show* on British television.

[108] A phrase from T. S. Eliot's *The Waste Land* (1922).

[109] Margaret Furse (1911–74), costume designer for *Anne of the Thousand Days*. She was to receive an Oscar for her work on this film. She had been costume designer on *Becket*.

[110] Hans Holbein the Younger (1498–1543), artist, who was King's Painter to Henry VIII.

[111] Gore Vidal wrote three novels between 1952 and 1954 under the pseudonym Edgar Box. Morpheus: the Greek God of sleep and dreams.

[112] Burton had played Heathcliff in a television production of *Wuthering Heights* for NBC in 1958

The girl is very small in every way, in height, in weight and vocally. I could out-project her with a whisper. Her face too is tiny but the eyes and mouth are good. In size and pertness only, she reminds me of the late and lamented Vivien Leigh. It's difficult to tell at a reading but I think she might have difficulty with long sustained speeches, but doubtless we'll be able to fiddle around that with judicious cuts to listening faces etc. and a spot of dubbing. She said one sensible thing à la Elizabeth: when they brought those inevitable tedious cardboard models of the sets around she said 'Those dolls houses mean absolutely nothing to me.' Quite right too. [. . .]

Thursday 22nd [. . .] Yesterday I rehearsed the song I have to sing in the film. It's very pretty but for an amateur, because of funny little stops in it, difficult to learn at such short notice. I record it this morning.

The doorbell rang yesterday morning about 11, and standing there was my niece Sian with an inevitable friend. Five minutes later another ring and it was Graham with an equally inevitable friend.[113] Why must they bring total strangers around with no advance notice? Showing off I suppose, but it shows a staggering amount of not understanding the kind of lives we are forced to live. E refused to come out to see them which is just as well because when she did come out later after the family had gone and Wynford Vaughan-Thomas and the director of the Investiture were here her cold charmlessness was ice-bergian.[114] Ordinary social charm is not E's strong suit. She was lovely with the Loseys who came for lunch, but there was an oddly constricted atmosphere even with them and there were rather forced silences when nobody seemed to have anything to say.

Every encounter indeed that day was so dispiriting that it put me in a foul mood. I went into the spare room and played the song over and over to myself singing with it until I thought I'd got it. Despite all that concentration however I can't remember a phrase of it this morning. It will all come back of course as soon as I listen to it once more. Elizabeth was as bare-toothed as a tigress when I went into the other room and said 'Surely you must know it by now!' This was delivered with sullen venom and set my ill-temper even more firmly. Thereafter we played an absurd game of Musical Rooms. I refused to be in the same room as E and she with me, but we kept on running into each other. Finally she went to bed in the spare room while I read in the other bedroom until the doctor came. I then woke her up, told her I was going to take two sleeping pills, that I was going straight to bed and not to bother me! And with that he swep' aht! What a fool I am.

---

[113] Siân Owen, daughter of Richard's sister Hilda.
[114] Wynford Vaughan Thomas (1908–87), broadcaster, at this time Director of Programmes for HTV. Mike Towers was the co-ordinating director for ITV.

How I could very well do without W. Vaughan Thomas. A pushy little man, though very bright. He means well but his ebullience makes me embarrassed. He's getting old of course. I remember how Dylan loathed him. [. . .]

Friday 23rd, London I did the song at 11 o'clock with no difficulty. [. . .] I was thinking yesterday, not for the first time of the fuss everyone makes of E and I. There are other so-called superstars but nobody, as a couple, get paid so much attention. At Shepperton they have given us the boardroom in the 'old house' with a private kitchen across the corridor.[115] The boardroom has been changed into the most elegant nineteenth century dining room with French windows leading onto one of those incomparable stretches of English lawn dotted with magnificent old trees. There, on fine days – and who knows that we might not be due for a good summer – the experts say it's due – E can hold court in the afternoons and retain her suntan for the winter ahead. In addition, they have supplied E with a private dressing room one floor up from the dining room if she wants to sleep. And they have knocked down three walls in the main block to make a more than adequate 'practical' dressing room for me. And we didn't ask!!

Everybody assured me that the run from Shepperton to Aston Clinton to meet Gwen and so on to Ivor, was only ½ hour to 35 minutes.[116] After an hour's hard driving we were nowhere near the place. When I finally did arrive at 1.15 instead of 12.20 I was a charming chap. I scowled at Norma Heyman who had been one of the informants and then called R. McWhorter and told him that by the time I returned after spending an hour with Ivor the working day would practically be over. He agreed and said that they all (Wallis, Jarrott) agreed that it was more important that I see Ivor.[117] So they rehearsed without me. [. . .]

The improvement in Ivor is considerable. He can wheel himself about in a motorized chair and seemed in very good spirits. We told various and sundry stories some of which made him laugh so much that we had to wipe the tears away from his eyes. Gwen's selfless devotion to him verges on the saint-like. What a marvellous woman. Old-fashioned self discipline, old-fashioned virtue, old-fashioned devotion to a loved one is not often seen. There's none of that 'fuck you Jack, I'm alright' stuff about her.

We go on the yacht tonight and stay for the week-end. [. . .]

---

[115] Shepperton Studios, Middlesex. The 'old house' is Littleton Park Manor, a seventeenth-century manor house.
[116] Aston Clinton, Buckinghamshire. The road distance between Shepperton and Aston Clinton is about 48 miles. Ivor was a patient at Stoke Mandeville Hospital, Aylesbury, location of the national spinal injuries centre. The hospital is about four miles from Aston Clinton.
[117] Hal Wallis (1898–1986), the producer. Charles Jarrott (1927–), the director.

Sunday 25th Princess Steps, **Kalizma** And they say that the world lacks romance. Ya Falaheen, Queen of the Islands, Denaud, White Sapphire, Rondoran, Makhala, Oranje, Shoshana, Silver Heron, Billet Doux [*sic*], Four rivers, Thelmarie, Painted Lady, Roding, White, Heron, Charade, Leonid, Minsquee, Corannanna [*sic*], Lady Holland <u>II</u>, Nordsee, La Sirena <u>II</u>, Eight Bells, Charis, Eros, Fordson, Pleasure Bound, The Joanne – a message for John Heyman perhaps – Minden Rose, Quicksilver, Kedidi <u>IV</u>, Poio, Olive Branch, Rowena, Nicomaa, Blackbird C., Perso, Druid Stone, Cassata, Oranya, Lady Tuht, London Pride, Jandora, Freeth, Tressares, Tara, Bankstone, Lilliana <u>II</u>, and erotically, Nun's Honey. All these are boats or ships that passed our ship in one hour between 9.15 and 10.15 yesterday morning.

What an extraordinary world it is. How do you live with one person for 13 years, and another for 8 and find both as alien as strangers. Elizabeth is an eternal one night stand. She is my private and personal bought mistress. And lascivious with it. It is impossible to tell you what is consisted in the act of love. Well I'll tell you, E is a receiver, a perpetual returner of the ball! I don't write about sex very often, because it embarrasses me, but, but, for some reason who knows why, whatever, is spared, original, strange. Counter. Felix Randall who hooved the horse his bright and battering sandal. Praise him.[118]

It's 7.30 in the morning and the world, little knowing that I am dying will persist in carrying on as usual. I watched two films with the baby last night.[119] They were not good, but they were cosy like bad but readable books. I love Elizabeth.

I love Joe Losey, not because he is a genius, but because he loves my wife. I love Patricia, not because she's a genius, but simply that she is a pleasure to be accommodated with.[120] I could spend a long time with her without a single interruption. They are coming to lunch today, which is not a fearsome idea. I think it's a diabolical idea.

How would you like to die on a boat on the Thames – a privilege not granted to many. I am stupefied with nostalgia. I am madly in love with the idea of remaining alive. I am agog with desire to see Elizabeth and Joe and that infinitely removed and eclectic Patricia. It's very rough in this world to find anybody that loves you, or anybody that you love. I think I'd better go back to bed. Don't you?

Where did they find the names. What funny people funny people are! Oh Bugger it. And my brother. And so to bed.

I never lie when I write. Honest. Though I'm not sure of that!

---

[118] This is a reference to the poems 'Pied Beauty' and 'Felix Randal' by Gerard Manley Hopkins (1844–89). 'Pied Beauty' includes the line 'All things counter, original, spare, strange' and ends with the line 'Praise him'. Felix Randal's last line is 'Didst fettle for the great grey drayhorse his bright and battering sandal!'

[119] 'The baby' is a reference to Elizabeth.

[120] Patricia, Joseph Losey's third wife.

Whit Monday, 26th, Kalizma, *Thames*

Yesterday's entry, as any man of discernment can tell at a glance, was written while under the strong influence of several vodkas. T. H. (Tim) White once wrote a poem for me and about me called 'Vodka Poem to Richard Burton.'[121] One night in New York when we [were] both suitably and idiotically drunk and I had given him the sword 'Excalibur' which I used in the play written from his *The Once and Future King,* and after he had insisted on knighting with full accolade many and various and bewildered New York cabbies, we repaired to my apartment on 81st Street on the West Park. There we wrote poems to each other. He kept both and some time later to my surprise and delight he had included the one to me in his last book of Poems.[122] Mine must be in his papers somewhere. Vodka is the operative word. Tim died in his late fifties. If I don't watch myself I'll be lucky to see my late forties. With his huge stature and white hair and beard it was some sight, as they say, to see Tim give the accolade to Harry Schwartz, and Sol Schmuck. Arise Sir Harry. Arise Sir Sol. A few of them actually knelt on the pavement! A barman, used to drunken eccentricity, knelt to be knighted with a glass of vodka in each hand. Quite a lot of actors were knighted also [on] that long-ago wild night. Jason Robards is about the only one I can remember.[123] He didn't bother to knight me he said, because ever since we had first met he had conferred a mental baronetcy on me. What a crying pity that he is dead. How E would have adored that madman. And he her. And what a maniacal and lovely mind! I once sat there bewitched while he spoke for a couple of hours on the subject of worms, how each wriggling thing had locked in side him the beginning and end of man, and that without worms we would all die. When you die, he said, give your body to the worms, they will be grateful. There is absolutely no reason to give it to fire, even the atmosphere might reject the noxious fumes from your burning body.

[. . .] The boat is a giggle. Almost everywhere one looks is a delight to the eye. Books in rows. Van Gogh and Picasso and Vlaminck and Howard behind the bar, I mean his painting, not the man himself, the only pretty TV set I've ever seen, the new carpet from Mexico, the pretty sheets on the bed, the immaculate and very gay bathroom, the cosy cabins down below. I tell you it's a floating palace. [. . .]

Tuesday 27th For the first time I enjoyed rehearsals of this epic, probably because there were a lot of actors there instead of the eternal girl and Quayle and Colicos only. Denis Quilley (who was my understudy in the dim days of

---

[121] Terence Hanbury White (1906–64), known as 'T. H.' or 'Tim', novelist, author of *The Once and Future King* sequence of four novels (1938–58), on which was based the musical *Camelot.*
[122] In *Verses* (privately printed, 1962). 'Vodka Poem To Richard Burton' is the last in the volume (p. 43).
[123] Jason Robards (1922–2000), actor.

The Lady's not for Burning and eventually took over), T. P. O'Connor, that marvellous Irish actor and in looks and manner a natural successor of Cusack's of whom he is a great friend I found out.[124] A splendid young man called, I think, Gary Bond, who is almost certain to become a very important actor and another good actor with whom I've worked before but cannot remember his name, he has a bitten, bitter, pock-marked face.[125] All cream and none of your skimmed milk. The girl too of course who boasted that she was taller than Elizabeth. T. P. O'Connor said: 'And so, d'you know, is Tina Louise.'[126] I think I'm going to like that chap a lot. [. . .]

Bernard (Greenford), Syb's brother-in-law was waiting for me when I finished. He has been squeezed out by his partner from the very lucrative chain of 'hairdressing salons' by his snake-in-the-grass partner André. This infuriates me, not simply because I like old Bernard, but because, without my backing in the early years the business would have folded. It was I who with a thousand quid here and a thousand quid there sustained the operation in its infancy. It was all paid back, but without the luck of the association, André and Bernard would have been Charlie and Harry back in Whitechapel where they started from. And I'm sodded if I allow Bernard, who mortgaged his mother's house to keep the thing going, to be struck off the register because of a sneaky jumped-up-jack of a fellow whose only desire in life is to belong to golf-clubs that don't allow Jews. I shall cable Aaron today to get our own back in operation. My darling girl, and why should she care?, has volunteered $50,000. [. . .]

I brought Bernard back on the boat without warning E. I took a chance that with her weakness for Jews he would be acceptable. She came up trumps as usual and asked him to stay for lunch as well as the offer of 50,000 smackeroos. He must have danced all night.

Today I rehearse in the morning and this afternoon Ron is going to muck about with my face and beard and try to make me look Tudorian. At the moment, with luck, I look like Sir Henry Morgan about to make someone walk the plank.[127]

I shall now sit here patiently and wait for her to get up. I am madly in love with the woman – even after 8 and getting on for 9 years. Now isn't that funny?

---

[124] Denis Quilley (1927–2003) played the part of Weston. Burton presumably means T. P. McKenna not O'Connor. McKenna (1929–2011) was playing the part of Norris. He would act alongside Burton again in *Villain*. However, Joseph O'Connor (1910–2001, sometimes O'Conor) was playing the part of Bishop Fisher in *Anne of the Thousand Days*. Cusack presumably refers to Cyril Cusack.

[125] Gary Bond (1940–95) played the part of Smeaton. He had appeared in *Zulu*. The unnamed actor might be Peter Jeffrey (1929–99), who played the part of Norfolk in *Anne of the Thousand Days*, and with whom Burton had worked on *Becket*.

[126] Tina Louise (1934—), actor, most famous for her role in the television series *Gilligan's Island*.

[127] Sir Henry Morgan (1635–88), Welsh buccaneer.

Wednesday 28th, Dorchester [hotel] [. . .] I sent a telegram off to Aaron asking him to fix up Bernard's financial predicament. I think it will cost about £50,000. Still, fly-on-the-wall as I would like to be, the thought of André's face when faced with implacable money-power does already in my imagination please me a great deal. I could, though I would not, be present at the confrontation with the board. Chuckle. Chuckle. Gurgle. Gurgle. Snigger. Snigger. V-Sign. V-Sign. Up Yours. Up Yours. I don't think that I am a nice man. But kick my dog, kick me.

I am drinking too much again and though I like to drink I have a fear that eventually it might affect my brain. Already, I've noticed, it has affected my memory. Or maybe I am getting old. Anyway I shall now, and hopefully for the rest of the film, slow down, and again hopefully, to a stop.

The film is important despite the fact that both Elizabeth's and my latest films are enormous financial successes. That is to say *Secret Ceremony* and *Where Eagles Dare*. Elizabeth, if you please and with her usual insouciance, impertinence and cheek has managed to win the French 'Oscar' for the former.[128] I am very proud of her because it was an immensely difficult part. I love the old girl very badly nowadays, though I've exactly been indifferent. The last phrase should read 'though I've <u>never</u> exactly been indifferent.' What the hell – it's very early in the morning.

I am very jealous of E. I'm even jealous of her affection for Dick Hanley, a 60 year old homosexual, and anybody she has lunch with. Girls, dogs – I'm even jealous of the kitten because her adoration of it is so paramount. They'll all die before me though, so I'll win in the end. [. . .]

Thursday 29th I danced all the morning with Gin [Bujold] and two ballet dancers. I must learn the elegant arrogance of the male ballet dancer. It could be very effective. As a result perhaps of an essentially masculine upbringing, surrounded by roaring miners, dinned with stories of feats of strength, I find myself slightly put out by the idea of doing a basse dance, with feline hand on the hip and swaying queerly from side to side. It will though, it <u>must</u>, be right on the night.

How drab people are, especially people from the Press. I lunched with a lady who calls herself Margaret Hinxman and who writes for the *Sunday Telegraph*.[129] I promised her the so far un-awarded Taylor-Burton 'Oscar' if she could ask me a question that neither E nor I had ever been asked before. She failed. Why didn't she take up the challenge and ask for instance: 'How often do you and your fabulous wife fuck? Do you confine it to weekends or do you have a fetish for Tuesdays?' Or 'How often do you masturbate?' Or 'Who do you think is most normal, you or John Gielgud?' Or 'Do you think, in the

---

[128] A César Award for Best Actress.
[129] Margaret Hinxman, journalist, film critic, novelist.

words of Carlyle, that we are living in the conflux of two eternities?'[130] Or 'bugger you baby, I find actors interminably boring, and you more than most, and now Lord Millionaire Richard, what do you have to say to that?' Anything would do of that nature, anything other than 'have you sold your soul to the films for the sake of filthy lucre?' Or 'what does it feel like to be famous, to have an even more famous wife, a private jet, a yacht on the Thames, a suite at the Dorchester, to have power, to be the compulsive centre of all eyes?' 'Do you believe in God?' 'What do you think when you read about yourself in the papers?' 'Are the Welsh people, and in particular your vast family, proud of you?' How does one reply to these inevitable banalities? Shit over the lot of them.

Barry Norman, another writer, for the *Daily Mail* and bright as a button, asked the unavoidable question. 'Why don't you come back to the theatre?' For some reason English people adamantly believe that acting in the theatre is superior (what a funny word) to acting in the films or TV. I've done all three with considerable success, and I'll tell you, Baby Barry, that they are all difficult but with the difference that after, shall we say, 10 weeks of playing *Hamlet* on the sage one's soul staggers with tedium and one's mind rejects the series of quotations that *Hamlet* now is. Has there ever been a more boring speech, after 400 years of constant repetition, than 'To be or not to be'? I have never played that particular speech, and I've played the part hundreds and hundreds of times, without knowing that everybody settles down to a nice old nap the minute the first fatal words start. E was quite savage with Norman, in defence of me, so much so that he perforce had tears in his eyes. So she gave him a kiss! Nobody will understand that I am unlike every actor I've ever met with the exception of Marlon Brando, without his extraordinary talent, but we are both bored!

[...] Marlon's and Elizabeth's personalities, to say nothing of their physical beauty, are so vast that they can and have got away with murder, but Elizabeth – unlike Marlon – has acquired almost by proximity to the camera, by osmosis, a powerful technique. Marlon has yet to learn to speak. Christ knows how often I've watched Marlon ruin his performance by under-articulation. He should have been born two generations before and acted in silent films. The worst thing that ever happened to him was Gadge Kazan, The Actors' Studio, and fantastic over-publicity when he was a baby.[131] I love the chap (though the reverse is lamentably not true) and I long to take him in my teeth and shake enthusiasm into him. But deep down in his desperate bowels he knows that like Elizabeth and myself it is all a farce. All three of us, in our

---

[130] From Thomas Carlyle's (1795–1881) *Signs of the Times* (1829): 'The poorest Day that passes over us is the conflux of two Eternities.'
[131] Elia 'Gadge' Kazan (1909–2003), director, producer, playwright, novelist, and co-founder of the Actors' Studio.

disparate ways, know that we are cosmic jokes. And all three know that 'dedi-cation' to the idea of the performing arts is an invention of envious journalists. It's alright for your Paul Scofield, or Gielgud or Larry Olivier or John Neville to 'dedicate' their lives to the 'theatre' but, poor sods, no other fucker will allow them on the phone.[132] I think essentially that if something comes too easily to you, you dismiss it as an accident. Marlon made that mistake. E didn't.

I love Elizabeth.

Friday 30th [. . .] We 'made' all the papers yesterday and Gin looked splendid in all of them, and apart from that idiot Fergus Cashin in the un-read *Sketch*, from which, I understand, he is being fired, the comments were universally favourable.[133] He never was much of a writer but being permanently drunk has made him worse. He has the lined and debauched face of an old man and he is, I believe, younger than I. Ah well, every man to his own destruction. I have to approve and correct an interview that I had with Ken Tynan some 3 or 4 years ago.[134] It is odd reading it how very pompous Ken sounds. Witty and devastating as he has been in print I wonder now if he has any sense of humour. He certainly doesn't have it about himself. He's always been very earnest of course. And star-struck. I remember introducing him to Humphrey Bogart at the now existless Pen and Ink Club, with the words: 'Bogie, this is a Mr Ken Tynan who wrote about you recently in the *Evening Standard*, and described your face as "a triumph of plastic surgery"'. Ken was devastated and though Bogie was easy on him he never recovered his aplomb and remained for the rest of the evening a stammering and stuttering skeletonic death's head. Ken has always looked like Belsen with a suit on. Dachau in Daks. Buchenwald in brown velvet.[135] An impedimented bone. John Heyman said yesterday that Ken has always written with a pen in one hand and *Roget's Thesaurus* in the other. And he may be right at that.

John himself, at the moment looks pretty emaciated. They recently had to remove a perforated ulcer and it became very dangerous. He had nearly destroyed himself over a girl called Joanna Shimkus, an actress who had left him for the Negro actor Sidney Poitier.[136] Sometimes I think that Jews are instinctive masochists, much as I admire them. Holy God, I could see what that girl was after five minutes. It took him three years and a smashed stomach. And almost his life. He is though a lovely man and loves my wife, in the best

---

[132] John Neville (1925–2011), who had acted with Burton in the Old Vic productions of *Hamlet, King John, Twelfth Night, Coriolanus, The Tempest, Henry V* and *Othello* in the mid 1950s.

[133] Fergus Cashin (1925–2004), then working for the *Daily Sketch*, who would become one of Burton's biographers.

[134] The interview appeared as 'Richard Burton with Kenneth Tynan', in Hal Burton (ed.), *Acting in the Sixties* (1970).

[135] All Nazi concentration camps.

[136] Sidney Poitier (1927—).

sense of the word of course, and is going to take her out to the cinema when I'm at work. Isn't it strange that the only two enthusiasms we do not share are fried chicken and films. I have learned to love bagels and Lox and hot dogs and she has learned to love caviare and rarish steaks.[137] But no accord have with fried chicken and films. I like her though, and God knows, she has a lot to put up with. I mean, there are times when I think I am slightly out of my mind. And there are times when I am. [. . .]

Saturday 31st, **Kalizma**, *Thames* [. . .] Yesterday was what one might call eventful. I tested at the studio, I danced with Gin who is, perhaps out of nerves, turning into a bit of a tiresome bore; I had lunch with E and C at the 'Guinea', I went to Berman's and fitted costumes; I went on the yacht; I was told by Gaston who was crying proper tears that 'Madame' didn't like him anymore because the Cadillac which she had given him and which he has apparently gone into business with Ron Ringer ensemble was being rented out to Elliott Kastner who in turn was assigning it to, of all people, the ineffable Claire Bloom.[138] E was in a rare tear. Gaston is a good chap but he made the fatal error of lying to her, I suppose. The French, with all their pretence to a perpetual renaissance of the brilliance in all forms of art etc. etc. really have never taken their eyes off the franc. It is, of course, fairly ridiculous that with four cars <u>one</u> has not been available to Mabel [Elizabeth] at all times. If I survive the day, which I doubt, I will start laying down the law. I mean, after all, that Bob Wilson, whom I love but is perfectly useless, has eternal use of E's Rolls. He shall be forced to ride in an Austin Princess.[139] Hardship. I'll give him black power. I'll give him Welsh Power. Note the difference in capitals.

Fortunately, towards the close of the day, Tim Hardy came on board.[140] His mind delights me and I forget, every so often, how much I adore and miss him. He talks as good as you can get, and has the charm of the angels. I think that I am, despite my ferocious attachment to the working-class, an admirer of the true aristocrat, particularly if he is cleverer than I am. And Tim after all is a direct descendant of Richard <u>III</u>. Honest. And he is cleverer than I am. What a terrible admission from a son of the soil. He is, I think, the 135th direct descendant of Alfred the Great, whereas the present Queen is only the 135th <u>indirect</u> descendant. He had come on board simply to tell me that Henry VIII was a great archer and show me exactly how to do it. Greater love hath no actor than that. Most people, he said last night when I expressed distaste for Buck's Club, love a Lord, but I love Dukes.[141] It gives me, he said, great pleasure

---

[137] Lox cured salmon fillet, typically served in a bagel.
[138] The Guinea Grill, Mayfair.
[139] A more modest (though still well-appointed) motor vehicle.
[140] Burton's friend the actor Robert Hardy.
[141] Buck's Club, a gentlemen's club established in 1919 and situated at 18 Clifford Street, London.

to dine at Buck's with a Duke in one corner and a Duke over my shoulder, and another Duke asking me if I could spare him a fiver. So there you are. Every man to his pleasure. I, personally, would prefer Welsh miners. But I'm perverse. Caroline stayed on the yacht. I love that child and forced to choose between a Duke and Caroline, I would take the latter. I'm not sure about a miner.

JUNE

Saturday 7th [. . .] I had a hard day yesterday. Gareth had come aboard with us the night before and we spent half the night sitting up and talking and drinking with me insulting E for most of the time.[142] Then off to work at the crack of dawn to face a long scene with Gin Bujold in which I had to do most of the talking. She'll be alright I suppose though she doesn't have enough dynamite and spit and venom and arrogance for the part, but of course I always am thinking in the remote rear of my cranium how marvellous E would be and how much better. I got through it well enough and then, Oh blessed relief, I had to work with Tony Quayle and Michael Hordern. Marvellous pair of pros and no rubbish and cunning as snakes. I held my own I think. They have every shrug, nod, beck, sideways glance and shifting of eyes ever invented. I said to the director that it was somewhat akin to playing between the frying-pan and the fire. All Michael Hordern had to say was 'Yes, your Grace.' He must have said four hesitant 'yours' and the three words, uttered in his inimitable way became slightly longer than *Hamlet*. Uncut. They both varied the time of their readings in an unconscious effort to 'throw' each other off, and me. But I'm too old a hand. I 'threw' them a couple of times too. None said a word to each other about it but all three old bastards knew bloody well that when that camera is purring it's every man for himself. Of course if you are the 'star' or the 'money' as the technicians call it you can afford to be magnanimous because the 'money' is almost automatically protected but it's as well to know what the hell you're up to. And to let them know that you know what they are up to. There is of course nothing malicious about it, but it is deep in the subconscious.

[. . .] The two babies arrived from La Suisse and I suddenly realized that after work on the film I had to do the narration for the investiture of the Prince of Wales. And after that Winston Churchill and 5 Dukes of Marlborough for the Son et Lumiere at Blenheim Palace.[143] Cor! Was I whacked. Liza is turning into a young lady and I don't think there's much wrong with Maria's intelligence. Thank God! It's the first time I've thought that she stands a chance in the rough world without us.

---

[142] Possibly Richard's nephew, Gareth Owen.
[143] Burton provided the narrative for the 1969 son et lumière at Blenheim Palace.

Sunday 8th [. . .] Yesterday was a soporific day. We lazed about all day with the din of a factory pump thumping in our ears. I called it Gorgonzola, because it went to the rhythm of that aromatic cheese: GORGONZOLA, GOR-GON-ZOLA etc. all day long. [. . .]

I cannot take my eyes off Liza. Her eyes are the most beautiful I've ever seen and I love her to the point of pain. Perhaps because she's so like her mother. And Maria, to repeat, is going to be alright, J'espere.

I had the frights again yesterday – the second weekend in a row, God Blast It! E and I were going to make love in the afternoon and while cleaning herself on the bidet, she began to bleed from her bumsie. And I mean BLEED. Not your pale pink variety but thick clots of blood that had to be fingered into disappearing down the drain. I sat with her and stroked her and tried to comfort her as best as I could. It finally stopped but I nightmared a great deal. In fact, after two weekends of torment on the yacht, I have mentally re-named the place 'Nightmare Stairs' and not Princes.[144] I searched E's bumsy very often to check up on its progress. It is an extraordinary thing to look up somebody's ass-hole, and a beautiful ass it is, and to do it not with lust or sex in mind, but with love.

And a little fear. I mean a great deal of fear. She is better this morning and the excrescences have receded a considerable amount, but I shall not feel safe until she's seen a Doctor though, <u>under no circumstances</u>, is the knife to be employed. There are other ways.

Wednesday 11th, Dorchester Yesterday the two girls, Liza and Maria, left to go back to school. Simmy has, in effect, been expelled from Montesano 'for' SHE SAYS 'being late for Sunday dinner and not being on time for roll-call!'[145] A likely story. Now we will have to employ all what little charm we have to get the Headmaster to change his mind so that she can at least finish the term. [. . .] Raymond, the chief steward told E, who didn't tell me until last night that once last term Simmy asked if she could bring some friends up to the chalet for tea. He said OK and she arrived with a boy of about 18 and another girl of her own age, which is 19. By the time they went back to school Simmy had imbibed a whole bottle of vodka. <u>Our</u> vodka. And the best of Samoan luck.

Scrumptious Kate is with us still and so far has come to work with me every morning, despite having to get up about 6 o'clock of a morning. All adore her and my leading lady in the film asked if she were for sale. I said that if she were I'd buy her myself.

[. . .] E looked very exciting in the shortest mini-skirt. The slightest inclination from the vertical and her entire bum was revealed to the admiring gaze.

---

[144] The *Kalizma* was berthed at Prince's Stairs, Rotherhithe.
[145] Institut Montesano, Gstaad, a girls' boarding school. Simmy: Simoleke Taylor.

Thursday 12th, **Kalizma,** *Thames* I have been up since 5.10. and obviously I caught the best part of the day since from 5 until 7 the boat was, and the river and shore, as quiet as a condemned cell, but now that infernal factory has started up again with its GOR-GON-ZOLA recurring and recurring. [. . .] Kate and Elizabeth are whole-fast asleep and it is hardly possible for any Prince to have greater love for a sleeping beauty than I have for them. Those. Two sleeping beauties.

[. . .] Kate went to see Ivor yesterday. I finished a little early on the film and went straight back to the hotel where, a little later, Kate joined us, and Michael Todd, and we all repaired to the yacht. Michael is a very rewarding and good and funny man and is a pleasure to be around. I hope that before long he will make an enormous success in his own right and not in the shadow of his father. It's a hell of a burden, I imagine, to have a famous father who was also a famous personality. In my case I have only the private memory of my father to compete against. [. . .]

[. . .] Elisheba, the dangerous woman, the Princess of Jugoslavia, is about to marry Neil Something-Or-Other, a charming English barrister, and they are due to come on board for lunch.[146] I utterly approve of the marriage, but I wouldn't like to be in his shoes. She is beautiful – about the only Princess who is – but she has a dismissive mind and tongue to match which can only come from a childhood of immense disillusions. She is as cynical as a freed slave, who rid of his master, finds that he was poorer than he was before. She would never marry Neil if she were a true Princess. They wouldn't allow her to.

Saturday 14th I love my wife. I love her dearly. Honest. Talk about the beauty, silent, bare ... Sitting on the Thames with the river imitating a blue-grey ghost. My God the very houses seem asleep. And all that mighty heart is ... lying still.[147]

My God, again, how easy it must have been in the early days of this language to write poetry. How easy to impersonate the false feelings of a shepherd like Wordsworth's 'Michael'.[148] Or impassive massive indifferent passion of my favourite lines. And I have felt a passion, a sense sublime, or something far more deeply interfused, whose dwelling is the light of setting suns, and the round ocean, and the living air, and the blue sky, and in the mind of men.[149]

---

[146] Neil Balfour.

[147] Burton is here referring to William Wordsworth's poem, 'Composed upon Westminster Bridge' (1802), which includes the lines 'The beauty of the morning: silent, bare', and 'Dear God! the very houses seem asleep; / And all that mighty heart is lying still!'.

[148] William Wordsworth, 'Michael: A Pastoral Poem' (1800).

[149] A reference to the lines from Wordsworth's 'Tintern Abbey' (1798): 'And I have felt / A presence that disturbs me with the joy / Of elevated thoughts; a sense sublime / Of something far more deeply interfused, / Whose dwelling is the light of setting suns, / And the round ocean and the living air, / And the blue sky, and in the mind of man'.

Among the extraordinary things that happened to me daily since I was a chuckle from the womb, yesterday the sound man asked me for a voice level. There were several hundred people around, Quayle said nothing [   ] The girl doesn't have a mind. Colicos is an invention of Churchill and is equally bereft. I mean as Quayle. Churchill himself would have given one a voice level which would have started a revolution in Scandinavia. I simply said: He had the ploughman's strength in the grasp of his arms. He could see a crow three miles away.[150] Did you ever look at Welsh mountains? We grow from sea-level. And one of them is a man. And the man happens to be a woman. And the woman is my wife. And she will sit there, eternally, forever, and hover over all of us.

The silence among these assorted Dukes and Dustmen was absolute. Everybody was fascinated but acutely embarrassed. So was I.

Sunday 15th I awoke this morning at about 7 o'clock. I stared at Elizabeth for a long time. I am worried about her and her little bum and the blood. I held her hand and kissed her very gently. Probably no woman sleeps with such childish beauty as my adorable difficult fractious intolerant wife. 'When in sorrow,' said T. H. (Tim) White, 'learn something new.' I decided to examine my reactions to all the men of talent I have ever met and which company would I prefer. After serious thought, lying on that silent bed, with that killing cigarette between my lips, how I love its round cool comfort, I dropped names all over my brain. Churchill? No! A monologist. Picasso? No! An egomaniac. Emlyn? No. A mind like a cut-throat razor and a tongue to match. Dylan? No! Brilliant but uncomfortable. William Maugham?[151] No! He cared only about playing bridge with losers. Gwyn Thomas? No! An impersonation of a chap who would like to be big strong and tough and who is actually fat weak and febrile. Camus?[152] Possibly. But he had the infernal impertinence to die young. John Osborne? No! No leavening of humour. Gielgud? A strong contender for the Burton stakes, but I have a feeling that he finds me uncomfortable. Edward Albee? No! A week with him would be a life-time, and he'd feel the same about me. Anyway, why go on? I reduced it to two people. Noel Coward and Mike Nichols. They both have the capacity to change the world when they walk into a room. They are instinctively and without effort and un-maliciously witty. They are both as bland as butter as brilliant as diamonds and never speak with the forked tongue. Noel is an old man and I think he plans to die shortly. Mike plans to out-last Methuselah. What they have, and what I envy, is their abso-lute assurance. They are totally unafraid. When Noel totters – and he actually does totter – into anyone's presence, their faces light up like lamps. Including

---

[150] A reference to lines from the poem 'Lost in France' by Ernest Rhys (1859–1946): 'He had the plough-man's strength / in the grasp of his hand; / he could see a crow / three miles away'.
[151] William Somerset Maugham. (1874–1965), novelist, short story writer.
[152] Albert Camus (1913–60), novelist.

mine. Including Elizabeth's. Both E and I have a remarkable capacity of inculcating the idea of fear into people. I have actually seen people shiver as they cross the room to be introduced to Elizabeth. What the hell is it? Who did it to us? I know that we are both dangerous people but we are fundamentally very nice. I mean we only hurt each other. And we never hurt other persons unless they hurt us first. Somebody once wrote [. . .] that when Elizabeth walked into a room for a press conference which he happened to be attending, she gave the impression that nobody else was there. She answered, as it were, from outerspace.

A tall slim beautiful girl has just decided to join me on deck and have some scrambled eggs. She happens to be my daughter I think, quite clearly, that she is no daughter, actually of mine but an invention, carved in living marble of Praxiteles.[153]

Monday 16th, Dorchester I am slowly coming out of my pit of despair. I am greatly helped by Elizabeth's understanding. I think that my daughter Kate loves me but is afraid of me whereas my wife loves me, j'espere, but is <u>not</u> afraid of me. Just afraid <u>for</u> me. Christ! I'm beginning to write like Queen Victoria. We are <u>not</u> amused. Take away our underlinings and our exclamation marks and we are illiterate. [. . .]

We went to Emma Jenkins' christening yesterday. She is the daughter of Wendy and Derek Jenkins, who, despite his name, is an Englishman.[154] She carried on like a she-wolf. The service was so banal that I approved of every scream and mentally applauded her total rejection of the vicar's platitudes. How can an intelligent man believe that tedious rubbish? I don't mean me. I mean the vicar. 'You god-parents must realize that it's not the physical [*sic*] of the child but also the spiritual.' The cracks were unquestionably directed at us. He was giving us a lesson. He was showing us that because we are rich and famous we are nevertheless not particularly desirable as parent in God. [. . .]

How can anybody believe such nonsense? I vomit from my brain such self-indulgent shit. You are invited to swear that you are a Christian, which I'm not, and E is a Jewess. I noticed that the vicar looked only at and directed his homily only at our party. Another child was also being wetted but she and her family might as well not have been there. But otherwise it was a day of pleasure. The baby, Emma, is enchanting. Elizabeth was an angel and looked like one. She suits a mini-skirt very well and I lusted after her. It was a warm and sunny day, there was a green garden hanging on to the house, and all the friends of Derek and Wendy are amiable. Gwyneth was so proud and nervous – she's the grandmother – and said to me at one point: 'If anything happens to one of those two,'

---

[153] Praxiteles, sculptor of Classical Greece, probably alive in the fourth century BC.
[154] Wendy and Derek Jenkins, the daughter-in-law and son of Gwyneth Jenkins, lived in East Molesey, Surrey.

meaning Elizabeth and Emma, 'I shan't know what to do.' How sweet of her to include E. [. . .]

Saturday 21st, Dorchester We arrived back in London last night after five pleasant days in Kent. We stayed at The Leicester Arms Penshurst.[155] They had done very hasty alterations to make a suite for us with a private bathroom. We worked at Penshurst Castle and later at Hever Castle both of which are a delight and the hosts – Astors in one case and I've forgotten who in the other – were equally delightful.[156] Kate was with us and was another delight. She was obviously fascinated by the whole business and was offered and accepted a role of a kitchen maid. [. . .]

JULY

Saturday 19th, Kalizma, Thames Christ Almighty, in whom I firmly believe not, what a week, what a fortnight, what a month. There is no question but that I must stop acting. It is dementing me. The thought of going to work in the intolerably early mornings is like a physical pain. It is all so perfectly boring. Anybody can play Henry VIII – I mean even Robert Shaw who should be consigned for the rest of his life to playing ping-pong against ageing former champions – has played it.[157]

There have nevertheless been a few rewarding things. Gielgud gave E an enchanting dog the day before yesterday which is described, discribed [*sic*] as a Shidzoo – at least that it how it is vaguely pronounced.[158] [. . .]

It is funny that a man who pretends to no recognition of the Holy Trinity will still refer to Christ and God – that is, I suppose, the weakness of background. Even the Holy Ghost. I suppose there is some atavistic fear bred in the bones that gives one a ridiculous prop to lean on, despite the fact that one doesn't believe a word of it. The American astronauts are due to land on the moon tomorrow sometime. I think there are three of them. If you combined all of their three brains together I doubt whether they could solve a quadratic equation – brave and stupid like Columbus who was so great a navigator that he never found himself in the same place twice.[159] He set out for Jamaica and found himself in Cuba. He set out for Cuba and found himself in somewhere like La Guaira.[160] I think he only found his way back to Spain by running

---

[155] The Leicester Arms Hotel, Penshurst, Tonbridge, Kent.
[156] Hever Castle was the childhood home of Anne Boleyn. In 1969 it was owned by the Astor family, William Astor (1951—) being the 4th Viscount Astor. Penshurst Castle is usually known as Penshurst Place and is owned by the Sidney family. In 1969 the head of the family was William Sidney, 1st Viscount De L'Isle (1909–91).
[157] Robert Shaw (1927–78) had played the role in *A Man For All Seasons*.
[158] Usually written Shitsu or Shih-tzu.
[159] Christopher Columbus (1451–1506), explorer.
[160] La Guaira, Venezuela.

aground in the middle of the night against a land mass which he thought was a new passage to the East Indies and China, and turned out to be Cadiz. The Welsh, of course, discovered the Americas. You know that, don't you? Can one imagine a mankind that has produced a Christ (there I go again) a Da Vinci, an Einstein, a Newton, a Darwin, an Erasmus, a Turgenev, a Shakespeare, a Pushkin, an Aristotle, a Pythagoras, a Freud, a Strindberg, a *Fleurs du Mal*, a Mallarmé, a Socrates, and endless others, including the multitudinous Huxleys, producing a product into outer space that can say nothing except 'A-O.K'.[161] They are nothing but humanized monkeys. Their wives and children would not agree with that. And so they shouldn't. Get there and get back boys. You worry me. You are doing a perfectly useless and perfectly splendid thing. I envy you your stupendous courage.

Liz, I mean Liz Williams, who is among the most delectable ladies in the world of being alive, tells me that her little baby, with the assistance of an operation might be alright.[162] How I am jealous of her hope, and Brook's. I would give half a soul to have Jess have the same hope. But it's hopeless, in my case, I mean with Jess. Quite hopeless. [. . .][163]

Tuesday 22nd, Dorchester The whole world, it seems, has gone mad because the American couple, Aldrin and Armstrong, have landed on the moon and got away again.[164] Myself included. I have read more about the moon and watched on TV more about the moon than in the rest of my life put together. The three moments of unforgettable tension were the count-down to the landing, the count-down to the blast-off and the coupling together of the moon-ship with the mother ship. Now all they have to do, <u>all</u> they have to do, is get home. In a week or less I suppose I shall be heartily sick of the whole thing as a great many people are already.

I have more or less stopped drinking and the shock to my system is obviously pretty profound. It didn't matter in Puerto V where I didn't have to work, but the effect at the studios, I mean on me, is awful. I am fundamentally so

---

[161] Leonardo Da Vinci (1452–1519), Renaissance man. Albert Einstein (1879–1955), physicist. Charles Darwin (1809–82), naturalist and scientist. Desiderius Erasmus (1466–1536), philosopher and theologian. Ivan Turgenev (1818–83), novelist. William Shakespeare (1564–1616), playwright. Alexander Pushkin (1799–1837), playwright, novelist, poet. Aristotle (384–322BC), philosopher. Pythagoras (c.570–c.495BC), mathematician and philosopher. Sigmund Freud (1856–1939), theorist of psychoanalysis. August Strindberg (1849–1912), novelist, essayist, playwright. 'Fleurs du Mal' is a reference to the poetry of Charles Baudelaire (1821–67). Stéphane Mallarmé (1842–98), poet. Socrates (469–399BC), philosopher. 'The Huxleys' is a reference to the multi-talented Huxley family, including Thomas Henry Huxley (1825–95), biologist, and his grandsons Julian Huxley (1887–1975), zoologist, biologist and humanitarian; Aldous Huxley (1894–1963), novelist and essayist; and Andrew Huxley (1917–2012), winner (together with two colleagues) of the 1963 Nobel Prize in Physiology or Medicine for research into the central nervous system.

[162] Liz Williams, Brook's wife, had a daughter from her previous marriage who suffered from cerebral palsy.

[163] Jessica had been diagnosed (in the mid-1960s) as suffering from severe autions and schizophrenia.

[164] Edwin 'Buzz' Aldrin (1930—) and Neil Armstrong (1930—) were members of the Apollo 11 moon landing mission and the first men to set foot on the surface of the moon, on 20 July 1969.

bored with my job that only drink is capable of killing the pain. The thought of doing a whole day's work with, for instance, John Colicos, which is my chore tomorrow, without at least half a bottle of vodka to ease back the yawns is like deliberately inciting a nightmare. It must however be done if I wish to live through the next fortnight. [. . .]

I have been like a mad and highly articulate bull in blinding flashes with all kinds of people that I normally have great respect for. I laid into Sheran yesterday at lunch for no good reason. I roughed up Brook and Bob Wilson and Jim Benton with a fine impartiality and to top it all I burned through and around E today at lunch, in front of the same Sheran, just after she had just come back from one of the most painful operations, the insertion of some dreadful machine up her behind. This is, or course, par for the course when I am drinking heavily, but I'm surprised that I still do it when sober. If it is still the same in a month I shall go back to old father booze and find out how long it will take him to kill me. I might as well enjoy what little might be left me. One of the oddities I've noticed before when I've stopped drinking is that when one starts again the smell of straight liquor is revolting, so much so that one either has to force it down like medicine to get over the initial shock, or mix it deeply with fruit juice or something that will camouflage the taste and smell. I made myself a martini before lunch today and could not drink it. I took one sip and shivered from top to toe. I've only been off it since Friday night and even now it is only withdrawal i.e. I still allow myself a couple of drinks a day. One forgets how delicious water is and milk. I shall continue these confessions of an alcoholic at a later date.

Wednesday 23rd [. . .] The 'moon-men' are already out of the headlines and poor Teddy Kennedy is in them.[165] I feel sorry for him and I suppose understand his panic and indeed it 'could happen to anybody' but unless he comes up with something extraordinary when he appears in court next week, he has had his presidential and possibly even his senatorial chips. The K family are of course notorious satyrs. (I was amazed when Bobby K took Margot Fonteyn off into a back bedroom at Pierre Salinger's house in B. H. and my asking Salinger, when they came back, 'where the hell have they been?' and Salinger's fat-faced reply which was a finger over the lips.)[166] It was undoubtedly a hot party and Kennedy may have tried to save his friends. I doubt that he lacks courage, maybe brains though. We shall never know I suppose. Maybe they, the Kennedys do believe that they can get away with anything. Gawd Help

---

[165] Edward 'Teddy' Kennedy (1932–2009), younger brother of John F. and Robert F. Kennedy, US Senator. In the early hours of 19 July 1969 he and his passenger, Mary Jo Kopechne (1940–69), had been involved in a car accident on Chappaquiddick Island, Massachusetts. Kopechne died and controversy surrounded Kennedy's actions in the immediate aftermath of the accident.
[166] Pierre Salinger (1925–2004), Press Secretary to John F. Kennedy and Lyndon Johnson, briefly US Senator, campaign manager for Robert F. Kennedy's campaign in 1968. B. H. being Beverly Hills.

him. The press are ready for the kill. (I know too that when Jack Kennedy was running for President and stayed with Sinatra at Palm Springs, that the place was like a whore-house with President Kennedy as chief customer. Christ the chances those fellers took.) But they all got away with it except the last remaining baby. Perhaps somehow or other he'll be able to get out of it. E and I like the Kennedys, though, except through a phone call and a couple of letters we do not know Teddy K.

I am waiting for Alex Cohen, who produced my last *Hamlet* in New York, to arrive.[167] I don't know what to say to him. I've changed my mind about doing another play. I don't deep in my heart want to do a play on the stage again for a long time, possibly never. I shall slide out with vague talk of other commitments etc.

I must start putting this diary together. I just slide it into the nearest drawer and so can't look back and find out what I wrote or didn't write about what or who or which. I mean, have I written about Gielgud or the dog he gave E. About my first time as a patient in hospital since I was 7 or 8? If I'm not called today I'll start assembling it. [. . .]

Thursday 24th [. . .] Confessions continued: Last night I fell by the wayside and became drunk. It didn't take much to make me so. Today I shall return to the pavement.

Being (relatively) sober for the last three or four days I have learned a great deal. Drink, for instance, is a great anodyne. I had forgotten how boring people are. I'd forgotten how afraid people are. I'd forgotten how boring I am. And how all of us lead lives of quiet desperation, and bugger you Thoreau.[168] [. . .]

I have since the above paragraph, taken a shower and washed my hands of [. . .], cleaned myself of every orifice, laboured over the cleansing of a body which will never be clean, examined a brain, some cells of which will never function properly again, and, in general, have dismissed me as a completely lost cause. There is no going back. There is no Isaiah's burning coal to cauterize a lifetime of self-indulgence.[169] What would you like to do Rich? You want a back room in Paddington with a gas-fire and bobs to put in it and no bath but a public one around the corner just off Praed Street? You want a good girl who thinks you are the world's best bank clerk and will defend you against any bank manager who cares to take you on at the staff party? Well, you won't find one, baby. You want Pontrhydyfen and the unbelievably bad weather and 10 quid a week and the lust for the pint that you can't afford and the other man

---

[167] Alexander H. Cohen (1920–2000).
[168] An adaptation of Henry David Thoreau's (1817–62) line, 'The mass of men lead lives of quiet desperation.'
[169] The Book of Isaiah 6: 6–7, in the King James version, 'Then flew one of the seraphims unto me, having a live coal in his hand, which he had taken with the tongs from off the altar: And he laid it upon my mouth, and said, Lo, this hath touched thy lips; and thine iniquity is taken away, and thy sin purged.'

has? You can't have it fellah. I mean you can have the pint but not the lust. Go home, said George Moore to John Millington Synge, Go home.[170] Well, I got news for you Thomas Wolfe, you can't go home no more [171]

It's 6.30 and Liza has just arrived sleepy-eyed and looking like bad breath and has just gone in to see her mother. The poor little girl is going through a bad time, a time that I don't understand and can therefore do nothing about. I hope her mother can. Her mother is also going through a bad time, but that she can cure herself. I am going through a bad time and already I've started to cure myself. I had forgotten how alien Americans are from me. They speak the same language, more or less, but it is utterly foreign. They are loose somewhere in the centre. It will not hold.[172] Rife with sentimentality, woolly-minded, and on the average, brilliant – at least their Jews are – like a vast race of Huns.

Saturday 26th, **Kalizma,** *Thames* [. . .] Liza went to see *Becket* the night before last and was I think surprised to see that her father could, despite his dissipation, play a saint. Now she wanted to see all the other films that E and I had done. We explained that a vast percentage of them were rubbish and not worth anybody's attention but that, however, there were some that would bear re-watching. Which ones, we asked ourselves? Now E has made around 50 films and I have made around 30. Let us say a rough total of about 80. I guessed that about 10 would bear re-examination. We tried to sort them out. In E's case:

> *National Velvet.*
> *A Place in the Sun.*
> *Cat on a hot tin roof.*
> *Butterfield 8.* (for her performance only, I understand.)
> *Suddenly Last Summer.*
> *Virginia Woolf.*
> *Boom!*
> *Secret Ceremony* (I think.)
> *Shrew.*
> *Faustus.* (For her eyes and her breasts alone.)

I'll think of something else in a minute but what is odd is, since actors are considered to be stupid, how E's best films have been made OUTSIDE the studio

---

[170] George Moore (1852–1933), novelist, poet, playwright, who wrote that 'a man travels the world in search of what he needs and returns home to find it'. John Millington Synge (1871–1909), playwright and poet.
[171] Thomas Wolfe (1900–38), novelist, author of *You Can't Go Home Again* (1940).
[172] A reference to the line in W. B. Yeats (1865–1939), *The Second Coming* (1919), 'Things fall apart; the centre cannot hold.'

to which she was contracted. And in my case the only films I've made that were any good were the films that I chose, again <u>outside</u> the influence of contracts. The only two watchable films that I ever made before the end of my 14 year contract with Fox and Warner Bros., were *Look Back in Anger* and *Alexander the Great*. After that, and because of the remarkable impact of E on my life, I have had virtually free choice. I have, except out of fear, hardly made a mistake. Since Elizabeth I have practically caught her up. I have done, now let's have a look:

Becket.
Woolf.
Spy.
Shrew.
Boom! (Support)
Iguana.
Faustus.
Staircase.

Not, if you have a careful look, a bad record, for two people, who happen to be in love, and compete with each other, and who have the same temperament.

So, in some way it proves that we have our own taste. And if they allow us free rein, we will manage not to let anybody down. I think we should revert to being splendid amateurs, and if E wants to shoot the love life of a turtle, with herself as the vet, we shall do exactly that. I'll be the turtle.

We are, for a minute or two, at the absolute zenith of our ragged professions. So they, before they start tearing us apart again, should gracefully withdraw. The last sentence does not make any kind of sense, so let us stop. NOW. It is still a beautiful morning. The Americans have arrived back safely from the moon. [. . .]

Sunday 27th I read a most enjoyable book yesterday by Laurie Lee. An account of a walk through Spain in the middle thirties with nothing to support him but the playing of a fiddle.[173] It showed remarkable enterprise in one so young – he was about 19 – and one who'd never been abroad and who moreover couldn't speak a word of the lingo. He has the same love for the Spanish people that I have. I once lived in and around Madrid for about six months and I remember that the minute I crossed the border from Lisbon driving alternately with Ivor a bright new red MG and a great grey ghost of a Jaguar, I felt at home.[174] Perhaps because the Spanish working man is small dark with cavernous

---

[173] Laurie Lee (1914–97), *As I Walked Out One Midsummer Morning* (1969).
[174] During the filming of *Alexander the Great*, which took place in Spain in 1955.

hollows under the cheek-bones and has a murderous death-wish humour. Just like my own people, and I don't mean the Welsh, I mean the South Welsh miner, the collier, or, as I discovered when I went to Somerset House to get a copy of my birth certificate, a 'coal hewer'. Was that my father who was determined to change the cliché? Or was it a clerk who fancied himself in the English language? 'Coal hewer' indeed![175] It sounds like my father I'm afraid. Or me. Nine tailors make a man, said Tommy Roblin, and ninety clerks make a tailor.[176] It therefore follows that . . . Roblin had had some trouble with some clerks at the Municipal Offices in Port Talbot. Roblin was responsible for some memorable lines. He is now an old man and a retired headmaster. 'How tall are you Mr Roblin?' ' Five feet six and a half inches, but stand me on the slimmest volume of human suffering and I will overtop the Himalayas.' 'The encroachment of this foreigner (he was talking about a man who'd bought the house next door to him) his proximity, his adjacency, has torn the compact metabolism of my land.' His 'land' was roughly $\frac{1}{8}$th of an acre! The 'foreigner' came from Cardiff and was as Welsh as Llywellyn ap Olaf.[177] But the poor sod couldn't speak Welsh. Roblin has red hair which stands up on end, even under water, with, as he says, 'the fury of my permanent sense of injustice.' Roblin was the local choir-master. In the choir were four, sometimes five, of my brothers. The choir was roughly forty strong. They used to practise twice a week, on Tuesday and Friday nights, in the local school in Cwmavon. And there, on his little podium with a thin baton in his hand stood the incomparable Roblin. I would sit with the bass section, oddly enough I am the only son of my father who has a bass voice, or a least a bass-baritone, – the rest are all tenors – and carefully watch myself in case I incurred the wrath of Sir Thomas Roblin. No shit was allowed by Roblin, none of those sickly ballads so beloved of drunks at closing-time, nothing but the best was allowed for Roblin and his ravaged nightingales. One Friday night, I must get E home to hear them one of these days before everybody dies, I sat there and listened and half joined in when I thought it was safe, as they sang the overture to the 3rd act of *Lohengrin* transposed by Roblin into human voice from German brass. 'No! No! No!' he roared, in his middle-of-the-night-dream of being Toscanini, 'No! Because you have vulgar souls, even him,' he said, pointing at me, 'playing as he is the great Welsh King Henry the Fifth at that monument to mediocrity, the Old Vic, even he is pandering to his own inferiority. Let me make it simpler gentlemen to you and for you,' and the forty colliers look at him with the sly

---

[175] Coal hewer is an acceptable term for one who cut the coal, an alternative to collier, and more precise in its specification of the task than 'coal miner'.
[176] Thomas J. Roblin, choirmaster of the Afan Glee male choral society, who lived in Cwmafan and taught at the Cwmafan Boys' School.
[177] Burton is presumably here referring to Llywelyn ap Gruffudd (1230–82), Welsh prince, also known as Llywelyn ein llyw olaf (Llywelyn our last prince or Llywelyn the last).

half-smile of pure delight, 'the last pause, despite the authority of baton was pure ostentation and self love'.[178]

I do believe, rubbish as a great deal of it is, that the half educated South Welshman speaks English with a verve a love and a vivacity unmatched anywhere. The peasant Irishman is lovely and mellifluous but as a result perhaps of over-exposure has played himself out. He is no longer unexpected. He is as predictable as dese dem and dose. The Scots, despite their gaunt and iron constitutions, are still as wayward as Burns. 'wee, slickit, timorous cowering beastie.' Can you imagine a Welsh miner calling a mouse a 'beastie'? Or a breast a 'breestie'? He would feed it, I mean the first, and feed from it, I mean the second, but he would never insult them with such diminutives. Even 'wee' is wee.[179]

But, to get back to the Spanish, the Spanish make me feel at home. They have the cruelty of children and the dumb acceptance of inevitability. Sitting in a desperate cafe once at a place called 'El Molar' about 30 or 40 miles outside Madrid, slightly drunk and in the company of the stunt-men from the film, we watched appalled as two Guardia came into the bar and started to beat a young man, sitting with a girl, about the head with their pistols.[180] I went mad and leapt across the room frightened and blood-red in the brain and stupefied and immunized by this affront to human dignity. Were it not for the fact that stuntmen were not strictly averse to a punch-up I have no doubt that I would be sleeping out now at 'El Molar'. The Molar. The Tooth. I remember Johnny Sullivan picking up one of the Guardia and slinging him through the door of the cafe which was a door made of long strings of coloured beads to keep out the flies (fat chance) and how one accidental string of beads nearly tore the man's lobe of his ear off.[181] Later when the Guardia had been driven away, we asked the two youngsters why they had been picked on. Only because I am with a pretty girl, said the boy. Well, Indeed To Christ! Come back with us to Madrid, we said, before they come back. They won't come back, said the boy. They have seen your great Rollas Royce (pronounced something like Royath Royth – it was the battle-grey Jaguar, actually) and they will not come back. And they didn't. I crept home at dawn and, sleepless, dreamt of killing Franco.[182]

Perhaps the feeling of helplessness and hopelessness of the Spanish, so reminiscent of the thirties in South Wales, endeared them to me. I dunno. Not

[178] Burton played Henry V at the Old Vic during the 1955–6 season. Arturo Toscanini (1867–1957), conductor. *Lohengrin* (1850), opera by Richard Wagner (1813–83).
[179] Robert Burns (1759–96). The reference is to the lines from Burns's poem 'To a Mouse' (1786): 'Wee, sleekit, cow'rin, tim'rous beastie / O what a panic's in thy breastie!'.
[180] El Molar, due north of Madrid.
[181] John Sullivan was a stuntman on *Alexander the Great*, also on *The Longest Day* and was Burton's stunt double in *Cleopatra*.
[182] General Francisco Franco (1892–1975), Head of State in Spain following the victory of the Nationalists over the Republicans in the Spanish Civil War in 1939.

that we were as badly off as the poor bloody Spanish. At this same El Molar we once employed most of the able-bodied as extras. They changed into Greek clothes in a large tent. The wardrobe man, a feller as queer as a river running up hill, came out ashen.[183] 'Come and have a look Richard,' he said, 'Come and have a look.' I went. I looked. Everybody, male, female, child and teenager had running eczema from the knees down. I killed Franco a few more times. Why does nobody kill these swine? Lincolns and Kennedys and Luther-Kings get themselves assassinated, why not a Hitler or a Macarthy or a Stalin or even a fart like Wallace?[184] What providence protects these pigs?

Monday 28th [. . .] The weekend has been delightful. Brilliant hot sunshine, E and Liza watching TV, me reading books. I read yesterday a book by Lord Kinross called *Between two Seas* a racy history of the building of the Suez Canal.[185] I had hazily got Lesseps all wrong.[186] I had always thought that he was an engineer. It turns out he was a French diplomatist, a consul. He was however a sort of Renaissance man and understood engineering. One reads the pig-headed British reaction to the canal, how they held it up for at least a decade out of sheer stupidity and non-knowledge, with a kind of despair. No wonder the French hate us. We lunched on the top deck, or 'brunched' rather and I over-ate. I remained bloated and belchy for the rest of the day. The pleasure boats came past packed to their taff-rails with red tourists, once every ½ an hour or so [. . .].[187] The 'sweet and rotten, unforgettable, unforgotten river smell' is certainly with us this morning.[188] Sweet Thames, run softly till I end my song, is a sewer.[189] [. . .]

I wrote a letter to the *Sun* newspaper yesterday offering to pay the expenses of a London boy who, a polio cripple, is walking on crutches from John O'Groats to Land's End.[190] He is moving towards Gloucester I suppose at the moment. He had said to the reporter who interviewed him that 'I hope somebody will be there to meet me when I arrive, just one or two. Nobody seems to know about me.' I told the Editor that E and the two girls, and if it were

---

[183] David Ffolkes (1912—) was in charge of costumes for *Alexander the Great*.
[184] A reference to the assassinations of President Abraham Lincoln (1809–65) in 1865, of President John F. Kennedy in 1963, of Robert F. Kennedy in 1968, and of Martin Luther King (1929–68), civil rights leader, in 1968. Macarthy is presumably Senator Joseph McCarthy (1908–57) of the 1950s anti-Communist witch-hunts, and Wallace is George Wallace (1919–98), Governor of Alabama (1963–7, 1971–9, 1983–7), 1968 candidate for the presidency. Wallace was the victim of an assassination attempt in 1972.
[185] Lord Kinross (1904–76), *Between Two Seas: The Creation of the Suez Canal* (1968).
[186] Ferdinand de Lesseps (1805–94), creator of the Suez Canal.
[187] The taffrail is the aftermost portion of the poop-rail of a ship.
[188] From Rupert Brooke's 'The Old Vicarage, Grantchester' (1912): 'To smell the thrilling-sweet and rotten / Unforgettable, unforgotten / River-smell'.
[189] From Edmund Spenser, *Prothalamion*: 'Sweet Thames, run softly, till I end my song'.
[190] David Ryder, a 21-year-old victim of polio, walked from the length of mainland Britain from John O'Groats to Land's End, leaving on 21 June and arriving on 22 August. An article featuring him appeared in the *Sun* on 26 July.

possible, I, given a couple of days' warning would be there to meet him. I hope to God the letter didn't sound unctuous. E says not. It will be interesting to see how the lad reacts and how the newspaper, which appears to be on its last legs, handles it. [. . .]

Tuesday 29th, Dorchester [. . .] It was an odd day. Sir Alan (A.P.) Herbert came to lunch with his grand-daughter, who is one of the ladies in waiting to Anne Boleyn.[191] He is old – coming up for 79 – and according to Gin Bujold, made a pass at her. It was probably wishful thinking as I didn't notice anything, but that's what she believes anyway. He is what one might describe as an enlightened Victorian. He refused, for instance to let anybody smoke between courses at lunch. On the other hand he said that the British should change to right side of the lane driving. He objects violently, on the second hand, to the introduction into England of the metric system.[192] Did you notice, he said, that over the weekend man achieved his greatest technological feat, that of landing on the moon, and everything was calculated in pounds feet, inches, miles and Fahrenheit and not in kilos, metres, centimetres, kilometres and centigrade. I hadn't thought of that and he was of course quite right. Note the reflectors that the Yanks put on the moon to catch the laser beams. When announcing the results, the Americans said that they could now measure distance from the Earth to the Moon within 7 inches. They didn't say 10 centimetres. So the old man has a point.

Tony Quayle revealed himself to me in a way that I would not have thought possible. He talked of the formative years of his childhood, spent in Wales at Pontypridd.[193] [. . .]

Wednesday 30th I knew there was something wrong yesterday. I could feel it in my primitive Welsh bones. E had gone into the surgery for her 3rd and last injection for her 'piles', and when by 2.30 I had not heard from her (a mistake I understand) and I couldn't get through to her, all kinds of horror began to pile up on me, if you'll pardon the pun. The first word I had was from her doctor, a minute Welsh Jew called Rattner, who, twixt lines as 'twere, made it blatantly clear that my baby child had nearly kicked it. Some doctor-idiot the last two words are virtually synonymous, had allowed the 'shot' to leak into her blood stream and the fools were standing by with heart shots etc. in case she started to die, which they feared she was actually doing. I can forgive a 'panel' doctor in South Wales making a mistake, seeing a miner every minute on the minute, because the pressures are so enormous, but I cannot forgive Harley

---

[191] Sir Alan Patrick Herbert (1890–1971), writer, novelist and politician.
[192] The metric system had begun to be introduced into the United Kingdom in 1965.
[193] Quayle's autobiography, *A Time to Speak* (1990), mentions a holiday he spent with his mother's lover in Pontypridd.

and Wigmore Streets.[194] They work hard of course, even they, but there is no excuse for treating so expensive and tender a mortal as Elizabeth with anything less than calculated care. I am still dazed by the potential enormities of their ill syringes. [. . .] Well she has defeated their best efforts to kill her many times. I wish she would realize, like me, that good doctors are as rare as good actors. I only know about ten of us, I mean actors, out of ten thousand, who are not derivative and repetitive and tedious and run-of-the-mill. Why should one expect a higher percentage from doctors? They continually make stupendous mistakes, mortal ones, and get away with it. The feller who buggered it up with E yesterday was already protesting that it was <u>her</u> fault not <u>his</u>! In case so celebrated a patient died as a result of his maladministration. I could beat him to death with an eye-lid.

Anyway, she's alright, though I am still night-mared. What could life possibly be without her? Where would I go? What would I do? Everybody else pales by comparison. It's no use picking up a mini-skirted chick of 18 – she wouldn't last a week, if that. I would die, I suppose, a greatly accelerated death. Anyway, she's alright. Bastards.

Because of my fear, relief, anxiety, etc. yesterday I went over the top in one scene. I had to say to an actor called Marne Maitland 'Get out! Limp back to Rome and tell His Holiness the Pope That I will have the marriage annulled. Get out. Get out Get out'.[195] The last 'get out' was delivered with such murderous virulence and at the top of my voice that Mr Maitland's feet left the ground and he tripped and fell down. It was somewhat embarrassing and we had to do the scene again. Not only doctors can make mistakes! I couldn't wait, you see, to get home.

Thursday 31st, Dorchester It's a cool grey dawn and E and I have just had a quarrel about who knows what. [. . .] If she'd only do some movement of some kind she could cure herself. But she slugs and slows and shrugs the world away. And she firmly believes in doctors rather than herself. Shots, shots, shots and pain-killers. And though she is not a Jewess by birth, she has acquired at second hand, not only their brilliance but their mass masochism. [. . .] As for me, the day and the days stretch before me like a vast steppe. I have mentioned many times that what kills me is boredom. I am perfectly happy to be alone with E or Liza, oddly enough I can't say that about anybody else except Kate – (note that they are all women) but the pity of me is that I pity everybody else. I cannot bear, and I have to bear it, members of the human race, who don't know where to turn or where to go. I have, despite my background, never lacked for money, and when I am confronted with a Tony Quayle or a Robert

---

[194] In London's Harley Street and Wigmore Street are to be found the practices of many leading doctors.
[195] Marne Maitland (1916–91) played the part of Campeggio. He had played the part of Euphranor in *Cleopatra*.

Beatty who cannot either separately or together afford the fare to Gibraltar or the Canary Islands I am suitably astounded.[196] I bet you that if the worst came to the worst and inevitably to the vast unknown, I could find a job that would feed and clothe my family. As long as I am alive, Ivor used to say, nobody shall go short.

This day is going to be a rough one but I shall be gentle. Liza is coming with me which is always a blessing. I love this child. I hope to Christ that she knows that I do. She must. She must. When this creature says something nice to me, un-asked for, I blossom like a cherry-tree. In spring. I mean Spring. And now the child-monster has arrived and is kissing her mother and it's time go to work.

Much love Elizabeth, and I'm sorry.

AUGUST

Friday 1st, Dorchester E was going to go away for the weekend [. . .] but I persuaded her not to. After all we both know we would be in agony without each other around. Little Liza behaved superbly with her mother and (on the telephone) with me, trying to reconcile us. She ordered E around. She made her eat breakfast. She made me ring up and apologize to E. She was every-body's minute mother. Instant wisdom. She is a hell of a child and I may be forced to keep her. Also she is going to be, and indeed already is, a knock-out as a beauty. She is a bloody 'Bramah' as we say at home.[197] Her teeth will have to be fixed one of these days otherwise she might become a little chinny and she walks like a duck but all those things can be corrected.' But her eyes, oh God, her eyes, fresh fire-coal etc. . . .'[198]

I suppose that deep down, though I hate to admit it, I am a proper actor and the parts I play do affect me slightly. There is always one part of me that is looking on and I am aware that I have become authoritative. Nobody is allowed to buy anything except me. I must give the drinks. I must pay for the lunch. My car, or one of them, must take you home. Mind, I've always been like that but playing a King, especially a man as demonic as Henry, has accentuated my natural assumption of superior means.

Aaron arrived at the studios yesterday. [. . .] I asked him how much money we have. Could we really afford to retire. He told me that in 'quick' money I have roughly 4 to 4½ to five million dollars, and E has slightly less. This is quick money and not to be confused with the various houses, the *Kalizma*, the paintings, the jewellery etc. which would amount to about 3 or 4 million more. If, I said, we stopped acting, what sort of income would we get without

---

[196] Robert Beatty (1909–92) had played the part of Cartwright-Jones in *Where Eagles Dare*.
[197] A colloquial Welsh term for a very attractive woman.
[198] A reference to a line in Gerard Manley Hopkins's poem 'Pied Beauty' (1877): 'Fresh-firecoal chestnut-falls'.

This studio portrait captures Richard at the very beginning of his acting career in the early 1940s, alongside his greatest mentor and the man whose surname he took, the English teacher and dramatist Philip Burton.

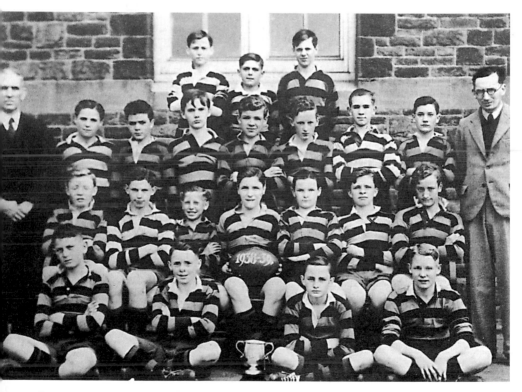

Port Talbot Secondary School's first fifteen (rugby union), 1938–9. Richard is in the middle row, second from right. According to legendary Welsh international Bleddyn Williams, 'Richard would have made as good a wing-forward as any we have produced in Wales!'

3 Richard and his father – 'Dic Bach' – walking across the tramroad viaduct in Richard's home village of Pontrhydyfen, in the direction of the Miners' Arms public house, 1953. Richard admired his father's physical strength and capacity for drink, but not much more.

4 Richard, studying the text of *Hamlet*, *c*.1953–4, in his London home at Lyndhurst Road, Camden, where he and his first wife Sybil lived from 1950 to 1957. On his bookshelves are a number of volumes about actors, acting and playwrights.

Richard, Sybil and their first daughter Kate, at their home – *Le Pays de Galles* – in Céligny, Switzerland, 1958.

Richard improving his French in conversation with owner/manager Paul Fillistorf at the Café de la Gare Céligny, *c.*1958. Richard would return to the Café's unpretentious comfort with regularity for the next arter century.

VODKA POEM TO
RICHARD BURTON.

7 T. H. White's gift of his 'Vodka Poem' is mentioned by Burton in his diaries, 26 May 1969. 'Richard ap Richard' is Welsh for 'Richard son of Richard'. 'Gwalia' is 'Wales'.

Richard ap Richard,
For you are
Your father and your son,
Are you the spendthrift and the spent,
The slayer slain in one?
Believer who does not believe,
Munificent and mean,
Trustless and Trusting, insecure,
How will you get you clean?
Do not. But suffer. Understand.
Mascara nor the dust of coal
Nor male nor female lashes fanned
Are Gwalia nor the whole.

HAM. I mean, HAMEN.

Tim

8 A month before the end of filming *Cleopatra*, Richard and Elizabeth spent time together on a yacht off the island of Ischia, Naples, June 1962. The paparazzi's long lenses revealed that 'le Scandale' had far from run its course.

Richard and Elizabeth were based in the small Mexican coastal town of Puerto Vallarta while Richard was filming *The Night of the Iguana* in autumn 1963. They bought Casa Kimberley and returned there frequently over the next decade.

0 Richard, Maria Burton, Liza Todd and Elizabeth at Chalet Ariel, Gstaad, December 1968. I am very excited at the thought of going home and seeing the two girls in their various [school] plays', Richard had written a few days earlier.

11 Richard and his older brother Ivor, whom he admired and respected greatly, in the mid-1960s. Ivor's death in 1972 precipitated a catastrophic decline in Richard's personal and professional fortunes.

12 Directed by John Gielgud, Richard's *Hamlet* ran for 134 performances on New York's Broadway in 1964, following a successful run in Toronto. A version was broadcast in cinemas across the USA and a long-playing record released.

13 While working on *The Comedians* in the South of France, Richard and Elizabeth discovered that Elizabeth had won her second Best Actress Oscar for *Who's Afraid of Virginia Woolf?* Richard's third nomination in three years for Best Actor was not successful.

14 Elizabeth shows off the 33.19 carat Krupp diamond, which cost $305,000, while in Britain for the filming of Harlech Television's 'Opening Night' in May 1968. Richard and Elizabeth were both directors of HTV.

15 Richard and Elizabeth arrive at RAF Abingdon, Oxfordshire in their Hawker Siddeley HS.125, in preparation for the film premiere of *Doctor Faustus*, October 1967. Elizabeth is wearing her *The Night of the Iguana* brooch, a present from Richard from four years earlier.

Richard and Elizabeth bought their yacht (renamed the *Kalizma*) in July 1967. They are pictured here e following month off the Capo Caccia peninsula, Sardinia, during the filming of *Boom!* Richard revelled the peace and isolation he found on his 'second home'.

17 Richard was nominated for the Best Actor Oscar for his performance as Henry VIII in *Anne of the Thousand Days*, but it was not a role he enjoyed – 'Anybody can play Henry VIII . . . even Robert Shaw'.

18 Richard and Elizabeth arrive at Heathrow Airport, London, in September 1970, prior to Richard filming *Villain*. He is carrying his new Olivetti typewriter, complete with Welsh flag sticker (see diary entry for 23 May 1970).

By 1974 Richard was drinking very heavily and his marriage to Elizabeth was in desperate trouble. Here is in California during the filming of *The Klansman* – one of his less successful screen appearances – here he met Jeanne Bell, who would share his life in 1975.

20 It's Perrier water in the ice bucket and Richard is enjoying his status as an honorary fellow at St Peter's College, Oxford. Richard had taken a wartime course in English at Exeter College, but had not returned to the university to complete a degree.

21 Richard met Susan (Suzy) Hunt in Switzerland early in 1976. Before August was out they were married in Arlington, Virginia, after Burton's successful return to Broadway in *Equus*.

"I had nothing to begin with except an unshakeable belief in my ability and the Richard Burton Divorce Contract. 23.2.82

2 Grenfell 'Gren' Jones drew for the *Western Mail* and *South Wales Echo*. He won the first of four awards or the best provincial cartoonist in Britain in 1983, the year that Richard was given a diary complete with ren' cartoons, one of which took him as its subject.

3 Richard's daughter Kate was erself a successful actress by e time *Private Lives* (starring ichard and Elizabeth) opened in ew York in May 1983.

24 Richard and Sally Hay married in Las Vegas in July 1983. Their marriage would last only thirteen months, but it brought Richard great stability and comfort.

5 Richard's passion for reading was life-long: here he is enjoying sunshine and scholarship at his home
Céligny.

26 'Looking forward to Switzerland and books and peace.' Richard's library, Céligny.

touching the principal. He said: At least ½ million dollars a year. Let us give away 100,000 of that in keeping R Hanley and Benton and Wilson in the style in which they are accustomed and all the godsons god-daughters nephews nieces and Howard and Sara and Will and schools. Let us give another 100,000 running the *Kalizma*. Let's allow another 50,000 for odds and ends and we, E and I, will have to make do on 250,000 a year. All the children are now rich, some more than other, and so we don't have to worry about them. Financially I mean. I think with some blank paper and a typewriter and some amiable but not furious vodka and Jack Daniels we could manage alright. [. . .]

Money is very important, not all important, but it helps a lot. That's why I have written about it so much today because it, if it means that E and I have the strength of mind to give up being famous we can at least live in more than lavish comfort. I might even be able to buy her the odd jewel or two. We'll spread our time between Gstaad the *Kalizma* and Puerto Vallarta. We'll nip over to Paris occasionally and give a party for the Rothschilds. We'll take the Trans-Siberian Express across Russia from Moscow to Vladivostok. We'll go to the hill stations in Kashmir. We'll muck around among the Greek Islands. We'll visit Israel and bury dead Egyptians. We'll re-visit Dahomey again and look at the washing on the line at the Palace – we can slide down the coast there in the *Kalizma*. And Spain and the West Indies and Ecuador and Paraguay and Patagonia and go up the Amazon. We'll take a month and do the Michelin Guide of France. There are many elsewhere, Coriolanus.[199] I can write pretty books with photos by E.

Sunday 3rd I went through a bad time yesterday, a time of enormous lassitude and indifference. I could barely bring myself, though I eventually did, to revise the enormous verbiage contained in the scenes I have to do this week. I tried to read a book about General Custer of Custer's Last Stand fame but found it un-readable. It is as if the writer was not only bad but a homosexual madly in love with Custer. The number of times he writes things like 'and so the American Mural stormed into battle with his golden locks flowing in the wind', or 'the impetuous young man his golden tresses flying with the urgency of his charge, this marvellous boy . . .' etc. Sick-making. How do writers like that get themselves published? The author's name is Van de Water.[200] I must carefully avoid him in future. [. . .]

Today, however, I have lost all sorrow for myself and am really thinking of stopping this acting lark altogether. I will go into it very carefully with Aaron

---

[199] The line is from Shakespeare's *Coriolanus*, Act III, scene iii, spoken by Coriolanus: 'There is a world elsewhere'.

[200] Frederick F. Van de Water (1890–1968), *Glory-Hunter: A Life of General Custer* (1934). Although these are not direct quotations, they are true to the flowery style of the original. For example, p. 67: 'Foremost rode the Michigan Brigade and at its head a youngster whose face was hardly less radiant than the newly risen sun.'

this week and find out exactly where our various obligations lie. It may mean working for another year and picking up an extra couple of million or so to pay everybody off that we feel responsible for. [. . .]

Acting is a funny thing. Yesterday I read an article by that tall girl, Philip Hope-Wallace about the Cleopatras he has seen.[201] Every one he mentioned (he was talking about Shakespeare's of course) was or is as ugly as sin. Tony Quayle, oddly enough, had said the day before at lunch. 'Why is it that all our so-called major actresses are so plain?' Why indeed? Let's have a look at the dames: Edith Evans, Ashcroft, Flora Robson and those who are semi dames like Maggie Leighton, Pamela Brown and that woman whose name I can never remember who's married to Larry Olivier – ah I have it – she is called Joan Plowright.[202] Vanessa Redgrave and Maggie Smith both tend to turn me agint sex.[203] He doesn't mention the only one who had the power or personality and physical beauty to destroy a man's life – Vivien Leigh. My wife was not considered of course because she is too beautiful and sensual. He talks of Peggy Ashcroft's exquisite care for the speaking of verse. Well Peggy speaks verse like an English mistress from Kensington. Fair dues the Hope-Wallace was only talking about stage performances.

Liza is quite hopelessly slap-dash. She has spent only two nights in the spare bedroom and where we share the bathroom and this morning it looked as if a tornado had hit it. Two pairs of under pants on the bathroom floor, her dress, shoes and socks in various corners of the bedroom, innumerable 'Charlie Brown' books scattered to the four winds.[204] What is this disease of sluttishness that possesses our children, boys and all? Well they are all past the age of curing so bugger it. But nobody shares the spare room with me again. I remember Simmy's room at Gstaad – the smell and chaos was so revolting that I couldn't go into it.

Monday 4th [. . .] I'm at my wit's end as to where to send Liza to school. She has the education of a child of 10 and is 12 years old. And she is very bright but wouldn't stand a chance of getting into any school where they demand the 11-Plus. I suppose we'll work something out.

[. . .] I loathe loathe loathe acting. In studios. In England. I shudder at the thought of going to work with the same horror as a bank-clerk must loathe that stinking tube-journey every morning and the rush-hour madness at night. I loathe it, hate it, despise, despise, for Christ's sake, it.

Well that has managed to get a little spleen out of [my] system.

---

[201] Philip Hope-Wallace (1911–79), music and theatre critic.

[202] Dame Peggy Ashcroft (1907–91) had appeared with Taylor in *Secret Ceremony*. Dame Flora Robson (1902–84). Joan Plowright (1929—), who was to be made a Dame in 2004, had married Laurence Olivier in 1961. She would appear with Burton in the film *Equus*.

[203] Maggie Smith (1934—), had appeared with Burton and Taylor in *The V.I.P.s*.

[204] 'Charlie Brown', the central human character in the *Peanuts* comic strip.

We must force ourselves to do something for Harlech TV though from all I hear from Stanley Baker, David Harlech and John Morgan the organization and the rivalry between the Welsh and English factions is as bad as I feared it would be when I first put E and my weight behind the effort to get the franchise. I should have had more sense. We'd better do something, much as I'd prefer to sell and get out. So far, every suggestion I've put to them not only has not been acted on but I've never even recieved, shit, received, that's better, any acknowledgement. They are quite hopeless.

So off to work and another round of repetition. 'I must have a son to rule England when I am dead. Find a way Cromwell. Find a way. The Pope. The Cardinal. Orvieto, My Lord Bishops. Divorce Katherine. Divorce Anne. Marry Jane Seymour.' I use every trick I know to make it credible but it's a losing battle. It's all mediocre rubbish. [. . .]

Tuesday 5th Yesterday was another depressing entry though it had a few rewarding moments. [. . .] I suppose I also found some pleasure in the discomfiture of a journalist-gossip-writer named David Lewin who has been so vicious to us, particularly Elizabeth, in the last few years. Actually I feel rather sorry for him. It seems that he's lost his job as head of the entertainment section of the *Daily Mail* and now tells me with a pathetic attempt at bluster that he is editing a magazine. 'Ah What magazine?' say I, with blue-eyed candour. '*Film Trade Review*,' says he. 'You really should subscribe to it.' This will make its circulation up to about six, I fancy – the other readers being his wife mother and children. Someone told me some time ago, I think it was Peter Evans of the *Express*, that his decline began with the pounding he took from Elizabeth on a TV interview at which he was idiotically present in company with an American Professor or Eng. Lit. Lord, and delicious, David Cecil, and our beloved N. Coghill. I have written about this encounter elsewhere in this diary. Why did a TV interview start his slide? 'Because,' said Peter Evans, 'the editor of the *Mail* presumably told him that he had disgraced the *Mail* by his persistent idiocy with me and E and that she had made a fool of him etc. etc.' The interview, unfortunately for him, was shown throughout the world. We, as a matter of fact, put it out as publicity for *Faustus*. Everybody exulted in E's anhiilation, how does one spell that word?, of him, though at the time I had the cold horrors and thought that in her tigeressish defence of me she was making a fool of herself. If he's any good he'll come back. But of course he's not good, is he? He writes in invisible ink.

We went to the Hornbys last night for dinner and took the kitten with us. Sheran took it bravely though apparently she doesn't like cats, at the same time not being an ailurophobe – pick the tad-pole out of that spawn. I was struck last night at the uncanny resemblance that Simon Hornby bore to Oscar Wilde. A taller version I suppose though not much, for Wilde was about 6 feet 2 inches tall. He has the same sort of hair, the same liquid eyes, the same long oval face, the same lavish lips and the same swaying elephantine hips. I never had the honour, of course, of being alive when the great Oscar was, but I've read endlessly about him and seen many cartoons and photographs.

Quip from Tony Quayle: 'Michael Redgrave is in love with himself but he's not sure if it's reciprocated. That's his problem.' I laughed for a long time.

Observation from John Colicos: 'My wife gave me a row on Saturday night because she said I was using words she'd never heard or read before, and that my attitudes had totally changed. I said that Burton not only was dynamic in himself but created dynamite in others. I blamed it all on you.'

I sound like that fool Richard Harris.[205]

Wednesday 6th Liza's Birthday.
We are confoundedly trying to find a hunter for L's birthday present. [. . .]

E said this morning that I lacked loyalty – simply because I said that Sheran is a snob and cultivates people only because they're temporarily 'in'. Now E is a bright bugger to talk about loyalty. The list of her dis-loyalties would fill the yellow pages of the New York Telephone Directory. Except of course to her children. And there she defeats me because I've been dis-loyal to mine.

Liza is very excited because she's just been told about the prospect of the horse. She's a lovely old kid and, despite my temper, I could spoil her almost as much as I spoil her mother. And that would take some spoiling. She is growing up at a fantastic rate and is tending to mother us all. She has latterly acquired the admonitory wagging of the finger with me and the 'now-you-relax-and-take-it-easy-he'll-come-to-his-senses-because-he-really-loves-you-and-cannot-live-without-you' sort of dialogue. It's a hot race in this family as to which is the most spoiled. But we all have instincts of generosity so I suppose we'll be alright. [. . .]

I muse that if the Hornbys had a child which seems to me to be unimaginable it would consist of one enormous buttock. All ass and no forehead. Their two bottoms side by side would fill the Albert Hall. We discussed sycophancy last night and nothing is as crawly as Simon's having to play golf with the new director of W. H. Smith's simply because he is the new director. He was also late for us at dinner and I cannot bear people being late. Except of course me.

Thursday 7th Well, I'll tell you. Liza's birthday is over and the change in her has been remarkable in the last 12 months and when other people take notice of it and tell me, not how beautiful she is which is self-evident, but how gracious and thoughtful she has become and how carefully she looks after weaker members of the family – like me – me or her mother or her sister for

---

[205] Richard Harris (1932–2002), actor, who would appear with Burton in *The Wild Geese*, and take over from him in the stage production of *Camelot* in 1981.

instance, and when they say, which is quite clearly impossible, that she sounds and even looks like me, I beam like a lighthouse.

I am in one of my idiotic moods and have kept the two little buggers awake far beyond their respective bedtimes. The two little buggers are E and L. When I say that she looks like me, or to be exact when they say she looks like, I don't mean for a second that it infers a physical resemblance but a trick of phrase, an oddity of expressions, a manner. She is vulnerable at this stage to any powerful influence and, I suppose, you could hardly come more powerfully than her mother and myself. If you know what I mean. We both have authority in our own rights and in very different ways. Anyway she is growing into a very special creature. Bill Squire said the other day, having met Liza for the first time, 'Good God, I would know she's Welsh from anywhere, she looks like us, she talks like us, she is us.'[206] I pointed out very carefully that she was about as Welsh as Josef Broz.[207] He was astonished. I suppose that is because one has forgotten how vast the changes are. The differences are day by day, week by week, month by month tiny but massive. And suddenly there is a different person.

I had been a little bit worried because it was quite obvious that people found Kate easier to handle and have around than Liza. But miraculously it seems, in the last month, Liza is running neck-and-neck with Kate and will, I guess, because the influences on Liza are more positive and because Liza's instincts are more generous, beat her (Kate) to the post. Understand that I love both children to the point of idolatry. She will never have charm in the ordinary sense of the word, she will never be, as Ivor says, and which I am, a 'shw'd ichi heddi', but, like her mother, she has the great virtue of honesty.[208] She enchants me because of course she is in any case a delightful child, she is her mother's daughter and because in the absence of her mother she lectures me exactly as if she were Elizabeth. She wags a self-conscious finger as portentously as Noël Coward. And she loves wicked and naughty words as innocently as her mother. She told me last night on her birthday if you please that she loved the word 'Shit'. I just love it she said. I just love it.

I remonstrated but to no avail.

Just like her mother.

Friday 8th, **Kalizma,** *Thames* It's 6 in the morning [. . .]. I am on a stand-by. I'd had very little sleep the night before (took a shower with my pyjamas on. Is't possible?) and for the rest of the day was like a somnambulist, drinking

---

[206] William Squire (1916–89) played Thomas More in *Anne of the Thousand Days*. Squire had been born in Neath, had played alongside Burton in the Stratford productions of *Henry IV (Part 2)* and *Henry V* in 1951, and in the Old Vic productions of *Hamlet, King John, Twelfth Night,* and *Coriolanus* in 1953–4. He had also played the part of Thomas in *Where Eagles Dare*.
[207] Josip Broz (1892–1980), Marshal Tito, President of Yugoslavia.
[208] *Shw'd ichi heddi* is Welsh for literally 'How are you today?' In this context it means someone of easy charm, with a hint of superficiality and insincerity.

steadily under the water until the exhausted and drunken body was given a succession of rockets from E and L on this yacht and ordered to go bed below decks. Example of dialogue with the two witches:

> *Me, in bed, with a book*: Liza, bring E'en So downstairs.
> *Elizabeth*: Get her yourself.
> *Liza*: Get her yourself.
> *Me*: Get me a sandwich.
> *Elizabeth*: Get it yourself.
> *Liza*: Get it yourself.

Outcome: A silent Liza appears with a tray of sandwiches and small exquisite tomatoes and spring onions with immense disapproval on the side. I gave her a sorrowful look with all the sly Celtic charm I could muster up, but it fell on deaf eyes. I think that child loves her mother. I hope she realizes that I do too. It's a shared privilege.

What a revelation Tony Quayle is? He's a sly-boots and perhaps he's mellowed with age, or perhaps I never knew him well enough but I'd either forgotten or didn't know how bright he is. And he can almost match me, said he with immense conceit, in knowledge of poetry. And reacts to it as immediately as litmus paper dipped in acid. What a strange thing for a man like Quayle to do. To stop being the boss of a great national monument like the Memorial Theatre and descend, for a few thousand quid, to playing opposite Gordon Scott in Tarzan.[209] And more than that. Stratford was a theatre that catered for actors who were not good enough for London, or amateurs straight down from the Marlowe Society or the OUDS.[210] T.Q. changed all that. For a torn second or two Stratford became the poshest theatre in the world. The ripped moment lasted for about 10 years and Quayle was the man who did it. He got Larry there, and Vivien, and Ralph (for better or for worse) and the tallest girl in the school Redgrave, and a host of unknowns who later became 'stars' like me for instance. And Gielgud. And Badel.[211] And the best wearer of costumes in the world, Harry S. Andrews.[212] It's quite something to have done. It's as, I think, Emile Zola said of a man's library: 'It was not a library in the ordinary sense of the word. It was an act of faith. It was a passion.'[213] Even that anonymous librarian probably did not know how unconsciously well he'd wrought. You don't write wrought very often do you? There's something wrong

---

[209] Anthony Quayle had a leading role in *Tarzan's Greatest Adventure* (1959), in which Gordon Scott (1926–2007) played the part of Tarzan.
[210] The Marlowe Society is the Cambridge University equivalent of OUDS.
[211] Alan Badel (1923–82) had appeared at Stratford with Burton in *Henry IV (Parts 1 and 2), The Tempest* and *Henry V*. He would also feature in *The Medusa Touch*.
[212] Harry Fleetwood Andrews (1911–89) had appeared at Stratford with Burton in *Henry IV (Parts 1 and 2)*. He had played alongside him in *Alexander the Great* and would do so again in *Equus*.
[213] Emile Zola (1840–1902), novelist.

with the syntax of the last but 7th sentence, but we'll let it go. It will amuse me to correct it in my old age which will arrive next week. It is the bloodiest thing but I am only at home with children of my own generation. If you don't know your Richard two-strokes or three or the Dane.[214] If you don't know that fool Dowson, or that lusting dying homosexual Housman, or Alexander Macgonical, then we have to begin from the beginning and re-educate ourselves.[215] Nothing will persuade me that accident is art. Don't give me your bloody Beatles.

[. . .] Quayle told me yesterday at lunch, and it needs somebody to lay down the law because one forgets the obvious, that art must have form. J. Gielgud had seen that thing of Peter Brook's of Marat? Sade? and they were all having dinner or supper or whatever the hell it was at The Mirabelle with Alec Guinness and Simone Signoret.[216] And Tony was in one of his recalcitrant moods. First: he hated the Mirabelle. Second: he wanted to find out something about Simone. Third: he hadn't seen the Brook thing. Fourth: he blew his top when J. G. said he'd been to see that particular production three or four times and though it was miraculous or marvellous or whatever the latest adjective was that he'd picked up that morning as he passed T. S. Eliot in St James' Park on his way to the nearest public lavatory. Well to cut a long diary short, Tony asked: 'But what was it about John?' John didn't know and again Quayle blew his top and embarrassed his wife, the waiters, and gentle Alec and presumably the baffled Simone Signoret.[217] And if I'd been there I would have blown my top too, except, of course that I wouldn't have the courage. But John, as Tony or I suggested, had deliberately become a send-up of himself. 'I am just a child of nature, I don't know what I'm doing. Give me the words and I'll get on with the job. Is the war over, I'm so glaaaaad.'

Elizabeth says that Tony does the best impersonation of Gielgud that's ever been, that's deliberate. Better than me. Better than the two Peters, Ustinov and Sellers. I promised that I would find for Quayle an observation of Bacon's. It goes like this: 'Reading maketh a full man; conference a ready man, and writing an exact man.'[218]

I am neither full, ready or exact this morning but I have created a base on which to work.

Saturday 9th, Dorchester Sadly I was called to work yesterday after all, and just for one line. 'All will be well now Anne, all will be well.' Today is Bob

[214] *Richard II, Richard III, Hamlet.*

[215] Ernest Christopher Dowson (1867–1900), poet. Alfred Edward Housman (1859–1936), poet. Burton presumably means William McGonagall (1825–1902), poet.

[216] *Marat/Sade*, the Peter Weiss play, translated into English and directed by Peter Brook in 1964, which ran on Broadway from 1965 to 1967. Peter Brook also directed the 1967 film version. Simone Signoret (1921–85), actor.

[217] Quayle's (second) wife was Dorothy Hyson (1914–96), actor.

[218] From Francis Bacon (1561–1626), *Of Studies.*

Wilson's and Gwladys's wedding.[219] I am to be best man and E the matron-of-honour or whatever the title is at Registry Offices. It is to be at Caxton Hall. I hope to god I don't get the giggles as I did at my first marriage at Kensington and E did at her marriage to Michael Wilding.

[. . .] Word came yesterday from the States that the children's film *Eagles* has grossed over $21m and is still going strong. That is in the United States alone. I don't know quite what it means but McKenna told me yesterday that it's been running for months in Dublin and if it goes on running much longer he'll be forced to see it. Cheek. In London it has been returned to Leicester Square from Coventry Street and is the only film in the recent heat-wave, not only to hold its own but to actually out-gross itself by £700 a week. So maybe retirement is a feasible idea after all. The film was a disappointingly slow starter but it is snow-balling along. If *Staircase* does half the business, I can probably employ J. Paul Getty as a butler and Onassis as a Greek chef.[220] Elizabeth top-less and mini-skirted, will serve me food and call me 'sir'. That'll be the day! Jackie Onassis can be the tweeny and get her orders from Elizabeth. Noel Coward will be brought in every night to be witty and sing us songs. We'll get us a defecting Russian pianist, one of the great ones, to play every night. In chains of course. We'll pour white confetti on his hair and tell him he's in Siberia. [. . .]

Sunday 10th, **Kalizma,** *Thames* The wedding went off without a hitch and there were a few moist eyes here and there. Quite a lot of photographers to give a tiny air of importance to the whole proceedings and last night we were all on the TV in the news. All good stuff and very nice for Bob and Gwladys. Not very nice however was the news that lovely Sharon Tate, wife of film director Roman Polanski, was one of the victims of a mass-murder in LA.[221] She was pregnant which somehow or other makes it worse. It is all very odd and perfectly like one of Polanski's films because all his films have bizarre sex killings etc. in them, and E wonders if it was some 'nut' who was carrying out in practice what Polanski preached in theory. In which case Elizabeth is due to be beheaded. The poor little thing was apparently strangled and then hung from a beam. We shall find out more details today from the newspapers. And then we must send off a letter of condolence to Polanski because E likes him very much and says he's a sweet little man. I do believe that Mrs Polanski is the only person I've ever met who was murdered. Friends of mine have been killed but not murdered.

I have arrived at the stage, which E tells me is predictable, of being thoroughly bored by what I'm doing. The next three weeks are going to be torture.

---

[219] Burton's nickname for Bob Wilson's wife Alice.
[220] J. Paul Getty (1892–1976), industrialist and multimillionaire.
[221] Roman Polanski (1933—). Sharon Tate (1943–69). Charles Manson (1934—) was the leader of the group that carried out the murders.

I have tried for several weeks, and all my friends have too, to make Gin Bujold feel like a desirable person. But it's a lost cause. It appears that she goes out to discotheques with her husband every night, ignores her child-son, and arrives at the studio looking like the end of the world. And smells like it. She is forever throwing up. She is only 27. She has re-invented biliousness. Why can't she learn to look splendid at 6 in the morning, even if she went to bed at 5.30. Elizabeth looks dew-dropped with 15 minutes sleep. [. . .]

Monday 11th It has been very humidly hot again over the week-end and promises to be so again today. This too is the day when I lie in bed with Gin Bujold which is not going to be cool. In fact it's likely to be somewhat sweaty.

Elizabeth has sweetly got up with me and is sitting opposite me at the moment making a deliberate nuisance of herself so I'll stop this entry right at this spot.

Monday 18th [. . .] E is going down to Cornwall today to meet the polio victim – he who has walked from John O'Groats to Land's End on crutches. She has a strange journey. London Airport to St Morgans by jet, then ten minute flight in a prop plane to somewhere else, then a 10 mile car drive to Land's End where she will be met by the Mayor of Penworth. Brook and the two babies will be going with her. I wish Brookie, who is among the world's nicest men would start writing. The work he is doing is nowhere near his intelligence, and from his brilliant wit – as witty as Emlyn but without the malice – and use of language I would guess that he could become a fine writer. [. . .]

Thursday 21st, Dorchester [. . .] Two events of family importance: An astonishing and lost and lonely and 'God-written' letter from young Michael in Hawaii.[222] [. . .] Poor little bastard. We must cwtch and cuddle him a lot when he arrives. We sent for him immediately. [. . .] I think we should keep him with us at Gstaad and/or the *Kalizma* for the next term and sort things out with him without too much of a rush.

Second event: A piece of crude but unsentimental doggerel from Kate which means, I hope to God, that she'll go on writing. She obviously has inherited the Jinks' gift for words. At least it's a gift, I hope.

Only a week to go now on the film and shan't I be glad.

Thursday 21st It's the same day but later of course, much later. I have finished work and am home and am supposed to go to a party given by Michael Hordern which surprisingly enough, knowing that we all in the film business have to get up at dawn or just after, doesn't start until 9 o'clock, which means

---

[222] In which Michael related the story of his thwarted attempt to leave Hawaii, his desire to rejoin Elizabeth and Richard in Europe, and his discovery of 'Jesus and Universal Love'.

10 o'clock if I know Elizabeth, and two o'clock if I know me. And if I really know me it might be 2 in the morning or straight to work. That kind of thing. And also after an orgy of story-telling and an eternal dressing-room full of people for weeks on end I prefer to settle down to a little, in my case, rare silence. And talking is a disease that somehow or other I have to cure. I find for the most part that if I have a room full of people which I invariably have, unless I talk nobody else will. And I'm damned if I'm going to go through it all again tonight. I will talk to this machine only. [. . .] The trouble with a diary is that you have to pound it out, slam it in, there is not time to make corrections. That's why I know E to be right when she says that I should pack it in for a bit – acting – and start to think. We both tend to forget, though we never really do, the tremendous combined impact of our arrogant personalities and fame and wealth on poor blokes who are just wondering where they can get the next job. I am quite sure, for instance, that, without meaning to, I, and in a supporting role, Elizabeth, have turned John Colicos into a drunken conceited maniac who believes himself to be as desirable an actor as I am and that his wife should be as desirable as Elizabeth. 'Vroom' as the Yankee comics say, and he has lost his wife and the next film. And a lot of money. It is only a question of time before he will elect to kill himself or somebody else, hopefully not one of us, and which river he will choose in which to hide the body. I feel immensely sorry for him but nobody else seems to share my sorrow. After all he has those two lovely little boys.[223] [. . .]

Friday 22nd Well, not long now boys, not long. One slight haul over the next hill and we're home again. I suppose there is no word quite as evocative in the English language as 'home', especially if you don't have one. Perhaps 'nevermore' is as good as any or 'over the hills and far away' or 'Will ye no come back again, son o' mine', or, my sister's favourite, 'Oh where is my wandering boy tonight, he is weary and far from home. Oh where is my boy tonight? For I love him he knows, wherever he goes. Oh where is my boy tonight.'[224] They used to sing the latter about my father when he disappeared for a few days or weeks and, we discover, not with women but, as Liza would appreciate, with horses. [. . .]

Sunday 24th, Liz and Brook's Cottage It's 7 o'clock and the place is as quiet as a country village which of course it is.[225] What a remarkable pleasure it is to be able to walk down the village street and stop at the tiny supermarket, minima-

[223] Colicos remained married to his wife, Mona McHenry, until 1981.
[224] 'Over the hills and far away' is an English song of the eighteenth century. 'Will ye no come back again' is a Scottish song, written in the nineteenth century, about the Jacobite Rebellion of 1745. 'Where is my wandering boy tonight' was a music hall song written by Clarence Wainwright Murphy and Albert Hall in 1894.
[225] Burton was at South Moreton, Oxfordshire.

rket, and buy a choc-ice or an iced lolly without anybody giving so much as a second glance. I played a great many games of 'pool' with Brook and munched a great deal of Lillabetta's food – she is a fine cook – and had Sherry off the wood at some friend's house and went to the pub and drank a vodka or so, and saw Brook's garage and met his partner in the enterprise which is bound to succeed and altogether had a splendid day. The nights are as chill as cuddling up. We will almost certainly meet Molly today, and possibly Emlyn.[226] It will be odd to see them or one or the other down here after all these years. It was only 1943, only 26 years ago, that's all, when I first came here. The little baby is a delight, helpless as she is, and I love her gurgles and hysteria as you wheel her in her pram over rough ground. And her delight in the sound of click and pot of pool and the harsh hurry of the balls to get back to the lower end of the table while she grinds her teeth and attempts to kick her fragile legs. I am in love with her. She has a mind and makes noises, unlike Jessica, poor bastard. I generally shut Jess out of my mind but sometimes she re-enters with staggering agony.

Well anyway, forget that. Ignore that. Obliviate that. Nowt you can do bachgen bach. Honest to God. All you can do is make her rich, Rich. And she is rich, Rich. [. . .]

Monday 25th, South Moreton To my delight Emlyn and Molly, both, came to lunch and to my added delight Emlyn and E got on very well. Emlyn was in first class order and as subtly wicked as ever. Age has not withered nor custom staled.[227] There was a good deal of give and take. It is a hard task not to be overwhelmed by Emlyn. The slightest suggestion of mock-modesty, of false values, of sentimentality and with a couple of words he will stab you right under the heart. But it is possible to retaliate if you keep your wits about you – but – of course they have to be well kept. [. . .]

So many delightful things happened yesterday that to write it all down would take a tome not much longer than *Paradise Lost*.[228] We went to the 'Bear' twice, the second time with the two Lizzes.[229] E played bar-billiards with a chap who said: 'Wait till I get home and tell my old woman who I've been playing bar-billiards with.' One youngish woman and her husband came up to me in the Bear and said how pleased she was to meet me, but added 'Do you know Virginia Woolf? 'Yes,' I said.' 'Well', she said, 'Jack or Sam or Charlie (or whatever his name was) saw the film the other night in Oxford, and we thought it was 'orrible.' Well there you are.

---

[226] Molly and Emlyn Williams, Brook's parents.
[227] An adaptation of Enobarbus's line about Cleopatra, in Shakespeare's *Antony and Cleopatra*, Act II, scene ii: 'Age cannot wither her, nor custom stale / her infinite variety'.
[228] John Milton's epic poem *Paradise Lost* (1667) runs to 10 or 12 books.
[229] The Bear at Home Inn, North Moreton.

Brook and I brought back home (actually he drove us) the boss of the Bear to have a frame or two of 'Pool' with us. He is as rotund as the idea of circles and handles a deft cue. He did a couple or more shots that put one in mind of Minnesota Fats.[230] [. . .]

Tuesday 26th, **Kalizma** Last night I went to the 'Talk of the Town' which used to be the London Hippodrome and introduced Sammy Davis Jr to the audience.[231] I have rarely been so nervous but managed to get me on with it alright. That kind of audience is a stranger to me and I wasn't absolutely sure that they wouldn't give me the bird but from the moment of the announcement and the reception I knew that I could handle them. I used E a lot. I said that I was wearing her frock (I wore the top half of a costume that I wear in the film – what we call the Nehru piece – with dinner jacket trousers) out of which she'd grown etc.[232] Liza and Brook came with me and both were marvellous. Ron and Vicky and Craig were also there. Sammy was as minute as ever and as clever as ever. [. . .]

Thursday 28th, **Dorchester** Michael arrived yesterday after a twenty hour journey from Hawaii. He didn't look at all tired and in fact looked the best I've seen him for a long time. He is now about 5ft 7 or 8 and looks like a very beautiful renaissance Christ. [. . .] I haven't really had a chance to talk with him yet to find out what's motivating him but I'm not as worried about him as I expected. He has matured vastly.

Despite my protestations E is still apprehensive about Gin Bujold. It is a dangerous situation but the danger lies to Miss Bujold and not to us. I imagine she is going to find it very difficult to go back to Montreal to the suburban house after the false glamour of this particular production. Well hew to my line and let the chips fall where they may.[233] Because of my insistence from the beginning that she must be given 'star' treatment, she has no idea how disliked she is. Because of their loyalty the lads, Ron, Jim, Bob (but not, repeat not, Gaston) have lunched her and dined her and wined her but they have palpably had it now up to the teeth. They will be as glad as I am when this show is ended and we can fold our tents and creep silently away.[234] With a loud roar! Oh monsieur, elle est laid. Elle ne pas laide mais chacun a son gout.[235] I will correct

---

[230] This may refer to the fictional pool player, who appeared in Walter Tevis's novel *The Hustler* (1959) and in the 1961 film of the same name, or it may refer to Rudolf Walter Wanderone (1913–96), who had been known as 'New York Fats' until the popularity of *The Hustler* encouraged him to change his nickname, and who had become a minor celebrity by the late 1960s.

[231] The Talk of the Town cabaret restaurant, on the corner of Charing Cross Road and Leicester Square.

[232] This a reference to a Nehru jacket, a very fashionable cut at the time with a mandarin collar, named after the first Prime Minister of India, Jawaharlal Nehru (1889–1964).

[233] 'Hew to the line, let the chips fall where they may!' Is the correct citation from *The Confessions of Aleister Crowley* (1875–1947).

[234] A reference to the 1844 poem 'The Day is Done' by Henny Wadsworth Longfollow (1807–82), which includes the lines 'shall fold their tents, like the Arabs, and quietly steal away.'

[235] Roughly, 'she is unattractive. She isn't unattractive but everyone to his own taste'.

that French one of these days. As a matter of fact I might get a tutor to refine my French during the next year off – and my Italian too. It will only cost me a few quid a lesson and it will help me at Oxford in '71 when I'm faced with all those smart-asses. Nevill Coghill has offered to come and stay with us and bone me up about tutorials etc. The lectures I shall manage. The tutorials are going to be a sod. All those hippy bastards with awkward questions. I hope anyway that I shall in the 3 months at Oxford find out what makes them tick because I'm damned if I do at the moment. I'll do my best.

Saturday 30th, **Kalizma** Well it's over. All I have is a couple of shots left to do and then I'll clean myself and go home and dry. I have rarely been so desperate. I remember waiting for the letter from Oxford and the terror of not being accepted. I remember the torment of choosing between Kate and Elizabeth. I chose the latter and perhaps I shall never forgive myself for it. Though I love them both very badly. E will not believe me but I have never done anything to betray her trust. Michael knows me not to be a liar and he believes me. [. . .]

G. Bujold is quite clearly a fool. She has upset all of us very badly. So perhaps she's not a fool. She may have meant to upset us. Well good luck to you baby because the only one who is going to be upset is you. Vulgar and rubbish and ambition. And I hate all three. [. . .]

Sunday 31st [. . .] Yesterday was another terrible day. I behaved in a way to make a banshee look kind good and sweet. Insulting Elizabeth, drunk, periodically excusing myself rather shabbily and then starting the rough treatment all over again. Sometimes I am so much my father's son that I give myself occasional creeps. He had the same gift for damaging with the tongue, he had the same temporary violence, he had the same fidelity to mam that I have to Elizabeth, he had the same smattering of scholarship, he had the same didactitism (bet I spelled that wrong),[236] we wave the same admonitory finger at innocence when we know bloody well when we are guilt-ridden, when we have to attack when we know we're in the defensive position. 'Banshee', incidentally, I have used badly – it actually means an Irish or West Scottish faery who screams and laments at the imminent death of any member of a family which she protects. And, despite *Staircase* I am not a faery.

Mike has turned into a very wise man I believe in love otherwise I'd have to throw myself overboard, but I cannot believe in that massive magician upstairs. At least he doesn't believe in organized religion. He's a lovely boy and I cannot believe I never knew him. I wish he were of my blood but perhaps it's better that he is not. His father is great and a gentleman. And I sure as hell am not.

Time to wake up Maisie. Life is a waste without her.

---

[236] Didacticism.

SEPTEMBER

Bank Holiday Monday 1st, Kalizma, *Thames*

Facts:

I don't have the shakes today.

I saw the film *Becket* last night. And I was obvious and terrible.

I heard Elizabeth say I was a bore. And right she is. When I'm drunk.

I've had a bath and shampooed my hair.

I've left my watch in the bathroom and the clock in the salon has stopped
    and so I don't know what time it is but it's perhaps about 9 in the morning.

My eyes are slits that only a locksmith could open.

I am going for a long walk all by myself.

Michael said that in *Becket* my hair was too short which is a fairly stupid
    remark.

He loves *The Prophet* which is a lousy lower-middle-brow piece of crap.[237]

I am fairly stupid myself.

It is a coldish but very beautiful morning.

If I walk long enough I may come back to my senses.

If I walk long enough I may lose them.

I must not talk.

Screw the other generation

The love of God

Is a sod

And God

Is a clod

We should not have such veneration.

No offence

But defence

Is the best form

Of attack

Jack.

Tuesday 9th, *Aston Clinton* Yesterday at last I finished the fucking film. You'd
think that would be a cause for rejoicing, but not a bit of it. It all started because
of my absolute, almost feminine [. . .] passion for neatness. The place we live in
is so small that all extras must be kept down to a minimum. Gaston came in like
a porter from Paddington station loaded down with cartons, bags, a box full of
booze. There were several of our own towels when all she has to is pick up the
phone and they'll bring her a hundred clean towels. Does she not realize that

---

[237] Khalil Gibran, *The Prophet*, (1923).

we have been paying the Bell Inn an average of £100 a week for a year to keep Gwen in comfort?[238] They'll turn cartwheels for us if you ask them. Well I went mad which ended up with Elizabeth smashing me around the head with her ringed fingers. If any man had done that I would have killed him, or any woman either, but I had sufficient sense to stop myself or I most surely would have put her in hospital for a long long time or even into the synagogue cemetery for an even longer time. I still boil with fury when I think about it. I took myself off on a long walk to some farms that are around the corner and thought of every possibility and its consequences. I decided that for a time anyway we are stuck with each other. I thought that what E needed was a long rest in a quiet place and that so did I and we might get together again. We are fighting and have been fighting for a year now over everything and anything. I have always been a heavy drinker but during the last 15 months I've nearly killed myself with the stuff, and so has Elizabeth. She has just come out to this minute back room where I type and we're at it again. Neither of us will give in and if one of us doesn't something is going to snap. And I'm not going to give in, I'm too small a man and not feminine enough. I prided myself on not having the shakes this morning but the minute E came out and sat down they started up again. Now what the fuck is the meaning of that? Anyway this naturally is one of the black Celtic melancholy days. I see nothing ahead of me but a long grey waste. This afternoon I may see a little colour in the desert and tomorrow perhaps even an oasis. But at the moment I am in despair. If we cannot understand each other or what is worst not stand each other we'd [better] go our separate ways pretty soon and go back to work . . . She'll film again and I'll write.

Thursday 11th, Bell Inn, Aston Clinton Missed yesterday. I suppose when you reach an oasis you don't write.

The children arrived in a heap and a tumble and we had a faintly hysterical lunch where everybody wanted to eat everybody's food except their own. Plates were exchanged, forksful of 'try this bit' were handed around and we generally left the bemused waiters cross-eyed [. . .]

I read most of the day and half the night (4.30 am) a book by Carlos Baker about Ernest Hemingway.[239] I have always loathed E.H.'s writing ever since I was a boy of about 14 I suppose and read *For Whom the Bell Tolls*.[240] The gross sentimentality of the man offended me, and still does. I cannot understand why 'critics' describe his 'harsh realism etc'. It seems to me he was a romantic shit. But this book, though too lyrical at times to be considered a work of scholarship, shows the man was the work. He himself was a shit of the first order and an Oscar winning sentimentalist. And yet everybody I know who

---

[238] The New Bell Inn, London Road, Aston Clinton.
[239] Carlos Baker, *Ernest Hemingway: A Life Story* (1969).
[240] Ernest Hemingway, *For Whom The Bell Tolls* (1940).

knew him adored him – even the mystic Archie MacLeish. I feel alternately sorry for him and contemptuous as I read this book and still, as they quote extracts from his writings as I go through the book feel slightly nauseated. I'll finish it today. One day, perhaps soon, I'll get all his works in paperback (he doesn't deserve hard-covers) and plough through him again. I'll choose a time when I'm constipated.

My shakes have practically gone! Ah what discipline! What Discipline? You may well ask. Well now, instead of 1½ bottles of vodka a day, it is now cut down to ½ a bottle. What's the next move? A descent and return to beer I think. Especially as I've lost my taste for it. I wonder if I can find barrelled beer in Suisse to keep in the house. I will ask the lady called 'Hedy' in Olden auberge in Gstaad if this is possible. I shall become fat but jolly and not frighten children no more. Any more. No more.

Friday 12th We leave today for London and on Monday for Paris and on Wednesday for Gstaad. What we do after that it is undecided but deliciously so. If the Med is nice and enjoying an Indian summer we will drive down in slow stages to the yacht at Cannes and cruise around for a bit. We may go to the party for 'Scorpions' given by the Rainiers at Monaco and live on the yacht and go by mini-moke to La Ferme, or La Réserve, or you name it. St Trop should be quiet at this time of year.[241] Corsica maybe? Calvi, Bonifacio, Costa Smeralda, Cappo Caccia? Potofino, Ischia, Porto Santo Stephano, Positano, Portofino?[242] Or other places we haven't discovered yet. All fair-weather or perhaps even to Mexico and the old regime. And in the new year, who knows?

Ivor came to have dinner and we ate in Michael Harris' mother's cottage (Harris is the owner of the Bell) and watched a ghastly but very enjoyable English film with Peggy Mount and David Kossoff etc. about cockneys taking over a country pub.[243] We had things called Bell Inn Smokies which are pieces of smoked haddock in a sauce with cheese on top in tiny individual casseroles. Mouth-watering. We must come back, if only for those.

Ivor will be coming over to Gstaad around about November with Robbie and the other girl. I must see Rossier in Geneva about getting all the equipment we can find to make life easier for everybody all round.[244] Electrical beds, pulleys and grips and any gadgets which will make everyone happier. If only we can get the strength back into Ivor's arms. He can move them now to a limited extent, which is a miracle in itself. We shall see what the year will bring. [. . .]

---

[241] St Tropez, Provence.

[242] Resorts in Corsica and Sardinia.

[243] *Inn for Trouble* (1960), directed by C. M. Pennington Richards (1911–2005), and starring Peggy Mount (1915–2001) and David Kossoff (1919–2005).

[244] Dr Alain Rossier (1930–2006), specialist in spinal injuries at Beausejour Hospital at the University of Geneva, himself paraplegic.

Sunday 28th, Gstaad We have been here for about two weeks – I will look up the exact date later – and already it has done me a world of good. Shortly after we'd arrived Lillabetta and Brook arrived with Marla. And we, i.e. D and I, have played badminton every day in the morning and occasionally in the afternoons. We have taken long fast five-mile walks and for about a week I was so still that I could barely turn over in bed and my hands shook so badly that drinks had to be held up to my lips by E. Now however I am as steady as a rock and [. . .] I am infinitely more limber than I have been for a long time. I have reduced my boozing to practically zero – by my standards. A vodka martini before lunch, and wine with dinner. And I frequently don't touch the wine. I have taken up the drinking man's diet again about three days ago. [. . .]

I have just finished a very readable Life of Mussolini, which depressed me so much that I hurriedly re-read Waugh's *Vile Bodies* to put me in a good frame of mind for sleep last night.[245] Poor man. What he lacked, it would seem when the chips were down, was moral fibre. L.M.F. He was a born coward with a woolly mind, a poseur, and a lousy actor if the many photos of him are to be taken as evidence. I sort of like him though, which one could hardly say of Hitler. It gave me a vindictive satisfaction to see the balloon of his pomposity pricked by the British and Yanks, both of which nations he had contemptuously dismissed in the days of his power before the Second World War as decadent layabouts. Never, I suppose, in the history of warfare has a nation been so derided for its inadequacy and general cowardice. Not only by its enemies, but by its allies.

Monday 29th [. . .] I fell off my disciplined waggon last night with a thunderous crash and sat up with Brook until 5.30 in the a.m. drinking in the mean-time a whole bottle of Scotch alone. I am feeling it today but have abandoned the diet and stopped all alcohol. I am topped up with milk and chocolate and two veganins and lots of water and health salts. And I had chips and fried eggs and grilled tomatoes and crunchy bread and butter for lunch and slept for about three hours while E was being massaged. I feel distant and distrait but not too bad, and I don't have the shakes. [. . .]

Brook became quite maudlin and lamented the fact that he had grown up in the shadow of his famous father, that it had crippled his spiritual and material life etc. I was fairly curt and told him not to blame his life on others, but to become his own boss. I suggested that he went into the garage business which he owns as a <u>working</u> partner with acting as a hobby. He says he couldn't afford it, but of course he could if he buckled down to it. Lillabetta is, I suspect a very good business manager and could, and does, I believe handle all the business side. Otherwise, even more than I have, he will suddenly find himself middle

---

[245] Many studies of Mussolini appeared in English in the 1960s. Evelyn Waugh, *Vile Bodies* (1930).

aged and looking back on a life-time of self-indulgent waste. I think Brook's ambition was and is to be a golf pro. He never keeps off the subject for long. Though he knows, good a golfer as he is, that he is not that good. He is such a marvellous chap and I hate to see his unhappiness. I think he could write too, far better than his boring brother Alan who writes 'tough' diluted James Bond novels, with a touch of Ambler and Graham Greene.[246] And with no shred of humour. But he cannot bring himself to settle before that awful blank sheet of paper. Anything is better than the indignity of being in effect a sort of super-extra with a few lines here and there as in *Eagles* and *Anne*. Even being a major actor like myself finds the profession insulting at times. [. . .] I am using Maria's room as a study until my room is ready downstairs. The book shelves have been made and in two or three days having shaved and polished the floor I shall start using it. Some years ago I was talking with E in the middle of the night about this and that and she asked me if I had any ambitions, minor, realizable ones. I thought and said that yes I had a small one but it was too late now. What was it she asked? I told her that it had been a childhood ambition to own the entire Everyman's Library. One thousand, numbered, gleaming, uniform books and from the age of about 12 I began to collect them. By the time I was in my twenties I had about 300 or so, and then, to my dismay Dent-Dutton changed the format and they were no longer uniform. Some were tall some were medium and some were the old size. Some, I said, must be in New York [. . .], some with Ivor in Hampstead, some in II Squire's Mount. Without saying a word to me she wrote to Dent-Dutton and asked if they could find all the books with the first pocket-sized uniformity. It took them a long time but they found them all. She then had them bound in several different colours of calf – red for novels, yellow for biography, green for poetry etc. etc. The whole thing cost her about £2,600. This was done five years ago and the books have been in packing cases ever since, but in two or three days they will be out and home on the shelves. It will be thrilling for me to see them again, especially the poetry section as it was from Everyman's that I first learned a body of poetry entirely on my own and without benefit of having it rammed down my throat for exams etc. in school. I know which sides of the pages my favourites lie on. It is a fantastic reference library with the index in my head. I shall browse in that place for the rest of my life. They will take up at least one wall of the room, and they should be a splendid sight.

I told E that while up at Oxford and in the RAF I would, when ever I could, go to London for the weekends and steal books from the giant Foyle's in Charing Cross Road. I told her how I used to do it. During the war, when I did my best stealing, there was an acute shortage of paper and Foyle's couldn't wrap the books up as they do nowadays. I would buy one book and pay for it.

---

[246] Alan Williams (1935—) had at this time published four thrillers. Eric Ambler (1909–98), author of espionage novels and screenwriter.

The assistant would give a receipt which I would ostentatiously leave hanging out of the pages of the legitimate purchase. Now whether one bought one book or ten you still had only the one slip of paper to show for it. I would then pick up one or two Everyman's, taking a long long time – as much as an hour sometimes before I sauntered quietly out of the shop. I must have stolen scores of Everyman's in this way. One day I was up to my usual tricks in Foyles when an Irish friend of mine called Mannock Quinn was doing likewise in the corner. I had been bold this day and had about five books in addition to the one I'd bought, when Mannock came and stood casually beside me. Out of the corner of his mouth he said softly: 'Put all the books back, Taffy. Put 'em all back.' Very slowly and acting the part of a man who could not make up his mind I, one by one, put them all back. Later on when we were safely away from the shop Mannock told me that he'd seen one of the male assistants go into the little glass walled office that Foyle's used to have then, put on a raincoat and follow me around. I never stole a book again, and indeed, within a year, having almost immediately become a 'star', I didn't need to anymore. But the story doesn't end there. After having told E the story of my only thieving she said that the next time we were in London we must go to Foyle's together. I said we would. And we did. Working there temporarily was Sybil's niece Helen Greenford. The shop had become bigger than ever and it was difficult to find her. Word, however had spread through the store like wildfire that we were there and she found us through the good offices of a shop detective. Nobody in our section was buying books anymore – they just stood and stared at us. Eventually when the press became too great and embarrassing I asked the manager if I might take my 'niece' around the corner for a cup of coffee for ten minutes. He agreed. People will agree to anything if you're famous enough. Helen left and we went home to the Dorchester. In the car, E opened her bag, and handed me a book. It was an old edition of the *Shropshire Lad*.[247] With all those hundreds of people around, to say nothing of store detectives watching for our safety, all of them staring and oohing and aahing over her beauty, she had stolen a book! I burst into a cold sweat I could see the headlines. 'Millionaire Couple Steal Book From Foyle's. "Book not worth more than five bob," says manager.' Christ. I gave her a terrible and rather pompous row but her delight was not to be crushed. It's the first and last thing she ever stole in her life, except of course husbands! [. . .]

OCTOBER

Wednesday 1st, Gstaad [. . .] Brook and Mike (on his motor bicycle) and I went down to the village to walk around Cadonau's where I ordered a

---

[247] A. E. Housman, *A Shropshire Lad* (1896).

table-tennis table and all the trimmings, where we bought a dozen books, all paperbacks. [. . .]

I did not know quite how significant the phrase 'blind drunk' was until a couple of weeks ago. I have played badminton since I was a boy in the secondary school and have no doubt that if I'd wanted to and had the proper coaching I could have become a champion of some minor sort. In fact nobody, except champions, has ever beaten me in thirty years. But the first few days here, playing Brook, I was continually beaten. I could not see the shuttle. Since stopping drinking however I can now see the shuttle right onto the racquet and am beating him more and more confidently every day. This ties in with Esmond Knight's telling me that the doctors had told him that he was losing what little sight he had in his one eye through booze.[248] (Teddy lost one eye during the war and the sight of the other was badly affected.) And Teddy has never been a heavy drinker – certainly not in my class. So 'blind drunk' means something after all. [. . .]

Thursday 2nd [. . .] I read a book called *The Center* by the Yankee political columnist Stewart Alsop, but fell asleep over it and slept for a couple of hours.[249] I finished the book later that day and learned even more about the mad intangibles of Washington politics. So haphazard is the choice of representatives of the people, not only in the USA, but elsewhere that it seems to me we are very lucky that some maniac hasn't had his finger on the button and sent us all into oblivion a long time ago.

[. . .] Today I am driving B and E to Geneva where we will spend the night at the Hotel President. This afternoon we shall visit the Art Gallery where they display some of E's collection and then to the Hospital to see Dr Rossier to arrange when he wants us to officially open the new apparatus which we bought for the Paraplegics ward – it cost us $50,000 I think – and to ask him if he can help us get the proper beds, pulleys etc. for Ivor's room here in Chalet Ariel.[250] It will give me a funny feeling going back to that hospital where we spent so many horrified and anxious days. [. . .]

Thursday 2nd, President Hotel, Geneva There is no way of knowing how infinitely nostalgic and irrevocable this street is. Jesus, when I remember how often and how long I paced this particular quai waiting and watching for a baby, both of whom are alive and one of whom is dead. And nobody knows the soft touch of a soft skin of a soft mind on a hard hand. An unsympathetic

---

[248] Esmond Knight (1906–87), who had acted with Burton in *The Spy Who Came in from the Cold* and *Anne of the Thousand Days*. He had been wounded while serving on the battleship the *Prince of Wales* during its encounter with the *Bismarck*.
[249] Stewart Alsop (1914–74), *The Center: People and Power in Washington* (1968).
[250] The Musée d'Art et d'Histoire, Geneva.

hand. A hand that doesn't understand. Wherever I turn I find that I don't know what exactly I'm doing.

That was written last night and indicates my temporary insanity. I was in a fearful state and I don't understand quite why. I didn't drink very much and apart from missing the autoroute after Bulle the day – physically at least – went smoothly enough. We arrived about 4.15, booked in at the Hotel which is nicer than I remember and took a cab to the Musee des Beaux Arts to look at E's paintings. Would you believe it but they were not on display but down in the basement. This angered us both, but E more than me. To make matters worse the oils we <u>did</u> see and which <u>were</u> hung were horrible. E's decided to take them out and hang them on the yacht, suitably weather-proofed by Sotheby's. Madame Favez, who showed us around the cellar-basement, was a shrill screaming harridan with a dreadful accent. She sounded like somebody from Tiger Bay.[251]

Afterwards we went to the hospital to see Rossier. He was very sweet and showed us the new machine we'd bought him. It really works. I asked him about arranging a bed for Ivor at Gstaad and he will start to work on it shortly. He let slip that the last time he talked to Walsh two weeks ago, they were worried about Ivor's heart.[252] He covered it up pretty quickly by saying what a remarkable recovery Ivor had made and how 'phenomenal' it was and so on but the knife had already gone deep into my stomach.

When we came out of the Beaux Arts the cab-driver had vanished, but he returned in a few minutes having very sweetly bought a single rose for Elizabeth. Somewhere between the hospital and dinner brooding set in. Between long silences deadly insults were hurled about. At one point E, knowing I was in a state of nastiness, said to me at the lousy Italian restaurant we went to: Come on Richard, hold my hand. Me: I do not wish to touch your hands. They are large and ugly and red and masculine. Or words to that effect. After that my mind was like a malignant cancer   I was incurable. I either remained stupidly silent or, if I did speak, managed an insult a second. What the hell's the matter with me. I love milady more than my life and I adore Brook. Why do I hurt them so much and spoil the day?

I am very contrite this morning but one of these days it's going to be too late cock, too late. E has just said that I really must get her the 69 carat ring to make her ugly big hands look smaller and less ugly! Nobody turns insults to her advantage more swiftly or more cleverly than Lady Elizabeth. That insult last night is going to cost me. Betcha! [. . .]

Friday 3rd, Gstaad [. . .] E says that last night in my sleep I was winding-up and pitching baseball, going through all the motions, spit-balls, change-ups,

---

[251] A reference to the docklands area of Cardiff.
[252] Dr J. J. Walsh, Ivor's doctor at Stoke Mandeville.

curves. All done in deadly seriousness, while fast asleep and lying on my back! It must have been occasioned by my explaining to Brook a couple of days ago some of the subtleties of baseball and pitching. In particular the latter. Thank God I wasn't playing rugby in my sleep or E might have been crash-tackled a few times.

Winter is definitely coming in with a decided nip in the air. It's early in the morning, not a cloud in the sky and the sun is just tipping the peaks, notably the snow capped Diableret, with blue-gold.[253] The table-tennis has arrived and we shall erect it to-day. The floor and bookcases are ready in 'Richard's Room' and the long hidden books will start to breathe again. I can't wait to see their serried ranks. (From the french verb 'serrer'; to squeeze or press. 'Serrez à droite.')

I am delighted to be home again after only one night away. The yacht is in Monte Carlo – our second home (the yacht, not Monte Carlo) and we join it there next month while we go to a party given by the Rainiers for Scorpios. Grace and I are both of that dangerous sign. Everybody has to be in black and white. It'll make a change for us to move in 'society' again and have a good laugh afterwards. [. . .]

Saturday 4th Yesterday I spent most of the day unwrapping the books. By some lucky guess the bookshelves, measured by guesswork on my part, accommodate the books almost perfectly, leaving half a shelf spare for any additions that Dent-Dutton may dream up. Now comes the task, looked forward to, of putting them in order, either alphabetically or by subject matter. Alphabetically by authors is probably the most practical, though E would prefer them in colours. I protest that they will look like a pretty wall-paper, a decoration reminiscent of those shops in London where one goes in and orders two yards of books without knowing or caring what's inside them. We have mild side-bets as to who has the most volumes under his name. It's probably Dickens but there are a quite a few dark horses like Walter Scott, Gibbon and Grote (*History of Greece*).[254] Shakespeare is in four volumes so he's out. The tomes are all beautifully bound in velvet green calf, red and blue calf, black and maroon morocco, grey calf. A sensuous delight just to hold and touch. There is a section for children, an encyclopedia, dictionaries of all kinds, history geography art science romances essays and all. The room when finished is going to be a dream and I shall probably spend most of my time there. There is a beautifully rough stone fireplace, log-burning, and the outside door leads directly into the garden. A couple of easy chairs, a small bar, a sofa, a desk and a chair and a couple of rugs thrown about the floor and a painting or two on the walls

---

[253] Les Diablerets (3,210m), south of Gstaad.
[254] Charles Dickens (1812–70). Sir Walter Scott (1771–1832). Edward Gibbon (1737–94). George Grote (1794–1871), whose *History of Greece* ran to 12 volumes in its original publication (1846–56).

and you have the best cell ever for a literary man. It's so particularly delightful to have the time and the leisure (and the money) to do it without having to rush off in 10 days to do some ghastly film chore.

The table-tennis has arrived and is installed in the long room. E wants to change that room into two rooms for the boys. I am trying to persuade her to leave it as a play-room and build a tiny two bedroom chalet adjacent to the house for the lads. [. . .]

Monday 6th I knew it would happen. I knew that there was only going to be a short time before I would want to show-off again. I knew that minor ambitions were going to be resolved. So here they are:

I shall play *King Lear* in East Germany with the Berliner Ensemble in German.[255] I shall write and ask my friends who translated it best, and learn it phonetically.

I shall play Sartre's piece *Le Diable et le Bon Dieu* in Paris, in French. And I shall ask Barrault to direct it.[256]

After all, I have sought for that play for a long time. I shall start learning it today. My accent, because Goetz is a German and not at all French, will be acceptable.[257] Now that I am an amateur, a dilettante, I can choose what I will.

And then, with a little assistance, I shall do readings of Tolstoy in Russian.[258]

Monday 20th, Gstaad We leave today for Geneva where we are guests of honour at some do with a lot of dignitaries and where I have to make a speech, God curse the mark, about the equipment we gave to the paraplegics section of the Hôpital Communal.[259] Christ what a boring prospect. The stuff cost $50,000 but I would gladly give a tip if it would let me out of the speech. And to such an audience. Got to be done though.

Tomorrow to England again and already I am depressed. A man who is tired of London is tired of life, said Johnson. Got news for you fatty. I am tired of London, and I am <u>not</u> tired of life.[260] I really cannot analyse why I find the place so dispiriting. Perhaps I know the wrong kind of people. Perhaps I need fresh minds around me, or no minds at all but just a lot of books. And the weather there, the climate and a whole nation suffering from permanent catarrh and all with prison-pallor. And the snide press and the lamentable TV

---

[255] Berliner Ensemble: German theatre company established by the playwright, theatre director and poet Bertolt Brecht (1898–1956).

[256] Jean-Paul Sartre (1905–80), writer and philosopher, recipient of the Nobel Prize for Literature, 1964. His play *Le Diable et le Bon Dieu* had been published in 1951. Jean-Louis Barrault (1910–94), French director and actor.

[257] Goetz is the central character in Sartre's play.

[258] Lev Tolstoy (1828–1910), novelist.

[259] Burton means L'Hôpital Cantonal.

[260] Samuel Johnson (1709–84). Line (from 1777) 'When a man is tired of London, he is tired of life; for there is in London all that life can afford.'

and we have to see Princess Margaret again at the opening night of *Staircase* and she is infinitely boringly uncomfortable to be around and I don't know how I can suffer to see myself in the film in front of such a snob-ridden load of shits as one always gets at premiers. Got to be done too I suppose. The following day we listen for the telephone call from NY to see if we have acquired the diamond or not. Then thankfully back home to walks, and cowbells and raclette and all that and the new, marvellous book-lined room. [. . .]

Tuesday 21st, President, Geneva [. . .] Christ what a night. All the things I dread came to pass. E and I went into a suffocatingly small room faced with scores of people and E with her usual aplomb looked cool and self-possessed. I, with my acute sense of physical inferiority became more and more nervous until every muscle in my body was quivering with panic. I felt like a small boy who has to walk down the aisle at morning assembly and explain to the whole school why he was late, or smoking in the lav. I made the proverbial aspen leaf look as steady as a rock.[261] The President of the St Vitus Club.[262] We paraded the paraplegic part of the hospital and it made us both desperate with pity. After a sweaty two hours – sweaty for me that is, everybody else was pretty cool to <u>look</u> at, at least – we went to dinner with Rossier and his wife in a splendid little restaurant which we must go to again. Faced with all that irrevocable tragedy I made a speech of stupendous banality blazing with failure.

To hell with it. There are so many things to record and I don't have the time.

NOVEMBER

Saturday 1st, Gstaad I haven't written for ten days in this thing and a great deal has happened. What an oddity it is that when events tumble over each other I don't write it down. And now I don't know where to begin. I must record that E started taking her hormone pills yesterday!

Well now, we went to the hospital in Geneva and stood like wooden statues in a small room, insufferably hot, while people made speeches. The ultimate speech was mine and I made a total failure. My French was hideous, my English worse. I am supposed to be the bloke who is glib and gifted with tongues of men and of angels but boy was I a cop-out that night! I stammered and stuttered, stuttered, and generally made a fool of myself. Nevertheless the evening was received with joy in the Swiss newspapers. [. . .]

Then to England and Ivor and he looked to me that he was dying fast. He is, of course, but I should expect it and not be as stricken as I was. It threw me for a long time lasting until this minute. I am not used to death and Ivor has

---

[261] The leaf of the aspen tree is renowned for fluttering in very light wind.
[262] A reference to St Vitus dance (also known as Sydenham's chorea), a complaint involving uncontrollable movements.

always been a kind of God to me. He never treated me harshly, despite his short-temper, all his life. He only hit me once and then I deserved it.

We are having desperate trouble with Michael. We do our damnedest to help him but it is impossible. We allow him every possible latitude but nothing avails. [. . .] At this moment I can hear mindless pounding music going on and on in his room. It says nothing, it means nothing but presumably fills up some void. All it creates in me is unspeakable fury. [. . .] So far it has been going on for two hours since we arrived back from lunch and has probably been going on for much longer before that. [. . .] However we will do our best and love him a lot and have patience with him as Phil instructed us in a sweet letter a couple of days ago.

But now on to other things: I bought the ring for Elizabeth. Its acquisition was a tremendous excitement. I had set a 'lid' on it of one million dollars if thou pleasest and Cartier outbid me by $50,000.[263] When Jim Benton called me and told me (we were at the Bell Inn visiting Ivor and Gwen) I turned into a raving maniac and insisted that he get Aaron on the phone as soon as possible. Elizabeth was as sweet as only she could be and protested that it didn't matter, that she didn't mind if she didn't have it, that there was much more in life than baubles, that she would manage with what she had. The inference was that she would make do. But not me! The relief in Jim's voice was unmistakable and, an hour later when I finally got him on the phone, so was Aaron's. I screamed at Aaron that bugger Cartiers, I was going to get that diamond if it cost me my life or 2 million dollars whichever was the greater. For 24 hours the agony persisted and in the end I won. I got the bloody thing. For $1,100,000. It will take two weeks or more to get here. In the meantime it is on view in Chicago and has been in New York and 10,000 people a day go to see it. It has also been a star on the Ed Sullivan Show and both Jim Benton and Aaron Frosch have entirely changed their mind about the wisdom of my buying it.[264] It turns out that one of my rivals was Ari Onassis but he chickened at $700,000. But apart from the fact that I am a natural winner, I wanted that diamond because it is incomparably lovely. And it should be on the loveliest woman in the world. I would have had a fit if it went to Jackie Kennedy or Sophia Loren or Mrs Huntingdon Misfit of Dallas, Texas.

Monday 17th, Monte Carlo It has been a very bizarre few days. First of all [. . .] there was the affair of the diamond! It created a sensation from the word 'go' starting with the fact that it was bought under strange circumstances, that Onassis was our chief rival, that Cartier out-bid me, that I got it from them, that Aaron, with his usual caution made the transaction on board a

---

[263] Cartier the jewellers. This was the 'Taylor-Burton' diamond of 69.42 carats.
[264] *The Ed Sullivan Show* was a variety show that screened on CBS on Sunday nights from 1948 to 1971, presented by Ed Sullivan (1901–74).

transatlantic airliner, that it arrived here to the *Kalizma* with several armed guards one of whom had a machine-gun.

Elizabeth's delight in it is a joy to behold and a very quaint thing to witness is the obvious pleasure that other people take in her wearing it. Even Hjordis Niven and Princess Grace, who are coldish fish, seemed to enjoy her enjoyment.[265] Even the ordinary public seem to like the idea. Even hard-boiled photographers applauded her and it. And of course, nobody can wear it better. The miraculous face and shoulders and breasts set it off to perfection. She made an enormous success and I am frantically proud of her. [. . .] It has also created a sensation in New York and Chicago where it has been on exhibition, without its wearer, naturally, for a few days in each town and where many thousands of people went to see it every day.

In complete contrast is the fact that my nephew, Anthony Cook, has been just sentenced to 3 years in prison for 'stealing cars in order to buy sex' – I quote the *Daily Mirror*.[266] He is a tall, handsome feller so why did he have to do that? [. . .]

Monday 17th, **Kalizma** [. . .] Prince Rainier and Grace and Grace's sister and a friend are coming to lunch today and Rainier is bringing either a tiger or a panther as a present for E. That's all I need. [. . .] What the hell are we going to do with a PANTHER or a TIGER? It means that we can never work in Britain again. Imagine a tiger or a panther in quarantine or on a yacht in the Thames? Many sailors would be eaten a day, several vets would be munched for lunch; I may be nibbled myself. Dead dogs and cats in Gstaad and Johann Sebastian Bach will be prostrate as he tries to water the flowers, and Raymond will be forced to play ping-pong with him. Brook Williams may tell the animal a joke or two but I bet the animal won't laugh. The only two persons who will survive it are going to be Elizabeth Taylor Burton and Liza Todd Burton. Liza will saddle him and ride him, and Elizabeth will insist that he sleeps in the bathroom, which means she has slept with me for the last time – it's the atom-bomb shelter for me! I'm sure that I'm going to love him or her but I insist it's by telephone. 'How big,' I said to Rainier yesterday at lunch, 'does a panther grow?' ' About this size,' he said, with a gesture that indicated something cosmic. I nearly struck him, but didn't because it would have been impolite, and also he might have struck me back. He had that look on his face which I can only describe as 'smug', that total assurance that the man to whom he is talking is absolutely terrified. I love the Prince and I love his wife and I love Monaco but if, every time we come here, we are going to be given a lion, I'd rather write bad books at home. And play with enormous jewels. [. . .]

---

[265] Hjordis Niven (1921–97), wife of David Niven.
[266] Cook, aged 23, of South Ruislip, Middlesex, had pleaded guilty to 11 charges of stealing cars and other property and asked for eight similar offences to be taken into consideration.

Tuesday 18th, **Kalizma, Monaco** This morning in the early hours the pot decided to have a go at the kettle and won handle down. E, the pot, gave this particular kettle, me, a savage mauling. I was coldly accused of virtually every sin under the sun. Drunkenness (true) mendacity (true) being boring (true) infidelity (untrue) killing myself fairly quickly (true) pride envy avarice (all true) being ugly (true) having once been handsome (untrue) and any other vice imaginable except homosexuality and ungenerousness. [. . .]

Grace, Rainier, Grace's sister, Peggy, and a Lady Fford (I think) came on board for lunch and stayed until 5 so they cannot have been displeased.[267] Also a 3 month old panther of great beauty but also of great wildness. Reluctantly we had to give him back to Rainier. Though, if we had a large enough piece of property for him to run around in I would have taken a chance and kept the little savage. [. . .]

DECEMBER

Friday 5th, **Gstaad** We leave for Paris tomorrow, regretfully. It is so beautiful here now – deep snow, brilliant sunshine, books to read and no work.

Yesterday we held Maria's birthday party prematurely as she was born on the 8th which we would not have been able to attend. We had four child guests from her school. [. . .] We gave Maria a stamp album with about four hundred stamps to put in it. She was busy all evening. [. . .]

Monday 8th, **Gstaad** [. . .] The thing we were supposed to do with Phil last night in New York, a special presentation to him or something, was called off because of the death of Mrs Winthrop Rockefeller's father.[268] [. . .] Now perhaps we can get out of it altogether. Why, I wonder, do I dislike being a public spectacle? Other actors love it – even Elizabeth doesn't mind tarting up for a premiere of one of our films. [. . .]

I will start early tomorrow and try and write all about the arrival of the diamond and the ball at Monaco's l'Hermitage.[269]

We arrived back last Tuesday from M.C. and waited for Ivor and Gwen to arrive from Stoke Mandeville.[270] [. . .] Ivor goes up and down, but catastrophically he had a stroke in his sleep last September, which was hidden from us. He has great difficulty in speaking and has retreated more and more into himself. Apart from an occasional spirited flash as of old, he has changed into another person. He is mortally afraid, he tells me, <u>not</u> of death itself but of leaving this

---

[267] Margaret Katherine Kelly, known as 'Peggy' (1925–91). Lady Fford is possibly Lady Jean Fforde (1920—), Countess of Arran.
[268] Winthrop Rockefeller (1912–73), Governor of Arkansas, whose second wife was Jeannette McDonnell.
[269] Hôtel Hermitage, Monaco.
[270] M.C.: Monte Carlo.

world and all its varying excitements. The physical pain of death he discounts. 'I will die in my sleep for sure anyway and won't know anything about it. My stroke in my sleep at Stoke Mandeville didn't wake me up and I didn't know anything had happened until the orderlies came in in the morning and I found I couldn't speak.' What a blow on a blow. He'd have lived until he was 90 were it not for that trip in the dark at Céligny. [. . .]

Wednesday 10th A choice of new furniture has arrived for the library. E and I are still in the top tens of the box-office which surprises me somewhat as, apart from *Secret Ceremony* for E and *Eagles* for me we didn't have anything out. *Staircase* hasn't been on general release yet so doesn't count. [. . .]

I am hovering around 176lbs in weight and it feels splendid but will try for 172 before I leave for New York next week. E is 127lbs. Lithe and limber we both are with murderous games of ping-pong to keep us that way.

Cocktail-time approaches, the fire roars, it is cold as cold can be outside.

Friday 12th Today we received a telegram from Ed Henry of Universal Pics saying that *Anne of the Thousand Days* has been shown to the press in NY and LA and the reaction is 'nothing short of sensational'. And 'superior to *Man for all Seasons* and *Lion in Winter*'.[271] We shall see Mr Henry, we shall see. It would be rather nice if it was a blockbuster as I have a hefty percentage of the gross. And rings and farthingales and things and hospital wings could be bought. It would be a good thing if Gin Bujold won an Oscar which, since she's unknown and if the film is as successful as Universal believe it's going to be and if she keeps her trap shut about how horrible a place Hollywood is, she is quite likely to do. If she does, or even if she doesn't come to think of it, I'd hate to be her next director or leading man. I think she firmly believes herself to be the legitimate heir to Rachelle and Bernhardt and Duse. She has all the power of a gnat. A dying one. I could whisper louder than her screams.

[. . .] We leave for New York in five days and I dread the journey or journeys involved. We go from there to LA, and from there to Hawaii. I long to see Hawaii but I loathe the means of getting there. It means in my case an entirely lost week before I have been able to re-adjust myself so I'm likely to be a moron through Xmas. I'll keep quiet and sleep in the sun, if any, and hide in corners with a bad book.

---

[271] *A Man For All Seasons* (1966), directed by Fred Zinnemann (1907–97), had won five Oscars. *The Lion in Winter* (1968), directed by Anthony Harvey (1931—), had won three Oscars.

1970

[Richard ceased making entries in his 1969 diary in mid-December. He did not begin his 1970 diary until late March.]

MARCH

Tuesday 24th, Puerto Vallarta It's a long time since I wrote in this thing. I fell by the wayside at the Sinatra house.[1] It must be confessed that he is a very unhappy man – apart from his fundamental moroseness he was at the time plagued by writs etc. by the State of New Jersey [. . .] about complicity with local gangsters. I believe Sinatra to be right that he was in no way implicated and we have read since that he finally appeared in New Jersey without the necessity of extradition or whatever they call it between state and state, and has been clean-slated.[2] So that's alright. His house is a kind of super motel in shape and idea. A series of very elaborate suites with every possible modern gadget included, vaguely surround a small swimming pool. There is what is known as the rumpus room which contains a pool table and a magnificent toy train set given to Frank by the manufacturers and which he has arranged to have transferred to some children's home or something. He is a very nice man in short doses but I imagine a bore to live with, especially now with the energy gone and where he is obviously watching his health. His library was quite extensive but 'Prince' Mike Romanoff told me that Frank had asked him to choose the books.[3] That may have been of course Mike's intellectual conceit, but I did see lots of copies of *Encounter* around and I'm bloody sure Francis doesn't read that.[4] Elizabeth made sheep's eyes at him the whole time, and sometimes he at her. I've never seen her behave like that before and apart from making me jealous – an emotion which I despise – I was furious that he didn't respond! We out-stayed our welcome and over-stayed it by three or four days, though I was longing to get away. Eventually we did and came back down here to Vallarta. We flew up to Palm Springs and back to LA in Sinatra's jet plane which is called a Gulf Stream jet or something like that. It's a lovely plane and

[1] Burton and Taylor had spent a few days staying with Frank Sinatra at his home at Rancho Mirage, California.
[2] Sinatra had been served with a subpoena by the New Jersey State Commission of Investigation and forced to appear before it in February.
[3] Mike Romanoff (1890–1971), former Hollywood restaurateur, actor.
[4] *Encounter* magazine (1953–91), co-founded by Stephen Spender.

E of course immediately wanted to buy a similar one. It costs no more than
$3¼m. That's all. What with that and a $1m hospital bill we'd be flat. And the
world has changed – I mean our world. Nobody, but <u>nobody</u>, will pay us a
million dollars a picture again for a long time. I've had two financial disasters
Staircase and *Boom!*, and Elizabeth *Boom!* and *Secret Ceremony. Anne* is going
steadily along and will more than make its money back. So is E's picture *The
Only Game* but *Anne* only cost $3½m whereas *The Only Game* cost $10 million
so that one will never get its money back under twenty years. I'm afraid we are
temporarily (I hope that it <u>is</u> only temporary) out in the cold and fallen stars.
We haven't of course fallen very far – we could doubtless still pick up $750,000
a picture which ain't chicken-feed. What is remarkable is that we've stayed up
there so long. Instance Julie Andrews who on the strength of <u>one</u> picture *The
Horrible Sound of Music* has stayed up for about 5 years but now the lads in
Hollywood tell me that as a result of two big failures she is really out.[5] Not only
that but she has had her head turned so it appears from her enormous initial
success and winning the Oscar etc., turning up late or not at all and sometimes
for days. Well she can always get Blake Edwards to write her a script and he
can produce and direct it.[6] How fast the moods change – two years ago she was
the darling of America and now she's hardly ever talked about. She doesn't
have our consistently antagonistic press and therefore the shocks are still
to come.

This is going to be a long entry presumably to be continued tomorrow.
[. . .] I went into Hollywood Presbyterian hospital to have a complete check-
up. And what a check-up! It took 24 hours which meant I had to stay the
night in the hospital. By the time they had made me get into bed, taken what
seemed like several pints of blood out of my [. . .] arm, [. . .] and Rex Kennamer,
the doctor, assuring me just by feel that I unquestionably had an enlarged liver
as a result of 30 years of excessive drinking. [. . .] Next day Kennamer came to
see me and told me that I simply had to stop drinking for at least 3 months.
Why, I asked? Because apparently, at my present rate of booze I would have
sclerosis of the liver within about five years which would get progressively
worse. Whether I drank or not. I mean after five more years. Very well, I
said, I shall stop drinking totally. I have done so before for an occasional week
and sometimes longer. This will be the longest time of the lot. This is my
10th day without booze of any kind and I must confess I feel immensely
healthier. [. . .]

---

[5] Julie Andrews (1935—). *The Sound of Music* (1965) directed by Robert Wise (1914–2005). Andrews
had won an Oscar for *Mary Poppins* (1964) and an Oscar nomination for *The Sound of Music*. She had
then starred in *Torn Curtain* (1966), *Hawaii* (1966), *Thoroughly Modern Millie* (1967), *Star!* (1968) and
Darling Lili (1969). The last two were not as successful as Andrews's previous films.
[6] Blake Edwards (1922–2010), director, and (from 1969), husband of Julie Andrews, who had directed
Darling Lili.

Wednesday 25th We are going fishing today and stopping for lunch with a man who lives in an Indian village half way between here and Jalapa.[7] He is a man called Richard Foot known to all as Don Ricardo. He is the only 'gringo' who lives in this particular village. He has reputedly built a school there and made a church. [. . .]

Thursday 26th We left the house at 10.15 and boarded a fishing boat [. . .] towards Foot's village [. . .]. It is a small pueblo and all the houses are the usual palapa except his of course which has every mod con, [. . .] full of fascinating bits and pieces from various but almost entirely Asiatic places.[8] Balinese, Japanese and Chinese and very fine copies of Spanish-Colonial cupboards and 'Welsh-Dressers' etc. with a garden, built on sand, which, were it not for the Bougainvillea could have been mistaken for an English garden in Kent. Beautiful roses etc. Much discussion on our return as to whether he was a genuinely good man, interested in the welfare, education etc. of his very back-ward village or whether he was merely playing God. He doesn't sound very intellectual and keeps on saying that he reads a great deal. I looked through his library which is small and contains very little that I haven't read and apart from a few pseudo-mystical books nothing that you wouldn't find in anybody's week-end cottage. On the table, opened and face down was a book called *Famous Stories of Sherlock Holmes*.[9] [. . .] We had raw grated fish marinated in lime juice to start, followed by clam chowder followed by grilled sierra with a tomato and cucumber salad. The two Chrisses also had lasagna and finished with what they said was cheesecake of the best kind they'd ever had.[10] [. . .] Elizabeth and Norma (Heyman that was), who has been staying with us for a couple of weeks escaping from her horrible lover [. . .] had had their 'Vallartans' which is the name we give to a drinking regime which means one drink before lunch and two before dinner. I am, of course, still not drinking anything at all except tea and occasionally coffee, which I don't normally drink except with brandy. [. . .] Since I stopped drinking I've become a bit of a gourmet myself, certainly were it not for stern self discipline, a gourmand. I have therefore formed the opinion that hard liquor in whatever form before eating is a taste-bud killer, though a burgundy rich and deep with beef and port with a powerful cheese is delectable. So is a good very dry light white wine with fish. [. . .]

Friday 27th Brook, Lillabette, and the three children – Liza, Maria and Liza's friend, Jennie, arrived last night 5 minutes before time. They all looked compared with us like suckling pigs or soft underbellies of slugs but today

---

[7] Yelapa, 20 miles south along the coast from Puerto Vallarta.
[8] A *palapa* is a house or hut with a thatched roof made of palm leaves. It is typically open-sided.
[9] Sherlock Holmes, fictional detective created by Sir Arthur Conan Doyle (1859–1930).
[10] Christopher Wilding and Christopher Taylor, Elizabeth's nephew.

already they are beginning to redden up. [. . .] I received a [. . .] letter from Tony Quayle who has a smash hit for himself in a play by one of the Shaeffer brothers called *Sleuth*.[11] [. . .]

I have decided to [do] an intensive 10 day course – self taught – in Spanish. I have avoided it for years in case it interfered with my beloved Italian, but since it seems that we shall be spending more time in Mexico than in Italy for the next few years I thought I would at least acquire the rudiments of the language, 'menu-Spanish' as they say. There are 45 lessons in my little book called *Madrigal's Magic Book of Spanish* and I did 5 lessons yesterday in an hour and got all the answers right.[12] [. . .]

I have heard nothing more about doing *The Defector* Charles Collingwood's book but doubtless a great deal will happen when I arrive in LA a week from today.[13] Peck and Elizabeth have agreed to do it. [. . .]

Today or tomorrow will make it a fortnight without drinking – the longest since I played *Camelot* and I haven't missed it at all but had a severe time at a party given by a family called the Gunsbergs, surprise luncheon birthday party for dear Phil Ober.[14] Everybody was stoned when we arrived, everybody was repetitious. I was vastly tempted to down a huge dollop of vodka and join the general boredom but desisted and smiled and smiled and hope for the best.

Saturday 28th It's a sod of a world today. I am extremely unhappy and as melancholy as a Sankey and Moody hymn.[15] My instinctive aversion and distrust of the human race is brought to a head periodically, drunk or sober. [. . .] The people around me in the house are all engaging but today, at least, I don't want to see any of them. I am writing this on the top private patio of the house wearing a Mexican hat, Mexican fashion over my nose because at the moment I could easily play Bardolph without any makeup.[16] It is Norma's birthday and she cried because everybody here had remembered it and kissed everybody indiscriminately, and each additional present wetted her eyes. She is 32 years old and a mess. But then so am I. So is practically everybody I know. Why do people weep on their birthdays. I noticed Phil Ober did the same the other day. The odd thing is that they seem to wail <u>not</u> out of self-pity at the miraculous addition of another year or the fear of old age, but out of happiness at being remembered. I remember that Dylan Thomas was almost embarrassingly sentimental about his birthday as indeed he shows in 'Poem in October'.

---

[11] Quayle won a Drama Desk Award (for 'excellence in theatre') for his role in the play *Sleuth*, written by Anthony Shaffer (1926–2001).
[12] The title was actually *Madrigal's Magic Key to Spanish*.
[13] Collingwood's novel *The Defector* had been published in 1970. There is no record of the film ever being made.
[14] Phil Ober (1902–82), actor.
[15] A reference to the evangelical hymns of Ira D. Sankey (1840–1908) and Dwight L. Moody (1837–99).
[16] The Shakespearean character Bardolph (*Henry IV* (*Part 1*)), who suffers from red blotches and carbuncles on his face.

'His tears burned my cheeks and his heart moved in mine.' 'The listening summertime of the dead.' 'It was my thirtieth year to heaven though the town below lay leaved with October blood.'[17] The trouble with total sobriety is that if you are a born misanthrope and if your base is an essential cynicism, and my birth and base are both, you do not see the world through a glass darkly (and in my case a glass of alcohol) but suddenly face to face. St Paul was talking about something on a slightly higher plane to put it mildly, he was looking for the face of God when he found the dark glass remove and the pure light of the love of God was revealed to him.[18] So he says anyway, the self hypnotized phony. But I find that, alcoholless, I have become for me relatively silent. I do not as before tell incessant stories, most of the audience having heard them before, especially poor Elizabeth who has had to suffer them endlessly for 8 or 9 years. There was an outburst at lunch today. Norma said how marvellous I was looking since I gave up booze – it's only been a fortnight for God's sake – and that when she arrived I looked so awful that she burst into tears (which she didn't) and I am reputed to have said to her 'It's only the booze love – I shall stop it.' This she does with that irritating impersonation of what she fondly thinks is a Welsh accent and the way I speak. I said it costs me no effort except when I am so bored that I lust for a second or two for a whopper of a Martini to kill the pain and the waste of time. They had all had their 'Vallartans' and Elizabeth was busily making one of Ray's specials which consists of iced coffee and milk or cream or ice-cream and some mild (55 proof) sweet Kalua – a dash of – and some rum to titch it up, because it was Norma's birthday. And I said 'there's someone who could never give up drink' pointing at E. Whereupon she said she (E) hated my guts and further more disliked me savagely. 'Ah,' said little stirrer-up Norma, 'but you do love him don't you? 'No,' said E, 'and I wish to Christ he'd get out of my life. It's been growing on me for a long time.' 'Piss off out of my sight,' she added. So like the Arab I picked up my tent and stole silently away up here – my tent being the type-writer, my sombrero and *Madrigal's Magic Key to Spanish*. She has said all those things before and I to her, but never before, as I recall, when sober and in front of people. It, of course she was sober. Raymond makes extremely powerful drinks. She has had the above outburst so often recently – going back about a year I would say that it undoubtedly smacks of the truth. The eyes blaze with genuine hatred and contempt and her lovely face becomes ugly with loathing. This hasn't happened for a long time, but I didn't care about the other girl much so it had very little impact on my vast ego except relief. I have to face the fact that E may be going to take off one of these days and perhaps sooner than

[17] The last quotation from Dylan (Marlais) Thomas's (1914–53) 'Poem in October' is inaccurate: 'It was my thirtieth / Year to heaven stood there then in the summer noon / Though the town below lay leaved with October blood.'

[18] A reference to Corinthians 1: 13.

I expect. I have known it deep down for some time but have never allowed it to surface. Well perhaps when we have all come out of this slough of despond we can still make it work. Tomorrow is always a surprise. Our quarrel sounded like the quarrels one hears from the next room in a cheap hotel by two middle-aged people, 20 years married and bored witless by each other. A good shouting match is sometimes good for the soul, cathartic, emetic, but I can't be bothered to shout back when I'm sober. Pity.

The woman who wrote Tim White's biography – and there was if you like a profound melancholic – wrote that he once said 'If you are unhappy, learn something.'[19] So I will learn some Spanish from *Madrigal's Magic Key* to same, and screw everybody.

Sunday 29th [. . .] I have now done 20 lecciones of the Madrigal Spanish. This morning [. . .] I shall revise and then take their examination, which is taken against time and is quite fun. So far according to the speed and accuracy which they deem average, above average, and superior, I am superior. It is a primitive grammar of course and the real work will start after I've finished the course, but I hear from other gringos around here who go to have Spanish lessons from a tutor that it takes them six months to do this particular book. [. . .]

Louise, I'm told by Foot who is a great friend, so he says, of the Collingwoods, is a hopeless lush and is far far gone in the liver department. She is 50 or about to be and any minute now is going to look 70. She said she'd come on the waggon with me but, like Maureen Stapleton, it only lasted the night.[20] She can't even stick to Vallartans like Elizabeth, though the latter exceeds her limit now and again.

As for E and I there is a kind of armistice. Both sides are fully armed, the bombs are ready to go off but so far nobody has pressed the button. The first six months of the sabbatical have been completely wasted. Except when we were alone we have bickered and quarrelled incessantly, and we have hardly ever been alone. Hawaii was a nightmare, Ivor's paralysis was a nightmare, Palm Springs and Los Angeles was a nightmare and there is more to come. I mean more Los Angeles nightmares. Anyway back to work soon thank God. Perhaps Europe and the *Kalizma* will rest us up for a bit after seeing Nevill off – if he can come, which now seems unlikely as his brother Paddy is dying.[21] And when *The Defector* starts [. . .] I am going to insist that everyone

---

[19] Sylvia Townsend Warner (1893–1978), whose *T. H. White* had appeared in 1967, quotes White's lecture 'The Pleasures of Learning' (1963): 'My parents loathed each other and were separated, divorced, when I was about fourteen or so. This meant that my home and education collapsed about my ears; and ever since I have been arming myself against disaster. That is why I learn.' Warner also explains that in the lecture White quotes from *The Sword in the Stone* the passage beginning, ' "The best thing for being sad", replied Merlyn, "is to learn something" '.

[20] Maureen Stapleton (1925–2006), actor, who suffered from alcoholism.

[21] 'Paddy' might refer to Sir Marmaduke Nevill Patrick Somerville Coghill (1896–1981), elder brother of Nevill and 6th Baronet Coghill.

must come to see me. I must have a look at Vietnam, just to see what it looks like and maybe I can get near enough to the DMZ to have a look at the famous bridge, but that shouldn't take more than a week or ten days.[22] Then a look at Taiwan and other places that supposedly look like, or near enough look like Vietnam. [. . .]

Monday 30th [. . .] Things seem to be more congenial around the house, largely because I kept out of the way of the family and guests practically all day. My teetotalism is inhibiting I can see. Every drink they take is almost apologetic which is silly. I am the one with the battered liver not they, though E will have to watch hers carefully by the time she's my age. [. . .] The dreaded trip to Los Angeles approaches fast. We leave on Friday and I present a prize to Army Archerd on Saturday at lunchtime.[23] I have never done such a thing before and certainly not sober. I am followed by Bob Hope, not an easy man to precede with his vast experience as an international toastmaster.[24] [. . .]

APRIL

Thursday 2nd [. . .] I did nothing all day except stare at the ocean and occasionally memorize some irregular Spanish verbs. I am well over half way through the Grammar at the moment and, given a little peace in LA I will have practically finished it by the time we return. I will then go through it again fast and translate the editorials from the most reputable Mexico City papers every day, in the meantime finding some intelligent bilingual Spaniard to make conversation with for an hour a day. The best man in town they say is a doctor who has already attended some members of the family and seems young and nice. David the Tutor goes to him and says he's not a good teacher and that his English is somewhat broken but I don't want a teacher, I want someone who will listen to me read to him and correct my accent and who will ask me questions in Spanish to which I shall give painfully slow but, I hope, grammatically correct replies.[25] I am pretty sure that in another month I shall be reasonably fluent. [. . .]

Another worry is that I have temporarily lost all sexual urge which is very frustrating for E. Presumably the terrific change in my body as a result of total abstinence for (now approaching) three weeks, after thirty years of steady and sometimes unsteady drinking is taking its time to re-assess itself. When it does come back it will be a vast explosion. If it does come back which it had better had.

---

[22] DMZ: the De-Militarized Zone between the states of North and South Vietnam. The Hien Luong Bridge crossed the Ben Hai River which formed part of the boundary between the North and the South.
[23] Army Archerd (1922–2009), Hollywood columnist for *Variety*.
[24] Bob Hope (1903–2003), actor and comedian.
[25] John David Morley (1948—), later to become a novelist.

I read last night Aaron's précis [. . .] of our respective financial positions. It seems that we have approx $5¼ million each but that our overheads are approx $600,000 a year. Insurance alone for jewellery and paintings is $200,000 a year. The *Kalizma* is 100,000. Vallarta is 20,000. Salaries and fees – lawyers etc. and agents Xmas bonuses et al. is 370,000. [. . .] I must find out from Aaron how we can cut down from $600,000 to about $400,000 a year. [. . .]

Friday 3rd, Beverly Hotels That's as much as I was able to write yesterday. We arrived smoothly from Vallarta in Sinatra's jet in 2½ hours. I have lost roughly 18lbs in two weeks on the Low Carbohydrate diet and have yet to have a drink in three weeks.

Saturday 4th, Beverly Hills Hotel [. . .] Yesterday I went for my fitting with Ron Poston who is supposedly the #1 tailor in LA and he found, not to his dismay that I had lost 3½ inches off my waist, and 1½ ins off my chest. This morning I discovered that I had lost yet another lb. Another two or three lbs and I shall be at my lightest since *Hamlet* and almost as light as I was when I was hard and fit and played rugby in my teens and early twenties.

Yesterday I went to a press lunch where I presented an award to Army Archerd, the columnist, which was well received. Almost all the other people went on far too long, particularly Anthony Quinn who went on and on with a typically verbose extract from Wolfe's *Time and the River*.[26] He also didn't know how to speak it. E made a surprise appearance at the end and had a standing ovation. Typical. We did all the work and she received all the applause. And where there had been no more than two or three photographers taking shots of the various candidates and donors, there were suddenly and from nowhere about forty or fifty of them. It must have astounded a French actress, said to be very good, called Jacqueline Bisset who had been sitting on my right throughout the proceedings on the dais, and who was also a giver of a prize.[27] [. . .]

Sunday 5th [. . .]I had a relentless and exhausting meeting with Lucy Ball who read out the script which we are going to do with her. The writing and situation will do and I shall change a great many of my own lines myself. Very nicely Brook is in it as well so will pick up a few dollars. Later that night we saw privately here at the B. H. projection room a film called *The Boys in the Band*.[28] Full of four letter words but not too much so as to offend and the performances are all good but a bit 'stagy' which is not surprising as it was

---

[26] Anthony Quinn (1915–2001), actor. Thomas Wolfe, *Of Time and the River* (1935).
[27] Jacqueline Bisset (1944—), is English, although her mother was part-French. Bisset was educated at a French school in London and speaks French fluently.
[28] *The Boys in the Band* (1970), directed by William Friedkin (1935—), based on the play by Matt Crowley (1935—), which dealt with issues of male homosexuality.

played by the original Broadway Cast. I doubt whether, like *Staircase*, it will do very well.

[...] Jonah Ruddy came at six to interview me about 'giving' such enormous gifts to E like the Krupp and Burton-Taylor diamond.[29] What did I think the taxi-driver and the bank teller think of such extravagance. It was boring and I could hardly defend myself by saying that we had given away or were owed nearly $2m, a half of which I doubt whether we will ever see again.

[...] We saw a film last night – one nominated for the Oscar – called *Z*.[30] It's in French about the Greek military junta. Not really a very good film but smacks of the truth about present Greece. And is therefore impressive. [...]

Monday 6th [...] I went this morning for a final fitting for my dinner jacket for the Oscars tomorrow night. There is apparently an outside chance I might win but I give it no mind or else I shall become morose if I'm a loser. I have now gone over 3 weeks without a drink and never give it a thought, though win or lose tomorrow night it's going to be another test of my will-power, because certainly everybody else will be intoxicated. It's one of those nights.

[...] My mind is obviously on other things because the preceding paragraph is about Saturday and not yesterday.

Now yesterday we sunbathed in the morning and at two o'clock Brook and I and E went to the rehearsals of the Oscars. There were a lot of people about, but I only knew a few by sight – Clint Eastwood was there and Jimmy Jones – the black actor of the great white hope and not Jimmy (*From Here To Eternity*) Jones.[31] Peck was charming and E found her speech for the presentation of the Best Picture Award too sententious and asked if she could re-write it herself, which she did last night so that they can put it onto the idiot boards.

[...] Later we watched the 'viewers' Oscars on TV horribly MC'd by Phyllis Diller – what a horror she is and Vincent Price who sounded terribly queer.[32] I wouldn't have thought that a man of such obvious taste in everything else would have allowed himself to get associated with such a farce. *Anne* won nothing. I hope it won't be the same tomorrow night.

Tuesday 7th Today is Hollywood's big day – the day of the Oscars. It's curious that the whole world makes fun of it, but that all actors want to win one and in the obituaries of actors it is invariably mentioned as the summit of their achievements. Even in *The Times* or the *Guardian*. For instance one of the reasons is that if the Oscar for leading actors is won tonight by John Wayne it will be out of pure sentimentality because, though I haven't seen his performance, I'm told

---

[29] Burton means Jo Roddy.
[30] *Z*, directed by Costa-Gavras (1933—), won the Oscar for Best Foreign Language Film.
[31] James Jones (1921–77), author of the novel *From Here To Eternity* (1951), made into a successful film in 1953.
[32] Phyllis Diller (1917—), actor. Vincent Price (1911–93), actor.

that it is little more than his usual walk through.[33] His performance is not comparable with Voight's or Hoffman's.[34] I haven't see O'Toole's and I am no judge myself.[35] The supporting actress will probably be won by one Goldie Hawn because she is a famous TV personality.[36] The leading actress will probably be Liza Minnelli because her mother died last year – Judy Garland a great and sentimental favourite here.[37] And so on. That's what makes it absurd and still it's coveted, even by me! My only chance is that I am a Kennedy-Adlai Stevenson associate and a 'Dove' while Wayne is a Republican, 'my country right or wrong' Birchite Hawk, and the 'artistic' Hollywood fraternity is usually very liberal.[38] Also, John Springer says that a great many people thought we wuz robbed when I didn't win for *Who's Afraid*. We shall see. [. . .] The rest of the day is going to be chaos and I look forward to Vallarta with longing. One more day.

Wednesday 8th Richard is the BEST

That was written in his sups and cups last night – I mean this morning at 4.30 by a pixilated Brook. But cups or not I think he means it so shall leave it in. [. . .]

John Wayne won the Oscar as predicted. We went to the party afterwards and sat with George Cukor the Pecks and the Chandlers (owners of the *LA Times*) but were surrounded by scores of photographers, who, to my delight, took very little notice of anybody else including the winners.[39] Barbra Streisand who fancies herself a big star was completely eclipsed. And a whole queue of people, literally hundreds, passed the table to stare at E and tell me that I was robbed and after all these protestations we began to wonder who in the world voted for Wayne.

We got out with a great difficulty because of the hordes of photographers, visiting Gig Young, who won best supporting actor, en route, who was stoned but sweet.[40] Hawn won the supporting actress, also as predicted. We couldn't find Duke Wayne so came home, [. . .] Later still came Wayne himself also very drunk but, in his foul-mouthed way very affable. I survived another night without booze [. . .]

---

[33] John Wayne (1907–79), actor, nominated for Best Actor for his performance in *True Grit*. Sometimes known as 'The Duke'.

[34] Jon Voight (1938—) and Dustin Hoffman (1937—), both nominated for Best Actor for their performances in *Midnight Cowboy*.

[35] Peter O'Toole was nominated for Best Actor for his performance in *Goodbye Mr Chips*.

[36] Goldie Hawn (1945—), nominated for Best Supporting Actress for her performance in *Cactus Flower*.

[37] Liza Minnelli (1946—), daughter of actor Judy Garland (1922–69) and Vincente Minnelli, nominated for Best Actress for her performance in *The Sterile Cuckoo*.

[38] Adlai Stevenson (1900–65), twice the Democratic candidate for the US presidency. 'Birchite' refers to the right-wing John Birch Society.

[39] The Chandler family had published the *LA Times* since 1917. Otis Chandler (1927–2006) was in control in 1970.

[40] Gig Young (1913–78) won Best Supporting Actor for his performance in *They Shoot Horses, Don't They?*

Anyway, I lost again, and am now the most nominated leading actor in the history of the Academy Awards who has never won. So I carved my tiny niche in the wall of Oscar's Wisden.[41]

Friday 10th, Puerto Vallarta We arrived yesterday [. . .] and are safe at home again. [. . .]

The day before yesterday was a right cock-up. We had arranged, win or lose, to have a 'Thanksgiving' dinner at 4.30 in the afternoon. This was to be for E's mother and Brook, Lilla, Norma, John Lee, Dick Hanley, Val Douglas, Jim Benton, George Davies, Aaron and so on. Afterwards, at six o'clock, we were to have a cocktail party for the 'losers'. The thanksgiving was to be held in a small room at the hotel and the party in our Bungalow. However, this was not to be. Elizabeth didn't turn up for the dinner until six, which meant that the cocktail guests had to be shunted over from the Bungalow to the main hotel and willy-nilly join with us for a combinatory mess-up. [. . .] Most of the losers turned up. Jon Voight and his girl friend Jennifer Salt (daughter of Waldo Salt who won the best screenplay Oscar) who looks 15 and is actually 25.[42] Rupert Crosse, negro supporting actor, Elliott Gould (didn't like him) Susannah York (very nice) Jane Fonda, who talked of nothing but the black panthers and got $3,000 each out of E and me, and Sylvia Miles, who was the only one I felt sorry for, a nice handsome negro called Otis Wilson and other people whose names I never found out.[43] It went on until 9.30. By this time we all thankfully returned to the Bungalow with everybody drunk except me of course (still no drink) and E really sloshed. [. . .] I went to bed and Elizabeth went to the bathroom. Then I heard her calling me and she was bleeding from her rectum, it turned out she'd had a burst 'pile'. I called Kennamer who told me to wrap some ice in a towel and for her to hold it against the bleeding. But she still wanted to see poor Kennamer, so I rousted the poor sod out of bed [. . .] and he came over within ten minutes. By this time naturally, it always happens, the bleeding had stopped. However he mucked about and put a bandage around her arse stayed for half an hour and talked about having just before us being sent for to the Hotel where John Lee, also pissed out of his mind, thought he was dying and Dick Hanley (drunk) had called for a priest to give the last rites. According to Kennamer the scene was so ludicrous that even the priest, a new young one, nearly laughed at the whole thing. What a lot.

---

[41] A reference to the annual almanac of cricket, *Wisden*.

[42] Jennifer Salt (1944—), who had acted alongside Jon Voight in *Midnight Cowboy*. Waldo Salt (1917–87), had won his Oscar for the same film.

[43] Rupert Crosse (1927–73), nominated for Best Supporting Actor for his performance in *The Reivers*. Elliott Gould (1938—), nominated for Best Supporting Actor for his performance in *Bob and Ted and Carol and Alice*. Susannah York (1939–2011). Jane Fonda (1937—), nominated for Best Actress for her performance in *They Shoot Horses, Don't They?* Sylvia Miles (1926—), nominated for Best Supporting Actress for her performance in *Midnight Cowboy*. The Black Panther Party was a Marxist organization which aimed to articulate the grievances of Black Americans, and which was at the height of its influence in the late 1960s.

We got off to Vallarta and the flight was quick [. . .]. And home in Vallarta, a game of ping-pong with Brook, fried fish for dinner, a few frames of Pool and off to bed with *Wellington: The years of the Sword*.[44] [. . .] I didn't do as much Spanish in LA as I hoped. I have 15 lessons to go to finish *Madrigal's Magic Key*. [. . .]

Sunday 26th, Guadalahara We are staying here at General García Barragan's house who, I'm told, in whispers and with much looking over the shoulder by a P.R.O. man called Martin Rodriguez, is the real power in Mexico.[45] He will decide, and has already perhaps decided, who will be the next President – it will be Echeverría apparently.[46] It is all very Graham Greenish. They, the family, have given E everything she's pointed at and said – 'It's yours.' A horse that she saw from their plane (actually an Army plane – a DC3) was given to her on the spot – a Palomino. But on second thoughts Barragan's son Oscar decided it wasn't good enough for her and gave her his own white stallion which we have yet to see.[47] I am left with the Palomino [. . .]. Tonight they gave her a splendid Mexican saddle. What is behind it all? [. . .]

Monday 27th This week-end has been intolerably long and none of us can wait to get home. The air of sinister politico-secret-police-Ambler-Greene has disappeared. Despite the fact that the house is continually surrounded by armed guards David Morley, the boys' tutor, managed to climb over the wall to get back in the house on a Friday night at about 2.00am! Now, instead of feeling stifled by the idea of so much hidden and arcane power, I'm beginning to feel somewhat sorry for them. They are irremediably middle-class in their reaction to our supposed fame and glamour. Though we have both said, almost to the point of vehemence in my case, that we hate, but HATE, meeting strangers and parties, they have had 12 to 14 people for lunch and dinner every day. That includes our lot of course which means that there are generally ½ of them and ½ of us.

[. . .] I read right through the night last night a biography of Ian (James Bond) Fleming. A thick paper-back with snapshots that I picked up in a giant store in town called Fabrica Francia I think.[48] [. . .]

It's a longish story about El General and our involvement with him. It involves a piece of land on a sweet-water lagoon made by a river called the 'Agua Caliente' and which comprises part of a big estate called El Tuacan

---

[44] Elizabeth Longford (1906–2002), *Wellington: The Years of the Sword* (1969).

[45] Garcia Barragán (1895–1979), Secretary of National Defense in Mexico (1964–70). By 'P.R.O.' presumably Burton means a public relations official. The city of Guadalajara, the capital of Jalisco, is about 160 miles east of Puerto Vallarta, and is over 5,000 feet above sea level.

[46] Luis Echeverría (1922—), President of Mexico (1970–76).

[47] Barragan's son's name was actually Carlos.

[48] By 1970 there were four biographies of Fleming in print, all published in 1965 or 1966. Fabrica de Francia is a department store chain.

which is the property of Barragan, the general. They have given us our choice
of a piece of land anywhere on the 10,000 acres which contains 5 miles of sea
front and goes 12 miles back into the interior. Many forests and another big
lagoon (salt water) which they plan to open to the sea so that small ships can
haven there. If we are left alone it could be a haven and a heaven. We both
chose, separately, a hill of tree-covered rock which plunges straight into the
lagoon and which is only about 50 yards – the lagoon – from the sea and at
high tide is frequently invaded by the ocean. There is an air-strip ½ mile away
which is to be extended to take jets. They are to put in a golf course and several
condominiums and small sky-scrapers, hotels and a shopping centre which is
sufficiently far away from us not to be a nuisance and at the same time highly
convenient for the comforts of bars and food etc. There will also be a group of
restaurants. They also plan an 18 hole golf course. I might even take it up
again. It's years since I played and it might be amusing again to become an
occasional 'mid-week' golfer. There is hunting – wild boar and deer – which
interests me not at all. But I think I'll get a gun and pot shot at tin cans. It is the
age of the private gun and I suppose I should have one. Their largesse is seemingly infinite and we can have all we want. [. . .] One thing is that it has spurred
me to new efforts of learning Spanish. The basic grammar is now under my
belt and I shall now extend my vocabulary for the rest of the year. It's sporadic
but progressive my self education in this language. My passive knowledge of it
is fairly good. Now I must read magazines etc. a lot with a dictionary and start
spouting forth. Apart from anything else it will make life much easier talking
to the Barragan family who speak nothing but Spanish. [. . .]

MAY

Sunday 3rd, Puerto Vallarta The boys and the tutor left last night for Mexico
City [. . .] The house feels very empty and quiet without them. [. . .]
     We spent the late morning and all the afternoon at the land in Bucerias – a
piece of land on the beach which we have leased for a 100 years or something.[49] It comprises many acres though I don't know exactly how many. All
of us are overlaid with red again. We have put up a palapa hut and a couple of
palapa umbrellas, one for drink and the other (when completed) will be
for food. We leave everything there unlocked and so far nothing has been
stolen.

Monday 4th [. . .] We went again to Bucerias today read, sunbathed, sea bathed
I did a double-crostic and read Alan Moorehead's book *Eclipse* about the fall
of Germany from Sicily on.[50] [. . .] The village is a couple of dust streets two

---

[49] On the northern shore of the Bahia de Banderas, 2 miles from Puerto Vallarta.
[50] Alan Moorehead (1910–83), *Eclipse* (1946; Burton was reading the 1967 abridged edition).

miles roughly from our property with 3 fairly raunchy little bars and pretty smelly with it. We had beer and coffee at one.

Tuesday 5th [. . .] We (Brook and I) went out shopping today and bought a very elaborate folding table and four unelaborate folding sit-up chairs and a machete each and 'espatulas' and barbecue forks and two bottles of olives for the martinis which I make every day for the family's 'Vallartan' at 6-ish every day. I regret that drink I must say. After the heat and the broiling sun and the frequent dips in the ocean and the hot-dogs and salad for lunch and a brisk mile sand walk the martini is fantastically tempting. But sternly I've refused. I shall take some coffee tomorrow with me and brew myself a cup during the 'Vallartans'. We shall all be very sorry to leave for LA. Sheerly for being left alone Bucerias is the best place we've found in 10 years.

Saturday 9th [. . .] Bucerias is rapidly becoming our favourite place. We barbecue every day there and read and I do double-crostics and swim and walk.
     [. . .] We leave for LA tomorrow and Lucy Ball's show, rehearsing Monday, Tuesday, Wednesday and shooting before a <u>live</u> audience on Thursday. Then E goes into hospital for the (we hope) final operation on her piles. Shall be very glad when that's all over for poor E. They say it is among the most sustainedly painful businesses. Nobody wants to go to LA but I must confess to a little excitement about the show because, I suppose, I haven't worked for so long. I'm told that L. Ball is very wearing to work with. [. . .]

Thursday 14th, Beverly Hills Hotel [. . .] Those who had told us that Lucille Ball was 'very wearing' were not exaggerating. She is a monster of staggering charmlessness and monumental lack of humour. She is not 'wearing' to us because I suppose we refuse to be worn. I am coldly sarcastic with her to the point of outright contempt but she hears only what she wants to hear. She is a tired old woman and lives entirely on that weekly show which she has been doing and successfully doing for 19 years. Nineteen solid years of double-takes and pratfalls and desperate up-staging and cutting out other people's laughs if she can, nervously watching the 'ratings' as she does so. A machine of enormous energy, which driven by a stupid driver who has forgotten that a machine runs on oil as well as gasoline and who has neglected the former, is creaking badly towards a final convulsive seize-up. I loathed her the first day. I loathed her the second day and the third. I loathe her today but now I also pity her. After tonight I shall make a point of never seeing her again. We work, or have worked until today which is the last thank God, from 10am to somewhere around 5pm, and Milady Balls can thank her lucky stars that I am not drinking. There is a chance that I might have killed her. Jack Benny, the most amiable man in the world and one of the truly great comedians of our time, says that in 4 days she reduced his life expectancy by 10 years. The hitherto impeccably professional Joan Crawford

was so inhibited by this behemoth of selfishness that she got herself stupendously crocked for the actual show and virtually had to be helped to her feet
and managed, not without some satisfaction I dare say, to bugger up the whole
show.[51] I said very loudly after yawning prodigiously and being asked by the
director, a nice but not overly brilliant man called Jerry Paris, whether I was
tired or bored or what, that I was not particularly any of those things but was
puzzled as to why anybody who didn't have to for financial reasons et al. would
submit themselves to this mindless routine week after week for 19 years.[52] Miss
Ball and her apology of a husband who were sitting beside me said nothing at
all. The husband is a man called Gary Morton, who laughs at all her 'takes' etc.
however often she does them and whether well or not.[53] I'm told he used to be
a 'stand-up' comic in lesser night-clubs, how good or bad I do not know, and
protects himself with standard jokes like: 'I hijacked Lucy from a Cuban'. It is
possible to imagine a series for a couple of years perhaps being reasonably
tolerable as a way of life and a way of money – enormous money it'd have to be
– with a congenial director and a happy few relaxed repertory of actors.

But for a life-time! Ah no. It is fascinating to watch her reaction to Elizabeth.
She calls her for the most part Mrs Burton or Miss Taylor and occasionally
Elizabeth but corrects it to the more formal immediately. She calls me in the
third person His Highness or Mr Burton and sometimes Mia. This is a joke
that E made on the first day when she, E, said that I had become so thin – I am
now about 160lbs – that sleeping with me was like sleeping with Mia Farrow
who is first cousin to a match-stick. She asked E yesterday how she felt. 'Fine
thank you,' said E., 'today my ass is not hanging out.' Miss Balls then went into
an embarrassing convulsion of hysterical laughter which terminated in her
throwing herself helplessly over the back of a sofa and drumming her legs
against the floor in a false ecstasy of amusement. It was acutely un-watchable
and we all avoided each other's eyes. At another point Lucy said to me 'We had
Ruthy Berle over to dinner last night – he wasn't there thank Christ, he's such
a goddam bore – and boy do you have a fan in her.[54] She went on and on about
you. Great actor. Great person and so on. Other people too. Roz Russell and
people.[55] Why do they do that?' She ignores Brook and her brilliant straight
man who's on, poor soul, week after week with her, a man called Gale Gordon,
and Cliff Norton who plays a small part and the director.[56] They don't exist off
camera. Sometimes on. Between shots yesterday she summoned us Norton,
Brook and myself to her dressing-room with a tap on each forehead – we were
all sitting down chatting with Hugh French – and proceeded to tell us how to

[51] Joan Crawford (1905–77), who had appeared on *Here's Lucy* on 26 February 1968.
[52] Jerry Paris (1925–86), director and actor.
[53] Gary Morton (1924–99), comedian and television producer.
[54] Ruth Berle (1921–89), wife of television comedian Milton Berle (1908–2002).
[55] Rosalind Russell (1907–76), actor.
[56] Gale Gordon (1906–95). Cliff Norton (1918–2003).

play the scene which we had just walked through. With faces as straight as freeways we then all proceeded to shout every line at each other in ludicrously loud voices. 'That's better, Richard, now I can hear that word, you're making me laugh.' And laugh she did, every time we did it and we did it about three times. Brook's face was a study in disbelief. The other actor was obviously used to it and took it all as if this were normal for an actor to tell other actors how to do a scene without the director being there. I warned the director to warn Jingle-Balls that if she tried any of that stuff on Elizabeth she would see, in person, what a thousand megaton hydrogen bomb does when the warhead is attached and exploded. It will all be over tonight and again Lucy will be lucky that I am temporarily such a little saint as normally I would probably let her have what the Yanks call 'the full shot' of my contempt. [. . .]

Dear Rich
I hit the sack at 3:30 – so lets sleep late, please!
You were so right on, so proud-making last nite – everything you did made everyone (like Lucy) look like peasants – Love you
[Elizabeth Taylor's hand]

Saturday 16th, Malibu We are staying here – with the inevitable Liz and Brook – for the week-end. It is Hugh French's house in the 'Colony' as it is known.[57] It is a Norman Rockwell cover of a place with a comfortably middle-class atmosphere.[58] [. . .]

We did the Lucy show to great acclaim from Lucy and the rest of the people and the audience. We were all apprehensive as to exactly what was going to happen. Ron and indeed all of us were firmly fearful that Lucy, with her superior experience with this kind of medium would swamp us with changes of pace and/or ad libs and other cheap tricks of that kind. Nothing of the sort happened. We swamped her. She was intensely nervous and I found immediately that I was in total control of the audience and her from the moment we appeared together. The same happened when E appeared – Lucy's timing and assurance which we had assumed was a built-in mechanism which was faultless went skew-whiff and E, as ever, took everything in her stride. Everything she did – E that is – worked like a charm, and the audience quite clearly adored her. Her stage presence (this the third time I've felt it happen) is quite electrifying. She held the audience like a vice in *Faustus* at Oxford, at the Poetry Reading in New York and now in the Lucy Show.[59] Now that we can afford it

---

[57] The Malibu Colony, Malibu, west of Santa Monica, California.
[58] Norman Rockwell (1894–1978), artist, in part famous for his covers for the *Saturday Evening Post*, which offered reassuring portrayals of American society.
[59] The poetry reading in 1964 at the Lunt-Fontanne Theatre, which was Taylor's first stage appearance.

though I will be as tense as a tigress with her young, she should try the living legitimate stage as they call it. Since she has decided to do it anyway there is no point in my getting in the way of a juggernaut, I talked to Ernie Gann yesterday about a stage adaptation of his forthcoming novel *The Antagonists* which is about the Masada, and it might be a good vehicle for her – and for me.[60] [. . .]

As a reaction from the nerve-rack of the Lucy show combined with E's fears of the surgical knife on Monday and my fears of her fears and my natural irascibility and impatience when not drinking led to two bitter exchanges yesterday. E's telling me to 'fuck off and get out of my sight' and me replying in kind. My disappointment at being offered a CBE (which nevertheless I accepted, though E wanted me to turn it down thinking only a knighthood good enough) and not the bigger prize. The trouble with a CBE is that it is so easily confused with the pathetic MBE and OBE in the public mind though it is a much more important honour. Like the OM and the CM it means nothing because though it is a title – I suppose one is entitled to be called 'Commander' – it doesn't have the nice rolling sound of Sir Richard and Lady.[61] I am nevertheless immensely pleased. Pleased that it wasn't a 'Beatles' award.[62] Pleased that it was obtained without any attempt on our part to get it. Pleased that it means we are no longer notorious but officially posh. Pleased that it will please the family. Pleased by the fact that a knighthood is not after all out of reach of a divorcee and a non-tax-paying citizen. [. . .] We might, in effect, have our cake and eat it at the same time. [. . .]

I was immensely pleased too – to revert back to the Lucy show, [. . .] that Brook had a success with his one scene in the Lucy Show. [. . .] He is terribly nervous, which worked in this part, but will have to learn very hard not to show it in other parts. Both E and I were too – particularly E as she had to wait for more than an hour before getting on stage, but it doesn't show. Everybody was amazed at our apparent relaxedness. James Stewart and Henry Fonda were overwhelmed by E's ability as a clown.[63] Since they didn't over-praise me I can only assume that they meant it! She was the star again. A bit sickening.

[. . .] It turns out that Frankenstein's first name was Richard.[64] This has been puzzling us for some time. Very odd timing to discover that, just when I'm behaving like his monstrous creation, we all thought. [. . .]

---

[60] Ernest K. Gann (1901–91), whose novel *The Antagonists* would be published in 1971. It became a TV mini-series (starring Peter O'Toole and Anthony Quinn) under the title *Masada* in 1981. Masada refers to Jewish resistance to the Roman Empire focused on the fortification of Masada in AD 72–73.
[61] All honours in the British honours system. CBE: Commander of the British Empire. MBE: Member of the British Empire. OBE: Order of the British Empire. OM: Order of Merit. It is not clear what Burton means by 'CM': it might be CMG: Companion of the Order of St Michael and St George.
[62] The four Beatles had been awarded the MBE in 1965. In 1969 John Lennon returned his in protest at American involvement in the Vietnam War and at British involvement in the conflict in Biafra.
[63] James Stewart (1908–97), actor. Henry Fonda (1905–82), actor.
[64] A reference to Mary Shelley's novel *Frankenstein, or the Modern Prometheus*, first published in 1818. In fact the original character is named Victor, although this did not remain consistent in all film versions of the story and its offshoots.

Sunday 17th [. . .] So far little attention has been paid to us and certainly no mob scenes. On Friday a big blonde woman or large girl passed us on a bike and said 'Look there's Kate's Daddy and this is her bicycle.' She said it to herself loudly as we took no notice of her. I talked to Kate on the phone yesterday and told her about it and she knew exactly who it was. She can be with us for a month this year so <u>that's</u> ok. I wonder if Liza will overlap with Kate's holidays. I love to see them together and to watch the competition.

Rex dined with us and told many fascinating stories of some of his patients and some who were not. An account of a few days with Nick Hilton a few months before he died was particularly hair-raising.[65] It seems that Hilton, towards the end of his relatively short life [. . .] became dominated by [. . .] a sort of quack trick-cyclist who had quit his medical training and turned psychiatrist when still an intern. Rex knew the analyst noddingly but had never met Nick Hilton. One day the quack called Rex and said that he had to leave town for a week or so and would he, Rex, act as locum while he was gone especially Hilton. This being apparently a common thing among doctors Rex agreed. Within a few hours of the psychiatrist's phone call there was another from the Hilton Mansion in Holmby Hills. The voice on the other end of the line asked him to come to the house immediately. Rex asked who was calling and the voice identified itself as a male nurse who was in attendance on Hilton. This surprised Rex who had been given no indication by the Hilton doctor that Nick was sick enough to warrant a male nurse. Off went Rex to the house and was met by Hilton's wife a woman or girl called Tricia who told him, again without a warning of any kind to go immediately to the bedroom.[66] Rex did so unaccompanied, knocked on the door, a voice told him to come in and in he went to find Nick Hilton sitting up in bed with a loaded gun pointing at him. There was no question, according to Rex, that Hilton was a lunatic – one glance was enough – and that the slightest mistake on Rex's part would have meant that he would be killed. There were three male nurses, not just one. There was nothing Rex could do except shiver in his shoes, stand there and suffer a torrent of vile abuse from the raving idiot in the bed. He got out as quickly as he could and sought information from the wife who said that Hilton had been like this for a long time, that there were loaded guns of all kinds all over the place and that the vanished head-shrinker was a terrible and evil influence over Hilton and stayed with him only to get his money. Rex went away convinced that Nick should be locked up as soon as possible. Thereafter he was called every hour or so by the wife or the male nurses until Rex himself began to think he was going to go mad. Eventually he called for assistance from a very famous and also very great LA psychiatrist who had given up his practice to teach at the University. Reluctantly and only as a favour to Rex the

---

[65] Conrad 'Nicky' Hilton (1926–69), socialite and businessman, Elizabeth Taylor's first husband.
[66] Hilton's second wife, Patricia (the marriage ended 1965).

great man went along with Kennamer to the house and, like Rex took one look at the patient and knew that he was far gone almost to the point of no return but that there was a chance that he could be helped. He told the wife that he was prepared to go into court the next morning and testify that the patient not only should but must be removed immediately to Menningers – the top place in the States apparently – by private plane.[67] That he should be either strong-armed into this and if necessary knocked out to get him there as soon as possible. The father Conrad Hilton was called who sent over his doctor.[68] This doctor in turn said that they shouldn't do this without consulting the doctor in nominal charge, i.e. the missing psychiatrist. 'But,' said Rex, 'nobody knows where he is.' 'I do,' pipes up Mrs Tricia Hilton the wife, 'he's here in town. He didn't go away at all. He just wanted to get away from Nick for a time.' So the dubious quack was called and eventually came over to the house. All this incidentally was taking place in the middle of the night. The arguments by the great doctor and the wife and Rex and to a lesser extent Conrad's doctor were presented to the vanishing doctor who replied coldly and precisely leaving no room for arguments that if these men and that woman went through that procedure the first thing that would happen would be that they would be slapped for millions of dollars of law-suits by his lawyers and Conrad Hilton's. The great one blew his top and threatened to have the man barred from the psychiatrics panel etc. or whatever it's called. The man however remained unmoved. The man was barred and is now according to rumour the private psychiatrist of Howard Hughes.[69]

Nick Hilton died six months later from unspecified causes.

Monday 18th [. . .] [Elizabeth] dreads hospitals so much and after 27 operations who wouldn't. Her greatest fear of all is the anaesthetics shoved into her body. And she tends to fight them like mad. I stayed with her in hospital until about 11.30 [. . .] I had a cup of tea and went straight to bed. I asked the operator to call me at 4.30am but awoke before the call [. . .] I [. . .] left for the hospital about 5.40, [. . .] I went in immediately to see E who was already awake. She told me that they had given her a sleeping pill or shot at about 4.30 and promptly woke her again to give her an enema. [. . .] Held Elizabeth's hand while she was given two or three pre-operative shots, [. . .] She gradually, while I held her hand sloped off into a semi-coma but awoke immediately when they came to take her away. That was ten minutes ago and presumably they are now hard at it. They said it would take no longer than a ½ hour and that she would be a further hour in the 'recovery room'. [. . .] I wonder how everything is

---

[67] The Menninger Psychiatric Hospital, Houston, Texas.
[68] Conrad Hilton (1887–1979), hotelier.
[69] Howard Hughes (1905–76), businessman who had been a film producer and film director and was by this time a notorious recluse.

going? The waiting after the endless wait in London when she had her hysterectomy, is the worst part for me. Always terrified that they'll make a mistake
and all the stories of simple errors made by surgeons – eminent ones, some of
them, come flooding back into my mind.

[. . .] The half-hour is up and over but no sign from Dr Swerdlow or Rex.
So keep on typing Rich Bach with crossed fingers. It's a lovely day, he said with
trembling chin and he has just noticed that a thriller story by John D.
Macdonald which he brought in for his wife to read when she is recuperating
is called *One Monday We Killed Them All.*[70] It is Monday today. Happiness is a
successful operation.

Dr Swerdlow has just come in to say that everything is perfect. I'm off to
have breakfast. Hip. Hip. Hooray. [. . .]

Tuesday 19th, Beverly Hills Hotel [. . .] PM Harold Wilson, finding himself
and party ahead on the public opinion polls, has announced an election for
the middle of June.[71] I wonder whether Emlyn will get a KBE in the birthday
honours announced just before and if so, whether my CBE and Emlyn's
KBE, if he is to have one, is some attempt to placate the Welsh Nationalist
Movement in Wales where at the last two elections they ate away at the labour
hegemony and even stole a seat in Carmarthen.[72] There are roughly 40 Welsh
constituencies I think and a switch of ten or so in a tight election could be
decisive.[73] Shall watch with interest. A win by Wilson would be the first time
this century that a PM has gone successfully three times to the country and
won. I hope he wins as he has taken a lot of stick from our loathsome Press,
predominantly Tory. If he wins he will prove himself the most adroit politician
of our time. The Tories have no real alternatives and Heath lacks even what
little stature as a world figure etc. that Wilson has.[74] They're all full of rubbish
of course and I love the hatred that the Tories must have for the unflappable
smugness of clever little Wilson. My hatred of Tories is unabated by long-term
membership of the rich class, and I hope they howl in the wilderness another
five years. It would pleasure me Aloysius, it would pleasure me to read the
outraged screams of the Tory Press, it would really pleasure me.[75] No legislation they might enact – the Tories – could ever make up for their intolerable
air of superiority over us lot in the years and years gone by. I hope they grovel
for evermore. [. . .]

---

[70] John D. Macdonald (1916–86), *One Monday We Killed Them All* (1961).
[71] Harold Wilson (1916–95), British Labour Party politician, Prime Minister 1964–70, 1974–76.
[72] Emlyn Williams had been appointed a CBE in 1962, but did not receive another honour. KBE: Knight
Commander of the British Empire. Plaid Cymru, the Welsh Nationalist party, had won the parliamentary seat of Carmarthen in a by-election in 1966.
[73] There were 36 parliamentary constituencies in Wales in 1970.
[74] Edward Heath (1916–2005), British Conservative Party politician, Prime Minister 1970–74.
[75] Aloysius is the name of Sebastian Flyte's teddy bear in Evelyn Waugh's *Brideshead Revisited* (1945).

Wednesday 20th [. . .] I spoke to Aaron for an hour yesterday about business and he told me that we were as usual overspending but no more than standard but this time without working and with no earned income and expenses. For the first time he may have to go into the income from the trusts we have set up for ourselves. I don't like that so therefore will go out and earn some more money. Next time we take a sabbatical and perhaps even when not I will squeeze in some time to write a book. If I write it in a certain way I can perhaps compromise with my conscience and deliberately write a best-seller. Have just talked to Elizabeth who has just had her first bowel movement since the operation. She says it is unbelievably painful and unfortunately occurred before anticipated by the doctors so she, as it were, did it all by herself without the assistance of lubricants and soothing laxatives etc. Result: Screaming agony. [. . .]

Must write an article for a book to be published marking the anniversary (100th) of the Rugby Union. Cliff Morgan is the demon-agent for this.[76] I know so much about rugby and so many stories that I don't know where to begin.

Thursday 21st [. . .] I wrote the first draft of the rugby article yesterday and shall try and complete it today. It looks awful in the cold light of dawn. Perhaps it will look better when it's all typed and neat. I have written a sort of account of the last game of rugby I ever played but have introduced elements from a lifetime of games in just such places. The place I physically think of is the awfulness of Tonmawr though I have never actually played there.[77]

Saturday 23rd This is a brand new Olivetti typewriter upon which I am writing given to me by Lil and Brook. It is sparkling and very loose compared with the Hermes Baby and it will take me a little time to bang away on it with the same abandon as I do on the old one which I shall keep anyway out of loyalty for many years of battered service. I shall retire the Baby to the library on the boat or at Gstaad. The machine is fire-engine red and I've pasted on it a Welsh dragon sent to us by a Welsh American firm that specializes in producing stickers for the various groups of Irish Scots English French Italian etc. descendants who like to remember their origins in Europe. [. . .]

I had lunch with Hugh French after having had my hair-cut by Ron B and after having signed and initialled lots of bumf for Aaron who, poor chap, is an old man 20 years before his time. [. . .] He will be a helpless cripple before long I'm sure. The forties are an odd and sad time because going going going are the old familiar faces. Indeed I am frequently surprised to find that people like

---

[76] Cliff Morgan (1930—), Welsh rugby player and broadcaster, was, with Geoffrey Nicholson, editing *Touchdown and other Moves in the Game,* to celebrate the centenary of the Rugby Football Union.
[77] Tonmawr: a mining community in the Pelenna valley a mile due north of Pontrhydyfen.

Binkie and John Perry and Dick Clowes and Stephen Mitchell are still alive.[78] All ghosts from my early years in the theatre. Even Emlyn can no longer remember his lines and had a sort of nervous breakdown last year. [. . .]

Sunday 24th

[Letter of farewell from Michael Wilding pasted in]

I wonder what the poor little bugger is going through – if anything. Is he or is he not a feckless cop-out? Time will tell if time will give us a chance to wait. This is a Sunday that feels like a Sunday. [. . .] I read *Reader's Digest* for half an hour – a publication I haven't looked at for years.[79] I read the sporting page and my favourite Jim Murray on Hank Aaron and have not even got round to the political pages which I hardly ever miss.[80] Re: politics: Brook was commenting yesterday on how the mighty had fallen in this case the mighty being the British. The announcement that Wilson had decided on a June election which was a front page photograph of Wilson in the *Times* with a hundred words on the subject, has not been followed up at all and on the news on TV that night was not even mentioned. Nobody gives a bugger. Pompidou and the French elections, Willy Brandt and the West Germans, received much much more attention.[81] Both of them lost the war and we won it. It is passing strange and a passing world. Always has been of course. I can imagine the various and vicious political machinations that are going on in the British press and the mud-slinging, not one smidgeon of which crosses the Atlantic to the ordinary papers or to the TV. The *Times* of NY doubtless has a column or two as will *Time* and *Newsweek*, but Wilson or Heath are not going to make the covers. [. . .]

Monday 25th [. . .] I watched a lot of television yesterday mostly sport. The Angels v The Twins (won 6–5 by the former) and golf from Atlanta (won by Tommy Aaron.)[82] I saw a much younger Clint Eastwood playing the piano and singing a love-song in a re-run of a series he used to do called *Rawhide*.[83] A rare sight. I wrote painfully inadequate letters to Liza and Maria – one page each – caught a glimpse of Boris Karloff and Bela Lugosi in a horror film.[84]

---

[78] Hugh 'Binkie' Beaumont (1908–73), theatre impresario and managing director of the H. M. Tennent theatrical agency, who had given Burton his first professional contract in 1948. John Perry (1906–95), playwright and theatre director, who adapted the Elizabeth Bowen play *Castle Anna*, in which Burton had starred in 1948.

[79] *Reader's Digest*: a monthly magazine.

[80] Jim Murray (1919–98), sports journalist writing for the *LA Times*. Hank Aaron (1934—), baseball player.

[81] Willy Brandt (1913–92), Chancellor of West Germany (1969–74).

[82] Tommy Aaron (1937—), golfer, won the Atlanta Classic tournament.

[83] *Rawhide* was a television series that ran from 1959 to 1965, and which starred Clint Eastwood as the character Rowdy Yates.

[84] Boris Karloff (1887–1969), actor. Bela Lugosi (1882–1956), actor. This might have been *The Body Snatcher* (1945), directed by Robert Wise.

The series is called *Creature Features*.[85] Ate two trout for lunch, raisin bran for breakfast and turkey with all the trimmings for dinner. Liquorice for dessert in bed while I tried to read a book, the *One Monday We Killed Them All* book I mentioned taking to the hospital last Monday. I read the political pages and found a spot about the British Elections. We came next after the Dominican Republic and the article says that it is likely to be the dirtiest election in modern times. It was very short. I read about Nixon [. . .], Cambodia, Kent State and the four students killed by the National Guard.[86] I read that all food regardless of how purely grown – even the much loved potato – contains powerfully toxic elements which in excess could kill us all. Air pollution and hard drugs and the population explosion and the trip-wire tension in the middle-east between Israel and its neighbours. And there is nothing about all these things that I can do anything at all about. I could, I suppose, buy an electric car to make my own personal protest against gasoline, but nobody has made one yet that is effective. That should be a simple matter I would have thought with modern technology, but what would Standard Oil think of such treachery? They wouldn't like that would they? The stock market is bad enough as it is. Perhaps I could buy a horse and cart and try the freeways, go only by train – electric of course and not fuel-burning – and nuclear submarine. Shit on the world. I'll sit on my hands and pray.

[. . .] Yesterday afternoon I took E'en So for a walk and was hailed by a man called Harry Guardino. He was in a car with two small girls. I had no idea who he was but he chatted with great familiarity. 'Who's that?' I asked. 'Harry,' he said 'Harry Guardino.' Who are the girls? My daughters. I was taking them for a drive as it's Father's Day. They don't remember me I said – meaning <u>my</u> daughters. 'The eldest one does,' he said, 'she recognized you first.' I went home and told the story and Brook said that this same Guardino is a well-known and very good actor and indeed he was on a TV re-run of a film that very night called *Hell is for Heroes*.[87] So now I know. Guardino must have thought me very up-stage but he probably doesn't know that I see very few films and never read the show-business page unless someone points out something funny about E or me or others

Tuesday 26th [. . .] We will [. . .] God willing after this week end, go to Palm Springs and sun there.[88] [. . .]

---

[85] *Creature Features* (1970–71).

[86] President Nixon had announced his decision to invade Cambodia in April 1970. This led to furious protests, including student demonstrations at Kent State University, Ohio. There the National Guard had opened fire on demonstrators on 4 May, killing four people.

[87] Harry Guardino (1925–95), actor, who appeared in *Hell is for Heroes* (1962), directed by Don Siegel (1912–91).

[88] The city of Palm Springs, Riverside County, California, about 110 miles east of Los Angeles.

The party was horrible if like me you were sober. E was in pain in the bed-room for most of the time. George Davies was drunk and silly by 8 o'clock and got drunker and sillier, Val was smashed, Guilaroff was catastrophically boring as ever and kept on telling endless tales to Brook of <u>his</u> massive operations.[89] Kennamer spent most of the time defending California's weather which I attacked and almost was reduced to tears at one point. His voice became very high.

Thursday 28th Lil and Jim have gone to Palm Springs today to look at a house which is for rent for $1,500 a month or is it $1,800? and to which we may move on Monday next. [. . .][90]

The market went up yesterday by a record number of points to everyone's surprise except mine. That is to say, I knew that it had to go up before long or go to war though by such a vast number of points and actually a record number of points in one day was not to be foreseen except by Getty.[91] A lot of people will be breathing a little easier today but I have an idea that it will drop again before it starts climbing steadily up hill.[92]

I have barely left the house except to take the dog for a walk and twice to shop at a super-market and buy books at an enormous book-shop called Pickwick's in Hollywood. Among other books I bought a very fat paperback called *University Hand-book for Readers and writers*. Flipping over the pages I came to 'Sir Henry Newbolt. (1862—)'. The book is the revised edition of 1965. Could Newbolt still be alive then? He must be sleeping there below by now surely.[93]

I finished the rugby article three days ago and asked Jim or George to type it up. For some reason it took two days to do this. I read it again last night and hate it so will write it all again.

Crisis or no crisis we are neck-deep in scripts some of which are not bad though none that are really worth doing. Haven't got through a third of them yet though there are two that sound interesting. *The Devils* of Aldous Huxley which was done as a play by the Stratford Company some years ago, and a script by Peter Shaffer's twin brother who is having a great success at the

[89] Sydney Guilaroff (1907–97), chief hairstylist at MGM studios, who had worked with Burton and Taylor on various films including *The Night of the Iguana*, *The Sandpiper*, and *Who's Afraid of Virginia Woolf*, and before that with Taylor on *Cat on a Hot Tin Roof* and *Butterfield 8*.
[90] Probably a reference to Elizabeth Taylor and Jim Benton.
[91] The Dow Jones average had hit bottom on 26 May, having lost 30% of its value since the beginning of 1969. On 27 May it closed 32 points up.
[92] It rose above 700 points on 29 May, and did dip below this in June, and again in July, but did not return to the low figure reached on 26 May, and from early July rose steadily.
[93] Sir Henry Newbolt (1862–1938), poet. Burton is making a reference to a line from Newbolt's 'Drake's Drum' (1897): 'Capten, art tha sleepin' there below?'

moment with a play in London called *Sleuth*.[94] He is not as fancy as his brother apparently. Good.

Friday 29th I cannot face the re-writing of the rugby piece, but it must be done. I must hypnotize myself into doing it somehow. I read somewhere once that all creation in art is induced by self-hypnosis which is almost sub-conscious. Well let's see if I can do it consciously and re-write 3000 lousy paroles about a game. [. . .] It must be done, Richard. I shall pretend that if I finish the piece and if it's good I shall be paid $2,000,000. That might get it done.

[. . .] I talked to Gwen yesterday. Ivor is back in hospital in Geneva. One kidney is mal-functioning. I wish him to die now. I can't bear to see him so helpless and childlike – not in his mind, that's all right – but in his querulousness, his hatred of being helped. And he is in continual pain since a kind of moribund life came back into the body. Why did that slip in the dark have to happen? So slight a slip, so gigantic a fall. A nightmare night that will haunt me forever. That whatever Gods may be for money. At least we don't lack that. He will die in first class which is the only way he has ever wanted to travel – a Pullman to the grave.

Saturday 30th Three men came to see me yesterday in the morning at 11 o'clock to discuss a sort of documentary of *Becket* in which I will be the story-teller and occasionally appear. It is to be anything from one to one-and-a-half hours long. It will take me 10 days in September. It will be an interesting bit of travelling at any rate. I shall own it for Great Britain and own 50% of it for the rest of the world. I shall insist too on the cassette rights. The plan is to take the itinerary that he took. [. . .] The men were Huw Davies, a very Welsh Welshman from the Gower, an American called Lou Solomon who started off his morning with the disastrous 'You don't remember me do you?' I didn't and said 'Remind me.'[95] He did and it turned out that he had written the first draft of *Elizabeth Taylor's London* and I made a faux pas when I blurted out 'but I thought Sid Perelman wrote that'.[96] Clang. He had the nervous idiocy to say the same to E on introduction and had the same blank reaction from her. Why do they do that? Mr Solomon has been in the business all his life and should know better. Doubtless he had boasted to the other two about how well he knew us, Dick an' Liz and all that, and had to get in fast. The third man is a very long haired dark eyed sallow Brooklyn boy who seems very nice, but I felt the smack of amateurism.

---

[94] Aldous Huxley's *The Devils of Loudon* (1952) had been written as a play (*The Devils*) by John Whiting (1917–63) and performed at Stratford in 1961. Anthony Shaffer (1926–2001), playwight, author of *Sleuth* (1970). Identical twin brother of Peter Shaffer (1926–), playwright, author of *Equus* (1973) which Burton would play on stage and on film.
[95] Louis Solomon (1911–81), screenwriter and producer.
[96] Burton is here referring to the 1963 CBS television documentary *Elizabeth Taylor in London*. Sidney Joseph Perelman (1904–79), author and screenwriter.

Brook has gone to watch the 'Indianapolis 500' in a cinema where it is shown on closed-circuit TV and while typing I am listening to it on the radio.[97] A dreadful cacophony, an assault on the ears. It is a very dangerous race apparently and is usually ignored by the great Grand Prix drivers though occasionally they have appeared here and won – the one I remember is Jim Clark the Scot, now dead.[98] [. . .] There is very little movement from Hathaway and Ed Henry re *Raid on Rommel*.[99] They must get cracking soon if they want to start on June 15th or thereabouts.

Sunday 31st Rex came to dinner last night. I went to bed at 1130 and left the family chatting with him and Brook and Elizabeth told me this morn that he had said categorically that no American had ever been wrongfully sentenced to death and/or executed for murder. God he is a simpleton. And as self righteous as only the genuinely stupid can be. He talks of Nixon as if he were a God. [. . .] He is a perfect fascist in embryo. Were Hitler to arise here he would think him a great man and would join the Nazi party like a flash. A good lecture on Racism would make him virulently anti-Semitic overnight and he would categorize them enthusiastically for the prison camps.

I lunched soberly with Harvey Orkin at the Cock n' Bull. He is a good sweet man and terribly muddled but could never become a Nazi or an anything-baiter.

I read all day apart from writing a couple of letters. When faced with this machine latterly I feel as dull as drinkwater. John.[100]

JUNE

Monday 1st, Beverly Hills Hotel We are flying to Palm Springs this morning at 11 o'clock though I won't believe it until we get there. Swerdlow and Kennamer came to probe around E and said she could 'dig ditches' now if she wanted to. I can't myself see E digging ditches but it's obviously doctors' idea of the acme of human good health that one is able to dig ditches. How about starting with a nice walk one asks one-self. Work it up to a slight sweat as 'twere. [. . .]

Tuesday 2nd, 925 Crescent Drive, Palm Springs We flew here yesterday morning in a De Havilland jet in 28 minutes. [. . .] It's a cheap house and has clearly just been repainted [. . .]. It is a bit short on baths but has three showers, a large kitchen and four bedrooms, a master bedroom for us, another with

[97] The Indianapolis 500 motor race, over a distance of 500 miles, held at Speedway, Indiana.
[98] Jim Clark (1936–68), Formula One racing driver and winner of two World Championships, competed in the Indianapolis 500 five times and won it in 1965.
[99] Henry Hathaway (1898–1985), director, who was to work with Burton on *Raid on Rommel*.
[100] A backhanded reference to John Drinkwater (1882–1937), playwright and poet.

twin beds for Liz and Brook one for Raymond and a spare one, sans toilet and bathroom for me and my typewriter and 'quarrels' as E says. She is actually there now in the 'quarrel' room but not from a quarrel, I was snoring last night she says and she couldn't stop me so sought sanctuary in the spare room. [. . .]

Wednesday 3rd, Palm Springs [. . .] There was much ado yesterday from Jim Benton and Dick Hanley and Springer in NY about an article in the current *Look* magazine about the sickness of E the fading film star and her insatiable demands for the most expensive things in the world including now if you please and above all things a $125,000 'coja'(?) mink given by the equally sick but presumably not fading husband, me. What a shame that I spoil the whole thing by not having given her the mink at all. It was paid for by posing for snaps for Neiman-Marcus and several cuts and bruises when E fell off a rock and landed awkwardly on a platinum beach location in Vallarta.[101] [. . .] The article is written by a singularly nice but singularly mediocre middle-aged man called Jonah Ruddy.[102] Nasty as the article is it only succeeds in perpetuating the legend of immense wealth and distant unattainability which is the very stuff of 'glamour'. [. . .]

Watched off and on the primary elections last night on TV. Politicians are really frightful people. God help us all.

Thursday 4th Elizabeth started bleeding yesterday from her behind, great gouts of blood which were frightening to behold. I cleaned it up periodically – on one occasion the bathroom floor was awash with it – and thanked the Lord that I was a non-drinking man and felt no nausea at all. I am convinced that were I a drinker as I used to be I would have thrown up convulsively. [. . .] The poor little thing had about 8 of these emissions before we finally got her to hospital. The unfortunate doctor – named Sisler, a relation of the hall-of-famer – gave her a sedative which only succeeded in making her very jumpy and nervous.[104] [. . .] Endless telephone calls were made to Kennamer and Swerdlow who both obviously thought that it was a minor thing and that she was trying to swing for some hard shots again. Finally we got Sisler, who has done a great deal of proctology and who is the doctor of and known to Dick Hanley to come over. After more phone calls it was decided to remove her to the Desert Hospital.[104] Swerdlow drove from LA in what must have been a hair-raising 90 minutes and waited to examine another dollop of blood. It was not long in coming and he decided to knock her out and have a look at least

---

[101] Neiman-Marcus, a luxury retail department store.
[102] The journalist was Jo Roddy, whose article 'How Do I Love Thee? Let Me Count the Ways', appeared in *Look*'s issue of 16 June 1970. Jonah Ruddy was Hollywood correspondent for the *New Musical Express*.
[103] George Sisler (1893–1973), baseball player, elected to the Baseball Hall of Fame in 1939.
[104] Desert Hospital, North Indian Canyon Drive, Palm Springs.

and see if she was haemorrhaging and she was knocked out and they wheeled her in to the theatre and found out that one of the stitches was ripped out, re-stitched it and she was all out in 30 minutes. I aged another ten years. She was pathetically frightened and kept on saying like a child as she was being wheeled down the corridor, 'I love you Richard.' 'I love you too, Baby.' And a baby she was, and a father I was. [. . .]

Friday 5th [. . .] E still in hospital but considerably more comfortable. She lost 'a unit and a half' of blood, i.e. about a pint-and-a-half, and is correspondingly weak and will have to take it nice and easy until she's built up her own blood again which will take from six to eight weeks.

[. . .] Last night I had a vivid nightmare in which our Michael was dead. He was a skeleton in a desert. I must have guilt about Mike because I kept on calling him Absolom in the dream and E – a vague figure – was accusatory.[105] What does it all mean. What's the meaning of this?

Sunday 7th I pulled myself together took my courage in both hands leapt the chasm and finally sent off the rugby article to Cliff Morgan. I hope it's acceptable. Awful if it's not. Will have to sell it to some other paper to salvage my pride. [. . .]

E still in hospital with her blood-count very low and weakening and depressing for her, but if the count has remained the same or gone up this morning she will come out today. She is to rest a lot and not strain herself or overtire herself etc. until the blood has been restored. This should take about 6–8 weeks. It means she won't be able to come to Mexico with me probably when I make the film.[106] It will be very strange without her but perhaps it's not altogether a bad idea as I shall be working terrible hours and will hardly see her at all, going to bed early and up at the crack of [dawn] in intense heat and so on. She might as well take it easy with somebody congenial in LA or Malibu. Female of course. Also, unlike E, once I start a film I want to get it over as soon as possible and will work any hours and seven days a week if necessary to do so. E, having grown up inside the MGM machine, gives them nothing free and considers adding to their costs fair game. I couldn't care less about that but with all the energy of a profoundly lazy man wish to get it over as soon as possible so that I can laze again or go to fresh fields. There is no film or play that I've ever been in that hasn't bored me after about six weeks so I like to get them over fast.

[. . .] I'm waiting anxiously for the phone call to find out if she's coming out or not. If not I shall sit there with her and do Spanish verbs. One a day keeps broken Spanish at bay. There are programmes on TV all day long here in

---

[105] Absalom, third son of David, King of Israel, who rebelled against his father and was killed in battle.
[106] Burton is referring here to his impending film. *Raid on Rommel* (1971), shot in Mexico.

that language but apart from the commercials, I have a terrible job trying to keep up.

Monday 8th Elizabeth came home yesterday at 4 o'clock, thank God, looking pale and wan but beautiful. Now for a slow but sure recovery. [. . .]

We watched the 'Emmys' on TV last night.[107] Horrible and shaming. A girl called Patty Duke who, when a small girl, was in *Wuthering Heights* with me and Rosemary Harris.[108] That enchanting child has turned into a dope-ridden idiot. Her acceptance of the Emmy was among the most embarrassing things I've ever seen. Clearly she was stoned witless. It made one want to crawl under the chair. What a mess.

Saw Charles Collingwood interviewing Speer about war crimes – his in particular.[109] Charles seemed a bit holier than thou to me and Speer came out of it better and made no excuses. He seemed thoroughly likeable. There was a slight air of kicking a man when he's down in Charles' attitude and more than a touch of self-righteousness. [. . .]

Tuesday 9th [. . .] I talked to Kate yesterday and she comes out to stay with us after school finishes, which is Friday so she'll be here on Saturday for which many thanks and general rejoicing. She is still a little girl and hasn't become a long-haired unkempt pot-smoking hippie yet at least. I also talked to Aaron re *Don Quixote* and *Defector* and the documentary *Becket*.[110] All as nebulous as ever. For *Quixote* I can get $½m in front as they say. The market is looking up a bit but nowhere near what it was.

I expect another couple of bad days from E before we turn the corner but nothing short of a catastrophe can be as bad as yesterday. The nervous tension created in me when she's in pain is quite extraordinary. I am incapable of dispassion and keep on thinking how nice it would be if I had the burden of pain instead, except that I'd be far worse than she.

Wednesday 10th Elizabeth in a complete reversal of form was bubbling over with joie de vivre all day yesterday and wanted to go out to a movie and/or go out for a drink. With memories of the last week's nightmares, fresh with haemorrhages and possible blood transfusions and hospitals and helpless pain, new in my mind, I said no. But perhaps, I said, tomorrow. [. . .] So if all proceeds at an even pace today we will go out to the cinema tonight. We have a choice of *Airport*,

---

[107] Emmys: the awards of the (America) Academy of Television Arts and Sciences.

[108] Patty Duke (1946—) received an Emmy for Outstanding Lead Actress for her role in *My Sweet Charlie*. *Wuthering Heights* had screened on NBC on 9 May 1958.

[109] Albert Speer (1905–81), architect, Nazi Germany's Minister of Armaments and War Production (1942–5), who had served 20 years' imprisonment for war crimes after being sentenced at the Nuremberg trials.

[110] None of these projects appear to have borne fruit.

Mash or *Marooned*.[111] It looks like *Airport*. I read a long piece in *Time* mag about Mike Nichols and *Catch 22* in which I am, as ever, misquoted.[112] I therefore assume that everybody else is. Mike, for instance, doesn't sound like Mike at all though if the writer is right Mike may have changed his attitudes to life and all that because of the profound impact on it of *Catch 22*'s despairing black humour. A book I couldn't abide and I have a treacherous feeling that I won't be able to abide the film either. We must get it run when we're back in LA. [...]

[...] Apart from my Spanish I cannot settle down to what is known as 'serious reading' but gobble up thrillers at the rate of knots. Have got some lovely books too, hanging around.

Thursday 11th [...] Received telegram from Cliff Morgan [...].[113] Gratifying. Cliff is no Connolly but gratifying.[114] [...] The best part of the day for me is usually the very early mornings – from 5.30–6.00 to about 9, but now the whole family has taken to getting up about 6.30–7.00 and it's bedlam. Lamentably here there is no place to hide, the house being so small. It'll be worse when Kate arrives. [...] Must learn to concentrate regardless of distractions. And they <u>will</u> read extracts from the newspapers to me in the middle of my typing. [...] I shall try typing outside on the patio beside the swimming pool tomorrow and see if I can get away that way.

Just had bacon and eggs and bangers which I didn't really want, but as I'm feeling churlish I took them with a reluctant 'thank-you'. Why don't they go back to sleep – they've got nothing else to do. I have heaps of things to do, heaps and heaps. [...]

---

[111] *Airport* (1969), directed by George Seaton (1911–79). *M*A*S*H* (1970), directed by Robert Altman (1925–2006). *Marooned* (1969) directed by John Sturges (1911–92).

[112] *Catch 22* (1970), directed by Mike Nichols, based on the 1961 novel by Joseph Heller (1923–99). The article 'Some are More Yossarian than Others' appeared in *Time* for 15 June 1970. The relevant paragraph states: 'Richard Burton remembers meeting Nichols and [Elaine] May [1932–, director, screenwriter, actor, who worked with Nichols] backstage when he was starring in Camelot. "Elaine was too formidable . . . one of the most intelligent, beautiful and witty women I had ever met. I hoped I would never see her again." Mike was less formidable, more agreeable. The mustard-colored eyes glinted, but the face had an unlined, almost feminine softness. The voice was as warm and resonant as a cello. Burton, who knows role playing when he sees it, was at first unconvinced by the proffered friendship and admiration. But eventually he enrolled Nichols in the Richard Burton fan club; it was an attachment that would one day pay off handsomely for Nichols.' Later in the article there is another passage: 'Richard Burton likes to retell the story of Walter Matthau, "a frenetic soul, and he finally blew his stack at Nichols' Odd Couple direction. 'You're emasculating me,' Walter cried. 'Give me back my balls!' From out front, Mike called back: 'Props.'"
'Mike was Burton's kind of boy. As the Liz–Dick scandal deepened during the filming of Cleopatra, Burton recalls, "Ninety percent of our friends avoided our eyes. Mike flew to Rome from New York to be with us." Nichols stayed by Elizabeth's side when Burton went off to make another film. Favors like that one remembers. In 1966, the Welshman and his lady were signed for Who's Afraid of Virginia Woolf?, and Elizabeth insisted on Nichols as director. Virginia Woolf could have been a mini-Cleopatra, but its below-the-belt punches intrigued critics and audiences.'

[113] Morgan accepted the article as it stood, terming it 'magic'.

[114] Cyril Connolly (1903–74), literary critic and essayist.

Friday 12th [. . .] I awoke at 4.45 this morn. Got up and made coffee. A quiet silver dawn. Dogs all sleeping and all the family. The lights in this house are so low and so few that at this hour of the morning I type in semi-darkness, a gloom. Had a reply from Emlyn Williams yesterday to my avuncular letter of advice and sympathy re his mental and physical collapse last year.[115] The letter [. . .] is very chipper and would seem to indicate that he's around the corner. His bad-taste revue number is not, however, up to standard. Of course, those numbers have to be acted not written. How long it is since Noel and Emlyn created the revue. The late King George VI singing 'K-K-K-Katie from the c-c-c-cowshed' and Kenneth Kent, Radie Harris and Herbert Marshall (all wooden-legged) doing a dance number called 'Touch Wood.'[116] Esmond Knight and Esmé Percy (both one-eyed) doing a number called 'I've got my eye on you.'[117] A chorus of skeletons dancing and singing 'Take me back to dear old Belsen, take me back to good old Buchenwald.' Those were the early ones, or some of them, and there have been hundreds since.

E had a good day, so much so that we decided to go out to dinner in the evening at a 'Steak House' but after ten minutes or so it was obvious that she was only barely hanging on and so I took her home and went back later to pick up Liz and a very drunken Brook. He had had a lot of Napa Valley claret during the ten minutes I was away – anyway, a huge jug of it was practically empty. He looks ugly when he's drunk, speaks very loudly and repeats himself a lot. Also he looks uncannily like Emlyn at such times and his mannerisms become absolutely and frighteningly the same. The rat-tat-tat nodding of the head before the witticism or the didactic finger-wag. The pursed lips. He went on and on about a British actor called Wilfred Hyde Whyte – who lives here in Palm Springs with his new and rich young wife – and what a swine he is to act with.[118] A laugh-killer and up-stager etc. He sounds a nasty piece of work to work with. All this cut-throatedness done with 'my dear boy' bonhomie. Oddly enough I have always defeated such actors by giving them everything and ultimately stealing every march on them. Instance Rex in *Staircase*. Rex was so busy getting his face into the camera that he forgot to play the part as well as he could. On the stage it's even easier than on the screen to break the back of such petty performers. Just give them their heads and they chop themselves off. I've always found it so childish anyway. [. . .] Kate arrives tomorrow at 2.15 LA time at LA. I shall drive in to pick her up. Longing to see her. Watched Mexico play Belgium in soccer at Azteca Stadium, Mexico City. It's

[115] This may refer to Emlyn Williams's unhappy experiences when taking over from John Gielgud in the part of the Headmaster in the play *Forty Years On* by Alan Bennett (1934—) at the Apollo. The play had run for nine months when Williams replaced Gielgud in September 1969, but it closed abruptly thereafter. Williams then spent some time in hospital undergoing an operation on his varicose veins.
[116] King George VI (1895–1952) suffered from a stammer. Kenneth Kent (1892–1963), actor. Radie Harris (1904–2001), Hollywood journalist. Herbert Marshall (1890–1966), actor.
[117] Esmé Percy (1887–1957), actor.
[118] Wilfrid Hyde-White (1903–91), who had married the actor Ethel Drew in 1957.

the world cup. Mexico won on a penalty.[119] I wanted to have the Belgians win. Silly. Just because they were Europeans I suppose and had to put up with the mindless antagonism of 100,000 screaming Mexicans. There might be trouble down there on a big scale before this competition is over. International sport on that level brings out the most virulent hatreds. I wouldn't enter myself. Soccer fans seem particularly idiotic even in England. I myself become a nervous wreck when watching Wales play rugby, though it expresses itself in silent writings internally with an occasional roar of relief or arbitrary remarks to perfect strangers and lots of pulls at the flask of whiskey or brandy. I'd rather not go any more. I cannot even read the accounts of a Welsh loss!

Saturday 13th [. . .] [Elizabeth] watched me in an old film last night – *The Rains of Ranchipur* – and said I was very handsome and sexy-looking and that the film was nothing like as bad as I said it was.[120] Perhaps it's mellowed with age. [. . .]

The *LA Times* today announce that Larry has been made a life peer [and] that Sybil Thorndike has been made a CH. Freddie Ashton the same. I am a CBE and David Frost an OBE.[121] Nothing still for Emlyn and he could have done with one. Larry told me years ago that he was determined to be the first 'actor-peer'. It was a reply to my asking him what worlds did he have left to conquer in our profession. He was in his cups and we were living together at Tower Road in Bev Hills and he was doing *Spartacus* and I was doing *Ice Palace* and neither of our careers were sparkling which is why we were doing such bad films.[122] Larry was tearful because he couldn't get backing for a film of *Macbeth* which he lusted to do, and I was contemplating retirement from acting and writing instead – not for a living, not for money. I was already a dollar millionaire and with the inexpensive Syb could have lived like a prince for the rest of my life. I wanted to write because I sought for some kind of permanence, a cover-bound shot at immortality and not a rapidly dating film and acting to match.[123] Well he's made his ambition to be a peer but not to film *Macbeth*. Perhaps one will follow the other now, but not if I can get in first. I'll be interested to see the reaction of the British Press to both Larry's peerage and my CBE. Larry's is so sensational an elevation that he might take the heat off my award and the stuff about me being a traitor to Britain for running away to Switzerland and not paying taxes. I remember being lumped with Chaplin and

---

[119] In a first round game in Group 1, the hosts Mexico beat Belgium 1–0 with a penalty scored in the 14th minute.

[120] *The Rains of Ranchipur* (1955), directed by Jean Negulesco (1900–93).

[121] Both the actor Sybil Thorndike (1882–1976), and the choreographer and dancer Sir Frederick Ashton (1904–88) were admitted to the Order of the Companions of Honour in 1970.

[122] *Spartacus* (1960), directed by Stanley Kubrick (1928–99). *Ice Palace* (1960), directed by Vincent Sherman (1906–2006).

[123] Cover-bound,' referring to book.

Noel and somebody else as instances of rats leaving a sinking ship and all that. If the press is quiet about this I might nip a knighthood one of these days. A couple of seasons at the Old Vic and a stint or two at Oxford and I could swing one fairly easily with a Labour government in power. We might however have all died of asphyxiation or world poison by then.

Shall send a cable to Olivier today.[124] It is a remarkable achievement considering that he has never been a 'clubbable' man in the Wolfit, Richardson or Guinness sense.[125] He has remarkable stamina and it's about time they separated him from the herd.

Sunday 14th Drove with Brook to LA yesterday to pick up Kate at the airport and it proved to be an eventful and very tiring journey. [. . .] At a place called Banning I was gonged down by a Highway Patrolman for exceeding the speed limit.[126] He said I was doing 80mph in a 70 zone. I didn't argue because I was actually going faster than that. Unfortunately I had no licence and no means of identification at all. Nothing in my pockets at all except cigarettes a lighter and about $300 in cash. I was forced to tell him that 'I'm quite a well-known actor, my name is Richard Burton.' He recognized me and I <u>did</u> have Dick Hanley's car-hire form and explained that he was my secretary. The boy was very polite but gave me a ticket nevertheless. [. . .]

Kate is already 5 ft 4 ins in height and is not yet 13 years old. She is as tall as Elizabeth. She is very white like all easterners and tells me to my surprise that she takes the sun very badly. Odd that, as both Syb and I take it very well. Throw-back to some funny gene somewhere.

E had had a rough day what with Sisler sticking a finger up her behind and wiggling it about to make sure that the passage was kept open. She shouted, she tells me, a great deal. Glad I wasn't here.

[. . .] Looks as if the film will start about the 25th–30th. Talk of P. Scofield playing the doctor.[127] He's quite wrong for it but he will help to give it 'class' as they say here. Will again make it 'a different ball of wax.'

[. . .] Will try to do some Spanish. Kate is reading *Jane Eyre* and announced fifteen minutes ago 'Rochester has just kissed Jane. Wow.'[128]

Monday 15th Have been up since 5.45 and for once was beaten to it by Kate and E and we all went to breakfast at the Dunes Hotel Coffee Shop driven by E in the golf-cart.[129] [. . .]

---

124 Reputedly the cable read 'By the Lord Harry, Larry'.
125 Sir Donald Wolfit (1902–68), actor and theatre manager, who had appeared alongside Burton in *Becket*.
126 About 23 miles west of Palm Springs.
127 The part of the medical officer in *Raid on Rommel* was to be played by Clinton Greyn (1936—).
128 Charlotte Brontë, (1816–55) *Jane Eyre* (1847).
129 Bermuda Dunes Hotel, Adams Street, Bermuda Dunes, Palm Springs.

Have read through some of the entries in this thing. It is stupendously tedious. But If I didn't do it I would feel guilty of something or other. So will slog away even though it is unreadable. It's some sort of writing at least. Perhaps I should do a daily thing like this and then write a Sunday précis in proper and considered English. Leave it till the end of the year and then turn it into one large book for my eyes only. Then there would be some purpose to these meanderings. Perhaps write my recollections of the year from memory alone. And then write what this book says and compare the two. Compare the anger of the day after with the dispassion of a year after. Recollect like Aunty Wordsworth in tranquillity.[130]

[. . .] I want to go to work for a time now, more than anything to find how I react in a sober way to the tedium of film-making. No drink to kill the pain. And an indifferent film to boot.

Tuesday 16th 7.30 and out on the concrete beside the pool in bathing costume and back to the sun. [. . .] Kate asleep still therefore am writing on this notepaper as my diary is in her room. I sleep tremendously heavily nowadays since the booze is working or has worked perhaps out of my system. The sleep is not long – 5 hours or 7 at the very most – but it is very concentrated. No dreams or nightmares or at least none that I can remember. I wonder if death is like that? If so it won't be at all bad. [. . .] Shopped at the bookstore and bought mags and a French/English version of Rimbaud.[131] Have never read him in the original. She [Kate] bought one for Jordan Xtoph Syb's husband.[132] I suspect she calls him 'Dad'. And feels guilty about it. I also suspect that he does not read poetry, though I may be wrong. Nobody has any opinion of the fellow at all, neither for nor against. He's nice and quiet, is about the only reaction I can get out of anybody. [. . .]

Dr Sisler's son watched me on *The David Frost Show* and heard me say that I used to learn the major classics of Shakespeare's by heart when I was a small boy.[133] Fired with ambition he has learned 'To be or not to be' or something and wishes to recite it to me. What can I say except yes? He is 12 years old. I shrink I flee I die but it has to be done. Marvellous what the public and press will persuade themselves of. I have this marvellous reputation as an actor of incredible potential who has lazed his talent away. A reputation which I enjoy, but which I acquired even when I was at the Old Vic those many years ago.

And unless I go back to England or the National Theatre in Cardiff etc. and slog away at the classics for a decade, that is the reputation I shall die with.

---

[130] A reference to William Wordsworth's preface to the 1802 edition of the *Lyrical Ballads*, in which he defined poetry as 'the spontaneous overflow of powerful feeling; it takes its origin in emotion recollected in tranquillity'.
[131] Arthur Rimbaud (1854–91), French poet.
[132] Jordan Christopher, Kate's stepfather.
[133] Burton and Taylor had appeared on *The David Frost Show* on 19 March 1970.

'Will you ever go back to your first love, the theatre?' they ask all the time. 'It's not my first love,' I snap. The theatre, apart from the meretricious excitement of the first night and the sometimes interesting rehearsals has always bored me and reading scripts has always bored me. I haven't read Shakespeare for years, except an occasional dip into *Lear* and a glance at *Macbeth*, though I will speak him for your entertainment endlessly. I do not wish to compete with Olivier or Gielgud and Scofield and Redgrave etc. as they are too 'actory' for my liking. Apart from occasional performances, few and far between, I don't believe a word they say. Larry is the past-master of professional artificiality. A mass of affectations. So is Paul. John is always the same and when it fits the part he is very watchable, but when it doesn't it can only be described as regrettable. They have splendid presences and are very hard-working and genuinely love their jobs. I cannot match the two latter qualities. And do not wish to. [. . .]

Wednesday 17th [. . .] Sisler's son came with mother and sister and Sisler himself and gave us his 'To be or not to be'. Sweet little boy and he read the speech very intelligently though he obviously mis-read a line which I told him about. I spoke a speech for him too. Elizabeth, in a fine frenzy, did a bit of the *Shrew*. Shook me and the family when she screamed 'Fie, Fie you s.o.b.'[134] Something like that. We all leapt a yard in the air. [. . .]

E had her bottom examined yesterday in the morning and she was a shaking mess for a long time afterwards with great outbursts about how bored she was having to stay in the house all the time because it was too hot outside, she couldn't read a book, she was sick of watching TV, she was sick of hearing us splashing in the pool while she was confined etc. I comforted her as best I could but I'm not very good at those sorts of things. [. . .]

Thursday 18th [. . .] Watched myself in old film called *Prince of Players* on TV last night. I had never seen it before. Can't think why it failed so badly when it came out in 1956 or whenever it was as it is more than averagely good.[135] I was surprised at the speed at which I spoke and the very obvious Welsh intonation on occasions.[136] Kate E. and I watched it together in the bedroom and E said she thought it was a fine film and Kate said she was proud of me. I must be getting calloused in my latter days because I wasn't in my usual despair after watching myself. Brook was a trifle sloshed, which he seems to be every night nowadays, and was a little sour-graped about the film saying, during one of the breaks, that Ron Berkeley clearly didn't do my make-up because my pock-marks were showing. E's loyal little face tightened in defence. Kate said to me

---

[134] The opening line of Kate's speech in *The Taming of the Shrew*, Act V, scene i: 'Fie, fie! Unknit that threat'ning unkind brow'.
[135] 1955.
[136] Despite playing the part of the American actor Edwin Booth, Burton hums the eighteenth-century Welsh love song 'Bugeilio'r Gwenith Gwyn' to his ailing wife Mary.

guilelessly afterwards 'you seem so different Dad, I mean you were so hand-some then.' Thank you I said. [. . .] It seems that I might do *Don Quixote* next year. I think I can do it by losing a really emaciating 15 pounds or so and getting a really fat Sancho Panza. Perhaps Ustinov or Alec Guinness. Or Zero Mostel.[137] If I do it we must get it out fast to beat the musical *Man of La Mancha*.[138] The deal is more or less fixed subject to my approval of the actor to play Sancho and the time slot. An interesting challenge, more so than Harry in *Staircase*.

Read Rimbaud yesterday for the first time in the original in one of those dual-language books. The translation is appalling. 'J'en ai trop pris' is rendered as 'I was fed up.' A lot of the nuance is lost to me, but I shall learn it slowly anyway and corner Enid Starkie or somebody and get myself a free lecture on the subtleties.[139]

The British elections are taking place today. We should have fairly positive results about 10 tonight our time here. Unless it's so close that they have to wait right down to the wire.

The next film is still amazingly vague. No script yet. A group of tailors bootmakers and hatters came down to the Springs the other day to measure me and Brook for the uniforms, but the costume director himself didn't know half the time what was what. It seems that I should be dressed roughly like George Peppard who was in the film *Tobruk* from which we have stolen the stock footage.[140] So, in effect, Peppard is my stunt double. It really is a film by computer and I shall record its idiocies with as faithful an accuracy as I can. The writing is to be 'dialogue sufficiently credible to get us from one explosion to another'. There is no overt attempt to give it any 'artistic' merit whatsoever. Any that comes will come if it comes from the personalities of the actors concerned so they must all be actors of the first rank. What is strangely ironic is that the film is based on a true story and the band of intrepid allies actually included an American, but we cannot use this because it would seem like an obvious gimmick to capture the American market. The fact is more a fantasy than the fiction. The schedule has been reduced again to 3 weeks and two days. If the film does a mediocre gross only, I shall pick up at least a million dollars. I could make as much as a million pounds. For 20 days' work. Morally indefensible. But at least I don't feel the guilt of taking a million dollars cash down for a film that might be a total failure. Here at least I'm gambling with my money to the same extent as the producers. [. . .]

---

[137] Zero Mostel (1915–77), actor.
[138] *Man of La Mancha* (1972), directed by Arthur Hiller (1923–), starring Peter O'Toole and Sophia Loren.
[139] Enid Starkie (1897–1970), fellow of Exeter College, Oxford, and an expert on Rimbaud. 'J'en ai trop pris' is perhaps better rendered as 'I have had enough'.
[140] George Peppard (1928–94), who starred in *Tobruk* (1967), directed by Arthur Hiller.

Friday 19th [...] There was a tremendous upset in the British elections yesterday and against all poll analysis the bloody Tories are in with a whacking majority.[141] The full extent of it is not known yet but it seems that it will be a very comfy 50 seats majority at least. I am furious. Those smug bastards are in again, and again we'll be run by the old school tie – not that we weren't before when the Labour boys were in power.

I did nothing, simply nothing all day long apart from a little light reading and a couple of pages of this. Watched a little on TV and chatted around with Kate and E and watched *Batman* and boxing from the Olympic auditorium.[142] [...]

Saturday 20th Leaving for Malibu today by jet at mid-day. [...]

Looks like the Tories are in by about 40 seats or so. That means that the Labour party can easily get back at the next election in five years time. So it's not too [*sic*] bad as it seemed.

[...] E lolling about on the bed watching TV. Asked me 'why are you being so bloody Welsh?' She is watching Cornel Wilde as Marco Polo in *Marco Polo*.[143] Funny we should think of the Italians as physical cowards but there's Marco Polo and Da Gama (or was he Spanish or P'guese) and Columbus.[144]

[...] I want to go home to Switzerland.

Sunday 21st, Malibu Colony Arrived here about 1.30. [...] Terrible silly quarrels for the rest of the day about who fries the chips for dinner. Said I wasn't because I didn't know how. E lost temper and said I'd been boasting for years as to how well I made chips. Told her it was a joke, the boasting. [...] Went to bed early and read a French roman policier by Japrisot.[145] Didn't get too far with it and fell asleep. [...] Went to the drug-store for breakfast with Kate. [...] Told her I was sick to death of the States and wanted urgently to get back to Europe though that continent was getting as bad as this. I suppose she'll end up being a Yank. For some reason being an American has always seemed to me to be unglamorous. Now why should that be? Is it natural British xenophobia? After all, they made it to the moon first and never stop

---

[141] In fact the Conservative Party won 330 seats against 287 for the Labour Party. With the support of the Ulster Unionists, Edward Heath (1916–2005) was able to form a government based on a parliamentary majority of 30.

[142] This could refer to the film *Batman* (1966), directed by Leslie Martinson (1915–), or to the television series of the same name, featuring some of the same cast as the film, which ran from 1966 to 1968. Possibly Burton is referring to the National Auditorium in Mexico City, which was the venue for gymnastics events at the 1968 Olympic Games, or to the Arena Mexico, the venue for the boxing tournament at the Olympics, which remained a major boxing venue for many years.

[143] Cornel Wilde (1912–89). Burton may be mistaken here. The 1962 film *Marco Polo* starred Rory Calhoun (1922–99) in the lead role. Marco Polo (1254–1324), explorer, traveller, merchant.

[144] Vasco De Gama (*c*.1460–1524), Portuguese explorer.

[145] Sébastien Japrisot (1931–2003), novelist.

propagating the 'greatness' of their country. I would still prefer being a Welshman or Irish or Scots. Even English, and even they're a pretty comical lot nowadays.

Have just had chat with Hugh French and Ronnie Lubin re *Don Quixote* to co-star Hoffman or Finney or Topol or somebody equally able and to be shot in Colombia as it will be too cold in Spain in the early part of next year but will be perfect in the former.[146] And cheaper. They want E to play Dulcinante but I don't think the part good enough for her.[147] However they have a lengthier script by the same Waldo Salt which I will read tomorrow or Tuesday. The present one is a little sketchy. We'll try and get a man called O'Steen to direct.[148] He has never done so before but cut *Woolf, Graduate* and *Catch 22*. So should know his stuff. [. . .]

Monday 22nd, Malibu This year drags on and on. Yesterday sat in the sun and read a bit. [. . .] Finished the Japrisot novel. Most improbable even for a detective thriller.

Am going to LA today, Western Costumes rather in Hollywood, to fit for clothes for this strange film I'm in. [. . .] An Englishman called Jacklin won the USA Open Golf Championship yesterday and delighted us all.[149] The first Englishman for 50 years and the first Britisher. Since he won the British Open last year it automatically puts him among the company of the great. He is only 25 and it's nice that somebody so young and seemingly deserving is successful at something so harmless. [. . .]

Dustin Hoffman I understand is either very fearful or very conceited as he says he cannot make up his mind whether to take the Sancho Panza or not as he's afraid that as Quixote I will steal the film from him. What a funny reaction from such a good actor. He obviously wants to play a one-man show where no other actor stands a chance. Reasoning that way, he would turn down Othello and/or Iago. I must be supremely self-confident as no such considerations cross my mind, or ever have.

Tuesday 23rd Another grey mist-enwrapped morning. Have just taken the girls to breakfast in the drugstore. Maria is a chatter-box, a 1000 words a minute type. When I remember that we were frightened that she would never speak. [. . .] She is a delight and as warm as kittens. She is nine years old. And not 10 as I thought. [. . .]

---

[146] Possibly Arthur Lubin (1898–1995), film director. Dustin Hoffman. Albert Finney (1936—), actor. Chaim Topol (1935—), actor.

[147] Burton means the character of Dulcinea del Toboso.

[148] Sam O'Steen (1923—), who had edited *Who's Afraid of Virginia Woolf, The Graduate* (1967) and *Catch 22* (1970), amongst other films, and who went on to direct, mainly films for television.

[149] Tony Jacklin (1944—), golfer, who had won the British Open in 1969, won his second (and final) 'major' at the US Open at Hazeltine in 1970.

B and I went to be fitted for our uniforms for the film yesterday at Western Costume co. in Hollywood. Hathaway was there. I have always thought of this film as a giggle but now that it gets nearer and nearer I am beginning to have qualms. I shall read what is supposed to be the final script today and see what I can salvage for myself from it. That's what comes of wanting to work for the sake of working and not for better reasons. [. . .]

Wednesday 24th [. . .] Went to see a bigger house along the beach. We have taken it. [. . .] We are moving in today. I read most of my next epic. I shall finish it today sometime. It is very laboured but I bet can be very watchable. I shudder to think what the posh critics will say. Well actually I don't shudder. I shall rather enjoy them. They are so serious or in a desperate attempt to send it all up they become comi-serio and snappish. There is a man called Morgenstern who writes for *Time* or *Newsweek* who is so pompous that he is a sure fire party piece when read aloud, especially about almost any foreign film.[150] He fairly bristles with insignificance, as indeed they all do. I suppose as a result of hob-nobbing with famous or notorious household words most of whom are incredibly stupid and having to see several films a week <u>and</u> writing about them must eventually stultify what small growths their minute minds are capable of.[151] Tynan started out with such a fine acerbic astringent flurry that I read his notices with glee and could even quote them. But the splendid frenzy is all but dead. He has become a plodder, a hack. Has no creative sense at all. I used to read them all and over all they have been excessively complimentary to me, but I have become perhaps so blasé in my old age that I find them unbearably tedious to read nowadays about anything or anybody. Somebody sent a me a long and breathtakingly adulatory article recently by Cecil Smith of the *LA Times* about me, and I couldn't get through it though the legend is that actors will read favourable notices about themselves for ever.[152] Not so in my case. I think I was badly hurt by my first batch of bad notices when I first played *Henry V* at Stratford and the callousing began then. That's twenty years ago and actually the notices weren't bad at all, but they didn't say I was the greatest etc. therefore they were bad as far as I was concerned. When notices are good they're not good enough and when they're bad they upset you. The worst notice of all of course is not to be noticed. Or 'Also in the cast were . . . . .'

I must strip my part in *Rommel* down to the bone. I talk too much in it and destroy what little mystery the part might be invested with.

Brook read the script yesterday and said he wanted to play Reilly, a nothing part, a man who drives the half-track and is in all the action and said 'The part of the C.O. disappears after one speech in the early pages. Says he won't be

[150] Joe Morgenstern (1932—), film critic for *Newsweek* (1965–83).

[151] Burton probably means 'household names'.

[152] Cecil Smith (1917–2009), by this time television critic for the *LA Times*, but previously drama critic.

involved in killing anyone and walks out of the film.' On the contrary I discovered that the C.O. seduces the Italian girl etc. and has the only 'love-interest' in the piece.[153] Reminds me of Jimmy Granger being sent the script of *Odd Man Out* by Carol Reed and flipping through the pages where he had dialogue, deciding that the part wasn't long enough.[154] He didn't notice the stage directions so turned it down and James Mason played it instead and made a career out of it. It's probably the best thing that Mason has ever done and certainly the best film he's ever been in while poor Granger has never been in a good classic film at all. Or, as far as I remember, in a good film of any kind. You could after all have a 'James Mason Festival' but you couldn't have a 'Stewart Granger' one. Except as a joke. Granger tells the story ruefully against himself. [. . .]

Thursday 25th This was our first night in the newly rented house and not a nice one. [. . .] There was a show on called the *Des O'Connor Show* which is enough to put you off to start with.[155] Immediately there was a reference to me. 'The crown jewels have been stolen.' Only one man can have done it. 'Who?' Richard Burton. 'He doesn't need them, he's got his own.' I had a shouting match with Ed Henry of Universal about Brook's pay for the film. They will not pay him more than $600 a week which is insulting. [. . .] I said how Brook had hung around to do the film and had turned down a play. Henry: 'Why didn't he take it?' Why not indeed. I understand that Colicos is in it.[156] I wonder how he'll like the non-drinking Burton. And how the non-drinking Burton will like him. [. . .] They want me to go up to Oxford for Michaelmas term October 11th to December 5th or Hilary in January until March. What am I going to lecture about? I must write today to Francis Warner and get some direction and hints. What, for instance, does he lecture about? It's a great platform to get rid of a lot of spleen. I can do lethal work on some public figures and clast a few icons. [. . .] I am very lazy. All work is a conscious effort and there is seldom any joy and enthusiasm in it. I could laze for a long time except that I would feel great guilt. I have dreams of living with Elizabeth on the *Kalizma* or a newer bigger vessel though the present one is perfectly adequate, and never living on land again. And moving all the time, a few days here a few days there. Make what is already a decent little library on the yacht into a really splendid one. Leave it only for a couple or three months a year while it's in dry dock and stay alternately in Vallarta and Gstaad. Just us and occasionally the children. Haunt the Mediterranean and search out all kinds of little ports that

---

[153] Brook Williams did play the part of Sergeant Joe Reilly. Christopher Cary (1930–2000) played the part of the 'C.O.' or conscientious objector, Corporal Peter Merrihew. He also played alongside Burton in *Camelot* on Broadway in 1960.

[154] Carol Reed (1906–76), who produced and directed *Odd Man Out* in 1947. Jimmy Granger being the actor Stewart Granger (1913–93), whose real first name was James, and who would play alongside Burton in *The Wild Geese*. James Mason played the leading role of Johnny McQueen.

[155] Des O'Connor (1932—) hosted seven American versions of his show in the summer of 1970.

[156] John Colicos (1928–2000) played Sergeant Major Al MacKenzie.

we've never seen. Work enough just to pay the overheads and only where we can live on the yacht. Seek the sun as much as possible and a little society now and again. Very little. The Rothschilds are our favourites and a weekend at Ferrières perhaps. Annual shopping sprees in Paris for E and gourmet journeys from the boat in the mini-moke. And then one year we could venture out into the Atlantic and work up the coast to Normandy and north to Scandinavia. But preferably remain in and around the countries where I speak the language. Italy Spain France. It costs roughly $110,000 a year to run the boat and keep it in good trim.

The world is in a terrible state of chassis as Joxer has it and I want to watch its chaos from a little distance and make a leisurely and I hope long preparation for death.[157] I love the world and its insanity and despite the fact that I am a highly romantic and passionate man, I find almost all things amusing – especially passion and romance in others. E's and my wildest quarrels are fundamentally ridiculously funny. Certainly in retrospect. And our leaders are without exception grotesquely and ludicrously comical. Brezhnev and Heath, Nixon and Agnew, Fred Kennedy and Humphreys and Pompidou and Willy Brandt and Mao Tse Tung and Cho en Lai and Nasser and Uncle Tom Cobley.[158] Watching Nixon making like a man of destiny on the TV talks to the nations about Cambodia is a divertissement unparalleled. Agnew's prolix and sententious rhodomontade is a national joke, and so is his audience.[159] Enoch Powell, so fantastically like Oswald Mosley intellectually and emotionally that I'm astonished that no one has remarked on it, is a howl.[160] Wilson wrapped in a cocoon of smugness, even in crushing defeat, is a howl. The idea of the queen and all her trappings is high comedy, which reminds me that I have a part in that show shortly when I receive the CBE. There is a great international madness and there always has been but the speed of modern communications accentuates its lunacy and those who don't laugh go mad. Student rebellions, an integral part of our natural history, are either frightening or funny depending on your reaction emotionally. To me they're funny because I know that all those shouting banner-waving little sods are with few

---

[157] A reference to Joxer Daly, a character in Sean O'Casey's (1880–1964) play *Juno and the Paycock* (1924), although the line (the final line in the play) 'th' whole worl's in a terrible state o' chassis' is spoken by Captain Boyle.
[158] Leonid Brezhnev (1906–82), General Secretary of the Communist Party of the Soviet Union (1964–82). Spiro Agnew (1918–96), Vice-President of the USA (1969–73). By 'Fred' Kennedy presumably Burton means Edward 'Ted' Kennedy. By 'Humphreys' presumably he means Hubert Humphrey. Mao Tse Tung (now usually written as 'Zedong') (1893–1976), Chairman of the Chinese Communist Party (1943–76). By Cho en Lai Burton means Zhou Enlai (1898–1976), Premier of the People's Republic of China (1949–76). Uncle Tom Cobley is a character from the song 'Widdecombe Fair' and is often used to suggest 'many others'.
[159] Rodomontade: a vainglorious boasting.
[160] Enoch Powell (1912–98), a Conservative MP and former minister who expressed strong opposition to immigration from Commonwealth countries into Britain, and who later moved to join the Ulster Unionists.

exceptions cop-outs and drop-outs. Like striking miners when I was a kid in the valleys. The union leaders had nothing to lose. The losers were the good miners, the lax and lazy ones were merely searching for a holiday – with no pay perhaps but there were always soup kitchens and a little casual labour building a new Co-op or something.[161] The people who died inside were people like my brothers who wanted to work. The most laughable strikes of all were those in the twenties when the miners went back after prolonged strikes to much less than they got before they struck.[162] The only strikes that really worked were wartime ones. And everybody can shout and bawl as much as they like but they won't change anything fundamental. They will be thrown a scrap or two to stop the barking but human nature is unchanged and unchangeable except over millions of years. There is no difference basically in humanity now than there was 5000 years ago. The same cruelty, the same vices and virtues as ever. The same stupidity and intelligence and in the same proportion. Who can possibly take seriously a student who says 'down with Nixon and Mao for ever' or vice versa. Both are clowns. Neither commands our gravity only our laughter. The 'thoughts of Mao Tse Tung' are a laugh a thought. Nothing can happen overnight.[163] The betterment of mankind will be a triumph of the inevitability of gradualness as the Baron of Passfield said in another context.[164] That is if there's to be a triumph at all. So far the gradualness has been so minutely graded that it is invisible to the naked eye. There must be a holocaust one day soon. All the practical man's hope can be is that he is not at its centre, that he is peripheral and do his duty to survive and if possible see that his family survives with him. Here is one man who firmly believes the world to be a delightful place nicely balanced by its horrors. Without sorrow there can be no joy. True happiness is as transient and as ephemeral as true misery, thank god. Plus ça change plus c'est la même chose.[165] The French, American and Russian revolutions changed nothing. Privilege and money still dominate mankind. 'The Great Experiment' in the USA is a whacking great spiritual and material failure.[166] A handful of men own the country and millions and millions are servants as near to automatons as you can get in a 'free' society. And nothing, but nothing at all can change that great amorphous mass, that limited sprawl, that defined shapelessness. It is not even influenced by the last argument it ever heard. It remains the same. This great anonymous multi-headed mob can not be moved to a new idea. It is impossible to persuade a southern redneck that a negro is a human being. They are

---

[161] Co-operative store.
[162] Burton is referring here to the industrial disputes of 1921 and 1926.
[163] Short quotations encapsulating the doctrine of Maoism were fashionable in leftist circles in the late 1960s and early 1970s.
[164] Sidney Webb, 1st Baron Passfield (1859–1947), Fabian socialist and Labour Party politician, who coined the phrase 'the inevitability of gradualness' in 1923.
[165] The more it changes the more it stays the same.
[166] A reference to the idealism of the founding of the American Republic.

uneducatable. You can only hope to change this atrophying muscle and make it limber by catching its offspring young. Keep a thing for seven years and you may find a use for it, as the proverb has it. Or the jesuitry 'Give me a child until its seven,' or is it 12, 'and he is mine for life'.[167] But even starting now today this minute the process of re-education will take a long time. Only a small percentage of the dumb will be taught to speak and the blind to see and the deaf to hear, therefore the process of re-education will take aeons and aeons. The very system of education must be torn out by the roots and made different, but that itself is so deeply ingrained that it seems impervious to surgery, or transplant. I am convinced that in any group of a hundred people less than a half dozen are capable of fundamental change. They can be easily swayed en masse – I've done it to myself and been swayed – but they are impervious to radical new thoughts. By 'new thoughts' I don't mean new in the sense of original – there is no new thought under the sun – but new in the sense of being new to them, to what they've grown up knowing or not knowing, believing or not believing. I read somewhere that the children of Republicans and Democrats and Tories and Labourites almost inevitably become Republicans and Democrats and Tories and Labourites respectively just like their dads. I remember that when it was rumoured in the family that my brother Dai the Policeman had turned Tory we all thought he'd gone mad. In the recent election in Britain which resulted in what the newspapers called sensationally a Tory landslide and sweeping victory an unprecedented volte face of the electorate turned out to be the indifference of the Labour turn-out.[168] Nobody had changed. Miners didn't go mad and vote for the Tories. They simply didn't vote at all. Labour will inevitably win again when they can get their supporters to get off their asses and away from the TV and make their marks in the appropriate space. Nothing has changed and regardless of any zeal he may possess Mr Heath will soon be sunk by the great apathy. We can be sure that if the world is still in existence in fifty years' time, we can be sure that nothing will have changed. You might be a little poorer or a little richer but nothing will have changed to humanity to any measurable extent.

Friday 26th Am writing this late in the afternoon having stayed upstairs and finished a book about golf and the professional golf tour in the USA called *Pro*

---

[167] A reference to the Jesuit maxim, 'Give me a child for the first seven years, and you may do what you like with him afterwards.'

[168] Turnout at the 1970 general election was 72%, as against 75.8% in 1966. It was to rise to 78.8% at the February 1974 general election. Labour support is generally thought to be more vulnerable than that of the Conservatives to a low turnout, and it was widely predicted by opinion pollsters during the campaign that there would be greater abstention amongst Labour supporters. In fact, as David Butler and Michael Pinto-Duchinsky note in their study *The British General Election of 1970* (1971) (p. 184): 'The actual voting figures . . . give no support to the idea that Labour abstention was the key factor in the results', and suggest that there was a differential turnout of only 1% in the Conservatives' favour.

by a pro golfer called Frank Beard.[169] [...] I was intrigued by the day to day struggle to win the expenses and by the fact that one could after sufficient mastery of the game become a millionaire as people like Palmer, Player, Nicklaus, Casper et al. have.[170] [...]

I read today in the *LA Times* that 'according to biological evolution both humans and sheep – as mammals – have evolved separately, but are derived from a common ancestor that lived aeons ago.' Very apropos of yesterday's entry.

The *Rommel* film is totally chaotic. Nobody knows when I start for sure. [...] I shall fly down on Tuesday which will give me a chance to see Liza before the work starts. [...]

Saturday 27th [...] I read after a month's procrastination the script called *Hammersmith is Out* which P. Ustinov had sent. It is very wild and formless but just the kind of thing that I would like to do at the moment. Particularly as it has a splendid part for E too, and a film for both of us is what we've been looking for for a long time. Ustinov is to direct so that should be alright. He should also play one of the smaller parts.[171] The whole thing begins and ends in a lunatic asylum and my role is a deadly and totally insane killer called Hammersmith. The idea is not new. Who are mad? Those inside the bin or those outside? In this case both. We might be able to shoot it this fall. I have a fear that I may have left it all too late. We shall know within the next few days I suppose. It should be wildly funny and fun to do, especially with somebody as congenial as Ustinov and as brilliant, and might be a big commercial success to boot and spur.

[...] French came to discuss business yesterday at our invitation and was dismissed by E in about three minutes flat. [...] Never mind about a year's time for Chrissake, she said – never taking her eyes off the TV screen where Astaire and Leslie Caron were giving us Daddy Long Legs – lay on *Hammersmith Is Out* and we'll play it by ear from there.[172] [...] She is wholly delightful lately and is beginning to read again. She finished a book for the first time since she went into hospital that age ago. I feel splendid myself as a result. [...]

It's difficult to know how far to go with the students at Oxford without becoming irresponsible and inciting the drop-outs again. I despise them and wish to concede them nothing but sweeping generalizations will include them. What thy hand findeth to do do it with thy might is really the burden of my message, for there is neither wisdom nor device nor knowledge in the grave

[169] Frank Beard (1939—), *Pro* (1970).

[170] Arnold Palmer (1929—); Gary Player (1935—); Jack Nicklaus (1940—); Billy Casper (1931—), all golfers.

[171] Peter Ustinov played the part of the doctor in *Hammersmith Is Out*. Elizabeth Taylor played the part of Jimmie Jean Jackson, and Burton that of Hammersmith.

[172] Leslie Caron (1931—), actor and dancer. *Daddy Long Legs* (1955), film directed by Jean Negulesco.

whither thou goest.[173] I wasted time, said Richard the Second, and now doth time waste me.[174] We have left undone those things we ought to have done.[175] Increasingly as I get older I regret the things that I should have done, regret the black spaces which I could have filled with some knowledge of no use to anybody except me and though I try to make up for lost time my mind is not what it was and its sponge-like ability to soak up new learning and retain it is sadly impaired by dissipation and age. And trying to concentrate is becoming more and more of a task. The imagination is a wilful creature and keeping it under control is an arduous task. [. . .]

Sunday 28th Two more days before I go to Mexico. Tales I hear of the place – San Filipe – are not too encouraging.[176] Mean temp 113. Only two restaurants. Population 800. Shark-infested waters. Hurricane season. Only 33 beds in the whole town for visitors, most people living in caravan trailers and tents. No telephone. Only expert pilots can land there. Otherwise OK.

[. . .] Saw or started to see film last night called *M.A.S.H.* Hated it and left after two reels. We had it shown here in the house [. . .]. The children for the most part enjoyed it – Kate and her friends from next door, two girls and a boy all about 12 to 15 years old. Maria hated it and had nightmares. There was a lot of blood on the screen since the whole thing took place in a Mobile Army Surgical Hospital in Korea and they showed operations and amputations and ligatures and spouts of blood and stitches. I was bored so left. Went to bed and read a 'Travis Magee' thriller by a very competent American writer called John D. Macdonald.[177] He is one of those prolific writers like Simenon and Erle Stanley Gardner and so on who seem to turn out a book a month.[178] Macdonald is a cut above most however and tries to be unsentimentally tough about the decaying morality and mass-production-mania and advertising nightmare of the American way of life. Ends up always with a lump in his throat about the occasional innate nobility of man. Magee is a thoroughly detestable man in his pretended cynicism and muscular pretension and despises with a tired dismissal anybody who is not 'machismo' and 'mucho hombre' and an inexhaustible stud. There are fairly sick-making lines like 'he patted her girl-rump' and 'he responded to the rampant woman in her'. Another occasion for bile is that this Magee – who is enormous 6ft 5 and as fast as a cat – is called 'Trav' by his friends. However, I've learned to skip the sermons when they come up and

---

[173] A reference to Ecclesiastes 9: 10: 'Whatsoever thy hand findeth to do, do it with thy might; for there is no work, nor device, nor knowledge, nor wisdom, in the grave, whither thou goest.'

[174] King Richard speaking in *Richard II*, Act V, scene v.

[175] General Confession from Morning Prayer in the *Book of Common Prayer* (1662): 'We have left undone those things which we ought to have done'.

[176] San Felipe, Baja California, Mexico.

[177] John D. Macdonald (1916–86), who wrote a 21-vol. series featuring the character Travis Magee.

[178] Erle Stanley Gardner (1889–1970), who published under many pseudonyms and created the character Perry Mason.

the yarns and the inconsequential but authentic seeming descriptive back-grounds are very readable. I envy anyone's capacity for such sustained and for the most part sound writing. If he wrote one book a year instead of ten he could be considerable. I don't think I could write a thriller. I don't think I want to even if I could. Such books are meant to be read, not written. Read fast and quickly forgotten and therefore readable again in a couple of years.

Oh to be in Europe, now that I have to go to work. I want to go everywhere at once. I want simultaneously to be watching the road to Santa Marguerita from Porto Fino through Zeiss binoculars while sunning on the poop deck of the *Kalizma*. I want to be sitting in front of a log fire in Gstaad in the library in the evening with a rich book in my lap and E in the chair beside me. Baked ham and au gratin potatoes in Gruyere in that hotel there. Trout at the top of Les Diablerets. Raclette in the Olden in Gstaad. More trout in Weissenbach in the restaurant by the river and the canopied wooden bridge. Saddle of lamb in La Réserve. Hors d'oeuvres in La Ferme above Beaulieu or in D'Chez Eux in Paris. Moules Marinieres in La Mediterranea opposite the Opera. Haddock filet a L'Anglaise at Fouquets. Omelette Arnold Bennett on the terrace of the Terrace Suite of the Dorchester on a fine day looking over the park on a Sunday with one powerful bloody Mary under my belt and that beauty always beside me and around. Raw fave and salami and white wine and a game of boule with E in the trattoria underneath the church on the hill outside Rome on the side road from De Laurentiis' studios to the Raccordo Annulare where the choir chants at 7 in the evening.[179] A car tour of the Michelin 3 star restaurants. Annecy and Beaumaniere and a couple of nights at The Hotel de la Poste at Avallon, can that be right?

Have just heard from Hugh French that Ustinov is ecstatic about our enthusiasm re *Hammersmith is Out*. Shall have a quick word with Peter's partner Alex Lucas, I think, today at lunch.[180]

JULY

Friday 3rd, San Felipe, Mexico Drove into Mexicali yesterday, took a room for the day at the Lucerna Hotel, phoned Elizabeth, borrowed a bell-boy from the hotel and raided supermarkets for food and bits and pieces for the apartment here.[181] It was delicious talking to E. I had wondered why I felt so peculiarly lost without her this time of parting as we have been apart before for a couple of weeks – when I was in Geneva two years ago and Ivor had his accident and two or three years before that when she went to California when her dad had his stroke and a few days when she went to Paris for the funeral of Gaston's

---

[179] By 'fave' Burton means fava beans, also known as broad beans.
[180] Alex Lucas would produce *Hammersmith Is Out*.
[181] Mexicali, state capital of Baja California, and on the border between Mexico and the USA.

son – but suddenly realized why I felt so lonely this time. Reason being that before we were always able to talk on the blower but not so from here. So for the first time in my life I appreciated the normally despised telephone, I talked to her twice in a couple of hours! She will be here in a couple of days. Hip! Hip! Michael! She said she missed me as badly as I missed her and that she mooned about at night and felt almost tearful over a pair of my socks that she saw hanging about. [. . .]

I feel extraordinarily fit since I talked to her and feel as young as 25 or something. Stopping drinking is the best thing I've ever done for my physical well-being. Twice since I arrived I was immensely tempted to have a drink – once when I was alone. This is the kind of place and the kind of situation where one is naturally driven to booze. Waiting for the film to start, waiting for the tanks and guns etc. to get here, the uncertainty of the Mexican immigration [. . .]

However, we do start work tomorrow so they told me last night.

I have been learning the German I have to speak in the film from a German actor who plays the part of Schröder.[182] He invented the reason for yawning. He is so boring that it is almost hypnotic. All I ask him to do is speak the lines for me and I will write it down phonetically in my own way and then learn the whole thing off like a machine-rattle. BUT he expatiates on every line. 'I do not zee Cherman think would say to a check-point man dese thinks mit deses words'. So doing a page of script consisting of perhaps 3 lines of German for me, takes a full hour. I faint with ennui. 'I disapproove of all military thinks and should not be doing ziss film but one must work I suppose and you are much admired in my country.' He has a great soft white face and refuses to go into the sun, and a large elephantine bum and belly. He is most unattractive and his smile is horrifying. He gives the impression of unredeemable smugness. But the new Burton says 'Yes, I see, of course, quite, See your point. Yes "krankenhaus" ' is right but you think a cultured German might say "Hospital" with the accent on the last syllable so good let's say that because our chief public for the picture are English-speaking and it's good if they recognize a word that is common to both languages.' instead of: 'Look, just speak the bloody lines for me and bugger off.' I am so tolerant and understanding that I frequently give myself a nasty turn.

I am still surprised and pleased at the impact of my name on people. I arrived (with Brook) at the Hotel in Mexicali, unannounced, yesterday and within minutes was waited on hand and foot. The people in the supermarkets – we went to three altogether – were without exception delighted to see me, and all proffered advice on where to go and what to buy and all seemed delighted that I spoke Spanish. I like being famous. I wonder how I'll feel when I'm not. After twenty years of it now and a further few years I suppose it will

---

[182] Karl-Otto Alberty (1933—) played the part of Captain Heinz Schröder. He would also play alongside Burton in *Bluebeard*.

feel very strange to be R. Jenkins again as it were. The manager of the hotel reserved a room for us at the hotel – a suite I mean, which is three rooms in effect, – even though it's his biggest week-end of the year, being the 4th of July. The young boy, terribly pretty and looking about 15 but is actually 21 and answering to the name of David was in his seventh heaven showing us around the shop calling out to his friends as we passed them in the hired Impala which I drove. 'Gustavo, Como 'sta?' He was a proper little lord for a day. 'I will be waiting for you when you come back and I will tresore your Elizabeth Taylor,' he assured me when I left.

Saturday 4th, San Felipe, Baja California [. . .] It's the first day of the film and everybody is more nervous than usual because of Hathaway's reputation as a shit of the first water once the film starts rolling. Yesterday he had a dress parade and it was every bit as realistic as a real inspection by a real commanding officer in a real war. The poor actors were terrified out of their wits. He bawled and screamed and cursed. Colicos was ordered to have his hair cut not once but three times. Side-boards had to be trimmed to the top of the ear-line which is difficult for some of the other actors as our film is so short in schedule and quite a few of them are off to do other films in which they wear long modern hair within a few weeks. [. . .]

We tried to go to dinner last night, Bob Wilson, Brook and Ron Berk, to a restaurant called 'Reuben's' which is in a trailer park on the beach on the far side of town, but curiosity-seekers and a group of hippies very high on pot drove us away and to the anonymity of our protected motel.[183] One immensely tall young man with the lost eyes of the hopelessly stoned tried like a man in a nightmare to put something in my pocket. Ron got him away. He was trying to give me a 'joint' i.e. a marijuana cigarette. Ron said to him after having wrestled him away 'It's very kind of you and Mr Burton appreciates it but he doesn't use them.' [. . .]

I was also driven off the beach yesterday where I was sitting reading a book called *An American Melodrama* by three English writers from the *Sunday Times* called Chester, Hodgson and Page.[184] Everything was alright for about two hours. I had walked with E'en So for a couple of miles along the beach and had had a couple of dips in the ocean, reading between times when suddenly I was surrounded by a crowd of people who simply stared. Jacques Charon (a French Professor of Art from Berkeley) came over [to] rescue me, and I went indoors for the rest of the day.

[. . .] A letter from Buck House arrived yesterday telling me of the investiture on the 28th of July.[185] I shan't be able to be there so other arrangements

---

[183] Ruben's Campground Hotel, San Felipe.
[184] Lewis Chester, Godfrey Hodgson and Bruce Page, *An American Melodrama: The Presidential Campaign of 1968* (1969).
[185] Buckingham Palace.

will have to be made. It can be done by a vice-consul I understand which will be much more satisfactory and much less fuss. I shall try to arrange that.

[. . .] I have become so obsessed lately with the hopelessness of any rebel-lion against authority that I can only assume that I have come to a sort of climacteric. I read the political page every day and am continually astounded by what I read. To read an intelligent man like William Buckley writing of Nixon with reverence![186] [. . .] I shall learn my languages, live at ease, look after my wife and family and deride all else. I love the world and shall be reluctant to leave it but if I take it seriously I shall go mad. I must regard it all as a vast cosmic joke. Even his infrequent bursts of nobility can be attributed to a self hypnotized conceit, – I mean man's. I am infinitely more lucky than billions of my fellow men and that is the only fact that awes me.

I am going out on the set to see the film begin and wish luck to my fellow prisoners. This film shows every sign of being the most eccentric I've been in for a long time. Perhaps since the *Night of the Iguana*. Hathaway said yesterday to a perfect stranger who was sitting in the bar: 'Get your goddamn hair cut and get rid of those goddamn side-boards. How many goddamn times do I have to tell you?' The innocent was an astonished tourist.

[. . .]

Sunday 5th, Lucerna Hotel, Mexicali Am in 'unit' 114 of the above hotel which is quite nice and air conditioned and room-serviced and indistinguishable from its USA counterpart.[187] [. . .] I talked immediately to Elizabeth when we got in. I'd forgotten what a sweet voice she has and how very young she sounds on the phone. She is coming on Tuesday with all the maniacs. I'm longing but longing to see her. [. . .] It seems that Hathaway gave the German actor Karl-Otto Something a dreadful time yesterday and did 57 takes on one scene, most of which takes were cut by Hathaway on the first line with suitable endear-ments like 'You are the goddamnest stupidest actor I've ever met.' Lucky I wasn't there. Such behaviour against a defenceless small-part player makes me angry to the point of blindness. Even a <u>German</u> small-part player. I talked on the beach to Greyn's girl friend who seems very nice and very intelligent and to Danielle De Metz who seems nice but not so intelligent [. . .].[188]

[. . .] This Hotel-Motel is very crowded and I had to settle for a room instead of a suite. What an eccentric idea of a holiday people have to spend it in a shabby hotel in the middle of a hideous town in intense airless heat with the only reliefs being to stay in the box-like rooms with the air-conditioning going full blast or to dip into the pool with scores of other people – the pool

---

[186] William F. Buckley (1925–2008), political columnist and writer.
[187] Hotel Lucerna, Boulevard Benito Juarez, Mexicali.
[188] Clinton Greyn (1936—), Welsh actor. Danielle De Metz (1938—) played the part of Vivi in *Raid on Rommel*.

being no larger than a very large bath-tub which is full of screaming children. Much better to camp out at San Felipe or stay at home and eat out of a can. The herd instinct is extraordinary. Like those people at home in Britain who will drive for hours bumper to bumper in a holiday traffic-jam to park finally on a grass verge take out the collapsible tables and chairs and picnic amongst the fumes while watching the jam go by before placidly joining it again. [. . .]

Monday 6th, San Felipe Talked to E again yesterday morning. She is coming in with kids on Tuesday and one would think I'd been away from her for ten years for I'm so excited. [. . .]

I feel terribly lazy. Having wanted to work theoretically for months I now don't want to do it at all. [. . .]

I read late last night – still that same book *An American Melodrama* which really should be called *An American Nightmare*. Politics is a filthy game but American politics are the filthiest of the lot I suppose because of the lip service that has to be paid to the American Dream and the anti-negro south. Lying is obligatory even from the most honourable men – at the very least even men like Adlai Stevenson and Eugene McCarthy had to lie by omission, if nothing else.[189] How could a Stevenson or a McCarthy or a Bobby Kennedy tolerate for one second the demagogues of the 'nigger-hating' South were it not for the fact that they had to garner Southern votes? The politician in Britain stands a slightly better chance of remaining honest but only slightly. Some of course are out-and-out liars on simple matters of fact, like Reagan for instance.[190] To quote him at a fund-raising dinner in Minneapolis he said 6 policemen had been killed in Chicago that year (1968) whereas it was actually one. This was pointed out to one of his spokesmen. 'Gov. Reagan stands by his text' was the reply.

[. . .] All the bars are closed because it's Election day. Luis Echeverria Alvarez is the President. Jim told me that General Barragan has given me a five-foot sword and that therefore I must do a costume picture in which I can use it. I shall wear it as Don Quixote and trip over it a lot. Jim also said that Echeverria was already and had been for a long time thoroughly 'bought'. 'What's new?' I said. Barragan is in Mexico City in case of student rebellion etc. Have heard nothing yet. I hope they keep quiet. It won't get them anywhere and he'll kill them for sure.

It's the usual glorious day. I am full of coffee and idleness and am writing this more to fill in space than anything else and to avoid reading the script and learning the German and my daily stint of Spanish. [. . .]

---

[189] Eugene McCarthy (1916–2005), US Senator (1959–71) and sometime candidate for the Democratic nomination for the presidency.
[190] Ronald Reagan (1911–2004), at this time Governor of California, former film actor, and future President of the United States (1981–9).

Tuesday 7th A typical film day. I went out twenty minutes before time and was at the location by 10.40. I waited until 5 o'clock in the afternoon before I worked. I drove a half-track pretending to be unconscious at the wheel and weaving my way across the desert.[191] It was my only shot. I was dismissed for the day and came straight home and under the shower. Did not feel like going out to the restaurant so stayed in and grapple-snapped and read the *LA Times* and switched between the political book and a thriller called *The Naked Runner*.[192] [. . .]

This Hathaway is fairly mindless as a director. He doesn't give the actors any respite between shots. Brook and the others sat on the back of a truck for several hours yesterday with a break only for lunch. Brook says that most of the time they weren't even seen. I simply don't understand that kind of mentality though I mentioned yesterday that a man who so patently couldn't care less whether he was liked or not couldn't be all bad.

[. . .] I have a lot to do in the mornings and if I don't work then I don't work for the rest of the day. I cannot, as some people, work between shots in the caravan. [. . .] I find it difficult even to do a crossword, though I will try today. Can't even read with enjoyment and it isn't as if I'm thinking about the next scene or something. I don't think about the film at all until I'm forced to. Not just this film – any film. Or play for that matter. Other actors fuss all day long and enjoy it. My heart sinks at the thought of a rehearsal. 'Where's the camera, where's my marks, what're my lines' is my attitude. Elizabeth's too as far as I know. Rex Harrison for instance will run lines all day long and, it seems to me, get more and more inhibited the more he rehearses. I have my first big scene today and have only read the scene twice. I have to lie there and pretend to be suffering from shock and dehydration. The scene is a couple of pages long and is likely to be uncomfortable in that heat though the more physically uncomfortable the better.

Somebody said what a thrill it was to act with me. 'Thank you,' I said lamely. I think you and Peter Ustinov and Orson Welles are the best actors in the world, they said. I thought you were marvellous in *Look Back in Anger* but obviously you walked through *Anne of the Thousand Days* didn't you. 'Well, not exactly,' I said, 'not – er – exactly.' Ah I could tell, said the other. [. . .] Gives one a bit of a turn, especially after the overpraise of the performance. [. . .]

Wednesday 8th A horrible day. The heat in the desert was insufferable and I spent half the day lying in the sand with my mouth agape pretending to be unconscious while the sand, stirred up by the wind which was blowing in exactly the wrong direction, blew up my nose and into my mouth. However

---

[191] The opening shot of the film.
[192] Francis Clifford, *The Naked Runner* (1965). 'Grapple-snapping': a family term for snacking from the refrigerator.

I was excited at seeing E so I was stoically good-natured. The plane carrying E and the kids and Norma buzzed a couple of times and I panted with impatience to finish and get home. Like all things too eagerly awaited the meeting was a fiasco. I arrived and tore into the 'suite' and there was nobody there! Kate came in and said 'Hi' and went out again. Somebody had turned the air-conditioning off and the living room was like an oven. E came prancing in and we hugged and kissed though I was filthy and covered with grease and sand and wasn't very huggable. Immediately everybody started making cracks about San Felipe and what a terrible place it was, and one would have thought they had attacked Pontrhydyfen – I was so defensive. Never has a man been so chauvinistic about a shit-house. I feebly pointed out the beauty of its beach, and lamely said the sea was wonderful. Kate said it was too warm and it was like taking a hot bath. I lamely and bravely said that there were horses for hire. I said it was much more cosmopolitan than Bucerias which is like saying that hell is better than purgatory. We went in a sullen silence to dinner at Reuben's [. . .]. E made me as jealous as vengeance earlier on by saying that she'd called Marlon on the phone and that they had talked for an hour and that he was very solicitous about me. He really is a smugly pompous little bastard and is cavalier about everybody except Black Panthers and Indians.[193] 'He's been keeping tabs on you,' said E. That infuriated me even more. That sober self-indulgent obese fart being solicitous about me. You can't get any of those surrounded-by-sycophants one-time-winners on the phone unless they want something from you. Sinatra is the same. Gods in their own mirrors. Distorted mirrors. [. . .]

Thursday 9th Yesterday was a lovely day. I left for work for the day at 7.00 and E came with me, despite the heat [. . .] she stayed until after lunch [. . .]. Everyone was delighted that she was there and everybody said afterwards that it was the best day they've had on the film yet. Hathaway was mellow by his usual standards and at one point when he started screaming at one of the actors I told him he was mistaken and that he had told the actor to move earlier. He said 'Goddamn it I did not.' 'Goddamn it, you did,' I said. 'I apologize,' he said to the actor. Everybody was astounded and one chap said to Ron that it was the first time in thirty years of working with Hathaway that he'd ever known him apologize to anybody. So I was a little hero, the leader of my little band, the little Robert Emmet.[194] Elliott Kastner arrived with 'Dirty' Brian Hutton who very sweetly drove the former all the way from LA in his Mercedes.[195] That's 6 to 8 hours hard driving. Both were exhausted particularly Elliott as he had flown over the Pole the same day I believe. Elliott brought a

---

[193] Marlon Brando gave financial support to the Black Panthers and also spoke out in support of the rights of Native Americans.
[194] Robert Emmet (1778–1803), United Irishman and leader of the 1803 Irish rebellion.
[195] Brian Hutton (1935—) had directed *Where Eagles Dare* and would direct Elizabeth Taylor in *X, Y and Zee*.

script called *Plea for Defense* or some courtroom title which is going to be changed.[196] It is a racy sadistic London piece about cops and robbers – the kind of 'bang bang – calling all cars' stuff that I've always wanted to do and never have. It could be more than that depending on the director. I play a cockney gangland leader who is very much a mother's boy and takes her to Southend and buys her whelks etc. but in the Smoke am a ruthless fiend incarnate but a homosexual as well.[197] All ripe stuff. And over in a minute. They can do me entirely in five weeks, possibly six. He has a much more significant piece for Elizabeth – an original screenplay by Edna O'Brien but it will not be finished until next week.[198] He says that E's could shoot at the same time as mine which wouldn't be a bad idea. It would also be in London. *Hammersmith Is Out* could go at the end of the year and E wants a bloke who is very hot at the moment called Robert Redford.[199] She says he's very good but won't be available until the end of the year which would be very suitable. London in the fall can be lovely and the thought of Europe is very stimulating. I shall watch us to note how soon we'll want to come back to this hemisphere again. We are both a pair of old nomads. Since taking our Sabbatical we have lived in Switzerland, France, (Evian), Monte Carlo, Hawaii, Vallarta, Beverly Hills, Vallarta again, Beverly Hills, Malibu, Beverly Hills, Palm Springs, Malibu and now San Felipe. Otherwise we haven't moved a step.

Buckley says in an article yesterday in the *LA Times*. 'If ever I saw firmness and justice tempered with mercy epitomized in one man, that man is Ronald Reagan.'

And talking of politics: Norma Heyman says that the feeling in the country at Wilson's defeat was indescribably joyous. She said it was like VJ day or something or Mafeking Night.[200] Everybody suddenly burst out singing type of reaction.[201] Poor old Wilson. I can't believe that the Labour rank-and-file felt like that and she is talking only of her particular social circle, which is not the most stable, but it is surprising nevertheless. She said that Heath, who has always been as dull as rust, positively sparkled when she saw him give a speech on TV. The office is making the man again I suppose, as so often before. [. . .] Modern politics is such that, if you never read the papers or watched TV and lived in a market town you would not have known or know which party was or had been in power in the last twenty years. The differences between them have been so indiscernible. The strikes show a fine impartiality, the cost of

[196] James Barlow's 1968 novel was called *The Burden of Proof.* The film title was changed to *Villain.*
[197] Southend-on-Sea, Essex. 'The Smoke': London.
[198] Edna O'Brien (1930—), novelist and screenwriter. This was published in 1971 under the title *Zee & Co* and became the film of that name (in the USA), titled *X, Y and Zee* in Britain.
[199] Robert Redford (1937—).
[200] VJ Day: to mark Victory over Japan in the Second World War. Mafeking Night refers to the celebrations in Britain when news was received in May 1900 of the relief of the British garrison of Mafeking during the South African War of 1899–1902.
[201] Refers to Siegfried Sassoon's poem, 'Everyone Sang' (1918).

living likewise, the unemployment figures remain the same, the health service and the railroads and the public services are the same with only tiny fluctuations. Once in the Common market if we ever go in, nobody will notice that there is much difference except that money is still hard to come by.[202] It's all a load of old cobblers as the boys say. [. . .]

Friday 10th [. . .]I did not work until after lunch [. . .]. Up and down a road waiting to be strafed by a plane – no plane will appear of course, that has already been shot. We had a full house yesterday morning with Kastner, Hutton, Romany Bain and Norma all in the one room.[203] Agreed to do Elliott's film subject to dates of *Hammersmith* which will be alright I should think to allow us to shoot former starting 14th September. Will do *Hammersmith* straight after presumably. He will get E's script to her shortly he says with Brian directing. Brook acquired himself a couple of extra lines yesterday by fast thinking. He had noticed that 'Brown' had a couple of lines to say to me but had been placed in another truck of the convoy.[204] Therefore when Hathaway said to Sevareid who was sitting next to me on the lorry 'D'you know the lines' Brook said 'I do Mr Hathaway.'[205] And they were his. He swapped places with the hapless Sevareid and got his face in lots more shots. Thinking all the time, that's our Brookie.

I lunched here at the motel with Bain and Elizabeth and the publicity man Walter. He is a negro and very pretty and intelligent. He says his wife has many white relatives and that the only time they acknowledge each other is when they commonly meet at funerals. The white half, when they have to, refer to the coloured half by their Christian names while they insist on being called by their surnames. Prejudice within the family because of different skin pigmentation is a new one on me. [. . .] The girls are full of giggles and are going through a dirty mind stage. Kate says things like 'Oh Pisspots' when she loses at Yahtsee. The film goes on apace and so far we seem to be well within schedule. [. . .] Hathaway is very careful of my comfort and, since I began shooting, has been pretty good with the first horrifying day with the German Karl Otto Alberty. He is still rough on the latter, but it has become a joke more than the terror that it was.

Kate leaves today to go to LA and tomorrow to NY. I can kiss goodbye to innocence. When we see her next she will be a teenager and the child will have gone for ever. It is unfortunate that sweet as Sybil can be that Kate picks up Syb's platitudinous lack of thought. One is aware all the time of half thought

---

[202] The 'Common Market' was a familiar phrase at that time, used to describe what was then termed the European Economic Community, which the United Kingdom would join in 1973.

[203] Romany Bain was a showbusiness journalist.

[204] This refers to the part of Brown played by Greg Mullavey (1932—).

[205] Michael Sevareid (1940—) played the part of Wembley, so it is likely that Burton is confused here over the real name of the actor playing Brown.

judgements on a great many things – from poetry to politics. I have told her that nobody knows what poetry is – she obviously could have a passion for it as I have, and has the ear – but that it can only be known to those who recognize it. She said that Rod McKuen was an awful poet.[206] I asked her if she'd read him. She said no she hadn't. Well, I told her she was quite right but that she should read him first and decide for herself. Pompous as pride I was and am. [. . .]

Saturday 11th 6.20 and the children are already over from their rooms so the usual morning peace is shattered. Liza wants to come to work with me principally I suppose because I said that yesterday I saw a mare with its foal standing under the shade of a tree in the desert on the road to the location. I took Kate to the plane – the airstrip is a dirt strip between the town and the mountains – and off she went. I felt a bit funny as ever. [. . .]

[. . .] A letter arrived from Cis saying how pleased she was with the CBE and saying that she enjoyed the 'Frost' show but that her grandchildren were annoyed that I described her as 'old'. [. . .]

It seems that we've been here for ten weeks and not ten days. The heat to which we are all thoroughly acclimatized is tremendous. And humid with it. Were it not for air-conditioning it would be a case of continual sweat morning noon and night. [. . .] The work consisted of throwing a German across a truck while four or five of my men render him unconscious. Next stint was jumping off the back of the lorry. Today there will be knifing in the back and lots of firing etc. Might even get to say a few jokes.

We dined at 'Arnold's' but almost as soon as we sat down to eat the main fuse blew and we ate in candlelight and air-conditionless until it became too insufferable.[207] As the waiters brought in the candles a cockney man called John Orchard sang 'Ave Maria'.[208]

Sunday 12th Woke early [. . .] from a dream in which E and I could not get anybody to put up money for any film we wanted to do. Refused to put up and actually withdrew money already committed if we had anything to do with a film. We were outcasts and were forced to go to the theatre, where again we were refused employment. The dream or nightmare wasn't as coherent as that and vivid faces came and went and was obviously prompted by 'producer's talk' yesterday with Harry Tatelman and Hathaway, but I was relieved to wake up.[209]

Yesterday was my first really full day on the film. I shot all day long, killing a man, firing machine-guns, jumping off half-tracks, jumping on lorries,

206 Rod McKuen (1933—).
207 Hotel Arnold's Del Mar, San Felipe.
208 John Orchard (1928–95) played the part of Dan Garth.
209 Harry Tatelman (1914–97), the producer of *Raid on Rommel*.

running across the sand in the boiling heat. It was an early day as the Mexicans insist on a straight through no-stopping-for-lunch-only-a-grabbed-sandwich day until 2.00. Starting shooting at 8am. This is a good day, and could well be done every day. A no-lunch day starting on the set at 8 in the morning and finishing at 3 in the afternoon would suit me fine. [. . .]

As for the nightmare – it cannot exist in reality for either of us – we are both too good at our jobs, and too rich and too famous. The producers are starting to line up again and 'stars' are coming back into fashion, after several failed attempts to repeat *Easy Rider* and other small-budget pictures.[210] Actually for people with our command we are just coming into the millennium. If this pic or the next or the one after gross an average of $4 million each which is pessimistic, I could 'walk away with' 3 or 4 million dollars. If they were biggish grossers I could take 5 or 6. If one of them was a smash I would make 7 or 8 millions. There is, in fact, no known series of accidents that I can think of that could impoverish us even if we never worked again. Even a large war – as long as it wasn't the ultimate catastrophe – if we survived it, would leave us rich, perhaps even richer in this insane world. Even if we both died this afternoon our children would be more than adequately provided for. Materialistically, we could hardly have done any better for our families. He said, smugly.

The present state of the industry is bad luck on the johnny-come-latelies unless they are quickly and enormously established. The latest 'stars' like Elliott Gould and Hoffman etc. have had bad luck in starting to hit the jackpot while it is empty. Hoffman of course is so brilliant that the state of the industry is a matter of indifference to him but people like Elliott Gould are by no means so clever and smack of being one-shot artists and might well fall on their asses. [. . .]

Liza is growing up into a sweet little lady and is going through a heart-breakingly vulnerable stage, very aware of boys and thinks she's ugly and unattractive and so on. I feel enormously protective and am worrying already that she is going to be hurt before long by some dashing idiot. She came to work with me yesterday and stayed the whole time despite the boredom and the fact that we couldn't find the horse and foal. She is frequently in day-dreams of some kind and has to be brought back to attention with an affectionate snap of the fingers. I wonder what she thinks about apart from the beloved Derby Day the VII.[211]

E is fat but happy. I suppose she'll have to start watching her weight before she starts the next film, but she's very jolly as she is. The camera is cruel however so five or ten pounds will have to come off.

---

[210] *Easy Rider* (1969), directed by Dennis Hopper (1936–2010).
[211] Possibly the name of Liza's horse. Taylor's second husband, Michael Wilding, had starred in the film *Derby Day* (1952).

Monday 13th [. . .] The rest of yesterday was a classical Sunday – a read and a doze and love in the afternoon, a crossword puzzle (Penguin *Sunday Telegraph* Collection) grapplesnaps and tea and an early dinner over in the restaurant and to bed about 9.00 with a John D. MacDonald and asleep by 10.30.

[. . .] There is a terrific amount of drunkenness in the bar after work is over, I'm told and two separate cliques have quickly formed. The Germans on one side and the British-Americans on the other. Brook says he wouldn't be surprised if there was a bit of a punch-up one of these days. Neither would I. Even in Stratford-upon-Avon I remember tempers getting frayed and a lot of snarling after the actors had been stuck together for ten months in one small town. Lucky it's only another three weeks or less here. I remember too in Tripoli doing *Bitter Victory* that I ended up by knocking Nigel Green about a bit, and he me.[212]

Elizabeth took the sun very well yesterday [. . .]. She has remarkable recuperative powers and has confounded the doctors [. . .]. When she loses a little flab she'll also look fitter than she has for years. Her sexual appetite is as eager as ever and so is mine though I don't think either of us attaches the urgent importance to it that we used to. I had a fear that the complete cessation of drink would decrease my sex desire, and so it did for a time probably because I concentrated so much on stopping the alcohol that everything else became diffuse – I had difficulty in concentrating on reading for instance – and I found that my mind raced and flitted from thing to object to idea at a bewildering speed. Now that the poison is nearly out of my system – I'm told it takes six months to dry out totally – I can think clearly again. I don't see the world whole, but I see it steadily. I have lost the hungover nightmarish fear of imminent disaster and early deaths and all its concomitants and am better balanced. [. . .] I think that in about two or three months I'll be able to settle down to a sustained piece of writing and in this new sober world I don't have the desperate urgency that I used to have that I would never do anything with any permanence, even semi-permanence. Now slowly, I believe I can, and not through writing novels which is a most unreal form to me. Novels are tricky and artificial and contrived and apart from the very great ones are all bedside reading. When I finish this piece I will try again.

Tuesday 14th [. . .] I worked until lunch-time yesterday [. . .]. I spoke my first German in the film and had a film-long speech and scene with Clinton Greyn who is not a very good actor I'm afraid. He is tall and good-looking in a kind of weak way with a voice that threatens to become prissy when he presses. I wish Hathaway would let him be more casual. I play my part with a ping-pong-no-damned-nonsense rapidity and he cannot match me when he tries to

---

[212] Nigel Green (1924–72) had played Private Wilkins in *Bitter Victory*. He had also appeared in *Zulu*.

do it. His voice is sibilant when he has a few esses flying about a sentence. Hathaway however is asking him to do things that don't accord with his personality – it's like asking the late Leslie Howard to be dynamic and harsh and clipped and furious.[213]

Today the film gets hot with guns firing, flame-throwers flaming hand-grenades grenading as I and the commandos teach the medics how to be men at arms. I heard good news yesterday that I may be out of here by the 26th of this month. That's a couple of weeks and will get us out of this long hot American summer and home to cool Europe. I am looking forward to going by train and lunch in the Pump Room in the Ambassador East in Chicago and paperbacks on the train and stupendous breakfasts while the States wheel by the windows. Read the various regional papers and all that and what comics do they have and which political boys do they syndicate.

[. . .] Last night I was lying on the bed doing a double-crostic and looked up a quotation in the paperbacked *Quotation Dictionary* that I carry around with me specifically for that purpose. I immediately became lost in the book and read all the Shakespeare ones right through very slowly. There was hardly a line there that I didn't immediately know but seeing the miraculous words in print again doomed me to a long trance of nostalgia, a stupor of melancholy, like listening to really massive music, music that moans and thunders and plumbs fathomless depths. I wandered through the book for a long time but no other writer hit me with quite the same impact as William S. What a stupendous God he was, he is. What chance combination of genes went to the making of that towering imagination, that brilliant gift of words, that staggering compassion, that understanding of all human frailty, that total absence of pomposity, that wit, that pun, that joy in words and the later agony. It seems that he wrote everything worth writing and the rest of his fraternity have merely fugued on his million themes. [. . .]

Wednesday 15th [. . .] Showered and shampooed after work and had an early dinner (7 o'clock) with Liza and Maria and Brook. [. . .] Then read on the bed while Maria did some sums in arithmetic and then read me a few pages from a book. She really does read now, not just remember from previous readings. I shall work with her every day and try to turn her into a bookworm. It would be nice to have a fellow bookworm in the family. She is a darling little child. I don't know why I worry about her so much.

I read yesterday in the *LA Times* that Frankie Sinatra has 'come out for Reagan'.[214] That's like Laurel coming out for Hardy. I shouldn't think either of them has had a thought of their own in their lives except about themselves.

---

[213] Leslie Howard (1893–1943), actor, renowned for playing archetypal English gentlemen.
[214] Sinatra had made a statement on 9 July that he was supporting Ronald Reagan in his bid for a second term as Governor of California.

Frank was asked by Haber of the *Times*, 'Knowing your justly deserved magnanimity and interest in charitable organizations and support for ethnic minorities and the under-privileged etc., how do you feel about Governor Reagan's slashing of the funds for the aged and the blind by $10 million?' 'Has he done that?' said Frankie, 'I must talk to him about that.'[215] Big, as they say, fuckin' deal. If we hear shortly that Reagan has only cut the aid-fund to $9,900,000 we shall know that Francis Albert Sinatra's fine Sicilian hand has been behind it again. All either of 'em can do is count – using their fingers of course. Hathaway suggests that it's pique on Frankie's part. He was given the brush-off by Jack Kennedy. 'Don't call us Frankie, we'll call you,' he is reputed to have said to Frankie who had been plaguing him with phone-calls after he was President. Even Frankie however, despite his monomania, should be able to see that Reagan is patched cardboard and dangerously stupid. Now let's hope that Jesse Unruh beats him in November and leaves Frank with egg on his face again.[216] Silly sod.

Read the first act of *Much Ado about Nothing* last night before turning out the lights. Delightful. I must <u>read</u> William more often and not merely quote him to myself. There is a peculiar and tangible satisfaction from actually seeing the words on the page defying mortality.

Thursday 16th [. . .] I worked steadily from 7.45 until just before 3 after noon, driving endlessly up and down a desert road chatting away to Clinton Greyn and John Colicos. It's odd that I cannot define what a good actor has, what quality or style but I can tell a bad actor immediately, and Clinton Greyn is bad. Colicos is slightly above average good and could in the right part be more than that, but Greyn is difficult to imagine good or forceful in anything. [. . .]

Elizabeth has been away for two days now and doesn't come back 'til Saturday and I miss her all the time. I love getting up in the morns and typing or reading to suddenly find that she's got up too and is having a screwdriver or a Bloody Mary or a salty dog. And generally making a nuisance of herself. [. . .]

Friday 17th [. . .] The acting in this film is very bad and I can only hope that there are enough explosions to kill the worst of it, or at least to take the attention away from it. Something better could be done with Greyn who is the worst offender but there is simply no time in a piece of this kind and there is the suspicion that it wouldn't improve things much anyway. He is, as Brook points out, a typically mediocre Rep actor and there's nowt one can do about that except re-write the entire thing to suit Greyn's personality. He should never have been cast in the first place. But nobody expects a masterpiece and

---

[215] Joyce Haber (1931–93), Hollywood columnist for the *LA Times*.
[216] Jesse Unruh (1922–87), Democratic politician in California (Speaker of the State Assembly, 1961–9) and in 1970 unsuccessful candidate for Governor.

by the time it's out I shall have forgottenabout it. Colicos is heavily dramatic all the time though he is much better than Greyn and can be directed quite quickly into a more casual approach. He'll be alright I suppose. Brook did a couple of good bits yesterday and I was very pleased.

Tomorrow comes Snapshot back to me and life will be richer again and a bit more mad. Without her I could quite easily become a recluse and be seen only fugitively, half glimpsed in distant villages like the Scholar Gypsy.[217] I dined with Liza, Brook and Maria (who forgot to come and do her lessons last night) and read *The Arms of Krupp* in bed until lights out at 10 o'clock.[218] The Krupp story is a fascinating story and in a sense is the history of modern Germany but Manchester, the writer, is a vulgarian and a cheap writer and the book suffers. A pity as it could have been a superb work and William Manchester obviously did extensive research. It's a shame when a man capable of such labour as Manchester is hasn't learned to write and doesn't have a friend who could edit it ruthlessly for him. Example: 'This Alfred (Krupp) found as funny as a crutch.'[219] Infuriatingly silly.

I was thinking yesterday as I saw everyone wilting in the heat and complaining about it how much stronger I feel than other people. I feel that I could go on for days while others fall beside the wayside, and have always thought so. I wonder if that accounts for Ivor's and my contempt and intolerance of weakness in others. Ivor's belief that one is ill only because one is mentally weak or masochistic has had a terrible retribution in his paralysis, but hasn't changed his belief. It hasn't changed mine either. But it is such a profoundly delicate subject that it is impossible to be adamant about it. Ivor's fall was an accident, or was it? Elizabeth's illnesses are bad luck or are they? If Ivor wasn't drunk he would not have broken his neck, or would he? Elizabeth's endless operations are the natural successors of indifferent eating and drinking habits and no exercise at all, or are they? There is no way of proving it one way or the other – one cannot set the clock back and say 'Try that walk again tomorrow night in the same conditions and without the booze and see what happens this time Ivor,' or, 'Let's go back ten years Elizabeth and run a mile every morning and play tennis or something or ride a horse for an hour a day and take no pills of any kind and only moderate drink and eat to a proper weight level and then let's see how you go.' If I have cancer of the lungs or throat tomorrow I have induced it by smoking too heavily haven't I? Or would I get it anyway? My father smoked all his life and didn't get it. Why should I? He lived 'til he was over 80. Why shouldn't I? We shall never know. [...]

---

[217] A reference to the poem 'The Scholar-Gypsy' (1853) by Matthew Arnold (1822–88).
[218] William Manchester (1922–2004), *The Arms of Krupp, 1587–1968* (1968).
[219] The actual reference is (p. 101): 'Now he [Alfred Krupp] was proposing to load his barrels from the *rear*. The officer corps considered the idea funny as a crutch.'

Saturday 18th Last day of the working week and it should be an early day, perhaps very early if Hathaway gives the new German actor who plays Rommel half a chance to speak his speeches trippingly off the tongue [220] I wonder if I should intercede on the German's behalf this morning before Hank destroys him before my eyes. I have no sympathy for any Germans but simply don't want to be bored by endless takes and mistakes from the actor – a Hun by the name of Wolfgang Preiss – pronounced Price. [221] I can tell that he's a good actor I think just by instinct. Hathaway said yesterday: 'Fuckin' Germans either want to be the bosses or kiss yer ass.' Churchill said the same thing about the odd humble-arrogance of the German people but in somewhat more classical terms: 'Germans are either at your throat or at your feet.' [222] Anyway, Hank's hatred of the Germans is not minced. He but hates them. I find them highly comical but as I would find the more amiable lunatics in an asylum comical, a laughter containing not a little pity and not a little fear that I may chortle myself to death. Of all the nations I have come to know reasonably well over the years the Germans are the nation who seem most the same, the most like each other, the most conformist. It is easy to see how they can become easily led. I cannot, simply cannot, like them though I have tried ever since Maria came into the family. Even when they are at their fat chuckling meerschaum-smoking jolly best I see the jew-baiting death's head under the jiggling flesh and the goose-step and the gas-chambers. [223]

Hathaway told me yesterday that many years ago he had an idea for a film – 'Christ as the unknown soldier'. He needed a writer to write it. He saw William Faulkner who thought it was a 'hell of an idea'. Faulkner went away and months later he called Hank and said I will write it as a book first, because I don't know how to write scripts and then we'll do it as a film. 'Great,' said Hank. 15 years later the book came out dedicated to Hathaway called *Fable*. [224] Hank asked me if I'd read it and I said yes. He had read it, he said, but couldn't get through it because 'it didn't have one, one single one of my goddamn ideas in it'. I told him I couldn't remember the book at all but remember only that it was very hard going. [. . .]

Sunday 19th Yesterday was a very early day indeed. We had four pages in the can, as they say, by 11 o'clock and I was back, showered and dressed by 12.30. I went to the airport 3 times in an hour before I met the right plane which disgorged Elizabeth. She looked fine but seemed from her talk to be a little

---

[220] This is a reference to *Hamlet*, Act III, scene ii: 'trippingly on the tongue'.
[221] Wolfgang Preiss (1910–2002) had previously appeared in *The Longest Day*, although not there playing the part of Rommel.
[222] Churchill had cited 'the saying', 'The Hun is always either at your throat or at your feet', in a speech before a Joint Session of Congress on 19 May 1943.
[223] A meerschaum is a name for an ornate pipe.
[224] William Faulkner (1897–1962), *A Fable* (1954), which won the Pulitzer Prize for Fiction and a National Book Award.

squiffy but I am now hyper-sensitive about drink. Anyway, one should have a drink before a tedious trip. Among other things she brought a tabloid newspaper which has a snap of us on the front page with a headline saying Elizabeth Taylor flies to save Burton's life. There was a magazine called *Look* containing letters about the 'Cojah' coat I am supposed to have bought E. I amused myself for a couple of hours writing a reply but it has become very long and could be developed into an article about money.[225] I'll keep on with it just for amusement. Might even place it somewhere. Perhaps even in *Look* magazine. Or I could incorporate it into the lectures in Oxford. Might amuse the lads. That's three 'amuses' in 5 lines. [. . .]

Monday 20th [. . .] E is going back to LA tomorrow for a complete job on her teeth, taking children and animals with her so I'll be alone again. It's hopefully only for a week so I'll be with them all shortly. In the meantime I have a hot few days ahead of me. Explosions and burning tanks and being inside a tank and flame-throwers again and running and shouting one-liners. 'Get the lead out, Garth', 'Over there Mackenzie' and similar deathless cries. Today however we simply have a talk scene with Rommel. Talking of Rommel and the actor Wolfgang Price [*sic*] – he is good as I suspected and to my delight Hathaway left him alone which was a boon and we didn't do more than three or four takes on any one scene, and apart from the weather that is the last obstacle left to the rapid completion of this great work. We are having lots of telegrams again about how good I and the film are which is faintly ominous as the same thing happened with *Staircase* which is the biggest failure with *Look Back in Anger* and *Faustus* that I've had.

I am still deep in the arms of Krupp. It's a long haul of a book and an astounding record of the collapse of all moral virtues among the Germans under Hitler with the Krupps showing all the signs even before the twenties and pre-Hitler thirties. It seems incredible that Adolf only came to power in '33 and was ready to go in '38 and actually went in '39. He was furious that Chamberlain appeased him at Munich. He didn't want to be appeased. He wanted war right then and there. What a clown. But it is genuinely astonishing that he could so revolutionize a whole country in so short a time. We and the Yanks can do it too. But only under the stimulus of war itself. If only we could harness and direct such vast forces in peacetime. We might achieve stupendous things, unbelievable changes for the good in a mere decade. Democracy, it seems, will not be hurried except in the agony of war when of course it ceases to be a democracy. It therefore follows that the swift implementation of the Civil Rights Bill in the States for example could only be brought about <u>quickly</u> by an immediate civil war, with Indians, Chicanos and Negroes on one side

---

[225] Burton means a Kojah mink pelt.

and the bewildered Wasps on the other. Fear is the key that will open the door. If such a thing happens I hope to be fishing in a remote Swiss lake. With all my family around me. No participation without representation is my cry. [. . .]

Tuesday 21st [. . .] Liza's report arrived and it is nice and affectionate but she is below average in practically everything due invariably to 'lack of concentration' and 'daydreaming'. She is a year younger than her classmates on the average so her position in the class, which is well in the lower half is partially understandable. However she is not the scholar type and as long as she keeps her end up vaguely, we don't really mind. Now that they are all coming into their teens or have arrived there I find all the children a pain in the neck and though there's no living without them, there's no living with them either. My idea of children is going to visit the grandchildren, when we have them, for Sunday lunch and a walk in the park and tea at 5 and home by six saying how charming they are and how nice they are to spoil while someone else does all the work of remonstration and correction and admonition. I haven't met a child yet that didn't bore the brains out of me in an hour – most can do it in 15 minutes. I would have made the worst teacher in the history of pedagoguery if there is such a word. The child that I was, I loathe. I prefer the man that I am, though not over-much. Of course we bore them too. Kate during her annual visits can't wait to get away from us and into the arms of her friends. Ditto Liza and Maria. Ditto the boys, though not so much as the girls. Christopher is the only one whose company I enjoy like that of an adult, largely because he's so very quick and so honest. All the rest are evasive and downright dumb about most things. [. . .]

Wednesday 22nd [. . .] Read a thriller by another MacDonald, Ross.[226] He is a good writer and very grey and despairing and weary. His detective Lew Archer is over forty and stolidly persistent and of course unostentatiously intelligent. He has no reason at all to be a detective – he could quite clearly succeed at anything. And no reason why he should be the hero of 'formula' detective stories, he could be the commentator on the mores morals and miracles of modern life in any other writing form. But this one is easier and more saleable I suppose.

I worked all the morning inside the mock-up of a tank with Johns Orchard and Colicos and Brook. It was very cramped and very hot and we were in there for a long time. It was less tedious than I anticipated however because I had imagined something much worse. I finished about 2 and was able to wave E and the children off from the airport. I felt very sad as the plane slowly rose, the undercarriage slowly pulling itself up into the belly when the small plane – a 4 seater twin engined Cessna – was barely off the ground. [. . .]

---

[226] Ross MacDonald (1915–83).

Everybody is convinced that our comical German – one Karl Otto Alberty – is either an amiable nut, solidly stupid or on drugs. Yesterday it seems he had to get hurriedly into a car and drive or be driven off at great speed in pursuit of me and my men. He hurried to the car alright but then did a kind of Charlie Chaplin high kick and gave a wild cry as he leapt into the car. Hathaway went 'spare' and bounced up and down in uncontrollable anguish. Everybody was so astounded that it wasn't until later that everybody laughed and were still laughing at ten o'clock at night.

'Do you know,' said Hathaway to me yesterday, 'what that stupid Kraut son-of-a-bitch did the other day?' 'What?' 'He drives up to the check-point, right?, and says did a British Medical Unit come through here? Then he's supposed to say Get me to Field Marshal Rommel. Right? No he says Follow the bloody British, he says. I went nuts. I said what the fuck d'yer think you're doing you Kraut bastard. He says, that's what I would do. I would chase the British. But you have a scene with Rommel, I says, it's in the script, d'yer want to miss your scene with Rommel? I says. I sweated right through my shirt. The guy's gor [sic] to be nuts.

Karl Otto dresses up every Saturday night in tight black 'charro' trousers, an ornamental black shirt of many silver decorations and a black sombrero low on the forehead.[227] It is an unbelievable sight as he is a very white man with a huge belly and a face like two melons one on top of the other joining around the eyes. No photograph can do justice to the idiocy of his appearance, and yet, if one didn't know his talent for unconscious buffoonery one might find his physical presence imposing, even distinguished. He becomes very wild when dancing in the bar and after 'dancing' with elephantine grossness and awkwardness one night he leaned ponderously over a table and said to the boys – Brook Ron and others – 'I wish people would learn to use their bodies with beauty' indicating the other dancers with scorn.

When he came into the restaurant last Saturday night where E and I were dining alone sitting by the window she said in genuine wonder: 'What is that?' 'That,' I said, 'is our tame German. That is our Karl Otto,' I added urgently, 'Do not look in his direction or we will have him for the night and he is unspeakably boring.' 'Hullo,' she said immediately, 'what a splendid costume you have on.' 'Sank Zew,' he said, 'I am always wearing dis on every Saturday night in honour of mein host country.' 'How thoughtful,' said milady. From there on neither she nor I understood a word he said. [. . .]

Thursday 23rd [. . .] Hathaway told me that we had six days left as from yesterday. The last few days always seem the longest in any film or play and yet time flies all the same. I am still reading Manchester's long tome about the

---

[227] 'Charro': Mexican horseman.

Krupps which I had neglected for several days. Virtually every paragraph contains an enormity. I wonder what I would have behaved like had I been a working-class German at that nightmare time, I don't think I could kill a child or a broken old man or an emaciated young one as they did, as one might swat a fly so to speak. But it was so much an ordinary day for so many Germans that I am riddled with possible guilt. No I couldn't do it and that's flat. More and more it seems ludicrous that we did not train and use a special force to kill Hitler himself sometime in the early forties. We could have saved two years of war with a little luck and millions of people would have been saved. I wonder if any of our special services ever seriously thought about it. It seems, in retrospect, an obvious thing to do. Difficult I know but with the disaffection of certain highly placed Germans, which Alan Dulles knew about in Switzerland early in the war, by no means impossible.[228] I suppose the obvious never occurs to the great minds that saw us through disaster after disaster.

Friday 24th [. . .] Yesterday was another very hot day for us actors particularly wearing our jackboots and high-neck uniforms and tight gun-belts and with the reflectors and the mini-arcs always on. Hotter 'n Hell as I say in the script and which might become the title of the film according to Hathaway. [. . .]

Saturday 25th This should be my last weekend here and a week tomorrow we should be on the Super-Chief steaming across the continent to New York and on to the *QE2* on the 6th August.[229] Keen looking forward. What shall I take to read I muse deliciously. *The Decline and Fall of the Roman Empire* which I have yet to read in its entirety.[230] Re-read Dickens favourites – *Bleak House, Dombey and Son Great Expectations, Tale of Two Cities.* Something like those and a mass of paperbacks for night reading in the swaying roaring train with the bedlight on. Breakfast with the local paper and the Pump Room in Chicago for lunch.

Alex Lucas, producer of *Hammersmith is Out* arrived unannounced yesterday morning as I was sitting on the beach. [. . .] He had brought two copies of the script with him one of which we gave to Frank Beeston to read with a view to his giving us a rough costing.[231] We want to shoot it without benefit of a studio and entirely on location if possible. I shall await Frank's reactions with interest. We shall take the same cameraman as we use on this probably, but I would like to see the work on this first before a definite commitment. [. . .]

---

[228] Allen Welsh Dulles (1893–1969), American intelligence operative in Switzerland during much of the Second World War, later the first civilian Director of the Central Intelligence Agency.

[229] *Super Chief*: passenger train from LA to Chicago. QE2: *Queen Elizabeth II*, ocean liner.

[230] Edward Gibbon's (1737–94) *The History of the Decline and Fall of the Roman Empire* (1776–89).

[231] Burton means Frank Beetson, unit production manager on *Raid on Rommel*.

Sunday 26th I was bloody irritated by work yesterday and this was surprising as this is the first film I've ever been in which didn't frustrate and bore me with the inevitable delays and hangings-about. My back muscles were aching a lot and it would be a day when I had to lie down with my head up and my spine hooped against the earth, the worst and most uncomfortable position for a pulled back muscle. [. . .] There were two journalists for interviews. One was called Leblanc and the other's name I don't recall. They were both bottom-of-the-barrel types, the nameless one being unbelievably square. He asked me – all his questions had been neatly written about beforehand – 'Do you think Mr Burton that there is a little of *Camelot* in every man?' 'Have you read a book called the *Peter Principle* the contention being that having achieved a certain plateau of incompetence you must then aspire to a higher plateau?'[232] No, I hadn't read the book but thought that in my profession one was almost always awarded a knighthood when the plateau had been reached, when 'they' were perfectly sure that you were not going to surprise them any more. What is the 'Peter Principle' I wonder? I suppose it's somewhere in the same school as Parkinson's Law.[233] I'll find it and read it up.

Only 3 or 4 more days now to the lovin arms of Sheba. Good idea to be away from her a little now and agin. Appreciate her more. Very strange to have no one to talk to and gossip with. Rather be home nevertheless Home being where she is. [. . .]

Apart from pulling that damned muscle I am pretty limber – largely from climbing in and out of tanks and lorries and running across the sand and diving into various holes when explosions are supposed to be going off. Hathaway said to me yesterday what a revelation I was to work with. He had heard, he said, that I was a consummate professional but that I was super-pro and super-on-time etc. I said how much I admired his thoroughness too and that we should try something really ambitious together one of these days. There was nothing he'd like more, he said. So there. How to make friends. [. . .]

Monday 27th Went out and sunbathed in the morning until too many people came on to the beach and then withdrew to the rooms at about one o'clock when Brook fried up some spam and sausage and scrambled some eggs. Went on to the bed to read but fell asleep and awoke to find Elizabeth standing in the doorway. It was very shocking and I was numbed with surprise. I am not very good at being surprised. I simply become very casual as if I had expected what the surprise was all the time. E was like Nellie Nemesis. Everything she had to tell me was instinct with near tragedy. Her teeth naturally had to be the ulti-

---

[232] Laurence J. Peter (1919–90) and Raymond Hull (1919–85), *The Peter Principle* (1969) suggested that 'in a hierarchy every employee tends to rise to his level of incompetence'.
[233] Cyril Northcote Parkinson (1909–93) expounded the notion, in his book *Parkinson's Law* (1958), that 'work expands so as to fill the time available for its completion'.

mate in difficulty and she had an allergy to something that nobody had ever had an allergy to before which took the form of a five minute 'tacky-cardy' attack which gave her acute St Vitus dance and frightened the shit out of her for the rest of the time. [...]

Then it turns out that E went out nightclubbing with Rex Kennamer and they were, on their way home to the hotel, chased and bothered by the attentions of some man in a Volkswagen who kept swerving the car across the road to try and stop them. [...]

Then E told me to my astonishment that she had gone to have dinner at Joyce Haber's house. Now Joyce Haber is the descendant of Hedda Hopper and just as stupid and virulent and snide.[234] I expressed surprise and asked what the devil she was doing at a gossip-columnist's house and she said she just tagged along with swinging Rex Kennamer to see a film. I asked since when she went to the homes of such people and she became very antagonistic and defensive and at one point started shouting and bawling about how lonely she was and that the dental work had shaken her up and she couldn't stand being alone in the bungalow etc. I gave up. [...]

Tuesday 28th [...] I only worked half the day yesterday with HH [Henry Hathaway] dismissing me at about 2 o'clock. In the meantime I had run and shouted and operated the flame thrower – once falling flat on my back while doing so and generally speaking being very hot. E came out about 11 and we lunched together and E drove me home with great élan in the Cadillac. [...] We are both looking forward to going home to Europe and the *Kalizma* and the journey on the *Chief* and the *QE2* is also looked forward to as a great treat. I hope the *Chief* is as good as it used to be. New York is likely to be hard work with Aaron around but perhaps I can do some of that work on the train which might give us some freedom in the big city before getting on to the blissful isolation of the *QE*.

Today I have lots of bits and pieces before a two page chat with Clinton Greyn and the end of the picture. I believe there will be no dubbing so I will be entirely finished as of tomorrow night, crossing my fingers.

Brother Graham, with his usual mindless bonhomie, folie de grandeur, and doubtless full of booze, had been entertaining the press again re my early life. The press concerned is that rag of all rags – the *People* newspaper. The ultimate in cheap journalism. They are about to do a several part article on my life and loves. This will be shame-making for a day and then will disappear into a just oblivion very rapidly, but it's a bore nevertheless. Why does little Graham do these things – even after the outrageous mess-up with the *News of the World* some years ago. He has entertained the writer of the article in his house

---

[234] Hedda Hopper (1885–1966), actor, radio and television host and Hollywood columnist for the *LA Times*. Haber (no relation) had taken up this post in 1968.

and taken them round to the other members of the family etc. and generally aided and abetted them in every way. He is a complete nincompoop and will never learn. I don't know whether I should write him a scathing letter or forget the whole thing. There is a letter from the *People* man to Aaron which indicates that he is in the same literary league as Graham and well down to barrel-scraping standards. Ah well. Ah well.

Wednesday 29th This is the last day of the film and we shall be back in the B. H. Hotel tonight and firmly planted in front of the TV set on which a splendid game of baseball will be going on if there's any justice in this world.

I wrote a page of remonstrance to Graham yesterday morning about the *People* and was going to finish it this morning but E pointed out sagely that my letter was so well written that it might over-impress Graham to the extent that 'the dummy might show it to the Press with a "hey look what my brother thinks about you lot". So I will write a shorter pithier one.

I got myself blown up yesterday and wounded in the leg and said the last immortal lines of the film which are 'Perhaps Rommel won't want to shoot two such devoted stamp-collectors as you and me.'

E came to lunch and made several oblique remarks which made me to realize that she had been reading this diary. I'm supposed to put in something nice today but am not going to. She's alright I suppose and is good at cards, though I reduced my losses to about $13 yesterday and I prefer having her around to not having her around, 'there's no living with her or without' her as the feller said, and she's very good-looking etc. and wears hardly any make-up and is a bit tubby but that in all honesty is about as far as I can go with praise. She fries a fair banger and grills an honest tomato and browns a nice onion perhaps. That'll do for now.

We are going to fly from here tonight in the twin-engined Cessna land at Mexicali or Calexico or both for clearance and fly on to Burbank and automobile it home to the B. H.[235] Everybody is very relieved to be finished and not many people, apart from me, will look back on this film with any particular pleasure. I think of it as an eye opener as to how efficiently – how much more efficiently – one can work with a skeleton crew. We have done the film for well under $1m. I should count my earnings as approx $½m certain with a probability of double or triple that and a possibility of five times that. Anyway enough to pay our expenses for a couple of years and live in the style to which we are accustomed.

Hathaway was at his most irascible yesterday, probably because the piece is coming to an end.

---

[235] Burbank Airport, Burbank, Los Angeles County, California.

Thursday 30th, Beverly Hills Hotel [. . .] Perversely having survived without any 'trots' etc. down in primitive little San Felipe I have them this morning in the Beverly Hills hotel. So badly indeed that there was nearly an horrendous accident in bed this morning. I made it in time, but it was touch and go. E was very nervous all the way up in the plane and held my hand several times en route. [. . .] With my new-found fatalism, or whatever this new placidity is, I was as relaxed as if in a train. I did the quite hopeless *LA Times* crossword. You might say that American crosswords are indicative of the national mind. They are all – even the *New York Times* uncomplicated synonyms except on Sundays when they are general knowledge tests and for the solving of which you must be armed with reference books. There are no plays on words, no puns, no anagrams. The only crossword I've come across in the USA that matches in any way the ingenuity of British puzzles is the Diacryptic of the *Saturday Review*, but its more popular one is the Double-Crostic which is straight synonyms or definitions. 'King of Westphalia – 1227 – 97.' That sort of thing. Occasionally a quotation with a blank space. In lesser papers like the *LA Times* and *The San Diego Union* which I've been reading in San Felipe they are child-like in their simplicity. In fact they can be difficult for the solver expecting subtleties. 'Industries (abb)' turns out to be 'Inds'. Honest to God. But I do them nevertheless, usually as a challenge against time. Once I did one as fast as I could write it down which would be about 3 to 5 minutes. Sometimes one is held up by a definition like 'root of indigenous Peruvian palm used in dyes' or something like that, but it is always multi-crossed with other clues so that its eventual solution is only a matter of time.

[. . .] E still asleep though she awoke in the middle of the night when I did and woke again at 7 when I nearly had my 'accident' and got up to type this and make myself some coffee. She looked very pale in the plane yesterday but looks better today. She's got that bloody dentist this afternoon. I shall sit in the waiting room and read and listen for distant groans and moans, though doubtless she'll make no sound. If there's a book shop near the dentist's I shall search out some literature for the train and boat. Now for some boiled eggs to bind me.

Friday 31st [. . .] Took E to the dentist at one o'clock and she was much less time than I anticipated – she was out by 3.15 and we were home by 4. Her poor little gums were all mauled about so she was in discomfort. She has to go back again today for a few minutes. There was a Thrifty drug store next to the dentist's building and I bought a few books for the long journey to Europe. [. . .] When we came out of the dentist's we looked up as we were walking to the car and the whole of the 2nd or 3rd floor of the block opposite was crowded with people all watching and waving at Elizabeth. Apparently they'd been there every time she went to the dentist but she hadn't noticed before. I was touched. And still surprised. And pleased.

[. . .] Granpa Wilding was buried yesterday and Dick Hanley and John Lee went to the funeral.[236] Mike Wilding had flown over from Europe for the thing and talked to E on the phone about Mike Junior who apparently is having a terrible time in Asia. Spat upon and insulted wherever he and his group go. I don't know quite why but chiefly out of xenophobia I think with the British refusal to let Indians and Pakistanis into Britain indiscriminately as we used to. He cannot get a visa to get into India. It is typical of Mike's airy-fairy woolliness that he never thought of that before he left. The same goes for the other people in his party. There probably isn't a practical man among them. Still, as long as Mike survives the experience will be invaluable and the lessons learned infinitely more various than he could get in any school curriculum. I wish he'd come home now for God's sake. He's not the adventurer type and he's not very sturdy, not the kind of man who pushes back frontiers and blazes trails. He's a nice feckless boy and may be meant for an artistic career either as a painter or writer. Unless he has the fatal lack of concentration which is the one ineradicable weakness of the lost.

Saw *Butch Cassidy and the Sundance Kid* last night.[237] A charming film very derivative of *Bonnie and Clyde*. The man Redford that I'd heard so much about is disappointingly ordinary and Newman is much more impressive. It is just as well that he has turned down *Hammersmith* as he has a quality of dullness and I can see quite easily why he has taken so long to become a star. I think he would have ruined our film simply because he seems so sluggish and certainly doesn't suggest for a second the kind of demonic idiot-ness that Billy Breedlove must have. Tonight we look at another highly touted 'star' called Beau Bridges.[238] Let's see what he's like.

AUGUST

Saturday 1st, Beverly Hills Hotel Saw yet another film last night. Called *The Landlord* with some very good stuff in it but tremendously derivative of *Graduate*.[239] Time and time again there were whole sequences reminiscent of the Nichols piece. I wasn't however bored which is a minor miracle in itself from a film as far as I'm concerned. The man Beau Bridges is nice and sloppy à la Dustin Hoffman but taller and just as plain. He won't do for our film – he's too young and too undynamic too undemonic. [. . .] I'm reading yet another diary-form book about sport – this time about baseball by a knuckleball pitcher called Jim Bouton [. . .] *Ball Four*.[240] I wouldn't like to have Bouton

[236] Henry Wilding, Michael's father.
[237] *Butch Cassidy and the Sundance Kid* (1969), directed by George Roy Hill (1921–2002) and starring Paul Newman (1925–2008) and Robert Redford.
[238] Beau Bridges (1941—) was to take the part of Billy Breedlove in *Hammersmith Is Out*.
[239] *The Landlord* (1970), directed by Hal Ashby (1929–88) and starring Beau Bridges.
[240] Jim Bouton (1939—), *Ball Four* (1969).

recording my every word in the free for all of a baseball locker room. Great stuff for the layman though.

Brook left for Chicago yesterday to stay with Cushman. He is a good guest but four months is a bit wearing on anyone. I'm glad he's gone. And it will be very nice to be alone together for a few days on train and boat. And then on boat again – the *Kalizma*.

Weather here is splendid and practically smog-free since we arrived and pleasantly warm, not overwhelmingly so as in San Felipe. Talked to Gwen who is back in Gstaad and Ivor is out of hospital. They had talked of going back to England but Ivor changed his mind and chose to stay in Switzerland. He is a long time a-dying poor old sod. I thought this to be his last few months once I heard that he was back in hospital again. The strain on Gwen must be well-nigh intolerable. Sent letter off to Graham with suitable admonitions re talking to the press. Hopeless I know as Graham is incapable of learning. He is a nice bloke though and you never know that he might not grow up one of these days.

Sunday 2nd, Super-Chief Have just had breakfast on the train and we are somewhere between Gallup and Alburquerque.[241] The weather is beautiful and the country looks like a million Cowboy and Indian movies. There is surely no more pleasant means of travel than to travel first class on this magnificent train. We have a drawing-room and a bedroom though actually we use the latter only to change in and sit when the steward is making up the beds or vice versa in the main room. All the terrible tales about the disintegration of the service on this railroad are totally unfounded – it's as good as ever and still the best train in the world. A private bathroom which is not a bathroom but a lavatory and sink. But will do. Tomorrow we can bathe and shower in the Ambassador East so dirty hair for one day.

I shall read *Airport* which is the current best-seller or was and feel very cosy knowing that I am on a train and not a nerve-racking plane.[242] Nice to be alone with E too. We worked out that it is the first time we've been without attendant guests or servants or both since this time last year. And we have more time on the QE2.

[. . .] Forgot momentous news. I had a Jack Daniels and Soda and two glasses of Napa Valley Red Wine last night with dinner. Felt immensely daring and all it did was make me feel very sleepy and not elated or anything like that. E had the giggles most of the time. Can't think why as I was in great control. Can't help if the train sways.

Monday 3rd, Super-Chief We are an hour and a half away from Chicago and it's been a very pleasant trip. Off to the Ambassador East for lunch and more

---

[241] Gallup and Albuquerque, both in New Mexico.
[242] Arthur Hailey (1920–2004), *Airport* (1970).

importantly a shower and shampoo. Typing this on my knees while the train sways around a lot. Ran along the Missouri for quite a time this morning and saw a paddle steamer. [. . .]

Ran most of yesterday through New Mexico which is very beautiful and even in the height of summer looks lush and pastured. Saw thousands of cows and scores of horses. Many streams and one-horse towns all of which looked delightful. Many eyesores however created by car dumps. [. . .]

We discussed whether we could live in the States somewhere in New Mexico or Colorado say. I said I could but would like to spend some time in Europe if possible. Also am afraid of the States – afraid of its corruptive influence and its lack of stability. But a small ranch near a small town with a few horses and somebody to run the whole thing and the family and a book and a typewriter would take some whacking I bet. A water-hole for the kids to swim in and winters in Vallarta and Spring visits to Europe. Not bad. [. . .]

Wednesday 5th, New York We arrived late in Chicago and rushed like mad to the Ambassador East and went straight into the Pump Room while they carried the bags upstairs. I had beef in the Polish fashion and E had calves liver and Canadian bacon. Delicious both with a bottle of Burgundy of superb quality. Upstairs and a bath for E and a shower for me, a complete change of clothes and we made it back to the *Broadway Limited* with about 5 minutes to spare.[243] The *Broadway* has run down though it was never much in the first place. We dined as we ran through Ohio and it was awful and there was nearly an incident when some black people came into the dining car to ask for autographs. It was alright for a time and then the headwaiter who on these trains is always white stopped others as the press became too great and a young negro started on Civil Rights and 'I can go anyplace I want to on this or any other goddamn train', etc. It passed off. Then a very drunken Mexican man and woman came and hovered pissedly over the table with the man saying 'Well there she is, are you satisfied now? And Ricardo too. Get their autographs.' 'I've been looking for you since Pasadena,' said the woman. 'I wanna tell you something . . .' long pause. 'I saw you in Pasadena and you're jus' beautiful. Great eyes. Hey, look at her eyes. How about that? Let me tell you something . . . I've been looking for you since Pasadena.' We got out of there in a hurry and to the isolation of our drawing-room. Finished *Airport* which I found very hard work to read. We were 40 minutes late getting into Penn Station[. . .][244] We were in the Regency by midday where we had a bloody Mary which I didn't like and I remember them being the best in the world.[245] Perhaps I've lost my taste for them anyway. We stayed in the rest of the day except for a

---

[243] The *Broadway Limited* was the passenger train operating between Chicago and New York.
[244] Penn Station, New York.
[245] Regency Hotel, Park Avenue, New York.

swift brunch at Rumpelmeyer's.[246] Aaron was there all the time and Phil came about 6 and stayed until about 8 when they both went off somewhere. I half watched a terrible film about the Black and-Tans and the Irish starring James Cagney.[247] [. . .]

Thursday 6th The newspapers made front page stuff yesterday of the fact that this hotel was robbed at 3 in the morning the night before – saying that the bandits were after E's Cartier-Burton and Krupp. Now we just so happened to have them with us up here on the 20th floor, every room of which is taken by guards etc. The strong boxes from the hotel vault had been brought up by the manager the day we arrived and were probably observed in the lobby by a member of the gang. What he didn't wait to see was that they were not taken back down again. The Krupp and Peregrina and lots of other pieces were in Dug's room in the strongbox under his bed where slept he and his son – also a cop. E was wearing the Cartier-Burton. So foiled again. I wonder how long we can keep up running this hideous risk without having genuine trouble one of these days.

The famed new white Cadillac containing every mod con for which we've been waiting for 18 months is a write-off before we've even seen it. It was badly smashed with Gaston driving it. His reasons all sound very dubious – the brakes went he says which seems unlikely in a brand new car – while the press say he crashed going the wrong way in a one-way street. We shall see. We don't even know where it occurred but it seems as if it were in the country around London. He'll have a volubly glib explanation and it wasn't his fault I bet. No use being angry about it but I am. Insurance will pay for it but it means another 18 months to get a new one so will abandon the idea.

We went to lunch at the Colony restaurant which is just around the corner from here.[248] We took Aaron and James Wishart with us. Aaron's sclerosis seems much worse while James has had a couple of mild heart attacks so we were with a right couple of athletes. [. . .] Today we're off to the *QE2* and looking forward to it. Shall go out and buy some books this morning. Letter from Alan Jay Lerner asking if I would be interested in doing the *Little Prince* of St Exupéry.[249] Might see him today on the ship to find out how he plans to do it. Might be good. Suggestion that Clint Eastwood might play in *Hammersmith*. Said yes if agreeable to Ustinov.[250]

---

[246] Rumpelmeyer's was located in the St Moritz Hotel, Central Park South and Sixth Avenue.

[247] *Shake Hands with the Devil* (1959), directed by Michael Anderson (1920–).

[248] The Colony Restaurant was at Madison Avenue and 61st Street, New York.

[249] Alan Jay Lerner (1918–86), writer and lyricist, co-author (with Frederick Loewe, 1901–88) of *Camelot* (stage play and film). Lerner wrote an adaptation of *The Little Prince* which Burton narrated in 1974. The original work was a novella, *Le Petit Prince*, by Antoine de Saint-Exupéry (1900–44) (1943).

[250] Clint Eastwood did not appear in the film.

Friday 7th, **Queen Elizabeth** We sailed yesterday at 5 o'clock. The ship is fine but horribly decorated. The British really have no sense of style, no sense of colour, no sense of line, of proportion, even of simple utilitarian sense. For instance, the door to the bedroom will not close unless you move the bed. The bed is fixed so the door remains permanently open. In both the bathrooms there are <u>three</u> sets of lavatory papers with the fitting fixed into the wall. In a desperate attempt to be 'with it' the decor has only succeeded in looking like 1925 German exhibition. It looks not unlike our little *Kalizma* before Elizabeth had it re-done. The tables in the Grill room are decorated with lamps about a foot high that look like blocks of box-flats lighted on the inside. The famous *Daily Telegraph* newspaper is a flimsy couple of sheets without even the virtue of the crossword puzzle which was a feature of the ship's paper on the old *Queens.* The passengers so far fit the decor – nobody seems first-class and we got the impression this morning when we went exploring around the deck at 7 o'clock that we were eternally wandering into the tourist section from the look of the passengers and the way they were dressed. We are still not sure. It may be a classless ship and we must ask and find out. She sails beautifully so far and there isn't a tremor from the engines and E became very nostalgic last night saying how unglamoured the whole thing was compared from her early journeys when First Class contained fabulous film stars and famous writers and crowned heads etc. And the engines really made the ship quiver and shudder. She became quite misty-eyed. I remember of course that the old *Queens* were pretty horribly decorated too, but at least it was substantial and expensively so. This ship gives the impression of being shoddy. But the rooms are pleasant and there are two little bars with all kinds of cute fittings and two small fridges – one in each bathroom. [. . .]

We both took a nap this morning mine unintended and short E's intended and long. I am reading a book by Le Carré called the *Looking-Glass-War* which is infinitely sad and depressing.[251] Le Carré writes about that clubby class of Englishmen as well as anybody I've ever read and I think him to be as good as Graham Greene without the mystic Roman Catholic stuff but with the dying mystique of Empire and fading old-school-tie virtues as a substitute. He really writes like an angel and understands his victims very well and has a marvellous ear for common speech.

Wednesday 26th, Portofino Yesterday was a day of frantic evasion tactics. We discovered that the bushes and road above our anchorage were infested with paparazzi – a mass of long-focus lenses everywhere one looked. They in turn must have passed the word around, though we were on the front page of the Genoa newspaper as well, with the result being that we were surrounded by

---

[251] John le Carré (1931—), *The Looking-Glass War* (1965). Le Carré had previously written the novel *The Spy Who Came in from the Cold* (1963).

craft of every conceivable description from about 10 in the morning until nightfall. Pedal-boats, smart and powerful Rivas, hard-rubber boats with outboard motors, boats from Santa Marguerita and Genoa and Rapallo, row-boats and even swimmers. If the novelty has not worn off today and we are not left alone, then we shall move tomorrow to Elba which we have never visited and where we should be tranquil enough. We were so ignored in Corsica and Sardinia a couple or three years ago and we may be lucky again.

[. . .] Last night we showed on board Elizabeth at 12 years old in a film called *National Velvet*.[252] An utterly improbable story about a horse winning the Grand National – never having run against anybody before – with E riding it. But nevertheless utterly enthralling and timeless. Elizabeth was enchanting with a face of such intensity and such love for the horse that it was almost heart-breaking at times. Though, oddly enough, the face remains the same twenty years later. By some trick of bone-work it still is the same face though the present one is more character-full with its over-lay of experience.

Interrupted by the necessity to have my hair dyed much darker than it has been, the reason being that everyone seems to think that in the next piece *Villain* I should be a black rather than a blond villain. [. . .]

Thursday 27th, Portofino – Elba 6.45 in the morning and we are about 2 hours out of Portofino en route to Elba. [. . .] The ship ploughs sturdily and I suppose steadily on to the beginning of Boney's One Hundred Days.[253] Have just finished reading White's *The Making of the President 1968* which I found very readable.[254] He, White, is obviously a good man. I am at the moment re-reading Machiavelli and it is extraordinary how all his dicta apply to the letter to the American Elections. A man must never lie to himself but must, if necessary, lie to the people if he thinks it is good for them. This both Humphrey, Nixon and Wallace did time and time again if only by omission. Lies that are lies repeated endlessly with adulatory listeners who believe the lies even if they were told the same lies in a bar by a friend who know them to be lies. [. . .] Elizabeth has gone back to bed reading Coward's *Hay Fever* which they've asked us to play on the stage and then make a film of. I've never read the play or seen it but Coward doesn't sound like our cup of tea. Mugs of beer or should I say ales are more in my line as an actor than pink champagne which is what Noel produces so beautifully. Still, I shall read it after Elizabeth and see if I can compromise and be black velvet.[255]

---

[252] *National Velvet* (1945), directed by Clarence Brown (1890–1987).
[253] A reference to the island of Elba, where Napoleon Bonaparte ('Boney') was exiled from April 1814 to February 1815. The 'hundred days' refers to Bonaparte's final campaign, which began with his escape from Elba on 26 February 1815 and ended shortly after his defeat at the Battle of Waterloo on 18 June 1815.
[254] Theodore Harold White (1915–86), *The Making of the President 1968* (1969).
[255] A blend of champagne and stout, usually Guinness.

Thursday 27th continued, at Sea [. . .] Yesterday was as mad as usual in Portofino – scores of small craft and one biggish one – about fifty feet, a largeish cabin-cruiser with a decadent looking white haired Italian owner about 55 years old or perhaps a well preserved 65 with lots of young girls – women – in bikinis, all very brown who had obviously come to look us over. We retreated inside to the salon. They got fed up in about an hour and a half and left. No people look quite as dissipated dissolute and handsomely debased as the rich middle-aged Latin. Vulpine creatures all coldly arrogant and generally with seedy titles and a powerful ambience of orgy. The women too with their lithe hard-eyed gigolos in disdainful condescending tow. They are virtually incapable of being affronted except by a whispered enormity from me in my vilest Italian as I pass within muttering distance. They are great fun to insult, because men of that age (I'm now talking only of the French and Italian Roués) remember only too painfully still the humiliations of the 39–45 war.

Gianni had a nasty little accident yesterday. He saw what he thought was a new kind of ball-point pen and fiddled with it to see how it worked. It was 'Mace' and he gave himself a faceful of it.[256] He cried gas tears for about an hour. It was our fault for leaving it lying about without telling everybody what it was. It was the kind that ladies carry in their handbags and had been accidentally unpacked by the stewardess Eugenie. Could have been much nastier. [. . .]

Friday 28th, San Ferraio, Elba[257] I slept for 10 hours last night. I have rarely felt so tired. We got here about 3 o'clock after a smooth journey. [. . .] This is the little place from which Napoleon set out for Waterloo. It's a bustling, beautifully sheltered little port with not a throttle of tourists but enough to make the stroll past the yacht and the stare at its occupants worth a walk they think. There are lots of those gaily decorated horse and carriages which trot back and forth which afford the dogs – our dogs – great opportunities for barking. I was so tired last night that I had a vodka martini but it was of no avail and I struggled through a modest dinner almost too tired to eat and went to bed at nine! We are moored right opposite a Bar Roma which is next door to a Hotel Darsena Ristorante announcing itself in large yellow letters. Higher above are the words 'Grand Hotel Darsena.' I love the little port already and hopefully we will only have people and no paparazzi which will make it a little heaven, and we <u>must</u> go and see Napoleon's Prison or whatever they call it.[258] Almost all the houses are pale yellow and all the shutters are green – without exception.

John Heyman found us here last night having come by Motoscafola from Piombino.[259] His news was that he had commissioned John Osborne to write

---

[256] A brand of tear gas, often used for personal defence.
[257] Burton means Portoferraio, Elba.
[258] Villa dei Mulini.
[259] Burton means '*motoscafona*' – motor boat. Piombino is the port on the Italian mainland closest to Elba from which ferry services operate.

two plays – a sort of *Rashomon* 1970 for E and I to do on TV for Harlech, which should get that lot off my back.[260] Osborne starts work on Monday. I wrote him a short delighted note. I hope it's some good. We passed a barren little rock half way here yesterday called Gargoni a most inhospitable looking place and a place of terror I've no doubt in earlier days and a haven for pirate vessels.[261] [. . .]

Saturday 29th, Portoferraio [. . .] We had lunch yesterday in a charming sea-side trattoria called very originally Ristorante della Mare – unhonoured by the Michelin Guide. The food was magnificent. We all decided to go off our various diets and to hell with it. We had mussels to start, dipping into hearts of artichoke, button-mushrooms, salami and other sausages the while, followed by a sort of thick clam and tomato soup followed by spaghetti with a sauce called something like 'pesti' – I mean something that sounded like that. It is a local herb, apparently, this 'pesti' slightly bitter but delicious – quite unlike any other taste that I can think of. I had four glasses of the local wine.

We bought in Portofino an immobile bicycle – one of those contraptions which when assembled presents you with a little bicycle on its own stand. One can adjust the height of handlebars and seat to one's own satisfaction. It has a kilometre attached which records your speed and after you've finished how much you have theoretically travelled.[262] Also attached is a clock which you set before you begin at the amount of time you wish to travel. When that time is up a bell rings. I started off four days ago with five minutes and am now doing 15 minutes. It seems a long and boring time and I am trying to find a music stand or something of that sort here in town which I can set up in front of the bike so that I can read. The problem is that as you pedal so the handlebars move forward and back. I might try reading by holding a book with one hand for five minutes and then changing to the other, in order to give each arm its own work-out. Because the arms work too. But more satisfactorily it would be a stand from which to read turning over the occasional page. I will try something this evening. Am now reading in tandem *The Tragedy of Lyndon Johnson* with Machiavelli.[263] The parallels are again very amusing. I will try and record some. [. . .]

Sunday 30th The sun is temporarily out but generally it looks like a continuation of yesterday, grey and dull. We went dutifully to Napoleon's house which was very pleasant and middle-class, not at all grand. A garden that could be lovely and a magnificent view of the ocean. The only place of real interest to

---

[260] *Rashomon* (1950), directed by Akira Kurosawa (1910–98).
[261] Burton must mean the island of Gorgona, approximately two-thirds of the way between Portofino and Elba.
[262] Burton means a milometer and speedometer.
[263] E. F. Goldman (1916–89), *The Tragedy of Lyndon Johnson* (1969).

me was the library but naturally, as in all such musées it was roped off. The bike is a marvellous idea. I 'rode' for twenty minutes this morning, sweated like a bull, and hot and cold showered for a further twenty. Makes one feel magnificently virtuous and fit. We are going by car, not our own – hired Hertz – to Rio Marina today and stopping somewhere en route for lunch.[264] [. . .] I have read so many books recently about Lyndon Johnson and nowhere does he seem a likeable man, with an ego so vast that it almost approaches mania, genuine madness. We are getting the English papers again and as before, after a long absence, they seem so stiflingly parochial. Huge headlines announce 'Mutiny in the Navy' and it turns out to be ½ dozen seamen who got stoned drunk and refused to obey orders and re-enacted Bligh and the *Bounty* taking all the parts between them.[265] Mutiny indeed. Picture of Onassis kissing Callas and a snidey-snidey article accompanying it. It is monstrous that such a magnificent pulpit as the press could be has such moronic preachers. Apart from a couple of sportswriters and the occasional political article and the literary critics there is hardly anybody who can write a plain English sentence. Even the *Times* has become a bit of a rag with gossipy columns yet! One can always rely of course on the crossword puzzles which maintain their standards!

SEPTEMBER

Tuesday 1st, Calvi, Corsica Missed yesterday as I was more less stupefied with drink all day long. We left Elba at 1 o'clock in the morning and the sea was as smooth as a dream. We watched the departure and the slowly disappearing lights of Portoferraio and then went to bed. Suddenly we were awoken by heavy pitching and an occasional combinatory roll and pitch. We dozed but were kept more or less awake by the occasional huge dip until suddenly again a particularly heavy wave broke over the bows and we had omitted to shut our forward port-holes as the sea had been so smooth when we set out and our air-conditioning had broken down – it is being repaired today here we hope – and burst into the bed-room so that our highly expensive pure wool carpet was awash. By this time the sea was really throwing us around and it was quite an effort to close the portholes against further inundation. We went out on the poop deck and or sat in the lounge. And that began my day of drinking. I had several straight martinis and goodbye yesterday. However I did my ten kilometres on the bike sweating like the tropics and then drank endless restoratives, alka salzer [*sic*] and some Italian equivalent that Gianni carries around with him. The day was superb, as indeed it is today, and the carpets are hanging out to dry having been washed again with fresh water, so that the damage might be negligible. One lesson learnt and a lesson that I knew but didn't

---

[264] Rio Marina, on the east coast of Elba.
[265] Burton is referring to a mutinous incident aboard HMS *Iveston*, berthed in Ullapool, Scotland.

apply. Never take the sea for granted. She can change from the sweetest smoothest lady into a mad termagant in two minutes. So always keep the port-holes closed while travelling - especially at night. We acquired however a new passenger, with the great wave into our bedroom came a tiny creature, some kind of sea-snail known already as Ari – after Onassis. He lives in a glass of salt water on the living-room table. This morning we found him outside the glass having obviously climbed out through the night. I was afraid I might kill him if I tore him away from the glass's side as he clung on very tenaciously, so Gianni found a jug which we filled with salt water and put the entire glass and snail inside. If this goes on we'll have to build him an entire aquarium all to himself.

We went to Rio Marina and had lunch in a restaurant 5km outside. It was a splendid lunch of antipasto followed by spaghetti alla marinare followed by delicious chicken flambée with brandy followed by the local cheese and grapes. I drank no wine but the others said it was delicious and they gave us a case for the yacht. Another restaurant not included in the Michelin Guide. Today we are going to lunch in town where we had a very good steak au poivre the last time we were here. I hope it's as good today.

[. . .] I discovered a way of passing the time while cycling. You prop a cross-word against the shaving mirror in the boys' room and do it in your head. The time flies by.

Read nothing yesterday – simply stared about in a generally stunned way. E was sweet and handled me with great affection and wisdom. She really is a superb woman. What I was suffering from was of course a slight case of guilt at not having closed those damned portholes. The drink compounded my irritation so that I was snarling at everybody. [. . .]

Wednesday 2nd, Calvi-Ajaccio [. . .] Went out for lunch yesterday to a hotel that we'd been to before called Les Aloes, I think.[266] Had what we hoped would be the same steak au poivre but the chef had obviously moved on to better places because the steak was indifferent. Bought a hammock for Elizabeth to lie on. Odd that we never had one before. Back in our own bedroom but it still ponks a little from the sea-depths. Afraid we'll have to have it all changed. Perhaps we can do it cheaply and temporarily in Ajaccio and do it up properly when we get to London. Little boats, mostly lobster fishers passing us all the time. Thought we might stop at Porto for lunch.[267] We have never visited the place, so it will be nice to see it.

Still hard at *Tragedy of Lyndon Johnson*. Surprisingly fat book. He does not get any more attractive [. . .]

---

[266] Hotel Les Aloes, Sal Les Aloes, Calvi.
[267] On the west coast of Corsica roughly equidistant between Calvi and Ajaccio.

Tuesday 8th, La Verniaz, Evian[268] We arrived here on Sunday having felt that we needed to be alone together if the paradox is pardoned – for a couple or three days before the hurly-burly of London and work again. A horrendous night on the yacht much compounded by a mighty sullen drunkenness on my part prompted us after hours of accusation and counter-accusation to a reconciliation and finally to a resolution that we were both happier when we are utterly alone. This done and agreed we ordered the jet and got out of Ajaccio and off the boat and into Geneva and onto a helicopter and are here at our favourite little hotel with our favourite little chef who flatters Elizabeth so. When we arrived and walked through the 'tea garden' we were applauded! [. . .] We have a little house – 3 bedrooms and a sitting room, standing in its own ground – about 200 yards from the main body of the hotel. It is a perfect place, the only nuisance being that we have to leave tomorrow to go and see Ivor and fly to London the following day as I have to be fitted with costumes etc. and begin the film with dread at the pit of my stomach – on Monday.[269] Be glad when the first day or so is over. Don't quite know what I'm going to do until I do it. It's about the only time when I miss rehearsals as in the theatre – the slow assimilation of the part, the pub in the breaks, the occasional small explosion of realization of what it's all about in a general mumbling of stage marks and lines imperfectly learned, the discarding of the book after a couple of weeks or three and BANG the whole thing falls into place. That's where it should end of course in a perfect actors' world, right there at the final dress rehearsal, no performance in front of an audience, no critics, three days' holiday and begin again on the next play. Or perhaps just <u>one</u> performance for friends. But on Monday, by 9.30am acting a strange part, peculiarly foreign to me, with actors that I think I've never met, there will be 30 seconds of my performance indelibly in the can, as they say. Perhaps I could persuade Elliott to persuade the director to persuade the actors to have a 'read-through' before Monday.[270] It will make me very unpopular with my fellow 'professionals' who want to play golf or screw women or each other but at least I'll know who everybody is. In the last couple of films I knew at least two or three of the company. In this one none.[271]

---

[268] Hotel La Verniaz, Neuvecelle-Eglise, Evian-les-Bains, on the southern shore of Lake Geneva.
[269] Burton is referring to the filming of *Villain*.
[270] Elliott Kastner was executive producer of *Villain*.
[271] Not entirely true, as also appearing in *Villain* were T. P. McKenna, Cathleen Nesbitt, and Brook Williams.

1971

[Richard ceased making entries in his 1970 diary in early September as he was about to start making *Villain* in London. On 6 October Richard and Elizabeth attended the wedding of Michael Wilding Jr and Beth Clutter at Caxton Hall Registry in London, Richard acting as Michael's best man. In the same month they appeared with Joseph Losey at the Round House Cinema City Exhibition before a showing of *Boom!*, after which they discussed their work with the audience. Conversations took place at this time between Burton and Laurence Olivier, about the possibility of Burton succeeding Olivier as Director of the National Theatre. On 10 November 1970 Burton attended Buckingham Palace to receive his CBE. Elizabeth's long-serving secretary, Dick Hanley, died in Los Angeles in January 1971, but Taylor, then filming *X, Y and Zee* in London, was unable to attend the funeral. Burton and Taylor spent part of January 1971 filming *Under Milk Wood* in the vicinity of Fishguard, Pembrokeshire, Wales. In May Richard and Elizabeth began filming *Hammersmith Is Out* in Cuernavaca in Mexico. Richard began his 1971 diary in late June.]

JUNE

Sunday 27th, Gstaad Feel inordinately lazy and somewhat disappointed as the Tito treatment is not very good.[1] A series of loud bangs like any other old war film. I will attempt to get them to make it more Tito than guns and local partisan heroics, which, though probably true, have been seen in every Hollywood film ever made. If they do not I shall have to withdraw. I will still struggle away with learning Serbo-Croat. I find it fascinating. [. . .]

Monday 28th Have been up since seven. Two cups of coffee and it is now eight-thirty. Can't get up steam to do anything except loaf around. I am going through that period which I call my crossword-puzzle time. Can't read a book of any kind except illustrated art books and such stuff. *Times, Telegraph* and a collected edition of double-crostics from the *Saturday Review* and the puzzles

---

[1] Burton was playing the part of Yugoslavia's Marshal Tito, born Josip Broz (1892–1980), President of Yugoslavia (1953–80), in a film recreating the 1943 battle of Sutjeska (also known as the fifth anti-partisan offensive) between Tito's Partisans and German forces.

from the *Times* and *Telegraph* are the present limit of my intellectual activity.[2] And a bit of Serbo-Croat thrown in for good measure.

Liza is at the most irritating and silly stage of her teens – at least I hope she is. It would be intolerable if it got worse. [. . .] Am getting another extra day off from Heathfield for Liza.[3] Don't like to do it but she is so persistent that I give in just for a quiet life. Like W. C. Fields I really have no patience with young people.[4] I find them all inordinately boring.

Must do something about Tito today or tomorrow. On reflection I think I could do something with it if I can persuade the writers to agree.

Wednesday 30th Missed yesterday as I have a gouty or arthritic left wrist, exquisitely uncomfortable. Usually I get it in the left ankle and foot. Better today but still uncomfortable and since Christy Brown wrote a whole and good book typing one letter at a time with one toe I argue that I should manage with one finger and an elbow.[5] Or rather two fingers.

Raymond found the lost volumes of diaries in the wine cellar where I had put them before leaving Gstaad last time for England and *Villain* which I think is a goodish film but so far isn't doing very well in the States but has not yet opened in Britain and the Commonwealth where it should do better I hope.

Liza left for school yesterday inevitably forgetting to take her passport and ticket. A car was sent after her with the documents but she missed the plane and took the next one. It is a good 2½ hour drive to Geneva from here. I hope Mrs Ladas (known and named by me 'Snakes and Ladas') will not be too cross.[6]

Have just had an offer, by letter, from Stan Stennett (very broad Welsh comedian) to play the Baron in a *Cinderella* pantomime to be staged in Porthcawl![7] Must say I'd love to be in a panto. I've done practically everything else. Impossible of course. [. . .]

JULY

1st, Gstaad [. . .] I was so uncomfortable last night that in bed the slightest movement made me to groan as if demented. Elizabeth says that I am the world's champion 'conyn' which is Welsh for moaning hypochondriac. [. . .]

---

[2] *Saturday Review* was an American weekly magazine published from 1924 to 1986.

[3] Heathfield School, London Road, Ascot.

[4] W. C. Fields (1880–1946), actor, comedian, writer. He is credited with a number of lines disparaging children, including 'I like children – fried'.

[5] Christy Brown (1932–81), novelist, poet and artist who suffered from severe cerebral palsy. His autobiography, *My Left Foot* was published in 1954, and in 1970 was used as the basis for Brown's novel *Down All the Days*.

[6] Mrs Diana Ladas (1913—), headmistress of Heathfield School.

[7] Stan Stennett (1925—), actor and comedian. Porthcawl is a seaside town in South Wales, eight miles south-east of Taibach.

To my delight we were able to watch the Wimbledon male semi-finals on our TV set here all bright and beautiful in colour on eurovision. The matches themselves were badly one-sided - Gorman losing to Stan Smith and the formerly great Rosewall losing to Newcombe.[8] The French announcer said they would, most of them, be playing at Gstaad next week so let us hope the weather keeps good.[9] [. . .]

It looks as if I will do a film written by Tony Shaffer, twin brother of the other playwright Shaffer, in September instead of Tito.[10] Perhaps the Jugs can shift the Tito affair to next spring when they could have a script with dialogue. If not will have to forgo same. Oddly enough Joe Losey called yesterday and asked if I would play Trotsky.[11] Trotsky and Tito in one week and both world famous communists. [. . .]

9th, Gstaad Wrote the [. . .] article for *Vogue* and at the behest of the editor, a lady called Beatrix Miller, who cornered me at the Snowdons' party a couple of weeks ago.[12] Left hand and wrist still gouty so am still typing with two fingers though can now use left hand for short periods. E did something bad to her back and is in agony. [. . .] We went out gouty and lumbered for half an hour to a cocktail party at the Palace hotel given for the tennis festival. There were no tennis players there as far as we could see but hordes of stupid middle-aged autograph hunters. E insisted on taking the masseur (Ulrich Behrens) and his wife to the party. They were frostily received by the management Messrs Scherz until they saw they were with us when their lofty scowls turned into beaming smiles of welcome. The Swiss are as snobbish as the British. You see Herr Behrens is a visiting masseur to the Palace Hotel. [. . .]

Sunday 11th Liza arrived yesterday evening accompanied by a large thunderstorm. [. . .] The weather until about four o'clock yesterday has been superb and I do most of my writing, Italian, French and Serbo-Croat in the sun. [. . .]

We go to see the tennis finals this morning. And then to lunch at the Palace perhaps. E's back much better. Liza looking like a cabbage out of which rises a beautiful face and wearing the most unflattering dress I've ever seen.

---

[8] Stan Smith (USA) (1946) beat Tom Gorman (USA) (1946), 6 3, 8 6, 6 2 and John Newcombe (Australia) (1944—) beat Ken Rosewall (Australia) 6–1, 6–1, 6–3.
[9] At the Swiss Open championships.
[10] Anthony Shaffer, author of the screenplay for what would become the film *Absolution*, in which Burton starred. His brother Peter (later Sir Peter) would write *Equus*, which Burton would act in on stage and on film.
[11] Joseph Losey would direct Burton in *The Assassination of Trotsky*, Burton playing the title role of Leon Trotsky (1879–1940).
[12] Beatrix Miller was the editor of the British edition of *Vogue* from 1965 to 1983. By the 'Snowdons' Burton means Princess Margaret and her husband, Antony Armstrong-Jones, the 1st Earl Snowdon. The article (which is bound amidst the pages of the diary) is a draft of 'My Day', an article that appeared in *Vogue*, 1 September 1971.

Monday 12th Went to see the men's singles finals. Newcombe of Australia and Okker of Holland. Newcombe won in five sets.[13] Half a dozen good rallies but mostly serve and volley. [. . .]

Played table tennis with Liza after breakfast and again after lunch. Her conversation is entirely standard cliché and platitude out of Heathcliff, I mean Heathfield. Her accent is awful at the moment, a terrible amalgam of Berks and Kensington refained. She is quite puppy fatted and pretends to be going on a diet with me and E but I don't think she'll stand it for very long. What she needs is a thumping lot of exercise. She went horse riding this morning and plays a couple of hours of ping pong a day with me which is a good thing for all concerned.

Wrote five letters yesterday and actually sent them off. Usually I write letters, which I like doing when in the mood and then find them in my briefcase six months later.

[. . .] Still not in a bookreading mood. Anything else will do. *National Geographic, Encyclopedia Britannica, Larousse*, painful reading of French and Italian. Well Italian is painful. French is ok reading one Maigret after another but not a sustained word in English. Heard in Cadonau's this morning that Julie Andrews is in town also that John Kenneth Galbraith has just left.[14] Wish it were the other way round.

15th It's afternoon and am sitting on the lawn outside the library. Julie Andrews and Blake Edwards (husband, film director) came to dinner. They seemed very nice together. He had sent a book the day before by Kingsley Amis called the *Green Man*.[15] It is, as one expects from Amis, expertly written but has 'don' written all over it. About ghosts which is never my cup of tea. But this one held my interest to the end which considering my inability to read at the moment is a fair old feat. They may use the house, this one at Xmas. Have ordered a lock-up filing cabinet to put away all the papers and diaries etc. Good idea anyway, even if we don't have visitors. Answered [. . .] letter from George Thomas, MP and wrote to David Harlech, Stan Baker and James Wishart passing on the message.[16] [. . .] Why do we send such obvious mediocrities to the Commons when there are such brilliant chaps on every street corner at home? I suppose we are all so bloody lazy that we let the dull and insignificant – like Lord Llew Heycock for

---

[13] John Newcombe (Australia) beat Tom Okker (Netherlands), 6–2, 5–7, 1–6, 7–5, 6–3 at the Swiss Open in Gstaad.

[14] John Kenneth Galbraith (1908–2006), economist and writer.

[15] Kingsley Amis (1922–95), *The Green Man* (1969).

[16] George Thomas (1909–97), Labour MP for Cardiff West, later Speaker of the House of Commons, and Viscount Tonypandy. Thomas had written to Burton in connection with the flotation on the Stock Exchange of HTV, asking Burton to use his influence to place HTV's business with the Hodge financial group, based in Cardiff.

Christ's sake – who are prepared to go to party meetings in vestries and half-empty halls, do the job for us.[17] [. . .]

16th Received [. . .] telegram yesterday from the editor of *Vogue*.[18] Why do notices and things similar about what little writing I do thrill me and notices for acting leave me totally indifferent? I was on air for the rest of the day after getting Miller's cable regardless of whether she has any judgement or not. Elizabeth played a trick on me which for a moment took me in completely. I [. . .] was awoken from a fairly deep nap by E brandishing the telegram and saying 'Your first rejection slip. I'm sorry Rich.' She said that my face for a second was a pathetic sight and 'all scrunchled up' as if I were about to burst into tears. Cheeky devil.

[. . .] I am slowly recording on a Philips tape machine the whole of Assimil in English for our German masseur and his wife who are very anxious to learn English.[19] The English is somewhat archaic – I imagine the text must be several decades old but it is good enough to start with. Also it means that I am getting a rough knowledge of German as I read the German listening to the English.

Sunday 18th [. . .] Very sad article yesterday in *Ici Paris* about the death of Maria's grandmother and the torment her mother and father have been suffering since allowing her to go for adoption.[20] Why don't the miserable French gutter press leave them alone. I have kept the article hidden away. Perhaps Maria will want to see such things one day.

Headlines in all the papers and front page that Nixon is going to meet Mao Tse Tung in Peking before next May.[21] Fancy Nixon graduating to statesmanship. Perhaps the office has made yet another man though I find it hard to believe. I dislike drunkards (and he was drunk as the devil the last time I saw him – before becoming President) having dominion over palm and pine and me and mine.[22]

Lovely down here in the library with the fire going and the beautiful books all around in disciplined ranks. [. . .]

We have our neighbours – who have been so generous with Maria, in for drinks tonight. They are Germans I think. [. . .]

Monday 19th [. . .] The German neighbours called Kehl, he's a banker in Dusseldorf and comes here for weekends only. She very outdoorsy looking,

[17] Llew Heycock (1905–90), a leading figure in the Labour Party in South Wales, who had been elevated to the peerage as Baron Heycock of Taibach in 1967.
[18] Telegram from Beatrix Miller enthusiastically accepting Burton's article.
[19] Assimil, a French publishing house specializing in language learning.
[20] *Ici Paris*: a weekly magazine.
[21] President Nixon (1913–94) would actually visit China in February 1972.
[22] A reference to the song 'California, sweet homeland of mine', which includes the lines 'Neath the palm of the sheltering pine / California, sweet homeland of mine'.

blonde and a little weathered though she can only be in her thirties. Skiers, horse-riders, early morning swimmers etc. and mountain walkers and pick-nickers. Nice enough. He with a loud cracked voice which seems typically Germanic and suggests an underlying nervousness. Perhaps hysteria. They must have a fair amount of money as the chalet next door, though smallish, must have cost a pretty penny and he flies to Gstaad from Dusseldorf every Friday and flies back again every Monday morning. Made fun of the German Swiss. Naturally. So did we rather lamely and affectionately. [...] Shall go shopping for odds and ends in a minute. I'm getting to the stage where I have a hatred of being stared at so the time for shopping for me is the early morning while the tourists are still a-bed and only the Swiss are around who couldn't give a cuss who you are. [...]

Wednesday 21st Spent most of yesterday with Jugoslavians about the Tito film. Lots of fascinating talk about Communism and Russia but mostly about Tito. Talked to Aaron who said it would be alright to postpone the other film[23] [...] We go, at Tito's invitation, to see him on the 28th instant. Should be very interesting to say the least. [...]

I start the film on the 15th of next month and the other film about the 15th of the month after. The former near Dubrovnik and the latter in Jersey.[24] Both places will be new to me and E.

[...] Have become very busy with my hands – gout and all – and managed to find out how to operate a very elaborate and very expensive Japanese TV machine which takes instant movies. Great fun fiddling about with it taking pictures of Liza and Maria on the trampoline, swings etc. [...]

Saturday 24th, Gstaad Leaving this morning by helicopter and plane for Nice and the *Kalizma*. [...]

Just discovered to my fury that Toronado, in perfect shape sold for 5000 Swiss francs. And who to? To Solowicz who was in charge of its sale.[25] Must investigate further.

Sat in sun yesterday and did nothing much except read the *Tribune de Genève* and listened to the Italian records.[26] Took Liza to the manege and walked E'en So for an hour while Liza went over the jumps.[27]

The pound of chocolate that I ate the day before last has had no effect on my weight as far as the scales go. Still around 174. Should drop before long to 170.

---

[23] This film is probably *Absolution*.
[24] Dubrovnik, city on the Adriatic coast, in the then state of Yugoslavia (now in Croatia). Jersey, the Channel Islands.
[25] Maurice B. Solowicz, Fert & Cie, Voyages/Transports, of Rue Fendt, Geneva, Burton's car dealer.
[26] *Tribune de Genève*: Geneva's daily newspaper.
[27] *Manège*: a riding school.

Am seeing Mazlanski, Shaffer, Berkeley and uncle Tom Cobly on the *Kalizma* on Tuesday re *Absolution*, the film.[28] [. . .]

Sunday 25th, Kalizma Journey here, both copter and plane very smooth and very fast. [. . .] E moaned all day long about the condition of the boat. Only two glasses out of scores left. Must have all been smashed I suppose. Big stain on the back of one of the chairs and two more on the bed-head and the facing wall. E tamping.[29] Raymond with a face as long as a yard of ale because quite clearly the steward and stewardess don't know their jobs. The former at least doesn't know how to serve table and his wife says, if you please that she doesn't launder. There is a perfectly good laundry on board. All she has to do is stick the stuff in the machine hang it on the line and iron it. The new cook is amiable and good so far and oldish but Raymond says he is dirty around the kitchen. We shall see. Moved the yacht immediately from Monaco to Villefranche to avoid the gawkers who were slowly gathering.[30] Parked a few hundred yards from the shore at Villefranche. Very pretty. Niarchos' 'Creole' is a hundred yards away.[31] E says that some one has bought it from him and he's going to buy another. [. . .]

Monday 26th, Monte Carlo Beth's baby was born yesterday at 2am.[32] A girl, as yet nameless. We didn't know until this morning as we spent Saturday and Sunday moored off Villefranche. Great excitement and I broke my drinking fast for the first time since June 15. Had a glass of nasty champagne and two or was it three stiffish martinis. Knocked me sideways and I slept for three or more hours this afternoon. We are off to London tomorrow morning and will stay until Thursday to muck about with the parents and baby.

Watched a very spectacular fireworks display tonight. This one put on by the Germans. The Portuguese and English still to come. They'll have to be good to beat the Germans. But then the Germans never play at anything and are always at war.

Telegram from Popovic to say we are expected in Pula at 10am Saturday 31st to meet Tito etc.[33] [. . .]

Tuesday 27th, Kalizma, Carlo Beautiful morning and early. [. . .] Excited at seeing the baby. Monte Carlo with all its new apartment blocks is becoming an eyesore. Towering block after towering block and also has become very noisy. [. . .]

---

[28] *Absolution* would eventually be made in 1978 but not released until 1981.
[29] 'Tamping' meaning mad, furious.
[30] Villefranche-sur-Mer: resort and port between Nice and Saint-Jean-Cap-Ferrat.
[31] Stavros Spyros Niarchos (1909–96), shipping tycoon. *Creole* was his luxury yacht, which he sold following the death of his wife in 1970.
[32] Beth Clutter, wife of Michael Wilding Jr.
[33] Nikola Popovic, producer of *The Battle of Sutjeska*.

There are a lot of things I can do in London – the meeting with Shaffer et al. Find out from Wishart and *Eagles* what the hell is going on at 2, Squire's Mount.[34] See Ivor and Gwen and depress myself. Call Kate if possible. Call Frosch if possible.

Both E and I in good humour so far. Will continue if she's on time. [. . .]

Have just received Deakin's book on Jugoslavia and the battle of Sutjeska.[35] Shall read it in London and on plane, though probably will do French and Italian via cassettes Assimil. Passes the time wonderfully.

Only one mention in the *Express* yesterday of the baby's birth. Thought there would be far more fuss. Might happen today with our arrival at London Airport. Just as well if there is none. [. . .]

Wednesday 28th, Dorchester [. . .] Yesterday, apart from the little baby – six pounds born – was a terrible day. Michael started it by announcing point-blank that he had no intention of continuing as Gianni Bozzacchi's assistant and that he was going to be a pop-group musician. Since he plays no known instrument with anything like proficiency and neither do any of his friends this is a hazardous prospect at the best. When he hurts and disappoints E as he does time after time I sometimes really feel physically violent. [. . .] The house is a mess apparently and is full of spongers and drifters. This we settle for but it hardly seems a fair place to take a child who is exquisite and Beth, also exquisite, who quite clearly loathes the atmosphere [. . .]. There is nothing to do but wait for him to grow up and think for himself. And the gaps in his knowledge are alarming. I had hoped that, when he quit school, that he would fill up the crevices by self-education but he still reads only what's currently fashionable among his friends. *Mad* Magazine and the inevitable Hesse, a phony, and Alistair Crowley, who is a joke.[36] He had professed a fascination with the Book of Revelations which I had talked to him about in Cuernavaca – particularly the 13th chapter.[37] He couldn't wait to read it he said. Yesterday I asked him if he'd thought about it any more, or if he'd read more Blacke.[38] Nothing. He had done nothing.

Ivor is very near the end. Death is written all over his face. He did not know me when I saw him yesterday. He can barely speak. He is already dead. I wish he were. The sight of Ivor, after the emotional disturbance of baby and Beth and Michael, finally reduced E to tears and she sobbed all the way back to the Dorchester and sometime afterwards. Liza was an angel to Elizabeth and

---

[34] Burton had owned 2, Squire's Mount Cottages, Hampstead, London since 1960, and it had been used as a home by Ivor and Gwen and, after Ivor's accident, by Gwen alone.

[35] Sir William Deakin (1913–2005), *The Embattled Mountain* (1971).

[36] *Mad*, a satirical magazine published in the USA. Hermann Hesse (1877–1962), novelist, perhaps most famous for *Steppenwolf* (1927). Aleister Crowley (1875–1947), writer on the occult, philosopher, mountain climber and explorer.

[37] Cuernavaca, Mexican city.

[38] By 'Blacke' Burton probably means William Blake (1757–1827), poet, mystical writer, artist.

cwtched her as the positions were reversed as 'twere and Liza was the mother and E the child. I love that child. She can be a bit of a bastard at times but she is fundamentally an angel and great in a crisis. So that was something splendid out of the day. Oddly enough the day had started in Monte Carlo by Liza and E having a quarrel about clothes which ended with E slapping Liza. Liza is going through a period where she thinks she is fat and ugly. Everybody but she thinks she is ravishing but there's no way of persuading her. And so to business and meeting Kate at Ivor's and buying books and thank the good God back to the *Kalizma* in the morning.

Thursday 29th, Dorchester A long long day. I waited for the Brass to turn up at 11 o'clock yesterday morning but they didn't and when I finally called I gave Ron Berkeley a severe tongue-lashing for making such a mess of the appointment.[39] I saw them at 6 instead and they were pleasant enough and it seems we shall go ahead with the film on September 15th as planned. Shaffer is a fat man biggish with prematurely grey hair and something wrong with his left eye. He told strange stories of being a Bevin boy in the last war but by no means an ordinary one – he was in intelligence and was a counter spy, he says, on the look out for infiltratory agents intent on sabotage.[40] Did you catch anybody asked somebody and if so what did you do with them? I shot them he said, or rather arranged for them to be killed. This is very easy in the mines he said. I didn't believe a word of it and said so. He said he had written it up he said but was not allowed to publish because of the official secrets act etc.[41] I shall see a lot of him in the next few weeks and shall delve further. It all seems a little too fantastic. But it could it seems be true. The British Secret Service is famous for its amateur idiocies. He insisted that it was still top secret and should not be repeated. But, I said, you have just told it openly to four perfect strangers. Yes but you must promise me not to tell any one else. I shall tell everybody immediately I said.[42]

Christopher Miles – brother of Sarah Miles, the actress – and the director of the film is a tiny fellow with bright sharp humouress eyes.[43] He looks as if he knows what he wants and will insist that he gets it. The film is to be shot in Jersey where I understand the natives are bilingual. It will be interesting I hope. The snaps they showed me of the locations seem quite right. Mazlanski seems to be out of his depth in the film world of high finance.

---

[39] By 'the Brass' Burton presumably means 'the top brass' – the highest-ranking officials.
[40] Bevin boys were men conscripted to work in the coal industry, as opposed to being enlisted into the armed forces, during the Second World War.
[41] The Official Secrets Act is a piece of legislation aimed at ensuring the restriction of sensitive information usually related to national security.
[42] For more, in the same vein, see Anthony Shaffer, *So What Did You Expect?* (2001), pp. 14–17.
[43] Christopher Miles (1939–). Sarah Miles (1941–). This could be intended to be either humourless or humorous.

The delightful Kate was with us from noon on and was her usual charming self. Giggles a great deal and pretends to be appalled by my occasional irreverencies. She is a joy and went to the hospital to see the nameless one while I went to Claude Gill's to buy books for the yacht.[44] Maria came with me and I bought a very catholic selection of books. A couple of Dickens and a few thrillers and horror stories for Liza and Hornblower for Chris and a few volumes of poetry in French, Welsh and English for myself. The French ones have prose translations which will save me a lot of bother. Also brought a lot of pocket dictionaries French Italian Spanish German. Also brought books for the chauffeur Charles Simpson's sons who are showing interest in school work.

Another telegram from Sarajevo [. . .] God knows what to expect in Brioni with Tito and his lads.[45] [. . .]

Saturday 31st, en Route to Lupa, Yugoslavia [. . .] Lupa which was variously announced as being 2½ hours by air then 1½ and now we are told 65 minutes away.[46] [. . .] Reading, in proof, Deakin's book about the partisans which is full of good stories. Must see him (Deakin) when we get back. [. . .]

Arrived safely and were taken by car – Mercedes-Benz – to and through Pula where a boat awaited us. A mass of photographers and journalists and TV people at the airport to meet us. Usual questions – 'What's it feel like to play a great man?' 'How much do you know about Tito?' They have given us a villa not far from Tito's. Very hot – no air conditioning. [. . .]

Madame Broz (she prefers to be called that to 'Tito') was at the villa to meet us.[47] Big woman and very peasant looking and utterly charming with a devastating smile. Speaks a little English and understands more. We were offered canapés (which I ate, removing the bread), and champagne which I refused and delicious Turkish coffee which I didn't refuse.

Our 'apartment' upstairs consists of a large bedroom and large sitting room with two huge bathrooms. We understand that this was Jane Swanson's family house when this belonged to Italy up to 1945. Jane Swanson is our secretary who lives on ½ pay when she doesn't work for us. We shall take pictures of the house to show her. Now off to lunch with Tito.

AUGUST

Sunday 1st, Brioni A long but enjoyable day spent apart from a short nap in the afternoon and until 7.30pm – with Tito. We went to his house – a few

---

[44] Claude Gill Books, Oxford Street. The 'nameless' one being the baby.
[45] The city of Sarajevo, Yugoslavia, today the capital of Bosnia-Hercegovina. By Brioni Burton means the Brijuni islands in the northern Adriatic, location of Tito's summer residences. Brioni is the Italian spelling.
[46] Burton probably means Pula, now in Croatia, a port on the mainland (with airport), close to the Brijuni islands.
[47] Tito's (third) wife, Jovanka Broz (1924—).

minutes from ours about midday. He and wife and cameras were waiting for us. (Later we saw ourselves on TV being greeted). We sat in one corner of a large room, one end of which was the dining area. There were two tables. We sat at one with the President and Madame Broz and two interpreters and a couple of other unidentified people. We presented the President and wife with our present from Van Cleef and Arpels – a chunk of pyrite (?) with a clock set into it.[48] I told Tito, after being asked what I thought of the script, that I thought he was weakly presented in it and should be stronger and that the part was too small. He said it was OK to make it larger which pleased the director Delić no end.[49] So perhaps I'll have something better to do than just stand around and look like a man of destiny.

The President is surprisingly small and delicate. Little short arms and legs and a small head with little features. He wears slightly tinted glasses and I can't really tell the colour of his eyes. He has quite a pot-belly but the rest of him is slim – no bottom and thin chest and legs. He walks slowly and with short steps. When he sits down behind a table he seems most formidable. I'm slightly put out by the nervousness with which the servants serve us all. They live in remarkable luxury unmatched by anything else I've seen and [I] can well believe Princess Margaret who says the whole business makes Buck House look pretty middle-class. After lunch the President and I talked a great deal about the war and Sutjeska in particular. I asked him if he liked Stalin. He took a long time to answer and finally said he 'liked him or rather admired him as a politician but disliked him as a man.' Most of the time he talked Serbo-Croat but when we were alone talked slow but adequate English. I said I had read that he was fluent in French and perhaps he would prefer to speak in that tongue but he appeared not to have heard me and continued in English until, with obvious relief, the interpreter rejoined us, and he rattled away in Serbo-Croat again.

He called for us at 4pm in a convertible Lincoln-Continental – 'a present from the people of Zagreb' I think he said – and started to drive – E in front beside him and me behind with Madame Broz. He immediately punctured the front right tyre by driving over a very sharp curbstone not 50 yards from the house. Instead of stopping and cutting the engine he revved-up and we jerked and jolted about for a nerve-racking 10 seconds or so. We left the car and went on foot to visit a small zoo with an elephant and ibex and elands etc. Gazelles too. He suddenly looked very old and even smaller after the car incident but was soon his old confident self again. He seemed a little apprehensive of the elephant when feeding it. To my horror – after about 15 minutes (and to E's horror too I found out later) – the Continental turned up again all mended and we took up the drive once more. He drove at a funeral's pace but my (and E's) heart was in my mouth for the rest of the journey, which was a tour of the

---

[48] Van Cleef & Arpels: French jewellery and watchmaking company.
[49] Stipe Delić (1925—).

entire island. I was very glad to get back to his villa. He was obviously used to power-steering and power-brakes and we all threatened to go through the windscreen every time he stopped to show us something or other. But he and Madame were so charming that one forgives them anything. He loves animals and trees and has a huge collection of both on the island and elsewhere, we gathered.

At one point I asked him what he would have done had Churchill had his way and instead of opening a Second Front gone straight up through the Balkans and Austria etc. and cut off the Russian advance.[50] He answered without hesitation: 'We would have stopped you. We had, by this time, 35 divisions, all battle trained, and a great deal of arms taken from the Italians and Germans.' I suppose he would have, at that and another war would have developed. Almost in the same breath he said that he trusted Churchill but not the British. Nobody it seems trusts the British. We really are, to the foreigner, 'perfidious albion.'[51]

We finally got home about seven and had yet another enormous meal. This time I weakened and had some ice-cream. Later, having already weakened, I ate two bars of choc while watching S. Tracy in a film – rather good – called *Bad Day at Black Rock*.[52] Scales show 79kg this morning 174lbs nearly. Saw many stills this morning. I looked very haggard. Perhaps I'm getting too thin. Tito looked rubicund and toby-juggish in comparison. I should film well though. Will certainly look hungry!

Monday 2nd Another day spent almost entirely with the President. I woke late – for me, 7.40. – and had breakfast down by the sea. As usual it was too much. Cold meats, ham, salami etc. Tea. An omelette. Hot sausage. Many sweet cakes. More tea. Then at 9.30 saw Delić, Popović and a P.R. man who asked me a lot of questions about why I was doing it all etc. For the umpteenth time I went through my stock verbiage. 'Great man', 'great opportunity'. 'Hope I can do justice' etc. I hope, more aptly, that they can do justice to me. Give me the tools, i.e. part, and I'll get on with the job.[53] Were it not, actually, for E's delight in the power and glory of it all I would do my best to cut and run – so great is the strain of boredom – especially the interminable translated conversation. Both Tito and Madame Broz tell long stories which they don't allow the interpreters to interrupt result being that by the time the latter have finished

---

[50] At the Tehran conference of November 1943, Churchill had suggested further Anglo-American operations in the eastern Mediterranean. US President Franklin D. Roosevelt (1882–1945) had raised the possibility of landing in Yugoslavia in order to lend support to Tito's partisans. Stalin resisted such proposals, which came to nothing.
[51] 'Perfidious Albion': a pejorative term for England (originally rendered in French – la perfide Albion), implying a lack of trustworthiness.
[52] Spencer Tracy starred in *Bad Day at Black Rock* (1955), directed by John Sturges.
[53] A reference to the speech of 9 February 1941 by Winston Churchill, which ended 'Give us the tools, and we will finish the job'.

one couldn't care less what the story is about. Madame has a very penetrating voice which, after a time, becomes extremely tiresome. And protocol demands that I'm always with her and the President with E. And they have a professional interpreter whereas I have a minister's wife whose English leaves a lot to be desired. Mrs Broz smiles all the time and so does the interpreter.

In the morning at precisely 9.50 we left the house for the President's villa. Then straight on to a small powerful yacht – 35 knots top speed, 160 tons, 120 feet – and went belting off down through all the hundreds of islands in this part of the world. Lovely towns and hundreds of spanking new hotels. The beaches, mostly rock, were crawling with tourists. They average 30,000,000 a year they kept on saying. Almost everybody waved at the Presidential Yacht and he waved back. So did E and Raymond. As soon as we were aboard drinks were served – whisky for the President and wife and E and local red wine for the others and a gin marguerita for some and the inevitable water for me. From then on the same booze was produced at regular intervals for the rest of the day. We disembarked at the President's villa after about two hours at sea during all of which time we were escorted by two torpedo boats and a police launch. The President proudly told me that his coast was the best defended in Europe and that guns, submarines and gunboats were hidden under all the cave-infested islands.

Occasionally through the binoculars which were amply supplied I would glimpse a sailor at attention on some remote hillock rigidly saluting. We had lunch on a little island facing Brioni, not without the excruciating examination of the house and grounds. 'This is from Indonesia from Sukarno himself.'[54] 'This is work from the people of Macedonia.' 'This is from the Sudan.' I noticed that most faces bore fixed smiles of boredom long before the end of lunch and despite the fact that they were drinking. E's face of course, was an exception. She is having a ball. It is as well that I'm not drinking or I might be asking some very awkward questions. There were occasional bright moments. Tito in English: 'I was very glad when my grandmother died.' E: 'Why?' Tito: 'Because it meant she stopped beating me.' E: 'That's an awful thing to say.' Tito: 'She was small but strong and always angry.' He met Churchill who was in the vicinity on Onassis's yacht. Winston C. accepted a very small whisky. Tito had his usual large one. 'Why so small a portion?' asked Tito. 'You taught me to drink large ones.' 'That was when we both had power,' said Winston C. 'Now I have none and you still have yours.'

Power does corrupt. I doubt whether Tito sees the ordinary Joe Soap from whom he came except when the latter waves a flag and carries a banner. At least he doesn't keep his people waiting. Last night we went to see a film in the Roman Theatre at Pula. The streets were lined with sailors rigidly at attention

---

[54] Sukarno (1901–70), President of Indonesia (1945–67).

behind them being masses of people who applauded the whole route. E was the star of the evening – much more so, or at least equal to Tito. When we entered the coliseum – 6000 people capacity – they all stood up and gave an ovation. E deeply thrilled. Me cynical as ever. The film was fun. The inevitable tray of drinks was presented at the same intervals throughout the film. We had earphones with an English translation. [. . .]

Tuesday 3rd Have just come back from the minute island of 'La Madonna' which is just off the front of our villa which I discover is called 'Jadaranda' I think. We see the President and Madame for the last time this trip at noon. It is now 11.30. We had a swim and breakfast on Madonna. I eat nothing and have, in fact, eaten nothing since lunch yesterday except one plum and a vitamin pill. Rarely have I stuffed myself as much as I did at lunch yesterday on the President's island – not Brioni, the other little retreat. Madame Broz likes to play practical jokes, so I understand but is restrained by the Marshal.

Had a 3 hour discussion with Tito about Sutjeska, Mihailović, Ćetniks, British, Churchill, Allies, Stalin and Uncle T. Cob. which I will type up later when I get back to the *Kaliz* this afternoon.[55] [. . .] Am still worried by the atmosphere of dread which surrounds Tito. Cannot understand it. Neither can the rest of us.

Thursday 5th, Villefranche Have been back since Tuesday. [Monte] Carlo a nuisance as usual so nipped over here for a slice of quiet. Michael Caine on board from his rented yacht – a veritable tub that bobs like a cork.[56] He has a nice girl with him called Suzy Kendall who is married and presumably separated from her husband who is a comedian called Dudley Moore.[57] Michael speaks in a shout which becomes a bit hard in a small room. He is very funny and very cockney most of his 'wit' being a regular and repeated pattern of catch-phrases. 'Black as your hat,' 'A turkish religion with a tip-up seat' etc. All repeated at various times during the day. Spends his time going to discotheques and parties of which, down here, there are hundreds. Many good reports of *XYZ* from all kinds of sources so E might have a big one again. [. . .]

Wednesday 11th, Kalizma We left Monte Carlo two or three days ago and went to Portofino which is as enchanting as ever and where of course we inevitably met Rex Harrison and his future wife Elizabeth Rees-Williams. She was

---

[55] Draza Mihailović (1893–1946), leader of the Serbian Ćhetnik movement, which opposed Tito's Partisans during the Second World War.
[56] Michael Caine (1933—), who had starred in *Zulu*, and who was playing opposite Elizabeth Taylor in *X, Y and Zee*.
[57] Suzy Kendall (1944—), actor. Her marriage to the comedian Dudley Moore (1935–2002) ended in divorce in 1972.

married to an actor – very good I believe, though I have never met him or seen him – called Richard Harris. Professional Irish type I gather, getting drunk and fighting when sufficiently so. Rex came on the *K* at cocktail time and was already paralysed with booze. So was the Rees-Williams. Acutely painful hour or so with Rex being endlessly repetitive and eventually tottering on the brink of outright rudeness. We all agreed after they had left that this couple were among the most unattractive we'd come across in a long time and the thought of their getting married before the end of the month a monstrous joke. She is a kind of brazen blonde type with a veneer of finishing school. I feel very protective about Rex as I fear this woman is not just a harum-scarum shouter and bawler like Rache but a devious minx on the make. She looked ugly with dissipation and so did Rex. His casual elegance was noticeably lacking and he has put on a lot of weight – tremendous pot and jowls. E and I sat up in bed after they had gone and after dinner and had a smug hour telling each other how lucky we are in that we have each other and that we like each other. And so on. And by god we are lucky in virtually every way. E kept on saying: How lucky we are to love each other. Too right.

We were hoping to get away from M.C. days before we did because there is no peace there and we were inundated with visitors. Niven, Van Cleef and Arpels from whom I bought a 'Leo' necklace with a lion pendant for E as a 'granny present'. It is very pretty and cost $27,000. She loves it. 'Leo' is the child's Zodiac sign. M. Caine and Suzy Kendall. Messages from Grace and Rainier asking us to come to the Red Cross Ball held outside the Opera. Tried like mad to get out of it but couldn't very well and anyway it turned out to be an entertaining evening. I had Grace one side of me and a young baroness the other who is Paul Gallico's daughter – or rather step-daughter – who was very sweet and thrilled and is going to be an actress.[58] She calls herself, for the stage, Ludmilla Kova I think.[59] Shouldn't think she'll get anywhere. Gallico, who is 74 and looks 55, impressed E very much but her favourite Rainier was as much fun as ever she tells me. He is an extraordinarily nice man and very bright which for some reason always surprises me in royalty.

We are half way between Portofino and Porto Santo Stefano where I shall see Losey as I've decided to do *Trotsky*. *Absolution*, for which I had high hopes has fallen through financially and I was forced to give it up and do *Trotsky* in between 'Tito' shooting. Got rid of Hugh French in as nice a way as possible and asked John Heyman to revert to his old job of agent for a while. He is in Belgrade at this moment chatting the Slav money boys up.

Thursday 12th En route to Porto Santo Stefano where we should have some or will have some word from Heyman. If all goes well I shall be playing Tito on

---

[58] Paul Gallico (1897–1976), novelist and sports writer.
[59] Possibly Ludmilla Nova (1949—), actor.

Monday though I'm so lazy and enjoying the bateau so much that wouldn't be averse to a few days or even a couple of weeks postponement. Wouldn't actually be suicidal if the whole thing were scrapped until next Spring, say, or scrapped altogether for that matter.

[. . .] Children and E watched a film of mine called *Prince of Players* which I made about seventeen years ago.[60] [. . .] I remember the high hopes I had of that film and my disappointment at its indifferent reception. The original script by Moss Hart was very good when I agreed to do it but a year later when I actually did it had been murdered by Zanuck and his hacks.[61] Some of it was saveable however which accounts for what little success we had. It seems to me that I was outrageously pretty in those days and much prefer my present hard and ravaged countenance. [. . .] Like last year, I am enjoying not drinking though there have been one or two close calls. [. . .] It is easy when I am alone with E as she rarely gets drunk. About the only time I get testy with E is when she has had a couple of drinks and has taken a 'pink' pill (a pain-killer) or prematurely taken a sleeping pill which are mild enough but in conjunction with the booze makes her speech funny and gives her a kind of false euphoria and she becomes sentimental and a bit reminiscent of her mother. Since her mother is the bore of all epochs this can be a bit hard.

We have had a tremendous amount of unsought for publicity in the last few weeks and publicity of the world-wide kind. The daggers incident.[62] The grandchild, Tito – which was news-reeled all over the world I understand – and guests-of-honour at Grace and Rainier's Red Cross Ball. One Italian newspaper yesterday said that La Taylor continues to astonish the world and can say to all her rivals that she is still the greatest headline maker of them all. Rubbish but pleasant. It is phenomenal the continued attention we get. Literally there must be millions of words written about us and hundreds of thousands of photographs. Once the girls thought that they would save all the photos of E or me or both on the covers of magazines and plaster them all over the wall of the games room in Gstaad – but there were so many, even in a short time, that they abandoned the idea as they decided they, the covers, would cover the whole house. [. . .]

Friday 13th, Porto Santo Stefano[63] Confusing telegram and messages from John Heyman. [. . .] Cable from Heyman says something like Expect conclude satisfactory deal this weekend. Popović says you (meaning me, RB) not interested in money and doing film because you are such a great fan of Tito's. You

---

[60] *Prince of Players* was released in 1955.
[61] Moss Hart (1904–61), playwright, screenwriter and theatre director.
[62] Richard and Elizabeth had apparently enjoyed a central role in a knife-throwing act at a Mexican circus, Richard having written about this in his article, 'My Day', for *Vogue*, 1 September 1971.
[63] Porto Santo Stefano, on the western coast of Italy, due east of Corsica, some 100km from Rome.

expected Dubrovnik Monday, and then four question marks. ???? [. . .] We are parked outside Stefano Harbour – there are two actually –and will go in with E and Raymond at 9 o'clock to phone [. . .] and find out what I can.

The other reason for going in is to visit the café where we had our first and near-fatal drink one near-dawn morning on our way to the next bay for a clandestine weekend. I had driven E from Rome in the small hours in a rented car – a small two-seater Fiat as I remember – in order to escape the paparazzi. The town was a grave at that hour and in the bar-cafe were only a couple of people and a boy and a dog and a waiter. All the world press were searching for us. We thought we had got clean away. One of the anonymous gentlemen in the bar was a newspaper man on a humdrum assignment to cover the arrival of Dutch royalty. And lo and behold there in front of his eyes were the 'hottest' and most scandalous couple in the world. We left the place after a coffee and cognac apiece or perhaps we had two and drove in smug blissfulness to the hotel who had set aside for us a half-finished and small villa which was half a mile from the hotel, looked stupendously over the sea and was completely isolated. We gambolled like children, scrambling down the rocks to the sea and enjoying ourselves as if it was the last holiday. We found out soon enough that every bush – and there were hundreds of them – contained a paparazzo. We were well and thoroughly trapped. The weekend turned immediately from an idyll into a nightmare. We drank to the point of stupefaction and idiocy. We couldn't go outside. We were not married. We were impregnated with guilt. We tried to read. We failed. We couldn't go out. We made a desperate kind of love. We played gin rummy. E kept on winning and oddly enough out of this silly game came the crisis. For some reason – who knows or remembers the conversation that led up to it? – E said that she was prepared to kill herself for me. Easy to say, I said, but no woman would kill herself for me etc. with oodlings of self-pity. Who knows what other kind of rubbish was said. Who remembers from so long ago with everything shrouded in a miasma of alcohol what was said. Out of it all came E standing over me with a bottle or box of sleeping pills in her hand saying that she could do it. Go ahead, I said, or words along those lines, whereupon she took a handful and swallowed them with gusto and no dramatics. I didn't believe that they were sleeping pills at first. For all I knew they could be Vitamin C or anything else. She then, I think, took herself off to bed in an adjoining room. From then I hardly remember any detail. Vague memories of trying to get her awake, of realizing that she wasn't joking, running around looking for that awful 'contessa' who, I discovered later was having an affair with our sometimes chauffeur Mario, searching also for the latter. Loading E into a car and a hair-raising drive to Rome and a hospital and hiding at home because officially E had a tummy complaint or some other excuse which the press told immediately to the Marines. Not being able to go to the hospital because of the snappers and not answering the telephone to all the disaster-lovers like Roddy McDowall and Manciewicz and almost everybody.[64]

So now we have just come back from the very same café where E had a cafe latte and a cognac as she did that time ago, and I noticed that it was Friday the 13th. I mean today and decided that I didn't want any repetition of that awful Easter. By God, what if she'd died. Worse, what if she'd lived with an impaired brain? I'm perfectly sure that I am incapable of suicide so presumably I would still be alive. What would I be doing? Maybe I would have drowned myself in booze by this time. Anyway, it's all over though never forgotten. It certainly has cured any thoughts of suicide from this family. In that year also Sybil had a go at knocking herself off. I was furious with her but not furious oddly enough with E. I suppose I must have been thinking of Kate being motherless and didn't think similarly of Liza, Maria et al. being likewise because they were still little-seen-known or loved by me at the time. [...]

Still Friday 13th, Approaching Anzio[65] [...] Tito told me that he never ever raised his voice above ordinary conversational level during his whole life, except where distances were involved – shouting across a valley for instance – and that he had always found it infinitely more effective and on occasions much deadlier than a Hitlerian or Mussolinian storm.

Kate and I discussed the day-to-day aspect of our lives and how strange it must be for people in ordinary jobs with a regular pay-packet to understand a life where, like today, we don't know whether we shall be in Jugoslavia tomorrow or Naples or both. Hopefully it will be Naples, or rather Ischia which is or was one of our favourite places.[66] I'm told though that it is now over-run with German tourists.

Almost in Anzio. Lovely dirty little port. And a working one to boot which I always love.

Saturday 14th, Anzio So at last the Tito deal has been fixed. I start a week on Monday – i.e. the 23rd of August and I am to be paid $50,000 expenses and $250,000 cash and vast percentages, starting at 10% of the first dollar and working up to 50% of the world grosses. I should end up with several hundred thousand dollars with an average return. A big hit of course could bring in untold monies though we are perfectly content with what we have. Heyman had just flown from the States which means that in less than a week, a week which he considers normal, he has flown from London to Nice, Nice to Rome, Rome to Belgrade, Belgrade to NY and New York to Rome and to us.[67] He flies

---

[64] Joseph L. Mankiewicz (1909–93), director of *Cleopatra*.
[65] Anzio, Italian port city, 56 km south of Rome.
[66] The island of Ischia, near Naples.
[67] Belgrade, then capital of Yugoslavia, now capital of Serbia.

back to Belgrade today and then from there to Messina (where we shall be) on Monday.[68] He is a very fast moving young man. He said the other day that he wants to retire from this business at 45, he is about 35, go into politics when his aim will be to abolish all forms of prejudice by way of a complete top to bottom revolution in education.[69] You might say he is a little ambitious.

My favourite kind of present, albeit a working present, was brought today by one of Losey's aides – a fat three volume paperback edition of Isaac Deutscher's *Trotsky*.[70] Days of splendid reading. And on a yacht too, at sea, with no telephone calls, no cables and all work set up for the next half year. Bliss.

[. . .] My refresher course in Italian has worked wonders and I find myself chatting away like mad. The Serbo-Croat has come to a stop as the discs they sent me have been completely fouled up in Nice by the man who transferred them to cassettes. Half the way through the first cassette the speakers go mad and jump from lesson to lesson like a back-played soundtrack.

Sunday 15th, Capri [. . .] E saw *Cleopatra* last night with all the kids. I popped in at one point for about ten seconds and went away and slept for another couple of hours. No reflection on the film! As a matter of fact E said this morning that the film is not at all bad – marvellous spectacle and all that. My lack of interest in my own career, past present or future is almost total. All my life I think I have been secretly ashamed of being an actor and the older I get the more ashamed I get. And I think it resolves itself into a firm belief that the person who's doing the acting is somebody else. That accounts presumably for my fury if anybody shows me anything about my acting in the magazines and journals. I don't mind the gossip stuff like 'seen walking on the Via Veneto last night' or 'The Burtons on their luxury yacht' etc. And I am equally angry whether I am praised or damned though mostly I'm praised. The press have been sounding the same note for many years – ever since I went to Hollywood in the early fifties, in fact – that I am or was potentially the greatest actor in the world and the successor to Gielgud Olivier etc. but that I had dissipated my genius etc. and 'sold out' to films and booze and women. An interesting reputation to have and by no means dull but by all means untrue. [. . .]

Monday 16th, Ischia Messina Sitting on the poop with a mug of real coffee [. . .] and the *Kalizma* steaming flat out with not a quiver on the waves. [. . .] Italians are shrieking on the radio and E is sitting opposite me having her 'breakfast' consisting of vodka and orange juice. A habit she picked up from me in my drinking days. A good start to the day if confined to one. In my case, sadly it had become as much as three and even more if there was anyone game

---

[68] Messina, Sicily.
[69] Heyman was 38.
[70] Isaac Deutscher's (1907–67) trilogy on Trotsky was first published in separate volumes in 1954, 1959 and 1963.

enough to join me. A bottle before lunchtime was by no means unusual and a pleasant but ruined morning behind me.

We left Capri, the Marina Grande, about 4 o'clock [in the] afternoon and sailed to Ischia where we parked off-shore from the Isabella Regina where we used to live in sin while locating for *Cleopatra*.[71] We went ashore to the pizzeria which we used to do then. Everybody had his or her pizza and then we attempted to do some shopping. I say attempted because the crowds became so great that we had to abandon it and run for the Riva and the *Kalizma*. [. . .]

As usual I am beginning to have butterflies in the belly at the thought of starting work again and don't even have the nerve-deadener of a script to learn as I know it is being entirely re-written. At least, I hope it is. So I continue with Italian and French and Frances Stevenson's [diary] re Lloyd George and Trotsky's life.[72] My ignorance of the latter was monumental. I didn't know that he was one of the Mensheviks, for instance, or that he vilified Lenin so harshly.[73] As for Frances Stevenson, her diary is sweet but she sometimes makes Lloyd George sound like a boastful little nothing.[74] Writing only his version of events and being constantly challenged by history in the shape of dry little footnotes by the editor, A. J. P. Taylor. [. . .]

Tuesday 17th, Ionian Sea [. . .] E read the diary yesterday and said I'd forgotten to mention the cig-holder given to her by Tito. It is the famous one, much cartooned, which he used to flourish a lot at the UN and other convocations holding it as if it were a pencil with hot end up. She passed many many remarks on its unusual beauty assuring him it must be a Fabergé.[75] It seems to me that no one there knew what a Fabergé was or is. However after two days of subtle brow-beating he gave it to her. She kissed him on both cheeks which gratified him enormously. He gave me a bunch of flowers. He also gave us a lot of his own home-produced wine made in his own vineyards. [. . .] There is some trouble brewing up again on his borders with Hungary, Romania and Bulgaria. Doubtless he'll be able to handle it. Geographically of course, he has that coveted access to the sea which all the land-locked have greedy eyes on. I understand a sight more about Russia's behaviour between the wars since reading *Trotsky* and for the first time Stalin's pogroms and purges take on a kind of historical inevitability. [. . .]

Wednesday 18th, Adriatic [. . .] Am still deep in *Trotsky* and so far the man who comes out as the most enigmatically fascinating is Stalin. I must get

---

[71] L'Albergo della Regina Isabella, Piazza Santa Restituta, Ischia.
[72] A. J. P. Taylor (1906–90) (ed.), *Lloyd George: A Diary by Frances Stevenson* (1971).
[73] Mensheviks: the moderate wing of the Russian Social Democrat Party, opposed to the Bolsheviks.
[74] Frances Stevenson (1858–1972), secretary to and second wife of British Prime Minister David Lloyd George (1863–1945).
[75] House of Fabergé, the Russian jewellery designers.

Deutscher's book about him as soon as I get back to an English library.[76] I
could order it to be sent to Rome for the start of the Trotsky film.

[   ] We are due in Dubrovnik in about four hours and am beginning to
feel nervous again about Tito. Jesus I hope they have a part for me to get hold
of. I have all rights outside Jug[oslavia] so I must do my best to get things done
so that I can re-cut and if necessary cut out some of the things they might get
up to. That is, if the director is as average as he seems to be. We shall soon find
out. How splendid it will be if the director is very good.

I want to persuade them – I have done so partially – to included a great
[deal] more stuff about the British Military mission's reaction to Tito and
his struggle. A lot more emphasis on his refusal to try and merely talk the
British – Deakin principally – into getting Allied support but to <u>show</u> them by
the deeds of his partisans that they were really fighting the German and Italian
and Bulgarian armies. I also want to show in as low-key a fashion as possible
Tito's life-long refusal to shoot captured enemies, even Ćetnik traitors. He told
me of one terribly bitter story. He had a few hundred German prisoners and
was at a point where he was forced to retreat. To carry the prisoners with him
would have been a tremendous strain on his ever-slender resources. So he
informed the senior German officer that he was releasing them to find their
own way back to their commands. They were astonished but delighted, naturally. The usual treatment in that kind of warfare was to shoot all prisoners. He
also hid his own injured men who were not able to move in what he thought
was a safe place. He found out later that the released Germans returned as
soon as he had disappeared and slaughtered the helpless partisans. Even so, he
never wreaked vengeance. The other day, I noticed that Mihaaelovic [sic], the
Royalist Ćetnik leader died of old age.[77] He had not been shot when he was
caught but given a trial, found justly guilty of collaboration with the enemy
and sentenced to life imprisonment (I believe) <u>but not shot</u>. When we were
with Tito he said how sorrowful he was that one of his favourites in the Sudan
coup which was happening then had shot out of hand scores of political and
military prisoners.[78] This had turned him off completely. I asked him if he had
ever lost his temper during those harrowing years of ravenous warfare. He said
he had only done so twice. Once when he and some of his men were trapped
in a cave and one by one tried to break out against heavy and concealed enemy
fire. He said he blazed away at a helplessly trapped company of Germans who
were in a captured jeep. Once when Deakin came to him to tell him that, after
the capitulation of Italy, all captured Italian arms, ammunition, tanks etc.
should be held and handled over to the Allies. Deakin mentions this in his

---

[76] Isaac Deutscher, *Stalin* (1949).
[77] It is not clear here what Burton is referring to. Mihailović had been shot in 1946.
[78] An unsuccessful Communist-backed coup, led by Hashem al-Atta, had been staged in the Sudan
from 19 to 22 July 1971. Hashem al-Atta was executed following the coup's failure.

book too saying it was the first time he, Deakin had seen the Marshal go mad with rage.[79] Among many little oddities I found from Tito [was] that he shaved everyday of the war except one day, the one day, when he was wounded in the left upper arm by bomb splinters. And that he dressed as impeccably as was possible throughout the whole madness. Another bit: he had sent a message to Stalin telling him of his release of the German prisoners. He received a brutally nasty telegram from Stalin in reply to which he sent a cold reply saying the unless Stalin could send him, Tito, material assistance, or at least the morale-lifting presence of a military mission, he should mind his own business. When later Tito went to Moscow to see Stalin there was a small party at which, among many others, was the dreaded Beria, chief of the Secret Police.[80] Many toasts were drunk and all inevitably to Stalin. Tito had not had a drink of any alcoholic kind during four years and the eternal vodka was hitting him very hard. When his turn to toast came he toasted the inevitable Stalin, whereupon Stalin said with deadliness 'Why do you toast me now after sending me that insulting telegram?' Tito mumbled some placatory answer but the atmosphere was charged with menace. Later feeling sick from the vodka Tito went out into the grounds to throw up. A shadow appeared among the trees. It was Beria who said: 'Don't worry, it is only your friendly policeman!'

Thursday 19th, Dubrovnik We arrived off Dubrovnik at 5.15 yesterday after-noon and waited for the pilot for whom we continued to wait and wait. [. . .] When the pilot finally appeared before our puzzled eyes he explained that there was an hour time difference between Italian and Jugoslavian time. Hence the muck-up.

To our surprise, puzzlement and delight there wasn't a soul to meet us. The wharf was a desert [. . .] After about half an hour the inevitable little John Howard appeared telling us that everybody was on tenterhooks waiting for us to come.[81] The radio and TV had been on about it for days. Were we coming by jet, private, or our yacht. We were due on Wednesday morning, Wednesday evening, we were coming by sea-plane on Thursday! Within half an hour they descended on us like Assyrians. Popović, Delić, Stepanjek, yet another inter-preter a General in full get-up – didn't get his name but sounded like Vuko something – the press representative.[82] [. . .] The Slavs seem unexpectedly to have a manana sense of time except so far Tito.[83] He was as fanatically on the dot as I am. [. . .]

[79] F. W. Deakin, *The Embattled Mountain* (1971), p. 115: 'This meeting was the only occasion since our arrival when Tito displayed, in my presence, an explosion of temper.'

[80] Lavrentiy Pavlovich Beria (1899–1953), head of the NKVD (People's Commissariat for Internal Affairs) in the USSR.

[81] John Howard: Australian photographer based in Rome.

[82] Stepanjek may be Branimir Šćepanović, the screenwriter. 'Vuko' is later adjusted by Burton to 'Vulkov'.

[83] *Mañana*: a tomorrow which may never arrive.

Friday 20th [. . .] The house is enormous and totally impersonal and it seems that we are the first people to sleep [there]. Despite its vastness it only contains four bedrooms, two of them gigantic and containing two equally gargantuan study-offices adjoining. The other two are your large but not awe-inspiring bedrooms. The groundfloor 'lounge' and dining-room which leads off from it is about the size of a tennis court. There are 17 servants only one of whom speaks English or Italian and badly at that. So I have temporarily married my Serbo-Croat phrase book. Have you . . . and nouns nouns nouns. Coffee, tea, onions, tomatoes.

Everybody means well but we shall quietly move back to live on the yacht. It is cooler and there is no language problem for E when I'm not around and the beloved books are ambient.

The yacht is parked very precariously near the steps leading up to the house and is potentially dangerous in case of a sudden sirocco so on local advice we are moving today to a little harbour about three miles away. Since leaving the yacht here is inviting everybody, and there are many many people around, to a perpetual 'open house', it is a good idea to get away. Yesterday we had Hardy Krüger and wife and children and the nanny and a Jug actress very young and a bit 'cute' called Neddy pronounced Naydee and probably written Nedj or something.[84] Krüger and wife are very German and very serious and determinedly intellectual. Somebody mentioned Visconti's *Death in Venice* and I said I hadn't seen it and – politely and totally without interest – asked if Mrs Krüger had seen it.[85] She had. What did she think of it? I said like a fool. Foolish, because then she proceeded to tell me and at length with a wealth of perfectly predictable criticisms of it because I too had read a few of the notices by accident, and saw them all coming like a Teutonic juggernaut. Phwew! Krüger himself who is one of those measured mental pipe-smoking meer-schaums went on for an equally long time about the vast problem of whether E should or should not play a small part in the film of a partisan lady-doctor who is conventionally brave and loses her legs in a battle and suitably dies heroically and so on. I said that I wouldn't dream of asking a major star like E or Loren or A. Hepburn to play such a minute and conventional role and that it demanded nothing of her while she, being a professional, would demand a great deal of them.[86] Well, Mr Krüger went on, now Stanislavski ('There are no small parts. Want a bet Stan?) Freud and Stephen Haggard (I would rather play a bad part in a good play than a good part in a bad play) and charity, as 'twere, her, E's contribution to the heroism of the Slav peoples by playing a

[84] Hardy Krüger (1928—). Krüger's wife at this time was the Italian painter Francesca Marazzi. Krüger and Burton would co-star in *The Wild Geese*, but Krüger did not appear in the final cut of *The Battle of Sutjeska*. Neda Arneric (1953—).
[85] *Death in Venice* (1971), directed by Luchino Visconti (1906–76).
[86] Audrey Hepburn (1929–93).

small part for nothing.[87] My syntax is all to hell as I am sitting on the poop and am continually distracted by Liza, Kate and E and Raymond.

I awoke this morning [. . .] and went downstairs to read the 'new' script. It is as far as I can remember the same as the previous one with the addition of a few large extracts from Tito's memoirs or speeches which read like memoirs or speeches and which I will change myself into believable jargon. As for the rest of it I have suggested that they employ a standard and inexpensive writer of English to put the translation into speakable terms. Example: young Partisan girl shouting to her companions in the midst of battle 'Remember the Dalmatians' which conjures up an image of a frenzied pack of Disney hounds.[88] I read out E's part to her as it came up. She is in 14 out of 214 which we have decided is not a dominating role especially as she is never mentioned throughout the other 200 pages. We have just heard from Ron that they are terribly disappointed but will search immediately for somebody else. Who do they have in mind, they were asked? Oh people like Jane Fonda, Simone Signoret, Vanessa Redgrave etc. They are breathtakingly unrealistic. But their innocence is so total that they might surprise us all by actually getting someone like that.

Anyway, and perfectly selfishly, if the film is a bust they have only one of us to blame because they always blame us for the failures and praise the director for our successes. I have lost count of the number of times I've read that 'Director X managed to wrest a brilliant performance out of Elizabeth Taylor.' This is particularly surprising to us because E and I in our combined careers don't recollect more than a dozen lines of direction all told from all directors. And specifically, since I reached my majority, so to speak, as an actor I don't remember any particular direction at all. The only people I remember actually evoking something in me as an actor which I didn't know was there are Phil, Emlyn and John Gielgud. All of which invaluable stuff I learned before I was 23 or so. Since, and sometimes with sad results, I have directed myself. The last man to give me direction which I found interesting and followable and some-times enthrallingly brilliant was Mike Nichols and that was in the comedy sequences in *Woolf*. A lot of people have said that my very long speech in that same film under the tree and on the swing outside the house is one of the best pieces of acting etc. I did it, I remember, in one take and without direction from Mike apart from things like 'maybe you should move from the swing to the tree'. And as for other 'great directors' like Marty Ritt, Mankiewicz, Babblin' Tony Richardson etc. I don't remember anything they said except idiocies which I ignored.

---

[87] Constantin Stanislavski (1863–1938), actor and director, usually credited with inspiring the 'method' approach to acting. Stephen Haggard (1911–43), actor, poet and writer.
[88] A reference to the Walt Disney film, *One Hundred and One Dalmatians* (1961).

Saturday 21st Beautiful morning as indeed all the mornings are here so far. Am sitting in a very smelly very noisy helicopter which is our transport to work in the mountains. The journey takes approx 45 minutes and unlike the many copters I have flown in hitherto there are only tiny little windows so there is – without a lot of contortion – no way of watching the lovely land underneath. Looking at it from above I wonder again at the tenacity of the Germans in being able to fight at all in these dreadful places. Crag and crevice, precipice and ravine, choked pass after choked pass, natural ambushes by the thousands and a people of murderous courage, and no victory to show for it as the Slavs would never face them in straightforward battle – hit and run, sabotage and hide, in and out of these endless hills. And what an admirable people the Jugoslavians are. Loveable and naive and quite clearly very different from the Latin and Anglo-Saxon. There is a lot of Asiatic fatalism combined with an almost Italian élan. I would guess.

[. . .] When I arrived in the mountains, a place called Zablijia pronounced Jabla (French 'J'), there were about a hundred press people, perhaps more.[89] This seemed odd as the copter landed in a field – actually it was a grass runway for light planes – and a scene one normally associates with big international airports took place on farm land. There were endless questions and only one which I'd never been asked before on this trip. To my carefully hidden astonishment a very sharp lady asked me how I felt playing Tito and was I also nervous because I was working with a director who'd never directed a film before. Since the Popović had given me the impression that Delić, the metteur, had done about 50 films and was the number one in Jugoslavia I was a little taken aback. I pointed out quite rightly that I had made three or four films with previously unknown directors and all those films had been successful: *Woolf* with Nichols, *Shrew* with Zeffirelli, *Anne* with Charles Jarrott and now *Villain* with whassisname.[90] Received a cable, incidentally, from Nat Cohen saying the notices for latter superb and great box-office, and another cable said we expect a million pounds from UK alone. That means about $½m for me if I remember correctly.

There is no accounting for the differing tastes of Yanks and English critics. *Villain* was received badly in the US and with rapture in the UK. I know it is cockney and therefore difficult for Yanks to follow but one would have thought the critics to be of sufficiently wide education to take it in their stride. The English critics, after all, are not embarrassed when they see a film made in Brooklynese. Anyway I am so delighted that it is doing well in UK. Otherwise I would have doubted E's and my judgement in such matters. I thought it was good and she said she knew it was good. The American reaction was therefore a surprise.

---

[89] Burton means Zabljak, now in Montenegro, which is at an altitude of 1,456 metres.
[90] The director of *Villain* was Michael Tuchner (1934—).

22nd, Zablja Came up last night in a helicopter to stay in a small house in this village. We have worked here for three days though me only for two as I have Sundays off. E [. . .] asked Gianni and Claudye to say with us though, thankfully they are going to the hotel today. Apart from the house being very small and despite the fact that they are nice people, neither of them are readers and E and I are. Also it means four people, all of whom get up at the same time, sharing one minute bathroom. [. . .] On Friday, I mean Saturday I spent my time apart from one tiny scene which contained dialogue narrowly escaping being blown up. Don't know what they'll look like on the screen but they – the explosions – looked bloody effective in reality. They had real planes too, trying to look like stukas – about 20 of them. Must have cost a fortune. And will look no better I suspect than an old Anglo-Saxon mock-up. At least to the ordinary public. [. . .]

It is magnificent country up here in the mountains – the famed Montenegrin mountains – and I could live here a long time if asked to. It is apparently cut off from the rest of the world completely in the depths of winter. I would like that. [. . .]

To my astonishment the actor with whom I have most to do in the film doesn't speak a word of English and was prepared to speak all his dialogue in Serbo-Croat. I refused to do this saying it would give the dubber into English an impossible task and ruin the film for distribution in the Western world. As it is, I don't see it having a chance even with them speaking all the dialogue in broken English with me speaking in perfect Oxford. We can, I think write this film off before we start. The Jugs are also particularly thick when one tries to explain this to them and I have almost given up. Even the Englishmen, Deakin, Stewart et al. are Serbs. It's hair-tearing. I plead with them that Deakin and Stewart are upper class British, one of them, Deakin, being an actual Oxford professor. But to no avail. Actually, assuming that they speak the English lines reasonably well they could be dubbable without it being too obvious but it will still look cheap.

I would willingly have learned my part in Serbo-Croat if they'd given me time but I cannot do it at short notice. I am in with a bunch of child-amateurs and must settle for it.

However it is lovely up here and the people are charming and willing and I must regard the whole thing as a working holiday. I'll do my best and hope for the best. [. . .]

23rd, Zablja [. . .] Have given up the film as a film and will now concentrate on doing my bit as well as possible. [. . .] If I'm not happy in a film it affects my whole attitude to everything. I am beginning to dislike this place and can't wait to get away from it though it is unquestionably delightful. There was a party given, I suppose, in honour of the film company which was friendly enough but my sour reaction was that all the actors there should be home learning their lines in English. Why the hell didn't they do it all in Serbo-Croat including an Yugoslav actor playing Tito instead of this half-assed thing that will appeal to neither the Slavs or the English audience! [. . .] I left the party early, unable to stand any longer the false bonhomie induced by showing off to the foreigners and the drunkenness. Being sober among a horde of drunks is exquisite torture. I slid quietly home and talked with Claudye for a while who had been as bored as I was and then tucked myself into bed with, surprisingly, a bad book by John D. Macdonald who usually can be relied on in his mock-tough-sentimental holier-than-thou way to be readable. [. . .]

24th, Cavtat-Stefani We are on the *Kalizma* en route to Stefani (I believe) where, we understand, Carlo Ponti and Sophia have a house.[91] It's supposed – the island I mean, not the Pontis' place – to be a location of staggering beauty. It is typical of us to be sailing in the dark to anchor at Stefani when we haven't yet seen the world-famous Dubrovnik which is a spit and a yard away from where we're living in Kupari.[92]

When we arrived at the *Kalizma* which is, was, moored at Cavtat there were a couple of hundred people standing on the pavement simply staring at the boat. They were delighted when we arrived and we were applauded royally. I was feeling terrible and for a second I had a feeling of panic but the crowd were so nice and friendly that I was alright immediately. E was very touched. We talked to Pedro who consulted the harbour pilot who told us that Stefani was about 3 hours away. We untied and left as soon as we could. The people waved and shouted us away as we stood beside the bridge. It was a good moment and we were both in a mood of divine content. [. . .] E is a magnificent midwife for the birth of the blues – it was her idea to go to the yacht as soon as we came down from the mountains. She didn't even consult me. And I was at bursting point. I had been very cruel to Liza this morning – viciously so. She had said that I ought to keep the film dog with me at all times while I was doing the work.[93] I said the bloody dog was so infatuated by his master that he would whine and scratch all night and in any case I said the bloody master was reluctant even to have me tickle his ears. Liza said 'But he's your dog.' And out of that cesspool of cold cruelty which some people call a brain came 'Don't be bloody stupid. He's no more my dog than you are my daughter.' Liza was as brave as hell and said with a strained little laugh 'That was very nice.' E was quite rightly livid and I wanted to cry or slit my jugular. I did neither except compound the crime by snarling at E upstairs that Liza was so insensitive that she was probably impervious to such an insult. I am so

---

[91] Cavtat, port south of Dubrovnik. Carlo Ponti (1912–2007), producer, and his wife Sophia Loren. Ponti was to produce *The Voyage*, co-starring Burton and Loren.
[92] Kupari, between Dubrovnik and Cavtat.
[93] The dog was playing the part of Tito's dog 'Lux'.

ashamed of myself for saying such a terrible thing to a creature that I love so blindingly and love her in a crazily compounded fashion. I love her for being Elizabeth's alter ego, for being lovely and so loving, for her pretty ruthless determination to get what she can get away with, for her genuine and occasionally staggering beauty and for the fact that though like me she cannot express it in so many words from some inborn refusal to give herself away I am pretty certain that she loves me. I could have cut out my vile tongue with a blunt razor. From what twisted root did that bastard tree grow? I do it again and again. In most cases where I maul and savage a victim I can generally account for it in some way. How can I attack myself so unbelievably – it is I who insists that she be Liza Todd Burton. It is I who boast about her beauty, her horsemanship, her good reports at school and even her bad ones. 'Her spelling is sometimes amusingly phonetic.' Just like her bloody mother to the T.

Eventually, I made it up with them both. But 'taint good enough.

Friday 27th, Kupari We spent yesterday in the bay of Kotor which Princess Margaret was so enthusiastic about.[94] [. . .] We entered through the straits of Verige – my little book tells me – so named because the locals would block the entrance in the middle ages with a chain and 'verige' is apparently the local word for chain.[95] The Turks appear to be the most persistent marauders and I wouldn't have thought that chains would have proved a very formidable obstacle to so tough a people. Anyway it appears that nobody over the centuries ever succeeded in penetrating into the city of Kotor. According to my little book Bernard Shaw thought it the most beautiful place on earth.[96] [. . .]

Wolf Mankowitz has arrived and has already re-written my part and simplified it. Good and hard-working man. But I think all to no avail. [. . .]

Sunday 29th, Fiord of Kotor [. . .] I said, at one point yesterday, that I thought the 'bungalow' arrangements were fine for an actor on location but that I found it surprising accommodation for the President of the country. Ah, they said, so do we, but it is to impress the people that he is still one of us. I said I thought it didn't work as far as I could see as the people are more impressed by our, E and me, display of enormous wealth – as they thought – and would be far less interested by a Ford, an arrival by Air Italia and a simple cotton frock than they are by a gleaming white yacht, a private jet and a giant Rolls-Royce. Of the scores of newspapers and magazines they bring to me occasionally which generally contain lots of pictures of me as Tito, E and me, E and me and

---

[94] The Bay of Kotor, often referred to as the Fjord of Kotor, 40 km south along the coast from Dubrovnik.
[95] The Verige strait is the narrowest section of the bay, separating the inner bay from the outer bay. A standard translation is 'trammel'.
[96] Shaw is usually credited with labelling Dubrovnik 'paradise on earth'.

Tito etc. there is invariably a very glam shot of the *Kalizma* and the Phantom 6 with a description of its inside, its TV etc. [. . .]

We steamed from Cavtat last evening as soon as I'd had time to arrive home from Sutjeska take my make-up off and shower and shampoo and get to the yacht. Liza left for England with wet eyes and much kissing from Mum and daughter, so Mum tells me, and weeping servants and all. We miss her already, rather more than usual as she has become more of a companion than hitherto and now, God be praised, has started to become our favourite thing – a book worm. *The Gabrielle Hounds* by Mary Stewart and *Rosemary's Baby* by Ira Levin which is a considerable advance over no books at all for thirteen years.[97] [. . .]

There is a big house opposite us that seems to be at least pre-war and has an air of neglect. Our Chekhovian imaginations run riot.[98] It could be very handsome if done up.

Monday 30th, Sutjeska There is no such definite locale as Sutjeska – the latter is the name of a river over which the Germans and the partisans fought so bitterly. Also here were the Italians but they are very much neglected both in history and in our script so I presume their contribution to the German slaughter of the partisans was probably as negligible as it was in every other theatre of the last war. Nearby – a short walk from this 'villa' which we are living in – is a very impressive monument to the Sutjeska dead, some 25,000 or 20–40,000 depending on which authority you listen to last, which is to be unveiled by Marshal Tito this week.[99] [. . .] There are many soldiers about who sing a lot around fires – a bit like my old Welsh lot. They seem very contented, or at least as contented as one can expect conscripted soldiers to be. [. . .]

Kathy Green, the giant daughter of Johnny Green – for many years head of the Music Dept of MGM – appeared on the set today with a man called Richard Chase.[100] I think the latter is a musician. However, while we were all waiting for the helicopter to arrive with E and Maria and Claudye aboard, she, Kathy, found a half-blind kitten, minute, in a hedge and kept it and gave it to E as she arrived. So now we have another member of the family, it seems [. . .]. It is already the centre of everybody's attention and is being fed with sugared water and milk and is being house-trained. It is a tom we think but no name has yet been chosen. I want to call it Jack. I've always like the name Jack. Dunno why really but possibly because it sounds honest and strong and masculine. Jack Stevens the Fruiterer who always thought the English language inadequate and added 'strengthening syllables' like collossical, majestical and monumentical

---

[97] Mary Stewart (1916—), *The Gabriel Hounds* (1967). Ira Levin (1929–2007), *Rosemary's Baby* (1967).
[98] Anton Chekhov (1860–1904), playwright and short-story writer.
[99] The memorial is at Tjentiste, now in Bosnia-Hercegovina.
[100] Johnny Green (1908–89), songwriter, composer, conductor, who was Music Director at MGM from 1949 to 1959.

etc. And Jack Jones Edwards, a rogue, smalltown politician in Cwmavon, and innumerably over-masculine Jack Joneses and Jack Jameses four square and brutally forward and overbearing affronters of pomposity and weak arguments. It looks however as if it might be called 'Sutjeska'. [. . .]

Tuesday 31st, Tjentiste I finally told Elizabeth this morning how ill her mother has been for the last nine days. I couldn't even confide my worry to this diary as E dips into it sporadically. Anyway her mother was operated on two days ago and the telegram we received yesterday said the five days following the operation are critical so now it's three days. [. . .] The latest telegram mentioned above was signed by some people called Karl and Mary Frances Voldeng, and of course Valerie who has been the signee for the past week and a bit.[101] [. . .] E has taken it all badly as she has a quite unjustified guilt complex re her mother. Nothing that can be reasoned out so I don't try. Also, I feel that I genuinely do not have the capacity for suffering that other people have and in particular Elizabeth. I am as dispassionate as it is possible for a human being to be and not be a machine, and what compassion I do have I find almost impossible to express. God knows what will be my feelings if anything happens to someone I greatly love but I generally console myself that I will have gone to my long home long before they. I am prepared for Ivor, even for Cis. But not for the children and above all E. If anything happens to E I am fairly positive that I won't be long after since I cannot believe that life will be worth living without her and indeed cannot believe that I ever did. I mean live without her. It was such a dreary plain with only an occasional high peak of excitement. [. . .]

SEPTEMBER

Wednesday 1st, Tjentiste [. . .] Yesterday was brilliant sunshine until lunch-time when a huge wind sprang up and by the time I finished work – about 4.30 – it began to rain and has continued to do so ever since with very few let-ups. It is pouring in torrents now at this moment and has been all night [. . .] I wonder if they can shoot in this monsoon weather. [. . .] I'd like to work because (a) I feel guilty when I don't as I cost so much money and (b) because I like these Yugoslavs so very much. I do not suffer any guilt pangs at all when working for a big studio though then I simply feel frustration at not getting the damned film finished as soon as possible. The thought of bad weather or bad luck causing a Zanuck a Warner or a Wasserman to cry into his Scotch gives me infinite pleasure.[102]

---

[101] Probably Karl E. Voldeng (1905–89) and his wife Mary Frances Voldeng.
[102] Jack L. Warner (1892–1978), executive producer at Warner Bros.

And still it rains and there are all our soldiers under canvas. Shades of Alun Lewis.[103] Unlightable fires and damp matches. Blue-cupped hands. Give us a light mate. [. . .]

It is now eight at night and still it rains and confuse it not with a drizzle. It is an unremitting Dickensian God-despairing world-ending Noachian deluge promising the end of the world by dawn. [. . .]

Thursday 2nd [. . .] The rain is coming down comme une vache qui pisse, a charming simile I learned yesterday from Claudye, and is not raining so much cats and dogs but mastodons and megathings and other prehistoric reptiles. [. . .]

Yesterday, while E stayed sensibly in bed and wrapped up, I went with Claudye, Gianni, Brook and E'en So to view the 'villa' up on the mountain called Bare. The situation is breathtaking. The house, very alpine looking on the very edge of a lovely little lake about 150 yards by 100. The road was unpaved and occasionally very dangerous, avalanche-prone, and interminable, hairpin after hairpin and in this torrential weather a real monster. We took no chances in the Phantom 6 and crept up. This meant a journey in pouring rain, of course, of just over an hour. Nevertheless I would have settled for the extra hour or so a day getting to work were it not for the fact that the interior of the house was a complete shambles. No heating except for a huge fireplace which could be jolly enough. No hot water, wood-burning kitchen stove, no electricity and no prospect of getting any as far as I could gather. Filthy, rusty bath and a blocked shower with a fin de siècle wood-burning stove to heat the water presumably. One of the ladies spoke a little French and was totally flabbergasted at the prospect of anybody staying there. But, we said, tout le monde dit que le President reste ici quelque fois. 'Jamais,' she said, 'he once came here and killed a bear, of whom the forest is full. But he has never stayed here.'[104] So thereby is killed another lie or, to be charitable, another bit of misinformation. [. . .]

Thursday 2nd, Kupari [. . .] Better and better news of Sara and hopes are now that it will not be necessary for either of us to fly to Arizona. We had more or less decided that E and Claudye would fly tomorrow. Temporarily, at least, that possibility is now in abeyance. [. . .]

Friday 3rd The Hitler War started 32 years ago today. A fine day like this I remember and a Sunday morning I think. I was excited, like all the other boys – I was 13 years old – and pleased enough that there was a real war, never dreaming that it would last long enough for me to be in the RAF toward the

---

[103] Alun Lewis (1915–44), poet.
[104] Everyone says that the President sometimes stays here. *Jamais*: never.

end of it.[105] The only disappointment was that I was quickly assured that the war meant I'd lost my chance for a schoolboy rugby 'cap' for Wales. I was an obvious certainty having been there or thereabouts the season before and was massive for my age – 12 stone and 5ft 8 or 9. I've hardly grown since. I might have got one as a grown-up largely through personality rather than genuine first class ability. I was a natural Captain wherever I played and might have sneaked a cap or two when one of the standard boys was crooked or something. I regret it a lot less than I used to do when I saw so many of my contemporaries getting caps while I was playing Shakespeare. Too late cock, too late. [...]

James Wishart expected any minute from London for me to sign some papers anent Harlech TV. It goes public shortly. I could make a fortune and pull out now but I suppose I shouldn't. Wait and see what James has to say. I wish he were a younger man and I wish he hadn't been so ill. Always affects people's judgements one way or the other.

Since writing the above we have been in to Dubrovnik again. [...] Bought books – not much choice but took everything unread. [...]

A letter from Liza [Todd]. How sophisticated her fist has become. Also one from Lil Williams who says that notices for *Milk Wood* are 'fabulous' and that one has to queue up to see *Villain* everywhere. Now if, as I expect, *XYZ* hits the jackpot too we shall have had a very good year. Even the joke film *Raid on Rommel* is surprising everybody. There's life in these old dogs yet.

Wishart's plane three hours late so shall see him tomorrow sometime. Going back up to Tjentiste tomorrow [...] to see Tito. Apparently he wants to see us before he sees all the other odds and sods. [...] And so, Samuel Pepys, to bed.[106]

Saturday 4th, Kupari James Wishart came with me [to Tjentiste] to tell me all the tales of Harlech TV. He seemed in good form and rubicund and jolly like an animated doll's head. He told me that the Harlech shares which we paid 2/6d a share for are likely to open on the market at a quid.[107] We could if we wished sell half the shares and pick up a half a million or so and still be rich holders – at the moment we are the principal shareholders by a considerable amount. I am accustomed to earning vast monies but they were earned. Picking up millions from an investment which was, I think, about £100,000 is fairy tale stuff. So after the horror of the first four days of this week everything is turning out golden again. Sara is going to be alright, God Willing, *Milk Wood* has had magnificent notices not only in London and Italy but now too in NY, *Villain* is packing them in in Britain and *Raid on Rommel* is doing

---

[105] Royal Air Force.
[106] Samuel Pepys (1633–1703), diarist, politician and public servant.
[107] £1.

likewise in Paris, Rome and Milan. And, most importantly of all E has come back to life again after being moribund for these horrific last few days.

In the car on the way up Wishart told me that he had guessed from various snippets of stock-exchange gossip that Stan Baker is having some financial difficulties.[108] I can't believe that hard-headed old Stan hasn't salted some nice sums away somewhere. He must have got himself into trouble with the tax people. He'll whistle his way out I'm sure.

We arrived at Tjentiste about 20 minutes early for Tito [. . .]. Then at eleven on the dot it seems we were summoned to the presence. For the first half hour or so it was just Tito and Madame and Popović and Delić and of course Tito's interpreter. We – Delić, Popović and I – all told Tito how good everything was. I said how efficient Popović was and he said how professional I was and I said what a splendid director Delić was and Delić said what a magnificent actor I was etc. Tito was in a very jolly mood putting what seemed like the fear of God or a firing-squad into the other two blokes when he said that he expected me to be in his old uniform tomorrow for the ceremony. They took him quite seriously until I said 'Come on, the President is pulling your leg!' Which of course he was. Afterwards all the other actors were presented to us and a dozen or so old comrades and I presume local big-wigs. From then on it was hard work for Tito, looking across the valley and at the mountains where he and his lads had fought so desperately 28 years ago, naturally began to reminisce and was so far gone in memories that he rarely gave his interpreter a chance to speak. This meant long periods of listening to stories in a completely alien tongue, only some of which were translated.

Sunday 5th Here we are again ready to set off for the dreaded Tjentiste <u>by helicopter</u> we hope this time. Today has all the hall-marks of being dreadful. Many thousands of people. Speeches. National Anthem. The Internationale.[109] And on top of it all they want me to work! Just so that Tito can see a bit of action. After all that they want us to fly to a place called Niš (pron Neesh) to the annual beano of the Yugoslav theatrical profession [110] We are expected to stay the night and come back tomorrow morning for work again. Strange behaviour. The film sometimes seems to be very much in second place to all kinds of social activities. [. . .]

<u>Later Today</u>:
Well, as prognosticated by Dr and Mrs Burton, it was a dreadful day though not as boring as I thought it might be. [. . .] First of all, we arrived in plenty of

---

[108] This may refer to some problems that Baker's company Oakhurst was encountering.
[109] The Internationale: the socialist anthem.
[110] The city of Niš, now in Serbia, the location of the Yugoslav National Theatre.

time to see Tito at eleven o'clock only to find out that His Excellency didn't expect to see us at all. It was the ineffable Popović who had insisted that we were there so early because of the danger of being delayed en route. [...] However we hung around the unfinished hotel and I drank coffee while E had a drink or two. Then suddenly there was a flurry of Generals and we were hastily put into cars and driven across fields where we were presented to the Marshal and Wife. Some bloke made a speech introducing the Tito I presume, whereupon the old man tore off up some steps to the podium, batteried with mikes and let us all have it for about 30 minutes. The crowd was huge. I guessed 50,000 trying vaguely to fit them into Cardiff Arms Park in my mind's eye.[111] 'Many more than that,' said the Generalissimo in English and quite sharply. In fact Tito seemed much less friendly today than he was yesterday. E remarked on it feeling a trifle miffed I suppose. I can only assume that his attitude changes subtly but definitely from public to private. There was none of the hugging and kissing of Brioni. Fact is that I was pretty well pissed off with the man-o-the-people because he didn't make more fuss of Elizabeth. He and Madame Broz did at least ask about her mother and at the end of the day when we had done a very actionful shot for their Majesties, Madame sent E her love and Tito said something which was I suppose 'hear hear' or something. And at the final handshake he said in English 'Hope to see you again.' You'll be lucky, mate. I swear to God there is more nonsensical protocol than with English royalty. [...]

After the speech which was apparently full of platitudes [...] about the heroism of the mighty dead and that the world and even their 'allies' – meaning Russia apparently – still did not believe the extent of the Jugoslavian sacrifice – we went back to the hotel not knowing whether we were invited to lunch with Tito or not. Not quite sure whether we wanted to be or not we put three tables together and ordered lunch at the hotel-restaurant. Five minutes later there was yet another panic and they came [...] in a sweat to say that we were expected to have lunch with Tito and the surviving partisans of the battle of Sutjeska. Furious [...] we got into the ever-present Mercedes and drove about 10 miles to the place. It was an open restaurant, obviously just shoved up for the day. We stood there, E and I and Maria and Vessna the new interpreter for 45 minutes signing endless autographs waiting for Tito to arrive. After all that we found we were not sitting with him but stuck with the scintillating Popović and Hardy Krüger. The latter obviously has a very nasty attack of jealousy and resentment of the red carpet treatment I get everywhere. He too is a bore and I hear from the other lads who live around the hotel with him that, typical Teuton, he bullies defenceless people like waiters etc. He works without cease on Wolf to write in flashbacks of Tito and himself enlarging his

---

[111] Cardiff Arms Park: the home of the Welsh rugby team.

part and enabling him to get to grips with R. Burton etc. and Wolf refuses and Krüger persists with Wolf saying; I wasn't paid to re-write the plot mate. I was hired to put the translation into palatable English. The insults began according to Ron and Brook. One sample: Krüger: 'You are a stupid man.' Wolf: 'And you're the Nazi Tab Hunter.'[112]

E is in the worst state of lassitude I ever remember of her. She has always been naturally somewhat indolent – not the kind of girl one finds rushing off to play golf and tennis, God Forbid – but now, I mean for the last couple of days, she can barely move one foot in front of the other. It's largely of course the reaction from the tension of the past week but it's bloody worrying. [. . .]

Monday 6th [. . .] The helicopters yesterday were the usual farce. For once we left on time but only seven people allowed again. From the air we could see huge concourses of people milling about before we landed and endless streams of buses. And thousands of cars. We landed on the football field where there was of course no one to meet us. [. . .] However [. . .] we were escorted to a car and drove off through dense crowds to the new hotel. [. . .] To add to the mania, incidentally, when E, bright with fury at the whole mess-up of the lunch came with me to location she sat down in my trailer on one of the banquettes and went right through it, legs kicking in the air. Nobody dared laugh or they would have been brained with a hand-bag but it was unquestionably funny. Ron had to leave the cabin. Once I knew she hadn't hurt her very vulnerable back I became faintly cracked myself. That sort of thing only happens when an entire day turns out to be a bastard.

Tuesday 7th, Tjentiste Am in Tito's hut and shall tonight sleep in his bed. For the first time it is really cold and fortunately the two little heaters from the other hut are with us and are going full blast. If the electricity fails again it will be mittens and woollen stockings all around. [. . .] As I say, once this lot get going they are very efficient but getting them going is torture. I doubt whether I've had more than five minutes on film in two weeks, and I have a definite stop-date. I am playing the part of a patient actor and hope to God I don't have to lose my temper. [. . .]

And now to await lunch and work and my lovely old E in the evening. It's not a bad life. Not really. Not like the other morning when I was figuring out the repercussions of my suicide on the people who like me.

Wednesday 8th [. . .] A miserable night in Tito's bed which for some reason, what I'm beginning to believe is typically Jugoslavian, refuses to have sheets or blankets which adequately cover the bed. This meaning a freezing shoulder or

---

[112] Tab Hunter (1931–), actor, perhaps renowned more for his looks than his talent.

a damp calf. Went in to get Maria's mug this morning – the only adequate drinking vessel we have – and she was completely covered with the clothes. Woke up with an awful feeling of deja vu. I was back in my cold damp childhood without even the prospect of a fire to light and leap and dance of burning anthracite. I shudder to be reminded of anything that happened to me before the age of about thirty and though I had a fantastically happy childhood I don't want to be reminded of Caradoc Street and that awful bathroom window which was broken by Rhys Oates' daughter when she was taking her monthly bath and which was never mended throughout my children [*sic*], and what is more ludicrous never allowed to be mended.[113] What a monster that Elfed was. Eleven years with the same broken window which would have cost sixpence and fifteen minutes to replace. If anybody had mended it he would have broken it again. What a foony mann. It is hard to remember that that idiot of my childhood is now a benign and elderly man. Had a bitter little contretemps with E this morning. [. . .] Ended up by her saying she would go on the boat and me saying good idea and her saying that when I was sober I was a pain in the ass and perhaps I should start drinking again. So you're damned if you do and you're damned if you don't. [. . .] We had the Bozzacchis all evening. They mean sweetly and Claudye helps to unpack etc. but it means eternal conversations and no long readings of books. I must have dropped hints by the thousand that my favourite occupation is sitting alone in a room with E drinking tea, me, and drinking, her or not drinking and simply and simple-mindedly reading books or occasionally chatting. But one might as well drop a canister of water on a prairie fire. [. . .]

Thursday 7th, Tjentiste[114] [. . .] Last night we sat and made our own supper. I looked up the various articles in the dictionary and asked for everything in Serbo-Croat. What's more, almost everything arrived as asked. I was flushed with success. E made some soup with an egg broken into it. Very good. I desserted on chocolate and fancy biscuits. [. . .]

Have just written a telegram to Kate who has a birthday on the 10th. She will be 14 years old. How she goes the time. And how she grows the girl. She is a head taller than Liza and as tall if not taller than E which makes her around 5'4". I hope she doesn't grow too tall. 5'6" is enough I think.

[. . .] How much happier E and I are when we are left alone. Last night, apart from the waiter, we saw nobody and it was delicious. People get on our collective nerves and as one attacks one of them the other defends. E attacks Brook. I defend. I attack Raymond. E defends etc. Fact is that we're wearing them all out. Raymond's relief when I say or we say that we shan't need him for

---

[113] Burton is referring here to one of his childhood homes in Caradoc Street, Taibach.
[114] Thursday was 9 September.

a few days is palpable. He can't wait to get away. He is rapidly getting old. Any minute or dark day now he is going to look his age. Terrible to be a middle aged pouff. He's actually 50 odd. I hope he's no longer in our employ when he's 60 odd. Still ogling fellow travellers. Creeps-giving. [. . .]

Received a cheque yesterday from Ron's Vicky for $3,350 which means $10,000 return on a $40,000 investment in about six years which is not bad. She is certainly the only one of our friends who has ever paid back anything. John Sullivan – over $100,000 and not a cent return. Heyman, ditto. Tim Hardy £12,000 and nil return. etc. etc. Including our various friends we must be owed a million dollars. Alexandre of Paris too yet owes us about $125,000. No sign of repayment – not even the interest. [. . .]

Friday 8th, Tjentiste[115] [. . .] Yesterday having sat around in make-up all day long I worked in Foca at 5.30pm. Did a scene with the girl who plays Vera who, of course, doesn't speak a word of English.[116] She shall be dubbed. However she was obviously experienced and had a go and was very nice. She had a 'film face' – a dark haired girl of about 30 that I'm pretty sure I shan't remember when next I see her where I saw her before. I mean if I saw her in the street. Or at a party or something like that. An oval face, regular features, a good standard voice. about 5'4", standard build. In short, like a thousand other actresses everywhere. [. . .]

We had sent Maria back to Kupari with Raymond the day before yesterday as she was quite clearly and understandably bored up here when the rain came down without stop. [. . .] So with everybody else congregating in the other hut and waiting for the call we sat and read all day. E reading thriller after thriller and me alternating between a 'Bony' thriller and a book called *Bridge over the Drina* described as Yugoslavia's 'greatest novel by Nobel Prizewinner Ivo Andrić' and good it is too though it's not a novel at all in the ordinary sense of the word so far anyway.[117] More a series of anecdotes loosely woven in and around the history of the bridge over a period of 300 years. I doubt if I would have read it with the same interest were it not that I am close to the actual scene of events. There is a description of an impalement, in detail, which horrified me. I didn't know that impaling was so exact a science. The 'master' impaler was able to so do his job that though the pointed stick went right through the body from bottom to shoulder through the anus it must avoid all the essential organs so that the poor bastard would live as long as possible, some for a few hours, some for as long as a day. [. . .]

---

[115] Friday was 10 September.
[116] Milena Dravić (1940   ).
[117] Arthur Upfield (1890–1964) wrote 29 novels featuring Detective-Inspector Napoleon Bonaparte, set mostly in the Australian outback. Ivo Andrić, *Bridge over the Drina* (1961). Andrić had won the Nobel Prize for Literature in 1961.

Saturday 9th, Kupari[118] [...] Am going into Dubrovnik to buy things. Don't quite know what. Lighters and lighter fluid and a book or two peut etre. [...]

Walked for an hour in Dubrovnik looking for a bacco shop. Finally found one and bought a gas lighter, cheap, and a pen-and-pencil case for E as an encouragement for her sudden letter-writing. Doubt if it will be used much but you never know.

Dubrovnik is made ugly by all its tourists. There are always thousands and I had an audience the whole time swelling to a hundred or so when I stopped to buy the lighter. I with Maria got out fast. Went in the mini-moke which is made for these narrow winding roads. I wish it had a little more power however. When I came back I saw John Heyman who stayed for a couple of hours chatting of this business and that business finally ending up chatting of cricket in the old days – i.e. the thirties. I told him of the enormous excitement of the 'bodyline' tour of my childhood when cricket made headlines not only on the sports pages but on the front pages and was the subject of editorials in solemn journals.[119] We shall never look upon its like again. Bradman and Larwood, Macabe and Voce, Ponsford and Hammond and Gubby Allen and Bowes bowling Bradman middle stump. And the imperturbable Jardine.[120]

Everybody, which means E principally, in a foul mood about going to Niš this afternoon for the bloody actors' do when we are presented with awards etc. and have to meet mayors and presidents of republics and cocktail parties and supposed to see a film in Serbo-Croat yet which we are determinedly holding out against seeing. And another cocktail party tomorrow morning at 10am if you please before flying back here. All the things in fact that we loathe most in this world but which have to be done. Sometimes.

If it were anything but a communist country, especially a nice one like this, they would be told in no uncertain fashion where to stuff their awards and cocktail parties and mayors and presidents. But we are being fixed-smile-diplomats. Shit.

Found about three books by unknown authors which will plough through if things get bad.

Heyman told me that everyone is agreed that The Burtons are as easy as pie to handle but that The Burtons' Entourage is a pain in the ass and every producer, when they are mentioned, hopes fervently that they will all die in the night of galloping heart attacks. Too bad, I said, though I agree about some. The great exception is of course Ron and though I like the others I don't think that any of them are necessary to me. I like Bob Wilson to be around and

---

[118] Saturday was 11 September.

[119] The 'bodyline' controversy (over what some felt was unnecessarily aggressive and intimidatory bowling) erupted during England's tour of Australia in 1932–3.

[120] International cricketers. Donald Bradman (1908–2001); Harold Larwood (1904–95); Stan McCabe (1910–68); Bill Voce (1909–84); Bill Ponsford (1900–91); Wally Hammond (1903–65); Gubby Allen (1902–89); Bill Bowes (1908–87); Douglas Jardine (1900–58).

be barman and man of distinction and Jim is useful with mail but lacks the charm so essential when handling so many different kinds of people. He's no Dick Hanley. Raymond, Claudye and Gianni actively bore me if they are around for any length of time. Brook is intelligent but is now so circumscribed by something, possibly E's and my hidden but perhaps not hidden enough distaste, that all his wit and humour seem to have fled except sporadically. He used to be very amusing.

Saturday 11th, Niš Same day and late at night – about 11.30 – and I've changed the date on the heading above as everybody assures me that it's not the 9th but the 11th. That means that all the dates for the last several days must be skew-whiff also. Probably came from making two entries on the same day – as today – and getting distracted or something.

Any road [. . .] the dreaded visit here didn't go too badly. At least we're home and safe. [. . .] there was the time-honoured conglomerate of stick mikes and TV cameras. They pounced and preyed on us of course immediately but we went straight into our car and then watched with astonishment the almost ludicrously old-fashioned posing of the German actor Hardy Krüger who really and truly struck dramatic attitudes – looking up at the sky and showing now this profile now the other. I could hardly credit my eyes while E had some very *XYZ* remarks to make re that particular kraut. When my baby don' take no fancy to somepoorbody she sure don' take no fancy. And the poor-spirited son of envy compounds his lack of charm at every opportunity. He can barely speak to or look at either of us. He reminds me oddly enough of a chap called Raymond St Jacques. A very handsome and some say homosexual American Negro actor who said in Cotonou that the waiters (all coal black) in the Hotel Croix de Sud were discriminating against black clients as for instance 'whenever the Burtons appear we might as well not exist even though we might have been sitting and waiting for 10 or 15 minutes.' 'Ah my friend,' said the delicious Roscoe Lee Browne, also a blackman, and who speaks as pedantically as a professor, 'Royalty itself has been known to wait when the Burtons are around. It is a fact of nature this attraction, like the moon's effect on the tide.'

Sunday 12th [. . .] After watching Krüger baring his profile, we left the airport, a military one by the look of it with no flare path and a dozen helicopters, we roared through the traffic with a police car leading us with its light flashing and its hooter going (the roof-top light being blue not red) and with a cop leaning out of one door with a round object on a stick waving all traffic to the side we swept into the oddest looking hotel that I'd ever seen. It was peculiar only in that it wasn't the hotel but a totally unannounced halt where we were made a speech to by a nervous and at the same time pompous manager about 'workers wanting to see other workers like ourselves even though the two workers her with them were a little better known than Jasha in the canteen' etc.

He gave us some presents and the factory workers presented E with lots of flowers and they pressed in on us from all sides feeling our faces and smoothing our hair, particularly E's. It was all terribly embarrassing as the factory had arranged a table with drinks, including Scotch, on it and there were canapés and cigs in boxes etc. all ready for a little cocktail party. All this time the TV cameras were going and the mikes and before we could attempt to make any sort of thank yous and how delighted we were to be one with the people we were whisked away [. . .] without giving us a chance to show something other than startled and bewildered shock. [. . .] From there we went to the hotel which was another mad-house, the police not being able to control the crowds at all. [. . .] After 45 minutes or so we were summoned down to the cocktail floor where the crowd outside in the square chanted our names. We stood there for some time on the balcony with E bravely and regally waving and me like some dumb Prince Albert giving an occasional half-hearted waggle myself.[121] We met the Mayor and I think two governors and other people who were never explained and then totally without warning there was a sort of native nightclub act. A horrible boy said into a mike that he represented the children of the world and proceeded to beat a funny little drum and hop around. There was no applause when he finished. Then a fat girl sang a couple of songs accompanied by a sort of flautist, a concertina, the boy on the small drum and a guitar. [. . .] After that [. . .] we went down to dinner. There was a long table seating about forty. We sat next to each other. E had the organizer of the Festival on her right and I had an actress-judge who spoke reasonable French on my left. Next to the actress, who seemed a nice woman there was a critic who spoke English. He was a crasher and talked about British theatre all the time. Since I've only seen two plays in England in 10 years I wasn't able to make much contribution. [. . .]

Airplane Sitting in the plane [. . .] having had yet another encounter with TV and radio and all its appurtenances. To my delight the Heavy Luger is late.[122] Presumably he wasn't informed. Have just been told that Luger has now got a snapper with him too just like Burtons have G. Bozzacchi. Am beginning to enjoy this. The poor sod has no chance of winning this somewhat unequal battle. Others have tried and failed. I learn now from E that the snapper is here to do the film, including me tomorrow he hopes, and not just the Bertha Krupp. They just happen to be all Germans together. The Panzer leutenant duly arrived and greeted everyone with a broad gesture and a 'Hi there'. There was no apology of any kind according to Radie Louella Hedda Taylor Burton.[123] [. . .]

---

[121] A reference to Prince Albert of Saxe-Coburg and Gotha (1819–61), husband of Queen Victoria and Prince consort.
[122] Heavy Luger, meaning Hardy Krüger.
[123] A reference to Radie Harris (1904–2001), Louella Parsons (1881–1972) and Hedda Hopper, gossip columnists.

After the dinner [. . .] we set off for the award-giving. I had also said that the best plan would be for us to arrive, be announced, and go straight onto the stage to take our bows and accept our awards which are called 'Constantines' the male award being called the Czar and the female the Czarina. And then, complete again with escort, bugger off back to the Hotel Ambassador and faint a lot.[124] [. . .] We were announced by the Festival's director and went on stage to a standing ovation. There were two microphones and the poor bloody Mayor read a speech of welcome to the great world renowned couple and then I was invited to give them a few deathless words. I was thinking of a few words rather on the lines of the Gettysburg Address but settled for 'Comrades, I am very nervous at the idea of my playing the greatest Jugoslavian (ovation) and probably the greatest Jugoslavian who ever lived. (Ovation) Especially as, if my work is not good today, he can have me deported tomorrow. (Laughter and applause) Thank you.'[125] Then came Female Lib herself, the Mrs Pankhurst of Culver City, who said: 'I love your country and your people.[126] (tumultuous rapture) I love your president and his lady (ecstasy) and would like to live here forever, if you would accept us.' (End of speech partially drowned by the ulti-mate in cosmic approval and the music of the spheres.) There goes, we both thought, our American visas! Quite genuinely though the audience were really moved. We then received our awards – E from a very good actor who had won the Grand Prix that night and I got mine from the actress equivalent. [. . .]

Monday 13th, Kalizma [. . .] Yesterday received a long and incoherent letter from Larry Olivier re the National Theatre.[127] He must have been very drunk the last times we talked to him as nobody could have turned down the job with more firmness. But he has obviously been persisting so I wrote a long letter, long-ish anyway, explaining that he mustn't worry about his not being able to get me the job and that I wouldn't take it if offered. Not at least unless there were drastic changes. That is to say, I couldn't see myself being overruled by a board of governors over some project I had in mind. As Larry was over the Hochhuth Churchill play [128] Granted the play was a travesty and badly written

---

[174] Ambassador Hotel, Trg Kralja Milana Bb, Niš.

[125] The Gettysburg Address was delivered by President Abraham Lincoln on 19 November 1863 when dedicating the Soldiers' National Cemetery at Gettysburg, Pennsylvania.

[126] Emmeline Pankhurst (1858–1928), suffragette. Culver City is in Los Angeles county and was home to the MGM studios.

[127] Laurence Olivier was a founder and the first Artistic Director of the National Theatre. In October 1970 he had impetuously suggested that Burton might take over from him, and Burton had been inter-ested in doing so, only to discover that the appointment was not in Olivier's gift. Olivier's letter, dated 16 July 1971, relayed the view of the Chairman of the National Theatre, Sir Max Rayne (1918–2003), that Burton did not have the appropriate experience to be seriously considered for the post. Rayne had in fact already identified Peter Hall (1930—) as his chosen successor to Olivier, this taking place in 1973.

[128] Rolf Hochhuth's play *Soldiers, Necrology on Geneva* (1967), was a controversial treatment of the Allied bombing of Hamburg in the Second World War and also of the alleged involvement of Winston Churchill in the death of the Polish leader General Sikorski (1881–1943). The National Theatre produc-tion of *Soldiers* in 1967 had been cancelled by the board of the National Theatre, against Olivier's wishes.

or translated or both but I would have resigned. He also said in the letter that they hadn't been allowed the money to put on *Guys and Dolls*.[129] Well, what sort of National Theatre is that? Those Old Etonians etc. would drive me mad in five months.[130] I love Larry but he really is a shallow little man with a very mediocre intelligence but a splendid salesman. But it is quite clear that when he is not active in the productions themselves the National loses all its glamour. It is impossible to get over-excited about people like Robert Stephens and his wife.[131] They are good but lack 'glamour'. And I don't mean 'glamour' in the vulgar sense of the word. I mean the sweeping grandeur of Edith or Gielgud or Larry himself.[132] The National should be full of the towering oaks of the profession. Scofield, Guinness, Redgrave should be permanent members of the company while those anonymous 'stars' like Stephens et al. should play the supporting parts with their usual brilliance. I saw both Stephens and Maggie Smith in the film of *Jean Brodie* and thought they were the dullest couple I've ever seen in an important film.[133] Also, alas, the National has lost its initial excitement and has become the Old Vic again – upsydownsy and again slowly being invaded by a younger generation of Paul Rogers and William Squires.[134] No offence to either of them but they do not illuminate Shakespeare with flashes of lightning. I told Larry also, to ease his conscience if any, that when I went back it would probably be to do something with the Drama Faculty at Oxford if and when it's created out of the *Faustus* monies. And indeed the latter is an attractive idea and a nice thing to do in my fifties. Keep me active but not too active and I would delegate like mad.

Evening

Sitting on the poop deck with my infinitely beloved wife who has acquired an even greater weight of love. I keep on mentally looking around to make sure she's there. For why this new and massive re-affirmation of adoration and worship and a promise to myself that I shall never be nasty to her ever again? I will tell you for why. For because for about three minutes this afternoon I thought that I was about to be killed instantaneously and at once, without time to re-tell her how much I love her, to apologize for breaking my contract to look after her forever, for letting her down with a bang (hysterical pun intended), and for having no time to tell her the million things yet to be told and for not realizing and demonstrating my full potential as husband, provider, lover and all.

---

[129] *Guys and Dolls*, a musical by Frank Loesser (1910–69) which had premiered in 1950.

[130] A reference to former pupils of the English public school, Eton College.

[131] Robert Stephens (1931–95) and his then wife Maggie Smith (1934—).

[132] Edith Evans.

[133] A reference to the film *The Prime of Miss Jean Brodie* (1969) which starred Robert Stephens and Maggie Smith. Smith had appeared with Burton and Taylor in *The V.I.P.s*.

[134] Paul Rogers (1917—); William Squire (1916–89).

I did not work today which is rapidly becoming the norm for this piece [. . .] finally and of course inevitably word came that work was over for the day and that it was 'a wrap' and so we set off back to the copter and Kupari. I settled in on the port side right behind the pilot while Vessna, the interpreter, sat beside me with Brook on her other side. Ron sat in the rear row with Gianni. And off we went. There was a low cloud ceiling which we went into immediately we'd gained some height and, as so many times before, we threaded our way through the vicious peaks to right and left. Suddenly and without warning we were completely blacked-out though I believe the technical description is 'whited out'. There was nothing to be seen outside the cabin of the chopper except nothing. A white nothing. On top of this it began to rain torrentially and the windscreen wipers whipped back and fore like insane crickets sharpening their legs. The co-pilot frantically tried to turn himself into a human demister. We flew like this for perhaps half a minute though it seemed like half an hour when there it was! We were going at an angle of about 45 degrees into a peak. The pilot, god bless his marvellous reflexes, flung the copter to the right and there appallingly was another rock face. The co-pilot slapped the pilot on the arm and we pulled away again to the left. I don't know how close we actually were but it seemed to be the length of a rotor-arm and six feet. Whatever the distance it must have been very very close otherwise we wouldn't have seen the two peaks at all. Still we ploughed on with everyone except Gianni and I – and the pilots of course – with their eyes closed tight. Ron I saw curl himself into a ball and cover his head and ears, with his knees on the floor waiting in what they say is the classical position for a plane crash. I stared to the side with hand ready poised to warn the pilot if anything appeared on our side. The pilot was straining his eyes forward. The co pilot was rubbing his side window with hand also poised to warn the pilot. Gianni just stared over Ron's semi-kneeling position like a man who saw nothing except eternity. Apart from my saying Holy Shit in a strangled whisper nobody uttered a sound. No sound, at least, that could be heard. So we continued to fly blind for another aeon (possibly a minute, possibly two, who knows?) dreading the head-on how-de-do from which there would be [no] way of turning. Then, the machine began to lose height pretty quickly. I could feel it though I daren't take my eyes away from the window to check the altimeter. I thought the pilot had gone mad. Later I found out why and how right he was. We dropped and dropped until there suddenly and miraculously was the much maligned road curling around the mountains. Rarely have I ever seen such a beautiful road, a masterpiece of the roadmaker's art, an example to the Romans of ancient time, I could not think how I had ever said that the road was a fucking nightmare and an elongated version of a shit-house, a ruined shit-house. I could have gladly apologized to every kilometre of its lovely length. The pilot had lost height, he said, to be able to see, to try and go above the clouds was certain suicide because in order to gain height quickly he would have had to circle and he knew, as indeed we all knew, that there were a hundred peaks of a different height width [sic] and also there was no knowing how high the cloud was. He was however fairly sure that the cloud base would not cover the bed of the valley. What is nightmarish on recollection is how many close shaves we must have had during those two or three minutes. Glimpses of eternity we have never seen.

What is also frighteningly revelationary [sic] too is the number of levels on which the mind functions at moments of imminent catastrophe. 'Believe me sir,' said Dr Johnson, 'when a man knows he is to be hanged tomorrow morning it concentrates the mind wonderfully.'[135] There was one blazing mental image that seemed to last right through the enormity. It was E lying in bed on the yacht with a book open at the page where she'd stopped reading with the title front cover and publisher's blurb on the other face up on the bed near her right hand which was out of the covers. She was wearing one of my favourite night-gowns, a blue thing and shorty which she may have been wearing this morning when I said good bye to her. (I've just asked her and she was.) She had one leg bent and the other straight. On another level I was telling her over and over again that I loved her, I loved her. At one fractioned [sic] point I kept trying to remember a line of Alun Lewis' – 'If I should go away, beloved, do not say . . .' and I couldn't remember the rest which I've known for 25 years or so. Immediately the crisis was over I remembered it immediately.

If I should go away,
Beloved,
Do not say,
He has forgotten me.
Forever you abide.
A singing rib within my dreaming side.[136]

The mind is a remarkable instrument. If I wrote down everything I could remember from those interminable seconds it would be a million words. It is in fact what James Joyce's *Ulysses* is all about except he took a whole day for Bloom while he could have taken three minutes because the mind concentrates so wonderfully.[137] A shorter catastrophe of this kind happened to me before when I was perhaps 19–20 years old but I hadn't learned to love then and to love obsessively. Going to stop now until tomorrow morning. I must read *Ulysses* again.

---

[135] Johnson is credited with saying 'when a man knows he is to be hanged in a fortnight, it concentrates his mind wonderfully'.
[136] This is the first half of Lewis's 'Postscript: for Gweno', which appeared in *Raiders' Dawn* (1942).
[137] James Joyce, (1882–1941), *Ulysses* (1922), the central character of which is Leopold Bloom.

Wednesday 15th, **Kalizma–Cavtat** Spent most of yesterday in a car – the Rolls-Royce. The weather was too bad to land in Tjentiste so we drove up. I sat in the back, put up the partition and settled down to *The Gingerbread Lady* a successful play by Neil Simon.[138] Simon is one of those playwrights who rarely is considered 'significant' by the critics, largely because he isn't, but who writes success after success. He also writes 'well-made plays' à la Rattigan.[139] In fact, he might be loosely described as a younger American version of Terry but much funnier. Some of the stuff I read in the car yesterday made me laugh out loud, which is very rare for me. They want E to it [sic] and she could have a good time in it and be very good to boot and also people forget how very funny her comedy is. Beloved old Maureen Stapleton played it on the stage and very brilliantly apparently and I can imagine her being very good. It's very sad that she photographs like a sack of potatoes. The story too is the story more or less of Maureen's life. A woman of superb talent – if she were British she would become an automatic dame – she is also a drunk and, like the woman in the play, it kills her career. Like the woman in the play she also becomes enormously fat and also has to go to a home to have a rest cure. Orkin and I watched her in and out of more alcoholic crises than one can imagine. I remember too, many years ago in Hollywood, her discovery of the joys of masturbation. 'Why the hell didn't someone teach me all about it when I was in that fucking convent?' she demanded. 'Think of all the emotional involvements I could have saved myself instead of having to get myself laid by guys I didn't even like just because I was horny. For Christ's sake I spent my youth looking for big cocks when I could have screwed myself with a brush handle.' And so on. All this revelationary [sic] talk took place in an apartment hotel, rather shabby, where most of the New York actors used to stay, on Sunset Boulevard. I think it's still going and is called the Sunset Towers.[140] In the middle fifties it was the thing to do if you were a New York stage actor, and to show your contempt for the contract stars, to stay there in that stucco monstrosity making it quite clear that you were your own man and not owned by some studio and the minute the fucking lousy film you were in was over you were going back to the great New York THEATRE where you re-found your soul as an artist and where the Real Work was done. I, because I was a real stage actor and had played your standard classics, was accepted there despite the fact that I had a million-dollar contract with Fox. Marlon and Monty Clift were habituees too for a time because they were always going to go back on the stage (and actually did for a second – Marlon did a couple of months in summer stock playing *Arms and the man* and Monty went back off-Broadway to do *The Seagull*) but gradually Marlon shifted further and further away until

---

[138] Neil Simon, (1927—), playwright and screenwriter. *The Gingerbread Lady* (1970).
[139] Terence Rattigan (1911–77), playwright.
[140] The Sunset Tower Hotel, 8358 Sunset Boulevard, West Hollywood.

he eventually had a permanent house of his own.[141] For Marlon, it must have been a harrowing time because he was their natural leader. They all worshipped him and comforted their own failure with 'Marlon is the greatest goddamn actor in the world and the greatest goddamn film star too but he's one of us and next season for Chrissake he'll be playing Richard III and Hamlet and fuck 'em all here in this shitty phony town.' But he never did and slowly he also began to fail even as a film star and the great disillusionment set in. Then it became fashionable to denigrate Marlon. 'He's sold out.' 'Let's face it, Marlon isn't any good unless Gadge [Kazan] is there to tell him what to do.' Etc. Arguments with which I'm only too familiar because I was the British version of Marlon. In my case it was even worse because I was, from the beginning, held up against Paul Scofield. We were the natural heirs to Gielgud and Olivier. Paul being Gielgud and me being Larry. 'But Burton let the side down etc.' What they don't seem to realize is that Paul tried like mad to be a film star. I remember him testing for film after film and being turned down largely because nobody knew how to photograph that magnificent face. It was the era of pretty boys: Rock Hudson, Jimmy Dean, Paul Newman and even Marlon and myself.[142] But, largely out of a kind of obligation to my background and because I felt that I owed it to Phil Burton to become a great classical actor I continually destroyed my film career by going back again and again to the theatre. And I did it against all odds. It was still, up to my middle thirties, 'Scofield and Burton'. But then everything changed. I went to live in Geneva, made me a million dollars quickly, did anything to get out of the contract with Fox even to the extent of doing two truly appalling films called *Bramble Bush* and *Ice-Palace* and, at last I was free to do anything I wanted and, more importantly, not do anything I didn't want to do. I spent a whole summer in Céligny blackening in the sun – it was a particularly splendid summer all over Europe – turning down film after film. I remember turning down an offer of $350,000 to play Christ in a film called *The King of Kings* that summer.[143] It was very tempting. Five months in my beloved Spain and though the script was unspeakable it was to be directed by Nick Ray who had after all made one good film *Rebel without a cause* and might pull it off again.[144] But I turned it down and just as well. Both Stratford and The Old Vic offered me whole seasons to myself. Play anything you like. Turned them down. I was offered plays by the score. The only thing I did for a whole year was the film of *Look Back in Anger* which was a flop and a TV special of another short Osborne play called *A Subject of Scandal and Concern* for the BBC. I stayed at the Savoy during rehearsals. It was for BBC TV and it seems ludicrous now to think that

[141] George Bernard Shaw, *Arms and the Man* (1894); Anton Chekhov, *The Seagull* (1896).
[142] Rock Hudson (1925–85); James Dean (1931–55); both of whom co-starred with Taylor in *Giant*.
[143] *King of Kings* (1961).
[144] *Rebel Without a Cause* (1955).

we had to hold a press conference with Tony Richardson, Osborne and myself while we defended the BBC against the fact that they were paying me £1000 – £1000 indeed to God – for an hour's play and three weeks rehearsal. The most ever paid before was 500. The thing was a huge success and I must try and get a copy for the boat. It seems odd too nowadays to think that the BBC solemnly warned all its viewers that the play was being put on deliberately late at night to give them, the viewers, a chance to put their young ones to bed as the play was about a man 'who didn't believe in God'.[145] Wow!

The fact is that I was in a very enviable position. Though I was knocked about by the press – British press particularly – for being a bloated millionaire and a traitor to my country for deserting a sinking British Empire on which the sun was at last setting, I was more courted than almost any actor in the world. I knew bloody well that I was not considered box-office after *Bramble Bush, Ice Palace* and *Anger* but I also knew that any film submitted to Marlon and turned down was automatically submitted to me and of course any play of significance came to me first and then went down another line of stage actors. I had an adorable girl baby, I was very fond of my wife, I was a millionaire, I had a sweet estate in Céligny. I had a superb convertible Cadillac (still among the favourite cars I ever had) a large library, an insatiable thirst for knowledge and the means to satisfy it and every opportunity to play anything I wanted and I was terribly unhappy.

And it was nothing to do with anything that I could fathom. Though the possibilities were endless, I had no ambitions at all in my own field of drama. I wrote a lot but never submitted anything for publication though I was asked to. The only piece I published was a couple of thousand words on Meredith Jones for the *Sunday Times* and I'm not sure whether I wrote that before or after my self-imposed exile.[146] Did I, deep down, regret having left England and all the things that would automatically come from a steady series of jobs in theatre and films? The inevitable knighthood perhaps. It, whatever it was, was not despair, nothing as dramatic as that. It was a strange vacuum. I wasn't interested in anything ordinary. That is to say that I wasn't interested in playing, shall we say, *Richard III* but might have been in *Richard II* in which I would have been very mis-cast. I did the Prince in Anouilh's *Time Remembered* in New York simply because everybody said that I didn't have the elegance to play a top-hat-and-tails part and because Paul had played it in London with considerable success.[147] I lost weight, cut down on my drinking, insisted on Sullivan and Williams flying over from London to make me the tails (I was sufficiently clever not to wear the top-hat) and the black riding-breeches and

---

[145] The subject of the play was the socialist, secularist, Owenite and co-operator George Jacob Holyoake (1817–1906).
[146] 'The Magic of Meredith Jones', *Sunday Times*, 17 June 1956.
[147] Burton played Prince Albert in *Time Remembered*. Paul Scofield had played the same part at the Lyric Theatre and New Theatre in London in 1954 and 1955.

jacket. I went every morning to the New York Athletic Club and 'worked out' and the play, which was supposed to be a vehicle for the new American Duse, Susan Strasberg, was a success for me but certainly not for her (in fact, it ended her career on the spot) and was a success for everyone except her.[148] Even Helen Hayes, who must be among the worst 'great' actresses ever, had good notices and I was nominated for a 'Tony' etc. and I was the only one who knew that 'they' were quite right. I am <u>not</u> a top-hat-and-tails actor.

My sense of chronology is hopeless and sometimes I put some plays and films in the wrong order but the next step I think was a film called *Bitter Victory* – a very good script – to be done with Alec Guinness and again Nick Ray directing. This was to be done in Libya, for the most part, with the studio work in Nice. Apart from its being a good script and a good director and the magnificent Guinness as co-star I had never been to the Sahara. So we were on. Alec couldn't do it at the last moment. I must ask him one of these days if he was ever offered it as people are so devious. Curt Jurgens stupendously miscast did it instead. There, at one stroke, went the film and following closely on *Anger*. I was at my lowest ebb as a film star. I didn't care very much – I won best-actor-of-the-year award somewhere, I think Venice – though I wasn't exactly pleased and was heart-broken by *Anger*'s failure – and then one day Lerner and Loewe and Moss Hart came en masse to see me. It was in Hollywood. Tower Road. They said they wanted me to play the lead in their new musical. It was based on T. H. White's *The Once and Future King* one volume of which – *The Sword and the Stone* – was and is among my favourite books.[149] With the condescension that seems axiomatic when writers talk to actors they started to tell me about the story. Quick as a flash <u>I</u> told <u>them</u> also saying that I personally <u>knew</u> Tim White. 'Tim?' they said. 'Why yes,' I said. 'His full name is Terence Hanbury White, but to his friends he is known as "Tim".' Squelch. In fact, I had never met Tim White but I knew a great deal about him from friends who knew him. I knew that he lived on the Channel Isle of Alderney. That he was a melancholic, that he drank himself into a stupor throughout the winters and sobered up in the Spring, started to bath again, and wrote during the summer. And that he was poor. I said that I would do it. They were thrilled. They asked me if I would sing something for them so that Fritz Loewe could note the range of my voice. I said sure thing and sat down very poshily at the piano and played a Welsh song and sang to my own accompaniment. They were pleased and said I was a natural baritone and the potential of my singing voice was immense and indeed I could have, with proper vocal training, made a living as a classical opera singer. 'Sure,' I said. 'Sure, kiddoes'. Would I go to so-and-so in London, or whassisname in Geneva, or ditto in Paris etc. wherever I might be in the next couple of years? It would

---

[148] Eleonora Duse (1858–1924), actor.
[149] T. H. White, *The Once and Future King* (1958). *The Sword and the Stone* (1938).

be a good idea too, since my voice was so rich so superbly natural Christ what a gift, an actor with such extraordinary vocal gift, such warmth such colour. So would I undergo voice training with any or all of the various names they had suggested? They would pay, of course. Would I do this as Rex Harrison had done.[150] 'NO' I said.

Now, two years later, not having heard a note of the music and not having read a word of the script, I was on my way to New York on the *Queen Mary* to play the piece.[151] I arrived in Manhattan to find (five weeks before the opening night in the O'Keefe Centre in Toronto) no script except a sort of treatment with occasional bits of dialogue thrown in. I went raving mad. Moss, sweet man that he was, tried his damnedest to calm me down. I called them every vile name I could think of. And it seems to me, even now, that I had justification. Lerner, Loewe and Hart's last collaboration had been *My Fair Lady* – the greatest success on any level and by any standards that had ever been. Rex had made the greatest success in his life. My leading lady was Julie who had also made the success of her life in *Lady*.[152] Our poor bloody piece, for God's sake, didn't even have a title!

Thursday 16th [. . .] For some reason, even more than usual, I made my entry in the diary yesterday like the beginning of a rather portentous autobiography, an apologia. Must save such fragments, properly written for the real thing which is about the only thing I'm ever likely to write – apart from the usual occasional snippet written for mags.

I read all day apart from the diary entry. Changing from the biography of Mussolini by somebody called John Collier – very journalisticky – with lots of ludicrous bits read out to E, and the first volume of Toynbee's *History* to Spengler's *Decline of the West* to a detective story by Erle S. Gardner.[153] [. . .] Have decided too, though whether I keep it up or not I don't know, that life is infinitely more rewarding without booze. At least my kind of boozing. It's been approx three months now I think though unless I look back in the diary, which I never do and can't anyway in this case as the preceding volume is in Gstaad, my estimation of time like estimating distances over water is absurdly inaccurate.

[. . .] the Italians are a race of opera-comics. [. . .] I pointed out to E that the more the Nazis bombed Britain the tougher morale became, and the more we bombed the Reich the tougher they became, but in the Musso book it says that when the first raid on Rome occurred, and compared with Dresden, Cologne

---

[150] For his part as Henry Higgins in *My Fair Lady* (1964).

[151] RMS *Queen Mary*, which operated between Southampton and New York from 1936 to 1967.

[152] Julie Andrews.

[153] Burton means Richard Collier, *Duce! A Biography of Benito Mussolini* (1971). Arnold Toynbee (1889–1975), *A Study of History* (1960 abridged edn). Oswald Spengler (1880–1936), *The Decline of the West* (first published in English in the 1920s, with further editions in the 1960s). Erle S. Gardner (1889–1970).

and Berlin it was a nothing, thousands of Italians ran out into the streets waving white flags improvised from pieces of stick and vests, shirts etc. but not, I'm sure, underpants which by this time would have been the wrong colour. I once saw a group of teenage Italians set on a lone colleague and finally get him on the ground. When he was down he put one hand over his face and one over his testicles and submitted. The others then proceeded to kick him but the kicks were unbelievably ineffective as they took turns to do running kicks at him but in their anxiety in case the man who was down happened to grab an ankle and pull one of them down with him they kicked from as far away as possible so that they couldn't possibly get any purchase, any power into the kicks. This was in or rather outside a bar somewhere in Rome many years ago and I was with Johnny Sullivan and a lot of other stuntmen who would have enjoyed joining in but the whole thing was so balletic and coy that all we could do was laugh. Of course the stories of Italian cowardice are legion – they even tell them against themselves – and indicate a highly civilized and very witty and healthy respect for life especially their own lives but, childishly, it's not a reputation I would like the British, and certainly not the Welsh to have. I was informed from birth that the toughest thing on earth was a Welsh miner. I believed it and it got me into more fights than one would have thought possible. I'm still likely to have a go though I know that at my age and condition I stand not a chance. I suppose that's what happens to the Irish too. The Scots are far more sensible, like the English they just know they are the best and don't bother to prove it.

Friday 17th [. . .] We sat and read again all day. [. . .] I finished off Mussolini. What an ignoble end to a fairly ignoble life. And extraordinary how his weaknesses, inferiority complexes, had the effect in other people's eyes, of giving him strength. He had the unthinking cruelty of a child and it seems that any really dirty work was unconsciously delegated and atrocities were committed without his knowledge. Fundamentally he was a weak but decent man. This man, Collier, though he mentions Mussolini's physical ailments, does not give them the importance they should have had in the book. Quite clearly, and I believe it more and more after that slight but important book *The Pathology of Leadership*, his physical illness had a great impact on his conduct of the war and in fact his going in to it at all.[154] I'm sure that Hitler wasn't at all pleased that Mussolini joined him in the war at all. It would have suited him much better to have Italy on the sidelines and supply him with materials, raw and finished. Some German General is asked before the war: 'Which side is going to win?' and the answer was 'The side that doesn't have Italy as an ally.' This gem is quoted in the book.[155] Yet another Italian-cowardice joke? Well let's see.

[154] Hugh L'Etang (1917–96), *The Pathology of Leadership* (1970).
[155] Collier, *Duce!*, p. 135, citing Field Marshal Werner von Blomberg.

If it were not for Italy's, or rather Mussolini's idiotic adventure into Greece – a blatant piece of idiocy to show Hitler that he too could go to war without informing his partner – there would have been no need for the Germans having to go into Jugoslavia to get at Greece. He could have chosen his own time later. Greece might never have come into the war at all as Turkey never did.[156] If the Eyties had not marched on the British and Egypt, Hitler need never have wasted his great troops in the long desert war.[157] When they were involved in the Russian War they were also having to defend Italy after her capitulation against the Allies. If Italy had stayed out of the war or come in on our side after she was sure, and everybody was, that the Democracies were going to win she would have had herself a seat at the carve-up table as a belligerent member of the winning side. She might even have kept Ethiopia. And Mussolini would have ended up with a state funeral amidst the weeping of a nation instead of being urinated on by Italian women in a square in Milan.[158]

Perhaps because it's my own time but this century's politics and wars seem to me to be the most fascinating of all time. Never in history have events followed so fast on each others' heels, never have politics been so copiously documented and never before has the final move, potential move so far meant the destruction of the entire human race and indeed all living things. Indeed the year of my birth is as good a time as any to begin a modern history. Because although the Great War was terrible and horrendous – more so perhaps than the second – the great disintegration of world values didn't begin until after the dust of the war had settled and the monsters began to appear. The new monsters.

[. . .] E still asleep and now must wake her up as she, at least, has to work today. She models for a furrier-artist so called, called Soldano who furs out of Genoa as one might say and who afterwards gives her the furs, and others, that she models.[159] Bozzacchi calculates that the furs on the market would bring in $150,000. I wonder what happened to the pledge that E signed in common with other famed ladies that she would never wear the furs of anything in future except pest furs and vermin. Must ask her and will record the answer tomorrow.

And now back to *The Decline of the West*.

Saturday 18th [. . .] E said that her declaration about furs, done through John Springer, was carefully worded. It said that she would continue to wear furs

---

[156] The Italian invasion of Greece in October 1940 had not gone to plan for Mussolini, and had necessitated, in April 1941, German intervention. This is widely believed to have delayed the onset of Operation Barbarossa, the German invasion of the Soviet Union, and thus to have played a critical role in determining that the Germans would not win the campaign on the Eastern Front.

[157] Eyties, (often 'Eyeties') is a derogatory term for the Italians.

[158] Mussolini was executed on 28 April 1945 and his body placed on public show in Milan, where it was subjected to public abuse.

[159] Sergio Soldano, furrier, clothes-designer, parfumier.

from vicious creatures like mink who were specially bred to be de-furred but would ban the buying, advertising or wearing of fur that came from genuinely wild creatures since, as a result of the trade in furs, they were in danger of extinction. She pointed out that she would wear Persian lamb since she still eats lamb chops. Personally, I said, I couldn't care less about the fate of wild animals and that I was far more concerned with the fate of wild human beings. And particularly with the fate of my wild human family. [. . .]

E did her fur reportage yesterday under great difficulties as they couldn't shoot out of doors as there was a continual downpour. I went over about 1.30 and was fitted for Trotsky and had a bite to eat. Couldn't wait to come back here to the warm intimacy of the yacht and with the two volumes of the *Shorter Oxford* on the sofa and *Decline of the West* across my knees I settled down together with endless cups of tea to a long read until E came home, quite late and slightly the worse for wear, about 7.30. She has just given me a graphic description of the delight of over-eating kippers and the particular joy of their repeating. She is the only person, certainly the only woman who will tell you – not anybody I mean, just me – details of the internal workings of her body. She knows it appals me which is why perversely she enjoys telling me. Liz la Perverse.

I'd forgotten how readable Spengler is even in translation or maybe the translation makes it more readable than the original. He really comes out with all guns firing. The fury in the professional philosopher world must have been joyful to watch. What, I wonder, did people like Bertrand Russell and lesser lights like C. E. M. Joad and economists like Keynes feel like when they read the cold dismissal of them all by our friend Oswald.[160] To turn from the vigorous dynamics of Spengler to the distant urbanity of Toynbee is almost comical. And so it was Spengler all afternoon and evening and Toynbee in bed and A. A. Fair for a night-cap.[161] [. . .]

Monday 20th [. . .] Did not write in this yesterday but spent a thoroughly lazy day reading *Palmerston* a biography by Jasper Ridley.[162] I didn't know much about Palmerston before and didn't know how loathsome he was. The kind of English that causes me bright fury and arouses all my usually sleeping hatred of the English. And now poor bastards they are worse than ever, their two or three centuries of arrogance as a right having turned into pathos. They flared up for a year or two as a result of Churchill and the war but the post-war debacles killed them stone dead. How I enjoyed Suez and the fools they made of themselves. How I enjoyed De Gaulle and his more English than the English

---

[160] Bertrand Russell (1872–1970), philosopher. C. E. M. Joad (1891–1953), philosopher. John Maynard Keynes (1883–1946), economist.
[161] A. A. Fair, one of the pseudonyms of the thriller writer, E. S. Gardner (1889–1970).
[162] Jasper Ridley (1920–2004), *Lord Palmerston* (1970).

'NO' to the Common Market.[163] I watch their every humiliation with great pleasure though I don't much like reading other people writing about them as I am now. [. . .]

Have worked and, as usual on this film, rather eccentrically. [. . .] Took off 9.50. [. . .] We understood from the pilot that we were flying right to the mountain-top for the location. However, to our surprise, he landed us at the bungalows and immediately took off again leaving us with three locked bungalows. Brook eventually found keys at the hotel. We opened up, put the heaters on, boiled water for coffee and sat in the sun by the window and I continued to read Solzhenitsyn's *One day in the life of* when the helicopter returned about 11.50 and we set off again.[164] It was a short trip as we circled the valley and landed again. Why? They wouldn't need me for another hour. More Solzhenitsyn and off we went again about 1.30 I suppose. Finally to work which consisted of being strafed by planes and explosions going off all over the place and is indeed the scene when I am supposed to be, i.e. Tito is supposed to be injured. Did it umpty-nine times. Became tetchy again when they pegged the poor Alsatian down and chloroformed it so that it would lie dead in the shot.

Home at last about 5 covered in mud and artificial blood. [. . .] was told that I too have to fly to Belgrade tomorrow to see Tito. I don't mind really but I feel guilty about the film again, though there is no way, short of insult, of getting Tito to let me off. We are taking him an Alsatian puppy of superior breeding from England.

Tuesday 21st, Aboard Presidential Plane On our way to see Tito complete with Alsatian dog [. . .]. The plane is very posh, very presidential – two apartments with beds and sitting accommodation for about 40 people I suppose.

This all came about when Tito told us in Tjentiste that his old Alsatian 'Tiger' had died and E suggested we get him a pup from England. He is very highly bred – the descendant of many champions including a few 'best dog of any breed at Crufts' and other 3 stars.[165] He is very good looking – a very blacky sort of brown.

It is also a good coincidence as Tito told us of Tiger II snarling and attacking the Russian Ambassador when he, the latter, brought the ultimatum from Stalin. Brezhnev arrives tomorrow for a state visit which I'm told by CBS and *NY Times* is a thinly disguised look-around for a possible puppet successor to Tito when the old man dies. So now he'll have another Tiger around. The western correspondents I've talked to – and because of the nature of the film and the part I'm

---

[163] President De Gaulle twice vetoed Britain's application to join the European Economic Community, in 1963 and 1967.
[164] Alexander Solzhenitsyn (1918–2008), *One Day in the Life of Ivan Denisovich* (published in English, 1963).
[165] Crufts is an annual international dog show which has been held in England since 1886.

playing all seem to be political rather than film commentators – say they expect a big explosion after Tito dies. All are worried that the various republics will want autonomy in which case they'll be dead ducks for Hungary, Roumania Albania etc. and ultimately, of course, Russia. We shall watch with more than fascination as we love this lot a lot and would hate to see them involved in another 'Hungary' or – even worse – another Czechoslovakia.[166] [. . .]

Wednesday 22nd, **Kalizma–***Cavtat* A horrendous journey back from Belgrade as E was in great pain throughout the journey. Bite-on-bullet, tearful type pain. [. . .] One of the famed pink pills seemed to help which I've told her to take even if she does get woozy oh willy-nilly-she's-a-ruby. Brilliant morn and God's in his heaven all's right with the world. [. . .]

Tito was obviously pleased with the puppy and chuckled richly when he saw it. The poor thing [. . .] followed him in from the garden once so that pleased him no end. I think he was genuinely moved. And so was the Madame Broz. He talked about Brezhnev coming today and how hard the work was going to be. E insisted that he, Tito, speak English for a while. He protested that he confused it with German but she would have none of it and indeed for about 10 minutes he laboured on in English. A few days and a few books and he'd be speaking it very well. We asked him the form for such visits and he sighed and said it would start with an hour or two tete a tete followed by lunch followed by a mass exchange between delegates from both countries. After this Brezhnev would lay a wreath on their cenotaph or visit a factory and then there would be a banquet in the evening. Fool! I would go mad. Three whole days of that with neither of them really saying anything and inferring mightily between the lines. He asked about the film and I told him that we'd been held up etc. but that the work we had done seemed to be good and that friends from London who'd seen the rushes dreamt of dollar signs. He said wickedly that dollar-signs weren't what they were. Well then I said 'Deutschmarks'. Must confess that I didn't think 20 years ago or even 20 weeks that I would choose to be paid in DMs rather than dollars. Oh what a fall was there my country-men.[167] I asked him about the Fitzroy Maclean story that 'you do this, and you that' was Ti, To and thereby came his name. I persisted and asked him if he'd told that to Maclean as a joke. No, he said, he'd never said anything of the kind but somebody else may have. He said that Tito was quite a common name in some parts, maybe his part of Jugoslavia. He mentioned some other name which was equally short like Nikki or taka or something which he could easily have become.

They want us to come back on Sunday to visit the War Museum but museums ought, as Dylan once said, to be put into museums and I can't think

---

[166] Burton is referring to Soviet interventions in Hungary (1956) and Czechoslovakia (1968).
[167] A reference to *Julius Caesar*, Act III, scene ii.

of anything more boring. One of the men there, a very suave under-secretary of the Foreign Office said that some ambassador had been to visit and after a couple of hours said that he had tears in his eyes. Lying bastard, I thought. Unless they were tears of boredom.

[. . .] E wrote two letters last night while I read *Dombey and Son*. Years since I read it but page after page comes back to my memory. We had several volumes of Dickens at home. They were won by my brothers, principally Ivor I think, for good attendance at Sunday School or day school.

Friday 24th Exhausting work up in the mountains, physically exhausting. Running about at a half crouch and diving into fox-holes at 9000 feet is not only wearying but boring. Seemingly endless explosions go off all around us and at the end of each day I am covered with dirt, some artificial put on by Ron and some, the most uncomfortable kind put on by nature in all the bombing and slithering about. By evening time I am a mass of aches from the use of unaccustomed muscles. So much so that I missed two days in this diary. Too stiff to be bothered. [. . .]

Still with *Dombey and Son*. Must confess that Dickens could do with some editing. Sometimes his discursiveness is charming but sometimes one is minded to skip. One can see him beginning a chapter with 'now let's start this with some fine writing!' Little Dombey is, let's face it, a bit of a pain in the ass. And the famous 'death of little Dombey' very contrived.[168] I'd forgotten how often people cry in Dickens. Tears are for ever starting from people's eyes. But it's all good reading nevertheless. [. . .]

We are going to go to an island supposedly very beautiful and sub-tropical 70% wooded etc. with interior lakes called Mljet.[169] We shall paddle around it. Tea and off again in the egg-beater. [. . .]

E told me tonight that she was always perfectly assured of herself in the early fifties when she knew that she was a sort of second string to Jean Simmons, Grace Kelly and Colleen Gray and Audrey Hepburn variously because deep down she could fall back on a sort of cultural or artistic background.[170] She is vague as to exactly what she means and so am I [. . .] but she thinks that growing up as she did surrounded as she was by great works of art, by your Van Goghs, Monets, Renoirs etc. gave her a sense of proportion about the relative insignificance of whether she played 'Young Bess' or whether somebody else did – in this case Jean Simmons.[171] E thinks that makes her sound like some kind of intellectual egotist but I don't think so at all. I was and to a certain extent still am, an awful academic snob. There was no mind, if

---

[168] The death of little Paul Dombey is a famous episode in Dickens's novel *Dombey and Son* (1847–8).
[169] Mljet, to the west of Dubrovnik.
[170] Coleen Gray (1922—), actor.
[171] *Young Bess* (1953), directed by George Sidney (1916–2002).

G. B. Shaw will forgive the paraphrase, that I didn't despise in the film business when I compared it with my own.[172] There was nothing much to compare it with. One can hardly describe Darryl Zanuck, Lew Schreiber, L. B. Meyer, Jack Warner and all their little satellites as being the owners of towering brains.[173] As E says, for her it was a harbour in which she could watch with some dispassion the busy toing and froing while for me, much more arrogantly, it was a mountain peak on which I could look down on the despicable ants.

I have been a little put out by something that Ron Berkeley told me and which I have yet to verify. I have predicated my still unwritten article or whatever it might turn out to be about Tito on the belief that he never ever ordered anyone, including captured Germans who had behaved with atrocity to his defenceless people and Chetniks who betrayed and murdered the partisans, to be shot. Now Ron tells me that he was in a bar in Dubrovnik the other night and in the course of conversation with a group of Jugoslavs he said that I was particularly fascinated by Tito because of this. Whereupon two men immediately stood up from the table and left the cafe-bar without a word. Ron asked why this, as Jugoslavs are generally polite. The proprietor who is a cockney Slav believe it or not said that the fathers of the two men had been shot in the Jugoslavian 'purge' of 1948.[174] I must now try and find out if these two killings (altogether, Ron says 41 people from Dubrovnik were shot at that time) were personal settling of scores or whether the orders came from the top. If so I shall be a disappointed man. I mean if the orders came from Belgrade. I must also find out if the people are willing to talk. So far, after countless conversations with all kinds of people I have never heard one bad word about Tito and very few pejorative remarks about communism, though quite a lot about bureaucracy and its attendant evils – particularly nepotism and the fact that a member of the party, though inferior in merit to a cardless Slav, will always get the vote. I asked Branko, a veteran Slav actor who speaks good English, why nobody, but simply nobody, spoke ill of Tito.[175] Was it caution or fear perhaps. Branko said that it was neither, that Tito was still a father-figure. To the older generation – people of my age and his (57? 62?) – he and Sava had been the legendary saviours and to the younger generation – those of 30 and under – there had never been any other President.[176] Tito and President had become synonymous. Rather, I suppose, the way in which Caesar came to mean King. Kaiser and Czar are probably etymologically derived from Julius and

---

[172] George Bernard Shaw, *Dramatic Opinions and Essays* (1907), vol. 2, p. 52: 'With the single exception of Homer, there is no eminent writer, not even Sir Walter Scott, whom I can despise so entirely as I despise Shakespeare when I measure my mind against his.'

[173] Lew Schreiber, the casting director of Twentieth Century-Fox. Louis Burt Meyer (1884–1957), film producer with MGM. Jack L. Warner (1892–1978), executive producer, Warner Bros.

[174] It is generally believed that no fewer than 50,000 people were killed during the 1948 'purge' of the Communist Party of Yugoslavia.

[175] Branko Spoljar (1914–85).

[176] A reference to Saint Sava (c.1175–1235).

his namesakes. The young ones know that he saved them from [the] Boche beast and the Red Bear and those who might have opposed him in the crisis of 1948 – if Ron's story in the pub is to be credited – were presumably knocked off or incarcerated. I must ask more of Branko and find out if I can detect in him any signs of caution or fear when next he chats at my instigation. I think I'll be able to tell. I must ask about Djilas and whether it would be possible for me to meet him or even whether it would be advisable of me to ask somebody like Popović who is a member of the party.[177]

Saturday 25th, Kalizma [. . .] I'd forgotten that *Dombey* was written in serial form which accounts, a great deal I imagine, for the incredibility of the plot which is really beyond belief. No question but that E. M. Forster was right (he is quoted in the afterword by Alan Pryce Jones) when he said that Dickens was the most popular novelist of the nineteenth century and its greatest humourist.[178] He is not however a great novelist because I don't believe half he says and his obvious 'set-pieces' set my nerves on edge and were it not for the fact that I am congenitally unable to skip passages I would have read the book in half the time. But he is good entertainment and ideal for reading on the daily helicopter trips and between shots on the film – something I was never able to do before. [. . .]

Having seen Tito on Tuesday we were more than interested in the report in yesterday's *Tribune* of the meetings between Tito and Brezhnev.[179] Looks like the old man is as tough and intractable as ever. He refuses to accept the idea of 'limited sovereignty' which is an absurd contradiction in terms anyway. Sovereignty is sovereignty and limited is limited and never the twain shall meet. The Orwellian double-think is evident in every arrogant word that Brezhnev says.[180] He denies that he meant by 'limited sovereignty' the status under which Czechoslovakia lived and the excuse for the invasion. It says that Mr Brezhnev and Tito were going on a hunting trip but owing to 'a slight cold' affecting Brezhnev the trip had been cancelled. How the Russian bosses must hate Tito and how they will exult when he dies. And there is no ear nose and throat specialist who can prescribe for the kind of cold that Brezhnev has. [. . .]

---

[177] Milovan Djilas (1911–95), Yugoslavian partisan and communist, who had fallen out of favour in the 1950s and served a number of prison sentences. He was by 1971 living in Belgrade, a renowned dissident.
[178] Burton is referring to E. M. Forster (1879–1970), novelist, biographer, essayist. However the Forster quoted (actually as saying that Dickens was 'the most popular novelist of the century, and one of the greatest humorists that England has produced'), was John Forster (1812–76), biographer. Alan Pryce-Jones (1908–2000), literary editor, critic and journalist. This is the 1964 edition of *Dombey and Son*, published by Signet.
[179] Presumably the *International Herald Tribune*.
[180] A reference to George Orwell's dystopian vision in *1984*.

Monday 27th, Cavtat [. . .] Flew by copter to the location – took about 40 minutes. Then were asked by Popović to go to Sarajevo to have a look at the inevitable 'Tito' house. It is the usual thing. A house divided into two floors the top one of which is two suites comprised of bathroom, bedroom with two single beds stuck together, and <u>two</u> minute sitting rooms for each suite. Why two? The helicopter attempted a landing in the grounds but it was impossible so we went off to the airport. [. . .] Knocked off three scenes as fast as I could and we were back on board the copter by 8.30pm. [. . .]

Tuesday 28th, Sarajevo Sitting here in my 'suite' in the house in Sarajevo. It is as far as one can get from the city without being in the country. The mountains go straight up a couple of hundred yards away. It is, this house and the surrounding ones, again one of those little estates which we have found by now everywhere we go which contain hotels and adjacent houses for the exclusive use of VIPs of the Party. Last night, for instance, one of the boys said that two men appeared unexpectedly and were shown into rooms on the ground floor. That floor has about 8 small bedrooms. So I suppose the VIPs don't bother to book into hotels when on business outside the big cities; they simply report to the nearest Commie-complex.

I finished work ridiculously early [. . .] about mid-day and was back here in the house by 1pm. Called E immediately at the house but it appears that she'd decided to stay on the *Kalizma*. Called again this evening after I'd been out shopping but couldn't get through. Will call again later. I feel terribly lonely without Elizabeth. Last night I had dinner as already said in previous entry and today I had lunch – wienerschnitzel, not bad, – just one course when Poppo [Popović] [. . .] turned up again with a very splendid brochure of an exhibition here called 'Art on the soil of Yugoslavia from prehistoric times to the present.' He is most insistent that E and I should pay a sort of state visit to it. I loathe the idea of a conducted tour around a museum. I loathe museums anyway and in my case they are a waste of time. The last one I went to was the big one in NY called the Metropolitan I think – it's on the east side of Central Park.[181] There were a lot of large Rodins about I seem to remember and I wandered about dutifully enough and was stopped by only one thing – a painting of a large forest, the shot, as 'twere, taken from one mountain top to another and in the far tree-covered mountain was a long thin waterfall. It was so excellently done that one wasn't sure whether it was smoke coming up from the bed of the valley or water streaming down. The woman I was with, a journalist who was supposed to be an aficionada, said it was a 'nothing picture'. And by a 'nobody'. So that was that. Next time I'm in New York I'll see if I can find it again.

---

[181] Metropolitan Museum of Art, Fifth Avenue, New York.

The shops close from noon to 4 and so this afternoon I read a book called *The French Connection* which is about the narcotics trade generally and about one case specifically.[182] Not very well written but informative and though written with the co-operation of the NY Police Department showed the Police up in an unattractive light. They seem to be so stupid. A clever man would be able to defeat them every time. The only reason they were successful in this particular case was, it seems to me, because the criminals were equally stupid.

Went out with Brook, Ron and Vessna the interpreter to buy books if any and biscuits and choc etc. for snacking. Found both. The bookshop, a small one was right near the University and was typical. There were many volumes of *Ulysses*, collected works of MacNeice, Auden, Keats, Byron, Shelley etc.[183] Many *Fowler's English Usage* and dictionaries and *Roget's* and to my delight two Rex Stouts which I don't think I've read and even more delightful four different Anthony Powells.[184] Also two Ngaio Marsh and *The Confidence Man* by Herman Melville which I've never read.[185] So for a small shop in the middle of Jugoslavia it was a considerable haul. Why do the idiotic profs in universities recommend *Ulysses* – you must know your *Ulysses* and your Eliot and Pound in your English course here, I gather from Vessna and Yasmin – which, unless you have a really wide and fairly deep knowledge of the language in which it is written must be impossibly difficult to read and certainly to enjoy. They'd even have difficulty with that last sentence of mine. [. . .]

Wednesday 29th Talked to E at last yesterday evening about 9 and we exchanged loneliness – one for the other. Ate many sweetmeats and drank much water and read Nero Wolfe. He writes so urbanely that after a diet of ordinary thriller writers he cuts the palate with a nice astringency, a neat pungency. [. . .]

I have decided, even though this is my first visit to a communist country, that the Slav is not made for Communism – at least, not the South Slav. I think it must be as atavistically alien to them as Puritanism would be to the South Irish. It doesn't seem to fit somehow. They seem uncomfortable in it. I have heard so many tales now of the really staggering rudeness of shop-keepers to people, particularly foreigners, that I can only think that they are a very unhappy lot. Raymond, for instance, went into a shop to buy something and when his turn came to be served he was asked for whatever it was he wanted and the shopkeeper said, What nationality are you and Raymond said Italian. Why don't you go and buy it in your own bloody country? was the gracious

[182] Robin Moore (1925–2008), *The French Connection: A True Account of Cops, Narcotics and International Conspiracy* (1969).
[183] George Gordon, Lord Byron (1788–1824); Percy Bysshe Shelley (1792–1822).
[184] *Roget's Thesaurus*. Rex Stout (1886–1975), crime writer, whose novels often featured detective Nero Wolfe. Anthony Powell (1905–2000), novelist.
[185] Ngaio Marsh (1899–1982), novelist. Herman Melville (1819–91) *The Confidence Man: His Masquerade* (1857).

response. They are just as bad to their own countrymen. Vessna went to buy some drawing pins in a shop and was kept waiting 1½ hours. The shop wasn't particularly crowded. The assistants simply took endless time, sometimes disappearing into a back room for 15 minutes in the middle of someone's order. Apart from the rudeness on the shopkeeper's part, where was Vessna's and the other people's independence? Where was the shouting and bawling which would have been automatic in any western country? She just shrugs. They also seem a most un-curious people. Though they have never been to the West, they have no curiosity about it. And those who have been to England or Italy or even, one or two like Vessna, to the USA, they never talk about it. [. . .]

I did a longish scene with two hopeless Jugo actors – hopeless in both languages – and then waited for hours for Heavy Luger to turn up. He had driven from Kupari and it had taken him about seven hours. In the meantime I finished my Nero Wolfe and started Anthony Powell's *A Question of Upbringing* which is very droll so far.[186] I've only read a chapter and a bit and I seem to remember that 'Witherspoon' or whatever his name is comes up again very largely in the later volume of *The Music of Time*.[187] It must be quite some time since I read that volume. I had a lot of coffee and had forgotten how shaky it makes you feel. However, nobody noticed and I used it in the scene to give a tensity to it which I hope will work. [. . .]

Thursday 30th [. . .] Finished the Powell and started another – got a little tired of that, I mean his style, – and changed to *Life at the Top* by John Braine.[188] Tired of that quickly too so tried a detective thriller. Got tired of that. So put out the light at 10 and went to sleep immediately. [. . .] Vessna and the chauffeur went out last night and bought two kinds of coffee and two tin jugs to boil water in and some strange looking tea so we'll be able to brew up on the mountain top. Also, from my memory of the bookshop, I wrote out a list of books for Vessna to buy which I suddenly decided would be a neat addition for the library on the *Kalizma*. I asked her to make it paperbacks as much as she could as 'good' books become mildewed from the salt air. So we now have a complete Shakespeare in separate paperbacked volumes, complete Keats, Shelley, Wilfred Owen, Louis MacNeice, Wystan Auden and a Larousse English dictionary which I can keep in the bedroom on the ship.[189] And a fat Penguin paperback of *Ulysses* which I read this morning and immediately after only four or five pages it brought back bleak memories of <u>having</u> to read it so many years ago. I have never looked at it since it was part of the syllabus laid out for me by Phil Burton. It's such a pleasure to read now knowing I won't

---

[186] Anthony Powell, *A Question of Upbringing* (1951).
[187] The character's name is Kenneth Widmerpool. There are 12 volumes in the *A Dance to the Music of Time* cycle.
[188] John Braine (1922–86), *Life at the Top* (1957).
[189] Wilfred Owen (1893–1918), poet.

have to answer questions about it. Having re-tasted it this morning, merely an aperitif of five pages, I shall devour it from time to time.

Ron came back by car last night as we were forced out of courtesy to invite Hardy (Heavy Luger) Krüger and wife to fly down with us in the copter and with Ron as well we would have been overloaded. [. . .]

Poppo has spent all day trying to persuade Brook, Vessna and Ron to persuade me to go to the Exhibition of Jug Art through the Ages. Normally I suppose I would have gone, but his persistence is so great and his urgency to have the Mayor there together with TV and snappers while I look at the exhibits has made me as recalcitrant as a wild horse. [. . .]

OCTOBER

Friday 1st, Sarajevo Have read myself into a stupor and practically a standstill. I tried all kinds of books last night and settled for thinking instead after throwing them all aside. I can't remember what I thought about altogether but I remember thinking how much I would like to have E there. I had gone for a walk through the forest – a planned walk laid out by the gardeners in gravel – and thought that much as I liked walking it is not quite as interesting if when you come back there is nobody to confide in. [. . .]

Sunday 3rd, Kalizma–Cavtat [. . .] it's a beautiful morning and I'm in love with my wife and apart from seeing a chap called Terence Baker at 10 o'clock I have a whole day with E and books ships and cabbages and kings.[190] It is also a sparklingly lively lovely day. And my rheumaticaly anthroidic but beautiful child is still a-slumber and E'en So is snoring and the boat moves in a slow circle on its anchor and now you see Dubrovnik and now you see the hotel here and the church-bells are ringing and a plane is coming in to land at Dub airport and I shall have a cup of tea or coffee and smoke a cig and read and waste myself indolently down the day.

Monday 4th Terence Baker, a large man with a lean face and a fat belly, somewhere in his thirties I suppose, came on board yesterday morn as expected and told me, as expected, that the company had not been paying me. I told him to tell the company that we had heard many tales of Yugoslavian perfidy in re the non-payment of actors or delayed payments of as much as 3 to 5 years that unless my money was in the bank on Monday (today) I would not work on Tuesday (tomorrow) and until the money has been paid would continue not to work. So that should be clear enough even to Poppo's muddy intelligence. [. . .] It is a shame that our dislike of the Poppo could mean a dislike of the entire Jugoslavian race

---

[190] A reference to Lewis Carroll's 'The Walrus and the Carpenter' (1872) which includes the lines 'Of shoes—and ships—and sealing–wax — / Of cabbages—and kings'.

were we dense enough to allow such an enormity. But from Tito on down we have found the South Slavs to be the most enchanting people it has been our pleasure to meet. They have only two rivals but the Italians are untrustworthy and will do almost anything for a fast lira and the Mexicans are so sad, so melancholy. And although the Jugoslavians are chauvinistic, they do not practise it as offensively as the French – particularly – and the English, Germans and Americans. [. . .]

Terence Baker is the brother of an actor – English – called George Baker who for a time was thought to be a promising piece of beef-cake but had no talent, even for that, and has drifted into obscurity.[191] T. Baker is a very different cup of cocoa and seems to live up to his reputation as a hard man with a contract. He is John Heyman's partner or assistant or co-producer or something of those and gives the impression that he will do well. He instructed Wolf Mankowitz to stay at home and not complete his assignment to finish writing the film as Wolf too has received not a penny-piece. In addition we have discovered that none of the lesser people, those being paid less money I mean, like Brook, Ron, Raymond, Gianni Bozz and, I expect, Vessna have been paid either. That is unforgivable. I could, after all, sell my paintings or E her jewels or something but what is Ron going to sell? His make-up box?

I have now finished three of the first four volumes of Anthony Powell's *Dance to the Music of Time* and have just started the fifth called *Casanova's Chinese Restaurant*.[192] He gives the impression of a deliberately distant artist. His canvas is large but he stands a long way off and paints with a remote brush only in the corners and only in miniatures. He is not exciting and his poetic impulse is firmly controlled. So much so, that it is rarely apparent. But he sticks with you and it is an interesting experiment in autobiography.

I wonder if I could use that form. I couldn't use the style which is abhorrent to me. He over-punctuates and is at times otiose and I cannot really believe Widmerpool. I cannot believe that a man so stupid could be so successful. But there are another five volumes to go I think. He is not a writer for any mood. There are times when I find him impossible to read and have to put him aside for a day. Also, his coincidences are too pat and occur too often. Though Evelyn Waugh pointed this out and then apologized on thinking of similar coincidences in his own and Powell's life, I think that Waugh was right in the first instance.[193] A coincidence that's true to life is not necessarily true to

[191] George Baker (1931–2011), whose greatest success was on British television portraying Inspector Reginald Wexford (1987–2000), created by Ruth Rendell (1930—).

[192] Anthony Powell, *Casanova's Chinese Restaurant* (1960).

[193] Burton refers here to Evelyn Waugh, *A Little Learning* (1964), p. 201, where Waugh writes of Powell: 'In reading his brilliant series of novels I have sometimes thought – and indeed, have been so foolish as to state as much in a review – that the recurring seemingly haphazard conjunctions of human life, which comprise his theme, pass beyond plausibility. His hero's passage through youth and early manhood is continually recrossed in improbable circumstances by the same characters. After I had written the review expressing doubts of the authenticity of so many coincidences, I began to reflect on my own acquaintance with him and understood that his was genuine social realism.'

fiction. Also, another weakness it seems to me is that the coincidences are predictable. 'Two people came into the room. Molly Blaides was going to marry a much younger man. The man turned and I saw it was ... Widmerpool.'[194] Don't believe you Tony bach.

A brilliant morning again. [. . .] It is very hot in the sun and people from the seafront hotels swim from morn 'til night. One massive German woman swam around the yacht yesterday for a couple of hours. She smiled at me so I waved at her and she answered me with a few gutturals and a wave that, perhaps accidentally, looked like a Nazi salute I swear to God. Who knows that the gutturals didn't contain a 'Heil Hitler' somewhere there.

E is a much cleverer reader than I am. She is currently reading a book called *Smith and Jones* by Nicholas Monsarrat.[195] It is quite a clever piece but she is asking me questions about certain anomalies in the writing which I don't remember asking myself. I read the book a week or so ago. I'll comfort myself by saying that she has a suspicious mind and I don't. I remember giving her *The Murder of Roger Ackroyd* of A. Christie and telling her that she would never guess the murderer.[196] She got it at the end of the second or third chapter. I was amazed and furious.

[. . .] There is a big 'spy' defector story in all the papers. A Russian has defected to the British.[197] Yesterday, I said he had 'defecated', which is a good Freudian slip.

[. . .]I did a scene this afternoon in which six planes, two at a time, dive-bombed us while we were crossing a very flimsy bridge across a roaring river. Explosions went off right, left and centre and were, of course, centred on me – we have to show the old man being under intense bombardment. So the bombs went off all over the place and many people were hit by 'shrapnel' one chap quite badly in the face and two men on the cameras were hit – Pinter in the belly – and several others got odd wounds while I, four times in the centre of the maelstrom, was only splashed with water. My family always told me from the toddling stage 'Ma' lwc y diafol arnat ti.' Touched with the Devil's luck. Keep it up oh diavolo!

Tuesday 5th, Mostar[198] [. . .] I went to sleep last night to the accompaniment of a very raucous 'group' playing the awful noise that passes for 'Mersey' sound I suppose.[199] [. . .]

---

[194] Burton is using poetic licence here. The relevant passage which inspires his invented quotation comes in the first chapter of Powell's fourth novel, *At Lady Molly's* (1957), in which Mildred Haycock, once Mildred Blaides, arrives at a party with her fiancé, who happens to be Kenneth Widmerpool, younger than Mildred by about ten years, and known to the narrator, Nicholas Jenkins.
[195] Nicholas Monsarrat, *Smith and Jones* (1963).
[196] Agatha Christie, *The Murder of Roger Ackroyd* (1926).
[197] Oleg Lyalin (1937–95) of the KGB (the Soviet intelligence service) had been revealed as a defector on 30 September.
[198] Mostar: north-west of Dubrovnik and inland, today in Bosnia Herzegovina.
[199] Pop music associated with Liverpool in the 1960s.

I am obviously still only half awake. Some of the sentences above are very oddly constructed. Beautiful day with a blue sky and a few white clouds. The moon was going down when I got up. The river, a very hurly-burly one is green in colour, like certain seas.

Wednesday 5th, Mostar[200] E arrived last evening earlier that I expected and all the better for that. She looked ravishing or perhaps she always looks startlingly beautiful when one hasn't seen her for even as short a time as 36 hours. Suddenly a bright room looks drab as she makes it by contrast. Received a message by phone which said: Terrance (sic) asks you to please <u>not</u> work Tomorrow or leave Mostar – Money not in Belgrad (sic). I was being interviewed by my Jugoslavian actor friend Basić (Pronounced Basheech) when the urgently awaited message arrived. I was very disappointed as the less I do now the more I shall have to do in December and bang goes Xmas in Vallarta for a start besides which I really am very sorry for the Director and all the other very nice people despite the fact that I was told [. . .] after I'd explained the situation, that they [. . .] would perfectly understand. [. . .] I had been warned [. . .] through Hugh French by Deakin that though he, Deakin, was greatly enamoured of the Slavs he was also very aware that in business they can be devious almost to the point of skulduggery. [. . .] What finally renders us all speechless is that the cost of sitting around with thousands of people on call must cost them far more than the relatively paltry sums they owe me and the rest of the lads. I am furious, all the same that I'm not working. How different it would be if I was holding up production on some cute little killer like Zanuck or Jack Warner or L. B. Meyer. I would give parties.

Last night after dinner Gianni Bozzacchi reduced me to tears of laughter when he told me some of the items put on our weekly bill at the house. Now, the number of people staying at the house is five – Gianni, Claudye, Raymond, E and myself, though E and I have spent very little time there as we usually stay at Cavtat in the *Kalizma* – and of those five only Elizabeth drinks <u>but</u> she drinks <u>only</u> booze brought from the boat, Smirnoff and Jack Daniels both of which products are unobtainable in Jugoslavia. So, in effect, nobody at the house of our party drinks at all. The bill however for one week had us down for 5,000 dinars, new dinars and the following week it had jumped to 8,000. I asked how much a bottle of Scotch was in dinars. Johnny Walker Red Label is 100 dinars. It therefore follows that <u>if</u> we were all drinking and <u>if</u> we drank only the most expensive drink obtainable which is Johnny Walker and other whiskies we would have drunk 50 bottles the first week and 80 the second. Again assuming we all drank the same amount it would mean that the first week we drank 1 and $\frac{3}{7}$ths of a bottle per day, and in the second week 2 and

---

[200] Wednesday was 6 October.

⅗ths of a bottle per day. Only five raving alcoholics of the classic pattern could keep up such a pace. I have in my time and at my best put away I'm sure the occasional 3 bottles of vodka a day but not for two or three days in a row and certainly not for a week or a fortnight. Otherwise it would be Dead Dad. No, that kind of consumption demands the presence of Bobby Newton, Bernie Lee, Trevor Howard, Errol Flynn and Jason Robards to name but a few of my friends only two of whom oddly enough are dead.[201] If we had taken the local, and apparently very drinkable wine which costs 10 dinars a bottle we would in two weeks have put away [. . .] 1,300 bottles. As for the food, it is a riot of over-charging. It is reminiscent of the time when Dick Hanley found that the monthly bill in the house in Rome on the Via Appia Pignatelli for bread alone was $500.

I wrote letters to Liza, Kate, Maria and Gwen and Ivor yesterday while E wrote two! One each to Liza and Maria. The pen-and-pencil set is practically smoking from use. [. . .]

Went to work at 12 noon as asked and did two shots both involving huge explosions and neither of which I enjoyed as I swear to God I am becoming shell-shocked. Also, it must be confessed that the explosions on this film are the heaviest by far of any film I've ever been on and I have made quite a few very noisy war-films – *Where Eagles Dare* must have the all time top of the decibel rating so far. But if this one is as loud in the cinema as it is to the naked ear *Eagles* will have to take second place. If it makes as much money as *Eagles* it can, for my part, get even noisier and I'll take a chance on being shell-shocked. For the first time in my life in war-films I jumped involuntarily at one particularly near and shattering explosion. Out of the corner of my eye I saw everybody else twitch too but they are not Tito and impassive. During the first series of explosions I am sending out a carefully worded call to Moscow to relay to 'Free Jugoslavia' a message to 'crush the vital forces of the enemy' with all the sang-froid of the typical Walter Mitty Englishman.[202] In this case I hope it's interpreted by the audience as Slavic fatalism. One of the decisions I had to make before the film started a personal one, as the director doesn't speak or understand English – was what accent to use for Tito. To speak English with a Slavic roll and rumbles was a temptation as critics and audiences tend to think of that as 'good acting' but I decided it was too obvious and might even, unless I was very careful, become comical in the wrong way. So I asked a lot of educated middle-class Jugoslavians whether there was a 'standard educated accent' in Serbo-Croat and they said yes and did Tito speak with such an accent and they said no but he was slightly off centre. Therefore I

---

[201] Robert Newton (1905–56), who had acted with Burton in *The Desert Rats*. Bernard Lee (1908–81), who had acted with Burton in *The Spy Who Came in from the Cold*. Trevor Howard (1913–88). Errol Flynn (1909–59).
[202] Walter Mitty is the daydreaming character in James Thurber's American short story, 'The Secret Life of Walter Mitty' (1939). It is possible that Burton means something else entirely.

thought I would speak my standard accent with the Welsh lilt occasionally thrown in as a shade, an almost elusive innuendo. I hope it will do. I was interviewed today for about half an hour by somebody [. . .] from *Newsweek* who was from Prague or Vienna or Budapest or somewhere in mittel europe with a mittel-european accent I think though it was so slight that it was difficult to place. [. . .] He was a political correspondent. What a relief they are after film writers. He asked me whether I thought the film had any political significance and I answered that of course it had. Apart from showing the fanatical courage of the Jugoslavian people it also showed its terrifying terrain and presumably, after seeing it, regardless of its artistic merit, anybody who planned Czechoslovakia here in my adopted country might well have second thoughts. The juggernaut could roll over the grass of Jugoslavia if it wished perhaps, but the grass would soon grow tall again and the Idol of Krishna would have to roll back and fore from coast to border for all eternity and still this particular grass would not lie down.[203] I also pointed out that I had the feeling that these people, like a certain kind of Celt – the industrial South Welsh, the Irish and the Scots – liked fighting, looked forward to fighting and even revelled in fighting. Not entirely comfortable people for a dove to live with but I would rather join them than fight them. If the Nazi Army, at the height of its power and already battle-hardened, couldn't defeat this, at first, People's Army accoutred with pitchforks and scythes and of course hammers and sickles, if the Germans – the formidable Army of modern times couldn't beat them and were indeed defeated by these same people eventually then, short of some new diabolical genocidal weapon, nobody could.

What will come out in the article as the reporter and I agreed after the automatons at *Newsweek* get at it is going to be of course something of stupendous banality attributed to me. Was it true, he asked me, that I was going to do a scene in front of Brezhnev which mentioned in more cryptic form the sentiments expressed above. I said that there was some talk of this but that something happened – perhaps the Russians got hold of it – and anyway it didn't come about. I said I regretted greatly that it hadn't.

Since the entire crew and all the actors were chuckling fiendishly at the idea of this sharp little sticloc [*sic*] to the vitals of Russian arrogance I have no doubt that the Russians <u>did</u> hear of it. I talked the standard replies to whether I liked Tito and Jugoslavia and so on and I said yes we had been with Tito the day before he had his 3 day meeting with Brezhnev and that no we hadn't had the temerity to ask Tito how he was going to handle the affair which was not strictly true.

[. . .] E will go back to Kupari tomorrow and I will get back on Saturday night which is going to be a charming six or seven hour drive in the dark down

---

[203] This is a rather oblique reference to the central character in the Indian Sanskrit epic The Mahabharata.

those interminably twisted roads. That will mean not getting back to the yacht before midnight possibly, then to Rome the following day and drawing a couple of hasty breaths hard and fast into Trotsky on Monday morning. I expect Joe will give me an easy first day or, with a bit of luck, it may be possible that I, or rather, they may not be ready to shoot so quickly after their long bout in Mexico. [. . .]

Thursday 7th [. . .] A lot of things happened to me – and us – in Rome and the old city is very much in my mind this morning. Perhaps because we are going there in three days' time. The first time I went there, sometime in the early fifties, everybody was on foot or push-bikes or bussed it or trammed. The second time was about '56 and push-bikes were losing out to Vespas and Corgis buzzing around the city like so many angry bees while the next time – the time of *Cleopatra* – the petrol bikes were being replaced by small, indeed the smallest, Fiats and Volkswagens all seemingly determined to become Fangios or Stirling Moss.[204] Now there are just as many of the latter I suppose but owned perhaps by the same people who have graduated to bigger and more middle-income cars while a lower group have taken over the Fiats etc. and the push-bikers to the Vespas have moved – why the German and Welsh syntax? – though the trams and buses must still be full. Since we were there last the Romans have passed laws restricting the traffic in some parts of the city. I think that some of the Piazzas are free from traffic – notably the Navona – but I wonder if the Vias Veneto and Sistinas and that street below the Spanish Steps are for pedestrians only. I shall find out by walking on Sunday mornings disguised in my John Heyman cap. I have been in only two towns where traffic is forbidden. One is Portofino and the other Dubrovnik. A traffic-less Rome would be a joy and an impossibility too since taxis and buses are essential.

Jane Swanson called yesterday from Rome to say that if I wanted my old dressing-room back at the De Laurentiis Studios I would have to pay $150 a week but that she didn't think it worth it as I spent most of the film on location! Nonsense, said I, Trotsky never leaves his house or hardly ever. Meanwhile I looked through the script and discovered that almost every scene I do takes place on 'The Patio of Trotsky's house'. So it appears that they must have taken a real house somewhere in the suburbs I presume and we will shoot it there. That will suit me fine if it's not too far from the city. It can't be in the heart because of the terrific traffic noise but also it can't be in the country as Trotsky's house was very definitely in Mexico City I think.[205] I'm not sure but I think I am looking forward to the film. Much more will depend on its ambience but I enjoy playing 'character' parts much more than 'straight' ones. Instance my intense enjoyment playing the bald homosexual in *Staircase*. I feel much more

[204] Juan Fangio (1911–95); Stirling Moss (1929—), racing drivers.
[205] Trotsky lived at Viena 45, Mexico City.

secure for some reason when the person played is not simply an extension of me. Also I feel that I'm a better character actor than a straight man. I loved doing Toby Belch and Caliban in my days at the Old Vic except for the laborious make-up, especially the latter.[206] Another good thing is that apart from 3 scenes I don't have to work with Delon who is so non-actor that I think I would be embarrassed.[207] He should be ok though in this part as E says he is marvellous at playing killer-gangsters and so on. Reading the script again this morning I think that Joe will have to move the camera around a lot in the big scenes – there are two of them – between Delon and Romy Schneider (odd that her name in German means Taylor – I mean Tailor) as they are very static non-committal scenes. Am also pleased that I have only one scene with Miss Schneider as from what I hear she is uneasy to work with.[208] [. . .] Ron, with his usual look of dark foreboding, says that she ruined the film they did in Israel for John Heyman with Richard Harris playing the star male lead and directing which Ron says was meant to be a sweet film about a small boy's adoration for a great veteran footballer but, he said, with more and more and darker and darker foreboding, she raped Mr Harris and by means of the bedroom literally fucked the film up into a love story between herself and Mr Harris, the footballer.[209] 'Keep,' says Ron, 'your eyes open and your wits about you. Beware the ides of October.' 'But surely Ron,' I say with wide-eyed innocence, 'it's Joe Losey who'll have to keep his hands on his zip-fly, I mean he's the director not me!' 'No offence, Rich,' he says with a look of age-old wisdom, 'you're an attractive guy and all that but Romy would give her eye-teeth to get you away from Elizabeth Taylor.' 'Very well Ron,' I say, 'I will have Elizabeth on set whenever I work with the dreaded Brunhilde and since I only work with her for two days at most and it's only one scene, I think we can safely say that we can consider that particular Biscay safely navigated.'[210] 'Ah,' he says, 'she's the kind who will come in on her days off like pretending that she wants to watch you work because you're a great actor and all that I'm telling you Rich you've got to watch it.' 'But Ron. I've met the woman and I thought she was pretty dog-like and wouldn't have been interested in her even in the old days.' 'Ah! But she has become very beautiful in the last few years. You wait 'til you see her.' 'OK Ron, OK.'

[. . .] Miss Schneider impressed me so much, and I saw her a lot when we were doing *Sandpiper* in Paris and she was doing *Pussycat* with the Peters O'Toole and Sellers and she was for ever in the bar and so were we, that

---

[206] Burton had played the part of Sir Toby Belch in the Old Vic production of *Twelfth Night*, and Caliban in the Old Vic production of *The Tempest*.

[207] Alain Delon (1935—), who would play Frank Jackson in *The Assassination of Trotsky*.

[208] Romy Schneider (1938–82), who would play the part of Gita Samuels in *The Assassination of Trotsky*. Delon and Schneider had been engaged from 1959 to 1963.

[209] The film is *Bloomfield* (1971), directed by Richard Harris and Uri Zohar (1934 –).

[210] Bay of Biscay.

I simply can't remember what she looks like. I have a vague memory of someone small, I think, and blonde but that's about all. I think Ron would be on more securely prophetic grounds if he warned me of Delon who apparently will go with a Swan to get on.[211] Now there's a bloke who would like to get Elizabeth Taylor away from Richard Burton if you like. And don't think Ron that he won't try. Look at the publicity for Chrissake, and in Rome too of all places. I mean, he would love to do a Burton on Burton. And I mean, this feller had a go at Elizabeth through an emissary when E and I were lovers in Rome and at the pinnacle of our scandal. Here is a man who will stop at very little. I don't know him and neither does E but I have an idea that I know his type very well. A sort of perennial juvenile delinquent who gets vicarious kicks out of hob-nobbing with the underworld. Very attractive to women. Not unlike Frank Sinatra and George Raft and Stanley Baker in their various milieux but without, in Frank's case at least, their talent. Actually, I know very little about his acting as I have, as far as I know, only seen him once in a film called *Rocco and his brothers* which must have been made about 1960.[212] A Visconti film, I think, in which Delon seemed as queer as an Arab but very very pretty and Visconti (with who, I hear, he set up house for a few years) and the camera lingered lovingly and almost lasciviously over his exquisite little bones in vast close-up after vast close-up. He must have had something though as he is the only thing I remember about the film despite the fact that it was another actor who made the biggest success in the film and won all the Awards and was critics pet etc. Recently – that is a year or two ago – he was involved with an underworld killing of some kind. His chauffeur-companion, a bad lot with a record who was Delon's 'bodyguard' as well was shot dead in Delon's house in Paris or maybe it was an apartment. It was news in France – front page stuff for *Paris Presse, Ici Paris, France Soir* etc. – but it all died down after a while and I don't know exactly how deeply Delon was compromised. Anyway, he wasn't locked up or anything but spent a lot of time being questioned by the police.[213]

Later.

Brook came upstairs in the house in Mostar this morning and gave me a twitch of the head indicating that he had something to tell me he didn't want E to hear. His face was ashen and he trembled. My heart stopped. What had happened? He led me into an office facing our suite where E was reading a

---

[211] A reference to Zeus as a swan seducing Lēda.

[212] *Rocco and His Brothers* (1960), directed by Luchino Visconti. Renato Salvatori (1934–88) won many plaudits for his part in the film.

[213] Delon had been questioned in connection with a police investigation into the murder of Stevan Marković (1937–68), one of his bodyguards, in 1968. Marković's body had been found outside Delon's Paris home. There had been a considerable press furore surrounding the murder, which had also involved Georges Pompidou.

book, closed the door and said that Mick Smith had just called from England to say that Liza had been thrown by her horse and was in hospital with a fractured skull and concussion but that she was alright and was conscious and was in no danger they thought but was very tearful and sorry for herself and asking for E. I was stupendously shocked. Despite Brook's playing down of the accident all I could see was his white face and all I could hear were the words 'fractured skull'. My first reaction was to literally tear my hair, a phenomenon which I'd heard of and read of but never seen and here was I putting the words into living practice. All I said was 'that horse, that fucking horse, why did I buy it for her?' I stopped behaving like Medea after a few seconds and asked Brook to tell me everything again.[214] Then my mind started functioning reasonably again. I asked Brook to phone Raymond and order the jet from Geneva and if unavailable at such short notice to get E on the plane from Dub to Rome at 2.20 and from Rome to London at 4. Failing that, try Jugoslavian charter. Failing that try Jane Swanson and Olympia jets in Rome and failing everything to try as a last resort to get Tito's Mr Protocol and an army jet or anything. In the meantime while waiting for the call I went in to tell Elizabeth, I prefaced everything by saying that there was no danger though, at that time, I was convinced that there was. E stared at me as if I was a stranger, her face went red then snow white. She moaned and cried but never became hysterical and never screamed or any of the things that lesser women do. We clung to each other and slowly, like a sleep-walker she began dressing and putting on her make-up. I made her a Jack Daniels and wrote Liza a letter for E to take with her and finally Raymond [Vignale] came on the blower. This was about 45 minutes after the news had come. Raymond was on the *Kalizma* and unreachable by phone. In the meantime E was ready to go and packed. We cleaved to each other again for a long time and then she was gone, her sweet eyes puffed with tears hidden by dark glasses. In that long hour before she left we hardly spoke at all. E wondered if she'd been thrown while crossing that dreaded road outside the school. I said I didn't think so. And it wasn't until after E had gone and I sat alone in my room did I begin to work out the timetable of the disaster saying to myself, quite logically: it happened yesterday obviously. Liz had tried to call us all morning and finally had left from the hospital leaving Mick to attempt the call which he succeeded in doing.[215] If therefore Liza was seriously injured and in a coma and all that they would somehow or other have got through last night. Liz and Mick had seen her conscious and though weepy and though the skull was fractured and though she had concussion she was unquestionably alright. On the way up in the car I reasoned all this out loud with Brook. We agreed that she was ok but all the

---

[214] Medea, Greek mythological princess of Colchis, with a reputation for hysteria vengeance and ruthlessness.
[215] Liz: wife of Brook Williams. Mick: business partner of Brook Williams.

time thinking – were they telling the truth. How can someone with a fractured skull be alright? [. . .] And then, oh happy day, I called E in Kupari. She had a jet for 6.15. She had talked to Liza! And Liza sounded as chipper as a chipmunk and couldn't think what all the fuss was about! She obviously doesn't remember how she felt when she was concussed. So now I'm back to reading again. For this relief muchas grazias.

Friday 9th, Sarajevo[216] [. . .] I have been reading all day a book which I started weeks ago and put down and remembering that I am Trotsky on Monday thought to take up again. It is or they are *The Memoirs of a Revolutionary* by Victor Serge.[217] A Russian by blood and temperament and a Belgian by birth and upbringing his is a depressing picture of man's inhumanity to man and nobody in my eyes, or capitalist, monarchist, Fascist or Communist comes out of it with any virtue. There are many tales of unfathomable courage for false or mistaken ideals but all it hammers home is pungent sentence after barbed comment.

After scathing sarcasm is the hopelessness of this frightful world – a world which has been so good to me personally and demanded so little in exchange that I hardly recognize the filthy reality of the evidence of my own mind and reading. In the book I came across the following passage: 'Sergei Yesenin, our matchless poet, has committed suicide . . . said good-night to his friends. "I want to be alone. . . ." In the morning he awoke depressed, and felt the urge to write something. No pencil or fountain pen was at hand, and there was no ink in the hotel inkwell: only a razor blade, with which he slashed his wrist. And so, with a rusty pen dipped in his own blood, Yesenin wrote his last lines:

Au revoir, friend, au revoir . . .
. . . There is nothing new about dying in this life
But there is surely nothing new about living either.'

Then Mr Yesenin hanged himself.[218] What a banal line to write with your own blood and how juvenile how undergraduate and in his own blood yet! I find it unspeakably vile to die with such lack of taste or genuine and proper despair. Yesenin was supposed to be a great lyric poet which judgement I shall never be able to test as I will never be able to read in the original. He was married 8 times so if he wasn't perhaps the greatest poet of all time, he must surely have been the most married. Since he died when he was only 30 years old perhaps all those marriages were behind the last line. Mr Serge says that it was the

---

[216] Friday was 8 October.
[217] Victor Serge (1890–1947), *Memoirs of a Revolutionary* (1963). Serge's real name was Victor Lvovich Kibalchich.
[218] The passage (reproduced accurately by Burton) is to be found on p. 195 of Serge's volume, and refers to Sergei Yesenin (1895–1925).

failure of the Glorious Revolution which drove him to suicide. Silly fool.[219] I imagine that by the time I finish with Trot and have come back here to finish with Tit I shall have had all this communist childishness up to my eyebrows. I am so far steeped in in Communistic lives and literature that all the capitalism in the rough rude West will be necessary to wash it out.

E is my only ism and a very nice purpose in life. Elizabethism. Do you have any firmly held belief or creed or politic Mr Burton? Yes, I believe in Elizabethism. Elizabeth the Great of course. Of course. End of interview. Next day's Headlines: BURTON CONFESSES TO BEING AN ELIZABETHIST.

E is in London and tomorrow, assuming I finish early enough and a plane can be found I shall be with her at the Savoy or the Dorchester. [. . .]

Saturday 10th[220] [. . .] Last day on the film and it's such a beautiful day that I think I will fly to London this afternoon, assuming that I finish in time and fly to Rome tomorrow morning. Talking of eccentricity, that is fairly good and since I am sick of reading about poverty and its accompanying miseries I shall behave like a mindless bloated plutocrat and scream from Sarajevo to Rome to London to Rome in 24 hours. Think of the money I'd save if I went by commercial jet to Rome only. How much would I save I wonder? About $400 I guess and what would I do with it? Give it to Marian. But I've already given her vast sums and she has a dead husband.[221] Add it to her Christmas Box. [. . .]

I talked to E last night. She sounded as disgruntled as a miner on a Monday morning and was obviously annoyed that I wasn't going to London which I was not last night, but have thought this morning that I really ought to see my daughter and want to see them both, I mean mother and daughter, and I will tell The Trot Company and M. Losey that I will do the make-up tests on Sunday evening. Good thinking Richard. Why can't a make-up test be done just as well in the evening as in the afternoon?

I tried to read a detective story last night in bed – one of my favourite men called Inspector Napoleon Bonaparte of the Australian Police. These books by a man called Upfield, an Englishman, are more than ordinarily interesting whodunits as there is a lot of cumulative bits and pieces about the Australian Aborigines. As far as I know he, Upfield, is the only popular writer who writes about them all the time. Therefore, for a lazy mind like mine he educates painlessly and entertainingly. But I think I have read so much about modern politics in the last three months that I find it difficult to switch to anything else. I felt awful last night and E didn't make me feel any better. Instead of being delighted about Liza being OK and being happy after having seen her she spent most of the time complaining about the hotel, about its distance to the

---

[219] Burton is referring to the direction taken by the Russian Revolution of 1917.
[220] Saturday was 9th October.
[221] Marian, Richard's cousin, whose husband Carl Mastroianni died in 1971.

hospital (45 minutes she said and since she is at Sunning and if it is the place I remember near Reading there must be some bad navigation on the chauffeur's part for it to be that long) that there was no telephone in her room but only in the bar and that the whole thing was unpleasant.[222] Also if people weren't so melodramatic E could have gone to see Liza at her leisure and certainly we would have both been spared half a day's spiritual agony because it turns out that, thank God the baby had not 'fractured her skull' but had taken a very heavy bump on the noggin and was correspondingly concussed. The words 'fractured skull' are so horrendous. One thinks of brain damage and smashed grey cells and all that while she has actually sustained an injury which, again thank God, is infinitely less dangerous than a broken arm or collar-bone etc. I know perfectly well and was therefore perfectly happy to know, that Liza was an island of content as long as her mother was there and since 'they' wanted me in Rome tomorrow afternoon and since last night I felt bone weary I thought there was no point in my going to London. But the weather is so lovely and I really want to see Elizabeth more than Liza I am ashamed to confess and I felt so much better this morning that I will flip over to London after all. It will be odd to start a film without E being there to give me moral support. I don't think it has happened in ten years. Ah! Yes it has. The immortal *Raid on Rommel* was started alone and also, double oddity, sober. [. . .]

[. . .] Ron is very nervous about the make-up and is beginning to make me so. He says, and I suppose, quite rightly, that the make-up is half the performance and that this is one film where I really should have been there a week or a few days before starting. It might take him, he says, 3 days to get the make-up exactly correct. [. . .] Also, he says morosely, that 'Joe doesn't like me you know, Rich'. He still believes, says Ron, 'that I poured that bottle of champagne over his head when we were all stoned in Cappo Cacia when it was Mcdonald all the time.'[223] 'Don't be silly Ron'. Ron may be right at that because I remember Joe coming to see me in some film or other, *Anne* perhaps, and saying 'Still keep your friends around you, I see.' Only Ron, who was making me up, was there at the time. It's true of course that Joe has no humour at all and is, apart from his work, hard going as a conversationalist. Time to go to work.

Later. London.

Flew today from Sarajevo directly to London – we were going to drop Ron at Rome but the pilot said that if we did we would almost certainly end up in Paris Amsterdam or Brussels or somewhere as there was a fog warning for London

---

[222] Burton may mean Sunningdale, near Ascot, in Berkshire, which is about 20 miles from Reading.
[223] Mcdonald may refer to the art director on *Boom!*, Richard Macdonald, who was production designer on *Secret Ceremony*, would be production designer on *The Assassination of Trotsky*, and later on *Exorcist II*.

for planes landing after dark. So despite Ron's anxiety to get to Rome because of somebody's – probably Joe's panic – I insisted he came to London with us and fly back with me in the morning. I can't understand this mad urgency for a make-up test. Ron is the best there is and has made old man make-ups on me before. I am very nervous about this film. John H[eyman]. suggests that Joe is drinking heavily. I wonder if Joe, in his middle sixties, has allowed the success of *Go-Between* to go to his old head.[224] 'Twould be funny. [. . .]

Sunday 10th, London Airport This morning, to my dismay, I awoke to find it was 10 to 8 and not my usual 6 or 6.30. Dismay because I had promised Gwen that I would be up in NW3 to see her and Ivor at 8.30. The shower in the Dorchester ran weak and cold (the hotel is really falling apart) and so I abandoned all thought of a shower and [. . .] tore off after a quick shave and a 'swill' and was up in 2, Squire's Mount a few mins after 8.30. Gwen looked much better than she did a couple of months ago and so, astonishingly did Ivor though for many weeks he has not been able to keep his food down and has an almost permanent high temperature. Any normal man would have been dead a long time but Ivor's stoical will to live is, and the doctors agree, phenomenal. His mind is still as lucid as ever. I started this page on the runways and now am half way to Rome [. . .]

Landed without incident at Ciampino, [. . .] I went immediately to the set which is about 10 minutes from the Studio and there was Rome as lovely mad as ever [. . .]. All seems well with the film and Joe was gentle and nervous and showed no signs of booze. Ron very seriously and very nervously did the make-up and though I think it looks as if I am a close relative of Ho Chi Minh everybody else was pleased as punch so assuming it pleases them as well on the screen as it did in the flesh that's one problem out of the way.[225] They will be able, miracles, to see the results tomorrow morning at 7 o'clock. I am called to rehearse at 9 without make-up. I am somewhat taken aback as it's so long since I've done a film in which I am required to rehearse. Got home about 6 and [. . .] I called E who sounded very chipper and was about to settle down and watch herself play *The Cat on the Hot Tin Roof* on TV in England.[226] I shall call her in ½ an hour or so to find out how she likes it and how she likes her pre-Burton self.

On the plane today Ron gave forth with yet another Jeremiad regarding the femme fatale Romy Schneider. This was, of course, after a couple of heavy libations which were by no means his first of the day I suspect. [. . .] Just talked to E who was watching *Laugh-In* and told her my love and devotion and she,

---

[224] Losey had directed *The Go-Between* (1970).
[225] Ho Chi Minh (1890–1969), Vietnamese revolutionary leader.
[226] *Cat on a Hot Tin Roof* (1958), directed by Richard Brooks (1912–92).

hers.[227] And now to read my favourite fairy-stories – the sports pages of the *Sunday Times*.

Monday 11th, Rome [. . .] Still don't know whether to play with an accent or not. What with the Frenchman and the German with accents and my wife – who is played by an actress who was somewhat distinguished in my early days – will play with an accent too. She is Valentina Cortese.[228] Much older than I, I would guess. Middle 50s or so betcha. So with all around me making mit the accent will I stick out like a sore thumb. I'll try both, that's what I shall do and see how it feels. That's three nights in a row without a proper sleep and it must be because E is not here. I go off like a log when she is. Extraordinary hold she has over me.

[. . .] Am about to have my second cuppa and will then read myself to work. I hate my work.

Saturday 16th Awoke at 5.30. Thought of getting up but decided to wait ½ an hour or so thereby falling asleep and not waking 'til 8.30. I was destined to meet a lady called Rosemary Bain – I mean Romany Bain – at 9 so called Bob Wilson on to put her off until 9.30. I showered, shaved and shampooed and had a cuppa before she arrived. She is not the most stimulating lady in the world but then her job is not exactly conducive to brilliance. She writes for *Woman's Own* and other such diabolically tedious mags though this interview was for *Cosmopolitan*, an American mag which is starting an English version. I answered the unanswerable questions like 'In what ways would you say you've changed since your first meeting and falling in love with Elizabeth 10 years ago in this very city?' with my usual non-committal circuitous tergiversation. She then interviewed E and she did more or less the same. Infinitely humdrum and heavy with humbug.[229] [. . .]

Monday 18th, Grand Hotel [. . .] Finished yet another volume of Powell's *Music of Time* and it's the first one that has made me laugh out loud. All that 'richly comic' stuff that I read in the extracts from notices is simply not there. I would say that he is quietly and perhaps cumulatively amusing. I still have difficulty in believing his coincidences.

Back to Trotsky this morning and that horrible scratchy beard with the gum offensively smelly and, even worse, the moustache. A real beard and moustache is bad enough – or in truth better than the false one during the day – but at least one can take the mock one off at the end of the day with

---

[227] *Rowan & Martin's Laugh-In* was an American television comedy show.
[228] Valentina Cortese (1923–) played the part of Natalia or Natasha Trotsky.
[229] This may be what appeared in *Harper's Bazaar* (April 1972), 126–9, as 'Ten Years Since Scandal Time'.

that equally horrible acetone, the smell of which would make a drinking me throw up.

A lovely day so I hope we'll be getting on with the film at a smart pace. I have to go back to Jugo after this and the sooner the better and the longer the holiday. Jugoslavia seems a long way off and already a long time ago. I'm looking forward to seeing it in the winter. Must wear long-johns or combs as the British call them. Since all these years with Elizabeth I am never quite certain whether a phrase, sometimes, is American or English. That's probably what's been happening to Wodehouse – about whom there is a great deal of fuss in the papers on his 90th birthday – for I find in his umpty-ninth 'Jeeves and Bertie' book that someone was 'as imperious as a traffic cop.'

Home now and it's evening. Have had a funny day. Called for 9.30 didn't work until 1.30 and not again until 5.30. Wrote letters to Kate and Val and started on Powell's *Military Philosophers*.[230] I don't yet have the last volume and I'm missing two of the others though I think I read one of them some time ago. [. . .]

Tuesday 19th, Rome Another scintillating day. [. . .] We shot, on my second day an establishing shot which covered a wide area and included my two co-stars Delon and Schneider. The sky was overcast. This means that all the following shots have to be in similar weather until I get inside the house. But the weather continues to sparkle. [. . .]

We were invited to have lunch with the King and Queen of Greece anytime we like this week or next Monday. I suppose they should be described as the ex-King and Queen.[231] I said that E and I would be delighted to meet them and have a noggin but that going to a lunch was awkward as I was covered with false beard and moustache. I wonder why they want to meet us. I am very suspicious of political royalty. Perhaps like the Shahrina of Persia they are simply star-struck but usually royalty are not. They've usually met so many. Talking of the Shahrina it appears that she reads everything about E and knows all the children's names and where they go to school and all that publicity in the journals.[232]

[. . .] My memory for words which has always been phenomenal had, in the last couple of years, become suspect. I found that I was taking longer than usual to learn lines but – probably as a result of abstinence – it has come back with all the tenacity of a steel trap. Very nice feeling. I have always said that if ever I got to the Noel Coward or Rex Harrison stage I would stop acting even if I wanted to.

---

[230] Powell, *The Military Philosophers* (1968).
[231] King Constantine II of Greece (1940—) and his wife Queen Anne-Marie (1946—), who had fled Greece in 1967. The Greek monarchy was abolished in 1973.
[232] Farah Pahlavi (1938—), Shahbanu (rather than Shahrina) of Iran.

Powell is a great user of archaisms. Yesterday I read 'the smell of eld'.[233] I rather like their use them myself.

The Soviet Premier, Kosygin, was physically attacked yesterday in Ottawa.[234] What, I wonder, would have been the effect on Anglo-Russian politics if he had been assassinated? A lot of big-sounding threats I expect gradually simmering down to cold tea.

Wednesday 20th, Grand Hotel I should not have spoken so soon about my memory being like a steel trap and all that mild boasting, as today I dried up in the middle of a long scene at least 15 times. Most unlike me. Actually the speech which threw me was an actual quote from Trotsky which Joe who has a predilection for such behaviour suddenly introduced into the scene. But that is no excuse really as I can normally learn a ten line speech in as many minutes. My real excuse is that it was a translation and the syntax was 'throwing'. The speech itself was easy apart from one line 'What aim could I possibly pursue in venturing on so monstrous so dangerous an enterprise.' Every so often I am – and all actors are – defeated by a speech. For years and God knows it <u>is</u> years – I must have learned it when I was about 15 – I have never been sure that I ever got my favourite speech from *Hamlet* absolutely correct. 'I have of late, but wherefore I know not, lost all my mirth foregone all custom of exercise etc.' God knows too how often I've said it and been paid to say it. There must have been with both the Old Vic and Gielgud NY production around 400 performances. Let's see if I can write it out correctly now and I'll check up when I go down to the yacht.

I have of late, but wherefore I know not, lost all my mirth, foregone all custom of exercise, and indeed it goes so heavily with my disposition that this goodly frame the earth look you, this brave o'er hanging firmament, this majestical roof fretted with golden fire, why it seems no other thing to me than a foul and pestilent congregation of vapours. What a piece of work is a man, in action how like an angel in apprehension how like a God in form in moving how express and admirable, the beauty of the world, the paragon of animals. And yet to me what is this quintessence of dust. How infinite in faculty in form in moving how express, should go after 'is a man.' Oh to hell with it. It should go after '... is a man. How infinite in faculty, in form and moving how express and admirable, in action how like an angel, in apprehension.' Now I really don't know.[235]

---

[233] It may have been 'the dust of eld', used in the first chapter of *The Military Philosophers*.

[234] Alexei Kosygin (1904–80) was attacked by Hungarian refugee Geza Matrai shouting 'Freedom for Hungary!'

[235] *Hamlet*, Act II, scene ii: 'I have of late – but wherefore I know not – lost all my mirth, forgone all custom of exercise; and indeed it goes so heavily with my disposition that this goodly frame, the earth, seems to me a sterile promontory, this most excellent canopy, the air, look you, this brave o'er hanging firmament, this majestical roof fretted with golden fire, why, it appears no other thing to me than a foul and pestilent congregation of vapours. What a piece of work is man! How noble in reason, how infinite in faculty, in form and moving how express and admirable, in action how like an angel, in apprehension how like a god! The beauty of the world, the paragon of animals – and yet, to me, what is this quintessence of dust?'

We are now having a dreadful time with Michael [. . .] Now he has assured Beth that he has got everybody out of the house in Hampstead and that he wishes to live with Beth and the baby alone. So, the innocent and her baby are flying back to the new Michael tomorrow. Elizabeth doesn't trust Michael an inch when he's under the influence of drugs which is now practically all the time. Just hoping and praying is all we can do. We both talked to Beth in Portland tonight and gave her what advice and blessings we could. I suggested that she go with the baby to London (she was going anyway) and that if Mike and his friends started his shenanigans again, they should go – she and the baby – hop on a plane to Rome. E is in a far worse emotional state than I as I, unlike E, am more optimistic about Michael keeping his word. [. . .]

And so to bed ere long. I feel very achy and I am expectorating great gobs.

Thursday 21st, Rome [. . .] I read a script called *The Savage is Loose* last night.[236] It is a very doable film but would need a very imaginative director with great patience with a boy actor and with many different animals including a panther, a python and a crane. A brilliant cameraman would also be top priority. E would have to lose weight and I would have to put on some muscle. The end is wrong but could be fixed. Will wait for E to read it and decide with her. It would certainly be a pleasant film to make and we could, according to Heyman, shoot it at home in P.V. [Puerta Vallarta] Having read the piece now I don't see why not. All you need is jungle a beach and an ocean all of which we have in abundance in P.V.

Have just started another piece – the long-promised play for TV of John Osborne's called *Separation*. Actually it's two pieces, one called 'His' and the other 'Hers'.[237] I gather it's about a marriage break-up, one play of an hour from her point of view and the other from his. We must do something for Harlech especially as it's made us some money, though that's incidental, and see if we can help keep the franchise or consortium or whatever they call it. Off to work. In case I hadn't mentioned it before I hate my work. Too strong a word – I dislike it.

Home from work at 6.00. Got through everything in takes one all day including a new scene with Valentine Cortese. Tomorrow I have yet another new scene to do with Cortese and two actors who play the Rosmers in the film.[238] The 'Rosmer' couple brought my (Trotsky's) grandson from Europe to see me in Mexico.[239]

There's been a man called Jeffrey Archer, MP plaguing the life out of me through Raymond for weeks.[240] I've always refused to talk to him and have told

---

[236] *The Savage is Loose* was made into a film in 1974, directed by George C. Slott (1927–99).
[237] This would become the film *Divorce His, Divorce Hers* (1973).
[238] Jean Desailly (1920–2008) played Alfred Rosmer and Simone Valère (1921–2010) played Marguerite Rosmer. Desailly and Valère were real life partners, later husband and wife.
[239] In fact it was Seva Trotsky, Trotsky's nephew, played by Marco Lucantoni.
[240] Jeffrey Archer (1940—), then MP for Louth.

Raymond to tell him to tell Raymond what he wants to talk to me about. This he has refused to do as it was very important stuff and had to do with Princess Margaret, HRH. Then would he write it as Mr Burton will not speak on the telephone? So the stuff comes. It is, if you please a Royal Command (according to Mr Archer) to appear in a TV play for Sir Lew Grade – a 90 minutes one – play under separate cover – and at the receipt of our agreement to perform this so far unread play, which incidentally we hear is dreadful, Sir Lew Grade would make over a cheque for £100,000 to the St John's Ambulance lot.[241] We would be paid nothing. Grade would have the right to sell it all over the world. I am absolutely staggered by Grade's effrontery. I await the play and John Heyman on Sunday. Her Majesty and His Royal Highness will find that they have commanded the wrong couple. I shall say that I'll do it for a KBE! Mr Archer hinted at it apparently to Raymond over the phone. He sounds a very ambitious little MP. We shall see.

Friday 22nd, Rome I am a very ignorant man. The front page of the Rome *Daily American* announces that the Nobel Prize for Literature for 1971 goes to a poet-politician called Pablo Neruda. He is 67 years old and the Chilean ambassador to Paris. A Communist and has the usual revolutionary's awful luck and life until of course the Communists under Allende attained power in Chile.[242] Having read a description of his poetry I have an idea that it wouldn't interest me very much – the content I mean. I can never really understand the poetry of another language, Welsh and English only. I suppose few men who are not genuinely bi or multi-lingual from birth can. I generally know the important writers of other cultures even if I've never read them but Signor Neruda is a new one. I was surprised to read that only 6 S. Americans have won Nobel Prizes. That includes that vast half continent from Mexico down and I seem to remember that the Americans and British between them have won over 200. I lump them together because frequently the British and Americans have shared Nobel Prizes like the two British and one Yank who created or discovered the design of a molecule or whatever it was about 10 years ago.[243] The Nobel Prize is a very funny one from the start. First of all Alfred Nobel, who started it all, was a Swede, I think, who invented gun-powder![244] It has given some hilarious awards. One of the funniest was to Winston Churchill. He won the 'Peace Prize'. Never has a politician, despite his outraged protestations, loved war as much as the old man. Peace Prize indeed![245]

---

[241] Lew Grade (1906–98), of Associated Television (ATV). St John Ambulance, a charity teaching first aid and offering ambulance services.
[242] Pablo Neruda (1904–73). Salvador Allende (1908–73), President of Chile.
[243] In 1962 the Nobel Prize for Physiology or Medicine was awarded to Francis Harry Compton Crick (1916–2004), James Dewey Watson (1928—) and Maurice Hugh Frederick Wilkins (1916–2004), 'for their discoveries concerning the molecular structure of nucleic acids'.
[244] Alfred Nobel (1833–96) invented dynamite.
[245] Winston Churchill actually won the Nobel Prize for Literature in 1953.

Sunday 23rd, Rome[246] We worked late last night and I didn't get home til after 7. E very impatient to see me as she'd had news that she valued from Brian Hutton who directed her in *XYZ*. He is normally a wry pessimist and not given, as most Americans in the film business are, to superlatives but E says that exhibitors are fighting for the privilege to show *XYZ* and that Harry Saltzman who had the taste to produce *Anger* and the lucky judgement to produce the James Bond films, has offered $6m for the film.[247] All this according to Hutton. I trust they won't accept the offer from Saltzman – I don't think that they can anyway without E's agreement – for if he offers 6 he must think it will gross more. Perhaps much more. At a sale of $6m I think that E could get about $1m guaranteed but at the end, since her percentage is of the gross absolute and for ever, Saltzman would still have to pay E the percentage. I must ask Aaron if E should persuade them to sell, pick up her guaranteed million and then sit back and – hopefully – watch the money roll in. We'll watch the outcome with great interest. There is even talk of Oscars and my lady must – if one can believe this pre-showing enthusiasm – should at least be nominated. That will bring her level with me said he with a sneering and somewhat bitter laugh. It is interesting to think that if one – only one – of the films we have made in the last 12 months or so hits the jackpot, the rewards will be fantastic. If *XYZ, Hammersmith, Tito* or *Trotsky* are blockbusters like *Cleo, Woolf* and *Eagles* the returns will have to be counted, for us, in many millions. Even if they are merely very big grossers – in the 10 to 20 million bracket – like *Becket, Sandpiper, Shrew, VIPs* it will still be considerable – far more than the old days of a million in front and 10% against the gross. I've worked out that if we'd no money in front and the same percentage deals as we've been having in the last 12 months, we would have made more money than we did on the old deals even with non-huge-grossing pics like *Ceremony, Spy* and *Iguana* all of which did 8–10 mils. It's more exciting this way all around. Against this argument is of course that for *Staircase* and *Only Game* we would only have received, as they were both massive flops, our expenses and, with luck a couple of 100 thousand.

The halcyon days for almost all actors except for the very very big stars or somebody who's had a recent big smash hit are over. I am being paid 5 thousand more in <u>expenses</u> for this film *Trotsky* than Rex Harrison is being paid in <u>salary</u> with <u>no</u> expenses and <u>no</u> percentage. This latter is an enormous drop from Rex's high time which was as recent as *Staircase* for which he was paid ¾ of a million and 10 against the gross. Rex is by no means alone. Anybody who is not in the 'superstar' category is getting the same kind of money or even less than the norm in the middle fifties – 150 to 250 thousand and no percentage.

---

[246] Sunday was 24 October.
[247] Harry Saltzman (1915–94), producer of *Look back in Anger*, and then all the James Bond films up to *The Man with the Golden Gun* (1974).

The most important thing of all from our point of view is of course that we try to do, at least, rewarding films in terms of the films themselves and not their financial returns, We are both rich enough for ever even despite an economic world-catastrophe. I would much prefer, for instance, that E and I won Oscars than that a film should gross like *Eagles* and have no importance at all. The fact is though that Oscars also, almost inevitably, go hand in hand with good box-office. Of all the films we've done since we were free of contracts, only two can I remember that we knew before starting were not serious. *Sandpiper* for both of us and *Raid on Rommel* for me. All the rest have been honest attempts at good movies including the flops au cinema like *Boom!*, *Staircase, Comedians* and *Only Game. Sandpiper* we did because we were afraid that we were going to be out of work and we wanted to work together, while *Raid on Rommel* was a joke. A joke that paid though. So did the other joke *Sandpiper*.

So enough of films. This was prompted by my excitement about *XYZ* [that it] will be a 'big one' for E. By talk of distinction and by talk of Oscars. I know she is brilliant in the film and I know the film is good but I thought almost as highly of *Boom!* and that went BOOM. [. . .]

Reading the *Times* this morning I came across a, to me, strange use of the word utter. In effect 'to utter' is to pass counterfeit coins. He uttered a lie now takes on more meaning.

[. . .] Yesterday's work was very strange as again – I thought I'd left all that kind of thing in Jugoslavia – for the second time this week I played a scene with two people who couldn't speak a word of English and who were found to be incapable of learning, even like parrots, the few lines they had to say. It was an all day agony of frayed nerves for everybody, including Joe, though we all kept our tempers and were very patient. But why did Joe cast them in the first place. Usually he is so keen on even the extras being accurate. Very odd indeed. I don't know whether Joe is ill or regards this piece as a failure before it starts or has simply run out of gas, but he is passing performances in this film which an amateur director of the annual church pageant would turn down with a shudder. With judicious cutting I don't suppose it will matter but it would be so much more professional not to have to depend on that. It is bad enough with Valentina Cortese who is a good enough actress but acts in clichés and because of her discomfort with the language makes the quoted banalities she is forced to utter even more banal. A line like the following when the Rosmers lament the fall of France becomes yawning chasm of boresville as a result of her infinitely slow and yet uncertain reading. 'Neither Weep Nor Laugh But Understand.'[248] I am beginning to wonder if the stuff they shot in Mexico with Delon and Schneider is equally bad. And that Joe has sort of given up. Because

---

[248] Baruch Spinoza (1632–77), *Tractatus Politicus* (1677), 'I have striven not to laugh at human actions, not to weep at them, nor to hate them, but to understand them.'

of its very nature the piece is rife with communist catch-phrases and the actors' job is to make them sound fresh and desperately intense. You can't do this unless your command of English is complete. I hope to God I'm being unduly pessimistic.

There was one very funny incident. Joe came in to me while I was being made up and said that the English of the two French actors was so bad that we might have to do it all in French or partly in French. A soon as he'd gone I translated my lines very quickly into French and with Gaston's help got the idioms and grammar right. When, about an hour later, Joe called me to shoot after rehearsing I told him that I knew it in French now. OK. So I started off in that language, going at a mile a minute, which is the way apparently Trotsky talked and was astounded to find that the French people were as bad in French as in English. Finally we stuck to English completely which they failed to get right. It is not even good enough to dub. They will have to [be] off-camera for almost every line they speak and on presumably when I speak. Shit and unnecessary shit and Joe Losey's mother. Anyway, it's a gorgeous day and we are off to lunch on the Via Appia Antica at L'escargot where they have a very good starter dish called Bouchee Caruso which is not too good for diets but undeniably this is a day off and I can watch waists tomorrow. Anyway I am back down to 165 and a bit. I might have a couple of glasses of Mouton or Lafitte or something.

Monday 25th, Rome I talked to Princess Margaret last night at about 7.25 – she had said 7.15 but not too bad for royalty, and amazingly for the Italian Telephone Service which gave us a very good line. She asked me whether [the] Lew Grade thing was acceptable and I told her that in principle the idea was fine though we thought the plays were not very good and we had two far better ones by John Osborne (I hope we have) and that we would do them in March next year and that the £100,000 would come anyway only simply from a different source. What did I mean? she asked. Well, I said, we had already contracted to do the two Osborne plays for Harlech TV and therefore Harlech had a prior call on our services and the plays were being, had already been financed by USA TV and that the 100,000 would come from us and not Lew Grade. Do you mean from Harlech, she asked? No, I said, from Elizabeth Taylor and Richard Burton. Good Heavens, M said, how very generous of you. I am absolutely staggered. Not at all, I said feebly. Pleasure I assure you. Delighted I'm sure and other fatuities. Then we went on to talk banalities about Tito and we must simply spend some time together when we were all back in England swap family albums and stories about Tito and Jugoslavia. She told me she had lost her voice and I thought that it was rather a good idea as she sounded so gentle and long-suffering. That's how I feel, she said. She sent her love to Elizabeth and I sent E's and mine back and to Tony as well I said. I shall give it to him when he comes back from America she said. Well goodbye I still can't get over your extraordinary generosity. Not at all. Goodbye. It was nice talking to you. Nice talking to you too. Goodbye then. Goodbye your Highness.[249]

I read a review in the *Paris Tribune* of a marvellous new-old book. Someone has published the entire *Oxford Dictionary* – all 17 volumes or whatever it is – in two microscopic volumes with a pull-out magnifier so that one can read the minute print.[250] E is buying me three sets for my birthday. One for Mexico, one for the yacht and one for Gstaad. I am genuinely excited. What a superb idea. The review goes on to say that the page titles can be seen with the naked eye and it's only the definitions that need magnification. What an even better idea if someone could do the *Britannica* as well. One would need nothing else on a desert island. I am waiting to see the *OED* with all the anticipatory pleasure of a small boy waiting for that engine-and-rails or this pair of ball-bearing roller-skates.

Suddenly bethought me that a few days ago the papers all carried front-page announcements that the royals were to get increases in salary and that Maggie's was to go up to £100,000. So we nonchalantly give away without so much as a wrinkled brow the equivalent of her annual income. I wonder if that crossed her mind and whether there might be a little pique that two commoners could be that rich.

Another superb day and Joe (Lucky) Losey should be happy. After my jeremiad the other day I had a letter from him Sat morn in which he said how marvellous it all looked – even the scene he wasn't sure about was splendid and he was herewith enclosing extra speeches about the theory of Art and the State which he had promised to find for me. I haven't looked at them yet but will.

Tuesday 26th, Rome A good day yesterday in which I did a long long speech while circumnavigating the lawn outside the house. Joe had made a sort of circular railway out of the tracks and the camera did a full 360 degrees. What one might call a typical Losey shot. To my delight Joe said that it was my only shot of the day, and it was. The shot demanded a nice series of movements on my and the camera's part but we got it correctly after a couple of false starts. Choreography in films. This took place in the morning and E was coming to lunch with Heyman and the new prospect as agent – a young man called Michael Linnit – nephew of Linnit (& Dunfee) who is the impresario.[251] He seems nice enough and we've decided to try him for 6 months or so. Bob called E for me and told her to wait for me at the Grand as I was finishing and I would take her out to the Flavia or whatever place she fancied. We went to

[249] Burton was agreeing to perform in a production for Harlech Television of what would become *Divorce His, Divorce Hers*.
[250] The *Compact OED* was published in 1971, reducing the original 13 volumes to two.
[251] Michael Linnit, theatrical agent. Linnit & Dunfee was a theatre management company.

the Rallye restaurant which is inside the hotel and probably has one of the best cuisines in Rome. I'd forgotten how good it was. Again I had two glasses of wine. It was fine but I fear the thin edge of the wedge. No more except for special occasions. Apart from anything else, it seems such a waste of good wine – and I only have the best – to have merely two glasses. The young potential agent pretended to a savoir faire at first which was somewhat and vaguely irritating but after a time the veneer disappeared and he became more himself. This was after E had sat beside him in the restaurant and applied her totally un-self-conscious charm. After that he didn't try to compete with the ambient worldliness but settled for it. I don't think he's very gifted – not in the same league as Heyman for instance – and will doubtless remain an agent all his life, probably not even having his own agency.

After finishing my film work for yesterday I did 15 minutes for the BBC *Tonight* programme or maybe it was *24 hours*. I talked at a mile a minute the usual guff about Tit and Trot. Then I shouted and bawled into a mike lots of speeches of Trotsky's for the background 'music' of some of the scenes. Joe still seems remarkably distrait. [...]

I started reading *Steppenwolf* which is very hard going.[252] I suppose it is more interesting in the original but in translation it seems so clichéd and juvenile and pseudo. He talks, for instance, of the importance of humour and how its possession is a potent weapon in the battle against the bourgeoisie and the smugly satisfied middle-class all the while demonstrating that he has none. Not a glimmer. Not a giggle. [...]

Wednesday 27th, Rome [...] Message from E came to say that Michael Beth and baby Leyla were coming to Rome [...]. Michael's philosophy is a complete balls-up at the moment. He doesn't want our money he says, but he lives in our house rent free. Again he wants to live the 'free life' without our money but with presumably Robin's.[253] So he is prepared to use us as suckers – his and his friends' use of the word – in taking the house. Then finding us not adequate he then uses his friend Robin as a 'sucker'. He is so exactly like his father that one cannot really blame him. It's bred in the bone. Whose money does he think he is using to fly to Rome? Whose money flew his wife to London? What a funny feller! Let's hope that there is enough of E's pride in him to adopt a more practical approach to life when he is older. Nobody expects him any more to <u>do</u> anything. We don't expect anything of him at all and will keep him in fags and pot forever if necessary as long as he doesn't hurt himself or others, <u>particularly the baby</u>. Now Chris is going to spend a week with him in London. Chris should hold his own I think and hope – a much more intelligent and stronger character altogether, but one can never tell.

---

[252] Hermann Hesse (1877–1962), *Steppenwolf* (1927; English translation 1929).
[253] Robin: Friend of Michael Wilding.

Yesterday, we worked well. [. . .] I worked with Romy Schneider for the first time. She is very arch. She displayed none of the 'temperament' which apparently manifests itself in screaming at the hairdresser, make-up man etc. and was, on the contrary the soul of modesty. [. . .]

Wednesday 27th, Rome Michael Beth and baby Leyla duly arrived having had a goodish journey I understand though an hour late. The baby doesn't like planes very much unlike Kate I remember at the same age who adored them – especially a rough ride. Gurgles galore while the adults tightened their sphincters. I did two scenes today one with Schneider and one with Delon. Delon is surprisingly small. From a distance he looks six feet but close to he is only about 5' 8". I finished with a close-up around 4.30 and was home before M and B and Leyla had arrived from the airport. They both, as usual with modern hippy clothes look unkempt and dirty but that's par for the course. The baby is a beauty and very well behaved and a mess of toothless grins and waving tight fists. She is very brown, and not from the sun. Some dark blood from one side of the family or other. [. . .]

Thursday 28th, Rome[254] What an enchanting evening yesterday's was. It was as if we'd turned the calendar back five years and Michael was himself again. He was loving with the baby, fun to talk to and to listen to. Elizabeth was as happy as only a grandmother can be. Beth was in good form. Even I was pleasant and though I longed to I daren't touch the baby as my cold [. . .] might have been given to her. She is the kind of baby that everyone should have. It kicks little legs and makes minute fists and blows spit-bubbles and smiles a lot but hardly ever cries. Everybody hates a crying baby – in fact distraught mothers, generally from the working classes have been known to kill them – and everybody loves a charmer as Leyla unquestionably is.

Elizabeth stopped her drinking dead in its tracks – or practically, as she did have one beer but that was not out of crying despair for alcohol but because it fitted with her food. You can't, after all, have orange juice or Pepsi Cola with pizza. I am marking the diary headings in red for every day she refrains from the demon drink. I am delighted. I've always wanted her to stop drinking occasionally as it must be good for the health and the mental well-being. The latter because it's good to know that one can stop, that one hasn't become an alcoholic, that one does not live by for and through booze. Usually, I take several days of cutting down before I stop altogether but E seems to be able to do it in one.

In addition to all yesterday's pleasantness came the news from New York and California that the showing of *XYZ* was received smashingly and all the distributors fought for it.

---

[254] The diary entries from this day until 10 November are either typed in red or underlined in red.

Another brilliant day and my call is for rehearsal at 9.30 and a continuation of the scene we did yesterday and then presumably I go into the first of my two scenes with Delon in the first of which he comes to kill me but doesn't, and the second when he does. Joe is definitely not himself. He doesn't seem to know the script as well as he usually does. Time and time again I, or the continuity girl, have to remind him of things that are very obvious. For instance: in one of the scenes I am pacing up and down and around the garden dictating. Every so often I pause as I hear myself talking to the now dead Sheldon Harte, killed in my defence.[255] I am remembering my last conversation with him. Joe asked me why I was pausing. I told him why. Oh really let me look at the script. Yes you're quite right. Yes. Very Odd.

Thursday 28th, Rome Worked all day until the light went. It's now 8.10am and delight of delights our Liza is arriving tonight at 10 o'clock and should be here about 11ish. Shall wait up. E has had three beers so far today but since I don't really consider beer a 'drink' unless many pints are taken I am allowing her a 'red' titled day. Mike and Beth and the luminous Leyla are still here and everything seems to go swimmingly. Oddly enough E had had only two beers when she saw that I had written three and decided to make the presumption a fact. Right now I mean.

Friday 29th, Rome E had a long heart-to-heart talk with Michael yesterday. Perhaps that's too intimate a word when one considers that Mike is in such a potentially explosive state that Elizabeth has to play him like a fish and every conversation has to be extremely circuitous and thin-ice-skating. [. . .]

Saturday 30th, Rome Very short entries. Largely because I'm not getting up early enough in the morning. [. . .] I worked with Delon all day yesterday. He is a much better actor than I believed. Quite sensitive and all that. Pleasurable surprise. Liza is here a little overweight with puppy-fat and a trifle spotty but all part of puberty or is it adolescence? Giggles a lot at bluish jokes which for some reason eggs me on to make endless juvenile and harmless and very bad sex jokes. Yesterday, I found a *Time* mag for April 1940 which was fascinating to read. Winston Churchill was described as 'Sandy Winston Churchill'.[256] One never thinks of Churchill with any particular hair or that it would be described as 'sandy'. One realizes what a silly magazine *Time* is. Their attitudes, even then, were of the most superficial. They had no more idea of the coming holocaust than I did. Just had a long talk with Liza about masturbation – prompted by a Dear Abby column she is just reading.[257] I told her that it was

---

[255] Sheldon Harte, the character played by Carlos Miranda.
[256] *Time*, 8 April 1940.
[257] 'Dear Abby' was a syndicated advice column written at the time by Pauline Phillips (1918—) using the pen name Abigail Van Buren.

a perfectly normal part of growing up – especially I said in boys. Why especially in boys? Because I said I knew about boys, having been one believe it or not but never having been a girl I wasn't too sure. I told her some of the frightful and stupid things I was told and heard as a kid. That you'd go blind and bald before you're 21 etc. All rubbish. Also told her that excessive masturbation might lead to an onanism which might spoil one for more normal sex though I wasn't too sure about that either.

NOVEMBER
.

Monday 1st, Anzio [. . .] I wonder if this film I'm doing is any good? I am not possessed by its success as E is with *XYZ* but would like it nevertheless. Don't really care though. Dangerous attitude to have. Where's your ambition man? Went and lost it a long time ago, sir. Tut-tut.

We moped around all day reading and eating and talking. We took a nap in the afternoon. I asked Liza whether, since she was so enamoured of horses, she would or had consider or considered spending the rest of her life with them. Would she like to breed them for instance? Or train them? I said that we could probably see her to a farm and stake her to a few livestock. I would rather, I said, like a farm in the family. Nice to visit. Smell of horses and brass and leather and a book-lined room for Dad and a large quiet bedroom for Liz and me with a good shower for Dad, very important a good shower, and walks along the woodland ride wearing white for Eastertide, and the morning men stumble out with their spades and all the woken farm at its white trades, and tea and crumpets and cucumber sandwiches in the summer, and a local quiet pub with cool beer frothed and quaffable and a nice walk before dinner and doubtless dogs in the yard, and a couple of superior cats, and why not have a farmhouse of mellowed brick with a chiming clock over the stables, and a rich smell of dung, and could we, do you think, get a couple of giant slow-moving dray horses and harness them up on occasions to some sort of shafted car and go for rides drawn by Dobbin and Robbin, with a market town nearby associated with minor history, with a wide main street and a graveyard beside the church where I could sit and read while waiting for E to finish shopping or examine the headstones and ponder on the monotony of death, and it would be nice to have a bustling W.H. Smith's with a serious nervous young man, thin with an Adam's Apple, weak-chinned and a-bristle with insignificance, a bad second at Oxford writing articles for the country newspaper. And a lot of local gossip and a scandal or two to titillate and who would have thought that the vicar's wife would have run away with a garage-hand 10 years her junior. He wasn't giving it to her, the vicar, couldn't get it up. Don't be disgusting from E and Oh Dad from Liza. There ought to be a train to London to see a play and the last train home after supper at the Savoy Grill or maybe we'll take the Harlequin Suite at the Dorchester and stay for a week while E raids Harrods and Selfridges and Cartiers with Liza and I rape Foyles and Cecil Gees looking for a second hand copy of the sermons of John Elias o Fon, and back to the farm and 7 o'clock breakfasts with the accentless tones of the BBC news at 7 and old films on the telly and Frankie Howerd getting older and dirtier with his odd air of soiled innocence, and Liza might get a child or two for me to shout at and spoil.[258]

Liza, in fact, has just arrived from the bowels of the ship and I've read her out the bit about the farm. I hope I've put the right idea into her head. [. . .]

Tuesday 2nd, Rome Worked a full day yesterday [. . .]. Bettina and her boy friend and Roddy Mann from the *Sunday Express* came to lunch with, as usual, E not turning up 'til 2pm. Fortunately I was able to squeeze in enough time between shots to go with them. [. . .] Today I do a scene with Val Cortese and then the mucky assassination starts with Delon. False blood all over the place.

We had one of those evenings yesterday. Liza was going back to school. She was arriving at London airport at 11 o'clock. Liz (Williams) was going to be there to meet her. Wouldn't it be better, E said, since Liza was going on a later plane than expected by Liz to have Charles Simpson pick her up in the chauffeured Rolls as Lil was a very busy woman and London airport was a monstrous thief of time making Dickens' procrastination a mere petty thief in comparison.[259] No, it's alright, said Liza flippantly, Lil will wait for me. She has to go up to London anyhow. But, we said, the airport is not in London, it is a long way from London. The upshot was that she became so adamant that she wanted Lil to pick her up that E became incensed and pinched Liza's arm. Liza dissolved in tears and left the room to sulk. She continued to sulk for 3 hours. Tear-stained face. Monosyllabic answers. Air of Tragedy. The only thing in this world I find totally unforgivable is the silent sulks. The sulker only looks a fool, and a stupid one, gets – from me at least – no sympathy at all after the 1st five minutes, and generally speaking is a crashing bore. E and I made a long-ago pact that regardless how flaming the quarrel, how bitter the recriminations that neither of us would ever mope and sulk. I remember Joy Parker telling me in the days of our friendship that she once had a quarrel with her husband Paul (Scofield) and that he sulked for a whole year. A whole year in which he never said anything outside the absolute necessities. Good morning. Good night. Shan't be home for supper. I would have shot him dead. Once I had a quarrel with E so vicious that I went for a long walk to cool my anger. I didn't sulk though. When I went back, we made it up immediately. That was in Aston Clinton, I think, at the Bell Inn. [. . .]

---

[258] Cecil Gee, a London menswear store. John Elias o Fon (1774–1841), a famous Welsh Nonconformist preacher. Frankie Howerd (1917–92), actor and comedian.
[259] Mr Micawber, in chapter 12 of Dickens's *David Copperfield*, says, 'My advice is, never do to-morrow what you can do to-day. Procrastination is the thief of time.'

Wednesday 3rd [. . .] Yesterday, had, as per usual its little crisis: Liza boarded a plane at Fumicino after a prolonged delay while officials went through every piece of baggage meticulously in the search for an IRA bomb.[260] Nothing found and off they went to England but not London airport. More IRA threats to blow up London airport had forced its closure so planes were being diverted to Stansted instead.[261] Widespread fury and I fancy the IRA are rapidly losing their romantic aura of Freedom Fighters for the ould sod.[262] Nobody likes a coward and the popular myth of fighting a merciless tyrant – the poor ineffectual English, if you please – is somewhat tarnished by acts of distant time-bombing. The Post Office tower was blown about a bit a couple of days ago, and shops and post offices in Ulster are forever going up in atoms.[263] I often wonder what I'd do if my Welsh extremists started the same thing. I wouldn't object very much to blowing up installations though I think it pretty childish but if they hurt anybody except themselves I would be red fury. I don't expect much from the Irish – a lot that I know so well that I despise them, everything about them, their posturing, the silly soft accents, their literature, especially Joyce, Synge but not including Yeats who writes like a great anglo – original spare strange – yes Hopkins – and I hate their genius for self-advertisement, their mock-belligerence, their obvious charm.[264] For the opposite of all these reasons I love the Scots and the South Welsh and even prefer the English b'god, especially the taciturn midlands and north country.

[. . .] With every excuse yesterday, E only had a beer and a glass of wine and so after a week of 'wagon' she has had a total of one glass of wine, one delicious Martini on Sunday as a reward from her proud spouse and about 10 bottles of beer. Somewhat of a drop from ½ or more of a bottle of hard liquor a day. As she says, the habit of drinking had become simply that – an odious habit in which the excitement of a good old booze-up was dissipated by the habit. We both agreed that the ice-cold vodka Martini on Sunday before lunch was all the better for being looked forward to and so on. E has just corrected me and reminded me that she had a vodka and orange sometime yesterday. So it's two vodkas in a week. Big deal.

[. . .] Tonight when I came home about 6 E was waiting for me and aglow with contentment. She had been out shopping to Gucci's and had a good time and there we were as happy as you like and looking forward to a nothing lovely evening, me with a crossword and E with a book and discussing whether we should go to Gstaad, Vallarta or – a sudden idea of mine – Quogue for Xmas. We also agreed to go the Rothschilds' (Ferrières) for a party on November 2nd

---

[260] Fiumicino airport, Rome.
[261] Stansted airport, Essex.
[262] The 'ould sod': Ireland.
[263] The Post Office Tower in central London was bombed by the IRA on 31 October 1971.
[264] James Joyce. Gerard Manley Hopkins, 'Pied Beauty', includes the line 'All things counter, original, spare, strange'.

which Guy and Marie-Hélène were giving, one of their truly posh ones which can be very amusing. Last time I sat with Madame Pompidou at dinner and drank with President Pompidou afterwards in the days of course when he was merely an ex-Prime Minister and in mild disfavour with De Gaulle. That night too I saw Brigitte Bardot for the first time since she was a young girl and married to or living with Vadim and not even remotely as famous as she is now.[265] I told Ron afterwards that I found it hard to believe that it was the same girl, so much so that I was almost tempted to think I had mis-remembered her name and that it was some other starlet of the time. Ah, Ron said, I expect you knew her when she still had projecting teeth. And that, of course, was probably the answer.

Thursday 4th, Grand Hotel [. . .] I read *Les Fleurs du Mal* of Baudelaire . . . Tout là-haut, tout là-haut, loin de la route sûre . . . Sous mes pieds, sur ma tête et partout, le silence, le silence qui fait qu'on voudrait se sauver, Le silence éternel . . . I slept fitfully and awoke every hour but I must have slept happily as E reports that I laughed a lot in my dreams.[266] I awoke to the alarm clock – a new and very expensive one which Frank Sinatra gave us for last Xmas. It makes a strange ullulating noise which is not very pleasant and is yet not harsh. I was very very sleepy and practically slept under the shower. I am dressed in outrageously expensive new trousers from some posh shop here in Rome. That's money that I do not like to spend – my idea of clothes is Ohrbachs or Vallarta where you can clothe yourself from top to toe, white thin shirt, white thin trousers and white sandals for an extravagant $8.[267] I wonder why Sinatra gave us so unexpectedly that expensive clock? What motive prompted the gift? What was going on in the poor man's Mafia mind? Had he realized perhaps at last that the painting we gave him – I've forgotten what it was – cost a great deal of money and told himself that he hadn't thanked us with sufficient grace? Whatever it was, the reason is likely to be vulgar.

Thursday 3rd, Grand[268] I wonder how long Frank will stay 'retired'.[269] What is he planning? I doubt that he can write and he doesn't have the sort of mind that makes you think so. Some people, Bob Mitchum and Marlon and Monty Clift and sometimes O'Toole in my profession, give me the feeling – in Monty's case past tense – that were they to set their minds to it and if they had discipline – that they are natural writers but the old Sinatra, the old sinner will I bet have

[265] Brigitte Bardot (1934–), actor and model. Roger Vadim (1928–2000), actor, director, husband of Bardot (1952–7), later of Jane Fonda (1965–73).
[266] Charles Baudelaire (1821–67), *Les Fleurs du Mal* (1857). These lines do not appear to be a direct quotation from *Les Fleurs du Mal*, although they may owe something to Baudelaire's 'Le Gouffre'.
[267] Ohrbach's: an American department store.
[268] Thursday was 4 November, as Burton had previously entered.
[269] Frank Sinatra had announced his retirement on 12 June 1971. He returned in 1973.

to be ghosted though if I know Francis as I think I do the ghost will be the most ephemeral of all his craft. Nobody will claim well actually I wrote it, it wasn't Frank at all. It is odd that Frank who interprets lyrics from common songs better than any of his rivals and is as I call him a fine interpreter of street corners poetry – one for my baby and one more for the road and other such good songs he can trick in such a way that they seem brilliant minor poetry but when faced with something massive – like for instance *Hamlet* – he is completely bewildered. I mention *Hamlet* because once when he was in the doldrums, becalmed in the ocean of Hollywood and unable to get work (somewhere in the early 50s) he asked me to read *Hamlet* with him as he was going to make a comeback through the classics yet and he'd show the mother-fuckers.

Friday 5th E said last night that I am very snobby about Sinatra and that he's really nice and means well. [. . .]

I had a most uncomfortable day yesterday. I did the assassination scene which involves a lot of blood. Ron clipped and concealed in my hair a thin rubber tube which went down my back to the floor. Delon strikes the blow and as I stand up and start screaming Ron, lying on the floor pumps the artificial blood through the tube. After one false start when Joe foolishly called cut after the false red stuff started to come through which meant an infuriating hour of cleaning up and re-doing the make-up, we did the whole bloody business in one. During it of course – because I am so lazily unfit – I pulled a muscle in my back or strained something with the result that this morning I am barely able to move. In addition the blood got into my eyes and I also swallowed some so that for a few hours afterwards my eyes were inflamed and my voice was practically lost and my throat was very sore. My eyes and throat are still sore this morning but not too badly. There will be more blood this morning though I fervently hope I don't have to do what we did yesterday all over again.

A group of Italians want me to play Mussolini!

I have been reading, in the last few weeks a lot of novels and enjoying them which is unusual for me – I mean the reading of novels not so much their enjoyment. The set which is a copy of Trotsky's house contains hundreds of books bought, I'm sure, in lots. I started reading them, some of them, at work between shots. I read for the first time *Adventures of The Scarlet Pimpernel* which I discovered is not the same as the famous book by Baroness Orczy which is simply *The Scarlet Pimpernel.*[270] Very entertaining, supremely snobbish rubbish. *Romance,* by Conrad and Ford Maddox Hueffer (later Ford Madox Ford), *Many Latitudes* by a vaguely familiar name F. Tennyson Jesse, a book of novelettes.[271] *Adam Bede* of Geo Eliot, *Malice Aforethought* by Francis

---

[270] Baroness Orczy (1865–1947), *The Scarlet Pimpernel* (1929). *Adventures of the Scarlet Pimpernel* was published in 1794.

[271] Joseph Conrad (1857–1924) and Ford Hermann Hueffer (later Ford Madox Ford) (1873–1939), *Romance* (1903). F. Tennyson Jesse (1888–1958), *Many Latitudes* (1928).

Iles and at home I've read a novel by Oxford colleague – we once played Shakespeare together – John Wain.[272] Another by the lady who wrote *The Severed Head* – a name I can never remember, Anglo-Irish, fiercesome looking – and a novel so old-fashioned, so *Woman's Own* and *Peg's Paper* that I found it hard to believe that anybody would seriously publish it, called *Virginia Perfect*.[273] Honest to God. My reading of novels is a change for me. Apart from reading my few modern favourites – Waugh, Greene, Powell, Huxley and Snow – my novel-reading is generally confined to re-reading books that I knew years ago. But now suddenly I want to read again books that I found unsympathetic to me but considered masterpieces by everybody else. I want to read, and will, Dostoevsky, Tolstoy, Proust, and I want to read, and will, Balzac, Dumas, Stendhal in the original.[274] Perhaps I will find the first three more to my liking than hitherto while the others I enjoyed in English and I thrill to the thought of reading them in the writer's own tongue. So much to do and not so little a time. I hope.

Just remembered the lady-writer's name. It is Iris Murdoch.

My chief joy at the moment is in reading Baudelaire. It is a magnificent thing to discover poetry in middle age. Most men take their quota of verse before the age of 25 and live on it for the rest of their lives – those, that is, who have a feeling for it at all. I mean, of course, to discover new poetry, new at least to them and not simply regurgitate the old and well-known. Baudelaire I had, of course, read in English, in which language he is unrecognizable. Why was I not properly educated in French in my early years though perhaps I should prefer it this way round. It is pretty astounding to find a whole new world of literature, discovering it, I may say, with all the enthusiasm of an undergraduate, at the ripe old age of 46 next week. Think of all those unworked seams of gold. Think of the incomparable treasure-trove to be still discovered in the immense store-house of French Literature. I can't wait for my next day off to augment my library. [...]

The blood didn't get into my eyes today so much though they are smarting again, and managed to keep it out of my mouth too so am in far better order than yesterday. [...] The screaming scene and the wrestle with Delon seems to be very effective so, thank the Lord, we don't have to do it again. [...]

Saturday 6th [...] Had lunch in a place called Passetto's. We apparently chose badly. My lamb – grilled and tasteless and dry. E's calf's liver and bacon – uninspired. I had cozze marinera to begin which was delicious. We shared a

---

[272] George Eliot (1819–80), *Adam Bede* (1859). Francis Iles (1893–1971), *Malice Aforethought* (1931). John Wain (1925–94) had by this time published five novels.
[273] Iris Murdoch (1919–99), *A Severed Head* (1961). Peggy Webling (1871–1949), *The Story of Virginia Perfect* (1909).
[274] Fyodor Dostoevsky (1821–81). Marcel Proust (1871–1922). Honoré de Balzac (1799–1850). Alexandre Dumas (1802–70) Gustave Stendhal (1783–1842).

bottle of Lafite 63. That was good. We had a couple of glasses each. It would seem that I have got the problem of drink licked, as they say. Yesterday is the fourth time in a month that I've had a glass or two of wine at lunch, and on one occasion a martini, without feeling it necessary to go on and drink down the day as in the old days.

The book about me by Cottrell and Cashin entitled simply *Richard Burton* arrived yesterday.[275] Again I tried to read it but could do no more than flick through the snaps and make fun of Claire Bloom. With the book came a letter from their agent suggesting that I might like to review it for a 'quality' weekly. I shall write back and say that from the bits I've looked at I feel certain that my review would be unfavourable and since I like the two writers and want them to have a success, it would be better if I kept silent. From the pictures in the book I found that the tiny boy in the middle of the back row in the under-14s Sec School Rugby Team is Freddy Williams who was the Speedway Motorbike Champion of the world some years ago. I'd forgotten that he was at the Sec. I thought we were at the Elementary School together – The Eastern. The only effect the book has had on me is to make me mildly determined to write my own story one of these days – in several volumes. I often think, when I'm reminded of my schooldays of a boy in school who seemed to us all at the time to be a god-given actor. His name was Morgan Griffiths I think. He was tall I believe and had a beautiful mellifluous voice, a real 'actor's voice' as we thought, tho there is no such thing of course. Actors' voices are as wide in variety as other people's and are equally badly produced from the lungs. Other than his acting, the boy was totally unmemorable, as dull as dust and as square as a table-top. But he played Magnus in *The Apple Cart* and Richard II with remarkable authority. At least, so it seemed to us. He had the look of someone who would go bald young. I wonder if he did. I believe he became a bank clerk. I believe also that he wrote to me about 10 years or so ago, no more than that, say 15, asking me to help him become an actor. I believe I replied as I've replied to all such letters that I would not encourage him to take the plunge and give up his security and pensions etc. but that once he had made the plunge I would help him in every way I could. The plunge was obviously never made as I would have heard from him again. But what dreams does that boy dream? What impossibilities disturb that middle-aged, bald gentleman. Is he the manager of the bank now. Did he continue to act with the YMCA or The Strolling Players or The Thespian Society. Does he dream of holding a great house in the palm of his hand and reducing it to his creature as he tots up the accounts. Does he lust for the standing ovation after a particularly electrifying performance as he stands in magnificent solitude against the front curtain of The Old Vic as a dirty old man lusts for the caress of voluptuous hands and the

---

[275] John Cottrell and Fergus Cashin, *Richard Burton* (1971).

succulence of young breasts. Perhaps not. I hope not. I wonder if he knows how monstrously unfair the business is. The man of thirty, his ambition still burning, bewildered by frustration when tall and graceful and full-voiced and handsome stands well-lighted on the stage and realizes, knows, that the audience are totally uninterested in him but in that other man, that thick graceless pockmarked man with a cracked voice. Why do the audience look at Alec Guinness and not me? Or Marlon Brando. Or Alan Badel. Or Paul Scofield. I mean look at Scofield. He walks like a pimp, he's got a patently false voice, he's elephant-arsed and thin-chested and minute-shouldered and here stand I the shining and superb son of a hundred earls and yet they look at Scofield and his apology for acting. And Larry, my dear, a Lord yet. I mean it's absurd. He's practically a dwarf. He has the most contrived voice, all affecta-tion. And that vulgar streak in him is shaming. As Othello I couldn't look at him. The audience could, of course. But then audiences are sheep, they believe the critics. Fools. And Brando. Have you honestly ever understood a word he's ever said? Be honest now. And as for Burton. Words almost fail me.

Sunday 7th, Rome [. . .] The virtual cessation of drink has made a terrific difference to E. She is more active, more spirited and at the same time more relaxed. And she looks even more beautiful than before. Her face has thinned very subtly and her ever present baby double chin is much less. Even with E there is bound to be a certain amount of bloat from booze. If she loses 5 or 6lbs with the diet she will look 25 again. And there is no doubt that less grey in the hair takes a few years off too. (For the first time in her life and after years of my refusing to let her have it done she has dyed her hair a bit, that is to say it has been 'streaked' leaving some of the grey). In the last two or three years and for the first time in her life E has looked a bit blotchy in the mornings when she first awoke. I told her so and for the first times ever had to suggest that she put some make-up on if someone was coming to visit us early. But now again the morning face is as fresh and glowing as the one that went to bed. I was going to say 'as a young girl's' but remembered that Liza and Kate too, both a mere 14 years old, look pretty ghastly in the mornings. We have to tell Liza frequently to go and splash water on her face. Mind you, in all fairness Liza's complexion is very different from E's, for E, tho she is Celtic dark has an underlying pigmentation of red whereas Liza tends to sallowness. Faintly yellow. Most women look fairly diabolical in the a.m. Syb was pretty good but a lot of other ladies I knew under those circumstances looked awful, even in their teens. Jean [Simmons] was alright, as I remember, and like E had no need of make-up at all tho she did wear it. Clara Cluck had to wear make-up all the time and not just in the morning.[276] She had, like so many women, a faintly

---

[276] Clara Cluck is a Disney character but this may well be a reference to Claire Bloom.

'bald' look without it. Some girls I knew looked so frightful under those circumstances that the 'intimacy' stopped right there. Hasty retreats in the cold cruel light of morning was often times the order of the day. The most rebarbative I ever remember was in Winnipeg, Canada. I had been stationed for 6 months at a place called Portage la Prairie, some 60 miles from Winnipeg.[277] I was 20 years old and it seemed to me that I had a permanent erection and could think of little else. Since a bad education had given me a guilt-fear of masturbation I only allowed myself recourse to it when I was truly desperate as, apart from the fore-written guilt fear, my own dignity screamed 'shame' at the prospect of frantically stroking myself in the squalid communal lavatory or in the RAF bed with thirty other men asleep around me. And the few women that were available were already spoken for. The WAAFs on the station and the women in the town, those who were ready and willing, had been serving the RAF for five years – it was 1945 – and were not likely to change a permanent member of the Station staff for chaps like us who were there only for a short course and then sent back to England.[278] It didn't matter that the girls were almost all vilely unattractive, all they had to be was clean and not actually cross-eyed and they were considered to be Hedy Lamarr.[279] Even with this collection of affronts to their own sex there was no hope. The incumbents exercised their territorial imperative with ruthlessness, and we hot boys had to content ourselves with wet dreams. Every 10 days we were given a 36 hour pass to Winnipeg and 60 panting young men walking on three legs would invade the infinitely dull city of Peg. Why, Oh Why could we not be stationed near Montreal. Why this town, clean and wide-avenued and built on grain, a great deal of which the citizens must have eaten as they all looked unattractively healthy, glowing with good thoughts and all descended from the British, not nice and dirty and hairy like French Canada. Since we were almost all Oxford and Cambridge undergrads we were 'placed' with good rich families who lived in wealthy suburbs with 'Aunties'. These were generally pretty well-to-do Canadian ladies with lovely Norman Rockwell houses with porches and rocking chairs and unfenced lawns sweeping down to the side-road on which they lived, mail-box on a pole, mosquito screens around the porch, decent 'best seller' libraries with, in one house, bound copies of the *Reader's Digest*, and they would invite round pretty blonde undergraduettes from the University who invariably either wanted to talk seriously about college subjects or – death of deaths and hell's destruction – would bring their boy-friends around with them.[280] It was a dry province so there was never any

---

[277] Portage la Prairie, Manitoba.
[278] WAAF: Women's Auxiliary Air Force.
[279] Hedy Lamarr (1914–2000), actor.
[280] This would appear to be an inaccurate reference to a line from the hymn 'Cwm Rhondda': 'death of death, and hell's damnation', although it is possible that Burton was familiar with a different translation from the Welsh.

alcohol to help reduce any defences and in any case there was simply no time. Thirty-six hours was cruelly inadequate. Once, at Aunt Elinor's – I had two aunts and alternated between them, the other one being Aunt Sally. Swear to God – she had a girl from the University who during the vac was jobbing as Elinor's maid – a nice sexy looking girl that I nearly managed to seduce but at the crucial moment she started to cry and I realized that the whole thing was too near home and gave up. One weekend however I decided to ignore Sally and Elinor and prowled the streets. Nothing, absolutely nothing doing. I tried parks and cinemas and the main streets. About 11 at night when I finally decided that the fucking town was hopeless and that it was the bloody YMCA after all I was walking down a side street of pretty lower-class houses when I heard the astonishing sound of revelry at night. Winnipeg went to bed at 10 o'clock in those days and was never given to revelry at any time and therefore the sound of singing and laughing at 11 at night was the equivalent of a wild party at 3 o'clock anywhere else. I located the heady sound finding that it came from a house with the blinds down but the lights on. I decided to 'crash' the party. There were about 8 people, all drunk and all older than grass – in those days that was about my age now, 45 or so – all soft with that peculiar North American obesity – and they greeted me with delight. I hadn't had a drink since arriving in Canada and was delirious with delight too when they told me to help myself. They were all drinking beer out of quart bottles. I was of course wearing my RAF uniform with a forage cap with the white band informing anyone that I was air-crew and a cadet officer. Usually Canadians hated RAF bods as we had been there for five years and like the GIs in Britain had more money and more glamour than the stay-at-homes and were thoroughly detested so I was surprised at their welcoming me so cordially. The reason for this change of heart was soon realized. We were sitting in a kitchen on kitchen chairs and a couple of chairs were brought in from another room. I was sitting on the draining board with my feet dangling. I asked what they were celebrating, whose birthday or what. Well we just fired off our new little 22 Browning, he said. I was completely bewildered though I pretended to know what they were talking about. Finally it dawned on me that we had dropped the Atom Bomb.[281] They then told me, when I asked, some of the details. I was delighted and wished I'd learned the news in better company the Canadians in that house being loathsome. I had only a vague idea of course in those days of its true horror. The evening wore on and eventually, about 12.30 I suppose I left and walked towards the city centre. I was fairly drunk. In one of the main streets I saw a woman alone. With the false effrontery of the drunk and the relieved – on the whole I decided that not having to fight the Japs was a good idea. A guaranteed life was somewhat more on the cards

---

[281] The first atomic bomb was dropped on Hiroshima on 6 August 1945, the second on Nagasaki on 9 August 1945.

than a guaranteed medal to go with it. I don't remember the exchange with the lady but I seem to remember that she looked reasonable enough and was I thought about 30. Old but not all that old. I had been told that there were no whores in Winnipeg and she was probably one of the many servicemen's wives who were celebrating the atom bomb and the imminence of the war's end. She took me home. It was a bed-sitter. We screwed. Can't very well say 'made love' under the circumstances. And slept. She also had some beer I think. The room was small and it was a double bed that dwarfed the room and there was no room for any other furniture except an upright chair. I awoke to the crying of a baby. It was very early in the morning and still only ½ light. I was for a long time unable to work out where I was. I then remembered. I turned and looked at the creature lying beside me. She was horrifically filthy. Vile. And old. Not thirty but fifty. And an old fifty. Under the dim street lights of the street and the darkness of her room she hadn't looked too bad. Also, I suppose, booze and indiscriminating lust had seen her with distorted myopia. Also she was heavily layered with a pound or so of make-up. Now there she lay in nightmare vomit, unspeakably repulsive. There was a minute bathroom which I had used the night before. I arrived there in time to be sick. After that and after dressing I pretended to a bonhomie that I didn't have and asked where the sound of the baby's crying had been coming from, it seemed very near. One corner of the room was curtained off. She withdrew the curtain. Behind the curtain was a cradle on a stand. In the cradle was her baby. I gave her some money and left.

Monday 8th, Rome Yesterday was for the most part unsatisfactory. Brook Williams came at 10 o'clock and J. Heyman at 11.20 [. . .]. It seems that I can delay going back to Jugoslavia until January and we have decided to do so and take a long seven week holiday. John Heyman's long disappearance can be attributed to – I had guessed so – to woman chasing. A particular woman called Suzy Kendall who is the girl who stayed with us on the yacht last summer with Mike Caine. We approve of her thoroughly though I am now finding it difficult to believe that neither Caine or Heyman (so he swears) have been to bed with her. She must either be that rare thing indeed – a truly chaste and virtuous girl – or that not so rare child – a girl who's not going to give herself unless the man is going to marry her, or that very common and to-be-pitied thing – frigid. Anyway, there goes Heyman with his tongue hanging out. Rather you nor me Johnny, rather you nor me. I must never have people around again on a Sunday morning. They destroyed the rhythm of the perfect Sunday, the reading of the papers with E reading me out choice bits from the cheap papers especially the *News of the World* while I work my way through the sports sections – Longhurst and McIlvanney and Parkinson and on to the politico pages with a final luxurious orgy in the book reviews with pencil and paper at the ready for books to buy immediately or shall we wait for them to come out in paperback.[282] I have long given up reading the theatre and film sections. I find them, and always have unless they concerned me, unreadable. When Tynan stopped flashing his naughtiness at us I stopped being interested. Apart from Hobson in theatre and Dilys Powell in films I don't even know the critics' names and I only know the two forementioned because they've been there ever since I was very young.[283] I've always been astounded actually that Hobson kept his job. He followed Agate and has always been considered a poor joke.[284] A good notice from Hobson was almost certainly the kiss of death unless you were already established. He is a tiny near-dwarf horribly disfigured by some cruel crippling thing or perhaps he was born that way. He walks with the aid of two sticks and seemed when I met him some years ago on a brains trust to be well under five feet. I was immensely nasty to him that night I remember. It was at Wyndham's Theatre. He had said in a recent article that though I was a great actor I was too short. Nobody else had thought I was too short either before or since and I am in fact the perfect size for an actor. At 5'10" I can be tall or shortish depending on what is wanted. Nevertheless I was still annoyed. When I met him, I said 'You are a bright bugger to describe someone as "lacking inches" aren't you. I must tell Mr Andrews about your breath-taking proportions when next I see him.' The very Sunday previous to this meeting he had described Harry Andrews as having the biggest chin in London with the possible exception of Mr Jack Hulbert.[285] And I knew Harry was very hurt, particularly so as Harry is a homosexual and like most of that company inordinately vain. He was, of course, still desperately trying – Hobson I mean – to match the much-quoted Agate's acid wit. Agate had described Neil Porter's nose as 'effectively bridging the gap between Roman and Modern times' in a performance of *Julius Caesar*.[286] And of another actor who was very fat and playing the *Merchant of Venice*: 'Mr So-and-so could very well afford to lose a pound of flesh.' And so on. Mr Hobson should have stayed in his former job which was, so I believe, soccer correspondent. Ken Tynan on the other hand was so good that Paul Scofield and I practically committed them to memory. He was at his very best when he began on the *Evening Standard*. Miss Anna Neagle took out her voice and shook it at the audience like a tiny fist.[287] There is nothing in Miss Audley's performance that fasting won't cure.[288] Except for flashes he never was that funny again and sadly ever as penetrating again. He is still though an exceptional writer and very disappointing at the

[282] Henry Longhurst (1909–78), golf columnist. Hugh McIlvanney (1933—), sports journalist. Michael Parkinson (1935—) wrote a sports column for the *Sunday Times* from 1965.
[283] Sir Harold Hobson (1904–92), drama critic of the *Sunday Times* (1947–76). Dilys Powell (1901–95), film critic of the *Sunday Times* (1939–76).
[284] James Agate (1877–1947), theatre and film critic.
[285] Jack Hulbert (1892–1978), actor.
[286] Neil Porter (1895–1944), actor and producer.
[287] Anna Neagle (1904–86), actor.
[288] Maxine Audley (1923–92), actor.

same time. He should never have allowed himself to be taken up with and by The National Theatre. He is now known as Ken (*Oh! Calcutta!*) Tynan.[289] A sad obituary.

I read David Niven's autobiography yesterday in one sitting.[290] It is very funny though not very well written and is, like all actors' biographies, very anecdotal and full of 'and then Mike Todd called me and said "Get your ass over here"' etc.[291] He describes one scene on Bogart's yacht which is not what happened at all as I was there. He describes Sinatra singing all through the night on a motor yacht with a lot of other yachts around 'awe-struck' he says.[292] Frankie did sing all through the night it's true and a lot of people sat around in boats and got drunk it's true but Bogie and I went out lobster-potting with Dumbum [. . .] while Frankie was singing kept on making cracks about Betty [Bacall] sitting on Sinatra's feet etc. and Frankie got really pissed off with Bogie and David Niv who describes himself as bewitched all through the night was trying to set fire to the *Santana* at one point, because nobody could stop Francis from going on and on and on.[293] I was drinking 'boiler-makers' with Bogie Rye Whiskey with canned beer chasers so the night is pretty vague but I seem to remember a girl having a fight with her husband or boy friend in a rowing dinghy and being thrown in the water by her irate mate. I don't know why but I would guess that she wanted to stay and listen to Frankie and he wanted to go. And Bogie and Frankie nearly came to blows next day about the singing the night before and I drove Betty home because she was so angry with Bogie's cracks about Frankie's singing. At that time Frankie was out of work and was peculiarly vulnerable and Bogie was unnecessarily cruel. But any way it is not at all like Niv's description. He's very sweet about E and indeed about practically everybody.

Alexandre has just arrived with a message from Marie Hélène Rothschild inviting us

Tuesday 9th, Rome (continued from yesterday) to a party at Ferrières on December 2nd and to stay the night before, which is a Wednesday, and to stay on over the following weekend. Now with the news about Jugoslavia, we are able to go. I had made it a condition of the party that we stayed at Ferrières the night before and after. Two reasons: I love Ferrières. And I don't have to worry about E being on time.

The first is the real reason. The vastness of the chateau and, at the same time, its cosiness gives me immense satisfaction. The grounds, seemingly

---

[289] Kenneth Tynan had joined the National Theatre in 1963 as its literary manager. He wrote *Oh! Calcutta!* (1969).

[290] David Niven, *The Moon's a Balloon* (1971).

[291] This passage is described on p. 297 of *The Moon's a Balloon*.

[292] The scene is described on pp. 292–3 of *The Moon's a Balloon* (1972). Niven uses the phrase 'the awed and grateful audience'.

[293] 'Dumbum' or 'Dum Bum' was Bogart's Danish crewman on his yacht the *Santana*.

endless, laked and forested and bridle-pathed are a huge world of their own and I walk around and about it for miles. Also I like the Rothschilds very much. I am not much given to 'Society' but Marie Helene and Guy will always command my respect and loyalty as they were so nice to us when nobody else was. During the time of the Scandale they went out of their way to be warmly polite to us when we were front-page and vulgar sensationalism every other day and every paper. Much lesser people cut us dead, even, if you please, people from our own profession. An idiot like Audrey Hepburn, for instance, a supposedly long time friend of E's was unobtainable on the phone and refused to acknowledge flowers that were sent her for her birthday. David Niven was toffee-nosed too, though he has apologized since. Grace wouldn't have been seen dead in our company though I'm sure now that Rainier didn't give a bugger. We didn't give a bugger either and were perfectly content to be left alone and therefore the nice attitude of Guy and M-H was of no real importance personally to our happiness, but it was a splendid smack in the eye for the black crows crowing at our 'disgrace'.

I gather that the party is in honour of the centenary of Proust's birth. Christ, he was dead in 1922 at 51 years of age and here I am only 5 years away from his death age without a book to my name. I have never liked his 7 volumes of *A la Recerche* but nevertheless recognize the enormity of the attempt.[294] Perhaps I will understand him and enjoy him better than I did when first I read him. I must have been in my teens. I will have another go when we get back to Gstaad.

The ladies are asked to dress in the style of the period with their hair in the period adorned only with 'flowers, feathers or diamonds'. The men are asked to wear tails! Marie Helene nearly got a 'go and take a running jump into Ferrières Lake' message in reply to the last request but E persuaded me otherwise. I am actually looking forward to it.

Yesterday was a blood and sweat day. Me being wheeled, dying from a terrible wound in my head, down a hospital corridor and in to the emergency operating theatre. A thoroughly messy day with false blood drying tackily in my hair and on my face and Cortese crying at my dying even in rehearsals. How I shrink from people who really 'act' like that. They are always so bad too. But they think they are being great instead of bloody idiots, self-indulgent idiots. Creepily embarrassing. E came in the afternoon to cheer me up. We worked at what was the Jewish hospital on the Isola Tiberina, a diabolical place to get to as the bridges Fabricio and Cestio are one permanent traffic jam. No wonder they've abandoned it as a hospital – an emergency patient would be killed by the traffic. Ponte Fabricio was built [in] 62BC with modern

---

[294] Proust's *A La Recherche du Temps Perdu* was published between 1913 and 1927. Burton considered a screenplay based on the novel, written by Harold Pinter (1930–2008), in 1972, but the film was not made.

traffic not being its main concern. The Ponte Cestio was built in AD192 and rebuilt last in 1890 so that too was made for horse and cart and pedestrians. We work there again today.

Brook told us on Sunday that Emlyn [Williams] wanted to sell his cottage at South Moreton and I immediately said we'd buy it. They want £16,000. It's a bit steep but is worth every penny and will be worth more in the years to come. Liza can have it when she's older. It is perfect for us for a weekend cottage. It is not far from a railway station and there is a good pub within walking distance and shops in the main street only a couple of hundred yards away and unlike Brook's cottage it is off the main street so that dogs and small children are fairly safe. A railway line runs between London and the West Country and Wales about a mile away and I've always loved the sound of trains at night. I prefer it to Sussex and Paul Scofield's part of the country while Kent, though lovely is a monster to get to. It is pretty convenient too for Shepperton and not outrageous for Elstree. All in all, I can't wait to work in England again. As long as it's summer time. I wrote to Emlyn this morning and Brook will take the letter back with him. I've told Emlyn that he can use the cottage whenever he likes for as long as he likes. We shall be there so seldom anyway. Did not note that on Sunday E and I had a martini each and two glasses of wine while yesterday E had a jack daniels. [. . .]

Wednesday 10th, Rome I am 46 years old today. I am sometimes surprised that I got so far. I always had the feeling that I would die in my thirties and in my twenties was firmly convinced that I would die at the age of 33. This belief was induced in me by an Irish (Welsh-Irish) idiot many years ago in the ML Club in London on a wet Sunday afternoon, late afternoon, when we were having a break from poetry reading. Dylan was there and Constant Lambert, Louis MacNeice and Esmé Percy – by God all of them are dead – and we were drinking well with no particular thought for the fact that we were broadcasting 'live' in an hour's time some intricate verse – at least Esmé and I were.[295] No we weren't, we were doing Thomas Love Peacock's *Nightmare Abbey*.[296] The ML Club was and is a most unattractive, badly run, filthy hole in a wall just off Upper Regent Street. I have never found out if I was a member though I must surely be one now as I 'loaned' them £500 last winter via John Dearth.[297] Its only use was as a place to drink when the pubs were closed. One never dreamt of going there if the 'George' was open a hundred yards away.[298] Anyway this particular afternoon we had the usual 'break 'til 6.30, run through until 7.30,

---

[295] Constant Lambert (1905–51), composer and conductor.
[296] Thomas Love Peacock (1785–1866), *Nightmare Abbey* (1818). Burton appeared in the BBC Radio production on 7 November 1949, playing the part of Scythrop Glowry, generally regarded as a depiction of Shelley.
[297] John Dearth (1920–84), who had played with Burton in *Look Back in Anger*.
[298] The George, Oxford Circus.

the red light comes on at 8' injuction and Esmé and I repaired to the ML. It was my idea of total bliss. A Sunday in London at the BBC on the Third Programme – surely the best radio channel in the world – playing Shelley in Peacock's marvellous piece, surrounded by a melodrama of brilliant English actors – Esmé himself, Count Robert Farquarson of The Holy Roman Empire who was reputed to be a Satanist, Ernest Thesiger, Andrew Cruikshank, Robert Speaight, Michael Hordern and sometimes Dylan and James Crock of Gold Stephens and always the BBC stock company one of whom was, if such a thing is possible on radio, a truly great actor – James McKechnie.[299] So there you are in my drab paradise of magnificent language for the speaking of which you were actually paid money, on a Sunday in Studio 8 of the BBC Portland Place, the Sunday papers strewn hither and thither and much chat between the boys who matched story after story and, because the competition is so intense, no one person was able to hold the floor for too long even if Dylan was there for Dylan – the most compelling talker I've ever met – was oddly constricted by these precise cold English actors with their impeccable accents. Lunch was at someone's club – I would sometimes go with Esmé to the Savile – but more often it was in the BBC canteen a hellish place appositely placed in the sub-basement of the huge building.[300] It was a serve-yourself cafe and a pretty sight it was to see the august Count Farquarson, cloaked like a bandit, and all the other great presences queueing up for the appalling BBC fare. The drinking men however lunched out of a bottle at the George or – not quite so popular as it was that bit further away – The Stag or The Roebuck or some such name. But it was the work itself that was the wonder. The audience was a minor consideration as it was so small. Apart from the fact that the channel for the Third Programme was unfindable in most of Great Britain this brainchild of the BBC would play plays in the original Greek and was indeed deliberately steered away from the mass audience. If they accidentally hit on a smash success it was almost always replayed on the Home Service or Light Programmes. The best work I have ever been associated with was with that programme. I did endless poetry readings there and every kind of adaptations from great works, particularly the lesser known stuff. Your *Hamlets* and *Henry Vs* were common fare and one did those on the vulgar airwaves but *'Tis Pity She's a Whore* and Love Peacock and Bussy D'Ambois and Chaucer and Jones' *In Parenthesis* and *Anathemata* and Joyce's *Finnegan's Wake* and *Ulysses* etc. were all done on 'our' programme.[301]

---

[299] Robert Farquarson (1878–1966). Ernest Thesiger (1879–1961), who co-starred with Burton in *The Robe*. Andrew Cruikshank (1907–88). Robert Speaight (1904–76). James Stephens (1882–1950), author of *The Crock of Gold* (1912). James McKechnie (1911–64).
[300] The Savile Club, Brook Street.
[301] John Ford (*c*.1586–*c*.1640), *'Tis Pity She's a Whore* (1633). George Chapman (*c*.1559–*c*.1634), *The Tragedy of Bussy D'Ambois* (1607). Geoffrey Chaucer (*c*.1343–1400). David Jones (1895–1974), *In Parenthesis* (1937); idem, *Anathemata* (1952). James Joyce, *Finnegans Wake* (1939).

Anyway this Cardiff Welshman – a feature of the sleazy drinking houses in those days and vividly remembered though I can't remember his name – a writer who never published and an actor who never acted elected to tell us from our hands when we were going to die. My father was up for a week from Wales and I'd taken him to the BBC to have a look at it and was going to send him back to Hampstead after the afternoon drinking session was told he was going to die when he was 81, Dylan when he was 39, Lambert when he was 55 and me when I was 33. I was very impressed – so much so that I have remembered it to this day. It was made more frightening as Dylan did die when I was 29 at the age of 39 and Dic my father died when I was about the same age at 81. My brothers say that my father was 83 but there has always been some confusion re the old man's age and in my case he was, the prophet, only a couple of years out.[302] Lambert died but I don't know at what age and I can't remember whether he foretold Esmé's death date, but Esmé also died. My behaviour to anyone who didn't know during my 33rd year to heaven was high comedy. I went by car and train and boat whenever I had to travel. I turned down a film in Durango with Burt Lancaster and Audrey Hepburn and directed by Huston because of the unavoidable flying.[303] Were it not for the fact that I was ashamed to tell anyone I would not have worked that year at all and celebrated my 34th birthday with a stupendous booze-up. I was already very rich and kept on saying to myself as the offers came up 'why should I risk my life for a mere $150,000 when I have a million in the bank, why don't I settle here in Céligny and never leave the grounds of the house even until the year is up. I can learn Hebrew or something. The thing is not to give the gods of retribution the slightest chance.' The anomaly is that I am not even mildly superstitious ordinarily and am certainly not a fatalist. I must find out, as a matter of mild interest at what age Lambert died. I wonder too if in death Lambert is still considered to be the genius he was thought to be when he was alive.

I have the day off today and tomorrow I think. I have received beautiful presents. E has given me two cigarette lighters – an exquisite one, very light and thin, of gold and polished walnut and a sturdier one for everyday use of heavy gold made for her especially by Braun of Germany – the best lighters in the world unfortunately. How the British have lost out to everybody not only in quantity but quality. Claudye and Gianni had a large brief-case made for me out of antique leather with many neat and practical compartments. My favourite kind of things.

E is still being a good drinker. Yesterday she had only a glass of wine at lunchtime and a Jack Daniels at night. She continues to look like several dreams of avarice and is happy.

---

[302] Burton's father was 81 when he died in 1957.
[303] *The Unforgiven* (1960), directed by John Huston and starring Burt Lancaster (1913–94) and Audrey Hepburn. It was filmed in Durango, Mexico.

Two books arrived from Jane Swanson and her daughter Sarah and Bob gave me a sweater from Battistoni's.[304] Several telegrams including one from Grace and Rainier and we realized that we haven't sent one to her and her birthday is about now too.[305]

I did an interview for *L'Express* yesterday for their cover story. My interviewer was an earnest young man with spectacles who spoke no English and talked a mile a minute and I virtually had to ask him to repeat every single question he asked me. This went on for an hour until I was practically screaming. In desperation I asked them to play some of the recording back for him to realize how impossible he was. He then confessed that he had never been so nervous in his life as he heard that I was an extremely dangerous person! [. . .]

Thursday 11th, Rome The discerning scanner will realize immediately that the title heading is not in red letters. My birthday was a semi-drunken one for both of us. The rot set in when I made a large martini each about 1 o'clock. Then I went down below to chat it up with a reporter from the *Daily Mirror* called Donald Zec.[306] Elizabeth was unbelievably late even for her and Mr Zec is very hard going so, fatally as it turned out, I had a 2nd Martini. Off we went to Valentino's for lunch. The latter is apparently a very swank haute couturier and is making E's frock for the Rothschild Ball.[307] I had invited myself together with Zec who was completely out of his depth and betrayed his discomfort by being a silly kind of smart-aleck while I, not unpleasantly, pretended with the assistance of several glasses of wine to anti-semitism, negro, anglo-saxon, American and anything else I could think of. In deference to my host I excluded the Italians and, for Claudye, Corsicans. The reaction set in later when I got back home refusing to fit for my new suits and slumping off to bed where I slept for a few hours. I was suitably grumpy and snarled at E a lot – one more indication that life is sweeter <u>off</u> the sauce. Today therefore I feel somewhat fragile while E, who decided that if you cannot fight 'em you might as well join 'em, has a monumental hangover. We both agree that heavy drinking doesn't suit us anymore at all.

Presents: Apart from the above-mentioned I was given a large soft leather travelling bag by Joe Losey and Patricia and a lot of Cashmere sweaters from Ron and Bob and Ray Stark who is in town trying to persuade E to do a film for him <u>but</u> the present of presents is the *Complete Oxford Dictionary* in microprint, the 17 (I think) volumes being reduced to two with a magnifying glass on a little wooden stand. You have to close one eye. To a bibliomaniac it is a

[304] Battistoni's boutique, Via Condotti.
[305] Grace Kelly's birthday was 12 November.
[306] Donald Zec (1919—) would publish a biography of Elizabeth Taylor in 1982.
[307] Valentino's, Via del Babuino.

thrilling present. Not to be all stingy about it E gave me three sets, one for Gstaad, one for the yacht and one for Vallarta.

An effusive letter came from Princess Maggie yesterday About the £100,000. Of course. Must write back.

We are all going to see *XYZ* at the Columbia private theatre tonight. We are trying to get a few people together to see it who have never seen it before, in the hope of finding out where the laughs come, but the place only holds 30 people.

Friday 12th, Grand Hotel Another non-red headline as E had a few beers and a bloody mary (at my insistence) and two Jack Daniels while I had a bloody mary. (E, I remember said she had only 1½ beers). This has been one of those mornings where through haste everything goes haywire. I didn't take a shower as not having been to bed until 3 I awoke by courtesy of E at 9 to be told immediately by Bob that I was wanted toute de suite. On opening the diary I dropped it and all the loose leaves fell out and had to be painstakingly put back in again. I tried to extract my vitamin pills from the box while holding a cigarette which dropped and burned my fingers while all the pills fell out on the bathroom floor. I managed to cut myself shaving – mildly it's true – but a considerable feat with an electric razor. I always order tea for two in the hope that E might join me. This morning I ordered only one – because I was in a hurry I guess – whereupon E arrived from the bedroom and asked for her tea. Not only had I not ordered my usual two teas but this morning she had asked for one. I hadn't heard her. The sun was brilliant when I first got out but is gone in again and today we must I think have sun. If Joe's and my luck hold we shall finish that shot today. If not it means working tomorrow and possibly even on Monday unless they can devise a shot without the sun's assistance. It is an awkward shot using a technique that I had never heard of. I talk of Stalin and pause to think and the technicians throw an image of Stalin onto space, suspended over my shoulder. I hope it's not too tricksy. Those are – there are a few such shots – the 'almost subliminal' shots described in the script and which I made so much fun of to Joe. So to work. Will write about the film which is, to me and will be I think to many people, absolutely shattering. I thought about it for several hours after the thing was over.

Evening.[308]

Well, we <u>had</u> the luck and I finished the film with two 'almost sublimal' shots in glorious technicolour and sunshine. Then the weather turned round and now it is grey-black and threatening again. There is a company party tonight down at Tor Vaianica but at the last moment we have decided not to go

---

[308] Heading in red type.

as (a) company parties are invariably as flat as pancakes especially as the company has to work some more tomorrow and the main reason is (b) it is 40 minutes in normal end-of-business-day traffic and likely to be much more on a Friday. Hence nous resterons chez nous tranquillement avec des livres, des journaux et cette machine a ecrire.[309]

The film I'm talking about above is of course *XYZ* which on seeing for the first time with everything finished – matching, music, titles (which I adored) and end titles etc. – I found more rewarding than ever. I am not much of a judge as I see so few films but I shall be very surprised if other people don't think E's performance to be one of the best ever given by anybody at any time. She runs the entire gamut from high comedy to knockabout prat-falls to pathos and near tragedy with dazzling brilliance. The film itself too is very and intriguingly beautiful I think and at one or two moments I had most unusual (for me) lumps in my throat. Especially when E was lonely and frightened. The remarkable thing too is that E emerges very sympathetically despite her stop-at-nothing ruthlessness to keep her man at any price. The others are good too but E completely out-dazzles them. Now watch for the reaction and I just hope we're not disappointed. I have never got *Staircase* and *Anger* out of my system. E's film *Gingerbread Lady* is postponed for a time – don't know how long – and Donen has been signed and E said that I shouldn't object too much as Donen's only good work has been with musicals. All this came from Swifty Lazar par telephone talk tonight.[310] I said if they could let me know in a week or so and if the music and script were ok I would try and fit it in next year. And so I will. It is a shame to do it with Donen who so thoroughly buggered up *Staircase*, no pun. And so to books.

Saturday 13th[311] [. . .] Awoke at 8 ordered tea and finished a long letter to Liza who has cleverly chosen Tito as her historical character for this term. She asked me for 'any information' on him so I tapped out three pages or so of a rough outline. Also told her that her penmanship was appalling and would alienate any examiner regardless of the excellence of her writing otherwise. A very slapdash young woman.

[. . .] Every day here seems to be a day of demonstrations. Yesterday it was something to do with the Coca-Cola factories which, presumably in despair with the endless strikes, have closed down entirely. This morning there was a tremendous hullaballoo about 'no repression in schools' which I don't understand and, since the local papers never or hardly ever mention the demonstrations (so many of them I suppose) I don't know what the protest marches are about. Italian friends confess to being equally baffled though

---

[309] We will stay at home quietly with books, newspapers and this typewriter.
[310] Irving Paul 'Swifty' Lazar (1907–93), talent agent.
[311] Heading in red type.

one can hardly expect couturiers like Valentino and Tiziani to be much interested in social disputes. They only deal with the very rich. I must ask Carlo
Cotti tonight when he comes.[312] He is the second assistant on the film and
appears to be a cut above the average in intelligence. He wants to talk to me re
Benito Mussolini I think for whom, I'm told, he has a great and relatively
unfashionable admiration. He is anxious for me to play the last days of
Mussolini in a film. Never know, it might be interesting and with E possibly
playing his mistress Clara Petacci it would certainly set all Italy by the ears.[313]
If we shot it cheaply and if it was well done it might be a knock-out. Why not
one asks oneself? Why not? This Carlo is reputedly a very rich young man. He
is certainly very richly dressed for a 2nd Assistant. [. . .]

Sunday 14th A black day again. E and I had martinis before lunch though E
only drank half of hers and we shared a bottle of Gewarstraminer at lunch
[. . .] with which [. . .] we washed down caviar blinis in my case, and some sort
of delicious veal with mushrooms in Elizabeth's.[314] After that I drank no more
for the rest of the day while E had a Jack Daniels and some wine at Joe Losey's
where we went for dinner. E is in rare form acting the goat and mucking about
and is generally very droll. [. . .]

Carlo Cotti came to see me yesterday to talk of Mussolini and he obviously
does know his subject and he is a neo-fascist. He made the point that since
Mussolini left us the Italians have not been governed at all and that Italy really
does need a strong central character, another Mussolini, another benevolent
dictator for they, the Italians, understand nothing else. He said that the cupidity
and villainy of his race demanded a police state and that the people demanded
by their very nature an organization which instilled fear. He wouldn't mind, he
said, if there was a strongly repressive Communist Government if only they
promised ruthlessness to tax evaders, brought back the death penalty and
more importantly corporal punishment – the lash, the cat, the birch. All this
from a young man of 32 with a sweet round face and curly hair and eyes of
liquid brown and a charming self-deprecating grin. The communists however
had behaved so stupidly and were so utterly alien to the Italian temperament
and, as a consequence, so weak, that he was constrained to advocate more
drastic means. He loved his people but they were en masse a silly mob of
disorganized undisciplined schoolchildren and like schoolchildren must be
threatened by dire punishment.

I sat back aghast. So much so that it took me 10 minutes to marshal my
liberal arguments against his. Better, I said, to have the economy collapse and
millions out of work and near starvation than the knout and the boot in the

---

[312] Carlo Cotti (1939—), who was proposing to act as director of a film on the last days of Mussolini.
[313] Clara Petacci (1912–45).
[314] Presumably Burton means Gewürztraminer.

face and the dreadful raid on your house in the small hours and imprisonment without trial and back to the torture chambers and the kneeling position and the bullet through the brain in secret executions. He was unmoved.

Deep in my heart of course I know he has a ruthless point but, like Communism, it is inapplicable to the Italians. I pointed out to him something that he had conveniently forgotten which is that Mussolini's Italy was as corrupt as the present Italy and that like this country today the Italy of the late thirties was also on the edge of bankruptcy.

Carlo later showed us a mink overcoat he'd made for himself and was not sure how his mother would take it and whether she would allow him to wear it. This information, together with his confession of wry idolatory for Franco Zeffirelli and his age and his bachelor status led us to suspect that he is either a Mama's boy or a homosexual. Oddly and perversely enough, with every pun intended, this belief was further strengthened by his political statements. Torture and manacling and gagged mouths being quite unfairly associated in my mind with sexual inversion.

We went to Joe Losey's last night for dinner. They live quite near the Tiber in a dark narrow street, three floors up which we laboriously climbed only to discover that there was a spanking new lift. It was a typical Roman apartment with very large rooms and glazed terra-cotta tiles, two feet square, on the floor, sparsely furnished and lofty ceilinged and as chilly as a hospital corridor. We imagined it being very cold in winter, for me uncomfortably cold and especially as Joe said the fireplace was ornamental only. They had a charming bearded long-haired male cook who went, as is the wont of all servants every-where, into conniptions at sight of Elizabeth. He was a very good cook though and why can't we ever find a cook like that instead of either lousy ones like the chap on the yacht or fellers who can only stay for 3 months and then have to go to the army or back to college or something equally frustrating. Mind you, I would rather not have a cook at all as one of us is always dickering with a diet and cooks become very put out if their creations are not eaten. Another thing with cooks is that they find it impossible to believe that one only wants one course. Their only virtue is when one has a large family gathering or a lot of people coming to eat. Eating with the Loseys alone or simply going to their home for a drink is always, to me, sort of Chekhovian. The conversation seems to have undertones and strange experiences between the lines, unspoken but guessed at. Joe is a bad conversationalist, a slow speech pattern with many pauses while he searches his vocabulary for the bon mot and a great deal of er-er-ers while Trapicia (E's spoonerism for Patricia years ago and which has stuck) talks in a mellifluous monotone the whole time with that kind of delivery that puts me – if I'm in a certain mood – into a species of trance where one listens, doesn't want the speaker to stop and where one doesn't want to interrupt in case the trance is broken. One gets it sometimes from a barber while one is getting a short-back-and-sides and the barber babbles cosily on and on. Minute and pleasant pulses tick softly in the temples as if there's pressure, very slight and euphoric pressure from soft strong fingers. I am very susceptible to this kind of mesmerism this kind of removal from the world. [. . .]

Joe has great charm despite his lack of humour especially about himself, a lack which was perfectly exemplified last night when he told us of a very savage telegram which he's sent off to a man called Bernard Delfont who 'produced' *The Go-Between* and who had put on the bill-boards his name in GIGANTIC LETTERS while Joe's name was tiny and Harold Pinter's wasn't on at all.[315] The telegram was something like 'What is the use of spending one's life producing artistic creations if in the end a shit like you has control etc.' Joe, like other humourless gents like Bill Wilder and Joe Manciewicz, will not realize that the general public do emphatically not go to see a Joe Losey Picture or a Joe Mank Picture or a Billy Wilder Picture but go to see that marvellous actor so-and-so or that great actress such-and-such or that screamingly funny whatchermaycallit.[316] It is true that there is a minute percentage who go more to see the director's work, the intelligentsia and other people in the profession who go more to see the director's work, the sort of people who belong to film clubs and love movies in foreign languages, than the actor's, but they don't need to see bill-boards to know it's a Losey picture. They will have read the information in *Sight and Sound*.[317] But there's no persuading them otherwise and I've long given up.

Monday 15th[318] A completely lazy day yesterday. Only 4 newspapers arrived: *News of the World, Express, Observer* and *Telegraph*. We always have bad luck with the *Observer* and wherever we are abroad we invariably seem to get the Scottish and Irish editions which means that the sports pages are devoted to Linfield versus Shamrock or whatever and not Arsenal v Leeds and Glasgow Academicals v Heriot F.P. instead of Harlequins v London Welsh or Blackheath. Very irritating. The *Sunday Times* is the most satisfying buy seeming to have more body to it than any other papers and I don't mean bulk but a way of presenting news in a chunkier form. There seem to be more solid columns and fewer snippets than others. Wilfred Wooller for instance in the *Telegraph* was given yesterday no more space than I have occupied writing this entry this morning.[319] That means, unless you write a sonnet, no space at all. But Parkinson and Longhurst and others have a thousand words and the political

---

[315] Bernard Delfont (1909–94), theatrical impresario. Harold Pinter, playwright, who had written the screenplay of *The Go-Between*. John Heyman and Norman Priggen (1924–99) were credited as producers of the film.
[316] Billy Wilder (1906–2002), producer.
[317] *Sight & Sound*, a monthly film magazine (1932–).
[318] Heading in red type.
[319] Wilfred Wooller (1912–97), international rugby player and sports journalist for the *Sunday Telegraph*.

columns and literary boys a fair space too. The *Express* also is a cut above the other rags and for the same reason. Hoby and Blanchflower have sizeable portions though I do wish they'd get someone other than Danny Boy to occupy that very desirable space – he so bristles with mediocrity and holier-than-thou humourless pretentiousness, pretending to a long range long viewed wisdom and a tedious philosophy where he is forever comparing the game of soccer with the 'game of life'.[320] Whereas Hoby is straightforward purple adjectived sensationalism. Peregrine Worsthorne has a beautiful lump in the *Sunday Telegraph* and is worth reading because of his almost amateur enthusiasm. A week ago he exultantly announced and explained the 'Death of the Labour Party' and that, short of a miracle, the Tories were going to be the masters for several generations. This week he threatened the Irish with Britain's hatred if they continued to tar and feather young girls who went a-courting with British soldiers. The British, he said, didn't hate easily but when they did . . . Oh Boy look out! Astonishingly, he said that during the last war the British didn't hate the Germans – quote – until we heard of the atrocities of the prison camps. Indeed, Worsthorne, indeed. Then, Cyril Connolly has a lot of space in the *Sunday Times* and Brandon from Washington while Toynbee and A. J. P. Taylor and Muggeridge get fair cracks of the whip too.[321] I wish though that the 'qualities' had proper, separate books sections like the *NY Times* and the old *Herald-Tribune*. The sort of thing you can keep in volumes and not the flimsy 4 pages the British have which includes travel and good food and wines and TV and theatre and films and art and ballet. The *Express* always has the unbelievable Mrs Grundy yclept John Gordon who is so ineffably self-righteous that he has the funniest column of the lot.[322] He has had several 'gos' at me over the years and I find it well-nigh impossible to be angry with him. 'Must we have again and again so much space in our newspapers devoted to the unimportant doings of Mr Richard Burton and his wife the much married Elizabeth Taylor. What are they after all but film stars who don't even have the sense of duty to pay their taxes. Who, after all, cares that Miss Taylor has a million dollar ring. I, for one and all of my friends find such ostentation boring and vulgar.' And then I'm very fond of Cross-Bencher in the *Express* who gnat-bites here thither and yon at front and back benchers alike with snide innuendo and arch imputation. 'Who is John Parrish who has been creating so much excitement in the drawing rooms of Conservative salons with his "I will stake my whole political future on the blazing belief that we

---

[320] Alan Hoby (1914–2008), sports journalist for the *Sunday Express*. Danny Blanchflower (1926–93), international footballer and sports journalist.

[321] Henry Brandon (1916–93), Washington correspondent for the *Sunday Times*. Philip Toynbee (1916–81), columnist for the *Observer*. A. J. P. Taylor (1906–90), historian, columnist for the *Observer* and the *Daily Express*.

[322] Mrs Grundy, a character in Thomas Morton, *Speed the Plough* (1798), taken to mean someone who is extremely strait-laced and conventional. John Gordon (1890–1974), columnist in the *Sunday Express*.

must, if we are not to commit political suicide, go whole heartedly into Europe." Why it is none other than Lord Ass-hole who before rejecting his hereditary title to sit in the Commons said on a famous occasion "As far as I'm concerned the Wogs begin at Calais."

We are going to have dinner tonight with Peter Sellers and an Indian Mystic who tells the future and who, Peter says, is called Gandhi.

Tuesday 16th, Rome We both fell off the waggon yesterday, me with a profound bump resulting in a pretty enjoyable but silly evening on my part. The usual drunken devil of impish perversity dominated my talk which since I didn't allow other people to talk much meant that I teetered on the edge of spoiling the night. However I wrote a letter of apology to Sellers and friends this morning together with the micro-*Oxford Dictionary* which E had promised to Peter last night.

Mr Gandhi was short and dark and spoke with the classic Indian-Welsh accent so outrageously impersonated by Peter in that record years ago.[323] I find it hard to believe that Peter cannot go back into England to see his wife in hospital who is suffering apparently from a severe attack of cerebral meningitis.[324] I told him that he should go ahead and do it quickly – in and out before anybody knows it – but I have a suspicion that he didn't want that advice. I hope I'm wrong but that marriage like his other two looks on the rocks. There was one startling moment which was missed unfortunately by E who was in the bedroom when, talking about the various legal suits we have all had against us he said that he and his former wife, Britt Ekland, were sued by Fox for breaking her contract which, he said, she broke at his insistence because 'I told her that I needed at least a year to educate her and teach her how to act and give her a knowledge of great world drama, before she was fit to face a major career.'[325] Neither E nor I think that little Miss Ekland needed much instruction from M. Sellers.

They talked, when I allowed them to, a lot about Yoga and meditation and vegetarianism and I told Pietro that I wanted to talk more about it and we are meeting tomorrow night on the yacht and will show, if we have it – it's in customs – *Under Milk Wood* which we have yet to see and which has been received so well. [. . .] I am genuinely interested in Yoga having read 3 or 4 books on the subject – only primitive stuff about weight and physical well being and diet and stuff – and would like to know more.

Zoe Sallis came too to the little party and it seems that she and Sellers hit it off very well indeed as we've just discovered from a phone conversation with Peter as he asked if she could be invited also tomorrow night.

---

[323] A reference to the 1960 Peter Sellers and Sophia Loren single 'Goodness Gracious Me'.
[324] Peter Sellers's third wife was Miranda Quarry (1948—).
[325] Sellers's marriage to Britt Ekland had ended in 1968.

I had a vodka and orange and a bloody mary at lunch time and have a martini in the fridge to titch me up before dinner – it's about 7.30 – and will revert to my sober behaviour tomorrow. I really don't like drinking at yesterday's pace and I'm silly to do it.

Zoe Sallis is a very attractive girl who has been John Huston's mistress for 10 years or so and we have known her since doing the film *Night of the Iguana* when she was living with John and their baby – then about 6 months old and now getting on for 9 and a breathless reminder of tempus will fugit – in Vallarta.[326] She now looks like a grown-up and not the child she looked then. She is about 30 I suppose and very dark and Indian looking. I think she said last night that she was Eurasian or perhaps she was only saying that to impress Sellers and 'Bert' (Seller's companion) and Ganh, Gandhi rather, who obviously are Indian lovers.[327] Shades of Anna Kashfi who used to be Marlon's wife and firmly convinced him that she was Indian when it turned out – to Marlon's fury and immediate divorce – that she was Cardiff Welsh.[328] I knew the minute I met her just after Marlon had married her that she was Welsh and said so to her and Marlon. She affected not to know what 'Welsh' was and asked if we were like the Irish and all that kind of rubbish. Marlon wasn't interested and only became so when he found out that he had been lied to – a heinous crime in Marlon's book. I still smile when I remember a picture of Kashfi's mother in the *Daily Express* or *Mail* with a real Celtic peasant look and wearing a 'pinny' and formidably Welsh look, sort of arms akimbo, with the caption 'Do I look Indian?' I laughed for a week. Later I teased Marlon about it until I realized that old fatty was not inclined to regard it or her in a humorous light. I haven't tried him on that affair since. I wonder how he would take it now. [. .]

Wednesday 17th, Grand [. . .] There has been a great deal of fuss and bother around the hotel for the last couple of days because President Franz Jonas of Austria is here on a state visit which consists of tea at the Quirinale with Saragat and tremendous traffic jams.[329] The streets around the hotel are one continuous cacophony of despairing horns and policemen's whistles and remarkably often the penetrating screams of ambulances. The Romans it seems are always in a rush to the grave. Yesterday too the sound of many horses set our dogs a-barking and there indeed was a pretty sight as one would want to see – several hundred horses riding four abreast caparisoned with riders dressed by Ivor Novello and all of them placed as to colour, a mass of

---

[326] Huston and Sallis's son Danny (now an actor) was born in 1962.

[327] Sallis is of mixed English and Indian descent.

[328] Anna Kashfi (1934—) was born Johanna O'Callaghan in Darjeeling, India. Her family moved to Cardiff in 1947. She and Brando were married from 1957 to 1959. She has claimed that her father William, a London Irishman, was her stepfather and that her biological father was Indian.

[329] President Franz Jonas (1899–1974). Giuseppe Saragat (1898–1988), President of the Italian Republic. Hotel Quirinale, Via Nazionale, Rome.

whites, a mass of blacks and a mass of browns.[330] E and Jane Swanson were watching it with delight from our balcony when Jane realized that all the onlookers had their binoculars trained on E and not the horses. Since E was in a dressing gown she fled inside. The concourse was endless and created, of course, the mother and father of all traffic jams. It was typical, I remarked to Jane, of the Romans to have a procession during the peak of the rush hour. She said that it was probably deliberate and that Italians love a mess so that they can have an excuse for tantrums. They are all natural thespians she said. Orson [Welles] once said that the Italians were the best actors in the world but unfortunately only the worst of them became professionals.

I'd forgotten to say that Robin Stafford of the *Express* came to visit us at the same time as Sellers.[331] He was the only journalist allowed at our wedding, not because he was a particular friend but because he was so quietly and charmingly persistent. It wasn't until we'd chatted for a long time that I thought to ask him if he were on a job or purely social visit. He is normally a diplomatic correspondent, political, and if there's a war, a war correspondent. It was clear that the job he's proudest of was the Six Day War. He told me many funny stories about it. The Israelis are a frighteningly pragmatic lot.

Thursday 7th, Yacht[332] [. . .] Sellers and 'Bert' whose other name is Mortimer and Zoe came on board as expected and dined and chatted a lot about Yoga.[333] Peter is surprisingly hard going to me with a strange self deprecation when telling a story – not necessarily about himself – in which he says things like, 'My boat is small, you know, and so I don't bother to have an extension for the telephone into the like this you know the thing where we're sitting now you know the er er salon because my boat well the er bridge is so er er thing you know and when Sam Spiegel came on the yacht he said can you get NY and thing and so on and how quick are you getting through to thing and thing . . .' and so on. Oddly irritating and smacking of false modesty as if to say I could of course speak with classic syntax and superb vocabulary but you know I could so I take that as read. It is now though a manner which he probably cannot get out of and therefore perfectly natural. I must deep down be a two-faced prude as I've quite gone off Zoe Sallis since she seems to be a lady of fairly easy virtue and is quite obviously having a er thing er you er know with er thing you know. Peter and Bert made a lot of sense about Yoga and we must try and find out more about it from a professional teacher when we get the chance – probably next year in Vallarta. He demonstrated a slow head-stand for us which seems absolutely beyond us both at this stage and possibly at any stage. Must try though.

---

[330] Ivor Novello (1893–1951), composer, actor, singer, whose musicals were renowned for their spectacular aspect.
[331] Robin Stafford, foreign correspondent for the *Daily Express*.
[332] The date is wrong. Thursday was 18 November.
[333] Bert Mortimer was Peter Sellers's valet and driver.

Under Milk Wood came through as something mysteriously else called *Daybreak at Sundown* or something equally funny and we consequently saw no film. [. . .]

Saturday 20th, Rome [. . .] This is our last few hours here in Rome. We leave at midday for Paris and from the airport straight to the clinic where the good doctor will remove a cyst from E's nose and a mole from my cheek. [. . .] After that to the Ritz at which we have never stayed as far as we can remember.[334] Since we have the original diamond as big as the Ritz it will be interesting to see if we can get inside.[335] We shall stay in Paris until Tuesday and then do a run for Gstaad which I'm longing to see.

A late birthday present arrived from Liza. Two books – one called *Roman Mythology* and one called the *Age of Revolution*. The first hard cover and expensive and the second a paperback. I was very moved and went around showing it to everyone. I was absurdly pleased that the return address was – in her own hand – Todd-Burton. The second has a note inside from Liza saying: See page 237. It was an index to Trotsky. I love that child surpassingly.

[. . .] I have put the title of this page in black since E is so anticipatorily anxious about her operation that I decided she should have the occasional drink until the ordeal is over. And yesterday I had a bloody mary and the day before a martini and a couple of glasses of wine.

Am reading for the first time for twenty years or more *A la recherche du temps perdu*. In English. I shall find a paperback French version in Paris and read them side by side. Scott Moncrieff together with the lesser known Gerard Hopkins are the best French translators I've come across.[336] I am enjoying the Proust far more than I remember from the last time – and I think it must have been at Oxford when I ploughed through him before. And 'ploughed through' is the operative word. It was deliberate labour as part of my education and all I can remember is that the only person I knew who had the complete set was Emlyn Williams who said I had to read them in his house as he was not letting them out of his sight. Under those circumstances it is not surprising perhaps that I thought the work pedestrian. They are anything but that as I read them now.

Bob has just brought me a telegram from Tony Richardson asking me to play with Vanessa Redgrave in *Antony and Cleopatra* 'early next year'. I said no. Politely. That man must have the thickest skin in and out of Christendom. This is his 2nd offer to me this year – the other being to do the film of *I, Claudius*.[337] After our bitter debacle about Nabokov's *Laughter in the Dark* one

---

[334] Ritz Hotel, Place Vendôme, Paris.
[335] A reference to *The Diamond as Big as the Ritz* (1922) by F. Scott Fitzgerald (1896–1940).
[336] Charles Kenneth Scott Moncrieff (1889–1930), translator of Proust. Gerard Hopkins, translator.
[337] Robert Graves, (1895–1985) *I, Claudius* (1934).

would think that he would be scared witless to approach me to play Scrabble.[338] But not our Tony. It's almost admirable. The fact that I was right about *Laughter* and he was shown to be catastrophically wrong should have made him even more shy in approaching me for anything else ever again as my attitude to him in any future co-labour would be savagely contemptuous. But ever since he first emerged from the OUDS he has shown total and ruthless selfishness in everything he has ever done. I know of no one who confesses either admiration or affection for him. Everyone is convinced that his good films have been accidents and that his bad ones are a just reflection of his abysmal talent. The cutter saved *Tom Jones*, they say while Ossie Morris and the continuity girl directed *Anger*.[339] He is slightly better than that. Totally unworthy of anyone's serious consideration, however, I would say. Certainly mine. [. . .]

Sunday 21st, Ritz Hotel, Paris[340] [. . .] E looks as if she's had a long gruelling 15 rounds with Clay while I simply have a bandage on my face which makes me look as if I have a huge wound when in actual fact – apart from the stitch there is nothing except a little hole to see. [. . .] We dined off 'Haddock poche a l'Anglaise et des pommes nature' and delicious it was.

Monday 22nd[341] [. . .] For the third time in my life I began to learn Spanish yesterday. Third time lucky I hope. It means wiping Italian out of my mind. No easy task. I am doing a grammar which is differently pronounced from Mexican but I can transfer the noises as I go along. I shall have every opportunity to use it at the new place in Bucerias and this time I shall do sternly what I do with the other tongues – which is to read a newspaper a day. Painful at first it soon becomes fluent.

There has been increasing pressure on me of late to play the last days of Mussolini and there are three different firms vying with each other. One neo-fascisti lot are after me and another lot Shaftel are running after me and Marlon while a third are trying for George Scott.[342] Soldati is writing one for me, he says, with Elizabeth for Clara Petacci.[343] Presumably nothing will come out of my participation. Tito, Trotsky and Mussolini would be a bit much in one year I guess. It would certainly be foolish to have three different Mussolinis come out together. The comparisons would give those covetous critics a field day.

I am going through one of my non-fiction reading moods again and apart from the always with me *Fleurs du Mal* I have nothing but fiction to read.

---

[338] The film project *Laughter in the Dark* from which Richardson had sacked Burton.
[339] *Tom Jones* (1963), which was edited by Antony Gibbs (1925—).
[340] Heading in red type.
[341] Heading in red type.
[342] Josef Shaftel (1919–96), director.
[343] Mario Soldati (1906–99), director, was writing the screenplay for the film on Mussolini.

Today, if E thinks my face good enough I shall dive across to W. H. Smith's and do one of my raids. There may be something downstairs in the foyer of this hotel. This is the first time I've ever stayed here so I know little about it. E too. So far I find it better than the Plaza Athenée and the Lancaster. The service is swift and the food, so far, of a good standard. I shall order me another cuppa immediately.

A letter was given us when we arrived from Hebe Dorsey who is an Arab French lady we have known for some time and who writes fashion columns for the *Herald Trib* here and 'fashionable' articles for many magazines about Princess Grace and Jackie Onassis and E and a few others. The letter complains of non-payments from a firm called Forum which is Gianni Bozzacchi's. She complains of non payments. She appeals to us as mutual friends to sort it out. Now, dear lady, what can I do?

[...] I have decided that Sunday Papers must arrive fairly early in the morning to be properly accorded the title – Sunday Papers. When they arrive, as they did yesterday, in the afternoon, they lose their status and are simply newspapers. One should read nothing but the Sundays on Sunday. The day is lost if one has started reading all manner of other things before they've arrived. The only Sundayish thing about yesterday's Sunday was that I turned on the hotel, in-built radio and found the BBC and a terrible voice saying: 'It is no use saying to one's conscience "go away you silly person, I have no wish to listen to you" because you are saying in effect "go away God, you are too awkward a customer and make too many demands on me."' For God's sake, said E, turn that bloody thing off. And so I did. It's hard to believe that such drivel is still being pumped out by the mile all over the country. The message is banal enough but the language it's clothed in is unspeakably arch, knowing and coy and stupendously vulgar. [...]

Tuesday 23rd[344] [...] Kurt (Stormtrooper) Frings came in about 6 and we discussed the script which I'd read in the afternoon. It's rubbish but it's something I've never done which is a 'horror film' and which the kids have been anxious for one or the other of us to do for many years. I play Bluebeard, a German or mittel-European Count or Marchese or something complete with Ruritanian or perhaps Transylvanian would be better castle. Booted and spurred and tails-clothed and impotent and kill eight wives – all of great beauty – the moment they expect me to go bed with them. There is a great deal of horror though everywhere. Can't make up my mind whether I should do it or not. Any road, if they wish to do it in January as they say they do, I must decline. Its other attraction is that they shoot in Hungary, to which country I've never been, and I could do with a little lightness after Tit and Trot. Am

---

[344] Heading in red type.

supposed to have lunch at Fouquet's with the director – one called Dmytryk who – I've only just discovered this morning – I've been confusing for years with a man called Siodmak.[345] Both have their similarities in that they started off well and then tapered off into the usual mediocrity.

I ambled through my Spanish lessons both in the morning and late at night – both of those times being the best possible time for me to learn things as I discovered in my examination-riddled childhood and youth. I should be able to read newspapers in about a month though probably the best thing to do would be to get hold of one of those Penguin dual language books which save you a hell of a lot of dictionary work. I love the latter so much that they are dangerous for me to use if I am really 'working' as I cannot resist scanning the page for another interesting word which may be lying around. This kills the pace. I shall go to Smith's after lunch perhaps and search me around. While I'm at it I might as well get a stock of holiday reading for Gstaad. [. . .]

Dirty Brian Hutton also popped in with Oscar Mayer bacon from the States. [. . .] He has brought a script for E by a man called Gibson – a better than average playwright who has written a couple of successful pieces or more the only one of which I can remember being *Two for the Seesaw* – called *A Cry of Players*.[346] I'm sure it was first written as a play and was sent to me 15 years ago perhaps with a view to my playing William Shakespeare and is indeed a play about Shakespeare and Anne Hathaway. Will and Anne. It has obviously been rewritten with modern 'permissiveness' in mind for E tells me that some of the dialogue is somewhat blue. I shall read this morn after my Spanish. Now, he sobbed, I am too old.

Frings wants to represent E again and me too now. We said he can go ahead with *Bluebeard* and *Under the Volcano* – the latter of particular import if there is a reasonable script.[347] The latter would be a good velocipede for us both. If well adapted, acted and directed, it could be a film of major interest – even perhaps as good as Lowry's novel which is a massive piece of work and, as I discovered when reading it again this year, ages magnificently. It needs a very fine director. [. . .]

Thursday 25th A pleasant enough day. I read E's script by W. W. Gibson.[348] It is the one I was sent 15 years ago and it is still not worth E's attention as it wasn't mine then. We went to lunch at the grill here in the hotel called L'Espadon which is a cosy little restaurant and the food is very good. We had a superb Coquille St Jaques to start which almost spoiled the equally splendid steak au poivre which followed. We had forgotten the joys of people-watching

[345] Edward Dmytryk (1908–99) would direct *Bluebeard*. Robert Siodmak (1900–73), director.
[346] William Gibson (1914–2008), *Two for the Seesaw* (1958). *A Cry of Players* (1968).
[347] Malcolm Lowry (1909–57), *Under the Volcano* (1947).
[348] Burton is confusing William Gibson with Wilfrid Wilson Gibson (1878–1962), the poet.

since we've been out so seldom. It is not easy to be a personality-watcher actually if you yourselves are so intently watched but there are some good things to be seen before you go to Paradise by way of Kensal Green.[349] There was a nervous high-pitched English, frightfully English lady of a certain age who talked out of nerves at the top of her voice. Unfortunately we were, I mean she was alone so we didn't hear as much as we should. She was placed in the middle of the room, having come in after us. After a time the waiter suggested that she should change her table to one against the window. She greeted this suggestion with a high pitched almost breathless enthusiasm – 'What a good idea, most frightfully thoughtful of you, my nerves were beginning to shriek, positively shriek, there in the midst of everybody and I did send a telex from London reserving my table. It's awfully good of you and frightfully intelligent. I shall enjoy myself so much more here. You are so terribly kind and I did send a telex all the way from London.' Why had she sent a telex to reserve a table in a not very popular and therefore hardly likely to be full restaurant. Why indeed had she flown from London to have lunch alone in L'Espadon, The Swordfish, in the Ritz Hotel Paris. She was about my age, brunette, with an aquiline nose that might have been Jewish but I don't think she was a Hebrew, and she used a lorgnette to study the menu. She was expensively but quietly dressed and was unquestionably a lady. E guessed she was a writer, and I agree that she looked very like all those unattractive lady-writers whose photos one sees on the backs of Penguins. Not unattractive exactly but one guesses at the unused flesh, the untidy bathing, the *Times* Crossword, and shrill conversations on the telephone and literary luncheons and all angularly sharp and feminist. Ugh somehow. There was another woman, American we guessed, with a ferocious face-lift, hard and predatory, vulpine and totally ignoring her husband staring, staring staring at E with malevolence, meanness, and murderous, envious hatred. E said that the loathing was so intense that it was tangible. She would have felt it, E went on, even were her back turned. Then there was a comic turn which E couldn't really see. A party of six came in dominated by a tall, dew-lapped loud-mouthed 60 year old central European speaking perfect and idiomatic English and French with a barely noticeable accent who said something like 'I guess we'll have one woman there and a guy there and another woman there and you Phil go there and that should about do it.' One of the women, a girl actually, writhed and suiggled and manoeuvred herself desperately towards a chair where she would be breathtakingly close to a profile shot of my fabled E. But there was another woman, ruthlessly middle-aged, very American, who stolidly held her ground. So at the next table were these two women, one in the awful position of being able to lust her eyes on E's profile but in doing so would look me straight in the eyes, while the other tried to

---

[349] A reference to the last line of the 1913 poem 'The Rolling English Road' by G. K. Chesterton (1874 1936).

turn into rubber to get fugitive glimpses at the back of E's head. Each time they managed either, they were faced with a knowing half-smile from me. At about this time, the Basilisk with the ignored and indifferent husband, one of the tight skull and the vicious envy left her husband calculating the pourboire and walked very deliberately and with no attempt at dissembling, straight across the room and turned the full glare of her gorgon gaze on Elizabeth. She left expressionlessly, her impassivity only matched by Elizabeth's.

[. . .] I am on my fifth Spanish lesson as well as listening to discs from the Assimil method.

Friday 26th, Ritz It was Thanksgiving Day yesterday and, foreign as I am, I eat turkey and giblet gravy and sweet corn and yams but not cranberry sauce. Delicious. Much debate as to whether the Americas had any original food. They argued that turkey, potatoes corn and cranberries were indigenous to the States and unknown in Europe. I agree with potato and corn but disagreed with turkey and cranberries. Must look it up at home. I seem to remember that 'cranberry' is originally Greek. My new *Oxford* will tell me all – and the *Britannica*. Brian Hutton and his girlfriend Tamara something came to dinner with us. Nice girl and surprisingly unflashy and that rare thing to me – a native Californian. I know only one other and that's Val Douglas. Ah yes, Budd Schulberg too but I don't count him as he has lived away from there so long.[350] Tamara who inevitably in this literate family creeps in with petty pace from day to day is that thoroughly nice thing – a well-educated clean looking intelligent middle-class girl finished educationally in Paris.[351] Almost old-fashioned. I would have thought that Brian would have more sultry ladies around, more obviously sexy and faintly dirty looking. I suspect though that underneath his talk of pot and 'taking trips' etc. that he is as square as a board. He says that the teaching system in his school in NY was so abominable that he was more or less illiterate until he was about 17 and didn't read his first book until he was 18. For somebody of his obvious intelligence it seems incredible to me. By that age I'd read and sometimes learned by heart half the world's classics. Perhaps he exaggerates a bit but he also averred that he was given an IQ test when he was about 15 and got a score of 5 points below 'Moron'. That I find hard to believe too. He may be over-compensating for slightly below average marks in exams by pretending he was an idiot. He failed to get his first job because he could not spell the opening words of an application 'To whom it may concern'. He got through 'whom' all right but couldn't be certain of 'may'. Was it 'mae' like Mae West or 'may' like the month or was it sneaky and neither of those but 'mai'. He gave up and left. [. . .]

---

[350] Budd Schulberg (1914–2009), writer, producer. He was actually born in New York.
[351] A reference to the line spoken by Macbeth in *Macbeth*, Act V, scene v: 'Creeps in this petty pace from day to day / To the last syllable of recorded time.'

I drank several glasses of nouveau Beaujolais last night at the Thanksgiving and though it seems innocuous it is not. I feel ghastly this morning despite tea and toast and copious swallows of coffee. Just had the bill from the hotel – $3000 approx. Staggering for just less than a week. They put up a buffet in Gianni's room for all the visiting couturiers and Van Cleef's and Alexandre etc. and it cost $500! Granted there were about 15 or 20 people but how could they eat and drink $500 worth of viands and vins especially when you think they barely had time to eat at all. Daylight bleeding robbery!

I wouldn't have had E's day yesterday for anything. She spent the entire day being dressed in what seems countless dresses and innumerable hair-dos. She looks dishy though and I pity those other poor bastards like Marie Helene. The latter is, if you please flying in Di Rossi from Italy (Rome) to do her make-up.[352] Nothing can help druan Rothschild – dim ond yr arglwydd.[353] A hopeless task.

E infuriatingly as bright as a button and aglow with youthful joie de vivre. I am tempted to kick her in the teeth. And so to Gstaad.

Saturday 27th, Gstaad The journey by Trans Europe Express was lovely. [. . .] We took some wine and, rare for me, a whiskey. We had a second half bottle in our seats. The various TEEs must be the most successful trains in the world – I have never seen an empty seat. But nevertheless, whether by train or plane, unless the helicopter is available, the last two hours or so depending on whether we car it from Geneva or Lausanne is tedious beyond words. By the time we'd arrived we had begun to get edgy with each other and by bedtime a flaming and quite childish row was in high dudgeon. Twice, I stormed off to the alternate bedroom. Twice I went back. All manner of little things were exacerbating our natural weariness. [. . .] The shutter to my room, the dreamt-of library was broken and therefore the room is in darkness and one of the things I looked forward to was seeing the library the next (this) morning with the sun striking along the edge of the garden beyond. [. . .] I'm writing this very slowly as I find myself so bewitched by the mountains and the brilliant sun on the virgin snow that I can't tear my eyes away from it. [. . .]

A bunch of letters (copies) from Aaron via Jane in Rome. One talks of a Mr Charles who, according to the biography of me now out, tried with the connivance of the rest of the village of Pontrhydyfen to 'soak me for £5000' for the purchase of 2, Danybont – the house where I was born and spent my happiest hours. The entire village and Mr Charles are furious and no wonder. I must do something about it.[354] But what. A letter to the *Guardian* and the

---

[352] Possibly by Di Rossi Burton means Grazia De Rossi, the hair stylist who had worked on the *Taming of the Shrew*.

[353] *Druan* is 'poor' in Welsh. *Dim ond yr arglwydd* is 'only the lord'.

[354] This appears to refer to the passage on p. 350 of Cottrell and Cashin's biography in which they write of Dan-y-bont coming on to the market.

Gazette?[355] A letter to the village? A letter to Mr Charles? Since I had nothing
to do with the attempted purchase of the house – Graham's big mouth at work
again I expect – it puts me in a funny position. I'd better do something. A
letter to Hilda would probably be the best way of letting everybody know in
Ponty, but apologies like Justice must not only be made but be seen to be made.
I could kill those two stupid failures who wrote the book. The only thing I
asked them to do was to make sure that nobody in the book was to be hurt by
it except myself. Bloody clowns of hell. [. . .]

Sunday 28th, Gstaad [. . .] It is very bright this morning but not the brilliant
sun of yesterday as expected. I sat and read in the sun yesterday wearing only
a light sweater for over an hour and was as warm as on a summer's day. The
sun must be pretty far away however as I only picked up a little colour whereas
in a hot sun one hour would turn me into a Mohican. I shall try the sun-lamp.
About my only vanity is to be tanned – on the face and upper body if possible.
For some reason it makes me <u>feel</u> better and healthier. If someone could or
would invent a really practical sunlamp I would use it summer and winter
rather than submit to the boredom of sun-worshipping. [. . .] Did not do my
espanol yesterday. Start again today.

Monday 29th [. . .] I had difficulty sleeping last night so – not to disturb E who
was quickly asleep – I slipped out to the kitchen made myself a sandwich of
ham and cheese and a cup of tea, then reading a book of John D. MacDonald's
I went into the other room and desserted on Rowntree's Pastilles, one and a
half packets no less and a packet of some other Swiss fruit pastilles. Result is
that on one scale I am 70 and the other 69. A long time since I was that weight
so will knock off a few pounds in the coming days. That means for me, strict
Drinking Man's Diet without the drink. I have been giving myself black titles
for too long a time anyway. I have got back into the habit of a drink before
lunch and dinner. So full stop again. Also I want to have my wits about me for
the Proust Ball for there will be fine things to see and a lot to be heard and I
want to see and listen and not be seen and listened to.

E and I are in the library which should always be the morning place as it
gives our old maid – I don't mean that she's not married, I mean that she's old
and a maid – Celina a chance to really 'do' the living room which she shows a
curious reluctance to do when we are about. Actually as to a question of
age – she is probably no more than about 50 but like most working-class Swiss
women seems much older. She is certainly as strong as an ox. She surprised me
yesterday when having asked where the two girls – Maria and Inge were – I
replied that they had gone first to church and then to school. To Church she

---

[355] The *Port Talbot Guardian* and *Glamorgan Gazette* newspapers.

said with great surprise and then 'ah but then all you Catholics have different hours from us Protestants.' What on earth supposed her to think we are Catholic? We have E – Jewish, Liza – nothing but Jewish by birth and C of E by school, Maria – wherever the school takes her which I believe is Protestant, Michael – nothing but a sort of Jesus lover mixed very woollily with anybody currently fashionable among his age-group like Hesse Tolkien and that huge idiot Alistair Crowley, Chris – non-committal but probably nothing.[356] Me – nothing. [...]

The devil over my shoulder, E, is trying to press me to have a martini before lunch because she wants one and doesn't like drinking alone. I'm dickering with the idea but think I will have one this evening if at all. As I've explained to E ad nauseam I find one drink simply not enough. I guess two or three stiff ones are what I'd find satisfactory but that means slowly reverting to being a drunkard again and I simply will not tolerate a return to that. [...]

Tuesday 30th[357] Raymond has arrived from London to sort out the chaos in the clothes dept. He has been a very ill man for a long time with absolutely crippling sciatica. After trying endless doctors of every nationality including Yugos, Italians, British, Yanks, French, Swiss and indeed every nationality in the various places we've been in the last few years he allowed himself at our continual insistence to submit, if necessary to surgery. He was very frightened as indeed why shouldn't he be – he is 52 and not brave anyway – but went through it. To our and his delight he didn't have to have surgery but last Friday he went to a hospital [...]. By, he gathers, using enormous pressures and bending his uncomplaining body hither, thither and yon they had forced the offending bone – whatever it was – smartly back into place. The acute, almost unbearable pain had gone and nothing remains but a mild ache in his left leg. The relief apparently enormous. Several times to me in the past few weeks he had thought of suicide if the horror persisted. Since he is a sprightly sort of feller normally with all the gaiety of the race this must have been pain indeed.

By his race I mean of course not his Italian-Swiss-French-German blood but the night-club dressed-up-to-the-tens-in-tight-tight-I-<u>will</u>-go-to-the-ball clothes and camping around with every conceivable signal of blatant homosexuality. [...]

Searching desperately, well not desperately but continually, for a book to write that would not be autobiographical, at least not overtly, I have come upon an excuse. I have been much impressed by a Jugoslav 'novel' called *The Bridge on the Drina* which I think I must have mentioned before in this haphazard daily exercise. For it is not a novel at all but a series of semi-legendary stories purporting to take place in and around the bridge. By this

---

[356] J. R. R. Tolkien (1892–1973), novelist, literary critic.
[357] Heading in red type.

means the author gives one a saga of the many invasions and changes of family and fortune, in small, of the entire south South Slavs of Jugoslavia. I thought of our pearl the famous or infamous Peregrina, and its extraordinary history.[358] Found by a slave in the sixteenth century or perhaps even the late fifteenth it was part of an argosy that took it to the Court of Spain. The slave who found it was given his freedom. Who was the slave? Are there any traceable descendants? Were the sons of slaves free too? Where were my ancestors at the time? Where were Elizabeth's? The tracing of the pearl's history will be complicated but much easier I would think but I shall have to imagine my and E's ancestors, unless E's mother's story that she is descended from Mary, Queen of Scots could be substantiated![359] That would be a great coup for the book. The thing would of course take years to write and would demand a great deal of specialized reading and almost certainly the employment of searchers, I believe they call them. It has been done before. There was a rather good film on the subject I remember – the object being a tail-coat. But the Pearl involved famous dynasties and is authentic history in itself. I could elaborate on my cynical-comical views of mankind and a small page or two of its history. The whole and vast personal question is do I have the intellectual stamina to sustain such a big undertaking and is my writing good enough? I shall need to be fairly near a great library which means Oxford or London. Not all the time but from time to frequent time at least. I think the first person to consult would be Nevill Coghill who would introduce me to the methods of scholarship, what sort of people to employ and consult. Now I will sleep on it for 6 months until we get to England again. [. . .]

DECEMBER

Wednesday 1st, Gstaad[360] A cold, very cold morning, with the sun just coming round the corner and I have just lighted the fire in the library and put the kettle on and the dogs E'en So and Daisy Mae are having a mock fight having been in the snow and all would be idyllic were it not for the fact that at 2pm we fly to Paris to the Ritz and tomorrow to the Rothschilds. The latter part is ok. It is simply the fact of disturbing the serenity of this place and being able to do what ever one wants without care to be social and having everything to hand. Still and however when we come back next Monday short of a death in the family which is, with Ivor and E's mother so perilously balanced between life and death, not at all unlikely, we should be here without interruption until the middle of January when it's Jugoslavia again. Also, yesterday, I took the

---

[358] Burton had bought the Peregrina pearl for Taylor in January 1969 at a cost of $37,000.
[359] Mary, Queen of Scots (1542–87), Queen of Scotland 1542–67, mother of James VI of Scotland and I of England.
[360] Heading in red type.

decision to do *Bluebeard*. I said I could do it in Feb–March-bit of April but that after that it would take too much chopping and changing for all concerned. They said they were prepared to shoot 'anywhere I want but preferably Hungary and next to that Spain and that I could make any changes I liked!' Well, well, I thought this is the lot who were so adamant that it must be shot in January. I said I thought Hungary would be the favourite as neither E nor I had ever been there but that we loved Spain too. I am to see Frings tomorrow morning. What I really must get after is *Under the Volcano*. That, if any film can be considered so, is an important piece.

Yves le Tourneur who is a salesman for Van Cleef and Arpel and 'covers' Switz, came from Geneva where he lives and mostly works bringing with him about $3m of gems. E had changed a gold belt she had bought from them – or I had rather when she was doing *XYZ* and he had come up with the new belt-cum-neck-lace in exchange. With us of course, and probably with everybody, he brought as I said an extra two or three millions in temptations. I was not to be drawn however except for a pair of matching earrings for the already bought necklace which E had been 'loaned' for some time and was naturally (sarcastically) attached to. That, by the way, is a good play of such people as Yves le Tourneur. They let you have a splendid but not overwhelmingly expensive piece on loan, or for a specific occasion, an opening night or the Rothschild party for instance, and hope that the wearer or the spectator, me, decides to buy it what the hell. The necklace and earrings are a perfect example since I bought the earrings. They cost about $6,000. [. . .]

Thursday 2nd, Ritz[361] We left the chalet at 1pm and were in Paris at 2.45pm. [. . .] Gianni and two Cadillacs were waiting and we were away to the Ritz. The radios and TVs told us or rather told them, Parisians I mean, that Le Grand Bal, le Bal du Siecle would be graced with unaccountable wealth and that there would be 500 guards around the house and la Reine elle-meme Elizabeth Taylor was apporting $3m from the neck up. True too, but who told them so exactly, they described the exact placing of all the nonsense. Van Cleef? Valentino? Alexandre? We arrived at the Ritz to find the place absolutely surrounded by large black bumper-to-bumper cars and found a hurly-burly reception on inside for the Republic of Congo and a great many black sleek gentlemen in diplomats' uniform, both the latter and the former as black as your hat in a coal-pit. And bowing and scraping and midst a brouhaha of c'est Liz Taylor et son mari Burton we entered the lift and ran up to the 3rd floor and found ourselves in a penthouse suite though the lift numbers definitely stated there was a 4th floor and therefore, having got off on the third and not having gone up a lot of stairs, how was it possible to be in the penthouse. The

---

[361] Heading in red type.

hotel is built oddly that's why. Some bits of it have 3 floors and some four. Carl Ritz who built it and whose son – very old I suppose – still lives here wanted to build a home from home for Gentlemen and obviously didn't have Conrad Hilton in mind as the corridors run in Euclidean nightmares and Pythagoras metempsychosis. This form would be turned into a brutish conglomeration of filled in erector set by a boy with a tidy mind and no imagination.[362] The suite was sweet and much prettier than the one we had last time and this one even includes a grand piano which I bet needs tuning though I haven't played it yet but will and E has just awoken and invaded the salon where I am typing this which is one reason why the other suite is more practical as I had a room between where I typed and where Elizabeth slept. But there, we are only here for one night this time, but if we stayed here a lot, I mean for a long time – as when making a fillum – I would ask for the room next door the other direction from the living room. That would stop my typing waking E too early and also give us a second bathroom. Very desirable this latter as after a day or two E reduces any bathroom to chaos. She carries around with her a cornucopian 'make-up' case that Malthea and Jupiter might have envied.[363] It measures a foot high to a foot wide to a foot and a few inches long I would guess and is 'hard'. That is to say it is not one of those bags that are soft-sided and topped and zipped but is solid and rigid and yet seems to contain endless things – eyebrow pencils, pens, the usual make-up things and deodorants and perfumes and what seems to be pills for any disease and malaises and balms and elixirs and you name it and that box contains it. It may even contain spare parts for the Rolls. Anyway the point is that after a day or two they gradually over-flow the bathroom like lava and there is no room for my pathetic collection of toothpaste and two brushes and deodorant and after-shave and razor and comb.

We established our corners, which means the small guest bedroom for me and my books and clothes, ordered tea and settled down to my Spanish Grammar which I am finding a bit of a bugger as I mix it up continually with Italian. Esta Questa Esto Questo. [. . .] E paraded in and out showing me the diamond headdress which she will wear tonight. Even my tasteless eye thought it superb. It was made especially for E by Van Cleef and Arpels and actually does cost well over £1m. Not dollars, POUNDS. Damned if I won't buy it one of these far-off days. It will always be a staggering sight and the knowledge of its cost adds to its beauty regardless of such Philistinism.

There were many telephone conversations twixt E and Marie Hélène and E and Grace who says that Rainier is going shooting and not at Ferrières and feels too shy to go alone to house Ferrières so would Elizabeth, asked

---

[362] César Ritz (1850–1918) built the Ritz Hotels in Paris and London. His son Charles C. Ritz (1891–1976) was President of the Ritz Chain from 1953 to 1976.
[363] Malthea is the name of the nymph who nursed the infant Jupiter.

Marie-Hélène, call Grace and ask her to come down with us and we still don't
know whether Rainier doesn't want to go to the do and Grace does but won't
go without him or whether Grace is uncertain of the protocol in case Mags
shows up and Marie-Hélène said rather frantically at one point to E 'you
simply must make her come, I mean I've even got a chair for her' which meant
that she (Grace) was to sit on Guy's right.[364] And my E told M-H that if she
(M-H) put E with a bunch of non-English-speaking idiots she (E) would never
speak to MH ever again. Grace said she would call E back before 11pm and tell
her what but she didn't and E, by this time fed up to the eyebrows being MH's
soc. sec'y said to hell with it and why didn't I (me) call up Grace and talk her
into coming. Why me? But I suppose I shall have to have a go. I just asked
where Grace was staying and to my astonishment they told me she was staying
at the Embassy. What Embassy asks I? The Monaco one. The Monaco one!
Anyway I just called and asked for Son Altesse but she is on the blower so the
lady said. She may decide to be 'occupie' all day. Fact is, I don't think either of
them, Rainier or Grace, feel too happy outside their realm as they can never
be sure how they are going to be treated, both of them terrified of being
comic-opera. Niven, all of whose stories have to be heard with suspicion and
delightfully so, says that once on the Côte d'Azur in some restaurant or other
a waiter didn't appear to have the proper deference and even though they
were supposedly incognito Rainier became extremely violent. I've forgotten in
what or which way but really nasty-violent.

   About 7 late night we suddenly realized that we had not eaten all day and
were mad with hunger so food was procured. [. . .] After which we watched
Inter-Milan play a German team in the quarter-finals of the European Cup.[365]
A nasty ill-tempered little match. Soccer seems to me a very boring spectacle
unless you see a genius at his best or you are desperate for one side to win. In
this case I couldn't have cared less about either team though the Germans
blond and clean looking looked nicer than the Eyeties, squat and hairy and
dark and thick thighed like pocket Welsh front-row forwards. And the incessant writhing about on the ground after every tackle, foul or fair, is stupefying
in its monotony. To my relief I have just heard that Grace _is_ coming and is
coming with us. So that's that. Phew! as they say in the comics. And it is
comical.

Friday 3rd – Saturday 4th, Ferrières[366] So the Ball was had. It was had until
7am when the music at last stopped and the do-or-die-ers crawled into their
cars and lumbered off with early morning traffic to Paris. We had come up

---

[364] Mags: possibly means majesties.
[365] Inter-Milan drew 0–0 with Borussia Mönchengladbach in the second leg of the quarter-final (played
in West Berlin) on 1 December 1971.
[366] Heading in red type.

from the party about 4.30am but, after packing away the 'big' jewellery and putting it in the house coffre, we sat and chatted desultorily away until the orchestra stopped at 7. I managed, though I was sorely tempted during dinner, not to have the mildest form of alcohol so despite only about 4 hours' sleep I feel as bright as a button. We have just had tea, as indeed we did at 5 this morn also. It is 1.15.

We picked up Grace at 32, Avenue Foche which doesn't seem to be the Embassy and I forgot to ask Son Altesse if it was or not. A very amiable Rainier brought Grace to the gate carrying her two small bags – a considerable difference from son altesse ETB even despite the fact that Grace was not staying the night. [. . .] Grace and E chatted away at the back of the car while I sat in front beside the driver. Grace was nice and relaxed and, after the initial awkwardness which I always feel with people like Grace who are in a somewhat false position and know it, everybody talked freely. Grace went into a blow by blow description of the Shah of Iran's famous or infamous party.[367] Grace defended its extravagance with extraordinary obtuseness though neither of us attacked it. It was meant, she said, as a tribute to the people of Persia and as self-advertisement for the Shah's magnificent governing which was bringing literacy to the illiterate and hygiene to the unwashed and culture to the brutish. She described the Shah as a marvellous man and once called him a great man which is going a titch too far. She said how monstrous it was of the Western Press to be so vulgarly cynical of the whole show, all of them she said she knew for a fact writing their stuff before the thing had really got going. E was sweet and said that yes I mean Tito and the Hungarians and other communist countries were there and didn't seem to be particularly put out by the obvious 'capitalism' of the whole thing. Absolutely said Grace and said it was a marvellous thing to see people of such enormous disparity in religions politics and races finally warming to each other after the birth-pangs of meeting and how a little chinaman who was stiff and unsmiling and reserved and talked only through an interpreter was by the last day chatting a mile a minute radiant with smiles in impeccable English to all and sundry. So there. It all goes to show that we are brothers under the skin. And why for heaven's sake doesn't the Western Press attack its own spending of zillions a year on advertisements, corrupting the minds of the young and the stupid with their idiotics. And so on. One didn't suggest that it might perhaps have been more helpful to his appallingly poor people if he had promoted a sort of World's Fair, an Expo 71 or something and have the other people pay for the advertising. The 'do' of the Shah's was supremely silly under any circumstances and if it was to celebrate the extraordinary advances made for the benefit of his people then it was inane to the point of simple-mindedness.

---

[367] The Shah of Iran (1919–80) had thrown a party in October 1971 to celebrate the 2,500th anniversary of the founding of the Persian Empire. It was estimated to have cost $100m.

Enough of the car journey. As we approached the last few miles to Ferrières there were policemen, mostly motorbiked every few hundred yards and learned later that Guy had arranged for a policeman or van every ½ mile from Paris. All the way from Paris!

Now President Pompidou used to be employed by Guy de Rothschild before and after he became Prime Minister and the new Prime Minister was also to be here last night but was unable to come and rang M-H this afternoon while we were there to apologize not only to M-H for not being able to come and telling the reason why but also asked the names of his two side by side companions in order to apologize to them too. Toujours la politesse. So it is no wonder that Guy can commandeer the entire Parisian Police force if he so wishes. As we turned into the drive the entire house faced us and for the first time since we've been coming here was lighted up. It looked magnificent and were it the clop-clop of horses and the smell of saddle leather and blankets round the knees and not the low hum of a heated Cadillac we could have been back a hundred years. The main entrance however was only for the herd – we entered by the side door as we usually do and went straight up to our rooms having some difficulty in finding out where was which and who was where. Sorted out finally we found ourselves in the Chambre Rose while Grace used the Chambres Balcon to change in and do her hair. We are changing from our chambre to the Balcon tonight while at dinner. The Rose while very nice and suitably rosy with all the decoration à la Wedgwood, panelling and all, has an outside bathroom which though exclusively for our use meant having to put on a dressing gown, if you happen to be in shorts in case of running into M. Olivier who lived next door and shared our little hallway. Also, to our surprise, we could hear everything in the two adjacent rooms quite clearly, it therefore following that everybody could hear us. So it will be nice to gossip at normal voice.

I sat around and waited for the girls to be ready – my girls including the Duchess of Windsor and The Princess of Monaco and of course my very own 'girl'. Grace was ready and waiting about 10 minutes before time and came to our room for a drink. E would have been ready but Alexandre, the hairdresser, took forever to arrive and longer to do M-H's hair-do. We had been told that we were to descend strictly at 9.10 and sit down to dinner at 9.30. We descended at 10.30 and sat down at 11pm. The great hall had been made into a dining room for the occasion and was impossible before we began. It took me 15 minutes to get to my table from the door – I timed it – and after having trod on endless trains and knocked aside several expensive coiffures, virtually climbing over half a dozen people, I found myself at table no 11 with madam de Montesquieu on my left and the former Mme Louis Malle on my right both of whom, thank God, I knew.[368] Now for an hour or more of absolute agony.

---

[368] Madame Louis Malle was Anne-Marie Deschodt who until 1967 had been married to the director Louis Malle (1932–95).

The waiters simply had no way of being able to get round the tables so most tables including ours elected one person to receive all the services and pass them on from hand to hand. The food was divine, or perhaps I was so hungry that it seemed better than it was, and I made an arrangement with Mme Malle who is a very beautiful but giant of a woman for her to pass me all her refills of water while I passed her all my wines. She must have a powerful head for she must have had well over a dozen glasses of various wines – champagne, a white wine, the inevitable Lafitte and a second white wine which I guessed from its viscousness was Chateau d'Yquem and it was. My attention was however riveted from the first by a man sitting opposite me.[369] He looked like a cadaver when still and a failure of plastic surgery when he moved which was seldom. He was eyebrow-less and eyelash-less and atrociously wigged or dyed with snow white hair at the front of his head and to the crown and nondescript brownish, rather like mine, hair at the back. His face was hideously pasted with make-up and had odd lumps on it, a face made of funny putty by an inept child. I had just asked in Mme Malle's ear who was that extraordinary thing over there when he leaned forward and said 'Where's my Elizabeth?' Ah, I said, well now, she is ah, over the other end of this ah sitting and ah eating indeed at the ah corresponding table to this but ah at the ah other end if you know what I mean. I wish she was here, said he, the inference being that far better her than me. So, as a matter of fact, do I, I said with a speed which would have done the Rev Sydney Smith no harm to admire.[370] [. . .]

After the strangely delivered question from Andy Warhol for that is who the horror film gentleman was, we all settled down to the battle of the food. I discussed on my left with Madame de Montesquieu who is indeed descended from the great Charles Louis Secondat, Baron de la Brede et de Montesquieu who wrote L'Esprit des Lois, poetry which all started by her saying that she had been at somebody's house and they had played records of me speaking The Ancient Mariner and how this woman who had given the party and played the record said that she had heard me speak poetry at the Rothschilds' 'and even Guy listened' and that she (the hostess) had gone out and found all the records she could find of me speaking verse.[371] I asked Montesquieu twice who the woman was and twice she told me but I should have written it down as I have forgotten it already, but would like to know who this lady is. Just out of curiosity. It wasn't Lili Rothschild who I know has some of my poetry things. So we talked about French poetry which I told her I was only just beginning to read and enjoy. She was rife with platitudes and has quite clearly inherited

[369] Andy Warhol (1928–87), the artist.
[370] Sydney Smith (1771–1845), clergyman and essayist, whose character Lady Holland in Memoir (1855) states that marriage 'resembles a pair of shears, so joined that they cannot be separated; often moving in opposite directions, yet always punishing anyone who comes between them'.
[371] Montesquieu (1689–1755). De l'Esprit des lois (1748). Burton's reading of Samuel Taylor Coleridge's The Rime of the Ancient Mariner (1798) had appeared on long-playing records in 1955 and 1960.

nothing from the great Baron except his name. She was, is, tall and blonde and retrousse-nosed and about 35. Mme Malle and her sideman were much more amusing and I think that E would like Malle. She, the latter is nicely unhappy, almost desperate I would guess and she and I and the man on her right discussed painting. I said my usual and quite true things about Art, that I didn't understand it at all and derived pleasure only from the occasional picture but that, quite clearly, I was artistically 'tone-deaf'. I said that we had what was by common consent a very fine Van Gogh but that though I was impressed by it I didn't know why it was remarkable and that to me the most impressive thing about it was its estimated value in cash which was enormous. Apart from the written and spoken word – preferably the former – the only other art-form that genuinely could disturb me was music, some cheap some deep. Malle and the man protested that music at its greatest was so much like painting at its greatest that I must try again with painting. I said I would.

Meanwhile at the other table E and Grace were having a marvellous time. The lucky bastards had Guy, the Duchess of Windsor, Maurice Herzog, Jean-Paul Binet and a few others.[372] The star turn according to E and Grace was the Duchess who is perhaps getting slightly ga-ga. She has an enormous feather in her hair which got into everything, the soup, the gravy, the ice-cream, and at every vivacious turn of her head it smacked Guy sharply in the eyes or the mouth and at one time threatened to get stuck in Guy's false moustache which was glued on. She made one bon mot which had Grace in tears. After having got her incredible feather into everything possible she then called in her very penetrating voice, having a desire to write down her tel no for E and me which has changed since they sold their house, Est-ce-que quelle-qu'n qui a une plume?[373] She was most insistent that E and I should see the Duke before we left for Gstaad giving E the feeling that he is probably on his last legs. We are going to dine with them on Monday night. Binet flirted blatantly with E but in the best French manner and they had the same hysteria with the serving of the food – Grace being the hander-over.

After the dinner, Guy asked E if she would help him remove his moustache which was now becoming a bore. They went into a gents lav, or rather a lav for either sex while a servant stood on guard outside. Bettina elected to choose this time to try and get into the same loo not knowing that E and Guy were inside. E had removed the moustache and was cleaning around Guy's mouth when Bettina finally burst past the servant and found them in this situation. It looked for all the world as if E and Guy had been having a necking session and E was now removing the evidence. Bettina was delighted by the whole thing.

---

[372] Maurice Herzog (1919—), Himalayan mountaineer and politician. Jean-Paul Binet (1917–86), eminent cardiovascular surgeon, pioneer of heart surgery, member of the Académie des Sciences and art collector.
[373] 'Est-ce-que quelle-qu'n qui a une plume?' (Has anyone got a feather?) A joke meaning an old style pen.

By this time the rest of the guests, as it were the 'b' list were arriving. They were announced in a stentor voice by a gentleman with a large voice and a large intricately carved staff – I've forgotten what they call those things – with which he pounded the floor and boomed that Madame et Monsieur Harry Dogface to which fascinating information nobody except the people who had just whispered their names to him paid the slightest attention. I squeezed past them followed by Mme Malle and her friend and Elsa Martinelli and somebody else (uninvited) to take them to the lav of our room.[374] E was already in the room repairing her maquillage with Bettina. I sat thankfully and smoked before we went back into the whirlpool below. We both sat for a time with Grace and Ricardo? of Madrid in the normally intimate corner of the first room. Scores, perhaps hundreds of people flocked past on some pretext or other to view E and Grace. I wandered about after a time talking to this one and that including Jaqueline de Ribes, Pierre Salinger and wife, Sam Spiegel and M-H's lovely big brother that we call 'Broken-nose' and occasionally I caught glimpses of E being avidly though covertly gazed at wherever she went.[375] And I congratulated Salinger on the success of his book and how much I'd enjoyed it and that I had read it in one sitting and had he yet sold it for a film and he had – to CBS – and we then talked of the splendid night in LA when Bobby Kennedy and I insulted each other's races bloody Irish v bloody Welsh and the usual Kennedy–Burton quotation match, and Rudi Nureyev and his wickedness and how horrified and struck dumb we all were by Bobby's assassination and how much we all loved him and later I found de Ribes flinging herself flatteringly into my arms socially acting as ever the Grande Dame with lovers and asked her how her love life was and she said she had a fantastic new lover and where was he said I and she looked and couldn't find him and how he had made her feel 18 again and I didn't say that 18 she might feel but 80 she looked, beautiful 80 but 80, and Broken-nose told me that Sam's film *Nicholas and Alexandra* was a slow film and very long but nevertheless very beautiful in it.[376] [. . .]

Have had a lunch, a too-much lunch for me of soup, lamb cutlets and boiled new pots in their jackets and string beans followed by a splendid gateau, and a sit-down. I told a lot of stories about the theatre and about British royalty. And after tisane which I drink here all the time, E and I and a lovely young girl, an English actress called Charlotte something went for a walk around the lake.[377] It was lovely and there were millions of birds chattering in a copse –

---

[374] Elsa Martinelli (1935—), who had played alongside Burton and Taylor in *The V.I.P.s*, and alongside Burton in *Candy*.

[375] Jacqueline de Ribes (1931—), fashion designer. Pierre Salinger (1925–2004), White House Press Secretary to Presidents Kennedy and Johnson. He had published *With Kennedy* (1966).

[376] Nureyev was friendly with the Kennedy family, and was particularly close to Princess Lee Radziwill (1933—), sister of Jacqueline Kennedy Onassis. *Nicholas and Alexandra* (1971), produced by Sam Spiegel, has a running time of 189 minutes.

[377] Charlotte Rampling (1946—), actor.

what kind of birds I have no way of knowing and the walk though pleasant didn't succeed in burning away my dinner.

... many other people told me of Sam's film and all of them reacted in more or less the same way. It is quite clearly an honest but rather dull film.

After a time wandering about Grace asked me to see her upstairs and help her remove her borrowed choker and get her to her car. I suppose it was about 1.30. This I did nearly strangling Grace to death while trying to get the necklace off. For a minute she was in bad trouble as the necklace got twisted up as a result of my inept handling of the clasp as the bloody thing was too tight in the first place and, in fact, I had told her before we went down to the ball that she ought to remove it telling her she didn't need it. However, we finally twisted it around so that she herself could see it in the mirror and finally we released her. Even when off it took considerable strength to unclasp it. So down the stairs we went together. At the bottom, alone, was Sam Spiegel. 'Where are you going you two?' 'For God's sake', said G, 'don't Sam say a word to Elizabeth. She's at the Ball, she's dancing, she's happy, let us go. Richard will let Elizabeth know. It's going to be a shock but ... these things happen.' Etc. For a full ½ minute Sam, because of Grace's normal seriousness and because of her very good piece of acting and my deliberately stricken-with-guilt face, was taken in. We made off. Found Grace's car after a lot of waiting in the piercing cold and she was gone. She was quite the nicest she's ever been and David Rothschild expressed astonishment that she could be so gay.[378] She had always he said been a bit of a dead weight. On the contrary, we said, but she does need a little drawing out. Actually it is the nicest she has been in all the years since we've known her as a Princess. At one moment during the choking choker episode I saw mental front-pages in *France Soir*'s and *News of the World*'s lurid headlines. Famed Actor Strangles Princess in Bedroom at Rothschild Mansion During Grand Ball.

For the rest of the evening we wandered about and ran into Audrey Hepburn and her ludicrously named Italian psychiatrist husband Doctor Dotti who is not very nice I think.[379] We had snaps taken of us by Cecil Beaton who is also not very nice in a different way.[380] Then in another room we had snaps with Audrey Hepburn and M Dotti and Doctor Troques and his wife and after an encounter, very strange, with M-H's sister-in-law Gabby Van Svillen who insisted that she was the Tsarina of All the Russias.[381] Did she, I asked politely feel this because she had in fact some Romanov blood – Mike Romanov blood, I added. No, she said, everybody is someone else and I am the Tsarinevitch. What about you? she said. I want to be a fellow of All Souls,

[378] David Rothschild (1942—).
[379] Andrea Dotti (1938–2007), Hepburn's second husband.
[380] Cecil Beaton (1904–80), photographer.
[381] Gabrielle van Zuylen (1933—), wife of Thierry Van Zuylen van Nijevelt.

I said.[382] A what? she asked and lost interest. I was saved by a man called Valery who is the son of the poet.[383] He was charming and again we discussed poetry. He told me of the time when everybody assured his father that he was a dead certainty to win the Nobel Prize for Literature that year and with what excitement, sitting in the garden, the maid came out in a hurry to say there was a long-distance call from Stockholm for him, he went bounding into the house to hear the great news only to find it was a wrong number. He never did get the Nobel Prize.

Then there was a young man with long blonde curly hair who followed E everywhere struck all of a heap with a mighty passion, dog-like in his adoration, looking a bit I thought like the American Pianist Van Cyburn, slavering at the jowls – of which he had none – in hopeless lust and writing her a note promising to dedicate his next novel to her.[384] His name is Francois-Marie Banier who has already made something of a stir with his second novel which he promised to send me or bring me I can't remember which to the Ritz on Monday.[385] He was engagingly eager and I shall read with interest.

At one moment Marie-Hélène came up to me at the bar where I was talking to Salinger's wife about Tours and the surrounding country which I love and blind as a bat as she looked me straight in the face at a distance of 1½ feet and said 'Where's Richard? There's a woman who's dying to meet him.' 'It is I, Hamlet, the Dane,' said I whereupon she screamed a little and went off at a tremendous pace forgetting to take me with her, and I never did meet the woman who was dying to meet me and Marie-Hélène has already forgotten who it was and indeed the entire incident. Salinger's wife asked me if people were always so cruel to Marie-Hélène. Cruel in what way, I asked, puzzled. Oh you know, she said, everybody thinks that she's a tremendous hypochondriac and once she fainted and fell off a chair in a restaurant and everybody carried on eating and talking as if nothing had happened and nobody picked her up. How, I said, extraordinary. Where did this happen? But then we were interrupted by someone and I never heard the details. I must find out next time I see her or Pierre.

Then at an earlier point of the evening that stupendous bore who is married to the sister of Guy's first wife I think came up to us and kissed E's hand with great unction and then Grace's very condescendingly and said – and there is nothing so intimidating – do you remember me, the many times we used to go to Lulatch's house. Who? asked Grace, genuinely puzzled. Lulatch, Lulatch, Lulatch, she loved you more than life, Lulatch, I'm terribly sorry said Grace but I'm sure I would remember that name. Lulatch, Lulatch, Lulatch, he said, she

---

[382] All Souls College, Oxford.
[383] Paul Valéry (1871–1945). He had two sons: Claude and François.
[384] Harvey Lavan 'Van' Cliburn Jr (1934—), pianist.
[385] François-Marie Banier (1947—), author of *Le Passé composé* (1971).

loved you and she died a terrible death eight years ago on the 27th of July but you have forgotten, it doesn't matter, ah if only we were here for 2000 years. Rather than just 1000 I said. Yes Yes Yes and I remember the night you and your superbe wife came to Eli Rothschild's house and we stayed up all night. And you made passes at me, said Elizabeth. And you and your superbe wife argued about poetry and she was right and you were wrong and it was a memorable evening. And you cried about the German Economic Miracle, I said. My god you're right, he said. What a memory. Quelle Memoire extraordinaire. What a memory, what a memory, the German economic miracle. What a memory. We got away from him somehow. A loathsome feller.

Sunday 5th, Ritz[386] Back at last at the Ritz though I could stay forever at Ferrières, and am feeling rather as if we've been on a personal appearance tour for the promotion of a film. This I supposed because one feels when there are a few strangers about, even though perfectly amiable, that something is expected of one and there is a slight suggestion of mildly self-conscious projection of oneself. There was a late lunch today – one of those splendid upper-class English brunches complete with small sausages on plats chauffand and big sausages and eggs labelled 2 minutes or 3 or 4 or 5, boiled of course and haddock poche a l'anglaise though the English could never do them so well and endless varieties of breads and biscuits and toasts (very un-Anglo-Saxon except for the last) and confitures – marmalade, strawberry – and fried bacon and fried bread but in croutons (also non English) and coffee and tea. Alex Rede and a beautiful Eurasian-looking lady was there as well as Etienne (reputedly M-H's lover though he may just be 'a good friend') and the blonde man – Olivier?[387] We talked of poetry again. Possibly because last night after dinner in the cosy corner room they asked me to speak some and I did and E says they were very impressed and talked of it when I left the room to go to the lavatory to pee which I seemed to be doing all evening. They seem, apart from the man called Etienne, to enjoy poetry when it is spoken for them but rarely to search it out themselves. I was a little cautious of speaking even a minute snippet from *Hamlet* with an audience consisting, among others, of two professional actresses – David's girlfriend, Marisa and Marisa's friend Charlotte – but E assured me that they too were held and agog. So that's alright. Also, both E and I are mean customers if there's ever the slightest suggestion of 'singing for our suppers'. Which there never is at the Rothschilds'. They really have – every one of them, including Philip (16) and the other 14 year old one – exquisite manners.[388] We discussed manners as an art in itself the night

---

[386] Word 'Ritz' in red type.
[387] Alexis von Rosenberg, Baron de Redé (1922–2004).
[388] Edouard Etienne de Rothschild (1957—) is Guy de Rothschild's son by his marriage to Marie-Hélène.

before for a time and we all agreed that the man with the most exquisite manners of any person we all of us knew was the Duke of Windsor. It was Guy who put him forward as the claimant. And though I'd never thought of him before as being so superbly well-mannered, I immediately agreed. It is a fact said I that manners are not the result of good breeding or intelligence for we know many well born and highly intelligent people who are boors, and that I personally knew many miners who have superb and quite un-self-conscious good manners and that manners, true good manners like charm you have or you don't. You cannot teach people to be charming and though manners may seem to be a question of opening and closing doors and holding chairs and standing up when a lady comes into the room etc. merely it is something that has to be done with an indefinably unobtrusive grace. Tim Hardy, for instance, whose manners are meticulous nevertheless manages to make himself faintly obtrusive, you are aware of his manners. So delicious were the Duke's that I hadn't thought of his being so until Guy pointed it out. I myself am incapable of such behaviour – and I am not being false cavalier – for I am simply not made properly. In fact, both Elizabeth's and my manners are appalling but E's obvious good nature and natural charm (if she likes you) and of course stunning beauty carry her through whereas I pretend to a gruff peasantness which (if I like you) carries me through. I hope. [. . .]

Monday 6th, Ritz[389] After having arrived back last afternoon I read papers and did yesterday's entry and read a book by Ross MacDonald and half watched TV and talked to Kurt Frings agreeing to see him and his lot today at 5 o'clock downstairs to 'discuss the script and read a note from a boy called Richard Sterne who addressed his note 'Most noble Richard of Burton' and ended 'Richard of Sterne'.[390] Surprising, this, as he has always struck me as being a most solemn feller and not given to even mild flights of fancy of this kind but he has been in Paris for a year or so as he says 'a great year here in Paris at the school of Marcel Marceau'. That's the mime chap I think.[391] And perhaps the air of Paris has gone to his head. He kept a diary and tape recorded a book called *John Gielgud directs Richard Burton* which I couldn't read but which other people obviously could as he says it is going into a second edition. He said he was below with 'Joanna the Piana' whoever that may be. Was there a girl in *Hamlet* called Joanna. Don't think so. The Sterne man played an infinitely small part but I can't remember which. He left his tel no. and I shall call him sometime if we stay longer in Paris as we may now as Losey wants me to do dubbing on Trot on the 13th in Rome and we are trying to get him to

---

[389] Heading in red type.
[390] Richard L. Sterne had had a part as a Player Musician in the Broadway production of *Hamlet* and had written a book, *John Gielgud Directs Richard Burton in Hamlet* (1967).
[391] Marcel Marceau (1923–2007), actor and mime.

change it to here. Going home to Gstaad and then packing again for Rome a couple of days later would be another trauma and drama. [. . .]

Tuesday 7th, Ritz[392] We shall be going to Rome, tomorrow night on the sleeper train leaving here at 6 and arriving in Rome at 9 the following morning. The motto is 'Bon soir, Paris – Bonjour Rome.' The Roman people said that they couldn't possibly get the loops ready by Thursday whereupon E said then very well he won't be able to come until the middle of January. Promptly they called back and said they'd be ready by Thursday.

Yesterday was one of those bitty days and today promises to be the same. [. . .] I went downstairs at 5 o'clock to talk to Dmytryk and about six other people including Frings who was the only one I knew and I said that E thought the end of the film too portentous and idiotic but that I didn't think a horror film should be taken too seriously either way as long as it was well done. We agreed on a venue outside Budapest and that we would live in a house if possible and a hotel if not. And they told me they had Virna Lisi and almost had Andress and Ann-Margret.[393] I couldn't care less but just to test their veracity Gianni called Lisi and I asked her if indeed she was in the film as I didn't trust anyone and she said yes but that she wanted to play the biggest part but they had said they had to have an American star for that because the man was probably going to be unknown and they needed Box Office but that now that I was the star who needed, she said and wanted an American star and would I mind if she tried for the biggest part now. Go ahead. Go ahead. And then there was talk about Brian doing a film with E and the TV films of Osborne's seem to be very confused. Nobody seems to know what is going on and there's a TV thing about Tennessee Williams directed by Hutton who is rapidly becoming a part of our lives and he wants and we want him to do the Osborne plays so we are all three likely to walk down the aisle before long and plight eternal troth.[394] And Stanley Donen of the squeaky voice called on the phone asking Comment va tu and I said Bene gracie and he's coming today at 2 o'clock for discussion re *Little Prince* which they want to do in the Spring and it all has to be fitted in with E and then there's also *Absolution* and I may kill myself on Christmas Day and screw everybody.[395]

We went to the Duke and Duchess' house last night for dinner with half a dozen of the most consummate bores in Paris. I don't know their names but I shall never need to remember them for I have an idea they are people who

---

[392] Word 'Ritz' in red type, date underlined in red.
[393] Ursula Andress (1936—). Ann-Margret Olsson (1941—).
[394] It is possible that this refers to the 1973 television documentary *Tennessee Williams' South*, which starred John Colicos, Maureen Stapleton and Michael York, and Williams himself. However it was written, directed and produced by Harry Rasky (1928–2007).
[395] Burton would eventually narrate *The Little Prince*, written by St Exupéry, which came out on a long-playing record in 1974.

only go to the Windsors and one of them – probably the old Duke – must die very soon – though it is she who is now nearly completely ga-ga. It was a sad and painful evening and needs a long time to write about and I haven't got the time. They both referred continually to the fact that he was once the King. 'And Emperor,' I said at one point. 'And Emperor,' she repeated after me, 'And Emperor, we always forget that. And Emperor.' He is physically falling apart, his left eye completely closed and a tremendous limp and walks with a stick. Her memory has gone completely and then comes back vividly in flashes. She derided Grace Kelly all night as being a boring snob. I defended but she would have none of it. I finally gave up as I knew that half the time she didn't know what she was saying. There was one woman there a French woman who protested violently that she was not Swiss – what's so wrong with being Swiss – and who is married to a Hungarian Count who obviously didn't realize that the Duchess was gone away from us and attempted pathetic rational argument. I gave the word. Her husband said that Tito was the natural son of a Hungarian Count who had exercised his Droit de Seignor or whatever that's called over Tito's mother's family. I said I would tease him with it when next we saw him. I doubt it. Both the allegation and that I would tease him.[396]

Wednesday 8th, Ritz[397] The Hungarian and his French wife were quite serious about Tito's illegitimacy and his being the natural son of a Hungarian nobleman as last night at Baron de Rede's supper for Liza Minnelli the wife slipped me a note with the name of Tito's father on it.[398] The father was a Count Erdody with an umlaut above the o, and he had fancied Tito's mother who supposedly a maid at Erdody chateau or castle or whatever the hell Hungarians have, was a pretty little thing, and was snapped up by the lechy count. Josip Erdody Tito. Pronounced Err-durdy. It might be possible to introduce it into conversation with Tito by saying something like 'My God, the Capitalist West and its decaying aristocracy claim even the foremost living Communist. D'you know sir, that they said of you quite seriously that . . .' and then duck or wait for the firing squad. The Count, the Parisian one I mean and not the dirty one who fathered Tito, said to me 'Has it ever occurred to you to wonder why these peasants, these Brozzes, managed to have such a beautiful family home? You must have seen it.' 'No,' I said, 'I haven't seen it but on reflection it does seem to be rather grand for poor people but I assumed that it had been tarted up by Tito after he became President. I have only seen still snaps of it in books.' 'My dear Burton, go and look at the house the next time you and Mrs Burton are in Jugoslavia. It's an easy trip after all. It has the best road in Jugoslavia leading to the god's birthplace. And it is not smartened up at all,

---

[396] Tito was the son of Franjo and Marija Broz.
[397] Heading in red type.
[398] Liza Minnelli, singer and actor.

except perhaps its immediate surroundings. It is as it was.' We will go if we have the chance. I'm sure that the Slavs will lay it on for us. It would weaken Tito immensely with the out and out extremely Lenin-Stalin Marxists to find him so tainted but I have an idea that any documentation will have been erased from all slates including living memory, if any. [. . .]

We went, E in a Caftan of Slav-Turkish origin and as heavy as lead with me in a dinner jacket with an all-black ruffled shirt with one brilliant diamond pin borrowed from Van Cleef mounting firmly to the chin. [. . .] Liza's opening numbers were frighteningly and intensely nervous and with the exception of Lena Horne (and possibly myself when boozing in a heat-wave) I have never seen anybody sweat so much.[399] After a time she settled down though I suffered agonies for the first 15 minutes. Rocky Brynner (Yul's son) sat in front of me and was so nervous for her, being her follower since childhood apparently, that he made me more nervous. However her shattering nervous energy finally communicated itself to her hopelessly dull audience until they went too far and would not let her leave the stage with a steady unisonic handclap and she did another number and still the now really silly audience asked for more and I told Rocky to wave her off – she was right near him – and off she went.

Alex de Rede's house is a museum and ought to be in one.[400] It was as intimate as a Maples show-window, but all done with superb and detailed taste.[401] It's a shame as well as a surprise to find out that it's not his house but is leased by him for 60 years so all that labour, and labour it is – he must have spent millions and travelled the world – will eventually fall under the auctioneer. Apart from some very discreet ceiling lights the whole place was lighted by candles and these were endlessly multiplied by mirrors. I sought the far room as soon as I arrived and sat there alone for ten minutes savouring a glass of Perrier – still liquor-less after an intensive 6 days of society – and I mean 'savouring' as I was terribly thirsty for some reason – and but for those concealed ceiling lights I could have been back in time a couple of hundred years. The same faces appear at all the parties. We talked to Salvador Dali for a time who clowned about charmingly as usual giving us his Catalanese pronunciation of 'butterfly' which cannot be impersonated in print.[402] The English live in fogs and therefore everything, including their language is rife with imprecision, including their language, he said, but our Catalan is sharp-edged and everywhere defined and sharply dominant, like our language. Nonsense I said. Your language with all its esses elided in eths sounds is liquid but not limpid, it is muddy like your minds. He left saying 'butterfly'. With him was a striking looking blonde, tall and thin, who stared at me all the time while

---

[399] Lena Horne (1917–2010), singer and actor.
[400] Hôtel Lambert, Paris.
[401] Maples was a well-known furniture store in Tottenham Court Road, London. It closed in the early 1990s.
[402] Salvador Dali (1904–89), artist.

at dinner and Guy (blonde hair always falling over his forehead) Barrault(?) was helpless with stoned laughter saying Tu as ton ticket, c'est drôle, tu as ton ticket et la dame est un homme.[403] And so she was. The girl was a man. [. . .]

We are off to Rome tonight on the train and I'm looking forward to it. I've had enough of French society. Also their faces were beginning to become familiar to me and indeed some of them began to acquire names as the same faces are seen at all parties. I want to retreat now into the silent world of the Alps and bury myself in walks and books and dogs and hibernate until the holidays, so loathed by me, are over. Messy Xmas trees that shed and the house running with people.

And now to meet someone called Robert (I think) Hakim, one of the innumerable Hakim (Egyptian) bros re *Under the Volcano*.[404]

Friday 10th, Grand[405] To work at 9 this a.m. and with a bit of luck I might be finished by lunchtime but I may become word-drunk around midday and it might be better to take a break before the final and last lap. Also I remember I have to do a lot of off-stage talking – nothing specific but the sort of diatribic stuff that Joe can shove in anywhere. Joe says that the visions over my shoulder things don't work and that he has cut them all out. Just badly done he says, the machine incompetently handled as he saw the same technique used on British TV only two nights ago absolutely brilliantly. Comes to something when the poor relation does technically better stuff than the rich Uncle. I thought at the time that the technical boys on the process were all too familiar to me, faces that I'd seen around for years in Italian films and guessed then that such a new process would demand, normally, new men – particularly the men who invented it, and usually young men. They were all old. That is at least my age – middle aged-ish.

E is eating as if she is about to acquire some dreadful disease which will include a loss of appetite, and so that while she is hungry she will eat and eat and eat. I keep on telling her that she is as round as she is tall which is a complete lie as apart from her impossible stomach and her hereditary double chin she is not really all that tubby. She is well covered though. She is one of those who can only diet when the mood takes her and then she goes too far. Since she doesn't have a weight problem of any consequence she could eat very well, not dieting and still remain trim without too much trouble, but milady has all the discipline of a mountain pony. I enjoy self imposed discipline, there must be a masochist hidden here somewhere, though in the matter of dieting I find it hardly any trouble at all. [. . .]

---

[403] Burton may possibly mean Jean-Louis Barrault (1910–94), actor, who had appeared with Burton in *The Longest Day*, although the description renders this unlikely.
[404] Robert Hakim (1907–92), producer. His brothers Raymond (1909–80) and André (1915–80) were also producers. Together they held an option on the film rights to *Under the Volcano*.
[405] Heading in red type.

<u>Evening</u>
I finished my so called two days' work in less than a day since yesterday we worked only from three 'til 5.45 and today I cleared the lot by lunchtime. Much private rejoicing as I hate that aspect of the work. After it was over I saw a reel of the film leading up to and including the assassination. It will look good I'm sure when all the thuds and noises are put in and the blood is very effective and will be more so in a good print.

Trap and Joe [Joseph and Patricia Losey] and the children are coming for dinner and I have just seen a pair of diamond earrings for a cool million dollars. They were two pendant diamonds 30 carats each and very beautiful and superbly cut but I told Gianni Bulgari's man that the price was outrageous and that I would find it nasty to buy them even at ½ half that cost.[406] Bet you an offer nearer the latter than the former will come through ere long.

Saturday 18th, Ariel[407] I stayed in bed for as long as I could bear it but finally – foot or no foot – I got me up and with cunning contortions managed to dress myself, sat me in a chair in the bedroom, placed another chair as a table and wrote yesterday's entry. I then began [. . .] the article for the *Mail*. I have a vague shape of it in my head and I did about 200 words though they have yet to be polished and balanced. At the moment I have only the vaguest idea as to how long it will be – anything from 1000 words to 3000 would be my guess.[408] [. . .]

Chris arrived last night very late and I was so bushed that I simply couldn't wait up for him. [. . .] Chris looks magnificent and is his usual sarcastic deni grating nothing-is-any-good self. Ron and E say that last night he excelled himself and Ron said, 'You'd better get him the hell out of that school in Krautland Richard – they're turning him into a Nazi.' I replied that nobody had to worry about his turning into Attila the Hun but Attila was the bloke to worry about. What did he say or do, I asked. They said that after he arrived Vicky asked him if he wanted to play Yahtsee and he replied: No, it's a boring repetitive and stupid game. Well, said I, in Chris' defence he's right and it is. However, I agreed he might have been slightly more non-committal as everybody else there was obviously enjoying the game. In any case I would prefer, in anybody, more jaundice and cynicism than over-sentimentality.

Sunday 19th, Gstaad[409] I went out last night to the Olden which was very crowded [. . .] Ron became sweetly and uncomfortably drunk very quickly and by uncomfortable I mean that I was afraid he was going to do something

---

[406] Gianni Bulgari, chief executive of Bulgari.
[407] Heading in red type.
[408] Burton had been invited to write an article for the *Daily Mail*'s Christmas number. It was published as 'A Story of Christmas, in the Twenties' on 23 December 1971.
[409] Heading in red type.

disastrous like fall off his chair or something. [. . .] we limped out and home in the car. Astonishingly after about 15 minutes at home and two games of table-tennis with Mike, Ron became merely pissed again instead of paralysed. [. . .]

Tuesday 21st, Ariel[410] Yesterday's entry is missing because I worked all day long, as I had most of the previous day and far into the night, on the story for the *Mail*. I read the first rough unhesitant plunging in up to the neck to Elizabeth who told me, though I was piqued at the time, but only for a second, that I must simplify it. So back I went to work, balancing and measuring and for the only time in my nothing writing life I looked up something in *Roget's* which I have never done before except for crossword puzzles and amusement. I can't remember what the word was that I was having difficulty with but in any case *Roget's* was no help and I ploughed on with my own built in one. I did almost all the work in long-hand, and not having written with pen and ink or pencil for many years I had the forgotten writer's cramp. It's very evident in the script, the writing starting off so neat and trim and mathematical and ending in huge drunken sprawling hieroglyphics. The deadline was this morning and assuming that I could send it by telex from the Palace Hotel I typed it laboriously out. Inevitably as I typed I deleted and added and changed the structure of sentences. I have never written anything so long (for publication I mean) in so short a time. The previous shortest for 2 or 3 thousand words was about 6 weeks. This one was 3,400 approx and in 3 days. Phew. I would have liked another week on it. E thinks it marvellous so that's ok and the Editor was bubbling over with words like Scoop. We all think it is a scoop. The staff are delighted etc. which is ok too. [. . .] I am worried about my sweet E. She doesn't seem to be at all well and her back is kicking up again like fury. It's a dreadful thing to think when we love this house so much but I am beginning to have the horrifying suspicion that the altitude is too much for her. She sparkled in Dubrovnik, she was radiant in Rome, she was a young girl in Paris but here she seems listless and slightly bored all the time, not just with me, but with everybody and everything. I think that already she is wishing that we were here just the two of us. We must use this time as a testing period for if it is the altitude then we must simply go lower down.

David Niven and wife Hjordis came up for an after lunch (at the Olden) drink and were in very good form and David, as usual, made us laugh a lot. He is tremendously excited about the success of his autobiography which is lovely to see and enjoy with him.

I feel so relaxed and almost smug about having got the article in on time and the *Mail's* liking it, but above all and especially E.

---

[410] Heading in red type.

Brook and Liza arrived last afternoon and Claudye and Gianni arrived today so the house is now bursting at the seams though the latter couple are not staying with us but at the Olden.

Liza is a bundle of energy and I spoil her with shamelessness though I have to mentally belt her now and again.

Brook is irremediably sad and lonely. And he is still a drunk though he claims that at home he only drinks at weekends and then only wine. I feel so sorry for him and wish I could help him more.

1972

JANUARY

Friday 28th, Phoenix[1] Yesterday we went to Sara's house for lunch and for the last time, thank God. It was the first time for me to see the place in daylight and it could be a very pleasant little abode were some money and taste expended on it. Sara's brother (80 next September) and his wife were there. He is a thin spare man with marvellous high Indian-looking cheek bones and Howard said of him: If you dip him in a barrel of salt water – clothes and all – then put him out in the sun to dry, he might approximate to looking like Sam. Sam was the pioneering adored grandfather.[2] [. . .]

Last night I had a unique experience – for me that is. I went to have dinner with the Voldengs in the swankest country club in Phoenix, or the richest, or both. However, the uniqueness was that I discovered towards the end of the dinner that the Club was restricted to gentiles only. NO JEWS ALLOWED. Mary Frances told me so.[3] She said that they, the Club, had told them, the Jews that there are just too many of you and before long you'll be running the place so why don't you form a club of your own. I was flabbergasted. I should have immediately announced this to the rest of the family and we would have undoubtedly swept out en masse. However I thought of Sara and that the only reason why we were dining with the Voldengs was to get her out as easily and unrancorously as possible, but I simply couldn't sit there and say nothing. She promptly gave me an opportunity to salvage my conscience as she said with twinkling glee 'And do you know Richard they ran into financial difficulties and had to appeal to us gentiles for help. What about that!' I swooped. 'How strange to hear that,' I said, 'our lot doesn't usually get into that kind of difficulty.' She took the blow with an air of not knowing quite whether I was making a little British joke or not. I now laid it on. 'Elizabeth, as you obviously don't know is a convert to Judaism and our daughter is of course a Jewess and my grandfather was a Jew'. She was helpless. She said 'Yes' but it had several additional vowels in it, impossible to write down but it was something like 'Yeaaeahowes.'

---

[1] All headings in this diary are in red with the exception of the last, the entire day's entry being hand-written in black pen. Richard and Elizabeth had travelled to Arizona early in 1972 to visit Elizabeth's mother.
[2] Sam Warmbrodt, Sara's father, a German engineer who migrated to the USA.
[3] Mary Frances Voldeng.

To reiterate here the platitudinous idiocies of their conversation would be tedious. E and I and Howard and Mara had gone there knowing what to expect but so exactly did they react to any given suggestion that they were little different from Pavlovian dogs. One rang the bell of this idea and they tolled the precisely expected answer. To the very anticipated word. We all agreed afterwards that they were so brain-washed that nothing, no argument, no appeal to intelligence, could possibly change them. For instance, and only one example will I give, Dr Voldeng said that the thing that had made this country great was that it was a melting pot for all the peoples of the world. Yawn. Yawn. But they had just said that Jews were not allowed in their club! There was therefore absolutely no point in asking about the blacks.

We reduced ourselves to hysteria in the course of the post mortem in our suite but under it all we were sick at heart. [...]

Saturday 29th, Beverly Hills Hotel An eventful day. One of those that despite much incident manage to be tedious. We left Phoenix at 2.14 in the GS2 [...] and we took 45 minutes to get to Air Research airport.[4] There, there was a hell of a problem with Sara who refused to lie down in the ambulance. I said I would ride with her if she would lie down but she wouldn't so I snapped off smartly into the Cadillac. She tried to get Howard and E to ride with her [...] but H nipped off as smartly as I and joined me in the car – then tore back to the ambulance which still refused to leave, grabbed E and brought her back and finally [...] we were under way. We arrived in the underground garage and I fled fast to the safety of Bungalow 5. The others came swiftly afterwards. Howard and E were already somewhat sloshed by this time but only my experienced eye could tell while Mara was trying to catch up. Howard and Mara told me that they never have a drink until the evening when they're at home and I know E barely has a drink before 6pm normally but seeing and being around Sara, said Howard, drink was the only defence. Yes sir. My way out was to eat ten lbs of chocolates and liquorice etc. washed down with many cups of tea. By about 8 o' clock at night all three were pixilated [...].

At one time Paul Newman came in and Howard and Mara carried on talking as if he was not there. I asked him what he was doing in town and he said he was there to see John Huston. 'Oh, I know him,' said Mara, 'he came to Kuwait once. He's got a patch over his eye and he's a film producer or something.' 'No,' says I, 'you're thinking of John Ford.'[5] That's right, she said. Sometimes I wonder whether Mara's defence mechanism against being impressed when she meets a famous and very distinguished man like Newman

---

[4] A GS-2 was a steam train operated by the Southern Pacific Company, although it was retired in the 1950s so Burton may be mistaken here.
[5] John Ford (1895–1973), director.

is a pretence of ignorance about all things filmic. She sees more films in three months than I see in ten years so it can't be ignorance. Paul is what I call a real actor. A nice man, extraordinarily youthful looking with a complexion so peaches and cream that at first I thought he had make-up on. Every move he makes is like one practising –with no need to look any more – in front of a mirror. I don't mean that unkindly. He doesn't even know he's doing it. He is a keep fit fanatic and my God the results are remarkable. He must be at least my age and yet with a little care around the eyes and a dye-job on the hair he could still pass for 24 or so.[6] I would hate to look like him. I did once before acne re-mapped my face and I hated it. I abhor mere prettiness.

Voldeng, while we were on the plane, quite blatantly asked E if she would contribute $5000 to the Orchestral Fund of Phoenix. E, caught in a corner said OK. In a minute he was sitting next to me in the rear compartment where he asked me the same. I said that we gave a considerable amount to charities but only with great suspicion and only to the lame and [. . .] the blind and the retarded etc. but that I would ask Aaron if it were possible to make an exception. I have no intention of giving $5000 to a group of anti-semitic idiots. What appalling effrontery.

I did something this morning which gave me immense satisfaction. I took the two dogs for a run on the lawns in front of the bungalows. [. . .] Suddenly I was aware that I was being shadowed from tree to bush to tree by some idiot photographer who fondly believed that I couldn't see him. I started to throw the ball harder and harder, followed by new friend. Suddenly I whirled and with all my strength threw the rubber ball with a baseball pitcher's action straight at the snapper hoping to hit the camera, instead of which I hit him square in the middle of his forehead. It's quite a heavy hard rubber ball with a bell inside it. It was only later that I realized that I could have taken his eye out if I'd hit him there and that if I'd missed I would have had to suffer the ignominy of having to cross the road to retrieve the ball. He said nothing but stared at me with under-privileged hatred. I stared back and said 'you're on private property, get off it.' He left.

Sunday 30th We ran *XYZ* yesterday afternoon and though I'd seen the film twice before (once a rough cut) and had seen sections of it ½ a dozen times I was still fascinated, though not so much when E was off-screen. There are always little subtleties in E's performance to be discovered anew whereas Caine and the girl are always carefully studied but obvious. What is that girl's name?[7] [. . .] I went to bed at 10.30 or thereabouts simply not being able to keep awake. [. . .] I awoke slightly in the middle of the night to find E snoring gently [. . .] and tipped her chin to stop her. She stopped.

---

[6] Newman was actually ten months older than Burton.
[7] Susannah York, playing the part of Stella.

Kurt Frings and his vapid little girlfriend came to the film and Alex Lucas and his wife (?) very very nervous girl Rex Kennamer (who again got pissed) and of course Sara and the two nurses and Jim and George. Half – more than half – the audience were seeing it for the first time and we at last got some idea of where the laughs come. I'm afraid that we have made a mistake with Frings. I cannot bring myself to like that man. He is monumentally ill-mannered and thick as a trunk. All he had to say about the film was that he wished that Maggie Leighton had a bigger part. Rex was staggering about with either drink or pot and endlessly cornered me (and before me Elizabeth) saying equally endlessly 'I know John Q Public better than you or Frings or anybody in the business. I listen to those old ladies talking and they say, "Is Liz Taylor really really beautiful?" and I think your John Springer should run a campaign saying, "Go and see the most beautiful woman in the world at her most beautiful," because these old ladies say, "you know, is she really beautiful or has she got old and fat," and I'm telling you Richard this is the most ravishing I've ever seen Elizabeth and I've seen everything she's ever done. You've gotta get Springer to do this because I know my John Q Public and I know them better than . . .' He doesn't know his John Q Public. Nobody does. If the film is a hit it's a hit and if it's a flop it's a flop and nobody can persuade John Q to go or not go by a piece of advertising. The most important advertisement in the business is unbuyable and it's called Word of Mouth. We shall not know for about three weeks whether – in the USA – we have a hit or a miss. I have an idea that the film will be immensely successful with sophisticated audiences but the hick may still be puzzled by the ending. Say and write what you will the small towner, the uneducated sticks, still don't know about lesbians. Howard and Mara Jim and George Alex Lucas know all about it and appreciated the ultimate horrendous trick that Zee plays but I can't see my brothers and sisters getting it. They'll just think that Zee has said something awful to Stella and be frustrated at not knowing what.[8] I may have underestimated the spread of sexual knowledge – God knows the papers never stop writing about sex and its aberrations – but I don't think so.

Mara and E came into the bedroom last night when they all got back from Sara's bungalow with some tale about the condescending rudeness of the room service manager as they had waited for over an hour for the food to come [. . .] I wasn't sure of what exactly went on. I'll get it straightened out this morning. [. . .] Once the waiters get their knives into you you might as well pack up and move to another hotel because they can make your life very uncomfortable. They can forget the sauce for the steak and the dressing for the salad and a million little inconveniences and since Sara relies on the room service to an unprecedented degree the waiters must be kept sweet. [. . .] I remember Ivor

---

[8] The film ends with Taylor's character (Zee) seducing Stella.

and I once in the Negresco being so fed up with the lousy waiter's lousy service combined with a 'fuck you' attitude that Ivor poured a bowl of chips over his head and while he was shouting and bawling I sketted him with a carafe of water.[9] We had the police an' all. Syb was pregnant with Kate at the time and while I had been at work apparently this waiter had been giving Gwen and Syb a rough time because they spoke no French and he didn't know who they were. Just two plain ladies from Wales I suppose he thought they were. We sorted him out alright. He was fired by the management for calling the police but, having withdrawn his charges I – against everybody's will – insisted that he was reinstated and that he continued to serve our suite. He became devoted to everybody and indeed used to send us postcards for a time until, not getting any back, he fell away.

Edie Goetz came with Mr and Mrs Arthur Hornblow to visit us last night at about 7.15.[10] The Hornblows left after half an hour [. . .] Edie stayed on. She looked alive and very well kept though she had on a pair of frightful eyelashes. [. . .] She, surprisingly to E and I both, boasted about the cost of her sable coat. It's Crown Sable she said and added $10,000 to the bill. After she left we both said how much we liked her whereupon Rex Kennamer, soberer now than he had been, began to attack her. It was all-embracing in its viciousness. He wouldn't allow her a single virtue. He said she thought of nothing but money and herself. That neither she nor Bill had ever given a penny to charity and that he had seen them stand up at fund-raising dinners and pledge money and then dishonour the pledge. That she has a daughter who has been desperately ill for two years and to whom she has given nothing except porcelain vases with potted plants inside, and that the girl is married to a not very successful agent and she needs money for hospital bills here are astronomical and don't we know that, and that she has fought for years to be LA's top hostess but has been out-ranked, flanked and buggered-up by a Mrs May (of May Company) who gives copiously to hospitals and was the force behind the building of the huge new cultural centre, and that she is obsessed by Frank Sinatra who, said Rex, pointing to his temples, is a sick man and if Frank ever drops her she will kill herself and that her obsession with Sinatra had made the last few years of her husband's life a torment as Frank had done a film for Goetz called *Capture of Queen* or something and that Frank had behaved so atrociously that he quadrupled the cost of the picture which was a majestic flop and he would normally never have had anything to do with Sinatra ever again but Edie ignored him and became Frank's slave despite Bill's protestations and so on and on and on.[11] [. . .] I said rather feebly [. . .] that she had always seemed very

---

[9] Hotel Negresco, Promenade des Anglais, Nice.
[10] Arthur Hornblow Jr (1893–1976), former film producer, and his wife Leonora.
[11] May's was a chain of department stores. Edie Goetz and Frank Sinatra were lovers. The film was *Assault on a Queen* (1966), starring Sinatra and Virna Lisi. The new cultural centre may be the Skirball Museum, established in 1972, now the Skirball Cultural Center.

nice to me. If I'd had a few argumentative drinks I would have challenged Rex all along the line but I decided he was drunk and therefore not a compos opponent. I shall ask him again when he is more measured in judgement. It was all fascinating – particularly the social aspect and it all seems so second class compared with Parisian society. Christ I'm a snob! How about, as they say, that?

Monday 31st 8am and we've all been up since 7 to see off Howard and Mara who have a pleasant 5 hour journey to Hawaii while we have an unpleasant 5 hours to NY on Wednesday and an equally unpleasant 7–8–9 hours to Rome the following day. [. . .] We went to see a James Bond film yesterday afternoon [. . .] called *Diamonds are Forever* which was good fun but surprisingly ill-acted and amateurish.[12] There are some good sequences – notably a car chase – but the plot, which as far as I can remember has nothing to do with the original, is very silly indeed.[13] It makes *Eagles* [. . .] look realistic by comparison. Sean has got potty and now really looks like a miner going to seed.[14] Which he is. [. . .] His Scots accent was more pronounced than ever – perhaps deliberately – perhaps indicating Home Rule for Scotland. He has become a devout nationalist. Anyway it was all good clean fun.

[. . .] I cannot make up my mind about Mara. One thing I'm certain of and that is that I couldn't live with her for more than two days. If one could only gag her it would be alright. E tells me how her father told her that he had long ago tuned off whenever her mother talked. Howard goes at it the other way. When <u>Mara</u> talks <u>he</u> talks, but louder, and the shriller she gets the more thunderous he becomes. I'm beginning to doubt whether they've had a proper conversation together for twenty years. In fact I can't imagine them having an ordinary chat as we have. The point about Mara is: is she stupid or not? Don't know. Is she silly or nasty or not? Don't know. If it were not for Howard I am pretty certain that E and I would make bloody certain that we were never in the same place as that most uncomfortable woman ever again. And it is not that I dislike her, it is simply that her manner and the content of her observations on life are so tremendously BORING. To the point of screaming. If only she could acquire the virtue of silence or force herself to listen when somebody anybody else is talking, she might be tolerable. There have been times when I longed to say 'shut your bloody trap for just 15 minutes, only 15 little minutes, while Howard talks or Elizabeth finishes that story'. She also has the most unfortunate accent and intonation. Sometimes I have – in the past week – asked her a direct question and listened to the answer and have realized after 10 minutes that I haven't known what she's been saying for

---

[12] *Diamonds are Forever* (1971), directed by Guy Hamilton (1922—).
[13] Burton means the original novel by Ian Fleming, published in 1956.
[14] Sean Connery (1930—), playing James Bond in the film.

the past five. My mind has wandered off. Some teachers and lecturers and most pulpit preachers were like that. That's the criminal thing about having children – they keep incompatible people together. I believe that I heard vaguely that Howard took off once with another woman maybe, or just took off. I bet that he would never have gone back were it not for the children. The same with Francis too, I guess. There must have been a time, before he got too old, when he wanted out. It's funny that both father and son married two non-stop talkers. You'd think that Howard would have chosen a quiet woman for a partner after a lifetime of Sara's endless gabble but he chose a lady who could if anything out-talk Sara. [. . .]

I've had a bellyful of the USA already and am ripe to go back to Europe though I will doubtless regret that after a few days behind the curtain and be lusting for the States again. Phoenix was a tremendous disappointment. I had a totally different picture of it in my mind. And I had no idea that it was such a huge city. I thought in terms of a 150,000 and not a million population as it is. When we left it we could see its great sprawl and there was the unmistakable smog. I had visions of Norman Rockwell far west with local drugstores and shops on the corner and the Town Hall with a church and a square and a drugstore and all that Andy Hardy stuff.

I talked to Kate last night. She sounded flip and cocky and I soon found out that the reason for that was that there was a girlfriend there so a little showing-off was going on. We will probably see her on Wednesday [. . .].

FEBRUARY

Tuesday 1st, Los Angeles A nice day yesterday. Howard and Mara arrived safely and I read and wrote practically all day long. The only cessation was in the afternoon when I talked with McWhorter and later with Alex Lucas. The first about the Canterbury Tales and the second about *Hammersmith*.[15] The former says he has three millions to do the former and the latter wants to get some control of *Hammersmith*. Good luck to both.

I popped up for about 15 minutes to see Sara with Elizabeth. The lady is still bonkers without any question. The entire bungalow apart from Sara's bedroom and sitting room [. . .] is stacked to the ceilings with bric a brac in boxes. And what rubbish! E found a packing case that appeared to contain nothing but tin-foil TV dinner plates [. . .]. Staggering idiocy. When E remonstrated with her about this she burst into large and, if E knows her, crocodile tears. [. . .] I told E last night that we must regard her as if she were a child of 10 years old and a very spoiled one. She must do what we – her parents say – and not what she whimsically feels like doing. [. . .] Val says that Robbie is

---

[15] This may refer to *The Canterbury Tales* (1972), written and directed by Pier Paolo Pasolini (1922–75).

weaving a web – his own words – around Sara to get her back to Phoenix. Well, in the immortal words of Zee, Scarlett, I couldn't give a sheeit.[16] [. . .]

Wednesday 2nd, Beverly Hills Hotel [. . .] We leave at 11 for NY and tomorrow night we leave NY for Rome in the evening. So we haul our indifferent bodies from yet one more continent to another. In a few days we shall be in Budapest and I am agog with curiosity. What will Hungary be like? It is impossible to find any literature on modern Hungary. Only a Fodor travel book which is hopeless and stops at '56. Will try again in NY. I can't believe that there is so little stuff about a famous modern state. Lack of interest must be the answer. Books on the impenetrable Red Chinese are all over the stalls, two of which I bought yesterday together with $150 worth of other books, mostly paperbacks with at least half being whodunits for the long stay in Budapest. The Cadogan diaries, the closing circle, the something foxes – highly recommended tome on international espionage – ecological books.[17] Barbara Tuchman's *Stilwell and the American experience in China* or some such title and a mass of Simenons and Creaseys and Helen Macguiness and A. A. Fairs and godknows what other readable rubbish.[18] But I guess that if there's so little about Hungary outside the country there'll be little about the West inside Hungary and without books of some kind E and I pine.

The one possible pleasure of the journey is that we may get a few hours of Kate in NY if Aaron can spring her from school for tomorrow. [. . .]

I am getting nearer and nearer to an attempt to give up cigarettes, not out of fear of cancer but simply because a) It's a filthy habit and b) I want to try and prove to myself that – as with booze – I am Henley and the master of my fate etc.[19] As for the fear of cancer I am one of those who believes they will either have found a cure by the time I get it or that, like my heavily smoking father, I won't get it at all but die like him at 83 of a stroke. I am determined to do it and will decide, after a suitable time period not yet decided precisely whether the effort is worth it. With alcohol it unquestionably is. [. . .]

Both of us are very glad to be on our way out of the States. Phoenix was the final straw that broke our camel's back. We had thought the American malaise to be possibly confined to big industrial centres, business centres, NY, Chicago, Detroit, Los Angeles etc. But it's everywhere. [. . .]

---

[16] A line uttered by the character Zee (played by Taylor) in *X, Y and Zee*, itself a reference to the line spoken by the character Rhett Butler (played by Clark Gable, 1901–60) in *Gone With The Wind* (1939).
[17] *The Diaries of Sir Alexander Cadogan, O.M., 1938–1945* (1972), ed. by David Dilks (1938–). Barry Commoner (1917), *The Closing Circle* (1971). The 'something foxes' was probably Ladislas Faragó (1906–80), *The Game of the Foxes: The Untold Story of German Espionage in the United States and Great Britain during World War II* (1971).
[18] Barbara Tuchman (1912–89), *Stilwell and the American Experience in China, 1911–45* (1971). 'Creaseys' are novels by John Creasey (1908–73), the crime and science fiction writer. By 'Helen Macguiness' Burton means Helen MacInnes (1907–85), the thriller writer.
[19] A reference to the 1888 poem 'Invictus' by W. E. Henley (1849–1903), which includes the lines 'I am the master of my fate: / I am the captain of my soul'.

Thursday 3rd, New York Airport We are at something called the International Hotel five minutes from the airport [. . .]. We are surrounded by a mass of Aaron's Praetorian guards, Tom Horan, Steve, Dug senior and junior and Rosemary, taking all the rooms around us and making sure that no wicked ones from the terrible city of NY will attack the Burtons. With justice too. The last time we were here we were very lucky to get safely away with our baubles intact. The gang – still at large and still operating – have pulled several jobs since they missed on us.

The journey was smooth [. . .]. There was a film called *Kotch* on which I could only watch for a time though E watched it all the way and said afterwards that it was beautifully done. After ten minutes however I could see the whole course of the movie and found reading more congenial.[20] [. . .] There were hordes of snappers when we came off the ship and they backed and clicked and attracted crowds so that the journey to the car went on and on for about what seems a good ½ mile but was probably only a ¼. I would have become angry in the old days were I drunk but I merely looked blank instead.

Tonight we're off again to Rome. [. . .] Have just read some more notices for *XYZ* which are all highly praised stuff for E but not so much for the film. The film is good so don't understand the carping at the film.

Have just been sent the script of a horrifying book of police corruption which I was sent to read three or four months ago. Will read it and decide. Rather like playing cockney thugs even though this one is supposed to be a policeman.

Friday 4th, Rome Late afternoon in a raining Rome. We flew from NY last night into the teeth of a howling 90mph gale. [. . .] The film we saw was called *The French Connection* which was done in a very mystifying fashion.[21] Elizabeth, who hadn't like me read the book, confessed herself utterly lost in the plot from time to time and because of the looseness of the direction wasn't sure sometimes who were cops and who were the baddies. Also the director having obviously decided that the original story was too quiet and tame, quite arbitrarily put in two episodes – a hair raising car versus electric train race with a mad killer aboard the latter, which had nothing to do with the film, and the final showdown was the olde classical gun-fight while in the original documented book, as I remember, there was no gunfight at all. Not one single shot fired as far as I can remember. Still, it was fast moving and interesting enough.

[. . .] I feel better already since coming back. I really am a little old European. We leave on Monday for Budapest. [. . .] I also have to ice skate, a little exercise I haven't done for years, and the return to that mildish form of exercise and balance is going to be very interesting.

---

[20] *Kotch* (1971), directed by Jack Lemmon (1925–2001).
[21] *The French Connection* (1971), directed by William Friedkin (1935—).

Damnedest thing about E's chimerical looks. She looked, in the USA the worst I've ever seen her. Tending to bloat, uncertain complexion, bags under the eyes – particularly the left, probably as a result of the cyst operation which is developing an internal keloid, and now suddenly this morning, in the plane she was back to being ravishing again when after two days of nightmarish travel she should have looked her all time worst. Funny woman. Actually I think that, at last, E now shows the effects of heavy drinking whereas Howard – apart from slightly bloodshot eyes in the first waking – still looks as if he's just come back from a health farm. Mara and I still look – as we always have – like the end of the earth. [. . .]

Saturday 5th [. . .] The top ten box office things have just come out in the States where I am not No 1 as in Europe but number 6 or 7.[22] E is ahead of me there so there must have been releases of some of her previous pictures. Any way the old firm is still way up there. My phraseology is becoming more and more transatlantic. That's what comes from being married to an American and being in America for ten days and reading American books.

I read a script in NY – the book of which I have already read – called *Sir, you bastard* and which is very and horribly compelling (about police corruption) but suffers from the same weakness as *Villain*.[23] It will not be understood by the yanks. And one can't make pictures nowadays for London only. [. . .]

Sunday 6th [. . .] I have so lost count of time and days that I had a lovely surprise – paradoxically an expected surprise if I'd known what day it was and that we were playing Scotland at Cardiff yesterday. Anyway, there were the lovely headlines. 'Welsh Crush Scots', 'King For A Day Gareth smashes Scotland', etc. We had beaten the Scots, strongly fancied in some quarters after beating the French by 20 points 4 weeks ago, by 35 to 12. Wales scored 5 tries to Scotland's one and three of the Welsh tries, one by Gerald Davies and two by Gareth Edwards had to be seen apparently to be believed.[24] I feel very strange about this Welsh team. It would appear that they are the greatest all round team since the 'Golden Age' from about 1900 to 1910 and like the golden men of that age, talked about with breathless awe by those who saw them, and again like those immortal ghosts, <u>I have never seen them play</u>.[25] I believe that I saw Gareth Edwards play for Millfield in a 'Sevens' many years ago but apart from him and possibly John Dawes playing for London Welsh I

---

[22] This refers to the *Motion Picture Herald*'s annual ratings.

[23] Gordon F. Newman, *Sir, you bastard* (1971).

[24] Scotland had beaten France 20–9 on 15 January. Gerald Davies (1945–), Gareth Edwards (1947–), Welsh rugby internationals and British Lions.

[25] The first 'Golden Age' of Welsh rugby began in 1900 and lasted until 1911. In that time Wales won the International Championship (played initially between the four home countries, joined by France in 1910) outright on six occasions, shared the title once, and also defeated New Zealand (1905) and Australia (1908).

have never even seen them play as individuals.[26] The Welsh this century, apart from a mediocre patch in the 20s, have always been able to produce very sound teams and nearly always hard to beat with an occasional match winner or two in the side, men out of the common mould like Bleddyn and the Cliffs Morgan and Jones, Tanner, Wooller, Watkins the forward before the 2nd War and Watkins the fly-half since, but since the Golden Age I cannot remember – on paper at least – a team that contained such a heavy percentage of 'geniuses' at the same time.[27] Morris of Neath, Mervyn Davies and John Taylor in the pack, Edwards and John at half back, John Williams at fullback, Gerald Davies on the wing and – in full cry – a virtually unstoppable Bevan on the other wing.[28] I have to guess that Bergiers and Lewis in the centre are sound, especially in defence.[29] What I should do is write to Cliff Jones and ask if I can buy 16mm copies of the matches played in the last 3 years including the tests against New Zealand and have myself a punny ball.[30] Must do so.

Tomorrow to Hungary. I am looking forward to it with excitement. The very name Budapest smacks of romance and tragedy and wild Magyar music. It cannot, simply cannot be dull, regardless of friends' warnings that it is the most depressing capital in Europe. I shall start out, at least, refusing to be talked into disliking it before I find out for myself. And again the Communist experiment is eternally fascinating. There must be some alternative to the idiocy and rat-race murderousness of 'democracy' and I'm pretty sure that Communism is not it but it is different so one more look at one more communist country.

I went to the 'Lion' book shop yesterday and bought yet another pile of books for the ten week stay in Buda and Pest. Cadogan's diaries, A. L. Rowse's two vols *The Early Churchills* and *The Later Churchills*, Solzhenitsyn's *Full Circle*, *Chosen Words* by Ivor Brown.[31] Two dual-language Penguins of Mallarmé and French Poetry of the 19th Century.[32] A book by Auberon

---

[26] Gareth Edwards had attended Millfield school. 'Sevens' is a rugby tournament where there are seven players on each team, rather than the usual 15, and the matches are shorter (usually seven minutes each way rather than 40) with more emphasis on running rugby. John Dawes (1940—), Welsh rugby international and British Lion who played for London Welsh Rugby Football Club.

[27] Welsh rugby internationals Bleddyn Williams (1923–2009), Cliff Jones (1914–90), Cliff Morgan, Haydn Tanner (1917–2009), Wilfred Wooler (1912–97), Edward Verdun Watkins (1916–95), who played at 'lock' forward in the second row, David Watkins (1942—), who played in the position of 'fly-half', also known as 'stand off' or 'outside half'.

[28] All Welsh rugby internationals. David or 'Dai' Morris (1941—), played mostly as a 'blind-side' wing forward, Mervyn Davies (1946–2012), played at 'Number Eight', John Taylor (1945—), played as an 'open-side' wing forward. Barry John (1945—), played at 'fly-half', outside Gareth Edwards at scrum-half. John 'J. P. R.' Williams, (1949—), played at full back. John Bevan (1950—), played on the left wing, Gerald Davies mostly on the right wing.

[29] Roy Bergiers (1950—) and Arthur Lewis (1941—) played in the centre.

[30] Cliff Jones (1914–90), former Welsh rugby international, chairman of the Welsh Rugby Union's coaching committee and a selector, later President of the WRU. In this context 'punny ball' would appear to mean 'have a great time'.

[31] A. L. Rowse (1903–97), *The Early Churchills* (1968) and *The Later Churchills* (1958); Alexander Solzhenitsyn (1918–2008), *The First Circle* (1968); Ivor Brown (1891–1974), *Chosen Words* (1961).

[32] Stéphane Mallarmé (1842–98), French poet. Possibly Burton is referring here to Anthony Hartley (1925–2000) (ed.), *The Penguin Book of French Verse, 3: The Nineteenth Century* (1957).

Waugh – son of Evelyn.[33] Isaac Deutscher *Red China Russia and the USA* – I think it's called.[34] A Hungarian Grammar. And a handful of thrillers. So we should have more than enough to get through ten weeks.

Monday 7th We leave this afternoon for Budapest flying at 3.30. The people are so adamant that we depart and arrive at the border, at the exact time <u>over</u> the border rather, that one gets the impression that if we are too early or too late we will be buzzed or shot down. This must be a very nervous frontier anyway since 1956 but particularly since they have a very nervous Jugoslavia nearby.[35] Joe and Patricia came for drinks and dinner last night and Joe, who has just come back from Jugland, said that the talk is that the dissident communists in Croatia are being financed and armed by either Nazi Jugoslavian exiles operating behind great wealth from South America or by Russia or both.[36] [...] I wonder if the old man is going to be forced to start shooting a few blokes at last.[37] If he doesn't and things get worse the Russians may come over the border 'to help out' as they did in Hungary in 56. Who knows? Merely taking political prisoners may not be enough. A few public trials and death sentences or forced exile may be called for. I hope the old man clears everything up shortly for out of sheer affection I'd not like to see his majestic and reasonably humane leadership of his marvellous little country fizzle out into a bewildered and helpless kow-tow to the Muscovites. Taking the long view it won't much matter historically if Jugoslavia becomes yet another satellite of the Kremlin's for nobody is going to be able to keep those people down for long.[38] It is writ down in corporal in the books for all to read, They cannot be a subject race for long. With the Mexicans I have never fallen so violently in love with a nation at first sight, as I have with the Jugoslavians. As for Hungarians, the only ones I have consciously known have been successful exiles – George Tabori and he who gave me his word and a contract for £100 per week while I was still slogging away in the theatre – the incomparable Alex Korda.[39] When I think of Hungarians I emblematize them in the person of that great scoundrel of ineffable charm, huge generosity and large lies, of living grandiosely beyond his means, of telling me of poverty in Paris where he lived at one time – he solemnly assured me – on one gigantic cake sent him by his mother, for 6 weeks. When, out of the blue, I was invited to have lunch with him at 146 Piccadilly which turned out not to be lunch at all but coffee and

---

[33] Auberon Waugh (1939–2001), novelist, poet, critic.

[34] Presumably Isaac Deutscher (1907–67), *Red China, Russia and the West: A Contemporary Chronicle, 1953–1966* (ed. Fred Halliday, 1970).

[35] A reference to the Soviet invasion of Hungary in 1956.

[36] Joseph and Patricia Losey.

[37] The 'old man' being Tito.

[38] 'Kremlin' meaning the government of the USSR.

[39] George Tabori (1914–2007), playwright and novelist, screenwriter for *Secret Ceremony*, also involved with *The Man From Nowhere* project and with *Boom!*

cigars, and he said in his growling Hoongarrian English, 'Would you like to work with me?' I stammered a sort of 'Yes, but of course I have to. . .' 'It will hardly inconvenience your stage career. In fact I insist that the theatre must come first. I am going to give you £100 a week for five years. I have never seen you act but I have heard from a friend or two that you are going to be an actor of importance. My friend and colleague Laurence Olivier told me that you are a natural aristocrat and now that I have seen you I know that he is right. I am therefore investing £5000 on a belief that Olivier and I are right. So learn all you can in the theatre. Try not to get in long runs, do as many plays as you can. Go to Stratford. Buy a car, get your wife a mink. Enjoy yourself.' I was in a daze of delight. I was about 24 – no 23 years old – and the most I'd ever earned was £12 a week. 'Sign this,' he said indicating one sheet of paper with only one side worded. I began to read it. 'Good,' he said: 'never sign any paper you haven't read and understood.' It said roughly that I was to be available to Sir Alexander Korda for a maximum of 12 weeks a year at <u>my</u> convenience, for a maximum of 5 years during which time – if I did a film for anyone else – I was to get my usual 5000 plus half of whatever price the other film company were prepared to pay. The other half was to go to Korda's company 'London Films'. I danced down Piccadilly to the nearest pub and phone. I called home and told Syb. I called Stanley Baker. I told the publican – a complete stranger. I called Ivor through Dai John Philips.[40] When the pub closed at 3 I suppose it was, I took a taxi, undreamt of extravagance, to the ML Club near the BBC where I was sure that there would be a few congenial well-wishing friends. To cap it all the late and beloved Dylan was there and the even later and equally beloved Louis MacNeice both of them well on the way to stupefaction. Vague figures loomed in the haze of smoke and alcohol and I had pretty well run through my first week's salary by the time I arrived home in the little hours.

This was an astonishing step forward. Many young actors, some of them good like Dirk Bogarde, Donald Houston, Andrew Crawford, Jimmy Granger – I think – and Jean Simmons were under horrible contracts to the Rank Organization but I was under contract to Sir Alexander Korda and his other contract actors were Olivier, Vivien Leigh, Ralph Richardson and a host of other giant names. A very much posher and distinguished lot than the Rank 'stable'. In the end I never did do a film for Alex. He loaned me out to Emlyn Williams and Tolly de Grunwald and then to Fox for a film called *My Cousin Rachel* with Olivia de Havilland as my leading lady.[41] I was still agent-less (unless one considers Korda as my agent) and Fox offered me $50,000. I had told Syb and the family that I was going to stick out for £7000. When the Fox representative, whose name oddly enough was Freddie Fox, offered me

[40] Dai John Philips, secretary of Aberavon Rugby Football Club.
[41] Anatole De Grunwald (1910–67), writer and producer, who worked with Burton on *The Last Days of Dolwyn* and *Now Barabbas* and with Burton and Taylor on *The V.I.P.s.*

roughly twice what I was so ruthlessly determined to hold out for I agreed at once. I must confess to lying about it all to my friends and saying that I had fought them every inch of the way to get that enormous sum. To ice the cake Korda said he was not going to take his cut but that I should go out and buy a Rolls-Bentley immediately. I bought a Mark 8 Jaguar instead.

But there was more to come. The man who insisted I played in the film was George Cukor, an infinitely wicked and loveable man as well as being, at his best, one of the very fine directors. He has seen me and was seeing me in a play of Lillian Hellman's yclept *Montserrat*.[42] I didn't think much of the book or the script but I thought a lot of Cukor and my leading lady was, he assured me, to be either Garbo (who told me mendaciously but charmingly some months later, having seen the film, that she would have done it had she known I was so good) or Vivien.[43] So I left with Syb and her brother Dai Mogs – just down from Cambridge with a deliberately indifferent degree – who was supposed to be my secretary though I ended up answering not only my own post but his too – on the *Queen Mary* first call and all found.[44]

By the time we got to NY 5½ days later Cukor had been either fired or had withdrawn (I never did find out which) and my leading lady was Olivia de Havilland who had just won two Oscars in three years and was in the language of Hollywood 'hot, hot, hot'.[45] She was married to a very eccentric man, very forgettable, who thought that his wife was the mid-century Duse and had a notice put on the board that all members of the crew and cast were no longer to call Olivia 'Livvy' which was her long-established diminutive in the industry, but as Miss De Havilland at all times.[46] I was also told by Zanuck's hatchet man [. . .] Lew Schreiber that Miss De Havilland would not permit me to have co-starring billing with her. I didn't mind about the billing a bit and to this day I have never cared about it but I did get the impression, later confirmed, that they were hoping I would do a Rex Harrison and arrogantly walk out as they wanted somebody else, or Miss De Havilland wanted somebody else – I seem to remember it was Greg Peck – to play my part.[47] I said somewhat testily to Schreiber that I had worked with the greatest living actors and actresses and they hadn't fussed about billing. So I stayed but with a little murder in my heart for Miss De H. The film, for some forgotten reason was delayed for 7 weeks and we lived in a small – large to us – duplex apartment on Charleville

---

[42] Burton played Captain Montserrat in *Montserrat*, written by Lillian Hellman (1905–84), which played at the Lyric Theatre, Hammersmith, in April 1952.
[43] Greta Garbo (1905–90), actor.
[44] David Morgan Williams, also known as 'Dai Mogs'.
[45] Olivia de Havilland had won the Best Actress Oscar for her performances in *To Each His Own* (1946) and *The Heiress* (1948).
[46] De Havilland's first husband was Marcus Goodrich (1897–1991), novelist.
[47] This may be a reference to Rex Harrison's troubled relationship with Twentieth Century-Fox, eventually terminated 'by mutual agreement'.

Boulevard. It was during those seven weeks that I started the hunt for Jean.[48] It didn't take long. What has this to do with Hungary? Well, eventually it will lead back to the loveable larcenous Sir Alex Korda. [. . .]

Tuesday 8th, Budapest We arrived yesterday at exactly 5pm [. . .] when I arrived a pimply bloke with a mike asked me why I had come to Budapest. I said 'You mean you don't know. I have come to do a film.' Yes please, he said, and what is the name of the film? 'Don't you read the papers?' I queried, and then, at a nudge and a look from E, added 'I have to do a film called *Bluebeard*.' 'What are you doing here Mrs Burton?' 'I am being Richard's wife' said E. End of interview. Budapest was shrouded in Danube damp, ghostlike like London sometimes and is still the same this morning. Pretty cold too, but the suite – The Presidential Suite of course – is about the best appointed of its kind I've ever seen anywhere.[49] It is enormous with an indoor garden and a massive balcony on which one could play tennis practically, certainly two games of table tennis. Additionally there is a heated indoor, glassed-in terrace. Two bedrooms, two bathrooms, a dining room, a largeish kitchen and enough space for all of E's clothes. Sensational. Its only drawback, which I shall try to rectify today is that at night the lights are so low powered that it is difficult to read. One has to sit directly under the lamps to read.

[. . .] There was much talk last night from Gianni, who is Jonah's half brother I swear, and Claudye about the recalcitrant intransigence of one of my ladies in the film. A lady I'd never heard of before this film called Joey Heatherton.[50] She has refused to work until her clothes which she wore in Paris and approved have all been re-done by someone other than Vicky who designed the first lot.[51] She sounds a frump but I shall be interested to find out if she carries on when I'm around. The probability is that she's talentless and knows it and is therefore frightened and hides behind a defensive cloak of 'temperament'. Why couldn't they get a good actress? There are a lot about.

The Danube – certainly not blue in this London weather – lies beneath us. It is as wide as the Thames at Westminster at this point I would guess. Perhaps a little less though I am a hopeless judge of water distances. The far 'Buda' side is thick with ice floes which are moving almost imperceptibly down river. It must be cold up in them thar hills.

So far all the Hungarians I've met are very solemn though I did get our evening waiter to crack a somewhat pained smile. The tragedy of '56 must still be a giant sorrow. I shall get to know them better once I start work. Gaston says they are much nicer than the Jugs. That must be very nice indeed.

---

[48] Charleville Boulevard, Beverly Hills. Jean Simmons, with whom Burton had an affair.
[49] The Duna Hotel, now the Budapest Marriott.
[50] Davenie Johanna or 'Joey' Heatherton (1944—), actor and singer, who played the part of Anne in *Bluebeard*.
[51] Vicky Tiel was costume designer for *Bluebeard*.

But back to Korda. As a result of the enormous success of the *Rachel* film and the one following it – a terrible thing called *The Robe* – Fox offered me a million dollars for 7 years for 7 films. It was only later that I found out that in addition to paying me a million they had – forced to because I was still under contract to Korda – paid him a ½ million on the side. A few years later, after I'd found this out, I went to have dinner with Alex in Millionaires' Row to which he had moved after living for years at Claridges taking his new wife with him. His brother had found a Canaletto and when I admired it Alex said, 'Enjoy it my boy, you paid for it.'[52] The new wife incidentally after Alex died married a tall thin chap with an enormous nose, very lah-di-dah and possibly titled, and, poor thing, committed suicide a few years ago. She was very rich apparently, very beautiful certainly while Lah-di-dah married a quite dishy French Countess later.[53] I always think of him with great suspicion as a sort of murderer once removed. Quite unjustified I suppose.

[...] I am cunningly, stealthily, thief-in-the-nightly trying to make the ultimate personal sacrifice. Today I am smoking only with a filtered cigarette holder – I have forgotten twice out of ten cigs so far this morning – and after some days I shall try and cut down to after breakfast, then after 10, then 11, then 12 and so on. If my desire to do it is great enough I should succeed unless some catastrophe intervenes. But can I do it while working? [...] Yes, of course Richard, you can do anything if you try hard enough except certain things like running 100 yards in even time. [...]

Wednesday 9th, Duna, Budapest [...] I am as happy as a scientist until Tommy Thompson of *Life* magazine and Eddie Dmytryk came to chat. It was alright for a bit but they – particularly Tommy sated us by staying on and on and we finally didn't have our pörkölt until nearly 10 o'clock.[54]

Both E and I did our going to bed exercises last night together. It is difficult to keep a straight face when she is doing her numbers as she goes at it with a solemn ferocity which is hilarious. It is especially droll when we do running on the spot as she has to hold her breasts – one hand on each – for firm as they are, really like a thirty-year-old's more than a nearly forty-year-old's, they are pretty big and the resultant wiggle-waggle would be pretty odd as well as bad for her. It's a very fetching sight and were it open to the public would fetch a lot of people. Like 10 million.

[...] yesterday I started out on the Hungarian language. It is the kind of potted grammar which I adore, somewhat like 'Hugo's' grammars, which have

---

[52] Giovanni Antonio Canal (1697–1768), artist, known as Canaletto. Alexander Korda's brothers were Zoltan (1895–1961) and Vincent (1896–1979). His 'new wife' was Alexandra Boycun (1928–66), whom he married in 1953.

[53] Alexandra Korda married David Metcalfe, whose father had been aide-de-camp to the Duke of Windsor. They were divorced in 1964. Her death in 1966 was due to an accidental overdose, not suicide.

[54] Pörkölt: Hungarian meat stew.

little vocabs and exercises at the end of each lesson with the answers in the back half, third, of the volume. And all my answers were alright. Since it is neither a slav or romance language the acquisition of the vocab alone is a formidable task. It has, the vocab, no association with anything I know.

I was up at 5.30 [. . .]. The bridges and the morning mist looked for all the world like a Whistler *Nocturne* except it was the Danube and not the Thames.[55]

Apparently, according to Dmytryk, the girl Heatherton is as good as gold and the reason for her tantrums is simply nerves. To my surprise, on the other hand, they said that Raquel Welch is a monster of egoism and difficulty.[56] For some reason, not ever except by accident reading the show pages of the various newspapers and mags I had the impression she was a nice and very pretty somewhat bewildered Marilyn.[57] According to Tommy Thompson and Dmytryk she is an arch fiend. Everybody expects me to control her. How? My only defence against 'temperament' – though oddly enough I have ever hardly come across it – is to laugh and leave the set until everybody has cooled off. They expect me to awe her and frighten her into good behaviour. I have no intention of doing anything of the kind unless she really does behave boringly in which case I will turn all my ice-cold intellectual guns on her. [. . .]

To my delight I got very good reception from the BBC on my little Philips Radio [. . .] I've looked again and it's not a Philips it's something called a Grundig. Inevitably German of course. When I turned it on at 6 there was a discussion going on about pornography. It was curious that the attackers were all lah-di-dah and cut-glass and chiffon and very pukka while the defenders – those who sold and published porno and made and showed the films were all provincially, mostly educated cockney accented. The pro-pornos in fact <u>sounded</u> dirty and salacious while the others with their Oxford and 'County' accents sounded faintly disgusted that they had to talk about such things at all may deah. It sounded in fact so funny that it might quite easily have been the *Goon Show* boys of delicious memory doing a send-up.[58]

E has been up, had a glass of grapefruit juice, read my last two entries, walked on the terrace and gone back to bed. [. . .]

Thursday 10th, Budapest I did not go to the studio at all yesterday. Elizabeth had to have a chat with Tommy Thompson of *Life* mag before her being snapped today by a very tall elegant – over elegant Englishman called Norman Parkinson (call me 'Parks' my dear) of whom neither of us had ever heard but who is apparently well known as a society photographer or something.[59] At

---

[55] A reference to the *Nocturne* series of paintings (many of the River Thames) by J. M. Whistler (1834–1903).

[56] Raquel Welch (1940—), who played Magdalena in *Bluebeard*.

[57] Marilyn Monroe (1926–62), actor.

[58] *The Goon Show*, British radio comedy programme (1951–60), one of whose stars was Peter Sellers.

[59] Norman Parkinson (1913–90), portrait photographer.

least I presume so as he snapped Princess Anne for the same distinguished mag a month ago.[60] He reminded us separately and together that we had all met some years ago. [. . .] Thompson is a nice enough man but a bad interviewer so just as he was due I sloped off into the smaller of the two bedrooms to read while he interviewed.

[. . .] Today I have to work. There is but no question that I am the laziest actor in the world with the possible exception of Marlon. My first scene today is merely to sit in front of the stage at the 'Moulin Rouge' and show myself attracted by the – as yet – unknown Miss Heatherton. I go to work at 11.30 to be ready at 1pm. I am so much more interested in *Volcano* that when I do think about my work at all it is always for the time being at least something that's in the future and not what I am presently doing. It has always been the case in my case. At Oxford if Chaucer was our task for that term I read Shakespeare, if Shakespeare I read the Metaphysicals, if the Romantics I read Eliot and Pound.[61] Yesterday I read – switching from one to t'other *Smokin' Joe* a book, very bad, about Frazier the current world heavyweight champ, a bit of *Volcano* and, in bed, *Hag's Nook* by Dr Fell, a John Dickson Carr whodunit.[62] The script stared at me from the coffee table all day long. It is still staring at me so will stop staring back and attack it at last. [. . .]

Saturday 11th[63] [. . .] I read in the local German–English paper that Sarah Jane Todd, wife of Mike Junior, had died suddenly of a heart attack. Totally unfair as unfairness goes in this world. Never drank, never smoked, adored and lived for by her husband, 6 children the oldest of whom must be about 16–17. She died on Monday but we got the news today only. Also we have to wait until tonight or late this afternoon to attempt at least to call him. Helpless feeling all round. I hope, no cynicism intended that he gets married in a couple of years.[64] He's a very married type and since he chose well the first time he probably will the second. [. . .]

I worked yesterday. It involved me sitting in a box and looking at a girl dancer on the stage played by the hitherto anonymous Heatherton and with her looking uncertainly back up at maniac with the blue beard.

Heatherton seems unbelievably ordinary which might be good for the part. She has one of those one-on-every-street-corner blonde rather common and at the drop of an insult I'm sure vicious bitchy faces. However the film comes first and I will do what I can to help her be good, because if she ain't good we

---

[60] Princess Anne (1950—), daughter of Queen Elizabeth II.
[61] Ezra Pound (1885–1972), poet.
[62] 'Smokin' Joe Frazier (1944–2011) had won the World Heavyweight Boxing Championship in 1968 and retained it until 1973. The book was probably Phil Pepe, *Come out Smokin'. Joe Frazier: The Champ Nobody Knew* (1972). John Dickson Carr's (1905–77) *Hag's Nook* (1933) features the detective Gideon Fell.
[63] Saturday was 12 February.
[64] Mike Todd Jr married again later in 1972 to Susan McCarthy.

only have half a picture. Dmytryk is very little and very brisk and light-voiced and intelligent and pretends to knowledge that he doesn't really have or has forgotten. The girl said that she had never been so nervous in her life at meeting anyone and that she had worshipped me ever since, as a schoolgirl (she was careful to point out) she had seen me in *Anger* and – wait for it – *Bramble Bush*. The first put her up in my estimation, the second sank her without trace. [...] Talk is that she is having a ding-dong, as the vernacular goes, with Dmytryk. I wouldn't be at all surprised as however else did she get the part? I mean, who had heard of her? And Ann-Margret who is currently fashionable, having made a success in Mike Nichols' film *Carnal Knowledge*, had offered to play in *Bluebeard*.[65] [...]

I dwell on 'Joey' as she is yclept, as until I read the script again yesterday I had forgotten what an enormous part and opportunity it is and gives. Also I've got to learn to act this kind of Maria in the Red Barn melodrama.[66] It has to be done with immense tongue in cheek. I try to remember how the master – whassisname – Vincent Price plays it. [...] Even voiced, measured in speech, purposeful in movement with the occasional violence in voice and movement. Must be funny serious. Shall know the minute I begin how to do it I hope. [...]

Keep on thinking about poor Mike Junior. His mother died when young as E pointed out.[67] His father died shockingly in an air-crash and they were very great friends. His wife dies after a skiing holiday at 41 years old. Rough on the poor little sod. Must try and talk to him tonight. <u>And he's such a nice man</u>. [...]

Sunday 13th [...] Had a telegram yesterday saying that Jim Benton was in Cedars of Lebanon Hospital having a bad case of infectious hepatitis and since we had [been] in contact with him 10 days ago it was necessary for us to have a shot of Gamma Globulin – if that's the word I'm searching for as Bertie Wooster might say – an operation that I always dread ever since I had a mass of typhoid, tetanus, yellow fever, Gdang fever and other assorted shots to go to work in Morocco in 1964 and lo and behold – after being as sick as a dog for a week with each inoculatory disease as they took turns, and having to work at the same time at the Vic I suppose – we shot the film (*Alex the Great*) in Madrid – in and around Madrid – instead.[68] [...]

I worked, as 'twere, for the first time yesterday. That is to say I did a full scene with the girl and her partner though he had nary a word to say and it seems to be alright. She has a natural hardness that might become effective as

---

[65] Ann-Margret had received an Oscar nomination as Best Supporting Actress for her performance in Mike Nichols's 1971 film *Carnal Knowledge*.

[66] A reference to the 1935 film *Maria Marten, or The Murder in the Red Barn*, directed by Milton Rosmer (1881–1971).

[67] Mike Todd's first wife, Bertha Freeman, died in 1946, when Mike Todd Jr was seventeen.

[68] Bertie Wooster is a character in the stories of P. G. Wodehouse. Burton means 1954.

she is the only lady of the 8 who manages to turn the tables on me and escape. I might enjoy this film and one of the ways is to work hard at it and not 'eef' it or 'wing' it as I had thought to do. First of all I can, I think, improve my dialogue by paraphrasing what they already have – I don't mean on the spot, waiting for the inspiration paraphrasing but pre-planned re-writing. Keeping it to myself and simply doing it when the time comes for I know that directors dearly love to 'kick it around a bit' when you suggest a change of dialogue. That can – and I'm pretty sure it applies to this man – mean a couple of wasted hours mucking about [. . .].

The minute people go away and leave E alone she is a different woman. She came to the studio yesterday afternoon and waited until the end and we went home together, and for the first time spent an evening together without inter-ruption from anybody except the waiter who unfortunately <u>will hang around</u> while we eat and though I'm sure he is not trying to listen to our conversation or any of that kind of spies everywhere rubbish it is still uncomfortable. We smile and nod and say that will be fine thank you, we'll help ourselves from now on and though he understands English perfectly, nevertheless it is cribbing cabining and confining.[69] [. . .]

We had our shots and E's left a lump like a goose egg whereas mine left nothing at all except a lot of blood on my underpants and pyjamas. I forgot to tell the Doctor that I am a bleeder. Whatever will the laundry think. [. . .]

Monday 14th [. . .] I am still slowly persisting with the Lingua Magyar but it is not so sweet now as twas before and I had asked the young doctor who comes in now regularly – whether asked or not it seems – if he could spare five minutes, to record some ordinary phrases into my tape-recorder which he did and I thanked him but on playing it back I must have buggered up the device as he sounds as if he's speaking Turkish on a bad line from Istanbul via Vladivostok.[70] I shall try again. [. . .] I don't ask much. I want to be able to ask for food and drink in the native tongue, acquire the numbers and the mone-tary system, and learn like a parrot about a page about any given current topic and show off. If anybody replies, I shall revert to English or if there's nobody around to understand it, Welsh.

Saw last night many lovely snaps of E taken by Norman Parkinson who turns out to be a very amusing <u>and</u> nice man and, indeed, of the scores of photographs, only about 5 or 6 made E's face look a little full. He must be used again. Those old aristos – Beaton and Parkinson, really know what they're doing. I suddenly realized the difference in quality between a Parkinson or a Beaton and a Gianni Bozzacchi and his kind. Not a brush of touch-up is

---

[69] A reference to Macbeth's line, Act III, scene iv, 'But now I am cabined, cribbed, confined, bound in to saucy doubts and fears.'
[70] A reference to a line from Duke Orsino's speech in *Twelfth Night*, Act I, scene i.

necessary. Partly by his lighting and mostly from E's having lost 8lbs or so I would say, the fullness of the chin – the underchin is never obtrusive.

He didn't make me look very fetching but I gather that he's not very good with gents. Anyway I've never been – at least not for 20 years or so – and am never likely to be the pin-up type. Too many excrescences and twisted bones. My hair is at last getting very thin though it still covers my whole scalp but when wet, soaking wet one can see its barrenness. Since it's such a bore to have Ron pencil in lines all over the place I think I might one of these days try one of those transplants. It won't be like those idiots who are really bald and on whom it is still obvious and I only need a few strands around the crown of the head. I don't think however that I will get a face lift like that abject Rod Steiger who not only admits to it but it makes him look like one half of a naked ass-hole.[71] In addition to which, he says, he can't get any jobs and will soon be broke. It might be because people don't want to be looking at a talking ass-hole. Now there's a man who really has worked very hard at his job all his life and at last, when he got an Oscar a couple of years ago, everybody thought well now at last he's a 'STAR'.[72] But he ain't and never was and never will be though with a harsh director he can still be very effective. He has the dreadful problem of believing himself to be a great actor – whatever that may be – and it shows in every thing he does. His Napoleon was merely silly.[73] Incidentally I sent off a telegram yesterday saying no to Nelson. Apart from the fact that Nelson bores me – unlike Napoleon – the film belongs to Lady Hamilton who if she's half a good actress will get an Oscar.[74] [. . .] The script is very able as usual as it comes from the fecund pen of Sir Terence Rattigan.[75] We really do have some very unlikely knights around nowadays. [. . .]

Tuesday 15th Started off in black and over-laid it in red. I am still as purely non-alcoholic as the scion of two AA's.[76]

Pouring with rain this morning and it rained all day yesterday too. I wish someone would reprint that slim volume of Alun Lewis which contains the poem 'All day it has rained' and 'For Gweno' etc., a companion of my teens, when I was more poet than most, indeed the time when I read and acquired by familiarity the vast store of memorized and memorable verse that still lies here in my head.[77]

---

[71] Rod Steiger (1925–2002), who had appeared like Burton in *The Longest Day* and with whom Burton would act in *Breakthrough*.

[72] Steiger had won Best Actor for his performance in *In the Heat of the Night* (1967), directed by Norman Jewison (1926—).

[73] Steiger had played Napoleon in *Waterloo* (1970), a role that Burton had considered.

[74] A reference to the film *Bequest to the Nation* (1973, US title *The Nelson Affair*), directed by James Cellan Jones (1931—), and starring Peter Finch as Nelson and Glenda Jackson (1936—) as Lady Hamilton.

[75] Terence Rattigan (1911–77) had written the play *Bequest to the Nation* in 1970.

[76] Alcoholics Anonymous. Burton is referring to the colour of the typewriter ribbon.

[77] Alun Lewis's poems 'All Day it has Rained' and 'For Gweno' appeared in the 1942 volume *Raiders' Dawn and other poems*.

[. . .] I awoke at 5 to 7 actually and did all my usual ablutions and exercised with the addition – very carefully for fear of my chipped base of spine and my tendency to lout gumbago and arturitis – Spooner and Mr Bindle – 10 sit ups the stomach muscles taking it very well.[78] I shall keep up twenty a day, 10 at night, 10 in the morning for a few days and see how it goes. Would like to work up to a hundred, 150, and lo those flat stomach muscles again. My stomach is flat at the moment but soft like a baby's. I wonder if I shall ever get those two parralel (still asleep) parallel ridges of vertical muscle that I used to pride myself on. Or am I now too old? [. . .] Yesterday I played organ (traditional for horror movies) while a hawk flew around – a falcon to be exact – and landed on my shouldders[79] (I really am only half awake) and a white cat streaked around. [. . .]

I work with 'Joey' again this day. She seems perfectly innocuous to me but everybody else seems to loathe her. She gets up to tantrums behind my back presumably that I never see. I must confess that she is about as stimulating an actress as the worst I've known but I keep on telling myself that it doesn't really matter. We can slide around her with cunning and girls in horror movies are always props after all. All they have to do is be pretty and dumb.

Am reading – at work – three books. In the upstairs dressing-room either *Volcano* or a novel by 'Hungary's greatest prose' writer Imre something and in the trailer and most fascinating a biog of Einstein.[80] At home it's a detective story in bed and a history of espionage in the Abwehr before during and slightly after the war.[81] Interesting that one of the so-called master spies was a Welsh Nationalist xenophobe – especially anglophobe – called Owens.[82] He is reputedly still alive. He is described as 'an excitable little Welshman' but he was a double spy used by the XX section of MI5 and the Germans. Some of the things he did were hair-raisingly courageous so he cannot have been all that excitable. I was told a long time ago that he was in South Ireland. I must try and seek him out. There might be a film on him as he reported to his German 'masters' that he had a whole ring of anglo-phobic Welshmen spying for him and therefore for them all around Britain including a former Chief Detective Inspector from Swansea. It could made a film and an odd one – perhaps even a funny one – as of course, the minute the Huns started out in earnest bashing us during the blitzes all the dissident malcontents in the Welsh Plaid Cymru turned double spies against their German friends. And deceived them throughout the war. A dirty game but fascinating nevertheless. [. . .]

---

[78] 'Spooner' is a reference to the Reverend W. A. Spooner (1844–1930) and his tendency to metathesis, the transposition of letters or sounds in a word, commonly known as 'Spoonerisms'. Mr Bindle is a cockney character in novels by Herbert Jenkins (1876–1923).

[79] There is an x typed over the second d in shouldders.

[80] Presumably Imre Kertesz (1929—), who would win the Nobel Prize for Literature in 2002. Albert Einstein (1879–1955), physicist.

[81] The Abwehr was a German military intelligence unit.

[82] According to Farago, *The Game of the Foxes*, p. 137, Arthur 'Johnny' Owens was freed in 1945 and went on to live in Ireland.

Friday 19th[83] [. . .] I read a lot of the biography of Einstein and indeed to God began to think that – poetically at least – I was understanding the relativity of time and space but very much through a glass darkly. Then I had several ½ hours of Wolf Mank and a man from the Jersey Islands who for some reason I didn't quite trust though he seemed nice enough.[84] I had no idea that the Channel Islands are so free of British rule and that they have their own tax laws. [. . .] Anyway if we do the *Canterbury Tales* there which I and E too probably will we might do worse than as twere case the joint as a possible home from home instead of Suisse. Geographically too I am moronic. I said the islands are midway in the channel or nearer France. Oh my God, he said, France of course – I frequently water ski there. Ah, said I. Dick Makewater was here too with the art director of *Shrew* or was it *Anne* who won an Oscar I think.[85] He is to direct. I wonder if he can. Wolfie was in one of his racier moods. 'My gawd you look smashing', he said, 'what's happened to you?' 'Dunno,' I said 'it can't be the loss of weight at I was this same weight approximately when we last saw each other in Bosnia.' 'Yeah I know,' he said, 'but you look more smashing, somethin's happened to you.' He kept on about it. [. . .] Anyway I said it was 'exercise'. 'Aw Chraist,' he said, 'I can never do anything physical for myself and to myself that I can imagine better.' He was at his most engagingly cockney and obviously adored Elizabeth who reciprocated and said, 'Now that's the kind of man I could love if you weren't around, I adore him.' 'Bloody daft thing to say,' I said, hurting. But good taste all the same I thought. Wolfie always looks hooded eyed and desperate and is always being hounded by some 'bird'. 'They're all fackin nuisances, they want to possess a man body and soul, won't leave you alone. Nasty dirty bastards. Hate the cunts.' Except Elizabeth apparently to whom he paid court all evening. There is always an oddity about people's preferences for types. I've always lusted for medium height dark haired Jewesses, or those who could be first racial cousins. Elizabeth has always fancied Jews period. She seems to have a rapport with them which she doesn't have with the ordinary Anglo Saxon. She and Wolf could obviously have talked all night. And about all kinds of things. They touched lightly on Wedgwood for instance last night [. . .].[86] And it has nothing to do – in E's case – with male beauty for Wolf is a mess, about my height with a great pendulous belly that is big enough to turn after the rest of his body has turned, double chinned, grubby looking without being unclean. But his mind is astringent. There is no shit about him and he is a renaissance man. He opens

---

[83] Friday was 18 February.
[84] Wolf Mankowitz (1924–98).
[85] Dick Makewater is Richard's nickname for Richard McWhorter. Lionel Couch (1913–89) was art director on *Anne of the Thousand Days*, for which he received an Oscar nomination for Best Art Direction.
[86] Mankowitz was an authority on antique porcelain, and had published *The Portland Vase and the Wedgwood Copies* (1953) and co-edited (with R. G. Haggar), *The Concise Encyclopaedia of English Pottery and Porcelain* (1957).

shop to sell Wedgwood having first made himself an expert on the subject, writing a lavishly illustrated book to prove his own provenance as an expert and then – as he just has – sold the shops owned by his sister and himself for half a million nicker tax free capital fackin gain. And who to, d'yer think? Fackin Wedgwood that's who.[87] He has now started or resurrected a small private printing press in Cork or Dublin – anyway in Eire somewhere – and his first publication is a book of his own poems.[88] Now he wants me to write for them. Anything he says, 'rondeaux, frigging triolets, belles lettres, the story of your life, graffiti, anything you like old mate.' He is superlatively intelligent with a considerable smattering of the poet about him. [. . .]

Saturday 20th[89] [. . .] Curious note: I sent a 'gram to Arthur Koestler (*Darkness at Noon*, a marvellous 3 volume autobiography and the latest *Case of the Midnight Toad*) expressing admiration for his work and asking him to come to the party with ulterior motive of possibility of film from *Midnight Toad*.[90] His reply said something like 'would love to come but climate there unhealthy for me. Happy 30th birthday to your wife.'[91] I am most surprised that he is still persona non grata after all these years. I wonder if he's melodramatizing the whole situation. After all, he reneged from the Party something like 35 years ago.[92] [. . .] The greatest monsters to the Jugoslavs were their former tyrannical Royalty and we heard from Tito himself that there was no objection to Elisheba coming back and at the Proust Ball I met Elisheba's (uncle)? cousin(?) who would be king were there a throne there to sit on and he told me that he'd been back as a tourist once and as a business man another time and everybody treated him with great bonhomie.[93] That's of course Jugland which is far more liberal than a Russian-run Hungary. Still, since *Darkness at Noon* Koestler has been harmless to them.[94] And even that, as I remember, didn't specify any particular country though it was obviously a Communist one. [. . .] Also, of course, I'm not sure how much pamphleteering Koestler has been up to through the years. It will be interesting to find out, for instance, if he's been read here at all since he changed colours. [. . .]

I did a longish scene with the girl yesterday and it seemed to go alright. This film might be amusant after all.

---

[87] Mankowitz had owned a shop selling porcelain in the Piccadilly Arcade in London.
[88] Mankowitz's *XII Poems* had been published in London by the Workshop Press in 1971, and the printing had been carried out in Dublin.
[89] Saturday was 19 February.
[90] Arthur Koestler (1905–83), author of the novel *Darkness at Noon* (1940), five volumes of autobiography published between 1937 and 1954 and *The Case of the Midwife Toad* (1971), a study of biologist Paul Kammerer.
[91] Elizabeth was of course about to turn 40.
[92] Koestler, who was born in Budapest, had been a member of the Communist Party (in Germany) from 1931 to 1938.
[93] Burton is referring here to Princess Elizabeth of Yugoslavia.
[94] *Darkness at Noon* has as its subject the Stalinist 'show-trials' of the 1930s.

E came in to the room for a half hour or so and has gone back to bed to read a script that I might do. It's *Sir, you bastard* and I want to find out if she understands it as I think it might be confusing unless, like me, you have read the book first. [. . .]

Saturday 26th A day of enormous excitement for all. Some 80 odd or so people arrived at various times of the day for the big weekend.[95] Chief pleasures were of course the families – mine and Elizabeth's or should I say rather ours and ours. The next were Grace who again qualified for five stars and Nevill Coghill and Spender and Mrs Ladas and Simon and Sheran. What exquisite manners they all have in their very different ways. I taught all the girls to curtsey and all the lads how to do a proper hand-shake with Royalty and each by each and one by one they all performed admirably. We had a cocktail party in our suite – hastily rearranged for the purpose – which went with a swing – at least the last reluctant group left at about midnight with Howard Mara and kids staying until the end as it was the only chance we had of talking properly to them. I had several clec-clecs with my lot in one of their rooms.[96] I took wee Maria along – not so wee, she is a very tall girl – and introduced her to her 1000s of heretofore unknown and un-met aunts and uncles and, completely forgetting, we went babbling on in Welsh until we suddenly all realized that Maria was completely bewildered. She had been told by me of course many times that certain percentages of Welshmen spoke a tongue entirely alien to English but I don't think, until she heard us all at it last night, that she realized quite how alien it actually was. I think that vaguely she thought it was the equivalent of an Irish brogue or a Highland Scottish. The family adored her of course because she looked so like Kate. In fact Will Cross-eyes and a couple of the others thought she was Kate.[97] There is superficially a fleeting resemblance. Round face, cherubic cheeks, same colouring. The family were in tremendous form – Tom at 71 being the dynamo. The flight was as smooth as silk and was a particular thrill for Verdun who had, to my astonishment, never been in an aeroplane in his life and a jet at that. That alone has been sufficient excitement for him. They, with their still retained sense of wonder, were bowled over by everything. The very bathrooms, the fact that there was a bar in each room the view of the legendary Danube, the meetings with Elizabeth and of course Grace were high points. Both E and Grace behaved superbly. [. . .] Little Mickey Caine had flown from LA with one of his exquisite 'birds', a Marlon Brando Asiatic as usual, and How and Mar and my lovely Layton and the equally lovely Chris and Aileen had come almost exactly half way around the world and are going to be a trifle jet-lagged today and

---

[95] Elizabeth's 40th birthday celebrations.
[96] *Clec-clecs* is a Welsh term for a chat or a gossip.
[97] Will Cross-eyes being Richard's brother Will, whose eyesight had been affected by a bullet wound he had suffered during the Second World War.

tomorrow I would guess but the parties will keep them going.[98] Victor Spinetti and boyfriend were, are here, and Ringo and wife and Susannah York and Mick and Liz and Brook and Grace's Lady-in-waiting a certain Mme Aurelli, Professor Warner and a lady –possibly his inamorata – called Anna Something, and Doris Brynner and Bettina and Marie Lou Tolo (one of the girls in the film), Yves Le Tourneur and wife, Vanhattan of Van Cleef – Cartiers NY I mean – Hebe Dorsey, Vicky Berkeley complete with Ron, Billy Williams and wife (Williams is the great cameraman who shot *XYZ*) and our very own Chris and Liza who gave me thunderous good night kisses several to each side of the face and Kurt Frings, John Springer and too many to recount them all.[99] Frings went into business as usual and after extracting a promise from me that I would not throw him into the Danube said that the Lerner–Loewe–Donen consortium were still desperate for me to play *Little Prince*. [. . .] He also said that representing E and I was the greatest experience of his life and that we didn't realize what magic our names were and that after *XYZ* E is hotter or as hot as she's ever been. And that the respect and even awe at the mention of our names in meetings is quite extraordinary, that he has been in the business forty years and that [the] plural noun 'Burtons' is almost synonymous with Royalty. Another incidental exchange in the brouhaha of the party was then Francis Warner said he would like to see me alone for ½ an hour or so today and I said I would call him as soon as I arrived back from the Studio. I didn't ask him what specifically about but he was obviously bursting to tell me and said something very quickly and in tone of espionage. 'Fellowship at Oxford'. I am intrigued. It could be a step towards a D.Litt., which is the only honour I really covet.[100] [. . .]

The world press is here in droves. From everywhere. Literally, it seems. Japanese, India, as well as every other place you can think of in the western hemisphere. I think I will have to talk to them today – perhaps en masse. Dread of dreads and hell's damnation.[101]

The brothers (and their women too for that matter) are agog about the Welsh rugby team of the last three years and have bought 16mm copies of 'highlights' of the All Blacks and various other games. Shall try and watch it all this afternoon while everyone else is kipping.

Graham got very sloshed very quickly. I had to pull him up once after having heard him introduce Ringo Starr and wife four times to Howard and Mara with a 'D'you know my brother-in-law Howard, these are friends of

---

[98] Michael Caine would marry Shakira Baksh (1947—) in January 1973. Layton is Howard and Mara Taylor's son. Christopher Wilding and Aileen Getty (1957—), who later married.
[99] By 'Professor Warner' Burton means Francis Warner. Marilu Tolo played Brigitte in *Bluebeard* and had also appeared in *Candy*. Billy Williams (1929—), cinematographer, who would also work with Elizabeth Taylor on *Night Watch*.
[100] Doctor of Letters: usually awarded for a substantial record of research and publication, it may also be an honorary degree.
[101] Another inaccurate reference to the line from the hymn 'Cwm Rhondda': 'death of death, and hell's damnation'.

mine called Starkie.' The latter is Ringo's real name and the joke once is ok.[102] Twice it's tedious. Three times it's rude. He is, poor boy very very star-struck. But lovely with it. S. Spender is anxious to talk to me too. I wonder what about. What is the Cause?

Monday 28th February 1972 Budapest Merely to record that I missed yesterday's entry out of sheer inability to get down to the job. The apartment seemed eternally full of various people from time to time on Saturday and again yesterday.

[. . .] Grace came to dinner last night just with Howard and Mara and us. I had three slices of layer cake and ice-cream and was so tired that I was to all intents and purposes drunk. As a matter of fact I did not have one single drink through all the endless weekend though it did cross my mind at one moment when my fatigue was so great that I could not think of another way to go. However I didn't succumb and just as well. A drunken me as well as a tired me would have been too much and possibly disastrous. The news is just about on. I have turned it off. The usual stuff. Nixon home claiming to have made no secret deal with China.[103] A protest march in Paris (including Simone de Beauvoir) re the shooting of a picketing striker at the Renault car factory.[104] They carried pictures of the dead man.

Francis Warner intimated at more than a fellowship but a doctorate and KBE.[105] We shall see. [. . .] I don't know what to do about *Little Prince*. I think I'd better listen to the tapes and decide for myself whether I can do it. [. . .]

The party was a huge success. That means four parties – the cocktail party when we arrived, the cellar party, the brunch party next day and the posh party at night. All apart from a nasty incident with Alan Williams at the cellar party went without a hitch.[106] There was a press conference which went alright. I had to do it alone. [. . .] I saw a couple of hours of Welsh and Lions rugby on 16mm and by god they were really good.

Both Grace and E turned out first class jobs, both looking pretty with E – at the last party particularly – looking absolutely dazzling. Raquel Welch arrived. She is very pretty though a trifle hard faced. I recounted our conversations to E who said 'She was making a pass at you.' I protested but E was adamant. [. . .] Stephen Spender gave me – or rather – us a volume of his latest verse and I gave him a cheque for £1000 and a promise to write an article for the magazine which will keep the world informed as to where the behind-the-iron-curtain

[102] Actually Starkey.
[103] President Nixon returned from a week's visit to China on 28 February 1972.
[104] Simone de Beauvoir (1908–86), writer, philosopher. Pierre Overney had been shot dead on 25 February during a demonstration outside the Renault factory.
[105] KBE: Knight Commander of the Order of the British Empire.
[106] Alan Williams, son of Emlyn, had objected to Burton and Taylor's lack of interest in the oppression of the Hungarian people by Soviet-directed communism.

writers are imprisoned so that they will at least know that the rest of the world knows that we know where they are and in some way we must let the incarcerated know that their names live on the lips and in the pen and ink of caring people outside their lands.[107]

[. . .] The weekend was an undoubted success. I am sure that were it not for the fantastic exuberance of my family that it would not have been half so good. They seemed to relax everybody and nobody has ever seen Grace let her hair down – literally and figuratively – as much as Grace. Her lady-in-waiting too a Mme Aurelia was a ball of fire. Grace confesses that she never knew she had it in her. She danced wild Hungarian dances and at one time as I was sitting in a booth with Frankie Howerd Susannah York and husband and Ladas and Spender the rest of the party swept past us doing the conga.[108] I was goggleeyed. Led by the family the whole thing passed before our eyes with Grace in the middle of it all. Unbelievable.

MARCH

Wednesday 1st, Budapest [. . .] St David's Day and they're all going to school in Wales bearing daffodils and leeks and there will be singing in the Assembly Hall and competitions and a great many will get drunk tonight except me of course.[109] [. . .]

It was nightmarish yesterday going into work and finding, as I walked on the set that the scene was yet another party, dinner jackets and ladies in evening dresses. For a second I thought that I was doomed to parties for the rest of my life. [. . .] I talked to Aaron and at last we have decided to return to England and pay our taxes. I also – they have come back to me with a bang – finally and irrevocably turned down *Petit Prince*. So my next definite stint is *Volcano*.

We have asked Simon and Sheran to look for a place near theirs and not too far from Oxford with plenty of ground to keep a horse or two and a large dog or two, so that I can nip in to Oxford when I feel like it.

I have to send telegrams etc. this morning setting the wheels turning for the return to England. We shall do our damnedest not to winter there though we shall pay the taxes.

Wednesday 15th It is our eighth wedding anniversary. By some standards that is nothing. By others it's a monumental achievement. During that time too we have the rare distinction – in our business – of having been faithful to each other and for three years approx before that. So it's unofficially 11 years.[110] And

---

[107] The volume was possibly Spender's *The Generous Days* (1971). The magazine was *Index on Censorship* (1972—).

[108] Susannah York's husband was Michael Wells.

[109] David is the patron saint of Wales.

[110] It was ten years, Burton and Taylor's romance having begun in 1962.

where do we think we shall celebrate tonight – in a small cafe, tete-a-tete, eyes misting over with memories, our favourite tunes playing on a gypsy violin, dancing cheek to cheek, alone together in a crowd. Ah no. We have something far better than that. We are going to be at the British Bloody embassy with their excellent bores the ambassador and dress.[111] A silly mistake on our parts and not to be repeated.

[...] E had bought me a score or more of books, many crazy pens and pencils, a mug for tea drinking – reputedly 150 years old – the perfect size. And an Art Nouveau picture frame, a small one for a desk. I have nothing for E except my presence.

E adores occasions. Wedding anniversaries, birthdays, Xmas, Thanksgiving etc. I loathe them except for personal things like the anniversaries. But commercialized things like Xmas and Mother's day and Father's day (yet) and so on give me a royal pain in the ass.

[...] Wish we didn't have to go out to the Embassy, especially as they think of actors and actresses as just so many clowns. Envying them just the same. Some ambassadors are very good company but they are few and far between. Some are even intelligent. I can't remember what this feller was like. Nothing stunning or I would have remembered him from the birthday party. A little gentle sending up is called for I think. After all, it's not their fault that they happened to ask us on our anniversary and it is my fault that I had forgotten that it was until too late. [...]

Thursday 23rd, Dorchester Hotel Back again to the somewhat dilapidated Dorchester in one of those horrible non-suites.[112] We flew from Budapest around 6pm and arrived about 8. [...]

We went straight to 2 Squires Mount where there were a great many people including Tom and Hyral, Will and son, Graham and son, Menna and husband, Wendy and Derek but no Cassie, Dai, Hilda, our Dai and Betty or Cis and Elfed.[113] They'll be alright and all there today. I am looking forward to being on the plane tomorrow morning though but not looking forward to Pest.

Sweet Liza is here which makes up for a great deal of the pain.

I don't think E should stay very long. She will go mad with boredom, for Gwen, much as I adore her, is not exactly a laugh a minute.

I couldn't sleep at all last night and feel like taking a swift kip now which would be catastrophic. Oh, that lovely Janine was there. Paul is apparently able to walk with the aid of crutches.[114]

Very warm. By English standards a heat wave. Too lazy to write more.

---

[111] The British Ambassador to Hungary was Derek Dodson (1920–2003). His wife was Julie Maynard Barnes. They attended the party.
[112] Ivor, Richard's brother, had died, and Burton and Taylor returned to England for the funeral.
[113] Wendy was another niece of Gwen. Her husband was Derek Jenkins.
[114] Paul and Janine Filistorf.

MARCH 1972–APRIL 1975

Richard Burton ceased keeping his 1972 diary in late March. For over three years he appears not to have made any attempt to maintain his personal record.

After Ivor's funeral Richard seemed to go into a deep depression. This was manifested both in a return to heavy drinking and in a cavalier attitude towards his marriage to Elizabeth. By May he may have been unfaithful, having affairs with some of his co-stars in *Bluebeard*, including Nathalie Delon. Elizabeth responded by being seen in public with Aristotle Onassis. Burton and Taylor spent an increasing amount of time apart: he had to return to Yugoslavia and to *The Battle of Sutjeska* while she made *Night Watch* in London. Burton did spend some time at St Peter's College, Oxford, but his plan to write a micro-history based on the Peregrina Pearl was not executed. Richard and Elizabeth teamed up once more in the autumn of 1972 to make the double TV film for Harlech Television *Divorce His, Divorce Hers*, shot in Rome and Munich. This was an unhappy experience and, again, did nothing for their critical reputation when it was broadcast the following year.

The year 1973 opened with Richard once more in Rome, making *Massacre in Rome*, while Elizabeth filmed *Ash Wednesday* in Treviso and in the ski resort of Cortina d'Ampezzo. By the summer the rift between them was serious. An attempt at reconciliation in New York failed and on 3 July 1973 their separation was announced. Elizabeth went to Beverly Hills, where she began a relationship with businessman Henry Wynberg. Richard initially based himself at Aaron Frosch's home at Quogue, Long Island, and then returned to Italy to start work on *The Voyage*, co-starring alongside Sophia Loren. Loren and her husband Carlo Ponti (who had produced *Massacre in Rome*) hosted him at their estate near Marino, where he was visited by Elizabeth in late July, but any attempt at reconciliation was short-lived. Divorce papers began to be drafted.

While filming *The Voyage* in Sicily in November, Richard learned that Elizabeth had been taken into hospital in Los Angeles, and he flew to California to be with her. Upon her recovery Elizabeth visited Richard in Naples, and over the following weeks they spent time together in New York, Hawaii and then in Gstaad. Early in 1974 they were together in Puerto Vallarta, and in March Richard began working on *The Klansman* in Oroville, near Sacramento, California. His disintegration was becoming a public spectacle, and rumours of liaisons with young women were widespread. In April he was taken into St John's Hospital in Santa Monica in order to 'dry out'. Elizabeth filed for divorce and this was granted at Saanen in Switzerland on 26 June 1974.

A single man for the first time in more than a quarter of a century Richard left hospital and sailed to Europe, staying for a while at his home in Céligny before travelling to Winchester to work alongside Sophia Loren once more in *Brief Encounter*. In October 1974 he became engaged to Princess Elizabeth of Yugoslavia (herself married to Neil Balfour), and began work on a drama documentary about Winston Churchill – titled *The Gathering Storm / Walk with Destiny*. A public furore followed the appearance of two articles by Burton in the *New York Times* and the American *TV Guide*, both of which were unrestrained in their attack on the former British Prime Minister. Shortly afterwards Richard's relationship with Princess Elizabeth collapsed, Burton having begun seeing Jeanne Bell, an African-American actor and former *Playboy* centrefold, whom he had first met on the set of *The Klansman*.

At the beginning of 1975 Burton, along with Bell (1943—), Charlotte Rampling and James Coburn, started filming *Jackpot* in Nice, but this project remained unfinished owing to financial difficulties. Burton returned to Céligny with Bell, and again took up his pen.

1975

APRIL

Friday 11th Taylors arrived from Leningrad.[1] [. . .] E has dysentery and may have to go to England.[2] Career sounds perilous if absence prolonged. Filming chaotic she says.

Monday 14th Jane Swanson arrived with clothes and papers to sign. Became thoroughly sloshed. [. . .]

Tuesday 15th, Céligny Brook arrived.[3] Very T and E by evening.[4] Film (*Jackpot*) still hanging on. Personally have no hope.

Wednesday 16th (78kg)[5] Brook left. T and E again. Went to see Maria's school. Welsh-speaking headmaster (Thomaster) seems efficient. Goes in next September together with friend Tournesol.[6]

Thursday 17th, Céligny (78kg) Sunbathed. Biked.

Friday 18th Fasted all day. While we biked to Founey, E'en So unprecedently walked to Café de la Gare.[7] Astonishing found eating in kitchen. Cycled from Nyon. [. . .]

Saturday 19th (77kg) Maria starts school tomorrow evening.

Tuesday 22nd (78kg) Talked E and Liza. Liza begs me to go see Elizabeth. Said would think about same.

Wednesday 23rd (77½kg) Fasted all day talked E in London hospital. Sounds v. little. Can't keep anything down. [. . .]

---

[1] Elizabeth was filming *The Blue Bird*, directed by George Cukor and shot on location in Leningrad and Moscow.
[2] Elizabeth was suffering from severe amoebic dysentery.
[3] Brook Williams.
[4] T and E presumably being 'tired and emotional', or drunk.
[5] Burton is keeping track of his weight.
[6] To the school at Tournesol.
[7] Burton must mean Founex, 3 kilometres south of Céligny.

Thursday 24th (76½kg) To Gstaad for the night. Drove M-Moke. Froze and wind-burned. Bed early with book. Felt terrible. Awoke feeling splendid. How and Mara talk and talk and talk.

Friday 25th, Gstaad Felt immensely better. Left Gstaad noon [. . .]. Bis still blowing but this time at my back so made good time.[8] Went ahead of hired Merc as latter so much faster. Had lunch between Vevey and Lausanne.[9] Good food. (Le Vieux Moulin) Place – village yclept Epesse.[10] Mara says Howard to give straight talk to E. Wish he w'nt [*sic*] put her misplaced loyalty on defensive.

Saturday 26th, Céligny (78½kg) Sunbathed all day. Read new sympathetic *Napoleon* also D. Francis thriller. JB, Maria and friend [. . .] came by train from Gstaad for weekend. [. . .][11]

Sunday 27th (78kg) Had a Gibson.[12] First for weeks. Hated it though well made by JB. Sunbathed, read, bicycled all day. Bise still blowing therefore weather perfect. Cold in the shade. Garden a riot of colour. Cherry, apple, pear, peach blossom. Talked E in hospital: Sounds much chippier. [. . .]

Monday 28th (77½kg) Yesterday sunned, read, new biography of Coleridge by one Fulman.[13] Fascinating. Rode on bike to Commugny and back.[14] Non-stop. Don't feel going on 50 at all. More like 40. [. . .] Had raclette at Village near Nyon.

Tuesday 29th, Céligny (77½kg) Yesterday sunned, read went to airport to see off Howard and family keeping Layton with us to take him interview at Int. School Gen.[15] Shopped in Nyon. Read Parkinson's book on footballer Best.[16] Horribly common. Talked to E last night. Sounds very depressed. Her film like mine seems doomed. [. . .]

Wednesday 30th, Céligny (77½kg) Yesterday saw Layton to school. Lunched at airport. [. . .] Bought JB watch (automatique) bought myself Power Certina for deep sea diving.[17] When I am going to do that nobody knows. New watch

---

[8] Burton means *bise*, the north wind.
[9] Vevey: 18 km east of Lausanne on the north shore of Lake Geneva.
[10] Restaurant Le Vieux Moulin, Route Cantonale, Epesses.
[11] The biography of Napoleon might have been Frank M. Richardson's *Napoleon: Bisexual Emperor* (1972), which is in Burton's library. Dick Francis (1920–2010), former jockey and thriller writer, who published *Knockdown* in 1974 and *High Stakes* in 1975. 'JB' Jeanne Bell (1943—), actor.
[12] A Gibson is a type of Martini cocktail.
[13] Norman Fruman, *Coleridge: The Damaged Archangel* (1971).
[14] Commugny, 4 km south of Céligny.
[15] The International School of Geneva, probably the La Châtaigneraie campus near Founex.
[16] George Best (1946–2005). Michael Parkinson, *Best: An Intimate Biography* (1975).
[17] A brand of Swiss watch.

stopped during night! Furious. Coffee'd and bicycled break-neck speed around block. Weather patchy. Read. *Times* crossword. Biked couple of miles. Martini at lunch. Ugh! Read. Read. Read no writing.

MAY

Thursday 1st, Céligny (77kg) Dinner with Stross and wife?[18] Yes. Their place 6.30. Perfect content. At peace. Film still on officially but personally give it no chance. Had above dinner with Strosses at Cully (Hotel de Raisin) good food and cosy room.[19] Stross same as all producers. Full of rubbish. Offered me another script. Will read. JB drove both ways. Early to bed.

Friday 2nd (76kg) [...] Rode bike to Founex for milk for JB's breakfast. Couldn't carry other odd and ends on bike so biked back and drove back to pick up goods. Had one martini (vodka). All fuzzy. Wrote Aaron. Wired Kate on acceptance in colleges. Am giving her car. Weather still miraculous though farmers want rain. Very sunburned. JB a delight.

Saturday 3rd (75½kg) Heard from Brook and (later) Solowicz that I start work again on Monday in Nice.[20] Mixed feelings but chiefly (a) money and (b) might as well get it over.
    Picked up Maria at Montreux. She is smoking very heavily. Bit much at her age – 14 – and shall say something though it's a bit kettle and pot. Watched West Ham beat Fulham in English Cup-final.[21] Soccer's very dull even on this occasion. Can't understand its popularity.

Sunday 4th (75½kg) Arrived Nice.

Tuesday 13th Arrived from Nice. Private jet. On health kick. Euphemism for on wagon.

Wednesday 14th, Céligny Had shock when Solowicz called and said they want me back in Nice tonight. Said NO! unless money actually in bank. Will await results today with trepidation. Wanna stay home and read and write!

Thursday 15th Phew! T. Young called Solowicz to tell me not come.[22] For this relief much thanks. Weather gorgeous.

---

[18] Raymond Stross (1915–88), film producer.
[19] Auberge du Raisin, Cully, east of Lausanne on the north shore of Lake Geneva.
[20] Maurice Solowicz, legal adviser.
[21] West Ham beat Fulham 2–0 in the FA Cup final.
[22] Terence Young (1915–94) was director of *Jackpot*.

Friday 16th Read all day. *Mosley* by one Skidelsky.[23] Talked E in Leningrad. Sounded fine. Her film moving at last. No news of mine. Hope there never is. Odd feeling reading *Mosley* corresponding so much to own childhood in 30s.

Saturday 17th Sunned, read, biked.

Sunday 18th Booze.

Monday 19th Booze.

Tuesday 20th Booze.

Wednesday 21st Booze.

Thursday 22nd Booze.

Friday 23rd Booze.

Saturday 24th Went into clinic late afternoon.

Sunday 25th Tests and books.

Monday 26th More tests hate clinics.

Tuesday 27th Home from three day check-up in clinic. OK everywhere except for slightly enlarged liver. No wonder.

Wednesday 28th Lunch and chat with one Goldman – potential producer of Dustman.[24] Dread it. Turned out to be nice but callow. Too much so for a producer perhaps. We shall see. Saw Leeds beaten by Huns.[25]

Thursday 29th Wrote E. Read and read. Strange request from Elish to deposit two books and script at Hotel President.[26] Puzzling. Weather bad. Might go to Gstaad. If weather good. Gareth asking for money again.[27] No chance.

Friday 30th Weather abominable practically confined to house [...]. Read three books. None much good but one (Warlock) readable. Another by Auchinloss. Lawyers and law etc.[28] Readable. Just.

---

[23] Robert Skidelsky, *Oswald Mosley* (1975).
[24] This was a film project that had been circulating since at least 1972.
[25] Leeds United lost 2–0 to Bayern Munich in the European Cup Final on 28 May 1975.
[26] Elish being short for Elisheba, Burton's nickname for Princess Elizabeth of Yugoslavia, although it might refer to Elizabeth Taylor. Possibly Hotel President Wilson, Geneva.
[27] Gareth Owen, Richard's nephew, who had already been financially supported in his business ventures.
[28] Possibly a book by Louis Auchincloss (1917–2010).

Saturday 31st, Céligny Walked, read, went to airport to pick up papers and lunched. Rain, rain, rain. Called Gstaad for Maria. All out on a 'course'. Weather same there. How weather affects my moods. Bad weather bad mood etc. Born of the sun despite the valleys.

JUNE

Sunday 1st, Céligny Read, read, biked. Latent (consciously latent) desire to write a book keeping me awake at nights. The creative, or may be the destructive urge is building up to a rape of words. I start and stop and start again. There is a furnace of ideas that must be put out. But what form do I take?

Monday 2nd Weather foul. Reading, as Somerset M. said is a disease.[29] Found paperback by Romain Gary called *White Dog*.[30] Brilliantly evocative. He writes with great facility. Wish I could. Every word I write I suspect the next day. Talked to Elisheba. Very self-sufficient. Brittle.

Tuesday 3rd This is like a ship's log. Weather half and half. Mont Blanc crystal clear. Shopped in Nyon for pens and drank tea while waiting for Anna to buy the staples. Talked to ETB.

Wednesday 4th Wrote, read, tried desperately to get Solowicz on phone to put bets on Derby.[31] To our fury Jeannie's horse an outsider would have won 4000 FRS with 500 each way. Great fun. Had one Martini which knocked my brains out combined with mild sleeping pill. Slept eleven hours!

Thursday 5th Brilliant weather. Sat in the sun and read. Listened to BBC. Found bright red face didn't realize I'd been out so long. Dined Hotel de Lac, Coppet.[32] [. . .] Still shaky from withdrawal. Very much better though. Reading new biography of Mao. More and more fascinated with China.

Friday 6th Sun, the great sun! Went to Geneva for physical check. All good. Got home about six o'clock to find Brook here together with 21 year old MG in very good nick both of them.[33] Got sloshed (not very) in celebration. JB took pictures of the car.

Saturday 7th Another brilliant day. Lay or sat in the sun all during its burning hours. Hid my face from it as am bright red. Brook feels helpless in a hopeless

---

[29] W. Somerset Maugham.
[30] Romain Gary (1914–80), *White Dog* (1970).
[31] Grundy won the Epsom Derby in 1975.
[32] Hotel du Lac, Grand Rue, Coppet.
[33] MG: a British sports car.

world. So do I. JB a gem. Vote yes or no for Europe, overwhelmingly in favour. Nobody seems to have realized that 'Yes' or 'No' is the same date as D-Day.[34] Very odd.

Sunday 8th Great sun. None of us went anywhere except JB to the airport for hot-dog (her) and newspapers for all. Otherwise got tanned again and read again but wrote nothing. I must start on something soon.

Monday 9th Discovered that JB leaves for LA tomorrow morning. Leaves Geneva at 8.50. Sad to see her go as adore the child – albeit 31 but has to be there for passport for son. Back in a week. Wrote letter to ETB but can't bring myself to send it.

Tuesday 10th Saw JB off. Lunched at La Réserve.[35] Took MG to be overhauled. Read, but still no writing. All this stuff bursting to come out but no response from the body – writing I mean. Weather at end of day turning around. Tomorrow likely to be lousy.

Wednesday 11th Boozed a bit.

Thursday 12th Nothing to report. Reminisced with Brook about things past. Drank wine.

Friday 13th Wined and am getting fat around the sides.

Saturday 14th Same again. Read a book but can't remember it.

Sunday 15th JB arrived back.

Monday 16th Brook left for London. Took MG in to be overhauled.

Tuesday 17th Read, wrote, biked. Still drinking but not much. Wine only.

Wednesday 18th Boozed mildly. Weather dreadful.

Thursday 19th Same.

Friday 20th Same.

---

[34] D-Day, the Allied invasion of Normandy, took place on 6 June 1944. The British referendum to ratify entry to the European Economic Community took place on 6 June 1975: the vote was 67% in favour and 33% against.
[35] La Réserve, Route de Lausanne, Versoix.

Saturday 21st Same. Starting to feel ill.

Sunday 22nd Going into DR tomorrow.[36]

Monday 23rd Verdun, wife, Hilda and husband arrived from Thun where they are on package tour.[37] Met them at Cornavin full of vitality.[38]

Tuesday 24th Weather good. Went round lake on ferry boat. Good time had by all. Drank beer.

Wednesday 25th Relatives stayed extra night.

Thursday 26th Up to Gstaad stayed one night. Gloomy place. Picked up Maria from school. Said farewell to staff at school.

Friday 27th Went to Thun. Lunched with family. Drove home. Lecture from Verdun on booze. Salutary.

Saturday 28th Stopped booze and Richard is his shaky self again. Dustman off as suspected.

Sunday 29th Booze or drug-ridden call from E to JB (who said I wasn't here) in which she told JB to leave me and Céligny was such a dull place. Is never going to call again. Well. Well.

Monday 30th Sober and shakeless. Report from Dr OK but must watch cholesterol count.

Blood group A-Neg. Never knew that before. Biked, played ping-pong with Troy.[39]

JULY

Tuesday 1st Biked and read am perfectly content when not boozing.

Wednesday 2nd Gained 2½kg. Back on diet. JB buying every conceivable gadget for kitchen. Biked to lake with Troy. Have taught him to drive Mini-Moke. Can't get him off it now. Must check on MG.

---

[36] Doctor.
[37] Thun, at the north end of the Thuner See, 28 km south of Bern.
[38] The Gare de Cornavin, railway station in Geneva.
[39] Troy Bell, Jeannie's son.

Thursday 3rd Arose at 6.30. Walked around block at spanking pace. Sun out so sat and read and pondered. Got rid of hired car. Biked in the evening with kids and JB. Read again until minuit.[40] Awoke at 6. Full of vitamins and fit as 30. Not a drink in sight for days.

Friday 4th Walked round block 7am. 28 minutes. Read Angela Davis' autobiography.[41] Not very impressed. Watched Wimbledon B. J. King whopped Goolagong 6–0 6–1.[42] Massacre. Went to bed early. Slept like proverbial log last night. One of the rewards of sobriety though Dylan told me otherwise. Over-ate.

Saturday 5th Walked block. Sat in watery sunshine. Solowicz came from town. Smug odious little man. Think might go to NY and LA 'to be seen' as they say. Much prefer solitude. [. . .] Dinner in Founex. Good. People at next table very German, very English, very loud.

Sunday 6th Sunned a bit read and read biked a bit. Bored. Troy drives moke all day long unless stopped. [. . .]

Monday 7th JB crashed into tractor from next door farm so sent for Hertz.[43] Lunched. Stopped at service station and found that MG was fully serviced so now have one crashed car, one wreck (temp I hope) and hired one. Talked to E and Liza (both in London). Liza expecting (hoping) to come here on Tuesday.

Tuesday 8th Made various arrangements with Kate who's in Paris and Liza. They arrive Tuesday. Brother Will and wife Betty plus Rhian (daughter) want to come but date not fixed yet. Gawd help me.

Wednesday 9th La Réserve for lunch. Very hot. Read [. . .] biography of one Hankey never heard of him.[44]

Thursday 10th Table tennised with Troy. He could become very good. Stiff as a brace afterwards. Weather brilliant but suddenly turned. [. . .] Am insane for sweets and ice cream. Can't stop and sleep a lot. Very bad.

---

[40] Midnight.
[41] *Angela Davis: An Autobiography* (1974).
[42] Billie Jean King (1943—) beat Evonne Goolagong (1951—) in two sets to win the women's singles championship at Wimbledon.
[43] Hertz car rental.
[44] Possibly Maurice Hankey (1877–1963), civil servant and politician, the subject of a biography by Stephen Roskill (*Hankey: Man of Secrets*, 3 vols, 1970–4).

Friday 11th Took crashed car and MG to carrosserie.[45] Meantime hired car again. Maddening. Read book by Shirley MacLaine.[46] Not very good but did increase interest in China. Must go there. Early to bed. Ate ice and chocs all day long again.

Saturday 12th Weighed 81kgs! 176lbs! 12st 8! Disgraceful. That's what Tete de Negre, Suchard, et al. can do to a slim lissome lithe limber 49 year old. Went on stringent diet (OK, WD[47] of low carb). Talked to Liza who wanted to get hold of Kate in Paris [. . .]. Biked to Grans beach with Troy.[48] Horrid. Lunched at Dominos.[49] Pedal boated. Swam in lake. T. Tennis with JB and Troy. Exhausted.

Sunday 13th, Céligny ETB returned Leningrad. She sounds a harassed mess. Wonder if I can put up with all that again. Try I suppose. Have an idea it won't last. Also she is beginning to sound like her mother at times. Frightening prospect. She denied what she'd said to JB about 'Why don't you leave. You're young and life must be boring in a Swiss village etc.' JB said nothing except let her ramble on.

Monday 14th (80kg) Glorious morn. Awoke at 5.30. [. . .] Very hot and sweaty. Couldn't read in the sun as sweat poured into my eyes. [. . .] Keep on dreaming that I've been drinking and then awake with delight to find I have not!

Tuesday 15th (79kg) Awoke at six. A beautiful morning. Hope weather holds. Kate arrived looking glorious. Hasn't grown which is a good thing. They, the females stayed up until 2.30 where I found them when I came down for ice cold water. Liza arrives to-morrow. Fullish house. Swam in lake at Céligny with Troy. Lunched at D'Alleves.[50] Table tennis with Troy. <u>LOST!</u> Now for Liza!

Wednesday 16th (79kg) Liza arrived à l'heure![51] Still short with yellow teeth but lovely nevertheless.

Thursday 17th (79kg) Kids settling sleeping arrangements. Maria has dreadful cough. Taking for X-ray. Turned out to be sinus. [. . .] Kate and Liza corporate devils. Troy very spoiled but not by me. Getting better. Bit of a smart-ass. He'll learn.

---

[45] A car body shop.
[46] Shirley MacLaine's *You Can Get There From Here* (1975) discussed her visit to China.
[47] 'WD' subscript under 'OK': meaning 'Will do'?
[48] Crans-près-Céligny.
[49] Au Domino, Coppet.
[50] Restaurant d'Allèves, Céligny.
[51] *à l'heure*: on time.

Friday 18th (79kg) Will Betty Rhian arrived 1½ hours too early. I was infuriated. Will in bad shape. Has become very old man. Wheel-chair, stick and all.

Saturday 19th Weather lousy. Will and I stayed all day together. Took girls and Troy to discotheque at Nyon. Danced! Twice. Left and took taxi home after 10 minutes. Sanka with cream and off to bed with Kipling (biography).[52]

Sunday 20th Awoke with the dawn. Sat on terrace and read tedious book by Michener clept *Drifters* what a poor mind he has![53] Played ping-pong. Sat in sun. Still on diet. Down from that appalling 81kg to 77. Will broke my sword-stick silly bastard and fell to boot. Putting in hospital tomorrow. He's a mess. Wife Bett f. stupid. Daughter fat and staggeringly tongue struck. K leaves tomorrow.

Monday 21st Sunned swam read – even letters. Aaron intolerably repetitive. Have dreams of firing him but after 26 years together with multiple sclerosis haven't the courage.

Tuesday 22nd Took Will to hospital. Endless corridors. Started smoking herbal cigs. Not bad. Girls went to discotheque in Geneva. Little ones not allowed in.

Wednesday 23rd (77+kg) Swam, biked, sat in sun with Liza, read visited Will in hospital. They may have found root of trouble. Hope to God yes.

Thursday 24th (77kg) Woke 6am spent all morning at hospital with Will in agony. Impossible to find doctor. Saw nurse. Insisted she gave him shot. Better after that. Went home after that in fury and as usual ate and ate chocs and ice-cream. Will show on scales tomorrow. Read sad and silly little book called *Exterminator*.[54] Re-reading *Golden Bough*.[55]

Friday 25th (77kg) Saw Will in hospital. Looks terrible and is in great pain all the time. Insisted they gave him stronger painkillers.

Friday [Saturday] 26th (77kg) Went to bring Will home from hospital.

Saturday [*Sunday*] 27th Took whole family to Rolle to eat, swim, row, sunbathe. Will much better.

---

[52] Sanka: decaffeinated coffee. The major biography of Kipling in print at this time was Charles Carrington, *Kipling: His Life and Work* (1955; new edn 1970), but Burton could also be refering to Kingsley Amis, *Rudyard Kipling and His World* (1975).
[53] James A. Michener (1907–97), *The Drifters* (1971).
[54] Probably William S. Burroughs (1914–97), *Exterminator!* (1974).
[55] James George Frazer (1854–1941), *The Golden Bough: A Study in Magic and Religion* (1890; abridged edn 1922).

Monday 28th Talked to Will all day practically. Surprising how little one knows about one's own brother.

Tuesday 29th Sunned. Had tea with producer [. . .] at D'Alleves. Very German. Have a feeling this film won't surface either. Has the same air as *Jackpot*. Takes place in Israel so I might see it at last.[56] [. . .]

Wednesday 30th Exercised but irritable all day. Liza going through yet another crisis with some bloke in Geneva via discotheque. Had eyes tested again. Bloke says I read too much. [. . .] Wish to Christ that Liza would grow an inch or two.[57] Talked to Gwen Gwyneth Kate. Norma. Brian Tashorne popped in to talk rugby. Told highly suspect story about Carwyn James and Llanelli.[58]

Thursday 31st
    Liza and Maria leave today for Leningrad. 33 days booze-less. I'm as brown as I can get so didn't court the sun yesterday. Read biography of Dorothy L. Sayers – *Such a strange Lady*.[59] Will still boringly ill some days.

AUGUST

Friday 1st National Holiday. Went shopping Geneva. Bought new typewriter.

Saturday 2nd Lindsay Anderson and Gottlieb arrive today.[60]

Sunday 3rd Glorious day. Liza, ETB, phoned. Latter finished on the 14th inst. Can't believe it and think of nothing else. What will it be like seeing her again. I'm a little scared. Jeannie Bell desperate. Keep my fingers crossed.

Monday 4th Very hot.

Tuesday 5th Sent telegram to Liza. ETB up to some game I don't quite understand.

Wednesday 6th Liza's birthday. Send another gram to Liza. Obtained temporary hearing-aid for Will. Revelation he says.

---

[56] The film project was *Abakarov*, to be filmed in Israel, but it was never made.
[57] Have inserted 'Christ' here – there is a mark which might be a cross.
[58] Carwyn James (1929–83), Welsh rugby international, coach of Llanelli Rugby Football Club and of the British Lions tour to New Zealand in 1971.
[59] Dorothy L. Sayers (1893–1957), crime writer, translator, playwright, essayist. The biography is by Janet Hitchman, *'Such a Strange Lady': An Introduction to Dorothy L. Sayers* (1975).
[60] Lindsay Anderson (1923–94), director.

Thursday 7th Talked Solowicz. Cannot find room anywhere for weekend for Jeannie and me.

Friday 8th Went 'La Réserve', Versoix for weekend with JB. Tiny room. Hated it.

Saturday 9th Weather uncertain. Under façade hotel is gimcrack. [. . .] Saw film in a cinema yet! English version Burt Lancaster and Paul Scofield. Indifferent thriller.[61]

Sunday 10th Went home to Céligny. Had left roof window in bathroom open. Place soaked by furious rains while away. Had to remove carpet.

Monday 11th Terrible weather. Stayed home all day apart from morning visit to Coppet for 'Boules des Berlin' – otherwise doughnuts fresh from oven. Talked Aaron. Sounded 100 years old. ETB did not call as promised. Troy very recalcitrant. Needs stiff discipline.

SEPTEMBER

Saturday 6th Céligny with ETB and Liza and friend Ali (Alexandra) Maria. Raymond took them all dancing. Both according to telegram should have arrived yesterday but muck up and arrive today. ETB got tearful about HW's father.[62] Good God the man is 80. Sq. for the 4 or 5th time. [*sic*] Still no booze.

Sunday 7th Troy arrives, Layton arrives. Both arrived! Tremendous thunderstorm. Phones have been dead for (so far) 16 hours. Maria, Ally (Liza's friend), Layton, Maria, Liza, so full house.

Monday 8th, Céligny Children back to School? [. . .] E and I more nervous than they. Bags, bikes E called HW. Long. E sounds so dramatic on telephone. She's just apologized by saying she has a lousy cold. [. . .]

Tuesday 9th Slept late. Went into Coppet for doughnuts. To Au Domino for E's handbag. Lunched D'Alleves. Kids have day off on Thurs. [. . .] Terribly sleepy all day after bad night. Article *McCall's* hanging over my head.[63]

Wednesday 10th Kate's birthday. One day's holiday for Troy, Layton, Maria.

---

[61] *Scorpio* (1973), directed by Michael Winner (1935—), starring Paul Scofield and Burt Lancaster.
[62] HW is Henry Wynberg (1935—) – Elizabeth Taylor's former consort.
[63] Burton was to publish 'My Life at 50' in *McCall's* (December 1975).

Thursday 11th Liza and Alessandra Mavroleon (Ally) left by train. [. . .]

Monday 15th – Wednesday 17th, Gstaad

Thursday 18th, Gstaad Brook arrived. Drove down to Geneva to pick him up. Looks very good.

Friday 19th, Gstaad Kids arrived for weekend.

Saturday 20th, Gstaad Kids and Gstaad. Troy cooked a supper that was an abomination to the Lord. The dessert was unspeakable.

Sunday 21st Children returned (train) to school. Going (us) to S. Africa on Wednesday. Reading up in *Encyclopedia Britannica*. My ignorance is appalling.

Monday 22nd Sunned. Read.

Tuesday 23rd, Gstaad-Céligny Left for Céligny with Brook and bike in exchange for Troy-Liza bike at school. Did it all in one fell swoop.

Wednesday 24th, Céligny Flew Geneve – Zurich. Zurich – Johannesburg. 14 hours.

Thursday 25th, Johannesburg Arrived Johannesburg. Many people at airport. Thousands I suppose.

Friday 26th Went to 'club' downstairs with creepy Peter Lawford.[64] [. . .] Terrible food danced with unknown girl. Press took pics. Also said I was drunk. Cheek. [. . .] Went to tennis. Pres and wife.[65] Usual agonizing boredom stiff with protocol.

Saturday 27th Tennis. Ugh! [. . .] Ringo out of his skull.[66] Very unhappy man.

Sunday 28th Went to 'Grand Bal'. Auctioned 'Hiz' and 'Liz' for 2000 Rand. Much the biggest buy of the evening. Went to bed at 6am.

Monday 29th, Johannesburg – Chobe Jet (Lear) to Chobe.[67] 1 hour 45 minutes. Landed on grass strip. Very bumpy. Saw elephants, baboons, buffaloes? Other people had terrible journey. [. . .] Married Elizabeth Zulu fashion.

---

[64] Peter Lawford (1923–84), actor.
[65] The President of South Africa at that time was Nicolaas Diederichs (1903–78), his wife Margaretha Potgieter.
[66] Ringo Starr's marriage to Maureen ended in divorce in July 1975.
[67] Chobe National Park, Botswana.

Tuesday 30th, Chobe Went up river with Fritz and Daniel (Black).[68] Fascinating encounter with bee-eating-birds troglodytes. Saw 30–40 elephants? Also fascinating. About 5–15 baboons surrounded our suite. We thought it normal but discovered that it was a phenomenon never seen before. It would of course occur when E was here. Hereforth to be known as Elizabeth's baboons. Strange. Richard Barrett (3 Degrees man) pestered us all evening.[69] Quite scary.

OCTOBER

Wednesday 1st, Chobe – Kruger[70] Land-Rovered through real bush. Non-tourist route to lose press. E took snap after snap of you name it she took it. Result – no film in the camera and eleven bruises around her body where she banged herself against the turret of Rover. She did it again!

Thursday 2nd, Kruger – Johannesburg Helicoptered over Kruger Park. Stampeded elephants and buffalo. Saw our second sable antelope – a very rare creature we're told. Eliz had immediate mutual love affair with cheetah – yclept Targa. Hope the pictures come out this time. Never seen E so happy but our hearts belong to Chobe. [. . .]

Friday 3rd, Johannesburg Jetted to J'burg. E was in agony to the point of tears which she hid from me but I am now unfoolable. I scratched her back and held her hand. Land-Rovered again with Targa or perhaps Tagra? Latter refused to hunt impala came back to Land Rover and E every time. Like Ferdinand the bull.[71] Though he <u>has</u> hunted and killed, his owner assured us. E went for X ray of ribs. No cracks but two spots on lung. We must make them go away.

Saturday 4th The most agonizing hour of my life ended at approx 1pm. Yesterday I mean. I had spent the previous hours back to approx 4pm Thursday in the most terrible fear for Elizabeth's and my life. Sleep was no palliative. I am still suffering from delayed shock and will in a lesser form, I think, continue to suffer for the rest of my life. E was incomparably brave. I love her mindlessly and hopelessly.[72]

---

[68] Fritz or Fred Knoessen, manager of the Chobe Game Lodge.
[69] Richard Barrett (1933–2006), music producer, singer and songwriter, manager of The Three Degrees girl group.
[70] The Kruger National Park, north-east South Africa.
[71] A reference to the children's book *The Story of Ferdinand* (1936) by Munro Leaf (1905–76), where the bull prefers flowers to fighting.
[72] Taylor suffered a temporary scare over her health when a chest X-ray was believed to reveal the possibility of lung cancer, only for this to be discounted within hours.

Sunday 5th We leave for Chobe tomorrow and will be in our small portion of the barren earth, paste and cover to our bones, for some days.[73] I am leaving the 10,000 rand I earned on Saturday morning for our return trips. And there shall be no mucking about at Kruger or the Cape. Chobe belongs to E and me. We love each other. It's very simple. [. . .]

Monday 6th E in splendid form and a trifle tiddly but sweetly so when we went to Sol's house for a late (very late!) lunch. Then E with what seems like aid and abettance from Adele (P.R.O. for Sunshine Hotels) that E and I should get married in Chobe this week I thought they were joking and said so.[74] But E and E turned out to be serious. Result the latter half of the day a series of ½ joking ½ bitter invective from E. I told her that I was <u>afraid</u>! Literally afraid, at the moment, that marriage might horrifyingly end in divorce. We will of course get married again if E so wishes but until I get over my fear and since I am, at least, deliriously happy at the moment why spoil it!

Tuesday 7th, Johannesburg – Chobe Grass landing. Slight brush with grim reaper. Left suspension, left wheel packed it in. Very rough landing. Guess that we were within 6–8–12 inches from kingdom come. Decided to get married here as soon as possible unless E (or I, for that matter) changes mind. Love her beyond measure and above anything. She fast asleep. Bathed and shamp in private pool. Shiver, shiver, shake shake. Can't wait for E to awaken! [. . .]

Wednesday 8th, Chobe Awoke at dawn. Went up river in the afternoon. Carmine breasted bee-eater chief delight. E talks endlessly about wedding. Can't make up my mind. Might be that cancer scare has given everything an unnatural shape. Also, like being hanged, it concentrates a man's mind wonderfully. All well.

Thursday 9th Stayed in bed all day yesterday. Read and slept. E fed me in bed lunch though had dinner in living room. Looks like marriage is on. I wonder why I am still doubtful. It doesn't seem right but I don't know why. Perhaps I'm afraid of legal responsibility. Also sex urge temporarily dormant. Very puzzling.

Friday 10th[75] Got shamefully sloshed and despite all my idiocies – nasty too – we are as happy as children. We catch our breaths every so often and say with a kind of smiling wonder and delight 'Hey!' Do you realize we are actually

---

[73] From *Richard II*, Act III, scene ii: 'And that small model of the barren earth / which serves as paste and cover to our bones.'

[74] Public Relations Officer.

[75] Elizabeth and Richard remarried on this day.

married?' We must have said it scores of times. I have never been so happy in my life. E cured me with loving even lavish attention. This is far better marriage than the first despite its silly (and dangerous) beginning [. . .]

Saturday 11th Woke up feeling very ill and to make sure that I would not get sloshed on 'livener' ETB gave me antabus which might quite easily have killed me feeling as I was.[76] However, despite physical ill-being felt emotionally very content. Worried about E. She not aware of it but sometimes, in a few seconds she changes colour. Much as I (and she) loves this place must get her back to somewhere sophisticated for a thorough check up. Sleep on it and tell her tomorrow perhaps. Nobody else seems to notice, but I watch my love intently without making [it] obvious. Please God she's OK. I'd die without her now.

Sunday 12th Went on picnic. Cucumber sandwiches on the marriage grounds. Cold wine, beer, champagne and cold chicken for the other. Coca-Colas and water for me. E still worrying me. So much so that I wonder if she thinks me a bit weird at times. She started talking oddly too now and again. [. . .] Went by Land Rover and returned by boat. Fritz (manager) Brian (white hunter) and wife.[77] [. . .] E came back into bedroom and fell fast asleep. Is asleep now. Will finish this tomorrow.

Monday 13th E arrived back from safari very late. [. . .] Black told me 'Madam sick,' she was too. Brian and Fritz with much difficulty, as there was no purchase at first got her out of Land Rover. Put her to bed. Undressed her. Said she was fine until she smoked cigarette then blacked out. Insisted she took shot. What is it? Nerves? Not enough exercise? Can't be lungs unless doctor an idiot. Liver? Want to take her back to England for check.

Tuesday 14th [. . .] E assiduously writing journal. Writes simply and well though spelling atrocious. She felt faint again twice after cigs. What the devil is it? Read hysterical book by one Douglas Reed called *Siege of S. Africa*.[78] Utterly absurd political rubbish for the most part but sometimes some truth to it. Must find out more about South Africa.

Wednesday 15th Got up early. Drank some wine while E asleep. Felt terrible. She took one look at me and put me to bed. I said it was malaria pills. She very not amused. Slept it off in a couple of hours. She still writing. Got the bug of writing. Told her the hard part was yet to come. News of wedding has broken earlier than expected. [. . .]

---

[76] Antabus or antabuse is the proprietary name for the drug disulfiram, used to combat alcoholism.
[77] Brian Graham organized wildlife tours from the lodge.
[78] Douglas Reed (1895–1976), *The Siege of Southern Africa* (1974).

Thursday 16th Press all over the place, so confined to camp. [. . .] Gavin enjoying himself hugely though pretends to great savoir faire.[79] E getting lazy again about writing. Loves Chobe (so do I) but would like to see and hear more – not animals but people of Botswana. One of them curtsied to E yesterday and she was frightened of the obsequity. They smile, she says, but hardly ever with their eyes. I must know more about them. How do they really think of white men? Of Europeans?

Friday 17th E didn't write at all yesterday. Gave her a mild row. Will not believe that she has anything to say and that she writes beautifully. Needs constant reassurance. Offers of money – quite large sums for her journal pouring in, so she may get her finger out again. [. . .] Press know all about wedding down to tiniest details that we worked out it can only be Ambrose (District Comiss) Masalila.[80] Wedding place has name apparently – Serendella, apparently.[81] Cannot blame him. Press very tenacious and insidious. Also obscure DC in obscure country doubtless enjoyed his hour upon the stage. Very unusual man if he didn't. Press searching for us everywhere. [. . .] Gavin beaming with long 'talks' on telex with J'burg. Must teach him not to get too funny with press. [. . .]

Saturday 18th E beginning to turn indifferent re HW.[82] Picknicked on marriage grounds. Bangers and Br and Butt.[83] Delicious! Fritz, Brian with us. E went away into a copse and sat writing sitting on a rock. Utter human stillness with air thrilled by bird-calls. Only Manley Hopkins could even attempt to catch in words the magic of this place. For a time we played Beethoven and Brahms for a time but they were an interference. Shut them up. Fritz and Brian read, Eliz wrote and I sat and the day wore exquisitely on. I swam in the Chobe for a time. E waded in boots. Result E lost one boot. That is it split at the seams and may or may not be rescue-able. Doubt it with local craftsmen. E very squiffy for first time for ages. And I don't know how. She had little to drink. I must stop worrying about her.

Sunday 19th American reporters here in force it seems. Therefore stayed in all day. Very hot. Our little monkeys (vemsets) didn't come to be fed yesterday.[84] E very disappointed. Read book entitled *Solo* re wild dog and runt of the pack,

---

[79] Gavin de Becker, Elizabeth's secretary.
[80] Ambrose Masalila, district commissioner.
[81] Serondela, in northern Chobe.
[82] HW: Henry Wynberg.
[83] Sausages, bread and butter.
[84] He may mean vervet monkeys.

very moving.[85] E not well at all. Don't know how to help except put her to bed and feed her. Honestly think before too late that she should go into sanato- rium. [. . .] Wonder if booze at fault though she doesn't drink much but if liver bad even a little is bad. Love her and cross fingers.

Monday 20th [. . .] Two little birds crashed into window. One merely stunned. Other looks dead. let him lie for a bit. Neck broken perhaps. Both on their feet after a while. One bird got himself up and away. Other on feet. Put food out for him. Took picture. Both OK and they flew away.

Tuesday 21st [. . .] Drank enormously and cheated when E wasn't looking. Don't remember much except falling a lot and suggesting divorce. Can't control my hands so cannot write any more. One word only. Very silly. Booze!

Wednesday 22nd, Chobe Having been so drunk yesterday felt terrible in morning and was desperately ill. Went quietly at 9.30 to find a double brandy. Bar closed until 10. Asked for Fritz (manager). Reluctantly he opened bar for me and suggested vodka as it wouldn't be so smelly when E had morning kiss. Drank it with very shaking hands. Have become a 'falling down'. [. . .] My hand writing indication of shakes. Painful knee, bottom, right elbow, back of head, right ear in great pain. [. . .] E an angel and looked like one. How does she do it? Look so well I mean for she had a lot to drink too. Fed monkeys who now come about 4–5 feet into room. Starting to tame them.

Thursday 23rd Two weeks married
    Still faintly dizzy if I make any sudden movement. Awoke at 5.15. E too and went lion hunting with Brian and his wife. Brian and E had seen a great beast last evening in all his glory. E agog with excitement. We searched for two hours with no success but saw everything else. Baboons, impala, kudus, buffalo, superb birds, the absurd undertaker storks that delight me with their parody of the human species. Read for the rest of the day. Marais *My Friends the Baboons*.[86] Powerfully and readably evocative. [. . .] Had to have helping hand to walk first few steps in any direction. Very disappointed in myself but periodically no doubt will fall into the trap.

Friday 24th Sat and read all day history of Zulus. *Washing of the Spears*.[87] Good history but sometimes hard work. Never moved out of the room. [. . .] E in good form and me much better though occasional wistful look at a bottle.

---

[85] Hugo van Lawick (1937–2002), *Solo: The Story of an African Wild Dog* (1974).
[86] Eugène N. Marais (1871–1936), *My Friends the Baboons* (1939).
[87] Donald R. Morris (1924–2002), *The Washing of the Spears: The Rise and Fall of the Zulu Nation* (1965).

Shen (Buddhist) and Fritz for drinks.[88] Told acting stories. They laughed a lot. Hope they enjoyed themselves. Made superb love to E in the afternoon. Gets better all the time if that's possible. Felt heavy weight of man's guilt at intervals. Very Celtic and Scandinavian. Thought about death too much. Much staring. [. . .]

Saturday 25th, Chobe Read and read as usual. Went to see potential water bore. Beautiful location. Am continually surprised by ignorance of people who live here as to primitive geology, flora, fauna etc. [. . .] Engrossed by Zulus. What a bureaucratic logistical mess on our part thrilling with personal bravery on both sides.[89]

Sunday 26th Stayed at home. Fritz's birthday (35). All went out on boat 4.30pm. Sans me. Just as well. All got sloshed except me naturally. Fritz especially falling down etc. Much baring of the soul. Was quiet and polite. Hard work. [. . .] Looking forward to Europe. First time since we arrived. Miss books – I mean mine – and children. Will doubtless miss Chobe as soon as we get home. [. . .]

Monday 27th Drank a lot. Don't remember anything, if at all.

Tuesday 28th Drank some more.

Wednesday 29th Ditto. Must stop!

Thursday 30th Shook and shivered all day long today. Read very dense history of Africa. Lost five days behind me. [. . .]

Friday 31st Felt inexplicably terrible last [night]. Slept badly. Actors' dreams. Went out on the tiny out-board motorboat. Very uncomfortable. Saw little but all made up for by a superb sunset. Read about Africa again. *Africa in History* by B. Davidson.[90] Africa now coming out of ears. Gavin upset about something. Long letter about how brilliant he is and how we don't appreciate him. [. . .] Off to Victoria Falls to stay for two days.[91] Then J'burg. Then home. [. . .]

---

[88] Burton means Chen Sam (d. 1996), who became Burton and Taylor's business manager and press spokesperson.
[89] This is probably a reference to the Anglo-Zulu War of 1879 and the battles of Isandhlwana and Rorke's Drift.
[90] Basil Davidson, *Africa in History* (1968).
[91] Victoria Falls, waterfall on the Zambezi river between Zimbabwe and Zambia.

NOVEMBER

Saturday 1st, Chobe – Victoria Falls [. . .] Flew to Victoria Falls. Very plush hotel called 'Elephant Falls.'[92] Naturally. Must write a thesis or at least article on subject of new hotels and why they won't learn from the failures of the older ones. [. . .] Air conditioning merely a noise and the hotel is not even finished yet. Took pills for bed dutifully but hopelessly awake. Put me into a fury that would not abate!

Sunday 2nd, Victoria Falls E practically sloshed all day on and off mostly because we got into bitter arguments about wording of invitation cards re my birthday party. At one point after I had been peculiarly destructive she went off in tears to 'Shen Buddhist's' room. I let her stay there for an hour or so and alternately read and wrote, very difficult stuff the latter because I know what I want to write but cannot decide on its form. Have decided that it must take two forms in two books. It means a year's work and a lot of research (which I will pay for). Finally went into SL. Budd's room where E was tearless but still sloshed. Later news came from Lantz that E's article accepted, bought for, by *LH Journal* for 25,000![93] [. . .] E screamed with delight and I mentally with relief. It would have hurt her if opposite and my judgement would have been suspect. [. . .]

Monday 3rd, Victoria Falls – Johannesburg Flew to J'burg. And off to the Landrost, where I spent the rest of the day reading.[94]

Tuesday 4th, Johannesburg Booze.

Wednesday 5th Booze.

Thursday 6th Booze.

Friday 7th Started antabuse. Absolute torture. Read books all day long and tried to sleep fitfully. [. . .]

Saturday 8th Big pull out from booze. Talked to Liza on phone. Very sweet. Doctors all over me taking blood tests, intravenous feeding etc. I look terrible and feel diabolical. Arranged for return of ring I bought E. Amicably arranged eventually.[95] Really must now never drink again except possibly a glass of wine with dinner.

---

[92] Elephant Hills Hotel, Victoria Falls.
[93] Robbie Lantz (1914–2007), agent to both Burton and Taylor. Elizabeth Taylor, 'Richard Again', *Ladies' Home Journal*, February 1976.
[94] Die Landdrost Hotel, Johannesburg.
[95] Richard had bought Elizabeth a pink diamond to mark their marriage. But she wished it to be returned and for the money to be used instead to finance a hospital-clinic in Botswana. Although the diamond was returned the clinic was never built.

Sunday 9th Feel better but curiously muted. Leave tonight for London. Started but for once will not finish a massive book by John O'Hara.[96] How that man wrote and wrote and wrote and he might easily have stopped with *Samarra* and no one would have noticed.[97]

Monday 10th, Johannesburg – London Lots of press. Usual fatuities. Long long journey. Found impossible to sleep. Thought I would sleep today for party tonight but out of question. Felt very nervous. Party well attended but felt remote from everything. Was glad to get away at 1.30? All sloshed. Still failed to sleep.

Tuesday 11th, London Heaps of presents. Can't be bothered opening them. Lots of lovely books including five copies of one. E as nervous as I am. Tomorrow evening present awards for *Evening News*.[98] Briefed by three gents about 5pm. All sounds simple. [. . .]

Wednesday 12th Did TV. Went alright. E looking splendid. Presented award to Albert Finney – a chap I've ever [*sic*] seen – but called him 'uniquely remarkable'.[99] Touch of hyperbole but better than the truth. Rather shabby affair and very provincial. [. . .]

Thursday 13th Had Antabuse and then tried one small vodka. Antabuse works! V. sick unto throws-up and the trots. Didn't feel right for hours. E went to have X-rays. Spots still there but inert as before. Thank God. She very ashamed of me with antabus and vodka. Quite right too. Saw A. Finney for first time in film *Orient Express*. Very amusing and obviously enjoyed by the cast. Tom very sick (75) and wife Hyral has terminal C.[100] Harvey Orkin died.[101] Loved that man. [. . .]

Friday 14th Saw F. R. Hauser and Alex Cohen at 10.[102] Stayed about one hour. Said I would read play *Kean* again down in the country.[103] Frank seems much the same. [. . .] Am thinking of coming back here to live. Haven't told E this though! Must find out about tax. Decision made to fire Gavin. When? Quite impossible PR man and useless secretary. Gets into panics about everything.

---

[96] John O'Hara (1905–70), novelist, short-story writer, screenwriter. Author of *Butterfield 8* (1935), later a film starring Elizabeth Taylor.
[97] *Appointment in Samarra* (1934).
[98] Burton means the Evening Standard British Film Awards.
[99] Albert Finney won the award for Best Actor for his performance in *Murder on the Orient Express* (1974), directed by Sidney Lumet (1924–2011), who would direct Burton in the film *Equus*. Burton presumably meant to write 'never seen'.
[100] Cancer.
[101] Harvey Orkin died on 3 November 1975.
[102] Frank Hauser (1922–2007), theatre director, based at the Oxford Playhouse from 1956 to 1973.
[103] Jean-Paul Sartre, *Kean* (1953).

No sense of humour either. [. . .] Slept like top but have cold caught from baby Naomi.[104] E's very bad. Had dinner at Scott's.[105] [. . .]

Saturday 15th E very bad cold. But went to Hackney anyway to open bazaar for youth club 'Pedro' one of Sheran's good works.[106] Lots of people. Very depressing. I have forgotten the class from which I come. Except that mine is Welsh – no difference. Thought of four to a room. Must go back there on an ordinary night. Do they have ping-pong, billiards etc. If not must buy same. Started to learn German. Not easy. No help from Latin or very little so far. Did two of twenty-six lessons. [. . .] Saw *Match of the Day*.[107] [. . .]

Sunday 16th, Pusey[108] [. . .] Still learning German. Liza here incl Lord Blandford (James) and Cliff Press Sarah Munster, Peggy Munster (Very young former Peggy – Simon's Aunt Peggy (70) no longer an invalid. (Manor House Bampton.)[109] Played and beat Sheran at Scrabble. Not easy. Did some German. Very cold. Walked with Liza and her alley-dog Tramp. Mutual admiration. [. . .]

Monday 17th Terrible weather. Stayed in all day. Francis Warner came in the morning stayed for lunch. Thinking of doing *Timon of Athens*. Found to my surprise that I'd never read it. Good sign. Had not read *Coriolanus* either. Oxford tomorrow. [. . .]

Tuesday 18th, Pusey – Wales Oxford all day. Lunched at Bear, Woodstock.[110] With David Masters (Finance) Elizabeth Sweeting, Francis Warner and Prof (bald) lady from St Anne's.[111] Terrible weather. Very wet cold. Froze all day. Visited Taylor-Burton.[112] Bought £17,500 piece of land for Buckminster Fuller Building.[113] Cheap. Everything very shabby. Clothes cars etc. Students unattractive. Beer warm. Depressing. Glad to get to bed. [. . .]

[104] Naomi, daughter of Michael Wilding and his girlfriend Johanna, had been born earlier in 1975.
[105] Scott's Restaurant, Mount Street, Mayfair, London.
[106] The Pedro Club, Rushmore Road, Hackney, established in 1929, and relaunched in the 1960s.
[107] *Match of the Day*, the BBC football highlights programme shown on Saturday evenings.
[108] Pusey, the home of Simon and Sheran Hornby.
[109] The Old Manor House, Bampton, Oxfordshire, to the north of Pusey. Lord Blandford (James) may be a reference to Jamie Spencer-Churchill, Marquess of Blandford (1955—).
[110] Bear Hotel, Park Street, Sunninghill, Woodstock, north-west of Oxford.
[111] Elizabeth Sweeting (1914–95), general manager of the Oxford Playhouse. Helen Gardner (1908–86), Merton Professor of English Literature (1966–75), was a Fellow of St Hilda's College, and held her chair in association with Lady Margaret Hall, both all-female colleges at this time.
[112] The Taylor-Burton building opened during 1976, an annexe to the Oxford Playhouse.
[113] This refers to unrealized plans (based on the concept of the geodesic dome, associated with the American scientist and designer Richard Buckminster Fuller, 1895–1983) for the building of the Samuel Beckett Theatre beneath a quadrangle in St Peter's College.

Wednesday 19th, Wales Drove to Neath Castle Hotel.[114] Terrible. Moved to 'Executive' Hotel, Aberavon.[115] Pretty bad too but had a bath to go with it. Tonight a suite. Meanwhile saw Tom in Cwmavon. Looks very ill. His wife in hospital with cancer. Weather wild and Welsh. Had beer and felt very ill. E nagged all day about Elisheba. Said I was ice cold. I'm not but hopeless to prove.[116]

Thursday 20th Sober and well. Weather good! No rain! Talbot very dramatic at night with huge furnaces going. Overall feeling of grime however despite clarity of air. Saw Dill Dummer and daughter. Told me Charlie Hock is in hospital.[117] Same age. 'But age with his stealing steps.'[118] Went to hospital see Hyral. Cancer ward. Hyral must realize she has it. Too intelligent not to. Tom better. Suite nice. Feel comfy for first time. Going to see Michael tomorrow. 2½ hours drive over Black Mountains.[119] Wild horses. Faggots and peas lunch. Fish and chips dinner [. . .].

Friday 21st Sober. Good Weather. [. . .] Drove to Michael's farm. Over Black Mountains. Wild Wales. Stopped for sust in Red Lion fifteenth century pub.[120] Black Mountains beautiful. Sheep cows wild ponies. M's place surprisingly well kept.[121] Huge fire. Ate there. Jo's cooking.[122] Divine impertinent boy yclept Ben. Hell on wheels. Very bright. Am going to invest £3000 in farm. [. . .] Inexpressibly pleased by atmosphere at farm. M. very sweet.[123] [. . .] Bad cold myself. Pontrhydyfen tomorrow.

Saturday 22nd, Wales Went to Pontrhydyfen. Lunched (Bara Lawr[124]) with Hilda. Half of Pontrhydyfen must have visited the house. Saw house where I was born. They've tarted it up. E still very ill. Puzzling. Gareth the villain was there with utterly spoiled child ('bratu') otherwise fine boy.[125] [. . .] Must earn some ready cash. Trusts inadequate. Looking forward to Switzerland and books and peace. Must write a book. Means another visit to Wales. Autobiog should make some money. Good Yarn! [. . .]

---

[114] The Castle Hotel, The Parade, Neath.
[115] Today the Aberavon Beach Hotel.
[116] This presumably refers to Burton's previous engagement to Princess Elizabeth of Yugoslavia.
[117] Charlie Hockin.
[118] The First Clown's line from *Hamlet*, Act V, scene i: 'But age with his stealing steps / Hath clawed me in his clutch'.
[119] Burton means the Black Mountain, the westernmost range of the Brecon Beacons.
[120] The Red Lion, Llangadog.
[121] Michael was living at Ffynnon-Wen, Goginan, Ponterwyd.
[122] Michael's girlfriend, Johanna.
[123] Michael.
[124] Bara Lawr: a laver bread recipe.
[125] 'Gareth the villain': probably reference to Gareth Owen, Richard's nephew. *Bratu*: Welsh for 'brat'.

Sunday 23rd, Wales – London [. . .] Went to Tom's lunch. T. H. J. (Tom)[126] very much better. Left for London 2pm. [. . .] Gavin must go and E must do the sending. Woe is me. Aaron going mad. Three films next year. Plus play. All TV. Very satisfactory. Lots of time off. Huge publicity re visit to Wales. Am feeling very fit and plan to ski over holidays. Can I now stop smoking? Can I diet? Liabilities £9000 car E. Loan £3000 Michael. Intake £150,000. Should manage. Money from writing too hope. German sporadic but coming along. Before long I will write though in that language. Wanna go home.

Monday 24th, Dorchester [Hotel, London] [. . .] Unusual 24 hours in which I slept 18–20 on and off. [. . .] E unhappy about something. [. . .] Talks about sex a lot. Just like Sara (Mom) sometimes. She in a quandary about piece of writing anent our marriage for which L's H. Journal has offered $25000. She very sensitive to criticisms. Warned her. Think she might expand into a book. Good idea! She is also upset that people might think I wrote it. Furious. She must get work soon as L. Olivier has offered TV film. She must do it. Do something. Have to fire Gavin today. Ugh. Liza to have car. Chosen Austin Mini. Long to drive it myself. Also MG should be ready. [. . .]

Tuesday 25th Cold, E in great form until about 8pm. Was then in terrible pain from neck and hands. Sent urgently for Tina Thatcher. Came within ½ hour. Manipulated neck. Greater pain. Tears. Unusual. Worried to death. Colds still bad. E very beautiful despite pain. Very sleepy (me) all day. Bought German cassettes. Hugo in 3 months. [. . .] Plucked up courage and fired Gavin verbally. Took it very well. Palliated pill with note asking him to work for us when we start independent TV. [. . .] Talked with Aaron. Sounded very coherent.

DECEMBER 1975–JUNE 1980

Richard Burton ceased keeping his 1975 diary at the end of November. With one exception, he did not resume his personal record until late June 1980.

After spending some time in a London clinic in December, Richard, together with Elizabeth, flew to Gstaad for Christmas. But their second marriage was already failing, and Richard became enchanted with Susan Hunt, wife of Formula 1 world champion, James Hunt (1947–93). The Hunts' marriage was itself in disarray. When Burton flew to New York early in 1976 to prepare for a return to the Broadway stage in the part of Martin Dysart in the Peter Shaffer play *Equus*, he was joined by Susan. Elizabeth stayed in Gstaad, and had a fling with businessman Peter Darmanin.

---

[126] T. H. J.: Thomas Henry Jenkins, Richard's brother.

Burton first appeared in *Equus*, succeeding Anthony Perkins (1932–92) in the part, in late February 1976. By this time he had met Elizabeth at the Lombardy Hotel in New York to tell her that he wanted a divorce. James Hunt agreed that he and Susan would divorce also. By mid-August both divorces had been processed and Richard and Susan married in Arlington, Virginia, on 21 August 1976. In October Elizabeth became engaged to US Republican Senator John Warner (1927—) and they married that December.

Following a successful, if brief, run in *Equus*, Richard filmed *Exorcist II: The Heretic* in Hollywood and then made a film version of *Equus* in Toronto in the autumn. He and Susan bought properties in Antigua and in Puerto Vallarta. Before the year was over he recorded *Chronicle of an English Crown (Vivat Rex)*, a 26-episode series for BBC radio about the history of the English monarchy. On 8 March 1977, while aboard a jet flying from Antigua to Switzerland, Burton made what was the only surviving diary entry of that year. Although one cannot be certain that it was part of a longer sequence, the fact that Burton did not therein comment on either beginning or ending this new diary suggests it may well have been one of a number of such entries, the rest of which have not survived.

MARCH [1977]

Tuesday 8th, British Airways, Atlantic[127] It's 4.45am. i.e. blackest night in an airplane somewhere over the Atlantic Ocean. We should be en-route to Geneva via London. Instead we <u>are</u> en-route to Geneva – yes – but via NY and London; possibly in the same plane with something replaced; probably in another. It is sufferable but only just. Susan was sad and almost tearful when she read news of a young racing driver – Tom Pryce – being killed outright in the SA Grand Prix. I was unmoved.[128] What a vast difference there is between lamenting the death of someone you know and one you don't. The bell doesn't toll for me.[129] A million people died of starvation yesterday and no one shed a tear. We are about two hours out of NY. What time we'll get to Geneva is anybody's guess. The best thing to do is not to. Guess, I mean. This too will pass.

We've had a long day and it's obviously going to be longer. We shan't get to Geneva for 10–12 hours surely.

We went in to St John's this morning (i.e. yesterday) heavy bag – books being the main weight – to be left behind in c/o architect Smith to be picked up by lawyer Fuller. Then went with former to see house of associate architect called Frazer. All very Edinburgh Scots with the innate neat smugness of

---

[127] Burton actually writes '1975' as the year, but the content of the entry indicates (along with a preceding marker in the original folder) that it was 1977.

[128] Tom Pryce (1949–77) was a Welsh racing driver killed on 5 March during the Formula 1 South African Grand Prix at Kyalami. Susan Burton (1948—), Richard's third wife.

[129] A reference to John Donne's poem, 'No man is an Island'. 'For whom the bell tolls' is the penultimate line.

those people. House nice enough but didn't fancy it myself. Small but lacked cosiness. The same applied to Mrs Frazer. I hope Susan's house will be grander and cosier. Don't know how one does that.

Am trying to keep awake until after NY then sleep to England. Can't read! Am, have been, trying to read a detective story by C. Day Lewis (N. Blake).[130] Won't hold my attention. Susan enclosed in blankets beside me – eyes closed but don't know if asleep. Every other berth in darkness. Stewardess ghost-like and the overhead light throws a shadow from my fist on to the paper so cannot literally read what I'm writing until several words are past. Not that it matters. Am drinking coffee and writing merely to pass the time.

I am glad to be going back to Europe for a short change but not to do looping on a lousy film.[131] Rome will be good to see again though I hope. News is that the paparazzi are a dying – if not dead breed. Hope so for Susan's sake. And mine. Ah what scenes I had with that lot. Endless maniacal chases down the Appia Antica and the Via Pignatelli(?).[132] Madness on wheels and no fun in it. The paparazzi were so humourless. How I hate and hated them. I see their empty endlessly mindless faces now, vacant and talentless and dirty, with their little chattering scooters and baby-pram Fiats. Auugh!

Somebody's holding back the dawn for surely it should be coming up now or am I going the wrong way? It's 5.35. Antiguan time. Still drinking coffee which I don't usually take in such quantities but I have to stay awake somehow. Smoking cigs. Stopping and staring out of the window over Susan's crouched and feline body. Can't be bothered to write more. Will smoke and doze.

This plane should have been getting us to London in three or four hours.

The summer of 1977 was spent filming *The Medusa Touch* at Pinewood Studios and then *The Wild Geese* at Pinewood and in the northern Transvaal, South Africa. *Equus* was released in October and earned Richard another Academy Award nomination for Best Actor, although in due course Richard Dreyfuss (1947—) won for his performance in *The Goodbye Girl*.

The years 1978 and 1979 passed relatively quietly. Burton narrated *War of the Worlds*, filmed *Absolution* (Shropshire, England), *Breakthrough* (Germany), *Tristan and Isolt* (Ireland) and *Circle of Two* (Toronto). Then in 1980 he returned to the stage again, this time reprising his role as King Arthur in *Camelot*, which opened its pre-Broadway run on 6 June at the O'Keefe Theatre Centre in Toronto. Then the company moved to New York, where Burton returned to his diary-keeping.

---

[130] Cecil Day Lewis (1904–72), who had been Poet Laureate (1968–72), published 20 detective novels under the pseudonym Nicholas Blake.
[131] Looping being the process whereby film dialogue is re-recorded after the original shoot.
[132] The Via Appia Antica and Via Appia Pignatelli, roads leading south-east from the city centre of Rome.

1980

JUNE

Sunday 29th, New York Today, like a man dying of thirst I slaked and lapped and wallowed in the *New York Sunday Times*. I haven't read a newspaper since leaving Geneva to come here – i.e. for about two months! Neither has Susan. The only encroachment from the outside world, outside the world of *Camelot* the musical, and King Arthur in particular, has been the occasional late-late-night film. I only remember one of them, chiefly because of a remarkable piece of acting by Dickie Attenborough in Greene's *Brighton Rock* yclept in Canada *Little Scarface*.[1] A rare picture of a shabby shop soiled, Roman-Catholic-haunted race-gang slasher. Very Graham Greene, very soul-stretched tight and grey with inarticulateness. For the rest of the time it seemed that I ate breathed dreamed and rode the nightmare of *Camelot*. We might be winning the race – I'm not sure – but, if the Toronto audience reaction is anything to go by, then we have a massive hit whatever the critics might say here in the Empire State. We open the previews in two days. [. . .] Susan went with Frank Dunlop to see a 'rock' show at Madison Square Garden.[2] S. returned looking shell-shocked. She had, she told me, never heard such a monstrous cacophony. Just imagine, she said, 19,000 people screaming manically for three non-stop hours. [. . .] Am having enormous difficulty sleeping. I suppose that when the play is definitely on the move I will sleep properly again. The lack of sleep is not helped by a bothersome and, by now, boring bursitis in my right bursar. Am going to see 'the daddy of all the "neck and shoulder"' doctors in the Western world. We shall see if I've torn something. Tomorrow also will be critical time for new costumes. Tomorrow, indeed, taken for all in all, is <u>not</u> a day I'm looking forward to.

JULY

Thursday 3rd, New York It's 4.15 in the morning. Last night we had our first NY preview. In the last 48 hours I have suffered an agony of brand-new

---

[1] Richard Attenborough (1923—). Graham Greene's 1938 novel *Brighton Rock* was made into a film in 1947, directed by John Boulting (1913–85), and released in North America with the title *Little Scarface*.
[2] Frank Dunlop (1927—) was director of *Camelot*. Madison Square Garden: an events arena on Eighth Avenue, New York.

costumes. John Barber of the London *Telegraph* and old friend and wisest and most compassionate of men (dispassionate too) David Rowe-Beddoe had (the former, Barber, by Frank Dunlop and the latter Rowe-Beddoe by Susan) been invited to look with new eyes at the production – we could no longer see the wood for the undergrowth.[3] Their observations were invaluable. And neither were sweeping generalizations but detailed analyses, scene by scene. Costumes worried them both. So they were changed. Why was I the only male member of the cast who didn't wear tights? asked Rowe-Beddoe. Had my legs suddenly, in middle-age become scrim-shanked. No, said I, spluttering at the very thought. I'll show you all by damn. And last night I did. All costumes had to be tightened up as I've lost 12–14lbs since we opened in Toronto. [. . .] Proper sleep – oh sleep it is a gentle thing beloved from Pole to Pole, To Mary Queen the praise be give she sent the gentle sleep from heaven that slid into my soul shall try again to sleep.[4] It's now 5.30. Come sealing night.[5]

AUGUST

Tuesday 12th So much for a daily report. The show is a super smash hit. Particularly, apparently, for me which is gratifying but surprising as only now, six weeks after the opening am I beginning to get the piece safely under my belt. We broke records week after week. [. . .] The show is still enjoyable. Long may it be so. I dread the time when I have exhausted its every possibility and go on automatic as 'twere. Thus far I haven't given the same performance twice. It is always different. It's unplanned – something curious comes from the audience and I instinctively respond – always, of course, within the frame-work of the play [. . .]. There have been a great many distinguished or notorious audiences I'll get to them by and by. I had one cauchemar, an appalling catastrophe which hardly bears thinking about. That too I will try to explain.[6] Politics are the talk of the times. Last night was the first night of the convention (Democratic) and Senator E. Kennedy is out!￼[7] There is a line or two in Kafka's letters that haunts me.[8] I read it years ago and was impressed by its perfection of style (even in translation) but only in the last four or five years

---

[3] John Barber (1912–2005), chief dramatic critic of the *Daily Telegraph* (1968–86). David Rowe-Beddoe (1937–), President of the cosmetics company Revlon at this time.

[4] Samuel Taylor Coleridge, *The Rime of the Ancient Mariner* (1798), part 5, includes the lines 'Oh Sleep! it is a gentle thing, / Beloved from pole to pole! / To Mary Queen the praise be given! / She sent the gentle sleep from Heaven, / That slid into my soul.' Burton had produced a long-playing record including this work in 1960.

[5] 'Come seeling night' are words spoken by Macbeth in Act III, scene ii.

[6] *Cauchemar*: nightmare. Burton does not return to this, which is a reference to his having to leave the stage after five minutes in New York in July on one occasion, an episode which prompted much speculation about his alcoholism.

[7] Edward Kennedy's bid for the Democratic nomination for the 1980 US presidential election ended with his withdrawal on 11 August.

[8] Franz Kafka (1883–1924), novelist.

has it meant anything to me – I mean only its horrifying and real meaning, personally applied, has it brutally come home to me after all these years in the smugness of the dark. [...] I am writing to please myself though there's a feeling in some place in my head [...] that this might be publishable. I haven't been writing for nothing. [...]

Thursday 14th Two shows yesterday and was I tired. Lots of people to see after the second performance. [...] Henry Kissinger's son, David, and a friend, Arnold Weissburger and Milton Goldman, Lucy Kroll, and others.[9] The dressing room is so small that I have to see them in the corridor outside. The newspapers – but nobody else I notice – agog with a 'great' speech by Edward Kennedy.[10] I read it and it is the usual fustian and good for his political future perhaps in 4 or 8 years time. He's a mere stripling of 48. Despite the polls I have a feeling that Carter will be re-elected.[11] Perhaps because I want him to be. Henry Kissinger who came to see the play with his wife Nancy a week or ten days ago said that the re-election of Carter would mean 'a world catastrophe' within a couple or three years.[12] Why? Because he (Carter) was totally ignorant of foreign politics. He was a peanut farmer and a fool and a megalomaniac. So, he said, was everyone else. Anderson (he'd seen him the night before in Washington) had a funny crazed look in his eye.[13] 'Messianical?' I asked. 'Yes.' Kissinger looked much the same as he did in Jerusalem in 1975 when we talked at the King David Hotel after one of his shuttle diplomacy days in the middle of the night.[14] A little less rotund perhaps and as witty and intelligent as ever [...] We supped at the '21'.[15] The Doctor had about 6 guards within shouting distance. I remembered the contrast. In Jerusalem I was told there were 750 guards. 250 Yanks, 250 Israelis, 250 Arabs – for <u>one</u> man. The conversation went on for hours (we closed the '21') although it was more a monologue by Kissinger. I was [...] the feed or stooge. 'The presidency is now open for any unemployed megalomaniac,' was one of his bon mots. He used the word megalomaniac many times. Anderson was, Carter was, everybody else was including, he said, for a short time, he himself. Nixon wasn't. Well-well.

[...] When we left I made as if to pay the bill as no one else seemed to be offering – I'm so accustomed to picking up the bills anyway but a shake of the

[9] David Kissinger, later a television producer, son of Henry Kissinger (1923–) (US Secretary of State, 1973-7) and his first wife Ann. Arnold Weissburger (1907–81), theatrical lawyer. Milton Goldman (1914–89), theatrical agent. Lucy Kroll (1910–97), talent agent.
[10] Kennedy's speech of 12 August at the Democratic Convention was hailed as one of his greatest.
[11] US President James Earl 'Jimmy' Carter (1924–), elected 1976, was defeated by Ronald Reagan in 1980.
[12] Second wife Nancy Kissinger (1934–).
[13] John B. Anderson (1922–), Illinois Congressman and Independent candidate at the 1980 US presidential election.
[14] Burton had met Kissinger while in Israel scouting locations for the film project *Abakarov*, which never materialized.
[15] The 21 Club, West 52nd Street, New York.

H. waiter indicated – I think – that the good Doctor had paid. We had paid for the house seats so it was a reasonable exchange. We later found out that the K's are very sensitive about this kind of thing as some actor had bitterly asked why he or the management always had to cough up money whenever Kissinger came to see a play.

Outside in the street Henry and David Kissinger announced that they were walking home to River House.[16] 'Take a couple of guards for God's sake,' I said. He did. [. . .]

Last night I ate dinner, half watched a film called *The Dam Busters*, read a little while Susan talked on the phone endlessly to Valerie in California, took a Mogadon and died for 7 hours.[17] Dreamless. Awoke at 9.30. Tonight we have what Susan calls a day off – meaning I don't have a matinee. After the show tonight we have supper with Richard Muenz and delightful girl Nana.[18] Muenz is an interesting boy. (Boy! He's 32) One other fascinating member of the company. Robert Fox.[19] Both heavily weighed down with chips on the epaulettes but interesting and moody. I barely know the rest of the cast, though I have a long time to get to do so. 40 weeks or more!

Saturday 16th Went to the Muenz flat. Delightful place, lovely, clean, Nana and Rich very good hosts. Muenz darkly funny at times. We talked into the small hours – of ghosts. [. . .]

Last night some strange man in the audience offered a thousand dollars if we would do the last act again as the audience had not understood me profoundly enough when I bellowed 'Long live the King.' Towards the very end of the play, when I had the boy Tom of Warwick (Thor) underneath my arm this same strange one came up on to the stage and tried to wrest the sword from one of the 'knights' saying 'I must have his eyes . . . I must have his eyes.'[20] And 'I have a message from God,' and finally 'I've failed. I've failed.' He was, apparently, taken away by the police. I kept on going willy-nilly. This almost child-like piece of Lerner and Loewe's has most extraordinary effects on people sometimes. Weirdly eerie. Some people, intelligent ones too, come backstage and are seemingly struck dumb, apparently speechless or incoherent with emotion. Others wait until they have stopped crying before they come to see me. Others though are untouched, or appear to be so and are as bland as bananas. One thing I've learned though or understood rather from personal experience: The emotional impact of a supple voice speaking lovely sounding banalities can shatter even the most cynical and blasé of audiences. They tell me that Lloyd George was a genius at it and I suppose too Senator Ed Kennedy's

---

[16] The Riverhouse building, Battery Park City, New York.
[17] *The Dam Busters* (1955), directed by Michael Anderson. Mogadon is a sedative.
[18] Richard Muenz (1948—) played Lancelot du Lac.
[19] Robert Fox played Mordred.
[20] Thor Fields (1968—) played the part of Tom of Warwick.

speech the other day was something of the same thing. Alex Cohen [. . .] said much the same thing. Oddly enough he (Alex) gave me a book by Tom Wicker which recalls that frightening Republican Convention when Eisenhower talked of the press and the 'media' as being enemies of 'the Party'.[21] Wicker says that the mass hatred of the conventioners was appalling and frightening. But then it is and always has been a frightening world. I am convinced that the self congratulatory, self and modestly named 'homo sapiens' is stark mad. Raving. And the beautiful Earth's greatest enemy. I hope we are a dying species, like dinosaurs and mastodons and brontosauruses, and that we will disappear in a few years, a few hundred years, a few thousand years or whatever so that some other sane species will evolve and nurture this heavenly accident we live on.

There is an idiotic amount of fuss going on twixt batteries of lawyers about the fact that the management are flogging T-shirts which bear my name and likeness and *Camelot*. [. . .] Lawyers are an abomination and should all be hurled into outer darkness.

Two shows today, one today and every day until we leave for Chicago. God save the mark.[22] Kafka and those lawyers haunt me still. I'll get on to Kafka tonight perhaps instead of watching the *Avengers* or Bogart or Clark Gable or *Cannon*.[23]

Sunday 17th, New York More strange behaviour in the audience yesterday afternoon at the matinee. Miss Linda Ronstadt a pop singer and her leading man, a Kevin Kline, came to see the play.[24] They had Christine's (Guenevere's) house-seats.[25] The cast were greatly excited. I am not much for pop singers but Miss Ronstadt sings one song which is very attractive called 'Blue Bayou' which I greatly admire so I was pleased too that she was in front. At the end of the performance when the tumult and shouting had died she apparently came to my dressing room door and was told I'd be ready in a few minutes. She stood there for a time [. . .] and suddenly turned and took to her heels, [. . .] on to the empty stage, leapt from the stage into the side aisle and ran through the theatre and out.[26] Her leading man (they are doing the *Pirates of Penzance* in the Park) also fled but re-appeared some time later and came into the dressing room to pay the usual compliments. I told him to tell Ronstadt that she was my favourite pop singer [. . .]. Robert Fox told me later that Kevin Kline was an

---

[21] Tom Wicker (1926–2011), political journalist. This refers to his *On Press* (1979), which opens with an account of the Convention.

[22] *Henry IV* (Part 1), Act I, scene iii: a line spoken by Hotspur.

[23] *The Avengers* was a British television series of the 1960s. It is likely that Burton was watching the 1970s series *The New Avengers* which was screening in the US from 1978. *Cannon* was an American television series of the 1970s.

[24] Linda Ronstadt (1946—) actor. Kevin Kline (1947—), actor. Ronstadt and Kline were appearing together in the New York Shakespeare Festival's production of Gilbert and Sullivan's *The Pirates of Penzance* in Central Park, which later transferred to Broadway.

[25] Christine Ebersole (1953—) played Guenevere.

[26] Jerry Adler (1929—) was production supervisor.

old friend of his who had recently become very successful but obviously regarded Fox as beneath him now that he, Kline, was a 'star'. [. . .]

My 'pinched nerve', now infamous in legend and story, went back on me last night and I played most of the play in considerable discomfort. It started when I was sitting off stage smoking a cigarette and waiting to go on for the chess scene with Paxton.[27] I handed the cigarette to Susan at exactly the wrong angle and the arm went berserk and played Hamlet with me, taking on a life – a spasmodic life – of its own. It's still a bit suspect today but much better and at least I can write this. [. . .]

Back to random wanderings: The audience reaction to the play: When we were in Toronto and we received <u>without fail</u> standing ovations at every performance I warned the cast not to take it for granted, that it would only happen occasionally, if at all, in NY. But I was wrong. The same thing happens here with unfaltering regularity. I used to get the occasional house to stand up for me in previous plays but now they always do. Will they in Chicago and the rest of the places? It's a phenomenon that I am puzzled by. Is it nostalgia? The roars I get when I take my second solo calls are almost exultantly savage. Is it a ferocious hunger for the past, a massive 'hiraeth', a sort of murderous longing for 'home' and security and simple peace.[28] I don't know. It cannot be simply the performance. Some nights unavoidably, though I try like the devil to climb to the audience's expectations every time I play, I am not so good – but the final reaction is exactly the same. Is it that the audience know so much about me – or think they do – from my highly publicized and infamous past? Is it because my performance is now truly dynamic but no, it can't be that because only in the last couple of weeks have I taken absolute control of myself on the stage. Is it a combination of all. I shall never know. But let me say at once that to this little shrinking Welsh violet it is highly gratifying. Today, a glorious one I may say, we have a matinee – a glorious summer Sunday matinee. Will the ovations continue? I will refer to them never again – unless they stop. [. . .]

Tuesday 19th 'Only our concept of time makes it possible for us to speak of the Day of Judgement by that name; in reality it is a summary court in perpetual session.'[29] That is from a letter of Kafka's. It haunts me. The supreme judge at that severe searching of the soul is oneself. It is I who act, I who do the deed or have the thought and it is I only who can judge the action or the thought. I am prosecutor and defender, Satan and Saint. I am totally responsible for all my sins and goodnesses. And I am alone. That great storehouse of knowledge and memory, ignorance and idiocy, brilliance and banality, good and evil is in my

---

[27] Paxton Whitehead (1937–) played King Pellinore.
[28] *Hiraeth* is a Welsh word which means a blend of nostalgia and longing.
[29] This aphorism is to be found in 'Reflections on Sin, Pain, Hope and the True Way, 1917–20', on p. 147 of Kafka's *The Great Wall of China, and Other Pieces* (1933; London, 1946 edn).

own brain and only my own brain can call itself to the bar for the agony of self examination. An endless, life-long viva voce. I wish I had more time to think. I wish I didn't have the nightly performance hovering over me day after day. Last night the audience was a phantom, now with you, now gone, a chimera of wrong responses. I felt angry with them and I'm afraid allowed it to show a few times. Afterwards we went to the John McClures' flat for supper.[30] We talked until 3.15am. Mostly about Lenny Bernstein.[31] How much we all loved him and how we loathed some of the things he does to himself and to other people. For Bernstein is indeed a fascinating creature, genius and dolt, a man and a woman. A boy and a girl. There is no personal hell quite like the hell Lenny lives through. All the time, all the time night and day there is the battle between his super ego and his utter self loathing – a Mahatma Miserable. I think that master means to die shortly unless the will to live reasserts itself. [. . .] I've written and thought myself into a state of depression. Ah! How I'd love the panacea of a drink now. A double ice cold vodka martini, the glass fogged with condensation, straight up and then straight down and the warm flood the pain-killer hitting the stomach and then the brain and an hour of sweetly melancholy euphoria. I shall have a Tab instead. Disgusting.

Friday 22nd Still finding new things in the play. We have had three 'bad' audiences in a row, 'bad' in the sense that they chuckle and don't laugh. But their silence which is sometimes very wearing explodes at the curtain calls into a roar. Rex's new Liza Doolittle (Miss Kennedy) who is British saw the play from the sound booth.[32] [. . .] I whispered to her 'Don't get upset when Rex (Harrison) loses his temper – he doesn't really mean it.' She said 'he's very charming and we have lots of laughs together.' Maybe the incomparable Rex has mellowed. If so he is not the Rex we have loathed and loved, lo, these many years.[33] He is coming to see *Camelot* on Saturday night. God save the mark!

Yesterday was our wedding anniversary – the fourth. Susan gave me a life-saving present. A portable book-case, immensely durably strong which, at a rough calculation will hold a hundred or so really heavy thick tomes and I suppose twice that number of paperbacks. She had conspired with the stage hands; props man and carpenter to make it. Was it not Francis Bacon who said that books make the best furniture.[34] He's right. I can't stop musing at it. It is painted <u>my</u> colour. Red. Very fetching and a delight. My beloved John Neville

---

[30] John McClure was sound designer on *Camelot*.

[31] Leonard Bernstein (1918–90), composer, conductor.

[32] Cheryl Kennedy (1947—).

[33] Luke 15: 29 includes the line 'Lo, these many years do I serve thee', as part of the parable of the Prodigal Son.

[34] Burton refers to Francis Bacon, but he may be thinking of Lady Holland's comment in Sydney Smith's *Memoir* (1855) 'No furniture so charming as books' or indeed the novel *Books Do Furnish A Room* (1971) by Anthony Powell. Producer and screenwriter Ernest Lehman (1915–2005) had given Burton an original edition of Bacon's essays at the end of the filming of *Who's Afraid of Virginia Woolf?* in 1965.

just phoned. He is coming to the play tonight. A remarkable man – brilliant actor, administrator, director and with the possible exception of John Gielgud and Larry Olivier knows more about the practical side of the theatre than anyone I know. I spoke in a whisper as Susan still asleep – she packed [...] yesterday and is very tired. [...] I am useless to help her as my right arm – which is now affecting my left arm as well – is dead for lifting the lightest weight beyond diaphragm height. After the show I can only eat food that is possible to lift to my mouth with one arm. Ridiculous.

[...] I was intrigued last night when one of the Chinese waiters after having asked me if the theatre had been full that night and my saying 'to the roof' he knocked on wood. I asked him if that was general in China. He said that it was. I said, 'How does one say "good luck" or "touch wood" "good health" in Chinese.' He said something that sounded like 'Hoo Toy'.[35] I'll try it out elsewhere to find out if he was pulling my leg. Which reminds me that Kissinger told us that the Chinese will still treat you as a President or Prime Minister or (in his case) Secretary of State <u>after</u> you have lost power – for ever. He instanced Edward Heath who was received with precisely the same courtesy and privileged treatment long after his fall from the highest office to the back-benches. They seem a very attractive people. Must go there one day.

There is something rotten in the State Theatre.[36] We are announced in the weekly *Variety* as grossing 98 or 99% capacity when we can see with our own eyes standing-room-only customers, together with collapsible, folding chairs down the aisles.[37] We know from Nancy Seltzer (who knows about such things) that people are sometimes paying $30 for standing-room night after night.[38] So where is that non-existent one or two per cent going to? It doesn't affect me financially as I have a fixed weekly wage but no percentage. What do the letters IRS mean to you at the Box Office?[39] Very curious. The two producers – Merrick and Gregory – plead, I believe honestly, that they cannot account for it. So who's robbing who? [...]

Talked to my younger brother Graham yesterday. Onllwyn Brace, famous ex-captain of Oxford and a Welsh International rugby player, is coming to Chicago to show me a documentary film of one hundred years of Welsh rugby.[40] It's our centenary and I am to narrate the film. It should be evocatively, perhaps tearfully good.[41] I look forward to it. Welsh rugby is a mystique

---

[35] Burton may mean 'Hao yun'.
[36] A reference to the line 'Something is rotten in the state of Denmark', Hamlet, Act 1, scence iv.
[37] *Variety* magazine, published weekly in New York. *Camelot* ran at the New York State Theatre from 8 July to 23 August.
[38] Nancy Seltzer, publicist.
[39] Internal Revenue Service.
[40] Onllwyn Brace (1932–), capped nine times for Wales, twice as captain, who succeeded Cliff Morgan as Head of Sport at BBC Wales.
[41] *Touch of Glory* screened on the BBC on 31 October 1980.

arousing in the Welsh a sort of madness when they play. I will write about it at length some day soon. It elevates us into ecstasy when we are at our brilliantly arrogant best and drives us to near suicide when we're not. [. . .]

Thursday 28th, Chicago Have been here since Monday. We have either stayed at home and slept and read [. . .] or rehearsed and played in this abysmal theatre.[42] It is enormous – seating 4,200 I'm told – and is atrociously designed. Endlessly long and thin and the audience seem a million miles away. [. . .] We must seem like ants to them and they seem to be from outer space to us. I know my eyesight is indifferent but I cannot even see the front row of the stalls especially because of the seeming blaze of the light on the orchestra. The first night [. . .] was funereal. F. Dunlop and M. Merrick et al. all assured us that the mass was enjoying it and laughing etc. but there was no hint of it on the stage. [. . .] The matinee yesterday was a little better and the response last night was almost riotous compared with the night before. But still it's very hard work. Susan went to the back of the stalls to check on her make-up of me. Especially the eyes, so vitally important to my kind of acting. She couldn't, she said, even see the expressions on my face – I was just a white amorphous blob – like Ralph Richardson thinks he looks like. 'I have seen better looking and more animated hot-cross buns,' he once told me of himself. Curious man Ralph. The official first night is tonight. [. . .] Talking of Ralph I had a note from J. Gielgud on Sunday last, written in his small fastidiously minute hand-writing saying he was sorry he'd missed me, had heard I was ill etc. I felt very guilty and hastened to phone him and ask him to come with us to the Kissingers' for drinks and dinner. He regretted that he couldn't come. There was a Cocteau film on that afternoon which he simply couldn't miss and there was dinner with friends which dear boy much as he'd love to . . .. and so on.[43] I mustn't be so remiss in future.

The Kissinger tea, cocktails and dinner was v. interesting though some-what nerve-wracking especially for Susan who didn't know who everybody was not having caught their names. I filled her in as quickly and as often as they were out of earshot. 'Joe Alcott famous, sometimes brilliant and always instinct with probity, political writer.' 'William F. Buckley (Bill), T.V. talk show star political writer too, brilliant too, not too sure of <u>his</u> probity.' Harry Evans we had to be told about as he was new to both of us.[44] Editor of London *Sunday Times* with a provincial accent. 42 years old or 44 I'm not sure. Irish-Welsh he said of himself. Did a very good Welsh accent. Mrs Buckley – sloshed.[45] 'Happy' Rockefeller – sloshed too but sweet and very <u>un</u>' happy.' Not surprising

---

[42] Arie Crown Theater, Chicago.
[43] Jean Cocteau (1889–1963), poet, playwright, novelist and filmmaker.
[44] Harold Evans (1928—), editor of *The Sunday Times* (1967–81).
[45] Patricia Buckley (1926–2007).

after the death of Nelson Rockefeller.[46] And the manner of his death. I spent a long time comforting her. Susan too. The Kissingers and Susan and thy humble servant all sober. Ed of the *Times* – careful. Joe Alcott a bit tight but impeccably spoken at all times. He spoke with a veddy veddy English upper class accent. 'Where on earth did you, a Yankee, get such an English accent?' I asked. 'I was very badly educated,' he replied. Buckley [. . .] very red in the face and tried desperately to make it a brilliant evening. Much talk of the Middle East. Only Jordan (the kingdom, not the politics) could solve the situation with the PLO etc.[47] 'Happy' Rockefeller said Buckley had no common-sense. She may have been right that night. We like the Kissingers more and more and Susan now feels at home with them. I always have done. I reasoned that after our first meeting in Jerusalem they wouldn't ask me back unless they liked me for my little timid self alone. Acting and actors were rarely if ever mentioned which is an enormous relief. I liked everyone there and, our hosts apart, 'Happy' and Joe Alcott the best. He has a wicked leprechaunish air about him and is deliciously acerbic – barbed at all points. 'Hiss was guilty as hell,' he said.[48] [. . .] 'I'm confused,' I said. I've over-read on that case. 'How can you be so sure?' 'Dean Acheson told me and my brother Stew,' he said.[49] 'In private, of course, in public he said that he would never turn his back on a friend.' He also said that Dean Acheson felt very uncomfortable with journalists – 'he accepted Stew and he accepted me with albeit some reluctance because we had aristocratic connections but he equated being a journalist as someone who was "in trade"'.

It never ceases to surprise me despite my wide reading of history and the inevitability of the class system in any form of government or society and their rigid adherence to their own shibboleths when the Americans show it at all levels. 'In trade' indeed? In the USA indeed? Yes indeed! Buckley is very American but European mostly in his way of thinking I believe – like his arch-enemy Gore Vidal.[50] [. . .]

All of them seemed to have read one or other of my occasional published writings and seemed to my relief far more interested in that part of me than the acting part. I couldn't have been better pleased. The Editor of the London *Sunday Times* suggested that I write about the American hinterland. I was going there for the first time – why didn't I make it a book? Any good and he would publish extracts in the *Sunday Times*. He'd paid £32,000 or was it

---

[46] Nelson Rockefeller (1908–79), US Vice-President (1974–77), whose death in January 1979 from a heart attack was surrounded in controversy, there being a strong suspicion that he had died in intimate circumstances with a young female aide. Margaretta 'Happy' Rockefeller (1926–) was his second wife.

[47] Palestine Liberation Organization.

[48] Alger Hiss (1904–96), US government servant convicted in 1950 of perjury.

[49] Dean Acheson (1893–1971) US Secretary of State (1949–53).

[50] Buckley and Vidal had a long-running feud dating from televised debates in 1968.

£38,000? to William Manchester for six or eight extracts from his latest.[51] Why not me? Why not indeed, I thought? I said I would ponder over it and perhaps send him a few thousand words to see if or how he liked it. I still don't know if I will but it's an intriguing temptation. But what can I do about getting out and around. I cannot sit in a public park or any public place, restaurant or bar or church without being recognized within minutes. Like Hamlet but not for the same splendid reasons I am the observed of all the observers[52] Being famous or infamous depending on whether you're Dean Acheson or Harry Goldberg the cab-driver has that disadvantage, and there are others but, I quickly must add, the advantages greatly out number the disadvantages. One curiosity about being as peculiarly well known as I am is that almost everywhere I go, it's the other people who change – not me. In the restaurant for instance, once it is known that I'm there and, gradually, Susan too, it's the other diners who begin to be self conscious and start unconsciously to act. Women especially become arch or arrogant, simpering or ultra-sophisticated [. . .] and every-body covertly, they think, stare at Susan – searching her hair, her jewelry, her clothes, her fingernails, face, figure legs and feet. A great many restaurants in these limited states have mirrors and it is sometimes amusing to sit at a mirrored bar with Susan beside me, while waiting for a table, [. . .] and watch the subtle changes of attitude and posture and pose and poise of the others. I taught Susan, who, unlike me, is shy almost to the point of being in pain, to watch them and I think it has greatly eased her shyness but she is still indig-nant that whenever she goes to the loo she is always followed by a gaggle of women who are hoping to see her at close quarters and her underclothes Bill Buckley would zengmatically say.[53] I got the impression from Buckley, oddly, that in his conversation and questions to Henry K he was anti-semitic. He used the word 'Israelis' for instance with greater assurance than the word 'Jewish' or 'Jews' and yet he said both with a kind of furtive defiance. I may have mistaken what was a slight awe of Kissinger, his fame and achievements with anti-semitism but I honestly don't think so. Coming from a minority myself and having been taught by Bob Wilson how to look out for the signs of prejudice I am pretty sure I was not mistaken. Wilson and I have been together for some 25 years. He is a negro or a black, take your choice, and his antennae are always miles out waiting for the signals. 'You see that guy,' he said of a white man at a party years ago, 'he hates my people's guts.' 'How do you know?' I asked. The fellow had been sitting beside us and seemed weak but pleasant enough. 'He's just asked me if I would let him freshen my drink. And I've let him.' 'So?' I said. 'He didn't ask if he could freshen yours.' It was true, for

---

[51] William Manchester's *American Caesar: Douglas MacArthur 1880–1964* had been serialized in the *Sunday Times* in 1979.
[52] A reference to *Hamlet*, Act III, scene i, where Ophelia speaks the line 'The observed of all observers'.
[53] Burton means zeugmatically.

I looked at my drink and saw the glass empty. Later on I came to know the man better – a theatre-buff in NY – and gradually I got him by very oblique statements, questions and answers to prove Bob right. He couldn't stand he told me finally 'uppity niggers.' It was a massive vindication of Bob's life-long experience. From then on, for some time I relied on Bob's judgements of people. He is always uncannily right. And though I think I'm pretty good myself now I always double check with Bob as I am still a little too naively trusting. I tell people, tongue slightly in cheek, that it's part of my charm but it is true. I am still appalled (at the age of 54) when I find out – and the evidence has to be overwhelming – that someone I like and trusted has lied to me, or stolen from me or cheated me. I lie quite freely myself but my lies are usually to make somebody else feel better and are rarely, if ever, egoistically prompted though some times egotistically so. Sometimes there is, to my sorrow, a touch of self aggrandizement in my talk. In vino which I never am nowadays I lose all control and will lie in my teeth about anybody or anything and viciously too. I am not a nice man at those times. I hope they never recur.

Susan has just come in to the room to talk to la concierge who is actually a Frenchwoman. The woman had asked me in rapid French if she could talk to Madame Burton. Obviously being tested I replied in equally rapid French that I would go and find her. Susan has just said that the concierge had asked if Susan would like her dead or dropping dying death's worst winding sheets tombs and worms and tumbling into decay flowers to be removed from the suite rooms, but her actual reason was to hear me talk.[54] 'Quelle voix extraor-dinaire! Ah!' 'Le Roi de Voix'. Now, peculiarly enough Susan who couldn't have a more different background from Bob Wilson has almost as quick and true an instinctive reaction to people as he does. At a party they will silently, across a crowded room, especially a crowded dressing room after a performance, agree or concur with minute eye-contacts and head-shakes of exquisitely impercep-tible signals who's 'class' and genuine or 'no class' and meretricious. Later they will give me the benefit of their combined instincts. Bob Wilson is 74 and Susan is 31. Bob is tall (6' 3") and Susan is tall (5' 10"), he is handsome, she is beautiful, they both speak differing forms of English but there the similarity ends. Bob is black. Susan is very white and blonde streaked. Bob worked on the railroads in Pittsburgh etc and his grandparents were slaves. Susan's father is Brigadier Frederick Miller and her mother Dierdre Wallis with some connections with the Duchess of Devonshire.[55] Bob learned the three 'R's. Susan grew up in Kenya, convent taught where her officially retired father was a lawyer and a judge. Bob's father is never mentioned and is still a mystery to

---

[54] A reference to Gerard Manley Hopkins's poem 'The Leaden Echo and the Golden Echo' (1882), which includes the lines 'drooping, dying, death's worst, winding sheets / Tombs and worms, and tumbling to decay'.
[55] Burton presumably means Georgiana Cavendish, Duchess of Devonshire (1757–1806).

me, his mother is still alive, immensely old and in a home. An absolutely impossibility for two such people to bridge that mighty chasm and understand each other even vaguely [. . .]. But on the contrary they understand each other perfectly and <u>did</u> from the first meeting 4½ years ago. I continue to be continually surprised by life. He Bob Wilson said to me one day quite recently that I had great taste in women. 'All your wives, Sybil, Elizabeth and Susan don't have an atom of prejudice in them. Neither does Valerie (Douglas) (my sister, my mother my baby and my Manager). Val may not like me but she hasn't got a prejudiced bone in her body.'

[. . .] Susan came into the room 15 minutes ago dressed for the party tonight. She is one of the few women in the world – certainly in my world – who could carry off such a fantasy of dress. Though 'dress' is the wrong word. It's actually black trousers, a kind of black 'merry widowish' top with a diaphanous black jacket that comes down to mid thigh. I should ravish her on the spot. I'll ask her if I may. On second thoughts I'll do it after the performance. Tiredly and gently.

Friday 29th, Chicago We opened last night and it went well. Christine, and Richard Muenz [. . .] were 'up' and so was I, though my shoulder gave me hell all night but surprisingly eased at the party afterwards. We arrived home at 2am and made cups of tea and grapple-snapped (Howard Taylor's, now the family's word, for raiding the refrigerator at sporadic intervals) [. . .]until long after dawn. And we talked and talked and talked – about Franz Allers and his delightful self adoration, about how old he was (74) and agreed that we loved him and his funny ways – about Eres McClure (John McClure's wife) and how earnest and subdued and intelligent she was last night.[56] She is a lovely woman, dark and high cheek-boned easily mistaken for an American Indian though she is in fact Israeli born and bred. [. . .] I took in the newspapers a couple of hours ago and saw a boxed announcement on the front page of one of them 'Burton regal in *Camelot*. See Page 22' or something like that. [. . .] I haven't read my notices for years but of course everybody else does. M. Merrick is amusingly predictable about them – he calls really vicious ones 'personal vendettas', bad ones 'constructive' and very good ones 'love letters.' I wonder why <u>he</u> is so worried about the critics. I'm not and he, I think, is uncertain as to whether I'm pulling his leg or not when I say simply and honestly 'How's the box-office?' or 'Are we sold out.' I mean it's no use having good notices and empty houses – much better to have stinkers and full houses. There is nothing, simply nothing that dispirits me more than to see great black blocked gaps in the audience like missing teeth. It's only happened to me once since I became a leading actor and it's an experience I didn't at all relish. (*Legend of Lovers*.

---

[56] Franz Allers (1906–95), Musical Director of *Camelot* in both 1960 and 1980.

Anouilh NY mid-fifties sometime.[57]) I've been very lucky in that way. A very different matter in films over which I have little or no control. We talked a lot too, in the small hours, of Elizabeth. We both are very fond of her and for some reason worry about her. I can't think why. She seems to be all right. It's the first time we've talked at length about her for a long time. Hope she's happy, as we are. Sounds fearfully smug which I suppose it is but it's true.

Susan awake (3pm) and has read the notices. I could feel her fury or disappointment. She said 'what did you say about the critics before we opened in Chicago.' I replied 'if they're good in New York they'll almost certainly be bad here.' Well, she said, I was right though they're actually a bit bland rather than bad, she said. 'Are they good for the kids?' I said meaning Christine, Richard Muenz in particular, but also Fox, Valentine and of course Paxton.[58] 'Yes,' she said. [. . .] She then said (God how I love this child) 'I am now going to have a bath and get myself <u>CLEAN</u>.' The 'clean' was said in majestically capital letters and victoriously underlined. So yet another first night is over and it seems that the houses – gigantic as they are – will be full ones. [. . .]

SEPTEMBER

Friday 5th, Chicago This city is very pleasing and unless I'm careful it will erode my affection for London and New York as being my first and second favourite cities. (Rome, LA, and Paris are villages avec beaucoup des banlieus.[59] Our day off (last Monday) co-incided with Columbus or Labor Day – which meant that the city was like London or New York on a Sunday – streets virtually deserted and very little traffic. [. . .] A lot of the restaurants were closed for the day but a few were not, including an Indian place called *The Khyber*. It was cool and pleasant and the food was good though no Indian restaurant have I found yet, anywhere, makes the spices hot enough. [. . .] I was surprised when I went to the lavatory that it [. . .] was filthy. [. . .] I am reminded of a story that D. M. Thomas told us about Caradoc Evans.[60] Now Caradoc Evans was a very Welsh Welshman who hated his own country and countrymen, hatred that was closely akin to love in its hostile virulence. He had written a famous diatribe against the Welsh in a book or a play called *Taffy* a pile of which books had been, so I'm told publicly burned in the towns of Aberystwyth Bangor Swansea and Cardiff by students.[61] Once below a time, as D. M. Thomas wrote,

---

[57] Burton appeared in an adaptation of Jean Anouilh's (1910–87) 1941 play *Eurydice*, retitled *Legend of Lovers* in New York in 1951–52.

[58] James Valentine played the Friar.

[59] Villages with lots of suburbs.

[60] Dylan Marlais Thomas. Caradoc Evans (1878–1945), short story writer, novelist, playwright, journalist.

[61] *Taffy* (1923), a play, certainly received a hostile reception from the London Welsh community (including Welsh students) when it premiered in London in 1923, and again when it was revived in 1925, although there is no record of Evans's works having been burned in public.

they, together with Augustus John and Louis MacNeice and others were drinking in a pub in Ceinewydd (New Quay) in Wales (a bewitching sailor's town) when Caradoc when offered a drink said darkly 'Where are your lavatories. I wish to inspect them.'[62] The barman an authentic cor blimey cockney said, 'they are outside turn left, left again and Bob's your uncle.' Caradoc left. Caradoc returned. He said 'I will have a drink now.' 'You must be a foreigner and not Welsh.' 'Well now,' said the sound of bow-bells, 'how did you guess that?' 'Because,' said Caradoc in a mighty voice, 'your urinals are clean!'[63]

It's 12.45 and Susan is still asleep. I have been awake and up and about and reading and writing this since about 10.30. We went to bed very late and I would guess that Susan didn't get to sleep until 7 or 8 or 9 o'clock this morning. She is dreadfully worried about her twin sister in South Africa.[64] We are trying to get her out of South Africa and to us here in Chicago without her husband's knowledge [. . .]. She has a 7 month old baby and the husband is found to be, I put it mildly, incompatible. [. . .] We are very anxious to get Vivvy and the child away before he does irretrievable damage to either or both. [. . .] We hope to fly her to Frankfurt where she will get a visitor's visa to these United States and fly on from there to us here in Chicago. We are continually on edge and will remain so until she and baby Vanessa arrives. Also excited at the prospect of having a small baby around. 1pm and time to awaken Susan who is going to see *The Empire Strikes Back* a sequel to *Star Wars*.[65] She goes with Bill Parry (Sir Dinidan in *Camelot* and my understudy) and two girls from the chorus Melanie and Laura.[66] I may go with them. They guarantee me bad acting which I enjoy.

[. . .] Yesterday, with Christine (Guenevere) Ebersole, I went on the *Donahue* talk show which is apparently unique among its kind in that it invites the audience to ask the interviewees questions.[67] It went along predictably enough. Same old questions. Same old answers. Booze, Elizabeth Taylor, which kind I prefer – stage or films etc? I felt sorry for Mr Donahue. He tried so hard to be provocative and had, fatal for an interviewer, got a couple of stock phrases locked into his brain in his exchanges with me which became almost uncomfortably ineffective as the hour wore on. [. . .] Susan listened and watched in the sound booth hoping that Mr Donahue would not ask about the booze and especially the one-night crack-up on Broadway. When, inevitably, he did, she said quietly 'Vulgarian.'[68] The technicians who had been talking

---

[62] A reference perhaps to the poem 'Once Below a Time' by Dylan Thomas, or to the same phrase used in Thomas's 'Fern Hill'. New Quay/Ceinewydd, on the Cardiganshire coast.

[63] Augustus John painted a portrait of Dylan Thomas, who married John's lover Caitlin Macnamara (1913–94).

[64] Vivienne Van Dyk.

[65] *The Empire Strikes Back* (1980), directed by Irvin Kershner (1923—), indeed a sequel to *Star Wars* (1977), directed by George Lucas (1944—).

[66] William Parry (1947—) played Sir Dinidan.

[67] *The Phil Donahue Show*, 1970–96, hosted by Phil Donahue (1935—).

[68] 'Vulgarian' superscript over 'you bum'.

like mad went absolutely silent. She also said that when I mentioned Dick
Cavett and Irv Kupcinet (two other talk-show hosts) they, the technicians, said
respectively 'shit' and 'son-of-a-bitch'.[69] I think of Donahue's job and shudder.
Every day, day after day, he has this shabby shop-soiled little show to do. The
strain must be enormous. Cavett really seems to enjoy his work but, on yesterday's evidence Mr Donahue does not. Later Christine said at the side of the
stage as we were due to go on in *Camelot*. 'You're such a gentle man (not
gentleman) that you made him look crass.' [. . .] Ah well. Kupcinet next. I
wonder if he'll be the same. In person he's a treasure – and his wife too. [. . .]

Thursday 18th 13 days since writing – at least in this apology for a journal.
Most importantly Vivvy and Vanessa [. . .] have arrived from J'burg. [. . .] Both
Susan and I and grandparents and Valerie and Bob immensely relieved. [. . .]
Now for the dreariness of divorce and who gets custody of the baby etc. That
could go on and on. But [. . .] – I am delighted with the child. I have played
with her for hours. And I'm trying to remember what my other babies were
like at that age – Kate, Jessica and Maria. I cannot remember of course.

[. . .] Susan and Vivienne and Baby and I and a brilliant sunny autumnal
day and full houses. What more could one euphorically want? And so to walk.

[. . .] As I entered the hotel I was greeted by a thunderous Welsh accent
saying 'Well look who's here by God Almighty. I heard you were about but
didn't think I'd see you.' I replied 'Sen he has all my brether ta'en He will nocht
let me live alane. Of force I man his nex' prey be Timor mortis conturbat me.'[70]
It was Ian Bannen, the very fine, highly eccentric Scots actor.[71] With him was
his wife. So he has married at last after years of living with this one and that
one. He must be 50 years old or so. I remember him first at Stratford-upon-
Avon at the Memorial Theatre (now called 'The Royal Shakespeare') and was
intrigued by the fact that he had a very (to me then) expensive two-seater
sports car despite the fact that he was a mere walk-on and understudy. Among
other roles, he understudied that of the Scot in *Henry V* in which I played the
King. One night the actor playing the Scot was off and this boy went on. To me
it was sensational – Bannen showed immediate, perhaps instinctive, dynamic
quality. Nobody else seemed to notice. It was therefore no surprise to me that
later he became one of the world's finest actors. He is, at the moment, doing
a personal appearance tour for *Tinker, Tailor, Soldier, Spy*.[72] [. . .] I'm very
fond of him. His wife is attractive and seemingly good and kind. He needs

---

[69] Dick Cavett (1936—), talk show host.
[70] The penultimate verse of Dunbar's 'Lament for the Makaris', which reads 'Sen he has all my
brether tane, / He will naught let me live alane; / Of force I man his next prey be: – / Timor Mortis
conturbat me.'
[71] Ian Bannen (1928–99), had starred alongside Burton in *The Voyage* and *Walk With Destiny*, also
known as *The Gathering Storm*. He had married Marilyn Salisbury in 1976.
[72] Bannen took the part of Jim Prideaux in the BBC television adaptation of Le Carré's 1974 novel
Tinker, Tailor, Soldier, Spy, which was subsequently broadcast in the US.

that – I would guess. The last time I worked with him I played Winston Churchill and he played Hitler. I thought he was splendid but the American producers thought he'd gone too far. I didn't think so and said that it was almost impossible to go too far with A. Hitler. They made him tone it down which I still think a shame. The show was for the *Hallmark Hall of Fame* yet! As they say. Very frightened people the latter lot. The *NY Times* had asked me to write about playing WSC and had published the article which wasn't entirely complimentary about 'the great man' on the Sunday of the TV premiere of the film in the USA.[73] I'm told that the *Hallmark Hall of Fame* people nearly had several heart attacks and seriously thought of cancelling the show.[74] So frightened indeed, is everybody in American TV [. . .] that one derogatory article in the August *NY Times* sends them immediately into conniptions. When one realizes that though the *NY Times* is read by a couple of million people and the viewing figures for a show of that magnitude are 60 or 70 or 80 millions who could not possibly be affected by what I wrote in the *NY Times* on the very day of issue and show one begins to wonder afresh at the sickness of our Western Society. Further, though I was very good in the part and would have been a certainty for the abominable *Emmy* (for make-up) if nothing else, my article struck at their fearless hearts and I wasn't even nominated. What should such creatures as they do, crawling between heaven and earth.[75] [. . .] Almost time to go to work. [. . .]

It's 11.55 and midnight is upon us again. In the car on the way home I saw what I thought with my bad eyesight, was the moon and muttered almost to myself: 'Regard the moon. La Lune ne garde aucune rancune, She winks a feeble eye, she smiles into corners, she smoothes the hair of the grass. A washed out small pox cracks her face.' Susan asked 'What's that you're saying?' I said that it was T. S. Eliot – a bit from 'Rhapsody on a Windy Night'.[76] When we were home, I said, I would try and remember the whole thing. I've tried (Susan is cooking supper) and can't get it all. Large lumps of it but not the whole thing. That means a walk to a book shop tomorrow. Unless midnight, '<u>this</u> midnight, tonight,' shakes the memory as a madman shakes a dead geranium.'[77] I must confess that some of Eliot's metaphors are hard wrought and sometimes unlikely and not at all evocative. 'Prufrock' for instance with 'when the evening is spread out against the sky, like a patient etherised upon

[73] Burton's article, 'To Play Churchill Is to Hate Him', appeared in the *New York Times* on 24 November 1974. It was extremely unflattering of Churchill and provoked a furious reaction in both the US and Britain.

[74] Hallmark Cards co-produced the play with the BBC. In the USA it appeared as part of the series 'Hallmark Hall of Fame'.

[75] A reference to Hamlet, speaking in *Hamlet*, Act III, scene i, 'What should such fellows as I do crawling between heaven and earth?'

[76] T. S. Eliot, 'Rhapsody on a Windy Night', first published in 1917, includes the lines 'Regard the moon, / La lune ne garde aucune rancune, / She winks a feeble eye, / She smiles into corners, / She smooths the hair of the grass. / The moon has lost her memory. / A washed-out smallpox cracks her face'.

[77] The line is 'Midnight shakes the memory / As a madman shakes a dead geranium.'

the table.'[78] Shocking then I suppose but a dead and very forced image now. [. . .]

Tuesday 23rd We are playing 13 days consecutively. Last night after a sleepless (who knows why?) night I laboured mightily through the piece with sudden turns of my head making me dizzy, both shoulders taut with pain, and legs of lead. [. . .] Came home immediately, dined while watching with dulled eyes Roger Moore in a *Saint* episode.[79] To bed and read and slept for ten solid hours. Consequent feeling of relief today almost amounting to joie de vivre.

I did the 'Kup show'[80] and though the questions were more or less the same as everybody else's they were framed with much more warmth and charm than most. We went well over the scheduled ½ hour to 42 minutes so the other guests, I understand, had to make do with what remained of the hour.

Last Friday night we supped after the show with a Mr Bricause and wife, Kup and wife, Forrest Tucker and daughter, and several other people – all unknown to me.[81] 'Tuck' boisterously drunk and loud. Nice man but can't hold the booze anymore. He shouted a lot and everybody except me was highly embarrassed. There but for the grace of Susan and God, thought I, goes I. Fortunately for the others he passed out early, in the middle, as 'twere, of a sentence and his daughter – a nice girl and as big as he is, took him home. To me, but hopefully not to himself, Forrest Tucker, is a minor tragedy. Very big personality, very big voice, handsome, very big man (6' 4–5", I would guess and heavy with it) and, as far as I know, never been out of work and, I would think, has made a lot of money in his time – for years he was in a TV series called *F TROOP*.[82] And yet he has never made the big scene, the big time. Far lesser people with far less talent have done far more. Where did it all go wrong? If he is happy with his lot then he's happy and he's been lucky. If he thinks of the other possibilities then he must be very unhappy. The 'other possibilities' are the doubtful privilege of a very thin company of actors or actresses, stage or screen. Those who for some reason create excitement wherever they appear, where audiences metaphorically – and sometimes literally – sit on the edge of their seats waiting for the ticking bomb to explode into a fury of interpretive creativity. Still and all, he works continually and is well paid which is a privilege in itself. So many thousands and thousands in my profession wear out

[78] The line from 'The Love Song of J. Alfred Prufrock' is 'When the evening is spread out against the sky / Like a patient etherised upon a table;'.
[79] Roger Moore (1927—), who had played alongside Burton in *The Wild Geese*, had previously played the character of Simon Templar in the television series *The Saint* (1960–69).
[80] The 'Kup show' was Irv 'Kup' Kupcinet's television talk show, which ran from 1959 to 1986. Richard appeared on 12th September 1980.
[81] Jack Brickhouse (1916–98), broadcaster, and his wife Pat. Forrest Tucker (1919—86), his daughter Brooke. Others present included Tony DeSantis (1914–2007), theatre owner, and his wife Lucille, and Mr and Mrs Bruce Goodman. The party was held at Café Angelo.
[82] *F Troop* ran for 65 episodes from 1965 to 1967 but was much shown thereafter.

legions of shoes, walking from agent to agent, from audition to audition for ever and ever. Poor sods.

Rex Harrison opens tonight – after a week of previews – in New Orleans in that jewel of a musical *My Fair Lady*. I'm told that his energy level and stamina are as electric as ever despite his advancing years (he's about 71, I think) and I pray for a repeat of his original smash hit in the same piece 25 odd years ago. Unlike most people so I understand I genuinely delight in the successes of my friends and do not exult in their failures. I think Rex is, of his genre, the greatest actor in the world – the highest of high comedians. No less a person than that delicious Noël Coward once said 'Rex is the greatest light-comedian in the world' – pause 'after me.' I would say they were at least even, with Rex having the edge. I shall be thinking of him all evening long. Both Susan and I have sent him telegrams separately and one to the entire company together. Rex's brand of acting and his off-stage personality are inextricably bound together. Most obviously, for instance Rex's normal private-life voice is the same as the voice on-stage – only projected a little more. I think mine is. So is George C. Scott's, so is Gielgud's, so was Coward's so is Jason Robards', so is Fonda's, so is Richardson's but Olivier's is totally different, and Scofield's, and Guinness'.[83] Alec and Paul tend to 'boom' on stage though cathedrically quiet off and Larry Olivier's develops a machine-gun metallic rattle with an occasional shout thrown in 'to keep,' as he said to me once 'the bastards awake.' I'm not quite sure whether Larry meant his fellow-actors or the audiences or both. But one has to be careful with Larry – he is a great dead-pan leg-puller and one is never quite sure whether he is probing very subtly for weak spots or majestically sending one up. Superb good value though all of them. O'Toole's voice too eccentrically accented in private is the same on the stage. I wonder what it means. Does it mean that Olivier, Guinness and Scofield are basically and essentially character actors while the rest of us mentioned above are simply extensions of ourselves. Well, the more I act and the more I think about it (which is not very often) the less I know of the heart of its mystery. Why one believes absolutely in one actor and knows he's blazingly honest and not in another equally dazzling player is beyond my competence to explain. I can only accept it and hope for the best.

Talking of O'Toole I only knew by chance that he had taken such a terrible hammering – a front-page hammering – from the British critics for his performance in *Macbeth*. I knew only because Onllwyn Brace came to supervise my narration in the documentary film about Welsh rugby football. 'Your pal O'Toole,' he said, 'has been murdered by the English critics.' 'For what?' asked I. 'For *Macbeth*,' said he. I phoned Peter that night as soon as the hours

---

[83] George C. Scott (1927–99), actor.

were right and managed to catch him before he'd left the Old Vic. I said, 'a couple of boys from the BBC were over today to record my voice and they told me you've had a bit of stick from the critics.' 'Yes.' 'How are the houses?' I asked. 'Packed.' 'Then remember this my boy,' I said (he is 4 years younger), 'you are the most original actor to come out of Britain since the war and fuck the critics.' 'Thank you.' 'Think of every four letter obscenity, six, eight ten and twelve letter expletives and ram it right up their envious arses in which,' I said, paraphrasing Robert Atkins, 'I'm sure there is ample room.'[84] 'Thank you.' 'Good night Peter. Don't give in and I love you.' 'I won't and it's mutual.' 'Good night again.' 'Good night Richard and thank you.'

That was the extent of our conversation but my fury at the critics took me through the night – another sleepless one – and I thought of all the things I should have said to Peter and didn't and thought I should write him a letter and didn't and prayed to God I hadn't sounded like a false sympathizer secretly rejoicing in his critical debacle. But no, I comforted myself, he knows I too have been through the fire and understand. And by God I have too. It's a phenomenon that is again inexplicable that a few of us – O'Toole, Sinatra, Brando, Elizabeth Taylor, Jane Fonda, Barbra Streisand et al. carry something sanguicolous and the parasite is called 'press-envy' – especially in our own countries. Why is it? Because we take risks and run against the conventional. It cannot be because we are, albeit patchily, successful and earn millions because one never hears of viciousness anent Robert Redford or Dustin Hoffman Paul Newman or De Niro or Jon Voight but one does <u>about</u> Al Pacino – my dear he has – an American Film Star yet – dared to play *Richard III*![85] And what's more – horror of horrors – he's going to have a go at *Othello*. Shakespeare's *Othello*, no less. I can hear the critics and gossip-mongers and the Sardi-Set already stirring up the vitriol.[86] Mr Pacino is certainly not lacking in courage – he has my deepest admiration. [. . .]

Monday 29th We shall be leaving at 1pm for the airport and so to Dallas. [. . .] Susan slipped while packing yesterday and gave herself a nasty bump on her middle spine. Both my shoulders have seized up again. [. . .] Vivienne very depressed yesterday and Susan had a weep – the shock of the fall didn't help. Vivvy said Susan was working too hard. I wonder if Vivvy realizes that she, Vivvy, has been the prime cause of Susan's high tension. Well now for three weeks alone with S. It's a curiosity that when Susan and I are apart from other people and only have each other we are perfectly happy. The intrusion of a third person, however affable and amiable begins to irritate

---

[84] Robert Atkins (1886–1972), actor.
[85] Robert De Niro (1943—). Al Pacino (1940—) played *Richard III* on Broadway.
[86] A reference to Sardi's restaurant, New York, frequented by movers and shakers in the theatre world.

us after a mere two days or so. We'll have to be careful of this. It could destroy us. [. . .]

We had dinner (supper) on Saturday night with the Kupcinets. Susan – as I hoped – has taken to them very much. What a pity that the people one really likes are almost always geographically very distant. [. . .]

Received an odd telegram from Tim Hardy (I presume) saying that he'd given a long interview to Paul Ferris – a South Welsh writer who's determined to write a book about me. I've tried to discourage him by total silence. Tim assures me that Ferris is a distinguished writer. Well, I've read his (Ferris') biog of Dylan Thomas and found it petty and silly. Fitzgibbon's book is far warmer and generous.[87]

We closed at the Arie Crown here on Saturday night to the usual non-audience <u>during</u> the show, sluggish and dull, and slow, but an ecstatically thunderous ovation at the end as ever. [. . .] Now we shall see how Texans – Dallas Texans in particular – respond. We are already completely sold out in Dallas, but they couldn't possibly be any nicer and generous than Chicagoans everybody, policemen, people in the streets, pubs and restaurants etc. have been overwhelmingly kind and it has been very gratifying to break every conceivable record, house, city and world records for attendance. [. . .]

How far away and unimportant everything else seems when one neither listens to the radio, watches TV or reads the newspapers. I discovered yesterday that there's a war on or something close to it between Iraq and Iran.[88] What's it all about Alfie?[89] Must get back to Keats' 'giant agony of the world' shortly.[90] The whole world's in a terrible state of chassis.[. . .]

My Fair Lady with the ineffable Rex H. opened in New Orleans last week and Rex, thanks to whatever Gods may be received an ovation. Diolch iddo byth am gofio.[91] If he hadn't bang! would have gone another friendship perhaps.

Vivienne and baby Vanessa leave for London this evening to start – yet again – divorce proceedings against Joe the husband. We shall win I'm sure. Muhammad Ali fights Larry Holmes on Thursday night. I wish he wouldn't. It genuinely frightens me.[92]

---

[87] Paul Ferris (1929—), *Dylan Thomas* (1977). Burton had reviewed Constantine Fitzgibbon, (1919–83) *The Life of Dylan Thomas* (1965) on publication. According to Ferris's biography of Burton (p. 181), Burton scorned the suggestion in Ferris's biography that Thomas had had homosexual experiences as a young man.
[88] Iraq invaded Iran on 22 September 1980. The war lasted until August 1988.
[89] The theme song for the film *Alfie* (1966), written by Burt Bacharach (1928—) and performed by Cilla Black (1943—), also covered by Dionne Warwick (1940—).
[90] The line 'the giant agony of the world' is from John Keats (1795–1821), *The Fall of Hyperion: A Dream* (1819).
[91] From the Welsh hymn 'Diolch iddo', the line translates as 'Thanks be to him for ever remembering'.
[92] World heavyweight champion Larry Holmes (1949—) stopped Muhammad Ali (formerly known as Cassius Clay) in ten rounds on 2 October 1980.

OCTOBER

Thursday 3rd, Dallas[93] Arrived here on Monday to very disappointing weather, overcast and Mancunianly depressing. [...]

We previewed the play on Tuesday night and despite being politely asked not to come – since previews, in our case, are to iron out the wrinkles and remove the gremlins attendant on opening in a new theatre with a much smaller stage [...] – the local critics were mule-headed and obdurately provincial and insisted on coming anyway and will-nilly. [...] The theatre, in comparison with the Arie Crown, was (is) a delight to play and long-forgotten laughs were back again. The notices incidentally [...] are fine according to Mike Merrick who phoned at 3am this morning to tell us so. I was very gruff and brusque. I was comfortably installed in bed complete with chocolates and Evelyn Waugh's *Black Mischief* when Merrick's call came through.[94] I talked, or replied rather in harsh monosyllables. 'Yes' 'No' 'Good' 'Bye' 'Thanks.' Susan asked from the bed when I re-entered the room [...] 'Who was that?' I said 'Mike Merrick.' She asked 'What did he want at this ungodly hour?' I said 'Wanted to tell us the notices were good.' Susan averred that my telephone manner was atrocious and she called Merrick back and apologized for me. I too apologized and Susan said how hopeless I was as my apology was gruffer than the original response. What is it about phones that makes me so antagonistic? I know I can sound reasonably nice on them if I'm prepared for a call but the unexpected ring infuriates me for some reason. [...]

Tuesday 7th, 0550 Greatly excited Sunday as Valerie arrived. She brought the inevitable 'goodies.' Yesterday, Monday, was a clear day off [...] I read, indoors, some of Peter de Vries *Consenting Adults; or, the duchess will be furious.*[95] Some of Kenneth Clark's *The Nude* – how beautifully and succinctly he writes [...] and Prufrockianly the comics and the sporting page, (and the politics) and watched the LA Dodgers v. the Houston Astros in a single game play off for the National League West.[96] Astros won rather dully. We the Yankees had already won our division on (Sat.)

McClure and wife Eres came to dinner on Friday night last. And were delightful. John drank a fair amount – enough to loosen him up to plunge into speaking verse by Edith Sitwell.[97] [...] McClure explained to me how D. H. Lawrence had changed his life.[98] Brought up as a WASP square and astonishing his people by preferring the piano to dating, smooching and necking

[93] Thursday was 2 October.
[94] Evelyn Waugh, *Black Mischief* (1932).
[95] Peter de Vries (1910–93), *Consenting Adults; or, The Duchess will be Furious* (1980).
[96] Kenneth Clark (1903–83), *The Nude: A Study in Ideal Form* (1956).
[97] Edith Sitwell (1887–1964), poet and novelist.
[98] D. H. Lawrence (1885–1930), novelist.

with girls and not being interested in going into business, he found himself the ultimate in intellectualizing every emotion, every lust, every desire.[99] Aldous Huxley, Eliot, Spender timidly cerebral, all added cold douches or water to his instinctive desires. He seemed potentially what V. S. Pritchett might call the inhibited descendant of late children of ancestors who had wasted the family lust and physical excitement before he McClure was unexpectedly born.[100] John is that rare combination – to me at any rate, of a man who's fascinated with technology – he must be one of the best 'sound' men in the world – Bernstein never moves without him, and from now on, neither will I. And at the same time <u>was</u> a potential concert piano pianist and is a fine harpsichordist [. . .]. He has met and known and worked with many people – some of whom we have in common – Stravinsky, Auden, Isherwood, Spender, and e. e. cummings.[101] Curiously enough the only time I met cummings he was very but coherently drunk but according to John, who visited him frequently in his deliberately primitive home somewhere in the Eastern States he, McClure, had never seen cummings even sip a glass of innocuous white wine. So now I am mystified as to why the only encounter I had with cummings he was so desperately drunk. Harvey Orkin, whom God preserve though now dead was with me. It was in the Brussels Restaurant [. . .].[102] In his cups John quoted him too [. . .]. After they left – 3 in the morning Susan and I talked ourselves into a profound melancholy and I added to it by speaking for her Eliot's the Journey of the Magi (Not a madly cheerful little number) 'A cold coming we had of it.'[103][. . .]

Eres is a rare creature in that she hardly ever [. . .] laughs out loud. But when highly amused by John's or Susan's or my sillinesses permits a fugitive shadow of humour to distort attractively one side of her face. Susan's smile is so open (and her mouth and teeth are magnificent) my smile and John's are charming so we're told – but Eres' slight readjustment of features is intriguing. Another unique, uncommon quality about Eres is that she hardly ever mentions that she is born and bred Israeli. None of that race's chauvinism, like the sometimes insufferable South Irish, is apparent in her for which respite many thanks.

I had been told that De Vries and Evelyn Waugh were similar – that in fact De Vries was the American Waugh. On the evidence of all of Waugh's work all of which I have read and re-read and I must confess so far only <u>one</u> book of Peter De Vries, the only comparison is that they both can be funny – funny to the point of making me laugh out loud – and fundamentally deeply serious

---

[99] WASP: White Anglo-Saxon Protestant.
[100] V. S. Pritchett (1900–97), short story writer, critic.
[101] Igor Stravinsky (1882–1971), composer, conductor, pianist. Christopher Isherwood (1904–86), novelist. edward estlin cummings (1894–1962), poet.
[102] Presumably the Brussels Restaurant, New York.
[103] T. S. Eliot, 'The Journey of the Magi', written in 1927 and published in 1930.

but otherwise, except superficially, poles apart. Before examining them against each other I must read and soak myself in De Vries. So now for a De Vries round-up.

[. . .] I shall try again to cut down on cigarettes. I know I can do it – stop smoking I mean, and not out of vanity either but I dislike being short of breath and who knows what other incidental damage it's doing to the body. But I have to be careful. The last time I tried (for five pathetic days) I turned into a monster and also completely lost my memory that is to say I had a five day blackout. That wouldn't do at all for *Camelot*.

[. . .] I have done a great deal of sleeping over the week-end – enough to keep me going over today and tonight I think, and have, for such a frugal eater, packed myself with food.

[. . .] The theatre in Miami is apparently another monster but I cannot think it will be as ugly as the Arie Crown. Also we have a house on the beach there, a private beach they say and there's no sound like the sea sound flowing like blood through the loud wound open wide to the winds the gates of the wandering boat for my voyage to begin to the end of my wound.[104]

I have been asked to be televiewed in Miami – CBS local. I suggested at once that P.H. should be on it but am beginning to have second thoughts about the whole thing.[105] I have been, in three last months or so on the widely (coast-to coast) viewed *Today* show (six days in a row) the *Donahue Show*, also coast to coast, and the *Dick Cavett Show*, another coast to coast, plus Kup's show which is apparently widely shown also but not nationally. Susan is afraid of over-exposure. I feel like a film in a camera. [. . .]

OCTOBER 1980–FEBRUARY 1983

Richard Burton ceased keeping his 1980 diary in early October. He did not resume his personal record until mid-February, 1983.

Richard continued to appear in *Camelot* throughout the remainder of 1980, the production visiting Miami Beach, New Orleans and San Francisco, and then going on in 1981 to Los Angeles. But the physical strain, evident in the diary entries for 1980, was too great and Burton had to withdraw from the production at the end of March. He was taken into St John's hospital in Santa Monica for spinal surgery in April. He emerged in time to provide television narration for the wedding of the Prince of Wales and Lady Diana Spencer on 29 July 1981, but was drinking again and the marriage to Susan

---

[104] Dylan Thomas, 'Lie Still, Sleep Becalmed' (1945), includes the following lines: 'Under the mile off moon we trembled listening / To the sea sound flowing like blood from the loud wound / And when the salt sheet broke in a storm of singing / The voices of all the drowned swam on the wind. // Open a pathway through the slow sad sail, / Throw wide to the wind the gates of the wandering boat / For my voyage to begin to the end of my wound'.

[105] P. H. Burton, by this time living in Florida.

was in dissolution. A further spell in hospital followed in October, by which time Susan had left to live in Puerto Vallarta. Their separation was finally announced in February 1982.

Apparently undaunted by this further setback in his personal life, Burton began 1983 with another major project: making the epic film *Wagner* which involved filming in a number of European cities. He was also drinking heavily. While on location in Italy he met continuity editor Sally Hay, and they began a relationship. Richard's health was not good – he spent more time in hospital – but he and Sally did find time to see Elizabeth Taylor in the London stage production of *The Little Foxes* in June. Over the summer Burton appeared alongside daughter Kate in a film adaptation of a stage production of *Alice in Wonderland*. In September it was announced that Burton and Taylor would appear together in a Broadway production of Noël Coward's *Private Lives* in the spring of 1983.

1983

FEBRUARY

Monday 14th Awoke as right as rainbows. Saw Pierre Koessler re: burglar alarms.[1]

Very complicated. Quite clearly security firms are in collusion with insurance companies. Said I will think about. Have lived here for twenty-odd years with not a blade of grass stolen. Anyway nothing here to steal. TV set, two or three radios, a couple of typewriters, a cheap clock. Ah well. Phone Rene and Berenice Weibel. Dinner at La Réserve on Wednesday. Shall ask him about it. Sally very depressed all day.[2] Worried about Haiti, divorce, NY and attendant publicity she thinks.[3] Poor thing. I went back to work.

Tuesday 15th S. still depressed and fed up. With being a slavey no doubt. Being with me is not as glamorous as people think. Did not get up until <u>2.35pm</u> put me into tearing fury. Very cold all the time and permanently overcast. What fools we are we could have been in Gstaad all this time where (according to D. Brynner) the weather has been fine all the time.[4] Half looking forward to, half dreading the Dearths.[5] Will I be able to handle John's very heavy drinking? Managing my own is a full-time job. Fury so great I didn't do any work at all. Cooled down after dinner but not entirely.

Wednesday 16th Sleepless until 5 or so. Got up at 12.30 or thereabouts. Verdun back in intensive care with yet one more heart attack. Will he repel the swine this time again? Pray that he does. He has been very overweight since he gave up fags. He is the linchpin of the family since Tom died.[6] His loss would be terrible. Took S out to dinner at La Réserve with Rene Weibel and Berenice and Janine Filistorf. Very pleasant. Rene has retired. Looks well. Talked to

---

[1] Pierre Koessler, architect, son of Edouard Koessler.
[2] Sally Hay (1948—), to become Burton's fourth wife.
[3] This refers to the forthcoming trip that Burton and Hay were planning to make to Haiti, to the intended divorce that Burton was seeking from third wife Susan Hunt, and the trip to New York to allow Burton to play in *Private Lives* with Elizabeth Taylor.
[4] D. Brynner is presumably Yul Brynner's second wife Doris, from whom he had been divorced in 1967.
[5] John and Joan Dearth were about to visit Richard and Sally.
[6] Brother Tom had died in 1980.

Milton Katselas.[7] J. Cullum to play Victor – Bravo.[8] ET going to be late for rehearsals. Three or four days. What's new?

Thursday 17th [. . .] Did three hours or so on *Lives* not far to go now. Telephoned J. Cullum to make sure they weren't fibbing to me. Phoned Aileen and Chris to get Mark Getty's telephone number.[9] Talked Graham. Verdun still in intensive care. Talked to Getty – latter sounded down in the mouth. Read awful book about G. Best (footballer) by M. Parkinson. I wonder if Parkinson knew he was writing about himself. Wine, women, TV star. Lost his talent as a promising writer as Best lost his genius. And for same reasons.[10]

Friday 18th Wishart and companion arrived. Quite clear from all his and her talk that going back to live in UK would be absurd – took them to dinner at 'La Réserve'. James became quite drunk. Did not drink at all.

Saturday 19th Took Wishart and Miss Hall to airport. Watched Ireland v. France. Heard Wales v. Scots not much in it either side could have won.[11]

Sunday 20th Picked up John and Joan [Dearth]. John looks terrible. Gave him lots of beer and wine. Joined him and hated myself.

Monday 21st Had Rene and Berenice Weibel to dinner. Excellent meal from Sally. Both of them very good with John. Latter had beer and wine all the live long day. I had none.

Tuesday 22nd Awoke late. John on the beer and later wine. Not very much though! Back to *Private Lives*. Early to bed but what time will I sleep? Home-made raclette for dinner. Ice cream and tinned fruit. [. . .]

Wednesday 23rd Took sun again. Went into Geneva in great excitement to get John Dearth machine to enable him to speak coherently when he hits the right spot on his neck. 'Twill take him a lot of practice to perfect. Also a rubber thing to cover the hole in his neck so that he can shower all over. [. . .]

Thursday 24th [. . .] Took Dearths to airport. Invaded by working-class schoolchildren. Must have signed 60–80 autographs on (most of 'em) the

---

[7] Milton Katselas (1933–2008) was the initial director of *Private Lives*, but would leave the production following disagreements with Taylor in Boston.

[8] John Cullum (1930—) was to play the part of Victor Prynne in the play. He had played with Burton in the 1960 production of *Camelot* and in the Broadway production of *Hamlet*.

[9] Mark Getty (1960—), businessman, brother of Aileen.

[10] Burton had read Michael Parkinson, *Best – An Intimate Biography* on its first publication in 1975.

[11] Ireland beat France 22–16 at Lansdowne Road, Dublin, and Wales beat Scotland 19–15 at Murrayfield.

dingiest pieces of torn bits of exercise books. Signed two cast legs (both 14 year old girls I would guess).

Heartbreaking to say goodbye to John. He still looks ghastly but better than London visit. Sorted out books for travelling library. Tried to make it lighter. Sally packed all afternoon. Sally all smiles because notices for *Profile of a Superstar* were very good apparently.[12]

Friday 25th [. . .] Milton Katselas (director) phoned to say rehearsals put two days forward so perhaps a longer stay in what we hope will be sun in Haiti. It is due for the first of the rainy seasons in Port au Prince. I wonder if ET is behaving herself in her film so hence the delay in beginning work.[13]

Sally worked like a miner all day long packing – quite a task as we're going to be away so long. All I did was pack the book bag with reference books and foreign grammars. And had at it with Noel again. Going through a blank and boring spot with it. Roll on work when it should all fall into place. Talked to Verdun. Seemed in good form.

Saturday 26th Left Geneva at 3.00 – 8 hours later, on the dot, in NY. [. . .] Place (airport) a madhouse but customs and immigration very amiable. Brook waiting [. . .] Straight to JFK Hilton. Bob and Alice came for sandwiches [. . .] Long for Port au Prince already.

Sunday 27th Port au Prince arrived. Very hot and humid. Sally enchanted by highly coloured buses jammed with people. Using the suite which the Pope will have when he arrives on the 9th.[14] [. . .] S and I eat too much. Very tired. Jetlag.

Mr and Mrs Vandal (lawyer and wife) for dinner.[15] Awfully hard to understand Haitian French especially with the nowadays eternal muzak in the background. Not their fault. Sally and I had to repeat things to each other and we sitting side by side. Might try to go to the sea today and see M. Silvera's other house.[16] Divorce papers finalized today.[17] Audience with President tomorrow I think.[18]

---

[12] *Profile of a Superstar* was a television film about Burton that screened on American television in 1983.
[13] Taylor was making a TV movie, *Between Friends*.
[14] Pope John Paul II visited Haiti in March 1983.
[15] M. Vandal was dealing with Richard's divorce.
[16] Albert Silvera, owner of El Rancho Hotel where Richard and Sally were staying in Haiti, who was attempting to persuade Burton to purchase his beach house.
[17] Burton's divorce from Susan Hunt.
[18] The President of Haiti was Jean-Claude Duvalier (1951—), also known as 'Baby Doc'.

Monday 28th Very appropriate – the cartoon opposite.[19] As I was divorced yet again today here in the Palais de Justice. Took ½ hour or so [. . .]. Delighted all over. Strongly tempted to buy a place here. Shall go to see some houses. People gay and delightful and no servant problem. Sally pleased too. And it's so helpful to know the language. Easier to get to than Mexico (PV) and only 3½ hours to NY.[20]

MARCH

Tuesday 1st Celebrated by over-eating – both the divorce and St David. Sudden qualm of conscience yesterday. Afternoon. I never ever (unless asked about her (rarely) or telling a story involving her), talk about poor little Susan [Hunt]. Or think of her. There's a self-defensive or self-serving thing in my brain that cuts out what I don't want in or consider an encumbrance. All have this quality but mine seems to be more highly developed than most. Not a commendable strain. [. . .]

Wednesday 2nd [. . .] Went to M. Silvera's house which was in an appalling state despite three servants on round-the-year pay. For this he wants $300,000. 50,000 would be more like it. Well over an hour from Port au Prince on a good road. No electricity. No phone. I wonder if he's bonkers. We shall look elsewhere as Sally and I like it here and the people are delightful. Painfully slow mentally – faster perhaps in Creole which is a curious lingo indeed. M. Silvera promises to find me a French–Creole book. [. . .]

Thursday 3rd Weather insy-outsy but only about noon by which time we had to leave for the Palace for pow-wow with M and Mme Le President Duvalier. She very bright and pretty. He obviously a powerful force. Audience lasted nearly 1½ hours which Brook was told was a world record for civilian visitors. Grandbaby Doc brought.[21] I held him for a few minutes. Snaps taken of course. Before audience. Went to American Consulate to thank them for H-I Visa. All charming. [. . .] Dinner with two consuls and a black (Haitian) producer-director-playwright. Seems very fond of lady consul and vice versa.[22] [. . .] We may look at some houses tomorrow. Longing to buy place here despite tonight's

---

[19] The cartoon was a 'Gren', (by the cartoonist Grenfell Jones (1934–2007) presumably from the Cardiff evening newspaper the *South Wales Echo*, dated 23 February 1982, in which a lawyer, sitting in a luxurious penthouse office suite, is explaining to a client, 'I had nothing to begin with except an unshakeable belief in my ability and the Richard Burton Divorce Contract.' The explanatory caption below the cartoon reads 'Yet another Richard Burton divorce is announced.'

[20] PV: Puerto Vallarta.

[21] Nicolas Duvalier, born 31 January 1983.

[22] François Latour (1944–2007), Haitian writer and actor. Leslie Gerson was US non-immigrant visa chief in Haiti. She and Latour subsequently married.

intimations of continued corruption in high places. Mme le President's brother in prison in USA for drug-smuggling.[23] [. . .]

Friday 4th [. . .] Slept like a rose. Awoke at 6am. Brilliant day. Lay in sun, had breakfast. Supine for a couple of hours going through *Private Lives* in my head after breakfast. Very hot. Frequent dips in the pool. [. . .] The black writer François Latour faithfully sent me Creole dictionary and phrasebook and grammar.[24] [. . .] I'm sure that with a little help I can get along in it. [. . .] Longing to have our own home in the sun for Sally. Second act of Noel's play contains second-hand moralizing that I find hard to learn because it's so specious. But he was very young.[25]

Saturday 5th Brilliant day again. Listened in frustrated agony to Wales–Ireland. Static terrible. But we won so all's well. Other match(?) was 9–6 to Scotland when last heard then we lost touch.[26] Went to see some land in splendid position. Looked to me about 3–4 acres. $75,000. Said we'd prefer to see house already built – found what seemed a beauty for $200,000.[27] Seeing more on Monday but they'll have to be good to beat that one at that price. Altogether successful day but for Sally cutting the top of her head on rusty barbed wire. Hope she's alright.

Sunday 6th Slept a lot and long. Poolside again after visiting the house very quickly to see where the sun hit it. OK. Approx 6 minutes from hotel. Went through inevitable *Private Lives* again for two-three hours. Dinner with manager and wife Chantelle(?).[28] Both assured me that our living here would help island enormously. No tax.

Monday 7th Sally feeling poorly tonight. Looks it too. Very sallow. Hope she'll sleep it off. It's not booze. Katselas phoned to say rehearsals postponed 'til Monday. ET tired or something! OK with me. Another week (nearly) in Haiti. Had American Consul and boyfriend (Latour) to dinner. He in love with her. He asked us to dinner on Wednesday as surprise for her. He drinks quietly but a lot. Wine. [. . .] Seems deal settled for new house. Sally having – apart from seems like 'flu – one of her self-doubting days. Nothing seems to reassure her. I hope those moods don't grow. I don't know how to handle them.

---

[23] The President's wife was Michele Bennett Pasquet (1950—). Her brother, Frantz Bennett, had been convicted of drug trafficking in Puerto Rico in 1982 and was serving a three-year term of imprisonment.
[24] Latour wrote in an accompanying letter (dated 4 March 1983), 'It is my pleasure to make it possible for you to have these books; I am so appreciative of the interest you are taking in my country.'
[25] Noel Coward wrote *Private Lives* in 1933, when he was 34.
[26] On 5 March Wales beat Ireland 23–9 at Cardiff, and Scotland beat England 22–12 at Twickenham.
[27] Burton was to purchase Habitation Courvoisier, l'Etang du Jone, Petionville.
[28] Willi Wichert, manager of the El Rancho Hotel, and his wife Chantal, sister-in-law to Albert Silvera.

Tuesday 8th A tedious day. Sally sick with migraine. [. . .] Spent a tedious ½ hour with the notary public – female, gaunt, 50, and appallingly freckled. Spoke like an automaton. [. . .] Pope arrives tomorrow. Must that silly old sod travel quite so much? He must cost each country he visits a bloody fortune. Everything here, for instance, stops for the whole day. No planes, no shops, no anything, and all for an idiot who says it's a sin for a man to <u>lust after his own wife</u>!

Wednesday 9th Slept 9–10 hours – not sure. Poolside until 3pm. Having another boring go at Noel. The more one steeps oneself in the play – the other parts as well – one realizes with dismay that a man one loved so much had such a slight mind. The Pope duly arrived at 2 o'clock and should leave at 2am. Thank whatever God may be for town completely disrupted. Police all over. Took us nearly 35 minutes to go to a place which normally would take 10 minutes. Went [to] Leslie Gerson's (American Consul). Goat was the first course. Watched Sally's face. She ate with gusto. So was the rest of the grub. Sally is going to try and steal her cook. The latter is intelligent and reads and understands French.

Thursday 10th Awoke at 6am. Found the BBC World Service but fell asleep on the sofa with the wireless on my belly. Sally knew – she was still in bed – that I must be asleep because the programme that followed the news was *Top of the Pops*.[29] Hardly my style. [. . .]

Friday 11th Very early again and brilliant weather. Too hot so into the pool every 15 minutes so it seemed. Malary (lawyer) turned up twice – once at 11.30 and again at 4.30.[30] Legally he's not allowed to say anything but pretty sure that everything's OK. Did TV interview. Appalling M.U. girl made me or tried to make me look like Roger Moore.[31] Ghastly. 5 minutes was it took [*sic*] – I mean – the actual interview but that hearty lady maqseuls slapped my sun burnt face a round as if she were playing handball.[32] [. . .] NY tomorrow. Don't know whether glad or sorry.

Saturday 12th Arrived NY on time. What a change in weather. [. . .] Had dinner with D. Rowe-Beddoe, plus Madeline, plus Valerie, Brook and Lisa Rowe-Beddoe.[33] Everyone drank except me. ET phoned in middle of dinner.

---

[29] *Top of the Pops*, the BBC TV pop music chart show.
[30] Guy Malary (1943–93), lawyer, assisting with the house purchase, later Minister of Justice (1991–3).
[31] M.U.: make-up.
[32] Burton presumably means *maquilleuse*, make-up girl.
[33] Madeleine Harrison, to marry David Rowe-Beddoe in 1984. Valerie Douglas. Lisa Rowe-Beddoe, eldest daughter of David Rowe-Beddoe.

Noise of clientele so loud that I could only get half of what she said. Will phone her or she me tomorrow sometime. Doesn't know a word says she.

Sunday 13th, New York, Lombardy [Hotel] Sunny day. Talked to Kate and coming over Monday night. Working off Broadway. Irish play.[34] Maria came over with baby.[35] Went with them to see ET who's using Rock Hudson's flat in Beresford.[36] Little or no library. Horrid flat. E's face OK but figure splop! Also drinking. Also has not yet read the play! That's my girl! Became very senti-mental. 'Please don't marry Sally for my sake for a long time' 'I have no dates.' She is very lonely. Buffman using her as is everybody else except us.[37] Feel sorry for her. A mass of mess. Poor thing. 'I have no dates' means 'nobody wants me for myself.' True too!

Monday 14th Began rehearsals. Arrived at 11.30 to find, as usual, that ET couldn't get there 'til noon. They had tried to phone me, they said, to stop my coming so early. Too late, tho! I was there. Director not very inspired. Perhaps he'll get more inventive. Kathryn Walker (Sybil) competent but not competi-tion.[38] [. . .] ET still drinking. Wine only she says. Honest Jack Daniels not too distant. ET bad. Couldn't even read the lines properly. Doubtless she'll come up to scratch eventually. ET as exciting as a flounder temporarily. [. . .] This is going to be a long long seven months. ET beginning to bore which I would not have thought possible all those years ago. How terrible a thing time is.

Tuesday 15th ET only 15 minutes late but then spent 15 minutes more doing her eyebrows. She stinks of garlic – who has garlic for breakfast? She is also on something or other because there are lines here and there which <u>she can't say at all</u>. Very worrying. It's appalling, but I'd not mind if she found she couldn't do it and we had to get someone else. She is also terribly low in energy. Tells me twice an hour how lonely she is. I pity that poor Buffman. Kate, Val, Alka, Lisa (Rowe-Beddoe) all here at one time.[39] K. unhappy I think. She and Lisa stayed for dinner. [. . .]

Wednesday 16th [. . .] ET one hour late today. Two vegann stuck in her throat and in trying to shift them (with Fernet Branca) she vomited. Then her car wouldn't start so mine was sent for her. On the white wine today. Bought me a quite unnecessary Cartier scarf 'Le Must.' Rehearsals with her very hard work.

---

[34] Kate Burton played the character of Mag in *Winners*, the first part of *Lovers* by Brian Friel (1929–), staged at the Roundabout Theatre, New York.
[35] Maria Burton, who had married Steve Carson in 1982, had given birth to Eliza in 1983.
[36] The Beresford, an apartment building on Central Park West, New York.
[37] Zev Buffman (1930–), producer of *Private Lives*, who had previously directed Taylor in *Little Foxes*.
[38] Kathryn Walker (1943–) played the part of Sybil Chase in *Private Lives*.
[39] 'Alka' was Richard's nickname for Nancy Seltzer, publicist, 'Alka Seltzer' being an effervescent antiacid compound used for indigestion, headaches and hangovers.

Stick it out Rich. Bought some books for bedtime. Dashiell Hammett, life of Kafka, and also Mark Twain and thrillers.[40] Michael Innes tonight but not for long. [. . .]

Thursday 17th St Pat's parade sent us off early to get through Fifth Avenue.[41] Result being we were at working theatre (the Cort) at about 11.20.[42] Ready for midday. ET had phoned earlier in her 'lolo little voice' full of brave self-pity to say she was very very sick and had the trots and vomits and she was very sorry but couldn't come to work. Sally and I exchanged looks directed at heaven. Anyway I worked 'til 4.30 straight. Without the book for the most part. [. . .]

Friday 18th Non-stop rain. Ran through the whole play or rather stumbled through it. All day. ET beginning to learn her lines. Kathryn Walker seems to know hers. J. Cullum, surprisingly is very hesitant. There are three or four exchanges that I'm a bit hazy on too. [. . .] By the end of next week I'll be itching for a real audience God willing. They are the only directors I can truly depend on. Milton alright but states the obvious with irritating predictability. Looking forward to Boston now.[43] Hope Sally will like it.

Saturday 19th Apparently according to Ron we might easily have won.[44]

Stumbles through the whole thing. I was the only one not holding a book though for some reason I couldn't remember the second act too well largely I think because of the staging. Went to Laurent for dinner. One large Martini, shared a lovely 1968 Lafitte, two brandies and was only mildly pissed.

Sunday 20th [. . .] Went to ET's for brunch. Eggs Benedict, chips, peas. All had Mimosas (Buck's Fizz) except me. Brook with us. Ran through second act with ET abysmal. She was quite crocked by this time and couldn't even read the lines let alone remember them. Sally spent her time in the next room with Chen Sam – also fried – and told Sally she is dying of leukemia. What a frightful liar she is. Among other fairy tales she told Sally of she'd nursed me through a bad bout of malaria in Botswana. I've never had malaria. ET gave me the terrors again. She is such a mess.

Monday 21st ET no better. Sally saw her have a Fernet Branca at 12.30pm then she drank white wine quite openly – lines getting better but not much. I mean

---

[40] Dashiell Hammett (1894–1961), crime writer. Fran 3 Kafka (1883–1924), novelist. The biography might have been Ronald Hayman, *Kafka: A Biography* (1982). Mark Twain (1835–1910), writer.
[41] 17 March is celebrated by people of Irish descent as St Patrick's Day, Patrick being the patron saint of Ireland.
[42] The Cort Theater, West 48th Street, New York.
[43] The play would start its run at the Shubert Theatre, Boston, on 7 April.
[44] Wales lost to France 9–16 at the Parc des Princes on 19 March 1983. Ireland beat England 25–15 at Lansdowne Road.

her text not her outline. Because she's struggling for words it makes for a very long day. Again she is terribly lacking in energy. Everything is an effort – even to get up from a chair. Talked to Kate on blower. She comes to the theatre tomorrow at 12 noon. Liza called and Sally talked to her. Gave birthday present to Lisa Rowe-Beddoe. $200 and a card chosen by Sally. Photo-call tomorrow. Gawd help us. Still I have Sally and will see Kate and Bob Wilson.

Tuesday 22nd Fury recollected in relative tranquilum. ET impossibly sloshed all day long. So much so she couldn't even <u>read</u> the lines. Same at dinner with the Sime Hornbys who are over on a flying visit.[45] They both sloshed and silly too – long and silly arguments over pronunciations of words. I won every one in the end – words in the play I mean. Had forgotten how ill-educated and stupid Sheran Cazalet is. Food good. La Lavendu yclept. But small and table not big enough for six. ET in hating and hatable mood – Buffman – an iron mouse. God were we glad to get home. Sally mentioned that Simon the Satyr did come on a bit strong.

Wednesday 23rd Worked from 12 noon 'til 7pm without ceasing. ET had an eternal costume fitting (2½ hours) so worked without her. Less sloshed but didn't know a single word of second act which Brook and I went over with her endlessly on Sunday last. Have been forced to promise to go to a memorial service (as 'one of the stars') for Tennessee Williams.[46] Did two films of his – both goodish I believe.[47] I didn't even like the chap. As a matter of fact I hardly ever saw him sober though we were together for months. A self-pitying pain in the neck. Also he made pass at my Chris when Chris was eight.[48]

Thursday 24th Usual day struggling with ET who is slowly getting the part in some sort of shambling shape. [. . .] I am still the only one without a book. I am immensely surprised at the lack of preparation but still we have four weeks before Broadway.[49] Very sunny.

Friday 25th No rehearsals – went for costume fitting. Usual tedium but Theoni Aldredge and tailor very sweet.[50] Did whole play at home and called ET in the a.m. to say that I wasn't going to Tennessee Williams' memorial – apparently a lot of crying went on. Geraldine Fitzgerald sang 'Danny Boy'![51] Sounded awful

---

[45] Simon and Sheran Hornby.
[46] Tennessee Williams had died on 25 February 1983 in New York.
[47] *The Night of the Iguana* and *Boom!*
[48] Christopher Wilding. If Burton is right then that would probably have been during the making of *The Night of the Iguana*.
[49] *Private Lives* opened at the Lunt-Fontanne Theatre, New York, on 8 May.
[50] Theoni V. Aldredge (1932—) was the costume designer for *Private Lives*.
[51] Geraldine Fitzgerald (1913–2005), actor.

– I mean the idea of it all. Kate went and came here to the hotel to give us a blow by blow. Funny child.

Saturday 26th Rehearsed from 11.30–7. ET a bit better in first act but still stuttery. So am I in bits. Long day and felt intensely nervous all day long. J. Breslin came for 10am coffee and to my surprise interviewed me.[52]

Sunday 27th ET tremendously better in first act – still rocky in second and reads third. For the first time in this piece I enjoyed rehearsals. Hope it continues. Home to the *Sunday Times* crostic. Did it quickly. Sally watching *Thorn-Birds*.[53] OK she says.

Monday 28th Kate here for dinner and is staying the night. Little sweetheart is suffering from pangs of disprised love.[54] I could kill the man. He's a stage-manager or something.[55] Rehearsals from 12–7. [. . .] Sally looking very tired tonight, though she bravely kept a good front up. I keep worrying that she's lost too much weight. She says it has plateau'd out. Hope so. 11.30 start tomorrow. [. . .]

Tuesday 29th [. . .] Technical people in front so all of us hyped up a bit. Everybody coming along well. Only worry is John Cullum who hasn't got hold of the essential 'squareness' of Victor. Katie and Sally to lunch together. ET's lethargy disappearing fast. She will be good I hope. So will I, I hope. Milton doesn't understand Coward. Suppose he's happier with American writers. [. . .]

Wednesday 30th Rehearsals ad nauseam. At very awkward stage and director is mildly irritating with continual and (it seems to me) sometimes idiotic suggestions. I don't think he understands comedies of manners at all and especially Noel. Suggested that I should play it with 'Welsh fire' and ET as Elizabeth (American) Taylor. I almost fell off my chair. I can't wait for a paying audience to teach me, in a few performances or so, what they want. Saw beloved Katie in Irish play *Winners*. She brilliant. Funny and moving.

Thursday 31st Most curious occurrence. Director went to lunch and came back exactly as if he were completely under the influence of booze (I thought). No smell on breath so I thought it must be 'speed' which is a habit he had once so he'd told me. ET and Brook thought he'd gone bonkers. We muttered under our breaths (ET and I) but said nothing. Thank God ET understands enough

---

[52] Jimmy Breslin (1930—), journalist, Hollywood columnist and writer, and friend of Burton.
[53] *The Thorn Birds* was a TV mini-series that screened over four nights from 27 March 1983.
[54] 'Pangs of disprised love' is a line from Hamlet's famous soliloquy in Act III, scene i.
[55] A reference to Michael F. Ritchie (1958—). He and Kate married in 1985.

Welsh to know when I'm telling her to control her temper. He stopped us every two lines or four sometimes <u>one word</u>. I nearly went mad. On top of all which ET lost a cap off her teeth. That means four teeth lost in the last five-six months in Sally's and my presence.

APRIL

Friday 1st Started 11. Mr Katselas the director made the mistake of insulting Kathryn first and ET second whereupon I turned on the heat. I blistered and blasted him. Theoni (dress designer) told me that director was almost certainly high on Scientology.[56] So ignorant am I that I didn't know what it meant. I'm still not quite sure. Anyway, end result was – so far – we did it our way and not his. Result: we went through it like whipped cream. He was very quiet for the rest of the day though ET continued to be sullen.

Saturday 2nd Two runs-through today and the difference in performances was sensational in comparison with a mere 1½ days ago. The play and players began to invent. J. Cullum now spot on. Odd man out is me at the moment. I suspect I'm too dangerous to play Noel. My bloody voice is too rich or something. Well, I'll see what I can do.

April 1983 – August 1984

Richard Burton ceased keeping his 1983 diary in early April. This was the last diary he compiled. On 8 May *Private Lives* opened on Broadway, and ran (in Philadelphia, Washington and Los Angeles) until October. It was not a success. On 3 July Richard and Sally married at the Frontier Hotel, Las Vegas. In late November Richard appeared in a televised event paying tribute to Frank Sinatra. On New Year's Eve 1983 Richard and Sally were amongst the guests of President Duvalier at his palace on Haiti.

In May 1984 Burton played the role of O'Brien in the film *1984*, based on the novel by George Orwell. This involved filming in London and in Wiltshire. Shortly after this Richard worked alongside daughter Kate in the TV mini-series *Ellis Island*, also filmed in England. Thereafter Sally and Richard returned to Céligny. On 3 August they entertained John Hurt who had taken the lead role of Winston Smith in *1984*.[57] The following morning Hurt left Burton reading the poetry of William Blake. On the morning of 5 August Richard, though breathing, did not awake. He had suffered a cerebral haemorrhage and died at 1.15p.m. in hospital in Geneva.

---

[56] Katselas had been a Scientologist since 1965.
[57] John Hurt (1940—), actor.

In accordance with his wishes Richard Burton was buried on 9 August in Céligny's Protestant cemetery. Two days later a memorial service was held at Bethel Baptist Chapel in Pontrhydfyen. On 24, 28 and 30 August respectively further memorial services were held at the Wilshire Theater in Beverly Hills, the Lunt-Fontanne Theater in New York and at St Martin-in-the-Fields, Trafalgar Square, London.

When he died Richard Burton left an estate valued at approximately £3.5 million. This was largely divided amongst his widow Sally, and his daughters Kate, Jessica and Maria. Smaller sums went to surviving family members, to Liza Todd, Christopher Wilding, Bob Wilson, Ron Berkeley, Valerie Douglas and Philip Burton.

BIBLIOGRAPHY

Archival Sources

Richard Burton Collection, Richard Burton Archives Swansea University
RWB 1 / 1: Diaries
RWB 1 / 2: Correspondence
RWB 1 / 3: Printed Items
RWB 1 / 4: Photographs
RWB 1 / 5: Film, Television and Audio Recordings, Documentaries and Interviews
RWB 1 / 6: Film Posters
RWB 1 / 7: Programmes and Scripts
RWB 1 / 8: Screenplays and Scripts
RWB 1 / 9: Press Cuttings and Publicity Material
RWB 1 / 10: Framed Prints and Pictures
RWB 1 / 11: Objects
RWB 1 / 12: Miscellaneous

Works of Reference

Chambers' Slang Dictionary
Collins Robert French–English English–French Dictionary
Encyclopedia of Wales
Halliwell's Film Guide
Halliwell's Who's Who in the Movies
Oxford Companion to Classical Civilization
Oxford Companion to English Literature
Oxford Companion to the Theatre
Oxford Dictionary for Writers and Editors
Oxford Dictionary of Foreign Words and Phrases
Oxford Dictionary of National Biography
Oxford Dictionary of Phrase and Fable
Oxford Dictionary of Quotations
Oxford Guide to Style
Shakespeare, William, *Complete Works*, ed. Jonathan Bate and Eric Rasmussen
   (Houndmills: Macmillan, 2007)
Shorter Oxford English Dictionary
Virgin Film Guide
Welsh Academy English–Welsh Dictionary
Y Geiriadur Mawr

Newspapers and Magazines

Esquire
Glamorgan Gazette
Guardian
Life
Look
New York Times

Observer
Port Talbot Guardian
Sunday Express
Sunday Times
Time
The Times
Vogue
Wayfarer
Western Mail

Audio Recordings

David Copperfield (1950)
Conversation Piece (1951)
Under Milk Wood (1954)
Homage to Dylan Thomas (1954)
The World of Dylan Thomas (1955)
Fifteen Poems by Dylan Thomas (1955)
The English Poets (1955)
Brad (1958)
The Love Poems of John Donne (1958)
The Poetry of Thomas Hardy (1958)
The Rape of Lucrece and Other Poems (1960)
The Rime of the Ancient Mariner (1960)
King Henry V (1961)
Camelot (1961)
Coriolanus (1962)
Henry V (1963)
Hamlet (1964)
Zulu (1964)
'A Married Man', *Baker Street* (1965)
The Days of Wilfred Owen (1966)
The Tragical History of Doctor Faustus (1966)
The Little Prince (1974)
A Personal Anthology: The Hound of Heaven and Other Poems (1978)
The War of the Worlds (1978)
'All on a Summer's Day', BBC, 31 December 1981
'Thanksgiving Service for the Life of Richard Burton', BBC, 30 August 1984
'Tribute to Richard Burton', BBC, 3 September 1984
Burton at the BBC (1995)
The Richard Burton Poetry Collection (2010)

Interviews

Richard Burton: My Time Again, BBC, 19 August 1965
24 Hours, BBC, 2 February 1966
Acting in the Sixties, BBC, 1 April 1967
Burton and Taylor at Oxford, BBC, 25 October 1967
Parkinson, BBC, 23 November 1974
Dick Cavett Show, PBS, 25 July 1980
Kane's Classics, BBC, 9 April 1998

Films and Television Appearances

The Last Days of Dolwyn (1949)
My Cousin Rachel (1952)
The Desert Rats (1953)

The Robe (1953)
Prince of Players (1955)
The Rains of Ranchipur (1955)
Alexander the Great (1956)
Sea Wife (1957)
Bitter Victory (1957)
Look Back in Anger (1959)
The Tempest (1960)
A Subject of Scandal and Concern (1960)
Dylan Thomas (1962)
The Longest Day (1962)
Cleopatra (1963)
The VIPs (1963)
Becket (1964)
The Night of the Iguana (1964)
Hamlet (1964)
What's New Pussycat? (1965)
The Sandpiper (1965)
The Spy Who Came in from the Cold (1965)
Who's Afraid of Virginia Woolf? (1966)
The Taming of the Shrew (1967)
The Comedians (1967)
Doctor Faustus (1967)
Boom! (1968)
Candy (1968)
Where Eagles Dare (1968)
Anne of the Thousand Days (1969)
Raid on Rommel (1971)
Villain (1971)
The Assassination of Trotsky (1972)
Hammersmith Is Out (1972)
Bluebeard (1972)
Under Milk Wood (1972)
The Battle of Sutjeska (1973)
Divorce His, Divorce Hers (1973)
Massacre in Rome (1973)
The Klansman (1974)
The Voyage (1974)
Brief Encounter (1974)
Exorcist II: The Heretic (1977)
Equus (1977)
The Medusa Touch (1978)
The Wild Geese (1978)
Breakthrough (1979)
Tristan and Isolt (1979)
Circle of Two (1980)
Absolution (1981)
The Fall Guy (1982)
Wagner (1983)
1984 (1984)
Ellis Island (1984)

Narrations

A Midsummer Night's Dream (1959)
Borrowed Pasture (1960)

Zulu (1964)
The Days of Wilfred Owen (1966)
Robert Kennedy Remembered (1968)
To The Ends of the Earth (1983)
Elizabeth R: A New Film Biography (1985)
Wales: Heritage of a Nation (1987)

Television Programmes and Films about Burton

In From The Cold? The World of Richard Burton, BBC/PBS (1989)
Richard Burton: An Actor's Life, A&E (1995)
Reputations: Richard Burton: Taylor-Made for Stardom, BBC (2001)
Welsh Greats: Richard Burton, BBC (2008)

Books, Chapters and Articles

This is a select listing of those volumes that have been most useful in the editing process. It is not a list of every work consulted. For readers seeking reliable biographical information on Burton, the best studies are those by Paul Ferris and Melvyn Bragg. Incisive, if brief, essays are provided by Peter Stead.

Alpert, Hollis. *Burton* (Toronto and New York: Paperjacks, 1987)
Amburn, Ellis. *Elizabeth Taylor: The Obsessions, Passions and Courage of a Hollywood Legend* (London: Robson, 2000)
Andrews, Julie. *Home: A Memoir of My Early Years* (Waterville, ME: Thorndike Press, 2008)
Babington, Bruce (ed.). *British Stars and Stardom: From Alma Taylor to Sean Connery* (Manchester: Manchester University Press, 2001)
Berry, David. *Wales and Cinema: The First Hundred Years* (Cardiff: University of Wales Press, 1994)
Bloom, Claire. *Limelight and After: The Education of an Actress* (London: Weidenfeld and Nicolson, 1982)
——. *Leaving a Doll's House. A Memoir* (London. Virago, 1996)
Bowyer, Justin. *Conversations with Jack Cardiff: Art, Light and Direction in Cinema* (London: Batsford, 2003)
Bozzacchi, Gianni. *Elizabeth Taylor: The Queen and I* (Madison, WI: University of Wisconsin Press, 2002)
Bragg, Melvyn. *Rich: The Life of Richard Burton* (London: Hodder and Stoughton, 1988)
Brodsky, Jack, and Weiss, Nathan. *The Cleopatra Papers* (New York: Simon and Schuster, 1963)
Burton, Hal (ed.). *Acting in the Sixties* (London: BBC, 1970)
Burton, Philip. *Early Doors* (New York: Dial Press, 1969)
——. *Richard and Philip: Burton – A Book of Memories* (London: Peter Owen, 1992)
Burton, Richard. 'The Magic of Meredith Jones', *Sunday Times*, 17 June 1956
——. 'A Candid Look at Becket and Myself', *Life*, 28 January 1964
——. 'Christmas Eve in Aberavon: A Memoir', *Glamour*, December 1964
——. *A Christmas Story* (London: Heinemann, 1965)
——. 'His Liz: A Scheming Charmer', *Life*, 24 February 1967
——. 'Who Cares about Wales? I Care', *Look*, 24 June 1969
——. 'The Last Time I Played Rugby', *Observer*, 4 October 1970
——. '"Le ma'r blydi film star 'ma?"', in Geoffrey Nicholson with Cliff Morgan and David Frost (eds), *Touchdown: And Other Moves in the Game* (London: Rugby Football Union, 1970)
——. 'The Last Game Richard Burton Lost', *Vogue*, 1 January 1971
——. 'Travelling with Elizabeth', *Vogue*, May 1971

——. 'The trials of travels with Liz', *Observer Review*, 13 August 1971
——. 'My Day', *Vogue*, 1 September 1971
——. 'A Story of Christmas: In the Twenties', *Daily Mail*, 23 December 1971
. 'The Immortal Dive of P. C. Mog', in *The Barry John Book of Rugby* (Swansea: Christopher Davies, 1972)
——. 'To Play Churchill Is To Hate Him', *New York Times*, 24 November 1974
——. 'The Shock of His Presence Was Like a Blow Under the Heart', *New York*, vol. 8 no. 3 (20 January 1975)
——. 'Aberavon', in J. Dolan (ed.), *The Wizards: Aberavon Football Club, 1876–1976* (Port Talbot: Aberavon Football Club, 1976)
——. 'Lament for a Dead Welshman', *Observer Review*, 11 July 1976
Burton, Sally. 'To Know the Library Was To Know the Man', *Life*, January 1985
Caine, Michael. *What's It All About?* (London: Random House, 1992)
Campbell, James. *Talking at the Gates: A Life of James Baldwin* (London: Faber and Faber, 1991)
Cardiff, Jack. *Magic Hour* (London: Faber and Faber, 1996)
Carpenter, Humphrey. *O.U.D.S. A Centenary History of the Oxford University Dramatic Society, 1885–1985* (Oxford: Oxford University Press, 1985)
Cashin, Fergus. *Richard Burton* (London, W. H. Allen, 1982)
Castle, Charles. *Noël* (London, W. H. Allen, 1972)
Caute, David. *Joseph Losey: A Revenge on Life* (London: Faber and Faber, 1994)
Chapman, Don. *Oxford Playhouse: High and Low Drama in a University City* (Hatfield: University of Hertfordshire Press, 2008)
Christopher, James. *Elizabeth Taylor: The Illustrated Biography* (London: André Deutsch, 1999)
Ciment, Michael. *Conversations with Losey* (London and New York: Methuen, 1985)
Clarke, Gerald. *Capote: A Biography* (London: Carroll and Graf, 2006)
Coleman, Terry. *Olivier: The Authorised Biography* (London: Bloomsbury, 2005)
Collins, Joan. *Past Imperfect: An Autobiography* (London: Coronet, 1985)
Cottrell, John, and Cashin, Fergus. *Richard Burton: A Biography* (London: Arthur Barker, 1971)
Coward, Noël. *The Noël Coward Diaries*, ed. Graham Payn and Sheridan Morley (Boston and Toronto: Little, Brown, 1982)
David, Lester and Robbins, Jhan. *Richard & Elizabeth* (New York: Funk and Wagnalls, 1977)
Downing, Christopher. *Burton Stories* (London: Futura, 1990)
Duncan, Paul (ed.), *Taylor* (Cologne: Taschen, 2008)
Dyffryn Grammar School, Port Talbot, 1912–1962
Edwards, Anne. *Callas: Her Life, Her Loves, Her Music* (London: Weidenfeld and Nicolson, 2001)
Evans, A. Leslie. *The Story of Taibach and District* (Port Talbot: 1963)
Fairweather, Virginia. *Cry God for Larry: An Intimate Memoir of Sir Laurence Olivier* (London: Calder and Boyars, 1969)
Falk, Quentin. *Anthony Hopkins: Too Good to Waste* (London: Virgin, 1989)
Farber, Manny. *Negative Space: Manny Farber on the Movies* (London: Studio Vista, 1998)
Farrow, Mia. *What Falls Away: A Memoir* (London: Doubleday, 1997)
Ferris Paul. *Richard Burton* (London: Weidenfeld and Nicolson, 1981)
——. *A Portrait of Richard Burton* (London: Weidenfeld and Nicolson, 1984)
Ffrancon, Gwenno. *Cyfaredd y Cysgodion: Delweddu Cymru a'i Phobl ar Ffilm, 1935–1951* (Caerdydd: Gwasg Prifysgol Cymru, 2003)
Findlater, Richard. *The Player Kings* (London: Weidenfeld and Nicolson, 1971)
Finstad, Suzanne. *Natasha: The Biography of Natalie Wood* (London: Century, 2001)
——. *Warren Beatty: A Private Man* (London: Aurum, 2005)
Fisher, Eddie. *Been There, Done That* (London: Hutchinson, 1999)

Forbes, Bryan. *That Despicable Race: A History of the British Acting Tradition* (London: Elm Tree, 1980)

Fothergill, Robert A. *Private Chronicles: A Study of English Diaries* (London: Oxford University Press, 1974)

Freedland, Michael. *Peter O'Toole* (London: W. H. Allen, 1983)

Gardner, Ava. *Ava: My Story* (London: Bantam, 1995)

Gielgud, John. *An Actor and His Time* (London: Sidgwick and Jackson, 1989)

Glenville, Peter. 'The Burtons', *Vogue*, 15 October 1967

Graham, Sheilah. *Scratch an Actor: Confessions of a Hollywood Columnist* (London: Mayflower, 1970)

Griffith, Kenneth. *The Fool's Pardon: The Autobiography of Kenneth Griffith* (London: Little, Brown, 1994)

Grobel, Lawrence. *The Hustons* (London: Bloomsbury, 1990)

Gussow, Mel. *Zanuck: Don't Say Yes Until I Finish Talking* (London: W. H. Allen, 1971)

——. *Edward Albee: A Singular Journey* (London: Oberon, 1999)

Hall, Sheldon. *Zulu: With Some Guts Behind It: The Making of the Epic Movie* (Sheffield: Tomahawk, 2005)

Hanson, J. Ivor. *Profile of a Welsh Town* (Port Talbot: 1969)

Harding, James. *Emlyn Williams* (London: Weidenfeld and Nicolson, 1993)

Harrison, Elizabeth. *Love, Honour and Dismay* (London: W. H. Allen, 1978)

Harrison, Rex. *Rex: An Autobiography* (London: Macmillan, 1974)

Hayman, Ronald. *Tennessee Williams: Everyone Else is an Audience* (New Haven and London: Yale University Press, 1993)

Heymann, C. David. *Liz: An Intimate Biography of Elizabeth Taylor* (London: Heinemann, 1995)

Hirsch, Foster. *Elizabeth Taylor* (New York: Pyramid, 1973)

Hordern, Michael. *A World Elsewhere: The Autobiography of Sir Michael Hordern* (London: Michael O'Mara, 1993)

Hotchner, A. E. *Sophia: Living and Loving – Her Own Story* (London: Michael Joseph, 1979)

Howerd, Frankie. *On The Way I Lost It: An Autobiography* (London: W. H. Allen, 1976)

Huggett, Richard. *Binkie Beaumont: Eminence Grise of the West End Theatre, 1933–1973* (London: Hodder and Stoughton, 1989)

Huston, John. *An Open Book* (London: Macmillan, 1981)

Isherwood, Christopher, *The Sixties: Diaries, Volume Two: 1960–1969*, ed. Katherine Bucknell (London: Chatto and Windus, 2010)

Jenkins, David. *Richard Burton: A Brother Remembered* (London: Random House, 1993)

Jenkins, Graham. *Richard Burton, My Brother* (New York: Harper and Row, 1988)

Jones, Sally Roberts. *The History of Port Talbot* (Port Talbot: Goldleaf, 1991)

Junor, Penny. *Burton: The Man Behind the Myth* (London: Sphere, 1986)

Kashner, Sam, and Schoenberger, Nancy. *Furious Love: Elizabeth Taylor, Richard Burton and the Marriage of the Century* (London: JR Books, 2010)

Kavanagh, Julie. *Rudolf Nureyev: The Life* (London: Penguin, 2007)

Kelley, Kitty. *Elizabeth Taylor: The Last Star* (London: BCA, 1981)

Kingsland, Rosemary. *Hold Back the Night: Memoirs of Lost Childhood, A Warring Family and A Secret Affair with Richard Burton* (London: Century, 2003)

Korda, Michael. *Charmed Lives* (London: Penguin, 1980)

Lambert, Gavin. *Natalie Wood: A Life* (London: Faber and Faber, 2004)

Lee, Hermione. *Biography* (Oxford: Oxford University Press, 2009)

Lesley, Cole. *The Life of Noël Coward* (Harmondsworth: Penguin, 1976)

Lycett, Andrew. *Dylan Thomas: A New Life* (London: Phoenix, 2004)

Macnab, Geoffrey. 'Valley Boys', *Sight and Sound*, March 1994

Maddox, Brenda. *Who's Afraid of Elizabeth Taylor? A Myth of Our Time* (London: Granada, 1977)

Mallon, Thomas. *A Book of One's Own: People and their Diaries* (St Paul, Minnesota: Hungry Mind, 1995)

Mann, William J. *How To Be A Movie Star: Elizabeth Taylor in Hollywood* (London: Faber and Faber, 2009)

Manso, Peter. *Brando* (London: Orion, 1995)

Matthews, Gethin. *Richard Burton: Seren Cymru* (Llandysul: Gomer, 2002)

McCann, Graham. *Frankie Howerd: Stand-Up Comic* (London and New York: Fourth Estate, 2004)

Minnelli, Vincente. *I Remember It Well* (New York: Doubleday, 1974)

Morgan, Cliff, with Nicholson, Geoffrey. *The Autobiography – Beyond the Fields of Play* (London: Hodder and Stoughton, 1996)

Morley, John David. *Encounters* (London: Bloomsbury, 1990)

Morley, Sheridan. *The Other Side of the Moon: The Life of David Niven* (Long Preston: Magna, 1985)

——. *Elizabeth Taylor: A Celebration* (London: Pavilion, 1988)

Moseley, Roy. *Rex Harrison: The First Biography* (Sevenoaks: New English Library, 1987)

Mosley, Leonard. *Zanuck: The Rise and Fall of Hollywood's Last Tycoon* (London: Granada, 1985)

Munn, Michael. *Richard Burton: Prince of Players* (London: JR Books, 2008)

——. *David Niven: The Man Behind the Balloon* (London: JR Books, 2009)

Nickens, Christopher. *Elizabeth Taylor: A Biography in Photographs* (London: Hutchinson, 1984)

Nolan, William F. *John Huston: King Rebel* (Los Angeles, CA: Sherbourne, 1965)

O'Connor, Garry. *Paul Scofield: The Biography* (London: Sidgwick and Jackson, 2002)

Parkinson, Michael. *Parky: My Autobiography* (London: Hodder and Stoughton, 2008)

Payn, Graham, and Morley, Sheridan (eds), *The Noël Coward Diaries* (Boston and Toronto: Little, Brown, 1982)

Phillips, Siân. *Private Faces: The Autobiography* (London: Sceptre, 1999)

——. *Public Places: The Autobiography* (London: Hodder and Stoughton, 2001)

Plowright, Joan. *And That's Not All* (London: Weidenfeld and Nicolson, 2001)

Podnieks, Elizabeth. *Daily Modernism: The Literary Diaries of Virginia Woolf, Antonia White, Elizabeth Smart and Anaïs Nin* (Montreal and Kingston: McGill-Queen's University Press, 2000)

Ponsonby, Arthur. *English Diaries* (London: Methuen, 1923)

Port Talbot Borough Council. *Port Talbot: The Official Guide* (Port Talbot: Port Talbot Borough Council, 1939)

Quayle, Anthony. *A Time to Speak* (London: Barrie and Jenkins, 1990)

Radovich, Don. *Tony Richardson: A Bio-Bibliography* (Westport, CT: Greenwood, 1995)

Read, Piers Paul. *Alec Guinness: The Authorised Biography* (London: Simon and Schuster, 2003)

Redfield, William. *Letters from an Actor* (New York: Viking, 1967)

Redgrave, Vanessa. *An Autobiography* (London: Hutchinson, 1991)

Richardson, Tony. *Long Distance Runner: A Memoir* (London: Faber and Faber, 1993)

Roberts, Peter (ed.). *The Best of Plays and Players, 1953–1968* (London: Methuen, 1988)

Roberts, Rachel. *No Bells on Sunday: The Journals of Rachel Roberts*, ed. Alexander Walker (London: Michael Joseph, 1984)

Rubython, Tom. *And God Created Burton* (London: Myrtle Press, 2011)

Seldes, Marian. *The Bright Lights: A Theatre Life* (Boston: Houghton Mifflin, 1978)

Sellers, Robert. *Hellraisers: The Life and Inebriated Times of Richard Burton, Richard Harris, Peter O'Toole and Oliver Reed* (London: Preface, 2009)

Shaffer, Anthony. *So What Did You Expect? A Memoir* (London: Picador, 2001)

Shail, Robert. *Stanley Baker: A Life in Film* (Cardiff: University of Wales Press, 2008)

Sheed, Wilfrid. 'Burton and Taylor Must Go', *Esquire*, October 1968

Sheppard, Dick. *Elizabeth: The Life and Career of Elizabeth Taylor* (London: W. H. Allen, 1975)

Spinetti, Victor. *Up Front* (London: Portico, 2008)

Spoto, Donald. *The Kindness of Strangers: The Life of Tennessee Williams* (London: Methuen, 1990)

——. *Elizabeth Taylor* (London: Little, Brown, 1995)

Stanley, Louis. *Sixty Years of Luxury: The Dorchester* (London: Pearl and Dean, 1981)

Stead, Peter. *Richard Burton: So Much, So Little* (Bridgend: Seren, 1991)

——. *Acting Wales* (Cardiff: University of Wales Press, 2002)

Sterne, Richard L. *John Gielgud directs Richard Burton in* Hamlet: *A Journal of Rehearsals* (London: Heinemann, 1968)

Steverson, Tyrone. *Richard Burton: A Bio-Bibliography* (Westport, CT: Greenwood, 1992)

Storey, Anthony. *Stanley Baker: Portrait of an Actor* (London: W. H. Allen, 1977)

Strasberg, Susan. *Bittersweet* (New York: Putnam, 1980)

Taibach and Port Talbot Co-operative Society Ltd. *Co-operative Jubilee, 1902–1952*

Taraborrelli, J. Randy. *Sinatra: The Man Behind the Myth* (Edinburgh: Mainstream, 1998)

——. *Elizabeth* (London: Pan, 2007)

Taylor, Elizabeth. *Elizabeth Taylor: An Informal Memoir by Elizabeth Taylor* (New York: Harper and Row, 1965)

——. *Elizabeth Takes Off* (London: Macmillan, 1988)

——. *My Love Affair with Jewelry* (London: Thames and Hudson, 2002)

Tynan, Kenneth. *The Diaries of Kenneth Tynan*, ed. John Lahr (London: Bloomsbury, 2001)

Ustinov, Peter. *Dear Me* (Harmondsworth: Penguin, 1978)

Vermilye, Jerry, and Ricci, Mark. *The Films of Elizabeth Taylor* (Secaucus, NJ: Citadel, 1976)

Wain, John. *Dear Shadows: Portraits from Memory* (London: John Murray, 1986)

Walker, Alexander. *Hollywood, England: The British Film Industry in the Sixties* (London: Harrap, 1986)

——. *Elizabeth* (London: Weidenfeld and Nicolson, 1990)

. *Fatal Charm: The Life of Rex Harrison* (London: Weidenfeld and Nicolson, 1992)

Wanger, Walter. *My Life with Cleopatra* (London: Transworld, 1963)

Warner, Sylvia Townsend. *T. H. White* (London: Jonathan Cape, 1967)

Waterbury, Ruth. *Richard Burton: His Intimate Story* (London: Mayflower-Dell, 1965)

Waterbury, Ruth, with Arceri, Gene. *Elizabeth Taylor: Her Life, Her Loves, Her Future* (New York: Bantam, 1982)

Wilding, Michael. *Apple Sauce: The Story of My Life* (London: George Allen and Unwin, 1982)

Williams, Bleddyn. *Rugger, My Life* (London: Stanley Paul, 1956)

Willoughby, Bob. *Liz: An Intimate Collection. Photographs of Elizabeth Taylor* (London: Merrell, 2004)

Wintour, Charles, et al., *Celebration: Twenty-Five Years of British Theatre* (London: W. H. Allen, 1980)

Woolf, Virginia. *The Death of the Moth, and Other Essays* (New York: Harcourt, Brace, 1942)

York, Michael. *Travelling Player* (London: Headline, 1992)

Zec, Donald. *Sophia: An Intimate Biography* (London: W. H. Allen, 1975)

——. *Liz: the Men, the Myths and the Miracle: An Intimate Portrait of Elizabeth Taylor* (London: Mirror, 1982)

Zeffirelli, Franco. *Zeffirelli: The Autobiography of Franco Zeffirelli* (London: Weidenfeld and Nicolson, 1986)

Internet Sources

Much of the research into the diaries would have been more difficult without the wealth of resources now available online. Particularly valuable were the following:

ESPN Scrum: www.espnscrum.com
Google Books: books.google.com
Google Maps: maps.google.com
Internet movie database: www.imdb.com

INDEX